Lecture Notes in Computer Science   11366

Commenced Publication in 1973
Founding and Former Series Editors:
Gerhard Goos, Juris Hartmanis, and Jan van Leeuwen

More information about this series at http://www.springer.com/series/7412

C. V. Jawahar · Hongdong Li ·
Greg Mori · Konrad Schindler (Eds.)

Computer Vision – ACCV 2018

14th Asian Conference on Computer Vision
Perth, Australia, December 2–6, 2018
Revised Selected Papers, Part VI

 Springer

Editors
C. V. Jawahar
IIIT Hyderabad
Hyderabad, India

Hongdong Li
ANU
Canberra, ACT, Australia

Greg Mori
Simon Fraser University
Burnaby, BC, Canada

Konrad Schindler 🄳
ETH Zurich
Zurich, Zürich, Switzerland

ISSN 0302-9743   ISSN 1611-3349   (electronic)
Lecture Notes in Computer Science
ISBN 978-3-030-20875-2   ISBN 978-3-030-20876-9   (eBook)
https://doi.org/10.1007/978-3-030-20876-9

LNCS Sublibrary: SL6 – Image Processing, Computer Vision, Pattern Recognition, and Graphics

This Springer imprint is published by the registered company Springer Nature Switzerland AG
The registered company address is: Gewerbestrasse 11, 6330 Cham, Switzerland

Preface

The Asian Conference on Computer Vision (ACCV) 2018 took place in Perth, Australia, during December 2–6, 2018. The conference featured novel research contributions from almost all sub-areas of computer vision.

This year we received a record number of conference submissions. After removing the desk rejects, 979 valid, complete manuscripts were submitted for review. A pool of 34 area chairs and 1,063 reviewers was recruited to conduct paper reviews. Like previous editions of ACCV, we adopted a double-blind review process to determine which of these papers to accept. Identities of authors were not visible to reviewers and area chairs; nor were the identities of the assigned reviewers and area chairs visible to authors. The program chairs did not submit papers to the conference.

Each paper was reviewed by at least three reviewers. Authors were permitted to respond to the initial reviews during a rebuttal period. After this, the area chairs led discussions among reviewers. Finally, a physical area chairs was held in Singapore, during which panels of three area chairs deliberated to decide on acceptance decisions for each paper. At the end of this process, 274 papers were accepted for publication in the ACCV 2018 conference proceedings, of which five were later withdrawn by their authors.

In addition to the main conference, ACCV 2018 featured 11 workshops and six tutorials.

We would like to thank all the organizers, sponsors, area chairs, reviewers, and authors. Special thanks go to Prof. Guosheng Lin from Nanyang Technological University, Singapore, for hosting the area chair meeting. We acknowledge the support of Microsoft's Conference Management Toolkit (CMT) team for providing the software used to manage the review process.

We greatly appreciate the efforts of all those who contributed to making the conference a success.

December 2018

C. V. Jawahar
Hongdong Li
Greg Mori
Konrad Schindler

Organization

General Chairs

Kyoung-mu Lee   Seoul National University, South Korea
Ajmal Mian   University of Western Australia, Australia
Ian Reid   University of Adelaide, Australia
Yoichi Sato   University of Tokyo, Japan

Program Chairs

C. V. Jawahar   IIIT Hyderabad, India
Hongdong Li   Australian National University, Australia
Greg Mori   Simon Fraser University and Borealis AI, Canada
Konrad Schindler   ETH Zurich, Switzerland

Advisor

Richard Hartley   Australian National University, Australia

Publication Chair

Hamid Rezatofighi   University of Adelaide, Australia

Local Arrangements Chairs

Guosheng Lin   Nanyang Technological University, Singapore
Ajmal Mian   University of Western Australia, Australia

Area Chairs

Lourdes Agapito   University College London, UK
Xiang Bai   Huazhong University of Science and Technology, China
Vineeth N. Balasubramanian   IIT Hyderabad, India
Gustavo Carneiro   University of Adelaide, Australia
Tat-Jun Chin   University of Adelaide, Australia
Minsu Cho   POSTECH, South Korea
Bohyung Han   Seoul National University, South Korea
Junwei Han   Northwestern Polytechnical University, China
Mehrtash Harandi   Monash University, Australia
Gang Hua   Microsoft Research, Asia

Rei Kawakami	University of Tokyo, Japan
Tae-Kyun Kim	Imperial College London, UK
Junseok Kwon	Chung-Ang University, South Korea
Florent Lafarge	Inria, France
Laura Leal-Taixé	TU Munich, Germany
Zhouchen Lin	Peking University, China
Yanxi Liu	Penn State University, USA
Oisin Mac Aodha	Caltech, USA
Anurag Mittal	IIT Madras, India
Vinay Namboodiri	IIT Kanpur, India
P. J. Narayanan	IIIT Hyderabad, India
Carl Olsson	Lund University, Sweden
Imari Sato	National Institute of Informatics
Shiguang Shan	Chinese Academy of Sciences, China
Chunhua Shen	University of Adelaide, Australia
Boxin Shi	Peking University, China
Terence Sim	National University of Singapore, Singapore
Yusuke Sugano	Osaka University, Japan
Min Sun	National Tsing Hua University, Taiwan
Robby Tan	Yale-NUS College, USA
Siyu Tang	MPI for Intelligent Systems
Radu Timofte	ETH Zurich, Switzerland
Jingyi Yu	University of Delaware, USA
Junsong Yuan	State University of New York at Buffalo, USA

Additional Reviewers

Ehsan Abbasnejad	Ognjen Arandjelovic	Nick Barnes
Akash Abdu Jyothi	Anil Armagan	Peter Barnum
Abrar Abdulnabi	Chetan Arora	Joe Bartels
Nagesh Adluru	Mathieu Aubry	Paul Beardsley
Antonio Agudo	Hossein Azizpour	Sima Behpour
Unaiza Ahsan	Seung-Hwan Baek	Vasileios Belagiannis
Hai-zhou Ai	Aijun Bai	Boulbaba Ben Amor
Alexandre Alahi	Peter Bajcsy	Archith Bency
Xavier Alameda-Pineda	Amr Bakry	Ryad Benosman
Andrea Albarelli	Vassileios Balntas	Gedas Bertasius
Mohsen Ali	Yutong Ban	Ross Beveridge
Saad Ali	Arunava Banerjee	Binod Bhattarai
Mitsuru Ambai	Monami Banerjee	Arnav Bhavsar
Cosmin Ancuti	Atsuhiko Banno	Simone Bianco
Vijay Rengarajan Angarai	Aayush Bansal	Oliver Bimber
Pichaikuppan	Dániel Baráth	Tolga Birdal
Michel Antunes	Lorenzo Baraldi	Horst Bischof
Djamila Aouada	Adrian Barbu	Arijit Biswas

Soma Biswas
Henryk Blasinski
Vishnu Boddeti
Federica Bogo
Tolga Bolukbasi
Terrance Boult
Thierry Bouwmans
Abdesselam Bouzerdoum
Ernesto Brau
Mathieu Bredif
Stefan Breuers
Marcus Brubaker
Anders Buch
Shyamal Buch
Pradeep Buddharaju
Adrian Bulat
Darius Burschka
Andrei Bursuc
Zoya Bylinskii
Weidong Cai
Necati Cihan Camgoz
Shaun Canavan
Joao Carreira
Dan Casas
M. Emre Celebi
Hakan Cevikalp
François Chadebecq
Menglei Chai
Rudrasis Chakraborty
Tat-Jen Cham
Kwok-Ping Chan
Sharat Chandran
Chehan Chang
Hyun Sung Chang
Yi Chang
Wei-Lun Chao
Visesh Chari
Gaurav Chaurasia
Rama Chellappa
Chen Chen
Chu-Song Chen
Dongdong Chen
Guangyong Chen
Hsin-I Chen
Huaijin Chen
Hwann-Tzong Chen

Jiacheng Chen
Jianhui Chen
Jiansheng Chen
Jiaxin Chen
Jie Chen
Kan Chen
Longbin Chen
Ting Chen
Tseng-Hung Chen
Wei Chen
Xi'ai Chen
Xiaozhi Chen
Xilin Chen
Xinlei Chen
Yunjin Chen
Erkang Cheng
Hong Cheng
Hui Cheng
Jingchun Cheng
Ming-Ming Cheng
Wen-Huang Cheng
Yuan Cheng
Zhi-Qi Cheng
Loong Fah Cheong
Anoop Cherian
Liang-Tien Chia
Chao-Kai Chiang
Shao-Yi Chien
Han-Pang Chiu
Wei-Chen Chiu
Donghyeon Cho
Nam Ik Cho
Sunghyun Cho
Yeong-Jun Cho
Gyeongmin Choe
Chiho Choi
Jonghyun Choi
Jongmoo Choi
Jongwon Choi
Hisham Cholakkal
Biswarup Choudhury
Xiao Chu
Yung-Yu Chuang
Andrea Cohen
Toby Collins
Marco Cristani

James Crowley
Jinshi Cui
Zhaopeng Cui
Bo Dai
Hang Dai
Xiyang Dai
Yuchao Dai
Carlo Dal Mutto
Zachary Daniels
Mohamed Daoudi
Abir Das
Raoul De Charette
Teofilo Decampos
Koichiro Deguchi
Stefanie Demirci
Girum Demisse
Patrick Dendorfer
Zhiwei Deng
Joachim Denzler
Aditya Deshpande
Frédéric Devernay
Abhinav Dhall
Anthony Dick
Zhengming Ding
Cosimo Distante
Ajay Divakaran
Mandar Dixit
Thanh-Toan Do
Jose Dolz
Bo Dong
Chao Dong
Jingming Dong
Ming Dong
Weisheng Dong
Simon Donne
Gianfranco Doretto
Bruce Draper
Bertram Drost
Liang Du
Shichuan Du
Jean-Luc Dugelay
Enrique Dunn
Thibaut Durand
Zoran Duric
Ionut Cosmin Duta
Samyak Dutta

Pinar Duygulu
Ady Ecker
Hazim Ekenel
Sabu Emmanuel
Ian Endres
Ertunc Erdil
Hugo Jair Escalante
Sergio Escalera
Francisco Escolano Ruiz
Bin Fan
Shaojing Fan
Yi Fang
Aly Farag
Giovanni Farinella
Rafael Felix
Michele Fenzi
Bob Fisher
David Fofi
Gian Luca Foresti
Victor Fragoso
Bernd Freisleben
Jason Fritts
Cheng-Yang Fu
Chi-Wing Fu
Huazhu Fu
Jianlong Fu
Xueyang Fu
Ying Fu
Yun Fu
Olac Fuentes
Jan Funke
Ryo Furukawa
Yasutaka Furukawa
Manuel Günther
Raghudeep Gadde
Matheus Gadelha
Jürgen Gall
Silvano Galliani
Chuang Gan
Zhe Gan
Vineet Gandhi
Arvind Ganesh
Bin-Bin Gao
Jin Gao
Jiyang Gao
Junbin Gao

Ravi Garg
Jochen Gast
Utkarsh Gaur
Xin Geng
David Geronimno
Michael Gharbi
Amir Ghodrati
Behnam Gholami
Andrew Gilbert
Rohit Girdhar
Ioannis Gkioulekas
Guy Godin
Nuno Goncalves
Yu Gong
Stephen Gould
Venu Govindu
Oleg Grinchuk
Jiuxiang Gu
Shuhang Gu
Paul Guerrero
Anupam Guha
Guodong Guo
Yanwen Guo
Ankit Gupta
Mithun Gupta
Saurabh Gupta
Hossein Hajimirsadeghi
Maciej Halber
Xiaoguang Han
Yahong Han
Zhi Han
Kenji Hara
Tatsuya Harada
Ali Harakeh
Adam Harley
Ben Harwood
Mahmudul Hasan
Kenji Hata
Michal Havlena
Munawar Hayat
Zeeshan Hayder
Jiawei He
Kun He
Lei He
Lifang He
Pan He

Yang He
Zhenliang He
Zhihai He
Felix Heide
Samitha Herath
Luis Herranz
Anders Heyden
Je Hyeong Hong
Seunghoon Hong
Wei Hong
Le Hou
Chiou-Ting Hsu
Kuang-Jui Hsu
Di Hu
Hexiang Hu
Ping Hu
Xu Hu
Yinlin Hu
Zhiting Hu
De-An Huang
Gao Huang
Gary Huang
Haibin Huang
Haifei Huang
Haozhi Huang
Jia-Bin Huang
Shaoli Huang
Sheng Huang
Xinyu Huang
Xun Huang
Yan Huang
Yawen Huang
Yinghao Huang
Yizhen Huang
Wei-Chih Hung
Junhwa Hur
Mohamed Hussein
Jyh-Jing Hwang
Ichiro Ide
Satoshi Ikehata
Radu Tudor Ionescu
Go Irie
Ahmet Iscen
Vamsi Ithapu
Daisuke Iwai
Won-Dong Jang

Kaimo Lin
Shih-Yao Lin
Tsung-Yi Lin
Weiyao Lin
Yuewei Lin
Venice Liong
Giuseppe Lisanti
Roee Litman
Jim Little
Anan Liu
Chao Liu
Chen Liu
Eryun Liu
Fayao Liu
Huaping Liu
Jingen Liu
Lingqiao Liu
Miaomiao Liu
Qingshan Liu
Risheng Liu
Sifei Liu
Tyng-Luh Liu
Weiyang Liu
Xialei Liu
Xianglong Liu
Xiao Liu
Yebin Liu
Yi Liu
Yu Liu
Yun Liu
Ziwei Liu
Stephan Liwicki
Liliana Lo Presti
Fotios Logothetis
Javier Lorenzo
Manolis Lourakis
Brian Lovell
Chen Change Loy
Chaochao Lu
Feng Lu
Huchuan Lu
Jiajun Lu
Kaiyue Lu
Xin Lu
Yijuan Lu
Yongxi Lu

Fujun Luan
Jian-Hao Luo
Jiebo Luo
Weixin Luo
Khoa Luu
Chao Ma
Huimin Ma
Kede Ma
Lin Ma
Shugao Ma
Wei-Chiu Ma
Will Maddern
Ludovic Magerand
Luca Magri
Behrooz Mahasseni
Tahmida Mahmud
Robert Maier
Subhransu Maji
Yasushi Makihara
Clement Mallet
Abed Malti
Devraj Mandal
Fabian Manhardt
Gian Luca Marcialis
Julio Marco
Diego Marcos
Ricardo Martin
Tanya Marwah
Marc Masana
Jonathan Masci
Takeshi Masuda
Yusuke Matsui
Tetsu Matsukawa
Gellert Mattyus
Thomas Mauthner
Bruce Maxwell
Steve Maybank
Amir Mazaheri
Scott Mccloskey
Mason Mcgill
Nazanin Mehrasa
Ishit Mehta
Xue Mei
Heydi Mendez-Vazquez
Gaofeng Meng
Bjoern Menze

Domingo Mery
Pascal Mettes
Jan Hendrik Metzen
Gregor Miller
Cai Minjie
Ikuhisa Mitsugami
Daisuke Miyazaki
Davide Modolo
Pritish Mohapatra
Pascal Monasse
Sandino Morales
Pietro Morerio
Saeid Motiian
Arsalan Mousavian
Mikhail Mozerov
Yasuhiro Mukaigawa
Yusuke Mukuta
Mario Munich
Srikanth Muralidharan
Ana Murillo
Vittorio Murino
Armin Mustafa
Hajime Nagahara
Shruti Nagpal
Mahyar Najibi
Katsuyuki Nakamura
Seonghyeon Nam
Loris Nanni
Manjunath Narayana
Lakshmanan Nataraj
Neda Nategh
Lukáš Neumann
Shawn Newsam
Joe Yue-Hei Ng
Thuyen Ngo
David Nilsson
Ji-feng Ning
Mark Nixon
Shohei Nobuhara
Hyeonwoo Noh
Mehdi Noroozi
Erfan Noury
Eyal Ofek
Seong Joon Oh
Seoung Wug Oh
Katsunori Ohnishi

Iason Oikonomidis
Takeshi Oishi
Takahiro Okabe
Takayuki Okatani
Gustavo Olague
Kyle Olszewski
Mohamed Omran
Roy Or-El
Ivan Oseledets
Martin R. Oswald
Tomas Pajdla
Dipan Pal
Kalman Palagyi
Manohar Paluri
Gang Pan
Jinshan Pan
Yannis Panagakis
Rameswar Panda
Hsing-Kuo Pao
Dim Papadopoulos
Konstantinos Papoutsakis
Shaifali Parashar
Hyun Soo Park
Jinsun Park
Taesung Park
Wonpyo Park
Alvaro Parra Bustos
Geoffrey Pascoe
Ioannis Patras
Genevieve Patterson
Georgios Pavlakos
Ioannis Pavlidis
Nick Pears
Pieter Peers
Selen Pehlivan
Xi Peng
Xingchao Peng
Janez Perš
Talita Perciano
Adrian Peter
Lars Petersson
Stavros Petridis
Patrick Peursum
Trung Pham
Sang Phan
Marco Piccirilli

Sudeep Pillai
Wong Ya Ping
Lerrel Pinto
Fiora Pirri
Matteo Poggi
Georg Poier
Marius Popescu
Ronald Poppe
Dilip Prasad
Andrea Prati
Maria Priisalu
Véronique Prinet
Victor Prisacariu
Hugo Proenca
Jan Prokaj
Daniel Prusa
Yunchen Pu
Guo-Jun Qi
Xiaojuan Qi
Zhen Qian
Yu Qiao
Jie Qin
Lei Qin
Chao Qu
Faisal Qureshi
Petia Radeva
Venkatesh Babu
    Radhakrishnan
Ilija Radosavovic
Bogdan Raducanu
Hossein Rahmani
Swaminathan Rahul
Ajit Rajwade
Kandan Ramakrishnan
Visvanathan Ramesh
Yongming Rao
Sathya Ravi
Michael Reale
Adria Recasens
Konstantinos Rematas
Haibing Ren
Jimmy Ren
Wenqi Ren
Zhile Ren
Edel Garcia Reyes
Hamid Rezatofighi

Hamed Rezazadegan
    Tavakoli
Rafael Rezende
Helge Rhodin
Alexander Richard
Stephan Richter
Gernot Riegler
Christian Riess
Ergys Ristani
Tobias Ritschel
Mariano Rivera
Antonio Robles-Kelly
Emanuele Rodola
Andres Rodriguez
Mikel Rodriguez
Matteo Ruggero Ronchi
Xuejian Rong
Bodo Rosenhahn
Arun Ross
Peter Roth
Michel Roux
Ryusuke Sagawa
Hideo Saito
Shunsuke Saito
Parikshit Sakurikar
Albert Ali Salah
Jorge Sanchez
Conrad Sanderson
Aswin Sankaranarayanan
Swami Sankaranarayanan
Archana Sapkota
Michele Sasdelli
Jun Sato
Shin'ichi Satoh
Torsten Sattler
Manolis Savva
Tanner Schmidt
Dirk Schnieders
Samuel Schulter
Rajvi Shah
Shishir Shah
Sohil Shah
Moein Shakeri
Nataliya Shapovalova
Aidean Sharghi
Gaurav Sharma

Pramod Sharma
Li Shen
Shuhan Shen
Wei Shen
Xiaoyong Shen
Zhiqiang Shen
Lu Sheng
Baoguang Shi
Guangming Shi
Miaojing Shi
Zhiyuan Shi
Takashi Shibata
Huang-Chia Shih
Meng-Li Shih
Sheng-Wen Shih
Atsushi Shimada
Nobutaka Shimada
Daeyun Shin
Young Min Shin
Koichi Shinoda
Tianmin Shu
Zhixin Shu
Bing Shuai
Karan Sikka
Jack Sim
Marcel Simon
Tomas Simon
Vishwanath Sindagi
Gurkirt Singh
Maneet Singh
Praveer Singh
Ayan Sinha
Sudipta Sinha
Vladimir Smutny
Francesco Solera
Amir Arsalan Soltani
Eric Sommerlade
Andy Song
Shiyu Song
Yibing Song
Humberto Sossa
Concetto Spampinato
Filip Šroubek
Ioannis Stamos
Jan Stuehmer
Jingyong Su

Jong-Chyi Su
Shuochen Su
Yu-Chuan Su
Zhixun Su
Ramanathan Subramanian
Akihiro Sugimoto
Waqas Sultani
Jiande Sun
Jin Sun
Ju Sun
Lin Sun
Min Sun
Yao Sun
Zhaohui Sun
David Suter
Tanveer Syeda-Mahmood
Yuichi Taguchi
Jun Takamatsu
Takafumi Taketomi
Hugues Talbot
Youssef Tamaazousti
Toru Tamak
Robert Tamburo
Chaowei Tan
David Joseph Tan
Ping Tan
Xiaoyang Tan
Kenichiro Tanaka
Masayuki Tanaka
Jinhui Tang
Meng Tang
Peng Tang
Wei Tang
Yuxing Tang
Junli Tao
Xin Tao
Makarand Tapaswi
Jean-Philippe Tarel
Keisuke Tateno
Joao Tavares
Bugra Tekin
Mariano Tepper
Ali Thabet
Spiros Thermos
Shangxuan Tian
Yingli Tian

Kinh Tieu
Massimo Tistarelli
Henning Tjaden
Matthew Toews
Chetan Tonde
Akihiko Torii
Andrea Torsello
Toan Tran
Leonardo Trujillo
Tomasz Trzcinski
Sam Tsai
Yi-Hsuan Tsai
Ivor Tsang
Vagia Tsiminaki
Aggeliki Tsoli
Wei-Chih Tu
Shubham Tulsiani
Sergey Tulyakov
Tony Tung
Matt Turek
Seiichi Uchida
Oytun Ulutan
Martin Urschler
Mikhail Usvyatsov
Alexander Vakhitov
Julien Valentin
Ernest Valveny
Ian Van Der Linde
Kiran Varanasi
Gul Varol
Francisco Vasconcelos
Pascal Vasseur
Javier Vazquez-Corral
Ashok Veeraraghavan
Andreas Velten
Raviteja Vemulapalli
Jonathan Ventura
Subhashini Venugopalan
Yashaswi Verma
Matthias Vestner
Minh Vo
Jayakorn Vongkulbhisal
Toshikazu Wada
Chengde Wan
Jun Wan
Renjie Wan

Baoyuan Wang
Chaohui Wang
Chaoyang Wang
Chunyu Wang
De Wang
Dong Wang
Fang Wang
Faqiang Wang
Hongsong Wang
Hongxing Wang
Hua Wang
Jialei Wang
Jianyu Wang
Jinglu Wang
Jinqiao Wang
Keze Wang
Le Wang
Lei Wang
Lezi Wang
Lijun Wang
Limin Wang
Linwei Wang
Pichao Wang
Qi Wang
Qian Wang
Qilong Wang
Qing Wang
Ruiping Wang
Shangfei Wang
Shuhui Wang
Song Wang
Tao Wang
Tsun-Hsuang Wang
Weiyue Wang
Wenguan Wang
Xiaoyu Wang
Xinchao Wang
Xinggang Wang
Yang Wang
Yin Wang
Yu-Chiang Frank Wang
Yufei Wang
Yunhong Wang
Zhangyang Wang
Zilei Wang
Jan Dirk Wegner

Ping Wei
Shih-En Wei
Wei Wei
Xiu-Shen Wei
Zijun Wei
Bihan Wen
Longyin Wen
Xinshuo Weng
Tom Whelan
Patrick Wieschollek
Maggie Wigness
Jerome Williams
Kwan-Yee Wong
Chao-Yuan Wu
Chunpeng Wu
Dijia Wu
Jiajun Wu
Jianxin Wu
Xiao Wu
Xiaohe Wu
Xiaomeng Wu
Xinxiao Wu
Yi Wu
Ying Nian Wu
Yue Wu
Zheng Wu
Zhirong Wu
Jonas Wulff
Yin Xia
Yongqin Xian
Yu Xiang
Fanyi Xiao
Yang Xiao
Dan Xie
Jianwen Xie
Jin Xie
Fuyong Xing
Jun Xing
Junliang Xing
Xuehan Xiong
Yuanjun Xiong
Changsheng Xu
Chenliang Xu
Haotian Xu
Huazhe Xu
Huijuan Xu

Jun Xu
Ning Xu
Tao Xu
Weipeng Xu
Xiangmin Xu
Xiangyu Xu
Yong Xu
Yuanlu Xu
Jia Xue
Xiangyang Xue
Toshihiko Yamasaki
Junchi Yan
Luxin Yan
Wang Yan
Keiji Yanai
Bin Yang
Chih-Yuan Yang
Dong Yang
Herb Yang
Jianwei Yang
Jie Yang
Jin-feng Yang
Jufeng Yang
Meng Yang
Ming Yang
Ming-Hsuan Yang
Tien-Ju Yang
Wei Yang
Wenhan Yang
Yanchao Yang
Yingzhen Yang
Yongxin Yang
Zhenheng Yang
Angela Yao
Bangpeng Yao
Cong Yao
Jian Yao
Jiawen Yao
Yasushi Yagi
Mang Ye
Mao Ye
Qixiang Ye
Mei-Chen Yeh
Sai-Kit Yeung
Kwang Moo Yi
Alper Yilmaz

Xi Yin

Zhaozheng Yin

Xianghua Ying

Ryo Yonetani

Donghyun Yoo

Jae Shin Yoon

Ryota Yoshihashi

Gang Yu

Hongkai Yu

Ruichi Yu

Shiqi Yu

Xiang Yu

Yang Yu

Youngjae Yu

Chunfeng Yuan

Jing Yuan

Junsong Yuan

Shanxin Yuan

Zejian Yuan

Xenophon Zabulis

Mihai Zanfir

Pablo Zegers

Jiabei Zeng

Kuo-Hao Zeng

Baochang Zhang

Cha Zhang

Chao Zhang

Dingwen Zhang

Dong Zhang

Guofeng Zhang

Hanwang Zhang

He Zhang

Hong Zhang

Honggang Zhang

Hua Zhang

Jian Zhang

Jiawei Zhang

Jing Zhang

Kaipeng Zhang

Ke Zhang

Liang Zhang

Linguang Zhang

Liqing Zhang

Peng Zhang

Pingping Zhang

Quanshi Zhang

Runze Zhang

Shanghang Zhang

Shu Zhang

Tianzhu Zhang

Tong Zhang

Wen Zhang

Xiaofan Zhang

Xiaoqin Zhang

Xikang Zhang

Xu Zhang

Ya Zhang

Yinda Zhang

Yongqiang Zhang

Zhang Zhang

Zhen Zhang

Zhoutong Zhang

Ziyu Zhang

Bin Zhao

Bo Zhao

Chen Zhao

Hengshuang Zhao

Qijun Zhao

Rui Zhao

Heliang Zheng

Shuai Zheng

Stephan Zheng

Yinqiang Zheng

Yuanjie Zheng

Zhonglong Zheng

Guangyu Zhong

Huiyu Zhou

Jiahuan Zhou

Jun Zhou

Luping Zhou

Mo Zhou

Pan Zhou

Yang Zhou

Zihan Zhou

Fan Zhu

Guangming Zhu

Hao Zhu

Hongyuan Zhu

Lei Zhu

Menglong Zhu

Pengfei Zhu

Shizhan Zhu

Siyu Zhu

Xiangxin Zhu

Yi Zhu

Yizhe Zhu

Yuke Zhu

Zhigang Zhu

Bohan Zhuang

Liansheng Zhuang

Karel Zimmermann

Maria Zontak

Danping Zou

Qi Zou

Wangmeng Zuo

Xinxin Zuo

Contents – Part VI

Oral Session O6: Vision and Language, Semantics, and Low-Level Vision

Poster Session P2

Revisiting Distillation and Incremental Classifier Learning

Khurram Javed[2]([✉]) and Faisal Shafait[1,2]

[1] Deep Learning Laboratory, National Center of Artificial Intelligence,
Islamabad, Pakistan
[2] School of Electrical Engineering and Computer Science,
National University of Sciences and Technology, Islamabad, Pakistan
{14besekjaved,faisal.shafait}@seecs.edu.pk

Abstract. One of the key differences between the learning mechanism of humans and Artificial Neural Networks (ANNs) is the ability of humans to learn one task at a time. ANNs, on the other hand, can only learn multiple tasks simultaneously. Any attempts at learning new tasks incrementally cause them to completely forget about previous tasks. This lack of ability to learn incrementally, called Catastrophic Forgetting, is considered a major hurdle in building a true AI system.

In this paper, our goal is to isolate the truly effective existing ideas for incremental learning from those that only work under certain conditions. To this end, we first thoroughly analyze the current state of the art (iCaRL) method for incremental learning and demonstrate that the good performance of the system is not because of the reasons presented in the existing literature. We conclude that the success of iCaRL is primarily due to knowledge distillation and recognize a key limitation of knowledge distillation, i.e., it often leads to bias in classifiers. Finally, we propose a dynamic threshold moving algorithm that is able to successfully remove this bias. We demonstrate the effectiveness of our algorithm on CIFAR100 and MNIST datasets showing near-optimal results. Our implementation is available at: https://github.com/Khurramjaved96/incremental-learning.

Keywords: Incremental learning · Catastrophic Forgetting · Incremental classifier · Knowledge distillation

1 Introduction

To understand incremental learning, let's look at a simple everyday example. Suppose that you are taking a walk in a garden and you come across a new kind of flower. You have never seen such a flower before and are intrigued by it, so you look up all the information regarding that flower, and learn everything you possibly can about it. You then continue your walk and come across a red rose; would you be able to recognize the rose? Assuming you have seen a rose in the past, the answer is a resounding yes. In fact, the question seems completely

© Springer Nature Switzerland AG 2019
C. V. Jawahar et al. (Eds.): ACCV 2018, LNCS 11366, pp. 3–17, 2019.
https://doi.org/10.1007/978-3-030-20876-9_1

unrelated to the task that you learned recently. However, if an Artificial Neural Network (ANN) was asked to do the same thing, it won't be able to answer the question. Even a network trained to recognize roses with an accuracy of 100% would fail to answer the question if it was not provided samples of roses at the exact moment it was learning about the new flower. This phenomenon is known as Catastrophic Forgetting and highlights a sharp contrast between the way humans and neural networks learn; humans are able to attain new knowledge without forgetting previously stored information. Artificial Neural Networks, trained using a variation of Gradient descent, on the other hand, must be provided with data of all previously learned tasks whenever they are learning something new (It should be noted that humans also have to revise old tasks eventually to be able to retain knowledge over long periods of times and that the new knowledge can in fact interfere with older knowledge [1]. However, the problem is not nearly as pronounced and debilitating in humans as it is in ANNs.). The goal of incremental learning is to bridge this gap between humans and ANNs.

The importance of incorporating incremental learning in ANNs is self evident; not only will it address a key limitation of ANNs and a fundamental AI research problem, but also provide countless practical benefits such as deploying ever evolving machine learning systems that can dynamically learn new tasks over time, or developing classifiers that can handle an ever changing set of classes (For example inventory of a store).

In this paper, instead of tackling the general problem of incremental learning of multiple tasks as described above, we limit our discussion to incremental classifier learning. We believe this is justified because incremental classifier learning presents most of the same challenges as the general incremental learning problem, and is at the same time easier to tackle given the current state of ANNs. Note that we are not the first one to limit ourselves to incremental classifier learning and as we shall see later in the paper, some of the most popular work on incremental learning made the same simplifying assumption.

1.1 Our Contributions

We make three main contributions in this work. First, we analyze the existing state of the art for incremental classifier learning, iCaRL [2] and make some insightful observations about the proposed approach. We then propose a novel Dynamic Threshold Moving Algorithm to address a well known issue of a popular knowledge transfer and preservation technique called Knowledge Distillation. Finally, we present a simple solution to address the major issue of lack of reproducibility in scientific literature.

1. **Analysis of iCaRL:** We thoroughly analyze the current state of the art incremental learning approach proposed by Rebuffi et al. [2] and show that some of the improvements resulting from this approach are not because of the reasons presented by the authors. More specifically, we show that NEM (Nearest Exemplar Mean) classifier is only effective because the classifier

learned through the training procedure is biased, and by either implementing threshold moving or using higher temperature distillation, it is possible to remove this bias. As a result, NEM classifier is not a necessary requirement for an incremental classifier. The author also proposed an exemplar set selection algorithm, called herding, well suited to approximate NCM (Nearest Class Mean) classifier. We failed to reproduce the effectiveness of herding in our experiments. In fact, herding did not perform any better than random instance selection. Wu *et al.* [3] also tried to independently reproduce the results of herding but failed.

2. **Dynamic Threshold Moving Algorithm:** We propose an algorithm for computing a scale vector that can be used to fix the bias of a classifier trained using distillation loss. The problem of bias resulting from distillation was first noticed by Hinton *et al.* [4] in their original work on knowledge distillation. However, in their work, they only showed the existence of a vector S that can be used to fix the bias. They did not provide a method for computing the said vector. Using our algorithm, on the other hand, it is possible to compute the said vector at no additional cost.

3. **Framework for Future Work:** We open-source an implementation of class incremental learning that can be used to quickly compare existing methodologies on multiple datasets. We develop our framework keeping in mind ease of extensibility to newer datasets and methods, and propose a simple protocol to facilitate quick reproducibility of results. We hope that future researchers would follow a similar protocol to complement the already positive trend of code, data, and paper sharing for quick reproducibility in the machine learning community.

We are confident that our work clarifies some of the uncertainties regarding incremental classifier learning strategies, and would act as a stepping stone for future research in incremental learning. We're also hopeful that our dynamic threshold moving algorithm will find other use-cases than that of training a classifier with distillation. One such potential use-case is to use dynamic threshold for removing bias when transferring knowledge to a student model from a larger, deeper teacher model.

2   Related Work

The problem of catastrophic forgetting was identified as early as 1989 by McCloskey *et al.* [5]. This led to preliminary work on incremental representation learning in the late 90s [6–8]. Later in 2013, Goodfellow *et al.* [9] extended the work to include current, deeper and more sophistical ANNs by presenting a thorough empirical analysis of Catastrophic Forgetting.

Methods for incremental classifier learning were also proposed quite early. For example, Mensink *et al.* [10] demonstrated that by fixing the representation and using NCM Classifier, it is possible to add new classes at zero additional cost. Lampert *et al.* [11] proposed a zero shot learning system that was able to classify new classes at no cost. However, in both of these methods, the feature extraction pipeline was not adapted to the new data, and only the classification algorithm was changed to incorporate new classes. This limited the performance of the system as feature extractor trained on one set of classes may not generalize to a newer set.

The remaining recent Incremental learning techniques can be categorized into (1) Rehearsal based and (2) Knowledge preserving incremental learning.

2.1 Rehearsal Based Incremental Learning

Rehearsal based incremental learning systems have a pipeline similar to joint training. They store the distribution of the data of the previously learned tasks in some form, and use samples from the stored distribution of the previous tasks to avoid catastrophic forgetting.

The most notable example of the rehearsal based system is iCaRL [2]. ICaRL stores a total of K number of exemplars from previously seen classes and uses distillation loss [4] in a way similar to Learning without Forgetting [12] to retain the knowledge of previous classes. Lopez-Paz and Ranzato [13] recently proposed a rehearsal based method that allows for positive backward transfer (i.e., the performance of the system improves on older tasks as it learns new tasks). However, they assumed that task descriptors are available at test time. This makes their problem statement only a very special case of ours.

GANs have recently become popular for storing distribution of the data. Venkatesan et al. [14] and Wu et al. [3] proposed incremental learning using GANs. Instead of storing K exemplars similar to iCaRL, they propose training a GAN that can generate data for the older tasks. They then use this GAN to generate images of older classes for rehearsal. However, because of the current limitations of GANs on complex datasets, purely GAN based approaches are not competitive yet.

2.2 Knowledge Preserving Incremental Learning

The second common category of techniques for incremental learning tries to retain the knowledge of the network when learning a new class. One recent approach, proposed by Rannen et al. [15] uses auto-encoders to preserve the knowledge useful for previous tasks. In this approach, the authors propose learning an under-complete auto-encoder that learns a low dimensional manifold for each task. When learning new tasks, the model tries to preserve the projection of data in this low dimensional manifold, while allowing the feature map to freely change in other dimensions. Oquab et al. [16] proposed that it is possible to minimize forgetting by freezing the earlier and mid-level layers of models. However, this limits the representation learning capability of the system for newer classes. Some researchers also proposed approaches that kept track of important weights for older tasks, and made it harder for the model to update those weights when learning new tasks [17,18]. Finally, distillation loss [4], inspired by the work of Caruana et al. [19], can be used for retaining older knowledge. For example, Li et al. [12] showed that by computing distillation using a copy of an earlier model, it is possible to retain knowledge of older tasks. Recently, Kemker and Kanan [20] proposed a methodology inspired by the human brain to solve incremental learning. However in their work, they use a pre-trained imagenet model as feature extractor and as a result, do not tackle incremental representation learning. Finally, Rusu *et al.* [21] and Xiao [22] proposed networks that grew as new classes were added to avoid changing weights important for older tasks. Their method is not memory bounded, however.

3 Overview of iCaRL

Algorithm 1. Herding Algorithm for Instance Selection

---

1 **Input:** Trained Model M, $C_i^j \in$ Images of class i, Size k;
2 **Output:** Set containing k instances of class C_i;
3 $\forall C_i^j \in C_i$, use M to get the feature map F_i^j;
4 Let S be a null set;
5 Compute the mean of all F_i^j. Let this be F_i^{mean};
6 Select F_i^j and add it in S such that mean of selected set is closest to F_i^{mean};
7 If $|S| < k$, repeat step 5. Else, return S.

In iCaRL, Rebuffi *et al.* [2] define an incremental classifier to satisfy two properties; First, at any time, the system should be able to give a reasonable classification performance for the classes seen so far. Secondly, the memory and computation requirement of the system should stay bounded. To specify the memory bound of the system, they propose a hyper-parameter K called the memory-budget of the classifier. This budget specifies how many instances of the old data, at max, the system is allowed to store at any given time.

In their implementation, they propose storing $\frac{K}{m}$ instances of each class where m is the number of classes. They call these instances the exemplar set, and use an algorithm called herding to construct the set. During an increment, they use both the new data and the stored exemplars to compute two kinds of losses. One is the standard classification loss computed using the ground truth of the images, whereas the other is a *variant* of the distillation loss proposed by Hinton *et al.* [4]. In their implementation of the distillation loss, they don't use the final softmax layer with softened distribution as originally proposed by G. Hinton. Instead, they use sigmoid activation for converting final values to probabilities.

To compute the targets for the distillation loss, they propose making a copy of the classifier just before an increment. Finally, they use the exemplar set to approximate the mean embedding of each class in the feature space, and use this approximate mean class embedding for classification at runtime.

3.1 Contributions of iCaRL

The authors claim that their systems work well because of three main contributions.

1. They use Algorithm 1 to construct an exemplar set that best approximates the real class means in the feature space.
2. They propose a new classification algorithm, called Neared Exemplar Mean (NEM) classifier, for classification. NEM is similar to the well known Nearest Class Mean (NCM) classifier, except that instead of using true class means for classification, it uses the mean of the exemplar set. The authors claim that NEM classifier gives better results compared to the naive classifier learned through back-propagation during training.
3. They use a variation of distillation loss [4] to transfer knowledge from an older network to the newer, incremented network. However unlike Learning without Forgetting [12], they distill knowledge without softening the target probability distribution from the teacher model.

In the following Sect. 4, we go over the implementation rationale and details of the iCaRL system, and in Sect. 5, we analyze the first two contributions made by iCaRL in detail.

4   Implementation Details

We re-implemented the iCaRL paper in PyTorch [23]. To validate our implementation, we compared our results with the ones reported in the iCaRL paper and compared our implementation with the open-sourced implementations of iCaRL. We reimplemented the paper for two main reasons.

First, our goal was to develop an extensible code base over which the research community can easily implement new ideas. To this end, we made sure that the algorithms, models, and datasets modules were decoupled, and that our design choices allowed for addition of new models, algorithms, and datasets without modification of the existing code.

Second, we wanted to introduce a protocol to facilitate quick reproducibility. To achieve this, our implementation automatically generates a meta-data file corresponding to every experiment. This file contains all the parameters that were used to run the experiment, and the hash of the version of the git repository used for the experiment. This means that the minuscule meta-data file contains all the information required to reproduce the results, and by simply sharing the meta-data file along with the paper, the authors would allow others to quickly reproduce their results.

4.1   Hyper-parameters Selection

For our experiments, we used a variant of Resnet32 [24] modified to work on CIFAR dataset [25] (Similar to iCaRL). Instead of modifying the model to work on MNIST [26], we rescaled MNIST images to 32×32 to work on the same model. All the experiments on CIFAR100 are run for 70 epochs per increment with an initial learning rate of 2.0 and a momentum of 0.9. The learning rate is reduced by a factor of five at epoch 45, 60, and 68. For MNIST, we only run experiments for 10 epochs with an initial learning rate of 0.1 reduced to 0.02 and 0.004 at epoch no 5 and 8. Memory budget of 2,000 is used unless mentioned otherwise.

5   Analysis of iCaRL

As discussed above, iCaRL makes three contributions. We discuss and analyze the first two contributions in Sects. 5.1 and 5.2 respectively.

5.1   Exemplar Selection Using Herding

iCaRL uses the herding algorithm (Algorithm 1) for selecting exemplars that approximate the true class mean. We implemented the herding algorithm and tested the performance of the system by toggling herding and keeping all other parameters the same. We discovered that there was no significant difference in the results with or without herding, and random instance selection worked as well as herding. Note that Wu *et al.* [3] also did a similar experiment and failed to reproduce any improvements resulting from herding. This goes to show that while the authors think that herding helps in choosing an exemplar set that gives an exemplar mean close to the true mean, this is in fact not the case. This makes sense because images chosen to give a good approximation of class mean at increment i will not necessarily give a good approximation at increment $i+1$ because the feature representation of each image would be different after the increment.

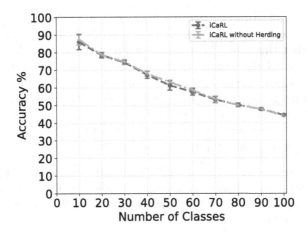

Fig. 1. Comparison of iCaRL results with and without herding. There is no significant difference between random exemplar selection and exemplar selection by herding for incremental classifier learning. Here initially the classifier is trained on the first ten classes of CIFAR100, and then ten new classes are added at each increment.

Experiment Design. We follow the same experiment design as iCaRL to compare our results. Initially, we train our classifier on the first p randomly chosen classes of CIFAR100 dataset. After training, we construct the exemplar sets by herding or random instance selection for all of the classes that the model has seen so far, and discard the remaining training data. Finally at each increment, we use the complete data of the new p classes, and only the exemplar set for the old classes.

Results. Result of our experiments on CIFAR100 with $p = 10$ can be seen in Fig. 1. By picking a different order of classes in different runs, we are able to get confidence intervals. Here the error bars correspond to one standard deviation of the multiple runs. Note that both random instance selection and herding give remarkably similar results showing that herding is not necessary for class incremental learning.

5.2 Classification Using Nearest Exemplar-Set Mean Classifier

The authors of iCaRL claim that an approximate variant of Nearest Class Mean (NCM) classifier that only uses the exemplar set for computing class mean (Let's call this NEM for Nearest Exemplar Mean) is superior to the classifier learned through back-propagation (Let's call this TC for Trained Classifier). To substantiate their claim, they experiment with both NEM and TC and demonstrate that NEM outperforms TC on a number of experiments. For smaller increments (two), NEM is particularly effective over TC in their experiments.

Hypotheses Development: Because NEM is just a special case of TC, and in theory, it is possible to learn weights such that TC and NEM are equivalent, we suspected that this large difference between the two might be because the newer classes contribute disproportionately to the loss (Because of the class imbalance; for older classes, we only have the exemplar set). To make matters worse, distillation is also known to introduce bias in training [4] because the distilled targets may not represent all classes equally.

Based on these observations, and the hypothesis that NEM performs better because of bias in training, we predict the following:

1. It would be possible to reduce the difference between TC and NEM by using higher temperature (T) when computing distillation. This is because higher values of temperature results in a softer target distribution that represents all classes more fairly.
2. It would be possible to improve TC by removing the bias by using some threshold moving strategy.

We tested both of our predictions experimentally and found conclusive support for our hypothesis.

Analysis of Prediction 1. First, we train an incremental classifier with temperature of 3 and an increment size of 2. Note that as per the authors of iCaRL, this is the worst case for TC and without the higher temperature, NEM outperforms TC by a large margin. With T = 3, however, we discovered that there was no difference between TC and NEM as shown in Fig. 2(a) (The performance was stable across a range of values of T from 3–10 in our experiments). In the original implementation of iCaRL without the temperature parameter, TC performed significantly worse as shown in Table 1.

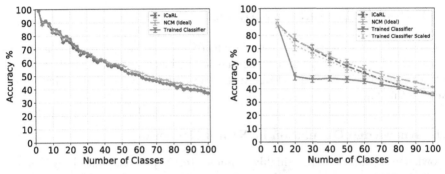

(a) Bias Removal by Temperature = 3   (b) Bias Removal by Threshold Moving

Fig. 2. (a) Comparison of iCaRL NCM with the softmax trained classifier. It is clear that by using temperature values of greater than 1, it is possible to remove the bias from the classifier and get results similar to NEM (iCaRL). (b) Effect of threshold moving (Scaling) using S on CIFAR100. We used memory-budget of 500 in this experiment to highlight the bias. Without scaling, iCaRL's NEM indeed does perform better.

Analysis of Prediction 2. Secondly, we ran an experiment with temperature = 1 but this time, we scaled the predictions of the model by a vector S to remove the bias of the classifier (We present the algorithm for computing S in Sect. 6). Without the scaling, NEM does indeed perform better as claimed by iCaRL. However with scaling, the difference between the two is insignificant. The results of the experiment are shown in Fig. 2(b).

Conclusion. From the two experiments, it is evident that while NEM does indeed perform better than TC in some cases, the difference is because of the learned bias of TC and not because NEM is inherently better for class incremental learning. This is an important distinction because in the original paper, the authors attributed the better performance of NEM to the fact that NEM classifier is not decoupled from the data representation. We show that this is not the case, and NEM performs better simply because it is more robust to the bias present at training time.

Table 1. By using softmax classifier with high temperature (T = 3), the trained classifier in our implementation performs as well as NEM. Note that we only show the results of the worst case scenario for us (i.e., the case when the difference between iCaRL and Trained Classifier was maximum).

Version	iCaRL (NEM)	Trained classifier
iCaRL implementation	57.0	36.6
Our implementation with T = 3	57.80	**58.21**

6   Dynamic Threshold Moving

In this section, we present a simple yet effective method for computing a vector for threshold moving to overcome the bias learned as a result of distillation. We first give an overview of knowledge distillation, and why distillation loss often leads to this bias.

6.1   Knowledge Distillation in Neural Networks

Knowledge distillation is a highly popular technique introduced by Hinton *et al.* [4] to train small networks with generalization performance comparable to a large ensemble of models. The authors showed that it is possible to achieve significantly better generalization performance using small neural network if the small network was optimized to approximate a pre-trained large ensemble of models on the same task. More concretely, given a large ensemble of models denoted by $F_{ens}(X)$ trained on x_i, y_i, where x_i and y_i, and a smaller neural network $F_{small}(X)$, it is better to train the smaller network on $(x_i, F_{ens}^T(x_i))$ instead of on the original data (x_i, y_i). Here parameter T denotes that the factor by which the pre-softmax output of the model is divided by before applying the final 'softmax'. In practice, it is better to jointly optimize to approximate the output of the larger model, and for the ground truth labels by a weighted loss function.

Why Distillation Can Introduce Bias: When computing distillation loss, we do not use the ground truth labels of the data points. Instead, we use the output of a model as labels. This can be problematic because the data corresponding to new classes can be more similar to some older classes than others. For example, if in an animal classifier one of the class is a whale, and others are terrestrial animals, and the new classes are also all of terrestrial animals, the older model would most probably assign a near zero probability of whale to the new images. This would introduce a bias against the whale class and result in poor performance of TC on whales. This problem of bias was noticed by Hinton *et al.* [4] in their original paper as well. However, instead of proposing a strategy to remove this bias in a practical setting, they were only interested in showing the existence of a vector that can be used to remove the bias. As a result, they found a scaling vector by doing a grid search over the *test* set. It's understood that we can not do such a search on the test set in a practical setting.

6.2   Threshold Moving

Threshold moving is a well-known technique to tackle the issue of class imbalance. Buda *et al.* [27] showed that threshold moving is effective in removing bias in ANNs. However, a measure of imbalance is required to apply the technique. In simple cases, the degree of imbalance can simply be measured by the frequency of instances of each class in the training set. In case of distillation, however, it is not clear how we can compute such a scaling vector because some classes might have zero frequency. Inspired by the loss function used for distillation, we propose that by simply measuring how much each class contributes to the target, it's possible to compute the scale vector.

6.3   Algorithm for Scale Computation

Let $F(x_i)$ be the model that outputs the probability distribution over N classes i.e., $\forall x_i \in X$, $F(x_i) = P(n|x_i)$ where $0 \leq n < N$. Suppose now that we want to find another model, $G(X)$, that gives a distribution over the old N classes and k new classes. Furthermore, we want to find G given only the data of the k new classes, and the original model $F(X)$. Finally, let y_i be ground truth of new classes and $\mathcal{D}$ be the training dataset. Li and Hoiem [12] showed that we can train such a model minimizing the following loss function:

$$\sum_{x_i, y_i \in \mathcal{D}} (1 - \gamma) \times C_{entropy}(G(x_i), y_i) + T^2\gamma \times C_{entropy}(G^T(x_i), F^T(x_i)) \quad (1)$$

where $C_{entropy}$ is the cross-entropy loss function, $\mathcal{D}$ is the training dataset and $G^T(x_i)$ is exactly the same as $G(x_i)$ except we scale the values of the final logit of the neural network by $\frac{1}{T}$ before applying the final softmax. Note that we multiply the distillation loss by T^2 as suggested by Hinton *et al.* [4] to keep the magnitude of gradients equal as we change the temperature T.

This loss function, however, results in a biased classifier as discussed above. We demonstrate that scaling the predictions of $G(X)$ by a scale factor $\mathcal{S}$ given by the following equation is effective for bias removal.

$$\mathcal{S} = \sum_{x_i, y_i \in \mathcal{D}} (1 - \gamma) \times y_i + T^2\gamma \times F^T(x_i) \quad (2)$$

Note that Eq. 2 for scale vector computation is very similar to the distillation loss described in Eq. 1. In fact, the scale vector is simply the sum of target probability distributions in the cross entropy loss.

Our final prediction $G'(X)$ is then given by:

$$G'(X) = G(x) \circ \frac{\|\mathcal{S}\|}{\mathcal{S}} \quad (3)$$

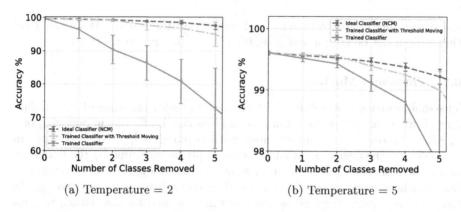

(a) Temperature = 2   (b) Temperature = 5

Fig. 3. Result of threshold moving with T = 2 and 5 on the unmodified test set of MNIST. We train our model after removing all instances of a certain no of classes (x-axis) from the train set, and only distill the knowledge of these classes from a teacher network trained on all data. Note that different scale is used for the y axis for a and b because using higher temperature results in softened targets and consequently, less bias.

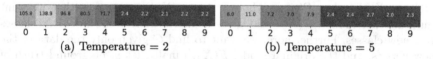

(a) Temperature = 2   (b) Temperature = 5

Fig. 4. Visualization of $\frac{\|\mathcal{S}\|}{\mathcal{S}}$ when the model is trained after removing first five MNIST classes using distillation. Note that the scaling factor is considerably larger for T = 2 than T = 5. This is because as we increase the temperature, targets are softened which reduces the bias.

where $\circ$ represents point-wise multiplication. Note that due the similarity between Eqs. 1 and 2, it is possible to compute $\mathcal{S}$ during training at no additional cost. A visualization of the scaling factor $\frac{\|\mathcal{S}\|}{\mathcal{S}}$ can be seen in Fig. 4.

6.4   Intuition Behind the Algorithm

An intuitive understanding of Eq. 2 is that we are measuring the relative representation of each class in the training targets. More concretely, we are computing the expected value of predictions made by a model trained using Eq. 1. When we scale our class predictions by the reciprocal of the expected value, we are effectively normalizing the class predictions such that expected value of predicting each class is equal. This in turn removes the bias introduced during training.

6.5   Experiment Design

To highlight and isolate the performance of our dynamic threshold moving algorithm, we first train a model on all the classes of MNIST dataset. We then train

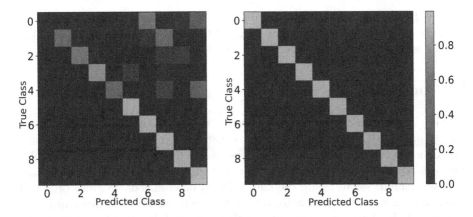

Fig. 5. Confusion matrix of results of the classifier with (right) and without (left) threshold moving with T = 2. We removed the first five classes of MNIST from the train set and only distilled the knowledge of these classes using a network trained on all classes. Without threshold moving the model struggled on the older classes. With threshold moving, however, not only was it able to classify unseen classes nearly perfectly, but also its performance did not deteriorate on new classes.

another randomly initialized model after removing p randomly chosen classes from the MNIST dataset and use the first model to distill the information of the older classes. Note that the second model does not see any examples of the removed classes at train time. Finally, we test the second model on all classes of MNIST. We run this experiment for T equal two and five (The difference is visible for other values of T as well; we only choose two due to lack of space).

6.6   Results

The results of the above-mentioned experiments can be seen in Fig. 3. As evident from the figures, the accuracy of the Trained Classifier drops significantly as we remove more classes. However by simply scaling the predictions of the classifier, it is possible to recover most of the drop in the accuracy and achieve near optimal NCM classifier results (Note that NCM Classifier uses training data of all the classes at test time to find the mean embedding and as a result, is an ideal classifier).

A more detailed picture of the bias can be seen in Fig. 5. The confusion matrix correspond to $x = 5$ in Fig. 3(a). It can be seen that without scaling, the model is struggling on the unseen classes. However after removing the bias, it can classify all 10 classes accurately. This is interesting because it shows that the model always had the discriminatory power to classify all classes and was performing poorly mainly because of the bias.

We further note that higher values of T results in smaller bias. Note that this is reflected in our computation of $\mathcal{S}$ in Eq. 2 where higher values of T lead to softened targets $F^T(x_i)$ resulting in $\mathcal{S}$ with values closer to one.

Finally, results of threshold moving on CIFAR100 are shown in Fig. 2(b). Again, we notice that our dynamic threshold algorithm is able to improve the performance of Trained Classifier to Trained Classifier Scaled.

7   Conclusion

In this paper, we analyzed the current state of the art method for class incremental learning, iCaRL, in detail. We showed that the primary reason iCaRL works well is not because it uses herding for instance selection, or Nearest Exemplar Mean classifier for classification, but rather because it uses the distillation loss on the exemplar set to retain the knowledge of older classes. We also proposed a dynamic threshold moving algorithm to fix the problem of learned bias in the presence of distillation, and verified the effectiveness of the algorithm empirically.

Finally, we release our implementation of an incremental learning framework implemented in a modern library that is easily extensible to new datasets and models, and allows for quick reproducibility of all of our results. We strongly believe that given the current state of research in the computer vision community, there is a strong need for analyzing existing work in detail, and making it easier for others to reproduce results and we hope that this work is a step in that direction. An anonymized version of our implementation is available at: https://github.com/Khurramjaved96/incremental-learning.

References

1. Wimber, M., Alink, A., Charest, I., Kriegeskorte, N., Anderson, M.C.: Retrieval induces adaptive forgetting of competing memories via cortical pattern suppression. Nat. Neurosci. **18**(4), 582 (2015)
2. Rebuffi, S.A., Kolesnikov, A., Sperl, G., Lampert, C.H.: iCaRL: incremental classifier and representation learning. In: Proceedings of the IEEE Conference on Computer Vision and Pattern Recognition, pp. 2001–2010 (2017)
3. Wu, Y., et al.: Incremental classifier learning with generative adversarial networks. CoRR abs/1802.00853 (2018)
4. Hinton, G., Vinyals, O., Dean, J.: Distilling the knowledge in a neural network. arXiv preprint arXiv:1503.02531 (2015)
5. McCloskey, M., Cohen, N.J.: Catastrophic interference in connectionist networks: the sequential learning problem. In: Psychology of Learning and Motivation, vol. 24, pp. 109–165. Elsevier (1989)
6. Ans, B., Rousset, S.: Avoiding catastrophic forgetting by coupling two reverberating neural networks. Comptes Rendus de l'Académie des Sciences-Series III-Sciences de la Vie **320**(12), 989–997 (1997)
7. French, R.M.: Catastrophic interference in connectionist networks: can it be predicted, can it be prevented? In: Advances in Neural Information Processing Systems, pp. 1176–1177 (1994)
8. French, R.M.: Catastrophic forgetting in connectionist networks. Trends Cogn. Sci. **3**(4), 128–135 (1999)

9. Goodfellow, I.J., Mirza, M., Xiao, D., Courville, A., Bengio, Y.: An empirical investigation of catastrophic forgetting in gradient-based neural networks. arXiv preprint arXiv:1312.6211 (2013)

10. Mensink, T., Verbeek, J., Perronnin, F., Csurka, G.: Metric learning for large scale image classification: generalizing to new classes at near-zero cost. In: Fitzgibbon, A., Lazebnik, S., Perona, P., Sato, Y., Schmid, C. (eds.) ECCV 2012. LNCS, pp. 488–501. Springer, Heidelberg (2012). https://doi.org/10.1007/978-3-642-33709-3_35

11. Lampert, C.H., Nickisch, H., Harmeling, S.: Attribute-based classification for zero-shot visual object categorization. IEEE Trans. Pattern Anal. Mach. Intell. **36**(3), 453–465 (2014)

12. Li, Z., Hoiem, D.: Learning without Forgetting. IEEE Trans. Pattern Anal. Mach. Intell. **40**(12), 2935–2947 (2018)

13. Lopez-Paz, D., et al.: Gradient episodic memory for continual learning. In: Advances in Neural Information Processing Systems, pp. 6470–6479 (2017)

14. Venkatesan, R., Venkateswara, H., Panchanathan, S., Li, B.: A strategy for an uncompromising incremental learner. arXiv preprint arXiv:1705.00744 (2017)

15. Rannen Triki, A., Aljundi, R., Blaschko, M.B., Tuytelaars, T.: Encoder based lifelong learning. arXiv preprint arXiv:1704.01920 (2017)

16. Oquab, M., Bottou, L., Laptev, I., Sivic, J.: Learning and transferring mid-level image representations using convolutional neural networks. In: 2014 IEEE Conference on Computer Vision and Pattern Recognition (CVPR), pp. 1717–1724. IEEE (2014)

17. Zenke, F., Poole, B., Ganguli, S.: Improved multitask learning through synaptic intelligence. arXiv preprint arXiv:1703.04200 (2017)

18. Kirkpatrick, J., et al.: Overcoming catastrophic forgetting in neural networks. Proc. Natl. Acad. Sci. **114**(13), 3521–3526 (2017)

19. Buciluă, C., Caruana, R., Niculescu-Mizil, A.: Model compression. In: Proceedings of the 12th ACM SIGKDD International Conference on Knowledge Discovery and Data Mining, pp. 535–541. ACM (2006)

20. Kemker, R., Kanan, C.: FearNet: brain-inspired model for incremental learning. arXiv preprint arXiv:1711.10563 (2017)

21. Rusu, A.A., et al.: Progressive neural networks. arXiv preprint arXiv:1606.04671 (2016)

22. Xiao, T., Zhang, J., Yang, K., Peng, Y., Zhang, Z.: Error-driven incremental learning in deep convolutional neural network for large-scale image classification. In: Proceedings of the 22nd ACM international conference on Multimedia, pp. 177–186. ACM (2014)

23. Paszke, A., et al.: Automatic differentiation in PyTorch (2017)

24. He, K., Zhang, X., Ren, S., Sun, J.: Deep residual learning for image recognition. CoRR abs/1512.03385 (2015)

25. Krizhevsky, A., Hinton, G.: Learning multiple layers of features from tiny images (2009)

26. LeCun, Y.: The MNIST database of handwritten digits. http://yann.lecun.com/exdb/mnist/

27. Buda, M., Maki, A., Mazurowski, M.A.: A systematic study of the class imbalance problem in convolutional neural networks. arXiv preprint arXiv:1710.05381 (2017)

Common Self-polar Triangle of Concentric Conics for Light Field Camera Calibration

Qi Zhang and Qing Wang[✉]

School of Computer Science, Northwestern Polytechnical University,
Xi'an 710072, China
qwang@nwpu.edu.cn

Abstract. Accurate light field camera calibration plays an important role in various applications. Instead of a planar checkerboard, we propose to calibrate light field camera using a concentric conics pattern. In this paper, we explore the property and reconstruction of common self-polar triangle with respect to concentric circle and ellipse. A light field projection model is formulated to compute out an effective linear initial solution for both intrinsic and extrinsic parameters. In addition, a 4-parameter radial distortion model is presented considering different view points in light field. Finally, we establish a cost function based on Sampson error for non-linear optimization. Experimental results on both synthetic data and real light field have verified the effectiveness and robustness of the proposed algorithm.

Keywords: Computational photography and video ·
Light field camera calibration · Common self-polar triangle

1 Introduction

Light field camera [23] captures spatial and angular information of light rays in the space, which provides multi-view observations of a scene with a single shot. Sophisticated post-processing techniques [14,22,27,31–33,38,39] ranging from digital refocusing to depth estimation have been introduced in decades. It is a crucial step to calibrate light field camera in various applications, such as registration [16], 3D reconstruction [36,37], light field stitching [1,9,26] and visual metrology [5,7].

In general, there are three popular types of meta-patterns for camera calibration, which are points, lines and conics. Existing approaches [2,3,6,15,29,30, 34,35] usually utilize checkerboard to detect corner points or line features for light field camera calibration. However, several open issues still remain. Firstly, it is difficult to extract accurate locations of corner points due to the effect of noise and the quality of sub-aperture image. Secondly, considering the fact that the line feature [2] is detected from micro-lens images in light field raw data

Supported by NSFC under Grant 61531014.

C. V. Jawahar et al. (Eds.): ACCV 2018, LNCS 11366, pp. 18–33, 2019.
https://doi.org/10.1007/978-3-030-20876-9_2

directly, the low resolution of micro-lens image affects the precision of line features. Thirdly, the 12-free-parameter intrinsic matrix proposed by Dansereau *et al.* [6] is redundant and dependent which makes it hard to represent the projection except points.

In this paper, a novel light field camera calibration method is proposed. Compared with point and line, conic has two advantages: one is that conic is well studied in mathematics and can be simply represented by a 3×3 matrix, the other is that conics can be detected and estimated robustly by existing algorithms. Although conic pattern has been used to calibrate traditional camera over decades, few attentions are drawn to light field camera calibration. In addition, several tradition camera calibration methods only consider the estimation of intrinsic parameters without distortion model and optimization, which is not appropriate for light field camera. The extrinsic parameters and distortion model are necessary for distortion rectification and 3D reconstruction. Consequently, instead of using the checkerboard, we creatively design a concentric conics pattern with known size (*i.e.* a circle and a ellipse with the same center) for light field camera calibration. We first exploit the property and reconstruction of self-polar triangle which is shared by concentric circle and ellipse. In addition, with the introduction of light field projection model, an effective linear initial solution for both intrinsic and extrinsic parameters is computed, making use of the property of common self-polar triangle. Furthermore, considering the effect of shifted view, a 4-parameter radial distortion model is defined. We present an effective Sampson cost function for optimization. Finally, we illustrate empirical performances in calibrating synthetic light field camera as well as commercial Illum light field cameras [20]. Quantitative and qualitative analyses verify the effectiveness and robustness of the proposed method.

Our main contributions are:

(1) The property of self-polar triangle which is common to concentric circle and ellipse is explored.
(2) A creative conics pattern which includes circles and ellipses is designed for light field camera calibration.
(3) An effective intrinsic and extrinsic calibration algorithm is proposed, including a linear initial solution, a 4-parameter radial distortion model for light field camera and a novel Sampson cost function for optimization.

2   Related Work

Light Field Calibration. Many research groups [2,3,6,15,29,30,34,35] have explored various light field camera calibration methods making use of the checkerboard or dot grid pattern in decades, where multiple viewpoints or micro-lens images are easy to be synthesized to describe the ray. A plane and parallax framework [30] is proposed to calibrate the camera array system. Johannsen *et al.* [15] exhibit metric calibration and depth distortion for the focused light field camera [25] through a dot grid pattern with know size. In addition, Thomason et al. [29] focus on geometrical distribution of micro-lens array and estimated its position and orientation.

Recently, Dansereau et al. [6] propose a light field camera model from a conventional pinhole lenslet and thin-lens model to calibrate light field camera through checkerboard pattern. They derive a 12-free-parameter intrinsic matrix to correspond recorded pixels to light rays in the 3D space (in nonlinear optimization, 10 intrinsic parameters and 5 distortion coefficients are finally estimated). Nevertheless, the calibration method is initialized by a traditional camera calibration algorithm which is not effective to generate all intrinsic parameters. More importantly, since the intrinsic matrix has redundancy and dependency, the decoded rays transformed through intrinsic matrix do not keep regular sampling. Differing from the calibration based on sub-aperture images, Bok et al. propose to directly extract line feature from the raw data for initial estimation of intrinsic parameters [2,3]. However, the detectability of line feature plays a crucial role to calibrate light field camera accurately (in practice, the checkerboard should be shot under an unfocused status in order to make the measurements detectable).

More recently, Zhang et al. [34] propose a simplified projective model on the reconstructed scene in the 4D light field. They established light field camera geometry for calibration by a 4-parameter model. In addition, a parallel bi-planar dot grid board is designed to provide prior scene points for calibration. This model just assumes that the image and view planes are Euclidean coordinates having equal scales in both axial directions. Nevertheless, there is additional possibility that light field camera contains non-square pixels. For this reason, unequal scale factors are introduced in each direction to explore the relationship between the pixels recorded by the camera and the decoded rays in the 3D space. Zhang et al. [35] propose a multi-projection-center model with 6 intrinsic parameters for light field camera. A 3D projective transformation is deduced to describe the relationship between geometric structure and the light field camera coordinates. Based on the camera model and projective transformation, a light field camera calibration method is proposed to verify the effectiveness of multi-projection-center model.

Conics for Calibration. Conic patterns have been utilized in tradition camera calibration over decades. Quan et al. [24] geometrically propose the invariants of two coplanar conics through the common self-polar triangle of two concentric circles. Kim et al. [17] explore the projective properties of the feature consisted of two concentric circles. They put algebraic and geometric constraints on the linear combination of two concentric circle images to recover the imaged circle center and circular points respectively. Previous approaches usually recover the center of conic and vanishing line in separate steps.

Recently, Huang et al. [12] explore properties of the common self-polar triangle of concentric circles. Making use of these properties, the imaged circle center and vanishing line of support plane can be recovered simultaneously. These properties can also be applied to estimate the intrinsic parameters of traditional cam-

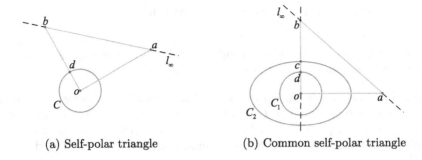

(a) Self-polar triangle   (b) Common self-polar triangle

Fig. 1. An illustration of self-polar triangle and common self-polar triangle. o is the center of conics, and l_∞ is the line at infinity. (a) $\triangle oab$ is the self-polar triangle with respect to C. (b) $\triangle oab$ is the common self-polar triangle with respect to concentric circle C_1 and ellipse C_2.

era. In addition, Huang *et al.* [13] investigate the location features of the common self-polar triangle of separate ellipses. Then, a novel approach for homography estimation is proposed. However, these methods only consider the estimation of intrinsic parameters. Little attention has been paid to estimate and optimize extrinsic parameters and lens distortion of light field camera based on concentric conics pattern simultaneously, which are also necessary for camera calibration. In the work, considering that the conic is well studied in mathematics and easy to be represented by matrix, we explore the property of concentric conics for light field camera calibration.

3   Common Self-polar Triangle of Concentric Conics

A point x and conic C define a line $l = Cx$ which is described as *pole-polar relationship* [11]. The line l is called the *polar* of x with respect to C, and the point x is the *pole* of l with respect to C.

    Self-polar triangle is defined as, just as Fig. 1(a) shown, the vertices of the triangle are the poles of a conic and their respective polars form its opposite sides [19,28]. A self-polar triangle which is shared by several conics is what we called *common self-polar triangle*, as shown in Fig. 1(b).

    Three theorems are illustrated for proving the property of common self-polar triangle.

- The polar line $l = Cx$ of the point x with respect to a conic C intersects the conic in two points. The two lines tangent to C at these points intersect at x.
- If a point x is on the polar of y, then y is on the polar of x.
- The circle has infinite self-polar triangles which are right triangles. These triangles share one common vertex and the opposite side of this vertex lies on the same line which are the center of circle and the line at infinity respectively.

3.1 Property of Common Self-polar Triangle

Property 1. The concentric circle and ellipse have and only have one common self-polar triangle which is right triangle. The three sides of this common self-polar triangle are major axis, minor axis and the line at infinity.

Proof. This property is elucidated in Fig. 1(b). Consider the point o denoting the center of concentric circle C_1 and ellipse C_2. Then, we obtain pole-polar relationships (*i.e.* $l_\infty \sim C_1 o$ and $l_\infty \sim C_2 o$, where $\sim$ refers to equality up to a scale) [11]. Obviously, o and l_∞ are a common pole-polar which is shared by C_1 and C_2.

Then, consider a point a on l_∞. The polars of a with respect to C_1 and C_2 are l_1 and l_2 respectively which go through the center of concentric conics (*i.e.* $l_1 \sim C_1 a$, $l_2 \sim C_2 a$). Consider l_1 and l_2 intersecting with C_1 and C_2 at points c and d respectively. It is noticed that l_1 and l_2 intersect at center point o. According to the theorem mentioned above, $\triangle oab$ is a self-polar triangle and a right triangle with the assumption that l_1 intersects with l_∞ at point b.

If $\triangle oab$ is the common self-polar triangle of C_1 and C_2, then l_1 and l_2 are common lines which intersect at b on infinite line. According to the theorem of self-polar triangle with respect to circle, we have

$$l_{oa} \perp l_{ob}, \ l_{ad} \perp l_{ob}, \ l_{ad} \parallel l_{ac} \Rightarrow l_{ac} \perp l_{ob}. \tag{1}$$

Meanwhile, l_{ac} is also the tangent line of ellipse C_2 which is orthogonal to l_{ob}. As a result, the line l_{ob} is the major or minor axis of ellipse C_2.

If l_{oc} is the major or minor axis of ellipse C_2, then we obtain

$$l_{ac} \perp l_{oc}, \ l_{ad} \perp l_{od}, \ l_{ad} \parallel l_{ac} \Rightarrow l_{oc} \parallel l_{od}. \tag{2}$$

Due to the same point o which is common to l_1 and l_2, $\triangle oab$ is the only one common self-polar triangle shared by concentric circle C_1 and ellipse C_2. □

3.2 Reconstruction of Common Self-polar Triangle

According to the *Property* 1, we find that the common self-polar triangle of concentric circle and ellipse has three special sides which are major axis, minor axis and the line at infinity. In addition, one vertex of this common self-polar triangle lies at the center of concentric circle and ellipse. In this section, we propose a method to reconstruct the only one common self-polar triangle of concentric circle and ellipse. Without loss of generality, the matrix representations of the circle C_1 and ellipse C_2 are

$$C_1 = \begin{bmatrix} 1 & 0 & -x_0 \\ 0 & 1 & -y_0 \\ -x_0 & -y_0 & x_0^2 + y_0^2 - r^2 \end{bmatrix} \text{ and } C_2 = \begin{bmatrix} \dfrac{1}{a^2} & 0 & -\dfrac{x_0}{a^2} \\ 0 & \dfrac{1}{b^2} & -\dfrac{y_0}{b^2} \\ -\dfrac{x_0}{a^2} & -\dfrac{y_0}{b^2} & \dfrac{x_0^2}{a^2} + \dfrac{y_0^2}{b^2} - 1 \end{bmatrix}, \tag{3}$$

where the center of concentric conics is $o = (x_0, y_0)$. The radius of C_1 is r, and the major and minor axes of C_2 are a and b respectively.

The *Property* 1 substantiates that C_1 and C_2 only have one common self-polar triangle. In other words, the concentric circle and ellipse have three common pole-polars. What is more, we assume that the point x and line l are satisfied with the pole-polar relationship of C_1 and C_2 (*i.e.* $l = C_1 x$ and $l = \lambda C_2 x$, λ is a scale factor). These relationships can be simplified as,

$$\left(\lambda I - C_2^{-1} C_1\right) x = 0, \tag{4}$$

where the x is the common pole for C_1 and C_2. The solutions of Eq. (4) are the eigenvectors of $C_2^{-1} C_1$. We obtain

$$\begin{aligned}
\lambda_1 = a^2 &\iff e_1 = (1,0,0)^\top, \\
\lambda_2 = b^2 &\iff e_2 = (0,1,0)^\top, \\
\lambda_3 = r^2 &\iff e_3 = (x_0, y_0, 1)^\top,
\end{aligned} \tag{5}$$

where λ_1, λ_2 and λ_3 are three different eigenvalues of $C_2^{-1} C_1$ and e_1, e_2 and e_3 are their corresponding eigenvectors. From Eq. (5), the only one common self-polar triangle of concentric circle and ellipse is reconstructed. The major and minor axes of ellipse are intersected with infinite line at the eigenvectors e_1 and e_2, which represent the direction of major and minor axes respectively. Due to different λ_1 and λ_2, the corresponding eigenvectors e_1 and e_2 are easy to distinguish for calculating the camera rotation parameters. What is more, the eigenvector e_3 is the center of concentric circle and ellipse.

4 Light Field Camera Calibration

4.1 Light Field Projection Model and Its Coordinates

Light field cameras, especially micro-lens array assembled inside, which are innovated from traditional 2D camera, record the 3D world in different but similar rays. With the shifted view, light field camera maps the 3D world to many sub-aperture images. In general, the ray recorded in the 4D light field is parameterized in a *relative* two-parallel-plane coordinates [18], where $Z = 0$ denotes the view plane and $Z = f$ for the image plane. According to the multi-projection-center model [35] which is proposed to describe light field camera, a 3D point $X = (X, Y, Z)^\top$ is mapped to the pixel (x, y) in the image plane,

$$\lambda \begin{bmatrix} x \\ y \\ 1 \end{bmatrix} = \begin{bmatrix} f & 0 & 0 & -fs \\ 0 & f & 0 & -ft \\ 0 & 0 & 1 & 0 \end{bmatrix} \begin{bmatrix} X \\ Y \\ Z \\ 1 \end{bmatrix}. \tag{6}$$

In addition, consider X_w denoting the scene point in the world coordinates, the transformation between world and camera coordinates is described by a rotation $R = (r_1, r_2, r_3) \in SO(3)$ and a translation $t = (t_x, t_y, t_z)^\top \in \mathbb{R}^3$, formulated as $X = R X_w + t$.

The ray captured by the camera is expressed as $p = (i, j, u, v)$ in term of pixel dimension, where (i, j) are the *absolute* indices of the view, and (u, v) are the *relative* pixel indices of sub-aperture image at the view (i, j). The light field $L(i, j, u, v)$ recorded by the camera is transformed into a normalized (*i.e.*, the spacing f between two planes is set to unit length for simplicity) undistorted physical light field $L(s, t, x, y)$ by a homogeneous decoding matrix $D \in \mathbb{R}^{5 \times 5}$ [35],

$$
\begin{bmatrix} s \\ t \\ x \\ y \\ 1 \end{bmatrix} = \underbrace{\begin{bmatrix} k_i & 0 & 0 & 0 & 0 \\ 0 & k_j & 0 & 0 & 0 \\ 0 & 0 & k_u & 0 & u_0 \\ 0 & 0 & 0 & k_v & v_0 \\ 0 & 0 & 0 & 0 & 1 \end{bmatrix}}_{=:D} \begin{bmatrix} i \\ j \\ u \\ v \\ 1 \end{bmatrix} = \begin{bmatrix} K_{ij} & O_{2 \times 3} \\ O_{3 \times 2} & K_{uv} \end{bmatrix} \begin{bmatrix} i \\ j \\ u \\ v \\ 1 \end{bmatrix}, \tag{7}
$$

where $(k_i, k_j, k_u, k_v, u_0, v_0)$ are intrinsic parameters of a light field camera. (k_i, k_j) are scale factors for s and t axes in the view plane and (k_u, k_v) for x and y axes in the image plane respectively. $(-u_0/k_u, -v_0/k_v)$ represent the coordinates of principal point in the sub-aperture image.

4.2   Initialization

The relationship between sub-aperture image pixel (u, v) and 3D world point X_w is extended by Eqs. (6), (7) and extrinsic parameters $[R|t]$,

$$
(u, v, 1)^\top \sim \underbrace{K_{uv}^{-1} [r_1, r_2, r_3, t - t_{st}]}_{=:P(s,t)} (X_w, Y_w, Z_w, 1)^\top, \tag{8}
$$

where $\sim$ refers to the equality up to a scale, $t_{st} = (s, t, 0)^\top$ and $(s, t)^\top = K_{ij}(i, j)^\top$. Moreover, the projection between the plane at infinity and sub-aperture image can be described by planar homography $H_\infty = K_{uv}^{-1} R$. Note that this projection is independent to the shifted view and the position of light field camera. Since the absolute conic Ω_∞ is on the plane at infinity [11], the sub-aperture image of absolute conic in light field can be described by the conic $\omega = K_{uv}^\top K_{uv}$. More importantly, $u_a^\top \omega u_b = 0$ only if the image points u_a and u_b correspond to the orthogonal directions.

Without loss of generality, we assume the conic pattern is on the plane $Z_w = 0$ in the world coordinates. Consequently, Eq. (8) is simplified as,

$$
(u, v, 1)^\top \sim \underbrace{K_{uv}^{-1} [r_1, r_2, t - t_{st}]}_{=:H_{ij}} (X_w, Y_w, 1)^\top, \tag{9}
$$

where H_{ij} is the planar homography. Supposing $\tilde{C}_1$ and $\tilde{C}_2$ represent the projections of concentric circle and ellipse in the sub-aperture image of the view (i, j), we have

$$
\tilde{C}_1 \sim H_{ij}^{-\top} C_1 H_{ij}^{-1} \quad \text{and} \quad \tilde{C}_2 \sim H_{ij}^{-\top} C_2 H_{ij}^{-1}, \tag{10}
$$

where C_1 and C_2 are described as Eq. (3) in the world coordinates respectively. Computing the product $\tilde{C}_2^{-1} \tilde{C}_1$, we obtain

$$
\tilde{C}_2^{-1} \tilde{C}_1 \sim \left(H_{ij}^{-\top} C_2 H_{ij}^{-1} \right)^{-1} \left(H_{ij}^{-\top} C_1 H_{ij}^{-1} \right) = H_{ij} \left(C_2^{-1} C_1 \right) H_{ij}^{-1}. \tag{11}
$$

As illustrated in Eqs. (5) and (11), $\widetilde{C}_2^{-1}\widetilde{C}_1$ is the similar matrix of $C_2^{-1}C_1$, which means they have the same eigenvalues (*i.e.*, λ_1, λ_2 and λ_3). In addition, the corresponding eigenvectors can be projected by H_{ij} (*i.e.*, $e_k^{(i,j)} \sim H_{ij}e_k$, $k = 1, 2, 3$). According to the *Property* 1 and Eq. (5), the only common self-polar triangle of sub-aperture image is reconstructed. Furthermore, the vanishing lines and center of concentric ellipse are recovered for light field camera calibration. More importantly, the major and minor axes (*i.e.*, $e_1^{(i,j)}$ and $e_2^{(i,j)}$) of ellipse in the sub-aperture image of the view (i, j) imply the rotation of light field camera. Due to different eigenvalues λ_1 and λ_2, the corresponding eigenvectors $e_1^{(i,j)}$ and $e_2^{(i,j)}$ are easy to distinguish for calculating r_1 and r_2 respectively.

Based on the theorem that there are infinite right self-polar triangles with respect to the circle, two self-polar triangles of the circle are randomly formed to generate the conjugate pairs with respect to ω,

$$u_a^\top \omega u_b = 0 \iff u_a^\top K_{uv}^\top K_{uv} u_b = 0, \tag{12}$$

where u_a and u_b are the points on the vanishing line. In addition, u_a and u_b represent the direction of two cathetuses with respect to self-polar triangle. Once ω is computed, it is easy to estimate K_{uv} to obtain intrinsic parameters except k_i and k_j by Cholesky factorization [10]. Besides, the rest intrinsic parameters and extrinsic parameters of different poses can be obtained as follows,

$$\tau = \sqrt{\frac{1}{2}\left(\frac{r^2}{|\lambda_{\widehat{C}_1}|} + \frac{b^2}{|\lambda_{\widehat{C}_2}|}\right)}, \quad \widehat{C}_1 = \frac{\hat{K}_{uv}^{-1}\widetilde{C}_1\hat{K}_{uv}}{\|\hat{K}_{uv}^{-1}\widetilde{C}_1\hat{K}_{uv}\|}, \quad \widehat{C}_2 = \frac{\hat{K}_{uv}^{-1}\widetilde{C}_2\hat{K}_{uv}}{\|\hat{K}_{uv}^{-1}\widetilde{C}_2\hat{K}_{uv}\|}, \tag{13}$$

$$\begin{bmatrix} I_{3\times3} & O_{3\times3} & O_{3\times5} \\ O_{3\times3} & I_{3\times3} & O_{3\times5} \\ & & \begin{array}{cc} -i & 0 \\ 0 & -j \\ 0 & 0 \end{array} \\ x_0 I_{3\times3} & y_0 I_{3\times3} & I_{3\times3} \end{bmatrix} \begin{bmatrix} r_1 \\ r_2 \\ t \\ k_i \\ k_j \end{bmatrix} = \begin{bmatrix} \dfrac{\hat{K}_{uv}e_1^{(i,j)}}{\|\hat{K}_{uv}e_1^{(i,j)}\|} \\ \dfrac{\hat{K}_{uv}e_2^{(i,j)}}{\|\hat{K}_{uv}e_2^{(i,j)}\|} \\ \tau\dfrac{\hat{K}_{uv}e_3^{(i,j)}}{\|\hat{K}_{uv}e_3^{(i,j)}\|} \end{bmatrix}, \tag{14}$$

$$r_3 = r_1 \times r_2, \tag{15}$$

where $\|\cdot\|$ denotes L_2 norm. $\hat{K}_{uv}$ is derived by intrinsic parameters in Eq. (12). $\lambda_{\widehat{C}_1}$ and $\lambda_{\widehat{C}_2}$ are the smallest eigenvalues of $\widehat{C}_1$ and $\widehat{C}_2$ respectively. τ describes the scale factor. (x_0, y_0) is the center of concentric conics in the world coordinates. $e_1^{(i,j)}$, $e_2^{(i,j)}$ and $e_3^{(i,j)}$ are the eigenvectors of $\widetilde{C}_2^{-1}\widetilde{C}_1$ on the view (i, j) corresponding to e_1, e_2 and e_3 depending on different eigenvalues (in Eq. (5)).

4.3 Distortion Model

In light field camera, there exists radial distortion on the image plane and sampling distortion on the view plane because of special sampling design of two-parallel-plane. In this paper, owing to the assumption that angular sampling is ideal without distortion, we only consider radial distortion on the image plane. The distorted $(\tilde{x}, \tilde{y})$ are rectified by the undistorted (x, y) under the view (s, t),

$$\begin{cases} \tilde{x} = (1 + k_1 r_{xy}^2 + k_2 r_{xy}^4)x + k_3 s \\ \tilde{y} = (1 + k_1 r_{xy}^2 + k_2 r_{xy}^4)y + k_4 t \end{cases}, \tag{16}$$

where $r_{xy}^2 = x^2 + y^2$ and the undistorted (x, y) are the projected points from the calibration pattern by intrinsic parameters (k_i, k_j) and extrinsic parameters according to Eq. (6). k_1 and k_2 regulate conventional radial distortion in light field camera. Compared with existing radial distortion of light field camera, k_3 and k_4 are added to represent the distortion affected by the shifted view. In summary, we utilize $\boldsymbol{k}^d = (k_1, k_2, k_3, k_4)$ to denote distortion vector.

4.4   Non-linear Optimization

The initial solution computed by the linear method is refined via non-linear optimization. We define a cost function based on Sampson error [11] to acquire the non-linear solution,

$$\sum_{p=1}^{\#pose} \sum_{n=1}^{\#conic} \sum_{i=1}^{\#view} \frac{\left| \tilde{\boldsymbol{u}}_i^\top \left(\mathcal{P}, \boldsymbol{k}^d, \boldsymbol{R}_p, \boldsymbol{t}_p, \boldsymbol{C}_{w,n}\right) \boldsymbol{C}_i \tilde{\boldsymbol{u}}_i \left(\mathcal{P}, \boldsymbol{k}^d, \boldsymbol{R}_p, \boldsymbol{t}_p, \boldsymbol{C}_{w,n}\right) \right|}{2 \| \left(\boldsymbol{C}_i \tilde{\boldsymbol{u}}_i \left(\mathcal{P}, \boldsymbol{k}^d, \boldsymbol{R}_p, \boldsymbol{t}_p, \boldsymbol{C}_{w,n}\right) \right) \|}, \tag{17}$$

where $\tilde{\boldsymbol{u}}$ is the projection of point on $\boldsymbol{C}_{w,n}$ according to Eqs. (6) and (7), followed by the distortion according to Eq. (16). $\boldsymbol{C}_{w,n}$ describes the conics in the world coordinates as Eq. (3). $\mathcal{P}$ and $\boldsymbol{k}^d$ represent intrinsic parameters and distortion vector respectively. Moreover, $\boldsymbol{R}_p$, $\boldsymbol{t}_p$ are extrinsic parameters at each position, where $\boldsymbol{R}_p$ is parameterized by Rodrigues formula [8]. In addition, the Jacobian matrix of cost function is simple and sparse. This non-linear cost function can be solved using Levenberg-Marquardt algorithm based on trust region method [21]. Matlab's lsqnonlin is utilized to carry out the non-linear optimization. The calibration algorithm of light field camera is summarized in Algorithm 1.

5   Experiments

5.1   Simulated Data

In order to evaluate the performance of the proposed method, we simulate a light field camera, whose intrinsic parameters are referred to Eq. (7) (*i.e.* $k_i = 1.4e{-}4$, $k_j = 1.5e{-}4$, $k_u = 2.0e{-}3$, $k_v = 1.9e{-}3$, $u_0 = -0.59$, $v_0 = -0.52$). These parameters are close to the setting of an Illum camera so that we obtain plausible input close to real-world scenario. Three types of calibration patterns are illustrated in Fig. 2.

Performance w.r.t. the Noise Level. In this experiment, we employ the measurements of 3 poses and 7×7 views to demonstrate the robustness of calibration algorithm with three types of calibration patterns. The rotation angles

Algorithm 1. Light Field Camera Calibration Algorithm.

Input: Concentric conics C_1 and C_2 and projected conics $\widetilde{C}_1$ and $\widetilde{C}_2$ in each view.
Output: Intrinsic parameters $\mathcal{P} = (k_i, k_j, k_u, k_v, u_0, v_0)$;
    Extrinsic parameters $\mathbf{R}_p, \mathbf{t}_p (1 \leq p \leq P)$;
    Distortion vector $\mathbf{d} = (k_1, k_2, k_3, k_4)^\top$.
1: **for** $p = 1$ to P **do**
2:     **for** each view (i, j) **do**
3:         Obtain the eigenvectors $(e_1^{(i,j)}, e_2^{(i,j)}, e_3^{(i,j)})$ of $\widetilde{C}_2^{-1}\widetilde{C}_1$.   ▷ Eq. (11)
4:     **end for**
5: **end for**
6: Obtain four intrinsic parameters (k_u, k_v, u_0, v_0) by Cholesky factorization ▷ Eq. (12)
7: **for** $p = 1$ to P **do**
8:     Get extrinsic parameters $\mathbf{R}_p$ and $\mathbf{t}_p$ ▷ Eqs. (13-15)
9: **end for**
10: Obtain other two intrinsic parameters (k_i, k_j) ▷ Eqs. (13,14)
11: Initialize distortion coefficient $\mathbf{d} = (0, 0, 0, 0)^\top$
12: Create the cost function according to intrinsic parameters, extrinsic parameters
    and distortion coefficient   ▷ Eq. (17)
13: Obtain optimized results using nonlinear LM algorithm

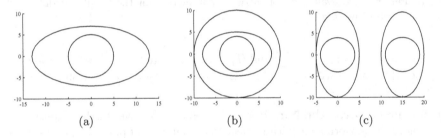

        (a)   (b)   (c)

Fig. 2. Three types of calibration patterns evaluated in experiments (unit: *cm*). (a) Two concentric conics. The major and minor axes of ellipse are 13 cm and 7 cm. The radius of circle is 5 cm. (b) Three concentric conics. The radiuses of big circle and small circle are 10 cm and 4 cm respectively. The major and minor axes of ellipse are 8 cm and 5 cm. (c) Two sets of concentric conics. The major and minor axes of ellipse are 8 cm and 5 cm. The radius of circle is 4 cm. The concentric center of right set is (15, 0).

of 3 poses are $(-21°, -14°, 6°)$, $(9°, 5°, 12°)$ and $(-12°, 11°, -4°)$ respectively. We choose 100 points on each conic image to fit the conics, which are projected from the calibration pattern by Eq. (6). Gaussian noise with zero mean and σ standard deviation is added to these points. We vary σ from 0.1 to 1.5 pixels with a 0.1 pixel step. For each noise level, 150 independent trials are conducted. The accuracy is evaluated by the average of relative errors with ground truth. As illustrated in Fig. 3, the errors almost linearly increase with noise level. When the level of noise is fixed, the relative errors are decreased with the number of conics. For the noise level $\sigma = 0.5$, which is larger than normal noise in practical

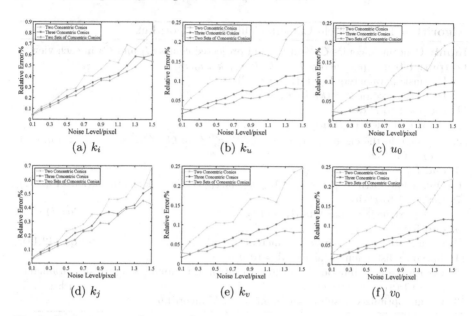

Fig. 3. Performance evaluation of intrinsic parameters on the simulated data with different levels of noise σ.

calibration, the errors of (k_i, k_j) and (k_u, k_v, u_0, v_0) are less than 0.28% and 0.1% respectively, which verifies the robustness of the proposed calibration method to high noise level.

Performance w.r.t. the Number of Poses and Views. In this experiment, we explore the performance with respect to the number of poses and views based on the calibration pattern in Fig. 2(a). We also choose 100 points on each conic. We vary the number of poses from 2 to 8 and the number of views from 3×3 to 7×7. For each combination of pose and view, 100 trails with independent poses are performed by adding the Gaussian noise with zero mean and a standard deviation of 0.5 pixel. The rotation angles are randomly generated from $-30°$ to $30°$. The average relative errors of calibration results with increasing measurements are shown in Fig. 4. The relative errors decrease with the number of views once the number of poses is fixed. Furthermore, the errors reduce with the number of poses. Especially, when $\#pose \geq 4$ and $\#view \geq 5 \times 5$, all relative errors are less than 0.5%, which further exhibits the effectiveness of the proposed method.

5.2   Real Data

The experimental data on real scene light fields are captured by Illum cameras. Two calibration patterns with different configurations and the number of conics are utilized, including a calibration pattern of two concentric conics (seeing Fig. 2(a)) for Illum-1 and Illum-2 and a calibration pattern of three concentric conics (seeing Fig. 2(b)) for Illum-3 and Illum-4. The configurations of two

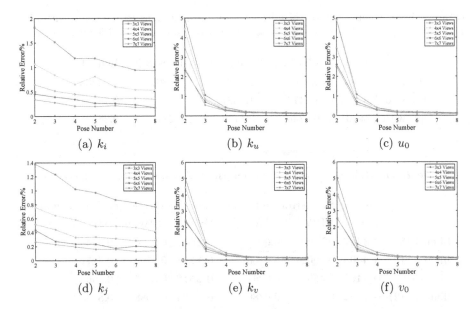

Fig. 4. Performance evaluation of intrinsic parameters on the simulated data with different numbers of poses and views.

patterns are also shown in Fig. 2. In the collected datasets, the range does not exceed 60 cm. A white image which is provided by camera is required for locating lenslet image centers and correcting vignetting. After the necessary preprocessing described in [6] (including demosaicing, aligning of the lenslet images and interpolation), the raw 2D lenslet image of light field camera is decoded to a 4D light field representation (*i.e.*, $L(i, j, u, v)$).

The Canny edge detector [4] is utilized to detect the conic from sub-aperture image on the view (i, j). Although the conics appear in all sub-aperture images, the middle 11×11 views are used (15×15 views in total) to produce accurate results. Table 1 summarizes the root mean square (RMS) Sampson errors, as described in Eq. (17), at three calibration stages. Considering the simpleness of conic detection, the proposed method provides an acceptable initial calibration performance. Furthermore, it is more important that the Sampson errors obviously decrease on the item of optimization without distortion, which verifies the effectiveness of cost function. It is noticed that the proposed method achieves smaller Sampson errors once the distortion model is introduced in the optimization. In addition, we compare the proposed method in RMS ray reprojection and re-projection error with state-of-the-art methods, including DPW by Dansereau *et al.* [6] and BJW by Bok *et al.* [3], as illustrated in Table 2. The intersections of major and minor axes with conics and the center of conics are utilized to calculate re-projection error and ray re-projection error. As exhibited in Table 2, the errors of the proposed method are obviously smaller than those of DPW and BJW. Consequently, such optimization results quantitatively substantiate the effectiveness and robustness of light field calibration using conic pattern.

Table 1. RMS Sampson errors of initialization, optimizations without and with distortion (unit: *pixel*). The (N) denotes the number of light fields used for calibration.

	Illum-1 (8)	Illum-2 (10)	Illum-3 (9)	Illum-4 (12)
Initial	5.2401	6.6361	4.1867	5.0426
Opt. w/o distortion	1.1173	1.1081	0.7818	0.7838
Opt. with distortion	0.1746	0.1778	0.2879	0.2889

Table 2. The RMS errors evaluation compared with state-of-the-art methods.

	Re-projection error unit: *pixel*			Ray re-projection error unit: *mm*		
	Ours	DPW [6]	BJW [3]	Ours	DPW [6]	BJW [3]
Illum-1 (8)	**0.3647**	0.5060	0.6084	**0.1692**	0.2736	0.3443
Illum-2 (10)	**0.3805**	0.4902	0.6156	**0.1788**	0.2704	0.3277
Illum-3 (9)	**0.4468**	0.4591	0.6947	**0.2512**	0.3007	0.3963
Illum-4 (12)	**0.4482**	0.4530	0.6780	**0.2471**	0.2988	0.8336

Table 3. Intrinsic parameter estimation results of our datasets.

	Illum-1	Illum-2	Illum-3	Illum-4
k_i	4.6247e−04	4.5028e−04	4.5230e−04	4.4933e−04
k_j	5.9420e−04	5.7428e−04	4.6485e−04	4.7185e−04
k_u	1.0227e−03	1.0541e−03	1.1112e−03	1.1063e−03
k_v	1.0174e−03	1.0493e−03	1.1062e−03	1.1019e−03
u_0	−0.3095	−0.3283	−0.3563	−0.3532
v_0	−0.2282	−0.2318	−0.3511	−0.3478
k_1	−0.3820	−0.3685	−0.1885	−0.1819
k_2	0.5574	0.5915	−0.8067	−0.8885
k_3	1.2206	1.2320	1.4064	1.3972
k_4	1.4654	1.4798	1.4242	1.4296

Table 3 shows the results of intrinsic parameter estimation. The results of Illum-1 and Illum-2 are similar due to the same camera configuration they have. Moreover, the same configuration of Illum-3 and Illum-4 which is different from Illum-1 and Illum-2 leads to similar results of intrinsic parameter estimation. Figure 5 illustrates pose estimation results on our collected datasets.

In order to verify the accuracy of geometric reconstruction of the proposed method compared with baseline methods, we capture a light field of real scene, then reconstruct several typical corner points and estimate the distances between them as illustrated in Fig. 6. The estimated distances between the reconstructed points are nearly equal to those measured lengths from real objects by rulers (*i.e.* Fig. 6(a)). In addition, Table 4 lists the comparisons of reconstruction results with state-of-the-art methods. The relative errors of reconstruction results demonstrate the performance of our method.

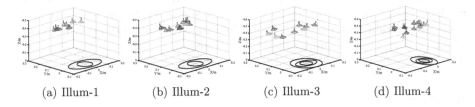

(a) Illum-1   (b) Illum-2   (c) Illum-3   (d) Illum-4

Fig. 5. Pose estimation results of our collected light field datasets.

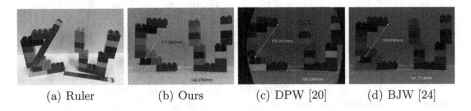

(a) Ruler   (b) Ours   (c) DPW [20]   (d) BJW [24]

Fig. 6. The evaluations of light field measurements. (a) shows distances between 3D points measured by rulers. (b–d) demonstrate the estimated distances using different calibration methods.

Table 4. Quantitative comparison of different calibration methods (unit: mm). The relative error is indicated in parentheses.

	Ruler	Ours	DPW [6]	BJW [3]
'C'	117.5000	117.2839 (**0.2%**)	103.2810 (12.2%)	119.6786 (1.9%)
'V'	144.0000	142.3753 (**1.1%**)	136.2380 (5.4%)	141.7118 (1.6%)

6 Conclusion

In the paper, instead of traditional checkerboard, a concentric conics pattern is designed for light field camera calibration. We firstly explore the property of common self-polar triangle on concentric conics and reconstruct this self-polar triangle. In addition, a light field projection model is utilized to acquire an effective linear initial solution for both intrinsic and extrinsic parameters, making use of the property. Finally, a 4-parameter radial distortion model and a Sampson cost function are defined to non-linearly optimize the 10-parameter model (6 for intrinsic and 4 for distortion). Qualitative and quantitative analyses on extensive experiments verify the effectiveness and robustness of the proposed method. In the future, we intend to concentrate on exploring a unified light field camera calibration method using different types of calibration patterns. The future work also includes conducting different conic detection algorithms to improve the effectiveness of initial solution estimation.

References

1. Birklbauer, C., Bimber, O.: Panorama light-field imaging. In: Computer Graphics Forum, vol. 33, pp. 43–52. Wiley Online Library (2014)
2. Bok, Y., Jeon, H.-G., Kweon, I.S.: Geometric calibration of micro-lens-based light-field cameras using line features. In: Fleet, D., Pajdla, T., Schiele, B., Tuytelaars, T. (eds.) ECCV 2014. LNCS, vol. 8694, pp. 47–61. Springer, Cham (2014). https://doi.org/10.1007/978-3-319-10599-4_4
3. Bok, Y., Jeon, H.G., Kweon, I.S.: Geometric calibration of micro-lens-based light field cameras using line features. IEEE T-PAMI **39**(2), 287–300 (2017)
4. Canny, J.: A computational approach to edge detection. In: Readings in Computer Vision, pp. 184–203. Elsevier (1987)
5. Dansereau, D.G., Mahon, I., Pizarro, O., Williams, S.B.: Plenoptic flow: closed-form visual odometry for light field cameras. In: IEEE IROS, pp. 4455–4462 (2011)
6. Dansereau, D.G., Pizarro, O., Williams, S.B.: Decoding, calibration and rectification for lenselet-based plenoptic cameras. In: IEEE CVPR, pp. 1027–1034 (2013)
7. Dong, F., Ieng, S.H., Savatier, X., Etienne-Cummings, R., Benosman, R.: Plenoptic cameras in real-time robotics. IJRR **32**(2), 206–217 (2013)
8. Faugeras, O.: Three-Dimensional Computer Vision: A Geometric Viewpoint. MIT Press, Cambridge (1993)
9. Guo, X., Yu, Z., Kang, S.B., Lin, H., Yu, J.: Enhancing light fields through ray-space stitching. IEEE T-VCG **22**(7), 1852–1861 (2016)
10. Hartley, R.: Self-calibration of stationary cameras. IJCV **22**(1), 5–23 (1997)
11. Hartley, R., Zisserman, A.: Multiple View Geometry in Computer Vision. Cambridge University Press, Cambridge (2003)
12. Huang, H., Zhang, H., Cheung, Y.M.: The common self-polar triangle of concentric circles and its application to camera calibration. In: IEEE CVPR, pp. 4065–4072 (2015)
13. Huang, H., Zhang, H., Cheung, Y.M.: Homography estimation from the common self-polar triangle of separate ellipses. In: IEEE CVPR, pp. 1737–1744 (2016)
14. Jeon, H.G., et al.: Accurate depth map estimation from a lenslet light field camera. In: IEEE CVPR, pp. 1547–1555 (2015)
15. Johannsen, O., Heinze, C., Goldluecke, B., Perwaß, C.: On the calibration of focused plenoptic cameras. In: Grzegorzek, M., Theobalt, C., Koch, R., Kolb, A. (eds.) Time-of-Flight and Depth Imaging. Sensors, Algorithms, and Applications. LNCS, vol. 8200, pp. 302–317. Springer, Heidelberg (2013). https://doi.org/10.1007/978-3-642-44964-2_15

16. Johannsen, O., Sulc, A., Goldluecke, B.: On linear structure from motion for light field cameras. In: IEEE ICCV, pp. 720–728 (2015)
17. Kim, J.S., Gurdjos, P., Kweon, I.S.: Geometric and algebraic constraints of projected concentric circles and their applications to camera calibration. IEEE T-PAMI **27**(4), 637–642 (2005)
18. Levoy, M., Hanrahan, P.: Light field rendering. In: ACM SIGGRAPH, pp. 31–42 (1996)
19. Liebowitz, D.: Camera calibration and reconstruction of geometry from images. Ph.D. thesis, University of Oxford (2001)
20. Lytro: Lytro redefines photography with light field cameras (2011). http://www.lytro.com
21. Madsen, K., Nielsen, H.B., Tingleff, O.: Methods for Non-linear Least Squares Problems, 2nd edn. Informatics and Mathematical Modelling, Technical University of Denmark, Kongens Lyngby (2004)
22. Ng, R.: Fourier slice photography. ACM TOG **24**(3), 735–744 (2005)
23. Ng, R.: Digital light field photography. Ph.D. thesis, Stanford University (2006)
24. Quan, L., Gros, P., Mohr, R.: Invariants of a pair of conics revisited. In: Mowforth, P. (ed.) BMVC 1991, pp. 71–77. Springer, London (1991). https://doi.org/10.1007/978-1-4471-1921-0_10
25. Raytrix: 3D light field camera technology (2013). http://www.raytrix.de
26. Ren, Z., Zhang, Q., Zhu, H., Wang, Q.: Extending the FOV from disparity and color consistencies in multiview light fields. In: Processing ICIP, pp. 1157–1161 (2017)
27. Si, L., Wang, Q.: Dense depth-map estimation and geometry inference from light fields via global optimization. In: Lai, S.-H., Lepetit, V., Nishino, K., Sato, Y. (eds.) ACCV 2016. LNCS, vol. 10113, pp. 83–98. Springer, Cham (2017). https://doi.org/10.1007/978-3-319-54187-7_6
28. Springer, C.E.: Geometry and Analysis of Projective Spaces, vol. 68. Freeman, New York (1964)
29. Thomason, C., Thurow, B., Fahringer, T.: Calibration of a microlens array for a plenoptic camera. In: AIAA, pp. 1456–1460 (2014)
30. Vaish, V., Wilburn, B., Joshi, N., Levoy, M.: Using plane + parallax for calibrating dense camera arrays. In: IEEE CVPR, pp. 2–9 (2004)
31. Wang, T.C., Efros, A.A., Ramamoorthi, R.: Depth estimation with occlusion modeling using light-field cameras. IEEE T-PAMI **38**(11), 2170–2181 (2016)
32. Wanner, S., Goldluecke, B.: Globally consistent depth labeling of 4D light fields. In: IEEE CVPR, pp. 41–48 (2012)
33. Xiao, Z., Wang, Q., Zhou, G., Yu, J.: Aliasing detection and reduction scheme on angularly undersampled light fields. IEEE TIP **26**(5), 2103–2115 (2017)
34. Zhang, C., Ji, Z., Wang, Q.: Rectifying projective distortion in 4D light field. In: IEEE ICIP (2016)
35. Zhang, Q., Zhang, C., Ling, J., Wang, Q., Yu, J.: A generic multi-projection-center model and calibration method for light field cameras. IEEE T-PAMI (2018). https://doi.org/10.1109/TPAMI.2018.2864617
36. Zhang, Y., Li, Z., Yang, W., Yu, P., Lin, H., Yu, J.: The light field 3D scanner. In: IEEE ICCP, pp. 1–9 (2017)
37. Zhang, Y., Yu, P., Yang, W., Ma, Y., Yu, J.: Ray space features for plenoptic structure-from-motion. In: IEEE ICCV, pp. 4631–4639 (2017)
38. Zhu, H., Wang, Q., Yu, J.: Occlusion-model guided anti-occlusion depth estimation in light field. IEEE J-STSP **11**(7), 965–978 (2017)
39. Zhu, H., Zhang, Q., Wang, Q.: 4D light field superpixel and segmentation. In: IEEE CVPR, pp. 6709–6717 (2017)

CubemapSLAM: A Piecewise-Pinhole Monocular Fisheye SLAM System

Yahui Wang[1], Shaojun Cai[2(✉)], Shi-Jie Li[1], Yun Liu[1], Yangyan Guo[3], Tao Li[1], and Ming-Ming Cheng[1]

[1] College of Computer Science, Nankai University,
Tianjin, China
{nkwangyh,lishijie,nk12csly}@mail.nankai.edu.cn,
{litao,cmm}@nankai.edu.cn
[2] UISEE Technology (Beijing) Co., Ltd., Beijing, China
shaojun.cai@uisee.com
[3] University of Chinese Academy of Sciences, Beijing, China
guoyangyan@semi.ac.cn

Abstract. We present a real-time feature-based SLAM (Simultaneous Localization and Mapping) system for fisheye cameras featured by a large field-of-view (FoV). Large FoV cameras are beneficial for large-scale outdoor SLAM applications, because they increase visual overlap between consecutive frames and capture more pixels belonging to the static parts of the environment. However, current feature-based SLAM systems such as PTAM and ORB-SLAM limit their camera model to pinhole only. To compensate for the vacancy, we propose a novel SLAM system with the cubemap model that utilizes the full FoV without introducing distortion from the fisheye lens, which greatly benefits the feature matching pipeline. In the initialization and point triangulation stages, we adopt a unified vector-based representation to efficiently handle matches across multiple faces, and based on this representation we propose and analyze a novel inlier checking metric. In the optimization stage, we design and test a novel multi-pinhole reprojection error metric that outperforms other metrics by a large margin. We evaluate our system comprehensively on a public dataset as well as a self-collected dataset that contains real-world challenging sequences. The results suggest that our system is more robust and accurate than other feature-based fisheye SLAM approaches. The CubemapSLAM system has been released into the public domain.

Keywords: Omnidirectional vision · Fisheye SLAM · Cubemap

1 Introduction

SLAM techniques have been widely applied in the robotics and automation industry. Specifically, Visual SLAM (**VSLAM**) is gaining increasing popularity,

This work is partially supported by the National Natural Science Foundation (61872200), the Natural Science Foundation of Tianjin (17JCQNJC00300) and the National Key Research and Development Program of China (2016YFC0400709).

because cameras are much cheaper than other alternatives such as differential GPS (D-GPS) and LIDAR. However, traditional VSLAM systems suffer from problems such as occlusions, moving objects and drastic turns due to the limited FoV of perspective cameras. In contrast, large FoV cameras significantly increase the visual overlap between consecutive frames. In addition, large FoV cameras capture more information from the environment, therefore making the SLAM system less likely to fail.

However, there are still many challenges in SLAM with large FoV cameras. The first challenge is that most of the widely-used feature descriptors are designed for low-distortion images. Some systems [21,24,26] choose more robust features such as SIFT [16] or design new features suited for highly distorted images [1,31], but they are too time-consuming to satisfy the real-time demands of many applications. Others [6,10,13] try to remove distortion effect by directly rectifying fisheye images into pinhole images, but the remaining FoV is much smaller after rectification. Multicol-SLAM [27] adapts ORB-SLAM [17] to operate on the raw distorted images, but the open-source version fails to achieve satisfying results.

In this paper, we redesign the pipeline of ORB-SLAM to fit the piecewise linear camera model that utilizes full FoV without introducing distortion. We thus propose an efficient and compact feature-based SLAM system dedicated to large FoV cameras. Our system achieves better performance than directly rectifying the fisheye image into a pinhole image and the other existing feature-based fisheye SLAM system [27]. Despite the limited angular resolution of a fisheye camera, we achieve comparable accuracy to ORB-SLAM with a pinhole camera while performing much more robustly. Specifically, our work has the following contributions:

1. We propose the first cubemap solution for feature-based fisheye SLAM. The piecewise-pinhole nature of the cubemap model is especially desirable for feature descriptors, and there is no need to retrain Bag-of-Words (**BoW**) [7] vocabulary for fisheye images.
2. In the initialization and point triangulation stages, we adopt a unified vector-based representation which efficiently handles the matches across multiple faces. Based on this representation, we propose a novel and systematic inlier checking metric for RANSAC with essential matrix constraint, and we provide a rigorous analysis of the correctness of this metric.
3. In the optimization stage, we carry out thorough comparisons of different error metrics, and we propose a novel reprojection error metric for the cubemap model that outperforms other metrics.
4. We present an extensive evaluation on public datasets, and a self-collected one containing typical outdoor driving scenarios. We also discover that by carefully choosing the camera mounting position, the problem of a low angular resolution in outdoor scenes mentioned in [30] can be greatly reduced.

1.1 Related Work

The VSLAM techniques have been widely used in various applications such as self-driving cars [14, 22, 32]. However, limited FoV of pinhole camera may cause the localization system to fail when there is little overlap between consecutive frames. Consequently, large FoV cameras are gaining attention. For instance, the V-Charge project [6, 13] builds a car surrounded with 4 synchronously triggered fisheye cameras modeled as a generalized camera [20]. In recent years, many works have discussed the methods to exploit large FoV cameras. [11] transforms the panoramas from the PointGrey LadyBug camera into cubic panoramas, but they aim to estimate poses of input cubic panoramas rather than build real-time SLAM system. A piecewise-pinhole model is presented in [29], but in the work the map needs to be built offline, and the local and global bundle adjustment as well as the loop closing based on the proposed model are not performed. A number of semi-direct or direct SLAM systems based on fisheye models have been proposed recently [9, 15]. In their works an adapted GPU-based plane-sweep stereo algorithm is used to find matching patches between stereo image from the raw fisheye images. Omni-LSD [3] also proposes a similar pinhole array model as part of the extension to origin LSD-SLAM [4]. While direct method is shown to be robust in scale-diverse environment, its performance in large outdoor environments is still unknown. To our knowledge, Multicol-SLAM [27] is the only existing feature-based fisheye SLAM, but it tries to extract features directly on highly distorted images, which may lead to false matches. Further comparison with MultiCol-SLAM will be presented in the experiment section.

In this work, we propose an efficient and practical cubemap SLAM solution aimed at large-scale outdoor applications. In the following sections, we will first introduce the theoretical adaptions we have made in order to maximally utilize the power of a cubemap model, and then we will demonstrate the advantage of our system in extensive large real-world experiments.

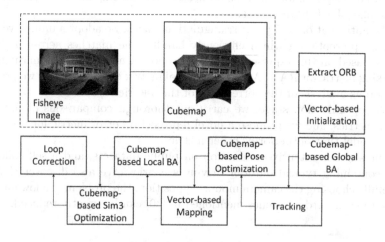

Fig. 1. System overview

2   Algorithm

In this section, we describe the pipeline of the proposed method. As shown in Fig. 1, we acquire cubemap image by calibrating the fisheye camera and mapping fisheye images onto a cube. A vector-based RANSAC is used to solve the essential matrix to recover camera motion and build the initial map. A cubemap-based global bundle adjustment is used to refine camera poses and the initial map. After initialization, the tracking thread estimates camera poses by tracking the local map and refines the poses with a cubemap-based pose optimization algorithm. When the tracking thread decides to insert current frame into the map as a keyframe, a vector-based triangulation algorithm is used to create new map points, and the frame is converted into BoW vectors for loop detection. When a loop is detected, a Sim_3 transformation for loop closing is computed by an adapted Sim_3 optimization algorithm and a loop correction is performed.

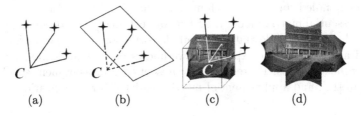

Fig. 2. A demonstration of projecting a fisheye image onto a cube. C are camera centers in the figures. (a) bearing vectors from fisheye image points. (b) project rays onto a single image plane. (c) project rays onto cube. (d) unfolded cubemap image

2.1   Fisheye Camera Model and the Cubemap Model

We choose the omnidirectional camera model from [23] to calibrate the fisheye camera in our work. By calibrating fisheye camera, we acquire a polynomial which transforms image points into bearing vectors as shown in Fig. 2(a). Since the bearing vectors are actually viewing rays, a pinhole image can be acquired by projecting the rays to an image plane with specified camera projection matrix, as in Fig. 2(b). However, projecting on a single pinhole plane would result in a much smaller FoV. To make full use of the large FoV of fisheye camera, we project bearing vectors to multiple image planes. For simplicity, we choose to project onto a cube where each cube face can be seen as an image plane of a virtual pinhole camera with 90° FoV, and the virtual camera shares the same camera parameters as in Fig. 2(c). After projection, we can get a cubemap image as in Fig. 2(d).

2.2   Initialization

Initialization is an important component in SLAM. In perspective camera situation, feature matching followed by RANSAC is used for solving the fundamental matrix F or the homography matrix H between two frames, and camera motion can be recovered afterwards.

Although the F and H models are widely used in SLAM for pinhole cameras, it is not possible to calculate them directly on the distorted fisheye images. Moreover, the F matrix does not exist because the pinhole camera projection matrix K, which is used to derive the F matrix, is undefined for fisheye cameras. To make use of the models, we can either rectify the fisheye images into multiple pinhole images that cover the full FoV, and model each pinhole image separately with F or H models, or transform the image points into bearing vectors through the calibrated fisheye model. For the former approach, we equivalently operate on a multiple pinhole SLAM system as in [5]. However, the inter-pinhole correspondence points have to be transformed to the same coordinate first before they can be handled correctly, which increase the complexity. For the latter approach, the essential matrix model E and H for vectors can be adopted in a vector form, and the intra-pinhole and inter-pinhole correspondences can be handled in a unified framework. In the experiment we find essential matrix model E works for most of the scenarios. Therefore, we represent each measurement as a bearing vector as in [12], and apply essential matrix model E for initialization.

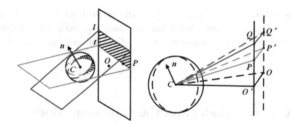

Fig. 3. Threshold of inlier checking in vector-based initialization. The left figure shows the corresponding inlier regions (the shadow areas) between the image plane and the unit sphere. The right figure shows the side view of the left figure. (Color figure online)

2.3   Epipolar Constraints on the Unit Sphere

For SLAM systems, epipolar geometry is used to check whether two points are in correspondence when the F matrix is known, or whether the F assumption is correct when the point correspondences are assumed to be right. To achieve an inlier probability of 95%, the following criteria are used for inlier checking,

$$\dot{\mathbf{p}}_2^T F \dot{\mathbf{p}}_1 < 3.84\sigma^2 \tag{1}$$

where $\dot{\mathbf{p}}_1$ and $\dot{\mathbf{p}}_2$ are homogeneous representation of the points p_1 and p_2 on the images, and σ is the variance of the measurement noise (cf. [8]). In Eq. 1, $F\dot{\mathbf{p}}_1$ can be geometrically explained as the epipolar line in the second image where p_2 belongs. Thus a product with $\mathbf{p}_2^T$ yields the distance of point p_2 to the epipolar line. Similarly, the essential matrix constraint can be written as

$$\mathbf{r}_2^T E \mathbf{r}_1 = 0 \qquad (2)$$

but $\mathbf{r}_1$ and $\mathbf{r}_2$ are bearing vectors rather than image points on the plane. We noticed that since E can be decomposed as $E = [t]_\times R$, where $E\mathbf{r}_1$ indicates the normal of the epipolar plane, the formula $\mathbf{r}_2^T E \mathbf{r}_1$ can be explained as the signed distance of $\mathbf{r}_2$ to the epipolar plane.

As shown in Sect. 2.1, for each vector, there is a corresponding image point on the cubemap. To find inlier threshold for measurements on the unit sphere, we propose to map the well-defined inlier region on image plane to the unit sphere as in Fig. 3. For simplicity, we only show the process on the front cubemap face. In Fig. 3, the sphere is the unit sphere with point C as camera center, and the plane in black is the front face of cubemap with point O as the center. Line l is the epipolar line from the intersection of the epipolar plane (red) and the image plane (black). $\mathbf{n}$ is the normal of epipolar plane. And we have

$$\mathbf{n} = E\mathbf{r}_1 \qquad (3)$$

as we mentioned above. A point P is considered as inlier if the distance to l is within a threshold as Eq. 1 indicates. The area within the threshold is represented by the shadow area with line t as boundary. We assume P is on the boundary line t to reveal the boundary conditions. For convenience we only draw area under l. The area above l can be handled in the same way. The mapped area on unit sphere is also shown in shadow, from which we can see that the corresponding threshold on unit sphere is not uniformly distributed. For area closer to the image plane, the threshold is larger, and for area further from image plane the threshold is smaller. Thus a constant threshold is not reasonable.

To illustrate the geometry relations of the threshold on the image plane and unit sphere, we show the side view of the model in the right figure of Fig. 3. In the figure, OQ' is perpendicular to the epipolar line QQ', and parallel to QO' which passes through P. The plane $OO'QQ'$ corresponds to the image plane in left figure. The line segment CO, which denotes the focal line, is perpendicular to the image plane and thus perpendicular to OQ'. Both $P'Q'$ and PQ indicate the threshold on image plane, thus the arc on unit sphere between QC and CP is the inlier region we demand. For simplicity, we notate $\angle PCO'$ as ϕ, $\angle QCP$ as θ, and length of QP as th, which is usually set to 1 pixel. We observe that:

$$\tan(\phi + \theta) = \frac{\|QO'\|}{\|CO'\|} = \frac{\|Q'O\|}{\|CO'\|} = \frac{\|th\| + \|PO'\|}{\sqrt{\|CO\|^2 + \|OO'\|^2}} \qquad (4)$$

$$\tan\phi = \frac{\|PO'\|}{\|CO'\|} = \frac{\|PO'\|}{\sqrt{\|CO\|^2 + \|OO'\|^2}} \qquad (5)$$

We notice in Eqs. 4 and 5 the length of OO' and PO' are the only unknowns. And $\mathbf{OP}$ can be derived immediately since the coordinates of the camera center O and image point P are already known. To calculate the length of OO' and PO', we can first solve the direction vector $\mathbf{e}$ of the epipolar line QQ'. Since QQ' is the intersection of the image plane and epipolar plane, $\mathbf{e}$ can be derived by the cross product of normals of the planes. By making

$$z = \frac{\mathbf{CO}}{\|CO\|} = (0,0,1)^T \tag{6}$$

as the normal of image plane, the direction vector $\mathbf{e}$ can be derived by:

$$e = n \times z \tag{7}$$

As a result we have:

$$\|OO'\| = \frac{|e \cdot \mathbf{OP}|}{\|e\|} \tag{8}$$

$$\|PO'\| = \sqrt{\|OP\|^2 - \|OO'\|^2} \tag{9}$$

We can derive $\tan(\phi+\theta)$ and $\tan\phi$ by substituting Eqs. 8 and 9 into Eqs. 4 and 5, we have:

$$\tan\theta = \frac{\tan(\phi+\theta) - \tan\phi}{1 + \tan(\phi+\theta)\tan\phi}, \sin\theta = \frac{\tan\theta}{\sqrt{\tan^2\theta + 1}} \tag{10}$$

Then from Eqs. 3 and 2, we get our inlier metric for the unit sphere as:

$$\left| \frac{\mathbf{r}_2^T E \mathbf{r}_1}{\|\mathbf{r}_2\| \|E\mathbf{r}_1\|} \right| = \left| \frac{\mathbf{r}_2^T \mathbf{n}}{\|\mathbf{r}_2\| \|\mathbf{n}\|} \right| \leq \left| \cos(\frac{\pi}{2} \pm \theta) \right| = |\sin\theta| \tag{11}$$

2.4   Optimization

To perform optimizations in vector-based vision systems, several metrics have been proposed. [12] proposes to minimize the angular error between bearing vectors, and [19] studies different metrics and shows that the tangential error has the best performance. Zhang et al. [30] evaluate the above metrics as well as a vector difference with a semi-direct VO [5]. Inspired by the multi-pinhole nature of cubemap, we propose to minimize reprojection errors of all cube faces as a multi-camera system.

The multi-camera model is used extensively in previous multiple-camera SLAM systems [5,6,13,27]. In the multi-camera model, a body frame B rigidly attached to camera frames is set as the reference frame. Transformations $T_{C_i B}$ from body frame to camera local frames C_i can be obtained by extrinsic calibration, where i represent the camera index. In cubemap model, different faces are equivalent to pinhole cameras as in Sect. 2.1. We set the front-facing virtual camera as the body frame, and all the pinhole cameras are transformed to the body frame by a rotation R_{C_iB}. The projection model of cubemap is:

$$u = KR_{C_iB}T_{BW}P \tag{12}$$

where $P = (x, y, z)^T$ is the 3D point in world frame, T_{BW} is transformation from world frame to body frame, and u is the local point coordinate in the image coordinate of each cubemap face.

We can represent $T \in SE_3$ with $\xi = (\phi^T, \rho^T)^T$ [2] and expand Eq. 12 into:

$$u = KP_1, P_1 = R_{C_iB}P_2, P_2 = T_{BW}P \tag{13}$$

The Jacobian of the measurement u to camera pose T therefore can be derived according to the chain rule:

$$J_\xi = -\frac{\partial u}{\partial P_1} \cdot R_{C_iB} \cdot [-P_2^\wedge, I_{3\times3}] \tag{14}$$

where $P_2^\wedge$ is the skew-symmetric matrix of P_2. The Jacobian for map point position is given by:

$$J_p = -\frac{\partial u}{\partial P_1} \cdot \frac{\partial P_1}{\partial P} = -\frac{\partial u}{\partial P_1} R_{C_iB}R_{BW} \tag{15}$$

where R_{BW} is the rotation part of T_{BW}.

To find the best metric for CubemapSLAM, we thoroughly evaluated the metrics. For convenience we keep the notation used in [30], where the angular metrics are denoted as r_{a1} and r_{a2}, and the tangential metric and vector difference metric are denoted as r_t and r_f respectively. The multi-camera model based metric is denoted as r_u. We compute the ATE RMSE (Absolute trajectory error) [25] of the system with different metrics in pose optimization. The evaluation is performed on a long straight track with local bundle adjustment disabled. In the result, r_t and r_f achieve errors as 11.27 m and 20.53 m and fail to keep the scale of the map, and r_{a1} and r_{a2} fail quickly after initialization. In contrast r_u achieves the most accurate result as 1.03 m, which indicates that the multi-pinhole model is more suitable for our system.

3   Experiments

We evaluate the performance of our system in the multi-fisheye dataset Lafida [28] as well as a dataset collected in large outdoor environments with our autonomous vehicle. In the Lafida dataset, we evaluate CubemapSLAM and Multicol-SLAM [27] on both accuracy and robustness. Then on the dataset collected by ourselves, we first evaluate the systems under two types of camera settings as in Sect. 3.2. We further investigate the effect of different mounting positions of the camera and loop closure. The result shows that our Cubemap-SLAM system performs consistently more robustly in all the experiments than the other ones, and it provides competitive accuracy.

3.1   Dataset

The Lafida dataset [28] is a multi-fisheye camera dataset collected for evaluating multi-fisheye SLAM systems. There are 6 sequences in total, which are *in_dynamic*, *in_static*, *out_static*, *out_static*2, *out_rotation* and *out_large_loop* captured from three rigidly mounted fisheye cameras. All the cameras share the same resolution of 754 × 480 pixels. As for our dataset, we equip the vehicle with two types of cameras: a pinhole camera with 80° FoV, and a fisheye camera with 190° FoV. Note that the pinhole camera and fisheye camera share the same model of sensor chip but use different lenses, so the pinhole and raw fisheye image have the same resolution of 1280 × 720 pixels.

The experiments on our dataset contain two camera settings. In the first setting, a pinhole camera and a fisheye are mounted at the frontal part of the vehicle (both facing front), and the other fisheye camera is mounted at the left side of the vehicle (facing left). In this setting, we choose various routes, including a large loop around an industrial park (*loop*1 sequence), a smaller loop inside the park with sharp turns (*loop*2 sequence), a large u-turn on the *loop*1 sequence (*uturn* sequence), a large sequence in a town with no loop but with traffic lights and traffic jams (*town* sequence), and a loopy route in an outdoor parking lot (*parkinglot* sequence). To further investigate the performance of the lateral mounting cameras, we create a second setting where a fisheye camera and a pinhole camera are both mounted laterally. We travel along the routes of *loop*1, *town*1 and *parkinglot* and recollect the data under the new camera setting. We name the collected data *loop*1_*c_clockwise*, *loop*1_*clockwise*, *town*_1 and *parkinglot*_1. *loop*1_*c_clockwise* and *loop*1_*clockwise* share the same route but drive in opposite directions. For all the sequences, D-GPS is used as groundtruth.

3.2   Baseline Comparison

We first compare our system with Multicol-SLAM [27] on the Lafida dataset [28], where Multicol-SLAM is sufficiently tested and well performed. For fairness, Multicol-SLAM is configured with one fisheye camera which is the same one as CubemapSLAM. For a comprehensive comparison, we set the resolution of the faces as 450×450, 550×550 and 650×650 pixels, respectively. In the experiment, both of the systems are configured to extract 2000 features, which we consider it is enough and representative for the dataset considering the image resolution.

On our dataset, the CubemapSLAM operates on the front (**Cube-F**) and left (**Cube-L**) fisheye cameras. We simply set the face resolution as 650 × 650 pixels. The first baseline comparison is to perform ORB-SLAM [18] on rectified fisheye images from front (**ORB-Rect-F**) and left (**ORB-Rect-L**) cameras. The rectified images are set to 100° FoV with a resolution of 775 × 775 pixels which share the same focal length with cubemap virtual cameras. Another baseline approach is to perform ORB-SLAM [18] on pinhole images from front (**ORB-Pin-F**) and left cameras (**ORB-Pin-L**). We also tested Multicol-SLAM [27] on the collected dataset. However, we find Multicol-SLAM fails soon after initialization stage in most of the sequences as it does in Lafida *out_large_scale* sequence, so we do not include trajectories of Multicol-SLAM in result comparison.

We first test the systems with loop closing thread disabled to evaluate system performance with only VO. In the experiments, all the systems are configured to extract 3000 features per image. For each output trajectory, we align it with the ground truth by a 7-DoF transformation since the scale is unknown. After that, we compute the ATE RMSE [25] of each trajectory for comparison. We also evaluate the tracking and mapping quality of all the systems by measuring the average number of tracked keypoints in each sequence. Note that for all the entries in the tables, we add a mark of *lost* in the entry if the system gets lost after finishing more than half of the sequence, and we add a mark of X if the system gets lost soon after initialization.

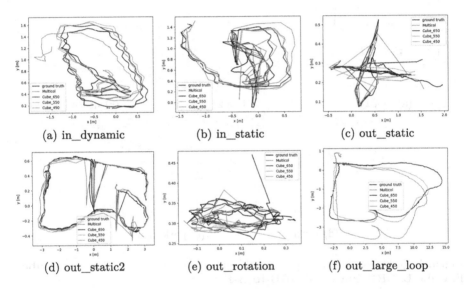

(a) in_dynamic   (b) in_static   (c) out_static

(d) out_static2   (e) out_rotation   (f) out_large_loop

Fig. 4. Trajectories on Lafida dataset [28] aligned to groundtruth with a 7-DoF transformation of Multicol-SLAM and CubemapSLAM with resolution of face as 450×450, 550×550 and 650×650 pixels, respectively.

Table 1. ATE RMSE and tracked frames (over all frames) on Lafida dataset [28] (m)

	in_dynamic	in_static	out_static	out_static2	out_rotation	out_large_loop
Multicol	0.78	0.32	0.07	0.31	0.05	0.06
	(880/899)	(1001/1015)	(**726**/755)	(1314/1642)	(397/779)	(202/3175)
Cubemap 650 × 650	**0.17**	**0.15**	**0.02**	0.14	0.06	**0.16**
	(**893**/899)	(997/1015)	(722/755)	(1604/1642)	(253/779)	(3111/3175)
Cubemap 550 × 550	0.28	0.16	0.03	0.15	0.10	0.44
	(**893**/899)	(**1006**/1015)	(717/755)	(1604/1642)	(399/779)	(**3132**/3175)
Cubemap 450 × 450	0.24	0.17	0.03	**0.13**	**0.04**	0.39
	(**893**/899)	(**1006**/1015)	(716/755)	(**1605**/1642)	(**743**/779)	(3129/3175)

3.3   Results on Lafida Dataset

We carefully evaluate both systems on all the six sequences, and the qualitative and quantitative results are shown in Table 1 and Fig. 4. The results show that the CubemapSLAM performs better than Multicol-SLAM in most sequences and the performance is stable with various face size. Also it should be noted that in *out_large_scale* although the error of Multicol-SLAM is slightly lower, the number of tracked frames are significantly less than ours. We've tested Multicol with several different start points for fairness, but the results do not show much difference. We notice Multicol-SLAM usually fails when the camera motion becomes large. However, large motions are very common in large-scale outdoor dataset.

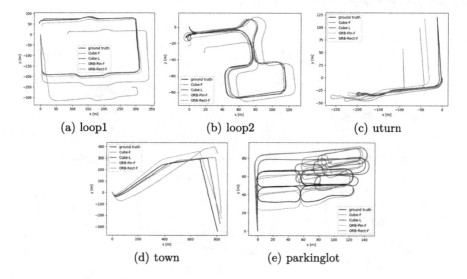

(a) loop1   (b) loop2   (c) uturn

(d) town   (e) parkinglot

Fig. 5. Trajectories aligned to groundtruth with a 7-DoF transformation of the **Cube-F, Cube-L, ORB-Pin-F** and **ORB-Rect-F**.

Table 2. ATE RMSE (m) and average number of tracked points (pt)

| | ATE RMSE | | | | Average number of tracked points | | | |
	Cube-F	Cube-L	ORB-Pin-F	ORB-Rect-F	Cube-F	Cube-L	ORB-Pin-F	ORB-Rect-F
loop1	22.73	**3.12**	3.92	121.14	194.21	198.73	**206.84**	190.73
loop2	2.68	**2.26**	2.54 (lost)	6.66 (lost)	210.64	229.35	**232.28**	201.45
uturn	12.14	**2.22**	7.99	27.85	196.78	**236.65**	176.74	150.93
town	57.32	23.58	**13.41**	207.15	256.06	**338.06**	222.50	207.29
parkinglot	16.47	9.54	**2.29**	16.92	170.34	**182.45**	148.36	164.34

3.4   Results of Setting1

The ATE RSME results for each method can be found in Table 2, and the comparison of the trajectories from different systems are shown in Fig. 5. In all the sequences, the ATE error of **ORB-Rect-F** is significantly larger than the other methods, which is the consequence of both a reduced FoV from the full fisheye image and a lower angular resolution than that of the pinhole camera. **ORB-Pin-F** has a low ATE RMSE in most of the sequences due to its higher angular resolution than fisheye image. However, in the *loop2* sequence, **ORB-Pin-F** fails to complete the entire trajectory due to a drastic turn at the end of the sequence. In contrast, both **Cube-F** and **Cube-L** successfully complete all the sequences including the difficult *loop2* with the help of a larger FoV. In addition, we find that in *loop1*, *loop2* and *uturn* sequences, **Cube-L** achieves the best result. In the *town* and the *parkinglot* sequences, as the feature points are relatively far from the camera, **ORB-Pin-F** outperforms **Cube-L** by a small margin, but we will show that the gap is significantly reduced after loop closure.

For the number of tracked keypoints, as in Table 2, **Cube-L** tracks the most points in *uturn*, *town* and *parkinglot*, and performs close to **ORB-Pin-F** in *loop1* and *loop2*. Note that besides the advantage of better tracking quality, more tracked keypoints also contributes to a denser and more structural map.

Table 3. ATE RMSE (m) and average number of tracked points (pt)

	ATE RMSE			Average number of tracked points		
	Cube-L	ORB-Pin-L	ORB-Rect-L	Cube-L	ORB-Pin-L	ORB-Rect-L
loop1_c_clockwise	**9.84**	15.60	X	**280.01**	215.06	241.97
loop1_clockwise	**8.94**	X	X	**136.99**	X	X
town_1	**14.75**	16.20 (lost)	6.94 (lost)	366.14	**379.21**	375.09
parkinglot_1	**5.44**	21.74 (lost)	X	**193.80**	191.01	152.76

3.5   Results of Setting2

To make the comparison fair for the lateral mounting cameras, we mount both types of cameras towards left and evaluate the performance respectively. Quantitative and qualitative results are shown in Table 3 and Fig. 6. In all the sequences, **Cube-L** outperforms the other two methods by a large margin. In the clockwise sequence where the cameras look outwards the park, both **ORB-Pin-L** and **ORB-Rect-L** get lost soon after initialization due to lack of texture and occlusions by objects close-by. We therefore do not compute the error and replace each field with a X. Also in *town_1*, both **ORB-Rect-L** and **ORB-Pin-L** get lost before finishing the sequence due to occlusion from cars passing by. In addition, we list the number of average tracked points in Table 3, in which **Cube-L** achieves better overall performance than the other systems.

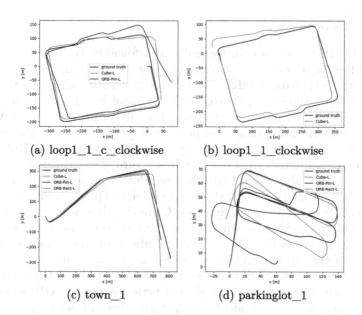

(a) loop1_1_c_clockwise   (b) loop1_1_clockwise

(c) town_1   (d) parkinglot_1

Fig. 6. Trajectories aligned to groundtruth with a 7-DoF transformation of the **Cube-L**, **ORB-Pin-L** and **ORB-Rect-L**.

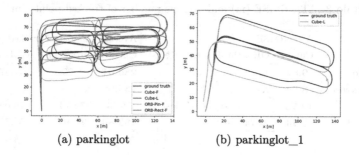

(a) parkinglot   (b) parkinglot_1

Fig. 7. Trajectories aligned to groundtruth with a 7-DoF transformation of the Cube-map and ORB-SLAM with loop closing.

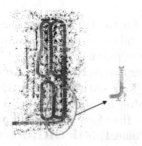

Fig. 8. Qualitative results of **Cube-F** (left) and **ORB-Pin-F** (right) on the *parkinglot* sequence with a lower frame rate by choosing one image from every three images.

Table 4. ATE RMSE with loop closure (m) on parkinglot and parkinglot_1 sequences

	parkinglot				parkinglot_1		
	Cube-F	Cube-L	ORB-Pin-F	ORB-Rect-F	Cube-L	ORB-Pin-L	ORB-Rect-L
w/o loop closing	16.47	9.54	**2.29**	16.92	**5.44**	21.74 (lost)	X
w/ loop closing	4.47	3.02	**1.69**	4.73	**2.41**	X	X

3.6 Results of Loop Closing

To evaluate system performance with loop closing thread enabled, we test the performances of the systems in both *parkinglot* and *parkinglot_1* sequences with and without loop closing. Results show that errors of **Cube-F** and **Cube-L** are greatly reduced and getting comparable to **ORB-Pin-F** with loop closing (see Table 4), and the robustness consistently outperform the rest. A qualitative result is shown in Fig. 7. To further reveal the advantage of a large FoV camera, we test **ORB-Pin-F** and **Cube-F** in the *parkinglot* sequence with a reduced frame rate by choosing one image out of three in the sequences. We find that **ORB-Pin-F** is hard to initialize and fails soon after initialization, while **Cube-F** is able to initialize fast, track stably, and successfully perform loop closing. A qualitative result of the trajectories is shown in Fig. 8.

4 Conclusions

This work presents a novel CubemapSLAM system that incorporates the cubemap model into the state-of-the-art feature based SLAM system. The cubemap model utilizes the large FoV of fisheye camera without affecting the performance of feature descriptors. In addition, CubemapSLAM is efficiently implemented and can run in real time. In the experiments, we extensively evaluate our systems in various challenging real-world cases and prove that our CubemapSLAM solution is consistently more robust than other approaches without losing accuracy. We also discover that by optimizing the mounting position of the fisheye camera and enabling the loop closing thread, CubemapSLAM can achieve even better accuracy than pinhole cameras, despite the limited angular resolution of the sensor. Overall, we provide an efficient and practical fisheye SLAM solution. Future work includes extending the cubemap model to stereo or multiple camera setting to further improve robustness as well as recover the absolute scale. The source code is available at https://github.com/nkwangyh/CubemapSLAM.

References

1. Arican, Z., Frossard, P.: OmniSIFT: scale invariant features in omnidirectional images. In: IEEE International Conference on Image Processing (ICIP), pp. 3505–3508. IEEE (2010)
2. Barfoot, T.D.: State Estimation for Robotics. Cambridge University Press, Cambridge (2017)

3. Caruso, D., Engel, J., Cremers, D.: Large-scale direct slam for omnidirectional cameras. In: IEEE/RSJ International Conference on Intelligent Robots and Systems (IROS), pp. 141–148. IEEE (2015)
4. Engel, J., Schöps, T., Cremers, D.: LSD-SLAM: large-scale direct monocular SLAM. In: Fleet, D., Pajdla, T., Schiele, B., Tuytelaars, T. (eds.) ECCV 2014. LNCS, vol. 8690, pp. 834–849. Springer, Cham (2014). https://doi.org/10.1007/978-3-319-10605-2_54
5. Forster, C., Zhang, Z., Gassner, M., Werlberger, M., Scaramuzza, D.: SVO: semidirect visual odometry for monocular and multicamera systems. IEEE Trans. Robot. **33**(2), 249–265 (2017)
6. Furgale, P., et al.: Toward automated driving in cities using close-to-market sensors: an overview of the V-Charge project. In: IEEE Intelligent Vehicles Symposium (IV), pp. 809–816. IEEE (2013)
7. Gálvez-López, D., Tardos, J.D.: Bags of binary words for fast place recognition in image sequences. IEEE Trans. Robot. **28**(5), 1188–1197 (2012)
8. Hartley, R., Zisserman, A.: Multiple View Geometry in Computer Vision. Cambridge University Press, Cambridge (2003)
9. Heng, L., Choi, B.: Semi-direct visual odometry for a fisheye-stereo camera. In: IEEE/RSJ International Conference on Intelligent Robots and Systems (IROS), pp. 4077–4084. IEEE (2016)
10. Heng, L., Li, B., Pollefeys, M.: CamOdoCal: automatic intrinsic and extrinsic calibration of a rig with multiple generic cameras and odometry. In: IEEE/RSJ International Conference on Intelligent Robots and Systems (IROS), pp. 1793–1800. IEEE (2013)
11. Kangni, F., Laganiere, R.: Orientation and pose recovery from spherical panoramas. In: IEEE International Conference on Computer Vision (ICCV), pp. 1–8. IEEE (2007)
12. Kneip, L., Furgale, P.: OpenGV: a unified and generalized approach to real-time calibrated geometric vision. In: IEEE International Conference on Robotics and Automation (ICRA), pp. 1–8. IEEE (2014)
13. Lee, G.H., Faundorfer, F., Pollefeys, M.: Motion estimation for self-driving cars with a generalized camera. In: IEEE Conference on Computer Vision and Pattern Recognition (CVPR), pp. 2746–2753. IEEE (2013)
14. Linegar, C., Churchill, W., Newman, P.: Work smart, not hard: recalling relevant experiences for vast-scale but time-constrained localisation. In: IEEE International Conference on Robotics and Automation (ICRA), pp. 90–97. IEEE (2015)
15. Liu, P., Heng, L., Sattler, T., Geiger, A., Pollefeys, M.: Direct visual odometry for a fisheye-stereo camera. In: IEEE/RSJ International Conference on Intelligent Robots and Systems (IROS) (2017)
16. Lowe, D.G.: Distinctive image features from scale-invariant keypoints. Int. J. Comput. Vis. (IJCV) **60**(2), 91–110 (2004)
17. Mur-Artal, R., Montiel, J.M.M., Tardos, J.D.: ORB-SLAM: a versatile and accurate monocular SLAM system. IEEE Trans. Robot. **31**(5), 1147–1163 (2015)
18. Mur-Artal, R., Tardós, J.D.: ORB-SLAM2: an open-source SLAM system for monocular, stereo, and RGB-D cameras. IEEE Trans. Robot. **33**(5), 1255–1262 (2017)
19. Pagani, A., Stricker, D.: Structure from motion using full spherical panoramic cameras. In: IEEE International Conference on Computer Vision Workshops (ICCV Workshops), pp. 375–382. IEEE (2011)
20. Pless, R.: Using many cameras as one. In: IEEE Computer Society Conference on Computer Vision and Pattern Recognition, vol. 2, pp. II-587. IEEE (2003)

21. Rituerto, A., Puig, L., Guerrero, J.J.: Visual SLAM with an omnidirectional camera. In: International Conference on Pattern Recognition (ICPR), pp. 348–351. IEEE (2010)
22. Ros, G., Sappa, A., Ponsa, D., Lopez, A.M.: Visual SLAM for driverless cars: a brief survey. In: Intelligent Vehicles Symposium (IV) Workshops, vol. 2 (2012)
23. Scaramuzza, D., Martinelli, A., Siegwart, R.: A toolbox for easily calibrating omnidirectional cameras. In: IEEE/RSJ International Conference on Intelligent Robots and Systems (IROS), pp. 5695–5701. IEEE (2006)
24. Scaramuzza, D., Siegwart, R.: Appearance-guided monocular omnidirectional visual odometry for outdoor ground vehicles. IEEE Trans. Robot. **24**(5), 1015–1026 (2008)
25. Sturm, J., Engelhard, N., Endres, F., Burgard, W., Cremers, D.: A benchmark for the evaluation of RGB-D SLAM systems. In: IEEE/RSJ International Conference on Intelligent Robots and Systems (IROS), pp. 573–580. IEEE (2012)
26. Tardif, J.P., Pavlidis, Y., Daniilidis, K.: Monocular visual odometry in urban environments using an omnidirectional camera. In: IEEE/RSJ International Conference on Intelligent Robots and Systems (IROS), pp. 2531–2538. IEEE (2008)
27. Urban, S., Hinz, S.: MultiCol-SLAM-A modular real-time multi-camera SLAM system. arXiv preprint arXiv:1610.07336 (2016)
28. Urban, S., Jutzi, B.: LaFiDa—a laserscanner multi-fisheye camera dataset. J. Imaging **3**(1), 5 (2017)
29. Ventura, J., Höllerer, T.: Wide-area scene mapping for mobile visual tracking. In: IEEE International Symposium on Mixed and Augmented Reality (ISMAR), pp. 3–12. IEEE (2012)
30. Zhang, Z., Rebecq, H., Forster, C., Scaramuzza, D.: Benefit of large field-of-view cameras for visual odometry. In: IEEE International Conference on Robotics and Automation (ICRA), pp. 801–808. IEEE (2016)
31. Zhao, Q., Feng, W., Wan, L., Zhang, J.: SPHORB: a fast and robust binary feature on the sphere. Int. J. Comput. Vis. (IJCV) **113**(2), 143–159 (2015)
32. Ziegler, J., et al.: Making Bertha drive—an autonomous journey on a historic route. IEEE Intell. Transp. Syst. Mag. **6**(2), 8–20 (2014)

Dense Light Field Reconstruction from Sparse Sampling Using Residual Network

Mantang Guo, Hao Zhu, Guoqing Zhou, and Qing Wang[✉]

School of Computer Science, Northwestern Polytechnical University,
Xi'an 710072, China
qwang@nwpu.edu.cn

Abstract. A light field records numerous light rays from a real-world scene. However, capturing a dense light field by existing devices is a time-consuming process. Besides, reconstructing a large amount of light rays equivalent to multiple light fields using sparse sampling arises a severe challenge for existing methods. In this paper, we present a learning-based method to reconstruct multiple novel light fields between two mutually independent light fields. We indicate that light rays distributed in different light fields have the same consistent constraints under a certain condition. The most significant constraint is a depth related correlation between angular and spatial dimensions. Our method avoids working out the error-sensitive constraint by employing a deep neural network. We predict residual values of pixels on epipolar plane image (EPI) to reconstruct novel light fields. Our method is able to reconstruct 2 to 4 novel light fields between two mutually independent input light fields. We also compare our results with those yielded by a number of alternatives elsewhere in the literature, which shows our reconstructed light fields have better structure similarity and occlusion.

Keywords: Dense light field reconstruction · Sparse sampling · Epipolar plane image · Residual network

1 Introduction

A dense light field contains detailed multi-perspective information of a real-world scene. Utilizing these information, previous work has demonstrated many exciting applications, including changing the focus [12], depth estimation [4,17, 19,21,30], light field segmentation [31] and stitching [14], aliasing detection and reduction [25], calibration [28] and saliency detection [9]. However, it is difficult

Supported by NSFC under Grant 61531014.

Electronic supplementary material The online version of this chapter (https://doi.org/10.1007/978-3-030-20876-9_4) contains supplementary material, which is available to authorized users.

© Springer Nature Switzerland AG 2019
C. V. Jawahar et al. (Eds.): ACCV 2018, LNCS 11366, pp. 50–65, 2019.
https://doi.org/10.1007/978-3-030-20876-9_4

for existing devices to properly capture such a large quantity of information. In early light field capturing methods, light fields are recorded by multi-camera arrays or light field gantries [23] which are bulky and expensive. In recent years, commercial light field cameras such as Lytro [10] and Raytrix [13] are introduced to the general public. But they are still unable to efficiently sample a dense light field due to their trade-off between angular and spatial resolution.

Many methods have been proposed to synthesize novel views using a set of sparsely sampled views in a light field [5, 22, 24, 29]. But, these methods only increase the view density in a single light field. Kalantari et al. [5] proposed a learning-based method to synthesize novel views at arbitrary positions by using views in the four corners of light field. Recently, Wu et al. [24] proposed a leaning-based method to synthesize novel views by increasing the resolution of EPI. These methods outperform other state-of-the-art methods [22, 29] on view synthesis. However, all these methods are only able to synthesize novel views in a single light field. Besides, in these methods, the baseline between sampled views has to be close enough. They cannot properly reconstruct a large quantity of novel light rays with wide baseline.

In this paper, we explore dense light field reconstruction from sparse sampling. We propose a novel learning-based method to synthesize a great number of novel light rays between two distant input light fields, whose view planes are coplanar. Using the disparity consistency between light fields, we first model the relationship between EPIs of dense and sparse light field. Then, we extend the error-sensitive disparity consistency between EPIs in sparse light field by employing ResNet [3]. Finally, we reconstruct a large quantity of light rays between input light fields. The proposed method is capable of rendering a dense light field by using multiple input light fields which are captured by commercial light field camera. In addition, the proposed method requires neither depth estimation nor other priors. Experimental results on real-world scenes demonstrate the performance of our proposed method. The proposed method is at most capable of reconstructing four novel light fields between two input light fields. Besides, in terms of the quality of synthesized novel view images, our method outperforms state-of-the-art methods on both quantitative and qualitative results.

Our main contributions are:

(1) We present a learning-based method for reconstructing a dense light field by using a sparse set of light fields sampled by commercial light field camera.
(2) Our method is able to reconstruct a large quantity of light rays and occlusion between two distant input light fields.
(3) We introduce a high-angular-resolution light field dataset whose angular resolution is the highest among light field benchmark datasets so far.

2   Related Work

Dense sampled light field is in need for many computer vision applications. However, it costs much time and space to acquire and store massive light rays by existing devices and algorithms. Many research groups have focused on increasing a camera-captured light field's resolution by using a set of samples [5,7,11,15, 16,18,22,24,26,27,29]. Here, we survey some state-of-the-art methods.

2.1   View-Based vs. EPI-Based Angular Interpolation

Wanner and Goldluecke [22] used the estimated depth map to warp input view image to novel view. However, the quality of synthesized view is easily affected by the accuracy of depth map. Levin et al. [7] used a new prior to render a 4D light field from a 3D focal stack. Shi et al. [16] took advantage of the sparsity of light field in continuous Fourier domain to reconstruct a full light field. The method sampled multiple 1D viewpoint trajectories with special patterns to reconstruct a full 4D light field. Zhang et al. [29] introduced a phase-based method to reconstruct a full light field from micro-baseline image pair. Schedl et al. [15] reconstructed a full light field by searching for best-matching multi-dimensional patches within the dataset. However, in these methods, due to the limitation of specific sampling pattern and algorithm complexity, they are unable to properly generate a dense light field. The angular resolution of synthesized light field generated by these methods is at most 20 × 20. Marwah et al. [11] proposed a method to reconstruct light field from a coded 2D projection. But it needs a special designed equipment to capture compressive light field.

Recently, learning-based methods are explored in light field super-resolution. Kalantari et al. [5] used two sequential networks to estimate depth and color values of pixels in novel view image. Srinivasan et al. [18] proposed a learning-based method to synthesize a full 4D light field by using a single view image. However, these methods heavily rely on the accuracy of depth map. Yoon et al. [26] trained several CNNs to increase spatial and angular resolution simultaneously. However, the method could only synthesize one novel view between two or four input views. Wang et al. [20] proposed a learning-based hybrid imaging system to reconstruct light field video. Although the work did not directly aim at novel view synthesis, it in fact had synthesized novel frames containing different views of a light field. In their proposed system, DSLR provided the prior information that was equivalent to the central view of each synthesized light field frame. Instead of using extra prior to guide light field reconstruction, our proposed method only use light fields which captured by commercial light field camera as input.

Apparently, EPI has a strong characteristic of linearity. Many methods explored light field processing based on EPI. However, there are fewer work focusing on angular interpolation of light field. Wu et al. [24] trained a residual-based network to increase angular resolution of EPI. They employ a 1D blur kernel to remove high spatial frequency in the sparsely sampled EPI before feeding to the CNN. Then, they carried out a non-blind de-blur to restore high spatial frequency details which were removed by the blur kernel. However, due to the limitation of blur kernel's size and interpolation algorithm in the preprocessing, the method also fails when the baseline of input views is wide.

2.2   View Synthesis vs. Light Field Reconstruction

Many methods focus on light field view synthesis, such as [5,7,11,15,16,18,22, 24,29]. The most important insight is that all these methods synthesize novel views in internal of a light field. Due to the narrow baseline among views of existing commercial light field camera, all the input view images in these methods have high overlapping ratio between each other. These methods use redundant information of input view images. Therefore, they are only able to synthesize novel views between input ones. On the contrast, we propose a novel method to reconstruct multiple light fields between two input light fields instead of reconstructing views inside a single light field. Therefore, our proposed method is capable of reconstructing a dense light field by using a sparse set of input light fields. Besides, the method is able to reconstruct a mass of occlusion in reconstructed light fields without requiring depth estimation.

We model novel light field reconstruction based on 2D EPI. Different from other light field view synthesis methods, our proposed method directly reconstructs multiple novel light fields, as shown in Fig. 1. Besides, view planes of input light fields are not overlapping. There are hundreds of missing views between two input light fields. Therefore, the difficulty lies in that it needs to reconstruct a large quantity of light rays and occlusion.

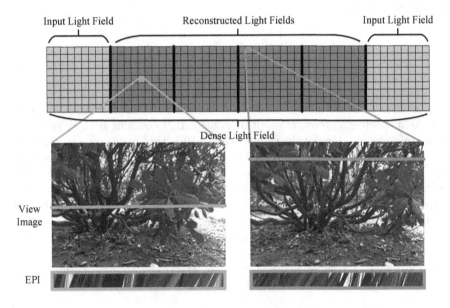

Fig. 1. An illustration of dense light field reconstruction (reconstruct 4 novel light fields between input light fields) from sparse sampling. The band on the top refers to the dense light field. Input light fields are denoted as pink, while reconstructed light fields are denoted as yellow. Our method employs a ResNet to reconstruct multiple light fields between input light fields. The view images are from two of reconstructed light fields. The EPIs are from two horizontal lines (red and blue) in dense light field. (Color figure online)

3 Problem Formulation

In the two-parallel-plane parameterization model, light field is formulated as a 4D function $L(u, v, s, t)$ [8], where the pair (u, v) represents the intersection of light ray and view plane, and (s, t) represents the intersection of light ray and image plane. In the paper, we assume that input light fields' view planes are coplanar (see Fig. 2). Besides, their view planes are non-overlapping. Our task is to reconstruct several novel light fields between these input light fields.

All views in a light field are assumed as perspective cameras with identical intrinsic parameters. The transformation between views within the same light field is merely a translation without rotation. Therefore, a 3D point $\mathbf{X} = (X, Y, Z)^\top$ in real-world scene is mapped to the pixel (s, t) in the image plane of light field as follows.

$$
\lambda \begin{bmatrix} s \\ t \\ d^{(s,t)} \\ 1 \end{bmatrix} = \begin{bmatrix} f & 0 & 0 & -fu \\ 0 & f & 0 & -fv \\ 0 & 0 & 0 & B \\ 0 & 0 & 1 & 0 \end{bmatrix} \begin{bmatrix} X \\ Y \\ Z \\ 1 \end{bmatrix} \tag{1}
$$

where B denotes a constant, $d^{(s,t)}$ refers to the disparity of (s, t), f is the spacing between view plane and image plane. Then, the constraints of a light ray in light field can be described as

$$
\begin{cases} u = X - \dfrac{B}{f} \dfrac{s}{d^{(s,t)}} \\ v = Y - \dfrac{B}{f} \dfrac{t}{d^{(s,t)}} \end{cases} \tag{2}
$$

In fact, Eq. 2 is the mathematical description of EPI which is a 2D slice cut from 4D light field. Its simple linear structure makes it easy to analyze in light field. As a specific representation of light field, EPI contains both angular and spatial information. One of the properties of EPI is that pixels on a straight line refer to different light rays emitting from the same scene point [1]. In fact, the slope of a line in EPI reflects the disparity of a point observed in different views. We define this linear constraint between u and s in EPI as disparity consistency, as formulated in Eq. 2. Based on disparity consistency, a EPI can be further formulated as

$$
epi(u, s) = epi(X - \frac{B}{f} \frac{s}{d^{(s,t)}}, s) \tag{3}
$$

For any two light fields in our assumption, the transformation between them is merely a translation without rotation

$$
\mathbf{X}' = [\mathbf{I}|\mathbf{t}]\mathbf{X} \tag{4}
$$

where $\mathbf{I}$ is an identity matrix, $\mathbf{t} = (t_x, t_y, 0)^\top$, $\mathbf{X}$ and $\mathbf{X}'$ are two scene points. Besides, the disparity of an identical scene point stays the same in multiple light fields. The transformation between EPIs of any two light fields in our assumption is formulated as

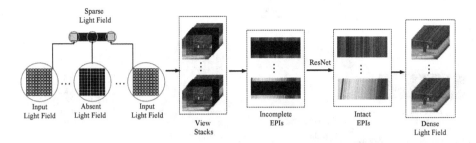

Input Light Field   Absent Light Field   Input Light Field

View Stacks   Incomplete EPIs   Intact EPIs   Dense Light Field

Fig. 2. The pipeline of the proposed method. Two input light fields' view planes are coplanar. The pixels' values in those absent light fields are initially set to zero. By employing ResNet to predict the residual values between intact EPI and incomplete EPI, all those zeroth pixels can be predicted.

$$
\begin{aligned}
epi'(u', s') &= epi'(X' - \frac{B}{f}\frac{s'}{d^{(s',t')}}, s') \\
&= epi(X + t_x - \frac{B}{f}\frac{s'}{d^{(s',t')}}, s') \\
&= epi(X - \frac{B}{f}\frac{s}{d^{(s,t)}}, s + \frac{f}{B}d^{(s,t)}t_x)
\end{aligned}
\tag{5}
$$

where $d^{(s',t')}$ is equal to $d^{(s,t)}$. Therefore, under the condition that two light fields' view planes are coplanar, their EPIs can represent each other through disparity consistency.

In our model, there are two kinds of light fields (see Fig. 2). One is the sparse light field which is made up by input light fields. The other one is the dense light field which is reconstructed based a sparse light field. In terms of the universe of light rays, the light rays in sparse light field are actually a subset of light rays in dense light field. Under our assumption, their view planes are coplanar. Therefore, their EPIs can also represent each other through disparity consistency.

$$
E_{sparse}(u', s') = E_{dense}(X - \frac{B}{f}\frac{s}{d^{(s,t)}}, s + \frac{f}{B}d^{(s,t)}t_x)
\tag{6}
$$

where E_{dense} is the dense light field's EPI, E_{sparse} is the EPI of sparse light field. Thus, we are able to reconstruct a dense light field by extending the disparity consistency in sparse light field.

4   Reconstruction Based on Residual Network

For gaining disparity consistency, disparity estimation is an error-sensitive solution with existing algorithms. In our proposed method, we extend the disparity consistency among light fields by employing a neural network.

Compared with dense light field, there are many light rays being absent in sparse light field which is composed by input light fields (see Fig. 2). Many entire

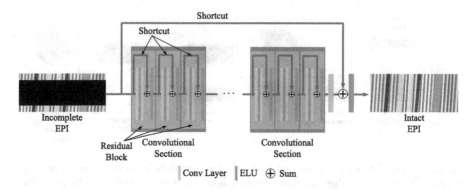

Fig. 3. The network contains 5 convolutional sections. Each section has 3 residual blocks which are defined in [3]. From the first section to the fifth one, the number of filters and filter sizes are configured as (32, 9), (64, 7), (128, 5), (256, 5), (512, 5) respectively. The input and output of the network is RGB incomplete EPI and intact EPI respectively. We use shortcut operation to maintain high frequency details of EPI during reconstruction. Each convolutional layer is followed by an exponential linear unit (ELU).

rows of pixels are needed to be reconstructed in its EPI. These missing rows form a blank band in EPI. We initially set these pixels' values to zero, as shown in Fig. 2. Our task is to find an operation that can predict the pixels' values in blank band.

4.1 Network Architecture

In fact, pixels' values of input light fields remain unchanged in the sparse light field's EPI during reconstruction. We only need to predict pixels' values in blank band. Therefore, we regard these pixels' values as the residual values between EPIs of dense and sparse light field:

$$Res = E_{dense} - E_{sparse} \tag{7}$$

where Res refers to the residual between E_{dense} and E_{sparse}. Thus, we employ ResNet [3] to predict the residual. Besides, due to particular residual blocks and shortcuts in the network, it only needs to consider the residual between input and output and preserves high frequency details of EPI. We reformulate the reconstruction of dense light field's EPI E_{dense} as follows:

$$\min_{res,\theta} \|E_{sparse} + res(E_{sparse}, \theta) - E_{dense}\| \tag{8}$$

where res refers to the operation of residual network that predicts residuals between input and output. θ refers to parameters of convolution layers in the network. Therefore, the residual between E_{sparse} and E_{dense} can be predicted by minimizing the difference between output and ground truth iteratively, which refers to $E_{sparse} + res(E_{sparse}, \theta)$ and E_{dense} respectively in Eq. 8.

The structure of supervised network is shown in Fig. 3. The network contains 32 convolutional layers. The input and output are single RGB images of incomplete EPI and intact EPI. The main part of the network contains 5 convolutional sections, and each section has 3 residual blocks demonstrated by He et al. [3]. The layers in the same section have the same number of filters and filter size. In order to preserve high frequency details in EPI, we cancel the pooling operation throughout the network and maintain the input and output at the same size in each layer.

4.2 Training Details

We have modelled light field reconstruction between input light fields as a learning-based end-to-end regression. In order to minimize the error between output and ground truth during training, we use the mean squared error (MSE) as the loss function,

$$L = \frac{1}{N} \sum_{i=1}^{N} \left\| E_{sparse}^{(i)} + res(E_{sparse}^{(i)}, \theta) - E_{dense}^{(i)} \right\|^2 \tag{9}$$

where N is the number of input EPIs. Since the training is a supervised process, we use EPI cut from the dense light fields in our dataset (see Sect. 5) as ground truth to guide the training.

In the training process, in order to converge our training model efficiently and improve the accuracy, we initialize parameters of network's filter by using Xavier method [2] and use the ADAM algorithm [6] to optimize them iteratively. Besides, to prevent the model from overfitting, we augment training data by randomly adjusting the brightness of EPIs and adding Gaussian noise to EPIs. Furthermore, we train the network with 5 epochs and each epoch contains 2256 iterations. The learning rate is set 1e−4 initially. Then, it is decreased by a factor of 0.96 every 2256 iterations so as to make the model converge more quickly. There are 30 EPIs in each batch in the training process. The training of the network takes about 23 h on 6 GPUs GTX 1080ti with the Tensorflow.

5 Results

In this section, we first explain the capturing process of our high-angular-resolution light field dataset. Then, we evaluate our proposed method on the light field dataset by using a sparse sampling pattern. In addition, we test our method's capacity of reconstructing dense light field with different sampling patterns.

Dataset. The angular resolution of existing light field datasets is too low to verify our proposed method. Since our training is supervised and need to be guided by ground truth dense light field, we create a dense light field dataset.

 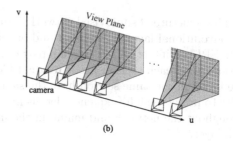

(a)   (b)

Fig. 4. (a) is the proposed capturing system of our method. The Lytro ILLUM is mounted on a translation stage in order to ensure all the captured light fields' view planes are coplanar; (b) models the capturing process. The camera moves on a straight line with a proper step size while capturing light fields. The view planes of each pair of adjacent captured light fields have overlaps.

The dataset composes of 13 indoor scenes and 13 outdoor scenes. It contains plenty of real-world static scenes, such as bicycles, toys and plants, which have abundant colors and complicated occlusion. Each scene in the dataset contains 100 light fields captured by Lytro ILLUM. There are 2600 light fields in total.

For each scene, in order to make all the captured light fields' view planes coplanar, we mount a Lytro ILLUM on a translation stage and move the camera along a line in the capturing process. Our capturing system is shown in Fig. 4(a). Furthermore, for the sake of gaining a dense light field from each scene, we set a proper step size for the camera's translation. It ensures that there is overlap between each pair of adjacent light fields' view planes, as shown in Fig. 4(b). In our experiment, there are 5 views that are overlapped between each pair of adjacent light fields. The camera focuses at infinity during the capturing. All the light fields are decoded by Lytro Power Tools [10]. For each light field, central 9×9 views are extracted from 14×14 views provided by raw data to maintain the imaging quality. Then, we fuse the overlapping views between each pair of adjacent light fields to merge all the light fields together. After merging, each scene is recorded by a 405 high-angular-resolution light field. From another perspective, the high-angular-resolution light field is composed by 45 9×9 low-angular-resolution light fields whose view planes connect with each other but have no overlapping views.

Real-World Scenes Evaluation. We design three sparse sampling patterns to evaluate the proposed method on our real-world dataset. With different sampling pattern, the number of light fields which need to be reconstructed between each pair of input light fields is different. First, we sample multiple light fields in each scenes's dense light field to make up a sparse light field. Then, we use the EPI of sparse light field as our network's input to generate the intact EPI and reconstruct a dense light field. The sampling patterns are shown in Fig. 6. We choose 20 scenes as the training data which contains 67680 EPIs. The other 6 scenes (see Fig. 5) are used to test our training model and other methods. For

Leaves	Books	Lego	Fruit	Bikes	Limb
Toys	Basket	Bicycle	Flower	Shrub	Hydrant

Fig. 5. The scenes in our light field dataset. The first row is a part of training data. The second row is testing data used to evaluate the proposed method.

our method, we reconstruct 2 novel 9×9 light fields between each pair of input light fields to verify the proposed method. The methods of Kalantari et al. [5] and Wu et al. [24] perform better than other state-of-the-art methods. Thus, we use them to evaluate the quality of views in reconstructed light fields. When we evaluate these two methods on our real-world dataset, we carefully fine-tune all parameters so as to gain the best experimental performance among their results. Furthermore, we set the same up-sampling factor in their code.

The average PSNR and SSIM values are calculated on each testing scene's reconstructed view images, listed in Table 1. In the method of Kalantari et al. [5], the quality of synthesized view is heavily dependent on the accuracy of depth map. It tends to fail in the Basket and Shrub data. Since these scenes are challenging cases for depth estimation. The method proposed by Wu et al. [24] uses the "blur-deblur" to increase the resolution of EPI instead of estimating depth. It achieves better performance than that of Kalantari et al. [5] on these. However, this method has to increase light field's angular resolution sequentially. The result of lower resolution-level's reconstruction is used as the input of higher resolution-level's reconstruction so that the constructing error is accumulated along with angular resolution's increasement. Our proposed method does not require error-sensitive depth estimation to reconstruct light field. Besides, all the light rays in the reconstructed light fields are synthesized at a time. Therefore, in terms of quantitative estimation, the results indicate that our proposed method is significant better than other methods on the quality of synthesized views.

Figure 7 shows view images in the reconstructed light field. The Toys scene contains plenty of textureless areas. Kalantari et al. [5]'s result shows heavy artifacts on the dog's mouth and the bottle, as shown in the blue and yellow boxes in the view image. The dog's mouth is teared up in their result while our result shows fidelity in these areas. The Basket scene is a challenging case due to the hollowed-out grids on the baskets. Plenty of occlusion is generated by the gridlines. The result of Kalantari et al. [5]'s method shows visual incoherency on grid area of baskets as shown in Fig. 7(b). The grids of the basket reconstructed by Wu et al. [24]'s method are also twisted. Besides, the synthesized views by Kalantari et al. [5]'s method and Wu et al. [24]'s method both show blurring

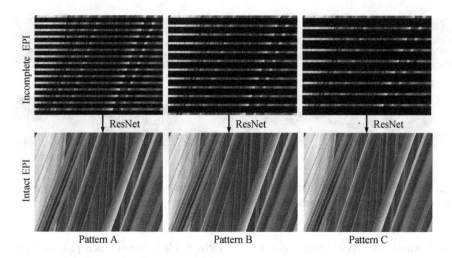

Fig. 6. The EPIs of sparse light field under different sampling patterns. The upper incomplete EPI with blank bands is cut from sparse light field. There is a certain number of light fields need to be reconstructed in blank band between each pair of input light fields. With incomplete EPI as input, our trained network outputs the lower intact EPI with all the blank bands filled in incomplete EPI. From pattern A to pattern C, the number of reconstructed light fields in each blank bands is respectively 2, 3, 4.

Table 1. PSNR and SSIM results of reconstructed light fields on real-world scenes with pattern A. The values are averaged over all the views in reconstructed light fields.

		Toys	Basket	Bicycle	Flower	Shrub	Hydrant
PSNR	Kalantari et al. [5]	34.42	30.26	30.64	31.50	28.55	31.82
	Wu et al. [24]	35.21	32.87	35.74	32.82	30.73	38.67
	Ours	**40.78**	**40.46**	**39.25**	**38.55**	**34.81**	**40.75**
SSIM	Kalantari et al. [5]	0.897	0.922	0.862	0.877	0.878	0.850
	Wu et al. [24]	0.919	0.958	0.943	0.904	0.910	0.947
	Ours	**0.942**	**0.987**	**0.949**	**0.943**	**0.932**	**0.958**

artifacts around the handle of basket, as shown in Fig. 7(b) and (c). However, our results show higher performance in those areas mentioned above. Moreover, our method has primely reconstructed high frequency details of the scenes. The Flower scene contains many leaves and petals with complex shapes which generates much occlusion. The results of Kalantari et al. [5] and Wu et al. [24] show ghost effects around the petals and occlusion edges. However, our method shows high accuracy in those occlusion and textureless areas, such as the place where two pedals with the same color overlap (see the yellow boxes of Flower scene in Fig. 7).

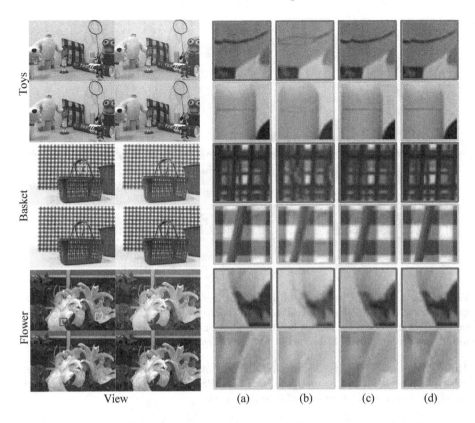

Fig. 7. The result of view images in reconstructed light field of 3 real-world scenes (reconstruct 2 novel light fields between each pair of input light fields). The first column shows view images. Upper left: ground truth. Upper right: Kalantari et al. [5]. Lower left: Wu et al. [24]. Lower right: Ours. From (a) to (d), the detailed results in the blue and yellow boxes are ground truth, Kalantari et al. [5], Wu et al. [24] and ours respectively. (Color figure online)

Figure 8 shows the details of reconstructed EPI on Flower case and Basket case. For our method, the EPIs in Fig. 8 is cropped from our results. The EPI in Flower scene contains many thin tube formed by pixels from the flower's stamen. These thin tubes are mixed together in Kalantari et al. [5]'s result. The result of Wu et al. [24]'s method shows cracked artifacts on EPI tubes. However, the EPI tubes in our results remain straight and clear. The Basket scene is a challenging case for EPI-based method. The grids on the basket also generate grids in EPI. Therefore, EPI-based method can be challenged by the complex structures in EPI. According to the results, Wu et al. [24]'s method shows many curved tubes in their result EPI. The result of Kalantari et al. [5] loses lots of details around tubes in EPI, while our result shows a structured EPI.

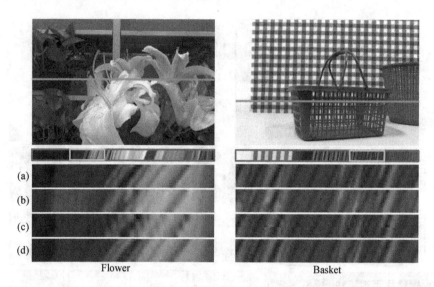

(a)

(b)

(c)

(d)

Flower   Basket

Fig. 8. The result of EPI of 2 real-world scenes. The EPIs enclosed by green box are the ground truth EPIs which are extracted from the green line in the view images. We up-sample each method's EPI result below for a better view. From (a) to (d), the detailed results are ground truth, Kalantari et al. [5], Wu et al. [24] and ours respectively.

Table 2. Comparison of reconstructing different number of novel light fields between two input light fields by our method. Time cost, PSNR and SSIM values are averaged on all reconstructed view images of 6 testing scenes.

	Pattern A	Pattern B	Pattern C
PSNR	39.10	37.08	36.04
SSIM	0.952	0.938	0.921
Time (sec)	34.26	33.61	33.44

Method Capacity. As shown in Fig. 6, with different sampling pattern, the number of light fields which need to be reconstructed between each pair of input light field is different. To test our method's capacity of reconstructing dense light field, we separately trained the network with different sampling patterns in Fig. 6 to reconstruct 2, 3, 4 novel light fields between each two input light fields. Then, we evaluate the results over 6 testing scenes. Table 2 indicates that time cost, PSNR and SSIM values average on 6 testing scenes decrease as the reconstructing number increases between each pair of input light fields. Figure 9 depicts L_1 error maps of the view images in reconstructed light field with different sampling patterns. It indicates that when the reconstructing number increases, the quality of reconstructed light fields also decreases. More results are shown in our supplementary material.

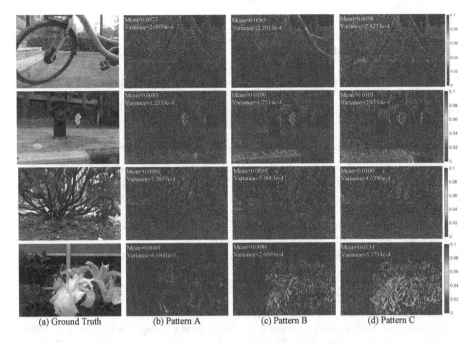

| (a) Ground Truth | (b) Pattern A | (c) Pattern B | (d) Pattern C |

Fig. 9. Reconstruction error analyses of different sampling patterns. (a) is ground truth view image. (b–d) are error maps and statistics under different light fields sampling patterns.

6   Conclusions and Future Work

We propose a novel learning-based method for reconstructing a dense light field from sparse sampling. We model novel light fields reconstruction as extending disparity consistency between dense and sparse light fields. Besides, we introduce a dense sampled light field dataset in which light field has the highest angular resolution so far. The experimental results show that our method can not only reconstruct a dense light field using 2 input light fields, but also extend to multiple input light fields. In addition, our method has a higher performance in the quality of synthesized view than state-of-the-art view synthesis methods.

Currently, our method is only able to deal with light fields which are captured along a sliding track without orientation change of principal axis. In the future, we will generalize our method to multiple degrees of freedom motion of light field camera. Furthermore, it would be interesting to choose suitable sampling rate of light rays automatically and reconstruct dense light field for a specific scene.

References

1. Bolles, R.C., Baker, H.H., Marimont, D.H.: Epipolar-plane image analysis: an approach to determining structure from motion. IJCV **1**(1), 7–55 (1987)
2. Glorot, X., Bengio, Y.: Understanding the difficulty of training deep feedforward neural networks. In: AISTATS, pp. 249–256 (2010)
3. He, K., Zhang, X., Ren, S., Sun, J.: Deep residual learning for image recognition. In: IEEE CVPR, pp. 770–778 (2016)
4. Jeon, H.G., et al.: Accurate depth map estimation from a lenslet light field camera. In: IEEE CVPR, pp. 1547–1555 (2015)
5. Kalantari, N.K., Wang, T.C., Ramamoorthi, R.: Learning-based view synthesis for light field cameras. ACM TOG **35**(6), 193 (2016)
6. Kingma, D.P., Ba, J.: Adam: a method for stochastic optimization. arXiv preprint arXiv:1412.6980 (2014)
7. Levin, A., Durand, F.: Linear view synthesis using a dimensionality gap light field prior. In: IEEE CVPR, pp. 1831–1838 (2010)
8. Levoy, M., Hanrahan, P.: Light field rendering. In: ACM SIGGRAPH, pp. 31–42 (1996)
9. Li, N., Ye, J., Ji, Y., Ling, H., Yu, J.: Saliency detection on light field. In: IEEE CVPR, pp. 2806–2813 (2014)
10. Lytro (2016). https://www.lytro.com/
11. Marwah, K., Wetzstein, G., Bando, Y., Raskar, R.: Compressive light field photography using overcomplete dictionaries and optimized projections. ACM TOG **32**(4), 46 (2013)
12. Ng, R.: Digital light field photography. Ph.D. thesis, Stanford University (2006)
13. RayTrix: 3D light field camera technology. https://raytrix.de/
14. Ren, Z., Zhang, Q., Zhu, H., Wang, Q.: Extending the FOV from disparity and color consistencies in multiview light fields. In: Proceedings of the ICIP, Beijing, China, pp. 1157–1161 (2017)
15. Schedl, D.C., Birklbauer, C., Bimber, O.: Directional super-resolution by means of coded sampling and guided upsampling. In: IEEE ICCP, pp. 1–10 (2015)
16. Shi, L., Hassanieh, H., Davis, A., Katabi, D., Durand, F.: Light field reconstruction using sparsity in the continuous Fourier domain. ACM TOG **34**(1), 12 (2014)
17. Si, L., Wang, Q.: Dense depth-map estimation and geometry inference from light fields via global optimization. In: Lai, S.-H., Lepetit, V., Nishino, K., Sato, Y. (eds.) ACCV 2016. LNCS, vol. 10113, pp. 83–98. Springer, Cham (2017). https://doi.org/10.1007/978-3-319-54187-7_6
18. Srinivasan, P.P., Wang, T., Sreelal, A., Ramamoorthi, R., Ng, R.: Learning to synthesize a 4D RGBD light field from a single image. In: IEEE ICCV, vol. 2, p. 6 (2017)
19. Wang, T.C., Efros, A.A., Ramamoorthi, R.: Depth estimation with occlusion modeling using light-field cameras. IEEE T-PAMI **38**(11), 2170–2181 (2016)
20. Wang, T.C., Zhu, J.Y., Kalantari, N.K., Efros, A.A., Ramamoorthi, R.: Light field video capture using a learning-based hybrid imaging system. ACM TOG **36**(4), 133 (2017)
21. Wanner, S., Goldluecke, B.: Globally consistent depth labeling of 4D light fields. In: IEEE CVPR, pp. 41–48 (2012)
22. Wanner, S., Goldluecke, B.: Variational light field analysis for disparity estimation and super-resolution. IEEE T-PAMI **36**(3), 606–619 (2014)

23. Wilburn, B., et al.: High performance imaging using large camera arrays. ACM TOG **24**, 765–776 (2005)
24. Wu, G., Zhao, M., Wang, L., Dai, Q., Chai, T., Liu, Y.: Light field reconstruction using deep convolutional network on EPI. In: IEEE CVPR, vol. 2017, p. 2 (2017)
25. Xiao, Z., Wang, Q., Zhou, G., Yu, J.: Aliasing detection and reduction scheme on angularly undersampled light fields. IEEE TIP **26**(5), 2103–2115 (2017)
26. Yoon, Y., Jeon, H.G., Yoo, D., Lee, J.Y., So Kweon, I.: Learning a deep convolutional network for light-field image super-resolution. In: IEEE ICCV Workshops, pp. 24–32 (2015)
27. Zhang, F.L., Wang, J., Shechtman, E., Zhou, Z.Y., Shi, J.X., Hu, S.M.: PlenoPatch: patch-based plenoptic image manipulation. IEEE T-VCG **23**(5), 1561–1573 (2017)
28. Zhang, Q., Zhang, C., Ling, J., Wang, Q., Yu, J.: A generic multi-projection-center model and calibration method for light field cameras. IEEE T-PAMI (2018). https://doi.org/10.1109/TPAMI.2018.2864617
29. Zhang, Z., Liu, Y., Dai, Q.: Light field from micro-baseline image pairs. In: IEEE CVPR, pp. 3800–3809 (2015)
30. Zhu, H., Wang, Q., Yu, J.: Occlusion-model guided anti-occlusion depth estimation in light field. IEEE J-STSP **11**(7), 965–978 (2017). https://doi.org/10.1109/JSTSP.2017.2730818
31. Zhu, H., Zhang, Q., Wang, Q.: 4D light field superpixel and segmentation. In: IEEE CVPR, pp. 6709–6717 (2017)

Exploring the Challenges Towards
Lifelong Fact Learning

Mohamed Elhoseiny[1(✉)], Francesca Babiloni[2], Rahaf Aljundi[2],
Marcus Rohrbach[1], Manohar Paluri[1], and Tinne Tuytelaars[2]

[1] Facebook AI Research, Palo Alto, USA
{elhoseiny,mrf,mano}@fb.com
[2] KU Leuven, Leuven, Belgium
{francesca.babiloni,rahaf.aljundi,tinne.tuytelaars}@esat.kuleuven.be

Abstract. So far life-long learning (LLL) has been studied in relatively
small-scale and relatively artificial setups. Here, we introduce a new
large-scale alternative. What makes the proposed setup more natural
and closer to human-like visual systems is threefold: First, we focus on
concepts (or *facts*, as we call them) of varying complexity, ranging from
single objects to more complex structures such as objects performing
actions, and objects interacting with other objects. Second, as in real-
world settings, our setup has a long-tail distribution, an aspect which
has mostly been ignored in the LLL context. Third, facts across tasks
may share structure (e.g., ⟨person, riding, wave⟩ and ⟨dog, riding, wave⟩).
Facts can also be semantically related (e.g., "liger" relates to seen categories like "tiger" and "lion"). Given the large number of possible facts, a
LLL setup seems a natural choice. To avoid model size growing over time
and to optimally exploit the semantic relations and structure, we combine
it with a visual semantic embedding instead of discrete class labels. We
adapt existing datasets with the properties mentioned above into new
benchmarks, by dividing them semantically or randomly into disjoint
tasks. This leads to two large-scale benchmarks with 906,232 images and
165,150 unique facts, on which we evaluate and analyze state-of-the-art
LLL methods.

1 Introduction

Humans can learn new visual concepts without significantly forgetting previously
learned ones and without necessarily having to revisit previous ones. In contrast,
the majority of existing artificial visual deep learning systems assume a replay-
access to all the training images and all the concepts during the entire training
phase – e.g., going a large number of epochs over the 1000 classes of ImageNet.
This assumption also applies to systems that learn concepts by reading the web

Electronic supplementary material The online version of this chapter (https://
doi.org/10.1007/978-3-030-20876-9_5) contains supplementary material, which is available to authorized users.

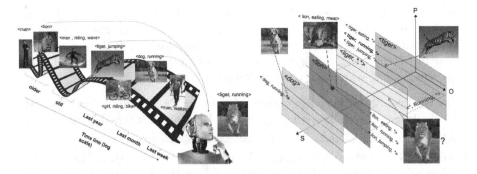

Fig. 1. Lifelong Fact Learning   **Fig. 2.** Structured fact representation

(e.g., [5,6,20]) or that augment CNNs with additional units to better transfer knowledge to new tasks such as [29].

To get closer to human visual learning and to practical application scenarios, where data often cannot be stored due to physical restrictions (e.g. robotics) or policy (e.g. privacy), the scenario of lifelong learning (LLL) has been proposed. The assumption of LLL is that only a subset of the concepts and corresponding training instances are available at each point in time during training. Each of these subsets is referred to as a "task", originating from robotics applications [27]. This leads to a chain of learning tasks trained on a time-line. While training of the first task is typically unchanged, the challenge is how to train the remaining tasks without reducing performance on the earlier tasks. Indeed, when doing so naively, e.g. by fine-tuning previous models, this results in what is known as *catastrophic forgetting*, i.e., the accuracy on the earlier tasks drops significantly. Avoiding such catastrophic forgetting is the main challenge addressed in the lifelong learning literature.

Lifelong Fact Learning (LLFL). Existing works on LLL have focused mostly on image classification tasks (e.g. [2,11,16,23,28,30]), in a relatively small-scale and somewhat artificial setup. A sequence of tasks is defined, either by combining multiple datasets (e.g., learning to recognize MITscenes, then CUB-birds, then Flowers), by dividing a dataset (usually CIFAR100 or MNIST) into sets of disjoint concepts, or by permuting the input (permuted MNIST). Instead, in this work we propose a LLL setup with the following more realistic and desirable learning characteristics:

1. *Long-tail:* Training data can be highly unbalanced with the majority of concepts occurring only rarely, which is in contrast to many existing benchmarks (e.g., [10,14,26]).
2. *Concepts of varying complexity:* We want to learn diverse concepts, including not only objects but also actions, interactions, attributes, as well as combinations thereof.
3. *Semantic and structure aware:* We want to connect semantically related visual facts. For example, if we have learned "lion" and "tiger" earlier, that can help

us later in time to learn a "liger" (a rare hybrid cross between a male lion and a female tiger), even with just a few examples. Relating this to point (2) above, this further allows *compositional lifelong learning* to help recognize new facts (e.g. ⟨dog, riding, wave⟩) based on facts seen earlier in time (e.g. ⟨person, riding, wave⟩ and ⟨girl, walking, dog⟩).

To the best of our knowledge, none of the existing LLL literature explored these challenges. We denote studying lifelong learning with the aforementioned characteristics as *lifelong fact learning* (LLFL); see Fig. 1.

A Note on Evaluation Measures. We argue that the evaluation of LLL methods should be reconsidered. In the standard LLL (with a few notable exceptions, such as [2,4]), the trained models are judged by their capability to recognize each task's categories individually assuming the absence of the categories covered by the remaining tasks – *not necessarily realistic*. Although the performance of each task in isolation is an important characteristic, it might be deceiving. Indeed, a learnt representation could be good to classify an image in a restricted concept space covered by a single task, but may not be able to classify the same image when considering all concepts across tasks. It is therefore equally important to measure the ability to distinguish the learnt concepts across all the concepts over all tasks. This is important since the objective of LLL is to model the understanding of an ever growing set of concepts over time. *To better understand how LLL performs in real world conditions, we advocate evaluating the existing methods across different tasks.* We named that evaluation *Generalized lifelong learning* (G-LLL), in line with the idea of Generalized zero-shot learning proposed in [3]. We detail the evaluation metric in Sect. 5.1.

Advantages of a Visual-Semantic Embedding. As illustrated in Fig. 1, we expect to better understand ⟨liger, running⟩ by leveraging previously learnt facts such as ⟨lion⟩, ⟨tiger, jumping⟩ and ⟨dog, running⟩. This shows how both semantics and structure are helpful for understanding. To our knowledge, such semantic awareness has not been studied in a LLL context. To achieve this, we use a visual-semantic embedding model where semantic labels and images are embedded in a joint space. For the semantic representation, we leverage semantic external knowledge using word embeddings – in particular word2vec [19]. These word embeddings were shown to efficiently learn semantically meaningful floating point vector representations of words. For example, the average vector of lion and tiger is closest to liger. This can help semantically similar concepts to learn better from one another, as shown in [7,31] in non LLL scenarios. Especially in our long-tail setting, this can be advantageous. Additionally, by working with an embedding instead of discrete concept labels as in [8,12,15,30], we avoid that the model keeps growing as new concepts get added, which would make the model less scalable and limit the amount of sharing.

Contributions. First, we introduce a midscale and a large scale benchmark for Lifelong Fact Learning (LLFL), with two splits each, a random and a semantic split. Our approach for creating a semantically divided benchmark is general and could be applied similarly to other datasets or as more data becomes available.

Table 1. Comparison of some existing task sequences. Split type is either S (Semantic), R (Random), or S&R (Both Semantic and Random splits are provided)

Dataset	Structured/Diverse	Long-Tail	Classes	Examples	Task Count	Split Type
MNIST	✗	✗	10	60000	2 to 5	R
CIFAR (used in [23,30,18])	✗	✗	100	60000	2 and 5	R
ImageNet and CUB datasets (used in [15])	✗	✗	1200	1211000	2	R
Scenes, CUB, VOC, and Flowers (used in [16,2,28])	✗	✗	122-526	5908-1211000	2	S
8 Dataset Sequence [1]	✗	✗	889	714387	8	S
CORe50 [17] / iCUBWorld-Transf([21]	✗	✗	10 (50)/15(150)	550/900 sessions	10	S
Our Mid-Scale LLFL Benchmark	✓	✗	186	28624	4	S & R
Our Large Scale LLFL Benchmark	✓	✓	165150	906232	8	S & R

Second, we advocate to focus on a more generalized evaluation (G-LLL) where test-data cover the entire label space across tasks. Third, we evaluate existing LLL approaches in both the standard and the generalized setup on our new LLFL benchmarks. Fourth, we discuss the limitations of the current generation of LLL methods in this context, which forms a basis for advancing the field in future research. Finally, this paper aims to answer the following questions: *How do existing LLL methods perform on a large number of concepts? What division of tasks is more helpful to continually learn facts at scale (semantically divided vs randomly divided)? How does the long-tail distribution of the facts limit the performance of the current methods?*

2   Related Work

Previous Evaluations of LLL. In Table 1, we compare some of the popular datasets/benchmarks used in LLL. As also noted by Rebuffi *et al.* [23], there is limited agreement about the setup. Most build a task sequence by combining or dividing standard object/scene recognition datasets. In the context of robotics, Lomonaco and Maltoni [17] introduced the CORe50 dataset which consists of relatively short RGB-D video fragments (15 s) of handheld domestic objects. They focus both on category-level as well as instance-level object recognition. With 50 objects belonging to 10 different categories it is, however, relatively small scale and limited in scope. Pasquale *et al.* with a similar focus proposed the iCUBWorld-Transf dataset [21] with 200 real objects divided in 20 categories. For CORe50 and iCUBWorld-Transf, the number of instances is shown in parenthesis in Table 1. In a reinforcement learning setup, Kirkpatrick *et al.* [12] and Fernando *et al.* [8] performed interesting LLL experiments using a sequence of Atari Games as tasks. In contrast to all of the above, we aim at a more natural and a larger-scale setup; see last two rows in Table 1. Our benchmarks are more structured and challenging, due to the large number of classes and the long-tail distribution.

Existing LLL Approaches. LLL works may be categorized into data-based and model-based approaches. In this work, we do not consider methods that require storing samples from previous tasks in an episodic memory [18,23].

In *data-based approaches* [16,25,28], the new task data is used to estimate and preserve the model behavior on previous tasks, mostly via a knowledge distillation loss as proposed in *Learning without Forgetting* [16]. These approaches are typically applied to a sequence of tasks with different output spaces. To reduce the effect of distribution difference between tasks, Triki *et al.* [28] propose to incorporate a shallow auto-encoder to further control the changes to the learned features, while Aljundi *et al.* [2] train a model for every task (an expert) and use auto-encoders to help determine the most related expert at test time given an example input.

Model-based approaches [8,12,15,30] on the other hand focus on the parameters of the network. The key idea is to define an importance weight ω_i for each parameter θ_i in the network indicating the importance of this parameter to the previous tasks. When training a new task, network parameters with high importance are discouraged from being changed. In *Elastic Weight Consolidation*, Kirkpatrick *et al.* [12] estimate the importance weights Ω based on the inverse of the Fisher Information matrix. Zenke *et al.* [30] propose *Synaptic Intelligence*, an online continual model where Ω is defined by the contribution of each parameter to the change in the loss, and weights are accumulated for each parameter during training. *Memory Aware Synapses* [1] measures Ω by the effect of a change in the parameter to the function learned by the network, rather than to the loss. This allows to estimate the importance weights not only in an online fashion but also without the need for labels. Finally, *Incremental Moment Matching* [15] is a scheme to merge models trained for different tasks. Model-based methods seem particularly well suited for our setup, given that we work with an embedding instead of disjoint output spaces.

3 Our Lifelong Fact Learning Setups

We aim to build two LLL benchmarks that consist of a diverse set of facts (two splits for large-scale and two splits for mid-scale). The benchmarks capture different types of facts including objects (e.g., ⟨lion⟩, ⟨tiger⟩), objects performing some activities (e.g., ⟨tiger, jumping⟩, ⟨dog,running⟩), and interactions between objects (e.g., ⟨lion, eating, meat⟩). Before giving details on the benchmark construction, we first explain how we represent facts.

A Visual-Semantic Embedding for Facts. Inspired by [7,22], we represent every fact for our LLL purpose by three pieces represented in a semantic continuous space. $\mathbf{S} \in \mathbb{R}^d$ represents object or scene categories. $\mathbf{P} \in \mathbb{R}^d$ represents predicates, e.g. actions or interactions. $\mathbf{O} \in \mathbb{R}^d$ represents objects that interact with $\mathbf{S}$. Each of $\mathbf{S}$, $\mathbf{P}$, and $\mathbf{O}$ lives in a high dimensional semantic space. By concatenating these three representations, we obtain a structured space that can represent all the facts that we are interested to study in this work. Here, we follow [7] and semantically represent each of $\mathbf{S}$, $\mathbf{P}$, and $\mathbf{O}$ by their corresponding word2vec embeddings [19].

$$\langle \mathbf{S,P,O} \rangle \text{ (e.g., <person, riding, horse>)}: \mathbf{t} = [\mathbf{t}_S, \mathbf{t}_P, \mathbf{t}_O]$$
$$\langle \mathbf{S, P,*} \rangle \text{ (e.g., <man, walking, *>)}: \mathbf{t} = [\mathbf{t}_S, \mathbf{t}_P, \mathbf{t}_O = *] \tag{1}$$
$$\langle \mathbf{S,*,*} \rangle \text{ (e.g., <dog, *, *>)}: \mathbf{t} = [\mathbf{t}_S, \mathbf{t}_P = *, \mathbf{t}_O = *]$$

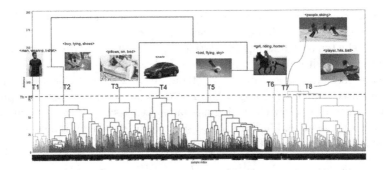

Fig. 3. Lifelong learning semantically divided benchmark: 8 tasks generated by agglomerative clustering in the semantic space of facts. The method is general and can be re-applied as more images and labels become available. (Color figure online)

where $[\cdot, \cdot, \cdot]$ is the concatenation operation and $*$ means undefined and set to zeros. The rationale behind this notation convention is that if a ground truth image is annotated as $\langle$man$\rangle$, this could also be $\langle$man, standing$\rangle$ or $\langle$man, wearing, t-shirt$\rangle$. Hence, we represent the man as $\langle$man, $*$, $*\rangle$, where $*$ indicates that we do not know if that "man" is doing something. Figure 2 shows how different fact types could be represented in this space, with **S**, **P**, and **O** visualized as a single dimension. Note that **S** facts like $\langle$lion$\rangle$ are represented as a hyper plane in this space. While $\langle$tiger, jumping$\rangle$ and $\langle$lion, eating, meat$\rangle$ are represented as a hyper-line and a point respectively.

3.1 Large Scale LLFL Benchmark

We build our setup on top of the large scale fact learning dataset introduced by [7], denoted as *Sherlock LSC* (for Large SCale). It has more than 900,000 images and 200,000 unique facts, from which we excluded attributes. The dataset was created by extracting facts about images from image descriptions and image scene graphs. It matches our desired properties of being *long-tailed* and *semantic-aware* due to its structure.

Given this very large set of facts and examples for each of them, we want to learn them in a LLL setting. This involves splitting the data into a sequence of *disjoint* tasks (that is, with no overlap in the facts learned by different tasks). However, due to their structured nature, facts may be *partially* overlapping across tasks, e.g. have the same subject or object. In fact, we believe that some knowledge reappearing across different tasks is a desired property in many real-life LLL settings, as it facilitates knowledge transfer. On the other hand, one could argue that the different tasks that real world artificial agents are exposed to, are likely to cover different domains – a setting more in line with existing LLL works. To study both scenarios, we built a semantically divided split (less sharing among tasks) and a randomly divided one (with more sharing).

Large Scale Semantically Divided Split. We semantically group the facts to create the tasks needed to build our benchmark, i.e. we cluster similar facts and assign each cluster to a task T_i. In particular, we first populate the structured embedding space with all the training facts and then cluster the facts semantically with a custom metric. Since our setting allows diverse facts where one or two of the three components might be undefined, we need to consider a proper similarity measure to allow clustering the facts. We assume that the structured fact space is Euclidean and has unit norm (i.e., cosine distance). Hence, we define the distance between two facts t_i and t_j as follows:

$$D(\mathbf{t}^i, \mathbf{t}^j) = \frac{w_S^{ij}\|\mathbf{t}_S^i - \mathbf{t}_S^j\|^2 + w_P^{ij}\|\mathbf{t}_P^i - \mathbf{t}_P^j\|^2 + w_O^{ij}\|\mathbf{t}_O^i - \mathbf{t}_O^j\|^2}{w_S^{ij} + w_P^{ij} + w_O^{ij}} \tag{2}$$

$$w_l^{ij} = 0 \text{ only if } \mathbf{t}_l^i = * \text{ or } \mathbf{t}_l^j = *, l \in \{\mathbf{S}, \mathbf{P}, \mathbf{O}\} \text{ and } w_l^{ij} = 1 \text{ otherwise.}$$

with w_l an indicator value distinguishing between singleton facts, pairs or triplets. The intuition behind this distance measure is that we do not want to penalize the $*$ (undefined) part when comparing for example $t_i = \langle\text{person}, *, *\rangle$ to $t_j = \langle\text{person, jumping}, *\rangle$. In this case the distance should be zero since the $*$ piece does not contribute to the distance measure. We rely on bottom-up hierarchical agglomerative clustering which clusters facts together monotonically based on their distance into disjoint tasks using the aforementioned distance measure. This clustering algorithm recursively merges the pair of clusters that minimally increases a given linkage metric. In our experiments, we use the nearest point algorithm, i.e. clustering with single linkage. An advantage of the agglomerative clustering algorithm is that the distance measure need not be a metric.

The result of the clustering is shown in the form of a Dendrogram in Fig. 3. By looking at the clustered facts, we choose a threshold of 85, shown by the red-dashed line, leading to $n = 8$ tasks in our work, as detailed further in Table 2. We attach in the supplementary a PCA visualization of the generated tasks using the word embedding representation of each fact and histogram over facts to illustrate the long-tail. We note that the number of facts and images is not uniform across tasks, and some tasks are likely easier than others. We believe this mimics realistic scenarios, where an agent will have to handle tasks which are of diverse challenges.

Table 2. Number of unique facts (i.e., Labels) and images in each of the 8 tasks for our semantically and randomly divided large-scale benchmark for $\langle S\rangle$, $\langle S, P\rangle$, and $\langle S, P, O\rangle$

	Random						Semantic					
Task	Facts-SPO	Facts-SP	Facts-S	images-SPO	images-SP	images-S	Task	Facts-SPO	Facts-SP	Facts-S	images-SPO	images-SP	images-S
1	19311	7100	1114	40244	41523	102605	1	6577	224	1	19311	41523	102605
2	16051	5926	961	35265	34234	99442	2	25552	2871	3	16051	34234	99442
3	14594	5305	796	27812	32215	58009	3	12400	517	250	14594	32215	58009
4	13430	4851	761	26069	24701	66355	4	7923	305	46	13430	24701	66355
5	8713	3255	524	18217	17588	100465	5	42264	24381	6321	8713	17588	100465
6	14125	5274	830	30827	32830	57656	6	2819	413	7	14125	32830	57656
7	16688	5935	876	34313	30582	55362	7	6917	1181	4	16688	30582	55362
8	13083	4845	802	28255	27525	366338	8	11543	12599	32	13083	27525	366338
Total	115995	42491	6664	241002	241198	906232	36	115995	42491	6664	115995	241198	906232

Large Scale Randomly Divided Split. We also introduce a randomly divided benchmark where the facts are divided randomly over tasks rather than based on semantics. The semantic overlap between randomly split tasks is expected to be higher than for the semantically-split tasks where the semantic similarity between tasks is minimized. Table 2 shows the task information some further information for both types of splits. For the random split, we make sure that the tasks contain a balanced number of facts and of corresponding training and test images by selecting the most balanced candidate out of 100 random trials. Hence, the random split is more balanced by construction in terms of training images per task. Since we split the data randomly into tasks, semantically related facts would be distributed across tasks.

3.2   Mid Scale Balanced LLFL Benchmark

Compared to the large scale dataset, this dataset is more balanced, with the long-tail effect being less pronounced. This allows us to contrast any change in the behavior of the LLL methods going from a uniform distribution to a long-tail distribution. We build the mid-scale LLFL dataset on top of the 6DS dataset introduced in [7]. It is composed of 186 unique facts and 28,624 images, divided in 14,599 training samples and 14,025 test samples. We divided this dataset randomly and semantically into 4 tasks.

Mid-Scale Semantic Split. We use the same mechanism for clustering as described above to create a benchmark of 4 tasks that are semantically divided. By visually analyzing the clusters, we find the following distribution: - *Task 1:* facts describing human actions such as ⟨person, riding bike⟩, ⟨person, jumping⟩, - *Task 2:* facts of different objects such as ⟨battingball⟩, ⟨battingstumps⟩, ⟨dog⟩, ⟨car⟩, - *Task 3:* facts describing humans holding or playing musical instruments, such as ⟨person, playing, flute⟩, ⟨person, holding, cello⟩, etc. - *Task 4:* facts describing human interactions such as ⟨person, arguing with, person⟩, ⟨person, dancing with, person⟩.

Mid-Scale Random Split. We followed the same procedure described in the large scale benchmarks to split the facts into 4 different random groups. Note that [1] evaluated image retrieval (with average precision) on a similar random-split of 6DS [7] while in this work we look at the task of fact recognition (measured in accuracy), which is meaningful for both the mid-scale and the large-scale benchmarks (our focus) since the vast majority of the facts has only one image example.

4   Lifelong Learning Approaches

In this section, we first formalize the life-long learning task, then we review the evaluated methods, and finally we explain how we adapt them to fact learning.

4.1   LLL Task

Given a training set $\mathcal{D} = \{(\mathbf{x}_k, y_k)\}_{k=1}^{M}$, we learn from different tasks $T_1, T_2, \ldots, T_N$ over time where $T_n \subset \mathcal{D}$. y_k in our benchmarks are structured labels. For most model-based approaches, we can formalize the LLL loss as follows. The loss of training the new n^{th} task is $L_n(\theta)$, where θ are the parameters of the network such that θ_i is the ith parameter of an arbitrary neural network (a deep neural network with both convolutional and fully connected layers, in our case). $L(\theta)$ is defined as $L(\theta) = L_n(\theta) + \frac{\lambda}{2} \sum_i \omega_i^{n-1}(\theta_i - \theta_i^{n-1})^2$, where λ is a hyperparameter for the regularizer, θ_i^{n-1} the previous task's network parameters, and ω_i^{n-1} a weight indicating the importance of parameter θ_i for all tasks up to $n-1$. Hence, we strongly regularize the important parameters at the previous time step (i.e., high ω_i^{n-1}) and weak regularization on the non-important parameters (i.e., low ω_i^{n-1}). This way, we allow changing the latter more freely. Under this importance weight based framework, Finetuning, Intelligent Synapses [30] and Memory Aware Synapses [1] are special cases.

4.2   Evaluated Methods

(1) **Finetuning** (FT): FT is a common LLL baseline. It does not involve any importance parameters, so $\omega_i^n = 0, \forall i$.

(2) **Synaptic Intelligence** [30]: (Int.Synapses) estimates the importance weights in an online manner while training based on the contribution of each parameter to the change in the loss. The more a parameter θ_i contributes to a change in the loss, the more important it is.

(3) **Memory Aware Synapses** [1]: (MAS) defines importance of parameters in an online way based on their contribution to the change in the function output. $\omega_i^n = \frac{1}{M_n} \sum_{k=1}^{M_n} \| g_i(x_k) \|$, where $g_i(x_k) = \frac{\partial (F(x_k;\theta))}{\partial \theta_i}$ is the gradient of the learned function with respect to θ_i evaluated at the data point x_k. F maps the input X_i to the output Y_i. This mapping is the target that MAS preserves to deal with forgetting.

(4) **ExpertGate** [2]: ExpertGate is a data-based approach that learns an expert model for every task $E_1, E_2, \cdots E_n$, where every expert is adapted from the most related task. An auto-encoder model is trained for every task $AE_1, AE_2, \cdots AE_n$. These auto-encoders help determine the most related expert at test time given an example input x. The expert is then to make the prediction on x. Note the memory storage requirements of ExpertGate is n times the number of parameters of a single model which might limit its practicality.

(5) **Incremental Moment Matching** [15] (IMM): For N sequential tasks, IMM finds the optimal parameter $\mu_{1:N}^*$ and $\Sigma_{1:N}^*$ of the Gaussian approximation function $q_{1:N}$ from the posterior parameter for each nth task, (μ_n, Σ_n). At the end of the learned sequence, the obtained models are merged through a first or second moment matching. Similarly to ExpertGate, IMM needs to store all models - at least if one wants to be able to add more tasks in the future. We find the mode IMM to work consistently better than the mean IMM so we report it in our experiments.

(6) **Joint Training** (Joint): In joint training, the data is not divided into tasks and the model is trained on the entire training data at once. As such, it violates the LLL assumption. This can be seen as an upper bound for all LLL methods that we evaluate.

4.3   Adapting LLL Methods to Fact Learning

We use the joint-embedding architecture proposed in [7] as our backbone architecture to compare the evaluated methods. We chose this architecture due its superior performance compared to other joint-embedding models like [9,13,24] and its competitive performance to multi-class cross-entropy. The main difference between joint embedding models and standard classification models is in the output layer. Instead of a softmax output, the last layer in a joint-embedding model consists of a projection onto a joint embedding space. This allows exploiting the semantic relation between facts as well as the structure in the data, as explained before. However, as discussed in the related work section, this is problematic for some of the LLL methods, such as [15,28] that assume a different output space for each task. This makes the problem challenging and may raise other forgetting aspects. Note that we used the same data loss term in all the evaluated methods in the previous section.

5   Experiments

We first present the evaluation metrics, then evaluate the different methods on our benchmarks and discuss the results, and finally we provide a more detailed analysis on long-tail, knowledge acquisition over time, and few-shot learning.

5.1   Fact Learning Evaluation Metrics

Evaluation Metric (Standard vs Generalized). A central concept of LLL is that at a given time n we can only observe a subset T_n of the labeled training data $T_n = \{(\mathbf{x}_k, y_k)\}_{k=1}^{M_n} \subset \mathcal{D}$. Over time, we learn from different tasks $T_1, T_2, \ldots, T_N$. The categories in the different tasks are not intersecting, i.e., if Y_n is the set of all category labels in task T_n then $Y_n \cap Y_{n'} = \emptyset, \forall n \neq n'$. Let $\mathcal{Y}$ denote the entire label space covered by all tasks, i.e., $\mathcal{Y} = \cup Y_n, \forall n$. Many existing works assume that one does not have to disambiguate between different tasks, i.e. for a predictive function $f_y : X \mapsto \mathbb{R}$, we compute $A_{T_n \to Y_n}$ as the accuracy of classifying test data from T_n (the nth task) into Y_n (the label space of T_n). The accuracy is computed per task.

Standard LLL (S-LLL) Accuracy: $A_{T_n \to Y_n} = \dfrac{1}{M_n} \sum_n^{M_n} 1[y_k = \arg \max_{y' \in Y_n} f_{y'}(x_k)]$

$$(3)$$

where y_k is the ground truth label for instance x_k. This metric assumes that at test time one knows the task of the input image. This is how most existing works are evaluated. However, this ignores the fact that determining the right task can be hard, especially when tasks are related. Therefore, we also evaluate across all tasks, which we refer to as *Generalized LLL*.

Generalized LLL (G-LLL) Accuracy: $A_{T_n \to \mathcal{Y}} = \frac{1}{M_n} \sum_{k}^{M_n} 1[y_k = \arg \max_{y' \in \mathcal{Y}} f_{y'}(x_k)]$

$$(4)$$

In the generalized LLL metric, the search space at evaluation time covers the entire label space across tasks (i.e., $\mathcal{Y}$). Hence, we compute $A_{T_n \to \mathcal{Y}}$ as the accuracy of classifying test data from T_n (the nth task) into $\mathcal{Y}$ (the entire label space) which is more realistic in many cases. In our experiments, $f_y(x)$ is a visual-semantic embedding model, i.e., $f_y(x) = s(\phi(x), \psi(y))$ where $s(\cdot, \cdot)$ is a similarity function between the visual embedding of image x denoted by $\phi(x)$ and the semantic embedding of label y denoted by $\psi(y)$. $\phi(x)$ is typically a CNN sub-network and $\psi(y)$ is a semantic embedding function of the label y (e.g., word2vec [19]). The above two metrics can easily be generalized to Top K standard and generalized accuracy that we use in our experiments.

For each metric, we summarize results by averaging over tasks ("mean") and over examples ("mean over examples"), creating slightly different results when tasks are not balanced.

Similarity Measure between Tasks (word2vec, SPO Overlap). As an analysis tool, we measure similarity between tasks in both the Semantic and the Random splits using two metrics. In the first metric, the similarity is measured by the cosine similarity between average word2vec representation of the facts in each task. In the second metric, we computed the overlap between the two tasks, separately for S, P, and O. For example, to compute the overlap in S, we first compute the number of intersecting unique subjects and divide that by the union of unique subjects in both tasks. This results in a ratio between 0 and 1 that we compute for subjects and similarly for objects and predicates. Based on these three ratios, we compute their geometric mean as an indicator for the similarity between the two tasks. We denote this measure as the SPO overlap.

5.2   Results

In this section we compare several state-of-the art LLL approaches on the mid-scale and the large-scale LLL benchmark which we introduced in Sect. 3. Tables 3 and 4 show the Top5 accuracy for the random and the semantic splits on the mid-scale dataset. Each table shows the performance using the standard metric (Eq. 3) and the generalized metric (Eq. 4). For the two large-scale benchmarks, the results are reported in Tables 5, 6, 7 and 8. Note that the reported Joint Training violates the LLL setting as it trains on all data jointly. Looking at these results, we make the following observations:

(1) The generalized LLL accuracy is always significantly lower than the standard LLL accuracy. On the large scale benchmarks it is on average several percent lower: 7.99% and 11.59% for the random and the semantic splits,

Table 3. Mid-scale dataset (random split) Top 5 accuracy

Random Split	standard metric						generalized metric						Drop (standard to generalized)	
	T1	T2	T3	T4	mean	mean over examples	T1	T2	T3	T4	mean	mean over examples	over tasks	over examples
ExpertGate	79.6	59.25	62.92	58.75	65.13	64.88	53.1	44.83	37.03	40.66	43.9	43.69	21.22	21.18
FineTune	76.41	46.18	52.44	88.32	65.84	66.11	42.06	22.5	17.84	83.15	41.39	42.02	24.45	24.09
IMM	85.2	75.15	83.66	69.27	78.32	78.15	63.39	62.13	67.58	43.06	**59.04**	**58.77**	19.28	19.38
Int.Synapses	82.31	65.28	68.64	87.03	75.81	75.94	49.37	39.92	38.45	74.52	50.57	50.95	25.25	24.98
MAS	86.76	70.89	75.87	85.06	**79.65**	**79.68**	55.23	48.62	51.1	71.72	56.67	56.94	22.98	22.74
Joint	88.66	78.38	87.82	75.91	82.69	82.57	75.81	68.45	79.03	60.82	71.03	70.87	11.67	11.7

Table 4. Mid-scale dataset (semantic split)

Semantic Split	standard						generalized						Drop (standard to generalized)	
	T1	T2	T3	T4	mean	mean over examples	T1	T2	T3	T4	mean	mean over examples	over tasks	over examples
ExpertGate	62.11	62.44	59.4	12.5	49.11	59.39	55.57	50.87	49.61	9.49	**41.38**	**51.83**	7.73	7.57
FineTune	16.24	35.63	31.71	15.19	24.69	21.3	8.25	0	0	15.19	5.86	6.07	18.83	15.24
IMM	64.26	87.52	63.27	12.82	**56.97**	**64.33**	38.75	30.16	43.28	8.70	30.22	37.31	26.74	27.02
Int.Synapses	16.48	35.69	32.01	8.54	23.18	21.23	8.25	0	8.54	4.2		5.77	18.98	15.46
MAS	28.19	47.91	34.8	12.97	30.97	30.96	8.34	0.13	0	12.97	5.36	6.04	25.61	24.92
Joint	80.14	53.12	81.47	21.2	58.98	74.75	77.34	39.55	79.2	18.99	53.77	70.87	5.22	3.87

Table 5. Large scale random split (standard performance) Top 5 accuracy

Random	T1	T2	T3	T4	T5	T6	T7	T8	mean	mean over examples
ExpertGate	16.37	20.49	28.36	22.2	37.75	12.52	14.14	24.37	22.02	20.95
Finetune	15.53	23.56	23.43	19.22	23.44	19.53	23.81	66.13	26.83	26.59
IMM	24.57	30.72	32.14	27.89	37.23	25	20.65	26.41	28.08	27.53
Int.Synapses	18.28	27.23	27.11	23.3	28.85	23.49	25.76	53.43	28.43	28.06
MAS	21.32	33.32	32.82	28.58	34.93	27.16	29.71	52.22	**32.5**	**32.00**

Table 6. Large scale random split (generalized performance) Top 5 accuracy

Random	T1	T2	T3	T4	T5	T6	T7	T8	mean	mean over examples
ExpertGate	12.99	20.77	25.19	17.72	35.17	9.62	11.64	21.75	19.36	15.34
Finetune	12.18	21.38	19.98	15.68	19.85	16.11	17.48	59.29	22.74	18.93
IMM	21.21	29.02	30.5	25.38	34.01	23.42	18.07	24.26	25.73	20.91
Int.Synapses	13.79	24.99	23.58	19.01	26.4	21.56	20.95	47.69	24.75	19.92
MAS	16.13	29.52	28.28	23.1	30.28	24.5	24.34	47.21	**27.92**	**22.48**

Table 7. Large scale semantic split (standard performance) Top 5 accuracy

Semantic	T1	T2	T3	T4	T5	T6	T7	T8	mean	mean over examples
ExpertGate	6.97	11.01	35.6	34.61	14.58	21.32	16.36	13.28	**19.22**	**20.15**
Finetune	5.55	11.17	13.65	24.04	10.84	12.68	19.41	39.41	17.09	17.91
IMM	9.49	9.25	16.90	30.95	11.05	33.92	18.2	10.99	17.59	14.81
Int.Synapses	5.47	13.3	14.95	25.23	12.43	14.4	20.18	29.8	16.97	17.49
MAS	6.36	14.16	19.51	26.25	13.25	15.22	20.57	28.59	17.99	18.75
Joint	11.62	5.90	36.26	37.56	28.16	16.16	14.32	12.85	20.35	23.41

respectively. While the large-scale benchmarks are more challenging than the mid-scale benchmarks, as apparent from the reported accuracies, the drop in performance when switching to the generalized accuracy on the mid-scale benchmarks is significantly larger: 20.59% and 18.16%, respectively. This could be due to more overlap between tasks on the large-scale dataset as we discuss later, which reduces forgetting leading to better discrimination across tasks.

Table 8. Large scale semantic split (generalized performance) Top 5 accuracy

Semantic	T1	T2	T3	T4	T5	T6	T7	T8	mean	mean over examples
ExpertGate	5.18	7.62	35.33	20.35	8.99	16.59	6.21	7.19	**13.43**	**14.91**
Finetune	1.58	8.56	0.07	2.06	5.88	2.86	4.77	37.9	7.96	9.75
IMM	8.34	5.06	0.18	13.27	0.52	21.48	11.21	3.26	7.91	4.15
Int.Synapses	1.71	10.82	0.22	2.84	5.87	4.77	6.36	28.26	7.61	8.70
MAS	1.79	11.35	0.64	4.25	4.76	5.36	6.2	27.35	7.71	8.54
Joint	10.20	4.86	37.71	33.52	25.09	3.17	4.83	8.43	15.98	20.68

Table 9. Large scale task similarities using average Word2vec space (top-part) and geometric mean S, P, and O overlap (bottom-part)

Semantic(0.07 mean similarity)								Random (0.96 mean similarity)							
x	T1	T2	T3	T4	T5	T6	T7	T8	T1	T2	T3	T4	T5	T6	T7	T8
T1	1	0.32	-0.28	-0.18	-0.45	0.23	0.16	0.15	T1	1	0.97	0.97	0.97	0.95	0.97	0.97	0.97
T2	0.32	1	-0.37	-0.11	-0.68	0.21	0.36	0.29	T2	0.97	1	0.97	0.95	0.95	0.96	0.96	0.96
T3	-0.28	-0.37	1	0.25	0.05	-0.26	-0.22	-0.52	T3	0.97	0.97	1	0.97	0.95	0.96	0.97	0.96
T4	-0.18	-0.11	0.25	1	-0.08	-0.01	-0.12	-0.41	T4	0.97	0.95	0.97	1	0.95	0.95	0.97	0.96
T5	-0.45	-0.68	0.05	-0.08	1	-0.26	-0.36	-0.04	T5	0.95	0.95	0.95	0.95	1	0.95	0.96	0.93
T6	0.23	0.21	-0.26	-0.01	-0.26	1	0.23	0.26	T6	0.97	0.96	0.96	0.95	0.95	1	0.96	0.96
T7	0.16	0.36	-0.22	-0.12	-0.36	0.23	1	0.35	T7	0.97	0.96	0.97	0.97	0.96	0.96	1	0.95
T8	0.15	0.29	-0.52	-0.41	-0.04	0.26	0.35	1	T8	0.97	0.96	0.96	0.96	0.93	0.96	0.95	1
Semantic (0.238 g-mean of S,P, and O overlap)								Random (0.453 g-mean of S,P, O overlap)							
T1	1	0.09	0.08	0.11	0.05	0.06	0.1	0.08	T1	1	0.39	0.38	0.38	0.35	0.39	0.4	0.38
T2	0.09	1	0.12	0.15	0.15	0.08	0.27	0.28	T2	0.39	1	0.38	0.37	0.35	0.37	0.38	0.38
T3	0.08	0.12	1	0.23	0.2	0.04	0.12	0.1	T3	0.38	0.38	1	0.38	0.36	0.38	0.4	0.38
T4	0.11	0.15	0.23	1	0.15	0.08	0.14	0.12	T4	0.38	0.37	0.38	1	0.37	0.37	0.37	0.37
T5	0.05	0.15	0.2	0.15	1	0.05	0.12	0.18	T5	0.35	0.35	0.36	0.37	1	0.36	0.37	0.36
T6	0.06	0.08	0.04	0.08	0.05	1	0.12	0.1	T6	0.39	0.37	0.38	0.37	0.36	1	0.38	0.38
T7	0.1	0.27	0.12	0.14	0.12	0.12	1	0.28	T7	0.4	0.38	0.4	0.37	0.37	0.38	1	0.38
T8	0.08	0.28	0.1	0.12	0.18	0.1	0.28	1	T8	0.38	0.38	0.38	0.37	0.36	0.38	0.38	1

(2) The LLL performance of the random split is much better compared to the semantic split. Note that the union of the test examples across tasks on both splits are the same. Hence, the "mean over examples" performance on the random and semantic splits are comparable. Looking at the performance of the evaluated methods on both random and semantic splits on the large scale dataset, the average relative gain in performance over the methods by using the random split instead of the semantic split is 61.74% for the generalized metrics. This gain is not observed for ExpertGate which has only 2.77% relative gain when moving to the random split (small compared to other methods). We discuss ExpertGate behavior in a separate point below. The same ratio goes up to 569.03% on the mid-scale dataset excluding ExpertGate. What explains these results is that the similarity between tasks in the random split is much higher in the large-scale dataset compared to the mid-scale dataset (i.e., 0.96 vs 0.22 using the word2vec metric and 0.84 vs 0.25 using the SPO metric – see Table 9 for the task correlation in the LSc dataset and the corresponding table for the mid-scale dataset in the supplementary. This shows the learning difficulty of the semantic split and partially explains the poor performance.

(3) ExpertGate is the best performing model on the semantic split. However, it is among the worst performing models on the random split. We argue that this is due to the setup of the semantic split, where sharing across tasks is

minimized. This makes each task model behave like an expert of a restricted concept space, which follows the underlying assumption of how ExpertGate works. However, this advantage comes at the expense of storing one model for every task which can be expensive w.r.t. storage requirements which might not always be feasible as the number of tasks increases. Additionally, having separate models, requires to select a model at test time and also removes the ability to benefit from knowledge learnt with later tasks, in case there is a semantic overlap between tasks. This can be seen on the random split on the mid-scale dataset (see Table 3) where ExpertGate underperforms several other LLL models: 43.69% generalized accuracy for ExpertGate vs 58.77% generalized accuracy for the best performing model. Similarly on the large scale dataset, ExpertGate performs significantly lower for the random split (15.34% generalized accuracy for ExpertGate vs 22.48% generalized accuracy for the best performing model); see Table 8. The shared information across tasks on the random split is high which violates the assumption of expert selection in the ExpertGate method and hence explains its relatively poor performance on the random split.

(4) For the *midscale dataset* and with the generalized metric, Incremental Moment Matching (IMM) is the best performing of the model-based methods using a single model (Finetune, IMM, Int.Synapses, MAS) on both the random and the semantic splits (see Tables 3 and 4). Only for the random split evaluated with the standard metric MAS is slightly better, indicating that MAS might be better at the task level. We hypothesize that IMM benefits from its access to the distribution of the parameters after training each task before the distributions' mode is computed. This is an advantage that MAS and Int.Synapses do not have and hence the IMM model can generalize better across tasks. For the *large-scale dataset*, we observe that MAS is performing better than IMM on both the random and the semantic split, but especially on the random split; see Table 6. This may be because MAS has a better capability to learn low-shot classes as we discuss later in our *Few-shot Analysis*; see Tables 11 and 12. This is due to the high similarity between the tasks as we go to that much larger scale; see Table 9. This makes the distribution of parameters that work well across tasks similar to each other and hence IMM no longer has the aforementioned advantage.

5.3   Detailed Analysis

Long-tail Analysis. We show in Fig. 4 on left and middle the head-to-tail performance on the random split and the semantic split respectively. Specifically, the figure shows the Top5 generalized accuracy over different ranges of seen examples per class (i.e., the x-axis in the figure). On the right, the figure shows the relative improvement of the model trained on the random split over the semantic split. Using the standard metrics, the head classes perform better using models trained on the semantic split compared to the random split. It also shows that the random splits benefit the tail-classes the most; shown in supplementary

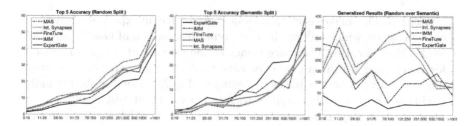

Fig. 4. LLFL benchmark long-tail analysis (generalized results). The x-axis in this figure shows the range of examples seen during training. On the left and middle: the y-axis shows the generalized Top 5 accuracy for the random and the semantic splits. On the right: The y-axis shows the Random split improvement over the random split for each range.

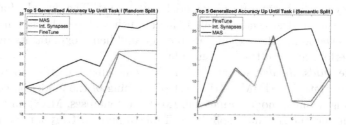

Fig. 5. Gained visual knowledge: the x-axis shows the task number i. The y-axis shows the Top5 generalized accuracy over the entire test set up until training task i, for the random (left) and semantic (right) split respectively.

materials (Sect. 4). However as shown on Fig. 4 (right), random split benefits everywhere with no clear relation to the class frequency (x-axis).

Gained Knowledge over Time. Figure 5 shows the gained knowledge over time measured by the generalized Top5 Accuracy of the entire test set of all tasks after training each task. Figure 5 (left) shows that the LLL methods tend to gain more knowledge over time when the random split is used. This is due to the high similarity between tasks which makes the forgetting over time less catastrophic. Figure 5 (right) shows that the models have difficulty gaining knowledge over time when the semantic split is used. This is due to the low similarity between tasks which makes the forgetting over time more catastrophic. Note that the y-axis in Fig. 5 left and right parts are comparable since it measure the performance of the entire test set which is the same on both the semantic and the random splits.

For a principled evaluation, we consider measuring the forward and the backward transfer as defined in [18]. After each model finishes learning about the task T_n, we evaluate its *test* performance on all N tasks. By doing so, we construct the matrix $R \in \mathbb{R}^{N \times N}$, where $R_{j,n}$ is the test classification accuracy of the model on task T_j after observing the last sample from task T_n. Letting $\bar{b}$ be the vector of test accuracies for each task at random initialization, we can define the backward

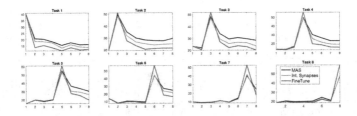

Fig. 6. Gained visual knowledge broken down for each task on the random split: The x-axis in each sub figure shows the task number i. The y-axis shows the Random Split Top5 generalized accuracy of the shown task after each task is learnt.

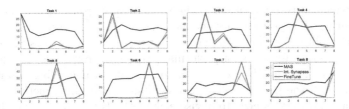

Fig. 7. Gained visual knowledge broken down for each task on the semantic split: The x-axis in each sub figure shows the task number i. The y-axis shows the Random Split Top5 generalized accuracy of the shown task after each task is learnt.

and the forward transfer as: **Backward Transfer:** $\text{BWT} = \frac{1}{N-1} \sum_{n=1}^{N-1} R_{n,N} - R_{n,n}$ and **Forward Transfer:** $\text{FWT} = \frac{1}{N-1} \sum_{n=2}^{N} R_{n,n-1} - \bar{b}_n$. The larger these metrics, the better the model. If two models have similar accuracy, the most preferable one is the one with larger BWT and FWT. We used the generalized accuracy for computing BWT and FWT.

Figures 6 and 7 show the performance of each task test set after training each task (from first task to last task). As expected the performance on the task n set peaks after training task n and the performance degrades after training subsequent tasks. Int.Synapses and Finetune show the best performance of training the current task at the expense of more forgetting on pre-

Table 10. Large scale benchmark forward and backward transfer for continual learning methods

Semantic	MAS	Int.Synapses	Finetune
Forward Transfer	0.24	0.08	0.06
Backward Transfer	-0.20	-0.37	-0.44
Random	MAS	Int.Synapses	Finetune
Forward Transfer	0.30	0.26	0.22
Backward Transfer	-0.22	-0.25	-0.35

vious tasks compared to MAS. Comparing the performance of task n at the nth task training to its performance after training the last task as a measure of forgetting, we can observe a lower drop on the performance on the random split compared to the semantic split; see the figures. This is also demonstrated by higher backward transfer on the random split; see Table 10.

Few-Shot Analysis. Now, we focus on analyzing the subset of the testing examples belonging to facet with few training examples. Tables 11 and 12 show

Table 11. Few-shot (≤ 10) generalized Top 5 accuracy, large-scale, semantic split

	T1	T2	T3	T4	T5	T6	T7	T8	average
ExpertGate	0.33	0.88	0.57	3.27	0.69	2.04	0	0.62	1.05
Finetune	0	0.65	0	0	0.3	2.04	1.76	10.14	1.86
IMM		1.3	0.03	0	0	0.04	2.65	0	0	0.5
Int.Synapses	0.11	0.37	0	0	0.28	2.65	1.14	4.91	1.18
MAS	0.11	0.31	0	0.05	0.22	3.67	1.24	4.58	1.27
Joint	5.55	2.65	4.79	6.27	2.85	10.9	8.88	3.7	5.7

Table 12. Few-shot (≤ 10) generalized Top 5 accuracy, large-scale, random split

	T1	T2	T3	T4	T5	T6	T7	T8	average
ExpertGate	1.54	1.41	2.51	1.69	0.9	1.58	1.13	0.91	1.46
Finetune	1.48	1.62	1.4	1.73	1.47	1.77	2.66	13.17	3.16
IMM	1.79	1.58	2.1	1.9	2.88	2.07	1.76	0.95	1.88
Int.Synapses	1.4	1.55	2.25	2.95	2.94	3.09	3	5.8	2.87
MAS	1.79	2.29	3.25	3.8	4.6	3.09	3.4	4.44	3.33
Joint	3.75	4.65	6.99	4.61	3.81	8.9	10.38	2.5	5.7

few-shot results on the semantic and the random split, respectively. As already observed earlier, the performance on the random splits is better compared to the semantic splits. We can observe here that finetuning is the best performing approach on average for few-shot performance on both splits. Looking closely at the results, it is not hard to see that the main gain of finetuning is due to its high accuracy on the last task. This shows that existing LLL methods do not learn the tail and there is need to devise new methods that have a capability to learn the tail distribution in a LLL setting.

6   Conclusions

In this paper, we proposed two benchmarks to evaluate fact learning in a lifelong learning setup. A methodology was designed to split up an existing fact learning dataset into multiple tasks, taking the specific constraints into account and aiming for a setup that mimics real world application scenarios. With these benchmarks, we hope to foster research towards more large scale, human-like artificial visual learning systems and studying challenges like long-tail distribution.

Acknowledgements. Rahaf Aljundi's research was funded by an FWO scholarship.

References

1. Aljundi, R., Babiloni, F., Elhoseiny, M., Rohrbach, M., Tuytelaars, T.: Memory aware synapses: learning what (not) to forget. In: Ferrari, V., Hebert, M., Sminchisescu, C., Weiss, Y. (eds.) ECCV 2018. LNCS, vol. 11207, pp. 144–161. Springer, Cham (2018). https://doi.org/10.1007/978-3-030-01219-9_9
2. Aljundi, R., Chakravarty, P., Tuytelaars, T.: Expert gate: lifelong learning with a network of experts. In: CVPR (2017)
3. Chao, W.-L., Changpinyo, S., Gong, B., Sha, F.: An empirical study and analysis of generalized zero-shot learning for object recognition in the wild. In: Leibe, B., Matas, J., Sebe, N., Welling, M. (eds.) ECCV 2016. LNCS, vol. 9906, pp. 52–68. Springer, Cham (2016). https://doi.org/10.1007/978-3-319-46475-6_4

4. Chaudhry, A., Dokania, P.K., Ajanthan, T., Torr, P.H.S.: Riemannian walk for incremental learning: understanding forgetting and intransigence. In: Ferrari, V., Hebert, M., Sminchisescu, C., Weiss, Y. (eds.) ECCV 2018. LNCS, vol. 11215, pp. 556–572. Springer, Cham (2018). https://doi.org/10.1007/978-3-030-01252-6_33

5. Chen, X., Shrivastava, A., Gupta, A.: NEIL: extracting visual knowledge from web data. In: 2013 IEEE International Conference on Computer Vision (ICCV), pp. 1409–1416. IEEE (2013)

6. Divvala, S.K., Farhadi, A., Guestrin, C.: Learning everything about anything: webly-supervised visual concept learning. In: Proceedings of the IEEE Conference on Computer Vision and Pattern Recognition, pp. 3270–3277 (2014)

7. Elhoseiny, M., Cohen, S., Chang, W., Price, B.L., Elgammal, A.M.: Sherlock: Scalable fact learning in images. In: AAAI, pp. 4016–4024 (2017)

8. Fernando, C., et al.: PathNet: evolution channels gradient descent in super neural networks. arXiv preprint arXiv:1701.08734 (2017)

9. Gong, Y., Ke, Q., Isard, M., Lazebnik, S.: A multi-view embedding space for modeling internet images, tags, and their semantics. Int. J. Comput. Vis. **106**(2), 210–233 (2014)

10. He, K., Zhang, X., Ren, S., Sun, J.: Deep residual learning for image recognition. In: Proceedings of the IEEE Conference on Computer Vision and Pattern Recognition, pp. 770–778 (2016)

11. Käding, C., Rodner, E., Freytag, A., Denzler, J.: Fine-tuning deep neural networks in continuous learning scenarios. In: Chen, C.-S., Lu, J., Ma, K.-K. (eds.) ACCV 2016. LNCS, vol. 10118, pp. 588–605. Springer, Cham (2017). https://doi.org/10.1007/978-3-319-54526-4_43

12. Kirkpatrick, J., et al.: Overcoming catastrophic forgetting in neural networks. Proc. Natl. Acad. Sci. 201611835 (2017)

13. Kiros, R., Salakhutdinov, R., Zemel, R.S.: Unifying visual-semantic embeddings with multimodal neural language models. arXiv preprint arXiv:1411.2539 (2014)

14. Krizhevsky, A., Sutskever, I., Hinton, G.E.: ImageNet classification with deep convolutional neural networks. In: Advances in Neural Information Processing Systems, pp. 1097–1105 (2012)

15. Lee, S.W., Kim, J.H., Jun, J., Ha, J.W., Zhang, B.T.: Overcoming catastrophic forgetting by incremental moment matching. In: Advances in Neural Information Processing Systems, pp. 4652–4662 (2017)

16. Li, Z., Hoiem, D.: Learning without forgetting. In: Leibe, B., Matas, J., Sebe, N., Welling, M. (eds.) ECCV 2016. LNCS, vol. 9908, pp. 614–629. Springer, Cham (2016). https://doi.org/10.1007/978-3-319-46493-0_37

17. Lomonaco, V., Maltoni, D.: CORe50: a new dataset and benchmark for continuous object recognition. In: Conference on Robot Learning (2017)

18. Lopez-Paz, D., Ranzato, M.: Gradient episodic memory for continual learning. In: Advances in Neural Information Processing Systems (2017)

19. Mikolov, T., Sutskever, I., Chen, K., Corrado, G.S., Dean, J.: Distributed representations of words and phrases and their compositionality. In: Advances In Neural Information Processing Systems, pp. 3111–3119 (2013)

20. Mitchell, T.M., et al.: Never ending learning. In: AAAI, pp. 2302–2310 (2015)

21. Pasquale, G., Ciliberto, C., Rosasco, L., Natale, L.: Object identification from few examples by improving the invariance of a deep convolutional neural network. In: 2016 IEEE/RSJ International Conference on Intelligent Robots and Systems (IROS), pp. 4904–4911, October 2016. http://ieeexplore.ieee.org/document/7759720/

22. Plummer, B.A., Mallya, A., Cervantes, C.M., Hockenmaier, J., Lazebnik, S.: Phrase localization and visual relationship detection with comprehensive image-language cues. In: Proceedings of the IEEE Conference on Computer Vision and Pattern Recognition, pp. 1928–1937 (2017)
23. Rebuffi, S.A., Kolesnikov, A., Lampert, C.H.: iCaRL: incremental classifier and representation learning. arXiv preprint arXiv:1611.07725 (2016)
24. Romera-Paredes, B., Torr, P.: An embarrassingly simple approach to zero-shot learning. In: International Conference on Machine Learning, pp. 2152–2161 (2015)
25. Shmelkov, K., Schmid, C., Alahari, K.: Incremental learning of object detectors without catastrophic forgetting. In: The IEEE International Conference on Computer Vision (ICCV) (2017)
26. Simonyan, K., Zisserman, A.: Very deep convolutional networks for large-scale image recognition. arXiv preprint arXiv:1409.1556 (2014)
27. Thrun, S., O'Sullivan, J.: Clustering learning tasks and the selective cross-task transfer of knowledge. In: Thrun, S., Pratt, L. (eds.) Learning to Learn, pp. 235–257. Springer, Boston (1998). https://doi.org/10.1007/978-1-4615-5529-2_10
28. Triki, A.R., Aljundi, R., Blaschko, M.B., Tuytelaars, T.: Encoder based lifelong learning. arXiv preprint arXiv:1704.01920 (2017)
29. Wang, Y.X., Ramanan, D., Hebert, M.: Growing a brain: fine-tuning by increasing model capacity. In: IEEE Computer Society Conference on Computer Vision and Pattern Recognition (CVPR) (2017)
30. Zenke, F., Poole, B., Ganguli, S.: Continual learning through synaptic intelligence. In: Proceedings of the 34th International Conference on Machine Learning, vol. 70, pp. 3987–3995. PMLR, 06–11 August 2017
31. Zhang, J., Kalantidis, Y., Rohrbach, M., Paluri, M., Elgammal, A., Elhoseiny, M.: Large-scale visual relationship understanding. arXiv preprint arXiv:1804.10660 (2018)

Geometric Image Synthesis

Hassan Abu Alhaija[1]([✉]), Siva Karthik Mustikovela[1], Andreas Geiger[2,3],
and Carsten Rother[1]

[1] Visual Learning Lab, Heidelberg University, Heidelberg, Germany
hassan.abu_alhaija@iwr.uni-heidelberg.de
[2] Autonomous Vision Group, MPI for Intelligent Systems, Tübingen, Germany
[3] University of Tübingen, Tübingen, Germany

Abstract. The task of generating natural images from 3D scenes
has been a long standing goal in computer graphics. On the other
hand, recent developments in deep neural networks allow for trainable
models that can produce natural-looking images with little or no knowledge about the scene structure. While the generated images often consist of realistic looking local patterns, the overall structure of the generated images is often inconsistent. In this work we propose a trainable,
geometry-aware image generation method that leverages various types
of scene information, including geometry and segmentation, to create
realistic looking natural images that match the desired scene structure.
Our geometrically-consistent image synthesis method is a deep neural
network, called Geometry to Image Synthesis (GIS) framework, which
retains the advantages of a trainable method, e.g., differentiability and
adaptiveness, but, at the same time, makes a step towards the generalizability, control and quality output of modern graphics rendering engines.
We utilize the GIS framework to insert vehicles in outdoor driving scenes,
as well as to generate novel views of objects from the Linemod dataset.
We qualitatively show that our network is able to generalize beyond the
training set to novel scene geometries, object shapes and segmentations.
Furthermore, we quantitatively show that the GIS framework can be used
to synthesize large amounts of training data which proves beneficial for
training instance segmentation models.

1 Introduction

Methods for generating natural images from noise or sparse input have gained
significant interest in recent years with the developments in Generative Deep
Neural Networks. Specifically, Generative Adversarial Networks (GANs) [13],
allowed for trainable models that can produce natural-looking images with little
or no prior knowledge input just by learning to imitate the distribution in a

Electronic supplementary material The online version of this chapter (https://
doi.org/10.1007/978-3-030-20876-9_6) contains supplementary material, which is available to authorized users.

© Springer Nature Switzerland AG 2019
C. V. Jawahar et al. (Eds.): ACCV 2018, LNCS 11366, pp. 85–100, 2019.
https://doi.org/10.1007/978-3-030-20876-9_6

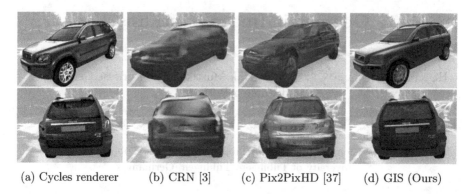

(a) Cycles renderer   (b) CRN [3]   (c) Pix2PixHD [37]   (d) GIS (Ours)

Fig. 1. (a) The result of a state-of-the-art Physically-based Renderer ("Cycle" Renderer). (b, c) Results of two other deep neural network based image generation methods [3,37]. While in both cases local image patches looks plausible the whole image does not look realistic. (d) Our GIS framework can realistically synthesize the car object with a specific pose using a deep neural network. (Color figure online)

target image set. While the generated images often consist of realistic looking local patterns, the overall structure of the images can be inconsistent. Using more sparse cues, like edge maps or semantic segmentation [18], introduces some local control over the output but doesn't address the global structure. Further, recent works have addressed the problem of global consistency by generating the image at different scales [3] or using two separate global and local networks [37]. These solutions, nevertheless, address the global 2D structure of the image but not the 3D structure of the scene. This is evident when trying to generate an object in a different pose than those present most commonly in the training dataset (see Fig. 1b and c). While image generation from semantic segmentation can produce visually impressive images, it is not clear whether it can produce new training data for other vision tasks. This could be attributed to two factors: (i) The sparse input makes the image generation problem largely under-constrained leading to inconsistent image structure; (ii) The lack of control parameters over the image generation process (e.g. Pose and color of objects) makes it hard to define the desired attributes of the output image.

On the other hand, generating natural images from known 3D geometry, texture and material properties through rendering engines has been widely used to generate training data for various computer vision tasks. While physically-based rendering engines aim at accurately reproducing the physical properties of light-material interactions, most available rendering engines use a set of carefully designed approximations, in order to reduce the computational complexity and produce results that are visually appealing to humans. Rendered images accurately matches the input scene structure but differ in local appearance from real images due the disparity between the real capturing process and the approximations in the software rendering pipeline. Previous works [32] pointed to the performance gap between synthetic and real data when used for training a task like semantic or instance segmentation. The other limitation of rendering engines is that they require accurate and complete information about the objects and the scene, namely, detailed 3D geometry, texture and material properties, lighting information, environment maps, and so on. This usually requires laborious manual work by experts to set up the 3D scene.

In this work, we propose a geometry-aware image generation method that leverages various types of scene information, like geometry and segmentation, to create realistic images which match the desired scene structure and properties. The network is trained with two objectives, the first is a supervised loss where the goal is to learn a mapping from the multi-channel input to an RGB image that matches the input structure. The second is an adversarial loss that learns to compare generated and real images enforcing the generator results to look similar to real data. We explore different input modalities like normals, depth, semantic and material segmentation and compare their usefulness. Using this rich input we are able to show visually a clear improvement over existing state-of-the-art image generation approaches, e.g. [3,18,37].

The goal of our approach is not only to generate visually realistic images, but also to explore whether the images generated can be useful for training other networks for various computer vision tasks. The advantage of using a trainable model instead of a software rendering engine is two-fold. Firstly, it can produce realistic looking images from geometry and segmentation while learning, from training data, to implicitly predict the remaining rendering parameters (e.g. material properties and lighting conditions). Secondly, the trainable model has the advantage of producing images that are fine-tuned to specific characteristics of the training dataset by leveraging the Adversarial loss. For instance, it can capture the specific noise distribution and color shifts in the data.

In order to demonstrate the abilities of our GIS framework, we perform two types of experiments. In the first, we utilize an augmented reality dataset where synthetic vehicles were realistically rendered into a scene using "Cycles renderer" from Blender [1]. We use the normals, depth and material labels as input and the rendered images as the target in the supervised loss, while using real car images to train the discriminator in the adversarial loss. In this way, our network is able to generate realistic looking images (see Fig. 1d and supplementary video[1]) similar to the rendered data from [1] (see Fig. 1a). In fact, we train the GIS network to give 9 diverse output-images and observed that each image captures a different lighting condition (e.g. direct sunshine, clear sky, or cloudy), all present in the training data. Using our trained network, we produce a new dataset of 4000 augmented images of car objects on top of real driving images. This dataset is used to train a state-of-the-art instance segmentation network, here Mask R-CNN [16]. This improves the performance of Mask R-CNN over the original augmented data [2]. In the second experiment, we demonstrate how our network can be trained directly using real images only. For that we utilize the Linemod dataset [17] that includes images of several objects and their 3D scanned models in addition to the corresponding 6D pose of the objects in each image. We show

---

[1] https://youtu.be/W2tFCz9xJoU.

that using our GIS Network we are able to generate large amount of training data that helps improve the performance of instance segmentation. To summarize, our **contributions** are as follows:

- We introduce a trainable deep neural network, called GIS, that is able to generate geometry-consistent images from limited input information, like normals and material segmentation, While the remaining aspects of the image, e.g. lighting conditions, are learned from training data.
- We qualitatively show that our framework generalizes to novel scene geometries, objects and segmentation, for both synthetic and real data.
- We quantitatively show that our network can synthesize training data that improves the performance of a state-of-the-art instance segmentation approach, here Mask R-CNN ([16]). To the best of our knowledge, this is the first time that synthesized training data from a Neural Network is used to advance a state-of-the-art instance segmentation approach.

2   Related Work

Synthetic Datasets. The success of supervised deep learning models has fueled the demand for large annotated datasets. An alternative to tedious manual annotation is provided by the creation of synthetic content, either via manual 3D scene modeling [28,41] or using some stochastic scene generation process [22,31,33,35]. Mayer et al. [20,21] demonstrate that simple synthetic datasets with "flying 3D things" can be used for training stereo and optical flow models. Ros et al. [28] proposed the SYNTHIA dataset with pixel-level semantic segmentation of urban scenes. In contrast, Gaidon et al. [10] propose "Virtual KITTI", a synthetic dataset reproducing in detail the popular KITTI dataset [12]. Richter et al. [25,26] and Johnson-Roberson et al. [19] have been the first to demonstrate that content from commercial video games can be accessed for collecting semantic segmentation, optical flow and object detection ground truth.

An alternative to synthesizing the entire image content is to render only specific objects into natural images. The simplest approach is to cut object instances from one image and paste them onto random background images [9] using appropriate blending or GAN-based refinement [39]. More variability can be obtained when rendering entire 3D CAD models into the image. Several works consider the augmentation of images with virtual [5,15] or scanned humans [4,34]. In contrast, Abu Alhaija et al. [1,2] consider the problem of augmenting scenes from the KITTI dataset with virtual vehicles for improving object detectors and instance segmentation algorithms. In particular, they have shown that a well performing instance segmentation method, here MNC [6], can be considerably improved by intelligently generating additional training data.

While great progress has been made in rendering photo-realistic scenes, creating the required content and modeling all physical processes (e.g., interaction of light) correctly is a non-trivial and time-consuming task. In contrast to classical rendering, we propose a generative feed-forward model which maps an intermediate representation of the scene to the desired output. The geometry and appearance cue of this intermediate representation are easily obtained using fast standard OpenGL rendering.

Conditional Adversarial Learning. Recently, generative adversarial networks (GANs) [13] have been proven to be powerful tools for image generation. Isola et al. [18] formulate the image-to-image translation problem by conditioning GANs on images from another domain and combining an adversarial with a reconstruction loss. Yang et al. [40] introduce an additional diversity loss to generate more diverse outputs. Wang et al. [36] propose a multi-scale conditional GAN architecture for generating images of up to 2 Megapixel resolution. Wang et al. [38] use a GAN to synthesize surface normals and another GAN to generate an image from the resulting normal map. GANs' major advantage is that they don't require matching source and target images but rather enforce the generator to produce images that match the target data distribution. We exploit this by adding an Adversarial loss in our GIS framework such that the generated images are realistic. Besides, we explore a richer set of input modalities compared to just raw images [7,24,38] or semantic segmentations [18,37,40] for generating higher-quality outputs. We demonstrate that our model compares favorably to the High-Resolution Image Synthesis model of Wang et al. [37] (see Fig. 1d).

Feed-Forward Image Synthesis. Dosovitskiy et al. [8] consider an alternative formulation to GANs using feedforward synthesis with a regression loss. Their work demonstrates that an adversarial loss is not necessary to generate accurate images of 3D models given a model ID and a viewpoint. In the same spirit, Chen et al. [3] consider the problem of synthesizing photographic images conditioned on semantic layouts using a purely feedforward approach. They demonstrate detailed reconstructions at resolutions up to 2 Megapixels, improving considerable upon the results of Isola et al. [18].

Our work also uses a feedforward formulation for the image synthesis problem. Unlike [3], however, our focus is on synthesizing controllable, high quality images. Thus, we consider 3D geometry and segmentation (semantic or material) as input, provided by a simple OpenGL rendering unit.

3   Method

A general image generation process can be defined as a mapping $\mathcal{F} : \{G, A, E\} \rightarrow I$ from scene description $\{G, A, E\}$ to an RGB image I. The scene description consists of three parts, (i) the geometry parameters G which include the poses and shapes of objects, (ii) the appearance parameters A which describe the objects' materials, textures and transparency and finally (iii) the environment parameters E which describe global conditions of the scene that affect all objects such as lighting, camera parameters, and the environment. In this work in contrast, our goal is to train a mapping $\mathcal{R} : \{G, S\} \rightarrow I$ that can produce natural images from a given geometry G and material segmentation S

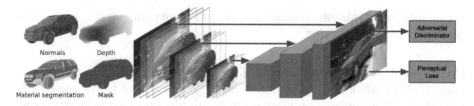

Fig. 2. Overview of our approach. We propose Geometric Image Synthesis framework, feed-forward architecture for synthesizing RGB images based on geometric and semantic cues. Here we show the case where a car is augmented onto an empty road. Compared to existing image synthesis approaches, our model benefits from a rich set of input modalities, while learning realistic mappings which generalize to novel geometries and segmentations, and integrate the objects seamlessly into provided image content.

only, without the knowledge of exact appearance A or environment parameters E. Similar to semantic segmentation, the material segmentation labels each pixel with a specific material label (e.g. metal, glass etc.) from a pre-defined set of materials without providing any properties or parameters of the material. The task of the network is to learn the unknown parameters from the training data directly and apply them to generate images from new input geometry.

The target image I, which is used for training, can either be a real image of a known scene geometry or a rendered synthetic image obtained through a high-quality software renderer. While learning image generation directly from real images is desirable, it is often difficult to obtain geometry and material labels which are pixel-accurately aligned with real-world images. For this reason, it is possible to exploit synthetically rendered data using a state-of-the-art physically based renderer as supervised target while using an adversarial loss with real images to acquire realistic looking results. Using realistically rendered images also gives us fine-grained control over the data, which we exploit to conduct various experiments for analyzing our model. Additionally, we demonstrate how our method can be trained directly using real images for the supervised loss when an exact 6D pose of the objects in the image is known.

3.1 Input Representation

Geometry plays a major role in defining the appearance of an object in an image since it defines its shape in addition to its shading through interaction with light. Providing the geometry as an input changes the learning objective from learning to create objects to learning a correlation between geometry and appearance. This makes the network more generalizable to new geometries as we show in later experiments. To use geometry in a deep neural network, it is important to find a compact representation of the object's 3D surface. While meshes are one of the most common representations for 3D objects, they are problematic in the context of convolutional neural networks due to their irregular 3D structure. Another popular representation of 3D objects are voxels. Voxel-based representations can be handled using 3D convolutions [27] but suffer from two shortcomings: high computational requirements and comparably low resolution.

A common 2D representation of 3D shapes is their depth in the camera view. The advantage of such an image-based geometry representation is that it can be directly processed with a regular 2D convolutional neural network. Nevertheless, the object appearance doesn't usually depend on its absolute depth except for secondary effects like lens blur and environmental distortions. Rather, it depends on the small changes in depth between neighbouring points which defines the relative surface orientation with respect to the light source. This can be better characterized by computing the surface normals in the camera coordinates system at each point of the visible surface.

The main advantage of learning the image generation from geometry compared to rendering is the ability to exploit high-level semantic and context cues to predict the appearance of an object. This allows it to *learn* non-geometric attributes of the object appearance such as material parameters, lighting, environment reflections and texture directly from data. Using semantic [3] or instance segmentation [37] can help the network to learn the appearance of semantically similar objects across multiple examples. Nevertheless, it can be challenging in cases where a semantic class has a large variety in appearance, e.g. cars with different models and colors. We propose in this work to use material segmentation instead. Each pixel in the segmentation input gets a label from a pre-defined set of materials (e.g. metal, plastic, glass etc.). This doesn't include any material properties or parameters. Rather, it groups parts made of similar materials together allowing the network to learn the material appearance model from multiple objects in different contexts, e.g. different lighting conditions. This results in more generalization power since the material appearance is often independent of the object class, pose or shape. We expect this labeling to be particularly effective when generating objects that consist of a small number of materials but vary significantly in shape, e.g., cars.

3.2   Network Architecture

We now define our network architecture in detail. As discussed before, our goal is to learn a mapping from an intermediate representation to a natural RGB image using a deep neural network. As input layers to our network, we use the normal map, the depth map, object mask and material segmentation of the object which can be easily obtained using OpenGL based rendering. Additionally, by providing the network with a background image I_{bg}, the network can learn to augment synthetic objects realistically into real images e.g. add shadows underneath a synthetic car and blending edges.

Figure 2 illustrates the input layers to our network. Let N, D, S be the 2D images representing the normal map, depth map and semantic segmentation of the input object respectively. Let M denote the material label where each pixel is represented by a one-hot encoding vector which identifies its material ID, see Fig. 2 for an illustration. We are now ready to formally represent the mapping as $\mathcal{R} : \{N, D, S, M, I_{bg}\} \rightarrow I$.

For our generator R, we follow Chen et al. [3] and use a feed-forward coarse-to-fine network architecture for image synthesis. More specifically, we leverage a cascade of convolutional layer modules C starting from a very low resolution input and growing to modules of higher resolutions (Fig. 2). Each convolutional module C_i has an input resolution of $w_i \times h_i$ and produces a feature map F_i of the same size. C_i receives the feature map F_{i-1} from the previous module, upsampled to $w_i \times h_i$, and concatenated with the input downscaled to the same resolution. The following layer, C_{i+1}, operates at twice the resolution of the previous layer ($2w_i \times 2h_i$), and receives the feature maps F_i and the input rescaled to $2w_i \times 2h_i$. Each convolutional module C_i consists of an input layer, intermediate layer and output layer, each of which is followed by a set of convolutions, a layer normalization and a leaky ReLU nonlinearity. The output layer of the final module is followed by a 1×1 convolution applied to the feature map and normalized to obtain the synthesized image. For the adversarial discriminator D, we adopt a fully convolutional network architecture consisting of 5 convolutional layers each followed by a leaky ReLU with a stride of 2 for all except the last layer. The discriminator's output is a 2D binary map where each value describes the discriminator classification of a patch as real or synthesized by the generator. This is specially useful when synthesizing objects into real images where the same image would contain both real and synthetic patches. To further stabilize the adversarial training, we employ the simple discriminator gradient regularization method proposed in [29].

3.3   Training

We train the generator R in our GIS framework to produce synthesized images I_s that resemble the target images I_t obtained using the "Cycles" rendering engine while at the same time being close in appearance to real images in order to "confuse" the adversarial discriminator. Effectively, the task of the network is to learn the process of generating images, directly from the target images, given $\{N, D, S, M, I_{bg}\}$ without information such as lighting, environment map or material properties. Those properties are estimated by the network during training and combined with the geometry and segmentation input to produce a high quality image. To achieve this, we choose to compute the perceptual loss (feature matching loss) as proposed in [11] between the generated and target image. The goal of the perceptual loss is to match the feature activations produced by I_t and I_s at various convolutional levels through a perception network, e.g., VGG. This helps the network to learn fine-grained image patterns while also preserving the global object structure. We use VGG pre-trained on ImageNet as our perceptual network. Let us denote this network by V, and let V_l denote a layer of this network. The loss between I_t and I_s is given by

$$\mathcal{L}^P = \sum_l S_l \lambda_l \left\| V_l(I_t) - V_l(I_s) \right\|_1$$

where $V_l(\cdot)$ denotes the feature activations of VGG at layer l and S_l is the binary mask of the object rescaled to the size of V_l. The GIS framework can also learn to synthesize objects on top of real images. In this case, our goal is to create augmented images by learning not just the target object appearance but also its interaction with the environment in the real image, including shadows, reflection and blending at the object's edges. Towards this goal, we add the background image to the input and train the network using an ℓ_1 loss for the background areas outside the object mask $\mathcal{L}^B = (1 - S)\|I_t - I_s\|_1$. The adversarial discriminator D_s is trained to segment the augmented images by the generator into real and synthetic parts using the Binary Cross-Entropy loss $\mathcal{L}^D = \mathbb{E}[\log(S - D_s(I_s))]$. By replace the synthetic object mask S with its inverse $(1 - S)$, we define an adversarial loss for the generator $\mathcal{L}^A = \mathbb{E}[\log((1 - S) - D_s(I_s))]$ that evaluates the realism of the synthesized objects.

3.4 Diversity

Synthesizing images from geometry and segmentation alone is an ill-posed problem. That is, for a specific set of inputs, there are infinite plausible outputs due to different possible lighting conditions, object colors etc. Thus, we task our network to produce K diverse outputs from the last layer using multiple-choice learning [3,14]. More specifically, we compute the loss for each of these outputs, but only back propagate the gradient of the best configuration for the foreground prediction, while averaging the background predictions as none of them should deviate from the input: $\mathcal{L} = w \min_k[\mathcal{L}_k^P + \mathcal{L}_k^A] + (1 - w)\frac{1}{K}\sum_k \mathcal{L}_k^B$. Where w is a weight inversely proportional to the number of pixels of the synthesized object(s). Note that only the foreground object with the smallest loss is taken into account, thus the min operator effectively acts as a multiple choice switch. This encourages the network to output a diverse set of images to spread its bets over the domain of possible images that could be produced from the current input. In all our experiments we use $K = 9$ as the number of diverse outputs, see Fig. 5 for an illustration.

4 Experiments

To demonstrate the ability of our GIS network to synthesize realistic images, we perform a set of experiments which assess the quality and generalization capacity of the method. We mainly focus on two scenarios, outdoor driving and indoor objects. Realistically synthesizing augmented objects like cars or obstacles into real-world scenes is an important feature for expanding manually annotated training datasets. In the case of indoor objects, a learned network can be used to synthesize novel views of objects to provide extensive training data for various tasks. In the following experiments, we show that our GIS framework produces better images for training an instance segmentation network compared to a state-of-the-art software rendering engine.

4.1 Augmentation of KITTI-360 Dataset

Introduced by Abu Alhaija et al. [1], the augmented KITTI-360 dataset features 4000 augmented images obtained from 200 real-world images through carefully rendering up to 5 high-quality 3D car models into each image using classical rendering techniques. The set of 28 car models have been manually created and placed to ensure high realism. Rendering was performed using the physically-based Cycles Renderer in Blender and followed by a manually designed post-processing pipeline to increase the realism of the output. Additional scene information like 360° environment maps and camera calibration has been used to ensure realistic reflections and good integration with the real image.

To train the GIS network, we use normals, depth, material segmentation and semantic masks of the augmented cars obtained using the augmented KITTI-360 pipeline. The material labels include 16 materials of different properties (e.g. plastic, chrome glass etc.) in addition to 15 car paint materials which differ only in color. We use the corresponding RGB images from augmented KITTI-360 as target images for training the parameters of GIS network. Mixing the real images with rendered cars presents an additional challenge since interactions between the inserted objects and the real background, e.g. shadows and transparencies, have to be taken into account. To deal with this, we input the background image to the network in addition to geometry and segmentation. The network's task is to learn the process of synthesizing cars realistically and blend them into the surrounding environment by appropriately adding reflections, shadows and transparencies, amongst others.

During inference, we obtain a new set of car model positions and orientations following the procedure in [1]. We render the mask, depth, normals and material labels from the camera viewpoint and use them as input to our GIS network. Note that during the inference phase, we do not require a sophisticated rendering pipeline, like "Cycles" renderer, since normals, depth maps and segmentations can be obtained directly using a simple OpenGL based renderer. We then leverage the trained GIS model to create a new dataset of 4000 augmented images with new car poses and combinations.

Qualitative Evaluation: Figure 3 shows augmented images produced by our GIS framework when trained on the augmented KITTI-360 dataset. Note that the synthesized cars exhibit realistic appearance properties like shading, shadows, reflections and specularity, despite the fact that this information is not provided to our model. The material labeling of the cars allows the model to tune the synthesis process to each material. Importantly, note that the material label is just a semantic label of material and does not contain any information with respect to the physical properties of the material. Interestingly, our model is able to learn the transparency property of the material with label "glass" from data, without providing any alpha channel or explicitly modeling transparency. Additionally, the model is able to replicate camera effects such as blur and chromatic aberrations, which are present in the augmented KITTI-360 dataset.

Quantitative Evaluation: To verify the effectiveness of data produced by our model, we train the state-of-the-art Mask R-CNN model [16] for car instance segmentation using the images produced by our network. Alongside, we also

Fig. 3. Images from KITTI-360 dataset augmented with cars synthesized using our GIS framework (Real image without augmentation in upper left corner).

train the same model with images from the original Cycles Rendering pipeline from [1] with the same 3D car models and poses, and a baseline model using the unaugmented real images from KITTI-360. We evaluate all models on the KITTI 2015 training set. The results are presented in Table 1. We observe that the model trained on images synthesized by the GIS network significantly outperforms the one trained only on real data, and marginally outperform the highly-tuned data from [1]. This clearly indicates that our model does not only learn to imitate the training data, but also the adversarial loss can contribute in make the resulting appearance more realistic and, therefore, more effective in training.

4.2 Generalization and Ablation Study

A key feature of our GIS framework is that it learns a mapping from any geometry to natural images and is not limited to a specific set of objects or shapes. In the following sections, we present an extensive experimental study to demonstrate that our model learns a generic image formation function and does not overfit or limit itself only to objects of certain geometry and material.

To show generalization ability, we present the network with two tasks: (i) synthesize seen objects with material combinations never seen before, and (ii) synthesize learned materials on new, unseen, geometries. In Fig. 4a we show the results of our model applied to the "Monkey" model from blender with different material labels applied to it. Our results clearly demonstrate that the material properties have been learned by the network independently from the geometry. In Fig. 4b we replace the car paint with the chrome material previously seen in the training data only on the car wheel rims. The resulting image looks realistic, demonstrating that the material properties learned from one part of the model can be transferred to other, geometrically different, parts by simply changing the material label. Using the diversity loss, described in Sect. 3.4, our GIS model produces 9 different possible images from the same input. The results in Fig. 5 show how the network can learn different lighting conditions (direct light, cloudy etc.) without providing any explicit lighting information.

(a)   (b)

Fig. 4. (a) GIS output for a monkey model with material labels: car paint, chrome and glass. (b) GIS output for a car with material label chrome.

Fig. 5. Three diverse outputs obtained from GIS on the KITTI-360 dataset. Note how the renderings vary in lighting conditions and reflections.

To better understand the importance of different input modalities, we perform an ablation study where we train the GIS model from scratch using all inputs excluding one at a time. We qualitatively compare the results in Fig. 6. When normals are not used for training, the output images become smooth and lack fine geometric details. Excluding depth maps from the input, on the other hand, leads to no noticeable difference. We hypothesize that this is due to the fact that most of the shading of the object can be modeled based on the local geometry cues that are expressed well in the normals, but little difference in appearance relates to the absolute depth of an object. In contrast, removing the material segmentation results in blurry images.

Table 1. Accuracy of Mask R-CNN when trained with real, augmented or GIS generated images.

Dataset	IoU 50%	AP
Real KITTI-360	58.80%	31.92%
Augmented KITTI-360	66.68%	37.88%
GIS (ours)	67.74%	38.69%

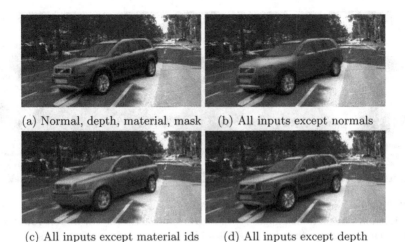

(a) Normal, depth, material, mask   (b) All inputs except normals

(c) All inputs except material ids   (d) All inputs except depth

Fig. 6. Output of GIS using various types of inputs. Note that GIS with all four inputs, or all inputs except depth, synthesizes realistic images.

4.3   Novel View Synthesis on Linemod Dataset

The Linemod dataset was introduced by Hinterstoisser et al. [17] for evaluating 6D object pose estimation algorithms. This dataset contains real images of multiple known objects, each of them annotated with a 6 degree-of-freedom pose. It provides 3D CAD models of all the objects in the dataset for which we annotated the materials present on each CAD model with a material label. Hence, using the 6D pose and the CAD model, we can obtain the normal map (N), material segmentation (S) and depth map (D) of objects.

The objective of this experiment is to use real images as target training data for our network with the corresponding geometric information (N, S, D) as inputs. Unlike the KITTI-360 dataset, where the target data is acquired using a manually designed rendering framework, the availability of real images as target data in this case allows the network to model real world images and their statistics directly. We use the objects $Ape, Can, Cat, Duck, Eggbox, Holepuncher$ each with 1200 images and their pose annotations. We use 600 images of each object for training and the rest for testing.

Due to the generalizability of our method, we can use the trained GIS network to generate new images of the objects in previously unseen poses. To demonstrate the efficacy of the images produced by our GIS network for training, we compare them to a training set generated using the traditional OpenGL rendering engine. To this end, we use the two kinds of datasets to train the Mask R-CNN. First, we crop the rendered images and place them at random locations on NYU dataset [30] images. We repeat the same process for object images generated by our network. To evaluate the performance of Mask R-CNN, we test it on Linemod-Occluded dataset, proposed by Michel et al. [23] (note that we do not use this data while training our GIS network). We observe that the Mask

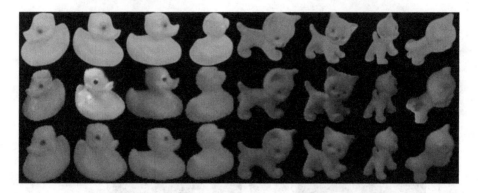

Fig. 7. Top row contains rendered images. Middle row contains real images in similar poses. Bottom row contains images synthesized by our network. The middle row images are not seen during training phase. GIS is still able to synthesize novel views of objects realistically.

R-CNN trained with rendered images performs at an average accuracy of 21.1% for all objects. On the other hand, the Mask R-CNN trained with our synthesized images performs at an average accuracy of 68.4%. This clearly indicates that the images synthesized by our network are highly realistic and are useful for training other deep networks which cannot be achieved with rendered data. Qualitatively, our GIS generated images appear more similar to real images as shown in Fig. 7.

5   Conclusion

In this we work, we have proposed GIS, a deep neural network which is able to learn to synthesize realistic objects by leveraging semantic and geometric scene information. Through various experiments we have demonstrated the generalization performance of our GIS framework with respect to varying geometry, semantics and materials. Further, we have provided empirical evidence that the images synthesized by GIS are realistic enough to train the state-of-the-art instance segmentation method Mask R-CNN, and improve its accuracy on car instance segmentation with respect to a baseline model trained on non-augmented images from the same dataset. We believe that our approach opens new avenues towards ultimately reaching the goal of photo-realistic image synthesis using deep neural networks.

Acknowledgments. This project has received funding from the European Research Council (ERC) under the European Unions Horizon 2020 programme (grant No. 647769) and by the Heidelberg Collaboratory for Image Processing (HCI).

References

1. Abu Alhaija, H., Mustikovela, S.K., Mescheder, L., Geiger, A., Rother, C.: Augmented reality meets deep learning for car instance segmentation in urban scenes. In: BMVC (2017)
2. Abu Alhaija, H., Mustikovela, S.K., Mescheder, L., Geiger, A., Rother, C.: Augmented reality meets computer vision: efficient data generation for urban driving scenes. IJCV **126**, 961–972 (2018)
3. Chen, Q., Koltun, V.: Photographic image synthesis with cascaded refinement networks. In: ICCV (2017)
4. Chen, W., et al.: Synthesizing training images for boosting human 3D pose estimation. In: 3DV (2016)
5. Cheung, E., Wong, T.K., Bera, A., Manocha, D.: STD-PD: generating synthetic training data for pedestrian detection in unannotated videos. arXiv:1707.09100 (2017)
6. Dai, J., He, K., Sun, J.: Instance-aware semantic segmentation via multi-task network cascades. In: CVPR (2016)
7. Denton, E.L., Chintala, S., Szlam, A., Fergus, R.: Deep generative image models using a Laplacian pyramid of adversarial networks. In: NIPS (2015)
8. Dosovitskiy, A., Springenberg, J.T., Tatarchenko, M., Brox, T.: Learning to generate chairs, tables and cars with convolutional networks. PAMI **39**(4), 692–705 (2017)
9. Dwibedi, D., Misra, I., Hebert, M.: Cut, paste and learn: surprisingly easy synthesis for instance detection. In: ICCV (2017)
10. Gaidon, A., Wang, Q., Cabon, Y., Vig, E.: Virtual worlds as proxy for multi-object tracking analysis. In: CVPR (2016)
11. Gatys, L.A., Ecker, A.S., Bethge, M.: A neural algorithm of artistic style. arXiv:1508.06576 (2015)
12. Geiger, A., Lenz, P., Urtasun, R.: Are we ready for autonomous driving? The KITTI vision benchmark suite. In: CVPR (2012)
13. Goodfellow, I.J., et al.: Generative adversarial nets. In: NIPS (2014)
14. Guzmán-Rivera, A., Batra, D., Kohli, P.: Multiple choice learning: learning to produce multiple structured outputs. In: NIPS (2012)
15. Hattori, H., Boddeti, V.N., Kitani, K.M., Kanade, T.: Learning scene-specific pedestrian detectors without real data. In: CVPR (2015)
16. He, K., Gkioxari, G., Dollr, P., Girshick, R.: Mask R-CNN. In: ICCV, pp. 2980–2988, October 2017. https://doi.org/10.1109/ICCV.2017.322
17. Hinterstoisser, S., et al.: Model based training, detection and pose estimation of texture-less 3D objects in heavily cluttered scenes. In: Lee, K.M., Matsushita, Y., Rehg, J.M., Hu, Z. (eds.) ACCV 2012. LNCS, vol. 7724, pp. 548–562. Springer, Heidelberg (2013). https://doi.org/10.1007/978-3-642-37331-2_42
18. Isola, P., Zhu, J., Zhou, T., Efros, A.A.: Image-to-image translation with conditional adversarial networks. In: CVPR (2017)
19. Johnson-Roberson, M., Barto, C., Mehta, R., Sridhar, S.N., Rosaen, K., Vasudevan, R.: Driving in the matrix: can virtual worlds replace human-generated annotations for real world tasks? In: ICRA (2017)
20. Mayer, N., et al.: A large dataset to train convolutional networks for disparity, optical flow, and scene flow estimation. In: CVPR (2016)
21. Mayer, N., et al.: What makes good synthetic training data for learning disparity and optical flow estimation? arXiv:1801.06397 (2018)

22. McCormac, J., Handa, A., Leutenegger, S., Davison, A.J.: SceneNet RGB-D: can 5M synthetic images beat generic ImageNet pre-training on indoor segmentation? In: ICCV (2017)
23. Michel, F., et al.: Global hypothesis generation for 6D object pose estimation. CoRR abs/1612.02287 (2016). http://arxiv.org/abs/1612.02287
24. Radford, A., Metz, L., Chintala, S.: Unsupervised representation learning with deep convolutional generative adversarial networks. arXiv:1511.06434 (2015)
25. Richter, S.R., Hayder, Z., Koltun, V.: Playing for benchmarks. In: ICCV (2017)
26. Richter, S.R., Vineet, V., Roth, S., Koltun, V.: Playing for data: ground truth from computer games. In: Leibe, B., Matas, J., Sebe, N., Welling, M. (eds.) ECCV 2016. LNCS, vol. 9906, pp. 102–118. Springer, Cham (2016). https://doi.org/10.1007/978-3-319-46475-6_7
27. Riegler, G., Ulusoy, A.O., Geiger, A.: OctNet: learning deep 3D representations at high resolutions. In: CVPR (2017)
28. Ros, G., Sellart, L., Materzynska, J., Vazquez, D., Lopez, A.: The SYNTHIA dataset: a large collection of synthetic images for semantic segmentation of urban scenes. In: CVPR (2016)
29. Roth, K., Lucchi, A., Nowozin, S., Hofmann, T.: Stabilizing training of generative adversarial networks through regularization. In: NIPS, pp. 2018–2028 (2017)
30. Silberman, N., Hoiem, D., Kohli, P., Fergus, R.: Indoor segmentation and support inference from RGBD images. In: Fitzgibbon, A., Lazebnik, S., Perona, P., Sato, Y., Schmid, C. (eds.) ECCV 2012. LNCS, vol. 7576, pp. 746–760. Springer, Heidelberg (2012). https://doi.org/10.1007/978-3-642-33715-4_54
31. de Souza, C.R., Gaidon, A., Cabon, Y., Peña, A.M.L.: Procedural generation of videos to train deep action recognition networks. arXiv:1612.00881 (2016)
32. Tremblay, J., et al.: Training deep networks with synthetic data: bridging the reality gap by domain randomization. arXiv preprint arXiv:1804.06516 (2018)
33. Tsirikoglou, A., Kronander, J., Wrenninge, M., Unger, J.: Procedural modeling and physically based rendering for synthetic data generation in automotive applications. arXiv:1710.06270 (2017)
34. Varol, G., et al.: Learning from synthetic humans. In: CVPR (2017)
35. Veeravasarapu, V.S.R., Rothkopf, C.A., Ramesh, V.: Model-driven simulations for deep convolutional neural networks. arXiv:1605.09582 (2016)
36. Wang, T., Liu, M., Zhu, J., Tao, A., Kautz, J., Catanzaro, B.: High-resolution image synthesis and semantic manipulation with conditional GANs. arXiv:1711.11585 (2017)
37. Wang, T.C., Liu, M.Y., Zhu, J.Y., Tao, A., Kautz, J., Catanzaro, B.: High-resolution image synthesis and semantic manipulation with conditional GANs. In: CVPR (2018)
38. Wang, X., Gupta, A.: Generative image modeling using style and structure adversarial networks. In: Leibe, B., Matas, J., Sebe, N., Welling, M. (eds.) ECCV 2016. LNCS, vol. 9908, pp. 318–335. Springer, Cham (2016). https://doi.org/10.1007/978-3-319-46493-0_20
39. Xu, W., Li, Y., Lu, C.: Generating instance segmentation annotation by geometry-guided GAN. arXiv:1801.08839 (2018)
40. Yang, Z., Liu, H., Cai, D.: On the diversity of realistic image synthesis. arXiv:1712.07329 (2017)
41. Zhang, Y., et al.: Physically-based rendering for indoor scene understanding using convolutional neural networks. In: CVPR (2017)

Partial Person Re-identification with Alignment and Hallucination

Sara Iodice$^{(\boxtimes)}$ and Krystian Mikolajczyk

Imperial College London, London, UK
s.iodice16@imperial.ac.uk

Abstract. Partial person re-identification involves matching pedestrian views where only a part of a body is visible in corresponding images. This reflects practical CCTV surveillance scenario, where full person views are often unavailable. Missing body parts make the comparison very challenging due to significant misalignment and varying scale of the views. We propose Partial Matching Net (PMN) that detects body joints, aligns partial views and hallucinates the missing parts based on the information present in the frame and a learned model of a person. The aligned and reconstructed views are then combined into a joint representation and used for matching images. We evaluate our approach and compare to other methods on three different datasets, demonstrating significant improvements.

Keywords: Partial person re-identification · Hallucination · Alignment

1 Introduction

Research in person re-identification (re-ID) has advanced with CNN-based methods and their performance on academic datasets almost saturated. However, these datasets do not reflect well typical application scenarios. Images in widely used benchmarks [1–3] have similar viewing angle, contain most of the human body, and are well aligned. Many of the state of the art methods assume full person view in both probe and the gallery. In real scenarios, a picture of a person often contains only a partial view, e.g., in crowded scenes. Partial person re-ID aims at recognizing or matching identities of people from frames containing only parts of human bodies, that are captured by different and non overlapping cameras. For example, in Fig. 1, real cases of people wanted by the police (top row) can be compared to samples from standard datasets such as CUHK03 (bottom row). Even with some body parts missing due to automatic person detector the views are still significantly more complete than the real cases. In addition, real case images are not aligned making the re-ID even more challenging.

Despite partial person re-ID being of high relevance to practical applications, it is still little addressed in the literature. Very few datasets were proposed for this task, such as simulated partial REID and partial i-LIDS [4], with a limited

© Springer Nature Switzerland AG 2019
C. V. Jawahar et al. (Eds.): ACCV 2018, LNCS 11366, pp. 101–116, 2019.
https://doi.org/10.1007/978-3-030-20876-9_7

Fig. 1. Example images or real police cases (top) and samples from academic datasets (bottom). Images in standard benchmarks such as CUHK03, have similar viewing angle, are better aligned and contain most of the human body.

number of pedestrians/frames, that are insufficient for training modern CNN-based models. In addition, the gallery set consists of full body views making it still distant from the practical scenarios.

To bridge the gap between the simulated and practical re-ID tasks, we generate new and more challenging datasets from the widely used CUHK03 [1]. Furthermore, to address the partial Re-ID task, we propose an approach based on two strategies, alignment and hallucination, that are motivated by the following observations. Firstly, alignment is a crucial process in human perception facilitating direct comparison between corresponding parts. Secondly, in human vision, missing content (e.g. due to the eye blind spot) is hallucinated in the brain based on the context and prior knowledge. Although the hallucinated part may not exactly correspond to the real view, it improves our ability to recognize objects. Similarly, we conjecture that alignment and hallucination may boost the recognition process in case of partial re-ID, by reconstructing missing coarse structures of the human body. From a practical perspective, CNN filters are adapted to spatial arrangement of parts and do not cope well with significant misalignment or large parts missing in some views, therefore we expect that providing full and aligned views should lead to improvements in partial person re-ID. We propose an architecture which is jointly optimized with real and hallucinated samples. To the best of our knowledge, this is the only work studying the impact of hallucination on human re-ID task. This idea has been exploited in face recognition [5] where real and hallucination face examples were used. In summary, we make the following contributions: (a) introduce an approach to partial re-ID that combines body joint detection, alignment, and hallucination; (b) demonstrate the impact of image alignment in case of partial views; (c) generate dataset *CropCUHK03*, which reflects partial re-ID scenario better than the existing datasets; (d) validate the approach in an extensive evaluation and comparison to several methods on three different datasets; (e) show that the proposed approach leads to significant improvements in partial person re-ID.

2   Related Work

Partial Person Re-ID. Whilst many works have focused on the traditional task of full person re-ID, the more challenging task of partial person re-ID has received little attention. Partial re-ID was recently introduced in [4] where partial observations of the query images were used, however, the gallery images contained full persons. Ambiguity-Sensitive Matching Classifier (AMC) [4] was also proposed with two matching approaches, i.e., a local-to-local based on matching small patches, and global-to-local with a sliding window search where the partial observation served as a template. The proposed approach was validated on small datasets, i.e., Partial Reid, i-LIDS and Caviar, and may not scale well to real scenarios due to the quadratic complexity. In another approach Deep Pixel Reconstruction (DPR) [6] reconstructs missing channels in the query feature maps from full observations in the gallery maps. Unlike these methods, we align and reconstruct missing body parts by using contextual and training samples only, without full body views in the gallery set.

Person re-ID with occlusion scenarios can be considered a particular instance of partial re-ID where other persons/objects are occluding the subject to recognize. Straightforward approach is to incorporate occluded samples during training as in [7], however, no results were reported on occluded cases and such an approach does not explicitly address occlusions. In [8,9] limited evaluations of hand-crafted solutions were performed on small synthetic datesets with occlusions similarly to [4]. An occlusion detector was proposed in [10], that may be incorporated in other re-ID methods as a pre-processing step, but not evaluations were done on person re-ID.

Person Re-ID. A number of CNN-based solutions have been proposed with diverse complexity of feature learning, or metric learning. Several works introduce specific layers and new components to learn strongest features against variations in people appearance across multiple cameras and misalignments. For example, [1,11–14] apply simple similarity metrics to discover local correspondences among parts. They assume misalignment within pre-defined strides or patches, therefore these methods do not work well for large misalignments. Next, attention models [14–17] focus on learning salient regions and extract strong activations in their deep feature maps. The selected regions lack semantic interpretation, therefore in case of severe misalignment they may correspond to different body or object parts and should not be directly compared. Methods from [18–21] rely on a body part detection, thus their performance depends on the accuracy of such detectors. Despite this issue, we believe that body part locations can be used to align pedestrian samples in a robust way. Moreover, body joint estimators are being improved for other applications, which also leads to better performance of re-ID methods relying on such detectors.

GAN [22] in Person Re-ID. One of the first attempts to adopt GAN-generated samples for training CNN embedding in re-ID was [23]. Furthermore, [24] improves the generalization ability of re-ID model by training with new generated poses. Other works, such as [25,26] propose a GAN model able to project pedestrian images between different dataset domains. Likewise, [27] focuses on camera style.

In contrast, to address partial re-ID problem, we propose to employ a body joint detector to align partial views and a GAN model to hallucinate body parts missing in the partial view.

3 Partial Matching Network

In this section, the proposed *Partial Matching Net (PMN)* is introduced with its three components, i.e., *Alignment Block (AB)*, *Hallucination Block (HB)* and *Feature Extractor Block (FEB)* as illustrated in Fig. 2. The alignment block *AB* detects human body joints and aligns the input image to a reference frame such that locations of body parts in different images correspond, which facilitates matching. Missing areas of the aligned example in the reference frame are zero padded. The hallucination block then reconstructs the pedestrian appearance in the padded areas based on the information present in the frame and a learned model of a person. Finally, a person representation is extracted from the reconstructed and aligned frames by *FEB*. In the following, we present the three components in more detail.

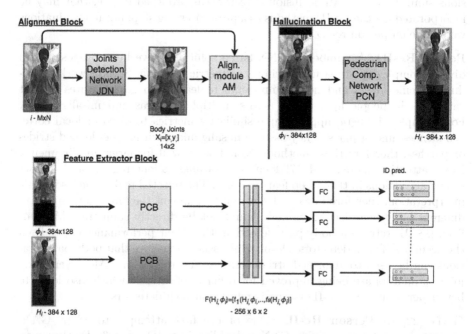

Fig. 2. Partial matching network. *Alignment Block (AB)* aligns the input example i of size $M \times N$, *Hallucinating Block (HB)* reconstructs missing parts and *Feature Extractor Block (FEB)* computes features from the aligned and reconstructed frames for several horizontal strides that are combined with fully connected layers.

3.1   Alignment Block

Based on the results reported in the literature, person re-ID is more reliable in images that are carefully cropped and person body parts are well aligned, in contrast to automatically detected bounding boxes with significant translation and scale change between different subjects or instances of the same ID. We therefore attempt to perform the alignment automatically by employing state of the art *Joints Detection Network (JDN)* [28] and then using the position of joints to align the input image in a reference frame. Specifically, JDN estimates positions $[x_k, y_k, m_k]$ of 14 body joints, corresponding to {head, neck, rightshoulder, rightelbow, rightwrist, leftshoulder, leftebow, leftwrist, lefthip, leftknee, leftankle, righthip, rightknee, rightankle}, where x_k and y_k are the joint coordinates, and $m_k \in [0, 1]$ is a confidence value for part k. From the training data, we estimate the average locations of body joints, which we use in a reference frame to which all examples can be aligned.

Based on the confidence value of each joint $[x_k, y_k, m_k]$, we select a subset of stable reference coordinates that are then used to estimate spatial transformation between the input frame and the reference frame. Specifically, we assume confidence values of each body joint in the training set follow a normal distribution, and we consider a joint as reliable if included within 3 standard deviations of the mean. As misalignment mostly derives from the inaccuracy of the pedestrian detectors and it is more significant along the y-direction, we assume it is a similarity transformation. In particular, parameters are estimated as follows: given the joints of the current sample X_i and the average coordinates of joints X_m, the parameters Φ_i of the similarity transformation are estimated with the least square solution $\Phi_i = \Phi_{\arg\min}||\Phi X_i - X_m||^2$.

Since the transformation to align input frames is estimated from detected joints, the accuracy mainly depends on JDN. Some examples are shown in Fig. 3, with successfully detected joints in left and failure cases in right images e.g. in the first failure example, elbows are classified as hips, and as a result, the frame is zoomed in rather than zoomed out. Note that JDN provides coordinates of body parts even if they are missing in the input image. We observe that the main misalignment in the input images is in the vertical direction, therefore

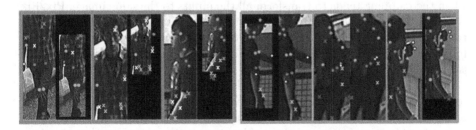

Fig. 3. Example pairs of partial views with detected and aligned joints: head (yellow), neck (sky blue), shoulders (pink), elbows (green), wrists (white), hips (grey), knees (turquoise) and ankles (red). (Left) Success cases. (Right) Failures. (Color figure online)

the transformation is typically a vertical translation and a scale change. Furthermore, the scale change is constrained to the same in vertical and horizontal direction to preserve the aspect ratio of the person. Missing areas in the aligned frame are zero padded. More examples can be found in Fig. 6.

3.2 Hallucination Block

Aligned examples are much better suited for extracting and comparing features between corresponding body parts. However, partial views may cover different body parts, therefore the similarity scores may vary not only due to viewpoint change, illumination, and occlusions but also due to the fact that a different number of filters is deactivated due to missing parts in different examples. One could address this issue by attempting to normalize the scores depending on what areas and parts are present. This however introduces more complexity to the re-ID process, and requires heuristic solutions rather than allowing the use of existing re-ID approaches. Instead, we introduce a hallucination block *HB* and propose to reconstruct the missing parts of the image. The advantage of our approach is that any state of the art person re-ID method can then be used. Moreover, given full views of pedestrians, it is straightforward to generate a large number of partial views avoiding manual annotation for training a hallucination network.

GAN Models. Impressive results have been achieved in image inpainting and generating new images with GANs, e.g., by synthesizing new views of pedestrians [24]. Partial views often contain useful information that allows to extrapolate the appearance of a person and reconstruct missing parts in a similar way humans do.

Pix2Pix [29] and Cycle-GAN [30] were recently introduced for transferring image appearance into a different weather, or generating realistic views from paintings and photo enhancement. These GANs learn a mapping function from domain Φ to H, such that the style of output images are indistinguishable from images in H. In Cycle-GAN, *"cycle consistency"* imposes that the transformed input image can be used to reconstruct the original version. In practice, this is implemented by introducing inverse mapping, i.e. another GAN, and then jointly training both models with a cycle consistency loss (cf. Fig. 4). This improves stability of the learning process and convergence by avoiding mode collapse i.e., when the mapping tends to transform all the inputs to the same image. Pix2Pix is designed for one-to-one corresponding instance pairs between the two domains, therefore intuitively, it seems more appropriate in our scenario, assuming that full view and partial (e.g. cropped) view of the same instance correspond to the two domains.

In our experiments with both models we observed that Cycle-GAN, leads to better results in person reconstruction. This may be due to the specificity of the pedestrian dataset containing articulated bodies. Also, although we can generate an infinite number of cropped image pairs the actual number of unique pedestrian images is limited in CUHK03. In Fig. 5, pix2pix is shown to introduce artifacts. Full Cycle-GAN (grey) shows better reconstructions than without the cycle (blue), e.g. preserving discriminative patterns.

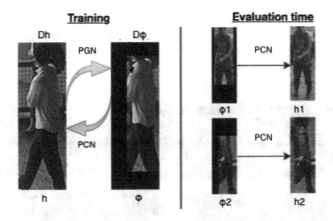

Fig. 4. PCN mapping from full body h to partial observations ϕ and reverse mapping PGN.

Fig. 5. Hallucination with GANs, (black) partial view; (red) pix2pix; (blue) no-cycle GAN; (grey) cycle GAN; (green) ground truth. Some artifacts (random pixels) in pix2pix outputs are pointed by yellow arrows. (Color figure online)

Pedestrian Completion Network. We therefore adapt Cycle-GAN by defining two mapping functions *Pedestrian Completion Network* (PCN) *and Partial Generation Network (PGN)*, as illustrated in Fig. 4. Our aim is to learn PCN that hallucinates missing parts of the image, given partially aligned samples $\phi \in \Phi$ and full body samples $h \in H$, and PGN only emulates a cropping operation to improve stability during cycle training. The model is optimized with the following objective:

$$\mathcal{L}_{tot} = \mathcal{L}_{GAN}(PGN, D_\phi, h, \phi) + \mathcal{L}_{GAN}(PCN, D_h, h, \phi) + \lambda \mathcal{L}_{cyc}(PGN, PCN)$$

$$(1)$$

where $\mathcal{L}_{GAN}$ are the adversarial losses, and $\mathcal{L}_{cyc}$ is the cycle consistency loss. Generators PGN and PCN aim to produce images that belong to domains Φ and H, respectively, while the discriminators D_ϕ and D_h try to distinguish real from fake samples in their respective domains. Finally, the cycle consistency loss is defined as

$$L_{cyc}(PGN, PCN) = |PGN(PCN(\phi)) - \phi|_1 + |PCN(PGN(h)) - h|_1 \quad (2)$$

that is the sum of l_1 norms between the reconstructed and the original samples. PCN model can then be applied independently, using aligned partial observation

ϕ as an input and generating a complete frame h with the missing parts hallucinated. Trained on a large number of examples the network learns to preserve the consistency of appearance between the partial views and the reconstructed parts.

Fig. 6. (Top) In green frame, examples of successful cases of aligned partial views and hallucinated full views from 50% area missing. In red frame, poor hallucination examples. (Bottom) Aligned and hallucinated examples from 75% area missing (Color figure online)

Some qualitative results of hallucinated outputs are shown in Fig. 6, in case of half and 3/4 of the original area missing. The task is significantly more challenging when only 1/4 of the original area is visible. In particular, the module is effective in reconstructing legs, head, and feet in examples shown in green frames, but it fails to reproduce fine details such as texture clothes in examples shown in red frames. The reason why some reconstructed regions are smooth and lack fine details may be due to the overfitting of the model to the visible region.

3.3   Feature Extractor Block

Both hallucinated and aligned frames are used as input to the feature extractor block (FEB). Thus, FEB includes two separate feature extraction networks, trained independently with aligned and hallucinated samples while using the same architecture in both. We experiment with two backbone networks, i.e., ResNet50 from [31], and PCB [14], that was recently designed for person re-ID. Given an input image i, PCB computes a 3D tensor of activations and then splits it into a number of column vectors by applying average pooling along the same horizontal strides. The dimension of each feature component is reduced and the resulting stripes are concatenated.

We propose to combine feature representations from the same stride in the hallucinated and the aligned frame using a fully connected layer. $F(h, \phi) = [f_1(h, \phi), \ldots, f_s(h, \phi)]$ as illustrated in Fig. 2. The model is then optimized by minimizing the sum of cross entropy loss over each concatenated feature component, related to the same horizontal stride. During the evaluation, we adopt $F(h, \phi)$ as final feature vectors and Euclidean distance as a comparison metric.

4 Experimental Results

In this section, we first present the implementation details and the datasets used for experiments and then we discuss our results, demonstrating the effectiveness of the alignment and hallucination in partial re-ID. Finally, we report the performance on standard benchmarks and compare our method against other re-ID systems for full [14,31] (without re-ranking) and partial views [4,6] over several settings and datasets.

4.1 Implementation Details

PCN network was trained with Adam optimizer and one partial observation per training sample with a learning rate of 0.0002 and linear decay to zero over 100 epochs. Other parameter settings can be found in [14].

FEB network was trained for 60 epochs according to dataset protocols. The base learning rate was initialized at 0.1 and kept the same for the first 40 epochs then decayed to 0.01. The model was pre-trained on ImageNet, and then, each PCB was trained either with partial or hallucinated samples. The number of horizontal strides is fixed to 6 and the final feature vector has 256×6 components. PCB networks for aligned and hallucinated frames were jointly fine-tuned for further 60 epoch with a learning rate 0.005, and decay by 0.01 after 40 epochs. The final feature vector $F(h, \phi)$ has dimensionality of $256 \times 6 \times 2$.

4.2 Datasets

We used three datasets in our experiments:

Partial REID [4] contains 600 images of 60 people captured from arbitrary viewpoints with different background/occlusions at a university campus. In particular, each person appears in 10 frames, including 5 partial observations and 5 full-body images.

Partial i-LIDS [4] is a simulated dataset derived from i-LIDS, originally including 476 pedestrian images of 119 people acquired by different and non-overlapping cameras with a significant amount of occlusion. The simulated partial version, named *Partial i-LIDS*, is achieved by generating query images as one partial observation for each pedestrian, i.e., by selecting the most occluded view and manually cropping the non-occluded part.

CropCUHK03 is our proposed generated dataset with partial observations from CUHK03 [1] of different size and overlap between views. Generating partial examples from widely used benchmarks has positives. The annotation is already available and the community is familiar with the data, thus one can easily interpret the results, compare to previous experiments or appreciate the difference

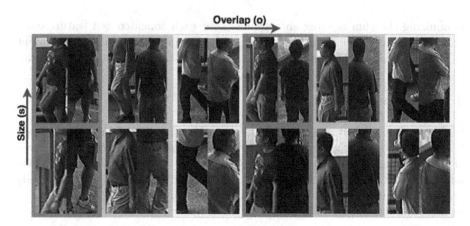

Fig. 7. Examples from CropCUHK03 datasets. (Bottom) 25% of full body view, $s = 0.25$, $o_{min} = [0, 0.5]$. (Top) 50% of full body views, $s = 0.5$, $o_{min} = [0.25, 0.5]$. The overlap is increasing from left to right. Even for humans it is very challenging to match some partial pedestrian images with little overlap between two camera views.

to the existing protocol. Note that a change of the evaluation protocol for full views in CUHK03 was also done in [31] to make it more challenging. Our new partial view protocol takes it a step further with CropCUHK03.

Originally the dataset contains 14,097 frames of 1467 pedestrians, captured with 2 different camera views and collected at CUHK campus. Several settings are generated maintaining the same number of individuals and frames as in CUHK03, which we refer to as $CropCUHK03_{(s,o)}$: $s \in \{0.25, 0.5\} \wedge o_{min} \in \{0.0, 0.5\}$, where s is the fraction of the area cropped from CUHK03 labeled frames, i.e., the maximum possible overlap between camera views, and o is the minimum overlap between image areas. Note that two crops from different views of the same ID do not need to fully overlap. The crops are generated from random locations by keeping the aspect ratio the same as the original frame and making sure that the overlap area between corresponding crops is at least o. This typically corresponds to less overlap than o between cropped parts as they come from different views. Figure 7, shows some examples from the generated partial views. The level of difficulty is controlled by parameters, e.g., for $s = 0.25$, $o_{min} = 0.5$ the crop is 0.25 of the full view and the overlap varies between 0.5 and 1 of the crop. The extreme cases are very difficult to match even for humans, given little overlap between camera views.

4.3 Evaluation on CropCUHK03 Datasets

Experimental Setting. We follow the new training/testing protocol [31], where training and testing sets have 767 and 700 identities, respectively, and using our generated datasets characterized by crops of increasing difficulty. We report results for a popular re-ID baseline Resnet50 [31] without re-ranking, and a recent architecture PCB [14]. All images are resized to 256×256 and 384×128 as input to the Resnet50 and PCB, respectively.

Evaluation of Individual Blocks. We carry out a systematic evaluation of the proposed approach, showing the effectiveness of the alignment, hallucination, and feature extractor blocks in the partial re-ID task.

Alignment. As discussed in Sect. 3.1, the main error comes from inaccurate joint detection. To measure the extent to which this affects the overall results we compare our method, termed *align*, to the case of manual alignment, which is the one in labeled original frames. Note that manually aligned (labeled) data is very common in person re-ID evaluations. Many relevant works e.g., [20,32] report final results on CUHK03 (labeled) where bounding boxes are manually cropped, or on datasets (e.g., MARKET) where the most misaligned cases are discarded. We also include a naive solution, denoted *baseline*, which simply re-scales the cropped views to the required input size.

Table 1 shows the results for different feature extractors, i.e., ResNet50 and PCB with varying overlap of partial views $s \in \{0.25, 0.5\}, o_{min} \in \{0.0, 0.25, 0.5\}$. The *baseline* corresponds to partial views resized to a fixed size as input. Manual alignment *man align* assumes correctly detected body joints, and alignment *align* uses JDN (joint detection network) for automatic alignment. First important observation is that PCB significantly outperforms ResNet50 in all experiments. Note that PCB extracts a feature vector per stride while ResNet50 computes global representation. Next, view alignment is effective when the misalignment is large, that is the overlap between partial views is small, i.e., $o_{min} \leq 0.25$, and brings an improvement regardless how much of the full frame was cropped. Resized *baseline* gives better results for overlap at least 0.5. This may be due to the filters that are deactivated by zero padding in the aligned views and general robustness of the networks to some misalignment. Finally, alignment

Table 1. Partial re-ID with alignment. Performances are shown in terms of r1 (rank-1), r5 (rank-5), r10 (rank-10), and map (mean average precision). The *baseline* corresponds to partial observations resized to a fixed size as input, manual alignment *manalign* assumes correctly detected body joints and alignment (*align*) uses JDN (joint detection network) for automatic alignment. PCB significantly outperforms ResNet50 (R50), and the benefits of alignment are visible when the overlap between views is small, i.e., $o_{min} < 0.25$. JDN introduces errors that affect the overall performance

Settings			Baseline				Man align				Align			
Mod	s	o_{min}	r1	r5	r10	Map	r1	r5	r10	Map	r1	r5	r10	Map
R50	.5	.5	11.8	22.9	31.2	10.7	11.5	23.1	29.8	10.3	8.2	17.8	23.6	7.1
PCB	.5	.5	**31.6**	**55.8**	**65.5**	**21**	**28.7**	**52**	**62.8**	**19.4**	**26.1**	**47.6**	**57.4**	**16.9**
R50	.25	.5	6.6	16.1	22.4	6.5	6.1	14.9	19.8	6.1	3.3	8.8	12.9	2.6
PCB	.25	.5	**23.7**	**45.7**	**55.8**	**16.7**	**15.4**	**33.9**	**43.7**	**10.2**	**10.8**	**24.7**	**33.8**	**6.9**
R50	.5	.25	9.6	19.7	27.8	9.3	11.2	22.1	29	10.4	7.3	15.4	21.8	6.1
PCB	.5	.25	**25.9**	**49.1**	**60.3**	**16.5**	**28.7**	**52.4**	**62.7**	**19.3**	**22.7**	**43.4**	**53.5**	**25**
R50	.25	0	5.9	14.2	20.3	5.2	6	14.7	20.3	5.7	1.9	6.2	8.9	1.9
PCB	.25	0	**11.8**	**27.2**	**36.2**	**7.2**	**12.3**	**27.3**	**36.3**	**7.9**	**7.7**	**18.4**	**25.1**	**4.5**

based on automatically detected joints by JDN [28] is less effective due to the errors introduced by JDN as discussed in Sect. 3.1. JDN was designed to detect a fixed number of parts, therefore it is forced to detect parts even when they are not present in the frames. This however shows that despite impressive results from recent human pose estimation networks there is still a gap to bridge before it can bring clear benefits to partial person re-ID.

Table 2. Partial re-ID with alignment and hallucination. Performances are shown in terms of r1 (rank-1), r5 (rank-5), r10 (rank-10), and map (mean average precision). Comparison to baseline as well as different variants of ResNet50 and our proposed approach. Combined alignment and hallucination consistently improves the results

Methods	CropCUHK03 .5,.25				CropCUHK03 .25,0			
	r1	r5	r10	Map	r1	r5	r10	Map
Res50+Eucl [31]	9.6	19.7	27.8	9.3	5.9	14.2	20.3	5.2
Res50+Eucl+re-rank [31]	11.6	19	24.4	12.8	6.8	12.9	18.4	7.2
Res50+XQDA [31]	16.6	30.7	38.4	14.5	8.9	19.7	26.4	7.4
Res50+XQDA+re-rank [31]	18.6	30	37.1	20	10.2	20	25.7	10.4
PCB baseline [14]	25.9	49.1	60.3	16.5	11.8	27.2	36.2	7.2
PCB align	20.1	40.2	50	13	6.4	16	22.5	3.7
PCB man align	28.7	52.4	62.7	19.3	12.3	27.3	36	37.9
PCB align+hall	15.4	32.3	41.3	9.3	3.2	9.7	14.8	1.7
PCB man align+hall	25	47.6	58.1	15.9	6.8	17.9	24.8	4
Our align+hall	22	42.5	52.5	14.4	5.4	14.5	20.6	3.1
Our man align+hall	**31.3**	**55.6**	**65.4**	**21.2**	**13.2**	**28.4**	**37.5**	**8.4**

Comparative Evaluation. Table 2 shows comparative results on the proposed CropCUHK03. We compare our approach with several other extensions of the backbone networks. We report results for the ResNet50 [31] and PCB [14] baselines, as well as extended with the automatic and manual alignment, XQDA feature projections, and re-ranking. In particular, XQDA feature projections and re-ranking have been successfully used in various re-ID systems which is also demonstrated by the results in Table 2. However, PCB baseline significantly outperforms ResNet50 with XQDA and re-ranking, which further validates its choice as the backbone for our approach. As reported in Table 1 automatic alignment with JDN introduces noise which affects the overall performance. There is a significant improvement though when the joints are correctly detected i.e., man align. Training and testing the PCB backbone only with hallucinated samples leads to a drop in re-ID rates (PCB man align+hall), probably due to overfitting to the hallucinated samples. Nevertheless, when FEB is applied to both, hallucinated and aligned samples (Our man align+hall), it brings an improvement of 2.6% compared to the alignment only (PCB man align) and by 5.4%

compared to the baseline (PCB baseline), showing the effectiveness of the hallucinated samples along with our feature combining strategy (FEB). Features from the hallucination and alignment blocks are processed through a fully connected layer, which emphasizes salient features and combines them into one representation. As expected, the results for 1/4 view and low overlap between views $s = 0.25, o_{min} = 0$ are significantly lower than for $s = 0.5, o_{min} = 0.25$ but our approach still improves upon the other methods. Specifically, $rank1$ increases by 1.5% compared to the PCB baseline.

In summary, our architecture jointly combines features from the aligned and hallucinated frames and significantly boosts the performance, e.g., our man align+hall improves rank 1 of PCB baseline from 25.9% to 31.3%.

4.4 Evaluation on Partial ReID and i-LIDS

In this section we present a comparison on existing Partial ILIDS and Partial ReID datasets [4].

Partial ReID. All our results are reported for single-shot setting, in which the gallery set includes only one image for each person. In Table 3, we compare our method against several other partial re-ID approaches, i.e., SWM [4], AMC [4], and DSR [6], which achieve rank-1 scores of 24.3%, 33.3% and 43%, respectively. Results show that our approach, assuming correctly detected body joints (PCB man align), gives significantly better score of 63%. There is still an improvement of 7% when the automatic JDN joint detector is used.

Table 3. Evaluation on Partial ReID and i-LIDS datasets. Performances are shown in terms of r1 (rank-1), r5 (rank-5), r10 (rank-10), and map (mean average precision). Our method performs best on Partial ReID but not on iLIDS due to low quality views and small training set

Method	Partial ReID				Partial iLIDS			
	r1	r5	r10	Map	r1	r5	r10	Map
SVM [4]	24.3	52.3	61.3	-	33.6	53.8	63	-
AMC [4]	33.3	52	62	-	46.8	69.6	81.8	-
AMC+SWM [4]	36	60	70.7	-	49.6	72.3	70.7	-
DSR (single-scale) [6]	39.3	65.7	76.7	-	51.1	70.7	82.4	-
DSR (multiple-scale) [6]	43	75	76.7	-	**54.6**	**73.1**	**85.7**	-
PCB baseline [14]	54.9	85.3	93.2	57.2	30.6	56.2	68.4	33.6
PCB man align [14]	61.7	89.7	95.9	63.8	35.5	61.7	74.9	37.4
PCB+align	49.6	82.3	92.2	52.2	35.3	62	73.6	37
PCB+align + hall	44.6	76.1	88.7	47.6	33.8	59.4	72.3	35.2
Our (man align + hall)	**63**	**89.1**	**95.3**	**64.7**	35.3	62.7	73.9	37.4
Our (align + hall)	50	82.3	92.2	52.7	38.4	64.5	76.1	39.3

Partial i-LIDS has lower quality images than other datesets, which is reflected in the performance of all compared methods. This dataset significantly differs from CUHK03, which we have adopted for pre-training the PCB. Furthermore, the number of samples of this dataset is too low to fine-tune our CNNs. In contrast, DSR implements a network of 13 layers only, i.e., fewer parameters, and training with small datasets such as Partial i-LIDS is more effective.

5   Conclusion

We have proposed an approach to partial person re-ID by combining body pose detection, spatial alignment, hallucination and feature extraction based on neural networks. We have extensively analyzed the impact of misalignment and hallucination in partial Re-id task, proving that view alignment is particularly effective in case image persons are severely misaligned regardless of how much content is missing in the partial observations. Furthermore, our proposed block (FEB) jointly combining features from the aligned and hallucinated frames significantly improve the performance. Finally, we have evaluated different variants of the approach and compared to state of the arts on three different datasets. The overall results with manual alignment demonstrate that hallucinating missing content from partial observation is an effective strategy for partial person re-identification. It shows the potential improvement that can be obtained by using more accurate human body part detectors.

Some possible improvements of the proposed PCN implementation include a refined loss function that could be designed to drive the Cycle-Consistency Adversarial Network to focus on missing regions of the frame, avoid local minima and to enhance the network ability to reconstruct fine details. Since we have observed the accuracy of JDN on cropped person images is limited, we hope this work would also encourage research community to improve human body joint detector to effectively work on such challenging cases.

Acknowledgment. This research was supported by UK EPSRC EP/N007743/1 grant.

References

1. Li, W., Zhao, R., Xiao, T., Wang, X.: DeepReID: deep filter pairing neural network for person re-identification. In: CVPR (2014)
2. Zheng, L., Shen, L., Tian, L., Wang, S., Wang, J., Tian, Q.: Scalable person re-identification: a benchmark. In: ICCV (2015)
3. Gray, D., Tao, H.: Viewpoint invariant pedestrian recognition with an ensemble of localized features. In: Forsyth, D., Torr, P., Zisserman, A. (eds.) ECCV 2008. LNCS, vol. 5302, pp. 262–275. Springer, Heidelberg (2008). https://doi.org/10.1007/978-3-540-88682-2_21
4. Zheng, W.S., Li, X., Xiang, T., Liao, S., Lai, J., Gong, S.: Partial person re-identification. In: ICCV (2015)

5. Xu, X., Liu, W., Li, L.: Face hallucination: how much it can improve face recognition. In: AUCC (2013)
6. He, L., Liang, J., Li, H., Sun, Z.: Deep spatial feature reconstruction for partial person re-identification: alignment-free approach. In: CVPR (2018)
7. Huang, H., Li, D., Zhang, Z., Chen, X., Huang, K.: Adversarially occluded samples for person re-identification. In: CVPR (2018)
8. Huang, B., Chen, J., Wang, Y., Liang, C., Wang, Z., Sun, K.: Sparsity-based occlusion handling method for person re-identification. In: He, X., Luo, S., Tao, D., Xu, C., Yang, J., Hasan, M.A. (eds.) MMM 2015. LNCS, vol. 8936, pp. 61–73. Springer, Cham (2015). https://doi.org/10.1007/978-3-319-14442-9_6
9. Wang, S., Lewandowski, M., Annesley, J., Orwell, J.: Re-identification of pedestrians with variable occlusion and scale. In: ICCV Workshops (2011)
10. Lee, S., Hong, Y., Jeon, M.: Occlusion detector using convolutional neural network for person re-identification. In: ICCAIS (2017)
11. Ahmed, E., Jones, M., Marks, T.K.: An improved deep learning architecture for person re-identification. In: CVPR (2015)
12. Varior, R.R., Haloi, M., Wang, G.: Gated Siamese convolutional neural network architecture for human re-identification. In: Leibe, B., Matas, J., Sebe, N., Welling, M. (eds.) ECCV 2016. LNCS, vol. 9912, pp. 791–808. Springer, Cham (2016). https://doi.org/10.1007/978-3-319-46484-8_48
13. Wu, L., Wang, Y., Li, X., Gao, J.: What-and-where to match: deep spatially multiplicative integration networks for person re-identification. Pattern Recogn. **76**, 727–738 (2018)
14. Sun, Y., Zheng, L., Yang, Y., Tian, Q., Wang, S.: Beyond part models: person retrieval with refined part pooling (and a strong convolutional baseline). In: Ferrari, V., Hebert, M., Sminchisescu, C., Weiss, Y. (eds.) ECCV 2018. LNCS, vol. 11208, pp. 501–518. Springer, Cham (2018). https://doi.org/10.1007/978-3-030-01225-0_30
15. Li, W., Zhu, X., Gong, S.: Harmonious attention network for person re-identification. In: CVPR (2018)
16. Zhao, L., Li, X., Zhuang, Y., Wang, J.: Deeply-learned part-aligned representations for person re-identification. In: ICCV (2017)
17. Guo, Y., Cheung, N.: Efficient and deep person re-identification using multi-level similarity. In: CVPR (2018)
18. Wei, L., Zhang, S., Yao, H., Gao, W., Tian, Q.: GLAD: global-local-alignment descriptor for pedestrian retrieval. In: ACM on Multimedia Conference (2017)
19. Su, C., Li, J., Zhang, S., Xing, J., Gao, W., Tian, Q.: Pose-driven deep convolutional model for person re-identification. In: ICCV (2017)
20. Zhao, H., et al.: Spindle net: person re-identification with human body region guided feature decomposition and fusion. In: CVPR (2017)
21. Xu, J., Zhao, R., Zhu, F., Wang, H., Ouyang, W.: Attention-aware compositional network for person re-identification. In: CVPR (2018)
22. Goodfellow, I., et al.: Generative adversarial nets. In: Advances in Neural Information Processing Systems (2014)
23. Zheng, Z., Zheng, L., Yang, Y: Unlabeled samples generated by GAN improve the person re-identification baseline in vitro. In: ICCV (2017)
24. Liu, J., Ni, B., Yan, Y., Zhou, P., Cheng, S., Hu, J.: Pose transferrable person re-identification. In: CVPR (2018)
25. Wei, L., Zhang, S., Gao, W., Tian, Q.: Person transfer GAN to bridge domain gap for person re-identification. In: CVPR (2018)

26. Deng, W., Zheng, L., Ye, Q., Kang, G., Yang, Y., Jiao, J.: Image-image domain adaptation with preserved self-similarity and domain-dissimilarity for person re-identification. In: CVPR (2018)
27. Zhong, Z., Zheng, L., Zheng, Z., Li, S., Yang, Y.: Camera style adaptation for person re-identification. In: CVPR (2018)
28. Wei, S.E., Ramakrishna, V., Kanade, T., Sheikh, Y.: Convolutional pose machines. In: CVPR (2016)
29. Isola, P., Zhu, J.Y., Zhou, T., Efros, A.A.: Image-to-image translation with conditional adversarial networks. In: CVPR (2017)
30. Zhu, J.Y., Park, T., Isola, P., Efros, A.A.: Unpaired image-to-image translation using cycle-consistent adversarial networks. In: ICCV (2017)
31. Zhong, Z., Zheng, L., Cao, D., Li, S.: Re-ranking person re-identification with k-reciprocal encoding. In: CVPR (2017)
32. Xiao, T., Li, H., Ouyang, W., Wang, X.: Learning deep feature representations with domain guided dropout for person re-identification. In: CVPR (2016)

FSNet: An Identity-Aware Generative Model for Image-Based Face Swapping

Ryota Natsume[1](✉), Tatsuya Yatagawa[1], and Shigeo Morishima[1,2]

[1] Waseda University, 3-4-1, Ohkubo, Shinjuku, Tokyo 169-8555, Japan
ryota.natsume.26@gmail.com, tatsy@acm.org, shigeo@waseda.jp
[2] Waseda Research Institute of Science and Engineering, Tokyo, Japan

Abstract. This paper presents FSNet, a deep generative model for image-based face swapping. Traditionally, face-swapping methods are based on three-dimensional morphable models (3DMMs), and facial textures are replaced between the estimated three-dimensional (3D) geometries in two images of different individuals. However, the estimation of 3D geometries along with different lighting conditions using 3DMMs is still a difficult task. We herein represent the face region with a latent variable that is assigned with the proposed deep neural network (DNN) instead of facial textures. The proposed DNN synthesizes a face-swapped image using the latent variable of the face region and another image of the non-face region. The proposed method is not required to fit to the 3DMM; additionally, it performs face swapping only by feeding two face images to the proposed network. Consequently, our DNN-based face swapping performs better than previous approaches for challenging inputs with different face orientations and lighting conditions. Through several experiments, we demonstrated that the proposed method performs face swapping in a more stable manner than the state-of-the-art method, and that its results are compatible with the method thereof.

Keywords: Face swapping · Convolutional neural networks · Deep generative models

1 Introduction

Face image editing has become increasingly prevalent owing to the growth of social networking services and photo-retouching software. To respond to the potential demand for creating more attractive face images with such photo-retouching software, many studies have been introduced for a range of applications including face image analysis [1–4] and manipulation [5–9] in computer vision and graphics communities. In such applications, face swapping is an important technique owing to its broad applications such as photomontage [5], virtual hairstyle fitting [9], privacy protection [6,10,11], and data augmentation for machine learning [12–14].

Electronic supplementary material The online version of this chapter (https://doi.org/10.1007/978-3-030-20876-9_8) contains supplementary material, which is available to authorized users.

C. V. Jawahar et al. (Eds.): ACCV 2018, LNCS 11366, pp. 117–132, 2019.
https://doi.org/10.1007/978-3-030-20876-9_8

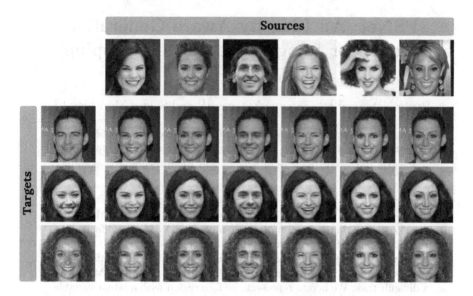

Fig. 1. Results of image-based face swapping using our method. In this figure, face regions of the target images in the left column are replaced with the faces of the source images in the top row. The supplementary document provides additional results for other input faces.

As its name indicates, face swapping replaces the face region of a target image with that in a source image. Traditional approaches [5, 15] uses three-dimensional morphable models (3DMMs) to estimate face geometries and their corresponding textures. Subsequently, the textures of the source and target images are swapped using the estimated texture coordinates. Finally, the replaced face textures are re-rendered using the lighting condition estimated from the target image. However, these methods are prone to fail in estimating the face geometries or lighting conditions in practice. The inaccurate estimations typically cause noticeable artifacts because human eyes can well detect slight mismatches of these geometries and lighting conditions.

In contrast to the methods above, several recent studies have applied deep neural networks (DNNs) to face swapping. Bao et al. [16] proposed a conditional image generation technique using a DNN, known as CVAE-GAN. They performed face swapping by considering face identities as image conditioners. A similar technique was used in "FakeApp" [17], an easy-to-use application software for image-based face swapping using a DNN. Korshunova et al. [11] considered face identities as artistic styles in neural style transfer [18], and performed face swapping by fine-tuning the pre-trained network using a dozens of images of an individual. Although these approaches facilitated the use of deep-learning techniques for face swapping, they share a common problem in that the users must prepare multiple input images of an individual. Meanwhile, Natsume et al. [19] proposed a DNN for face image editing that only uses a single source image and a single target image. Even though their method can be applied to a wide range of applications including face swapping, the hair regions of their face-swapped results are no longer the same as those in the original images.

To address the problems above, we propose FSNet, a novel DNN for image-based face swapping. The proposed method disentangles face appearance as a latent variable that is independent of the face geometry and the appearance of the non-face region, including hairstyles and backgrounds. The latent variables for the two face appearances of two input images are swapped, and are combined with the latent variables for the non-face parts of the counterpart images. Once the network of FSNet is trained using a large-scale face image dataset, FSNet does not require any additional fine-tuning and performs face swapping only with a single source image and a single target image. As shown in Fig. 1, the faces are swapped appropriately in that face identities in the source images are preserved well and composed naturally with the non-face regions of the target images. In this study, we evaluated the face-swapping results using a number of image assessment metrics and demonstrated that FSNet achieves more stable face swapping than the state-of-the-art methods. In addition to the stability, the quality of the FSNet results is compatible to the methods thereof. The technical contributions of FSNet are summarized as follows:

1. It is a new DNN for image-based face swapping that uses only a single source and a single target images, and does not require any additional fine-tuning.
2. While face swapping, it well preserves both the face identity in a source image and the appearances of hairstyle and background region in a target image.
3. It performs high-quality face swapping even for typical challenging inputs with different face orientations and with different lighting conditions.

2   Related Work

Face swapping has been studied for a range of applications including photomontage [5], virtual hairstyle fitting [9], privacy protection [6,10,11], and data augmentation for large-scale machine learning [14]. Several studies [7,10] have replaced only parts of the face, such as eyes, nose, and mouth between images rather than swapping the entire face. A popular approach for face swapping is based on the 3DMM [5,15]. Fitting a 3DMM to a target face yields the face geometry, texture map, and lighting condition [1,2]. A face-swapped appearance is generated by the replacement of the face textures and the subsequent re-rendering of the face appearance using the estimated lighting condition.

The primary drawback of these approaches is the difficulty in the accurate estimation of three-dimensional (3D) face geometries and lighting conditions from single images. The failure estimation often causes noticeable visual artifacts. To alleviate this problem, Bitouk et al. [6] proposed an image-based face swapping without the 3DMM. To avoid the estimation of face geometries, they leveraged a large-scale face database. Their system searches a target image whose layout is similar to that of a source image. Subsequently, these face regions of two similar images are swapped using boundary-aware image composition. A more sophisticated approach was recently proposed by Kemelmacher-Shlizerman [9]. She carefully designed a handmade feature vector to represent face image appearances and improved the accuracy of searching similar faces successfully. However, these methods do not allow the users to choose both the source and target images; therefore, they are not applicable to arbitrary face image pairs.

Several recent studies have applied deep neural networks for image-based face swapping. Bao et al. [16] indicated that their conditional image generation technique can alter face identities by conditioning the generated images with an identity vector. Meanwhile, Korshunova et al. [11] applied the neural style transfer [18] for face swapping by considering the face identities as the artistic styles in the original style transfer. However, these recent approaches still have a problem. They require at least dozens of images of an individual person to obtain a face-swapped image. Collecting that many images is possible, albeit unreasonable for most non-celebrities.

Another recent study [20] proposed an identity-preserving GAN for transferring image appearances between two face images. While the purpose of this study is close to that of face swapping, it does not preserve the appearances of non-face regions including hairstyles and backgrounds. Several studies for DNN-based image completion [21,22] have presented demonstrations of face appearance manipulation by filling the parts of an input image with their DNNs. However, the users can hardly estimate the results of these approaches because they only fill the regions specified by the users such that the completed results imitate the images in the training data.

3   FSNet: A Generative Model for Face Swapping

The architecture of FSNet is shown in Fig. 2. The network is separated into two parts and each of them performs one of two different tasks. The first part, i.e., encoder-decoder network in Fig. 2(a), disentangles a face appearance as a latent variable from a source image. The architecture of this part is based on the variational autoencoder [23] (VAE), and the latent variable can be obtained from the middle layer of the network. The second part, i.e., generator network in Fig. 2(b), synthesizes a new face part such that it fits the non-face part of a target image. The architecture of this part is based on the U-Net [24] and it synthesizes the face part by concatenating the latent variable with the feature map provided in the middle layer of the network. In the following subsections, we first elaborate the two partial networks; subsequently, we describe an image dataset for training the networks. In addition, we provide the detailed network architecture of FSNet in the supplementary document. The notations used in this paper are also summarized in the supplementary document.

3.1   Encoder-Decoder Network

The training of FSNet requires sampling the full face image x_θ and three intermediate images as in Fig. 2. Here, $\theta \in \{s, t\}$, and x_s and x_t represent a source

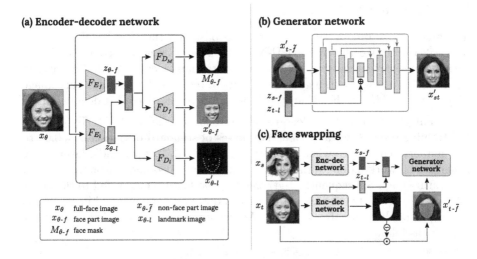

Fig. 2. Network architecture of FSNet. The network consists of two partial networks, i.e., (a) encoder-decoder network, and (b) generator network. The encoder-decoder network obtains a latent variable for a face appearance that is independent of the face geometry and appearance of the non-face part. The generator network synthesizes a face-swapped result from the latent variable and non-face part of another image.

and target image in face swapping, respectively. The three intermediate images, i.e., face mask $M_{\theta\text{-}f}$, face part image $x_{\theta\text{-}f}$, and landmark image $x_{\theta\text{-}l}$, will be compared to the outputs from the encoder-decoder network.

As shown in Fig. 2(a), the encoder-decoder network outputs face mask $M'_{\theta\text{-}f}$, face part image $x'_{\theta\text{-}f}$, landmark image $x'_{\theta\text{-}l}$, and non-face part image $x'_{\theta\text{-}\bar{f}}$. In the encoder-decoder network, the full face image x_θ is first encoded by two different encoders F_{E_f} and F_{E_l}. Following the standard VAEs, these encoders output the means and standard deviations of the corresponding standard normal distributions. Subsequently, the latent variables $z_{\theta\text{-}f}$ and $z_{\theta\text{-}l}$ are sampled from the following distributions:

$$z_{\theta\text{-}f} = \mathcal{N}\left(\mu_{\theta\text{-}f}, \sigma_{\theta\text{-}f}\right), \quad \left(\mu_{\theta\text{-}f}, \sigma^2_{\theta\text{-}f}\right) = F_{E_f}(x_\theta),$$
$$z_{\theta\text{-}l} = \mathcal{N}\left(\mu_{\theta\text{-}l}, \sigma_{\theta\text{-}l}\right), \quad \left(\mu_{\theta\text{-}l}, \sigma^2_{\theta\text{-}l}\right) = F_{E_l}(x_\theta),$$

where μ_θ and σ^2_θ are the mean and variance of z_θ. The three decoders F_{D_M}, F_{D_f}, and F_{D_l} reconstruct face mask $M'_{\theta\text{-}f}$, face image $x'_{\theta\text{-}f}$, and landmark image $x'_{\theta\text{-}l}$, respectively:

$$M'_{\theta\text{-}f} = F_{D_M}(z_{\theta\text{-}f}, z_{\theta\text{-}l}), \quad x'_{\theta\text{-}f} = F_{D_f}(z_{\theta\text{-}f}, z_{\theta\text{-}l}), \quad x'_{\theta\text{-}l} = F_{D_l}(z_{\theta\text{-}l}).$$

To encode only geometry-independent information in $z_{\theta\text{-}f}$, we input both $z_{\theta\text{-}f}$ and $z_{\theta\text{-}l}$ to F_{D_f} and F_{D_M}, similarly for F_{E_f}.

3.2   Generator Network

The architecture of generator network G is based on the U-Net [24], as shown in Fig. 2(b). Unlike the original U-Net, the generator network receives latent variables and concatenates them with a feature map given in the middle layer of the network. Moreover, the generator network receives the non-face part image $x'_{t\text{-}\tilde{f}} = x'_{t\text{-}f} \odot \tilde{M}'_{t\text{-}f}$ rather than the full-face image x_t. Here, $\odot$ denotes pixel-wise multiplication and $\tilde{M}$ denotes an inversion of the mask M. To stabilize the training process, we add Gaussian noises of standard deviation $\sigma = 0.05$ to the non-face part image when the network is trained. In the middle layer of the generator network, latent variables $z_{s\text{-}f}$ and $z_{t\text{-}l}$ are tiled and concatenated with the feature map. Subsequently, the concatenated feature map is fed to the latter part of the U-Net structure. Finally, we can obtain a face-swapped image x'_{st} as an output of the generator network. We denote the operation of the generator network as follows:

$$x'_{st} = G(x_{t\text{-}\tilde{f}}, z_{s\text{-}f}, z_{t\text{-}l}).$$

When the two same images x_s and x_t ($s = t$) are input to the proposed network, the generator network should reproduce the input full-face image x_s ($= x_t$). We denote the reconstructed image as x'_s. It is noteworthy that the masked image $x'_{t\text{-}\tilde{f}}$, which is one of the inputs of the generator network, is computed by the encoder-decoder network only using the full-face image x_t. Therefore, face swapping can be performed with only the source and target image themselves, and the user need not prepare intermediate images used in the training.

3.3   Training

The proposed network is trained similarly as VAE-GAN [25]. In other words, the two partial networks are trained with VAE objectives and GAN objectives, separately. In addition, the proposed network is also trained with an identity loss to preserve the face identities in the face swapping results. We define the identity loss using the triplet loss [26]. Therefore, we sample a triplet of images consisting of anchor sample x_{s_1}, positive sample x_{s_2}, and negative sample x_t. The anchor and positive samples are used as source images, and the negative sample is used as a target image. The different identities in these three images are ignored when we evaluate the VAE and GAN objectives.

VAE Objectives: For three outputs $M'_{\theta\text{-}f}$, $x'_{\theta\text{-}f}$, and $x'_{\theta\text{-}l}$, we define the reconstruction losses using the corresponding ground truth images in the training data. We evaluate the cross entropy losses for the face masks and landmark images and an L1 loss for the face part images:

$$\mathcal{L}^{rec}_{\theta\text{-}M} = \mathbb{E}[L_{CE}(M_{\theta\text{-}f}, M'_{\theta\text{-}f})],$$
$$\mathcal{L}^{rec}_{\theta\text{-}f} = \mathbb{E}[\|x_{\theta\text{-}f} - x'_{\theta\text{-}f}\|_1],$$
$$\mathcal{L}^{rec}_{\theta\text{-}l} = \mathbb{E}[L_{CE}(x_{\theta\text{-}l}, x'_{\theta\text{-}l})],$$

where L_{CE} denotes a function for the cross entropy loss. In addition, we define another reconstruction loss $\mathcal{L}_\theta^{rec}$ between the full-face image x_θ and its corresponding reconstruction x'_θ as well. For imposing more reconstruction loss for the pixels in the foreground region, i.e., the face and hair regions, we define the loss with the foreground mask $M_{\theta\text{-}FG}$ as follows:

$$\mathcal{L}_\theta^{rec} = \mathbb{E}\left[\left\|\left(x_\theta - x'_\theta\right) \odot \left(M_{\theta\text{-}FG} + \beta(1 - M_{\theta\text{-}FG})\right)\right\|_1\right].$$

In our implementation, we used the parameter $\beta = 0.5$ to halve the losses in the background. To evaluate the means and standard deviations given with the encoders, we employed a latent classifier as in α-GAN [27] rather than evaluating the Kullback-Leibler loss in the standard VAEs. Let C_ω be the latent classifier and $z \sim \mathcal{N}(0,1)$ be a random vector sampled with the standard normal distribution. Therefore, we can define the latent classification loss as follows:

$$\mathcal{L}_{\theta\text{-}f}^{lat} = -\mathbb{E}[\log C_\omega(z_{\theta\text{-}f})] - \mathbb{E}[\log(1 - C_\omega(z_{\theta\text{-}f}))].$$

Equally, $\mathcal{L}_{\theta\text{-}M}^{lat}$ and $\mathcal{L}_{\theta\text{-}l}^{lat}$ are defined for $z_{\theta\text{-}M}$ and $z_{\theta\text{-}l}$.

GAN Objectives: As the standard GAN, both the encoder-decoder and generator networks are trained adversarially with several discriminators. To evaluate the real and synthesized images, we used two discriminators, i.e., global discriminator D_g and patch discriminator D_p. The global discriminator distinguishes whether an image is a real sample or a synthesized image. The patch discriminator, which is originally introduced as a part of PatchGAN [28], distinguishes whether a local patch of the image is from a real sample or a synthesized image. In addition to x_θ and x'_θ, we also synthesize images with a random face using normal random vectors instead of $z_{\theta\text{-}f}$ and $z_{\theta\text{-}l}$. Let $\hat{x}'_\theta$ be such a random face image, we define global and patch adversarial losses $\mathcal{L}_\theta^{adv\text{-}g}$ and $\mathcal{L}_\theta^{adv\text{-}p}$ as follows:

$$\begin{aligned}
\mathcal{L}_\theta^{adv\text{-}\{g,p\}} = &- \mathbb{E}\left[\log D_{\{g,p\}}(x_\theta)\right] \\
&- \mathbb{E}\left[\log(1 - D_{\{g,p\}}(x'_\theta))\right] \\
&- \mathbb{E}\left[\log(1 - D_{\{g,p\}}(\hat{x}'_\theta))\right].
\end{aligned}$$

Identity Loss: In the CelebA dataset, which we used in the experiments, identity labels are assigned to all the images. A straightforward method to evaluate the identity of a synthesized image is to train an identity classifier. However, human faces are typically similar between two different people. We found that training by this straightforward approach is unstable and can be easily stuck in a local minimum. Alternatively, we employed the triplet loss [26] to evaluate the similarity of identities in two face images. The triplet loss is defined for a triple of image samples, i.e., anchor, positive, and negative samples. These samples are first encoded to the feature vectors; subsequently, the distances of the feature vectors are computed for the anchor and positive samples, and the anchor and negative samples. The triplet loss is defined to broaden the difference between these distances. To train the network, we generate two face-swapped results

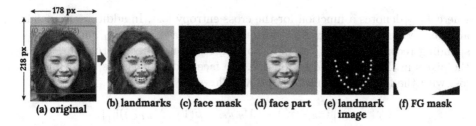

Fig. 3. Dataset preparation from each image in CelebA [3]. To reduce the size of the dataset, we include only (a), (c), (e), and (f) in the dataset, and other intermediate images are computed while training FSNet. (Color figure online)

$x'_{s_1 t}$ and $x'_{s_2 t}$ from three input images x_{s_1}, x_{s_2}, and x_t. The triplet losses are defined for the triplets $\{x_{s_1}, x_{s_2}, x_t\}$, $\{x'_{s_1 t}, x_{s_1}, x_t)\}$, and $\{x'_{s_2 t}, x_{s_2}, x_t\}$, where images in each triplet denote {anchor, positive, negative} samples. For a triplet $\{x_{s_1}, x_{s_2}, x_t\}$, the triplet loss is defined using a feature extractor $F_{E_{id}}$ as in the original study [26]:

$$
\mathcal{L}^{id}_{\{s_1, s_2, t\}} = \min\left(0, \|F_{E_{id}}(x_{s_1}) - F_{E_{id}}(x_{s_2})\|_2^2 + \alpha_1 - \|F_{E_{id}}(x_{s_1}) - F_{E_{id}}(x_t)\|_2^2\right) \\
+ \alpha_3 \min\left(0, \|F_{E_{id}}(x_{s_1}) - F_{E_{id}}(x_{s_2})\|_2^2 - \alpha_2\right).
$$

In our implementation, we set the parameters as $\alpha_1 = 1.0$, $\alpha_2 = 0.1$, and $\alpha_3 = 0.5$. To normalize the color balances in the face images, we subtract the average pixel colors from the image and divide it by the standard deviation of the pixel colors before feeding the images to $F_{E_{id}}$.

Hyper Parameters: The overall loss function for training FSNet is defined by a weighted sum of the loss functions above:

$$
\begin{aligned}
\mathcal{L} = {} & \lambda_f^{rec} \mathcal{L}_f^{rec} + \lambda_M^{rec} \mathcal{L}_M^{rec} + \lambda_l^{rec} \mathcal{L}_l^{rec} \\
& + \lambda^{lat}(\mathcal{L}_f^{lat} + \mathcal{L}_M^{lat} + \mathcal{L}_l^{lat}) \\
& + \lambda^{adv\text{-}g} \mathcal{L}^{adv\text{-}g} + \lambda^{adv\text{-}p} \mathcal{L}^{adv\text{-}p} \\
& + \lambda^{id} \mathcal{L}^{id}
\end{aligned}
$$

In this equation, we simply wrote $\mathcal{L}$ as an average of the corresponding losses for s_1, s_2, and t for VAE and GAN objectives, and $\mathcal{L}^{id}$ as the sum of all the triplet losses for the identity losses. We empirically determined the weighting factors as $\lambda_f^{rec} = \lambda_M^{rec} = 4{,}000$, $\lambda_l^{rec} = 2{,}000$, $\lambda^{lat} = 30$, $\lambda^{adv\text{-}g} = 20$, $\lambda^{adv\text{-}p} = 30$, and $\lambda^{id} = 100$. In our experiment, the loss functions were minimized by mini-batch training using the ADAM optimizer [29] with an initial learning rate of 0.0002, $\beta_1 = 0.5$, and $\beta_2 = 0.999$. A mini-batch includes 20 images for each of x_{s_1}, x_{s_2}, and x_t; therefore, the size of the mini-batch was 60.

3.4   Datasets

The dataset for training FSNet includes four types of images, i.e., the original full-face image (Fig. 3(a)), face mask image (Fig. 3(c)), landmark image (Fig. 3(e)), and foreground mask (Fig. 3(f)). All these images are generated computationally for each image in CelebA.

For an original full-face image, we first extract 68 facial landmarks (Fig. 3(b)) with Dlib [30], which is a typically used machine-learning library. A convex hull is computed from the 41 landmarks that correspond to the eyes, nose, and mouth, which are indicated with blue circles in Fig. 3(b). The convex hull is stretched to obtain a face mask (Fig. 3(c)). The hull is stretched 1.3 times along the horizontal direction and 1.4 times along the vertical direction.

Subsequently, we dilate the mask by 3% of the image width to ensure that the mask boarders are slightly inside the face contours and include the eyebrows inside the mask. The face part image (Fig. 3(d)) is obtained by applying the face mask to the input image. We use landmarks on the eyes instead of the eyebrows because the eyebrows are often hidden by bangs. Compared to the eyebrows, the landmarks on the eyes are less likely to be hidden, and the face masks can be more appropriately defined with them.

The landmark image Fig. 3(e) includes 5 landmarks inside the face region and 17 landmarks on the face contour. The top two internal landmarks correspond to the eye center positions, and are calculated by averaging the position of the eye landmarks. That in the middle corresponds to the nose position, and is represented by a landmark on the tip of nose. The two bottom ones correspond to the mouse position and are represented by two landmarks on two ends of the mouse. The 17 contour landmarks are represented by those on the face contour among the original 68 landmarks. These 22 landmarks are splatted on the landmark image as circles with a radius of 3% of the image width. Finally, The foreground mask (Fig. 3(f)) is detected using a state-of-the-art semantic segmentation method, PSPNet [31]. Pixels labeled as "person" are used as the foreground mask.

All of these images are cropped from 178×218 pixel region of the original image by a square of 178×178 pixels whose top-left corner is at $(0, 20)$. We used the cropped images after resizing them to 128×128. While processing images in CelebA, we could extract facial landmarks properly for 195,361 images out of 202,599 images. Among these 195,361 images, we used 180,000 images for training and the other 15,361 images for testing.

4   Results

This section presents our face swapping results for various face images. The proposed method was implemented with TensorFlow in Python, and executed on a computer with an Intel Xeon 3.6 GHz E5-1650 v4 CPU, NVIDIA GeForce GTX TITAN X GPU, and 64 GB RAM. We trained the proposed network over 180,000 global steps. The training required approximately 72 h using a single

Fig. 4. Face swapping between images with different face orientations. The left group shows the swapping results from frontal faces to lateral faces, while the right group shows those from lateral faces to frontal faces.

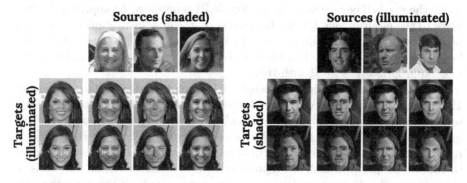

Fig. 5. Face swapping between images with different lighting conditions. The left group shows the swapping results from shaded faces to uniformly illuminated faces, while the right group shows those from uniformly illuminated faces to shaded faces.

GPU. All the results herein were generated using test images not included in the training data.

Figure 1 shows the face swapping results for several face images. In this figure, the source images are in the top row and the target images are in the left column. As shown in this figure, face swapping is performed appropriately for such a variety of inputs. In addition, we tested the input images with several challenging cases to demonstrate the robustness of the proposed method. First, we swapped faces between images with different face orientations. The results are shown in Fig. 4. In this figure, one of the sources or target images shows a frontal face and the other shows a lateral face. As shown in this figure, the face appearances including their identities are transferred appropriately to the target image even though the face orientations differed significantly. Next, we tested the images with different lighting conditions. As shown in Fig. 5, one of the sources or target images shows a uniformly illuminated face while the other shows a face lit from the side. When shaded faces are transferred to uniformly illuminated faces, the

Sources   **Sources**

Fig. 6. Face swapping between images of the same person. The four images in each group are those of an individual.

shades are removed appropriately from the faces. Furthermore, when uniformly illuminated faces are transferred to shaded faces, the overall appearances of the results are natural whereas the shades in the target images are not necessarily observed in the results. Thus, the proposed method achieves face swapping even in such challenging cases.

We also evaluated the capability of preserving face identities by swapping faces of a single individual using the proposed method. The results are illustrated in Fig. 6. In this figure, each group of images includes two input images for source images and the other two for target images. All of these four images show the faces of a single person. As shown in this figure, the second and third rows in each group are almost identical. These results demonstrate that the proposed network can preserve the facial identities in the input images appropriately.

To evaluate the proposed method quantitatively, and compare it with prior approaches, we conducted two experiments using four different metrics, as shown in Table 1. Two of these metrics are for measuring the capability of identity preservation, and the other two are for measuring the output image quality.

In these experiments, two previous studies: VAE-GAN [25] and α-GAN [27] were used as baselines. Although these studies were not originally for face swapping, we performed face swapping with them in three steps. First, we compute a face mask similarly as in our dataset synthesis. Next, the face region of the source image in the mask is copy and pasted to the target image such that the two eye locations are aligned. Finally, the entire image appearance is repaired by being fed to each network. In addition to these baseline methods, we compared the proposed method with a 3DMM-based state-of-the-art method by Nirkin et al. [15]. In each experiment, we sampled 1,000 image pairs randomly.

In the first experiment, we swapped the faces between two different images of a single individual. Subsequently, we calculate the absolute difference and MS-SSIM [32] between the input and swapped images. The results are shown in the third and fourth columns of Table 1. In the second experiment, the faces of two

Table 1. Performance evaluation in capabilities of identity preservation and image qualities.

		Same person		Different people	
		Abs. errors	MS-SSIM	OpenFace	Inception score
VAE-GAN [25]	Avg.	0.115	0.619	1.591	2.142
	Std.	0.041	0.105	0.499	0.137
α-GAN [27]	Avg.	0.099	0.705	1.353	2.056
	Std.	0.040	0.099	0.487	0.082
Nirkin et al. [15]	Avg.	0.024	0.956	0.811	2.993
	Std.	0.010	0.025	0.749	0.229
FSNet	Avg.	0.030	0.936	0.883	2.846
	Std.	0.007	0.029	0.829	0.116
FSNet (for images Nirkin et al. failed)	Avg.	0.031	0.933	0.888	(1.235)
	Std.	0.006	0.025	0.837	—

different people were swapped by each method. To evaluate how the identities are preserved after face swapping, we calculated a squared Euclidean distance of two feature vectors for an input and a face-swapped result using OpenFace [33], which is an open-source face feature extractor. In addition, we computed the inception scores [34] to measure the capability of our face swapping method when applied to a broad variety of individuals. The results are shown in the fifth and sixth columns of Table 1.

From these experiments, Nirkin et al. [15] demonstrated the best scores for all the metrics in Table 1, and the proposed method follows it closely. However, Nirkin et al.'s method sometimes fails to fit the 3DMM to one of the sources or target images, and could generate the results for only approximately 90% of the input pairs. Meanwhile, the proposed method and the other baseline methods could generate the results for all the input pairs. Thus, the robustness of Nirkin et al.'s method can be problematic in practice. We also calculated each score with FSNet for the images whereby Nirkin et al.'s method could not generate the results. The scores in the bottom rows indicate that each of them is almost identical to that calculated with all sample images. These results demonstrate that the proposed method is advantageous because it can well generate high-quality results for arbitrary pairs of input images.

To elaborate the comparison with the method of Nirkin et al., we present the typical failure cases of their method and our FSNet in Fig. 7. In this figure, the first two cases exhibit the limitations of Nirkin et al.'s method, and the last one case for FSNet. First, their method and also other methods based on the 3DMM often demonstrate the inaccurate segmentation of face areas. While Nirkin et al. proposed the occlusion-aware segmentation of the face areas, its accuracy is still limited. In their results in Fig. 7(a), the left eye of a target person remained in our face swapping result. The proposed method and other image-based method using

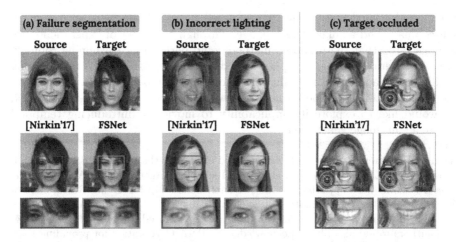

Fig. 7. Typical failure cases of Nirkin et al.'s method [15] and FSNet. (a) Failure segmentation and (b) incorrect lighting estimation are those for Nirkin et al.'s method and (c) occluded target face is that for proposed FSNet. (Color figure online)

DNNs do not require such a fragile segmentation process. Next, the estimation of lighting condition from a single image is a challenging task. The failure estimation drives the 3DMM-based methods in inappropriate face appearances. As in Fig. 7(b), the face color in the results of Nirkin et al. was attenuated unexpectedly, and the details around eyelashes became blurry. The DNN-based methods, including FSNet, were not strongly affected by such lighting conditions, as shown in Fig. 5. Meanwhile, the proposed method cannot properly swap faces when a part of the face region is occluded. As shown in Fig. 7(c), the camera and left hand in front of the face were lost in the face swapping result. This is because only a limited number of image samples are available for such occluded faces in the training dataset. Recently, several approaches [15,35] have augmented an image dataset by artificially adding random obstacles to the images, and separated face regions occluded by such obstacles successfully. Although this approach can likely be applied to the face image synthesis, we will leave it for future work owing to its uncertain applicability. It is noteworthy that the proposed method can consider a face occluded by hair as in Fig. 7(a) because such hairstyles are included in the training data.

5   Conclusion

We proposed FSNet, a deep generative model for image-based face swapping. The encoder-decoder part of the proposed network disentangles a face appearance as a latent variable that is independent of the face geometry and appearance of non-face parts. The latent variable was composed together with the non-face part of the target image, and a face-swapped image was generated by the generative network. In contrast to previous methods, our method used neither the 3DMM nor any additional fine-tuning. It performed face swapping only with a single source image and a single target image. Through a number of experiments, we demonstrated that the proposed method could perform face swapping robustly even for several challenging inputs with different face orientations and lighting conditions. In addition, the quality of the results is comparable with the state-of-the-art method [15] and performed face swapping more stably. For future work, we would like to explore its applicability to movies by introducing temporal coherency in image generation.

Acknowledgments. This study was granted in part by the Strategic Basic Research Program ACCEL of the Japan Science and Technology Agency (JPMJAC1602). Tatsuya Yatagawa was supported by the Research Fellowship for Young Researchers of Japan's Society for the Promotion of Science (16J02280). Shigeo Morishima was supported by a Grant-in-Aid from Waseda Institute of Advanced Science and Engineering. The authors would also like to acknowledge NVIDIA Corporation for providing their GPUs in the academic GPU Grant Program.

References

1. Blanz, V., Vetter, T.: A morphable model for the synthesis of 3D faces. In: Proceedings of the 26th Annual Conference on Computer Graphics and Interactive Techniques, pp. 187–194 (1999)
2. Cao, C., Weng, Y., Zhou, S., Tong, Y., Zhou, K.: FaceWarehouse: a 3D facial expression database for visual computing. IEEE Trans. Vis. Comput. Graph. **20**, 413–425 (2014)
3. Liu, Z., Luo, P., Wang, X., Tang, X.: Deep learning face attributes in the wild. In: IEEE International Conference on Computer Vision (ICCV), pp. 3730–3738 (2015)
4. Zhang, K., Zhang, Z., Li, Z., Qiao, Y.: Joint face detection and alignment using multitask cascaded convolutional networks. IEEE Signal Process. Lett. **23**, 1499–1503 (2016)
5. Blanz, V., Scherbaum, K., Vetter, T., Seidel, H.P.: Exchanging faces in images. Comput. Graph. Forum **23**, 669–676 (2004)
6. Bitouk, D., Kumar, N., Dhillon, S., Belhumeur, P., Nayar, S.K.: Face swapping: automatically replacing faces in photographs. ACM Trans. Graph. (TOG) **27**, 39:1–39:8 (2008)
7. Yang, F., Wang, J., Shechtman, E., Bourdev, L., Metaxas, D.: Expression flow for 3D-aware face component transfer. ACM Trans. Graph. **30**, 60:1–60:10 (2011)
8. Chai, M., Wang, L., Weng, Y., Yu, Y., Guo, B., Zhou, K.: Single-view hair modeling for portrait manipulation. ACM Trans. Graph. **31**, 116:1–116:8 (2012)
9. Kemelmacher-Shlizerman, I.: Transfiguring portraits. ACM Trans. Graph. **35**, 94:1–94:8 (2016)
10. Mosaddegh, S., Simon, L., Jurie, F.: Photorealistic face de-identification by aggregating donors' face components. In: Cremers, D., Reid, I., Saito, H., Yang, M.-H. (eds.) ACCV 2014. LNCS, vol. 9005, pp. 159–174. Springer, Cham (2015). https://doi.org/10.1007/978-3-319-16811-1_11
11. Korshunova, I., Shi, W., Dambre, J., Theis, L.: Fast face-swap using convolutional neural networks. arXiv preprint arXiv:1611.09577 (2016)
12. Hassner, T.: Viewing real-world faces in 3D. In: IEEE International Conference on Computer Vision (ICCV), pp. 3607–3614 (2013)

13. McLaughlin, N., Martinez-del Rincon, J., Miller, P.: Data-augmentation for reducing dataset bias in person re-identification. In: IEEE International Conference on Advanced Video and Signal Based Surveillance, pp. 1–6 (2015)
14. Masi, I., Trần, A.T., Hassner, T., Leksut, J.T., Medioni, G.: Do we really need to collect millions of faces for effective face recognition? In: Leibe, B., Matas, J., Sebe, N., Welling, M. (eds.) ECCV 2016. LNCS, vol. 9909, pp. 579–596. Springer, Cham (2016). https://doi.org/10.1007/978-3-319-46454-1_35
15. Nirkin, Y., Masi, I., Tran, A.T., Hassner, T., Medioni, G.: On face segmentation, face swapping, and face perception. In: IEEE Conference on Automatic Face and Gesture Recognition (2018)
16. Bao, J., Chen, D., Wen, F., Li, H., Hua, G.: CVAE-GAN: fine-grained image generation through asymmetric training. In: IEEE International Conference on Computer Vision (ICCV), pp. 2745–2754 (2017)
17. FakeApp (2018). https://www.fakeapp.org/
18. Gatys, L.A., Ecker, A.S., Bethge, M.: Image style transfer using convolutional neural networks. In: IEEE Conference on Computer Vision and Pattern Recognition (CVPR) (2016)
19. Natsume, R., Yatagawa, T., Morishima, S.: RSGAN: face swapping and editing using face and hair representation in latent spaces. arXiv preprint arXiv:1804.03447 (2018)
20. Bao, J., Chen, D., Wen, F., Li, H., Hua, G.: Towards open-set identity preserving face synthesis. In: IEEE Conference on Computer Vision and Pattern Recognition (CVPR) (2018)
21. Iizuka, S., Simo-Serra, E., Ishikawa, H.: Globally and locally consistent image completion. ACM Trans. Graph. **36**, 107:1–107:14 (2017)
22. Chen, Z., Nie, S., Wu, T., Healey, C.G.: High resolution face completion with multiple controllable attributes via fully end-to-end progressive generative adversarial networks. arXiv preprint arXiv:1801.07632 (2018)
23. Kingma, D.P., Welling, M.: Auto-encoding variational bayes. arXiv preprint arXiv:1312.6114 (2013)
24. Ronneberger, O., Fischer, P., Brox, T.: U-Net: convolutional networks for biomedical image segmentation. In: Navab, N., Hornegger, J., Wells, W.M., Frangi, A.F. (eds.) MICCAI 2015. LNCS, vol. 9351, pp. 234–241. Springer, Cham (2015). https://doi.org/10.1007/978-3-319-24574-4_28
25. Larsen, A.B.L., Kaae Sønderby, S., Larochelle, H., Winther, O.: Autoencoding beyond pixels using a learned similarity metric. arXiv preprint arXiv:1512.09300 (2015)
26. Cheng, D., Gong, Y., Zhou, S., Wang, J., Zheng, N.: Person re-identification by multi-channel parts-based cnn with improved triplet loss function. In: IEEE Conference on Computer Vision and Pattern Recognition (CVPR), pp. 1335–1344 (2016)
27. Rosca, M., Lakshminarayanan, B., Warde-Farley, D., Mohamed, S.: Variational approaches for auto-encoding generative adversarial networks. arXiv preprint arXiv:1706.04987 (2017)
28. Isola, P., Zhu, J.Y., Zhou, T., Efros, A.A.: Image-to-image translation with conditional adversarial networks. In: IEEE Conference on Computer Vision and Pattern Recognition (CVPR) (2017)
29. Kingma, D.P., Ba, J.: Adam: a method for stochastic optimization. arXiv preprint arXiv:1412.6980 (2014)
30. King, D.E.: Dlib-ml: a machine learning toolkit. J. Mach. Learn. Res. **10**, 1755–1758 (2009)

31. Zhao, H., Shi, J., Qi, X., Wang, X., Jia, J.: Pyramid scene parsing network. arXiv preprint arXiv:1612.01105 (2016)
32. Wang, Z., Simoncelli, E.P., Bovik, A.C.: Multiscale structural similarity for image quality assessment. In: The Thirty-Seventh Asilomar Conference on Signals, Systems & Computers, pp. 1398–1402 (2003)
33. Amos, B., Ludwiczuk, B., Satyanarayanan, M.: OpenFace: a general-purpose face recognition library with mobile applications. Technical report, CMU School of Computer Science (2016)
34. Salimans, T., et al.: Improved techniques for training GANs. In: Advances in Neural Information Processing Systems (NIPS), no. 29, pp. 2234–2242 (2016)
35. Saito, S., Li, T., Li, H.: Real-time facial segmentation and performance capture from RGB input. In: Leibe, B., Matas, J., Sebe, N., Welling, M. (eds.) ECCV 2016. LNCS, vol. 9912, pp. 244–261. Springer, Cham (2016). https://doi.org/10.1007/978-3-319-46484-8_15

A Data-Driven Approach for Direct and Global Component Separation from a Single Image

Shijie Nie[1,4], Lin Gu[1(✉)], Art Subpa-asa[2], Ilyes Kacher[1], Ko Nishino[3], and Imari Sato[1]

[1] National Institute of Informatics, Chiyoda, Japan
{nsj,ling,ilyeskacher,imarik}@nii.ac.jp
[2] Tokyo Institute of Technology, Meguro, Japan
art.s.aa@m.titech.ac.jp
[3] Kyoto University, Kyoto, Japan
kon@i.kyoto-u.ac.jp
[4] Department of Informatics,
SOKENDAI (The Graduate University for Advanced Studies), Hayama, Japan

Abstract. The radiance captured by camera is often under influence of both direct and global illumination from complex environment. Though separating them is highly desired, existing methods require strict capture restriction such as modulated active light. Here, we propose the first method to infer both components from a single image without any hardware restriction. Our method is a novel generative adversarial network (GAN) based networks which imposes prior physics knowledge to force a physics plausible component separation. We also present the first component separation dataset which comprises of 100 scenes with their direct and global components. In the experiments, our method has achieved satisfactory performance on our own testing set and images in public dataset. Finally, we illustrate an interesting application of editing realistic images through the separated components.

1 Introduction

When there is a light source, the radiance captured by camera is actually the sum of both direct and global components. The direct component is the direct reflectance of the light from source on the surface (Fig. 1(3)). The global component is the indirect lighting from complex phenomena such as inter-reflection, subsurface scattering, volumetric scattering and diffuse (Fig. 1(4)).

Traditionally, separating above two components requires multiple images taken under specific setting such as high frequency light patterns [1,10,18,29, 35,36,43]. In this paper, we separate the two components directly from a single image without any hardware constraints. We also present a dataset including 100 scenes with their direct and global components.

Since each separated component carries much information about both the scene and environment, our method and the dataset would benefit both computer

© Springer Nature Switzerland AG 2019
C. V. Jawahar et al. (Eds.): ACCV 2018, LNCS 11366, pp. 133–148, 2019.
https://doi.org/10.1007/978-3-030-20876-9_9

vision and graphic community. For example, the direct component conveys the information about interaction between material properties, geometry and the lights. Obtaining pure direction component would enhance the computer vision task such as material recognition [22], depth recovery [14], shape reconstruction [24] and colour constancy [49]. For the global component, it plays an important role in rendering realistic scenario [5]. This knowledge would also endow us a better image manipulation algorithm [4]. What is more, since global component reflects complex interaction amid the environment, separating it could also reveal the surrounding environment [8] by treating the foreground object as a complexly shaped and far-from-perfect mirror.

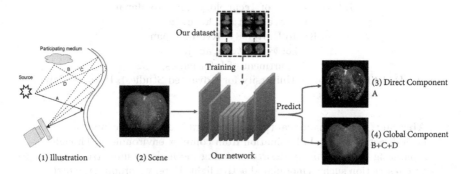

Fig. 1. (1) The captured radiance of scene is due to direction illumination (A) from source and global illumination (B + C + D). The global illumination may arise form volumetric scattering (B), subsurface scattering (C) and subsurface scattering (D). (2) A scene lit by a single light source. (3) Direct component directly from the light source. (4) Global component arising from complex global illumination effects.

To facilitate the research of single-image global and directional component separation, we present the first dataset with measured two components. We captured 100 controlled indoor scene covering various objects like plastic toys, translucent objects, foods, *etc*. Each scene has a triple of images: normal observed image, direct component and global component.

Based on this dataset, we propose the first method to directly separate the two components from a single image without any hardware constraints. We achieve this through a novel generative adversarial network (GAN) based networks. Specifically, we introduce an inverse loss which explicitly imposes prior physics knowledge into the network to force a physically plausible component separation. This allows us to separate components on general images even under different capture setting of training set. With the separated components, we show some interesting image manipulating result to exhibit some potential application. As illustrated in Fig. 2, we manipulate the appearance of the image by simply changing the weight of global and direct component. In the separated global

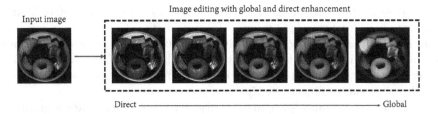

Fig. 2. From left to right: input image, direct component, edited result with linear mixture weight (direct, global): (0.7, 0.3); (0.5, 0.5); (0.3, 0.7), global component (Color figure online)

component, the color looks more saturated due to multiple bounces inside the fruit. By adding more global component, we make the fruits in Fig. 2 looks more sweet.

In summary, we have made following three major contributions:

1. We propose the first method to separate the direct and global component from a single image without hardware constraints.
2. We collected the first dataset for the quantitative analysis of single-image global and direct component separation.
3. We have shown a potential application of components separation in physically plausible image editing.

2   Related Works

The very first approach [29] separates the direct and global components by capturing multiple images under high frequency light patterns and compare the pixel with or without the light. Assuming neighbouring points share the same direct and global components, this approach could work on single image at the cost of lower resolution. This is also sensitive to the violation assumption such as sharp depth or colour variance.

Gu *et al.* [10] reduce the number of required images to three by simultaneously projecting multiplex sinusoid light patterns. Achar *et al.* [1] allow images captured by human held device by compensating the small motion. By synchronising illumination and project defocus, Gupta *et al.* [14] separate the global component before recovering the depth. Similarly, with coaxial camera setup, O'Toole *et al.* [34,36] also propose a system to modulate both the light and the camera to selectively probe the light transport matrix. Gupta *et al.*, Reddy *et al.* [13,39] further separate the global component into near range and far range by projecting multiple binary [13] or sinusoid patterns [39]. Recently, Subpa-asa *et al.* [43] propose a method for separating global and direct components on a single image without any resolution loss, but still rely on high frequency lighting.

Noted that above methods treat the subsurface scattering as a whole rather than decompose it into more details [50], some recent efforts focus on the light transport subsurface scattering. By analysing the side slice of the surface illuminated with high-frequency light source, Mukaigawa *et al.* [25] manage to image n-bounce subsurface scattering. Tanaka [46] decompose the appearance of a surface seen from above into a few layers at various depths. Apart from the subsurface scattering, there are more researches on other components such as volumetric fluid [12], translucent object [26,27].

Apart from reflectance phenomenon discussed above, there are a group of algorithms which attempts to separate the foreground reflectance before the glass and the transmitted background after the glass. Most of these algorithms either require multiple images [6,20,51] or user interactions [19]. Recently, a new benchmark [47] for single-image based method on this task has been proposed. However, the physic foundation of reflectance removal is totally different from our direct and global component separation task. The reflectance and transmission of former occurs on the glass-air interface while later is more complex that involves the volumetric scattering, inter-reflection, subsurface scattering and translucency *etc.*

3   Benchmark Dataset

For this research, we collect a dataset of 100 controlled indoor scenes along with their direct and global components. The captured scenarios cover a wide range of daily-life objects including plastic, food and sweets (fresh fruits, vegetables, bread), synthetic fabrics and wooden object *etc.* There are 13 translucent items among 100 items, including common objects such as ceramic, jade, glass, various minerals and candy *etc.* Each scene is of a triplet of images: 1. Scene image (Fig. 1(2)), 2. Direct component (Fig. 1(3)) and 3. Global component (Fig. 1(4)). In all, our dataset contains $3 \times 100 = 300$ images.

3.1   Data Collection

The data capture setup involves one projector, one camera and a scene of one or multiple objects. For each scene, we collect the data in two steps: 1. We at first capture the scene image using a white background projected by the projector. 2. Then we measure the direct and global components in the way of [28].

As Nayar *et al.* [28] suggested, each scene was lit using a checkerboard pattern projected by the projector when calculating the global and direct component. A checker pattern size of 8×8 pixels was used for the experiment with a shift of 2 pixels 8 times in each of the two dimensions.

We denote L^+ as the image under a high-frequency illumination that half of the image is lit. L^- is the image under the complementary illumination. For any pixel i lit in L^+ and deactivated in L^-, as proved in [28], it should follow $L^+[i] = L_d[i] + (1+b)\frac{L_g[i]}{2}$ and $L^-[i] = bL_d[i] + (1+b)\frac{L_g[i]}{2}$, where $L_d[i]$ is the direct component and $L_g[i]$ is the global one. b represents the deactivated source element brightness on the pixel i. In theory, two images are sufficient to calculate the separation if digital projector is able to project an ideal high-frequency pattern. In practise [1, 10, 29], capturing more images would significantly relieve this issue. For each pixel i, we use the minimum and maximum measured brightness $L_{min}[i]$, $L_{max}[i]$ instead of $L^-[c, i]$, $L^+[c, i]$ to compute the separated components. For each scene, we captured 64 images to ensure the reliable separation of direct and global components.

Throughout the data collection, two projectors and two cameras were utilised to simulate various capture setting. For example, we use BenQ PJ projector for half of scene and DLP Light Commander for the remainder. Similarly, the Nikon 40S camera was used to capture half of scene regardless the selection of projector while the rest were captured by Grasshopper 3. To maximise the diversity, we change the position of projectors, the camera and the target objects for each scene.

4   Global and Direct Component Separation

Generative adversarial network (GAN) [9] has achieved impression result in image generation such as image reconstruction [2], biological image synthesis [33], image style transfer [15], shadow detection [30], and future video frame prediction [21]. In this paper, we propose a novel GAN based network architecture for recovering the direct and global component from a single image. Inspired by cycleGAN [54], as illustrated in Fig. 3, our network introduces an inverse operation which imposes physical prior knowledge to enforce a physically plausible separation.

Instead of treating neural networks as 'black box', more and more research [7, 17, 31, 42] attempted to embed domain knowledge in deep learning models. This would not only help to compress large parameter searching space but also provide meaningful results. For example, by assuming a object is moving at a constant velocity, Stewart et al. [42] proposed a method to supervise convolutional neural network to detect and track objects without any label. Video frames could be predicted by forcing pixels with physics dynamics [7]. Another example is to embed relationships between density, depth and temperature of lake with known physical equation in a physics-guided neural network [17].

Since our mapping from direct/global components to input image is defined by physical Eq. 3, we replace the G_x of standard cycleGAN [54] that maps domain Y to domain X with a linear mapping layer as shown in Fig. 3. This architecture allows us to reduce complexity need and get a realistic solution for components separation.

4.1   Overview

Our architecture is shown in Fig. 3 for single-image components separation.

The input is a single RGB image X and output Y is a concatenation of global component Y_1 and direct component Y_2: $Y = Y_1 \| Y_2$. Let the G, D denote a generator (G) and a discriminator (D) respectively for the sake of simplicity.

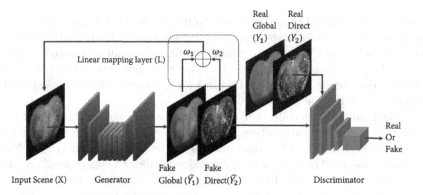

Fig. 3. Our models contains three functions: a generator (G), a linear mapping layer (L), a discriminator (D). For a scene X, we concatenate global and direct component image together as Y. We add a linear mapping layer to regularise prediction Y to the physical constraint [28]: $\hat{X} = w1 * \hat{Y}_1 + w2 * \hat{Y}_2$ and add $Loss_L = L1(X, \hat{X})$ to the final loss function.

For our specific problem, we introduce a linear mapping layer L and encourages $L(G(x)) \simeq x$ to force the generated global and direct component to follow physics model of Eq. 3.

4.2   Network Architecture

Our network module is formed as follows: 2D convolution-BatchNorm-Relu. The generator takes scene image of size $256 \times 256 \times 3$ as input and finally produces the corresponding global and direct images of size $256 \times 256 \times 6$. Let Ck denote a convolutional block including one convolutional layer with k filters, one leakyReLU activation layer, one BatchNormalization layer. The convolutional layer in each Ck has 3×3 sized kernels with stride 2. The downsampling factor is 2 with proper zero padding to edges. The α parameter in the leakyReLU layer is set to 0.2. CDk denotes the same block as Ck, except that the convolution layer is replaced by the deconvolution layer which upsamples the input by a factor of 2. A dropout layer with 50% dropout rate is added after each block. The generator architecture is composed as: C64-C128-C256-C512-C512-C512-C512-CD512-CD512-CD512-CD256-CD128-CD64-CD6.

Compared to a standard U-net, we modify its final layer from 3 channels to 6 channels. The discriminator takes $256 \times 256 \times 9$ as input image, which is concatenation of generator input and output. The final layer of discriminator adopts sigmoid active function. The structure is composed as: C9-C64-C128-C256-C512-C1.

4.3 Network Design for Components Separation

The objective of traditional GAN is defined as:

$$Loss_{GAN}(G, D) = E_{Y \sim P_{data}(X,Y)}[log D(X, Y)]$$
$$+ E_{X \sim P_{data}(X), Z \sim P_Z(Z)}[log(1 - D(X, G(X, Z)))], \tag{1}$$

where Z is a noise vector.

Pix2pix, a generic GAN method [15] found that mixing $Loss_{GAN}(G, D)$ with generator loss $Loss_{L1}$ would be beneficial as L1 produces less blurring results:

$$Loss_{L1}(G) = E_{X,Y \sim P_{data}(X,Y), Z \sim P_Z(Z)}[||Y - G(X, Z)||_1]. \tag{2}$$

The generator loss requires G to not only fool discriminators D but also to provide more traditional loss, in order to get similar images compared to ground-truth images. In the current setting, we find L1 distance would deliver more clear result.

However, $Loss_{GAN}(G, D)$ and $Loss_{L1}(G)$ does not consider the physics relation between global image Y_1 and direct image Y_2. According to [28], the input image X is under the linear relation:

$$X = w_1 Y_1 + w_2 Y_2 \tag{3}$$

where w_1, w_2 is the weight of two components. Therefore, we add this prior knowledge by defining a linear mapping layer $L(Y) = \sum_{n=1}^{2} w_n Y_n$. We propose the inverse cost to impose the physics regulation:

$$Loss_I(G, L) = E_{X,Y \sim P_{data}(X,Y), z \sim P_Z(Z)}[||X - L(G(X, Z))||_1] \tag{4}$$

Finally, the objective function of network is defined as:

$$Loss = \arg \min_G \max_D Loss_{GAN}(G, D) + \lambda_1 Loss_{L1}(G) + \lambda_2 Loss_I(G, L) \tag{5}$$

Where λ_1 controls the relative importance of reconstruction loss while λ_2 determines the weight of inverse loss. In this paper, we set the λ_1 and λ_2 to 100.

5 Evaluation

5.1 Experiment Setting

In this evaluation, the whole dataset was randomly split into training/testing set. The training set includes 80 scenes while the testing set takes the rest 20. During the training, we at first resize each image into 1500 * 1500. Then, it was randomly cropped into 256 * 256 patches with affine transform, rotation and shearing as data augmentation. Rotation range is $-20°$ to $20°$ while shearing range is $-10°$ to $10°$.

During the testing process, we at first crop the input scene image into overlapping 256 * 256 patches before feeding into the trained generator. The overlapping part of each patch is 200 pixel in horizontal an vertical direction separately. When knitting the patches back into image, we calculate the pixel value of overlapping part by taking average of corresponded image piece.

5.2   Visual Quality Evaluation

We compare our separated components with the groundtruth in Figs. 4 and 5.
The comparison shows that our method successfully separates most details of
components from a single image.

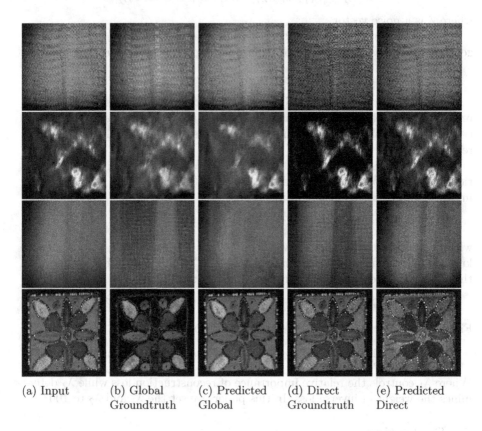

(a) Input   (b) Global   (c) Predicted   (d) Direct   (e) Predicted
                 Groundtruth   Global   Groundtruth   Direct

Fig. 4. The exemplar components separation of real scattering materials.

We also compare our result with the baseline pix2pix [15] that works without
physical constraints. As shown in Fig. 6, the baseline method pix2pix2 often
delivers striped distortion or blurry results, especially at the object boundary
and background area. However, with our proposed network, these artefacts are
avoided as shown in Fig. 6.

With the proposed dataset, our method is able to work on the general images
without strict capture setting requirement. As illustrated in Fig. 7, we also apply
our trained model on the images in public dataset such as CAVE [52]. The
images in CAVE are captured under a neutral daylight illuminant (CIE Standard
Illuminant D65). The image size are of 512 * 512 resolution and it was cropped
into 256 * 256 pieces to feed into our pre-trained network. The output are tilled

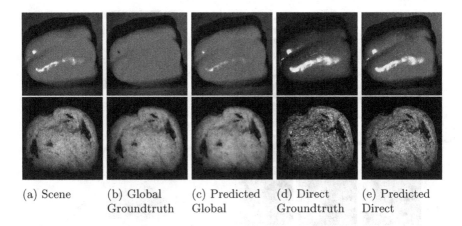

| (a) Scene | (b) Global Groundtruth | (c) Predicted Global | (d) Direct Groundtruth | (e) Predicted Direct |

Fig. 5. The exemplar components separation on food.

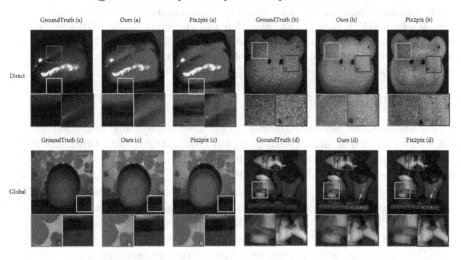

Fig. 6. The first row shows the comparison of our method and pix2pix for direct generation, the second row shows the comparison on global generation. Note that pix2pix sometimes provides striped distortion as shown in (a, b, d) and more blurry result as shown in (c). We adjust the brightness and contrast for better visualization.

with 100 pixel to fit original input size. Figure 7 shows our method could achieve reasonable performance even for images captured under different setting from that of training set. We also tested our method in improving the computer vision application such as shape from shading (SFS) [38]. One example is given in Fig. 7. Our global component SFS results is more accordance with real geometry by removing the specular part in direct component.

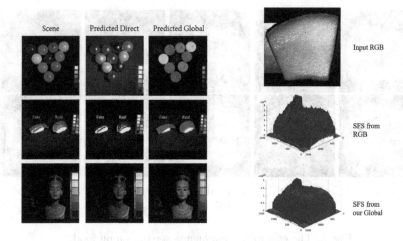

Fig. 7. Left-hand part: we test our method to separate global and direct components in images from CAVE dataset [52]. From left to right: input single RGB scene under neutral illumination, predicted direct component, predicted global component. The right-hand part is shape from shading result compared with baseline.

5.3   Quantitative Result

In this analysis, we adopted three metrics when comparing recovered global and direct component image with provided ground-truth: structural similarity (SSIM) [48], structure index (SI) [44], Inception Score (IS) [41]. We did not use the evaluation metrics such as L2 (RMSE), L1 or PSNR because they prefer a blurring result rather than the one with highly accurate textures [16,37,53]. Mean pixel-wise Euclidean distance is minimized when result averages all plausible outputs. Therefore, we select SI,SSIM, Inception score which are more widely used for quality assessment of generative model application such as [3,11,23,32].

SSIM [48] evaluates the human visual perception on luminance, contrast and structure. However, this does not consider correlations between pixels, which carries structure information of an object in a scene. Thus, we also suggest structure index (SI) [44] which only focus on structure relation between recovered image I and groundtruth I^*. The SI is defined as: $SI = \frac{2\sigma_{I,I^*}+c}{\sigma_I^2+\sigma_{I^*}^2+c}$, where σ_I, σ_{I^*} stands for the variance of I, I^*, σ_{I,I^*} stands for the covariance of I and I^*. c is a constant. The higher SSIM and SI score indicates less structure distortion and better quality.

The Inception Score (IS) is a metric for evaluating the quality of image generative models [41], which used an Inception v3 network [45] pretrained in ImageNet [40]. IS was shown to correlate well with human judgment of realism [41]. High score means better result.

We report the baseline, which is the result of our proposed method compared with pix2pix [15] of SSIM, SI, IS on the test set of this dataset as shown in Table 3. We also report quantitative result for individual image in Tables 1 and 2.

Table 1. SSIM, SI for direct component reconstruction. Superscript * stands for the result of pix2pix baseline.

Number	1	2	3	4	5	6	7	8	9	10	11	12	13	14	15	16	17	18	19	20
SSIM(0.)	7.9	5.0	**9.0**	8.2	9.3	**9.5**	**8.8**	**9.2**	**9.4**	**9.3**	**9.3**	**8.5**	**8.7**	**7.8**	**9.0**	9.1	7.2	**9.4**	**9.1**	9.2
SSIM*(0.)	8.1	5.3	8.8	7.9	9.4	9.3	8.3	9.1	9.2	9.1	9.1	8.0	8.5	7.7	8.4	9.1	7.2	9.2	9.0	9.2
SI(0.)	**9.6**	**9.2**	9.8	**9.0**	9.8	9.9	9.5	9.4	9.9	9.8	9.7	9.6	**9.7**	9.5	**9.7**	9.8	7.3	9.8	9.8	9.8
SI*(0.)	9.5	9.1	9.9	8.9	9.8	9.9	9.5	9.5	9.9	9.9	9.7	9.6	9.6	9.5	9.5	9.8	7.4	9.8	9.8	9.8

Table 2. SSIM, SI for global component reconstruction. Superscript * stands for the result of pix2pix baseline.

Number	1	2	3	4	5	6	7	8	9	10	11	12	13	14	15	16	17	18	19	20
SSIM(0.)	**9.0**	**8.2**	**5.7**	8.4	**9.1**	9.3	5.5	9.6	8.5	**9.1**	**6.6**	9.4	7.5	**5.3**	**8.1**	4.2	**8.5**	**8.0**	8.1	**5.2**
SSIM*(0.)	9.1	8.2	5.5	8.7	9.0	9.3	5.5	9.7	8.8	8.9	6.3	9.5	7.5	5.2	8.0	4.3	8.5	7.6	8.1	4.7
SI(0.)	9.8	**9.2**	**9.6**	9.5	9.8	9.9	6.0	9.9	9.4	9.6	**8.2**	9.9	9.0	5.7	**9.4**	5.5	9.7	**9.3**	9.4	8.2
SI*(0.)	9.8	9.1	9.5	9.6	9.8	9.9	6.0	9.9	9.4	9.6	8.1	9.9	9.0	5.7	9.2	5.6	9.7	9.2	9.5	8.3

On all of the three metrics, our methods outperforms pix2pix. This is accordance with our observation in Fig. 6 that the components separated by our method are with less structure distortion and of more natural looking.

Table 3. Quantitative results of global and direct separation on our dataset.

Method	Ours	Pix2pix [15]
SSIM	0.823	0.812
SI	0.924	0.922
IS	2.24	2.21

6 Image Editing by Enhancing Direct and Global Components

Nayar *et al.* [29] showed that linearly mixing direct and global components with different weights is effective for image editing. In this paper, we further explore physically plausible material editing by manipulating our direct/global separation results with different linear weights.

Figure 8 shows image editing by manipulating the weights of direct and global components separated by our approach from the single input image. We can see that object impression changes according to the weight. For instance, we show a hard-to-soft transition in Fig. 8(a): as we increase the weight of the global components, the objects look softer. Metallic/non-metallic transition in (b) where objects look more metallic with higher weights of direct components. Interestingly, the visual freshness of food can also be controlled with different weights in Fig. 8(c). The proportion of specularity due to its subsurface scattering seems to be essential for us to recognize food freshness.

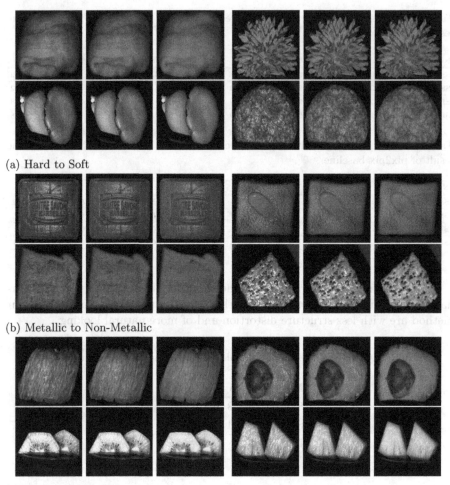

(a) Hard to Soft

(b) Metallic to Non-Metallic

(c) Freshness of food

Fig. 8. Image editing with direct and global enhancement. The appearance of objects changes according to different linear mixing applied to direct and global components. The weights (direct, global) used for (a) and (b) are (0.9, 0.1); (0.6, 0.4); (0.3, 0.7) from left to right. In (c) the weight used are (0.8, 0.2); (0.5, 0.5); (0.2, 0.8) from left to right.

7   Conclusion

In this paper, we propose the first method to separate direct and global components from a single image without hardware constraints. This model embeds physical prior knowledge into the GAN based network to achieve single-image components separation. To train and evaluate this model, we also present the first dataset which comprises of 100 scenes with their groundtruth direct and global components. Our method has been shown to successfully work on our own testing set and general images from public dataset. Finally, we demonstrate how the separated components could be used for realistic image editing.

References

1. Achar, S., Nuske, S., Narasimhan, S.: Compensating for motion during direct-global separation. In: IEEE International Conference on Computer Vision (ICCV), pp. 1481–1488, December 2013. https://doi.org/10.1109/ICCV.2013.187
2. Alvarez-Gila, A., van de Weijer, J., Garrote, E.: Adversarial networks for spatial context-aware spectral image reconstruction from RGB. In: IEEE International Conference on Computer Vision Workshop (ICCVW 2017) (2017)
3. Berthelot, D., Schumm, T., Metz, L.: BEGAN: boundary equilibrium generative adversarial networks. arXiv preprint arXiv:1703.10717 (2017)
4. Boyadzhiev, I., Bala, K., Paris, S., Adelson, E.: Band-sifting decomposition for image-based material editing. ACM Trans. Graph. 34(5), 163:1–163:16 (2015)
5. Debevec, P.: Rendering synthetic objects into real scenes: bridging traditional and image-based graphics with global illumination and high dynamic range photography. In: ACM SIGGRAPH 2008 Classes, SIGGRAPH 2008, pp. 32:1–32:10. ACM, New York (2008)
6. Farid, H., Adelson, E.H.: Separating reflections and lighting using independent components analysis. In: Proceedings of the 1999 IEEE Computer Society Conference on Computer Vision and Pattern Recognition (Cat. No PR00149), vol. 1, p. 267 (1999)
7. Finn, C., Goodfellow, I., Levine, S.: Unsupervised learning for physical interaction through video prediction. In: Neural Information Processing Systems (NIPS), pp. 64–72 (2016). https://papers.nips.cc/paper/6161-unsupervised-learning-for-physical-interaction-through-video-prediction
8. Georgoulis, S., Rematas, K., Ritschel, T., Fritz, M., Tuytelaars, T., Van Gool, L.: What is around the camera? In: The IEEE International Conference on Computer Vision (ICCV), October 2017
9. Goodfellow, I., et al.: Generative adversarial nets. In: Advances in Neural Information Processing Systems, vol. 27, pp. 2672–2680 (2014). http://papers.nips.cc/paper/5423-generative-adversarial-nets.pdf
10. Gu, J., Kobayashi, T., Gupta, M., Nayar, S.K.: Multiplexed illumination for scene recovery in the presence of global illumination. In: IEEE International Conference on Computer Vision (ICCV), pp. 1–8, November 2011
11. Gulrajani, I., Ahmed, F., Arjovsky, M., Dumoulin, V., Courville, A.C.: Improved training of Wasserstein GANs. In: Advances in Neural Information Processing Systems, pp. 5767–5777 (2017)
12. Gupta, M., Narasimhan, S., Schechner, Y.: On controlling light transport in poor visibility environments. In: IEEE Conference on Computer Vision and Pattern Recognition (CVPR), pp. 1–8, June 2008. https://doi.org/10.1109/CVPR.2008.4587763
13. Gupta, M., Agrawal, A., Veeraraghavan, A., Narasimhan, S.G.: A practical approach to 3D scanning in the presence of interreflections, subsurface scattering and defocus. Int. J. Comput. Vis. 102(1–3), 33–55 (2013)
14. Gupta, M., Tian, Y., Narasimhan, S., Zhang, L.: A combined theory of defocused illumination and global light transport. Int. J. Comput. Vis. 98(2), 146–167 (2012). https://doi.org/10.1007/s11263-011-0500-9

15. Isola, P., Zhu, J.Y., Zhou, T., Efros, A.A.: Image-to-image translation with conditional adversarial networks. arXiv, p. 16 (2016). http://arxiv.org/abs/1611.07004
16. Isola, P., Zhu, J.Y., Zhou, T., Efros, A.A.: Image-to-image translation with conditional adversarial networks. In: CVPR (2017)
17. Karpatne, A., Watkins, W., Read, J., Kumar, V.: Physics-guided neural networks (PGNN): an application in lake temperature modeling (2017). http://arxiv.org/abs/1710.11431
18. Kubo, H., Jayasuriya, S., Iwaguchi, T., Funatomi, T., Mukaigawa, Y., Narasimhan, S.G.: Acquiring and characterizing plane-to-ray indirect light transport. In: 2018 IEEE International Conference on Computational Photography (ICCP), pp. 1–10. IEEE (2018)
19. Levin, A., Weiss, Y.: User assisted separation of reflections from a single image using a sparsity prior. IEEE Trans. Pattern Anal. Mach. Intell. **29**(9), 1647–1654 (2007)
20. Li, Y., Brown, M.S.: Exploiting reflection change for automatic reflection removal. In: 2013 IEEE International Conference on Computer Vision, pp. 2432–2439, December 2013
21. Liang, X., Lee, L., Dai, W., Xing, E.P.: Dual motion GAN for future-flow embedded video prediction. In: Proceedings of the IEEE International Conference on Computer Vision, October 2017, pp. 1762–1770 (2017). https://doi.org/10.1109/ICCV.2017.194
22. Liu, C., Sharan, L., Adelson, E.H., Rosenholtz, R.: Exploring features in a Bayesian framework for material recognition. In: 2010 IEEE Computer Society Conference on Computer Vision and Pattern Recognition, pp. 239–246, June 2010
23. Mao, X., Li, Q., Xie, H., Lau, R.Y., Wang, Z., Smolley, S.P.: Least squares generative adversarial networks. In: 2017 IEEE International Conference on Computer Vision (ICCV), pp. 2813–2821. IEEE (2017)
24. Morris, N., Kutulakos, K.: Reconstructing the surface of inhomogeneous transparent scenes by scatter-trace photography. In: IEEE 11th International Conference on Computer Vision (ICCV), pp. 1–8, October 2007. https://doi.org/10.1109/ICCV.2007.4408882
25. Mukaigawa, Y., Yagi, Y., Raskar, R.: Analysis of light transport in scattering media. In: 2010 IEEE Computer Society Conference on Computer Vision and Pattern Recognition, pp. 153–160, June 2010. https://doi.org/10.1109/CVPR.2010.5540216
26. Mukaigawa, Y., Suzuki, K., Yagi, Y.: Analysis of subsurface scattering based on dipole approximation. Inf. Media Technol. **4**(4), 951–961 (2009)
27. Munoz, A., Echevarria, J.I., Seron, F.J., Lopez-Moreno, J., Glencross, M., Gutierrez, D.: BSSRDF estimation from single images. Comput. Graph. Forum **30**(2), 455–464 (2011). https://doi.org/10.1111/j.1467-8659.2011.01873.x
28. Nayar, S.K., Krishnan, G., Grossberg, M.D., Raskar, R.: Fast separation of direct and global components of a scene using high frequency illumination. ACM Trans. Graph. **25**, 935 (2006). https://doi.org/10.1145/1141911.1141977
29. Nayar, S., Krishnan, G., Grossberg, M.D., Raskar, R.: Fast separation of direct and global components of a scene using high frequency illumination. ACM Trans. Graph. **25**, 935–944 (2006). (also Proceedings of ACM SIGGRAPH)
30. Nguyen, V., Vicente, T.F.Y., Zhao, M., Hoai, M., Samaras, D., Brook, S.: Shadow detection with conditional generative adversarial networks. In: ICCV 2017, pp. 4510–4518 (2017)

31. Nie, S., Gu, L., Zheng, Y., Lam, A., Ono, N., Sato, I.: Deeply learned filter response functions for hyperspectral reconstruction. In: Proceedings of the IEEE Conference on Computer Vision and Pattern Recognition, pp. 4767–4776 (2018)
32. Odena, A., Olah, C., Shlens, J.: Conditional image synthesis with auxiliary classifier GANs. arXiv preprint arXiv:1610.09585 (2016)
33. Osokin, A., Chessel, A., Salas, R.E.C., Vaggi, F.: GANs for biological image synthesis (2017). http://arxiv.org/abs/1708.04692
34. O'Toole, M., Mather, J., Kutulakos, K.N.: 3D shape and indirect appearance by structured light transport. IEEE Trans. Pattern Anal. Mach. Intell. **38**(7), 1298–1312 (2016)
35. O'Toole, M., Achar, S., Narasimhan, S.G., Kutulakos, K.N.: Homogeneous codes for energy-efficient illumination and imaging. ACM Trans. Graph. (ToG) **34**(4), 35 (2015)
36. O'Toole, M., Raskar, R., Kutulakos, K.N.: Primal-dual coding to probe light transport. ACM Trans. Graph. **31**(4), 39:1–39:11 (2012)
37. Pathak, D., Krahenbuhl, P., Donahue, J., Darrell, T., Efros, A.A.: Context encoders: feature learning by inpainting. In: CVPR, June 2016
38. Ping-Sing, T., Shah, M.: Shape from shading using linear approximation. Image Vis. Comput. **12**(8), 487–498 (1994)
39. Reddy, D., Ramamoorthi, R., Curless, B.: Frequency-space decomposition and acquisition of light transport under spatially varying illumination. In: Fitzgibbon, A., Lazebnik, S., Perona, P., Sato, Y., Schmid, C. (eds.) ECCV 2012. LNCS, vol. 7577, pp. 596–610. Springer, Heidelberg (2012). https://doi.org/10.1007/978-3-642-33783-3_43. http://graphics.berkeley.edu/papers/Reddy-FSD-2012-10/
40. Russakovsky, O., et al.: Imagenet large scale visual recognition challenge. Int. J. Comput. Vis. **115**(3), 211–252 (2015)
41. Salimans, T., Goodfellow, I., Zaremba, W., Cheung, V., Radford, A., Chen, X.: Improved techniques for training GANs. In: NIPS, pp. 1–9 (2016). arXiv:1504.01391, http://arxiv.org/abs/1606.03498
42. Stewart, R., Ermon, S.: Label-free supervision of neural networks with physics and domain knowledge, vol. 1, no. 1 (2016). http://arxiv.org/abs/1609.05566
43. Subpa-asa, A., Fu, Y., Zheng, Y., Amano, T., Sato, I.: Direct and global component separation from a single image using basis representation. In: Lai, S.-H., Lepetit, V., Nishino, K., Sato, Y. (eds.) ACCV 2016. LNCS, vol. 10113, pp. 99–114. Springer, Cham (2017). https://doi.org/10.1007/978-3-319-54187-7_7
44. Sun, S.H., Fan, S.P., Wang, Y.C.F.: Exploiting image structural similarity for single image rain removal. In: 2014 IEEE International Conference on Image Processing, ICIP 2014, pp. 4482–4486 (2014). https://doi.org/10.1109/ICIP.2014.7025909
45. Szegedy, C., Vanhoucke, V., Ioffe, S., Shlens, J., Wojna, Z.: Rethinking the inception architecture for computer vision. In: Proceedings of the IEEE Conference on Computer Vision and Pattern Recognition, pp. 2818–2826 (2016)
46. Tanaka, K., Mukaigawa, Y., Kubo, H., Matsushita, Y., Yagi, Y.: Recovering inner slices of layered translucent objects by multi-frequency illumination. IEEE Trans. Pattern Anal. Mach. Intell. **39**(4), 746–757 (2017). https://doi.org/10.1109/TPAMI.2016.2631625
47. Wan, R., Shi, B., Duan, L.Y., Tan, A.H., Kot, A.C.: Benchmarking single-image reflection removal algorithms. In: 2017 IEEE International Conference on Computer Vision (ICCV), pp. 3942–3950, October 2017. https://doi.org/10.1109/ICCV.2017.423

48. Wang, Z., Bovik, A.C., Sheikh, H.R., Simoncelli, E.P.: Image quality assessment: from error visibility to structural similarity. IEEE Trans. Image Process. **13**(4), 600–612 (2004). https://doi.org/10.1109/TIP.2003.819861
49. van de Weijer, J., Gevers, T., Gijsenij, A.: Edge-based color constancy. IEEE Trans. Image Process. **16**(9), 2207–2214 (2007). https://doi.org/10.1109/TIP.2007.901808
50. Wu, D., O'Toole, M., Velten, A., Agrawal, A., Raskar, R.: Decomposing global light transport using time of flight imaging. In: 2012 IEEE Conference on Computer Vision and Pattern Recognition, pp. 366–373, June 2012
51. Yang, J., Li, H., Dai, Y., Tan, R.T.: Robust optical flow estimation of double-layer images under transparency or reflection. In: 2016 IEEE Conference on Computer Vision and Pattern Recognition (CVPR), pp. 1410–1419, June 2016. https://doi.org/10.1109/CVPR.2016.157
52. Yasuma, F., Mitsunaga, T., Iso, D., Nayar, S.K.: Generalized assorted pixel camera: postcapture control of resolution, dynamic range, and spectrum. IEEE Trans. Image Process. **19**(9), 2241–2253 (2010)
53. Zhang, R., Isola, P., Efros, A.A.: Colorful image colorization. In: Leibe, B., Matas, J., Sebe, N., Welling, M. (eds.) ECCV 2016. LNCS, vol. 9907, pp. 649–666. Springer, Cham (2016). https://doi.org/10.1007/978-3-319-46487-9_40
54. Zhu, J.Y., Park, T., Isola, P., Efros, A.A.: Unpaired image-to-image translation using cycle-consistent adversarial networks (2017). http://arxiv.org/abs/1703.10593

ScoringNet: Learning Key Fragment for Action Quality Assessment with Ranking Loss in Skilled Sports

Yongjun Li[1,3], Xiujuan Chai[1,2], and Xilin Chen[1,3]

[1] Key Lab of Intelligent Information Processing of Chinese Academy of Sciences (CAS), Institute of Computing Technology, CAS, Beijing 100190, China
{yongjun.li,xiujuan.chai}@vipl.ict.ac.cn, xlchen@ict.ac.cn
[2] Agricultural Information Institute, Chinese Academy of Agricultural Sciences, Beijing 100081, China
[3] University of Chinese Academy of Sciences, Beijing 100049, China

Abstract. Nowadays, scoring athletes' performance in skilled sports automatically has drawn more and more attention from the academic community. However, extracting effective features and predicting reasonable scores for a long skilled sport video still beset researchers. In this paper, we introduce the ScoringNet, a novel network consisting of key fragment segmentation (KFS) and score prediction (SP), to address these two problems. To get the effective features, we design KFS to obtain key fragments and remove irrelevant fragments by semantic video segmentation. Then a 3D convolutional neural network extracts features from each key fragment. In score prediction, we fuse the ranking loss into the traditional loss function to make the predictions more reasonable in terms of both the score value and the ranking aspects. Through the deep learning, we narrow the gap between the predictions and ground-truth scores as well as making the predictions satisfy the ranking constraint. Widely experiments convincingly show that our method achieves the state-of-the-art results on three datasets.

Keywords: Action quality assessment ·
Key fragment segmentation · Ranking loss

1 Introduction

The sports in which athletes have to complete the specified actions are called skilled sport. In these sports, the process can be divided into several stages and only key stages determine scores according to sports rules. Referees will give three kinds of scores including "Difficulty" score (fixing agreed-upon value based

This work was partially supported by 973 Program under contract No. 2015CB351802, Natural Science Foundation of China under contracts Nos. 61390511, 61472398, 61532018.

on specified action type), "Execution" score (judging quality of an action) and the final score. The final score can be obtained with the other two scores, such as adding them. These sports includes all diving events, all gymnastics events, equestrianism, synchronised swimming and so on.

In real life, it is very time consuming to train a qualified referee of skilled sports because they must go through long-term training to get familiar with all specified actions. Hence replacing manual scoring with an automatic scoring system is a trend in the future. On the other hand, the manual judgement is subjective. The automatic scoring system could be used as a trusted impartial opinion to avoid scoring scandals where the partiality of judges is questioned [1]. Nowadays, there have been some organizations trying applying automatic scoring systems in real sports competitions. For example, the international gymnastics federation (FIG) plans to introduce artificial intelligence technology to assess the quality of gymnastic in the 2020 Tokyo Olympics. Although there is a pressing need for the automatic scoring system, its application is impeded by two major obstacles. (1) A skilled sport usually contains a series of complicated motion fragments. So how to model a skilled sport video and obtain effective features are difficult. (2) The predictions should not only have small difference from the ground-truth scores but also satisfy the ranking constraint. How to make reasonable predictions to accomplish the two goals at the same time is non-trivial.

To overcome the aforementioned obstacles, we introduce the ScoringNet, as shown in Fig. 1, which consists of KFS and SP to realize action quality assessment in skilled sports. Inspired by the deep learning breakthroughs in the video domain [13, 23–25] where rapid progress has made in feature learning, we build the ScoringNet on top of the 3D convolutional neural network to extract discriminative features. But the sport videos are usually untrimmed and have some noise fragments, extracting features from an untrimmed video is unreasonable. What's more, not all fragments of trimmed video have contribution to the score, such as the fragment where athletes are in run-up of diving. Hence we design the learning-based KFS to perform semantic video segmentation in the ScoringNet. Then the 3D convolutional neural network will only extract features from the key fragments which determine scores. In [5], Pirsiavash *et al.* first proposes to divide a video into fragments in action quality assessment, but they segment a video along the temporal dimension evenly. Most importantly, we fuse ranking loss into traditional loss function to make the predictions satisfy the score value constraint and the ranking constraint at the same time effectively. Additionally, the ScoringNet assesses athletes' performance more carefully by generating "Difficulty" score, "Execution" score and the final score instead of only the final score.

To summarize, our main contributions are as follows:

- We design the learning-based KFS in the ScoringNet to filter irrelative fragments and obtain key fragments by semantic video segmentation to ensure the effectiveness of features.

– The ranking loss are integrated with traditional loss function to form a powerful combined loss function which takes account of both the score value constraint and the ranking constraint.

2   Related Works

In action quality assessment, previous works fall into two categories, i.e. sports [5–7,9,12,14] and medicine [8,10,11] according to the application scenarios. Concerning the method, there are regression-based method [5,6,9,14,31] and classification-based method [8,10,12,30].

The regression-based method directly predicts a continuous score to evaluate the quality of an action. In [5], Pirsiavash *et al.* introduce a general learning-based framework to automatically assess actions' quality from videos. The framework uses a pose estimator to extract both low level and high level features of each frame. Then a support vector regression model (SVR) is trained to predict the final score. The results show that their approach is significantly better at assessing an action's quality than a non-expert human. Literature [7] proposes a recursive neural network that leverages growing self-organization for efficient learning of body motion sequences. The quality of an action is then measured in terms of how much a performed action matches the correct continuation of a learned sequence. In [31], they first use the similar way to segment videos into five stages. Then they employ P3D [24] to extract the body-pose features of fragments. Finally, SVR is implemented to regress the score.

While for the classification-based method, the quality of an action will be classified into different grades. In [8], Parmar and Morris examine the assessment of quality of large amplitude movement (LAM) actions designed to treat cerebral palsy (CP) in an automatic fashion. They transform both joint positions and angles to frequency domain by taking the discrete cosine transform (DCT). Each data variation then be used as the input feature vector for classifier. The task is regarded as a classification problem that whether the quality of an action is good or not. Literature [10] presents an automatic framework for surgical skill assessment. They first use Spatio-Temporal Interest Points (STIPs) [28] to get the feature from video data. Then they also transform motion data into frequency domain and finally the skill classification.

There are also some works combining the two methods. In [16], Chai *et al.* develop a system on sign quality evaluation with both classification and regression model. The system first determines whether a sign is the appointed one by the classification model. For the sign which passes the verification, the regression model will give a score.

Both [5] and [9] are comprehensive and pioneering works on action quality assessment in sports. However, their methods are traditional. Although [9] using deep learning to obtain features, they divide the whole process into feature extraction and score prediction instead of an end-to-end process. In score prediction, they assess the quality of an action only by the final score and their loss functions ignore the ranking constraint. In [9], they also divide a video into fragments, but the segmentation is even along the temporal dimension and not semantic.

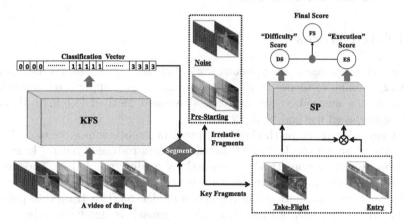

Fig. 1. The pipeline of the ScoringNet. DS, ES and FS represent "Difficulty" score, "Execution" score and the final score respectively. Pre-Starting, Take-Flight and Entry are the stages of a dive.

3   Our Method

In this section, we give detailed descriptions of the ScoringNet. The ScoringNet is composed of key fragment segmentation (KFS) and score prediction (SP). KFS is in charge of semantic video segmentation and obtaining key fragments. SP is employed to regress scores of the given sport videos. Firstly, the untrimmed video is sent into KFS to generate a classification vector whose value on each dimension represents the class. Then, all frames are classified into several fragments according to the vector. The irrelative fragments are dropped and the key fragments are sent to SP to predict "Difficulty" score and "Execution" score. Finally, the final score is obtained by fusion of the two scores.

3.1   Key Fragment Segmentation

Inspired by the idea that FCN [22] segments images by classifying each pixel, we design KFS for semantic video segmentation. KFS classifies all frames by sport stages and noise, the frames in the same class form a fragment. Only the key segments will be preserved. In general, a deep 2D convolutional neural network [19,26,27,29] is widely used for image classification. However, they may not generalize well to video-frame classification because of their limited access to temporal context. In a video, the contents of many frames at different times may be similar. The temporal context can help to distinguish these similar frames.

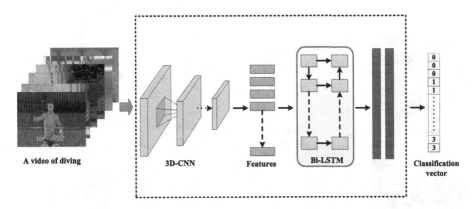

Fig. 2. The structure of KFS. The input and output of KFS are a video of diving and classification vector respectively.

Hence KFS consists of a 3D convolutional neural network, a Bidirectional LSTM (Bi-LSTM) network [21] and two fully connected layers, as Fig. 2. The 3D convolutional neural network processes short-temporal context and the Bi-LSTM is mainly for long-temporal context.

To clearly illustrate KFS. We can formulate KFS as Eq. 1,

$$C = T_{kfs}(X; W_{kfs}, B_{kfs}) \tag{1}$$

where $C = \{c_1, c_2, c_3...c_l\}, c_i \in \mathbb{R}^0, C \in \mathbb{R}^{l \times 1}$. c_i is the classification result of *ith* frame in the video. $X = \{x_1, x_2, x_3...x_l\}, x_i \in \mathbb{R}^{h \times w \times c}, X \in \mathbb{R}^{l \times h \times w \times c}$. x_i is the *ith* frame in the video. h, w and c are the height, width and channel of a frame respectively. l is the length of the video. T_{kfs} is a function representing operations on X in KFS. W_{kfs} and B_{kfs} are the hyper-parameters of T_{kfs}.

The Bi-LSTM we employ is the same as [21]. For the 3D convolutional neural network, we modify C3D [13] by the following two steps: **(1)** removing the fully connected layers of C3D and flatting the output of pool5 layer into a 4096-dim vector. **(2)** removing the temporal max-pooling operation to maintain the length of the video.

3.2   Score Prediction

In skilled sports, we just need to predict "Difficulty" score and "Execution" score. The final score can be obtained by them according to sports rules.

Thus SP, as Fig. 3, includes two branches and parallelly predicts the two kinds of scores. These two branches have the same structure but don't share weights. In each branches, a C3D extractor is adopted for the feature extraction, which consists of the first 12 layers of C3D. Once the feature is extracted, it will go through the score regressor which consists of two convolution layers (followed by Relu and $3 \times 3 \times 3$ Max-pooling) and three fully connected layers (followed by Relu and Dropout) to regress the score.

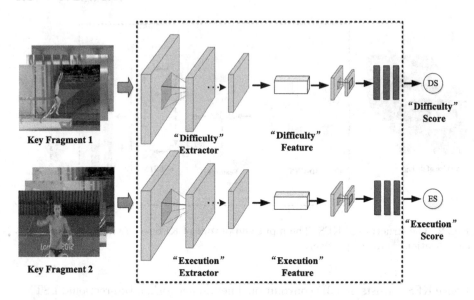

Fig. 3. The structure of SP. The input and output of SP are key fragments and scores respectively.

The SP can be formulated as Eqs. 2–4. For one branch predicting "Difficulty", we can formulate it as Eq. 2,

$$S_d = T_{spd}(D; W_{spd}, B_{spd}) \tag{2}$$

where $D = \{d_1, d_2, d_3...d_m\}, d_i \in \mathbb{R}^{h \times w \times c}, D \in \mathbb{R}^{m \times h \times w \times c}$. d_i is the ith frame in the key fragment which determines the "Difficulty" score. m is the length of the key fragment. T_{spd} is a function, with hyper-parameters W_{spd} and B_{spd}, which represents operations in SP. S_d is the "Difficulty" score prediction. Similarly, we can get another branch as Eq. 3,

$$S_e = T_{spe}(E; W_{spe}, B_{spe}) \tag{3}$$

where $E = \{e_1, e_2, e_3...e_t\}, e_i \in \mathbb{R}^{h \times w \times c}, E \in \mathbb{R}^{t \times h \times w \times c}$. e_i is the ith frame in the key fragment which determines the "Execution" score. t is the length of the key fragment. T_{spe} is a function, with hyper-parameters W_{spe} and B_{spe}, which represents operations in SP. S_e is the "Execution" score prediction.

Finally, according the rules, the finally score can be obtained by Eq. 4. In diving, F is the sum function of two scores while F represents quadrature function of them in vault.

$$S = F(S_d, S_e) \tag{4}$$

3.3   Loss Function

The loss function mainly consists of two parts in which one is for KFS and the other is for SP.

For KFS, we use standard categorical cross-entropy loss as the loss function, as Eq. (5),

$$L_{ce} = -\frac{1}{n \times l} \sum_{i=1}^{n \times l} (y_i \ln(p_i) + (1 - y_i) \ln(1 - p_i)) \tag{5}$$

where n is the size of a batch. y_i and p_i are the *ith* ground-truth label and prediction label respectively. l is the length of the video.

For SP, MSE is widely adopted as the loss function to constrain score value, as Eq. (6),

$$L_{mse} = \frac{1}{2n} \sum_{i=1}^{n} (s_i - g_i)^2 \tag{6}$$

where g_i and s_i are the *ith* ground-truth score and prediction respectively. However, the performance of an automatic scoring system depends on whether the predictions satisfy both the score value constraint and the ranking constraint. So we add the ranking loss to make the predictions meet the ranking constraint. The ranking loss for a batch of data is defined as Eq. (7),

$$L_{rk} = \sum_{i=1}^{n} \sum_{j=1, j>i}^{n} RELU(-(s_j - s_i)sign(g_j - g_i) + \delta), \delta > 0 \tag{7}$$

where $RELU(\cdot)$ is a rectified linear unit activation and δ works as the margin for the ranking loss. When the predictions violate the ranking constraint, the ranking loss will generate a punishment term. On the contrary, the value of the ranking loss is zero. Further, the combined loss function for SP can be written by Eqs. (8) and (9),

$$L_d = L_{mse}^d + \alpha L_{rk}^d + \beta ||w^d||^2 \tag{8}$$

$$L_e = L_{mse}^e + \alpha L_{rk}^e + \beta ||w^e||^2, \alpha > 0, \beta > 0. \tag{9}$$

where L_d and L_e are the loss functions for two sub-architectures in SP respectively. $||w||^2$ is L2-regularization term, α and β are parameters used to balance these three terms.

Our final loss function includes two combined loss functions and the categorical cross-entropy loss as Eq. (10),

$$L = L_d + L_e + L_{ce} \tag{10}$$

4   Experimental Results

In this section, we evaluate our method on two sports (diving and vault) from three public datasets, i.e. Mit-Diving Dataset [5], UNLV-Diving Dataset [9] and

UNLV-Vault Dataset [9]. Firstly, we make a simple introduction of the three datasets. Secondly, the experimental configuration and the evaluation metric are given. Thirdly, we give the way of selecting key fragments and verify the correctness of this way. Then three experiments are conducted on the latter two datasets to evaluate our method. After this, the qualitative analysis is given to explain why our method works well. Finally, we compare our method with other state-of-the-art methods on the three datasets.

4.1 Datasets

Mit-Diving Dataset: This dataset contains 159 videos of London Olympic men's 10-m platform, each has roughly 150 frames. The size of all frames is 320×240. The annotation includes "Difficulty" score (varying between 2.7 and 4.1) and "Execution" score (varying between 6.0 and 29.0). The final score (ranging from 21.6 to 100.0) is determined by the product of "Difficulty" score multiplied by "Execution" score.

UNLV-Diving Dataset: This dataset, which is extended from the Mit-Diving Dataset, includes 370 videos from London Olympic men's 10-m platform. Apart from the number of videos, everything else is the same as the Mit-Diving Dataset.

UNLV-Vault Dataset: This dataset includes 176 videos with an average length of about 75 frames. The frame size is 320×240. The annotation includes "Difficulty" score (varying between 4.6 and 7.4) and "Execution" score (varying between 7.38 and 9.67). The final score (ranging from 12.30 to 16.87) is generated by adding "Execution" score and "Difficulty" score. These videos are shot from 5 international competitions and the view variation is quite large among these videos making it a more difficult dataset to score.

Since the Mit-Diving Dataset is a subset of the UNLV-Diving Dataset, we perform the detailed evaluation on the UNLV-Diving Dataset while only give the comparison results on the Mit-Diving Dataset. In experiments on the UNLV-Diving Dataset and UNLV-Vault Dataset, we follow the testing scheme in [9]. In [9], they perform a random data split and release the split result. The training/testing split is 300/70 on the UNLV-Diving Dataset and 120/56 on the UNLV-Vault Dataset.

4.2 Experimental Setting and Evaluation Metric

To mitigate the risk of over-fitting from the limited training data source, we pre-train the C3D in KFS and two extractors in SP with UCF-101 [15]. Further, all videos are augmented by shifting the start frame with a random number within $[0, 5]$. In the training process, the learning rate is initialed as 10e−4 and decreases to its 0.45 every 600 iterations. The optimization algorithm is Adam [18]. In the loss function, α is set to 5 and 10 empirically for two diving datasets and the vault dataset respectively. Meanwhile β is set to 0.0005.

To measure the performance of our method, the spearman rank correlation (SRC, as Eq. 11) and mean euclidean distance (MED, as Eq. 12) are adopted as the our criterion.

$$SRC = 1 - \frac{6 \times \sum\limits_{i=1}^{n} h_i^2}{n \times (n^2 - 1)} \tag{11}$$

$$MED = \frac{1}{n} \sum\limits_{i=1}^{n} |s_i - g_i|, \tag{12}$$

where h_i is the difference between the two ranks of each observation. $|\cdot|$ represents absolute function. SRC is a nonparametric measure of rank correlation. We utilize it to measure the statistical dependence between the ranking of the predictions and the ground-truth scores. The larger the SRC, the higher the rank correlation. For MED, the smaller MED represents that the predictions are more close to the ground-truth scores.

In all experiments, we calculate "Difficulty" score SRC (D-SRC), "Execution" score SRC (E-SRC) and the final score SRC (F-SRC). For MED, there are also three kinds of MED (D-MED, E-MED, F-MED) accordingly.

4.3 Which Are Key Fragments

KFS is a learning-based method and need to be trained with videos which have labelled fragments. So we have to determine which fragments are key fragments.

In diving rules [3], the diving can be divided into 4 consecutive stages, namely the Pre-Starting, the Take-Off (including the starting position and the approach), the Flight and the Entry. We regard the Take-Off and the Flight as one stage called the Take-Flight because they determine "Difficulty" score together. Then, we divide each diving video into four fragments including all three stages and the noise. According to diving rules [3,4], the Take-Flight determines "Difficulty" score while the Take-Flight and the Entry contribute to "Execution" score together, so the Take-Flight and Entry are two key fragments while the Pre-Starting and the noise are irrelative fragments. Consequently, we employ the Take-Flight to predict "Difficulty" score while the Take-Flight and Entry are for "Execution" score prediction. Similarly, a vault video can be divided into four fragments which are the Pre-Flight, the Posting-Flight (including the Support), the Landing and the noise [2]. The Posting-Flight and Landing are two key fragments while the Pre-Flight and noise are irrelative fragments. According to vault rules [2], we use the Posting-Flight to predict "Difficulty" score. Meanwhile the Posting-Flight and Landing are for "Execution" score prediction.

To validate the way of selecting key fragments, we employ different ground-truth fragments to predict the two kinds of scores and compare performances of them. In this experiment, the loss function for SP is MSE for simplicity. As Table 1 shows, The Take-Flight and Take-Flight+Entry are the most suitable for "Difficulty" score prediction and "Execution" score prediction respectively on the UNLV-Diving Dataset. The similar results are reported in Table 2 on the UNLV-Vault Dataset. So, in the following subsections, we select key fragments according to sports rules.

Table 1. Validation on the way of selecting key fragments on the UNLV-Diving Dataset.

SRC	Pre-Starting	Take-Flight	Entry	Take-Flight+Entry
D-SRC	0.12	**0.64**	0.3208	0.56
E-SRC	0.08	0.52	0.82	**0.85**

Table 2. Validation on the way of selecting key fragments on the UNLV-Vault Dataset.

SRC	Pre-Flight	Posting-Flight	Landing	Posting-Flight+Landing
D-SRC	0.20	**0.53**	0.25	0.43
E-SRC	0.13	0.3475	0.38	**0.41**

4.4 Effect of Key Fragment Segmentation

In this subsection, we compare KFS against other networks and verify the effectiveness of KFS on the UNLV-Diving Dataset and the UNLV-Vault Dataset. Since there are no frame-level labels in these two datasets, we assign the label for each frame manually by stages and noise. Firstly, we compare KFS with ResNet50 and the Modified C3D respectively. The Modified C3D is obtained by two steps in Sect. 3.1. Figure 4 reports that the Modified C3D outperforms ResNet50 and KFS achieves the best performance. The results suggest both the short and the long contextual information can indeed help to classify frames. Additionally, we observe that the three results are very close on diving. The reason is that the contents of diving frames in different stages are distinct and easy to be classified. Further on, we show the accuracy on each class of two actions in Table 3.

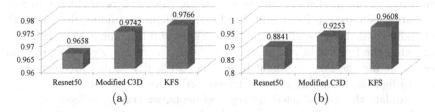

Fig. 4. Exploration of different networks for semantic video segmentation on the UNLV-Diving Dataset and the UNLV-Vault Dataset. (a) The accuracy of classification on UNLV-Diving Dataset. (b) The accuracy of classification on the UNLV-Vault Dataset.

Table 3. The accuracy on each class of two actions.

UNLV-Diving	Noise	Pre-Starting	Take-Flight	Entry
Acc	0.97	0.95	0.99	0.97
UNLV-Vault	Noise	Pre-Flight	Posting-Flight	Landing
Acc	0.96	0.81	0.97	0.97

Secondly, we verify the effectiveness of KFS. In this experiment, we drop KFS and take the untrimmed video as the input to SP directly. We also employ MSE as the loss function for SP in this experiment. Table 4 shows that the performance drops sharply without KFS. The results show that KFS has a strong positive effect for score prediction.

Table 4. Validation on the effectiveness of KSF on UNLV-Diving Dataset (represented by Diving) and UNLV-Vault Dataset (represented by Vault). −KFS refers to the experiment without KFS and +KFS refers to the experiment with KFS.

Method	D-MED	E-MED	F-MED	D-SRC	E-SRC	F-SRC
−KFS (Diving)	0.16	1.75	6.78	0.35	0.78	0.71
+KFS (Diving)	0.13	1.50	5.95	**0.57**	**0.82**	**0.79**
−KFS (Vault)	0.53	0.86	1.35	0.48	0.33	0.61
+KFS (Vault)	0.49	0.64	1.04	**0.51**	**0.38**	**0.68**

4.5 Evaluation on Different Loss Functions

We compare the performances of different loss functions which are MSE and the combined loss on the UNLV-Diving Dataset and the UNLV-Vault Dataset. This experiment is carried out with KFS. Table 5 reports the results. Our results show SRCs obtain the significant improvement while MEDs retain relatively small value, suggesting that the combined loss is capable of making the predictions satisfy the score value constraint and the ranking constraint as the same time.

In order to illustrate the effectiveness of the ranking loss explicitly, we choose three samples from UNLV-Diving Dataset (their ground-truth "Execution" scores: sample1 13.00, sample2 15.50, sample3 16.00) and record their "Execution" score predictions every epoch in the experiment with MSE (Fig. 5(a)) and the experiment with the combined loss (Fig. 5(b)) respectively. As shown in Fig. 5(a), only using MSE, three curves are interlaced. What's more, the predictions of sample2 and sample3 are in wrong order as they have close ground-truth scores. When MSE are combined with the ranking loss, as shown in Fig. 5(b), these three curves are separated and the predictions are in right order from very early and keep it afterwards. That shows the powerful effectiveness of the ranking loss in the ranking constraint.

Table 5. Comparison of different loss functions on the UNLV-Diving Dataset (represented by Diving) and the UNLV-Vault Dataset (represented by Vault).

Method	D-MED	E-MED	F-MED	D-SRC	E-SRC	F-SRC
MSE (Diving)	0.13	1.50	5.95	0.57	0.82	0.79
The combined loss (Diving)	0.11	1.55	5.36	**0.79**	**0.86**	**0.84**
MSE (Vault)	0.49	0.64	1.04	0.51	0.38	0.68
The combined loss (Vault)	0.55	0.45	1.11	**0.57**	**0.57**	**0.70**

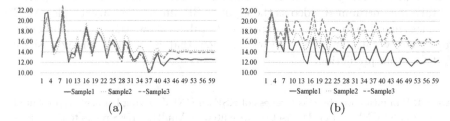

(a)   (b)

Fig. 5. Illustration about effectiveness of the ranking loss (a) The predictions of three samples in the experiment with MSE. (b) The predictions of three samples in the experiment with the combined loss. In the two diagrams, Y-axis represents the value of the predictions and X-axis represents the number of epochs.

4.6 Qualitative Analysis

In order to further clarify the effect of KFS and Ranking loss. We make the following qualitative analysis. There are three models which are baseline model (M-b), the model with KFS (M-k) and the model with both KFS and ranking loss (M-kr). We predict the "Difficulty" score of a test video by these three models respectively. The ground truth score is 3.7 and three predictions are M-b:3.40, M-k:3.47 and M-kr:3.64 respectively. Then we show the feature maps (Fig. 6, the lighter the gray scale, the larger the activation value.) from conv1-layer of the three models. We infer that KFS removes redundant temporal information and makes the model focus on current frame (the legs in current feature map of M-b include the information of two frames before and after). Meanwhile, ranking loss is a powerful constrain and is able to eliminate the redundant spatial information, such as background.

Fig. 6. (a) A frame from the test video. (b) The 8th feature maps of conv1-layer from three models (left to right: M-b, M-k, M-kr). (c) The 44th feature maps of conv1-layer from three models (left to right: M-b, M-k, M-kr).

4.7 Stability of Our Method

We perform 6 random data splits to exclude the influence of data split and verify the stability of our method. This experiment is carried out with KFS and the combined loss is the loss function for SP. Table 6 shows the average value and standard deviation over 6 random data splits on the UNLV-Diving Dataset and the UNLV-Vault Dataset respectively. The high average value and small standard deviation of SRCs suggest the strong stability of our method.

Table 6. Verification on the stability of our method on the UNLV-Diving Dataset (represented by Diving) and the UNLV-Vault Dataset (represented by Vault). The AVG and the STD mean average value and standard deviation respectively over the results of 6 random data splits.

Method	D-MED	E-MED	F-MED	D-SRC	E-SRC	F-SRC
AVG (Diving)	0.10	1.32	5.60	0.77	0.85	0.79
STD (Diving)	0.01	0.11	0.46	0.05	0.03	0.04
AVG (Vault)	0.48	0.81	1.08	0.61	0.50	0.68
STD (Vault)	0.07	0.16	0.12	0.04	0.07	0.05

4.8 Comparison with Other Methods

We compare our method with other state-of-the-art methods on the three Datasets. In previous methods, they only predict the final score, so we adopt F-SRC as evaluation metric. All results are shown in Table 7.

For the UNLV-Diving Dataset and the UNLV-Vault Dataset, we adopt the same split as [9]. They also test Pose+DCT with the same split. The results of Pose+DCT on the UNLV-Diving Dataset and the UNLV-Vault Dataset are extracted from [9].

For MIT-Diving Dataset, [5] uses 200 random data splits on this dataset and averages the results. The training/testing split is 100/59. The results of ConsISA

Table 7. Comparison of our method with other state-of-the-art methods on the three datasets

	UNLV-Diving	UNLV-Vault	MIT-Diving
Pose+DCT [5]	0.53	0.10	0.35
ConsISA [17]	-	-	0.19
ApEnFT [14]	-	-	0.45
C3D+LSTM [9]	0.27	0.05	0.36
C3D+SVR [9]	0.78	0.66	0.74
Ours (MSE+Ranking loss)	**0.84**	**0.70**	**0.78**

and ApEnFT are also extracted from [5]. Since the limited computing resources, our results are obtained by averaging the results from 6 random data splits.

As shown in Table 7, our method outperforms others tremendously and achieve the state-of-the-art results on these three datasets.

5   Conclusion

Automatically assessing an action's quality is a pressing need in skilled sports. But the two obstacles of extracting effective feature and making reasonable predictions prevent it being realized. In this paper, we present the ScoringNet, an end-to-end framework that aims to realize the action quality assessment in skilled sports. As demonstrated on three public datasets, our work has brought the state-of-the-art to a new level. This is largely ascribed to KFS and the combined loss, which overcome the two obstacles. The former provides an effective way to remove irrelative fragments and obtain key fragments to ensure the effectiveness of features, while the latter makes more reasonable predictions with satisfying the score value constraint and the ranking constraint as the same time.

References

1. List of Olympic Games Scandals and Controversies. https://en.wikipedia.org/wiki/List_of_Olympic_Games_boycotts. Accessed 26 Mar 2018
2. Vault. https://en.wikipedia.org/wiki/Vault_(gymnastics). 2.1.2. Accessed 4 June 2018
3. FINA Diving Rules. http://www.fina.org/sites/default/files/2017-2021_diving_16032018.pdf. D8.1.3. Accessed 12 Sept 2017
4. FINA Diving Rules. http://www.fina.org/sites/default/files/2017-2021_diving_16032018.pdf. APPENDIX 4. Accessed 12 Sept 2017
5. Pirsiavash, H., Vondrick, C., Torralba, A.: Assessing the quality of actions. In: Fleet, D., Pajdla, T., Schiele, B., Tuytelaars, T. (eds.) ECCV 2014. LNCS, vol. 8694, pp. 556–571. Springer, Cham (2014). https://doi.org/10.1007/978-3-319-10599-4_36
6. Tao, L., et al.: A comparative study of pose representation and dynamics modelling for online motion quality assessment. Comput. Vis. Image Underst. **148**, 136–152 (2016)
7. Parmar, P., Morris, B.: Human motion assessment in real time using recurrent self-organization. In: 25th IEEE International Symposium on Robot and Human Interactive Communication, New York, USA, pp. 71–76 (2016)
8. Parisi, G., Magg, S., Wermter, S.: Measuring the quality of exercises. In: 38th Annual International Conference of the IEEE Engineering in Medicine and Biology Society, Florida, USA, pp. 2241–2244 (2016)
9. Parmar, P., Morris, B.: Learning to score olympic events. In: 30th IEEE Conference on Computer Vision and Pattern Recognition Work Shop, pp. 76–84. IEEE, Hawaii (2017)
10. Zia, A., Sharma, Y., Bettadapura, V., Sarin, E.L., Clements, M.A., Essa, I.: Automated assessment of surgical skills using frequency analysis. In: Navab, N., Hornegger, J., Wells, W.M., Frangi, A.F. (eds.) MICCAI 2015. LNCS, vol. 9349, pp. 430–438. Springer, Cham (2015). https://doi.org/10.1007/978-3-319-24553-9_53

11. Baptista, R., Antunes, M., Aouada, D., Ottersten, B.: Video-based feedback for assisting physical activity. In: 12th International Conference on Computer Vision Theory and Applications, Porto, Portugal, pp. 430–438 (2017)
12. Carvajal, J., Wiliem, A., Sanderson, C., Lovell, B.: Towards Miss Universe automatic prediction: the evening gown competition. In: 23rd International Conference on Pattern Recognition, pp. 1089–1094. IEEE, Cancun (2016)
13. Du, T., Bourdev, L., Fergus, R., Torresani, L., Paluri, M.: Learning spatiotemporal features with 3D convolutional networks. In: International Conference on Computer Vision, pp. 4489–4497. IEEE, Santiago (2015)
14. Venkataraman, V., Vlachos, I., Turaga, P.: Dynamical regularity for action analysis. In: 26th British Machine Vision Conference, pp. 67.1–67.12. British Machine Vision Association, Swansea (2015)
15. Soomro, K., Zamir, A., Shah, M.: UCF101: a dataset of 101 human actions classes from videos in the wild. arXiv preprint arXiv:1212.0402 (2012)
16. Chai, X., Liu, Z., Li, Y., Yin, F., Chen, X.: SignInstructor: an effective tool for sign language vocabulary learning. In: 4th Asian Conference on Pattern Recognition, Nanjing, China (2017)
17. Le, Q., Zou, W., Yeung, S., Ng, A.: Learning hierarchical invariant spatio-temporal features for action recognition with independent subspace analysis. In: 24th IEEE Conference on Computer Vision and Pattern Recognition, pp. 3361–3368. IEEE, Colorado Springs (2011)
18. Kingma, D.,Ba, J.: Adam: a method for stochastic optimization. arXiv preprint arXiv preprint arXiv:1412.6980 (2014)
19. He, K., Zhang, X., Ren, S., Sun, J.: Identity mappings in deep residual networks. In: Leibe, B., Matas, J., Sebe, N., Welling, M. (eds.) ECCV 2016. LNCS, vol. 9908, pp. 630–645. Springer, Cham (2016). https://doi.org/10.1007/978-3-319-46493-0_38
20. Szegedya, C., et al.: Going deeper with convolutions. In: 28th IEEE Conference on Computer Vision and Pattern Recognition, pp. 1–9. IEEE, Boston (2015)
21. Huang, Z., Xu, W., Yu, K.: Bidirectional LSTM-CRF models for sequence tagging. arXiv preprint arXiv preprint arXiv:1508.01991 (2015)
22. Long, J., Shelhamer, E., Darrell, T.: Fully convolutional networks for semantic segmentation. In: 28th IEEE Conference on Computer Vision and Pattern Recognition, pp. 3431–3440. IEEE, Boston (2015)
23. Carreira, J., Zisserman, A.: Quo vadis, action recognition? A new model and the kinetics dataset. In: 30th IEEE Conference on Computer Vision and Pattern Recognition, pp. 4724–4733. IEEE, Hawaii (2017)
24. Qiu, Z., Yao, T., Mei, T.: Learning spatio-temporal representation with pseudo-3D residual networks. In: International Conference on Computer Vision, pp. 5534–5542. IEEE, Venice (2017)
25. Simonyan, K., Zisserman, A.: Two-stream convolutional networks for action recognition in videos. In: 21st Conference on Neural Information Processing Systems, pp. 568–576. MIT Press, Montreal (2014)
26. Krizhevsky, A., Sutskever, I., Hinton, G.E.: ImageNet classification with deep convolutional neural networks. In: 19th Conference on Neural Information Processing Systems, pp. 1097–1105. MIT Press, Lake Tahoe (2012)
27. Simonyan, K., Zisserman, A.: Very deep convolutional networks for large-scale image recognition. In: International Conference on Learning Representations (2015)
28. Laptev, I., Lindeberg, T.: On space-time interest points. Int. J. Comput. Vis. **64**, 107–123 (2005)

29. Huang, G., Liu, Z., Laurens, V.D.M., Weinberger, K.Q.: Densely connected convolutional networks. In: 30th IEEE Conference on Computer Vision and Pattern Recognition, pp. 2261–2269. IEEE, Hawaii (2017)
30. Doughty, H., Damen, D., Mayol-Cuevas, W.: Who's better? Who's best? Pairwise deep ranking for skill determination. In: 31st IEEE Conference on Computer Vision and Pattern Recognition. IEEE, Salt Lake City (2018)
31. Xiang, X., Tian, Y., Reiter, A., Hager, G.D., Tran, T.D.: S3D: stacking segmental P3D for action quality assessment. In: IEEE International Conference on Image Processing. IEEE, Athens (2018)

Style Transfer with Adversarial Learning for Cross-Dataset Person Re-identification

Furong Xu[1], Bingpeng Ma[1(✉)], Hong Chang[2], Shiguang Shan[2], and Xilin Chen[2]

[1] School of Computer and Control Engineering,
University of Chinese Academy of Sciences, Beijing 100049, China
xufurong17@mails.ucas.ac.cn, bpma@ucas.ac.cn
[2] Key Lab of Intelligent Information Processing of Chinese Academy of Sciences
(CAS), Institute of Computing Technology, CAS, Beijing 100190, China
{changhong,sgshan,xlchen}@ict.ac.cn

Abstract. Person re-identification (ReID) has witnessed great progress in recent years. Existing approaches are able to achieve significant performance on the single dataset but fail to generalize well on another datasets. The emerging problem mainly comes from style difference between two datasets. To address this problem, we propose a novel style transfer framework based on Generative Adversarial Networks (GAN) to generate target-style images. Specifically, we get the style representation by calculating the Garm matrix of the three-channel original image, and then minimize the Euclidean distance of the style representation on different images transferred by the same generator while image generation. Finally, the labeled source dataset combined with the style-transferred images are all used to enhance the generalization ability of the ReID model. Experimental results suggest that the proposed strategy is very effective on the Market-1501 and DukeMTMC-reID.

Keywords: Person re-identification · Style transfer · Adversarial learning

1 Introduction

Person re-identification (ReID) [31] is a challenging image retrieval task, which amis to match persons in the different places/time under non-overlapping cameras. It is obvious diversity between different images of the same identity because of various viewpoint, body structures, and occlusion (see Fig. 1). Although existing many supervised deep learning approaches [22,28] have achieved significant performance on the single dataset, it is worth noting that manually annotating a new dataset is expensive and impractical.

Many approaches perform well on one person dataset but fail to generalize well to another dataset [7]. Difference between different datasets mainly comes

© Springer Nature Switzerland AG 2019
C. V. Jawahar et al. (Eds.): ACCV 2018, LNCS 11366, pp. 165–180, 2019.
https://doi.org/10.1007/978-3-030-20876-9_11

Fig. 1. Examples of person re-identification datasets. The left is selected from the Market-1501 and the right is selected from the DukeMTMC-reID.

from light conditions and backgrounds (we call it style), which results in poor performance under cross-dataset ReID. For example, as shown in Fig. 1, Market-1501 dataset is collected in summer with strong lighting, but the DukeMTMC-reID is collected in winter. Therefore, the seasonal difference causes different styles of dressing. A single dataset often has its own style characteristics, and the model is easy to overfit on the style of the dataset. Considering this matter, some approaches [21, 26] employ unsupervised dictionary learning to acquire a dataset-shared space, Xiao et al. [24] design a Domain Guided Dropout (DGD) classification model to learn generic feature representations with multiple datasets. Recently, several works [6, 23] adopt domain adaptation method based on Cycle-GAN [34] to translate the labeled source dataset to target domain, and then the transferred images are used to train ReID models.

As reported in [9], the images can be composed of the content and the style. Therefore, the features extracted by the ReID model will consist of both the style representation and the content representation, any poor representation will affect the final accuracy. To ensure performance of the cross-dataset ReID, it is quite important to extract the dataset-invariant content representation, as well as to obtain the consistent style representation between the source dataset and the target dataset. Some works [21, 23, 26] have committed to learning the shared features across all datasets. However, none of these methods focuses on pushing the style consistency between datasets.

To explicitly address these issues of the cross-dataset ReID, we propose a novel style-transferrable framework based on CycleGAN to generate target-style images for learning discriminative features. Generally speaking, the style representation can be extracted by looking at the spatial correlation of the values within a given feature map, which is available by calculating Gram matrix of the feature map, and the feature map is usually the output of the network middle layer [9, 10]. Inspired by their style representation way, we calculate the Gram matrix of the three-channel original image to get the style representation, rather than the feature map of the network middle layer, because the original image contains all the style information. In the image generation process, we constrain the Euclidean distance of the style representation to be minimized, the constrained objects are different images generated by the same generator. We call this structure Style-consistent, Identity-consistent, Cycle-consistent Generative Adversarial Network (SICGAN). After we get the transferred target-style images, considering that ID-related information is preserved between the original images and the corresponding generated images, we use the style-transferred image together with the original image as a training set to train the ReID model in supervised learning, which enables the model to learn discriminative features. Extensive experimental results show that our method can achieve consistent and competitive ReID accuracy on two large-scale datasets.

2   Related Work

In this section, we first review some related works in person ReID, especially some methods about single-dataset and cross-dataset, then we introduce a few image generation works related to our method, such as style transfer and image-image translation.

2.1   Person ReID

Single-Dataset ReID. Single-dataset ReID means that both training and testing are in the same dataset. Recently, deep learning based person ReID approaches [1,18,29] have achieved great success through simultaneously learning the person representation and similarity within one network on a single-dataset. These methods usually learn the ID-discriminative Embedding (IDE) feature [31] via training a deep classification network. In addition, some works try to introduce the pair-wise contrastive loss [5], triplet loss [14,27] and quadruplet loss [4] to further enhance the IDE feature. There are currently some methods that achieve good performance in single-dataset. AlignedReID [28] introduces a feature matching method to align different body parts. [3] uses manifold-based affinity learning for postprocessing. These deep learning methods can achieve considerable results in large-scale datasets [17,20].

Cross-Dataset ReID. Cross-dataset ReID is very close to the realistic scenarios, which trains on one dataset and tests on another. Many transfer learning methods [11,24,25] have been adopted for cross-dataset ReID in the hope that labelled data from other datasets can provide transferable identity-discriminative information for the given target dataset. Peng et al. [21] use unsupervised multi-task dictionary learning (UMDL) to learn discriminative representation. Yu et al. [26] use unsupervised camera-specific projection to get the shared space. Generative Adversarial nets (GAN) [12] has also gained promotion in the ReID task recently. Deng et al. [6] propose a similarity preserving generative adversarial network (SPGAN) for domain adaptation. Wei et al. [23] propose a Person Transfer Generative Adversarial Network (PTGAN) to bridge the domain gap between different datasets which relieves the expensive costs of annotating new training samples. Different from [6,23], our SICGAN use extra style consistency constraints to ensure the style-transferred images can be applied to cross-dataset model training.

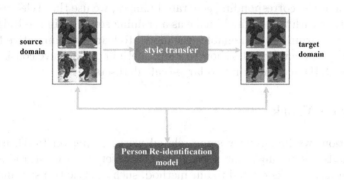

Fig. 2. Pipeline of our framework. First we transfer the style of the target dataset to the source dataset, and then use the style-transferred images together with the source dataset to train the ReID model.

2.2   Image Generation

Style Transfer. Style transfer is the task of generating a new image, whose style is equal to a style image and whose content is equal to a content image. Some works [9,10] have a clear definition of the style and content representation of an image. In [9], Gatys et al. study how it is actually possible to transfer artistic style from one painting to another picture using convolutional neural networks. Frigo et al. [8] propose an effective style transfer algorithm fully based on traditional texture synthesis method. Inspired by [9,10], we use Gram matrix at the image level to represent the style of image.

Image-Image Translation. Recently, there are some methods [16,34] based on Generative Adversarial Networks (GANs) [12] for image-level domain translation. In [34], Zhu et al. present an approach to translate an image from a source domain to a target domain in the absence of paired examples. Image analogy [15] aims to learn a mapping between a pair of source images and target stylised images in a supervised manner. Aytar et al. [2] use a weight-sharing strategy to learn a common representation across domains. Different from the previous methods which mainly consider the quality of the generated samples, some works [6,23] aims at using the style-transferred samples to improve the performance of ReID. However, our method introduce extra style consistency constraints during image generation for cross-dataset ReID.

3   Our Proposed Method

Our method transfers the style of the target dataset to the source dataset, and then uses the source dataset combined with the style-transferred images to learn discriminative feature for ReID. The framework of the proposed approach is shown in Fig. 2, including image generation and feature learning.

Fig. 3. Visual examples of image-image translation. The left five columns map DukeMTMC-reID images to the Market-1501 style, and the right five columns map Market-1501 images to the DukeMTMC-reID style. From top to bottom: (a) original image, (b) output of CycleGAN, (c) output of SICGAN. Images produced by SICGAN are further constrained by style loss.

3.1   CycleGAN Revisit

CycleGAN, as one of the image generation technique, has achieved good performance in many tasks, such as collection style transfer, object transfiguration, season transfer and photo enhancement. It mainly consists of two generator-discriminator pairs, $\{G, D_T\}$ and $\{F, D_S\}$. Generator G is used to translate the source dataset to the target-style. Discriminator D_T is used to determine the real and fake of the target dataset and the G generated images. Similarly, F and D_S complete the reverse transfer and discrimination. The adversarial loss of generator G and discriminator D_T is:

$$L_{Tadv} = E_{y \sim p_y}[(D_T(y) - 1)^2] + E_{x \sim p_x}[(D_T(G(x)))^2] \tag{1}$$

The adversarial loss of generator F and discriminator D_S is:

$$L_{Sadv} = E_{x \sim p_x}[(D_S(x) - 1)^2] + E_{y \sim p_y}[(D_S(F(y)))^2] \tag{2}$$

Where p_x and p_y denote the sample distributions in the source and target dataset.

For the purpose of reducing the space of possible mapping functions, Cycle-GAN also introduces a cycle-consistent loss, which attempts to recover the original image after a cycle of translation and reverse translation. The cycle-consistent loss is:

$$L_{cyc}(G, F) = E_{x \sim p_x}[||F(G(x)) - x||_1] + E_{y \sim p_y}[||G(F(y)) - y||_1] \quad (3)$$

Apart from cycle-consistent loss and adversarial loss, CycleGAN proposes an additional identity loss to encourage the mapping to preserve color composition between the input and output. The identity mapping loss is:

$$L_{identity}(G, F) = E_{x \sim p_x}[||F(x) - x||_1] + E_{y \sim p_y}[||G(y) - y||_1] \quad (4)$$

As shown in Fig. 3(b), CycleGAN can generate relatively realistic images and preserve most ID-related information of original images, which improved the performance of cross-dataset ReID to a certain extent. However, there is still a certain style bias between the generated images and the corresponding dataset, and we can further improve performance by reducing style differences.

3.2 SICGAN

Generally speaking, the images generated by CycleGAN are realistic and preserve a large amount of ID-related information about the original image, but the change in style is not very obvious. As shown in Fig. 3(b), CycleGAN slightly fades the background and changes the lighting. Considering that the decrease in performance of cross-dataset is mainly due to style divergence between different datasets, in order to generate images that can improve the performance of the ReID model, the following requirements should be met: (1) the style-transferred images are realistic. (2) preserve ID-related information between the style-transferred images and the original images, so that they can be used to train the ReID models as the same ID. (3) the style of style-transferred images is consistent with the target dataset. CycleGAN can solve the first two requirements, therefore, we focus on the style transfer between the source dataset and the target dataset. For the purpose of generating target-style images, we propose Style-consistent, Identity-consistent, Cycle-consistent Generative Adversarial Network (SICGAN). Our SICGAN based on CycleGAN pay attention to the style consistency constraints of different images generated by the same generator.

For style constraints, we first need to extract the style representation of the image. Gatys et al. [9,10] found that the extraction of style representation can be done by looking at the spatial correlation of the values within a given feature map, the feature map is usually the output of the network middle layer. Inspired by their style representation manner, we calculate the Gram matrix of the three-channel original image to get the style representation. Different from [9,10], we believe that the original image contains more style information than feature map, which guarantees a better extraction of the style representation of the image. Specifically, in the image generation process, we constrain the Euclidean distance of the style representation from different images generated by the same generator to be minimized. The style loss is:

$$L_{style}(G, F) = \frac{1}{c * m * n}[||M(F(x)) - M(F(y))||_2 + ||M(G(x)) - M(G(y))||_2]$$
(5)

where $M(.)$ is used to get the Gram matrix, c is the number of channel of the image, m is the height of the image, and n is the width of the image. In our setting, they are 3, 256 and 128 respectively. In order to get the Gram matrix of fake image $F(x), F(y), G(x), G(y)$, the two-dimensional pixel value of each channel is expanded into a one-dimensional vector by row. Then each channel vector of a image is dot-producted each other to obtain a $c*c$ matrix. The specific calculation formula is as follows:

$$M_{ij} = \sum_k A_{ik} A_{jk}$$
(6)

where A_{ik} represents the k-th pixel value of the i-th channel in channel vector. During the data generation phase, the overall loss function can be written as:

$$L = L_{Tadv} + L_{Sadv} + \lambda_1 L_{cyc}(G, F) + \lambda_2 L_{identity}(G, F) + \lambda_3 L_{style}(G, F)$$
(7)

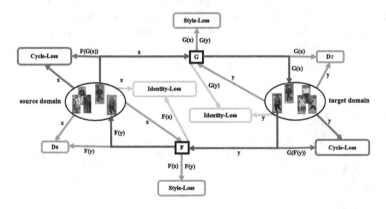

Fig. 4. Our SICGAN consists of two generator-discriminator pairs, $\{G, D_T\}$ and $\{F, D_S\}$. G is used to generate the target-style image, F is the opposite. The adversarial loss, cycle-consistent loss and identity loss here are the same as those used in Cycle-GAN, our style loss is used to constrain the style representation of different images generated by the same generator, such as G(x) and G(y).

where λ_1, λ_2 and λ_3 correspond to the weight of cycle-consistent loss, identity loss and style loss respectively. The image generation process is shown in Fig. 4. To get images that meet the requirements, the parameters of generators G, F and discriminators D_S, D_T are adversarially optimized step by step, and style loss is only used to update the parameters of generator. The image generated by SICGAN is shown in Fig. 3(c). When testing, target-style and source-style images are generated by well-trained generators G and F.

3.3   Feature Learning

Following the pipeline [6], feature learning is the second step for cross-dataset person ReID. But Deng et al. only use the transferred images for feature learning. Considering that the generated image preserves the ID-related information of the original image, we employ the labeled original images and style-transferred images together to learn discriminative features, which makes full use of the original image information and reduce the impact of generating less realistic images. Our pipeline is shown in Fig. 2. Similar to [31], we train a classification network named IDE for ReID embedding learning. The base model is ResNet-50 [13], we retain layer4 of ResNet-50 and its previous structure, adding the global average pooling (GAP) layer and fully-connected (FC) layer whose output dimension is the number of training identities. When testing, given an input image of query, we can extract the 2,048-dim feature after GAP to calculate Euclidean distance from the gallery.

Bottleneck. In order to confirm the performance of the generated image does not depend on the model, we also adopt an improved version of the classification network. Similar to [33], we add a bottleneck after the layer4 of ResNet-50. The bottleneck includes (1) global average pooling (GAP), (2) fully connected layer (FC), (3) batch normalization (BN), (4) ReLu activation function (ReLu), (5) dropout (DP), which used to fuse the learned features. The network structure after adding the bottleneck is shown in Fig. 5. It differs from IDE in that the FC, BN, ReLu, and DP layer of the network structure are newly added. Generally speaking, its performance is higher than IDE.

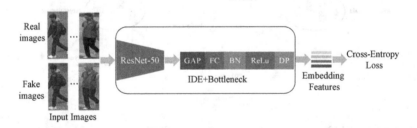

Fig. 5. ReID network structure with bottleneck. Compared to IDE, fully-connected (FC), batch normalization (BN), ReLu activation function (ReLu), and dropout (DP) are newly added layers.

4   Experiment

4.1   Dataset

We evaluate our method on the Market-1501 and DukeMTMC-reID, because both datasets are large-scale and have different styles. Sample images of the two datasets are show in Fig. 1. Their amount of data can train deep learning methods, and different styles can strongly prove the effectiveness of our method. For both datasets, we use rank-1, rank-5, rank-10 accuracy and mean average precision (mAP) for result evaluation.

Market-1501. [30] is collected from six cameras in front of a supermarket in Tsinghua University, and contains 32,668 annotated bounding boxes of 1,501 identities. For evaluation, we employe the same settings as [30], 12,936 images from 751 identities are used for training, and 19,732 images from 750 identities plus some distractors form the gallery. Moreover, 3,368 hand-drawn bounding boxes from 750 identities are used as queries to retrieve the corresponding person images in the gallery. We use the single-query evaluation in our experiment.

DukeMTMC-reID. [32] is a ReID version of the DukeMTMC dataset, which recorded outdoors on the Duke University campus with 8 synchronized cameras. It contains 34,183 image boxes of 1,404 identities. Similar to the division of Market-1501, the dataset contains 16,522 training images from 702 identities, 2,228 query images from another 702 identities and 17,661 gallery images.

4.2 Experiment Settings

The entire experiment includes two steps. Firstly, SICGAN generates realistic images that preserve the ID-related information of the source images and have the same style as the target dataset. Secondly, the original images and the generated images are used together as a training set to train the ReID model. In the second step of training, the generated images and the corresponding original images maintain the same ID.

SICGAN Model. We implement SICGAN with PyTorch to achieve image-image translation. To prove the validity of our method, we adopt the network structure of CycleGAN released by its authors, which consists of a series of building block based on ResNet [13]. When training SICGAN model, we use the training set of Market-1501 and DukeMTMC-reID as transfer objects, the inputs images are resized to 256×128. In all experiment, we empirically set $\lambda_1 = 10, \lambda_2 = 5, \lambda_3 = 5$ in Eq. (7). We make the initial learning rate 0.0002, batch size is 1, and the model stop training after 10 epochs. For generator and discriminator, we use Adam optimizer with the default hyper-parameters $(\eta = 10^{-8}, \beta_1 = 0.9, \beta_2 = 0.999)$. During the testing procedure, we employ the Generator G to get fake DukeMTMC-reID images of Market-1501 style, the Generator F to get fake Market-1501 images of DukeMTMC-reID style.

ReID Model. To test the effectiveness of the generated images, we train a classification network named IDE [31] for ReID embedding learning. The input images are resized to 256×128, and random horizontal flipping for data augmentation are employed during training. We use ResNet-50 as backbone, in which the last fully connected layer has 751 and 702 units for Market-1501 and DukeMTMC-reID, respectively. We set the batch size to 32 and use the SGD (momentum $= 0.9$, weight_decay $= 5e{-}4$, nesterov $=$ True) optimizer to train ReID model. The learning rate starts with 0.001 for ResNet-50 base layers and 0.01 for the full connected layers, and divided by 10 after 40 epochs. We train 60 epochs in total. In testing, we extract the output of the global average pooling (GAP) layer as image descriptor (2,048-dim) and use the Euclidean distance to compute the similarity between images. For ReID network structure with bottleneck, we have the same settings with IDE. Additionally, the output units of FC in bottleneck is 512, the dropout probability is 0.5 and the learning rate of new layer starts with 0.01.

4.3   Evaluation

Evaluate the Effect of CycleGAN. In our experiment, there is a large performance drop when directly using a source-trained model on the target dataset. As show in Table 1, the ReID model trained and tested on Market-1501 achieves 79.16% (IDE(Market)) in rank-1 accuracy, but drops to 43.34% when trained on DukeMTMC-reID and tested on Market-1501 (IDE(Real)).We can see the same phenomenon in Table 2. Following the pipeline of [6], we first translate the labeled images from the source dataset to the target dataset and then use the translated images to train ReID models. We achieve significant performance improvements, training with generated fake DukeMTMC-reID of Market-1501 style (*e.g.*, Table 1 (IDE(Fake))) improved by 7.51% and 3.17% in rank-1 accuracy and mAP compared to direct testing (IDE(Real)). A similar improvement can be observed on DukeMTMC-reID, after the Market-1501 is translated by CycleGAN, the performance gain is +6.35% and +2.75%. This shows that the image generated by CycleGAN has a certain effect on accuracy improvement of the cross-dataset ReID. It is consistent with the experiments reported in [6].

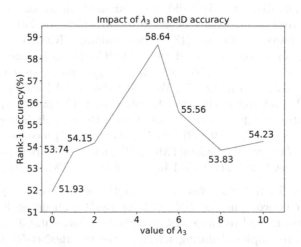

Fig. 6. λ_3 (Eq. 7) *v.s* ReID Rank-1 accuracy of IDE model on Market-1501. A larger λ_3 means larger weight of style loss.

Evaluate the Effect of SICGAN. On top of the CycleGAN baseline, we add style loss to optimize generators. The effectiveness of the proposed SICGAN can be seen in Tables 1 and 2. Compared with CycleGAN, our SICGAN leads to +2.56% and +4.24% in rank-1 accuracy and mAP on Market-1501, and +2.6% and +2.96% on DukeMTMC-reID. The coherent improvement suggests that style consistency constraints on the different samples generated by the same generator are necessary. Our SICGAN generate the target-style images, so that the ReID model can learn the style representation feature of the target dataset. Example of transferred images by SICGAN are show in Fig. 3(c).

Table 1. Comparison of various methods on the Market-1501 dataset. The Market in parentheses indicates that the model is trained using the training set of Market-1501, the Real indicates the training set using the original DukeMTMC-reID, and the Fake indicates the training set using the style-transferred DukeMTMC-reID.

Generate	ReID	Top1	Top5	Top10	mAP
-	IDE(Market)	79.16	87.32	89.28	59.34
-	IDE(Real)	43.34	61.52	68.97	17.31
-	Bottleneck(Real)	46.76	66.27	72.26	20.39
CycleGAN	IDE(Fake)	50.85	66.92	73.29	20.48
CycleGAN	IDE(Real+Fake)	51.93	68.85	76.33	22.85
SICGAN	IDE(Fake)	53.41	70.81	77.19	24.72
SICGAN	IDE(Real+Fake)	58.64	74.94	81.79	26.68
SICGAN	Bottleneck(Real+Fake)	**60.18**	**75.92**	**82.21**	**29.00**

Table 2. Comparison of various methods on the DukeMTMC-reID dataset. The Duke in parentheses indicates that the model is trained using the training set of DukeMTMC-reID, the Real indicates the training set using the original Market-1501, and the Fake indicates the training set using the style-transferred Market-1501.

Generate	ReID	Top1	Top5	Top10	mAP
-	IDE(Duke)	70.94	80.87	84.65	53.49
-	IDE(Real)	36.47	52.51	58.79	19.30
-	Bottleneck(Real)	38.01	53.05	59.91	21.83
CycleGAN	IDE(Fake)	42.82	55.79	61.98	22.05
CycleGAN	IDE(Real+Fake)	43.96	58.25	63.60	23.65
SICGAN	IDE(Fake)	45.42	61.23	66.53	25.01
SICGAN	IDE(Real+Fake)	48.42	63.57	69.27	27.85
SICGAN	Bottleneck(Real+Fake)	**49.82**	**65.66**	**70.86**	**29.23**

Evaluate the Effect of Training Together. Wei et al. [6] only use the generated images to train the ReID model. However, in view of the following fact: (1)

the most ID-related information is retained during image generation, (2) there is always a gap between the generated image and the real image. In view of the above-mentioned facts, we use the original images and the style-transferred fake images together as training set to train the ReID model. As show in Tables 1 and 2, for CycleGAN, we gains +1.08% and +2.37% in rank-1 accuracy and mAP on Market-1501, +1.14% and +1.6% on DukeMTMC-reID. For SICGAN, the gains are 5.23% and 1.96% on Market-1501, 3% and 2.84% on DukeMTMC-reID. When training together, the images generated by SICGAN combined with the original images will get a more significant performance improvement, indicating that the style of images generated by SICGAN is closer to the target images, and the two styles of images together help to learn discriminative features.

Comparison of Different Feature Learning Methods. In this paper, we use two feature learning methods. For comparison with [6], we use the more common IDE [31]. In order to better prove that generated images by SICGAN can effectively improve performance, and do not depend on the selected ReID model, we employ an improved version of the IDE as well. After adding the bottleneck show in Fig. 5, we achieve better accuracy as [33]. As show in Tables 1 and 2, our network achieves 60.18% rank-1 accuracy and 29.00% mAP on Market-1501, 49.82% rank-1 accuracy and 29.23% mAP on DukeMTMC-reID, both higher than IDE, which is consistent with direct testing (Bottleneck(Real)).

Sensitivity of SIGAN to Key Parameters. The weight λ_3 of style loss in Eq. 7 is a key parameter. If $\lambda_3 = 0$, the style loss is not back propagated. If λ_3 gets larger, the weight of style differences in loss calculation increases. We do experiment to verify the impact of λ_3, and results are shown in Fig. 6. When increasing λ_3 to 5, we have much superior accuracy. It indicates that the style loss and the identity loss are equally important.

Table 3. Results on the Market-1501 dataset.

Methods	Top1	Top5	Top10	mAP
BOW [30]	35.8	52.4	60.3	14.8
LOMO [19]	27.2	41.6	49.1	8.0
UMDL [21]	34.5	52.6	59.6	12.4
PUL [7]	45.5	60.7	66.7	20.5
CAMEL [26]	54.5	-	-	26.3
Direct transfer	43.34	61.52	68.97	17.31
SPGAN [6]	51.5	70.1	76.8	22.8
SICGAN(Fake)	53.41	70.81	77.19	24.72
SICGAN(Real+Fake)	58.64	74.94	81.79	26.68
SICGAN(Real+Fake+Bottleneck)	**60.18**	**75.92**	**82.21**	**29.00**

Table 4. Results on the DukeMTMC-reID dataset.

Methods	Top1	Top5	Top10	mAP
BOW [30]	17.1	28.8	34.9	8.3
LOMO [19]	12.3	21.3	26.6	4.8
UMDL [21]	18.5	31.4	37.6	7.3
PUL [7]	30.0	43.4	48.5	16.4
Direct transfer	36.47	52.51	58.79	19.30
SPGAN [6]	41.1	56.6	63.0	22.3
SICGA(Fake)	45.42	61.23	66.53	25.01
SICGAN(Real+Fake)	48.42	63.57	69.27	27.85
SICGAN(Real+Fake+Bottleneck)	**49.82**	**65.66**	**70.86**	**29.23**

4.4 Comparison with State-of-the-Art Methods

We compare the proposed method with the state-of-the-art unsupervised learning method and cross-dataset methods on Market-1501 and DukeMTMC-reID in Tables 3 and 4, respectively.

Market-1501. On Market-1501, we first compare our results with two hand-crafted features, *i.e.*, Bag-of-Words (BoW) [30] and local maximal occurrence (LOMO) [19]. Those two hand-crafted features are directly applied on test dataset without any training process, their inferiority can be clearly observed. We also compare existing unsupervised methods, including the Clustering-based Asymmetric MEtric Learning (CAMEL) [26], UMDL [21], and the Progressive Unsupervised Learning (PUL) [7]. In addition, we compare to data augmentation method for cross-dataset ReID, such as SPGAN [6]. In the single-query setting, our SICGAN achieves 60.18% rank-1 accuracy and 29.00% mAP. It outperforms the second best method (CAMEL) by +5.68% in rank-1 accuracy and +2.70% in mAP. In order to compare with the similar method SPGAN, we use the same settings, using IDE to train the generated image, we get 53.41% and 24.72% in rank-1 accuracy and mAP with fewer model parameters, both higher than SPGAN. The comparisons indicate the competitiveness of the proposed method on Market-1501.

DukeMTMC-reID. On DukeMTMC-reID, we compare the proposed method with BoW [30], LOMO [19], UMDL [21], PUL [7] and SPGAN [6] under the single-query setting. Our proposed method achieve 49.82% in rank-1 accuracy and 29.23% in mAP. Compared with the second best method, *i.e.*, SPGAN, our results are +4.32% higher in rank-1 accuracy and +2.71% in mAP under the same settings. Therefore, the superiority of SICGAN can be concluded.

5   Conclusions

This paper focuses on generating target-style images for cross-dataset person ReID. Models trained on one dataset often failed to generalize well on another due to style diversity. To achieve improved performance in the new dataset, we propose a novel style-transferrable framework to generate target-style images for style adaption. Specifically, we get the style representation by calculating the Gram matrix of the three-channel original image, and then minimize the Euclidean distance of the style representation on different images transferred by the same generator during image generation. Finally, the labeled source dataset combined with style-transferred images are both used for training the ReID models to enhance the generalization ability. We show that the images generated by SICGAN allow the model to learn more discriminative features and yield consistent improvement on different ReID model.

Acknowledgment. This work is supported in part by National Basic Research Program of China (973 Program): 2015CB351802, and Natural Science Foundation of China (NSFC): 61390501, 61876171 and 61572465.

References

1. Ahmed, E., Jones, M., Marks, T.K.: An improved deep learning architecture for person re-identification. In: IEEE Conference on Computer Vision and Pattern Recognition, pp. 3908–3916 (2015)
2. Aytar, Y., Castrejon, L., Vondrick, C., Pirsiavash, H., Torralba, A.: Cross-modal scene networks. arXiv preprint arXiv:1610.09003 (2016)
3. Bai, S., Bai, X., Tian, Q.: Scalable person re-identification on supervised smoothed manifold. In: IEEE Conference on Computer Vision and Pattern Recognition, pp. 2530–2539 (2017)
4. Chen, W., Chen, X., Zhang, J., Huang, K.: Beyond triplet loss: a deep quadruplet network for person re-identification. In: IEEE Conference on Computer Vision and Pattern Recognition, pp. 403–412 (2017)
5. Chung, D., Tahboub, K., Delp, E.J.: A two stream siamese convolutional neural network for person re-identification. In: IEEE Conference on Computer Vision and Pattern Recognition, pp. 1983–1991 (2017)
6. Deng, W., Zheng, L., Ye, Q., Kang, G., Yang, Y., Jiao, J.: Image-image domain adaptation with preserved self-similarity and domain-dissimilarity for person reidentification. In: IEEE Conference on Computer Vision and Pattern Recognition, pp. 994–1003 (2018)
7. Fan, H., Zheng, L., Yang, Y.: Unsupervised person re-identification: clustering and fine-tuning. arXiv preprint arXiv:1705.10444 (2017)
8. Frigo, O., Sabater, N., Delon, J., Hellier, P.: Split and match: example-based adaptive patch sampling for unsupervised style transfer. In: IEEE Conference on Computer Vision and Pattern Recognition, pp. 553–561 (2016)
9. Gatys, L.A., Ecker, A.S., Bethge, M.: A neural algorithm of artistic style. arXiv preprint arXiv:1508.06576 (2015)
10. Gatys, L.A., Ecker, A.S., Bethge, M.: Image style transfer using convolutional neural networks. In: IEEE Conference on Computer Vision and Pattern Recognition, pp. 2414–2423 (2016)

11. Geng, M., Wang, Y., Xiang, T., Tian, Y.: Deep transfer learning for person re-identification. arXiv preprint arXiv:1611.05244 (2016)
12. Goodfellow, I., et al.: Generative adversarial nets. In: Advances in Neural Information Processing Systems, pp. 2672–2680 (2014)
13. He, K., Zhang, X., Ren, S., Sun, J.: Deep residual learning for image recognition. In: IEEE Conference on Computer Vision and Pattern Recognition, pp. 770–778 (2016)
14. Hermans, A., Beyer, L., Leibe, B.: In defense of the triplet loss for person re-identification. arXiv preprint arXiv:1703.07737 (2017)
15. Hertzmann, A., Jacobs, C.E., Oliver, N., Curless, B., Salesin, D.H.: Image analogies. In: Conference on Computer Graphics and Interactive Techniques, pp. 327–340 (2001)
16. Isola, P., Zhu, J.Y., Zhou, T., Efros, A.A.: Image-to-image translation with conditional adversarial networks. In: IEEE Conference on Computer Vision and Pattern Recognition, pp. 1125–1134 (2017)
17. Ji, R., Liu, H., Cao, L., Liu, D., Wu, Y., Huang, F.: Toward optimal manifold hashing via discrete locally linear embedding. IEEE Trans. Image Process. **26**, 5411–5420 (2017)
18. Li, W., Zhao, R., Xiao, T., Wang, X.: DeepReID: deep filter pairing neural network for person re-identification. In: IEEE Conference on Computer Vision and Pattern Recognition, pp. 152–159 (2014)
19. Liao, S., Hu, Y., Zhu, X., Li, S.Z.: Person re-identification by local maximal occurrence representation and metric learning. In: IEEE Conference on Computer Vision and Pattern Recognition, pp. 2197–2206 (2015)
20. Liu, H., Ji, R., Wang, J., Shen, C.: Ordinal constraint binary coding for approximate nearest neighbor search. IEEE Trans. Pattern Anal. Mach. Intell. (2018). https://doi.org/10.1109/TPAMI.2018.2819978
21. Peng, P., et al.: Unsupervised cross-dataset transfer learning for person re-identification. In: IEEE Conference on Computer Vision and Pattern Recognition, pp. 1306–1315 (2016)
22. Wang, G., Yuan, Y., Chen, X., Li, J., Zhou, X.: Learning discriminative features with multiple granularities for person re-identification. arXiv preprint arXiv:1804.01438 (2018)
23. Wei, L., Zhang, S., Gao, W., Tian, Q.: Person transfer GAN to bridge domain gap for person re-identification. In: IEEE Conference on Computer Vision and Pattern Recognition, pp. 79–88 (2017)
24. Xiao, T., Li, H., Ouyang, W., Wang, X.: Learning deep feature representations with domain guided dropout for person re-identification. In: IEEE Conference on Computer Vision and Pattern Recognition, pp. 1249–1258 (2016)
25. Yosinski, J., Clune, J., Bengio, Y., Lipson, H.: How transferable are features in deep neural networks? In: Advances in Neural Information Processing Systems, pp. 3320–3328 (2014)
26. Yu, H.X., Wu, A., Zheng, W.S.: Cross-view asymmetric metric learning for unsupervised person re-identification. In: IEEE Conference on Computer Vision and Pattern Recognition, pp. 994–1002 (2017)
27. Yu, R., Dou, Z., Bai, S., Zhang, Z., Xu, Y., Bai, X.: Hard-aware point-to-set deep metric for person re-identification. arXiv preprint arXiv:1807.11206 (2018)
28. Zhang, X., et al.: AlignedReID: surpassing human-level performance in person re-identification. arXiv preprint arXiv:1711.08184 (2017)

29. Zhao, L., Li, X., Wang, J., Zhuang, Y.: Deeply-learned part-aligned representations for person re-identification. In: IEEE International Conference on Computer Vision, pp. 3219–3228 (2017)
30. Zheng, L., Shen, L., Tian, L., Wang, S., Wang, J., Tian, Q.: Scalable person re-identification: a benchmark. In: IEEE International Conference on Computer Vision, pp. 1116–1124 (2015)
31. Zheng, L., Yang, Y., Hauptmann, A.G.: Person re-identification: past, present and future. arXiv preprint arXiv:1610.02984 (2016)
32. Zheng, Z., Zheng, L., Yang, Y.: Unlabeled samples generated by GAN improve the person re-identification baseline in vitro. In: IEEE International Conference on Computer Vision, pp. 3754–3762 (2017)
33. Zhong, Z., Zheng, L., Zheng, Z., Li, S., Yang, Y.: Camera style adaptation for person re-identification. In: IEEE Conference on Computer Vision and Pattern Recognition, pp. 5157–5166 (2018)
34. Zhu, J.Y., Park, T., Isola, P., Efros, A.A.: Unpaired image-to-image translation using cycle-consistent adversarial networks. In: IEEE International Conference on Computer Vision, pp. 2223–2232 (2017)

Automatic Graphics Program Generation Using Attention-Based Hierarchical Decoder

Zhihao Zhu, Zhan Xue, and Zejian Yuan$^{(\boxtimes)}$

Institute of Artificial Intelligence and Robotics,
School of Electronic and Information Engineering,
Xi'an Jiaotong University, Xi'an, China
{zzh123,xx674967}@stu.xjtu.edu.cn, yuan.ze.jian@xjtu.edu.cn

Abstract. Recent progress on deep learning has made it possible to automatically transform the screenshot of Graphic User Interface (GUI) into code by using the encoder-decoder framework. While the commonly adopted image encoder (e.g., CNN network), might be capable of extracting image features to the desired level, interpreting these abstract image features into hundreds of tokens of code puts a particular challenge on the decoding power of the RNN-based code generator. Considering the code used for describing GUI is usually hierarchically structured, we propose a new attention-based hierarchical code generation model, which can describe GUI images in a finer level of details, while also being able to generate hierarchically structured code in consistency with the hierarchical layout of the graphic elements in the GUI. Our model follows the encoder-decoder framework, all the components of which can be trained jointly in an end-to-end manner. The experimental results show that our method outperforms other current state-of-the-art methods on both a publicly available GUI-code dataset as well as a dataset established by our own.

1 Introduction

Using machine learning technologies to generate codes of Graphic User Interface automatically is a relatively new field of research. Generally, implementing the GUI is often a time-consuming and tedious work for the front-end developers, which disputes them from devoting more time to developing the real functionalities and logics of the software. So developing systems to transform the GUI mockup into programming code automatically shows a very promising application potential.

Recent examples of using machine learning technologies to automatically generate programs in a human-readable format are [4,5], who use gradient descent

---

This work was supported by the National Key R&D Program of China (No. 2016YFB1001001) and the National Natural Science Foundation of China (No. 91648121, No. 61573280).

C. V. Jawahar et al. (Eds.): ACCV 2018, LNCS 11366, pp. 181–196, 2019.
https://doi.org/10.1007/978-3-030-20876-9_12

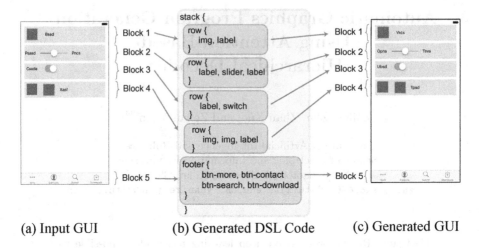

(a) Input GUI   (b) Generated DSL Code   (c) Generated GUI

Fig. 1. An example of the code generated by our model given an input GUI screenshot. (a) gives an example of how a GUI is divided into blocks. (b) shows the generated DSL code. (c) is a rendered GUI based on the generated DSL code.

to induce source code from input-output examples via differentiable interpreters. However, their performance has been proven by [11] to be inferior to discrete search-based techniques that are widely used by the programming language community. Another work is the DeepCoder [2], a system attempting to generate computer programs by leveraging statistical predictions to augment traditional search techniques. Its ability to model complex programming languages is however limited by its reliance on the *Domain Specific Languages (DSL)*, which are designed only for a specialized domain.

In the task of generating codes from visual inputs, there has been only a few numbers of works [3,8], among which, pix2code [3] is the most similar to ours. [3] employs a feedback mechanism, where decoding process can be proceeded iteratively with two different levels of LSTMs: an "encoding" LSTM for encoding the already generated code sequence to reduce the "decoding" LSTM's burden for learning long sequence relationships. The "decoding" LSTM is for the code sequence generation, and it then feeds the decoded token sequence back into the "encoding" LSTM to form a feedback loop. By employing the feedback mechanism, [3] is able to generate much longer word/token sequence than other single-pass based methods. However, their method needs to pre-fix the maximum sequence length that the "encoding" LSTM can generate. In other words, the range of the code length should be pre-specified, which reduces their method's extensibility and generalization ability. Another apparent defect of their methods is that they didn't take into consideration the hierarchical structure of GUI and its code, which limits their performance in generating accurate graphics programs.

To tackle the above problems, we propose a new method for automatic graphics program generation. It not only can well solve the long-term dependency problem, but can also capture the hierarchical structure of the code by explicitly representing the code generation process in a hierarchical approach. Our method reasons about the code sequence using a hierarchical decoder, generating graphic programs block by block. Figure 1 shows an example of GUI and its corresponding code, as well as the approach for dividing the GUI into blocks. The detailed DSL code generation process is as follows: first, a first-stage LSTM is used to decode image's visual contents in the block level, with its every hidden state containing general context information of that block. Then, we feed the first-stage LSTM's hidden state as well as image's convolutional features into an attention model to select the most important parts of the convolutional features, which are then input into the second-stage LSTM as context information to generate code tokens for the corresponding block.

The experimental results on a benchmark dataset provided by [3] well demonstrate the effectiveness of our method: we perform better than current state-of-the-art methods across all three sub-datasets: iOS, Android, and Web. Besides, to further illustrate our proposed model's advantage in dealing with more complex GUIs, we establish a new dataset containing GUI screenshots that have more graphic elements and more diversity in graphic elements' style and spatial layout. On this dataset, our method outperforms the compared methods even by a larger margin.

2 Related Work

Automatically generating code for the GUI screenshot is very similar to the task of image captioning [9,10,16,17,21–23], both of which need first to understand image's visual contents, and then interpret them into the language form. Our proposed method for generating GUI code follows the encoder-decoder framework and incorporates the attention mechanism. So we mainly introduce the related work about automatic GUI code generation with them.

Most recent neural network-based methods for generating image descriptions follow the encoder-decoder framework, which first uses a deep CNN to encode an image into an abstract representation, and then uses a RNN to decode that representation into a semantically-meaningful sentence which can describe the image in details. Chen et al. [7] learned a bi-directional mapping between images and their sentence-based descriptions using RNN. Mao et al. [15] propose a Multimodal Recurrent Neural Network (MRNN) that uses an RNN to learn the text embedding, and a CNN to learn the image representation. [20] and [18] show that high-level semantic attributes can boost the image caption generation performance. Inspired by the successful application of attention mechanism in machine language translation [1], spatial attention has also been widely adopted in the task of image captioning [6,14,19]. However, due to the limited capability of a single LSTM to learn the long sequence dependency, the above methods are not able to generate very long image descriptions. It's also a bottleneck of these

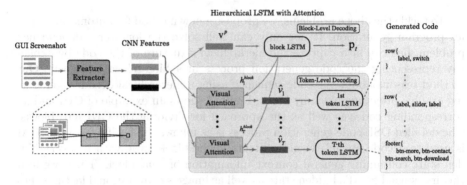

Fig. 2. Overview of our proposed model for automatic graphics program generation. The input GUI screenshot is first fed into a CNN to obtain high-level visual features. All the visual features are projected to $\mathbb{R}^D$, pooled to give a compact image representation, and is then fed into block LSTM as input. Block LSTM determines the number of blocks to generate based on p_t, and generates the guiding vector $\boldsymbol{h}_t^{block}$, which is fed into the attention model for selecting CNN features to feed into t-th token LSTM to generate codes for the t-th block.

methods for interpreting more complex GUIs into codes, which usually contain hundreds of thousands of tokens.

To tackle the above issue, Jonathan et al. [13] employ the hierarchically structured LSTMs, and their model is able to generate paragraph-level image descriptions. Basically, in their work, two levels of LSTM-based language decoders are used: a first-stage LSTM captures the general information of the image and stores context information of each sentence in its hidden states. Then, a second-stage LSTM is used to decode the first-stage LSTM's hidden states into different sentence in a paragraph. Our method for automatic GUI code generation also employs a similar hierarchical approach. However, in our method, first-stage LSTM's hidden states are only used in the attention network to help select the CNN features, which are then fed into the second-stage LSTM for code generation. Our experimental results show that the first-stage LSTM's hidden states, which only contain a coarse level of visual information, are insufficient for guiding the second-stage LSTM to generate accurate token sequences. We do obtain better results by feeding the more information-carrying raw CNN features into the second-stage LSTM.

The contributions of our work are as follows: (1) We are the first to propose using a hierarchical approach for generating programs from the graphics user interface. (2) We propose a new method to integrate attention mechanism with hierarchical LSTM, which outperforms current state-of-the-art methods that also use hierarchical LSTM. (3) We introduce a new dataset named PixCo-e *(details in Sect. 4.1)*, which contains GUI-code examples from three different platforms: iOS, Android, and Web.

3   Proposed Method

3.1   Overview

Our method takes a GUI screenshot as input, generating a body of programming languages to describe it, and is designed to take advantage of the hierarchical structure of both the GUI and the graphics programs. Figure 2 provides an overview of our attention-based hierarchical code generation model. We first use the intermediate filter responses from a Convolutional Neural Network (CNN) to build a high-level abstract visual representation of the image, denoted by ν, which are then taken as input by a hierarchical LSTM composed of two levels: a block LSTM and a token LSTM. The block LSTM receives the image's visual features as input, and decides how many code blocks to generate in the resulting program. The hidden state h_t^{block} of the block LSTM at each time step t is then fed into an attention model as a guiding vector to select the most important sub-regions in the visual feature map. Given the selected visual features as context, a token LSTM generates the code for the corresponding block.

3.2   Vision Encoder: Convolutional Features

We first follow [3] to design a lightweight *DSL* to describe GUIs. Generally, our method generates a computer program as a long sequence of 1-of-K encoded tokens:

$$q = \{\mathbf{q}_1, \mathbf{q}_2, ...\mathbf{q}_C\}, \quad \mathbf{q}_i \in \mathbb{R}^K,$$

where C is the total number of tokens in the program, and K is the size of the token vocabulary.

We use a convolutional neural network as the image encoder to extract a set of visual feature vectors $\nu = [\mathbf{v}_1, \mathbf{v}_2, ..., \mathbf{v}_L]$, and each $\mathbf{v}_i$ is a D-dimensional representation corresponding to a certain part of the image. To obtain a correspondence between the feature vector and each sub-region in the 2-D image, we extract features from a lower convolutional layer instead of using the final fully connected layer.

Region Pooling: We want to aggregate all the visual features $\nu = [\mathbf{v}_1, \mathbf{v}_2, ..., \mathbf{v}_L]$ into a single pooled vector $\mathbf{v}^p \in \mathbb{R}^D$ that compactly describes the content of the image, which later will be fed into the block LSTM as context. The pooled vector $\mathbf{v}^p$ is computed by taking an element-wise maximum on each channel: $v^{p,c} = max\{v_1^c, v_2^c, ..., v_L^c\}$, where $v^{p,c}$ and v_i^c represent the c-th channel of $\mathbf{v}^p$ and $\mathbf{v}_i$, respectively.

3.3   Attention-Based Hierarchical Decoder

The extracted visual features are fed into a hierarchical visual decoder model composed of two modules: a block LSTM and a token LSTM. The block LSTM is responsible for determining the total number of blocks that the entire program will have, and for generating a H-dimension guiding vector for each of these blocks. Given the guiding vector, the token LSTM then uses the attention mechanism to select the most important visual features as the context information at each time step to generate code tokens of that block.

Block LSTM. The block LSTM is a single-layer LSTM with a hidden size of $H = 512$. Its initial hidden state and cell state are both set to zero. The block LSTM receives the pooled feature vector $\mathbf{v}^p$ as the initial input, and in turn produces a sequence of hidden states $\boldsymbol{H}^{block} = [\boldsymbol{h}_1^{block}, \boldsymbol{h}_2^{block}, ...]$, each corresponds to a single block in the program. The overall working flow of the block LSTM is governed by the following equations:

$$\boldsymbol{x}_0 = W_{x,v} \cdot \mathbf{v}^p, \tag{1}$$

$$\boldsymbol{x}_t = W_{x,o} \cdot \boldsymbol{o}_{t-1}, \tag{2}$$

$$\boldsymbol{h}_t^{block} = LSTM(\boldsymbol{h}_{t-1}^{block}, \boldsymbol{x}_t), \tag{3}$$

$$\boldsymbol{o}_t = \sigma(W_{o,h} \cdot \boldsymbol{h}_t^{block}), \tag{4}$$

where Ws denote weights. $\sigma(\cdot)$ stands for sigmoid function, and $\boldsymbol{o}_t$ is the output of block LSTM at each time step. For clearness, we do not explicitly represent the bias term in our paper.

Each hidden state $\boldsymbol{h}_t^{block}$ is used in two ways: First, a linear projection from $\boldsymbol{h}_t^{block}$ with a logistic classifier produces a distribution p_t over the two states {CONTINUE $= 0$, STOP $= 1$}, which determine whether the t-th block is the last block in the program. Second, the hidden state $\boldsymbol{h}_t^{block}$ is fed into an attention network to select specific CNN features, which are input into the following token LSTM as context information. Each element $\boldsymbol{h}_i^{block}$ in $\boldsymbol{h}^{block}$ contains information about the input visual features with a strong focus on parts surrounding each specific block.

Token LSTM. Once the block LSTM's hidden states are obtained, we use the following approach to select the CNN features to feed into the token LSTM: We first reshape the convolutional visual features $\nu = [\mathbf{v}_1, \mathbf{v}_2, ..., \mathbf{v}_L]$ by flattening its width W and height H, where $L = W \cdot H$. Then, we use a multi-layer perceptron with a softmax output to generate the attention distribution $\boldsymbol{\alpha} = \{\alpha_1, \alpha_2, ..., \alpha_L\}$ over the image regions. Mathematically, our attention model can be represented as:

$$e_t = f_{MLP}((W_{e,v}\boldsymbol{v}) + (W_{e,h}h_t^{block})) \tag{5}$$

$$\boldsymbol{\alpha}_t = softmax(W_s e_t) \tag{6}$$

$$\widehat{\mathbf{v}}_t = \sum_{i=1}^{L} \alpha_{i,t}\mathbf{v}_i \tag{7}$$

Where $f_{MLP}(\cdot)$ represents a multi-layer perceptron. We follow the "soft" approach as illustrated in Eq. (7) to gather all the visual features using the weighted sum, and $\hat{\mathbf{v}}_t$ stands for the selected visual features that will be fed into the t-th token LSTM as context information.

The token LSTM is a two-layered LSTM with hidden size of $H = 512$. Notice that there are multiple token LSTMs, and the total number of token LSTM equals the total number of blocks. Each token LSTM receives the selected visual features $\hat{\mathbf{v}}$ as its initial input, and is responsible for generating code for a block. Token LSTM's subsequent inputs are the embedding form of the output token generated in the previous time step. The hidden state h_t^{token} of the second LSTM layer is used to predict a distribution over the tokens in the vocabulary, and a special END token signals the end of a block.

After each token LSTM has generated the codes of their corresponding blocks, these blocks of code are concatenated to form the complete GUI program.

3.4   Training

The use of hierarchical LSTM makes it possible to train the entire model in an end-to-end manner. Training data consists of (x, y) pairs, where x represents the input GUI screenshot and y is the code for that GUI. Different from [3], who used a fix-sized sliding window to obtain slices of code to feed into their "encoding" LSTM at different training iteration, our method only needs to feed the entire body of code into the model once.

Because we use the same *DSL* as the intermediate programming language to describe GUIs across all three platforms, we follow a consistent rule to divide the codes in the training dataset into blocks: we first ignore the "stack" token at the beginning of each program body, as well as its corresponding open brace "{" and ending brace "}". Besides of these two special braces, each one of the other open braces signals the beginning of a block, and the corresponding ending brace signals the end of that block. We then manually insert a BLOCK-END token at the end of each block. After the division, we assume that the whole program contains S blocks, and the i-th block has N_i tokens, and y_{ij} is the j-th token of the i-th block.

We then unroll the block LSTM for S time steps, providing a distribution p_i over the {CONTINUE $= 0$, STOP $= 1$} states for each block. Each block LSTM's hidden state is used for selecting the visual features, which are later fed into S copies of token LSTM to produce distribution q_{ij} over each token. Our training loss for the example pair (x, y) is a sum of two cross entropy functions: a block loss l_{block} on the stopping distribution p_i, and a token loss l_{token} on the token distribution q_{ij}:

$$L = \sum_{i=1}^{S} l_{block}(p_i, g_i) + \sum_{i=1}^{S} \sum_{j=1}^{N_i} l_{token}(q_{ij}, y_{ij}) \tag{8}$$

where g_i is the groundtruth distribution of the {CONTINUE $= 0$, STOP $= 1$} states for i-th block, and y_{ij} is the groundtruth distribution over j-th token in i-th block.

4   Experiment

4.1   Setup

Data: We implement the proposed automatic graphic program generation model on two datasets, both of which are composed of GUI screenshots and the corresponding source codes.

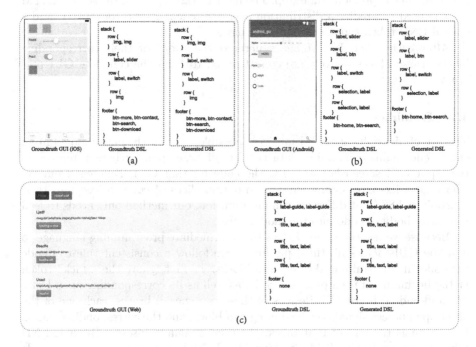

Fig. 3. Qualitative results of our model on the PixCo dataset. DSL code generated by our method (black), groundtruth DSL code (blue), GUI screenshots are shown. (a), (b), (c) represent examples from iOS, Android and Web platforms respectively. (Color figure online)

(1) The first one is a public dataset[1] provided by [3]. For readability, we denote this dataset as PixCo dataset. It consists of three sub-datasets, corresponding to the GUI-code pairs in three different platforms: iOS, Android, and Web. Each sub-dataset has 1500 GUI-code pairs for training and 250 GUI-code pairs for testing.

(2) The second one is our own dataset: PixCo-e dataset. The reason for establishing this new dataset is that the GUI examples in the PixCo dataset are relatively too simple, while the real-world GUIs contain much more graphic elements, and

---

[1] https://github.com/tonybeltramelli/pix2code/tree/master/datasets.

have more complex visual layout. The GUIs in our PixCo-e dataset keep all the basic graphic elements used in the PixCo dataset, such as labels, sliders, switches, but the difference is that each GUI in our PixCO-e dataset contains much more graphic elements and the visual layout is more complex *(examples can be seen in Figs. 5 and 6)*. Similar to PixCo, PixCo-e is also composed of three sub-datasets of GUI-code pairs corresponding to iOS, Android, and Web platforms. Each subset is comprised of 3000 GUI-code pairs for training and 500 GUI-code pairs for testing.

Note that we follow the same rule illustrated in *Sect.* 3.4 to divide the codes into blocks for both datasets. *(The code and dataset are published in[2])*

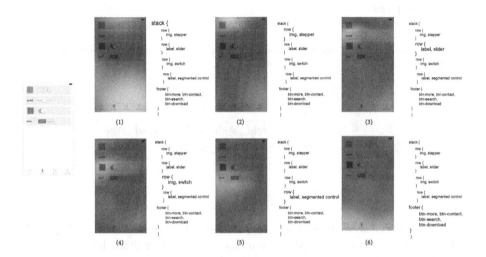

Fig. 4. Attention over time. As the model generates each block, its attention changes to reflect the relevant parts of the image. Brighter areas indicate where the attentions are paid, while darker areas are less attended. The orange noted codes are the blocks generated at the current step. (Color figure online)

Implementation Details: We first re-size the input images to 256 × 256 pixels and then the pixel values are normalized. For the encoding part, for a fair comparison, we employ the same CNN-based encoder architecture adopted by [3], which consists of three convolutional layers, with widths of 32, 64 and 128, respectively, and two fully-connected layers. For the decoding part, the dimensions of both block LSTM's and token LSTM's inputs are set to 512, and *sigmoid* is used as the nonlinear activation function. Moreover, as the size of our token vocabulary is small, we directly use the token-level language modeling with a discrete input of one-hot encoded vector.

In the training procedure, we use Adam algorithm [12] for model updating with a mini-batch size of 128. We set the model's learning rate to 0.001 and the

---

[2] https://github.com/ZhihaoZhu/Auto-GUI-Code-Generation.

dropout rate to 0.5. Using a single NVIDIA TITAN X GPU, the whole training process takes about three hours on the PixCo dataset and six hours on our PixCo-e dataset.

Baseline Methods: To demonstrate the effectiveness of our method, we also present the results generated by two baseline methods. Notice that two baseline methods are trained and tested on the same datasets, and all the hyper-parameters and CNN architectures remain the same for the two baseline models.

(Baseline-1:) The first baseline method follows a simple encoder-decoder architecture, where a CNN is used to encode the pixel information into the high-level visual features, and a single-layer LSTM is used to decode these features into the token sequence.

Table 1. Comparison of the performance in block partitioning accuracies on PixCo and PixCo-e datasets by baseline-2 method and our method.

Dataset type	Accuracy of block partitioning (%)					
	PixCo			PixCo-e		
	iOS	Android	Web	iOS	Android	Web
Baseline-2	90.2	91.4	93.3	84.4	85.1	90.0
Ours	90.7	91.9	94.0	85.1	85.9	91.5

(Baseline-2:) The second baseline method follows the hierarchical LSTM-based architecture. It also first encodes the image's pixel information into high-level visual features. Then, the visual features are pooled to obtain a more compact representation, which is then fed into a two-stage hierarchical LSTM. Compared to ours, the only difference of the hierarchical LSTM used in baseline-2 is that the first-stage LSTM's hidden states at each time step are directly fed into the second-stage LSTM as context, without passing through any other modules.

4.2   Effect of Block LSTM

As both of our method and the baseline-2 method generate programs in a block-by-block way, we first want to test two methods' accuracy in partitioning programs into the right number of blocks. We calculate the block partitioning accuracy A_{bp} by following equations:

$$A_{bp} = \frac{1}{G} \sum_{i=1}^{G} f(c_p^i - c_{gt}^i), \tag{9}$$

$$f(x) = \begin{cases} 1, & |x| = 0 \\ 0, & other \end{cases}, \tag{10}$$

where G represents the number of examples in a dataset. c_p^i is the generated number of blocks, and c_{gt}^i is the ground-truth number of blocks.

Table 1 illustrates the block partitioning accuracies achieved by the baseline-2 method as well as our method. We note that two methods can both partition the program into blocks in a satisfying manner. And the performance of two methods are very close, which can be explained as follows: two models' ability in correctly partitioning the programs is mainly trained via minimizing the block loss l_{block} as in Eq. (8). During training, this loss is directly passed to the first-stage LSTM without going through models' other modules (e.g., Attention network, second-stage LSTM...), where lies two models' main structural differences. Thus, by trained on the same dataset, the first-stage LSTMs in two models are equipped with very similar capabilities in correctly partitioning programs into blocks.

Table 2. Performance of our proposed method on the test dataset, comparing with the baseline-1, baseline-2 and pix2code [3] methods. All four methods use the greedy search strategy.

Dataset type		Error (%)			
		pix2code [3]	baseline-1	baseline-2	Ours
PixCo	iOS	22.73	37.94	20.90	**19.00**
	Android	22.34	36.83	21.72	**18.65**
	Web	12.14	29.77	11.92	**11.50**
PixCo-e	iOS	36.4	53.21	29.43	**26.79**
	Android	36.94	54.75	29.11	**26.10**
	Web	29.47	43.60	22.70	**18.31**

Table 3. Comparison of our method's performance by using different search strategies: "greedy" represents greedy-based method, "beam-3" and "beam-5" stand for beam search strategy using beam size of 3 and 5, respectively.

Dataset type		Error (%)		
		Ours		
		greedy	beam-3	beam-5
PixCo	iOS	19.00	**17.90**	17.43
	Android	18.65	18.20	**16.31**
	Web	11.50	11.23	**10.88**
PixCo-e	iOS	26.79	**23.40**	23.62
	Android	26.10	27.20	**26.78**
	Web	18.31	17.25	**16.11**

4.3   Quantitative Evaluation Results

Table 2 compares our method to the pix2code [3] and two baseline methods on the PixCo dataset as well as our PixCo-e dataset. The quality of the generated code is evaluated by computing the classification error for each sampled token. While the length of the generated token sequence might differ from the ground truth, we still count those unmatched tokens as errors.

When comparing our method with pix2code [3], we first note that our method outperforms theirs across all three sub-datasets on the PixCo dataset. It's worth noting that on the web sub-dataset, the performance difference between the two methods is very minor. Actually, the average *HTML/CSS* code length used to implement web GUI is much shorter (37 tokens/GUI) than the *storyboard* code for iOS (51 tokens/GUI) and *XML* code for Android (53 tokens/GUI). The better performance in the iOS/Android platforms who have longer code length demonstrates our model's advantage in interpreting more complex GUI and handling longer sequence dependency. This can be further illustrated by our model's even lower error rates across all three platforms in the PixCo-e dataset. Note that compared to the PixCo dataset, the average code length in PixCo-e dataset is much longer: iOS (109 tokens/GUI), Android (112 tokens/GUI) and web (86 tokens/GUI).

When comparing our method to the baseline-2 method, which also employs a hierarchical architecture, we note that our method still performs better across all the platforms in both two datasets. This well demonstrates that when using the same CNN, adding attention mechanism can boost the hierarchical model's performance in generating accurate token sequences.

Table 3 compares the performance of our method when using different search strategies during sampling. We note that better performance is achieved by using the beam search strategy.

4.4   Qualitative Evaluation Results

Figure 3 shows examples of the GUI screenshots, ground-truth DSL codes as well as the DSL codes generated by our model. What's more, we also show in Fig. 4 the intermediate dynamic attention process during the code generation. As we can see, the model is able to learn proper alignments between the code blocks and their corresponding spatial areas in the GUI screenshot.

To better compare the qualitative results achieved by our method and the current state-of-the-art method, we render the DSL codes generated by two methods into GUIs. Figures 5 and 6 show the examples of iOS and Web examples. Note that we use the same approach as [3] to ignore the actual textual value and assign the text contents in the label randomly. We observe that on the PixCo dataset, despite some occasional problems like misplacement and wrong styles of certain graphic elements, the results output by pix2code [3] and our model are both very close to the ground truth. This proves that two

(a) Groundtruth GUI

(a) Groundtruth GUI

(b) Generated GUI by Pix2code [3]

(b) Generated GUI by Pix2code [3]

(c) Generated GUI by Ours

(c) Generated GUI by Ours

Fig. 5. Experiment samples from the web-based GUI dataset. The examples on the left column are form the PixCo dataset and the examples on the right column are from the PixCo-e dataset.

models can both learn simple GUI layout in a satisfying manner. However, on the PixCo-e dataset where the GUIs get more complicated, we note that the quality of the GUIs generated by pix2code [3] drops drastically and is clearly inferior to ours: many graphic elements from the input GUI are even not presented in the GUI generated by [3], while our model can preserve and recover most of the visual details in the input GUI. Qualitative evaluation results on two different datasets demonstrate our model's advantage in interpreting more complex GUIs.

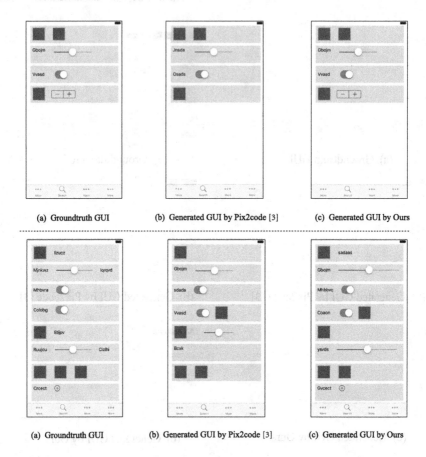

(a) Groundtruth GUI   (b) Generated GUI by Pix2code [3]   (c) Generated GUI by Ours

(a) Groundtruth GUI   (b) Generated GUI by Pix2code [3]   (c) Generated GUI by Ours

Fig. 6. Experiment samples from the iOS-based GUI dataset. The examples on the upper row are form the PixCo dataset and the examples on the bottom row are from the PixCo-e dataset.

5   Conclusion

In this paper, we propose a novel method for automatically generating the code of GUI. Our method is able to achieve state-of-art performance on a benchmark GUI-code dataset as well as a dataset established by our own. Our model used a hierarchically-structured decoder integrated with attention mechanism, capable of better capturing the hierarchical layout of the GUI and the code. Our method is proven to be very effective in solving the long-term dependency problem and is able to generate codes for complex GUIs accurately. For the next steps, we plan to experiment with new methods that can recognize and segregate the overlapped graphic elements and generate the correct code to describe them.

References

1. Bahdanau, D., Cho, K., Bengio, Y.: Neural machine translation by jointly learning to align and translate. CoRR abs/1409.0473 (2014)
2. Balog, M., Gaunt, A.L., Brockschmidt, M., Nowozin, S., Tarlow, D.: Deepcoder: learning to write programs. CoRR abs/1611.01989 (2016)
3. Beltramelli, T.: pix2code: generating code from a graphical user interface screenshot. CoRR abs/1705.07962 (2017)
4. Bosnjak, M., Rocktäschel, T., Naradowsky, J., Riedel, S.: Programming with a differentiable forth interpreter. In: Proceedings of the 34th International Conference on Machine Learning, ICML 2017, 6–11 August 2017, Sydney, NSW, Australia, pp. 547–556 (2017)
5. Bunel, R.R., Desmaison, A., Mudigonda, P.K., Kohli, P., Torr, P.H.S.: Adaptive neural compilation. In: Advances in Neural Information Processing Systems 29: Annual Conference on Neural Information Processing Systems 2016, 5–10 December 2016, Barcelona, Spain, pp. 1444–1452 (2016)
6. Chen, L., et al.: SCA-CNN: spatial and channel-wise attention in convolutional networks for image captioning. In: 2017 IEEE Conference on Computer Vision and Pattern Recognition, CVPR 2017, 21–26 July 2017, Honolulu, HI, USA, pp. 6298–6306 (2017)
7. Chen, X., Zitnick, C.L.: Learning a recurrent visual representation for image caption generation. CoRR abs/1411.5654 (2014)
8. Ellis, K., Ritchie, D., Solar-Lezama, A., Tenenbaum, J.B.: Learning to infer graphics programs from hand-drawn images. CoRR abs/1707.09627 (2017)
9. Fu, K., Jin, J., Cui, R., Sha, F., Zhang, C.: Aligning where to see and what to tell: image captioning with region-based attention and scene-specific contexts. IEEE Trans. Pattern Anal. Mach. Intell. $39(12)$, 2321–2334 (2017)
10. Gan, Z., et al.: Semantic compositional networks for visual captioning. CoRR abs/1611.08002 (2016)
11. Gaunt, A.L., et al.: TerpreT: a probabilistic programming language for program induction. CoRR abs/1608.04428 (2016)
12. Kingma, D.P., Ba, J.: Adam: a method for stochastic optimization. CoRR abs/1412.6980 (2014)
13. Krause, J., Johnson, J., Krishna, R., Fei-Fei, L.: A hierarchical approach for generating descriptive image paragraphs. In: 2017 IEEE Conference on Computer Vision and Pattern Recognition, CVPR 2017, 21–26 July 2017, Honolulu, HI, USA, pp. 3337–3345 (2017)
14. Lu, J., Xiong, C., Parikh, D., Socher, R.: Knowing when to look: adaptive attention via a visual sentinel for image captioning. In: 2017 IEEE Conference on Computer Vision and Pattern Recognition, CVPR 2017, 21–26 July 2017, Honolulu, HI, USA, pp. 3242–3250 (2017)
15. Mao, J., Xu, W., Yang, Y., Wang, J., Yuille, A.L.: Deep captioning with multimodal recurrent neural networks (m-RNN). CoRR abs/1412.6632 (2014)
16. Rennie, S.J., Marcheret, E., Mroueh, Y., Ross, J., Goel, V.: Self-critical sequence training for image captioning. In: 2017 IEEE Conference on Computer Vision and Pattern Recognition, CVPR 2017, 21–26 July 2017, Honolulu, HI, USA, pp. 1179–1195 (2017)
17. Wang, Y., Lin, Z., Shen, X., Cohen, S., Cottrell, G.W.: Skeleton key: image captioning by skeleton-attribute decomposition. In: 2017 IEEE Conference on Computer Vision and Pattern Recognition, CVPR 2017, 21–26 July 2017 Honolulu, HI, USA, pp. 7378–7387 (2017)

18. Wu, Q., Shen, C., Liu, L., Dick, A.R., van den Hengel, A.: What value do explicit high level concepts have in vision to language problems? In: 2016 IEEE Conference on Computer Vision and Pattern Recognition, CVPR 2016, 27–30 June 2016, Las Vegas, NV, USA, pp. 203–212 (2016)
19. Xu, K., et al.: Show, attend and tell: neural image caption generation with visual attention. In: Proceedings of the 32nd International Conference on Machine Learning, ICML 2015, 6–11 July 2015, Lille, France, pp. 2048–2057 (2015)
20. Yao, T., Pan, Y., Li, Y., Qiu, Z., Mei, T.: Boosting image captioning with attributes. In: IEEE International Conference on Computer Vision, ICCV 2017, 22–29 October 2017 Venice, Italy, pp. 4904–4912 (2017)
21. Zhou, L., Xu, C., Koch, P.A., Corso, J.J.: Watch what you just said: image captioning with text-conditional attention. In: Proceedings of the on Thematic Workshops of ACM Multimedia 2017, 23–27 October 2017, Mountain View, CA, USA, pp. 305–313 (2017)
22. Zhu, Z., Xue, Z., Yuan, Z.: Think and tell: preview network for image captioning. In: British Machine Vision Conference 2018, BMVC 2018, 3–6 September 2018, p. 82. Northumbria University, Newcastle (2018)
23. Zhu, Z., Xue, Z., Yuan, Z.: Topic-guided attention for image captioning. In: 2018 IEEE International Conference on Image Processing, ICIP 2018, 7–10 October 2018, Athens, Greece, pp. 2615–2619 (2018)

Occlusion Aware Stereo Matching via Cooperative Unsupervised Learning

Ang Li and Zejian Yuan$^{(\boxtimes)}$

Institute of Artificial Intelligence and Robotics, Xi'an Jiaotong University,
Xi'an, People's Republic of China
bennie.522@stu.xjtu.edu.cn, yuan.ze.jian@xjtu.edu.cn

Abstract. Occlusion as a core challenge for stereo computation has attracted extensive research efforts in the past decades. Apart from its adverse impact, occlusion itself is a crucial clue which has not been exploited in the field of CNN based stereo. In this paper, we argue that a deep stereo framework benefits from reasoning occlusion in advance. We present an occlusion aware stereo network comprising a prior occlusion inferring module and a subsequent disparity computation module. The occlusion inferring module is a sub-network that directly starts from images, which averts the sophisticated procedure to iteratively estimate occlusion with disparity. We additionally propose cooperative unsupervised learning of occlusion and disparity, based on a different hybrid loss enforcing them to be consensus and trained alternatively to reach convergence. The comprehensive experimental analyses show that our method achieves state-of-the-art results among unsupervised learning frameworks, and is even comparable to several supervised methods.

Keywords: Stereo · Occlusion detection · Unsupervised learning

1 Introduction

Stereo computation has long been a primary and attractive topic in the community of computer vision. It is the task of finding the disparity, i.e., the pixel-to-pixel correspondence from a stereo image pair. State-of-the-art methods extensively adopting convolutional neural networks (CNN) achieve a dramatic performance improvement. Despite the tremendous advances, stereo matching still suffers from problems caused by occlusion, noise, and texturelessness.

Occlusion is one of the most challenging situations. One reason is that it is the area that inherently violates the fundamental corresponding constraint. In the absence of matching evidence, estimating disparities in occlusion is arduous. The other is that the ambiguous matching in occlusion can potentially be propagated to affect other regions. Restraining these adverse impacts of occlusion conduces to accurate disparity estimation [9,24,31].

Supported by the National Key R&D Program of China (No. 2016YFB1001001) and the National Natural Science Foundation of China (No. 61573280, No. 91648121).

C. V. Jawahar et al. (Eds.): ACCV 2018, LNCS 11366, pp. 197–213, 2019.
https://doi.org/10.1007/978-3-030-20876-9_13

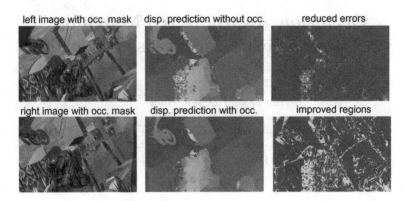

Fig. 1. *A Toy Example.* We use the matching part in PSMNet [3] to compute disparity from images and ground-truth occlusion augmented images. From left to right: an input image pair with occlusion visualized on it; the predicted disparity from different inputs; the reduced error map (the warmer, the larger) and the regions that are improved using the occlusion-augmented input compared to using the raw input

However, the effect of occlusion to stereo computation is more than harmful. As early as a couple of decades ago, Nakayama and Shimojo [21] have found that monocular occlusion can induce the perception of depth, they call this form of depth information *da Vinci stereopsis*. They have demonstrated that occlusion geometry gives rise to qualitative as well as quantitative depth percepts. Computer vision researchers make positive use of the informative occlusion cue to facilitate calculating disparity [27,28]. However, current CNN based stereo methods have not ever exploited the rewarding role of occlusion. It provokes us into thinking the way for these methods to benefit from occlusion

We argue that one could reason occlusion in the early stage of a network to serve subsequent disparity computation. As suggested in [15], occlusion is a coarse depth representation, which can be taken as prior knowledge for fine stereo matching. Interestingly, psychological experiments presented by Anderson and Nakayama [2] also indicate that there exist structures specialized to sense occlusion during the earliest stages of the binocular visual system. In a toy experiment visualized in Fig. 1, we compare the resultant disparities calculated from images and from occlusion-augmented images. The significant improvement brought by the input occlusion experimentally verifies the rationality to specially infer occlusion ahead of stereo matching.

A critical technical barrier to take advantage of occlusion lies in its chicken-and-egg relationship to stereo. Acquiring occlusion always relies on a precomputed disparity, making it tedious for occlusion, in turn, to assist with disparity estimation. Thanks to a recent study which breaks this deadlock by inferring occlusion directly from images based on CNN [15], we consider it possible to estimate occlusion and aid stereo matching in a non-iterative fashion.

We incorporate occlusion detection into an unsupervised framework. This is for three considerations. First, unsupervised learning has a great generalization ability which is favorable to practical applications. Secondly, knowing occlusion is vital for unsupervised learning of stereo matching. Since the widely used training losses, which penalize reconstruction error and left-right inconsistency, do not work at occluded regions. Furthermore, many popular stereo datasets do not provide dense, perfect disparity ground-truth, resulting in no access to true occlusion.

Taken the above together, we propose an occlusion aware stereo matching network (*OASM-Net*). The network comprises a prior module to reason occlusion and a succeeding module to compute disparity from images and the predicted occlusion. We further introduce a cooperative unsupervised learning scheme with a new hybrid loss. The loss enforces the estimated occlusion and disparity to be consensus, which enables the network to cooperatively learn two tasks and lead to coherent improvement. To reach convergence, we train alternatively between occlusion and disparity.

The major contributions of this paper are three-fold:

- This work is, to the best of our knowledge, the first to integrate a specialized occlusion reasoning machine into a stereo network to investigate the positive role of occlusion.
- We introduce an unsupervised scheme for cooperatively learning occlusion and disparity.
- We carry out extensive experiments to verify our network design and the learning mechanism.

2   Related Work

Occlusion is always detected as a by-product of disparity or motion. Ordering constraint detector [10,23] is one of the earliest detection methods which judges a pixel as occlusion when the relative order in a scan line is inconsistent between two views. This method fails to handle narrow objects. Left-right cross checking methods [9,24] are based on the definition of occlusion to find the regions which have no correspondence cross view. Disparity discontinuity detection [27,28] locates occlusion at edges where the disparities are discontinuous. All of these detectors rely on a preceding disparity estimation. A recent CNN based method [15] frees occlusion detection from stereo matching to directly infer from stereo inputs. We follow this methodology to detect occlusion. Nevertheless, the detector is trained unsupervised in our framework, so as to adaptively cope with diverse data under different camera configurations.

Existing stereo approaches treat occlusion in two ways. The first group of methods manage to prevent the unreliable estimations in occlusion from polluting the overall performance. Among this group of methods, some [9,31] regard occlusion as outliers and interpolate disparity values here afterward. This kind of methodology is simple and flexible, widely used in local matching algorithms and in the post-processing. Other methods [8,24] explicitly model occlusion with disparity and neglect to penalize the disparities at the occlusion regions. These methods can obtain the optimal disparity directly without additional processing

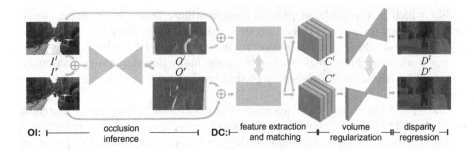

Fig. 2. *Network architecture.* The OI sub-network is a 2D hourglass architecture to regress occlusion from stereo images. The DC sub-network starts with occlusion-augmented images to regress final disparities. Network weights are shared between left and right in DC. $\oplus$ is the concatenation operation

for the occluded area. The second group of methods take advantage of occlusion geometry to better constrain disparity. Yamaguchi et al. [27,28] use occlusion boundaries to help locate disparity discontinuities. Our method handles occlusion from both sides. We employ a deep network to estimate disparity with the help of occlusion. Compared to using a manually designed model to represent the relationship between disparity and occlusion geometry, we are able to explore more sophisticated auxiliary information with the great representational power of CNN. Besides, we mimic prior methods to suppress the harmful effect of occlusion through the proposed hybrid loss.

CNN based stereo methods mainly focus on suppressing the adverse impact of occlusion. Deep matching methods [18,22,31] select corresponding pairs from non-occluded regions to train the feature net and refine the occluded disparity in post-processing. Zhou et al. [33] iteratively utilize confidential matches which are likely non-occluded to guide training. iResNet [16] utilizes a CNN based refinement module to modify the disparity estimations with large reconstruction error, which may arise from the occlusion. In a similar case of motion estimation, Wang et al. [29] control the effect of occlusion through loss function. In the context of unsupervised learning, [33] and [29] deterministically infer occlusion from disparity estimation, and impose constraints essentially only on the learning of disparity. [25] is based on the confidence to select reliable disparity estimation as supervision signals, which may avoid training from the erroneous matchings in occlusion. Our OASM-Net is more on utilizing the favorable impact of occlusion to further improve disparity. We antecedently estimate occlusion through a specialized module. The estimated occlusion serves as an important depth cue fed to a subsequent module to facilitate stereo matching. Moreover, we propose to cooperatively learn occlusion and disparity without ground-truth supervision based on their corresponding relationship.

3   Occlusion Aware Stereo Matching Network

Given a stereo image pair I^l and I^r, we aim at estimating dense disparity maps D^l and D^r. The proposed network comprises an occlusion inference module (OI) and an occlusion-aided disparity computation module (DC). OI takes the stacked stereo images $\{I^l, I^r\}$ as input to simultaneously regress occlusion probability maps O^l and O^r for both views. The normalized occlusion maps are then augmented to the original images as $\{I^l, \hat{O}^l\}$ and $\{I^r, \hat{O}^r\}$, acting as inputs for DC to compute final disparities. The overview of our whole architecture is illustrated in Fig. 2. Table 1 summarizes the detailed layer-by-layer definitions.

3.1   Occlusion Inference

We follow SymmNet [15] using a hourglass network to infer the occlusion maps for both views in OI. This module takes a stacked stereo image pair as input. With the aim of encoding large structures, the input image features are spatially contracted through a serial of 2D convolutional layers with strides of 2. To obtain pixel-wise predictions with the original input resolution, we further expand the down-sampled features by deconvolutional layers. Skipping additions connect lower level features with higher level decoding part to keep fine local information. Each convolutional layer is followed by a ReLu in case of gradient vanishing.

Unlike SymmNet which regards occlusion detection as a binary classification problem, we regress the probability of a pixel to be occluded. This is for the purpose that we can directly feed the output of OI to the subsequent module and train the whole network in an end-to-end fashion. We accordingly modified the output channel size of the last prediction layer to 2, rather than a size of 4 used in SymmNet. The final prediction layer is followed by a tanh to output $\hat{O}^l$ and $\hat{O}^r$, which range in $[-1, 1]$. Then a simple linear transformation rescales $\hat{O}^l$ and $\hat{O}^r$ to the range of $[0, 1]$, as the final occlusion prediction O^l and O^r. With the linear operation, the predictions can be interpreted as probability and trained properly. Following the instructions from LeCun et al. [14], we feed the zero-mean outputs $\hat{O}^l$ and $\hat{O}^r$ to the following layers, for faster convergence.

3.2   Disparity Computation

To take advantage of the occlusion information, we make DC module start from a stacked image-occlusion pair. The pre-computed occlusion probability map serves as an augmented channel to the image, indicating whether a pixel is binocularly visible. A unary feature network acts on the occlusion-augmented image to extract deep features. Left and right features are shifted and matched to form a 4D feature volume. Following that, a 3D hourglass network further regularizes the feature volume. Left and right streams are symmetrically calculated with shared network weights. Finally, regression is applied to predict the output disparity for both views.

Table 1. *Architecture summary.* Each layer except for the prediction layer *pr1* and *pr2* is followed by ReLU. *pr1* layer is followed by *tanh* and linear transformation, *pr2* layer is followed by *softmax* to generate probability. This table is arranged from top to bottom, left to right. The layers in the same line are sequential

Name	Layer		Input	Name	Layer		Input
	OI				**DC**		
input1	stacked stereo image pair			input2	stacked image-occlusion pair		
dnsp1	8×8 c16 $s2$,	3×3 c16	input1	conv0	$[3 \times 3$ c32$] \times 3$ $s2$		input2
dnsp2	6×6 c32 $s2$,	3×3 c32	dnsp1	conv1_x	$[3 \times 3$ c32, 3×3 c32$] \times 3$		conv1_x-1
dnsp3	6×6 c64 $s2$,	3×3 c64	dnsp2	conv2_x	$[3 \times 3$ c64, 3×3 c64$] \times 16$ $s2$		conv2_x-1
dnsp4	4×4 c128 $s2$,	3×3 c128	dnsp3	conv3_x	$[3 \times 3$ c128, 3×3 c128$] \times 3$		conv3_x-1
dnsp5	4×4 c256 $s2$,	3×3 c256	dnsp4	conv4_x	$[3 \times 3$ c128, 3×3 c128$] \times 3$ $d2$		conv4_x-1
dnsp6	4×4 c512 $s2$,	3×3 c512	dnsp5	branch_x	$[3 \times 3$ c32$] \times 4$ $ap2^{x+2}$		conv4_3
upsp5		4×4 c256 $s2$	dwnsp6	fusion	3×3 c128,	1×1 c32	$\oplus$branch_x
upsp4	3×3 c256,	4×4 c128 $s2$	dnsp5+upsp5	fv	construct feature volume		
upsp3	3×3 c128,	4×4 c64 $s2$	dnsp4+upsp4	3Dconv0	$[3 \times 3 \times 3$ c32$] \times 4$		fv
upsp2	3×3 c64,	4×4 c32 $s2$	dnsp3+upsp3	3Ddnsp1	$[3 \times 3 \times 3$ c64$] \times 2$ $s2$		3Dconv0
upsp1	3×3 c32,	4×4 c16 $s2$	dnsp2+upsp2	3Ddnsp2	$[3 \times 3 \times 3$ c64$] \times 2$ $s2$		3Ddnsp1
upsp0	3×3 c16,	4×4 c8 $s2$	dnsp1+upsp1	3Dupsp2	$3 \times 3 \times 3$ c64 $s2$		3Ddnsp2
				3Dupsp1	$3 \times 3 \times 3$ c64 $s2$		3Dupsp2+3Ddnsp1
				3Dout	$3 \times 3 \times 3$ c32,	$3 \times 3 \times 3$ c1	3Dupsp1+3Dconv0
pr1	3×3 c4,	3×3 c2	input0$\oplus$upsp0	pr2	upsampling,	regression	3Dout

Feature Extraction and Matching. We extract unary features through a number of 2D convolutional layers followed by a spatial pyramid pooling module (SPP) as in [3]. To reduce the computational demand, an initial convolutional layer with a stride of 2 firstly down-samples the features to half resolution. Then, a cascade of basic residual blocks make the features go deeper for a stronger ability of representation. At the same time, unary features are further down-sampled to a quarter resolution. SPP is applied after that for the sake of rich contextual information at different spatial levels. Features flow through four fixed-size average pooling branches in SPP, i.e., 8×8, 16×16, 32×32, and 64×64, then converge to form the final unary features.

Features from the reference view are concatenated with the corresponding ones from the target view across each disparity level, resulting in a 4D feature volume. This operation inherits the geometry knowledge of stereo vision, as well as preserves the unary representations from the last stage [12].

Feature Volume Regularization. Even with deep features, matching from unaries is far from reliable. It is necessary to further regularize the feature volume. Due to our limited computational capability, we employ one of three 3D hourglass networks that are in the original PSMNet [3] to incorporate context information and improve this volume. Two layers of 3D convolution with strides 2 down-sample the volume by a factor of 4, reaching 1/16 of the initial spatial size of the image. This enables us to leverage context with a large field of view while prevents the computational demand from overgrowth. The volume is then up-sampled to quarter resolution through a series of 3D deconvolutions. To retain fine-grained details, we add lower level feature maps before up-sampling. Finally, we apply a bilinear interpolation on the volume to make dense predictions with the original input resolution.

Disparity Regression. We calculate the final outputs by employing a differential disparity regression operation with a soft argmin proposed in [12]. The matching cost $C_{\dot{d}}$ for each disparity $\dot{d}$ computed from the last stage is converted to probability by a softmax operation $\sigma(\cdot)$. Then the predicted disparity $D(\mathbf{p})$ at location $\mathbf{p}$ is calculated as the expected disparity value, as

$$D(\mathbf{p}) = \sum_{d=0}^{D_{max}} \dot{d} \times \sigma\left(-C_{\dot{d}}(\mathbf{p})\right). \tag{1}$$

4 Cooperative Unsupervised Learning

We cooperatively learn occlusion and disparity without ground-truth. A hybrid loss is imposed which takes the interaction between disparity and occlusion as the supervision signal to train OI and DC. To ensure training convergence, we decouple the twined tasks and learn them alternatively. The learning scheme is illustrated in Fig. 3.

4.1 Hybrid Loss

The loss L consists of four terms,

$$L = \omega_{rc}L_{rc} + \omega_{lr}L_{lr} + \omega_{s}L_{s} + \omega_{oreg}L_{oreg}. \tag{2}$$

Reconstruction loss L_{rc} prefers the non-occluded regions in an image can be reconstructed from the fellow image. Left-right consistency loss L_{lr} enforces the left and right disparities are consistent except for the occlusion area. Smoothness loss L_s encourages adjacent pixels to have similar disparity and occlusion values. Occlusion regularization term L_{oreg} prevents the occlusion prediction from meaninglessness. $w.$ are the weights harmonizing each term. All these terms of both left and right views account for the total loss L. Here we only explain the left losses due to the length limitation.

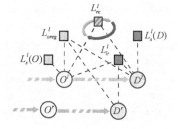

Fig. 3. *Learning diagram.* Input images, network, and losses of the right stream are omitted here for clarity

Reconstruction Loss. The non-occluded area of an image should be able to reconstruct from the other view. Based on this assumption, we introduce a loss to penalize the reconstruction error. Inspired by [6], we enforce the observation and the reconstruction have color appearance similarity by L1 loss and structure similarity by an SSIM term [26] S. The reconstruction loss L_{rc}^l for the left view hereby is derived as:

$$
L_{rc}^l = \frac{1}{N} \sum_{\mathbf{p}} \left(\alpha \frac{1 - S(I^l(\mathbf{p}), \hat{I}^l(\mathbf{p}))}{2} + (1 - \alpha)\|I^l(\mathbf{p}) - \hat{I}^l(\mathbf{p})\| \right) \bar{O}^l(\mathbf{p}), \quad (3)
$$

where $\bar{O}^l(\mathbf{p}) = 1 - O^l(\mathbf{p})$, $\hat{I}^l$ is the reconstructed image, N is the pixel amount.

Given disparity D^l and image I^r, the reconstructed image $\hat{I}^l$ is computed by linear sampling mechanism [17], $\hat{I}^l(\mathbf{p}) = v_l I^r(\mathbf{t}_l) + v_r I^r(\mathbf{t}_r)$. $\mathbf{t}_l$ and $\mathbf{t}_r$ are the left and right neighbors of $\mathbf{t}$, where $\mathbf{t}$ is $\mathbf{p}$'s corresponding position in I^r based on $D^l(\mathbf{p})$ calculated by $\mathbf{t} = \mathbf{p} - (D^l(\mathbf{p}), 0)^\top$. $v.$ are the interpolation weights that are inversely proportional to their distance to $\mathbf{t}$, and $v_l + v_r = 1$. The sampler is locally fully differentiable, such that loss can be back-propagated along the estimated disparities.

Left-Right Consistency Loss. Corresponding disparities, except the occluded ones, should have a unique value for both stereo views. We use an LRC loss to minimize the discrepancy between the disparities of each non-occluded pixel $\mathbf{p}$ in the left image and its corresponding position $\mathbf{t}$ in the right image,

$$
L_{lrc}^l = \frac{1}{N} \sum_{\mathbf{p}} |D^l(\mathbf{p}) - D^r(\mathbf{t})| \bar{O}^l(\mathbf{p}). \tag{4}
$$

The disparity value $D^r(\mathbf{t})$ at non-integer position $\mathbf{t}$ can be obtained by linear sampling as used in Eq. 3.

Smoothness Loss. We desire that the predicted disparity field changes smoothly except at image discontinuities. Also, we encourage neighbor pixels to have similar occlusion assignments. To this end, an edge-aware penalty based on the image gradient ∇I [7] is imposed on the disparity gradient ∇D, and an L1 loss is applied on the occlusion gradient ∇O,

$$
L_s^l = \frac{1}{N} \sum_{\mathbf{p}} |\nabla_x D^l(\mathbf{p})| e^{-\|\nabla_x I^l(\mathbf{p})\|} + |\nabla_y D^l(\mathbf{p})| e^{-\|\nabla_y I^l(\mathbf{p})\|}
$$
$$
+ \frac{1}{N} \sum_{\mathbf{p}} |\nabla_x O^l(\mathbf{p})| + |\nabla_y O^l(\mathbf{p})|, \tag{5}
$$

where ∇_x and ∇_y are gradients in the x and y directions respectively.

Algorithm 1. Alternative Training Scheme

---

initial $O = \mathbf{0}$
for $t = 0 \ldots T$ **do**
    Minimize $L_{D^t|O}$ w.r.t DC with fixed OI
    Minimize $L_{O^t|D^t}$ w.r.t OI with fixed DC
    if $t > T_0$ **then**
        $O = O^t$
    end if
end for

Occlusion Regularization Loss. Minimizing the losses above leads to an all-one occlusion map. A regularization term is necessary to keep the occlusion estimation meaningful. We directly utilize the disparity inconsistency to restrict the value of occlusion map,

$$L^l_{oreg} = \frac{1}{N} \sum_{\mathbf{p}} \left| O^l(\mathbf{p}) - \left(1 - e^{-|D^l(\mathbf{p}) - D^r(\mathbf{t})|} \right) \right|. \tag{6}$$

With an exponential acting on the negative difference of corresponding disparities, occlusion can be regressed near an approximate binary value. Unlike the commonly used regularization as in [34] which enforces the estimation everywhere to be close to 0, we relax the constraint to mitigate the conflict between those losses. The relaxation, however, increases the risk of approaching all-one. To resolve it, we propose a training scheme which will be introduced in Sect. 4.2.

Discussion. Our hybrid loss enables the network to cooperatively learn to predict occlusion and disparity. For learning disparity, occlusion masks the regions where the reconstruction and the left-right consistency constraints are invalid. For learning occlusion, it is enforced to be intrinsically consensus to the disparity. Two tasks lay restraints on each other and can be jointly improved.

4.2 Alternative Training Scheme

With the proposed hybrid loss, the network is theoretically end-to-end trainable. However, it is not easy to directly learn a desirable result in practice due to three possible reasons. (1) The tightly coupled disparity and occlusion make it difficult to find a reasonable solution. (2) It is empirical and cumbersome to determine the weights $\omega.$, who balance the trade-off between losses. Specifically, LRC loss contributes to accurate disparity estimation but tends to drive the network unstable. Thus choosing ω_{lr} is of particular importance. (3) It is an underlying trend to get all-one occlusion with the relaxed regularization term L_{oreg}. To overcome them, we propose an alternative training scheme, inspired by the optimization strategy widely used in multi-task frameworks [24,32].

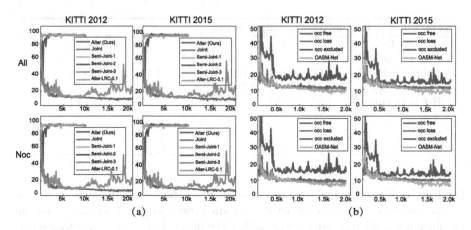

Fig. 4. *3px-error Curves with the KITTI 2012 and 2015 validation set.* (a) The convergence performance (b) Unsupervised results with different occlusion configurations

Instead of directly optimizing the problem above, we alternate between two sub-tasks: training disparity and training occlusion. By fixing OI, training disparity is to minimize a disparity loss $L_{D|O}$ w.r.t DC,

$$L_{D|O} = \omega_{rc}L_{rc} + \omega_{lr}L_{lr} + \omega_s L_s. \tag{7}$$

For training disparity, L_{oreg} acts similarly as L_{lr}. Hence we discard L_{oreg} here to weaken their impact. Vice versa, training occlusion is to minimize an occlusion loss $L_{O|D}$ w.r.t. OI with fixed DC,

$$L_{O|D} = \omega_{rc}L_{rc} + \omega_{oreg}L_{oreg} + \omega_s L_s. \tag{8}$$

Starting from an all-zero occlusion initialization, we first train DC without seeing the actual OI output for the first several iterations. Occlusion is alternatively trained to convergence conditioned on a gradually finer disparity estimation. As the occlusion results get stable, they are allowed to participate in disparity computation and the loss $L_{D|O}$. The training procedure is continued alternatively until reaching a maximum iteration step, as summarized in Algorithm 1.

Our alternative training scheme decouples the challenging problem into two training tasks, and each is relatively easier to converge. The loss is accordingly simplified by rejecting terms which may confuse training. Moreover, we interfere in the training flow to prevent the network moving towards a wired solution.

5   Experiment

We conduct cross-dataset validation to test our method. We train our model on SceneFlow training set [19], while we validate the model on the training set from KITTI stereo 2012 [5] and KITTI stereo 2015 [20]. The large-scale SceneFlow dataset contains 35454 training and 4370 test stereo pairs. The images are rendered from three different synthetic scenes, covering ordinary objects, nonrigid motions, and driving scenarios. Dense, accurate ground-truth disparity maps are equipped for both views. KITTI 2012 and KITTI 2015 comprise street images with semi-dense ground-truth disparity for the left view. KITTI 2012 contains 194 training and 195 test image pairs, while KITTI 2015 contains 200 training and 200 test image pairs. Unlike KITTI 2012, KITTI 2015 contains densely labeled vehicles with CAD models. This leads to the fact that vehicles count as a major part when evaluating results on KITTI 2015.

Our architecture is implemented using PyTorch. All models are optimized with Adam [13] ($\beta_1 = 0.9$, $\beta_2 = 0.999$). For the first 500 training iterations, we block the path from OI to DC. After 500 iterations the occlusion predictions gradually converge, DC is allowed to be trained conditioned on the outputs of OI. We train the model for 30k iterations. The learning rate begins with 0.01 and then is reduced by 10 times at the 5k-th and 2k-th iterations. Loss weights in Eq. 2 are set empirically: ω_{rc} and ω_{oreg} share a maximum value of 1. We allow a small degree of smoothing to set ω_s to 0.001. To avoid a trivial solution, LRC weight ω_{lr} is set to 0.05 in the first 1k iterations and increased to 0.1 after that. α in Eq. 3 is set to 0.9 for a large ratio of structure feature term to improve the robustness. We train with a batch size of 1 using a pair of randomly cropped image patches in size of 256×512. The training process takes about 18 h on a single Nvidia GTX-1080 GPU.

For evaluation, we report two kinds of metrics commonly used in the field of disparity estimation. The end-point-error (EPE) measures the averaged erratic difference between the estimation and ground-truth. The $x$px-error measures the percentage of bad pixels whose error is larger than x pixels. Metrics are evaluated over the whole image (All) and the non-occluded regions (Noc).

5.1 Convergence Analysis

We experimentally analyze the convergence of our cooperative training scheme. The possible factors considered to affect the convergence are three-fold: the coupling of occlusion and disparity, the left-right-consistency constraint, and the regularization term. Our training scheme is designed according to the three factors. To test the design, we compare the validation results during training with the proposed training scheme and with several relaxed schemes.

- *Alter*, our alternative training scheme. Occlusion predictions are fed to DC and $L_{D|O}$ at the 500-th iteration. ω_{LRC} is increased from 0.05 to 0.1 at the 1k-th iteration.
- *Joint*. Jointly train OI and DC. Occlusion predictions are fed to DC at the beginning. The totally coupled loss L in Eq. 2 is used for training. ω_{LRC} is increased from 0.05 to 0.1 at the 1k-th iteration.
- *Semi-Joint-1*. Occlusion predictions are fed to DC at the 500-th iteration. OI and DC are jointly trained with the loss L. ω_{LRC} is increased from 0.05 to 0.1 at the 1k-th iteration.

Table 2. *Supervised Results on the SceneFlow test set with different occlusion configurations.* Our proposed model performs best among variants

Setting		1px-error		3px-error		EPE	
		All	Noc	All	Noc	All	Noc
Matching	Occ Free	19.94	11.65	11.65	4.98	3.06	1.50
	Occ Loss	18.13	8.31	12.07	3.06	4.68	0.93
	Occ Excluded	29.34	21.98	16.47	8.62	7.76	2.88
	Ours	13.20	4.22	9.23	**1.09**	3.99	**0.43**
Matching + Regularization	Occ Free	12.98	6.65	6.08	2.43	1.46	0.76
	Occ Excluded	14.27	7.48	6.52	2.93	1.71	0.79
	Ours	**8.92**	**4.06**	**4.06**	1.30	**1.13**	0.49

- *Semi-Joint-2.* Occlusion predictions are fed to DC at the 500-th iteration. OI and DC are jointly trained with loss L, while ω_{oreg} is reduced from 1 to 0.1. ω_{LRC} is increased from 0.05 to 0.1 at the 1k-th iteration.
- *Semi-Joint-3.* Occlusion predictions are fed to DC at the 3k-th iteration. OI and DC are jointly trained with loss L, and ω_{oreg} is set to 0.1. ω_{LRC} is increased from 0.05 to 0.1 at the 4k-th iteration.
- *Alter-LRC-0.1*, the alternative training scheme. ω_{LRC} is fixed to 0.1 from the beginning.

Figure 4(a) shows the 3px-error curves on the validation set during training. We achieve reasonable results within 4k iterations by using our alternative training scheme. On the contrary, jointly train occlusion and disparity easily results in model divergence (Joint, Semi-Joint-1 and Semi-Joint-2 curves). We attribute this phenomenon to the highly coupled two modules with a loose regularization term L_{oreg}. With the two ingredients carefully balanced by hand (Semi-Joint-3), the model converges temporarily, while becomes unstable with further iterations. Our alternative training scheme, however, alleviates this fussy tuning procedure and reaches steady performance.

Training with a large proportion of the LRC term at the very beginning cannot make the model converge as well (Alter-LRC-0.1 curve). At the early stage during training, the network is unable to predict a reasonable occlusion map. With the ridiculous occlusion mask, enforcing left and right disparity to be consistent easily blows the model away from a rational solution. It suggests that our occlusion-aware model together with the cooperative training scheme provides a sensible way to take advantage of LRC constraint for unsupervised stereo matching.

5.2   The Effectiveness of Occlusion

Our disparity estimation method benefits from the occlusion in two aspects: the occlusion clue fed to DC and the occlusion mask in the loss function. To verify the effectiveness, we compare our model with three variants. *Occ Free* is a model entirely free from occlusion either at the input stage of DC or in the disparity

Table 3. *Comparison with supervised methods on KITTI 2015.* Zhou *et al.* -S is the work of Zhou *et al.* [33] trained under supervision. Our unsupervised method is comparable to other supervised methods

Methods	2px-error		3px-error		4px-error		5px-error		EPE		Runtime(s)
	All	Noc	All	Noc	All	Noc	All	Noc	All	Noc	
MC-CNN [30]	15.83	13.20	13.21	11.35	11.67	11.14	11.59	10.11	4.55	3.41	23
Deep Embed [4]	11.26	9.81	8.51	7.29	7.32	5.83	6.48	5.26	2.65	1.92	3.1
Content-CNN [18]	11.37	10.10	8.55	7.14	751	5.74	6.49	5.41	2.76	1.91	0.34
DispNet [19]	**10.74**	9.56	8.23	7.19	7.55	6.01	6.98	5.16	2.55	1.82	0.12
Zhou *et al.* -S [33]	10.96	**9.23**	**7.29**	**6.81**	7.28	5.55	6.22	5.01	2.29	1.57	0.39
OASM-Net	11.54	9.99	8.21	6.65	**6.65**	**5.12**	**5.69**	**4.20**	**1.73**	**1.35**	0.73

Table 4. *Comparison on 3px-error with unsupervised methods on KITTI 2015 and KITTI 2012.* Our method performs the best

		KITTI 2015			KITTI 2012	
		USCNN [1]	Yu *et al.* [11]	Zhou *et al.* [33]	OASM-Net	OASM-Net
Train	All	18.12	22.69	9.41	**8.21**	8.79
	Noc	12.41	15.32	8.35	**6.65**	6.69
Test	All	16.55	19.14	9.91	**8.32**	8.60
	Noc	11.71	8.35	8.61	**6.86**	6.39

loss $L_{D|O}$. *Occ Loss* only utilizes the occlusion information in the loss function. *Occ Excluded* is the same model to ours except that the input of DC in it is not the occlusion-augmented images. Instead, images with zero values at occlusion are taken as inputs here.

We first test on the SceneFlow dataset. We train our model and variants in a *supervised* manner. OI and DC modules are trained with ground-truth occlusion and disparity respectively. We investigated two kinds of architecture when calculating disparity: a matching-only architecture and a matching with regularization architecture[1]. The variant Occ Loss is only tested for the matching-only architecture. This is because matching the pixels in occluded regions is meaningless, akin to the situation of unsupervised learning. As listed in Table 2, integrating occlusion into the loss improves all the metrics on non-occluded regions compared to Occ Free. Performance gets bad with Occ Loss when evaluating over the whole image. We ascribe this phenomenon to the lack of supervision in the occluded regions. Occ Excluded directly removing the occluded regions from images leads to the poorest results. With the augmentation of the occlusion feature to the input, performance is significantly improved.

Figure 4(b) illustrates the 3px-errors of the variants based on our complete *unsupervised* model with the KITTI validation sets. The curves point to the

---

[1] The matching with regularization architecture is exactly the one we used in our DC module.

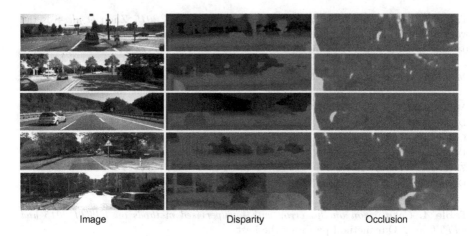

Image   Disparity   Occlusion

Fig. 5. *Example results.* The first three rows are examples from KITTI 2015, and the last two rows are examples from KITTI 2012. The lighter in occlusion results means a higher probability to be occluded. Our method can estimate disparity with details, and an approximate binary occlusion map

same conclusion as we find in the supervised experiment above. This shows that our hybrid loss suppresses the adverse effect of occlusion. More importantly, occlusion as a depth cue assists with disparity estimation.

5.3   Overall Performance

To obtain the final model for submission, we augment SceneFlow dataset with the training set from KITTI 2012 and KITTI 2015. We prolong the training process for another 30k iterations. Figure 5 shows some example results.

Following Zhou *et al.* [33], we compare our results with several existing supervised and unsupervised methods. We directly quote their results reported in [33]. For a fair comparison, all the results are raw-network output without any post-processing. Compared with supervised methods, as shown in Table 3, our unsupervised method without seeing any ground-truth achieves comparable results. A comparison with existing unsupervised methods is given in Table 4. [1] and [11] are unsupervised optical flow methods adapted to the stereo problem by Zhou *et al.* [33]. Our method outperforms all the prior studies. Especially over the non-occluded regions, we surpass the others by a noteworthy margin.

5.4   Limitations and Future Work

In our work, occlusion is trained on the basis of the uniqueness constraint. In fact, the geometry relationship between occlusion and disparity can also be considered to restrain occlusion better. For example, the occlusion boundary should coincide with disparity discontinuity. It would be interesting to investigate these potential interactions. Besides, our model is trained offline. Online training with test data can be developed to make the model handle various situations.

6   Conclusions

We have first presented a stereo matching network with occlusion cue exploited in advance. The network comprises a functional module for estimating occlusion and a following module for calculating disparity from input images and the estimated occlusion. Accurate disparity estimation is obtained with the aid of occlusion prior. Then, we have accordingly proposed to cooperatively learn occlusion and disparity without ground-truth. A hybrid loss makes occlusion and disparity constrain each other, reaching coherent improvement during learning. The two sub-tasks are trained alternatively to ensure convergence. Cross-dataset validations have shown the rationality of our designs. Our results on benchmarks are superior to current unsupervised methods.

References

1. Ahmadi, A., Patras, I.: Unsupervised convolutional neural networks for motion estimation. In: Proceedings of IEEE International Conference on Image Processing, ICIP (2016)
2. Anderson, B.L., Nakayama, K.: Toward a general theory of stereopsis: binocular matching, occluding contours, and fusion. Psychol. Rev. **101**(3), 414 (1994)
3. Chang, J.R., Chen, Y.S.: Pyramid stereo matching network. In: Proceedings of the IEEE Conference on Computer Vision and Pattern Recognition, CVPR (2018)
4. Chen, Z., Sun, X., Wang, L., Yu, Y., Huang, C.: A deep visual correspondence embedding model for stereo matching costs. In: Proceedings of IEEE International Conference on Computer Vision, ICCV (2015)
5. Geiger, A., Lenz, P., Urtasun, R.: Are we ready for autonomous driving? The KITTI vision benchmark suite. In: Proceedings of IEEE Conference on Computer Vision and Pattern Recognition, CVPR (2012)
6. Godard, C., Mac Aodha, O., Brostow, G.J.: Unsupervised monocular depth estimation with left-right consistency. In: Proceedings of IEEE Conference on Computer Vision and Pattern Recognition, CVPR (2017)
7. Heise, P., Klose, S., Jensen, B., Knoll, A.: PM-Huber: PatchMatch with Huber regularization for stereo matching. In: Proceedings of IEEE International Conference on Computer Vision, ICCV (2013)
8. Heitz, F., Bouthemy, P.: Multimodal estimation of discontinuous optical flow using Markov random fields. IEEE Trans. Pattern Anal. Mach. Intell. PAMI **15**(12), 1217–1232 (1993)
9. Hosni, A., Bleyer, M., Gelautz, M., Rhemann, C.: Local stereo matching using geodesic support weights. In: Proceedings of the IEEE International Conference on Image Processing, ICIP (2009)
10. Intille, S.S., Bobick, A.F.: Disparity-space images and large occlusion stereo. In: Eklundh, J.-O. (ed.) ECCV 1994. LNCS, vol. 801, pp. 179–186. Springer, Heidelberg (1994). https://doi.org/10.1007/BFb0028349
11. Yu, J.J., Harley, A.W., Derpanis, K.G.: Back to basics: unsupervised learning of optical flow via brightness constancy and motion smoothness. In: Hua, G., Jégou, H. (eds.) ECCV 2016. LNCS, vol. 9915, pp. 3–10. Springer, Cham (2016). https://doi.org/10.1007/978-3-319-49409-8_1

12. Kendall, A., Martirosyan, H., Dasgupta, S., Henry, P.: End-to-end learning of geometry and context for deep stereo regression. In: Proceedings of the IEEE International Conference on Computer Vision, ICCV (2017)

13. Kingma, D.P., Ba, J.: Adam: a method for stochastic optimization. arXiv preprint arXiv:1412.6980 (2014)

14. LeCun, Y.A., Bottou, L., Orr, G.B., Müller, K.-R.: Efficient backprop. In: Montavon, G., Orr, G.B., Müller, K.-R. (eds.) Neural Networks: Tricks of the Trade. LNCS, vol. 7700, pp. 9–48. Springer, Heidelberg (2012). https://doi.org/10.1007/978-3-642-35289-8_3

15. Li, A., Yuan, Z.: SymmNet: a symmetric convolutional neural network for occlusion detection. In: Proceedings of the British Machine Vision Conference, BMVC (2018)

16. Liang, Z., et al.: Learning for disparity estimation through feature constancy. In: Proceedings of the IEEE Conference on Computer Vision and Pattern Recognition, CVPR (2018)

17. Liu, M., Salzmann, M., He, X.: Discrete-continuous depth estimation from a single image. In: Proceedings of IEEE Conference on Computer Vision and Pattern Recognition, CVPR (2014)

18. Luo, W., Schwing, A.G., Urtasun, R.: Efficient deep learning for stereo matching. In: Proceedings of the IEEE Conference on Computer Vision and Pattern Recognition, CVPR (2016)

19. Mayer, N., et al.: A large dataset to train convolutional networks for disparity, optical flow, and scene flow estimation. In: Proceedings of IEEE Conference on Computer Vision and Pattern Recognition, CVPR (2016)

20. Menze, M., Geiger, A.: Object scene flow for autonomous vehicles. In: Proceedings of IEEE Conference on Computer Vision and Pattern Recognition, CVPR (2015)

21. Nakayama, K., Shimojo, S.: Da vinci stereopsis: depth and subjective occluding contours from unpaired image points. Vis. Res. 30(11), 1811–1825 (1990)

22. Shaked, A., Wolf, L.: Improved stereo matching with constant highway networks and reflective confidence learning. In: Proceedings of the IEEE Conference on Computer Vision and Pattern Recognition, CVPR (2017)

23. Silva, C., Santos-Victor, J.: Intrinsic images for dense stereo matching with occlusions. In: Vernon, D. (ed.) ECCV 2000. LNCS, vol. 1842, pp. 100–114. Springer, Heidelberg (2000). https://doi.org/10.1007/3-540-45054-8_7

24. Sun, J., Li, Y., Kang, S.B.: Symmetric stereo matching for occlusion handling. In: Proceedings of IEEE Conference on Computer Vision and Pattern Recognition, CVPR (2005)

25. Tonioni, A., Poggi, M., Mattoccia, S., Di Stefano, L.: Unsupervised adaptation for deep stereo. In: The IEEE International Conference on Computer Vision, ICCV (2017)

26. Wang, Z., Bovik, A.C., Sheikh, H.R., Simoncelli, E.P.: Image quality assessment: from error visibility to structural similarity. IEEE Trans. Image Process. TIP 13(4), 600–612 (2004)

27. Yamaguchi, K., Hazan, T., McAllester, D., Urtasun, R.: Continuous Markov random fields for robust stereo estimation. In: Fitzgibbon, A., Lazebnik, S., Perona, P., Sato, Y., Schmid, C. (eds.) ECCV 2012. LNCS, vol. 7576, pp. 45–58. Springer, Heidelberg (2012). https://doi.org/10.1007/978-3-642-33715-4_4

28. Yamaguchi, K., McAllester, D., Urtasun, R.: Efficient joint segmentation, occlusion labeling, stereo and flow estimation. In: Fleet, D., Pajdla, T., Schiele, B., Tuytelaars, T. (eds.) ECCV 2014. LNCS, vol. 8693, pp. 756–771. Springer, Cham (2014). https://doi.org/10.1007/978-3-319-10602-1_49

29. Wang, Y., Yang, Y., Yang, Z., Zhao, L., Wang, P., Xu, W.: Occlusion aware unsupervised learning of optical flow. In: Proceedings of the IEEE Conference on Computer Vision and Pattern Recognition, CVPR (2018)
30. Zbontar, J., LeCun, Y.: Computing the stereo matching cost with a convolutional neural network. In: Proceedings of IEEE Conference on Computer Vision and Pattern Recognition, CVPR (2015)
31. Zbontar, J., LeCun, Y.: Stereo matching by training a convolutional neural network to compare image patches. J. Mach. Learn. Res. **17**, 65:1–65:32 (2016)
32. Zhang, C., Li, Z., Cheng, Y., Cai, R., Chao, H., Rui, Y.: MeshStereo: a global stereo model with mesh alignment regularization for view interpolation. In: Proceedings of IEEE International Conference on Computer Vision, ICCV (2015)
33. Zhou, C., Zhang, H., Shen, X., Jia, J.: Unsupervised learning of stereo matching. In: Proceedings of the IEEE International Conference on Computer Vision, ICCV (2017)
34. Zhou, T., Brown, M., Snavely, N., Lowe, D.G.: Unsupervised learning of depth and ego-motion from video. In: Proceedings of IEEE Conference on Computer Vision and Pattern Recognition, CVPR (2017)

Background Subtraction Based on Fusion of Color and Local Patterns

Md Rifat Arefin, Farkhod Makhmudkhujaev, Oksam Chae, and Jaemyun Kim(✉)

Department of Computer Science and Engineering,
Kyung Hee University, Yongin-si, Gyeonggi-do 17104, Republic of Korea
{rifat.arefin,farhodfm,oschae,jaemyunkim}@khu.ac.kr

Abstract. Segmentation of foreground objects using background subtraction methods is popularly used in a wide variety of application areas such as surveillance, tracking, and human pose estimation. Many of the background subtraction methods construct a background model in a pixel-wise manner using color information that is sensitive to illumination variations. In the recent past, a number of local feature descriptors have been successfully applied to overcome such issues. However, these descriptors still suffer from over-sensitivity and sometimes unable to differentiate local structures. In order to tackle the aforementioned problems of existing descriptors, we propose a novel edge based descriptor, Local Top Directional Pattern (LTDP), that represents local structures in a pattern form with aid of compass masks providing information of top local directional variations. Moreover, to strengthen the robustness of the pixel-wise background model and get benefited from each other, we combine both color and LTDP features. We evaluate the performance of our method on the publicly available change detection datasets. The results of extensive experiments demonstrate the better performance of our method compared to other state-of-the-art unsupervised methods.

Keywords: Background subtraction · Directional Pattern ·
Foreground segmentation

1 Introduction

Detection of objects from video sequences is one of the active research areas in computer vision for a large number of applications such as video-based surveillance, object tracking, activity recognition, and so on [1,5,14,23,27]. The fundamental task is to segment the foregrounds (i.e., moving objects) from the

This research was supported by the MSIT (Ministry of Science and ICT), Korea, under the Grand Information Technology Research Center support program (IITP-2018-2015-0-00742) supervised by the IITP (Institute for Information & Communications Technology Promotion), and the National Research Foundation of Korea (NRF) grant funded by the Korea government (MSIT) (No. NRF-2015R1A2A2A01006412).

C. V. Jawahar et al. (Eds.): ACCV 2018, LNCS 11366, pp. 214–230, 2019.
https://doi.org/10.1007/978-3-030-20876-9_14

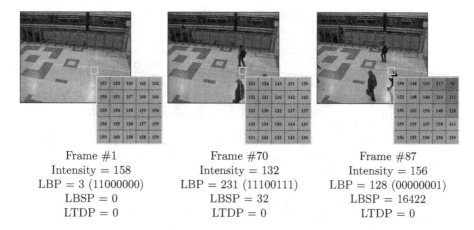

Frame #1
Intensity = 158
LBP = 3 (11000000)
LBSP = 0
LTDP = 0

Frame #70
Intensity = 132
LBP = 231 (11100111)
LBSP = 32
LTDP = 0

Frame #87
Intensity = 156
LBP = 128 (00000001)
LBSP = 16422
LTDP = 0

Fig. 1. Intensity and local descriptor variations at (485, 375) in three different frames of PETS2006 dataset. Frame 1, 70 and 87 represent background, shadow and background near foreground objects respectively. In these cases, our descriptor is robust while color, LBP and LBSP are representing changes which result in false detections. (Color figure online)

background in various scenes. Background subtraction is one of the widely used methods to do this task. This method requires to create a background model without any moving object which captures background variations so that changes occurred by the foregrounds of incoming frames can be detected. For constructing the background model, one of the naive approaches is to directly store the pixel values of a frame, and then detect objects by comparing the pixel values of the new frames with the model [3, 20]. However, this approach is impractical in most of the cases since videos of real scenarios may contain noise, dynamic elements like illumination variations, shadows and so on, which produce changes in the later frames yielding to inappropriate detections. One of the ways to alleviate the effect of these unreliable conditions is to model the background by using local descriptors.

Over the years, numerous local descriptors have been proposed for background modeling [4,11,19,31]. One of them is Local Binary Similarity Pattern (LBSP) [4] which is a variant of Local Binary Pattern (LBP). LBSP encodes the similarity among center and neighbor pixels based on a threshold by taking absolute differences. Charles *et al.* [24] improved LBSP by calculating this threshold dynamically, and used in combination with color features in sample consensus based background modeling derived from ViBe [3]. More recently, Charles *et al.* proposed SuBSENSE [25], an enhanced version of the previous method which dynamically adjusted internal parameters, and showed state-of-the-art results. Although LBSP descriptor is robust to illumination variations, it performs poorly in flat areas and results in holes in foreground objects. Moreover, it is over-sensitive to local changes because of being deteriorated by the

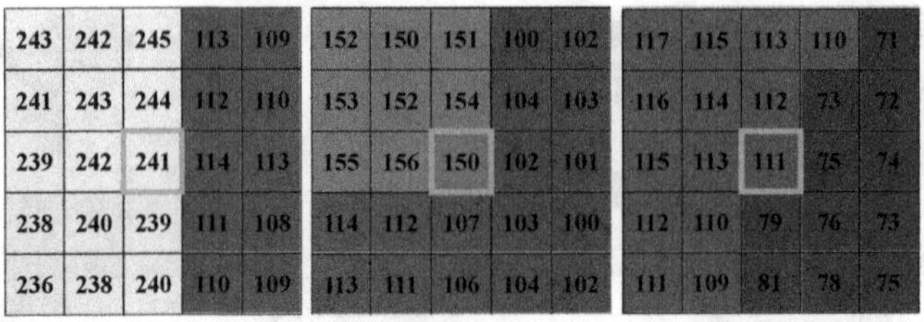

243	242	245	113	109
241	243	244	112	110
239	242	241	114	113
238	240	239	111	108
236	238	240	110	109

152	150	151	100	102
153	152	154	104	103
155	156	150	102	101
114	112	107	103	100
113	111	106	104	102

117	115	113	110	71
116	114	112	73	72
115	113	111	75	74
112	110	79	76	73
111	109	81	78	75

	Straight Edge		Corner		Curved Edge
LBP	56	LBP	56	LBP	56
LBSP	56118	LBSP	56118	LBSP	56118
LTDP	156	LTDP	147	LTDP	153

Fig. 2. Shortcoming of LBP and LBSP descriptors. Failing to differentiate Straight edge, Corner, and Curved edge. (Color figure online)

neighborhood information as shown in Fig. 1. Furthermore, it is found to be less discriminative in a various local structures. Figure 2 demonstrates such example.

To solve the above-mentioned issues, we propose a novel edge based descriptor for modeling the background, Local Top Directional Pattern (LTDP), which encodes top directional information of local structures. The proposed LTDP descriptor makes use of compass masks to extract different directional edge variations accurately. Hence, it can discriminatively extract various local structures like straight edges, corners, curved edges and so on. Moreover, since edge information (i.e., direction and response) are less sensitive to lighting changes, and proposed descriptor employs them after applying edge strength threshold, LTDP is robust to illumination variations and discriminative as shown in Figs. 1 and 2. Besides, we utilize ViBe like sample consensus-based method to model the background pixel-wise as it has shown noteworthy performance. To take advantage of both the features, we use a weighted combination of both color and LTDP features in pixel-wise background model. Furthermore, we also adapt dynamic parameter update strategy introduced in SuBSENSE, so that our method can adaptively overcome unexpected conditions. In order to evaluate the performance of our background subtraction method, we perform experiments on the publicly available change detection datasets (CDnet 2012 and 2014) [8,29]. Experimental results demonstrate that our proposed method outperforms SuBSENSE and other unsupervised state-of-the-art methods.

In this paper, we present a background subtraction method based on a robust and efficient descriptor which encodes directional information. The key contributions of this paper are: (1) we propose a descriptor simultaneously working with a color feature for background modeling; (2) we introduce a weighted fusion of color and our proposed descriptor to get benefited from each other; (3) we achieve state-of-the-art performance on benchmark datasets.

The rest of the paper is organized as follows. Section 2 describes the related works of different background subtraction methods and existing descriptors.

Section 3 introduces our background subtraction framework. Section 4 shows the experimental results on the CDnet 2012 and 2014 datasets. Finally, conclusions are given in Sect. 5.

2   Related Work

The most important task in background subtraction is to build a reliable background model. Traditional methods suffer if the model is created with moving objects or scenes containing illumination variations, shadows, dynamic backgrounds like moving trees and rippling of water, etc.

To overcome these problems, a wide number of studies have been conducted over the years. The contributions of these works are mainly focused on developing more complex and robust background subtraction methods or representing models with more powerful and sophisticated features. From the motivation of representing each pixel in the model by some distribution, unimodal Gaussian distribution was used in [30]. However, it is hard for a single model to capture all the variations in a complex scene which may produce poor segmentation results. To solve this problem, Gaussian Mixture Model (GMM) was proposed to model the background variations in multivariate environments [26]. In addition, to generate stable background model in presence of motions, several methods have proposed the idea of representing the distribution by a weighted mixture of Gaussian observed over times [13,18,32].

However, a Gaussian assumption for pixel color or intensity distribution does not hold in real-world scenarios. Hence, a non-parametric approach using Kernel Density Estimation (KDE) was proposed in [7]. This method estimates the probability density function directly from the observed data without any prior assumptions. However, this approach is time-consuming and updates the model based on first-in-first-out (FIFO) strategy, thus unable to model the periodic events. To solve the problems of KDE, an alternative idea was proposed in [17] where a code-book was built for each pixel, consisted of multiple code-words which were created by clustering the observations. In terms of memory, the code-book representation of the model is efficient compared to other traditional models but requires extra computations for clustering.

Another pixel-wise background modeling technique named ViBe was proposed in [3], which stores several samples to represent each pixel of the model. If a pixel in the new frame matches some of the background samples, it is classified as background. It integrates new information caused by background variations into the model over time, by using a stochastic update strategy. Moreover, to maintain spatial consistency, a spatial information propagation strategy was also introduced. Although ViBe provides several benefits, it produces false detections in shadows, illumination variations and dynamic backgrounds as the model is constructed based on only color information and parameters of the method are manually adjusted.

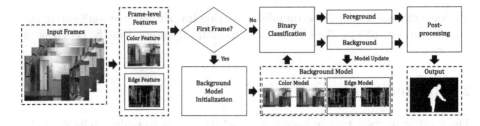

Fig. 3. Overview of the proposed background subtraction method.

Alongside the effective models, powerful feature representations are also introduced to better adapt the challenging situations. The Local Binary Pattern (LBP), is a well-known texture feature which was introduced for background modeling in [11]. LBP is robust to monotonic illumination variations but at the expense of sensitivity to subtle local texture changes. An improved version of LBP called the Scale-Invariant Local Ternary Pattern (SILTP) was proposed in [19], which is more tolerant to noise and computationally efficient. Another texture based descriptor named Local Binary Similarity Pattern (LBSP) proposed in [4], was demonstrated to perform better than color features. Apart from the fact that LBSP is robust to illumination variations, it performs poorly in flat regions and thus produces holes in foreground objects. Moreover, it is over-sensitive to subtle texture changes which result in false detections.

Besides, some authors combined different features in their background model to get benefits from each other. For instance, Han *et al.* [10] proposed background modeling with color, gradient, and Haar-like features. Some authors introduced background subtraction methods by constructing models using color and texture features [24,25,31]. Also, Local Hybrid Pattern (LHP) [15] was proposed by Kim *et al.* where each pixel of the background model was represented by color and edge information. Moreover, some authors tried to combine color and edge features using gradient magnitude based weighting mechanism [16,21].

3   Methodology

Although color features are widely used in background modeling, their limitations are observed in camouflages, shadows, and illumination variations. Spatial features can solve these problems to some extent. Thus, for improving the performance of background modeling, we introduce a spatial descriptor to model the background which will be described in this section. Furthermore, we also discuss our background initialization, update, and foreground segmentation strategies. We perform very simple post-processing operation to get rid of some noisy segmentation as well. Figure 3 demonstrates the work-flow of our method.

$$\begin{bmatrix} -3 & -3 & 5 \\ -3 & 0 & 5 \\ -3 & -3 & 5 \end{bmatrix} \begin{bmatrix} -3 & 5 & 5 \\ -3 & 0 & 5 \\ -3 & -3 & -3 \end{bmatrix} \begin{bmatrix} 5 & 5 & 5 \\ -3 & 0 & -3 \\ -3 & -3 & -3 \end{bmatrix} \begin{bmatrix} 5 & 5 & -3 \\ 5 & 0 & -3 \\ -3 & -3 & -3 \end{bmatrix}$$
$$\qquad M_0 \qquad\qquad M_1 \qquad\qquad M_2 \qquad\qquad M_3$$

$$\begin{bmatrix} 5 & -3 & -3 \\ 5 & 0 & -3 \\ 5 & -3 & -3 \end{bmatrix} \begin{bmatrix} -3 & -3 & -3 \\ 5 & 0 & -3 \\ 5 & 5 & -3 \end{bmatrix} \begin{bmatrix} -3 & -3 & -3 \\ -3 & 0 & -3 \\ 5 & 5 & 5 \end{bmatrix} \begin{bmatrix} -3 & -3 & -3 \\ -3 & 0 & 5 \\ -3 & 5 & 5 \end{bmatrix}$$
$$\qquad M_4 \qquad\qquad M_5 \qquad\qquad M_6 \qquad\qquad M_7$$

Fig. 4. Kirsch Masks in all eight directions.

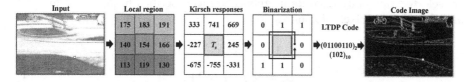

Fig. 5. LTDP code generation.

3.1 Local Top Directional Pattern (LTDP)

Our proposed Local Top Directional Pattern (LTDP) is an 8-bit binary code, assigned to each pixel which is computed by comparing the relative edge responses of a pixel in different directions. The edge response values of a particular pixel are calculated using Kirsch masks. The Kirsch masks are used to detect edge responses in all eight directions of a compass. One mask is denoted as $M_i(x)$ for $i = 0, 1, ..., 7$ and rotated 45° incrementally through all eight compass directions as shown in Fig. 4.

Among these eight edge responses, top responses (at-most four for reliable code) are selected irrespective of their sign if their strengths are significant and their positions are encoded by setting them to 1 in 8-bit binary code. And, rest of the positions in the binary code are set to 0. Finally, LTDP code is calculated through

$$LTDP(x) = \sum_{i=0}^{7} S(m_i) \times 2^i, \qquad (1)$$

$$S(m_i) = \begin{cases} 1 & m_i \geq T_s \\ 0 & otherwise, \end{cases} \qquad (2)$$

where x denotes central location, m_i corresponds to i^{th} direction edge response, and T_s is the edge strength threshold. We adaptively change T_s in different scenarios so that it can be sensitive to local changes. To do that, T_s is adjusted relative to central location pixel value, c. Specifically, T_s is computed using c by multiplying with a factor, f which is in the range of 0–15. We have experimentally chosen 2 as the value of f. The proposed descriptor achieves robustness to noise based on the strength of T_s threshold that omits noise corrupted edge responses. Example of code generation for a particular pixel of the frame is illustrated in Fig. 5.

3.2   Background Modeling

As a background modeling technique, we use a sample consensus-based method like ViBe. In this technique, several samples are stored in the background model for each pixel. A given pixel on an incoming frame is classified as either background or foreground based on its similarity to the background samples. In particular, our per-pixel background model is composed of N samples, where each sample uses color and LTDP features as the core component. The model is initialized using the first frame of a video, where N samples for each pixel are selected randomly from its neighborhood as described in [3]. We define the model B at each pixel location as

$$B = \{B_0, B_1, ..., B_{N-1}\}, \tag{3}$$

$$B_i = \{C_i, LTDP_i\}, \tag{4}$$

where, C_i and $LTDP_i$ are color and LTDP codes respectively. We incorporate color and LTDP features into our background model, so that model containing these two information can take benefit from each other in various situations. For instance, a color feature is helpful in the case of pixels from flat regions, whereas descriptor information is not reliable. On the other hand, LTDP is a useful feature to overcome the unexpected effects of illumination variations, soft shadows, and noises. Thus, in (4), we use RGB color space values alongside LTDP features. Although YCbCr and HSV are robust to illumination changes, the former one might have a problem in poor color discrimination cases, whereas latter one is prone to noise due to its description in polar coordinate [22]. Moreover, the use of these color spaces increases computation cost.

3.3   Foreground Segmentation

To segment foreground objects, we match each pixel of the incoming frame with all background samples corresponding to that pixel. If the pixel matches with a required number of background samples, it is classified as background, otherwise foreground. To find the match between an observed pixel and the background model, the distance measure is applied.

As we are using color and LTDP descriptor for background modeling, for each pixel we compute a color distance D_c and descriptor distance D_d while matching with all the background samples corresponding to that pixel. Specifically, to calculate the color distance D_c, we utilize L1-distance by using

$$D_c(C_o, C_s) = |C_o - C_s|, \tag{5}$$

where D_c refers to the distance between observed color C_o and background sample color C_s. We have also experimented with L2-norm and Minkowski-norm for distance calculation. However, compared to L1-norm, in most of the cases, overall results were worse as well as having extra computation cost. Thus, we have stuck to straightforward L1-norm.

In order to calculate the descriptor distance between the observed pixel and background sample, we make use of bit-wise Hamming Distance as follows

$$H(a, b) = \sum_{i=0}^{n-1} D(a_i, b_i), \tag{6}$$

$$D(a_i, b_i) = \begin{cases} 1 & a_i \neq b_i \\ 0 & otherwise, \end{cases} \tag{7}$$

where a_i and b_i represent the ith bit of a and b descriptor codes respectively.

Hence, the distance of LTDP features, D_d can be calculated using (6) as follows

$$D_d = H(LTDP_o, LTDP_s), \tag{8}$$

where $LTDP_o$ and $LTDP_s$ are the observed and background sample LTDP code respectively.

In segmented images, a problem of holes appears due to the texture-less inner regions of the foreground which is similar to the background. In such case, color is a complementary information where descriptor fails. However, it is noteworthy to mention that we are not directly dependent on color as the proposed method makes a decision based on the combination of descriptor and color distances, where the latter one provides complementary information for better segmentation. In particular, to get benefited from both color and LTDP features, we combine their distances by using weighted sum in the following way

$$D_{comb} = \alpha \cdot D_d + (1 - \alpha) \cdot D_c, \tag{9}$$

where α is the weight, and its value is selected 0.4 experimentally.

At final step to classify pixel to either background or foreground, we apply separate thresholds for combined distance (D_{comb}), and descriptor distance (D_d). Algorithm 1 demonstrates the foreground segmentation process for each pixel of video frames.

In statement 3 of the algorithm, we are performing a search among all samples (N) of background model to find matches between current observation and background samples till the required minimum number of background matches, R_{min}, are found for a pixel to be classified as background. To make the matching process faster, we apply a channel-wise threshold in statement 8 and 13, whereas in statement 19, we utilize the aforementioned two thresholds for background matching. These two thresholds, T_{comb} and T_{desc}, mainly complement each other and calculated dynamically using the idea demonstrated in [25], which helps to gain better detection rate. In particular, T_{comb} helps to detect foreground pixels by rejecting matches with background samples when descriptor distance cannot pass T_{desc} due to the texture-less inner regions both in foreground and background model (e.g., holes), whereas T_{desc} serves to detect foreground when combined distance matches with background samples in case of camouflages.

Algorithm 1. Foreground/Background classification process for each pixel

---

Require: Input pixel, $p_{x,y}$ and N background samples for location (x, y) from Background model B

Ensure: $S :$ *Foreground or Background*

 1: *Sample iteration,* $i \leftarrow 0$
 2: *Match count,* $m \leftarrow 0$
 3: **while** $i \leq N \wedge m < R_{min}$ **do**
 4:　　$TotCombDist \leftarrow 0$
 5:　　$TotDescDist \leftarrow 0$
 6:　　**for** $c \leftarrow 1 : TotNumChannels$ **do**
 7:　　　　$ColDist \leftarrow$ *Compute* D_c *for channel* c *& sample* i *using* (5)
 8:　　　　**if** $ColDist > T_{comb}/2$ **then**
 9:　　　　　　go to *FailedMatch*
10:　　　　**end if**
11:　　　　$DescDist \leftarrow$ *Compute* D_d *for channel* c *& sample* i *using* (8)
12:　　　　$CombDist \leftarrow \alpha \times DescDist + (1 - \alpha) \times ColDist$
13:　　　　**if** $CombDist > T_{comb}/2$ **then**
14:　　　　　　go to *FailedMatch*
15:　　　　**end if**
16:　　　　$TotDescDist \leftarrow TotDescDist + DescDist$
17:　　　　$TotCombDist \leftarrow TotCombDist + ColDist$
18:　　**end for**
19:　　**if** $TotCombDist > T_{comb} \vee TotDescDist > T_{desc}$ **then**
20:　　　　go to *FailedMatch*
21:　　**end if**
22:　　$m \leftarrow m + 1$
23:　　*FailedMatch* :
24:　　　　$i \leftarrow i + 1$
25: **end while**
26: **if** $m < R_{min}$ **then**
27:　　*return Foreground*
28: **else**
29:　　*return Background*
30: **end if**

3.4 Background Model Update

Illumination variations over time can generate changes in background. To get accurate segmentation results, the background model needs to be updated so that it can capture the changes introduced in the background. As we keep several samples for each pixel, it is difficult to know which background sample should be updated or replaced when a new one comes. The simplest way is to replace the oldest sample. However, there is no special benefit or logic behind this strategy. Instead of utilizing this type of approaches, our update mechanism follows a random selection strategy demonstrated in [3]. This policy randomly picks one of the samples and replaces it with the new one.

Another important aspect is the time to update the background model. One widely used strategy is a conservative update where a pixel can be included in the background model only when it has been classified as background. This update policy never includes a pixel in the model if it is classified as foreground which helps to capture only the background variations. Although such an update mechanism is straightforward, it has some drawbacks where we can be stuck to deadlock situations or everlasting ghosts. For instance, if some background pixels keep being incorrectly classified as foregrounds, then the conservative update strategy will not allow the model to be updated leading to permanent miss-classification. To solve such problems, spatial diffusion [3] was introduced in update strategy where a new background sample of a pixel should also update the models of neighboring pixels under the assumption that neighboring background pixels share similar temporal distribution. So considering different scenarios, in our background subtraction method for updating the background model, we use the conservative update strategy with random selection and neighborhood diffusion.

3.5 Post-processing

Our segmentation result is not heavily dependent on post-processing but to avoid some unwanted detections, we perform very simple processing after segmentation. To filter out the effect of unreliable noise in the form of blinking pixels (salt-and-pepper noise) existing in the segmentation results, we make use of a median filter of 9×9 size as a post-processing operation. Subsequently, we perform morphological closing operations with a structural element of size 3×3 to fill some of the holes of foreground objects. Both median filter and structural element sizes are chosen empirically.

4 Experimental Results

4.1 Dataset

To evaluate the proposed background subtraction method, we perform experiments on change detection datasets, CDnet 2012 [8] and CDnet 2014 [29]. These datasets provide real-world challenging videos, which have diverse scenes captured by CCTV cameras. They have been selected to cover a wide range of detection challenges. The CDnet 2012 dataset includes the following categories of scenes: baseline (BL), dynamic background (DB), camera jitter (CJ), intermittent object motion (IOM), shadow (SH) and thermal (TH); whereas CDnet 2014 expands CDnet 2012 by including to it categories like bad weather (BW), low frame rate (LFR), night videos (NV), PTZ and turbulence (TU). Each category is accompanied by ground-truth segmentation masks of foreground objects in all the frames of a video.

4.2 Evaluation Metrics

We apply F-measure (FM) metric in our performance evaluation. F-measure can be calculated by using Precision (Pr) and Recall (Re) as a consequence of

computing True-Positive (TP), False-Positive (FP), True-Negative (TN) and
False-Negative (FN) rates. We provide the results of our method by calculating

$$Pr = \frac{TP}{TP + FP},$$ (10)

$$Re = \frac{TP}{TP + FN},$$ (11)

$$FM = \frac{2 \times Pr \times Re}{Pr + Re},$$ (12)

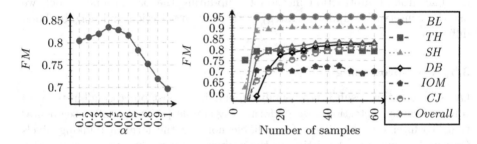

Fig. 6. The effect of varying α (left) and number of samples (right) to the performance
of proposed method in all CDnet 2012 dataset.

4.3 Parameter Settings

Our method is derived from ViBe same as SuBSENSE which has several parameters. As we combine color with LTDP feature, we have carefully adjusted the
parameters to achieve optimal results. Specifically, the value of α in (9) is one
of the important parameters as it controls how much information we allow to
convey in color and descriptor. As can be observed from Fig. 6 (left), high or low
α values affect classification. Based on this, we found that $\alpha = 0.4$ produces the

Table 1. Average performance comparison of different feature combination. (Note
that, bold entries indicate the best results in the corresponding columns)

Feature combination	Pr	Re	FM
Color	0.842	0.670	0.709
Color + LBP	0.721	0.783	0.714
Color + SILTP	0.748	0.802	0.730
Color + LSSD	0.777	**0.861**	0.795
Color + LBSP	**0.856**	0.831	0.826
Color + LTDP	0.843	0.856	**0.834**

Table 2. Average results of proposed method in all CDnet 2012 dataset (left) and new categories of CDnet 2014 dataset (right). Overall 2014 represents average results of all categories of 2012 and new categories of 2014

Category	Pr	Re	FM
BL	0.941	0.961	0.951
TH	0.878	0.756	0.794
SH	0.871	0.949	0.905
DB	0.854	0.823	0.823
IOM	0.729	0.804	0.726
CJ	0.785	0.842	0.807
Overall	0.843	0.856	0.834

Category	Pr	Re	FM
BW	0.963	0.549	0.671
LFR	0.783	0.774	0.762
NV	0.606	0.605	0.544
PTZ	0.265	0.794	0.31
TU	0.951	0.841	0.889
Overall 2014	0.784	0.791	0.744

Table 3. CDnet 2012 per-category and all datasets average F-measure comparisons. (Note that, bold entries indicate the best results in the corresponding columns)

Method	FM_{BL}	FM_{TH}	FM_{SH}	FM_{DB}	FM_{IOM}	FM_{CJ}	FM_{all}
Proposed	**0.951**	0.794	**0.905**	**0.823**	**0.726**	0.807	**0.834**
SuBSENSE [25]	0.950	0.817	0.899	0.818	0.657	**0.815**	0.826
LSSD [31]	0.936	0.813	0.871	0.744	0.609	0.780	0.792
CwisarD [6]	0.908	0.762	0.841	0.809	0.567	0.781	0.778
DPGMM [9]	0.929	0.813	0.813	0.814	0.542	0.748	0.776
PBAS [12]	0.924	0.756	0.860	0.683	0.575	0.722	0.753
LOBSTER [24]	0.924	**0.824**	0.872	0.567	0.577	0.742	0.752
ViBe+ [28]	0.871	0.665	0.815	0.720	0.509	0.754	0.722
KDE [7]	0.909	0.742	0.803	0.596	0.409	0.572	0.672
ViBe [3]	0.870	0.665	0.803	0.565	0.507	0.600	0.668
GMM [26]	0.825	0.662	0.737	0.633	0.520	0.597	0.662

best performance where increasing it leads to poor results since high α values penalize color more that leads to decrease the importance of color, where too low one allows to contribute more so that color can take initiative over descriptor. In the result generation, we have kept all the manual parameters same for all the datasets. In particular, our parameter set is defined in the following way. The minimum number of matching samples required to classify a pixel as background like ViBe is $R_{min} = 2$. During the classification, we apply two thresholds: T_{comb} and T_{desc}. The values of these thresholds are calculated based on the dynamic update strategy described in SuBSENSE. Another important parameter is N, a number of samples to model the background for each pixel. Figure 6 (right) shows the relation between the number of samples and their average F-measure in each category and overall CDnet 2012 dataset. From Fig. 6 (right) we can observe that after 35 samples the performance almost stabilizes in almost all categories. But, if we increase the size of N, then it helps to produce more precise segmentation. Therefore, we have selected $N = 45$ in our method.

Table 4. CDnet 2014 per-category and all datasets average F-measure comparisons. (Note that, bold entries indicate the best results in the corresponding rows)

FM	CNN [2]	SubSENSE [25]	PBAS [12]	GMM [26]	Proposed
FM_{BL}	**0.958**	0.9503	0.9242	0.8245	0.951
FM_{DB}	**0.8761**	0.8177	0.6829	0.633	0.823
FM_{CJ}	**0.899**	0.8152	0.722	0.5969	0.807
FM_{IOM}	0.6098	0.6569	0.5745	0.5207	**0.726**
FM_{SH}	**0.9304**	0.8986	0.860	0.737	0.905
FM_{TH}	0.7583	**0.8171**	0.7556	0.6621	0.794
FM_{BW}	0.8301	**0.8619**	0.7673	0.738	0.671
FM_{LFR}	0.6002	0.6445	0.5914	0.5373	**0.762**
FM_{NV}	**0.5835**	0.5599	0.4387	0.4097	0.544
FM_{PTZ}	0.3133	**0.3476**	0.1063	0.1522	0.31
FM_{TU}	0.8455	0.7792	0.6349	0.4663	**0.889**
FM_{all}	**0.7458**	0.7408	0.6416	0.5707	0.744

Table 5. Approximate processing speed and memory usage comparison (using same parameters for all methods)

Method	Average FPS (320×240)	Required bits per pixel sample
Our	16.0133	48
SuBSENSE	20.7938	72
ViBe	47.6727	24

4.4 Result Analysis

We demonstrate the effectiveness of our main contribution of LTDP features. Table 1 shows the performance comparison of our descriptor with other existing works. Although the precision and recall performance of our descriptor with color is less than other ones, it surpasses other descriptors in F-measure as precision and recall values are closer to each other. In Table 2, we present average results in terms of F-measure in each category, and overall datasets. Table 3 shows the performance comparison of our method with some of the state-of-the-art methods in each category and overall CDnet 2012 dataset. Results demonstrate that our method outperforms other ones in most of the categories and overall dataset. Although the performance of the proposed method is marginally better than SuBSENSE, still this result is achieved with lesser memory consumption as each background sample in the proposed method consists of 24 bit per color and descriptor whereas SuBSENSE defines 24 and 48 bit for color and descriptor respectively. Moreover, we have performed experiments on CDnet 2014 by using the same parameters chosen for CDnet 2012 dataset. Table 4 also shows better performance of the proposed method compared to existing meth-

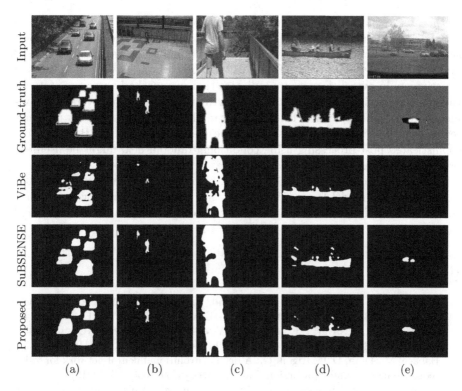

Fig. 7. Segmentation results of various sequences. (a) Highway, (b) PETS2006, (c) Overpass, (d) Canoe, (e) Parking from CDnet 2012 dataset.

ods. Furthermore, it is noteworthy to mention that on CDnet 2014, proposed method demonstrated a comparable performance (FM difference is 0.0023) to a recent deep learning-based supervised method [2] without the process of additional background image generation, and at the low computational cost. We also provide qualitative results in Fig. 7 which advocates our better performance compared to other existing methods.

Finally, we compare the processing speed and memory usage of our method with ViBe and SuBSENSE as our method is derived from these two. We have run the methods on Intel core i5 CPU (3.40 GHz) with a video of 320×240 frame size by keeping the parameters common for all the methods. From Table 5, we can observe that even though our method requires less memory than SuBSENSE, it is slower than others. However, it is very possible to decrease the time necessary for code generation by optimizing the implementation.

5   Conclusions

In this paper, we have presented a background subtraction method for foreground segmentation based on a highly efficient and robust descriptor. This method represents the background model by combining color and our proposed Local Top Directional Pattern (LTDP) which unambiguously characterizes local shape information while showing robustness to illumination variations. We have evaluated our method on the CDnet 2012 and 2014 datasets, and the results of experiments in overall F-measure indicates that our method surpasses state-of-the-art unsupervised methods. It is noteworthy to mention that several improvements are still possible which can make our method more powerful. For instance, region level analysis could improve the shape of segmented objects. Besides, more sophisticated post-processing using conditional random field might be useful to provide better results. In addition to these, as we are calculating 8-directional responses for encoding the descriptor code, high-speed parallel implementations would make the model faster. We believe that this kind of improvements may encourage and derive one to achieve outstanding results in the background subtraction.

References

1. Aggarwal, A., Biswas, S., Singh, S., Sural, S., Majumdar, A.K.: Object tracking using background subtraction and motion estimation in MPEG videos. In: Narayanan, P.J., Nayar, S.K., Shum, H.-Y. (eds.) ACCV 2006. LNCS, vol. 3852, pp. 121–130. Springer, Heidelberg (2006). https://doi.org/10.1007/11612704_13

2. Babaee, M., Dinh, D.T., Rigoll, G.: A deep convolutional neural network for video sequence background subtraction. Pattern Recogn. **76**, 635–649 (2018)

3. Barnich, O., Van Droogenbroeck, M.: ViBe: a universal background subtraction algorithm for video sequences. IEEE Trans. Image Process. **20**(6), 1709–1724 (2011)

4. Bilodeau, G.A., Jodoin, J.P., Saunier, N.: Change detection in feature space using local binary similarity patterns. In: 2013 International Conference on Computer and Robot Vision (CRV), pp. 106–112. IEEE (2013)

5. Bouwmans, T., Silva, C., Marghes, C., Zitouni, M.S., Bhaskar, H., Frelicot, C.: On the role and the importance of features for background modeling and foreground detection. Comput. Sci. Rev. **28**, 26–91 (2018)

6. De Gregorio, M., Giordano, M.: A WiSARD-based approach to CDnet. In: 2013 BRICS Congress on Computational Intelligence and 11th Brazilian Congress on Computational Intelligence (BRICS-CCI & CBIC), pp. 172–177. IEEE (2013)

7. Elgammal, A., Duraiswami, R., Harwood, D., Davis, L.S.: Background and foreground modeling using nonparametric Kernel density estimation for visual surveillance. Proc. IEEE **90**(7), 1151–1163 (2002)

8. Goyette, N., Jodoin, P.M., Porikli, F., Konrad, J., Ishwar, P.: Changedetection.net: a new change detection benchmark dataset. In: 2012 IEEE Computer Society Conference on Computer Vision and Pattern Recognition Workshops (CVPRW), pp. 1–8. IEEE (2012)

9. Haines, T.S., Xiang, T.: Background subtraction with dirichletprocess mixture models. IEEE Trans. Pattern Anal. Mach. Intell. **36**(4), 670–683 (2014)

10. Han, B., Davis, L.S.: Density-based multifeature background subtraction with support vector machine. IEEE Trans. Pattern Anal. Mach. Intell. **34**(5), 1017–1023 (2012)

11. Heikkila, M., Pietikainen, M.: A texture-based method for modeling the background and detecting moving objects. IEEE Trans. Pattern Anal. Mach. Intell. **28**(4), 657–662 (2006)
12. Hofmann, M., Tiefenbacher, P., Rigoll, G.: Background segmentation with feedback: the pixel-based adaptive segmenter. In: 2012 IEEE Computer Society Conference on Computer Vision and Pattern Recognition Workshops (CVPRW), pp. 38–43. IEEE (2012)
13. KaewTraKulPong, P., Bowden, R.: An improved adaptive background mixture model for real-time tracking with shadow detection. In: Remagnino, P., Jones, G.A., Paragios, N., Regazzoni, C.S. (eds.) Video-Based Surveillance Systems, pp. 135–144. Springer, Boston (2002). https://doi.org/10.1007/978-1-4615-0913-4_11
14. Kalaivani, P., Vimala, D.: Human action recognition using background subtraction method. Int. Res. J. Eng. Technol. (IRJET) **2**(3), 1032–1035 (2015)
15. Kim, J., Ramirez Rivera, A., Ryu, B., Chae, O.: Simultaneous foreground detection and classification with hybrid features. In: Proceedings of the IEEE International Conference on Computer Vision, pp. 3307–3315 (2015)
16. Kim, J., Rivera, A.R., Kim, B., Roy, K., Chae, O.: Background modeling using adaptive properties of hybrid features. In: 2017 14th IEEE International Conference on Advanced Video and Signal Based Surveillance (AVSS), pp. 1–6. IEEE (2017)
17. Kim, K., Chalidabhongse, T.H., Harwood, D., Davis, L.: Real-time foreground-background segmentation using codebook model. Real-time Imaging **11**(3), 172–185 (2005)
18. Lee, D.S.: Effective Gaussian mixture learning for video background subtraction. IEEE Trans. Pattern Anal. Mach. Intell. **27**(5), 827–832 (2005)
19. Liao, S., Zhao, G., Kellokumpu, V., Pietikäinen, M., Li, S.Z.: Modeling pixel process with scale invariant local patterns for background subtraction in complex scenes. In: 2010 IEEE Conference on Computer Vision and Pattern Recognition (CVPR), pp. 1301–1306. IEEE (2010)
20. McIvor, A.M.: Background subtraction techniques. Proc. Image Vis. Comput. **4**, 3099–3104 (2000)
21. Roy, K., Kim, J., Iqbal, M.T.B., Makhmudkhujaev, F., Ryu, B., Chae, O.: An adaptive fusion scheme of color and edge features for background subtraction. In: 2017 14th IEEE International Conference on Advanced Video and Signal Based Surveillance (AVSS), pp. 1–6. IEEE (2017)
22. Sajid, H., Cheung, S.C.S.: Universal multimode background subtraction. IEEE Trans. Image Process. **26**(7), 3249–3260 (2017)
23. Senior, A.W., Tian, Y.L., Lu, M.: Interactive motion analysis for video surveillance and long term scene monitoring. In: Koch, R., Huang, F. (eds.) ACCV 2010. LNCS, vol. 6468, pp. 164–174. Springer, Heidelberg (2011). https://doi.org/10.1007/978-3-642-22822-3_17
24. St-Charles, P.L., Bilodeau, G.A.: Improving background subtraction using local binary similarity patterns. In: 2014 IEEE Winter Conference on Applications of Computer Vision (WACV), pp. 509–515. IEEE (2014)
25. St-Charles, P.L., Bilodeau, G.A., Bergevin, R.: SuBSENSE: a universal change detection method with local adaptive sensitivity. IEEE Trans. Image Process. **24**(1), 359–373 (2015)
26. Stauffer, C., Grimson, W.E.L.: Adaptive background mixture models for real-time tracking. In: IEEE Computer Society Conference on Computer Vision and Pattern Recognition, vol. 2, pp. 246–252. IEEE (1999)
27. Tian, Y., Senior, A., Lu, M.: Robust and efficient foreground analysis in complex surveillance videos. Mach. Vis. Appl. **23**(5), 967–983 (2012)

28. Van Droogenbroeck, M., Paquot, O.: Background subtraction: experiments and improvements for viBe. In: 2012 IEEE Computer Society Conference on Computer Vision and Pattern Recognition Workshops (CVPRW), pp. 32–37. IEEE (2012)
29. Wang, Y., Jodoin, P.M., Porikli, F., Konrad, J., Benezeth, Y., Ishwar, P.: CDnet 2014: an expanded change detection benchmark dataset. In: Proceedings of the IEEE Conference on Computer Vision and Pattern Recognition Workshops, pp. 387–394 (2014)
30. Wren, C.R., Azarbayejani, A., Darrell, T., Pentland, A.P.: Pfinder: real-time tracking of the human body. IEEE Trans. Pattern Anal. Mach. Intell. **19**(7), 780–785 (1997)
31. Zeng, D., Zhu, M., Zhou, T., Xu, F., Yang, H.: Robust background subtraction via the local similarity statistical descriptor. Appl. Sci. **7**(10), 989 (2017)
32. Zivkovic, Z.: Improved adaptive Gaussian mixture model for background subtraction. In: Proceedings of the 17th International Conference on Pattern Recognition, ICPR 2004, vol. 2, pp. 28–31. IEEE (2004)

A Coded Aperture for Watermark Extraction from Defocused Images

Hiroki Hamasaki[1], Shingo Takeshita[1], Kentaro Nakai[1], Toshiki Sonoda[2],
Hiroshi Kawasaki[2], Hajime Nagahara[3], and Satoshi Ono[1(✉)]

[1] Kagoshima University, Kagoshima, Japan
ono@ibe.kagoshima-u.ac.jp
[2] Kyushu University, Fukuoka, Japan
[3] Osaka University, Osaka, Japan

Abstract. Barcodes and 2D codes are widely used for various purposes, such as electronic payments and product management. Special code readers, and consumer smartphones can be used to scan codes; thus concerns about fraud and authenticity are important. Embedding watermarks in 2D codes, which allows simultaneous recognition and tamper detection by simply analyzing the captured pattern without requiring an additional device is considered a promising solution. However, smartphone cameras frequently suffer misfocus especially if the target object is too close to the lens, which makes the captured image defocused and results in failure to read watermarks. In this paper, we propose the use of a coded aperture imaging technique to recover watermarks. We have designed a coded aperture that is robust against defocus blur by optimizing the aperture pattern using a genetic algorithm. In addition, we have developed a programmable coded aperture that includes an actual optical process that works in an optimization loop; thus, the complicated effects of the optical aberrations can be considered. Experimental results demonstrate that the proposed method can extend the depth of field for watermark extraction to 3.1 times wider than that of a general circular aperture.

Keywords: Coded aperture · Digital image watermark ·
Two-dimensional code · Extended depth of field ·
Device-based optimization · Genetic algorithm

1 Introduction

There is strong demand for machine recognition of artificial patterns such as alphanumeric characters, traffic signs, barcodes and two-dimensional (2D) codes. Various studies have explored recognition of such artificial patterns, and most of these studies assumed that the patterns are captured in focus. If this assumption does not hold due to defocus or motion blur, the recognition rate deteriorates. Therefore, some attempts have been made to read such patterns from blurred

© Springer Nature Switzerland AG 2019
C. V. Jawahar et al. (Eds.): ACCV 2018, LNCS 11366, pp. 231–246, 2019.
https://doi.org/10.1007/978-3-030-20876-9_15

images. Digital image watermarks, which are widely used for copyright protection, tamper detection, and authenticity verification, are also machine-readable artificial patterns.

In the last couple of years, 2D codes have become widely used for electronic payments using smartphones to scan 2D codes. Embedding watermarks in 2D codes allows simultaneous recognition and tamper detection without any additional operations, with the exception of scanning the code. However, smartphone cameras frequently misfocus if the target code is too close to the camera lens. In addition, watermarks are typically designed for low-visibility and it is difficult to focus using a camera's auto focus mechanism. Thus, compared to special equipment, such as barcode readers, the smartphone cameras easily cause defocus blur and fail to read watermarks. Extracting watermarks from blurred images is a formidable challenge, and very few studies have addressed the problem of extending the depth of field for watermark extraction.

In this study, we use coded aperture imaging for watermark reading under the defocus condition. We introduce a coded aperture that considers the spatial frequency characteristics of the watermark to prevent loss of watermark components caused by photographing and to restore them by deconvolution and frequency transformation. However, when the distance between a sensor and target changes, the amount of blur and the target image size change; thus, the coded aperture must deal with a broader band than the frequency wavelengths of the original watermark pattern.

There, we propose an aperture pattern design method that increases comprehensive optimization in consideration of photographing to postprocessing. The proposed method is based on a genetic algorithm (GA) [18] and designs a pattern that maintains watermark components even when the capturing distance changes while suppressing the occurrence of artifacts caused by deconvolution.

In addition, conventional methods [1–5] for coded aperture optimization are based on only simulation that cannot completely imitate an actual camera's optics, such as aberration. Therefore, we also propose an optimization method that incorporates an actual camera into an optimization loop for objective (cost) function calculation. A camera with a programmable aperture enables us to realize device-based optimization.

The main contributions of this paper are as follows:

- To the best of our knowledge, this study is the first attempt to realize coded aperture imaging for watermark extraction. The proposed method is robust against defocus blur, scale changes, and the camera-capture process, which is a serious attack against image watermarks [6,7].
- We propose a coded aperture design optimized for watermark detection under defocus conditions.
- In addition to simulation, we also optimize the coded aperture pattern using a camera in the loop. This approach can include the effects of optical aberrations for coded aperture optimization.

2   Related Work

2.1   Coded Apertures

Recently, computational photography (CP), i.e., technologies for digital image capture with postprocessing, has attracted increasing attention. Representative technologies include *coded apertures (CAs)*, which are non-circular 2D pattern masks inserted into the aperture position of a camera [1–5], *coded exposures*, [8] in which the shutter open/close pattern is coded along the time axis, and *light field cameras* that capture the direction and intensity of light rays [9].

Recently, CAs have been investigated relative to deblurring, super-resolution, and all-focus image production [1–5]. Correcting defocus blur is a major purpose of CAs. It can be described by a point spread function (PSF) that depends on the shapes of the camera aperture and lens. When using a general circular aperture, defocus blur damages the high frequency components of a captured image because the frequency components of the PSF of the circular aperture involve many zero-crossings in the frequency domain. On the other hand, a CA controls PSF shape and its frequency components and therefore avoids information loss. For example, Zhou et al. proposed a method to design CA for defocus deblurring [1]. In addition, Levin et al. proposed an aperture for simultaneous reconstruction of a deblurred image and depth information [2], and Veeraraghavan et al. proposed a coded aperture to synthesize refocused images [4].

2.2   Applications of Computational Photography to Pattern Recognition

Recently, some studies have attempted to apply coded aperture techniques to pattern recognition, where the targets involve known artificial patterns. Iwamura et al. proposed a recognition framework of known patterns such as characters and traffic signs [10], which uses Veeraraghavan's aperture to recover a less-degraded image from defocused images while estimating depth. It experimentally demonstrated that this framework achieved fast and robust recognition against defocus and scaling. Sakuyama et al. proposed a recognition method for alignment marks for assembly and inspection by industrial machines [11]. Compared to natural images, the target alignment images involve a strong spectrum in the low frequency range; therefore, they designed a target-oriented coded aperture using a GA and demonstrated that the designed aperture allowed higher accuracy alignment than that of conventional aperture patterns. Kawamoto et al. designed a coded aperture pattern for object recognition, such as printed barcodes, and showed that the designed aperture successfully extended the depth of field for recognition [12]. In addition, Masoudifar et al. designed an aperture for license plate recognition and demonstrated the effect of DoF extension compared to a circular aperture [13].

In contrast, other CP techniques have been applied to pattern recognition tasks involving barcodes and 2D code decoding. For example, Hashimoto et al. proposed a method to extend DoF for barcode decoding using wavefront coding, which allows a PSF to be depth invariant [14]. Tisse et al. applied a method

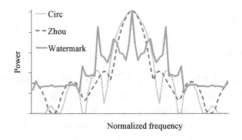

Fig. 1. 1D slices of fourier transforms of watermark components and some aperture patterns. (Color figure online)

where specific lens flaws are introduced during lens design to increase the DoF for barcode reading and natural image capturing [15], and McCloskey et al. proposed a method to decode barcodes using a light field camera [16].

Few studies have investigated the application of CP to extract watermarks from blurred images. Pramila et al. proposed a method to extract watermarks from images captured with wide angles by reconstructing an all-focus image [6,7]; however, this method requires capturing a focal stack and time-consuming postprocessing involving focal stack optimization, image registration, and image fusion.

This paper addresses the problem where watermarks are difficult to read under defocus conditions. We use coded aperture imaging to robustly capture and decode it. The proposed method uses a single image and simple computation, while a previous method using a focal stack or light field requires multiple images or higher computation. In addition, the proposed coded aperture design framework produces an optimized aperture pattern appropriate to a target watermarking scheme, where a certain combination of frequency coefficients is selected to embed watermark information.

3 Overview of the Proposed Method

3.1 Difficulty of Designing Aperture Patterns for Watermark Extraction

The purpose of this study is to realize a watermark extraction method for defocus-blurred images using CA. Note that it is only necessary to preserve the frequency coefficients corresponding to the watermark and suppress the occurrence of artifacts that affect the watermark. If the frequency coefficients of the watermark are not maintained when captured, it is difficult to reconstruct watermark information even by deconvolution in postprocessing. Figure 1 shows example frequency components of a watermark, as well as circular and CA [1]. If an aperture has zero-crossing or low response, such as that shown in green in Fig. 1 at the frequency where the watermark power peaks, it is difficult for the aperture to hold the frequency coefficients of the watermark.

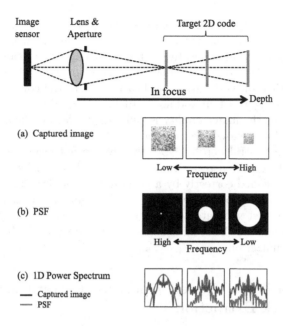

Fig. 2. Difficulty to extract watermark. (Color figure online)

The difficulty in designing a blur-invariant aperture arises from asynchronous changes to the image resolution and the degree of blur. Figure 2 shows an optical configuration, including changes to the captured image sizes (Fig. 2(a)), the PSF depending on the depth (Fig. 2(b)), and the power spectra of the PSFs and captured images involving the watermark (Fig. 2(c)). In this study, we focus on the out-of-focus area, i.e., areas shifted from the focal plane. When the target 2D code moves away from the camera beyond the focal plane, the resolution of the captured image is reduced, as shown in Fig. 2(a); thus, high frequency components in the aperture are required, as shown by the gray lines in Fig. 2(c). However, the defocus blur scale increases, as shown in Fig. 2(b); therefore, the aperture frequency response is reduced, as shown by the blue lines in Fig. 2(c). On the other hand, when the target moves from the focal plane toward the camera, the captured image gets larger and the amount of blur increases. Although the necessary frequency component gets lower in both cases, the change rates of the frequency bands differ. To achieve blur-invariance relative to depth, the frequency characteristics in the inverse direction must be considered, which makes it difficult to design an effective aperture pattern.

3.2   Basic Idea

To design a coded aperture pattern that satisfies the requirement discussed in Sect. 3.1, this paper proposes a global optimization method that comprehensively takes from photographing to postprocessing. The proposed method utilizes a GA that allows the design of an aperture in which appropriate frequency bands appear depending on the distance from the focal plane. We assume that the frequency bands that include the watermark components are known; thus, the aperture pattern should retain the watermark components from defocus blur while preventing artifacts that damage the watermark. Conversely, since we assume a 2D code authentication verification application where the cover image is a 2D code that is robust against blur and noise [16,17], the quality of the image can be sacrificed; however, the image quality is sufficient to decode the cover 2D code.

The proposed GA-based optimization method maximizes the watermark extraction rate at several depths. Note that we do not evaluate reconstructed image quality. The only constraint the proposed method considers is if the cover 2D code can be decoded correctly by a general 2D code decoder. Since the proposed optimization method is applicable to both simulation- and device-based optimizations, we first generate aperture candidates via simulation-based optimization. We then refine the obtained candidates and select the best pattern via device-based optimization.

4   Optimization of Coded Aperture Pattern for Watermark Extraction

4.1   Process Flow

Figure 3 shows the process flow of the proposed aperture design method. The proposed method is based on a GA [18], and the algorithm framework is the same as that of previous work [1] but differs in the evaluation process relative to two points, i.e., the proposed method

- evaluates potential solutions using actual devices and optical simulation (Sect. 5), and
- introduces fitness sharing [23] to avoid premature convergence (Sect. 4.5).

At initialization, N_P potential solutions, which correspond to aperture pattern candidates, are generated at random. In the case of refinement using actual devices, the final solution candidates obtained by the previous optimization via simulation are used as the initial population.

The main loop of the proposed algorithm primarily comprises solution evaluation and reproduction. The difference between simulation- and device-based optimizations is the evaluation process. The right part of Fig. 3 shows the evaluation process based on simulation. A watermarked image is virtually photographed by convolving its original image with a simulated PSF distorted by free form deformation (FFD) to consider the distortion of the actual device, and by subsequently adding Gaussian noise. Then, the virtually captured image is deconvolved. Finally, the watermark components are extracted via frequency transformation and compared to an original watermark pattern for fitness calculation. In

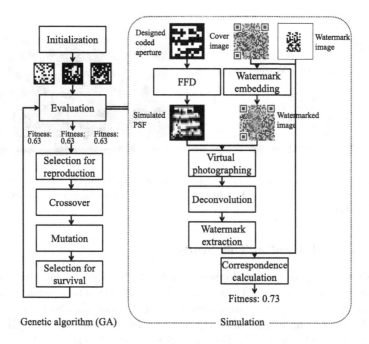

Fig. 3. Process flow of the proposed aperture design method.

case of refinement, a camera equipped with a programmable aperture captures the watermarked image.

After evaluation, new solution candidates are generated in the same manner as the general GA. Parent solutions are selected at a probability proportional to their fitness. The selected parents produce two offspring by crossover, where subsolutions trimmed by a randomly-selected rectangle region are exchanged between the parents. A mutation operator is then applied to generate new offspring.

Next, solution evaluation by simulation and solution reproduction based on objective function values are iterated. Details about the simulation are given in Sect. 4.4, and the objective function of the GA is described in Sect. 4.5.

4.2   Solution Representation

Designing an aperture is a combinatorial optimization problem whose search space size is $2^{N_a \times N_a}$, where $N_a \times N_a$ is the number of binary aperture patterns of side length N_a. According to the previous work [1], here, N_a is set to 11. By considering surrounding closed cells, this results in a 13×13 pattern as a coded aperture.

(a) Cover code   (b) Watermark

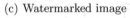

(c) Watermarked image

Fig. 4. Example images of cover code, watermark, and watermarked 2D code (LH1 and LH2).

Fig. 5. Experimental environment with a programmable-aperture camera.

4.3 Watermark Used in This Study

This study utilizes a frequency domain-based watermarking scheme relying on a Haar-based Discrete Wavelet Transform (DWT) [19–21]. The proposed method embeds the watermark image into a combination of subbands obtained by DWT, i.e., low-horizontal high-vertical (LH), high-horizontal low-vertical (HL), and high-horizontal high-vertical (HH) frequencies for each level.

A watermarked image Y can be obtained by the following DWT:

$$Y(x,y) = \frac{1}{\sqrt{MN}} \sum_m \sum_n \bar{d}_\phi(j_0,m,n)\phi_{j_0,m,n}(x,y)$$

$$+ \frac{1}{\sqrt{MN}} \sum_{i \in \{H,V,D\}} \sum_k \sum_m \sum_n \bar{d}_\psi^i(j_0-k,m,n)\psi_{j_0-k,m,n}^i(x,y) \quad (1)$$

where, $\phi_{j,m,n}(x,y)$ and $\psi_{j-k,m,n}^i(x,y)$ indicate scaling and Wavelet functions, j_0 is a starting scale, and (M,N) indicates a target image size. $\bar{d}_\phi$ and $\bar{d}_\psi$ denote coefficients that the corresponding watermark component is added. Figure 4 shows examples of a cover image, a watermark pattern image, and a watermarked 2D code image whose LH1 and LH2 subbands are used to embed the watermark.

Assuming a 2D code verification application, we use a 2D code as a cover image and we refer to it as a cover 2D code. For the cover 2D code to include frequency components in various directions, its module has a circular shape (rather than the commonly used rectangle), and its edges are slightly blurred by applying a Gaussian filter.

4.4 Simulation for Watermark Extraction

Generally, a captured image Y' is represented by the following equation:

$$Y' = Y \otimes PSF + N \quad (2)$$

where Y denotes an original image, $\otimes$ denotes convolution, N denotes Gaussian noise, and PSF denotes the blur kernel. Theoretically, the aperture pattern can be used as a PSF; however, they do not correspond exactly due to distortion caused by the optical system.

The proposed method defines its simulation model and represents a captured image Y' as follows:

$$Y' = D(PSF) \otimes Y + N \tag{3}$$

As described in Sect. 6, the proposed method employs LCoS-based programmable aperture; thus, distortion introduced by this aperture should be modeled. The proposed method models optical distortion $D(\cdot)$ that represents non-linear response between the aperture pattern and the PSF by free form deformation [22].

4.5   Objective Function

The proposed method maximizes the amount of extracted watermark defined as the bit correct ratio (BCR) [21]. The objective function f of potential solution I is calculated as follows:

$$f(I) = \sum_{d \in S_d} \sum_{a \in S_a} \mathrm{BCR}\left(W, W_{d,a}^{\mathrm{cap}}(I)\right) \tag{4}$$

where W is an original watermark image, S_d and S_a are sets of depth and rotation angles around the axis perpendicular to the screen in which images used for solution evaluation are captured, and $W_{d,a}^{\mathrm{cap}}$ denotes the watermark image extracted from $Y_{d,a}^{\mathrm{cap}}$, which is a target 2D code image captured at depth d and angle a. $Y_{d,a}^{\mathrm{cap}}$ is obtained by simulation using I as an aperture.

The BCR is calculated as follows:

$$\mathrm{BCR}(W, W') = 1 - \frac{\sum_{w=1}^{w_W} \sum_{h=1}^{h_W} \left(W_{w,h} \oplus W'_{w,h}\right)}{w_W h_W} \tag{5}$$

where $W_{w,h}$ and $W'_{w,h}$ denote intensity values at the position (w, h) in the original and extracted watermark images, $h_W \times w_W$ denotes watermark image size and $\oplus$ denotes exclusive OR operator.

The proposed method adopts a simple GA, a generation alternation model, and employs fitness sharing [23] to compensate for a drawback of the generation alternation model, i.e., the fitness value of a potential solution I is degraded if there exist other potential solutions $S_{I_{\mathrm{sim}}}$ near I and I is not the best in $S_{I_{\mathrm{sim}}} \cup I$.

$$f_{\mathrm{sh}}(I) = \begin{cases} \dfrac{F(I)}{|S_{I_{\mathrm{sim}}}| - T_{S_{\mathrm{sim}}} + 1} & \text{if } I \text{ is not the best} \\ & \text{and } |S_{I_{\mathrm{sim}}}| > T_{S_{\mathrm{sim}}} \\ F(I) & \text{otherwise} \end{cases} \tag{6}$$

where $|S_{I_{\text{sim}}}|$ is the number of potential solutions in $S_{I_{\text{sim}}}$, and $T_{S_{\text{sim}}}$ is a parameter that determines the number of solutions permitted to exist in a single neighborhood.

5 Photographing Environment with Programmable Aperture Camera

In this study, a programmable aperture camera [24] captures the watermarked 2D codes. This camera utilizes liquid crystal on silicon (LCoS) as an aperture. Compared to a LC display (LCD)-based device, the LCoS-based camera can attenuate diffraction caused by driving circuits between LC elements in the LCD. The camera does not require any mechanical operation to change the aperture patterns. Only electrical operations are required, e.g., uploading aperture patterns to the camera. Therefore, when validating various aperture patterns, all other experimental parameters can be constant.

The proposed method refines the aperture pattern candidates obtained through simulation-based optimization by including the actual optical process using the camera in the evaluation process in an optimization loop. Simultaneously, to capture a watermarked image with a candidate aperture pattern, its PSF, which is used for deconvolution process, is captured by photographing a pseudo point light source, i.e., a small dot displayed on a smartphone. Here, a motorized stage is used to perform photographing and calculate the watermark extraction rate under several different distances and rotation angles. The above device-based optimization allows the proposed method to consider the complicated effects of the optical aberrations, thereby resulting in designing a coded aperture that is adapted to the camera.

6 Evaluation

6.1 Experimental Setup

Experiments were conducted to evaluate the effectiveness of CA for watermark extraction from blurred images. This study utilized a Haar-based DWT [19–21]. In addition, we employed a programmable-aperture camera (Sect. 5), a Point Grey CCD sensor (1/3 in. CCD; $1,384 \times 1,036$ pixels; 30 fps), and a TAMRON C-mount lens (8 mm, F/1.8). In addition, we used a smartphone ($720 \times 1,200$ pixels resolution, 4.6 in. LCD) to display a watermarked 2D code[1]. The smartphone was set on a motorized stage that can change both the distance between the camera and the smartphone and the rotation angle around the axis perpendicular to the screen (Fig. 5). Here, the smartphone was set in a direction unaffected by polarized light when not rotated. Note that, when rotating $-30°$, the photographed images became somewhat dark due

---

[1] Note that the watermark can be extracted from the 2D codes printed on papers. Under such scenarios, the 2D code needs to be illuminated.

to the influence of the polarized light. This environment does not require mechanical operation to change aperture patterns and watermarked images; thus, all other experimental parameters can be constant. We set the focal plane of the camera to 50 mm from the front of the lens.

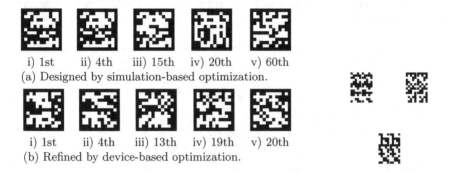

i) 1st   ii) 4th   iii) 15th   iv) 20th   v) 60th
(a) Designed by simulation-based optimization.

i) 1st   ii) 4th   iii) 13th   iv) 19th   v) 20th
(b) Refined by device-based optimization.

Fig. 6. Designed apertures by the proposed method.

Fig. 7. Watermark patterns for test.

6.2 Aperture Pattern Optimization

We attempted to design an aperture that expands the DoF for watermark extraction in two cases, i.e., with and without deconvolution. To facilitate simple analysis, the watermark image was embedded into the LH1 and LH2 subbands with a watermarking strength level of 192. The proposed GA-based method with a population size of 100 first designs aperture pattern candidates via simulation-based optimization over 600 generations, and then refines them via device-based optimization over 50 generations. In both the simulation- and device-based optimizations, the proposed method attempted to maximize the BCR at three depths (70, 80, and 90 mm) and three rotation angles (0, −15, and 15°). To prioritize the extraction rate when not rotating, seven points were used for the objective function calculation, i.e., $(S_d$ mm$, S_a$ degrees$) \in \{(70, 0), (80, 0), (90, 0), (70, -15), (90, -15), (70, 15), (90, 15)\}$. In the simulation-based optimization, the noise level σ was set to 0.0001. The deformation model $D(\cdot)$ used to simulate PSF distortion was generated at a depth of 80 mm by capturing a 3×3 grid pattern. In the device-based optimization, for each candidate aperture pattern, the PSF was captured using a point light source from the smartphone displaying a small rectangle (2×2 pixels) at depths of 70, 80, and 90 mm.

Figure 6(a) shows example aperture patterns designed by simulation-based optimization, and Fig. 6(b) shows examples refined by device-based optimization. Overall, simulation-based optimization tended to produce aperture pattern candidates involving narrow linear openings; however, when mounted on the programmable aperture camera, such openings were collapsed and the aperture pattern shape changed. Therefore, during the refinement with the camera, narrow linear openings such as ones contained in apertures shown in Fig. 6(a)(i) and (ii) were widened and high frequency patterns were added as shown in Fig. 6(b)(i) and (ii). In contrast, the aperture patterns with both blob-like opening shapes and diagonal patterns, as shown in Fig. 6(a)(iii) and (v), demonstrated watermark extraction rates similar to that of the simulation, leading to the occurrence of the good apertures, as shown in Fig. 6(b)(iii) and (iv), which were different from the top elites.

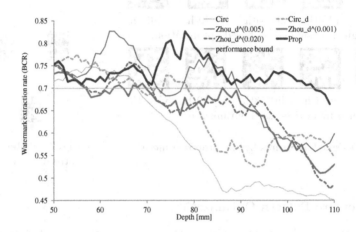

Fig. 8. Watermark extraction rates (BCR) without rotation on the actual environment.

6.3   Comparison with Conventional Apertures

The aperture designed by the proposed method ($Prop_d$) was compared in a real environment with a circular aperture (Circ and $Circ_d$) and CAs for deblurring [1] with different three noise levels of 0.001, 0.005, and 0.020 ($Zhou_d^{(0.001)}$, $Zhou_d^{(0.005)}$, and $Zhou_d^{(0.020)}$). $Prop_d$ is shown in Fig. 6(b)(iv), which was selected among the top 20 aperture patterns because it demonstrated a stable extraction rate throughout the entire range, while the others adapted excessively to depths of 70 through 90 mm. We applied Wiener deconvolution with the kernels that were captured PSF using a point light source while changing the distance to it. All apertures were evaluated with the target at distances between 50–110 mm from the camera lens in intervals of 1 mm using the motorized stage.

Figure 8 shows the watermark extraction rates (BCR) on the actual environment when the target watermarked 2D code was not rotated. In this comparison, three test watermark images (Fig. 7), which differ from the one used in the optimization, were used to observe the averaged BCR values. Circ and $Circ_d$ show the results of the circular aperture without and with deconvolution, respectively. Here, the differences demonstrate the effect of deconvolution. $Zhou_d^{(0.001)}$, $Zhou_d^{(0.005)}$, and $Zhou_d^{(0.020)}$ show the results obtained using CAs.

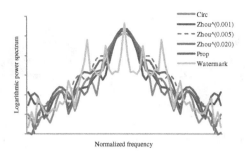

Fig. 9. 1D slice of power spectra at 80 [mm] depth.

As can be seen, the watermark extraction rate improved at certain ranges, such as 58–72 mm and 78–99 mm with $\sigma = 0.005$

Overall, $\mathrm{Prop_d}$ demonstrated almost the best BCR values at approximately 72–110 mm, which includes the target depths of the optimization. Originally, Zhou's apertures have less zero-crossings and were expected to be effective at removing the blur of the cover code; however, $\mathrm{Zhou_d}$ showed worse performance than $\mathrm{Prop_d}$ because it was designed assuming greater photographic distance and is inappropriate for the environment employed in this study. Figure 9 shows the 1D slice of the power spectra of the tested apertures obtained from the PSFs at 80 mm. At this depth, $\mathrm{Prop_d}$ demonstrated the best performance and $\mathrm{Zhou_d^{(0.001)}}$ and $\mathrm{Zhou_d^{(0.020)}}$ showed the worse because, as shown in Fig. 9, they have lower responses than others in the frequencies corresponding to the watermark.

For 2D code authentication, a BCR value of 0.7 is sufficient to extract the entire watermark information because a 30% decoding error[2] can be corrected using Reed-Solomon coding at the expense of embedded information capacity. Therefore, decoding with the proposed aperture at 50–105 mm from the front of the lens can be considered as a success, whereas the general circular and Zhou's apertures allowed extracting the watermark up to 58 and 72 mm, respectively. Using a focal length of 50 mm as a reference, the aperture designed by the proposed method successfully expands the DoF for watermark extraction by 3.1 times compared to the circular aperture.

6.4 Robustness Against Rotation

To facilitate simple analysis, the watermarking scheme used in this experiment embeds watermark information into LH1 and LH2, and seems to be sensitive to the target rotation. To evaluate the robustness against rotation of the apertures designed by the proposed method, the watermark extraction rates were compared while rotating a target watermarked 2D code on the axis perpendicular to the smartphone screen. The same apertures compared in Sect. 6.3 were evaluated by changing the rotation angles from −30 to 30° in intervals of 15° while changing

---

[2] 30% error correction is the same capacity as QR code [25].

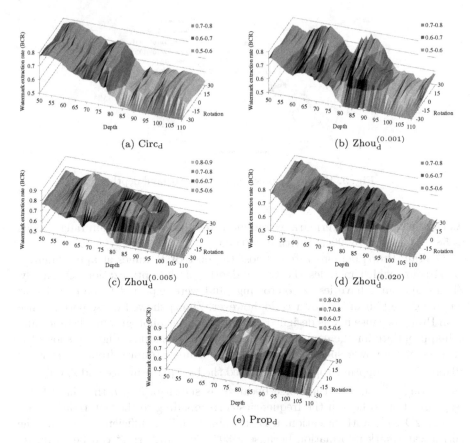

Fig. 10. Watermark extraction rates (BCR) with rotation.

the distance between the camera and the rotated target from 50–110 mm in intervals of 1 mm using the motorized stage. As with the experiment discussed in Sect. 6.3, the three watermark patterns shown in Fig. 7 were tested.

Figure 10 shows the average BCR value for each depth and rotation angle. The graph in Fig. 10(e) clearly shows that the aperture designed by the proposed method was as robust against target rotation within the tested angle range as the other apertures, whereas the DoF of the proposed aperture was broader than the other apertures. When the smartphone was rotated at −30°, BCR values deteriorated due to the influence of the polarized light.

7 Conclusion

This paper has proposed a method to design CAs that allows watermark extraction from blurred images. The proposed method first designs CA candidates via simulation-based optimization and then refines them via device-based optimization to consider the complicated effects of the optical aberrations. Experimental results demonstrate that the aperture designed by the proposed method successfully extended the DoF for watermark extraction while maintaining robustness against rotation. In future, we plan to focus on simultaneous optimization of the aperture and watermarking scheme.

Acknowledgements. This study was partially supported by JSPS KAKENHI Grant Numbers JP15H02758 and JP16K12490.

References

1. Zhou, C., Nayar, S.: What are good apertures for defocus deblurring? In: IEEE International Conference on Computational Photography (ICCP), pp. 1–8. IEEE (2009)
2. Levin, A., Fergus, R., Durand, F., Freeman, W.T.: Image and depth from a conventional camera with a coded aperture. ACM Trans. Graph. (TOG) **26**, 70 (2007)
3. Zhou, C., Lin, S., Nayar, S.: Coded aperture pairs for depth from defocus. In: IEEE 12th International Conference on Computer Vision, pp. 325–332 (2009)
4. Veeraraghavan, A., Raskar, R., Agrawal, A., Mohan, A., Tumblin, J.: Dappled photography: mask enhanced cameras for heterodyned light fields and coded aperture refocusing. ACM Trans. Graph. **26**, 69 (2007)
5. Gottesman, S.R., Fenimore, E.: New family of binary arrays for coded aperture imaging. Appl. Opt. **28**, 4344–4352 (1989)
6. Pramila, A., Keskinarkaus, A., Takala, V., Seppänen, T.: Extracting watermarks from printouts captured with wide angles using computational photography. Multimed. Tools Appl. **76**, 16063–16084 (2017)
7. Pramila, A., Keskinarkaus, A., Seppänen, T.: Increasing the capturing angle in print-cam robust watermarking. J. Syst. Softw. **135**, 205–215 (2018)
8. Raskar, R., Agrawal, A., Tumblin, J.: Coded exposure photography: motion deblurring using fluttered shutter. ACM Trans. Graph. (TOG) **25**, 795–804 (2006)
9. Ng, R., Levoy, M., Brédif, M., Duval, G., Horowitz, M., Hanrahan, P.: Light field photography with a hand-held plenoptic camera. Comput. Sci. Tech. Rep. CSTR **2**, 1–11 (2005)
10. Iwamura, M., Imura, M., Hiura, S., Kise, K.: Recognition of defocused patterns. IPSJ Trans. Comput. Vis. Appl. **6**, 48–52 (2014)
11. Sakuyama, T., Funatomi, T., Iiyama, M., Minoh, M.: Diffraction-compensating coded aperture for inspection in manufacturing. IEEE Trans. Ind. Inform. **11**, 782–789 (2015)
12. Kawamoto, Y., Hiura, S., Miyazaki, D., Furukawa, R., Baba, M.: Design and evaluation of the shape of coded aperture for the recognition of specific patterns (in Japanese). J. Inf. Process. **57**, 783–793 (2016)
13. Masoudifar, M., Pourreza, H.R.: Coded aperture solution for improving the performance of traffic enforcement cameras. Opt. Eng. **55**(10)
14. Hashimoto, W., Sugita, H., Komatsu, S.: Extended depth of field for laser-scanning barcode reader with wavefront coding. In: 2015 20th Microoptics Conference (MOC), pp. 1–2 (2015)
15. Tisse, C.L., Nguyen, H., Tessières, R., Pyanet, M., Guichard, F.: Extended depth-of-field (EDoF) using sharpness transport across colour channels. In: Proceedings of SPIE, Novel Optical Systems Design and Optimization XI, vol. 7061 (2008)

16. McCloskey, S., Miller, B.: Fast, high dynamic range light field processing for pattern recognition. In: 2016 IEEE International Conference on Computational Photography (ICCP), pp. 1–10 (2016)
17. Yang, G., Liu, N., Gao, Y.: Two-dimensional barcode image super-resolution reconstruction via sparse representation. In: Proceedings of International Conference on Information Science and Computer Applications (2013)
18. Goldberg, D.E.: Genetic Algorithms in Search, Optimization, and Machine Learning. Addison Wesley, Reading (1989)
19. Kundur, D., Hatzinakos, D.: A robust digital image watermarking method using wavelet-based fusion. In: 4th IEEE International Conference on Image Processing, pp. 544–547 (1997)
20. Kundurf, D., Hatzinakos, D.: Digital watermarking using multiresolution wavelet decomposition. In: Proceedings of the 1998 IEEE International Conference on Acoustics, Speech and Signal Processing, vol. 5, pp. 2969–2972 (1998)
21. Ono, S., Maehara, T., Minami, K.: Coevolutionary design of a watermark embedding scheme and an extraction algorithm for detecting replicated two-dimensional barcodes. Appl. Soft Comput. 46(C), 991–1007 (2016)
22. Sederberg, T.W., Parry, S.R.: Free-form deformation of solid geometric models. SIGGRAPH Comput. Graph. 20, 151–160 (1986)
23. Horn, J., Nafpliotis, N., Goldberg, D.E.: A niched pareto genetic algorithm for multiobjective optimization. In: Proceedings of the First IEEE Conference on Evolutionary Computation, IEEE World Congress on Computational Intelligence, pp. 82–87 (1994)
24. Nagahara, H., Zhou, C., Watanabe, T., Ishiguro, H., Nayar, S.K.: Programmable aperture camera using LCoS. In: Daniilidis, K., Maragos, P., Paragios, N. (eds.) ECCV 2010. LNCS, vol. 6316, pp. 337–350. Springer, Heidelberg (2010). https://doi.org/10.1007/978-3-642-15567-3_25
25. Information Technology: Automatic identification and data capture techniques - QR Code 2005 bar code symbology specification, ISO 18004 (2000)

Towards Locally Consistent Object Counting with Constrained Multi-stage Convolutional Neural Networks

Muming Zhao[1,2], Jian Zhang[2], Chongyang Zhang[1(✉)], and Wenjun Zhang[1]

[1] Shanghai Jiao Tong University, Shanghai 200240, China
sunny_zhang@sjtu.edu.cn
[2] University of Technology, Sydney, Sydney, NSW 2007, Australia

Abstract. High-density object counting in surveillance scenes is challenging mainly due to the drastic variation of object scales. The prevalence of deep learning has largely boosted the object counting accuracy on several benchmark datasets. However, does the global counts really count? Armed with this question we dive into the predicted density map whose summation over the whole regions reports the global counts for more in-depth analysis. We observe that the object density map generated by most existing methods usually lacks of local consistency, i.e., counting errors in local regions exist unexpectedly even though the global count seems to well match with the ground-truth. Towards this problem, in this paper we propose a constrained multi-stage Convolutional Neural Networks (CNNs) to jointly pursue locally consistent density map from two aspects. Different from most existing methods that mainly rely on the multi-column architectures of plain CNNs, we exploit a stacking formulation of plain CNNs. Benefited from the internal multi-stage learning process, the feature map could be repeatedly refined, allowing the density map to approach the ground-truth density distribution. For further refinement of the density map, we also propose a grid loss function. With finer local-region-based supervisions, the underlying model is constrained to generate locally consistent density values to minimize the training errors considering both the global and local counts accuracy. Experiments on two widely-tested object counting benchmarks with overall significant results compared with state-of-the-art methods demonstrate the effectiveness of our approach.

Keywords: Crowd counting · Constrained multi-stage CNN · Local consistency

1 Introduction

Automatic object counting in images using computer vision techniques plays an essential role in various real-world applications such as crowd analysis, traffic control and medical microscopy [23], and hence has gained increased attention

© Springer Nature Switzerland AG 2019
C. V. Jawahar et al. (Eds.): ACCV 2018, LNCS 11366, pp. 247–261, 2019.
https://doi.org/10.1007/978-3-030-20876-9_16

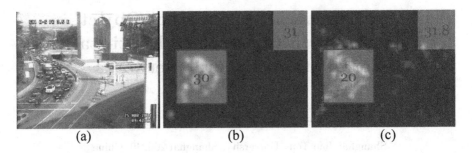

Fig. 1. Illustration of a locally inconsistent density map prediction. (a) to (c): the original image, the ground truth and the estimated density map. We observe that although the estimated total count (shown in the upper right box) is very close to the ground truth, the quality of prediction is not satisfactory with observation of obvious background noise and count errors of local regions (shown in the red-line-framed boxes). (Color figure online)

in recent years. Currently, the density-map-estimation based counting framework [11] learns to regress a spatial object density map instead of directly estimating the global counts, which is further reported by the summation of pixel values over the whole region on the density map. Due to its effective exploitation of the spatial information, this paradigm has been adopted by most later counting methods [4,17]. Recently the prevalence of deep learning combined with the density-map-estimation paradigm has largely boosted the counting accuracy on several benchmark datasets [16,19,22,25,26,28]. However, does the global counts really count? Our observation is that despite the improved global counting accuracy, significant local counting errors exist when diving into the predicted density map. This phenomenon has been reported in [6,23], however, it has not been sufficiently investigated and explicitly addressed.

Here we term this problem as *local inconsistency*. This is to denote the fact that, although a predicted density map can report accurate global count for an input image, the quality of prediction is not good from local perspectives: errors arise when counting objects in subregions of the image. This can be mainly attributed to the various object scales for most images taken in surveillance scenes with perspective distortion. With this property, the model is usually difficult to generate density values which adapt to the drastic changing scales. An example of a locally inconsistent prediction of density map is shown in Fig. 1. It can be observed that the estimated global count (*31.8*) is very close to the ground-truth (*30*). However, errors are exposed to the selected ROI and background regions. For the ROI area with objects, the predicted local count is only *20*, which is far more satisfactory compared to its real value (30). At the same time, the predicted count (*11.8*) for the background region takes a nearly 30% proportion of the estimated global count (*31.8*), whose influence to the counting accuracy should not be neglected. The Existence of local inconsistency of the predicted density map not only degrades the reliability of the finally reported object count, and also limits the quality of predicted object density distribution for related higher-level tasks [23]. In Sect. 3 we mathematically demonstrate that for an image the local object counting errors decide the upper bound of the global counting errors. In this way, pursing a locally consistent density map which aims to decrease local counting errors as much as possible is a reliable way to help improve the global counting accuracy.

In this paper, we start from this observation of locally inconsistent problem and propose a joint solution from two aspects. Current existing CNN-based methods handle object scale variations mainly by engineering multi-scale features either with multi-column architectures [9,19,28] or with multi-resolution inputs [16]. We differently exploit a simple yet effective stacking formulation of plain CNNs. Benefited from the internal multi-stage learning process, the feature map is repeatedly refined, and the density map is allowed to correct its errors to approach the ground-truth density distribution. The multi-stage network is fully convolutional and can generate corresponding-sized density map for an arbitrary-sized input image. We also propose a grid loss function to further refine the density map. With finer local-region-based supervisions, the model is constrained to generate locally consistent density values to help minimize the global training errors. The grid loss is differentiable and can be easily optimized with the Stochastic Gradient Descent (SGD) algorithm.

We summarize our main contribution as follows:

- For the observed local inconsistency problem, we propose a constrained multi-stage Convolutional Neural Networks (CMS-CNN) for jointly handling from two aspects.
- We exploit the multi-stage formulation to pursue locally consistent density map through repeatedly evaluation and refinement, and we also propose a grid loss function to further constrain the model to satisfy the demanding of locally consistent density values.
- Experiment results on two widely-adopted datasets demonstrated the effectiveness of the proposed method.

2   Related Work

Traditional detection-based counting methods mainly rely on the performance of object detection algorithms [5,13,20] and are usually fragile especially in crowded scenes with limited object sizes and severe occlusions. Alternatively, early regression approaches directly learn a mapping function from foreground representations to the corresponding counts [2,8], avoiding explicit delineation of individuals. However, this global regression approach ignores the useful spatial information. Towards this goal, a novel framework is proposed in the seminal work [11], which formulates object counting as a spatial density map prediction problem. With a continuously-valued density assigned for every single pixel, the final object counts can be obtained by summation of the pixel values over the whole density map. Enabling the utilization of spatial information, counting by density map prediction has been a widely-adopted paradigm for later counting approaches [4,17]. However, the representation ability of hand-crafted features limits the performance of those methods, especially for more challenging situations with severe occlusions and drastic object scale variations. Following our analysis in Sect. 1, our solution to the local inconsistency problem is related to those counting methods handling the object scale variation, which we will give a detailed discussion below.

Recently the prevalence of deep learning technique has largely boosted the counting performance [16,19,22,25,26,28]. Along with several newly-emerged datasets [1,6,26,28] which contain extremely dense crowd in clutter background with large perspective distortion, the drastic object scale variation has been one of the most important problems which hinders the counting accuracy. Several deep learning based counting methods are proposed to deal with this situation. To overcome the object scale variations, one of the earliest works [26] propose a patch-based convolutional neural network (CNN) to process normalized patches for object density map estimation. Given an image, patches are extracted at a size proportional to their perspective values and then are normalized into one same scale. In this way, object scale distinctions in the input patches are alleviated during the training data preparation stage, which relieves the burden applied to the regression model on various scale handling. However, with the normalization procedure objects in the image may be distorted [7]. To improve training and inference efficiency, later methods shift their focus to in-network handling of the scale variation. In [28] a multi-column neural network [3] (MCNN) is proposed to incorporate multi-scale features for density map estimation. The network consists of three columns with small, medium and large kernel sizes respectively. Feature maps from the three sub-models are then aggregated to generate the final object density map. To further improve the multi-scale feature fusion efficiency, an improved work is proposed in [9] where the MCNN is viewed as three experts to handle objects in each of the three scales respectively, and another gating CNN is proposed to decide the confidence of the generated feature map by each expert for an input image. The confidence is learned and formulated by the gating CNN as the weights applied for feature map fusion to estimate final object counts. Furthermore, in [19] the authors propose to leverage the internal object density distinctions and assign the three columns of networks in MCNN to process image patch other than the whole image. A switch network is proposed to relay each image patch to the best-suited model for density map estimation. With a similar strategy to the MCNN [28], in [16] a Siamese CNN is employed to receive multi-resolution input to generate corresponding multi-scale features for density map estimation.

To the best of our knowledge, most existing methods on object scale variations handling mainly rely on the formulation of multi-scale feature either with the multi-column architecture [3] or using the multi-resolution input [16]. In this paper, we start from our observation with the local inconsistency problem and propose a joint solution from two aspects. First, we resort to a completely different formulation with previous methods which stacks multiple plain CNNs to handle the scale variation. Benefited from the internal multi-stage inference mechanism [15], the feature is repeatedly evaluated for refinement and correction, allowing the estimated density map to approach the ground-truth density distribution gradually with local consistent density values. In the other aspects, we propose a grid loss function to further constrain the model to adjust density values that are not consistent with local object counts. The multi-stage mechanism has been proven effective in various computer vision tasks like face detection [18], semantic segmentation [12], and pose estimation [15]. In this paper, we exploit the multi-stage mechanism with the proposed grid loss towards locally consistent object counting. Our model is trained end-to-end efficiently, with validated effectiveness on two publicly available object counting datasets.

3 Relationship Between Global Counting Errors and Local Counting Errors

Given a pair of ground truth and predicted density map $\{D_{gt}, D_{es}\}$ of an image I, we manually divide the map into T non-overlap grids denoted as $B = \{b_1, b_2, \cdots, b_T\}$. Mean Absolute Error (MAE) is used to measure the global counting accuracy, i.e., $E_I = \left| \sum_{i=1}^{N} D_{gt}(p_i) - \sum_i D_{es}(p_i) \right|$, where N is the pixel number in image I. Reformulate above equation in terms of subregions will obtain:

$$E_I = \left| \sum_{j=1}^{T} \sum_{i \in b_j} (D_{gt}(p_i) - D_{es}(p_i)) \right| \tag{1}$$

$$= \left| \sum_{j=1}^{T} E_{b_j} \right| \leq \sum_{j=1}^{T} \left| E_{b_j} \right|, \tag{2}$$

where E_{b_j} denotes the MAE of the object count in local region b_j. From Eq. (2) it can be concluded that summation of MAE of object counts in each non-overlap subregions is an *upper bound* of the MAE of the global object counts in the whole image. From this perspective, pursuing a locally consistent density map which aims to decrease local counting errors will help improve the reliability as well as drive the accuracy of the global object counts.

4 Constrained Multi-stage Convolutional Neural Networks

Our overall model consists of two components, *multi-stage convolutional neural network* and the *grid loss*. Since the grid loss provides additional supervisions, it can be viewed as constraints to the proposed multi-stage network. Before presenting the details, we first give the formulation of density-map-prediction based object counting paradigm.

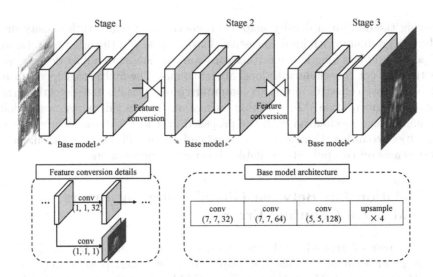

Fig. 2. Architecture of the multi-stage convolutional neural network. We stack several base models sequentially with feature conversion blocks which (i) perform feature dimension alignment of feature maps between two adjacent base models, and (ii) generate a prediction for each base model to enable intermediate supervision. The first base model accepts the input image, and the rest base models in the following stages accept feature maps which comes from the previous feature conversion block.

4.1 Density Map Based Object Counting

In this work, we formulate the object counting as a density map prediction problem [11]. Given an image I with the dotted annotation set A_I for target objects, the ground truth density map D_{gt} is defined as the summation of a set of 2D Gaussian functions centered at each dot annotation, i.e., $\forall p \in I, D_{gt}(p) = \sum_{\mu \in A_I} \mathbb{N}(p; \mu, \Sigma)$, where $\mathbb{N}(p; \mu, \Sigma)$ denotes a normalized 2D Gaussian kernel evaluated at p, with mean μ on each object location and isotropic covariance matrix Σ. Total object count C_I for image I can be obtained by summation of pixels' values over the density map. Note that all the Gaussian are summed to preserve the total object count even when there are overlaps between objects [16].

Given this counting framework, the goal of our work is to learn a mapping function from an input image I to its estimated object density map D_{es}, i.e., $\forall p \in I, D_{es}(p) = F(p|\Theta)$, where the underlying model is parameterized by Θ.

4.2 Multi-stage Convolutional Neural Network

To generate locally consistent density values, we resort to the stacking formulation of plain CNNs. We exploit the internal multi-stage inference mechanism to repeatedly evaluate the feature map and allow the generated density map to be refined to figure out the best-suited density values. Mathematically, For each pixel p in the training image I, we learn the mapping function $F(p|\Theta)$ in a compounded way with a series of functions from different stages:

$$F(p|\Theta) = f_K(\cdot|W^K) \circ \cdots \circ f_s(\cdot|W^s) \circ \cdots \circ f_2(\cdot|W^2) \circ f_1(\cdot|W^1), \qquad (3)$$

where $\{f_s, s = K, K-1, \cdots 2, 1\}$ represents the base model parameterized by W^s in the s stage, and $\circ$ denotes the function compounding operation. With this decomposition, we can add intermediate supervisions [10] to each base model f_s to facilitate the training process. A pixel-wise $L2$-norm loss function can be applied for training:

$$L(W, D_{es}) = \frac{1}{N} \sum_p \sum_s \alpha_s \|D_{es}^s(p) - D_{gt}(p)\|_2^2,$$

$$= \frac{1}{N} \sum_p \sum_s \alpha_s L_p^s \qquad (4)$$

where $D_{es}^s = f_s(X^{s-1}|\widehat{W^s})$ is a side output density map of base model f_s, X^{s-1} are feature maps produced by the model f_{s-1} in the previous stage, $W = \{W^s, \widehat{W^s}\}_{s=1,\cdots,K}$ are parameters of the whole model, N is the number of pixels in image I and α_s is the weight for the side output loss of base model f_s.

Figure 2 illustrates the proposed multi-stage model, where the base model is formulated as a fully convolutional neural network [14]. For a convolution (conv) layer, we use the notation (h, w, d) to denote the filter size $h \times w$ and the number of filters d. Inspired by [26] the convolution part of our base model contains three convolution layers with sizes of $(7, 7, 32)$, $(7, 7, 64)$ and $(5, 5, 128)$ respectively, each followed by a ReLu layer. Max Pooling layer with 2×2 kernel size is appended after the first two convolution layers. Considering the input image is downsampled by a stride of 4, we add a deconvolution layer at the end of each base model to perform in-network upsampling to recover the original resolution. The resulted feature maps of each base model are fed into the subsequent stage after dimension alignment with a 1×1 convolution layer of the feature conversion block. Inspired by the success of training CNN models with deep supervisions [10, 15], another 1×1 convolution layer is appended on the feature maps to predict a side output of density map, where the intermediate supervision will be then applied. Applying supervisions on each base model help facilitate the learning process of the whole network. The feature conversion and intermediate supervision block are illustrated in Fig. 2. Except for the first base model that accepts the input image, the first convolution layers of the following base models are modified to be consistent with the dimensions of previously generated feature maps.

4.3   Grid Loss

To further refine the density map to generate accurate global counts as well as the local counts, we also propose a grid loss function as the supervision signal. With the consideration of training error in local regions, the model is constrained by the grid loss to correct those density values which result to severely conflicts of estimated local counts with the ground truth.

Divide an image into several non-overlapping grids, and the grid loss can be depicted with local counting errors in each sub-region. The traditional pixel-wise loss (Eq. (4)) measures pixel-level density divergence while the grid loss reflects region-level counting difference. Considering the numerical gap between the numerical value between the global and local counting errors, we depict the grid counting loss with the average density loss for pixels within each specific area. This is based on the assumption that within a relatively small area, it has a great chance that pixels' density values are very similar. Then it can be regarded that every single pixel within this area has a density loss which contributes to the total count loss. By distributing the total count loss to each pixel, the grid loss help drive the correction of most violated density values and improve regression accuracy. Following previous notation in Eq. (4), for a group of non-overlap grid set $B = \{b_1, b_2, \cdots, b_T\}$ in the predicted density map D_{es}, the grid loss is defined as

$$L_{grid} = \sum_{j=1}^{T} \left\| \frac{1}{|b_j|} (\sum_{p \in b_j} D_{es}(p) - \sum_{p \in b_j} D_{gt}(p)) \right\|_2^2, \tag{5}$$

where $|b_j|$ denotes the pixel number in this grid. Reformulation of the grid loss for the multi-stage model will be

$$\widehat{L}_p^s = (1 - \lambda^s) L_p^s + \lambda^s L_{grid}^s, \tag{6}$$

where λ^s is a weight scaler applied to trade off between the estimator, i.e., the traditional pixel-wise loss and the modulator, i.e., the proposed grid loss. Substitute L_p^s in Eq. (4) with Eq. (6) will derive the final grid loss used to supervise the whole network. With this formulation, it can be observed that each pixel is not only supervised by the original density loss, and is also additionally regularized by the average density loss of the block it belongs to. This will drive the model to correct those density values that are not consistent with local object counts and improve final counting accuracy. In Fig. 3 a sample image is given to show the effects of the grid loss on a three-stage model. It can be seen that training the multi-stage model with grid loss is able to drive the model to correct regression errors and obtain more accurate object counts.

5   Experimental Results

5.1   Experiment Setting

Training Details. Our model is implemented using MatConvNet [24] with the SGD optimization. The hyper-parameters of our network include the mini-batch size (64), the momentum (0.9) and the weight decay (5×10^{-4}). We experimentally set the weights for each intermediate supervision α_i to be 1 and the weight for grid loss λ_i to be 0.5. Detailed analysis of λ_i in the grid loss is given in Sect. 5.3. The grid size is set according to the average object size in the dataset, and is 56 for an 224×224 image. Training starts from an initial learning rate of 1×10^{-6}, which is divided by 10 after the validation loss plateaus.

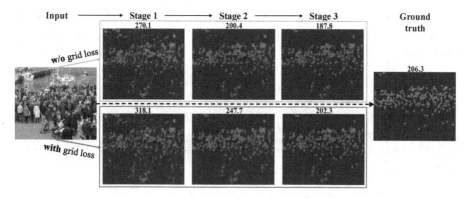

Fig. 3. Effects of the grid loss on a three-stage model. It can be observed that training with grid loss drives the model to learn to correct the regression errors and produce more accurate object counting results.

Model Initialization. Considering the difficulty to train a deep model from scratch, we take advantage of the widely-used pre-training strategy. The base CNN model is first trained and then is duplicated to construct the multi-stage network. Additional weights, e.g., the feature alignment layers between adjacent base models are randomly initialized. Finally, the whole model is fine-tuned end-to-end.

Data Augmentation. During training, 20 image patches with a size of 224 × 224 are randomly cropped from each training image for data augmentation. Randomly flipping and color jitter are performed for data augmentation. Note that the ground truth density map is a combination of 2D Gaussian functions, and their numeric values are very small (10^{-3}–10^{-5}) to enable effective learning. For this reason, we magnify the ground truth density map by a factor of 100 during the training process.

Running Time. With end-to-end training, it takes about 15 h to train a 3-stage CNNs on a single NVIDIA TITAN X GPU. For testing it takes about 0.15 s for an image of size 576 × 720.

5.2 Evaluation Metrics

Given a test image I, we directly use the output from the last stage of the network as the density map prediction. Three standard metrics are utilized for evaluation: mean absolute error (MAE), mean square error (MSE), and the grid average mean absolute error (GAME). For a dataset with M test images the MAE is defined as $MAE = \frac{1}{M}\sum_{i=1}^{M}\left|C_{es}^{i} - C_{gt}^{i}\right|$, where C_{es}^{i} and C_{gt}^{i} are the predicted and the ground truth object counts for the i-th image. MSE measures the robustness of the predicted count, which is defined as $MSE = \sqrt{\frac{1}{M}\sum_{i=1}^{M}(C_{es}^{i} - C_{gt}^{i})^2}$.

MSE and MAE evaluate the global object counts while ignoring the local consistency of predicted density maps. We additionally include the Grid Average

Mean Absolute Error (GAME) [6] as a complementary evaluation metric. After dividing a density map into 4^L non-overlapping regions, GMAE for level L is defined as:

$$GAME(L) = \frac{1}{N} \cdot \sum_{i=1}^{M} \left(\sum_{l=1}^{4^L} |C_{es}^{il} - C_{gt}^{il}| \right), \qquad (7)$$

where C_{es}^{il} and C_{gt}^{il} denotes the predicted and ground truth counts within the region l respectively. The higher L, the more restrictive this GAME metric will be on the local consistency of the density map. Note that the MAE metric is a special case of GAME when $L = 0$.

5.3 Hyper-Parameter Selection in Grid Loss

There are three hyper-parameters in the proposed grid loss function: the grid size, the loss weights α for each base model and the weights λ to balance the pixel-wise loss and grid loss. We experimentally fix α to be 1 across different stages and study the effects of another two parameters. The grid size denotes the number of blocks divided in the image. The weighting scaler λ is in charge of the modulation degree of a block count loss on its inner pixels. We conduct experiments comparing the MAE of applying grid loss to a 2-staged model with different hyper-parameter settings of grid size $1, 2, 4, 8, 16$ and $\lambda = 0.9, 0.5, 0.1, 0.01$.

Experimental results show our method performs best with $\lambda = 0.5$ and block size of 4. We use this setting across all our experiments unless otherwise specified. $\lambda = 0.9$ degrades the original performance for almost all the grid size settings, which implies that large weighting scaler may disturb the normal density learning process. As λ further decreases, the network converges to the performance training with the pixel-wise loss. When the grid size is too big, each grid area will become too small to effectively include objects, and the performance starts to degrade to the per-pixel density loss.

5.4 Ablation Experiments

We perform extensive ablation experiments on ShanghaiTech Part-A dataset to study the role of the multi-stage convolution network and the grid loss separately play in the whole constrained multi-stage networks. Results of alternative design choices are summarized in Table 1. For simplicity, we denote the multi-stage model with n stages as MS-CNN-n, and the corresponding constrained model trained with grid loss as CMS-CNN-n.

From Table 1 several observations could be drawn. First, the multi-stage formulation of plain CNNs (compare between a, c, e) and the proposed grid loss (compare a and b, c and d, e and f) both demonstrate effectiveness in improving counting accuracy. Second, the overall MAE performance of the constrained multi-stage CNNs (CMS-CNN) can be improved by adding stage by stage. We observe the MSE performance of MS-CNN-3 degrades the performance of CMS-CNN-2 a little bit. We suspect this may be the reason that with more stages added, the model becomes deeper to be well optimized.

Table 1. Performance of ablation experiments for network structures and supervisions.

Index	Design choices	MAE	MSE
a	MS-CNN-1 (the base model)	107.7	173.2
b	CMS-CNN-1	101	160.4
c	MS-CNN-2	82.3	140.4
d	CMS-CNN-2	74.2	127.6
e	MS-CNN-3	74.4	129.7
f	CMS-CNN-3	73	128.5

5.5 Comparison with the State-Of-The-Arts

ShanghaiTech. The ShanghaiTech dataset [28] is a large-scale dataset which contains 1198 annotated images. It is divided into two parts: there are 482 images in part-A and 716 images in part-B. Images in part-A are collected from the Internet and the part-B are surveillance scenes from urban streets. We follow the official train/test split [28] which is 300/182 for part-A and 400/316 for part-B. For validation, about 1/6 images are randomly selected from the original training data to supervise the training process.

Table 2 reports the comparison results with five baseline methods: Crowd-CNN [26], MCNN [28], Cascaded-MTL [21], Switch-CNN [19], CP-CNN [22]. On Part-A our methods achieves best MAE among all the comparison methods, and the second-best MSE. We observed that most images in Part-A are extremely crowded and also have pretty uniform object scales within the image, where the context information matters much compared to considering object scale variations to derive accurate counting results. In [22] the counting method is proposed from the perspective of context information modeling, which better suits the situation on Part-A. On Part-B our method outperforms all other methods and evidences a 40% improvements in MAE over CP-CNN [22]. Figure 4 illustrates the inference process in each stage with the CMS-CNN-3 model of two sample images from ShanghaiTech dataset. For the first image, it can be observed that the total object counts gradually approaches the ground truth. What's more, errors exist in the upper left background region are gradually refined and the local counting accuracy is also gradually improved. The similar situation can be observed for the second image, where the predicted density map is becoming more consistent with the ground-truth density distributions.

TRANCOS. We also report our results on another dataset for car counting to validate the effectiveness of the proposed method. TRANCOS [6] is a publicly available dataset which contains 1244 images of different traffic scenes obtained by surveillance cameras. An ROI map is also provided for each image. We strictly follow the experimental setup proposed in [6] for training and testing, where there are 403, 420 and 421 images are settled for train, validation and test, respectively.

Table 3 reports the comparison performance on this dataset with four state-of-the-art approaches: density MESA [11], regression forest [4], Hydra CNN [16]

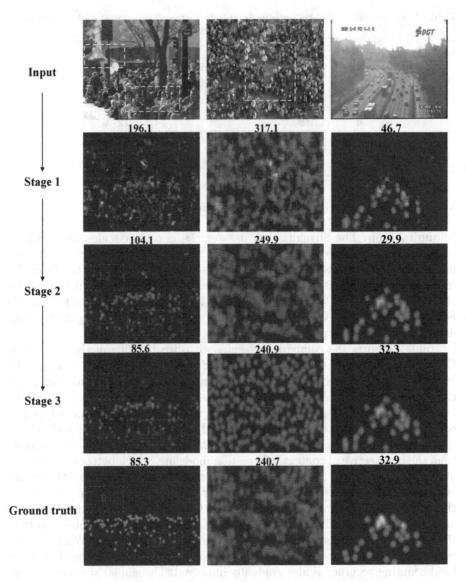

Input

Stage 1

Stage 2

Stage 3

Ground truth

Fig. 4. Density map prediction results as input images proceed through the multi-stage convolution model. The first row lists images sampled from the ShanghaiTech dataset (first two) and the TranCos dataset (last one). The second to the fourth rows show the intermediate outputs from the first two stages and the final prediction of the last stage, respectively. The ground truth density maps are shown in the last row. Object count derived from the density map are labeled on top of each prediction result. For the first two crowded sample images we also randomly select several subregions to track the local object counts, which are shown in the red boxes. (Color figure online)

Table 2. Comparison results on the ShanghaiTech dataset.

Method	Part-A		Part-B	
	MAE	MSE	MAE	MSE
Crowd-CNN [26]	181.8	277.7	32.0	49.8
MCNN [28]	110.2	173.2	26.4	41.3
Cascaded-MTL [21]	101.3	152.4	20.0	31.1
Switch-CNN [19]	90.4	135.0	21.6	33.4
CP-CNN [22]	73.6	**106.4**	20.1	30.1
CMS-CNN-2 (ours)	74.2	127.6	15.0	25.8
CMS-CNN-3 (ours)	**73.0**	128.5	**12.0**	**22.5**

and MCNN [28]. The GAME metric with $L = \{0, 1, 2, 3\}$ is utilized for evaluation. Across all the levels of GAME, our method achieves the best results compared to other approaches. There is another work [27] reporting their GAME~0 result of 5.31 on this dataset. However, the other three metrics (GAME~1, 2, 3) are unavailable for direct and effective comparison. A qualitative result for a sample image from the TRANCOS dataset is shown in Fig. 4 (the third column). It can be seen that the model is able to generate accurate global counting errors with obvious improvements stage-by-stage to become consistency with ground-truth density map.

Table 3. Comparison results of GAME on the TRANCOS dataset.

Method	GAME 0	GAME 1	GAME 2	GAME 3
regression forest [4]	17.8	20.1	23.6	26
density MESA [11]	13.8	16.7	20.7	24.4
Hydra CNN [16]	11	13.7	16.7	19.3
MCNN [28]	9.9	13	15.1	17.6
CMS-CNN-2 (ours)	7.79	9.81	11.57	13.69
CMS-CNN-3 (ours)	**7.2**	**9.7**	**11.4**	**13.5**

6   Conclusions

We propose a joint solution to address the local inconsistency problem of existing density map predictions from two aspects. We exploit a different formulation to stack multiple plain CNNs. Benefited from the internal multi-stage inference, the feature map is repeatedly evaluated and thus the density map can be refined to approach the ground-truth density distributions. To further refine the density map, we propose a grid loss function. With local-region-level supervisions, the model is constrained to correct density values which violate the local counts.

Extensive experiments on two public counting benchmarks and comparisons with recent state-of-the-art approaches demonstrate the effectiveness of the proposed method.

Acknowledgments. This work was partly funded by NSFC (No. 61571297, No. 61420106008), the National Key Research and Development Program (2017YFB-1002401), and STCSM (18DZ2270700).

References

1. Chan, A.B., Liang, Z.S.J., Vasconcelos, N.: Privacy preserving crowd monitoring: Counting people without people models or tracking. In: 2008 IEEE Conference on Computer Vision and Pattern Recognition, CVPR 2008, pp. 1–7. IEEE (2008)
2. Chen, K., Loy, C.C., Gong, S., Xiang, T.: Feature mining for localised crowd counting. In: BMVC. vol. 1, p. 3 (2012)
3. Cireşan, D., Meier, U., Schmidhuber, J.: Multi-column deep neural networks for image classification. arXiv preprint arXiv:1202.2745 (2012)
4. Fiaschi, L., Köthe, U., Nair, R., Hamprecht, F.A.: Learning to count with regression forest and structured labels. In: 2012 21st International Conference on Pattern Recognition (ICPR), pp. 2685–2688. IEEE (2012)
5. Gao, C., Li, P., Zhang, Y., Liu, J., Wang, L.: People counting based on head detection combining adaboost and CNN in crowded surveillance environment. Neurocomputing **208**, 108–116 (2016)
6. Guerrero-Gómez-Olmedo, R., Torre-Jiménez, B., López-Sastre, R., Maldonado-Bascón, S., Oñoro-Rubio, D.: Extremely overlapping vehicle counting. In: Paredes, R., Cardoso, J.S., Pardo, X.M. (eds.) IbPRIA 2015. LNCS, vol. 9117, pp. 423–431. Springer, Cham (2015). https://doi.org/10.1007/978-3-319-19390-8_48
7. He, K., Zhang, X., Ren, S., Sun, J.: Spatial pyramid pooling in deep convolutional networks for visual recognition. In: Fleet, D., Pajdla, T., Schiele, B., Tuytelaars, T. (eds.) ECCV 2014. LNCS, vol. 8691, pp. 346–361. Springer, Cham (2014). https://doi.org/10.1007/978-3-319-10578-9_23
8. Kong, D., Gray, D., Tao, H.: A viewpoint invariant approach for crowd counting. In: 18th International Conference on Pattern Recognition (ICPR 2006), vol. 3, pp. 1187–1190. IEEE (2006)
9. Kumagai, S., Hotta, K., Kurita, T.: Mixture of counting CNNs. Mach. Vis. Appl. (2018). https://doi.org/10.1007/s00138-018-0955-6
10. Lee, C.Y., Xie, S., Gallagher, P., Zhang, Z., Tu, Z.: Deeply-supervised nets. In: Artificial Intelligence and Statistics, pp. 562–570 (2015)
11. Lempitsky, V., Zisserman, A.: Learning to count objects in images. In: Advances in Neural Information Processing Systems, pp. 1324–1332 (2010)
12. Li, K., Hariharan, B., Malik, J.: Iterative instance segmentation. In: Proceedings of the IEEE Conference on Computer Vision and Pattern Recognition, pp. 3659–3667 (2016)
13. Lin, Z., Davis, L.S.: Shape-based human detection and segmentation via hierarchical part-template matching. IEEE Trans. Pattern Anal. Mach. Intell. **32**(4), 604–618 (2010)
14. Long, J., Shelhamer, E., Darrell, T.: Fully convolutional networks for semantic segmentation. In: Proceedings of the IEEE Conference on Computer Vision and Pattern Recognition, pp. 3431–3440 (2015)

15. Newell, A., Yang, K., Deng, J.: Stacked hourglass networks for human pose esti-
    mation. In: Leibe, B., Matas, J., Sebe, N., Welling, M. (eds.) ECCV 2016. LNCS,
    vol. 9912, pp. 483–499. Springer, Cham (2016). https://doi.org/10.1007/978-3-319-
    46484-8_29
16. Oñoro-Rubio, D., López-Sastre, R.J.: Towards perspective-free object counting
    with deep learning. In: Leibe, B., Matas, J., Sebe, N., Welling, M. (eds.) ECCV
    2016. LNCS, vol. 9911, pp. 615–629. Springer, Cham (2016). https://doi.org/10.
    1007/978-3-319-46478-7_38
17. Pham, V.Q., Kozakaya, T., Yamaguchi, O., Okada, R.: Count forest: co-voting
    uncertain number of targets using random forest for crowd density estimation.
    In: Proceedings of the IEEE International Conference on Computer Vision, pp.
    3253–3261 (2015)
18. Qin, H., Yan, J., Li, X., Hu, X.: Joint training of cascaded CNN for face detec-
    tion. In: Proceedings of the IEEE Conference on Computer Vision and Pattern
    Recognition, pp. 3456–3465 (2016)
19. Sam, D.B., Surya, S., Babu, R.V.: Switching convolutional neural network for
    crowd counting. arXiv preprint arXiv:1708.00199 (2017)
20. Sidla, O., Lypetskyy, Y., Brandle, N., Seer, S.: Pedestrian detection and track-
    ing for counting applications in crowded situations. In: 2006 IEEE International
    Conference on Video and Signal Based Surveillance, p. 70. IEEE (2006)
21. Sindagi, V.A., Patel, V.M.: CNN-based cascaded multi-task learning of high-level
    prior and density estimation for crowd counting. In: 2017 14th IEEE International
    Conference on Advanced Video and Signal Based Surveillance (AVSS), pp. 1–6.
    IEEE (2017)
22. Sindagi, V.A., Patel, V.M.: Generating high-quality crowd density maps using
    contextual pyramid CNNs. In: IEEE International Conference on Computer Vision
    (2017)
23. Sindagi, V.A., Patel, V.M.: A survey of recent advances in CNN-based single image
    crowd counting and density estimation. Pattern Recogn. Lett. 107, 3–16 (2018)
24. Vedaldi, A., Lenc, K.: MatConvNet: convolutional neural networks for MATLAB.
    In: Proceedings of the 23rd ACM International Conference on Multimedia, pp.
    689–692. ACM (2015)
25. Xie, W., Noble, J.A., Zisserman, A.: Microscopy cell counting and detection with
    fully convolutional regression networks. Comput. Methods Biomech. Biomed. Eng.
    Imaging Vis. 6(3), 283–292 (2018)
26. Zhang, C., Li, H., Wang, X., Yang, X.: Cross-scene crowd counting via deep con-
    volutional neural networks. In: Proceedings of the IEEE Conference on Computer
    Vision and Pattern Recognition, pp. 833–841 (2015)
27. Zhang, S., Wu, G., Costeira, J.P., Moura, J.M.: Understanding traffic density from
    large-scale web camera data. arXiv preprint arXiv:1703.05868 (2017)
28. Zhang, Y., Zhou, D., Chen, S., Gao, S., Ma, Y.: Single-image crowd counting via
    multi-column convolutional neural network. In: Proceedings of the IEEE Confer-
    ence on Computer Vision and Pattern Recognition, pp. 589–597 (2016)

An Improved Learning Framework
for Covariant Local Feature Detection

Nehal Doiphode[1], Rahul Mitra[2(✉)], Shuaib Ahmed[3], and Arjun Jain[2]

[1] University of Pennsylvania, Philadelphia, USA
lahen@seas.upenn.edu
[2] Indian Institute of Technology Bombay, Mumbai, India
{rmitter,ajain}@cse.iitb.ac.in
[3] Mercedes-Benz Research and Development India Private Limited, Bengaluru, India
shuaib.ahmed@daimler.com

Abstract. Learning feature detection has been largely an unexplored area when compared to handcrafted feature detection. Recent learning formulations use the covariant constraint in their loss function to learn covariant detectors. However, just learning from covariant constraint can lead to detection of unstable features. To impart further, stability detectors are trained to extract pre-determined features obtained by hand-crafted detectors. However, in the process they lose the ability to detect novel features. In an attempt to overcome the above limitations, we propose an improved scheme by incorporating covariant constraints in form of triplets with addition to an affine covariant constraint. We show that using these additional constraints one can learn to detect novel and stable features without using pre-determined features for training. Extensive experiments show our model achieves state-of-the-art performance in repeatability score on the well known datasets such as Vgg-Affine, EF, and Webcam.

Keywords: Local features · Covariant detection · Deep learning

1 Introduction

Representing an image as a collection of local features is important in solving computer vision problems like generating point correspondences between images [4] and subsequently used in Structure From Motion (SFM) [15], image stitching [3], image retrieval [20] and image registration [23]. Hence, detecting local features from images which are invariant towards viewpoint and illumination changes has been actively pursued by the research community.

A *good* local feature is characterized by two properties. First, the feature point should be discriminative from its immediate neighborhood, which ensures that these points can be uniquely identified which is essential in many vision

---

N. Doiphode—Work done as student in IIT Bombay.

© Springer Nature Switzerland AG 2019
C. V. Jawahar et al. (Eds.): ACCV 2018, LNCS 11366, pp. 262–276, 2019.
https://doi.org/10.1007/978-3-030-20876-9_17

algorithms. The second property is the ability of a feature point to be consistently detected in images which differs vastly in terms of geometric and photometric transformations. This property is termed as *covariant* constraint in the literature [6]. There have been comparatively fewer learning based detector compared to hand-crafted ones. Early learned detectors [12], focused on learning to extract discriminative points. Recently, convolutional neural network (CNN) based methods [6,21] coupled with covariant constraint as a loss term while training has been proposed. The method defined in [6] with their CNN model DDET ensures extracted features are covariant to geometric changes without handling discriminativeness. However, as shown in [21], the feature points predicted by DDET are not stable due to the nature of covariant constraint loss. In order to predict stable features DDET was extended in COVDET [21] by learning to pick pre-determined good features along with maintaining covariance. However, by regressing to pre-determined features extracted from a base detector, the learned model does not get an option to discover possibly more stable feature locations. It also inherits the nuisances of the base detectors.

To alleviate the issues faced by DDET and COVDET, we introduce a novel training framework which tries to combine the advantages of both DDET and COVDET. In our framework, we added additional geometric constraints in the form of loss functions to ensure stability of extracted features. In particular, translation covariance is enforced in multiple patches sharing a common feature point. We further incorporate affine covariance in our training procedure to increase stability towards affine transforms which is found in abundance in real image pairs. Extensive experiments show that our proposed model out-performs other approaches in three well known publicly available datasets in terms of *repeatability* scores.

The contributions of this paper are the following:

- We introduce a novel learning framework for covariant feature detection which extends the two existing frameworks by incorporating two different types of geometric constraints. This enables the detector to discover better and stable features while maintaining discriminativeness.
- The model trained with our proposed framework achieves state-of-the-art performance in *repeatability* score on well known publicly available known benchmarks.

2   Related Work

Detecting interest points in images have been dominated by heuristic methods. These methods identify specific visual structures, between images which have undergone transformations, consistently. The visual structures are so chosen to make detection covariant for certain transformation. Hand crafted heuristic detectors can be classified roughly into two category based on the visual structure they detect: (i) points and (ii) blobs. Point based detectors are covariant towards translation and rotation, examples include Harris [5], Edge-Foci [22].

Scale and affine covariant version of Harris [5] are proposed in [8] and [9] respectively. Blob detectors include DoG [7] and SURF [2] are implicitly covariant to scale changes by the virtue of using scale-space pyramids for detection. Affine adaptation of blob detection is also proposed in [9].

There are fewer learning based approaches compared to hand-crafted ones. The most common line of work involves detecting anchor points based on existing detectors. TILDE [18] is an example of such detector that learns to detect *stable* DoG points between images taken from the same viewpoint but having drastic illumination differences. A point is assumed to be *stable*, if it is detected consistently in most images sharing a common scene. By additionally introducing locations from those images where these *stable* points were not originally detected into the training set, TILDE outperforms DoG in terms of repeatability. TaSK [16] and LIFT [19] also detects anchor points based on similar strategies. The downside of such approaches is that the performance of the learned detector is dependent on the anchor detector used, i.e for certain transformations the learned detector can also reflect the poor performance of the anchor detector. Another area focuses on increasing repeatability of existing detectors. An instance being FAST-ER [13] improves repeatability of FAST [12] key-points by optimizing its parameters. In Quad-Network [14] an unsupervised approach is proposed where patches extracted from two images are assigned a score and ranking consistency between corresponding patches helps in improving repeatability.

More recently, Lenc et. al [6] proposed a Siamese CNN based method to learn covariant detectors. In this method, two patches related by a transformation are fed to the network which regresses two points (one for each patch). Applying a loss ensuring that the two regressed points differ by the same transformation, lets the network detect points covariant to that transformation. However, a major drawback of the method is the lack of ensuring the network regressing to a *good* and *stable* feature point. This method can lead to the CNN model being trained sub-optimally. In order to alleviate the drawback, Zhang et. al [21] proposed a method using standard patches to ensure that the network regress to the keypoints. The standard patches are centered around a feature detected by detectors such as TILDEP24 [18]. Though, this method of standard patches is generic in nature, the transformation extensively studied is translations.

3   Fundamentals of Covariant Detection

3.1   Preliminary

Let $\mathbf{x}$ be an image patch from a set of all patches $\mathcal{X}$. A feature $\mathbf{f} \in \mathcal{F}$ is represented by a point (position w.r.t center of the patch) or a circle (position and scale) or an ellipse (position, scale, shape). Let $\mathbf{g}$ be a function representing geometric transformation belongs to a group of transformation G. Let $\mathbf{f_0}$ be a fixed canonical feature positioned at the center point of the patch and unit scale. When $\mathcal{F}$ resolves $\mathcal{G}$, there will be a bijective mapping between $\mathcal{F}$ and $\mathcal{G}$ [6,21]

With this setting, instead of feature detector, it is possible to work with transformations and a function $\phi(\cdot)$ usually represented by a CNN can take a patch $\mathbf{x}$ as input and regresses a transformation $\mathbf{g}$ that brings a *good* feature positioned at $\mathbf{f}$ to $\mathbf{f_0}$. In other words, $\phi(\mathbf{x}) = \mathbf{g}$; $\mathbf{f_0} = \mathbf{g} \otimes \mathbf{f}$, $\otimes$ is an operator used to transform $\mathbf{f}$ using $\mathbf{g}$. Now, the function $\phi()$ respects covariant constraints for a class of transformations G when the Eq. 1 holds for all patches and all transformations belonging to the class.

$$\phi(\mathbf{g} * \mathbf{x}) = \mathbf{g} \circ \phi(\mathbf{x}); \; \forall \mathbf{x} \in \mathcal{X}, \forall \mathbf{g} \in G \tag{1}$$

In the above equation $*$ symbolizes warping of patch $\mathbf{x}$ with transformation $\mathbf{g}$ and $\circ$ stands for composition of transformations.

3.2   Covariant Constraint

In Lenc et al. [6] a Siamese network takes two patches $\mathbf{x}$ (reference patch) and $\mathbf{x'} = \mathbf{g} * \mathbf{x}$ and uses the covariant constraint mentioned in Eq. 1 as the loss function. The optimum regressor $\phi(\cdot)$ is obtained as,

$$\phi = \underset{\phi}{\operatorname{argmin}} \sum_{i=1}^{n} \|\phi(\mathbf{g_i} * \mathbf{x_i}) - \mathbf{g_i} \circ \phi(\mathbf{x_i})\|^2. \tag{2}$$

However, just using the covariant constraint makes the learning objective have multiple solutions as mentioned in [21]. This can makes learning ambiguous and the can lead the regressor to choose non-discriminative points.

3.3   Standard Patches

In order to avoid the above mentioned limitations of only using covariant constraints, Zhang et. al. [21] introduced the concept of *standard patches* and shown that the function $\phi(\cdot)$ trained only with such patches is sufficient to mitigate the limitation. The standard patches $\mathbf{x}$ are reference patches centered around any feature detectors such as TILDEP24 [18] points. An additional loss term(*identity loss*) is incorporated which ensures $\phi(\cdot)$ regresses to the center point in $\mathbf{x}$. The optimization objective including both the covariant loss and the identity loss is shown in Eq. 3.

$$\phi = \underset{\phi}{\operatorname{argmin}} \sum_{i=1}^{n} \|\phi(\mathbf{g_i} * \mathbf{x_i}) - \mathbf{g_i} \circ \phi(\mathbf{x_i})\|^2 + \alpha \sum_{i=1}^{n} \|\phi(\mathbf{x_i})\|^2 \tag{3}$$

The network architecture used in [21] along with the loss terms is shown in Fig. 1. Both DDET [6] and COVDET [21] limits the class of transformations to translations. This implicitly makes the network to regress to same feature point which is shared among adjacent patches as shown in Fig. 2.

While extracting features from an image, the entire image is forwarded through the network. The network being fully-convolutional, outputs the translations to feature points relative to 2D grid of every 4 pixels (since both DDET and

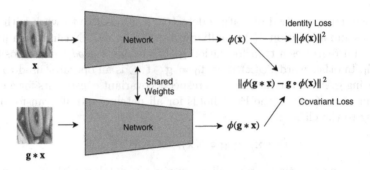

Fig. 1. The Siamese architecture along with the *covariant* and *identity* loss used in [21].

Fig. 2. The 3 adjacent patches outlined in red, blue and green sharing a common good feature point marked in yellow. The dotted lines are predicted translations of the feature point from the center of their respective patch. (Color figure online)

COVDET has two 2×2 pool layers) taken as centers. The predicted translations are added to their respective center pixels to get final positions of the regressed points. A vote-map is generated by bi-linear interpolation of the regressed locations to its 4 nearest pixels and accumulating the contributions. Since, grid points sharing a good feature point regress to its location, the vote-map exhibits high density at locations of these points. Finally, similar to many feature point detection algorithms, non-maximal suppression is used to select points with local maximum. In Fig. 3(a) and (b) predicted translations for each grid point and the generated vote-map is shown respectively. Figure 3(c) shows the final selected points after non-maximal suppression. The usage of standard patches improves the repeatability and matching score of the learned detector when compared to DDET [6].

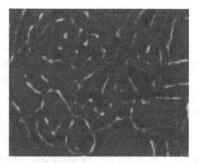

(a) Predicted 2D translations   (b) Generated vote-map

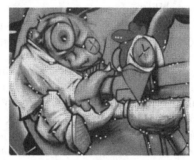

(c) Final extracted points

Fig. 3. Output of different stages of feature extraction pipeline for a full image. (a) Shows the predicted 2D translations for every 4th pixel. (b) Shows the bi-linearly interpolated votemap (c) Shows the final detected features.

4 Proposed Method

The method described in [6] and its extension [21] suffer from a few drawbacks as follows:

- Using only a covariance loss between the reference patch and translated patch can introduce instability in the learning procedure as mentioned in Sect. 3.1. The regressed points are also not ensured to be discriminative.
- Regressing to pre-determined feature points extracted by a base detector resolves issues of instability but makes the model susceptible to the vulnerabilities of the base detector.

To overcome the drawbacks, we extend the work of [21] by introducing a novel training framework which incorporates multiple neighborhood patches sharing a *good* feature while designing the covariant constraint. Affine covariance between reference patch and affine warp of it is also introduced. The additional geometric constraints enforces the network to choose points which are stable to such transformation and in effect reducing the regression space. In addition to the above, the proposed model is not explicitly enforced to regress to pre-computed

TILDE [18] points. This is done in accordance with observations in [19] where the authors observed sub-optimal performance when only selecting points retrieved by SFM rather than treating the location as latent variable and letting the model discover more reliable points in the vicinity.

The proposed training framework, in essence, similar to descriptor training frameworks L2-Net [17] and Hardnet [11] where the loss functions are formulated by coupling together a batch of triplets. Their modified framework outperforms Tfeat [1] which trains using triplets independently. The reason attributed to the improvement in performance is increase in context which in case of descriptor training comes with gradients from several coupled triplets. In our case, additional geometric constraints obtained from coupling all the pairs serves as the extra context needed for stability.

In the proposed extension, a triplet of patches x_1, x_2, x_3 from a reference patch x is generated by translating x by t_1, t_2, t_3 respectively. Translation covariance is enforced between any of the two patches taken in order in the learning framework. Further a fourth patch x_A which is an affine warp (using affine transform A) of x is created to ensure the regressed point is stable towards affine transformations. It should be noted that the reference patch does not necessarily have *good* feature point at the center. The advantage of our approach over DDET [6] which also does not regress to pre-determined features is the enforcement of additional geometric constraints by introducing multiple covariance constraints patches, x, x_1, x_2, x_3 and x_A. These additional constraints ensures selection of more stable features than DDET. Since, the learned regressor should obey Eq. 1 for all the pairs formed by the reference patch and the generated patches, we have the following set of equations,

$$\phi(x_1) = \phi(x) + t_1 \qquad (4a)$$
$$\phi(x_2) = \phi(x) + t_2 \qquad (4b)$$
$$\phi(x_3) = \phi(x) + t_3 \qquad (4c)$$
$$\phi(x_A) = A * \phi(x) \qquad (4d)$$

The covariant constraint between any two of the patches from the generated triplet along with reference patch is given in Eq. 5,

$$\alpha\phi(x_1) - \beta\phi(x_2) = (\alpha - \beta)\phi(x) + t_{12} \qquad (5a)$$
$$\alpha\phi(x_2) - \beta\phi(x_3) = (\alpha - \beta)\phi(x) + t_{23} \qquad (5b)$$
$$\alpha\phi(x_3) - \beta\phi(x_1) = (\alpha - \beta)\phi(x) + t_{31} \qquad (5c)$$

The above equation is obtained from the first 3 sub equations of Eq. 4. t_{ij} in the above equations equals $\alpha t_i - \beta t_j$. The constants α and β are chosen to be 2 and 1 respectively. Higher values of α and β led to instability in training due to high gradient flows.

Our loss term has 2 components, the first component comprises of the translation covariant terms which are derived from Eq. 5 and formulated in Eq. 6.

$$\ell_{cov-tran} = \|\alpha\phi(\mathbf{x_1}) - \beta\phi(\mathbf{x_2}) - (\alpha - \beta)\phi(\mathbf{x}) - \mathbf{t_{12}}\|^2$$
$$+ \|\alpha\phi(\mathbf{x_2}) - \beta\phi(\mathbf{x_3}) - (\alpha - \beta)\phi(\mathbf{x}) - \mathbf{t_{23}}\|^2$$
$$+ \|\alpha\phi(\mathbf{x_3}) - \beta\phi(\mathbf{x_1}) - (\alpha - \beta)\phi(\mathbf{x}) - \mathbf{t_{31}}\|^2 \quad (6)$$

In addition to the above, a second loss term ensuring affine covariance between reference patch $\mathbf{x}$ and its affine warp $\mathbf{x_A}$ is defined in Eq. 7.

$$\ell_{cov-aff} = \|\phi(\mathbf{x_A}) - A * \phi(\mathbf{x})\|^2 \quad (7)$$

The total loss is given in Eq. 8,

$$\ell_{total} = \ell_{cov-tran} + \ell_{cov-aff} \quad (8)$$

Our training framework is shown in Fig. 4. It takes a tuple of 5 patches and passes each of them through a network of same configuration and sharing weights. The outputs of the triplet patches contribute to the translation covariant loss term while that of the affine warped patch to affine covariant term. The output of the reference patch is utilized in both the loss terms. We restrict to training on tuple of 5 patches as increasing the number leads to a combinatorial increase in the number of terms in the loss function which are difficult to converge during training.

5 Experimental Setup

Details of implementation and training procedure are mentioned in Sect. 5.1. Section 5.2 explains the different evaluation protocols and characteristics of test-datasets used.

5.1 Implementation and Training Details

For fair comparisons, the same network architecture and training data used in [21] has been used. The input patches are of size 32×32 pixels. Table 1 gives the different layers of the network used in [21]. In Table 1, A max pool layer with kernel 2×2 is used after convolution layers 1 and 2. After each convolution layer except the last layer, ReLU activation is used. As in [21] only position is regressed, hence the output of the last layer is 2.

For generating the patches for training, the same set of standard patches which are used in [21] is used. These patches are extracted from the *Mexico* scene of the Webcam Dataset [18]. The same set of perturbation applied to the reference patch is maintained like scaling both axes uniformly within $[0.85, 1.15]$, shearing both axis within $[-0.15, 0.15]$, and uniform rotation between $[0°, 360°]$. Additionally, to ensure that the reference patch does not necessarily have a good feature point at the center, the reference patch is translated randomly by $[-5, 5]$ in both directions. To generate the triplet of patches $\mathbf{x_1}, \mathbf{x_2}, \mathbf{x_3}$ mentioned in Sect. 3, the reference patch is randomly translated between $[-6, 6]$. For affine

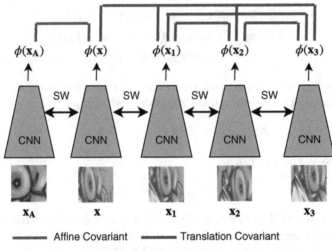

Fig. 4. Training framework of our proposed approach. The green lines connect outputs which are used in the translation covariant loss terms while outputs connected by the red line contribute in the affine-covariant loss term. (Color figure online)

Table 1. The configuration of the different convolution layers used in the CNN.

Layers	1	2	3	4	5
Kernel, #feats	5, 32	5, 128	3, 128	3, 256	1, 2

covariance, the patch x_A is generated by applying another affine warp to the reference patch with the scale, shear, and rotation values sampled ranges mentioned earlier. A 256,000 samples of the tuple x, x_1, x_2, x_3, x_A has been generated for our training. The model is trained for 10 epochs with batch size of 128. For the first 5 epochs the affine loss term (Eq. 7) is turned off and trained with only translation covariance loss (Eq. 6). For the next 5 epochs, both the loss terms are used. It has been observed that training with both the translation and affine loss terms from the beginning gives sub-optimal results. One possible explanation would be that the affine loss is difficult to satisfy for an untrained network. For optimization, SGD with momentum 0.9 and initial learning rate 0.1 is used. The learning rate is exponentially decayed with a decay rate of 0.96 after every epoch.

5.2 Evaluation Protocols

Two publicly available datasets are used for evaluation purposes,

- **VggAffine** dataset [10], contains 8 scenes or sequences with 6 images per sequence. The images are numbered 0 through 5 and the image with serial 0 in the sequence is the reference image. The amount of transformation increases in the image with increase in its serial number. The transformations are related by ground truth homography. Each sequence exhibits either geometric or illumination transforms.

– **Webcam** dataset [18], contains 6 sequences with 80, 20 and 20 images for training, testing and validation respectively, per sequence. All images in a sequence is taken from the same viewpoint. The images are in different times of days and at different seasons providing extreme illumination and appearance changes.

– **EF** dataset [22], contains 5 scenes or image sequences showing simultaneous variation in viewpoint, scale, and illumination. Like Hpatches, images in a sequence are related by homography.

As with COVDET [21], *repeatability* and *matching score* are used as the metrics for quantitative evaluation of the proposed approach and for comparison against others.

– **Repeatability:** It is the same evaluation procedure detailed in [10]. In this procedure, regions around extracted feature points are considered instead of using only the location. The size of the regions depends on the scale at which the feature was extracted. Two regions R_A and R_B from images A and B are said to correspond when the overlap between R_A and projection of R_B into image A is more than 40%. Since repeatability score for a detector is sensitive to the number of points extracted per image, all models are evaluated twice by fixing the number of points extracted to 200 and 1000.

– **Matching score:** repeatability of a detector although useful cannot quantify the discriminative nature of the extracted points. One way to evaluate discriminativeness of the extracted points is to compute descriptors of regions around the points and use them for matching using nearest neighbors. The protocol used in Tfeat [1] has been followed where in-order to eliminate any bias between certain image pairs, 1000 points are extracted from each image and SIFT [7] descriptors are computed. Matching score is the fraction of correct matches to the total number of points extracted. Out of any two detectors having comparable repeatability, the one with more discriminative feature points will have a better matching score.

6   Results

This section discusses about the comparative results of other popular approaches against our proposed in the two evaluation criteria mentioned in Sect. 5.2. Table 2 provides an ablation on the two different component of our loss terms. Additionally, a model trained using the training framework of COVDET [21] but with twice the amount of training pairs is also compared. We call this model as COVDET++. Comparison with this model is done to understand the effect of training with additional data. *Trip* represents the model trained using only loss mentioned in Eq. 6. *Cov + Aff* represents a model trained with loss which is a

combination of one translation covariance term and the affine loss term. *Trip +
Aff* is our proposed method and trained with the loss given in Eq. 8. The mean
and standard deviation of repeatability score of each model from 5 training runs
is reported. 1000 points were extracted from each image. As can be seen from
Table 2, our proposed approach of combining translation covariance with affine
covariance clearly outperforms other variations. The superior performance of our
proposed method along with low standard deviation values validates the need to
have additional geometric constraints to extract points stable towards geometric
covariance.

Table 2. The mean ± std.dev of repeatability on all datasets for various modifications
of proposed approach.

Method	Vgg-Aff	EF	Webcam
COVDET++	58.14 ± 0.12	36.41 ± 0.05	51.39 ± 0.05
Trip	54.65 ± 1.34	32.10 ± 0.30	48.45 ± 0.30
Cov + Aff	59.72 ± 1.15	34.14 ± 0.20	50.23 ± 0.30
Trip + Aff (proposed)	**63.12 ± 0.20**	**36.50 ± 0.05**	**51.40 ± 0.05**

Table 3 provides a comparative measure of repeatability on all the 3
datasets mentioned in Sect. 5 for our proposed approach against other popular
approaches. Our proposed approach either outperforms or performs comparably on the all the three benchmark datasets. The performance gap is higher in
case of 200 points than for 1000 points which in line with the observations of
COVDET [21].

Table 3. Comparing repeatability % of different methods on all the datasets. 200 and
1000 represents the number of features extracted per image.

Method	Vgg-Affine		EF		Webcam	
	200	1000	200	1000	200	1000
TILDEP24 [18]	57.57	64.35	32.3	45.37	45.1	61.7
DDET [6]	50.9	65.41	24.54	43.31	34.24	50.67
COVDET [21]	59.14	68.15	35.1	46.10	50.65	**67.12**
Proposed	**63.12**	**69.79**	**36.5**	**46.49**	**51.4**	65.0259

As discussed in Sect. 5, repeatability does not takes into account the dis-
criminitiveness of the extracted feature points. Matching feature points using a
feature descriptor gives an estimate of feature discriminativeness. Table 4 reports
the matching score coupling SIFT [7] as feature descriptor with different feature
extractors. We observe that our proposed model clearly outperforms DDET [6],
while performing comparably or marginally below COVDET [21]. These results
translates that the feature points detected by the proposed models are better
discriminatable than DDET and comparable to COVDET.

Table 4. Comparing matching score of different methods on all the datasets

Method	Vgg-Aff	EF	Webcam	Average
TILDEP24 [18]	36.13	5.50	13.41	18.34
DDET [6]	37.09	4.15	12.56	17.93
COVDET [21]	41.79	**6.15**	19.19	22.37
Proposed	**41.81**	5.85	**20.14**	**22.60**

(a) Extracted feature points from 'img5' of *Wall*. Left: proposed, Right: COVDET

(b) Extracted feature points from 'img6' of *Wall*. Left: proposed, Right: COVDET

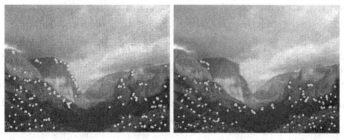

(c) Extracted feature points from 'img6' of *Yosemite*. Left: proposed, Right: COVDET

Fig. 5. Features extracted from the *Wall* sequence from Vgg-Affine [10] and *Yosemite* sequence from EF [22] dataset.

7   Qualitative Analysis

In this section, visual differences between extracted features of our proposed model with that of COVDET and TILDE is analyzed.

A visual comparison between extracted feature from images of *Wall* and *Yosemite* sequence is shown Fig. 5. It can be observed that our proposed method have extracted features which are far more spread out in the images than the ones by COVDET. Also, from visual inspection most of the points extracted by our model lies inside discriminative areas.

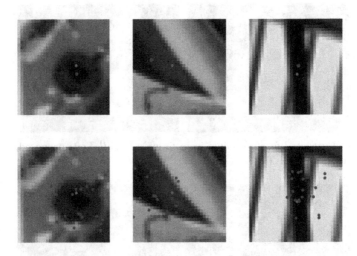

Fig. 6. The top row shows 25 points predicted by the model trained with affine covariance loss while the bottom shows the predictions for the model trained without affine covariance loss. The points marked in red is a pre-determined feature point. The points marked in blue are predicted by the model. (Color figure online)

In order to visualize the impact of using the affine covariance loss, two models were trained, which regresses 25 points instead of 1, for a given patch. Both the models are trained using the *Mexico* scene of the *Webcam* dataset. Covariant losses are applied individually to each of the 25 points. The only difference between the two models is that, one is trained with additional affine covariance and the other one without. Figure 6 investigates the distribution of the points regressed by the two models on unknown test patches containing a predetermined feature point. We can see that all the points regressed by the model trained with the affine loss collapses into a single point close to the feature point there by enforcing the stability of that point. We can see quite the opposite for the model trained without affine loss with point scattered around.

8   Conclusion

The existing learned covariant detectors have the drawbacks of detecting either unstable features or constraint themselves not to detect novel features. In this work, we have addressed these limitations by proposing an approach that uses covariant constraints in a triplet fashion and also incorporates an affine constraint for robust learning of the keypoint detector. Multiple neighborhood patches sharing a *good* feature has been incorporated, while designing the covariant constraint. As a result, the proposed network learned novel features on its own further resulting in an improvement in the repeatability measure on state-of-the-art benchmarks. Lower standard deviation in the repeatability score for multiple runs validates the stability of the features detected. From these observation, we conclude that the proposed method including affine loss term guides the regressor in choosing a stable and novel features. Future approaches may include to extract both shape and position information from a single network.

References

1. Balntas, V., Riba, E., Ponsa, D., Mikolajczyk, K.: Learning local feature descriptors with triplets and shallow convolutional neural networks. In: BMVC 2016, pp. 119:1–119:11 (2016)
2. Bay, H., Tuytelaars, T., Van Gool, L.: SURF: speeded up robust features. In: Leonardis, A., Bischof, H., Pinz, A. (eds.) ECCV 2006. LNCS, vol. 3951, pp. 404–417. Springer, Heidelberg (2006). https://doi.org/10.1007/11744023_32
3. Brown, M., Lowe, D.G.: Automatic panoramic image stitching using invariant features. IJCV **74**, 59–73 (2007)
4. Brown, M., Szeliski, R., Winder, S.: Multi-image matching using multi-scale oriented patches. In: CVPR 2005, pp. 510–517 (2005)
5. Harris, C., Stephens, M.: A combined corner and edge detector. In: Alvey Vision Conference 1988, pp. 147–151 (1988)
6. Lenc, K., Vedaldi, A.: Learning covariant feature detectors. In: Hua, G., Jégou, H. (eds.) ECCV 2016. LNCS, vol. 9915, pp. 100–117. Springer, Cham (2016). https://doi.org/10.1007/978-3-319-49409-8_11
7. Lowe, D.G.: Distinctive image features from scale-invariant keypoints. IJCV **60**, 91–110 (2004)
8. Mikolajczyk, K., Schmid, C.: Indexing based on scale invariant interest points. In: ICCV 2001, pp. 525–531 (2001)
9. Mikolajczyk, K., Schmid, C.: Scale & affine invariant interest point detectors. IJCV **60**, 63–86 (2004)
10. Mikolajczyk, K., et al.: A comparison of affine region detectors. IJCV **65**, 43–72 (2005)
11. Mishchuk, A., Mishkin, D., Radenovic, F., Matas, J.: Working hard to know your neighbor's margins: local descriptor learning loss. In: NIPS 2017 (2017)
12. Rosten, E., Drummond, T.: Machine learning for high-speed corner detection. In: Leonardis, A., Bischof, H., Pinz, A. (eds.) ECCV 2006. LNCS, vol. 3951, pp. 430–443. Springer, Heidelberg (2006). https://doi.org/10.1007/11744023_34
13. Rosten, E., Porter, R., Drummond, T.: Faster and better: a machine learning approach to corner detection. PAMI **32**, 105–119 (2010)
14. Savinov, N., Seki, A., Ladicky, L., Sattler, T., Pollefeys, M.: Quad-networks: unsupervised learning to rank for interest point detection. In: CVPR 2017, pp. 3929–3937 (2017)
15. Snavely, N., Seitz, S.M., Szeliski, R.: Photo tourism: exploring photo collections in 3D. In: ACM SIGGRAPH 2006, pp. 835–846 (2006)

16. Strecha, C., Lindner, A., Ali, K., Fua, P.: Training for task specific keypoint detection. In: Denzler, J., Notni, G., Süße, H. (eds.) DAGM 2009. LNCS, vol. 5748, pp. 151–160. Springer, Heidelberg (2009). https://doi.org/10.1007/978-3-642-03798-6_16

17. Tian, Y., Fan, B., Wu, F.: L2-Net: deep learning of discriminative patch descriptor in euclidean space. In: CVPR 2017, pp. 6128–6136 (2017)

18. Verdie, Y., Yi, K.M., Fua, P., Lepetit, V.: TILDE: a temporally invariant learned detector. In: CVPR 2015, pp. 5279–5288 (2015)

19. Yi, K.M., Trulls, E., Lepetit, V., Fua, P.: LIFT: learned invariant feature transform. In: Leibe, B., Matas, J., Sebe, N., Welling, M. (eds.) ECCV 2016. LNCS, vol. 9910, pp. 467–483. Springer, Cham (2016). https://doi.org/10.1007/978-3-319-46466-4_28

20. Zhang, H., Zha, Z.J., Yang, Y., Yan, S., Gao, Y., Chua, T.S.: Attribute-augmented semantic hierarchy: towards bridging semantic gap and intention gap in image retrieval. In: ACM MM 2013, pp. 33–42 (2013)

21. Zhang, X., Yu, F.X., Karaman, S.: Learning discriminative and transformation covariant local feature detectors. In: CVPR 2017 (2017)

22. Zitnick, C.L., Ramnath, K.: Edge foci interest points. In: ICCV 2011, pp. 359–366 (2011)

23. Zitova, B., Flusser, J.: Image registration methods: a survey. Image Vis. Comput. **21**, 977–1000 (2003)

Better Guider Predicts Future Better: Difference Guided Generative Adversarial Networks

Guohao Ying[1], Yingtian Zou[2], Lin Wan[1(✉)], Yiming Hu[1], and Jiashi Feng[2]

[1] Huazhong University of Science and Technology, Wuhan, China
wanlin@hust.edu.cn
[2] National University of Singapore, Singapore, Singapore

Abstract. Predicting the future is a fantasy but practicality work. It is the key component to intelligent agents, such as self-driving vehicles, medical monitoring devices and robotics. In this work, we consider generating unseen future frames from previous observations, which is notoriously hard due to the uncertainty in frame dynamics. While recent works based on generative adversarial networks (GANs) made remarkable progress, there is still an obstacle for making accurate and realistic predictions. In this paper, we propose a novel GAN based on inter-frame difference to circumvent the difficulties. More specifically, our model is a multi-stage generative network, which is named the Difference Guided Generative Adversarial Network (DGGAN). The DGGAN learns to explicitly enforce future-frame predictions that is guided by synthetic inter-frame difference. Given a sequence of frames, DGGAN first uses dual paths to generate meta information. One path, called Coarse Frame Generator, predicts the coarse details about future frames, and the other path, called Difference Guide Generator, generates the difference image which include complementary fine details. Then our coarse details will then be refined via guidance of difference image under the support of GANs. With this model and novel architecture, we achieve state-of-the-art performance for future video prediction on UCF-101, KITTI.

1 Introduction

Predicting the future has drawn increasing attention due to its great practical value in various artificial intelligence applications, such as guiding unmanned vehicles, monitoring patient condition, to name a few. In this paper, we consider the task that learns from the prior video frames to predict the future frames. Some previous distinguished works which aim to predict the low-level information like action [24], the flow [13,25], or skeleton [1,27] have shown remarkable success. The limitation is that they do not predict the holistic information. To ameliorate it, we adopt this strategy which develop a model that can acquire complete future RGB-images of the future not just one-sided information. The images can then be transferred to other video analysis tasks such as action recognition or utilized for models based on reinforcement learning.

© Springer Nature Switzerland AG 2019
C. V. Jawahar et al. (Eds.): ACCV 2018, LNCS 11366, pp. 277–292, 2019.
https://doi.org/10.1007/978-3-030-20876-9_18

However, the generation of realistic frames is a challenging task, especially when it is required to generate the whole foreground/background and unambiguous motion dynamics. Intuitively, for the sake of obtaining accurate prediction under the precondition of realistic generation, one has to delve deeper into previous adjacent frames. Some existing methods directly generate future frames by encoding context information using generators like CNNs [20], LSTM [3,18] Auto-Encoder [23] or GANs [2,16,20,28]. Unfortunately, those methods often suffer from blurry problem. To alleviate the issue, a more elegant method is to introduce a motion field layer under the assistance of auxiliary information. Those layer can produce motion dynamics, which transform pixels from previous frames to future frames [17]. practical end-to-end fashions [16,27] usually incorporate auxiliary information such as optical-flow, skeleton-information through neural networks. They acquire complete clear frames from combination of the previous frames and auxiliary information. Nevertheless, complicated loss to control the matrix transformation is ineluctable when most of above models aim at transform the given frames to future frames. Following this inspiration, guiding by an efficient auxiliary information is the keystone and a easier implement method is better. Consequently, we aim at developing a better "guider" that predicts future more accurately and relieve the blurry problem.

To acquire this better guider, we resort to a strong motion information map, the Inter-Frame Difference Image. In particular, we propose the Difference Guided Generative Network (DGGAN) model that learns to generate the predicted frames and the difference frames which encode the difference between adjacent frames. To get over the hurdle of blurry problem, we deploy the predicted inter-frame difference as the guider for future frame prediction. Combining the guider with the previous frames, in that way we can apply pixel-shift from prior distributions instead of generating images from random-noise. The proposed model finally obtains the future frames with fine details and proper smoothness. Our end-to-end trainable model deploying this strategy achieves the state-of-the-art performance on multiple video benchmark datasets without complicated computing on transformation.

In summary, our main contributions are three-folds:

- We proposed DGGAN model which can generate inter-frame difference image and complete future frame. In single future image prediction, DGGAN achieve the state-of-the-art on UCF-101, KITTI.
- Inter-frame difference is a neglected powerful guider in motion video analysis. To our best knowledge, we are the first to introduce it into future prediction where the guider compels motion information become dominant.
- Learning from [2,4] we propose a multi-stage model which will lessen the mistiness after single stage. And we experimentally demonstrated that our Refine Network is efficacious on improving the coarse prediction generated by GAN.

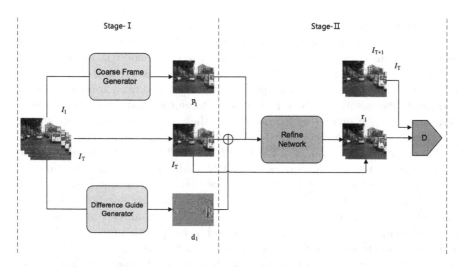

Fig. 1. Overview of Difference Guide Generative Adversarial Network (DGGAN). The Coarse Frame Generator generates the coarse result of $T+1$ frame, p_1. Difference Guide Generator generates the difference image d_1 of I_{T+1} and I_T. During stage-II, p_1 will be concatenated with I_T "$\oplus$" by d_1 and then input to Refine Network where "$\oplus$" means pixel-wise sum. A discriminator will adversarial train the Refine Network to output the final result r_1 which is the fine prediction of $T + 1$ frame.

2   Related Works

Video prediction has been more popular since it can be used in various of areas including self-driving, medical monitoring, or robotics. One way to make a simple prediction is predicting the future frames. Subsequently we will introduce some prominent existing Network Architectures for future frames prediction.

Video frame prediction is a challenging task due to the complex appearance and motion dynamics of natural scenes. Early approaches only use the RGB-frames [3,18] as input information, using CNN, RNN or LSTM to handle multi-frames input, and generate at least one future frame. Further notice, as Generative Adversarial Networks [7] showing good performance compared with traditional generating works, [16,20,22,28] utilize GANs to achieve better generation. To obtain more effective information from previous scenario, they also take low-level features such as optical flows or separating the foreground and background as auxiliary information.

A series of works above attempt to propose more effective networks to generate the future frames pixel directly. But the output is often blurry and training is costly, which usually spends a long time. An alternative approach to alleviate those problems is copying pixels from previous frames [13,16,23,27]. Patraucean *et al.* [23] use optical flows to encode a grid to transform the front one frame to the next one frame [23]. And the work of Jin *et al.* [13] define a Voxel Flow which is coded from the previous frames to transform the front frames to the new one. Liang *et al.* [16] use a dual Motion GAN to generate optical flow and frames, they make use of the optical flow to warp the last one frame from the input frame-sequences to the next new one frame. At the same time, they use the generated frame connected with the last one frame to encode optical flow. They have two discriminators, which are used to control the generating of optical flow and frames [16]. Xiong et al. [30] apply multiple GANs on raw frames for generation and refinement. Although most of the aforementioned networks have good performance when predicting future frames, they may suffer from sophisticated transformation and need complicated loss for controlling the images generation. Another contemporary model of Liang *villegas*. make use of the fusion of skeleton and previous adjacent frames instead of sophisticated transformation and need complicated loss. But the limitation of this model is that it can be only utilized for the prediction of foreground including different human actions, and the variation of background is hard to predict. Zhao et al. [31] use highly specific motion information such as 3DMM based face expression motion and human body keypoints motion for face and human video generation. In this sense, their method [31] is cumbersome than as it needs to manually select motion cues for generating videos of different themes.

Our networks makes full use of the advantages of the above model and avoids their weakness as much as possible. Our approach exploit simple loss to make the machine learn the coarse predicted frame and Difference Guide (DG) information which contain the variation of foreground and background from the previous frames to the new frames. Then the fusion of DG and previous adjacent frames can help getting over the problem of blurry. In addition our ultimate prediction is refined via GANs. To achieve more stable and superior training results, we use WGAN-GP [8] in combination with CGAN [21] instead of original GANs.

3   Difference Guided GAN

As mentioned above, predicting clear and accurate future frames has been attracting lots of attention. Though several works begin to employ various credible auxiliary information as the guide [16,22,23,27], their performance is still not satisfactory. In this work, as shown in Fig. 1, we devise a multi-stage generative network based on a better guide—the difference image, to effectively overcome their limitations. Concretely, during stage-I, we introduce the dual-path networks—one path contains the Coarse Frame Generator and the other one contains the Difference Guide Generator. The upper path generates the coarse result of future predicted frame while the lower path generates the difference image between last frame and predicted frame which we regard it as the guide. To adequately learn the context, we set multi-frames as the input sequence where the recent frames will serve as constraints. Besides, we use additional losses to constrain the generation of difference image and coarse predicted frame. At stage-II, the coarse predicted frame, difference image and last frame will be fused by Refine Network. There is a discriminator that adversarially trains the Refine Network to enhance reality of the synthetic image. Reasons for this design are: (1) difference image compels motion information become dominant; (2) under the guidance of difference motion information, we could refine our obscure results. In this way, we could get clear and accurate predicted image (Fig. 2).

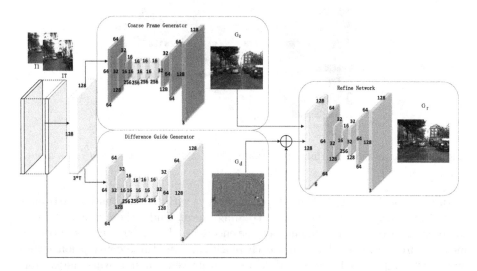

Fig. 2. Frameworks of generators. Firstly, the sampled frames sequence of length T are contacted together, where each frame contain 3 channels. There are two input paths that identical sequence is fed into Coarse Frame Generator (CFG) and Difference Guide Generator (DGG) simultaneously. The CFG and DGG have the same structure which includes three convolutional layers, three res-block layer, and three deconvolutional layers. But the different generation target that produce Coarse Frame G_c and Difference Image G_d respectively. Then pixel-wise adding G_d and I_T to get $\tilde{G}_d$. $\tilde{G}_d$, G_c will be fed into Refine Network (RN). Finally, the RN refine those afferent features to ultimate accurate prediction G_r.

3.1   Coarse Frame Generator

As shown in Fig. 1, the Coarse Frame Generator (CFG) in the upper path predicts coarse information in future frames. CFG is structurally similar to the Transform Net in [14], which contains an encoder, a res-network and a decoder. The encoder contains three convolution layers, each of which is followed by a Batch-norm layer [11] and a LeakyReLU [19] layer. In contrary to encoder, the decoder has three deconvolution layers, and all the convolution or deconvolution layers utilize 4×4 filters and stride 2 to process input feature maps. At the end of decoder, we add *tanh* activation function for normalization. More formally, let $S_I = \{I_1, I_2, \ldots, I_T\}$ denotes the input sequence of T frames and I_{T+1} denotes the future frame. After encoder, we can get features $O_1 = f_{conv}(S_I)$. With only three convolution layers, O_1 is a poor representation in such a difficult task. As each S_I contains consecutive frames which may include the same I_t, such as $S_I = \{I_1, I_2, \ldots, I_T\}$ and $\hat{S}_I = \{I_2, I_3, \ldots, I_{T+1}\}$. Besides, each I_t have similar

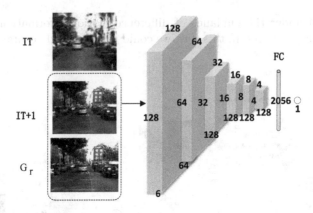

Fig. 3. Frameworks of discriminator. Taking I_{T+1} or G_r contacted with I_T as input.

features. Thus if we deepen the net, inconspicuous variation in consecutive frames may cause the gradient vanishing in training phaze. Under these circumstances, we insert the res-networks [9] between the encoder and decoder. The res-networks include three residual blocks and each block contains three convolution layers which use simple 1×1 filters and stride 1 to process input feature maps., followed by a Batch-norm layer [11] and a ReLU. When passing through the blocks, we can get feature maps $O_2 = f_{res}(O_1)$ where $f_{res}(O_1) = \mathcal{F}(O_1, \{Wi\}) + O_1$. Deconvolution layers in decoder will then up-sample O_2 to be the same size with input frames. In a nutshell, the CFG learns to produce coarse predicted frame G_c.

At this stage, we simplify the awkward task that we don't need to predicted the ultimate clear and realistic frame in one step. At the beginning, DGGAN only need to learn to fit the distribution of raw data. The fitting is important for providing structural information for our last refined prediction. There, we use the Mean Square Error (MSE) loss function to train the CFG:

$$\mathcal{L}_{cf}(G_c, I_{T+1}) = \sum_{i \in I} (G_c(i) - I_{T+1}(i))^2, \tag{1}$$

where $G_c(i)$ and $I_{T+1}(i)$ means the i-th pixel value of coarse predicted frame G_c and real predicted frame I_{T+1}.

3.2 Difference Guide Generator

In the lower path, the inter-frame difference is generated by Difference Guide Generator (DGG). As it shown in Fig. 3, the identical input $S_I = \{I_1, I_2, ..., I_T\}$ have two paths, lower of which will then be processed by the encoder and decoder of DGG. As for the encoder and decoder, DGG and CFG share the same structure. What distinguishes them is the different learning objective that target of DGG is generating Difference Image. First of all, we need to get real difference image $\hat{D}$, where $\hat{D}_T = I_{T+1} - I_T$. Through the DGG, we obtain the predicted difference image G_d. Generating this sparse image G_d is an easier task compared to generating realistic image which is dense. Thus, we introduce the L_1 loss to constrain the generation which outperform the MSE Loss when dealing with the generation of sparse image:

$$\mathcal{L}_{dg}(G_d, \hat{D}_T) = \sum_{i \in \hat{D}} \left| G_d(i) - \frac{\hat{D}_T(i)}{2} \right| \tag{2}$$

where $G_d(i)$ and $\hat{D}_T(i)$ denote the i-th pixel value of generated difference image sequences G_d and real difference image sequence $\hat{D}_T$. Note that we take *tanh* activation function to normalize our output, but the ground-truth of difference image $\hat{D}_T$ is between $[-2, 2]$. So we divide $\hat{D}_T$ by factor 2 to nondimensionalize the $\hat{D}_T$. Difference image plays a guide role in the following stage. Contrary to generating predicted frames directly, generating the sparse motion information is easy to converge. This well-trained information will guide coarse prediction to produce more accurate result.

For stage-I, the CFG and DGG generate coarse predictions G_c and difference images G_d respectively at each time step. A MSE penalty item constrains the CFG and L_1 penalty item constrains the DGG. In summary, the holistic penalty of stage-I is:

$$\mathcal{L}_{stage-I} = \mathcal{L}_{cf}(G_c, I_{T+1}) + \mathcal{L}_{dg}(G_d, \hat{D}_T) \tag{3}$$

From the (6), it suggests that CFG and DGG are synchronously trained under their own objective. The targets of stage-I are making coarse result approach to the future frame and generating more accurate difference image.

3.3 Refine Network

After stage-I, we can obtain coarse predicted frame G_c and difference guide G_d. As "$\oplus$" shown in Fig. 3, the guide G_d pixel-wise plus I_T will synthesize the guided image $\hat{I}$ where $\hat{I}_{T+1} = G_d \times 2 + I_T$.

Coarse predicted frame G_c have blurry problems which is far short of generating the realistic images. On the other side, $\hat{I}$ of combining the difference image and previous adjacent frame directly have abundant artifacts. Thus we define a Refine Network (RN) in stage-II to smooth the predicted frame. It has the analogic function with Auto-Encoder which learns to compress data from the input layer into a compact code, and then recover the original data from the code. To fuse the frame $\hat{I}_T$ and G_d, we set the guide as a condition. They are taken as the input of RN. RN merely has a simple structure which consists of three convolutional layers and three deconvolutional layers.

We add Batch-Norm layer and a LeayReLU layer following the convolution and deconvolution layer. And at the last output, we use *tanh* activation function to normalize. After RN, the coarse prediction G_c will be refined to a high visual quality prediction G_r with reduced blurriness or artifacts.

3.4   Adversarial Training

Since the GANs [7] has achieved tremendous success on generating of realistic images, we adopt GAN-based training strategy to refine our coarse results. As the original GAN suffers from several training difficulties such as mode collapse and instable convergence. In DGGAN, we adopt WAGN-GP [8] as our learning tactic. The WAGN-GP theoretically solve problems of original GAN mentioned before by minimizing an approximated Wasserstein distance and remedy the limitation of weight clipping about WGAN via the utilization of more advanced gradient penalty. In order to attain the goal of predicting, we also control our generation with the restrictions of given information like the principle of CGAN. As the Difference Image to be a condition guiding the generating, that's why we call Difference guide. As shown in Fig. 1, discriminator (D Net) located at the end of model is used for training the refined results. D Net has five convolutional layers with 4×4 filters and stride 2 to process input feature maps and one fully connection layers. Follow the WGAN-GP [8], we use layer-norm layer instead of batch-norm layer.

Training of the Discriminator. When training the discriminator, we regard the refined output G_r stacked with last frame I_T as negative example where the I_T is the condition. Analogously, we can get positive example by concatenate real image I_{T+1} with I_T. The optimization objective of discriminator can be written as:

$$\mathcal{L}_{adv}^{D} = E_{r \sim \mathbb{P}(Gr|I_T)}[D(r)] - E_{I \sim \mathbb{P}(I_{T+1}|I_T)}[D(I)]$$
$$+ \lambda E_{\hat{x} \sim \mathbb{P}_{\hat{x}}}[(\|\nabla_{\hat{x}} D(\hat{x})\|_2 - 1)^2] \quad (4)$$

where the $\mathbb{P}(I_{T+1}|I_T)$ is the distributions of real future frames in combination with conditions, the $\mathbb{P}(Gr|I_T)$ is the distributions of synthesized prediction in combination with conditions, $\hat{x}$ is the random samples between I_{T+1} and G_r and λ is the coefficient. $\hat{x}$ helps us to circumvent tractability issues by enforcing such a soft version of the constraint with a penalty on the gradient norm which lessen the distraction and burden from generating realistic images.

In this way, our discriminator learn to distinguish the ground-truth and refined generation with the condition of previous adjacent frame.

Training of the RN. Contrary to discriminator, we regard the refined output G_r stacked with last frame I_T as positive input. Keeping the weights of D fixed, and we perform an optimization on RN:

$$\mathcal{L}_{adv}^{RN} = -E_{r \sim \mathbb{P}(Gr|I_T)}[D(r)] \quad (5)$$

By minimizing the above two loss criteria (4), (5), RN trying to confuse the generated frames and real future frames. Meanwhile the ability of D that distinguish the synthesized frames and the real future frames is promoting. At last, the D can no longer make sure the source of input frames, and the output prediction of RN will be realistic to the real future frames.

In summary, the optimization target of stage-II is:

$$\mathcal{L}_{stage-II} = \mathcal{L}_{adv}^{RN} + \mathcal{L}_{adv}^{D} \quad (6)$$

3.5 Multi-frame Generation

Our model can be competent at Multi-frame Generation. We take the generated frame G_{r1} combined with previous $\{I_2, ..., I_{T+1}\}$ as the new input sequence, then use it to generated r_2 which is closed to real-frame I_{T+2}. By repeating the above operation, we can acquire a sequence of frames $S_r = \{G_{r1}, G_{r2}, ..., G_{rn}\}$ where n is the length of multi-frames. Because all the following prediction are influenced by the first frame prediction, our main target is making the one-frame prediction as accurate as possible.

4 Experiments

4.1 Experimental Set-Up

Datasets. We evaluate our proposed model in three different real-world scenarios, UCF-101 dataset [26], KITTI dataset [6] and Human 3.6M dataset [12]. The UCF-101 dataset, which contains 13320 annotated videos, include many human's activities. It was split to three subsets. We take the first subset as our training set and testing set. In KITTI dataset, it includes many driving-scenarios from different road conditions. Training set and testing set are from two categories: road and cars. Human 3.6M dataset is formed by various videos which consists of plentiful motions of humans. We extract these video to frames as well. In those dataset, to produce examples, we extracted every 5 continuous frames each step. We give the front four frames as input, and then try to predict the next one frames which is similar to the last one. The data patches are firstly normalized to the range $[-1{:}1]$ so that their values are equal to the generation interval of *tanh*.

Quality Evaluation. To quantify the comparison with State-of-the-Art methods, we use Structural Similarity Index (SSIM) [29], Mean Squared Error (MSE) [18] and Peak Signal-to-Noise Ratio (PSNR) [10] evaluation prototypes to assess the image quality of the results. SSIM is used for measuring the similarity between two images and higher value of SSIM means better accuracy of predicting. The MSE represents the quality of predicted frames. It is always nonnegative and value closer to zero is better. PSNR is similar to MSE, which can assess approximation to human perception of reconstruction quality, and higher value means better results.

Training Details. We use the Adam [15] to optimize DGGAN at the batch-size of 8 in both two stages. In stages-I, Both CFG and DGG use the same learning rate which is set to 0.001 and gradually decreased to 0.0001 over time. It takes about 100 epochs to reach convergence.

In stage-II, keeping the weight of that networks in stages-I fixed, the learning rate about Refine Network and the discriminator is set to 0.0001 and gradually decreased to 0.00001 over time. It takes about 200 epochs to reach convergence. We also set the weighting parameter $\lambda = 10$ in L_{adv}^D.

4.2   Comparison with the State-of-the-Art

As shown in Tables 3–2, we list our results and other State-of-the-Art approaches in detail.

Comparison on UCF-101. Firstly, We assess our model on UCF-101. We equally spaced sample from videos and choose examples from part-one as train and test datasets. The frames are resized to 128×128. Table 1 displays the results compared with other methods.

We take the one-frame prediction experiment results illustrated in Deep Multi-stage (DMS) [2]. For multi prediction setting, there is no data reported in [17].

Note that in single-frame prediction, our network surpasses the state-of-the-art comprehensively and transcends Deep Voxel Flow (DVF) 2% on SSIM and 10.6 on PSNR. For second frame prediction, DGGAN transcends the state-of-the-art 2%, 5.6 on SSIM, PSNR respectively. To our knowledge, we have achieved the state-of-the-art on UCF-101 on these two different settings. In another point, our approach is similar to DVF who generates a motion information (Voxel Flow) to guide the input frames. But DGGAN guiding by Difference shows the better performance than DVF. That's we think Difference has a stronger lead than Vodel Flow.

Table 1. Comparison of performance for different methods using SSIM/PSNR scores for the UCF-101. Value in "()" means score of second frame r_2. "*" This score is provided by [2] which predicted four frames once a time, but we only compare with the first frame of it. "$\sqrt{}$" means the model based on GAN.

Method	GAN	SSIM(2nd frame)	PSNR(2nd frame)
BeyondMSE [20]	$\sqrt{}$	0.92(0.89)	32(28.9)
DVF [17]	$\times$	0.96(-)	35.8(-)
*DMS [2]	$\sqrt{}$	0.95(0.93)	38.2(36.8)
Ours	$\sqrt{}$	**0.98(0.95)**	**46.4(42.3)**

Comparison on KITTI. Secondly, we assess our model by training on the KITTI dataset and testing on the CalTech Pedestrian dataset from "city", "Residential", and "Road". Frames from both datasets are center-cropped and down-sampled to 128×160 pixels. Different from previous dataset, the KITTI dataset have obvious background pixels changing. Nonetheless, our model can be capable of the prediction task. Table 2 shows all the consequence compared with other methods. All the score are provided by the Dual Motion Gan (DMG) [16]. Our model excess BeyondMSE [20], PredNet [17] and DMG [16] on SSIM. On MSE, we also have the minimum error. In particularly, compared with DMG which take optical flow as "guider", the results confirm the superiority of difference image. More intuitive performance are shown in Fig. 4. In spite that KITTI has

T-1   T   T+1   Ours   BeyondMSE

Fig. 4. Results in KITTI. From column 1–3 are past frames $T-1$, T and ground truth of frame $T+1$. Column 4 in blue is our prediction of frame $T+1$. Column 5 in blue is the result of BeyondMSE [20]. These three narrow columns in red are zoom in details of the $T+1$ real frame, our prediction and result of BeyondMSE respectively. (Color figure online)

greater variation between frames, we still anticipate the precise position about streetlight, cars and windows. And in comparison with BeyondMSE, our generated images are clearer significantly, and boost the image quality conspicuously.

Table 2. Comparison of different methods using SSIM/MSE scores for the KITTI.

Method	SSIM	MSE($\times 10^{-3}$)
BeyondMSE [20]	0.881	3.26
PredNet [17]	0.884	3.13
DMG [16]	0.899	2.41
Ours	**0.902**	**2.18**

Comparison on Human 3.6M. We assess our model in Human 3.6M at last. We extract frames from video and choose 100000 frames which contain a mass of consecutive motions randomly as the training set, and we take 10% of entire dataset as testing set. All of frames are down-sampled to 64×64. As seen in Table 3, it reports the quantitative comparison with the state-of-the-art methods from BeyondMSE [20], DNA [5] and Full Context (FC) [3]. We re-implement the result of BeyondMSE according to [20] that minimizes the loss functions in BeyondMSE (ADV+GDL) under the same setting with our model. And the result about DNA and FC refer to the experimental results shown in their papers. Since the dynamic regions in Human 3.6M are the central human movings, and usually the background is static, the difference guide have shown improvement in local variation of pixels. Under the guiding of it, our model significantly outperform BeyondMSE. And because DNA and FC need ten frame as input but our model just use four frame as input, we can also compete within them in a comprehensive way.

Table 3. Comparison of different methods using PSNR/SSIM scores for the Human 3.6M.

Method	SSIM	PSNR
BeyondMSE [20]	0.90	26.7
DNA [5]	0.992	42.1
FC [3]	**0.996**	**45.2**
Ours	0.990	44.1

T+1	CFGAN	DGN	DGGAN	PDI

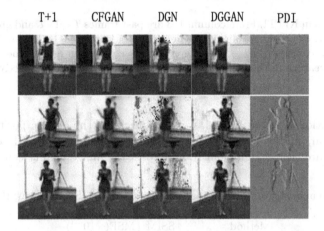

Fig. 5. Visual presentation of one-frame prediction on Human 3.6M. From left to right are ground truth of frame T+1, results of Coarse Frame Generative Adversarial Network (CFGAN), Difference Guided Net (DGN), our proposed model (DGGAN) and Predicted Difference Image (PDI).

4.3 Evaluation on Effectiveness

In order to evaluate our model, we set three baselines to prove the effectiveness of DGGAN in Table 4. In general, the copy of last frame I_T(Copy) is a significant reference. Without the guide, we append a discriminator to upper path which only contains the CFG as the second baseline named Coarse Frame Generative Adversarial Network (CFGAN). For third baseline, we directly apply the guide G_d into the last frame I_T to generate the prediction. There is a striking enhancement when comparing the Copy(Row 1) and DGN(Row 3). Accordingly, the difference image's intrinsic motion guidance is ideally suited for future prediction.

Drill down further to analysis the Table 4, the gap between DGGAN and CFGAN tells that multi-stage and dual path GAN is more effective than plain GAN. Especially on KITTI, conspicuous variation between inter-frames, copying pixels from last frame(Row 1) have a poor performance than DGN(Row 3) that indicates it is vital to utilize motion guider. Furthermore, DGGAN also exceeds three benchmarks on all the evaluation indexes. The results of these contrast

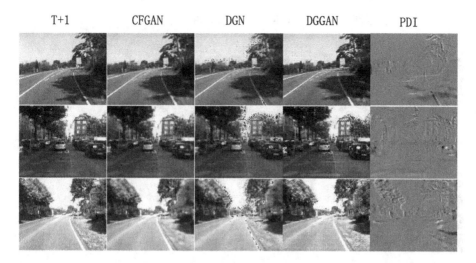

Fig. 6. Visual presentation of one-frame prediction on KITTI. The label means the same thing as Fig. 5

Table 4. Comparisons of our ultimate network with other two path methods in stage-I on Human 3.6M, UCF-101 and KITTI. The order of magnitude in "MSE" column is $(\times 10^{-3})$.

Model	Human 3.6M			UCF-101			KITTI		
	SSIM	PSNR	MSE	SSIM	PSNR	MSE	SSIM	PSNR	MSE
Copy	0.90	-	-	0.80	-	-	0.67	-	-
CFGAN	0.87	29.4	3.9	0.89	31.5	4.2	0.79	28.4	5.26
DGN	0.97	41.6	2.1	0.96	44.7	2.9	0.86	35.6	2.9
DGGAN	**0.99**	**44.1**	**1.8**	**0.98**	**46.4**	**2.4**	**0.90**	**37.5**	**2.1**

experiments illustrate that our proposed DGGAN has a reasonable structure. Both on guiding the motion information prediction and refining the synthetic image, DGGAN has shown its potential and superiority in this field.

More Intuitive performance are shown in Figs. 5, 6 and 7. Owing to the hard task that CFGAN need to generate the whole future frames directly, it's inevitable that generated frames are a bit blurry. On the contrary, our DGGAN focus on the variations between inter-frames under the guide of difference images and show better performance on generation. Beyond that, the similarity of Real Difference Image (PDI) and Predicted Difference Image (PDI) show the validity of task that using L1 loss to control the generation of sparse difference image. In addition, as we can see, the use of difference images directly will produce the images with lots of artifact and the RN can solve this problem by refining the images effectively.

Fig. 7. Visual presentation of one-frame prediction on UCF-101. The label means the same thing as Fig. 5. Besides, Real Difference Image (PDI) means the ground truth of difference image between I_T and I_{T+1}

5   Conclusion

In future prediction, we proposed a novel and reasonable methodology, Difference Guide Generative Adversarial Network (DGGAN). This method can refine the synthetic predicted image under the guiding of difference image. Although recent works provide plenty of alternative strategies such as leveraging optical flow to guide the prediction. DGGAN still stands out through a better guide. To explore effectiveness of DGGAN, we conducted a serials of experiments on comparing the state-of-the-art and our benchmarks. As we expected, DGGAN experimentally and theoretically demonstrated its excellent capacity which could be further applied to action analysis and video generation.

References

1. Barsoum, E., Kender, J., Liu, Z.: HP-GAN: Probabilistic 3D human motion prediction via GAN. arXiv preprint arXiv:1711.09561 (2017)
2. Bhattacharjee, P., Das, S.: Temporal coherency based criteria for predicting video frames using deep multi-stage generative adversarial networks. In: Advances in Neural Information Processing Systems, pp. 4271–4280 (2017)
3. Byeon, W., Wang, Q., Srivastava, R.K., Koumoutsakos, P.: Fully context-aware video prediction. arXiv preprint arXiv:1710.08518 (2017)
4. Denton, E.L., Chintala, S., Fergus, R., et al.: Deep generative image models using a Laplacian pyramid of adversarial networks. In: Advances in Neural Information Processing Systems, pp. 1486–1494 (2015)
5. Finn, C., Goodfellow, I., Levine, S.: Unsupervised learning for physical interaction through video prediction. In: Advances in Neural Information Processing Systems, pp. 64–72 (2016)

6. Geiger, A., Lenz, P., Stiller, C., Urtasun, R.: Vision meets robotics: the KITTI dataset. Int. J. Robot. Res. **32**(11), 1231–1237 (2013)
7. Goodfellow, I., et al.: Generative adversarial nets. In: Advances in Neural Information Processing Systems, pp. 2672–2680 (2014)
8. Gulrajani, I., Ahmed, F., Arjovsky, M., Dumoulin, V., Courville, A.C.: Improved training of wasserstein GANs. In: Advances in Neural Information Processing Systems, pp. 5769–5779 (2017)
9. He, K., Zhang, X., Ren, S., Sun, J.: Deep residual learning for image recognition. In: Proceedings of the IEEE Conference on Computer Vision and Pattern Recognition, pp. 770–778 (2016)
10. Huynh-Thu, Q., Ghanbari, M.: Scope of validity of PSNR in image/video quality assessment. Electron. Lett. **44**(13), 800–801 (2008)
11. Ioffe, S., Szegedy, C.: Batch normalization: Accelerating deep network training by reducing internal covariate shift. arXiv preprint arXiv:1502.03167 (2015)
12. Ionescu, C., Papava, D., Olaru, V., Sminchisescu, C.: Human3. 6m: Large scale datasets and predictive methods for 3D human sensing in natural environments. IEEE Trans. Pattern Anal. Mach. Intell. **36**(7), 1325–1339 (2014)
13. Jin, X., et al.: Predicting scene parsing and motion dynamics in the future. In: Advances in Neural Information Processing Systems, pp. 6918–6927 (2017)
14. Johnson, J., Alahi, A., Fei-Fei, L.: Perceptual losses for real-time style transfer and super-resolution. In: Leibe, B., Matas, J., Sebe, N., Welling, M. (eds.) ECCV 2016. LNCS, vol. 9906, pp. 694–711. Springer, Cham (2016). https://doi.org/10.1007/978-3-319-46475-6_43
15. Kingma, D.P., Ba, J.: Adam: A method for stochastic optimization. arXiv preprint arXiv:1412.6980 (2014)
16. Liang, X., Lee, L., Dai, W., Xing, E.P.: Dual motion GAN for future-flow embedded video prediction. arXiv preprint (2017)
17. Liu, Z., Yeh, R., Tang, X., Liu, Y., Agarwala, A.: Video frame synthesis using deep voxel flow. In: International Conference on Computer Vision (ICCV), vol. 2 (2017)
18. Lotter, W., Kreiman, G., Cox, D.: Deep predictive coding networks for video prediction and unsupervised learning. arXiv preprint arXiv:1605.08104 (2016)
19. Maas, A.L., Hannun, A.Y., Ng, A.Y.: Rectifier nonlinearities improve neural network acoustic models. In: Proceedings of ICML, vol. 30, p. 3 (2013)
20. Mathieu, M., Couprie, C., LeCun, Y.: Deep multi-scale video prediction beyond mean square error. arXiv preprint arXiv:1511.05440 (2015)
21. Mirza, M., Osindero, S.: Conditional generative adversarial nets. arXiv preprint arXiv:1411.1784 (2014)
22. Ohnishi, K., Yamamoto, S., Ushiku, Y., Harada, T.: Hierarchical video generation from orthogonal information: Optical flow and texture. arXiv preprint arXiv:1711.09618 (2017)
23. Patraucean, V., Handa, A., Cipolla, R.: Spatio-temporal video autoencoder with differentiable memory. arXiv preprint arXiv:1511.06309 (2015)
24. Rezazadegan, F., Shirazi, S., Davis, L.S.: A real-time action prediction framework by encoding temporal evolution
25. Sedaghat, N.: Next-flow: Hybrid multi-tasking with next-frame prediction to boost optical-flow estimation in the wild. arXiv preprint arXiv:1612.03777 (2016)
26. Soomro, K., Zamir, A.R., Shah, M.: Ucf101: A dataset of 101 human actions classes from videos in the wild. arXiv preprint arXiv:1212.0402 (2012)
27. Villegas, R., Yang, J., Zou, Y., Sohn, S., Lin, X., Lee, H.: Learning to generate long-term future via hierarchical prediction. arXiv preprint arXiv:1704.05831 (2017)

28. Vondrick, C., Pirsiavash, H., Torralba, A.: Generating videos with scene dynamics. In: Advances in Neural Information Processing Systems, pp. 613–621 (2016)

29. Wang, Z., Bovik, A.C., Sheikh, H.R., Simoncelli, E.P.: Image quality assessment: from error visibility to structural similarity. IEEE Trans. Image Process. **13**(4), 600–612 (2004)

30. Xiong, W., Luo, W., Ma, L., Liu, W., Luo, J.: Learning to generate time-lapse videos using multi-stage dynamic generative adversarial networks. In: Proceedings of the IEEE Conference on Computer Vision and Pattern Recognition, pp. 2364–2373 (2018)

31. Zhao, L., Peng, X., Tian, Y., Kapadia, M., Metaxas, D.: Learning to forecast and refine residual motion for image-to-video generation. In: Ferrari, V., Hebert, M., Sminchisescu, C., Weiss, Y. (eds.) ECCV 2018. LNCS, vol. 11219, pp. 403–419. Springer, Cham (2018). https://doi.org/10.1007/978-3-030-01267-0_24

Guided Feature Selection for Deep Visual Odometry

Fei Xue[1,4(✉)], Qiuyuan Wang[1,4], Xin Wang[1,4], Wei Dong[2], Junqiu Wang[3],
and Hongbin Zha[1,4(✉)]

[1] Key Laboratory of Machine Perception (MOE), School of EECS,
Peking University, Beijing, China
{feixue,wangqiuyuan,xinwang_cis}@pku.edu.cn, zha@cis.pku.edu.cn
[2] Robotics Institute, Carnegie Mellon University, Pittsburgh, USA
weidong@andrew.cmu.edu
[3] Beijing Changcheng Aviation Measurement and Control Institute, Beijing, China
jerywangjq@foxmail.com
[4] Cooperative Medianet Innovation Center, Shanghai Jiao Tong University,
Shanghai, China

Abstract. We present a novel end-to-end visual odometry architecture
with guided feature selection based on deep convolutional recurrent neural networks. Different from current monocular visual odometry methods, our approach is established on the intuition that features contribute
discriminately to different motion patterns. Specifically, we propose a
dual-branch recurrent network to learn the rotation and translation separately by leveraging current Convolutional Neural Network (CNN) for
feature representation and Recurrent Neural Network (RNN) for image
sequence reasoning. To enhance the ability of feature selection, we further introduce an effective context-aware guidance mechanism to force
each branch to distill related information for specific motion pattern
explicitly. Experiments demonstrate that on the prevalent KITTI and
ICL_NUIM benchmarks, our method outperforms current state-of-the-
art model- and learning-based methods for both decoupled and joint
camera pose recovery.

Keywords: Visual odometry · Recurrent neural networks ·
Feature selection

1 Introduction

Visual Odometry (VO) and Visual Simultaneous Localization and Mapping (V-
SLAM) estimate camera poses from image sequences by exploiting the consistency between neighboring frames. As an essential task in computer vision, VO

Supported by the National Key Research and Development Program of China
(2017YFB1002601) and National Natural Science Foundation of China (61632003,
61771026).

C. V. Jawahar et al. (Eds.): ACCV 2018, LNCS 11366, pp. 293–308, 2019.
https://doi.org/10.1007/978-3-030-20876-9_19

has been widely used in autonomous driving, robotics and augmented reality. Features play a key role in building consistency across images, and have been widely used in current VO/SLAM algorithms [10,26,28]. Despite the success of these methods, they ignore the discriminative contributions of features to different motions. However, if specific motions, especially rotations and translations, can be recovered by related features, the problems of scale-drifting and error accumulation in VO can be mitigated.

Unfortunately, how to detect appropriate features for recovering specific motions remains a challenging problem. Handcrafted feature descriptors such as SIFT [24] ORB [31], *etc.* are designed for general visual tasks, lacking the response to motions. Instead, geometry priors such as vanishing points [21], planar structures [19,32], and depth of pixels [17,30,33] are used in VO algorithms for camera pose decoupling. These methods provide promising performance in certain environments. However, they have limited generalization ability and may suffer from noisy input.

Rather than handcrafted features, Convolutional Neural Networks (CNNs) are able to extract deep features, which can encode high level priors and can be fed into Recurrent Neural Networks (RNNs) for end-to-end image sequences modeling and camera motion estimation. A few methods based on regular Long Short-Term Memory (LSTM) [14] have been proposed for camera motion recovery, such as DeepVO [35] and ESP-VO [36]. While achieving promising performances, they did not take into account the different responses of visual cues to motions, thus may output trajectories with large error.

In this paper, we aim to explore the possibility to select features with high discriminative ability for specific motions. Therefore, we can relax the assumptions of scenes required in previous works. We present a novel context-aware recurrent network that learns decoupled camera poses using selected features, as shown in Fig. 1. The main contributions include:

- We propose a dual-branch recurrent network with convolutional structure underneath for decoupled camera pose estimation, enabling the model to learn different motion patterns via specific features.
- We incorporate a context-aware feature selection mechanism to steer the network explicitly for distilling motion-sensitive information for each branch, using previous output as guidance spatially and temporally.
- Our experiments on the public benchmarks show that the proposed approach outperforms state-of-the-art VO methods for both joint and decoupled camera pose prediction.

The rest of this paper is organized as follows. In Sect. 2, related works on monocular VO and context-aware learning strategy are discussed. In Sect. 3, we introduce the architecture of our Guided Feature Selection for Deep Visual Odometry. The performance of the proposed approach is compared with other state-of-the-art methods in Sect. 4. We conclude the paper in Sect. 5.

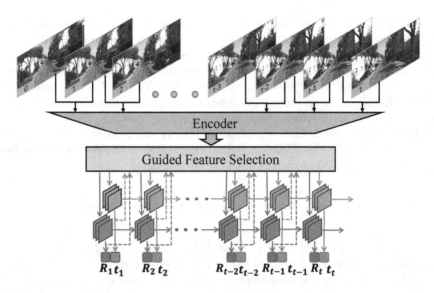

Fig. 1. An overview of our architecture. Rotation and translation are estimated separately in a dual-branch recurrent network. The specific motions are calculated using corresponding features selected with the guidance of previous output.

2   Related Work

2.1   Visual Odometry Based on Joint Pose Estimation

Traditionally, VO algorithms can be roughly categorized into feature-based and direct methods. Feature-based approaches establish correspondences across images via keypoints. VISO2 [10] utilizes circle matching between consecutive frames to realize an efficient monocular VO system. Since outliers and noises are unavoidable, all VO algorithms suffer from scale-drift and error accumulation. The problems can be partially solved in SLAM algorithms such as ORB-SLAM [26] by introducing pose graph optimization. Feature-based methods suffer from heavy time cost for feature extraction, and can fail in environments with limited texture information. Direct methods [7,8] recover poses by directly minimizing photometric error. These methods do not require expensive feature extraction, yet are sensitive to illumination variations. DSO [7] alleviates this problem by integrating a full photometric calibration. Up to now, both feature-based and direct methods are designed for static scenes and may face problems encountering dynamic objects. Moreover, absolute scale cannot be recovered in these methods without auxiliary information.

Recently, due to the advances of deep learning for computer vision tasks, CNNs and RNNs have been utilized for pose estimation. DeMoN [34] estimates depth and motion from two consecutive images captured by monocular cameras. SfmLearner [43] and its successors [22,38] recover depth of scenes and ego-motions from unlabeled sequences with view synthesis as supervisory signal.

DeepVO [35] learns camera poses from image sequences by combining CNNs and RNNs. It feeds 1D vectors learned by an encoder into a two-layer regular LSTM to predict motion of each frame and builds the loss function over the absolute joint poses at each time step. ESP-VO [36] extends DeepVO by inferring poses and uncertainties directly in a unified framework. VINet [4] fuses visual and inertial information in an intermediate representation level to eliminate manual synchronizations and performs sequence-to-sequence learning.

The methods above, however, consider measly the response of visual cues to different motion types. Besides, spatial connection is ignored in approaches based on regular RNNs, such as DeepVO and ESP-VO.

2.2   Visual Odometry Based on Decoupled Pose Estimation

Generally, instead of sharing the same features with translation, rotation can be recovered via geometric priors of certain scenes. Vanishing point [16,21] and planar structure [18,19,32,44] are two kinds of frequently-used visual cues. [18,32,44] decouple the rotation and translation to estimate orientation by tracking Manhattan frames. [19] extends to compute translational motion in VO system by minimizing de-rotated reprojection error given the rotation. [1] exploits vanishing points to recover the absolute attitude, and uses a 2-point algorithm to estimate translation for catadioptric vision. [17,33] select features for specific motion estimation according to depth values, since points at infinity are hardly influenced by translation, and hence are appropriate to estimate orientation. The strategy is also adopted in stereo SLAM systems [26].

Methods relying on Manhattan World assumption or depth of features achieve promising results in limited scenes but at a cost of reduced generalization and heavy noise. Instead, our method partially solves these problems by leveraging CNNs to extract features explicitly, and effectively.

2.3   Context-Aware Learning Mechanism

Contextual information is helpful in improving the performance of networks. It has been widely utilized in many computer vision tasks. Specifically, TRACA [3] uses the context of coarse category of tracking targets and proposes multiple expert auto-encoders to construct context-aware correlation filter for real-time tracking. PiCANet [23] learns to selectively attend informative context locations for each pixel to generate contextual attention maps. EncNet [41] uses the semantic context to selectively highlight the class-dependent feature-maps for semantic segmentation. CEN [25] defines the context as attributes assigned to each image and model the bias for image embeddings.

Our model benefits from the *small motion* between two consecutive views in an image sequence and exploits context i.e. continuity of neighboring frames in content and motion, to infer camera poses in a guided manner.

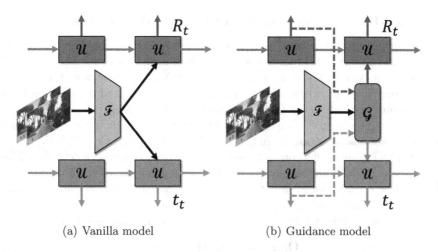

(a) Vanilla model   (b) Guidance model

Fig. 2. An illustration of two structures for decoupled motion estimation. A vanilla structure (a) feeds feature-maps into a ConvLSTM unit directly, while the guided model (b) utilizes previous output as guidance for feature selection.

3   Guided Feature Selection for Deep Visual Odometry

In this section, we introduce our framework (Fig. 1) in detail. First, the model encodes RGB images to high-level features in Sect. 3.1. Then, a context-aware motion guidance is adopted to recalibrate these features in Sect. 3.2. After that, the feature-maps are fed into two branches for learning rotation and translation in Sect. 3.3. Finally, we design a loss function considering both the rotational and translational errors in Sect. 3.4.

3.1   Feature Extraction

We harness the CNN to learn feature representation. Recently, plenty of excellent deep neural networks have been developed to deal with computer vision tasks such as classification [15], objection detection [12], semantic segmentation [2] by focusing on appearance and content of images. The VO task, however, depends on geometrical information in input sequences. By taking the efficiency of transfer learning [39] into consideration, we build the encoder based on Flownet [6] proposed for optical flow estimation. We retain the first 9 convolutional layers, as [35,36], encoding a pair of images into a 1024-channel stacked 2D feature-maps. The process can be described as

$$\mathbf{X}_t = \mathcal{F}(I_{t-1}, I_t; \theta_{\mathcal{F}}), \tag{1}$$

where I_{t-1}, I_t are consecutive frames. $\mathbf{X}_t = [\mathbf{X}_t^1, \mathbf{X}_t^2, ..., \mathbf{X}_t^C] \in \mathbb{R}^{H \times W \times C}$ is the extracted features with channel C and size $H \times W$. $\mathcal{F}$ maps raw images to high-level abstract 3D tensors through parameters $\theta_{\mathcal{F}}$. Different from DeepVO [35] and ESP-VO [36], we keep the structure of feature-maps for retaining the spatial formulation rather than compressing features into 1D vectors.

3.2 Dual-Branch Recurrent Network for Motion Separation

VO algorithms aim to recover camera poses from image sequences by leveraging the overlap between two or several consecutive frames. It's reasonable to model the sequences via LSTM [14], a variation of RNN. In this case, the feature flow passing through recurrent units, carries rich accumulated information from previous observations to infer current output. Unfortunately, standard units of LSTM utilized by DeepVO [35] and ESP-VO [36] requires 1D vector as input, and thus break the spatial structure of features. We rather adopt ConvLSTM [37], an extended LSTM unit with convolution embedded preserving more detailed visual cues to form a two-branch recurrent model. Since *gates* in ConvLSTM unit such as *output gate, input gate, forget gate* can be thought intuitively as regulators of the flow of values going through the connections, features are filtrated and reorganized to fit relevant motions. The process can be controlled by

$$\mathbf{O}_t, \mathbf{H}_t = \mathcal{U}(\mathbf{X}_t, \mathbf{H}_{t-1}; \theta_{\mathcal{U}}), \tag{2}$$

where $\mathbf{X}_t, \mathbf{O}_t$ and $\mathbf{H}_t$ denote the input, output and hidden state at current time point, respectively. $\mathbf{H}_{t-1}$ is the previous hidden state. Note that $\mathbf{X}_t, \mathbf{O}_t$ are both 3D tensors, so are the hidden states $\mathbf{H}_t, \mathbf{H}_{t-1}$. $\mathcal{U}$ plays the role of recurrent units of ConvLSTM [37] with $\theta_{\mathcal{U}}$ representing its parameters.

We create a two-branch recurrent model for decoupled motion prediction, enabling each branch to control corresponding feature flow for one type of motion. In general, a vanilla model feeds extracted features $\mathbf{X}_t$ into each branch directly, using the recurrent units for information selection, as show in Fig. 2(a). The unit, however, may be inefficient in feature selection due to finite capacity. Amount of redundant information may ulteriorly aggravates the situation, and hence degrades the accuracy.

Intuitively, previous output contains valuable visual cues for corresponding motion estimation, and thus can serve as a supervisor. In our model, raw feature-maps $\mathbf{X}_t$ are reconsidered before fed into each branch as depicted in Fig. 2(b). Thereby, each motion pattern can be learned from most related features, as discussed in Sect. 3.3. The process can be described as

$$\mathbf{O}_t^{motion}, \mathbf{H}_t^{motion} = \mathcal{U}(\mathbf{X}_t^{motion}, \mathbf{H}_{t-1}^{motion}; \theta_{\mathcal{U}}), \tag{3}$$

where $\mathbf{X}_t^{motion}, \mathbf{H}_t^{motion}$ and $\mathbf{O}_t^{motion}$ denote the recalibrated features, hidden state and output for specific *motion*. $\mathbf{H}_{t-1}^{motion}$ is the previous hidden state for the *motion* branch. Here, *motion* indicates *rotation* and *translation* specifically in our work. Obviously, the model is flexible to accept various motion patterns according to tasks.

3.3 Guided Feature Selection

To achieve the purpose of generating related information for each branch, our approach benefits from *small* motion between neighboring views by incorporating a guidance module to selectively distill features for current pose inference adaptively as

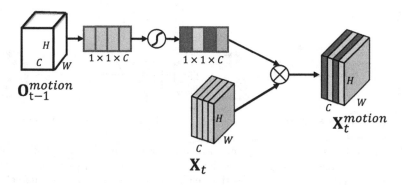

Fig. 3. SENet-like guidance module. Encoded features are scaled along channel dimension according to only previous output without the participation of current input.

$$\mathbf{X}_t^{motion} = \mathcal{G}(\mathbf{X}_t, \mathbf{O}_{t-1}^{motion}; \theta_{\mathcal{G}}). \tag{4}$$

Here, $\mathcal{G}$ is a function that maps features $\mathbf{X}_t$ to motion-sensitive tensors $\mathbf{X}_t^{motion}$ with the supervision of previous output $\mathbf{O}_{t-1}^{motion}$. $\theta_{\mathcal{G}}$ denotes the weights of $\mathcal{G}$. We introduce two strategies for context-aware guidance considering the connections in temporal and spatial domain. The first one is a SENet-like guidance, and the second one is a correlation-based guidance.

SENet-like Guidance. Inspired by the work of SENet [15], in which a *Squeeze-and-Extinction* block is implemented to *self-recalibrate* channel-wise feature responses. Rather than self-adjusting the weights, we focus on the relationship in temporal domain. The previous output is first passed through a global average pooling (GAP) layer to yield a channel-wise descriptor. Two Fully-Connected (FC) layers are followed to learn inner channel dependence and produce scale values. Then, a sigmoid layer normalizes these values to [0, 1]. The final output is obtained by rescaling features along the channel dimension. A diagram of channel-wise guidance is shown in Fig. 3. The process is formulated as

$$\mathbf{s}^{motion} = \sigma(\mathbf{W}_2\delta(\mathbf{W}_1 GAP(\mathbf{O}_{t-1}^{motion}) + \mathbf{b}_1) + \mathbf{b}_2), \tag{5}$$

$$\mathbf{X}_t^{motion,c} = \mathbf{X}_t^c \cdot s_c^{motion}, \tag{6}$$

where $\mathbf{W}_1, \mathbf{W}_2$ denote the two FC layers with $\mathbf{b}_1, \mathbf{b}_2$ as biases. σ, δ indicate the sigmoid and ReLU [27] activation functions. $\mathbf{s}^{motion} = [s_1^{motion}, s_2^{motion}, ..., s_C^{motion}]$ is the obtained scale vectors. $\mathbf{X}_t^c, \mathbf{X}_t^{motion,c}$ are feature-maps of $\mathbf{X}_t$ and $\mathbf{X}_t^{motion}$ of channel c.

Note that, SENet aims to exploit contextual interdependencies of $\mathbf{X}_t$, while our algorithm focuses on temporal consistency by filtering $\mathbf{X}_t$ according to the proposal of $\mathbf{O}_{t-1}^{motion}$.

Correlation-Based Guidance. SENet-like subnetwork produces relatively coarse scalars in temporal domain without considering spatial relationship between $\mathbf{O}_{t-1}$ and $\mathbf{X}_t$. Since the detail information is not kept, the performance

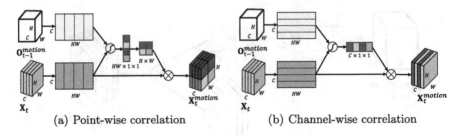

(a) Point-wise correlation   (b) Channel-wise correlation

Fig. 4. An illustration of two types of correlation-based guidance. Point-wise correlation (a) takes values at the same position of all 2D feature-maps as a unity, while channel-wise correlation (b) computes the weight for feature-map of each channel.

is not satisfying. We further explore the guidance at a finer level from the aspect of correlation between $\mathbf{O}_{t-1}^{motion}$ and $\mathbf{X}_t$, as depicted in Fig. 4.

Since $\mathbf{X}_t$ and $\mathbf{O}_{t-1}^{motion}$ are both 3D tensors of stacked 2D-features, there are two different approaches to calculating the cross-correlation parameters by taking each pixel position along channel dimension as a column (Fig. 4(a)) or each feature-map as a unity (Fig. 4(b)). In the first form, we compute the cosine similarity of each corresponding column first, and normalize the weight next. We have tried the sigmoid and softmax for normalization. The sigmoid function gives better performance in our experiments. The process can be described as

$$s_{(u,v)}^{motion} = \sigma\left(\frac{\mathbf{X}_{t,(u,v)} \cdot \mathbf{O}_{t-1,(u,v)}^{motion}}{||\mathbf{X}_{t,(u,v)}||_2 \cdot ||\mathbf{O}_{t-1,(u,v)}^{motion}||_2}\right), \tag{7}$$

$$\mathbf{X}_{t,(u,v)}^{motion} = \mathbf{X}_{t,(u,v)} \cdot s_{(u,v)}^{motion}, \tag{8}$$

here $\mathbf{X}_{t,(u,v)}$ and $\mathbf{O}_{t-1,(u,v)}^{motion}$ are vectors with size of C at each point of $\mathbf{X}_t$ and $\mathbf{O}_{t-1}^{motion}$ indexed by u, v. $s_{(u,v)}^{motion}$ is the scale for re-weighted tensor $\mathbf{X}_t^{motion}$ at (u, v). Intuitively, if current vectorial feature $\mathbf{X}_{t,(u,v)}$ is close to previous output $\mathbf{O}_{t-1,(u,v)}^{motion}$, it should be assigned a larger weight, otherwise a smaller one.

In the second type, 2D feature map of each channel is unified as a vector, on which we compute the correlation as

$$s_c^{motion} = \sigma\left(\frac{Vec(\mathbf{X}_t^c) \cdot Vec(\mathbf{O}_{t-1}^{motion,c})}{||Vec(\mathbf{X}_t^c)||_2 \cdot ||Vec(\mathbf{O}_{t-1}^{motion,c})||_2}\right), \tag{9}$$

where $Vec(\cdot)$ reshapes a 2D feature map into a vector for correlation computation. $\mathbf{X}_t$ is re-weighted adaptively for each branch according to the correlation parameters as (6).

Context-aware motion guidance scheme brings better performance for our model with a limited time cost. We analyze the boosted efficiency in Sect. 4.

3.4   Loss Function

Our architecture learns rotation and translation in two individual recurrent branches separately, hence the final loss consists of both rotational and translational errors. We define the loss on the absolute pose error of each view using the L_2 norm. The loss functions are formulated as

$$\mathcal{L}_i^{rot} = ||\hat{\phi}_i - \phi_i||_2, \tag{10}$$

$$\mathcal{L}_i^{trans} = ||\hat{p}_i - p_i||_2, \tag{11}$$

$$\mathcal{L}_{total} = \sum_{i=1}^{t} \frac{1}{i}(\mathcal{L}_i^{trans} + k\mathcal{L}_i^{rot}). \tag{12}$$

Here $\hat{p}_i, p_i, \hat{\phi}_i$, and ϕ_i represent the predicted and ground-truth translation and rotation (Euler angles) of the i-th view in world coordinate. $\mathcal{L}_i^{rot}$ and $\mathcal{L}_i^{trans}$ denote the rotational and translational error of the i-th frame, respectively. The final loss, $\mathcal{L}_{total}$ sums the averaged loss of each time step. t is the current frame index in a sequence. k is a fixed parameter for balancing the rotational and translational errors. It is set to 100 and 10 in experiments on KITTI and ICL_NUIM dataset respectively.

4 Experiments

We first discuss the implementation details of our network in Sect. 4.1, and introduce the datasets used in Sect. 4.2. We compare the effectiveness of variations of our network, RNN for the regular recurrent network, SRNN for the dual-branch recurrent model, SRNN_se for dual-branch network plus senet-like contextual mechanism, SRNN_channel for dual-branch network plus channel-wise correlation, and SRNN_point for dual-branch network plus point-wise correlation, in Sect. 4.3. Next, we compare our proposal with current methods on the KITTI dataset [9] in Sect. 4.4, and ICL_NUIM dataset [11] in Sect. 4.5.

4.1 Implementation

Training. Our model takes monocular image sequences as input. The image size can be arbitrary because the model has no requirement of compressing images into vectors. We use 7 consecutive frames to construct a sequence considering the time cost, yet our model can accept dynamic lengths of inputs.

Network. Weights of recurrent units are initialized with MSRA [13], while the encoder is based on pre-trained Flownet [6] to speed up convergence. Our networks are implemented by PyTorch [29] on an NVIDIA 1080Ti GPU. We employ the poly learning rate policy [2] with power = 0.9 and initial learning rate = 10^{-4}. Adam [20] with $\beta_1 = 0.9, \beta_2 = 0.99$ is used as optimizer. The networks are trained with a batch size of 4, a weight decay of 10^{-4} for 150,000 iterations in total.

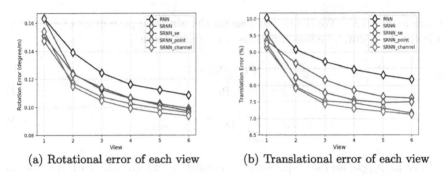

(a) Rotational error of each view   (b) Translational error of each view

Fig. 5. Rotational (a) and translational (b) errors along each view of the network for joint motion prediction, vanilla and guided models for separate pose recovery.

4.2 Dataset

KITTI. The public KITTI dataset is used by both model- [10,26] and learning-based methods [35,36,43]. The dataset consists of 22 sequences captured in urban and highway environments at a relatively low sample frequency (10 fps) at speed up to 90 km/h. Seq 00-10 provide raw data with ground-truth represented as 6DoF motion parameters by considering the complicate urban environments, while Seq 11-21 provide only raw sensor data. In our experiments, the left RGB images are resized to 1280×384 for training and testing. We adopt the same train/test split as DeepVO [35] by using Seq 00, 02, 08, 09 for training and Seq 03, 04, 05, 06, 07 and 10 for quantitative evaluation.

ICL_NUIM. The ICL_NUIM dataset [11] consists of 8 sequences of RGB-D images captured within synthetically generated living room and office. Images in this dataset meet the Manhattan World assumption. The dataset is widely used for VO/SLAM [18,19,44] and 3D reconstruction [5]. ICL_NUIM dataset is synthesized by a full 6DoF handheld camera and thus is challenging for monocular VO methods due to complicated motion patterns. Our model is trained on kt0, kt3 and evaluated on kt1, kt2 on the living room and office datasets, respectively. Only RGB images with size of 640×480 are used in our experiments.

4.3 Evaluation of Context-Aware Mechanism

We first evaluate the efficiency of *context-aware* strategies by analyzing rotational (Fig. 5(a)) and translational (Fig. 5(b)) errors along each view of the sequence on KITTI test datasets. We adopt the orientation and position drift errors divided by traveling length as metric. In Fig. 5, we observe that results of the vanilla network are remarkably improved by the context-aware guidance, and meanwhile, networks with different contextual modules behave diversely.

Among the models with guidance, SRNN_se extends the self-recalibration of SENet [15] by introducing temporal relationship, leading to improvement

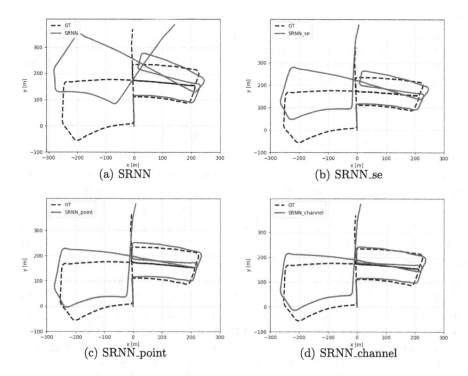

Fig. 6. Qualitative comparison of the trajectories of the vanilla and three guided models for separate motion estimation on the KITTI Seq 10.

in decoupled motion learning. Compared with SRNN_se, the superior performance of SRNN_point and SRNN_channel suggests that correlation may be more effective in feature filtration for the VO task. The results of SRNN_channel are slightly better than SRNN_point. We explain that keeping the interdependence of feature-map in each channel may be a better manner for the guidance (Fig. 6).

4.4   Results on KITTI Dataset

We compare our framework with model- and learning-based monocular VO methods on the KITTI test sequences. The error metrics, i.e., averaged Root Mean Square Errors (RMSEs) of the translational and rotational errors, are adopted for all the subsequences of lengths ranging from 100, 200 to 800 m.

Most monocular VO methods cannot recover absolute scale, and their results require post alignment with ground-truth. Therefore, the open-source VO library VISO2 [10] estimating scale according to the height of camera is adopted as the baseline method. The results of both monocular (VISO2-M) and stereo (VISO2-S) versions are provided. Table 1 indicates that our models, even the vanilla version, outperform VISO2-M in terms of both rotation and translation estimation by a large margin. Note that the scale is learned during the end-to-end

Table 1. Results on the KITTI dataset. DeepVO [35], ESP-VO [36] and our models are trained on Seq 00, 02, 08 and 09. SfmLearner [43], UndeepVO [22] and Depth-VO-Feat [40] are trained on Seq 00–08 in an unsupervised manner. The best results of monocular VO methods are highlighted without considering stereo ones including VISO2-S, UnDeepVO and Depth-VO-Feat.

Method	Sequence											
	03		04		05		06		07		10	
	t_{rel}	r_{rel}	t_{rel}	r_{rel}	t_{rel}	r_{rel}	t_{rel}	r_{rel}	t_{rel}	r_{rel}	t_{rel}	r_{rel}
VISO2-S [10]	3.21	3.25	2.12	2.12	1.53	1.60	1.48	1.58	1.85	1.91	1.17	1.30
UnDeepVO [22]	5.00	6.17	5.49	2.13	3.40	1.50	6.20	1.98	3.15	2.48	10.63	4.65
Depth-VO-Feat [40]	15.58	10.69	2.92	2.06	4.94	2.35	5.80	2.07	6.48	3.60	12.45	3.46
VISO2-M [10]	8.47	8.82	4.69	4.49	19.22	17.58	7.30	6.14	23.61	19.11	41.56	32.99
SfmLearner [43]	10.78	3.92	4.49	5.24	18.67	4.10	25.88	4.80	21.33	6.65	14.33	3.30
DeepVO [35]	8.49	6.89	7.19	6.97	**2.62**	3.61	**5.42**	5.82	3.91	4.60	8.11	8.83
ESP-VO [36]	6.72	6.46	6.33	6.08	3.35	4.93	7.24	7.29	3.52	5.02	9.77	10.2
RNN	6.36	3.62	5.95	2.36	5.85	2.55	14.58	4.98	5.88	2.64	7.44	3.19
SRNN	5.85	3.77	4.22	2.79	5.33	2.36	13.60	4.21	4.62	2.48	7.08	2.79
SRNN_se	5.45	3.33	4.11	1.70	4.74	2.21	12.44	4.45	4.23	2.67	6.79	2.91
SRNN_point	5.64	**3.06**	3.98	1.79	3.71	1.70	9.16	3.27	3.57	2.53	6.77	2.82
SRNN_channel	**5.44**	3.32	**2.91**	**1.30**	3.27	**1.62**	8.50	**2.74**	**3.37**	**2.25**	**6.32**	**2.33**

t_{rel}: average translational RMSE drift (%) on length from 100, 200 to 800 m.
r_{rel}: average rotational RMSE drift (°/100 m) on length from 100, 200 to 800 m.

training without any post alignment or relying on priori knowledge such as the height of camera used by VISO2-M. VISO2-S gains superior performance due to the advantages of stereo image pairs in scale recovery and data association. Note that, our SRNN_channel achieves very close performance to VISO2-S provided solely monocular images. Qualitative comparisons are shown in Fig. 7. Our approach outperforms VISO2-M especially in handling complicated motions.

Besides, we compare our approach against current learning-based supervised methods DeepVO [35] and ESP-VO [36], both of which are implemented on a single branch with standard LSTM for coupled motion estimation. Table 1 illustrates the efficiency of our vanilla model. The improvement of this version is slight. We assume that extracting motion-sensitive features from encoded

Table 2. Evaluation on the ICL_NUIM dataset. Results of DRFE, DEMO, DVO and MWO are taken directly from [19].

Sequence	SRNN_channel	SRNN	DFRE [19]	DEMO [42]	DVO [18]	MWO [44]
lr kt1	**0.009**	0.010	0.021	0.020	0.023	0.100
lr kt2	**0.019**	0.019	0.031	0.090	0.084	0.052
of kt1	**0.011**	0.015	0.014	0.054	0.045	0.263
of kt2	0.019	0.019	0.021	**0.015**	0.079	0.065	0.047

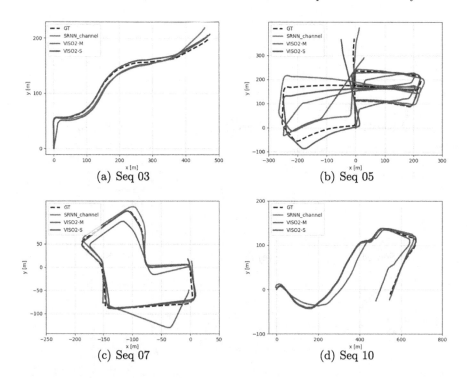

Fig. 7. The trajectories of ground-truth, VISO2-M, VISO2-S and our model on Seq 03, 05, 07 and 10 of the KITTI benchmark.

feature-maps directly may limit the accuracy. Fortunately, the deficiency is compensated by the context-aware feature selection mechanism. Our models with guidance outperform DeepVO and ESP-VO consistently. Meanwhile, out method achieves superior performance than unsupervised monocular approach, SfmLearner [43], and yields competitive results than stereo methods such as UnDeepVO [22] and Depth-VO-Feat [40].

We intensively test our model in various scenes with complicate motions on Seq 11–21. The trajectories of results are illustrated in Fig. 8. In this case, our network is trained on all the training sequences (Seq 00–10), providing more data to avoid overfitting and maximize the ability of generation. We use the accurate VISO2-S [10] as reference due to the lack of ground-truth. Our model also obtains outstanding results. The appearing performance of our method reveals that the model generalizes well in unknown scenarios.

4.5   Results on ICL_NUIM Dataset

We further compare our model with methods on the challenging ICL_NUIM dataset [11]. We test our networks on the living room and office datasets individually. The baseline methods include algorithms for both joint (DEMO [42],

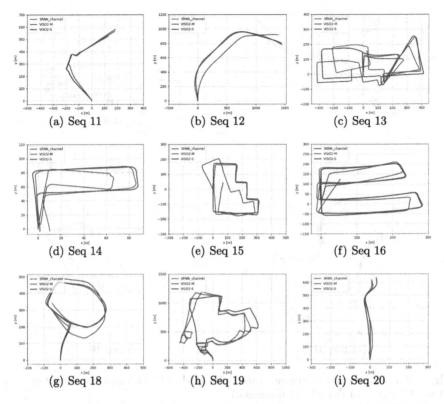

Fig. 8. The predicted trajectories on KITTI sequences 11–20. Results of VISO2-S are used as reference since ground-truth poses of these sequences are unavailable.

DVO [18]) and separate (DRFE [19], MWO [44]) pose recovery. The error metric for qualitative analysis is the root mean square error (RMSE) of the relative pose error (RPE), used in [19]. Table 2, indicates that the best performing SRNN_channel yields lower errors in relative pose recovery on three among the four sequences. Note that all the four baselines use depth information while only monocular RGB images are used in our networks. The remarkable results suggest the potential ability of our proposal in dealing with more complicated motion patterns generated by handheld cameras or moving robotics.

5   Conclusions

In this paper, we propose a novel dual-branch recurrent neural network for decoupled camera pose estimation. The architecture is able to estimate different motion patterns via specific features. To enhance the performance, we incorporate a context-aware feature selection mechanism in both spatial and temporary domain, allowing the network to suppress useless information adaptively. We evaluate our techniques on the prevalent KITTI and ICL_NUIM datasets, and results demonstrate that our method outperforms current state-of-the-art learning- and model-based monocular VO approaches for both joint and separate motion estimation. In the future, we plan to visualize the features used by specific motions. We will also explore the relationship between visual cues and more specific motion patterns such as rotation in different directions.

References

1. Bazin, J.C., Demonceaux, C., Vasseur, P., Kweon, I.: Motion estimation by decoupling rotation and translation in catadioptric vision. CVIU **114**, 254–273 (2010)
2. Chen, L., Papandreou, G., Kokkinos, I., Murphy, K., Yuille, A.: DeepLab: semantic image segmentation with deep convolutional nets, atrous convolution, and fully connected CRFs. TPAMI **40**, 834–848 (2018)
3. Choi, J., et al.: Context-aware deep feature compression for high-speed visual tracking. In: CVPR (2018)
4. Clark, R., Wang, S., Wen, H., Markham, A., Trigoni, N.: VINet: visual-inertial odometry as a sequence-to-sequence learning problem. In: AAAI (2017)
5. Dai, A., Nießner, M., Zollhöfer, M., Izadi, S., Theobalt, C.: Bundlefusion: real-time globally consistent 3D reconstruction using on-the-fly surface reintegration. TOG **36**, 76a (2017)
6. Dosovitskiy, A., et al.: Flownet: learning optical flow with convolutional networks. In: ICCV (2015)
7. Engel, J., Koltun, V., Cremers, D.: Direct sparse odometry. TPAMI **1**, 4 (2017)
8. Engel, J., Schöps, T., Cremers, D.: LSD-SLAM: large-scale direct monocular SLAM. In: Fleet, D., Pajdla, T., Schiele, B., Tuytelaars, T. (eds.) ECCV 2014. LNCS, vol. 8690, pp. 834–849. Springer, Cham (2014). https://doi.org/10.1007/978-3-319-10605-2_54
9. Geiger, A., Lenz, P., Urtasun, R.: Are we ready for autonomous driving? The KITTI vision benchmark suite. In: CVPR (2012)
10. Geiger, A., Ziegler, J., Stiller, C.: Stereoscan: dense 3D reconstruction in real-time. In: IV (2011)
11. Handa, A., Whelan, T., McDonald, J., Davison, A.J.: A benchmark for RGB-D visual odometry, 3D reconstruction and SLAM. In: ICRA (2014)
12. He, K., Gkioxari, G., Dollár, P., Girshick, R.: Mask R-CNN. In: ICCV (2017)
13. He, K., Zhang, X., Ren, S., Sun, J.: Delving deep into rectifiers: surpassing human-level performance on imagenet classification. In: ICCV (2015)
14. Hochreiter, S., Schmidhuber, J.: Long short-term memory. Neural Comput. **9**, 1735–1780 (1997)
15. Hu, J., Shen, L., Sun, G.: Squeeze-and-excitation networks. In: CVPR (2018)
16. Jo, Y., Jang, J., Paik, J.: Camera orientation estimation using motion based vanishing point detection for automatic driving assistance system. In: ICCE (2018)
17. Kaess, M., Ni, K., Dellaert, F.: Flow separation for fast and robust stereo odometry. In: ICRA (2009)
18. Kerl, C., Sturm, J., Cremers, D.: Robust odometry estimation for RGB-D cameras. In: ICRA (2013)
19. Kim, P., Coltin, B., Kim, H.J.: Visual odometry with drift-free rotation estimation using indoor scene regularities. In: BMVC (2017)
20. Kingma, D.P., Ba, J.: Adam: a method for stochastic optimization. In: ICLR (2015)

21. Lee, J.K., Yoon, K.J., et al.: Real-time joint estimation of camera orientation and vanishing points. In: CVPR (2015)
22. Li, R., Wang, S., Long, Z., Gu, D.: UnDeepVO: monocular visual odometry through unsupervised deep learning. In: ICRA (2018)
23. Liu, N., Han, J.: PiCANet: learning pixel-wise contextual attention in ConvNets and its application in saliency detection. In: CVPR (2018)
24. Lowe, D.G.: Distinctive image features from scale-invariant keypoints. IJCV **60**, 91–110 (2004)
25. Mac Aodha, O., Perona, P., et al.: Context embedding networks. In: CVPR (2018)
26. Mur-Artal, R., Tardós, J.D.: ORB-SLAM2: an open-source SLAM system for monocular, stereo, and RGB-D cameras. T-RO **33**, 1255–1262 (2017)
27. Nair, V., Hinton, G.E.: Rectified linear units improve restricted boltzmann machines. In: ICML (2010)
28. Newcombe, R.A., Lovegrove, S.J., Davison, A.J.: DTAM: dense tracking and mapping in real-time. In: ICCV (2011)
29. Paszke, A., Gross, S., Chintala, S., Chanan, G.: Pytorch (2017). https://github.com/pytorch/pytorch
30. Paz, L.M., Piniés, P., Tardós, J.D., Neira, J.: Large-scale 6-DOF SLAM with stereo-in-hand. T-RO **24**, 946–957 (2008)
31. Rublee, E., Rabaud, V., Konolige, K., Bradski, G.: ORB: an efficient alternative to SIFT or SURF. In: ICCV (2011)
32. Straub, J., Bhandari, N., Leonard, J.J., Fisher, J.W.: Real-time Manhattan world rotation estimation in 3D. In: IROS (2015)
33. Tardif, J.P., Pavlidis, Y., Daniilidis, K.: Monocular visual odometry in urban environments using an omnidirectional camera. In: IROS (2008)
34. Ummenhofer, B., et al.: DeMoN: depth and motion network for learning monocular stereo. In: CVPR (2017)
35. Wang, S., Clark, R., Wen, H., Trigoni, N.: DeepVO: towards end-to-end visual odometry with deep recurrent convolutional neural networks. In: ICRA (2017)
36. Wang, S., Clark, R., Wen, H., Trigoni, N.: End-to-end, sequence-to-sequence probabilistic visual odometry through deep neural networks. IJRR **37**, 513–542 (2017)
37. Xingjian, S., Chen, Z., Wang, H., Yeung, D.Y., Wong, W.K., Woo, W.C.: Convolutional LSTM network: a machine learning approach for precipitation nowcasting. In: NIPS (2015)
38. Yin, Z., Shi, J.: GeoNet: unsupervised learning of dense depth, optical flow and camera pose. In: CVPR (2018)
39. Zamir, A.R., Sax, A., Shen, W., Guibas, L., Malik, J., Savarese, S.: Taskonomy: disentangling task transfer learning. In: CVPR (2018)
40. Zhan, H., Garg, R., Saroj Weerasekera, C., Li, K., Agarwal, H., Reid, I.: Unsupervised learning of monocular depth estimation and visual odometry with deep feature reconstruction. In: CVPR (2018)
41. Zhang, H., et al.: Context encoding for semantic segmentation. In: CVPR (2018)
42. Zhang, J., Kaess, M., Singh, S.: Real-time depth enhanced monocular odometry. In: IROS (2014)
43. Zhou, T., Brown, M., Snavely, N., Lowe, D.G.: Unsupervised learning of depth and ego-motion from video. In: CVPR (2017)
44. Zhou, Y., Kneip, L., Rodriguez, C., Li, H.: Divide and conquer: efficient density-based tracking of 3D sensors in Manhattan worlds. In: ACCV (2016)

Appearance-Based Gaze Estimation Using Dilated-Convolutions

Zhaokang Chen$^{(\boxtimes)}$ and Bertram E. Shi

The Hong Kong University of Science and Technology, Kowloon, Hong Kong SAR
{zchenbc,eebert}@ust.hk

Abstract. Appearance-based gaze estimation has attracted more and more attention because of its wide range of applications. The use of deep convolutional neural networks has improved the accuracy significantly. In order to improve the estimation accuracy further, we focus on extracting better features from eye images. Relatively large changes in gaze angles may result in relatively small changes in eye appearance. We argue that current architectures for gaze estimation may not be able to capture such small changes, as they apply multiple pooling layers or other downsampling layers so that the spatial resolution of the high-level layers is reduced significantly. To evaluate whether the use of features extracted at high resolution can benefit gaze estimation, we adopt dilated-convolutions to extract high-level features without reducing spatial resolution. In cross-subject experiments on the Columbia Gaze dataset for eye contact detection and the MPIIGaze dataset for 3D gaze vector regression, the resulting Dilated-Nets achieve significant (up to 20.8%) gains when compared to similar networks without dilated-convolutions. Our proposed Dilated-Net achieves state-of-the-art results on both the Columbia Gaze and the MPIIGaze datasets.

Keywords: Appearance-based gaze estimation · Dilated-convolutions

1 Introduction

Gaze tracking has long been considered as an important research topic, as it has various promising real-world applications, such as gaze-based interfaces [5,20], foveated rendering in virtual reality [19], behavioral analysis [11] and human-robot interaction [12]. Early gaze tracking techniques required strong constraints, e.g., facing the tracker frontally and keeping the positions of eyes inside a certain region. These constraints limited the applications to relatively controlled environments. In order to apply gaze tracking in real-world and more flexible environments, researchers proposed many novel methods to alleviate these constraints and move towards unconstrained gaze tracking, e.g., [1,6,21,22,27,28,36].

Supported by the Innovation and Technology Fund of Hong Kong under grant ITS/406/16FP.

© Springer Nature Switzerland AG 2019
C. V. Jawahar et al. (Eds.): ACCV 2018, LNCS 11366, pp. 309–324, 2019.
https://doi.org/10.1007/978-3-030-20876-9_20

Unconstrained gaze tracking refers to calibration-free, subject-, viewpoint- and illumination-independent gaze tracking [21]. Appearance-based gaze estimation is a promising approach to unconstrained gaze tracking. It estimates the 2D gaze target position on a given plane or 3D gaze angles based on the images captured by RGB sensors. The key advantage of this method is that it does not require expensive custom hardware but off-the-shelf cameras, which are inexpensive and commonly available nowadays. However, it is a very challenging problem as it needs to address several factors, such as differences in individual appearances, head-eye relationships, gaze ranges and illumination conditions [36].

In recent years, with the success of deep convolutional neural networks (CNNs) in the field of computer vision, researchers have started to apply deep CNNs to appearance-based gaze tracking. Thanks to the large number of publicly-available high quality real and synthetic datasets [8,15,23,25,27,34], deep CNNs have demonstrated good performance, but there is still room for improvement.

In this article, we propose to improve the accuracy of appearance-based gaze estimation by extracting higher resolution features from the eye images using deep neural networks. Given the fact that eye images with different gaze angles may differ only by a few pixels (see Fig. 1), we argue that extracting features at high resolution could improve accuracy by capturing small appearance changes. To extract high-level features at high spatial resolution, we applied dilated-convolutions (alternatively, atrous-convolutions), which efficiently increase the receptive field sizes of the convolutional filters without reducing the spatial resolution. The main contributions of this article are that we propose Dilated-Net and quantitatively evaluate the use of high resolution features on the Columbia Gaze [25] and MPIIGaze datasets [34] through Dilated-Net. In cross-subject experiments, the proposed Dilated-Net outperform CNNs with similar architecture significantly from 3.2% to 20.8% depending on the task. It achieves state-of-the-art results on both datasets. The results demonstrate that the use of high resolution features benefit gaze estimation.

2 Related Work

2.1 Appearance-Based Gaze Estimation

Methods for appearance-based gaze estimation learn a mapping function from images to gaze estimate, where the estimation target is normally defined as either a gaze target in a give plane (2D estimation) or a gaze direction vector in camera coordinates (3D estimation). Appearance-based methods are attracting more and more attention as they use inputs from off-the-shelf cameras, which are widely available. Given enough training data, they may be able to achieve unconstrained gaze estimation.

Several methods in computer vision have been applied to this problem, e.g., Random Forests [27], k-Nearest Neighbors [22,27], Support Vector Regression [22] and, recently, deep CNNs. Zhang et al. proposed the first deep CNN to estimate 3D gaze angles [34,36]. Their network takes the left eye image and

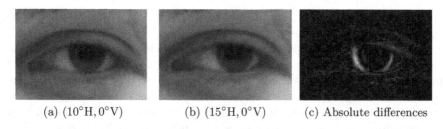

(a) $(10°H, 0°V)$ (b) $(15°H, 0°V)$ (c) Absolute differences

Fig. 1. Images of two left eyes and their difference from the Columbia Gaze dataset [25]. (a) Left eye image with $10°$ horizontal and $0°$ vertical gaze angle. (b) Left eye image with $15°$ horizontal and $0°$ vertical gaze angle. (c) The absolute difference between (a) and (b) (scaled for better illustration).

the estimated head pose angles as input. They showed that the use of deep CNNs trained on a large amount of data improved accuracy significantly. To employ information outside the eye region, Krafka *et al.* proposed a multi-region CNN that takes an image of the face, images of both eyes and a face grid as input to estimate the gaze target on phone and tablet screens [15]. Zhang *et al.* proposed a network that takes the full face image as input and uses a spatial weights method to emphasize features extracted from particular regions [35]. This work has shown that regions of the face other than the eyes also contain information about gaze angles. To further improve the accuracy, other work has concentrated on estimating the head-eye relationships. Ranjan *et al.* applied a branching architecture, where parameters are switched by clustering head pose angles into different groups [21]. Deng and Zhu trained two networks to estimate the head pose angles in camera coordinates and gaze angles in head coordinates separately. The final gaze angles in camera coordinate were obtained by combing the estimates geometrically [6].

Instead of estimating the continuous gaze directions, some work considered gaze tracking as a classification problem by dividing the gaze directions into certain blocks. For example, George and Routray applied a CNN to classify eye images into 3 or 7 target regions [9]. The binary classification problem, referred as gaze locking or eye contact detection, detects whether the user is looking at the camera. A Support Vector Machine (SVM) [25], Random Forests [31] and a CNN with multi-region input [18] have been applied to this problem.

While the recent trend has been to investigate how information from regions other than the eyes can benefit gaze estimation [6,21,35], here we focus on how better features extracted from the eye images can be used to benefit multi-region networks.

2.2   Dilated-Convolutions

Dilated-convolutions were first introduced in the field of computer vision to extract dense features for dense label prediction, i.e., semantic segmentation [3,32]. Given a convolutional kernel of size $N \times M \times K$ (*height $\times$ width $\times$ channel*), the key idea of dilated-convolutions is to insert spaces (zeros) between the weights so that the kernel covers a region larger than $N \times M$. Therefore, dilated-convolutions increase the size of receptive field without reducing the spatial resolution nor increasing the number of parameters. Comprehensive studies of dilated-convolution in semantic segmentation were reported in [4, 29], where the results show that dilated-convolutions improve performance significantly. Recently, Yu *et al.* proposed dilated residual networks [33] and showed that they outperform their non-dilated counterparts in image classification and object localization on the ImageNet dataset [7].

3   Methodology

3.1   Issue of Spatial Resolution

When a person looks at two different locations with his/her head fixed, the appearance of the eyes changes. However, these differences can be subtle, as shown in Fig. 1. A 5° horizontal difference only results in differences at a few pixels. Other small changes, e.g., in the openness and the shape of the eyes, also contain information about gaze direction. Intuitively, extracting high-level features at high resolution will better capture these subtle differences.

Most current CNN architectures use multiple downsampling layers, e.g., convolutional layer with large stride and pooling layers. In this article, we use max-pooling layers as an example for discussion because they are commonly used both in general and in gaze estimation [6, 15, 21, 35, 36]. Similar considerations apply for convolutional layers with large stride. The use of max-pooling layers progressively reduces the spatial resolution of feature maps. This enables the networks to tolerate small variations in position, increases the effective size of receptive field (RF) at higher layers and reduces the number of parameters in the networks. However, the drawback is that spatial information is lost during pooling. For example, 75% of activations will be discarded if a 2×2 pooling window with a stride of 2 is used. To better illustrate, Fig. 2a shows the RFs resulting from first applying 3×3 convolution, followed by 2×2 max-pooling with stride of 2, followed by 3×3 convolution. Inserting a pooling layer increases the size of RF. A 3×3 kernel on the higher-level feature map has an 8×8 RF on the lower-level feature map. However, the lower level locations that pass on information to the higher levels varies with the input. Successively applying max-pooling layers results in a loss of important spatial information, which we expect will degrade the performance of gaze estimation.

3.2   Dilated-Convolutions

Dilated-convolutional layers preserve spatial resolution while increasing the size of RF without a large increase in the number of parameters. Given an input feature map (U), a kernel of size $N \times M \times K$ (with weights W and bias b)

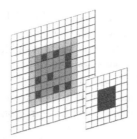

(a) 3×3 convolution $+ 2 \times 2$ max-pooling $+ 3 \times 3$ convolution

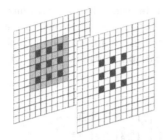

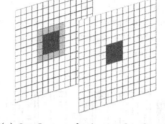

(b) 3×3 dilated-convolution $(1, 1)$ $+ 3 \times 3$ dilated-convolution $(2, 2)$

(c) 3×3 convolution $+ 3 \times 3$ convolution

Fig. 2. Receptive fields for three different combinations of layers. The grid on the left represents the lower-level feature map. The grid on the right represents the output of the max-pooling (a) or the convolution (b, c). Locations in dark blue show locations weighted by the convolution operating on the right grid, and the corresponding locations in the left grid. Light blue shows the effective size of the RF in the lower layer due to the first convolution. The strides for convolutions and dilated-convolutions are 1 and the stride for max-pooling are 2. (Color figure online)

and dilation rates (r_1, r_2), the output feature map (V) of a dilated-convolutional operation can be calculated by

$$v(x, y) = \sum_{k=1}^{K} \sum_{m=0}^{M-1} \sum_{n=0}^{N-1} u(x + nr_1, y + mr_2, k)w_{nmk} + b, \qquad (1)$$

where $(x, y[, k])$ represents the position in the corresponding feature map. Equation (1) shows that the dilation rates (r_1, r_2) determine the amount by which the size of RF increases. Dilation rates which are larger than one allow the network to enlarge the RF without decreasing the spatial resolution (compared to the use of pooling layers) or increasing the number of parameters.

Figure 2b shows the RF resulting from a 3×3 dilated-convolutional layer with dilation rates $(1, 1)$ followed by a 3×3 dilated-convolutional layer with dilation rates $(2, 2)$. Because of the $(2, 2)$ dilation rates, a 3×3 kernel applied to the higher-level feature map corresponds to a 7×7 RF on the lower-level feature map. Spatial resolution is preserved. The lower level locations feeding into the higher level units are also constant, independent of the input.

Figure 2c shows the result of successively applying two 3×3 convolutional layers while maintaining spatial resolution. The corresponding RF on the lower level map is only 5×5. Stacking convolutional layers only increase the size of RF linearly, which makes it hard to cover large regions at higher layers.

3.3   Dilated-Nets

Multi-region Dilated-Net. Our proposed architecture, which we refer to in our results as **Dilated-Net (multi)**, is shown in Fig. 3. It takes an image of the face and images of both eyes as input and feeds them to a face network and two eye networks, respectively. The general architecture is inspired by iTracker [15]. However, here the eye networks adopt dilated-convolutional layers to extract high resolution features.

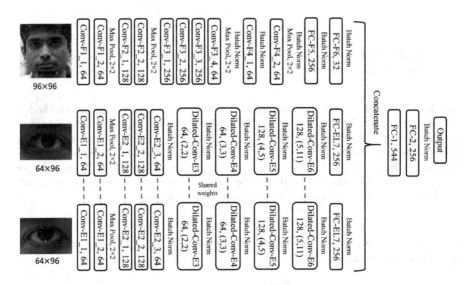

Fig. 3. Architecture of the multi-region Dilated-Net. The numbers after convolutional layers (Conv) represent the number of filters. The numbers after dilated-convolutional layers (Dilated-Conv) represent the number of filters and dilation rates. 3×3 filter size is used except that Conv-F3_4 and Conv-E2_3 use 1×1. FC represents fully connected layer.

The face network is a VGG-like network [24] which consists of four blocks of stacked convolutional layers (Conv) followed by max-pooling layer, as well as two fully connected layers (FC). The weights of the first seven convolutional layers are transferred from the first seven layers of VGG-16 pre-trained on the ImageNet dataset. We insert a 1×1 convolutional network (Network in Network [16]) after the last transferred layer to reduce the number of channels.

The two eye networks have identical architecture and share the same parameters in all convolutional and dilated-convolutional layers. The network starts with four convolutional layers with a max-pooling layer in the middle, followed by a 1×1 convolutional layer, four dilated-convolutional layers (dilated-Conv) and one fully connected layer. The dilation rates of the layers are $(2, 2)$, $(3, 3)$, $(4, 5)$ and $(5, 11)$, respectively. These dilation rate are designed according to the hybrid dilated convolution (HDC) in [29] so that the RF of each layer covers a square region without any holes in it. The weights of first four convolutional layers are transferred from the first four layers of VGG-16 pre-trained on the ImageNet dataset.

We concatenate the output of FC-F6, FC-EL7 and FC-ER7 to combine features from different input. This is fed to FC-2 and then an output layer.

We use the Rectified Linear Unit (ReLU) as activation function for all convolutional and fully connected layers. Zero padding is applied to convolutional layers to preserve dimension. No padding is applied to dilated-convolutional layers to reduce the output dimension and computation. We apply the batch renormalization layers (Batch Norm) [13] to all layers trained from scratch. Dropout layers are applied to all fully connected layers.

Single-Eye Dilated-Net. To compare with the networks which only use the left eye image and estimated head pose as input, e.g., [21, 36], we shrunk the Dilated-Net (multi) in Fig. 3 down to only one eye network and concatenated the estimated head pose angles with FC-EL7. In our results, we refer to it as **Dilated-Net (single)**.

CNN Without Dilated-Convolutions. To show the improvement achieved by dilated convolutions, we use a deep CNN that has similar architecture but no dilated-convolutions. It replaces the four dilated-convolutional layers by four convolutional layers and three max pooling layers located at the beginning, in the middle and at the end of the four convolutional layers, respectively. The size of final feature maps is the same as the one in Dilated-Nets, and this CNN has the same number of parameters as the corresponding Dilated-Net.

One key difference between the CNN and the Dilated-Net is shown in Fig. 4, where we show the sizes and centers of RFs of the third max-pooling layer in the CNN and of the Dilated-Conv-E4 layer in Dilated-Net. In the CNN, the progressively use of max-pooling results in larger distance (8 px) between two centers of RFs. For Dilated-Net, the distance between two centers is preserved (2 px).

3.4 Preprocessing

We apply a two-step preprocessing method. In the first step, We apply the same image normalization method used in [21, 35, 36]. This method virtually rotates

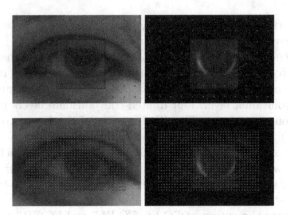

Fig. 4. Size (blue square) and centers (white dots) of the receptive fields. Top row: the third max-pooling layer in our CNN (36 × 36 with distance 8). Bottom row: the Dilated-Conv-E4 layer in our Dilated-Net (34×34 with distance 2). (Color figure online)

and translates the camera so that the virtual camera faces the reference point at a fixed distance and cancels out the roll angle of the head. The reference point is set to be the center of the left eye for Dilated-Net (single) and the center of the face for Dilated-Net (multi). The images are normalized by perspective warping, converted to gray scale and histogram-equalized. The estimated head pose angles and the ground truth gaze angles are also normalized.

In the second step, we obtain the eyes images and face image from the warped images based on facial landmarks. For automatically detected landmarks we use dlib [14]. Then, for each eye image, we use the eye center as the image center and warp the image by an affine transformation so that the eye corners are at fixed positions. For the face image, we fix the position of the center of two eyes and scale the image so that the horizontal distance between the two eye centers is a constant.

4   Experiments

4.1   Cross-Subject Evaluation

We performed cross-subject experiments on the Columbia Gaze dataset [25] for eye contact detection and the MPIIGaze dataset [34] for 3D gaze regression.

Columbia Gaze Dataset. This dataset was collected for a task to classify whether the subject is looking at the camera (gaze locking). It comprises 5880 full face images of 56 people (24 female, 21 with glasses) taken in a controlled environment. For each person, images were collected for each combination of five horizontal head poses $(0°, \pm 15°, \pm 30°)$, seven horizontal gaze directions $(0°, \pm 5°, \pm 10°, \pm 15°)$ and three vertical gaze directions $(0°, \pm 10°)$. Among the

Table 1. Results on the Columbia Gaze dataset.

Name	Method	Input	Training set	PR-AUC	Best F1-score
GL [25]	PCA+MDA+SVM	Two eyes	Columbia	0.08	0.15
	PCA+SVM	Two eyes	Columbia	0.16	0.25
OpenFace [1]	Model-based	Two eyes	SynthesEyes [30]	0.05	0.10
CNN (single) (ours)	CNN	Left eye + estimated head pose	Columbia	0.40	0.44
Dilated-Net (single) (ours)	Dilated-CNN	Left eye + estimated head pose	Columbia	0.42	0.48
CNN (multi) (ours)	CNN	Two eyes + Face	Columbia	0.48	0.52
Dilated-Net (multi) (ours)	Dilated-CNN	Two eyes + Face	Columbia	**0.58**	**0.62**

105 images of each person, five are gaze locking (0° horizontal and 0° vertical gaze direction).

For cross-subject evaluation, we divided 56 subjects into 11 groups, where ten groups contained five subjects and one group contained six. The numbers of male/female subjects with/without glasses were balanced among different groups. We conducted leave-one-group-out cross-validation. In each fold, if a validation set was needed, we randomly select one group from the training set. Since the ratio between negative and positive samples is unbalanced (20 : 1), we upsampled the positive examples to balance positive and negative examples by randomly disturbing the facial landmarks.

We used a sigmoid function as output. During training, we used cross-entropy as loss function and stochastic gradient descent with momentum (0.9) to train the network (mini-batch size 64). We used an initial learning rate of 0.01 and multiplied it by 0.5 after every 3000 iterations.

We re-implemented the gaze locking method (GL) [25] as baseline, which reduces the intensity features by Principal Component Analysis (PCA) and Multiple Discriminant Analysis (MDA), and uses an SVM [2] as the final classifier. We applied OpenFace 2.0 [1] to estimate 3D gaze vectors and calculated the cosine of the angular error from the ground truth.

We present the average testing results over 11-folds by the precision-recall (PR) curve in Fig. 5. We also report the value of area under curve (PR-AUC) and the best F1-score in Table 1. OpenFace performs the worst, mostly because it is a model-based method and trained on another dataset. All deep networks performed better than the two SVM methods, indicating that deep networks have better capacity for appearance-based gaze estimation.

Among the four deep networks, Dilated-Net (multi) performed the best and CNN (single) performed the worst. The degradation of single-eye networks from

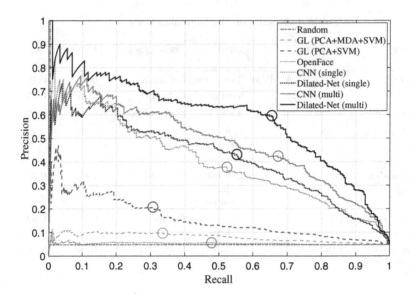

Fig. 5. Precision-recall curve of different models on the Columbia Gaze dataset. The circle on each curve indicates the location where the best F1-score is obtained.

multi-region networks is because the CNN captures better and more information from the face, which is consistent to [35]. When comparing our Dilated-Net (multi) with the second best model, i.e., CNN (multi), Dilated-Net (multi) outperformed by 0.10 (20.8%) in terms of PR-AUC and by 0.10 (19.2%) in terms of best F1-score. Figure 5 shows that Dilated-Net (multi) achieves higher precision for nearly all values of recall, indicating that it generally achieves a better trade-off between precision and recall.

MPIIGaze Dataset. The MPIIGaze dataset [34] was collected for a task to estimate the continuous gaze direction angles. It contains $213,659$ images of 15 subjects (six female, five with glasses). It provides an "Evaluation Subset", which contains $3,000$ randomly selected samples for each subject with automatically detected (manually annotated) facial landmarks. As in [21,35,36], we trained and tested our Dilated-Net on this "Evaluation Subset", which we refer to as MPIIGaze (MPIIGaze+).

We conducted leave-one-subject-out cross-validation. During each fold, we randomly chose the data from three subjects in training set for validation. We trained all our networks with the same validation set in each fold. We used a linear layer to output estimated yaw and pitch gaze angles. The Euclidean distance between the estimated gaze angles and the ground truth angles in normalized space was used as the loss function. We trained all the networks using the Adam optimizer with a mini-batch size 64. An initial learning rate of 0.001 was used. The learning rate was multiplied by 0.1 after every 8000 iterations.

Table 2. Mean angular errors in normalized space using eye center as origin.

Name	Architecture	Input	Pre-train	MPIIGaze	MPIIGaze+
GazeNet [36]	VGG-16	Left eye + estimated head pose	ImageNet	5.5°	5.4°
Branched CNN [21]	AlexNet	Left eye + estimated head pose	ImageNet	5.88°	5.88°
			RFC [26]	5.56°	5.38°
			RFC + 1M Synth	5.38°	5.3°
	AlexNet + branch	Left eye + estimated head pose	ImageNet	5.77°	5.63°
			RFC	5.49°	5.46°
			RFC + 1M Synth	5.48°	5.42°
CNN (single) (Ours)	VGG-16	Left eye + estimated head pose	ImageNet	5.45°	5.35°
Dilated-Net(single) (Ours)	Dilated-CNN	Left eye + estimated head pose	ImageNet	**5.21°**	**5.12°**

Table 3. Mean angular errors in original space using face center as origin.

Name	Architecture	Input	Pre-train	MPIIGaze+
GazeNet [34]	AlexNet	Left eye + estimated head pose	ImageNet	6.7°
iTracker [15,35]	AlexNet	Two eyes + face	ImageNet	5.6°
Spatial weights CNN [35]	AlexNet	Face	ImageNet	5.5°
	AlexNet + spatial weights	Face	ImageNet	**4.8°**
CNN (multi) (Ours)	VGG-16	Two eyes + face	ImageNet	5.4°
Dilated-Net (multi) (Ours)	Dilated-CNN	Two eyes + face	ImageNet	**4.8°**

For the networks that use a single eye image and estimated head pose as input, we compared with the GazeNet [36] and the state-of-the-art branched CNN [21]. For the networks that use images of the full face, we compared with a re-implementation of iTracker [15] reported in [35] and the state-of-the-art spatial weights CNN [35]. Note that [21,36] reported the angular errors in the normalized space and [35] reported the results in the original space (the camera coordinates).

We present the mean angular errors across 15 subjects in Tables 2 and 3. In Table 2, our Dilated-Net (single) achieved the best performance. It achieved 5.21° on MPIIGaze and 5.12° on MPIIGaze+. It outperformed the second best method, the branched CNN without head-pose-depending-branching, by 0.17° (3.2%) on MPIIGaze and by 0.18° (3.4%) on MPIIGaze+, even though the branched CNN were pre-trained on more related RFC and 1M synthetic images. The gain was higher if we only considered the networks that were pre-trained on ImageNet. In this case, it outperformed the second best network, CNN (single), by 0.24° (4.4%) on MPIIGaze and by 0.23° (4.3%) on MPIIGaze+.

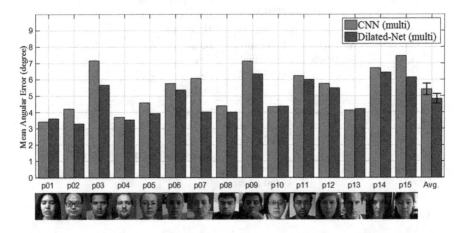

Fig. 6. Mean angular error of different subjects on the MPIIGaze dataset in original space. Error bars indicate standard errors computed across subjects.

Similar results can be observed in Table 3. When compared to the networks that use similar input (face + two eyes), our proposed Dilated-Net (multi) outperformed iTracker (AlexNet) by 0.8° (14.3%) and CNN (multi) by 0.6° (11.1%). In Fig. 6, we further compare the average error for each subject. Dilated-Net (multi) outperformed CNN (multi) for 12 out of the 15 subjects. Dilated-convolutions improves accuracy for most subjects, despite variations in individual appearance.

Finally, we would like to note that our Dilated-Net (multi) achieved the same results as the state-of-the-art spatial weights CNN. Compared to the spatial weights CNN, our Dilated-Net has several advantages including smaller input size (96 × 224 v.s. 448 × 448), lower (64%) input resolution, and much smaller number of parameters (~ 5 M v.s. ~ 196 M). This suggests that the Dilated-Net might achieve better performance for low resolution images.

4.2   Comparing Dilated-CNN with CNN

To better understand the differences between Dilated-Net (multi) and CNN (multi), we studied the features learned by the final convolutional layers and evaluated their importance. Both networks have 4 × 6 × 128 final feature maps. The sizes of the RFs are also similar (76 × 76 for the CNN and 70 × 98 for the

Dilated-Net), but they are centered at different locations. The center locations of the CNN units spread over the entire eye image (white dots in Fig. 7a), but the center locations of the Dilated-Net are concentrated at the center (red dots).

We performed an ablation study to determine the contribution of features from different spatial locations, where we only retrained the parameters of the fully connected layers. We left the face network unchanged and evaluated on MPIIGaze+. The average angular errors are presented in Fig. 7b for three cases: (1) using all 4×6 spatial locations, (2) eliminating the boundary locations and using only the 2×4 array in the center, and (3) using only the 2×2 array in the center. For the CNN, eliminating the boundary features actually improves performance. This may be due to the removal of person-specific features, enabling better generalization. For the Dilated-Net, we see a degradation in performance as features from different locations are removed. This indicates that despite the significant overlap of the RFs due to the close center spacing, the features at different locations are not redundant. Note that Dilated-Net only using features in 2×2 center region still outperforms the best performing CNN.

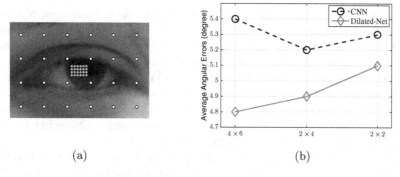

(a)   (b)

Fig. 7. (a) The corresponding center locations of the learned features of the final (dilated-)convolutional layers of the CNN (white) and the Dilated-Net (red); (b) The average angular errors as a function of the remaining features. (Color figure online)

We applied t-Distributed Stochastic Neighbor Embedding (t-SNE) [17] to reduce the feature dimension at each location from 128 to 1, and used Pearson's r to evaluate the linear correlation between these 1D features and the horizontal gaze angles with fixed head poses and vertical gaze angles. The CNN features were less correlated with gaze. Even restricting attention to the central 2×4 array, correlation coefficients ranged from 0.59–0.82, whereas for the Dilated-Net, they ranged from 0.74–0.86 for all 24 locations.

4.3   The Effect of Landmarks Precision

To evaluate the influence of facial landmark detection, we randomly disturbed the landmarks by 7%–10% of a 64×96 eye image in each direction. In cross-subject evaluation of MPIIGaze+, performance of the Dilated-Net (multi) degrades by $0.4°$ to $5.2°$ from $4.8°$. CNN (multi) degrades by $0.2°$ to $5.6°$ from $5.4°$. While the Dilated-Net is more sensitive to landmark detection, it is still robust and maintains the performance gains over the CNN.

4.4   The Use of ResNet

To study whether a similar improvement can be obtained using a more advanced architecture, we trained a modified ResNet-50 [10] and a Dilated-ResNet on the MPIIGaze+ and tested them on the Columbia Gaze dataset. We changed the stride of the first layer to one and modified the last two residual blocks to dilated-residual blocks. The average angular errors are $6.1°$ (Dilated-ResNet), $6.3°$ (Dilated-VGG), $6.5°$ (ResNet) and $7.2°$ (VGG). While we can achieve improvement by replacing VGG with the more advanced ResNet, greater improvement is achieved by using dilated-convolutions on VGG. In addition, our results indicate that introducing dilated-convolutions to ResNet further improves performance.

5   Conclusion

We applied dilated-convolutions in deep neural networks to improve appearance-based gaze estimation. The use of dilated-convolutions allows the networks to extract high level features at high resolution from eye images so that the networks can capture small variability. We conducted cross-subject experiments on the Columbia Gaze and the MPIIGaze datasets. Our results indicated significant gains from the use of dilated-convolutions when compared to CNNs with similar architectures but without dilated-convolutions. These high resolution features improve the accuracy of gaze estimation. Our proposed multi-region Dilated-Net achieved state-of-the-art results on both datasets.

Moving forward, we plan to apply our gaze estimation in real-world settings for human-machine interaction and human-robot interaction. As gaze trajectory is an excellent cue about user intent, the results of gaze tracking or eye contact detection can be used to estimate the user intent. This estimated intent enables the systems to react more naturally and to provide appropriate assistance.

References

1. Baltrusaitis, T., Zadeh, A., Lim, Y.C., Morency, L.P.: OpenFace 2.0: facial behavior analysis toolkit. In: IEEE International Conference and Workshops on Automatic Face and Gesture Recognition, pp. 59–66. IEEE (2018)
2. Chang, C.C., Lin, C.J.: LIBSVM: a library for support vector machines. ACM Trans. Intell. Syst. Technol. **2**(3), 27 (2011)
3. Chen, L.C., Papandreou, G., Kokkinos, I., Murphy, K., Yuille, A.L.: Semantic image segmentation with deep convolutional nets and fully connected CRFs. arXiv preprint arXiv:1412.7062 (2014)
4. Chen, L.C., Papandreou, G., Kokkinos, I., Murphy, K., Yuille, A.L.: Deeplab: semantic image segmentation with deep convolutional nets, atrous convolution, and fully connected CRFs. IEEE Trans. Pattern Anal. Mach. Intell. **40**(4), 834–848 (2018)

5. Chen, Z., Shi, B.E.: Using variable dwell time to accelerate gaze-based web browsing with two-step selection. Int. J. Hum.-Comput. Interact. **35**, 240–255 (2018)
6. Deng, H., Zhu, W.: Monocular free-head 3D gaze tracking with deep learning and geometry constraints. In: IEEE International Conference on Computer Vision, pp. 3162–3171. IEEE (2017)
7. Deng, J., Dong, W., Socher, R., Li, L.J., Li, K., Fei-Fei, L.: Imagenet: a large-scale hierarchical image database. In: IEEE Conference on Computer Vision and Pattern Recognition, pp. 248–255. IEEE (2009)
8. Funes Mora, K.A., Monay, F., Odobez, J.M.: EYEDIAP: a database for the development and evaluation of gaze estimation algorithms from RGB and RGB-D cameras. In: ACM Symposium on Eye Tracking Research & Applications, pp. 255–258. ACM (2014)
9. George, A., Routray, A.: Real-time eye gaze direction classification using convolutional neural network. In: International Conference on Signal Processing and Communications, pp. 1–5. IEEE (2016)
10. He, K., Zhang, X., Ren, S., Sun, J.: Deep residual learning for image recognition. arXiv preprint arXiv:1512.03385 (2015)
11. Hoppe, S., Loetscher, T., Morey, S.A., Bulling, A.: Eye movements during everyday behavior predict personality traits. Front. Hum. Neurosci. **12**, 105 (2018)
12. Huang, C.M., Mutlu, B.: Anticipatory robot control for efficient human-robot collaboration. In: ACM/IEEE International Conference on Human Robot Interaction, pp. 83–90. IEEE (2016)
13. Ioffe, S.: Batch renormalization: towards reducing minibatch dependence in batch-normalized models. In: Advances in Neural Information Processing Systems, pp. 1942–1950. MIT Press (2017)
14. King, D.E.: Dlib-ml: a machine learning toolkit. J. Mach. Learn. Res. **10**(Jul), 1755–1758 (2009)
15. Krafka, K., et al.: Eye tracking for everyone. In: IEEE Conference on Computer Vision and Pattern Recognition, pp. 2176–2184. IEEE (2016)
16. Lin, M., Chen, Q., Yan, S.: Network in network. arXiv preprint arXiv:1312.4400 (2013)
17. van der Maaten, L., Hinton, G.: Visualizing data using t-SNE. J. Mach. Learn. Res. **9**(Nov), 2579–2605 (2008)
18. Parekh, V., Subramanian, R., Jawahar, C.V.: Eye contact detection via deep neural networks. In: Stephanidis, C. (ed.) HCI 2017. CCIS, vol. 713, pp. 366–374. Springer, Cham (2017). https://doi.org/10.1007/978-3-319-58750-9_51
19. Patney, A., et al.: Towards foveated rendering for gaze-tracked virtual reality. ACM Trans. Graph. **35**(6), 179 (2016)
20. Pi, J., Shi, B.E.: Probabilistic adjustment of dwell time for eye typing. In: International Conference on Human System Interactions, pp. 251–257. IEEE (2017)
21. Ranjan, R., De Mello, S., Kautz, J.: Light-weight head pose invariant gaze tracking. In: IEEE Conference on Computer Vision and Pattern Recognition Workshops, pp. 2156–2164. IEEE (2018)
22. Schneider, T., Schauerte, B., Stiefelhagen, R.: Manifold alignment for person independent appearance-based gaze estimation. In: International Conference on Pattern Recognition, pp. 1167–1172. IEEE (2014)
23. Shrivastava, A., Pfister, T., Tuzel, O., Susskind, J., Wang, W., Webb, R.: Learning from simulated and unsupervised images through adversarial training. In: IEEE International Conference on Computer Vision, pp. 2242–2251. IEEE (2017)
24. Simonyan, K., Zisserman, A.: Very deep convolutional networks for large-scale image recognition. arXiv preprint arXiv:1409.1556 (2014)

25. Smith, B.A., Yin, Q., Feiner, S.K., Nayar, S.K.: Gaze locking: passive eye contact detection for human-object interaction. In: ACM Symposium on User Interface Software and Technology, pp. 271–280. ACM (2013)
26. Su, H., Qi, C.R., Li, Y., Guibas, L.J.: Render for CNN: viewpoint estimation in images using CNNs trained with rendered 3D model views. In: IEEE International Conference on Computer Vision, pp. 2686–2694 (2015)
27. Sugano, Y., Matsushita, Y., Sato, Y.: Learning-by-synthesis for appearance-based 3D gaze estimation. In: IEEE Conference on Computer Vision and Pattern Recognition, pp. 1821–1828. IEEE (2014)
28. Wang, H., Pi, J., Qin, T., Shen, S., Shi, B.E.: SLAM-based localization of 3D gaze using a mobile eye tracker. In: ACM Symposium on Eye Tracking Research & Applications, p. 65. ACM (2018)
29. Wang, P., et al.: Understanding convolution for semantic segmentation. arXiv preprint arXiv:1702.08502 (2017)
30. Wood, E., Baltrusaitis, T., Zhang, X., Sugano, Y., Robinson, P., Bulling, A.: Rendering of eyes for eye-shape registration and gaze estimation. In: IEEE International Conference on Computer Vision, pp. 3756–3764. IEEE (2015)
31. Ye, Z., Li, Y., Liu, Y., Bridges, C., Rozga, A., Rehg, J.M.: Detecting bids for eye contact using a wearable camera. In: IEEE International Conference and Workshops on Automatic Face and Gesture Recognition, pp. 1–8. IEEE (2015)
32. Yu, F., Koltun, V.: Multi-scale context aggregation by dilated convolutions. arXiv preprint arXiv:1511.07122 (2015)
33. Yu, F., Koltun, V., Funkhouser, T.: Dilated residual networks. In: IEEE International Conference on Computer Vision, pp. 636–644. IEEE (2017)
34. Zhang, X., Sugano, Y., Fritz, M., Bulling, A.: Appearance-based gaze estimation in the wild. In: IEEE Conference on Computer Vision and Pattern Recognition, pp. 4511–4520. IEEE (2015)
35. Zhang, X., Sugano, Y., Fritz, M., Bulling, A.: It's written all over your face: full-face appearance-based gaze estimation. In: IEEE Conference on Computer Vision and Pattern Recognition Workshops, pp. 2299–2308. IEEE (2017)
36. Zhang, X., Sugano, Y., Fritz, M., Bulling, A.: MPIIGaze: real-world dataset and deep appearance-based gaze estimation. IEEE Trans. Pattern Anal. Mach. Intell. **41**, 162–175 (2017)

Deep Clustering and Block Hashing Network for Face Image Retrieval

Young Kyun Jang, Dong-ju Jeong, Seok Hee Lee, and Nam Ik Cho[✉]

Department of Electrical and Computer Engineering INMC,
Seoul National University, Seoul, Korea
{kyun0914,jeongdj,seokheel}@ispl.snu.ac.kr, nicho@snu.ac.kr

Abstract. This paper presents a new hashing method to learn the compact binary codes for implementing a large-scale face image retrieval system. Since it is very difficult to deal with the inter-class similarities (similar appearance between different persons) and intra-class variations (same person with different pose, facial expressions, illuminations) in face-related problems, we propose a new deep clustering and block hashing (DCBH) approach to alleviate these issues. The network we adopt for the feature extraction is the VGG, where we design a new loss function to learn the robust and mulit-scale facial features for addressing the above-stated problems. Specifically, we design a center-clustering loss term to minimize the distance between the image descriptors belonging to the same class. Besides, the classification errors of the image descriptors and the learned binary codes are minimized to learn the discriminative binary codes. In addition, we introduce a block hashing layer for reducing the redundancy among hash codes and the number of parameters simultaneously without loss of similarity. Extensive experiments on two large scale face image datasets demonstrate that our proposed method outperforms the state-of-the-art face image retrieval methods.

Keywords: Center-clustering loss · Block hashing layer

1 Introduction

In recent years, a tremendous amount of images that contain faces are being uploaded to the Internet everyday. For many applications and services that use the faces, the required fundamental technologies are the face detection, facial feature extraction, analysis, etc. An interesting application based on these techniques is the face image retrieval, which finds similar faces on the Internet or database to the query face [20].

The most important factors for an efficient image retrieval system are the searching time, storage cost, and the results robust to various changes of the objects in a search. To be specific with the face image retrieval, there are some inter-class similarities (different persons with similar appearance) and intra-class variations (the same person with different makeup, outfit, pose, facial expressions, illuminations, etc.) as shown in Fig. 1, which make it more difficult to find

© Springer Nature Switzerland AG 2019
C. V. Jawahar et al. (Eds.): ACCV 2018, LNCS 11366, pp. 325–339, 2019.
https://doi.org/10.1007/978-3-030-20876-9_21

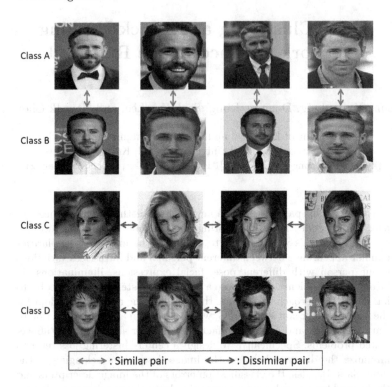

Class A

Class B

Class C

Class D

⟷ : Similar pair   ⟷ : Dissimilar pair

Fig. 1. Example of inter-class similarities and intra-class variations of face images

similar faces to the query. Hence, it is important to develop small but effective facial features and their descriptor that can well reflect the inter-class differences, which is also robust to intra-class variations.

As convolutional neural networks (CNNs) demonstrate superior performance to the conventional methods in visual recognition [12], they have been widely used in many computer vision tasks including face recognition [17,18,23] and image retrieval [8,15,25]. Recently, deeper network architectures, such as VGG [19] and Residual Networks (ResNets) [6], have proven that more enriched features can be extracted as the number of channels grows larger. Based on this, several researchers have proposed to aggregate the deep features to represent a whole image with global features from the CNNs [1,5,10]. Although the CNN-based features can be considered the generalized features for image retrieval, they are not practical for large database systems due to their huge dimension.

As a progressive solution to this high-dimension problem, the hashing approaches are proposed to map an image to a compact binary code rather than a real-valued vector [9,22]. Using the binary descriptor has some advantages that we need less memory when building the database and also that we need a simple logical operation when measuring the difference between the images. Also, some recent researches [3,8,15,25,26] have shown that feature representation and hash coding can be jointly learned by using deep neural networks. For some specific examples of this approach, the CNN-based hashing (CNNH) [25] consists of two stages: the first learns the approximate binary codes by preserving the pairwise similarity and the second learns the hash function. The Deep Supervised Hashing (DSH) proposed in [15] learns the binary hash codes by exploring the supervised information in terms of pairs (similar/dissimilar) of training images. The Supervised, Structured Binary Code (SUBIC) in [8] uses block-*Softmax* non-linearity and batch-based entropy losses to make each block contain a single active bit.

For the importance of face-related applications, there are also several deep-learning based hashing methods that focus on the retrieval of face images rather than the general ones [2, 14, 20, 21]. To be specific, the Deep Hashing based on Classification and Quantization errors (DHCQ) [20] jointly learns the feature representation and binary hashing codes by optimizing an objective function which is defined over the classification and quantization errors. The Discriminative Deep Hashing (DDH) in [14], which is similar to [13], incorporates the divide-and-encode module to generate compact hash codes. The Discriminative Deep Quantization Hashing (DDQH) [21] introduces a batch normalization quantization (BNQ) module to improve the retrieval accuracy. In [2], they introduced a compact deeply transferred description (CDTD) method which not only reduces the dimension but also exploits the distinctive capability of semantic facial attributes.

In this paper, we propose a new face image retrieval method which is devised to alleviate the above-stated intra-class variation and inter-class similarity problems, while compactly encoding the high-dimensional deep features into the hash codes. For this, we propose a deep network structure based on the VGG and a new block hashing layer, and also design a new loss function for training the network. To alleviate the intra-class variation problem, we introduce a center-clustering loss term that minimizes the distance between the input image descriptor and the cluster-center of the descriptors that belong to the same class as the input. This makes the final binary code of a face closer to the center of its class so that both of intra-class variation and inter-class similarity problems are alleviated. Also, to further differentiate the different labels, i.e., to alleviate the inter-class similarity problem further, we add a cost function that measures both the hash codes' and image descriptors' differences. Extensive experiments on two widely-used face image datasets [14, 20, 21] show that the proposed method brings improvements compared to the current state-of-the-art hash-based face image retrieval methods.

2   Related Work

2.1   Binary Hashing via Deep Learning Network

Deep learning has been used to learn the efficient and effective image hashing schemes for the large-database image retrieval system. For some examples, CNNH [25] decomposes the hash learning process in two stages: to learn the hash codes and the hash functions. It learns approximate hash codes by preserving the supervised pairwise similarity, followed by a stage of fine-tuning the image features and hash functions simultaneously. In [13], this scheme is further improved by exploiting a divide-and-encode module, which divides the intermediate image features into multiple branches and introduces a triplet ranking loss function to preserve the relative similarities. The DSH proposed in [15] learns hash codes from the input pairs for preserving the similarity. The SUBIC in [8] learns the block-structured features in a supervised manner by means of a block-wise *Softmax* non-linearity along with two entropy-based penalties. Inspired by [8,13], we propose a block hashing layer that slices the image descriptor into fixed-size blocks containing the high-dimensional facial expression. As the *Softmax* function squashes an M-dimensional vector into a real value in the range of $(0,1)$, we employ *Softmax* function for each block to obtain the desirable length of vector.

2.2   Face Feature Representation via Deep Learning Network

Like most of computer vision tasks, the performances of face-related problems have been significantly improved by using the deep CNN. For example, CNN-based features are used for the face recognition in [17,18,23]. In [17], an end to end learning architecture is designed, along with the triplet-loss training scheme. In the case of FaceNet in [18], they provided a method to learn a mapping from a face to a point in the Euclidean space, by using a deep neural network with a harmonic triplet loss function. The "center loss" has been proposed in [23], which simultaneously learns a center for deep features of each class and penalizes the distances between the deep features and their corresponding class centers.

The researches on face image search have also been advanced by using the deep learning [2,14,20,21]. In the case of DHCQ algorithm [20], they proposed a deep hashing based on classification and quantization errors, by jointly learning feature representations and binary hashing codes. This method is further improved in [14], by incorporating divide-and-encode module to reduce the redundancies among hash codes and the network parameters simultaneously. Furthermore, DDQH in [21] expanded the number of channels in layers, removed divide-and-encode module and applied batch normalization quantization module (BNQ) instead for further improvement. Meanwhile, since using the CNN-based descriptors usually demand high computational power and storage space, a compact yet discriminative subset of raw deep transferred CNN descriptors (CDTD) had been proposed to add the scalability to the task of face image retrieval [2].

3   Deep Center Clustering and Block Hashing

Given a face image $\mathbf{I}$, our goal is to learn a mapping

$$f \colon \mathbf{I} \to \hat{b} \in \{-1,1\}^K \tag{1}$$

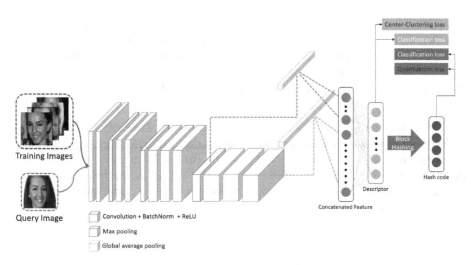

Fig. 2. The network architecture of the proposed DCBH.

that encodes an input image into K-bit binary hash code $\hat{b}$. For the effective face image retrieval, the hash codes should preserve semantic information of face images and be discriminative. For this purpose, we design a deep network shown in Fig. 2 which consists of the conventional VGG followed by a fully connected network with our contributions in loss function design. Specifically, we design (1) a center-clustering loss and classification loss for the face image descriptor to alleviate inter-class similarities and intra-class variations, (2) a block hashing layer to generate optimal hash codes from face image descriptors, and (3) a quantization loss for controlling hashing quality by imposing a regularizer.

Network Architecture. As shown in Fig. 2, the first part of our architecture is a conventional VGG network for the robust facial feature extraction [19]. The VGG part consists of ten convolutional layers with 3×3 kernels and the number of channels doubles after the max pooling layer. Each max pooling layer reduces the size of the image by half, by extracting the maximum value of the 2×2 kernel with stride 2. Like many other deep neural networks, we employ the rectified linear unit (ReLU) [12] as the activation function. Additionally, to accelerate the training of our proposed network, batch normalization layer [7] is employed between the convolutional layer and the activation function layer. Weights are initialized by Xavier initialization [4]. Different from the conventional VGG, we replace the fully connected layer with global average pooling layer from the bottom of the network to enhance the generalization and reduce the number of network parameters. Outputs of the 3rd max pooling layer and the last convolutional layer turn into one-channel vector after the global average pooling layer. To extract robust and multi-scale facial representations, both one-channel vectors are concatenated. A fully connected layer and block hashing layer are placed at the last stage as shown in the figure, where the fully connected layer obtains the length-scalable face image descriptors and the block hashing layer encodes this high-dimensional face image descriptor into a compact hash code. Then, hash codes are relaxed by tanh function to approximate the thresholding procedure. Finally, hash codes are thresholded to be $+1$ or -1 by using the $sign(\cdot)$ function to obtain binary hash code $\hat{b} \subset \mathbf{B}$.

Center-Clustering and Classification Loss from Descriptor. As shown in Fig. 1, face images have large intra-class variations. Therefore, class-specific facial features should be clustered. We handle this problem by reducing the $l2$-distance between the face image descriptors ($\mathbf{D} = [\hat{d}_1, \ldots, \hat{d}_N]$ where N is the number of training images) of the same class by using the center-clustering loss function inspired from [23]:

$$\mathcal{L}_{center} = \frac{\alpha}{2} \sum_{i=1}^{N} ||\hat{d}_i - \hat{c}_{y_i}||_2^2 \tag{2}$$

The centers are initialized on the look-up-table with Xavier initialization [4], which makes them follow Gaussian distribution. In every iteration, each center is updated by subtracting the distance between the center and the features of corresponding classes from the center. In addition, to keep the features of different classes as far as possible, we introduce an additional cross entropy loss:

$$\mathcal{L}_{cls:\mathbf{D}} = -\sum_{i=1}^{N} log \frac{\exp\left(W_{D_{y_i}}^T \hat{d}_i\right)}{\sum_{j=1}^{L} \exp\left(W_{D_j}^T \hat{d}_i\right)} \tag{3}$$

where y_i denotes the i-th label, $\hat{c}_{y_i}$ indicates the y_i-th class center and $W_{D_{y_i}}$ denotes the weight for the linear prediction of the L-class label by using $\hat{d}_i$. Let us denote the vector of weights $W_{D_{y_i}}$ as $\mathbf{W_D}$. The centers of the classes are saved in a look-up-table for the mini-batch based updating, because updating the centers at every iteration is inefficient and impractical. We use a non-negative hyper-parameter α to control the influence of the center loss.

Block Hashing Layer. The last element of our architecture in Fig. 2 is the "Block Hashing," which converts a large real-valued feature vector into a binary hash code. The structure of the block hashing is detailed in Fig. 3, which receives the descriptor as the input and produces the hash code as the output. The final hash code is set to have K bits where K can be set bigger for the larger database. For the pre-defined hash size K, we set the size of the fully connected layer to $K \times M$ where M is called the block size. As shown in the figure, we divide the $K \times M$ descriptor ($\hat{d} = [d_1, \ldots, d_{K \times M}]$) into M blocks, and we extract the maximum of the $Softmax$ of the elements in the i-th block as

$$z_i = \max(Softmax(\text{elements of descriptor in the } i\text{-th block})). \tag{4}$$

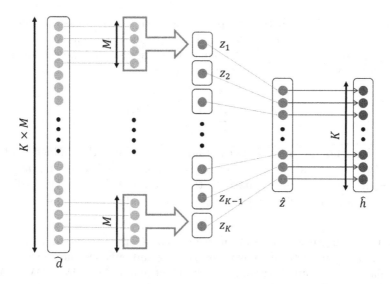

Fig. 3. Block hashing layer

Then, these are concatenated to be a vector $\hat{z} = [z_1, z_2, \cdots, z_K]$, and the final hash code $\hat{h}$ is obtained as

$$\hat{h} = [h_i \mid h_i = \tanh(z_i - \beta), \ i = 1, \ldots, K] \tag{5}$$

where β is a balancing parameter.

In this approach, each block is generated from a face image descriptor of a separate slice. Hence, blocks can effectively contain some characteristics of facial representations which are less relevant to each other. Unlike divide-and-encode module in [13], our block hashing layer does not have any trainable parameters, which can greatly reduce the redundancy. In addition, since we extract the maximum of the block-wise output during the back propagation, the gradient from the next layer is passed back to only that neuron which achieved the max. As a result, discriminative information of the large real-valued descriptor is well maintained while each element of the block is effectively trained to be a representative value of the block according to the classification result of the descriptor.

Classification and Quantization Loss from Hash Code. In order to get discriminative hash codes ($\mathbf{H} = [\hat{h}_1, \ldots, \hat{h}_N]$), we design the classification error as the cross entropy loss:

$$\mathcal{L}_{cls:\mathbf{H}} = -\sum_{i=1}^{N} log \frac{\exp{(W_{H y_i}^T \hat{h}_i)}}{\sum_{j=1}^{L} \exp{(W_{H j}^T \hat{h}_i)}} \tag{6}$$

where $W_{H y_i}$ denotes the weight for the linear prediction of the L-class label by using $\hat{h}_i$. Let us denote the vector of the weights $W_{H y_i}$ as $\mathbf{W_H}$ for the later use.

Our final goal is to learn a mapping function, which turns an image into a binary hash code that constitutes of discrete values. Therefore, we introduce another regularizer on $\mathbf{H}$ to make the continuous values approximate the discrete values. Formally, this regularizer is expressed as

$$\mathcal{L}_Q = \gamma \sum_{i=1}^{N} |||\hat{h}_i| - \beta \cdot \mathbb{1}||_1| \tag{7}$$

where γ is a non-negative hyper-parameter to adjust the influence of the quantization loss and $\mathbb{1}$ is a vector of ones. Since $\mathbf{H}$ is in the range $(\tanh(-\beta), \tanh(1-\beta))$, minimizing the absolute value of the $l1$-distance between $|\hat{h}_i|$ and $\beta \cdot \mathbb{1}$ efficiently guarantees discrete-like hash codes.

Regularization Loss. In addition, we employ $l2$ regularization with a non-negative hyper-parameter δ to avoid overfitting and enhance the generalization by calculating Frobenius norm of network weight matrix $\mathbf{W} = \mathbf{W}_D \cup \mathbf{W}_H \cup \mathbf{W}_L$, where $\mathbf{W}_L$ is a collection of weight matrix for each network layer. To be specific, this regularization is formulated as

$$\mathcal{L}_{reg} = \frac{\delta}{2}(||\mathbf{W}||_F^2 + \epsilon) \tag{8}$$

From the Eqs. 1 to 8, the loss function of our network is summarized as

$$\mathcal{L} = \mathcal{L}_{cls:\mathbf{D}} + \mathcal{L}_{center} + \mathcal{L}_{cls:\mathbf{H}} + \mathcal{L}_Q + \mathcal{L}_{reg}$$
$$= -\sum_{i=1}^{N} log \frac{\exp(W_{D_{y_i}}^T \hat{d}_i)}{\sum_{j=1}^{L} \exp(W_{D_j}^T \hat{d}_i)} + \frac{\alpha}{2} \sum_{i=1}^{N} ||\hat{d}_i - \hat{c}_{y_i}||_2^2 \tag{9}$$
$$- \sum_{i=1}^{N} log \frac{\exp(W_{H_{y_i}}^T \hat{h}_i)}{\sum_{j=1}^{L} \exp(W_{H_j}^T \hat{h}_i)} + \gamma \sum_{i=1}^{N} |||\hat{h}_i - \beta \cdot \mathbb{1}||_1| + \frac{\delta}{2}(||\mathbf{W}||_F^2 + \epsilon).$$

4 Experiments

4.1 Experimental Setting

Datasets. Well-organized large scale face image datasets are essential for both model training and evaluation. For the fair comparison, we conduct experiments on two datstets [16,24] following the experimental protocol proposed by Lin and Li [14]. Specifically, the first dataset is *YouTube Faces* [24] which is a database of face videos designed for studying the problem of unconstrained face recognition. The dataset contains 3,425 videos of 1,595 different people. Each subject has been shown in average number of 2.15 videos and the average length of video clip was 181.3 frames. We take 63,800 images for training with randomly selected 40 face images per person and 7,975 images with 5 images per person for testing. The second is *FaceScrub* [16] which consists of total of 106,863 face images of 530 male and female celebrities, with about 200 images per person retrieved from the Internet and are taken under real-world situations. 2,650 images are used for test data (5 images per person), and the remainder are used as the training set. All face images are resized to 32×32.

Evaluation Metrics. The retrieval results are evaluated based on whether the returned images and the query image have the same semantic labels or not. To each testing query image, we rank all the images according to Hamming distance. Then, we select the top M images from the ranked list as retrieval results and then compute the mean Average Precision (mAP) over all the testing images. In our experiment, M is set to 50. In addition, we illustrated precision curves with Hamming distance 2, precision curves with respect to different numbers of top returned images and precision-recall curves (48-bit) to make a precise comparison.

Training Details. We adopted Adam [11] as our optimization algorithm, starting with an initial learning rate of 0.001 and reducing it by a factor of 10 at every 10K iterations. We fixed the batch size as 256 during the training and for the parameters α, β, γ and δ, we set them to 0.0002, 0.5, 0.1 and 0.0002 respectively. All the experiments for our method are implemented based on the Tensorflow framework. The length of binary codes is set to 12, 24, 36 and 48 bits.

4.2   Optimal Network Architecture

Depth of the Network. To find the optimal number of channels to get the best performance from the proposed face retrieval framework, we conduct experiments on the network architecture shown in Table 1. For the details, we fixed block size as 6 and all the other parameters (α, β, γ and δ) as mentioned above.

Table 1. Networks with varying depths for comparison according to network depth. The '#cha' and 'size' represent the number of output feature maps and size of output feature maps, respectively. Also, 'conv' and 'max' represent the convolutional layer and max-pooling layer respectively. We employed ReLU activation and batch normalization layer at the end of each convolutional layer.

		1	2	3	4	5	6	7	8	9
Shallow	Layer	$2\times$conv	max	$2\times$conv	max	$3\times$conv				
	#cha	64	64	128	128	256				
	size	32	32	16	8	8				
Mid	Layer	$2\times$conv	max	$2\times$conv	max	$3\times$conv	max	$3\times$conv		
	#cha	64	64	128	128	256	256	512		
	size	32	32	16	8	8	4	4		
Deep	Layer	$2\times$conv	max	$2\times$conv	max	$3\times$conv	max	$3\times$conv	max	$3\times$conv
	#cha	64	64	128	128	256	256	512	512	512
	size	32	32	16	8	8	4	4	2	2

Table 2. mean Average Precision (mAP) of 'Shallow', 'Mid' and 'Deep' on the *YouTube Faces* and *FaceScrub* datasets.

	YouTube Faces				FaceScrub			
	12-bit	24-bit	36-bit	48-bit	12-bit	24-bit	36-bit	48-bit
Shallow	0.8908	0.9451	0.9688	0.9806	0.6882	0.7054	0.7313	0.7608
Mid	**0.9753**	**0.9899**	**0.9914**	**0.9922**	**0.7182**	**0.7317**	**0.7696**	**0.7862**
Deep	0.9304	0.9772	0.9846	0.9907	0.7167	0.7290	0.7468	0.7659

Each network has two global average pooling layers. In the case 'Shallow' in Table 1, the outputs of 4-max pooling layers (8×8 feature maps with 128 channels) and 5-convolutional layers (8×8 feature maps with 256 channels) are global average pooled. For the case of 'Mid,' much smaller feature maps with the larger numbers of channels are used, and outputs of 6-max pooling layer (4×4 feature maps with 256 channels) and 7-convolutional layer (4×4 feature maps with 512 channels) are global average pooled. Lastly, 'Deep' uses the most smaller feature maps and the largest number of channels that global average pools from the outputs of 8-max pooling layer (2×2 feature maps with 512 channels) and 10-convolutional layer (2×2 feature maps with 512 channels).

As shown in Table 2, the features extracted from the 6-max pooling layer and 8-max pooling layer outperform others from all bit-lengths. This is because 'Mid' is considered to hold the low-level features and high-level features appropriately. Therefore, we used the network architecture of 'Mid' for the rest experiments.

Block Size of the Network. In face image retrieval, increasing the dimension of a descriptor can contain more information, however, there is a trade off due to the increased computational complexity and redundancy. Consequently, we proceeded experiments on the same parameters as mentioned above with 'Mid' architecture to find the optimal dimension of a descriptor. As can be observed in Fig. 3, we can easily handle the dimension of descriptor by adjusting the size of block M. For the fixed size bit length K, we conduct experiments with changing the block size from 4 to 10 with the intervals of two (e.g. for 48-bit, descriptor dimension from 192 to 480). Finally we chose the block size 6 for the proposed network from the result shown in Table 3.

Table 3. Networks with varying block size for comparison according to the dimension of a descriptor. mAP on the two face datasets according to block size.

Block Size	YouTube Faces				FaceScrub			
	12-bit	24-bit	36-bit	48-bit	12-bit	24-bit	36-bit	48-bit
4	0.9662	0.9850	0.9894	0.9913	0.7033	0.7212	0.7564	0.7668
6	**0.9753**	**0.9899**	**0.9914**	**0.9922**	**0.7182**	**0.7317**	**0.7696**	**0.7862**
8	0.9513	0.9890	0.9911	0.9917	0.7113	0.7234	0.7580	0.7707
10	0.9455	0.9861	0.9904	0.9910	0.7164	0.7293	0.7424	0.7691

Influence of the Center-Clustering Loss. To verify the effectiveness of the center-clustering loss term, we investigate three different schemes: (1) Block hashing layer without center-clustering and classification loss from descriptor, (2) Block hashing layer and classification loss from descriptor without center-clustering loss and (3) Block hashing layer with center-clustering and classification loss from descriptor. We conducted experiments on the same parameters as mentioned above with 'Mid' architecture and block size 6. The results presented in Table 4 demonstrates that the proposed loss terms significantly improve performance in face retrieval for binary code of all lengths, especially for 12-bit.

Table 4. Network performance comparison based on presence of center-clustering loss and classification loss from descriptor by calculating mAP on both face datasets. The 'Clu' and 'Cla' represent center-clustering loss and classification loss from descriptor, respectively.

Clu	Cla	YouTube Faces				FaceScrub			
---	---	12-bit	24-bit	36-bit	48-bit	12-bit	24-bit	36-bit	48-bit
X	X	0.7631	0.8455	0.9152	0.9833	0.6234	0.6454	0.6872	0.6962
X	O	0.8423	0.9263	0.9611	0.9863	0.6615	0.6814	0.6998	0.7224
O	O	**0.9753**	**0.9899**	**0.9914**	**0.9922**	**0.7182**	**0.7317**	**0.7696**	**0.7862**

Balancing Parameter β. To investigate the effect of the balancing parameter β, we change it to 0.25, 0.5 and 0.75 and the result was best at $\beta = 0.5$ that has even distribution of positive and negative numbers. The derivative of quantization loss function proposed in [14] approaches zero as the input value increases,

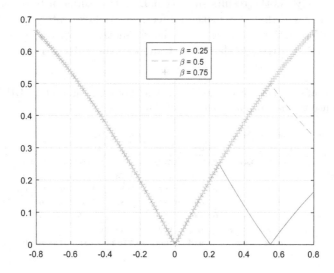

Fig. 4. Different quantization loss functions for different parameter β

which results in decreasing the convergence speed of the objective function. From Eq. 7, our proposed quantization loss function does not decrease the convergence speed regardless of the change in β, because the derivative does not converge to zero within a fixed domain as illustrated in Fig. 4.

4.3   Comparison to Other Methods

From the extensive experiments conducted on 4.1 and 4.2, we found the best architecture of our DCBH network. To validate the effectiveness of DCBH, its performance is evaluated in terms of mAP at top 50 images on the *YouTube Faces* and *FaceScrub* dataset. The same experiments are also conducted on DSH [15], DHCQ [20], DDH [14] and DDQH [21]. Since DCBH has much deeper network architecture than others, we employed the same deep network architecture based on VGG [19] for DDH and DDQH (which we called DDH-Deep and DDQH-Deep) to verify the performance of our proposed block hashing layer and loss terms. The corresponding results are presented in Table 5.

Observed from the results in Table 5, our proposed method outperforms all the compared methods. In some cases, the performance of other deep hashing methods with longer binary codes are still worse than the performance of DCBH with shorter binary codes, which indicates that DCBH encodes hash codes more efficiently and compactly. Besides, DDH-Deep achieves superior performance to its original DDH, as expected. However, in the case of DDQH-Deep, it does not always improve the performance compared to its original version, which demonstrates that the deeper network does not necessarily bring better results.

We also evaluate the performance by using the metrics of precision curves with Hamming distance 2, precision curves with respect to different numbers of top returned images and precision-recall curves (48-bit) as illustrated in Figs. 5 and 6, respectively. As the results show that DCBH is superior to other hashing methods, we can see that our method effectively reduces inter-class similarity and intra-class variation to learn more discriminative hash codes. The source code is available at https://github.com/youngkyunJang/DCBH.

Table 5. mAP of different hashing approaches on both face datasets. DDH-Deep and DDQH-Deep use the network architecture of 'Mid'.

Methods	YouTube Faces				FaceScrub			
	12-bit	24-bit	36-bit	48-bit	12-bit	24-bit	36-bit	48-bit
DSH	0.1355	0.4111	0.5319	0.5708	0.0419	0.0886	0.1020	0.1142
DHCQ	0.2501	0.4892	0.6813	0.7682	0.1873	0.2113	0.2406	0.2810
DDH	0.4029	0.8223	0.8457	0.9068	0.0650	0.1103	0.1437	0.1889
DDQH	0.6322	0.9720	0.9780	0.9852	0.1185	0.2682	0.3410	0.4523
DDH-Deep	0.6121	0.8658	0.9005	0.9584	0.6074	0.6285	0.6643	0.6862
DDQH-Deep	0.6521	0.8972	0.9418	0.9623	0.6213	0.6315	0.6704	0.6793
DCBH	**0.9753**	**0.9899**	**0.9914**	**0.9922**	**0.7182**	**0.7317**	**0.7696**	**0.7862**

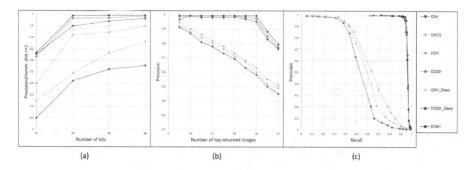

Fig. 5. Results on the *YouTube Faces* dataset. (a) Precision curves with Hamming distance 2. (b) Precision curves with 48 bits with respect to the number of top returned images. (c) Precision-recall curves of Hamming ranking with 48 bits.

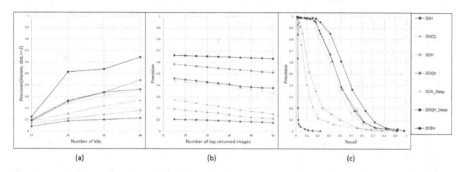

Fig. 6. Results on the *FaceScrub* dataset. (a) Precision curves with Hamming distance 2. (b) Precision curves with 48 bits with respect to the number of top returned images. (c) Precision-recall curves of Hamming ranking with 48 bits.

5   Conclusion

We have presented a new hashing method named Deep Clustering and Block Hashing network for a large-scale face image retrieval. To alleviate the problems due to the inter-class similarity and intra-class variation in face images, we introduced center-clustering loss and block hashing layer for the network training. Experimental results on two widely used face image datasets show that the DCBH method achieves the state-of-the-art performance.

Acknowledgements. This work was supported by Institute for Information & communications Technology Promotion (IITP) grant funded by the Korea government (MSIT) (No. 1711075689, Decentralised cloud technologies for edge/IoT integration in support of AI applications).

References

1. Babenko, A., Lempitsky, V.: Aggregating local deep features for image retrieval. In: Proceedings of the IEEE International Conference on Computer Vision, pp. 1269–1277 (2015)
2. Banaeeyan, R., Lye, H., Fauzi, M.F.A., Karim, H.A., See, J.: Semantic facial scores and compact deep transferred descriptors for scalable face image retrieval. Neurocomputing **308**, 111–128 (2018)
3. Erin Liong, V., Lu, J., Wang, G., Moulin, P., Zhou, J.: Deep hashing for compact binary codes learning. In: Proceedings of the IEEE Conference on Computer Vision and Pattern Recognition, pp. 2475–2483 (2015)
4. Glorot, X., Bengio, Y.: Understanding the difficulty of training deep feedforward neural networks. In: Proceedings of the Thirteenth International Conference on Artificial Intelligence and Statistics, pp. 249–256 (2010)
5. Gordo, A., Almazán, J., Revaud, J., Larlus, D.: Deep image retrieval: learning global representations for image search. In: Leibe, B., Matas, J., Sebe, N., Welling, M. (eds.) ECCV 2016. LNCS, vol. 9910, pp. 241–257. Springer, Cham (2016). https://doi.org/10.1007/978-3-319-46466-4_15
6. He, K., Zhang, X., Ren, S., Sun, J.: Deep residual learning for image recognition. In: Proceedings of the IEEE Conference on Computer Vision and Pattern Recognition, pp. 770–778 (2016)
7. Ioffe, S., Szegedy, C.: Batch normalization: accelerating deep network training by reducing internal covariate shift. arXiv preprint arXiv:1502.03167 (2015)
8. Jain, H., Zepeda, J., Pérez, P., Gribonval, R.: SUBIC: a supervised, structured binary code for image search. In: Proceedings of International Conference on Computer Vision, vol. 1, p. 3 (2017)
9. Jegou, H., Douze, M., Schmid, C.: Product quantization for nearest neighbor search. IEEE Trans. Pattern Anal. Mach. Intell. **33**(1), 117–128 (2011)
10. Jeong, D.j., Choo, S., Seo, W., Cho, N.I.: Regional deep feature aggregation for image retrieval. In: 2017 IEEE International Conference on Acoustics, Speech and Signal Processing (ICASSP), pp. 1737–1741. IEEE (2017)
11. Kingma, D.P., Ba, J.: Adam: a method for stochastic optimization. arXiv preprint arXiv:1412.6980 (2014)
12. Krizhevsky, A., Sutskever, I., Hinton, G.E.: ImageNet classification with deep convolutional neural networks. In: Advances in Neural Information Processing Systems, pp. 1097–1105 (2012)
13. Lai, H., Pan, Y., Liu, Y., Yan, S.: Simultaneous feature learning and hash coding with deep neural networks. arXiv preprint arXiv:1504.03410 (2015)
14. Lin, J., Li, Z., Tang, J.: Discriminative deep hashing for scalable face image retrieval. In: Proceedings of International Joint Conference on Artificial Intelligence (2017)
15. Liu, H., Wang, R., Shan, S., Chen, X.: Deep supervised hashing for fast image retrieval. In: Proceedings of the IEEE conference on Computer Vision and Pattern Recognition, pp. 2064–2072 (2016)
16. Ng, H.W., Winkler, S.: A data-driven approach to cleaning large face datasets. In: 2014 IEEE International Conference on Image Processing (ICIP), pp. 343–347. IEEE (2014)
17. Parkhi, O.M., Vedaldi, A., Zisserman, A., et al.: Deep face recognition. In: BMVC, vol. 1, p. 6 (2015)

18. Schroff, F., Kalenichenko, D., Philbin, J.: FaceNet: a unified embedding for face recognition and clustering. In: Proceedings of the IEEE Conference on Computer Vision and Pattern Recognition, pp. 815–823 (2015)
19. Simonyan, K., Zisserman, A.: Very deep convolutional networks for large-scale image recognition. arXiv preprint arXiv:1409.1556 (2014)
20. Tang, J., Li, Z., Zhu, X.: Supervised deep hashing for scalable face image retrieval. Pattern Recogn. **75**, 25–32 (2018)
21. Tang, J., Lin, J., Li, Z., Yang, J.: Discriminative deep quantization hashing for face image retrieval. IEEE Trans. Neural Netw. Learn. Syst. (2018)
22. Wang, J., Kumar, S., Chang, S.F.: Semi-supervised hashing for large-scale search. IEEE Trans. Pattern Anal. Mach. Intell. **34**(12), 2393–2406 (2012)
23. Wen, Y., Zhang, K., Li, Z., Qiao, Y.: A discriminative feature learning approach for deep face recognition. In: Leibe, B., Matas, J., Sebe, N., Welling, M. (eds.) ECCV 2016. LNCS, vol. 9911, pp. 499–515. Springer, Cham (2016). https://doi.org/10.1007/978-3-319-46478-7_31
24. Wolf, L., Hassner, T., Maoz, I.: Face recognition in unconstrained videos with matched background similarity. In: 2011 IEEE Conference on Computer Vision and Pattern Recognition (CVPR), pp. 529–534. IEEE (2011)
25. Xia, R., Pan, Y., Lai, H., Liu, C., Yan, S.: Supervised hashing for image retrieval via image representation learning. In: AAAI, vol. 1, p. 2 (2014)
26. Zhu, H., Long, M., Wang, J., Cao, Y.: Deep hashing network for efficient similarity retrieval. In: AAAI, pp. 2415–2421 (2016)

Learning Energy Based Inpainting
for Optical Flow

Christoph Vogel[1(✉)] ⓘ, Patrick Knöbelreiter[1] ⓘ, and Thomas Pock[1,2] ⓘ

[1] Graz University of Technology, Graz, Austria
{christoph.vogel,patrick.knobelreiter,thomas.pock}@icg.tugraz.at
[2] Austrian Institute of Technology, Vienna, Austria

Abstract. Modern optical flow methods are often composed of a cascade of many independent steps or formulated as a black box neural network that is hard to interpret and analyze. In this work we seek for a plain, interpretable, but learnable solution. We propose a novel inpainting based algorithm that approaches the problem in three steps: feature selection and matching, selection of supporting points and energy based inpainting. To facilitate the inference we propose an *optimization layer* that allows to backpropagate through 10K iterations of a first-order method without any numerical or memory problems. Compared to recent state-of-the-art networks, our modular CNN is very lightweight and competitive with other, more involved, inpainting based methods.

Keywords: Optical flow · Energy optimization · Deep learning

1 Introduction and Related Work

The computation of optical flow, the apparent 2D motion field between two consecutive frames of a temporal image sequence, is one of the most investigated problems in computer vision. Optical flow possesses a vast number of applications, among others, video processing for action detection or activity recognition, autonomous driving [22] or medical imaging. Similarly, there are multiple methods, to compute the optical flow field. Energy based techniques that were popular in the past, are now outperformed and replaced by approaches that solely rely on convolutional neural networks (CNNs) [11,21]. Despite their great performance on benchmark data sets, these networks often lack interpretability – often it remains unclear, apart from input and loss function, how the network internally models the flow problem. In this work we seek to combine both ideas. We propose to utilize an energy based optimization problem suitable for the computation of optical flow and let the network learn the input to the energy.

Supported by the ERC starting grant 640156, 'HOMOVIS'.

Electronic supplementary material The online version of this chapter (https://doi.org/10.1007/978-3-030-20876-9_22) contains supplementary material, which is available to authorized users.

We then minimize the energy to produce the flow field by unrolling the iterations of a first-order algorithm. Our energy is convex but non-smooth and hence demands for a large number of iterations. To address the memory and numerical problems that occur when running backpropagation for more than 10K iterations on the GPU, we propose an *optimization layer*, that handles these problem in an efficient GPU implementation using *checkpointing* [8,14] and buffering of intermediate solutions in double precision. Our energy minimizing network layer is related to ideas proposed in [3]. Compared to [3], we solve a non-linear and non-smooth problem, but similarly facilitate to backpropagate through the minimization process. However, our experiments indicate that the increased robustness provided by the non-smooth formulation is beneficial for our optical flow problem. A combination of CNNs and energy optimization was also proposed by [30,34,39]. Here, we seek to run our optimization until near convergence. Our optimization layer allows us to unroll 4 orders of magnitude more iterations than [30,39].

For our model we consider a class of algorithms that treat the computation of optical flow as a form of *inpainting* or sparse-to-dense interpolation problem. Possibly the most prominent representative of these methods is [28] that tackles the problem in many different steps, including sparse matching [36], edge detection [10], computing super-pixels [1], variational refinement [6], and various post-processing steps. Here, we simplify the inpainting process to its core, feature generation to build a cost volume for image matching, selection of supporting matches and inpainting via energy minimization. We tackle the problem via deep learning and propose a network structure that still delivers interpretable intermediate results, and allows for training in end-to-end fashion. In contrast to other inpainting based optical flow methods, we start our process from dense matching. Consequently, we are not committed to a pre-selection of, possibly incomplete or unmatchable interest points [36,40], but can select the supporting pixels *after* matching. Compared to nearest neighbor field methods [18,35], we make use of a complete cost-volume and avoid a coarse-to-fine scheme or hashing. To that end, we make use of a recent result [23] that allows for a low memory footprint of the cost volume. In contrast to network based solutions to inpainting [40], we maintain the interpretability of an energy based framework.

The core idea of our algorithm is closely related to diffusion based inpainting for image compression [12]. Here, the compression ratio is mainly dependent on the selection of *supporting points* from which the image is then inpainted. Given the image to be compressed, this selection process can be formulated as a bi-level optimization problem [9,25]. Unfortunately, we have no knowledge of the ground-truth reconstruction and have to select the supporting points from a large number of possible matches per pixel. Here, our method estimates the confidence of the different matches per pixel. In the context of stereo matching confidence estimation is a well studied problem [16]. Lately also CNN based solutions have been proposed [2,26]. Compared to the general problem, our solution is directly task related. We are not interested in providing a confidence for each pixel, but also have to consider the relevance of a pixel to our inpainting task. Our selection process has to balance the added information content and robustness of the match on a per pixel basis. This is addressed by learning confidence estimation and inpainting in end-to-end fashion.

In this paper, we propose a novel, 'from scratch' algorithm for inpainting optical flow. We reduce the process to its core: feature computation and matching, selection of supporting pixels and energy based inpainting. Compared to recent state-of-the-art networks, our CNN is lightweight with only 450K parameters. We introduce a novel *quad-fitting* layer that can learn features for sub-pixel accurate matching, while still allowing for large displacements and finally propose an *optimization layer* to solve the energy minimization problem. Here, we show that a tailored GPU implementation can lead to memory and numerical efficiency and facilitate backpropagation over more than 10K iterations.

2   Method

In this work we consider the estimation of optical flow, the 2D motion field that describes the movement of pixels between two consecutive frames $I^0, I^1 \in \Omega \subset \mathbb{R}^2$ of an image sequence defined over the domain Ω. Formally, we define the optical flow field as $\mathbf{u} := (u_0, u_1)^\mathsf{T}$, consisting of a vertical and a horizontal component given by the functional $u_i : \Omega \to \mathbb{R}, i \in \{0, 1\}$. Here, we let super-indices encode the time step and sub-indices the motion direction. We formulate the task of estimating such motion field as a classical inpainting/denoising problem:

$$\min_{u_i} \mathcal{R}_1(u_i) + \int_\Omega c(x)|u_i(x) - \hat{u}_i(x)|\mathrm{d}x, \quad \text{with} \quad \mathcal{R}_1(u_i) := \int_\Omega |W^{\frac{1}{2}}\nabla u_i|_\delta \mathrm{d}x, \quad (1)$$

which corresponds to weighted Total Variation [31] regularization with a robust weighted ℓ_1 data fidelity term, known to lead to piecewise constant solutions. Here, $|\cdot|_\delta$ denotes the Huber-norm $|\cdot|_\delta := \frac{1}{2}|\cdot|_2^2 + \frac{1}{2}\delta^2$, if $|\cdot|_2 \leq \delta$ and $\delta|\cdot|_2$ else. Likewise, we also consider a variant corresponding to weighted Total Generalized Variation [5] of second order, were we replace the regularization term by:

$$\mathcal{R}_2(u_i) = \min_{w_i = (w_{i,0}, w_{i,1})^\mathsf{T}} \int_\Omega |W^{\frac{1}{2}}\nabla u_i - w_i|_\delta + \beta(|\nabla w_{i,0}|_\delta + |\nabla w_{i,1}|_\delta)\mathrm{d}x, \quad (2)$$

where $w_{i,j} \in \Omega \to \mathbb{R}, i, j \in \{0, 1\}$ represent auxiliary variables. In contrast to (1), (2) prefers a piecewise affine solution for the flow components u_i. Both cases require a good guess for the initial flow $\hat{\mathbf{u}} := (\hat{u}_0, \hat{u}_1)^\mathsf{T}$, the *diffusion tensor* $W := \mathrm{diag}(\omega_0, \omega_1)$, c.f. [37] and the *confidence score* $c \in [0, 1]$ that locally ties the solution $\mathbf{u}$ to the initial estimate $\hat{\mathbf{u}}$. To compute $\mathbf{u}$ we use a CNN that is split into different parts to deliver the inputs for our optimization stage solving (1) or (2). In particular, we perform dense pixel-wise matching using network generated features, refine the matches by locally fitting a quadratic to the cost and employ the arg min cost solution as initial estimate. Diffusion Tensor W and confidence c are provided by 2 sub-networks. All these CNNs are rather small, with around 150k parameters each. To solve our optimization problem we employ a special

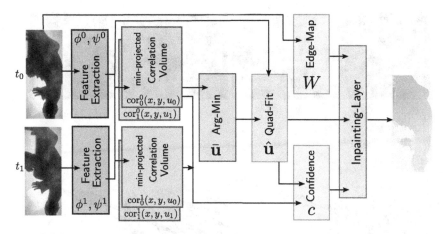

Fig. 1. The overview of our pipeline. Feature vectors are generated from the input images. Per view, in forward and backward direction, two (see Sect. 2.1) correlation volumes are built. A preliminary solution $\hat{u}$ is obtained by refining the flow at minimal (negative) correlation $\bar{u}$ in the *quad-fitting layer* (see Sect. 2.2). Afterwards, a confidence c is computed for each flow vector obtained from the fitting. In parallel, a diffusion tensor or edge-map W is generated (Sect. 2.3). Confidence, tensor and preliminary solution $\hat{u}$ are fed into our optimization layer (Sect. 2.5) that solves problem (1) or (2).

custom layer that allows to accurately minimize convex, non-smooth problems in the form of (1) or (2) and provides a simple, memory efficient and accurate way to backpropagate through them and, thus, learn its input parameters.

An overview of our method and the progression of our framework is provided in Fig. 1. The input images pass the feature extraction stage from which the cost volumes are constructed. We employ the method of [23] and generate 2 3D volumes from one complete 4D cost volume (c.f. Sect. 2.1). This allows to train the feature generation step on whole images instead of small patches and also enables us to compute cost volumes in forward and backward direction, which are later used for our confidence estimates. To keep the network simple and small we do not consider filtering of the cost volumes, e.g. [15,29,32]. Instead, we directly use the solution with maximal correlation for both forward ($\bar{u}$) and backward direction ($\bar{u}^{BW}$). Our *quad-fitting* layer (Sect. 2.2) delivers sub-pixel accurate matches, by fitting a quadratic function to the local feature cost. The computed pixel-wise estimates $\hat{u}$, along with some extra features like the softmax-probabilities are fed into a network to compute the confidence scores c, c.f. Sect. 2.4. Further, we generate the diffusion tensor, or edge-map, W applying a network that receives the images as input, described in Sect. 2.3. The initial estimates $\hat{u}$ the confidence scores c and the diffusion tensor W are the fed into our optimization layer to compute the final solution (Sect. 2.5).

Following the flow of our pipeline, we now consider each of its stages in detail.

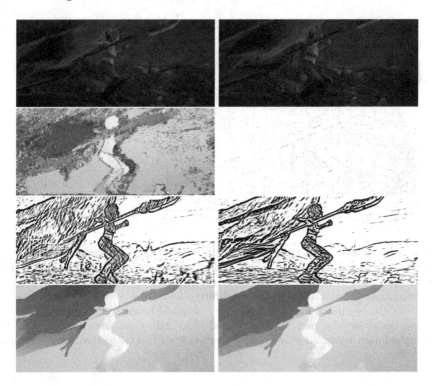

Fig. 2. *Top*: input images at time step 0 (left) and time step 1 (right). *Second row*: data term $\hat{\mathbf{u}}$ (left) and confidence map c (right), where black means high and white low confidence. *Third row*: diffusion tensor W. Horizontal edges, W_0 (left) and vertical edges, W_1 (right). Here white means strong and black weak regularization. *Bottom*: the ground truth solution (left) and the output of the optimization layer.

2.1   Feature Generation

For feature generation we follow [23] and employ a Siamese network consisting of two convolutional branches with shared parameters. In our implementation we utilize a feed forward network comprised of 5 convolutional layers with a filter size of 3×3 and 64 channels, followed by a single 1-D convolution. After each stage we apply a tanh non-linearity. Further, we utilize dilated filters [38] of sizes $1, 2, 4, 1, 4$ and 1 in the stages. In the fourth layer we apply a striding of 2 and reduce the feature maps by a factor of 2 in each dimension of our domain Ω. We retain the feature maps (ψ^0 and ψ^1) after the third layer for our sub-pixel refinement step described in Sect. 2.2. The final feature maps ϕ^0 and ϕ^1 of the two frames are fed into a correlation layer that generates four 3D cost volumes:

$$\text{cor}_i^j(x, y, u_i) := \min_{u_{1-i} \in H} -\langle \phi^j(x, y), \phi^{1-j}(x + u_0, y + u_1) \rangle, \quad i, j \in \{0, 1\}. \quad (3)$$

$H := \{-d, \dots, d-1\}$ denotes our range of integer displacements, which effectively correspond to a twice as large displacement at the original resolution due to the striding. Note that we explicitly consider the forward (cor_i^0) and backward direction (cor_i^1) and split the full 4D cost volumes $\text{cor}^j(x, y, u_0, u_1)$ into two directional ones, c.f. (3). To that end, [23] proposes to use *min-projection* to eliminate one of the motion directions via: $\text{cor}_i^j(x, y, u_i) := \min_{u_{1-i} \in H} \text{cor}^j(x, y, u_0, u_1)$. Most prominently this reduces the memory complexity of storing the cost volume from quadratic to linear. Our initial discrete motion estimates can then be found as $\bar{u}_i := \arg \min \text{cor}_i^0(x, y, u_i), i = 0, 1$. Note, that the arg min remains untouched by the *min-projection* operation applied beforehand on the cost volumes. Further, we can define a probability for each pixel and possible displacement via the usual *softmax* function for the reference view 0:

$$p_i(x, y, u_i) := \exp(-\text{cor}_i^0(x, y, u_i)) / \sum_{u_i \in H} \exp(-\text{cor}_i^0(x, y, u_i)), \text{ for } i = 0, 1. \quad (4)$$

Those (pseudo-)likelihoods, evaluated at the preliminary motion estimate $\bar{u}$, are used as input for our confidence network and for training the data term via a maximum likelihood criterion (c.f. Sect. 2.6).

2.2   Quad-Fitting

Our procedure above limits our candidate flow to take only even integral values, due to the sampling and additional striding imposed on the feature maps. While the striding increases the admissible motion magnitude of our cost volume, the local (sub-)pixel accuracy suffers. Our solution is to refine the location by fitting a quadratic at the predicted motion and return its arg min and cost. To that end, we up-sample and scale the preliminary motion estimates $\bar{u}$ and fit the quadratic in the vicinity of the initial match. Using nearest neighbor interpolation we can – at each non-boundary pixel – identify 4 motion candidates in the up-sampled motion field that are investigated for a refinement. Here, we fit a quadratic at the position (of the 4 candidates) of minimal cost and update the displacement to sub-pixel accuracy by solving the quadratic equation. To fit the quadratic, we utilize the high-resolution feature maps ψ, acquired before the striding in the feature generation takes place. We use a 5 stencil around the predicted match that is given by $(\bar{v}_0, \bar{v}_1) := \arg \min_{v_0 \in \{2\bar{u}_0, 2\bar{u}_0 + 1\}, v_1 \in \{2\bar{u}_1, 2\bar{u}_1 + 1\}} - \langle \psi^0(x, y), \psi^1(x + v_0, y + v_1) \rangle$. We fit a quadratic function $f(\mathbf{v}) := \sum_i a_i v_i^2 + b_i v_i + c$ to the (negative) correlation $q_{x,y,v_0,v_1} := -\langle \psi^0(x, y), \psi^1(x + \bar{v}_0 + v_0, y + \bar{v}_1 + v_1) \rangle$ between the respective feature vectors in both images. Abbreviating the negative correlation cost with q_{x,y,v_0,v_1} the solution to the fitting problem becomes:

$$a_0 = \frac{q_{x,y,+1,0} + q_{x,y,-1,0} - 2q_{x,y,0,0}}{2}, \quad b_0 = \frac{q_{x,y,+1,0} - q_{x,y,-1,0}}{2}, \quad c = q_{x,y,0,0} \quad (5)$$

$$a_1 = \frac{q_{x,y,0,1} + q_{x,y,0,-1} - 2q_{x,y,0,0}}{2}, \quad b_1 = \frac{q_{x,y,0,1} - q_{x,y,0,-1}}{2} \quad \text{and solution} \quad (6)$$

$$v_0 = \frac{-b_0}{2a_0}, \quad v_1 = \frac{-b_1}{2a_1} \quad \text{with } f(v_0, v_1) = a_0 v_0^2 + b_0 v_0 + c + a_1 v_1^2 + b_1 v_1. \quad (7)$$

If the fitting fails, the motion estimate $\bar{\mathbf{v}}$ is not a local minimum of the cost w.r.t. ψ and we return the integral flow $\bar{\mathbf{v}}$ and cost at that pixel. Otherwise we set $\hat{\mathbf{u}} := \bar{\mathbf{v}} + \mathbf{v}$. The second row of Fig. 2 shows a typical result for $\hat{\mathbf{u}}$ of our fitting layer. Subpixel accuracy can only be achieved if the initial discrete flow $\bar{\mathbf{u}}$ returned as the arg min solution of the correlation volume is close to the ground-truth. We embed our fitting procedure into a single network layer. Backpropagation only requires us to compute the derivatives of the expression above w.r.t. the feature vectors ψ. Empirically, compared to directly matching features at the finest resolution, our combination of striding and quad-fitting leads to a smaller sized correlation volume and sub-pixel accuracy.

2.3 Diffusion Tensor

To compute the diffusion tensor, we apply a simple 4 layer feed-forward network with 64 channels and relu non-linearities between 3×3 convolutions with dilations of size $1, 2$ and 4 on the input image I^0. By using dilations we operate at the finest resolution, but aggregate information of a larger spatial context [38]. To obtain values between 0 and 1 for our 2D tensor W, a final 1×1 convolution is followed by a sigmoid activation function. Figure 2 (3rd row) shows a typical tensor obtained from an image of the Sintel benchmark. The regularization force is only low near image edges. Otherwise the regularizer of (1) operates at full strength.

2.4 Confidence Estimate

Again we prefer a simple network to produce a single confidence estimate per pixel. The input to this stage are the upsampled pseudo-likelihoods (4) of the preliminary motion estimates $\bar{\mathbf{u}}$, the upsampled distances between forward and backward flow vectors, $d(\bar{\mathbf{u}}, \bar{\mathbf{u}}^{\mathrm{BW}})$, the distance to the boundary of the warped pixels, $b(\hat{\mathbf{u}})$, and the costs after the quadratic fit (7). The forward-backward distance is computed by linear interpolation of the backward flow vectors, i.e. $d(\bar{\mathbf{u}}, \bar{\mathbf{u}}^{\mathrm{BW}}) := |\bar{\mathbf{u}}(x, y) - \bar{\mathbf{u}}^{\mathrm{BW}}(x + \bar{u}_0, y + \bar{u}_1)|$. Assuming images of $N \times M$ pixels the distance to the boundary is given by $b(\hat{\mathbf{u}}) := \max(0, \min(x + \hat{u}_0, y + \hat{u}_1, N - x - \hat{u}_0, M - y - \hat{u}_1))$. We further apply non-minimum suppression on the high resolution confidence map. Of the four pixels covered by one pixel of the low dimensional feature map, we only allow $c > 0$ for the one of maximum confidence.

We posit, that all inputs to the network contribute some independent information that can be exploited for our confidence score: a forward-backward check can identify occlusions and demand consistency, the arg min flow can lead to higher confidence in smooth regions than in noisy ones, a criterion also investigated in e.g. [16]. By design, the softmax-probabilities are directly related to the confidence, whereas the fitting score can provide similar information, but in a more local vicinity. The network architecture is again given by a sequence of dilated 3×3 convolutions with relu activations, followed by a single 1×1 convolution with a sigmoid activation function. We employ seven layers with empirically chosen dilations of size $1, 2, 4, 8, 4, 2$ and 1 for the final 1×1 convolution that produces the 1D confidence signal. Figure 2 (2nd row, right) visualizes the confidence scores for the example. We observe that confident pixel are rare, and that those occur mostly close, but in some distance to the edges in the image.

2.5   Optimization Layer

Given the input from the stages above we can compute the solution to (1) or (2) by unrolling iterations of a first-order algorithm. The non-smooth convex problem has a composite (smooth plus non-smooth) structure that allows the application of FISTA [4], which has optimal convergence rate $\frac{1}{k^2}$ after k iterations [24]. Yet, the very sparse data term (c.f. Fig. 2), leads to a situation that requires many iterations to achieve convergence for our diffusion like algorithm with local updates. A naive implementation in a high-level language like Tensorflow or Theano [33], would demand $O(KNM)$ memory to perform backpropagation over K iterations and NM pixels, which is too much to handle for current GPU hardware. Likewise, accumulating gradients over many iterations in single precision can be numerically troublesome. Here, we show that it can be beneficial to implement the optimization stage of such first order algorithms, including backpropagation, within in a single layer in order to reduce memory overhead and make end-to-end training feasible. To that end, we combine two simple ideas, the gradient checkpointing technique [14] and accumulating the gradients into a buffer of double precision, such that the core of our algorithm can still run in the much more efficient single precision on the GPU. Checkpointing reduces the memory requirements to $O(\sqrt{K}NM)$ at the cost of a second forward pass. At $K \sim 10^4$ this leads to savings of a factor of 100 and, hence, we can backpropagate gradients over 10000 iterations without numerical problems. In practice, we introduce $O(\sqrt{K})$ checkpoints every $\lceil k\sqrt{K} \rceil, k = 0 \ldots \lfloor \sqrt{K} \rfloor$ iterations at which we store the necessary information to reproduce a forward pass from $\lceil k\sqrt{K} \rceil$ to iteration $\lceil (k+1)\sqrt{K} \rceil$. This procedure demands $O(\sqrt{K}NM)$ storage. To perform backpropagation, we go backwards from checkpoint to checkpoint and recover the information needed to perform backpropagation between two checkpoints with a second forward pass. Again, this requires $O(\sqrt{K}NM)$ intermediate memory, which can be released afterwards. We then compute the gradients of this stage and, at the end, accumulate them into buffers of double precision.

We focus our analysis on the TV like inpainting functional (1). After discretization on a cartesian grid of size $N \times M$, the problem to determine $u_i \in \mathbb{R}^{NM}$, the pixelwise flow in each coordinate direction $i = 0, 1$ can be written as

$$\min_{u_i} \|\sqrt{W}Du_i\|_\delta + \|u_i - \hat{u}_i\|_c. \tag{8}$$

The linear mapping $D : \mathbb{R}^{NM} \to \mathbb{R}^{2NM}$ approximates the spatial gradient of the flow per direction via finite forward differences and $W : \mathbb{R}^{2NM} \to \mathbb{R}^{2NM}$ represents the discretized diffusion tensor and accordingly weighs the contribution of each local gradient per direction. The Huber norm $\|\cdot\|_\delta$ operates on each local gradient individually. The norm $\|\cdot\|_c$ denotes the ℓ_1 norm weighted by the confidence c.

Our optimization procedure can be described by the following FISTA step:

$$u_i^{k+0.5} := v_i^k - D^\mathsf{T} \frac{W}{\max(1, |\sqrt{W}Dv_i^k|_2/\delta)}Dv_i^k \tag{9}$$

$$u_i^{k+1} := \begin{cases} u_i^{k+0.5} - c \text{ if } u_i^{k+0.5} - c > \hat{u}_i \\ u_i^{k+0.5} + c \text{ if } u_i^{k+0.5} + c < \hat{u}_i \\ \hat{u}_i \quad\quad \text{else} \end{cases} \tag{10}$$

$$v_i^{k+1} := u_i^{k+1} + \frac{t^k - 1}{t^{k+1}}(u_i^{k+1} - u_i^k), \tag{11}$$

which is executed for $i=0,1$ in parallel and K iterations. The solution returned, u_i^K, is one of the components of $\mathbf{u}$, and $t^k \in \mathbb{R}$ denote the step-sizes. In contrast to [34] we leave learning the step-sizes for future work and use $t^k := \frac{1+\sqrt{1+4t^{k-1}}}{2}$ for $k > 0$ and $t^0 := 1$, as advocated in the original FISTA paper. This scheme guarantees a $\frac{1}{k^2}$ convergence rate [4]. We can incorporate the Lipshitz constant L into our Tensor $W := 1/L \cdot W$. Later, the gradients $\frac{\partial f}{\partial W}$ w.r.t. W have to be adjusted accordingly, we simply return $L\frac{\partial f}{\partial W}$. Here, L is the maximal eigenvalue of our system matrix $D^\mathsf{T}WD$, e.g. for TV we have $L = 8$. Given the gradient of some loss function f on our returned solution u^K from the forward pass, $\frac{\partial f}{\partial u^K}$, we have to compute the gradients w.r.t. our parameters $W, \hat{u}$ and c (and β for TGV-inpainting). Our backward algorithm is composed of the following steps and returns $\frac{\partial f}{\partial \hat{u}_i}, \frac{\partial f}{\partial c}, \frac{\partial f}{\partial W}$ and $\frac{\partial f}{\partial u^0}$, the gradient w.r.t. the initial solution u^0.

$$\frac{\partial f}{\partial \hat{u}_i} := \frac{\partial f}{\partial \hat{u}_i} + \frac{\partial f}{\partial u_i^{k+1}} \text{ if } c < |\hat{u}_i - u_i^{k+0.5}| \tag{12}$$

$$\frac{\partial f}{\partial c} := \frac{\partial f}{\partial c} + \text{sign}(\hat{u}_i - u_i^{k+0.5})\frac{\partial f}{\partial u_i^{k+1}} \text{ if } c \geq |\hat{u}_i - u_i^{k+0.5}| \tag{13}$$

$$\frac{\partial f}{\partial u_i^{k+0.5}} := \begin{cases} \frac{\partial f}{\partial u_i^{k+1}} \text{ if } c \geq |\hat{u}_i - u_i^{k+0.5}| \\ 0 \quad \text{else} \end{cases} \tag{14}$$

$$\frac{\partial f}{\partial v_i^k} := \left(I - \frac{\partial}{\partial v_i^k}\left(\frac{W}{\max(1, |\sqrt{W}Dv_i^k|_2/\delta)}Dv_i^k\right)\right)^\mathsf{T} D\frac{\partial f}{\partial u_i^{k+0.5}} \tag{15}$$

$$\frac{\partial f}{\partial W} := \frac{\partial f}{\partial W} + \frac{\partial}{\partial W}\left(\frac{W}{\max(1, |\sqrt{W}Dv_i^k|_2/\delta)}Dv_i^k\right)^\mathsf{T} D\frac{\partial f}{\partial u_i^{k+0.5}} \tag{16}$$

$$\frac{\partial f}{\partial u_i^k} := \frac{\partial f}{\partial u_i^k} + \left(1 + \frac{t^{k-1}-1}{t^k}\right)\frac{\partial f}{\partial v_i^k} \tag{17}$$

$$\frac{\partial f}{\partial u_i^{k-1}} := -\frac{t^{k-1}-1}{t^k}\frac{\partial f}{\partial v_i^k}. \tag{18}$$

Here, we use the outer products in (15, 16) to achieve a compact notation. In our implementation, we exploit the extreme sparsity of the resulting matrix.

Most of the above lines are a direct application of the chain rule, however, we briefly show how to arrive at (16). Looking at a single gradient of index l, $\frac{\partial f}{\partial W_l}$, the chain rule suggests that $\frac{\partial f}{\partial W_l} = \sum_k \left(\frac{\partial f}{\partial u_i^{k+0.5}} \right)^{\mathsf{T}} \frac{\partial u_i^{k+0.5}}{\partial W_l}$ and $\frac{\partial u_i^{k+0.5}}{\partial W_l} = D^{\mathsf{T}} \left(\frac{\partial}{\partial W_l} \frac{W}{\max(1,|\sqrt{W}Dv_i^k|_2/\delta)} \right) Dv_i^k$. While this justifies our summation over the iterations, we also observe that $\frac{\partial}{\partial W_l} (\frac{W}{\max(1,|\sqrt{W}Dv_i^k|_2/\delta)})$ is the zero matrix except at indices l and $l+1$, where we assume wlog. that $l+1$ indicates the co-dimension of the diffusion tensor at the pixel. If we let W_l^{l+1} denote the 2×2 submatrix at row and column indices $l, l+1$ of the diagonal matrix $\frac{W}{\max(1,|\sqrt{W}Dv_i^k|_2/\delta)}$, we find $\frac{\partial f}{\partial W_l} = \left((D\frac{\partial f}{\partial u_i^{k+0.5}})_l^{l+1} \right)^{\mathsf{T}} \left(\frac{\partial}{\partial W_l} W_l^{l+1} \right) (Dv_i^k)_l^{l+1}$, which equals $\frac{\partial f}{\partial W}$ of (16) at the respective index l. Finally, note that the matrix in (15) also has non-zero entries for – in backward direction – horizontal and vertical neighbors of a pixel.

Algorithmically backpropagation works as follows. Our checkpoint variables are u_i^k and v_i^k from which we recover all $u_i^{k+0.5}$ and v_i^k for a whole stage. Given $\frac{\partial f}{\partial u^K}$, we once apply (12–14) to initialize $\frac{\partial f}{\partial u^{K-0.5}}$ along with $\frac{\partial f}{\partial u_i}$ and $\frac{\partial f}{\partial c}$. Per iteration k we already know $\frac{\partial f}{\partial u^{k+0.5}}$, $u_i^{k-0.5}$ and v_i^k and can execute Eqs. 15–18 followed by Eqs. 12–14 for iteration number $k-1$ to recover $\frac{\partial f}{\partial u^{K-0.5}}$ and we can continue with the next iteration by repeating these steps. Because $\frac{\partial f}{\partial u_i^{k-1}}$ from (18) is required in (17) the values have to be kept in memory for one iteration.

The TGV case (2) is slightly more involved, but the derivations are similar. Discretization leads to the objective:

$$\min_{u_i} \min_{w_i=(w_{i,0},w_{i,1})^{\mathsf{T}}} \|\sqrt{W}(Du_i-w_i)\|_\delta + \beta(\|Dw_{i,0}\|_\delta + \|Dw_{i,1}\|_\delta) + \|u_i - \hat{u}_i\|_c, \quad (19)$$

with auxiliary variables $w_{i,j} \in \mathbb{R}^{NM}$, $i,j \in \{0,1\}$. We define the operator $B : \mathbb{R}^{3NM} \to \mathbb{R}^{6NM}$ by stacking the linear operations in (19) into a single mapping and likewise define the matrices $V_\beta : \mathbb{R}^{6NM} \to \mathbb{R}^{6NM}$ and $V : \mathbb{R}^{6NM} \to \mathbb{R}^{6NM}$. With I denoting the identity mapping, $I : \mathbb{R}^{4NM} \to \mathbb{R}^{4NM}$, we define V_β by stacking the W and βI into a single diagonal matrix. To construct V we omit the multiplication of the unit matrix I with β. As before, the Lipshitz constant $L = \max(12, 8\beta)$ is incorporated into the operators V_β and V and the respective gradient $\frac{\partial f}{\partial V_\beta}$ is adjusted; again we return $L\frac{\partial f}{\partial V_\beta}$. Then the forward path becomes:

$$(u_i^{k+0.5}, w_i^{k+1})^{\mathsf{T}} := (v_i^k, q_i^k)^{\mathsf{T}} - B^{\mathsf{T}} \frac{V_\beta}{\max(1,|\sqrt{V}B(v_i^k,q_i^k)^{\mathsf{T}}|_2/\delta)} B(v_i^k, q_i^k)^{\mathsf{T}} \quad (20)$$

$$u_i^{k+1} := \begin{cases} u_i^{k+0.5} - c & \text{if } u_i^{k+0.5} - c > \hat{u}_i \\ u_i^{k+0.5} + c & \text{if } u_i^{k+0.5} + c < \hat{u}_i \\ \hat{u}_i & \text{else} \end{cases} \quad (21)$$

$$(v_i^{k+1}, q_i^{k+1})^{\mathsf{T}} := (u_i^{k+1}, w_i^{k+1})^{\mathsf{T}} + \frac{t^k - 1}{t^{k+1}}((u_i^{k+1}, w_i^{k+1})^{\mathsf{T}} - (u_i^k, w_i^k)^{\mathsf{T}}), \quad (22)$$

The complete backward path for TGV inpainting is presented in the supplementary material. Algorithmically we operate in the same manner as described for the TV case. In both cases we set δ to 0.1. Please note that instead of learning a single scalar β, the algorithm can be extended to learn a pixel-wise diffusion tensor that operates on the auxiliary variables w_0, w_1 in (19).

Hierarchical Optimization. Although we do not experience problems when training our network for 10K iterations at full resolution, a simple hierarchical strategy proves to be more efficient. At first we solve (8) at a lower resolution, using down-sampled versions of c, W and $\hat{u}$ to initialize u^0. At the next level c, W and $\hat{u}$ are set accordingly, but u^0 is initialized by up-sampling the solution of the coarser level. Requiring fewer iterations at the finest level, this strategy accelerates the optimization. Here, we use 3 levels with 2K, 2K and 4K iterations.

2.6 Training

We start with the feature generation and pretrain this part of the network. Apart from the log-likelihood term (4), our loss function also considers the quad-fitting procedure. Given the ground-truth flow $\mathbf{u}^*$, we define the loss function

$$L_{\mathrm{cor}}(\hat{u}_0, \hat{u}_1) := \sum_{(x,y)\in\Omega} \log p_0(x, y, u_0^*) + \log p_1(x, y, u_1^*) + \alpha \min(1, |\hat{\mathbf{u}} - \mathbf{u}^*|_\epsilon), \quad (23)$$

where we use $\epsilon = 0.01$ for the Huber-norm and define the lookup by rounding the continuous $\mathbf{u}^*$ and set $\alpha = 0.1$. Further, we use the up-sampled softmax probabilities in (23) and take care to not pass the gradients implied by the quad-fit through to the arg min lookup and correlation volume. Equipped with a trained and, in this work from now, fixed feature generation part, we further train the rest of the network by measuring the Huber-norm w.r.t. the ground truth. We set our displacement range to $d = 96$ in each direction and note that it is effectively doubled, due to our striding/quad-fitting methodology. All our trainings are run on full images without down-sampling or cropping the input.

3 Evaluation

We train our networks with the Theano package [33] on a machine equipped with a NVIDIA Titan X GPU with 12 GB of RAM. Our training data consists of either the artificial Sintel data set [7] or both of the KITTI [13, 22] data sets. KITTI targets an automotive setting and provides real world scenes, but only sparse and approximately correct ground truth. When training on Sintel we use 441 of the 1041 images for training and use the other images for validation and evaluation. The KITTI data is divided in a similar manner. An implementation of our custom layers (quad-fitting, TV/TGV inpainting) can be found online[1].

Memory and Runtime. Overall our network has 450K parameters. Training the feature generation on full sized Sintel images requires 4 GB, the same amount is used for training the full inpainting network with backpropagation disabled for

---

[1] https://github.com/vogechri/CustomNetworkLayers.

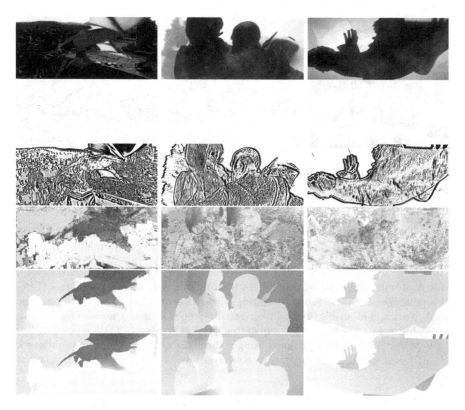

Fig. 3. Example results from the Sintel training data set [7]. From top to bottom: input image I^0, confidence c, horizontal component of the diffusion tensor W, arg min solution, solution after the optimization layer and the ground truth.

the pretrained part. In both cases, most of the memory is used by the correlation volumes, despite min-projection and down-sampling. A full joint training is left for future work. Our optimization layer proves to be a lightweight contribution to the network, requiring only additional 600 MB of GPU memory at training time. A forward pass of the network requires 0.4 s on a full sized image.

3.1 Qualitative Evaluation

We show a few results in Fig. 3 for the TV based inpainting on Sintel and in Fig. 4 for our TGV model on KITTI. The hard Sintel examples lead to a noisy arg min solution (4th row) and confident pixels (2nd row) are rare. The network appears to prefer only few correct matches, which in turn demands many iteration to spread the information. For the simpler left example the confident pixels outline the image and arg min-flow edges (zoom in). Interestingly, compressive inpainting models [8] also prefer those kind supporting matches for their diffusion process. Those appear to possess the highest information content. The KITTI examples

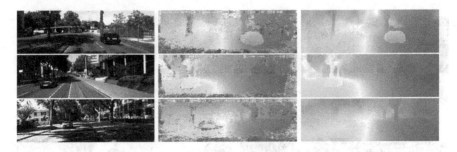

Fig. 4. *Left*: example from the KITTI training set [22]. *Middle*: the arg min solution, û, used as input to the optimization layer. *Right*: our inpainted solution (TGV variant).

possess less sharp edges than the results on Sintel. We suspect the sparse ground truth, lacking information at object edges, to cause this phenomenon.

Table 1. Results on the Sintel training set (final). Displayed are end-point error (EPE) and percentage of outliers (Out), deviating >3 pixels from the ground truth for unoccluded (Noc) and all pixels (Occ). Investigated methods include *Quad-fit*: results after the quadratic fit, *TV-Model*: TV inpainting (1), *TGV-Model*: TGV inpainting (2), $n \times$ *TV-Model*: TV inpainting trained using n times the default number of iterations in (9-11), L_2^2-*Reg*: quadratic regularizer, L_2^2-*All*: quadatric on confidence and regularizer.

Model	EPE (Noc)	>3px. (Noc)	EPE (Occ)	>3px. (Occ)
Quad-fit	11.27	17.16%	-	-
TV-Model	1.64	7.63%	2.48	10.29 %
TGV-Model	1.81	7.79%	2.68	10.42 %
$0.1\times$ TV-Model	3.11	10.01%	5.69	13.79 %
L_2^2-Reg.(TV)	2.21	8.38%	3.02	11.06 %
L_2^2-All (TV)	2.56	9.29%	3.70	12.23 %

3.2 Quantitative Evaluation

We start with the results for the Sintel data set in Table 1. The TV-model can improve the 'matching only' solution after quad fitting by a significant amount. TGV performs about 10% worse than TV. Note that for TGV more correct matches (3) are required to inpaint an affine motion in a segmented region than for TV (only 1). Training a TV-model with 10 times less iterations leads to significantly worse results. We observe that the higher the number of iterations, the sparser the confidence can be chosen; in other words, the stricter the selection becomes. Finally, we also investigate if it is worthwhile to use a robust, non-smooth energy model or whether a linear model, as used in, e.g., [3] already suffices. In the fifth row we replace the Huber norm in (1) with a quadratic

Table 2. Results on the Kitti training set. Investigated methods include. *TGV-Model*: TGV inpainting (2). *bi-Laplacian*: Inpainting based bi-Laplacian described in the text.

Model	Noc				Occ			
	EPE	3px	4px	5px	EPE	3px	4px	5px
TGV-Model	1.73	8.16%	6.33%	5.26 %	3.36	12.83%	10.52%	9.06 %
TV-Model	1.85	9.90%	7.71%	6.36 %	6.93	23.53%	19.43%	16.53 %
bi-Laplacian	2.19	10.42%	8.07%	6.53 %	4.17	15.70%	12.97%	11.38 %

Table 3. Results on the Sintel [7] (final) and KITTI [22] test sets. Displayed are end-point error (EPE) for Sintel and percentage of outliers for KITTI. Investigated methods include our submissions *(TV)* and *(TGV)* and related methods from the benchmark.

	(TV)	(TGV)	[17]	[40]	[28]	[15]	[20]	[32]	[27]
[7] EPE (Noc)	2.70	-	2.77	2.79	3.06	2.62	2.4	2.4	4.5
[7] EPE (Occ)	6.12	-	5.62	6.04	6.29	5.73	5.4	5.0	8.4
[22] % >3px. (Noc)	-	10.8	10.3	13.6	16.7	12.4	5.5	5.1	26.7
[22] % >3px. (Occ)	-	15.6	18.8	22.8	26.3	21.2	9.4	7.9	35.1

term. In the last row we introduce the square also on the ℓ_1 term in (1). The results gradually worsen the smoother the energy becomes. The complete linear model delivers results that are about 50% worse. The network seems unable to compensate the lost robustness via diffusion tensor and confidence map alone.

On KITTI (Table 2) the TV based model cannot compete with the piecewise affine TGV model. We also compare inpainting with the robust TGV model (2) with a well studied bi-Laplacian model: $\arg\min_{u_i} \int_\Omega |W^{\frac{1}{2}}\Delta u_i|_2^2 + c|u_i - \hat{u}_i|_2^2 \mathrm{d}x$, $i = 0, 1$, where Δ is the Laplacian matrix. Again the linear model performs worse than our robust model, trailing its results by about 20%.

Table 3 compares our submitted models with a selection of inpainting based competitors on the official test set of both benchmarks. At first we notice a significant performance drop for both benchmarks, compared to the training set. On KITTI our network outperforms all three inpainting models Epic-Flow [17, 28] and the inpainting network of [40] by a large amount, although all either employ an affine model [17, 28] or can learn one [40]. Our method even outperforms [15], who process the cost volume with a MRF model, before using [28] for inpainting. On Sintel our model performs on par or better than competing methods, but only for non occluded regions. Measuring all pixels our method trails [17] and [15]. However, recall that [17] starts from a much better initial flow [19] that is already on par with our approach in this metric. In fact many methods on the benchmark are not stand-alone, but utilize some well performing model for initialization or employ multiple post-processing steps. Here, our optimization layer could serve as a differentiable inpainting algorithm within a larger network.

Our model trails the current state-of-the-art [20,32] as shown Table 3. Yet, we use 10 [20] or 17 [32] times less parameters. Even [27] uses more than twice the number of parameters and clearly performs worse. Further, our model is minimalistic by design, employs no post-processing and can be used as complementary step for other methods, i.e. by replacing our initial flow $\hat{u}$ with theirs.

4   Conclusion

We proposed a simple model for the accurate inpainting of optical flow, using an interpretable network to deliver the inputs for an optimization stage. In the course of this work we proposed two non-custom layers, one for subpixel-refinement and one for optimization of our inpainting energy. For the latter, we showed that we can run and backpropagate through 10K iterations, which allows to accurately solve our energy problem. While the layer itself could be useful for various tasks, the lessons learned can also be transferred to similar problems.

In the future we would like include 3D cost volume filtering and train the full model end-to-end, including feature generation. Further we believe that learning a selection mechanism for a joint TV/TGV regularization will be of benefit.

References

1. Achanta, R., Shaji, A., Smith, K., Lucchi, A., Fua, P., Susstrunk, S.: SLIC superpixels compared to state-of-the-art superpixel methods. IEEE Trans. Pattern Anal. Mach. Intell. **34**, 2274–2282 (2012)
2. Agresti, G., Minto, L., Marin, G., Zanuttigh, P.: Deep learning for confidence information in stereo and tof data fusion. In: The IEEE International Conference on Computer Vision (ICCV) Workshops, October 2017
3. Barron, J.T., Poole, B.: The fast bilateral solver. In: Leibe, B., Matas, J., Sebe, N., Welling, M. (eds.) ECCV 2016. LNCS, vol. 9907, pp. 617–632. Springer, Cham (2016). https://doi.org/10.1007/978-3-319-46487-9_38
4. Beck, A., Teboulle, M.: SIAM J. Imaging Sci. A fast iterative shrinkage-thresholding algorithm for linear inverse problems **2**, 183–202 (2009)
5. Bredies, K., Kunisch, K., Pock, T.: SIAM J. Imaging Sci. Total generalized variation **3**, 492–526 (2010)
6. Brox, T., Bruhn, A., Papenberg, N., Weickert, J.: High accuracy optical flow estimation based on a theory for warping. In: Pajdla, T., Matas, J. (eds.) ECCV 2004. LNCS, vol. 3024, pp. 25–36. Springer, Heidelberg (2004). https://doi.org/10.1007/978-3-540-24673-2_3
7. Butler, D.J., Wulff, J., Stanley, G.B., Black, M.J.: A naturalistic open source movie for optical flow evaluation. In: Fitzgibbon, A., Lazebnik, S., Perona, P., Sato, Y., Schmid, C. (eds.) ECCV 2012. LNCS, vol. 7577, pp. 611–625. Springer, Heidelberg (2012). https://doi.org/10.1007/978-3-642-33783-3_44
8. Chen, T., Xu, B., Zhang, C., Guestrin, C.: Training deep nets with sublinear memory cost. CoRR abs/1604.06174 (2016)
9. Chen, Y., Ranftl, R., Pock, T.: A bi-level view of inpainting - based image compression. CoRR abs/1401.4112 (2014)

10. Dollár, P., Zitnick, C.L.: Structured forests for fast edge detection. In: CVPR, ICCV 2013, pp. 1841–1848. IEEE (2013)
11. Dosovitskiy, A., et al.: FlowNet: learning optical flow with convolutional networks. In: ICCV (2015)
12. Galić, I., Weickert, J., Welk, M., Bruhn, A., Belyaev, A., Seidel, H.P.: Image compression with anisotropic diffusion. J. Math. Imaging Vis. **31**(2), 255–269 (2008). https://doi.org/10.1007/s10851-008-0087-0
13. Geiger, A., Lenz, P., Urtasun, R.: Are we ready for autonomous driving? In: CVPR (2012)
14. Griewank, A., Walther, A.: Algorithm 799: revolve: an implementation of checkpointing for the reverse or adjoint mode of computational differentiation. ACM Trans. Math. Softw. **26**(1), 19–45 (2000)
15. Güney, F., Geiger, A.: Deep discrete flow. In: Lai, S.-H., Lepetit, V., Nishino, K., Sato, Y. (eds.) ACCV 2016. LNCS, vol. 10114, pp. 207–224. Springer, Cham (2017). https://doi.org/10.1007/978-3-319-54190-7_13
16. Hu, X., Mordohai, P.: A quantitative evaluation of confidence measures for stereo vision. IEEE Trans. Pattern Anal. Mach. Intell. **34**(11), 2121–2133 (2012)
17. Hu, Y., Li, Y., Song, R.: Robust interpolation of correspondences for large displacement optical flow. In: CVPR. IEEE (2017)
18. Hu, Y., Song, R., Li, Y.: Efficient coarse-to-fine patchmatch for large displacement optical flow. In: The IEEE Conference on Computer Vision and Pattern Recognition (CVPR), June 2016
19. Hu, Y., Song, R., Li, Y.: Efficient coarse-to-fine patchmatch for large displacement optical flow. In: CVPR. IEEE (2016)
20. Hui, T.W., Tang, X., Change Loy, C.: Liteflownet: a lightweight convolutional neural network for optical flow estimation. In: CVPR (2018)
21. Ilg, E., Mayer, N., Saikia, T., Keuper, M., Dosovitskiy, A., Brox, T.: Flownet 2.0: evolution of optical flow estimation with deep networks. In: CVPR (2017)
22. Menze, M., Geiger, A.: Object scene flow for autonomous vehicles. In: CVPR (2015)
23. Munda, G., Shekhovtsov, A., Knöbelreiter, P., Pock, T.: Scalable full flow with learned binary descriptors. In: Roth, V., Vetter, T. (eds.) GCPR 2017. LNCS, vol. 10496, pp. 321–332. Springer, Cham (2017). https://doi.org/10.1007/978-3-319-66709-6_26
24. Nesterov, Y.: A method of solving a convex programming problem with convergence rate $O(\frac{1}{k^2})$. Sov. Math. Dokl. **27** (1983)
25. Peter, P., Hoffmann, S., Nedwed, F., Hoeltgen, L., Weickert, J.: From optimised inpainting with linear PDEs towards competitive image compression codecs. In: Bräunl, T., McCane, B., Rivera, M., Yu, X. (eds.) PSIVT 2015. LNCS, vol. 9431, pp. 63–74. Springer, Cham (2016). https://doi.org/10.1007/978-3-319-29451-3_6
26. Poggi, M., Tosi, F., Mattoccia, S.: Quantitative evaluation of confidence measures in a machine learning world. In: ICCV, October 2017
27. Ranjan, A., Black, M.J.: Optical flow estimation using a spatial pyramid network. In: CVPR (2017)
28. Revaud, J., Weinzaepfel, P., Harchaoui, Z., Schmid, C.: Epicflow: edge-preserving interpolation of correspondences for optical flow. In: CVPR. IEEE (2015)
29. Rhemann, C., Hosni, A., Bleyer, M., Rother, C., Gelautz, M.: Fast cost-volume filtering for visual correspondence and beyond. In: CVPR, pp. 3017–3024. IEEE (2011)

30. Riegler, G., Rüther, M., Bischof, H.: ATGV-Net: accurate depth super-resolution. In: Leibe, B., Matas, J., Sebe, N., Welling, M. (eds.) ECCV 2016. LNCS, vol. 9907, pp. 268–284. Springer, Cham (2016). https://doi.org/10.1007/978-3-319-46487-9_17
31. Rudin, L.I., Osher, S., Fatemi, E.: Nonlinear total variation based noise removal algorithms. Phys. D Nonlinear Phenom. **60**, 259–268 (1992)
32. Sun, D., Yang, X., Liu, M.Y., Kautz, J.: PWC-Net: CNNs for optical flow using pyramid, warping, and cost volume. In: CVPR (2018)
33. Theano Development Team: Theano: a Python framework for fast computation of mathematical expressions. CoRR (2016)
34. Vogel, C., Pock, T.: A primal dual network for low-level vision problems. In: Roth, V., Vetter, T. (eds.) GCPR 2017. LNCS, vol. 10496, pp. 189–202. Springer, Cham (2017). https://doi.org/10.1007/978-3-319-66709-6_16
35. Wang, S., Fanello, S.R., Rhemann, C., Izadi, S., Kohli, P.: The global patch collider. In: CVPR. IEEE, July 2016
36. Weinzaepfel, P., Revaud, J., Harchaoui, Z., Schmid, C.: DeepFlow: large displacement optical flow with deep matching. In: ICCV. IEEE, Sydney, December 2013
37. Werlberger, M., Trobin, W., Pock, T., Wedel, A., Cremers, D., Bischof, H.: Anisotropic Huber-L1 optical flow. In: BMVC (2009)
38. Yu, F., Koltun, V.: Multi-scale context aggregation by dilated convolutions. In: ICLR (2016)
39. Zheng, S., et al.: Conditional random fields as recurrent neural networks. In: ICCV (2015)
40. Zweig, S., Wolf, L.: InterpoNet, a brain inspired neural network for optical flow dense interpolation. In: CVPR, pp. 6363–6372 (2017)

Learning Background Subtraction by Video Synthesis and Multi-scale Recurrent Networks

Sungkwon Choo, Wonkyo Seo, Dong-ju Jeong, and Nam Ik Cho[✉]

Seoul National University, Seoul, Korea
{chewry,cusisi,jeongdj}@ispl.snu.ac.kr, nicho@snu.ac.kr

Abstract. This paper addresses the moving objects segmentation in videos, *i.e. Background Subtraction* (BGS) using a deep network. The proposed structure learns temporal associativity without losing spatial information by using the convolutional Long Short-Term Memory (LSTM). It learns the spatial relation by forming various-size spatial receptive fields through the various scale recurrent networks. The most serious problem in training the proposed network is that it is very difficult to find or make a sufficient number of pixel-level labeled video datasets. In order to overcome this limitation, we generate many training frames by combining the annotated foreground objects from some available datasets with the background of the target video. The contribution of this paper is to provide the first multi-scale recurrent networks for the BGS, which works well for many kinds of surveillance videos and provides the best performance in CDnet 2014 which is widely used for the BGS testing.

Keywords: Background subtraction · Convolutional LSTM ·
Video augmentation

1 Introduction

Background Subtraction (BGS) is one of video understanding tasks, which is to find areas of moving objects in a video. This task is similar to video object segmentation, but BGS focuses on segmenting *moving* objects from *stationary* background while general video object segmentation focuses on finding any (predefined) objects regardless of background properties. Hence, the BGS is more suited for security applications where camera is fixed. It also is focused on developing methods to find the exact regions of moving objects which need to be robust to camera jitters and background clutters (such as randomly moving leaves due to the wind, waves in the water, or flashing lights at night). Most of the existing BGS algorithms first learn background at the beginning of the video. Then, they classify the non-stationary areas as the foreground in the test phase, and update the background in an appropriate online manner.

© Springer Nature Switzerland AG 2019
C. V. Jawahar et al. (Eds.): ACCV 2018, LNCS 11366, pp. 357–372, 2019.
https://doi.org/10.1007/978-3-030-20876-9_23

Recently, deep convolutional neural networks (CNNs) have been tried in almost all fields of computer vision. They generally show superior performance to the previous non-CNN studies. Convolutional networks have also been tried for BGS or video segmentation [1,13,20,23,24,26], but they have some problems as follows:

1. Most deep learning methods use CNNs as the baseline architecture because the CNNs have been very successful in feature learning and image understanding tasks. Specifically, they tried the image-based (frame by frame) learning, by stacking the randomly shuffled (often unrelated) frames as the mini-batch. However, sequential movements cannot be learned by training the frames without temporal continuity.
2. There are some studies that attempted to learn the sequential information [13,24], but they also have some problems. In the case of [13], it uses the insufficient information to convey the state since there is only one BG model that is generated from an unsupervised method and fed to the network for the training. The structure that adds a convolutional LSTM at the end of the CNN structure is often used in other video applications [20,23], but only a partial experiment is presented in the case of applying this network for BGS.
3. There are also some problems with the training data. Since existing BGS datasets are prepared for unsupervised methods, there are not many datasets with pixel-level ground truth. Therefore, some supervised BGS learning algorithms use the test phase data for training and evaluated the results without differentiating them. For practical use and also for fair comparisons, it is desired to consider cross-validation by splitting the video datasets into test/training ones or to learn the network by using the data out of the test datasets. Although there was a research [13] that proceeded as the former method (cross-validation), they did not show the validation results in the experiments. The latter method (using the totally different video sets for the training) is ideal, but there is not enough sequentially annotated data. Also, it is difficult to supplement video annotations because it requires much more efforts than the image annotations.

In order to overcome the above-stated problems, we propose a new network structure to learn sequential relations and a technique that can produce sufficient learning data. The contributions of this paper are as follows.

1. A multi-scale convolutional LSTM structure with various spatiotemporal receptive fields is proposed. Since the moving objects in a video experience various types of spatial and temporal changes, the network must have a structure that can learn such variations. In the proposed method, a convolutional LSTM is arranged for each scale by modifying an encoder-decoder model that spatially covers a wide range. Through skip connections which connect the layers of the same scale, the stacked recurrent neural network can have flexible temporal receptive fields to learn both spatial and temporal associations.
2. We propose a method to generate lucid synthetic videos that can be used as training data with minimum effort. Specifically, we generated a training

video by combining the background of the training frames with the foreground objects from the irrelevant dataset. As a result, it is possible to obtain rich data to train the network.

2   Related Work

The proposed structure uses the convolutional LSTM as a building block to keep the sequential and spatial information simultaneously. In order to train this structure for BGS, data augmentation which simulates real video is designed. This section describes the previous works related to our structure, data, and algorithm.

2.1   Dense Prediction

Dense prediction is to find the pixel-wise labels for a given image. In general image classification problems, it is important to grasp information of the entire image. Hence, the size of a feature is gradually reduced to make the receptive field larger, and finally the fully connected layer, which combines all the spatial regions, is arranged. Conversely, for the dense prediction, it is important to keep the local information at every scale and location. For this purpose, [14] proposed a method which uses only the convolutional layer (without the fully connected layer) for the first time. In this approach, it is necessary to preserve the feature size to achieve high accuracy. However, several studies have proposed encoder-decoder architectures [2,5,17] because learning with the CNN alone has some limitations due to a limited receptive field. These structures reduce the size of the feature in the encoder part to acquire a sufficient receptive field and then restore the size of the feature in the decoder part. Several studies have also been done to add skip connections to the symmetric layers [16,21] to further reduce the loss of information. The overall architecture of our method is in the form of the encoder-decoder structure, where each layer in our method is a recurrent network instead of plain convolutions.

2.2   Convolutional RNN

The convolutional RNN was developed for capturing the temporal relationship in addition to the spatial information. The convolutional RNN has been applied for many tasks [20,23,24], where the most common form is to append the RNN at the end of the pre-trained CNN. Since the CNN parts are already trained, the overall network usually converges fastly and yields some additional gain. However, since only one RNN layer is added at the end of the convolutional layer where the only high-level feature is left, it is difficult to accurately find a pixel-level result. In the case of [15], they utilized long temporal dependency of stacked RNN which learns low-level features directly through a raw image and predicted the next frame through unsupervised learning with an autoencoder structure. In [10], they proposed a recursive network for a single image through a feedback loop. This is different from our study because it is to improve the outcome through repeated inference on multiple tasks rather than learning about temporal associations. In our method, we also propose structural design which multi-scale RNNs directly view the raw image (not through the pre-trained CNN). In this design the pixel-level classification is performed through supervised learning of overall networks.

2.3 Image Synthesis for Data Augmentation

In recent video object segmentation researches [8,12], they developed a method to generate lucid synthetic images in order to compensate for the lack of training data. By training the network with synthetic data, they showed good results in the 2017 DAVIS Challenge on Video Object Segmentation [19]. In this approach, the foreground is extracted from the image of the labeled region, and the area is composited into the background-only image by inpainting. After generating pure foreground/background images, they can be combined with arbitrary image transforms to create an annotated image dataset that simulates various situations. They also generated optical flows for a pair of composite images, allowing the network to learn both types of information. Their composite images and optical flows can be used for the training of deep convolutional networks, but a pair of images (two frames) is not enough for training the recurrent networks. Hence, we propose a video synthesis method that shows a plausible continuous motion of foreground objects.

2.4 Background Subtraction

Background subtraction algorithms have been developed for decades where most of them are unsupervised learning methods and a few are deep learning approaches. For the CDnet 2014 dataset, which is commonly used for the test of BGS algorithm, the best performing method is the STSOM algorithm [6], which is an unsupervised method using spatiotemporal self-organizing map (SOM). In this study, the SOMs learned by unsupervised learning are stacked so that they learn the background and the rest are filtered out as the foreground. SemanticBGS [4] also performs well by using semantic segmentation results learned through PSPNet [27] and the IUTIS-5 [3]. The IUTIS-5 is the algorithm that also shows high performance for the CDnet 2014 [25], which actually is the ensemble of 5 different algorithms. In [13], they proposed a supervised method using a structure that appends a decoder to the VGG-19. The pixel-level mask can be obtained through the decoder and the background is updated to adapt it to the changing scenery. The network proposed in [26] learns the foreground/background with a sliding window input and a binary labeled output pair. It shows near-human labeling accuracy, but the training data is manually selected from the timeline of videos and the remaining frames are used as the test data. For the first time, we train a network in a supervised manner without any information about the test phase.

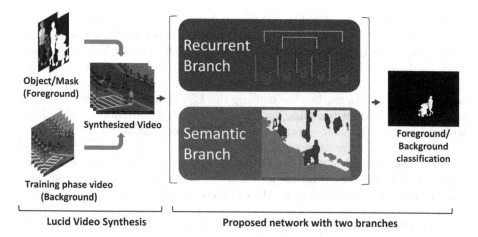

Fig. 1. Overview of the proposed network. In the video synthesis on the left, stationary background video (from CDnet 2014 dataset) and annotated foreground objects (from DAVIS 2016 [18] dataset) are synthesized. The proposed network is trained to classify each pixel of the synthesized video through the recurrent and semantic branches. The recurrent branch is constructed by stacking multi-scale convolutional LSTMs. In the semantic branch, the DeepLabv3+ trained for the ADE20K dataset [28, 29] is used for the semantic prediction

3 Proposed Method

3.1 Architecture

The overview of the proposed method is shown in Fig. 1 and Algorithm 1. The proposed structure can be divided into two branches. The recurrent branch learns the spatiotemporal information by stacking the convolutional LSTM in the form of multi-scale encoder-decoder. The semantic branch extracts visual information from each frames. The tensors of the two branches are piled in the original resolution of the image and classified as foreground/background according to the softmax value at each pixel. We can create a binary label through our augmentation, but it is not possible to synthesize semantic and optical flow labels with unlabelled training phase video. Hence, the semantic branch is also trained for Background Subtraction. The pre-trained network DeepLabv3+ [5] is used for network initialization. If we train the entire branch, the network is not well trained because it has much more parameters than other branches. We have added only bottleneck part to trainable parameters in the network. This method allows the network to transmit necessary information without degrading performance of feature extraction and refinement. In the experiment, we use pre-trained parameters for ADE20K dataset [28, 29].

The architecture of the recurrent branch is the encoder-decoder structure which is widely used for dense prediction. Each layer consists of convolutional LSTMs instead of CNNs. In the layers of the encoder section, the spatial size of the output is reduced by half, so the spatial receptive field is widened. In the layer of the decoder section, spatial size of the output is doubled to increase the resolution of the result. Furthermore, the output of the encoder having the same shape as the shape of the decoder portion is stacked so that necessary information is not lost due to space reduction and layer depth. We use asymmetric kernels to reduce computational burden because the LSTM requires 4 times as many parameters and more computation than the conventional convolutional layer with the same depth. Through this decomposition, the convolutional LSTM layer can obtain the same receptive field with complexity of $O(2/k)$ against original $k \times k$ convolution operation, where k is kernel size. To avoid the effect of kernel order and direction, we compute all cases exists to obtain the gates and cells. The asymmetrical convolution for the cell state update can be expressed as

$$g = \left[\mathrm{sigm}(W_{k \times 1}^{g,0} * W_{1 \times k}^{g,0} * [x_t; h_{t-1}^l]); \mathrm{sigm}(W_{1 \times k}^{g,1} * W_{k \times 1}^{g,1} * [x_t; h_{t-1}^l]) \right]. \quad (1)$$

where g is for input, output, forget gates and for new cell state, sigm is replaced by tanh. Since each asymetric kernel is different, we have numbered them to avoid ambiguity.

The recurrent branch is made with 5 convolutional LSTM layers which are shallower than widely used networks such as ResNet [7] and VGG [22]. Deep structures have advantages in learning high-level features in images. However, in the case of BGS, a shallow network is suggested because it is important to understand the changes at raw pixel-level. From the extensive experiments, we decided that constructing the branch with only recurrent networks is more stable and provides good performances. Thus, our structure consisting only of recurrent networks is close to the general stacked RNNs except for the spatial dimension. Ours also have a long temporal dependency which is an advantage of a stacked recurrent structure. We design the network to have 16, 64, 128 hidden units at each depth in the encoder and the decoder is designed to be symmetrical to this.

As a prior, we provide a median image of the training phase videos. The temporal median operation selects middle value at each pixel location from a sequence of images. It provides a stationary region for a video. Before learning, the temporal median image is calculated and fed to the network as a stacked tensor with each video frame.

3.2   Augmentation

As a way to train the proposed structure, we synthesize the videos by referring to the Lucid Data Dreaming method [8] mentioned in Sect. 2.3. For generating lucid *sequential* data by expanding this method, we propose a modified synthesis method with additional annotation and consecutive parameters.

Unlike the video object segmentation task, BGS dataset does not provide a labeled pair for the first frame but instead provides a video section called training phase. This video section has a relatively small foreground, but not all of it is background area. Since both the foreground and the background are not explicitly given, it is impossible to synthesize the correct training data from

Algorithm 1. Foreground/Background Classification

Input: Sequential *images* of the video, previous *states* of the convolutional LSTMs
Output: Updated *states*, pixel-level foreground/background *logitBinary*

1: **function** BACKROUNDSUBTRACT(*images, states*)
2:     *logitSemantic* ← semanticBranch(*images*)
3:     *net* ← *images*
4:     **for** i ← 1 to $nEncLayer$ **do**
5:         *net*, *states*$_{enc,i}$ ← convLSTM$_{enc,i}$(*net*, *states*$_{enc,i}$)   ▷ stride=2
6:         *skip*$_i$ ← *net*
7:     **end for**
8:     **for** i ← $nDecLayer$ to 1 **do**
9:         *net* ← resizeBilinear(*net*)   ▷ ratio=2
10:         *net*, *states*$_{dec,i}$ ← convLSTM$_{dec,i}$(*net*, *states*$_{dec,i}$)
11:         *net* ← concatenate(*net*, *skip*$_i$)   ▷ skip connetions
12:     **end for**
13:     *net* ← transposeConv(*net*)   ▷ stride=2
14:     *net* ← concatenate(*net*, *logitSemantic*)
15:     *net* ← convolution(*net*)   ▷ pixel-wise
16:     *logitBinary* ← pixelwiseSoftmax(*logit*)
17:     **return** *states*, *logitBinary*
18: **end function**

these alone. We solve this problem by acquiring the foreground and background with external data. First, annotated objects in the Densely Annotated Video Segmentation (DAVIS) 2016 dataset [18], are used as the artificial foreground. For the background, we find intervals with only a background in the training phase videos and use only these annotated intervals for synthesis. This is the only part of our method that requires additional effort by the user.

Using the foreground/background obtained above, we synthesize the video with continuous motion. The background region comes directly from the sequential frame of the training phase, and the foreground F with mask M is put on the background sequence B_t with the consecutive transform parameter T_t for smooth motion. The *similarity transform* is used to transform the scale, rotation, and translation. The motion of the synthesized video I_t is not realistic, but it provides spatiotemporal variations similar to the real video through non-stationary objects and stationary backgrounds in the view of the local region. In order to simulate various motions sufficiently, the synthesized frames are generated on-the-fly through random parameters without precomputing. The synthesis is expressed as

$$I_t = B_t \odot (1 - M) + T_t(F) \odot M. \tag{2}$$

Fig. 2. An example of the video synthesis. Red boundaries outline the ground truth segments. Since characteristics of the foreground are not taken into account in the synthesis process, the videos that do not fit the situation is generated (a ship on the snow road), but the object and the background are distinguished from each other. In the generated videos, the foreground moves continuously. Note that the background is moving in every frame, but is stationary relative to the foreground (Color figure online)

3.3   Two Stage Training Procedure

The proposed method carries out a two-step training process. In the first stage (Stage I), all synthesized data is used as a training set to train the network. Training at the first stage shows good performance on average for all the videos. However, since the videos of the dataset have very different noise and color characteristics, training them at once is a halfway learning to satisfy all the videos.

To compensate for this, we add separate training for each of the videos to make the network learn scene-specific characteristics. In the second stage, the network is initialized to the learned state of the previous step, and only synthesized data of the target sample is learned. This method is also referred to as *video fine-tuning* and has the advantage of being able to adapt the network by learning new videos which may be different from the video of the dataset.

There is an experiment [8] that training with a specific video shows better segmentation results than training with multiple scenes. However, they trained only with two adjacent frames without a recurrent network. However, the network trained with a video is not helpful for inferring other videos. On the other hand, since the proposed structure is trained with a long range of consecutive frames, it can learn motion information which can be helpful even for the visually different videos.

The optimizer for the training is Adam [9] and the learning rate is $1e-4$. The classification loss is measured by binary cross entropy. By setting a time step to 20, the recurrent networks can learn longer associations by backpropagation through time (BPTT). Experiments on the effect of time step length are presented in Table 3, where it can be seen that the performance decreases with short time step. The network is trained about 40,000 loops in 20 sequential frames at a time and the network parameter is selected to be the best performance in the last few states. Since large memory is required for containing 20 frames to train, the input size is decimated to 320×240 and the BGS results are interpolated back to the original size.

In the second stage of the training, the learning rate of $1e - 5$, which is lower than the first stage, is used to limit the deviation from the trained parameters at the first stage. Here, we train with a loop of about $1/100$ in the first stage. Although scene-specific training can be performed in the same way as in the first stage, we train with different learning rate of the recurrent branch and the other parts, taking into account that the distribution of visual and kinetic characteristics between videos is different. The visual characteristics of the foreground and background are that their features do change significantly between the videos, regardless of their motion. Changing the trained parameters (by training a network for another specific video) can make the network to forget the general visual feature and miss a foreground withe similar appearance of a specific background. However, the motion characteristics of the background tend to vary from video to video, and is hardly changed in the synthesized video created with the training phase and later in the test phase. Therefore, scene-specific training for the recurrent networks helps to increase the performance. The learning rate for the parameters of the semantic bottleneck is set to 100 times smaller value. If the bias-corrected first moment of θ is $\hat{m}$ and second order moments is $\hat{v}$, then the update formulas for each parameter of the recurrent, semantic branches are as follows:

$$\theta_{recurrent} \leftarrow \theta_{recurrent} + \frac{\eta}{\sqrt{\hat{v}_{recurrent}} + \epsilon} \hat{m}_{recurrent} \tag{3}$$

$$\theta_{semantic} \leftarrow \theta_{semantic} + 0.01 \cdot \frac{\eta}{\sqrt{\hat{v}_{semantic}} + \epsilon} \hat{m}_{semantic}. \tag{4}$$

In the course of scene-specific learning, it is found that the performance for the "thermal" video and "turbulence" in CDnet 2014 becomes significantly lower than before. This phenomenon is due to the fact that these videos consist of gray images, whereas the synthetic foreground objects are color. To ensure proper training, we need to set the synthetic objects also gray images when the target video is a gray one.

4   Experiments

4.1   Evaluation

For the evaluation, we use the CDnet 2014 dataset as it contains diverse videos and thus has been used in most of existing BGS researches. This dataset has 53 videos classified into 11 categories. The category is a classification of videos according to the situation in which the BGS is vulnerable. It is helpful to identify the tendency of the technique in each condition. To be specific, in the CDnet 2012, which is the previous version of 2014, there are 6 categories: *baseline* which contains the easiest cases where foreground is easily distinguished from the background, *dynamic background* (DynamicBg.) which contain somewhat moving backgrounds such as water and leaves due to the wind, *camera jitter* means the camera is shaking, *intermittent object motion* (Intermit.ObjectMotion) which contains go-stop objects, *shadow* has strong shadows of objects, and *greyscale* thermal video. In CDnet 2014, 5 categories are added to the dataset. The added categories consist of the videos of *bad weather*, *low frame rate*, *night scene*, *pan-tilt-zoom* (PTZ) camera moving a wide range of angles, and *turbulent* situation, in which the shape of the object is hard to recognize. Among the categories of CDnet 2014, PTZ is excluded because our network is to learn the background and thus covering the PTZ may need additional techniques. To be precise, the recurrent branch of our network is a shallow one which is designed to learn only the locally stationary regions. Also, making a synthetic training set for the dynamically changing background needs more efforts, and thus we leave the research on the dynamic background as a future work.

Unlike the training process, the test uses stateful LSTM which is the opposite of stateless LSTM, by leaving the LSTM cell and state uninitialized for one batch and the next. Because the learning process does not know whether the state being passed is correct, training to deliver it can be adversely affected by performance. However, in the test procedure, if the previous state is not conveyed, it is necessary to perform a redundant operation with a sliding window inference like the convolution operation, and there is a disadvantage that only a short interval information is obtained. Through the stateful method, the proposed network can transmit the state from the beginning to the end of the video and perform the fast test without repetitive operations. In addition to training, we test with multiple scaled inputs, which are often used in semantic segmentation, to further enhance the performance. Robust results can be obtained over various sizes of objects through the input of various sizes. In multi-scale testing, inputs are scaled to $0.5\times$, $1\times$, and $1.75\times$ of the input size (320×240) used in the training. We also perform experiments with dense conditional random field (DenseCRF) [11] to refine the result. However, since the video used in the experiment has low resolution, a lot of noise and compression artifacts, it is difficult to obtain additional gain using the edges, and post-processing with DenseCRF degrades the performance. The results are summarized in the Table 1. We will make the code and results of our network publicly available[1] for further researches.

4.2   Comparison

As in the Table 1, there are various metrics for BGS evaluation. In most studies, the criterion for evaluating the performance of the BGS algorithm is the

---

[1] https://github.com/chewry7/MSRNN.

Table 1. Results of the proposed network on the CDnet 2014 benchmark dataset. In addition to the F-measure, performance is measured with Precision, Recall, Specificity, False Positive Rate (FPR), False Negative Rate (FNR), Percentage of Wrong Classifications (PWC).

Category/Metric	Recall	Specificity	FPR	FNR	PWC	Precision	F-measure
Baseline	0.9962	0.9981	0.0019	0.0038	0.1964	0.9265	0.9595
DynamicBg	0.9300	0.9990	0.0010	0.0700	0.1507	0.9018	0.9135
CameraJitter	0.9042	0.9983	0.0017	0.0958	0.4921	0.9545	0.9246
Intermit.ObjectMotion	0.8790	0.9966	0.0034	0.1210	0.8079	0.8760	0.8717
Shadow	0.9885	0.9973	0.0027	0.0115	0.3074	0.9267	0.9557
Thermal	0.8256	0.9959	0.0041	0.1744	1.1420	0.8745	0.8483
BadWeather	0.8931	0.9982	0.0018	0.1069	0.3276	0.8943	0.8874
LowFramerate	0.8767	0.9978	0.0022	0.1233	0.4516	0.8174	0.8435
NightVideos	0.7516	0.9803	0.0197	0.2484	2.5312	0.5313	0.5576
Turbulence	0.7552	0.9994	0.0006	0.2448	0.1332	0.8868	0.7998
Overall	0.8800	0.9961	0.0039	0.1200	0.6540	0.8590	0.8562

average F-measure for each category. This metric is useful for evaluating the robustness of algorithms in various situations, rather than measuring the performance of each video. We also compare the performance based on this metric. Performance comparisons with other methods are shown in Table 2. The performance of the first stage training (Stage I) is also presented. The performance of the proposed methods is measured by the multi-scale test. The results of not performing a multi-scale test are also shown in Table 3. All the cases in the table are the results of algorithms that do not use data from the test phase at all. The results of the proposed network show the best overall performance. The proposed method outperforms STSOM [6], which is the state-of-the-art, by 1.39% on the F-measure, and is 4.30% better than the next best method. Our overall performance is also better than combining the best performance of three algorithms (IUTIS-5 [3], SemanticBGS [4], STSOM [6]).

The proposed method has increased performance in several categories without significant performance degradation through scene-specific learning. The order of categories with significant performance improvements is lowFramerate, dynamicBackground, intermittentObjectMotion, and cameraJitter. There is no particular difference in the image quality or the appearance of the object when looking at the commonality of these categories compared to the baseline, but as the name suggests, they are videos that show global or local movements different from the baseline. In contrast, shadow, thermal, badWeather, nightVideos, and turbulence are challenging videos that are difficult to distinguish between the background and the foreground visually, but the motion of objects is a simple pattern of moving at a constant speed. This performance

Table 2. Results on CDnet 2014 benchmark comparing with the state-of-the-art method. Average F-measure of each category is shown. The metrics of other methods are from each paper. Note that only our results are tested on multi-scale.

Category/Method	IUTIS-5	SemanticBGS	STSOM	Stage I	Proposed	Difference
Baseline	0.9567	0.9604	0.9576	0.9511	0.9595	+0.0084
DynamicBg	0.8902	0.9489	0.9235	0.8499	0.9135	+0.0636
CameraJitter	0.8332	0.8388	0.8881	0.8949	0.9246	+0.0297
Intermit.ObjectMotion	0.7296	0.7878	0.8357	0.8408	0.8717	+0.0309
Shadow	0.9084	0.9478	0.9003	0.9609	0.9557	−0.0052
Thermal	0.8303	0.8219	0.8488	0.8404	0.8483	+0.0079
BadWeather	0.8289	0.8260	0.8926	0.8879	0.8874	−0.0005
LowFramerate	0.7911	0.7888	0.8125	0.7067	0.8435	+0.1368
NightVideos	0.5132	0.5058	0.5631	0.5617	0.5576	−0.0041
Turbulence	0.8507	0.6921	0.8009	0.7847	0.7998	+0.0151
Overall	0.8132	0.8118	0.8423	0.8279	**0.8562**	+0.0283

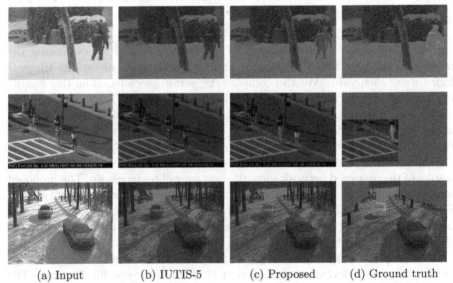

(a) Input   (b) IUTIS-5   (c) Proposed   (d) Ground truth

Fig. 3. The qualitative comparison of the IUTIS-5 and our network. Each row shows a single frame result from the videos, which are skating (BadWeather), sidewalk (cameraJitter), winterDriveway (intermittentObjectMotion)

enhancement demonstrates that scene-specific learning adapts the network to match the motion characteristics of the video.

In addition to the quantitative comparison, the resulting images are also compared in Fig. 3. Only the results of IUTIS-5 are compared because the resulting images of STSOM and SemanticBGS are not fully available.

4.3   Ablation Study

This section describes the experimental results and results of variants of the proposed architecture to analyze which elements of the proposed structure affect the results. Ablation has proceeded from several perspectives. In order to investigate whether the proposed stacked convolutional LSTM structure is useful for continuous information learning, we experiment by changing the number of recurrent layers. Based on the proposed 5 convolutional LSTM structure, the LSTM layer is removed symmetrically from the far side of the bottleneck. The removed recurrent layer has been replaced by a convolution network with the same kernel so that the overall scale and parameters do not differ significantly. By removing the convolutional LSTMs from the network with this removal method, the number of LSTMs is reduced to 3, 1, 0. We summarize the experiment by using the number of LSTM as LSTM item in the Table 3. Regardless of whether the semantic information is used or not, the performance improvement is the largest in a network where one recurrent network is added compared to a network without a recurrent layer. It can be interpreted that the LSTM structure improves the performance through the temporal association learning that CNNs can not. However, stacking the LSTMs does not always improve the performance. In the experiment using semantic information, performance increases continuously as more convolutional LSTM is accumulated. Conversely, in the experiments without semantic information, performance increases up to 1 LSTM and performance decreases as LSTM accumulates. To analyze this phenomenon, more experiments are needed. It is assumed that the learning performance for the spatial feature is limited as the convolutional LSTM accumulates and substitutes the CNN because the temporal and spatial information should be grasped only by the shallow network in the absence of the semantic branch. These ablation experiments of the recurrent network and time step confirm that the proposed multi-scale recurrent networks, under the condition that the visual and global information is assisted, learn the complex temporal associations of videos at the deeper depth with the longer time step.

Next, we measure the performance difference caused by removing each branch and confirm their influences. In the experiment of removing the recurrent branch, only the learning of the semantic bottleneck and 1×1 pixel-wise convolution results in a high classification result for some simple videos. Conversely, when we remove the semantic branch and experiment with various conditions for the recurrent branch, all experiments show the better performance than experiments using only the semantic branch. This result supports that low-level features are better suited for the background subtraction than high-level features.

We experiment with additional training on the seen foreground to see how the training of the test phase images, like the existing supervised learning, would improve the performance. Experiments are carried out in the same way as the proposed method by replacing the foreground for video synthesis with one object picked in the test phase. This approach obviously improves the performance much better than a method that does not use test video information for learning at all. In our experiments, we can also see that the performance is improved by synthesizing one of the forthcoming objects. If we use multiple objects in the test phase for synthesis, the network will be able to learn more foreground ahead of time, which will increase the performance gain.

Table 3. Ablation study of training variants. ✓ in LSTM means the proposed 5 layers convolutional LSTM. The result of training with synthesized video of the foreground of the test phase (Seen foreground) is also presented.

Aspect	Variant	LSTM	Semantic	Time step	Finetune	Multi-scale	F-measure
Ours		✓	✓	20	✓	✓	0.8562
		✓	✓	20	✓	✗	0.8391
No fine-tuning		✓	✓	20	✗	✓	0.8279
		✓	✓	20	✗	✗	0.8102
Recurrent depth	3 ConvLSTM	3	✓	20	✗	✗	0.7983
	1 ConvLSTM	1	✓	20	✗	✗	0.7942
	Fully conv	0	✓	20	✗	✗	0.7543
	3 ConvLSTM	3	✗	20	✗	✗	0.7268
	1 ConvLSTM	1	✗	20	✗	✗	0.7616
	Fully conv	0	✗	20	✗	✗	0.6609
Branch	No recurrent	✗	✓	20	✗	✗	0.6349
	No semantic	✓	✗	20	✗	✗	0.6839
Time step	10 frames	✓	✓	10	✗	✗	0.7691
Seen foreground (1 object)		✓	✓	20	✓	✓	0.8728
		✓	✓	20	✗	✓	0.8543

5   Conclusions

In this paper, we have proposed multi-scale recurrent networks for background subtraction in video sequences, as well as a video synthesis method which can enrich the training dataset for deep learning based video applications. The proposed multi-scale RNNs learn the complex temporal associations of the videos while preserving its spatial size. Also, by modifying the existing synthesis method to fit the video task, the proposed video synthesis allows the training of the network by generating rich, continuous frames without using test data. This approach is the first supervised training method that can be compared with the same criteria as the existing algorithms, and it shows the best performance on the benchmark dataset (CDnet 2014).

Acknowledgement. This research was supported in part by Projects for Research and Development of Police science and Technology under Center for Research and Development of Police science and Technology and Korean National Police Agency (PA-C000001), and in part by Institute for Information & communications Technology Promotion (IITP) grant funded by the Korea government (MSIT) (No. 1711075689, Decentralised cloud technologies for edge/IoT integration in support of AI applications).

References

1. Babaee, M., Dinh, D.T., Rigoll, G.: A deep convolutional neural network for video sequence background subtraction. Pattern Recogn. **76**, 635–649 (2018)
2. Badrinarayanan, V., Kendall, A., Cipolla, R.: Segnet: a deep convolutional encoder-decoder architecture for image segmentation. IEEE Trans. Pattern Anal. Mach. Intell. **39**, 2481–2495 (2017)
3. Bianco, S., Ciocca, G., Schettini, R.: How far can you get by combining change detection algorithms? In: Battiato, S., Gallo, G., Schettini, R., Stanco, F. (eds.) ICIAP 2017. LNCS, vol. 10484, pp. 96–107. Springer, Cham (2017). https://doi.org/10.1007/978-3-319-68560-1_9
4. Braham, M., Piérard, S., Van Droogenbroeck, M.: Semantic background subtraction. In: IEEE International Conference on Image Processing (ICIP), Beijing, China, pp. 4552–4556, September 2017
5. Chen, L.C., Zhu, Y., Papandreou, G., Schroff, F., Adam, H.: Encoder-decoder with atrous separable convolution for semantic image segmentation. arXiv:1802.02611 (2018)
6. Du, Y., Yuan, C., Hu, W., Maybank, S.: Spatio-temporal self-organizing map deep network for dynamic object detection from videos. In: IEEE Conference on Computer Vison and Pattern Recognition 2017. IEEE Computer Society (2017)
7. He, K., Zhang, X., Ren, S., Sun, J.: Deep residual learning for image recognition. In: Proceedings of the IEEE Conference on Computer Vision and Pattern Recognition, pp. 770–778 (2016)
8. Khoreva, A., Benenson, R., Ilg, E., Brox, T., Schiele, B.: Lucid data dreaming for multiple object tracking. arXiv preprint arXiv:1703.09554 (2017)
9. Kingma, D., Ba, J.: Adam: a method for stochastic optimization. arXiv preprint arXiv:1412.6980 (2014)
10. Kong, S., Fowlkes, C.C.: Recurrent scene parsing with perspective understanding in the loop. In: The IEEE Conference on Computer Vision and Pattern Recognition (CVPR), June 2018
11. Krähenbühl, P., Koltun, V.: Efficient inference in fully connected CRFs with gaussian edge potentials. In: Advances in Neural Information Processing Systems, pp. 109–117 (2011)
12. Li, X., et al.: Video object segmentation with re-identification. In: The 2017 DAVIS Challenge on Video Object Segmentation - CVPR Workshops (2017)
13. Lim, K., Jang, W.D., Kim, C.S.: Background subtraction using encoder-decoder structured convolutional neural network. In: 2017 14th IEEE International Conference on Advanced Video and Signal Based Surveillance (AVSS), pp. 1–6. IEEE (2017)
14. Long, J., Shelhamer, E., Darrell, T.: Fully convolutional networks for semantic segmentation. In: Proceedings of the IEEE Conference on Computer Vision and Pattern Recognition, pp. 3431–3440 (2015)
15. Lotter, W., Kreiman, G., Cox, D.: Deep predictive coding networks for video prediction and unsupervised learning. arXiv preprint arXiv:1605.08104 (2016)
16. Mao, X., Shen, C., Yang, Y.B.: Image restoration using very deep convolutional encoder-decoder networks with symmetric skip connections. In: Advances in Neural Information Processing Systems, pp. 2802–2810 (2016)
17. Noh, H., Hong, S., Han, B.: Learning deconvolution network for semantic segmentation. arXiv preprint arXiv:1505.04366 (2015)

18. Perazzi, F., Pont-Tuset, J., McWilliams, B., Van Gool, L., Gross, M., Sorkine-Hornung, A.: A benchmark dataset and evaluation methodology for video object segmentation. In: Computer Vision and Pattern Recognition (2016)

19. Pont-Tuset, J., Perazzi, F., Caelles, S., Arbeláez, P., Sorkine-Hornung, A., Van Gool, L.: The 2017 davis challenge on video object segmentation. arXiv:1704.00675 (2017)

20. Qiu, Z., Yao, T., Mei, T.: Learning deep spatio-temporal dependency for semantic video segmentation. IEEE Trans. Multimed. **PP**(99), 1 (2017)

21. Ronneberger, O., Fischer, P., Brox, T.: U-Net: convolutional networks for biomedical image segmentation. In: Navab, N., Hornegger, J., Wells, W.M., Frangi, A.F. (eds.) MICCAI 2015. LNCS, vol. 9351, pp. 234–241. Springer, Cham (2015). https://doi.org/10.1007/978-3-319-24574-4_28

22. Simonyan, K., Zisserman, A.: Very deep convolutional networks for large-scale image recognition. CoRR abs/1409.1556 (2014)

23. Tokmakov, P., Alahari, K., Schmid, C.: Learning video object segmentation with visual memory. In: ICCV (2017)

24. Valipour, S., Siam, M., Jagersand, M., Ray, N.: Recurrent fully convolutional networks for video segmentation. In: 2017 IEEE Winter Conference on Applications of Computer Vision (WACV), pp. 29–36. IEEE (2017)

25. Wang, Y., Jodoin, P.M., Porikli, F., Konrad, J., Benezeth, Y., Ishwar, P.: CDnet 2014: an expanded change detection benchmark dataset. In: Proceedings of the IEEE Conference on Computer Vision and Pattern Recognition Workshops, pp. 387–394 (2014)

26. Wang, Y., Luo, Z., Jodoin, P.M.: Interactive deep learning method for segmenting moving objects. Pattern Recogn. Lett. **96**(Suppl. C), 66–75 (2017)

27. Zhao, H., Shi, J., Qi, X., Wang, X., Jia, J.: Pyramid scene parsing network. In: The IEEE Conference on Computer Vision and Pattern Recognition (CVPR), July 2017

28. Zhou, B., Zhao, H., Puig, X., Fidler, S., Barriuso, A., Torralba, A.: Semantic understanding of scenes through the ADE20K dataset. arXiv preprint arXiv:1608.05442 (2016)

29. Zhou, B., Zhao, H., Puig, X., Fidler, S., Barriuso, A., Torralba, A.: Scene parsing through ADE20K dataset. In: Proceedings of the IEEE Conference on Computer Vision and Pattern Recognition (2017)

Universal Bounding Box Regression
and Its Applications

Seungkwan Lee, Suha Kwak, and Minsu Cho[✉]

Department of Computer Science and Engineering,
POSTECH, Pohang, Korea
{seungkwan,suha.kwak,mscho}@postech.ac.kr

Abstract. Bounding-box regression is a popular technique to refine or predict localization boxes in recent object detection approaches. Typically, bounding-box regressors are trained to regress from either region proposals or fixed anchor boxes to nearby bounding boxes of a pre-defined target object classes. This paper investigates whether the technique is generalizable to unseen classes and is transferable to other tasks beyond supervised object detection. To this end, we propose a class-agnostic and anchor-free box regressor, dubbed *Universal Bounding-Box Regressor* (UBBR), which predicts a bounding box of the nearest object from any given box. Trained on a relatively small set of annotated images, UBBR successfully generalizes to unseen classes, and can be used to improve localization in many vision problems. We demonstrate its effectiveness on weakly supervised object detection and object discovery.

Keywords: Bounding box regression · Transfer learning · Weakly-supervised object detection

1 Introduction

The recent advances in object detection have been driven mainly by the development of Deep Neural Networks (DNNs) [11,12,16,24,32–34]. Especially, one crucial component that allows DNNs to localize object bounding boxes precisely and flexibly is the Bounding Box Regressor (BBR) originally proposed in [12]. As a part of object detection networks, BBR refines off-the-shelf object proposals [11,12] or anchor boxes with fixed positions and aspect ratios [24,32,34] so that the refined ones localize nearby objects more accurately. For this purpose, BBRs are tightly coupled with other components of object detection networks, and trained to localize predefined object classes better. That is, they have been developed typically for supervised object detection where ground-truth bounding boxes for target classes are given.

This paper studies BBR in a direction different from the conventional one. Specifically, we propose a BBR model that is class-agnostic, even well generalizable to unseen classes, and transferable to multiple diverse tasks demanding accurate bounding box localization; we call such a model *Universal Bounding*

© Springer Nature Switzerland AG 2019
C. V. Jawahar et al. (Eds.): ACCV 2018, LNCS 11366, pp. 373–387, 2019.
https://doi.org/10.1007/978-3-030-20876-9_24

Box Regressor (UBBR). UBBR takes an image and any arbitrary bounding boxes, and refines the boxes so that they enclose their nearest objects tightly, regardless of their classes. The model with such a simple functionality can have a great impact on many applications since it is universal in terms of both object classes and tasks. An example of the applications is weakly supervised object detection where box annotations for target object classes are not given. In this setting, object bounding boxes tend to be badly localized due to the limited supervision [3,20,36], and UBBR can help to improve the performance by refining the localization results. In this case, UBBR can be considered as a knowledge transfer machine for bounding box localization. Also, UBBR can be used to generate object box proposals. Given boxes uniformly and densely sampled from image space, UBBR transforms them to approximate the boxes of their nearest objects, and the results are bounding boxes clustered around true object boxes. In this case, UBBR can be considered as learning-based object proposal methods [28,29,38].

This paper introduces a DNN architecture for UBBR and its training strategy. Our UBBR has a form of Convolutional Neural Networks (CNN), trained with randomly generated input boxes. It successfully generalizes to unseen classes, and can be used to improve localization in various computer vision problems, especially when bounding box supervision is absent. We demonstrate its effectivenss on weakly supervised object detection, object proposal generation, and object discovery. Main contribution of this paper is three-fold:

- We present a simple yet effective UBBR based on CNN, which is versatile and easily generalizable to unseen classes. We also present a training strategy to learn such a universal model.
- A single UBBR network achieves, or help to achieve, competitive performance in three different applications: weakly supervised object detection, object proposals, and object discovery.
- We provide an in-depth empirical analysis for demonstrating the generalizability of our UBBR for unseen classes.

The rest of this paper is organized as follows. Section 2 overviews previous approaches relevant to UBBR, and Sect. 3 presents technical details of UBBR and a strategy for training it. UBBR is then evaluated on three different localization tasks in Sect. 4, and we conclude in Sect. 5 with brief remarks.

2   Related Work

Conventional BBR in Object Detection: BBR has been widely incorporated into DNNs for object detection [11,12,24,32–34] for precise localization of object bounding boxes. Initially it was designed as a post-processing step to refine off-the-shelf object proposals boxes [11,12]. Recently, it directly estimates bounding boxes of nearby objects from each cell of an image grid [33], or aims to transform a fixed set of anchor boxes to cover ground-truth object boxes accurately [24,32,34]. Here the anchor boxes, also known as default boxes, are pre-defined bounding boxes that are sampled on a regular grid with a few selected scales and aspect ratios [24,33,34] or estimated from ground-truth object boxes of training data [32]. Thus those BBRs are trained to be well harmonized with other components of object detection networks, and are dependent on a few pre-defined object classes and characteristics of anchor boxes. On the other hand, our UBBR is designed and trained to be class-agnostic, transferable to unseen classes, and free from anchor boxes. These properties of UBBR allow us to apply it to multiple diverse applications demanding accurate bounding box localization, beyond the conventional object detection.

Object Proposal: Our UBBR is also closely related to object proposals since it naturally generates accurate object candidate boxes given uniformly sampled boxes as inputs. Well-known early approaches to object proposal are unsupervised techniques [18,26]. Motivated by the fact that typically an object box include a whole image segment rather than a part of it, they draw bounding boxes encompassing image segments obtained by hierarchical image segmentation methods. Since there is no supervision for object location and image segmentation results often fail to preserve object boundary, the unsupervised techniques are limited in terms of recall and localization accuracy. Supervised approaches for object proposals have been actively studied as well, and exhibited substantially better performance. Before the era of deep learning, there have been proposed object proposal techniques generating object candidate boxes [38] and masks [2], which are trained with object boundary annotations. Recently, Pinheiro et al. [28,29] introduce DNNs for generating and refining class-agnostic object candidate masks.

Learning-based proposals, including ours, require strong supervision in training. One may ask, if such bounding box annotations are given, why not directly learning an object detector instead of proposals? We would like to argue that the learning-based proposals are still valuable if they are class-agnostic, well generalizable to unseen classes, and universally applied to various applications. Note that existing datasets provide a huge amount of readily available annotations, especially for bounding boxes; there is no reason to avoid them when localizing objects of unseen classes in the context of transfer learning.

Transfer Learning for Visual Recognition: Oquab et al. [27] demonstrated that low-level layers of a CNN trained for a large-scale image classification can be transferred to classification in different domains or even different visual recognition tasks. Since that, transferring low-level image representation has been a common technique to avoid overfitting in various visual recognition tasks like object detection [11,12,16,24,32–34] and semantic segmentation [6,25,35]. While these approaches focus on transferring low-level image representation between different tasks, UBBR is to transfer the knowledge about *how to draw bounding boxes to enclose an object*. In that sense, UBBR also has a connection to TransferNet [15], which transfers the segmentation knowledge to object classes whose segmentation annotations are not available.

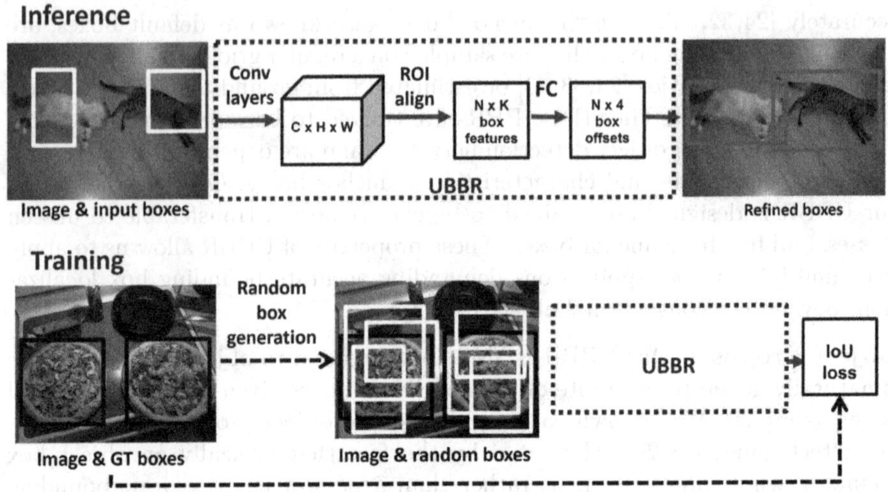

Inference

Image & input boxes   Refined boxes

Training

Image & GT boxes   Image & random boxes

Fig. 1. Illustration of UBBR's architecture. In inference time, the network takes an image with roughly localized bounding boxes and refine them so that they tightly enclose nearby objects. N is the number of input boxes and K is the dimensionality of box features. In training time, the network takes bounding boxes randomly generated around ground-truth boxes, and is learned to transform each input box so that Intersection-over-Union between the box and its nearest ground-truth is maximized.

3   Universal Bounding Box Regressor

3.1   Architecture

The architecture of UBBR is similar with conventional object detectors (*e.g.*, Fast R-CNN [11]) which consist of convolutional layers for feature representation, a region pooling layer for extracting region-wise features, and fully-connected layers for box classification and regression. Figure 1 illustrates training and inference stages of the UBBR network. The architecture first computes a feature map of an input image with the convolutional layers, and a feature vector of a fixed length is extracted for each input box through the RoI-Align layer [13]. Each of the extracted box features is then processed by 3 fully-connected layers to compute a 4-D real vector indicating the offset between the corresponding box and its nearest object. Note that UBBR is designed to use input boxes with arbitrary shapes and object classes unlike those of most conventional object detection networks [11,34]. Hence, the UBBR network is trained in a anchor-free and class-agnostic manner as will be described in the following.

3.2   Training

Dataset: Since UBBR predicts object boxes, it demands images with ground-truth object boxes during training, and any existing datasets for object detection

Fig. 2. Example of randomly generated bounding boxes for training UBBR. Black boxes are ground-truths and yellow ones are randomly generated boxes.

can meet the need. Note that since UBBR is class-agnostic, class labels of the box annotations are disregarded in our case.

Random Box Generation: UBBR takes as its inputs not only image but also (roughly localized) boxes that will be transformed to enclose nearby objects tightly. Thus, each training image has to be served together with such boxes. Furthermore, the boxes fed to the network during training should be diverse for universality of UBBR, but at the same time, have to be overlapped with at least one ground-truth to some extent so that UBBR can observe enough evidences about target object. To this end, in training time we generate input bounding boxes by applying random transformations to ground-truth boxes.

Let $g = [x_g, y_g, w_g, h_g]^\top$ denote a ground-truth box represented by its center coordinate (x_g, y_g), width w_g, and height h_g. Transformation parameters for the four values are sampled from uniform distributions independently as follows:

$$
\begin{aligned}
t_x &\sim \mathcal{U}(-\alpha,\ \alpha), \\
t_y &\sim \mathcal{U}(-\alpha,\ \alpha), \\
t_w &\sim \mathcal{U}(\ln 1 - \beta,\ \ln 1 + \beta), \\
t_h &\sim \mathcal{U}(\ln 1 - \beta,\ \ln 1 + \beta).
\end{aligned}
\tag{1}
$$

Then a random input box $b = [x_b, y_b, w_b, h_b]^\top$ is obtained by applying the sampled transformation to g:

$$
\begin{aligned}
x_b &= x_g + t_x \cdot w_g, \\
y_b &= y_g + t_y \cdot h_g, \\
w_b &= w_g \cdot \exp(t_w), \\
h_b &= h_g \cdot \exp(t_h).
\end{aligned}
\tag{2}
$$

Also, if Intersection-over-Union (IoU) between b and g is less than a pre-defined threshold t, we simply discard b during training. α and β are empirically set to 0.35 and 0.5 respectively. The effect of α, β, and t on the performance of UBBR is analyzed in the next section. Figure 2 shows examples of random box generation.

Loss Function: For the regression criterion, IoU loss [37] is employed instead of conventional ones like L_2 and smooth L_1 losses. The drawback of the conventional losses in bounding box regression is that the bounding box transformation

---

Algorithm 1. IoU loss

Input : Two bounding boxes $u = [x_u, y_u, w_u, h_u]^\top$, and $v = [x_v, y_v, w_v, h_v]^\top$
Output: loss $\mathcal{L}$
Function IoU-loss(u, v):

$A_u = w_u \cdot h_u$
$A_v = w_v \cdot h_v$
$I_w = \min(x_u + 0.5 \cdot w_u, \ x_v + 0.5 \cdot w_v) - \max(x_u - 0.5 \cdot w_u, \ x_v - 0.5 \cdot w_v)$
$I_h = \min(y_u + 0.5 \cdot h_u, \ y_v + 0.5 \cdot h_v) - \max(y_u - 0.5 \cdot h_u, \ y_v - 0.5 \cdot h_v)$
$I_w = \max(I_w, \ 0)$
$I_h = \max(I_w, \ 0)$
$I = I_w \cdot I_h$
$U = A_u + A_v - I$
$IoU = \frac{I}{U}$
$\mathcal{L} = -\ln(IoU + \epsilon)$
return $\mathcal{L}$

---

parameters (t_x, t_y, t_w, t_h) are optimized independently [37] although they are in fact highly inter-correlated. IoU loss has been proposed to address this issue, and we observed in our experiments that IoU loss allows training more stable and leads to better performance when compared to smooth L_1 loss.

The procedure for computing IoU loss between two bounding boxes is described in Algorithm 1, where A_u and A_v are the areas of u and v, and I_w and I_h means the width and height of their intersection area. Note that we add a tiny constant ϵ to IoU value before taking logarithm for numerical stability. The image-level loss is then defined as the average of box-wise regression losses as follows:

$$L_{\text{IoU}} = \frac{1}{N} \sum_{n=1}^{N} \text{IoU-loss}\Big(f\big(b_n, \text{UBBR}(b_n)\big), g_n\Big), \tag{3}$$

where b_n is an input box and g_n is the ground-truth bounding box that is best overlapped with b_n in terms of IoU metric. Also, $\text{UBBR}(b_n)$ is the offsets predicted by UBBR and f is the transformation function that refines b_n with the predicted offset parameters.

4   Experiment

In this section, we first describe implementation details, then demonstrate the effectiveness of our approach empirically in three tasks: weakly supervised object detection, object proposal, and object discovery.

4.1   Datasets

To demonstrate transferability of UBBR, we carefully define source and target domains. Basically, we employ COCO 2017 [23] as source and PASCAL VOC [10] as target. Then all images containing the 20 PASCAL VOC object categories are

Table 1. Average precision ($IoU > 0.5$) for weakly supervised object detection on PASCAL VOC 2007 test set. For baseline model, we train OICR using published code and extract detection results from it. We refer to this model as OICR-ours. t is IoU threshold for random box generation. The models trained with smooth L1 and IoU losses are denoted by UBBR-sl1 and UBBR-iou, respectively.

Method	aer	bik	brd	boa	btl	bus	car	cat	cha	cow	tbl	dog	hrs	mbk	prs	plt	shp	sfa	trn	tv	mAP
OICR-paper	58.0	62.4	31.1	19.4	13.0	65.1	62.2	28.4	24.8	44.7	30.6	25.3	37.8	65.5	15.7	24.1	41.7	46.9	64.3	62.6	41.2
OICR-ours(baseline)	61.2	64.6	41.3	24.1	10.4	65.7	62.3	32.6	23.1	48.0	35.3	29.3	43.8	63.9	14.1	24.0	41.3	50.5	61.1	61.1	42.9
OICR + UBBR-iou($t=0.5$)	66.0	58.0	50.8	31.3	17.9	71.1	66.6	47.7	26.2	59.1	40.6	40.6	54.8	63.4	23.3	25.3	51.1	57.7	68.0	66.3	49.3
OICR + UBBR-iou($t=0.3$)	66.3	56.9	53.9	32.4	22.4	71.3	67.3	53.4	25.5	60.0	40.4	47.0	61.6	64.0	28.3	25.5	51.4	61.1	67.7	67.6	51.2
OICR + UBBR-sl1($t=0.5$)	65.7	57.0	49.9	30.5	18.7	69.5	66.2	45.6	25.6	58.9	40.9	39.9	56.9	65.2	21.7	25.5	50.7	56.8	67.7	65.9	48.9
OICR + UBBR-sl1($t=0.3$)	65.2	52.1	53.7	30.3	22.2	71.4	66.8	52.6	23.6	60.5	37.5	47.1	61.9	63.7	27.3	24.4	51.4	58.5	69.3	66.2	50.3

Table 2. Performance improvement of iterative refinement.

Method	aer	bik	brd	boa	btl	bus	car	cat	cha	cow	tbl	dog	hrs	mbk	prs	plt	shp	sfa	trn	tv	mAP
OICR + UBBR($t=0.5$) 1 iter	66.0	58.0	50.8	31.3	17.9	71.1	66.6	47.7	26.2	59.1	40.6	40.6	54.8	63.4	23.3	25.3	51.1	57.7	68.0	66.3	49.3
OICR + UBBR($t=0.5$) 2 iter	63.9	50.4	53.8	32.1	23.3	73.3	66.9	52.6	25.9	59.4	38.1	47.3	58.6	62.7	27.0	23.2	55.2	60.2	68.6	66.3	50.7
OICR + UBBR($t=0.5$) 3 iter	59.9	48.3	55.4	34.9	24.6	73.8	66.8	60.7	25.5	63.5	35.1	51.4	59.5	62.9	31.0	22.0	56.1	60.8	69.6	66.2	51.4
OICR + UBBR($t=0.3$) 1 iter	66.3	56.9	53.9	32.4	22.4	71.3	67.3	53.4	25.5	60.0	40.4	47.0	61.6	64.0	28.3	25.5	51.4	61.1	67.7	67.6	51.2
OICR + UBBR($t=0.3$) 2 iter	63.2	47.2	55.2	33.8	27.4	71.7	67.5	67.9	24.0	62.6	33.1	58.6	63.2	63.4	35.7	19.1	52.9	58.3	67.8	63.9	51.8
OICR + UBBR($t=0.3$) 3 iter	59.7	44.8	54.0	36.1	29.3	72.1	67.4	70.7	23.5	63.8	31.5	61.5	63.7	61.9	37.9	15.4	55.1	57.4	69.9	63.6	52.0

removed from the COCO 2017. As a result, there remain 21,413 training images and 900 validation images of 60 object categories in the source domain dataset. Note that we train a single UBBR with the above dataset, and apply the model to all applications without task-specific finetuning.

4.2 Implementation Details

The training is carried out using stochastic gradient decent with momentum and weight decay. The momentum and weight decay multiplier are set to 0.9 and 0.0005, respectively. The learning rate initially starts from 10^{-3} and is divided by 10 when the validation loss stop improving. We stop the training when the learning rate become 10^{-6}. In all experiments, we employ ResNet101 [14] (upto conv4) pre-trained on ImageNet as backbone convolutional layers. The fully-connected layers are composed of three linear layers with ReLU activations. The weight parameters of fully connected layers are randomly initialized from zero-mean Gaussian distributions with standard deviation 0.001, and their biases are initialized to 0. For both training and testing, input images are rescaled using bilinear interpolation such that its shorter side becomes 600 pixels. We generate 50 random bounding boxes for each ground-truth object.

4.3 Weakly Supervised Object Detection

To demonstrate the effectiveness of UBBR, we apply our model as a post-processing module of weakly supervised object detection. The goal of weakly supervised object detection is to learn object detectors only with image-level class labels as supervision. Due to the significantly limited supervision, models

Iterative refinement

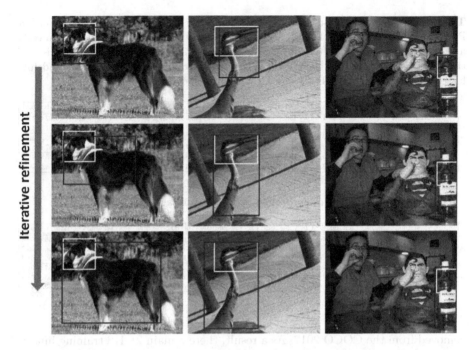

Fig. 3. Qualitative results of (OICR + UBBR) on PASCAL VOC 2007 test set. Yellow boxes are detection results of OICR and blue boxes are refined bounding boxes. From top to bottom, each row is the result of 1, 2, and 3 iterative refinement respectively. (Color figure online)

in this category often fail to localize the entire body of target object but cover only a discriminative part of it. Thus, UBBR can help to improve localization by refining bounding boxes estimated by weakly supervised object detection model. This setting also can be considered as transfer learning for weakly supervised object detection, where UBBR transfer the bounding box knowledge of source domain to target domain.

We use OICR [36] as a baseline model for weakly supervised object detection, and apply UBBR to the output of OICR. The quantitative analysis of the performance on PASCAL VOC 2007 is summarized in Table 1, in which one can see that UBBR improves the object localization quality substantially. We also validate the effect of the threshold t by applying UBBR models learned with two different values of t. In general, the model with a smaller t performs better than that with a larger t since UBBR is able to learn from more various and challenging box localization examples by decreasing t during training. Also, we report the performance of the models learned with conventional smooth L_1 loss. Figure 3 presents qualitative results of our approach.

Besides the above straightforward application of UBBR, we further explore ways to better utilize UBBR and provide more detailed analysis on its various aspects in the context of weakly supervised object detection as follows.

Fig. 4. Box refinement examples of bike class. Yellow boxes are detection results of OICR and blue boxes are refined bounding boxes. From top to bottom, each row is the result of 1, 2, and 3 iterative refinement respectively. Left three examples are failure cases, and right two examples are successful cases. (Color figure online)

Iterative Refinement: UBBR also can be applied multiple times iteratively so that localization is progressively improved. That is, for each iteration, bounding boxes refined in previous step are fed into the network again. Through this strategy, we can obtain better localization results. It is important to note that, for efficiency of overall procedure, we reuse the convolutional feature map of the backbone network. As can be seen in Table 2, we can further improve the localization performance by iterative refinement, and the effect was consistent up to the third iterations.

Limitation: As Table 1 shows, the quality of refined localization of *bike* class is worse than baseline. Furthermore, the iterative refinement makes the quality even worse as shown in Table 2. This means UBBR rather degrades localization of *bike* class, and we found that it is because of a side effect of the class-agnostic nature of UBBR. Figure 4 shows box refinement examples of *bike* class. Left three examples are failure cases, and right two examples are successful cases. Most of failure cases of *bike* class occur when there is a person riding the bike. Because UBBR predicts class-agnostic bounding box, it does not distinguish *bike* and *person* and recognizes them as a single object in the examples. As illustrated in two rightmost columns, when there is no person on the bike, it successfully localizes the bikes.

Generalizability: The previous experiments already validated that our approach is generalizable to unseen object classes of the target domain. To further

Table 3. Average precision ($IoU > 0.5$) for weakly supervised object detection on PASCAL VOC 2007 test set. COCO-60 is our main dataset excluding 20 categories from original COCO 2017 dataset. COCO-21 and COCO-40 are more reduced datasets which contain 21 and 40 categories respectively. COCO-full is the original COCO 2017 train set which contains 80 categories.

Method	aer	bik	brd	boa	btl	bus	car	cat	cha	cow	tbl	dog	hrs	mbk	prs	plt	shp	sfa	trn	tv	mAP
OICR-ours(baseline)	61.2	64.6	41.3	24.1	10.4	65.7	62.3	32.6	23.1	48.0	35.3	29.3	43.8	63.9	14.1	24.0	41.3	50.5	61.1	61.1	42.9
COCO-21(t=0.5)	65.2	66.6	46.0	31.2	19.2	67.0	65.7	36.6	26.3	51.5	35.7	32.9	49.5	66.0	16.1	25.0	43.6	56.2	62.0	65.1	46.4
COCO-21(t=0.3)	63.8	67.7	48.9	30.7	21.5	67.2	66.2	37.8	25.2	52.1	38.9	34.8	48.9	65.2	18.8	23.9	38.2	57.5	62.4	65.4	46.8
COCO-40(t=0.5)	65.4	65.9	50.6	30.7	18.8	66.9	65.7	44.4	26.2	55.1	38.8	36.8	54.1	66.4	17.8	24.8	46.9	56.1	63.7	63.9	48.0
COCO-40(t=0.3)	65.2	63.7	50.4	30.4	23.3	69.8	66.0	46.3	25.7	56.9	41.8	42.7	56.6	65.3	21.3	24.1	46.4	59.8	62.2	63.9	49.1
COCO-60(t=0.5)	66.0	58.0	50.8	31.3	17.9	71.1	66.6	47.7	26.2	59.1	40.6	40.6	54.8	63.4	23.3	25.3	51.1	57.7	68.0	66.3	49.3
COCO-60(t=0.3)	66.3	56.9	53.9	32.4	22.4	71.3	67.3	53.4	25.5	60.0	40.4	47.0	61.6	64.0	28.3	25.5	51.4	61.1	67.7	67.6	51.2
COCO-full(t=0.5)	66.4	64.5	51.4	34.2	19.7	72.0	67.0	47.7	26.3	56.9	41.4	38.7	57.0	65.5	26.8	26.4	50.7	56.5	70.8	64.4	50.2
COCO-full(t=0.3)	67.6	63.9	54.1	33.0	24.1	72.7	69.0	53.4	26.1	59.1	42.1	47.7	63.1	65.6	38.4	28.1	51.9	60.0	70.7	66.6	52.9

Table 4. Effect of box generation parameters α and β on the performance of weakly-supervised object detection. $\alpha = 0.35$ and $\beta = 0.5$ are used in all other experiments.

	$\beta = 0.35$	$\beta = 0.5$	$\beta = 0.65$
$\alpha = 0.25$	49.0	51.2	51.7
$\alpha = 0.35$	48.9	51.2	52.0
$\alpha = 0.45$	49.0	50.7	51.8

demonstrate the generalizability, we analyze the performance of UBBR models trained with even a smaller number of object classes. To this end, we build two additional training sets by reducing the number of object classes. COCO-40 is composed of 40 categories excluding animal, accessory, electronic, and appliance classes from the original training data. Also, COCO-21 consists of 21 classes and is obtained by further excluding furniture, indoor, and food classes from COCO-40. The original training dataset is denoted by COCO-60. Moreover, to eliminate the effect of dataset size, we make the sizes of COCO-40 and COCO-21 identical to that of COCO-60 by randomly sampling 21,413 images containing at least one object belonging to the categories of interest.

We report the performance of UBBRs learned with COCO-40 and COCO-21 in Table 3. Although the models trained with these datasets perform worse due to lack of diversity in their training data, they still improve localization performance substantially. An interesting observation is that they improve localization of animals although their training datasets do not include animal classes. The results indicate that UBBR can be generalizable to unseen and unfamiliar classes well. We also report the performance of UBBR models learned with full COCO 2017 train set, which is denoted by COCO-full and contains all PASCAL VOC classes. It is natural that UBBR trained with COCO-full outperforms the others, but their differences in performance are marginal.

Box Generation Parameters: The box generation parameter α and β are chosen empirically to generate diverse and sufficiently overlapped boxes. Table 4

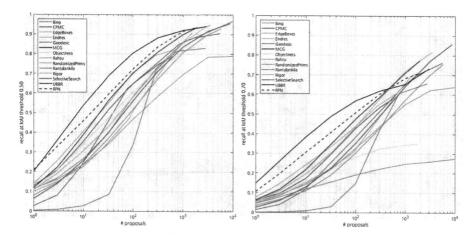

Fig. 5. Recall of box proposals on the PASCAL VOC 2007 test set. (*left*) recall@IOU = 0.5. (*right*) recall@IOU = 0.7.

shows how these parameters affect the performance of weakly-supervised object detection when t is 0.3. As shown in the table, the performance is not very sensitive to both parameters. In all other experiments, $\alpha = 0.35$ and $\beta = 0.5$ are used. Note that we did not optimize those parameters using the evaluation results.

4.4   Object Proposals

For the second application, we employ UBBR as a region proposal generator. Similarly to RPN [34], we generate seed bounding boxes of various scale and aspect ratio and locate them in image uniformly. We feed them into UBBR so that each seed bounding box encloses its nearest object. To select object proposals from the refined bounding boxes, we assign score s_n to each bounding box b_n. In assumption that the refined bounding boxes will be concentrated around real objects, s_n is initially set to the number of adjacent bounding boxes whose IoU with b_n is greater than 0.7. After that, we apply non-maximum suppression (NMS) with IoU threshold 0.6. In NMS procedure, instead of removing adjacent bounding boxes, we divide their scores by 10, which is similar to Soft-NMS [4]. In Fig. 5, performance of proposals generated by our method are quantified and compared with popular proposal techniques [1,2,5,7,9,17,18,21,26,30,31,38]. The performance of UBBR clearly outperforms previous methods in comparison. Note that unlike many other methods (except SelectiveSearch [18]), UBBR does not use any images from PASCAL object classes for training. We also evaluate RPN [34] in the same transfer learning scenario with ours, where we train RPN with COCO-60 dataset and evaluate it on PASCAL VOC dataset. Note that we use the same backbone network for both of RPN and UBBR. As shown in Fig. 5, UBBR outperforms RPN in particular with a tighter IOU criterion. Note

Fig. 6. Visualization of top-10 region proposals generated by the proposed method.

Table 5. Object discovery accuracy in CorLoc on PASCAL VOC 2007 trainval set.

Method	aer	bik	brd	boa	btl	bus	car	cat	cha	cow	tbl	dog	hrs	mbk	prs	plt	shp	sfa	trn	tv	Avg
Cho *et al.* [8]	50.3	42.8	30.0	18.5	4.0	62.3	64.5	42.5	8.6	49.0	12.2	44.0	64.1	57.2	15.3	9.4	30.9	34.0	61.6	31.5	36.6
Li *et al.* [22]	73.1	45.0	43.4	27.7	6.8	53.3	58.3	45.0	6.2	48.0	14.3	47.3	69.4	66.8	24.3	12.8	51.5	25.5	65.2	16.8	40.0
Ours	47.9	18.9	63.1	39.7	10.2	62.3	69.3	61.0	27.0	79.0	24.5	67.9	79.1	49.7	28.6	12.8	79.4	40.6	61.6	28.4	47.6

that the x axis of the figure starts from recall at 10^0 proposal rather than 10^1 proposals. Figure 6 presents qualitative examples of object proposals obtained by our method.

4.5   Object Discovery

For the last application, we choose the task of object discovery that aims at localizing objects from images. Since most of previous methods consider localization of a single foreground object per image, the object discovery can be viewed as an extreme case of object proposal generation where only top-1 proposals are used for evaluation. The correct localization (CorLoc) metric is an evaluation metric widely used in related work [8,19,22], and defined as the percentage of images correctly localized according to the PASCAL criterion: $\frac{area(b_p \cap b_{gt})}{area(b_p \cup b_{gt})} > 0.5$, where b_p is the predicted box and b_{gt} is the ground-truth box. For evaluation on the PASCAL VOC 2007 dataset, we follow to use all images in PASCAL VOC 2007 trainval set discarding images which only contain 'difficult' or 'truncated' objects. We report the performance in Table 5. The performance of UBBR significantly outperforms the previous approaches to object discovery [8,22], which implies that generic object information can be effectively learned by UBBR and transferred to the task of object discovery.

5 Conclusion

We have studied the bounding box regression in a novel and interesting direction. Unlike those commonly embedded in recent object detection networks, our model is class-agnostic and free from manually defined anchor boxes. These properties allow our model to be universal, well generalizable to unseen classes, and transferable to multiple diverse tasks demanding accurate bounding box localization. Such advantages of our model have been verified empirically in various tasks including weakly supervised object detection, object proposal, and object discovery.

Acknowledgements. This research was supported by Samsung Research and also by Basic Science Research Program through the National Research Foundation of Korea funded by the Ministry of Science, ICT (NRF-2018R1A5A1060031, NRF-2017R1E1A1A01077999).

References

1. Alexe, B., Deselaers, T., Ferrari, V.: Measuring the objectness of image windows. TPAMI **34**, 2189–2202 (2012)
2. Arbeláez, P., Pont-Tuset, J., Barron, J.T., Marques, F., Malik, J.: Multiscale combinatorial grouping. In: CVPR (2014)
3. Bilen, H., Vedaldi, A.: Weakly supervised deep detection networks. In: CVPR (2016)
4. Bodla, N., Singh, B., Chellappa, R., Davis, L.S.: Soft-NMS - improving object detection with one line of code. In: ICCV (2017)
5. Carreira, J., Sminchisescu, C.: CPMC: automatic object segmentation using constrained parametric min-cuts. TPAMI **34**, 1312–1328 (2012)
6. Chen, L.C., Papandreou, G., Kokkinos, I., Murphy, K., Yuille, A.L.: DeepLab: semantic image segmentation with deep convolutional nets, atrous convolution, and fully connected CRFs. TPAMI **40**, 834–848 (2017)
7. Cheng, M.M., Zhang, Z., Lin, W.Y., Torr, P.: BING: binarized normed gradients for objectness estimation at 300fps. In: CVPR (2014)
8. Cho, M., Kwak, S., Schmid, C., Ponce, J.: Unsupervised object discovery and localization in the wild: part-based matching with bottom-up region proposals. In: CVPR (2015)
9. Endres, I., Hoiem, D.: Category-independent object proposals with diverse ranking. TPAMI **36**, 222–234 (2014)
10. Everingham, M., Van Gool, L., Williams, C.K., Winn, J., Zisserman, A.: The pascal visual object classes (VOC) challenge. IJCV **88**, 303–338 (2010)
11. Girshick, R.: Fast R-CNN. In: ICCV (2015)
12. Girshick, R., Donahue, J., Darrell, T., Malik, J.: Rich feature hierarchies for accurate object detection and semantic segmentation. In: CVPR (2014)
13. He, K., Gkioxari, G., Dollár, P., Girshick, R.: Mask R-CNN. In: ICCV (2017)
14. He, K., Zhang, X., Ren, S., Sun, J.: Deep residual learning for image recognition. In: CVPR (2016)
15. Hong, S., Oh, J., Han, B., Lee, H.: Learning transferrable knowledge for semantic segmentation with deep convolutional neural network. In: CVPR (2016)

16. Huang, J., et al.: Speed/accuracy trade-offs for modern convolutional object detectors. In: CVPR (2017)
17. Humayun, A., Li, F., Rehg, J.M.: Rigor: reusing inference in graph cuts for generating object regions. In: CVPR (2014)
18. Uijlings, J.R., van de Sande, K.E., Gevers, T., Smeulders, A.: Selective search for object recognition. IJCV **104**, 154–171 (2013)
19. Joulin, A., Tang, K., Fei-Fei, L.: Efficient image and video co-localization with frank-wolfe algorithm. In: Fleet, D., Pajdla, T., Schiele, B., Tuytelaars, T. (eds.) ECCV 2014. LNCS, vol. 8694, pp. 253–268. Springer, Cham (2014). https://doi.org/10.1007/978-3-319-10599-4_17
20. Kantorov, V., Oquab, M., Cho, M., Laptev, I.: ContextLocNet: context-aware deep network models for weakly supervised localization. In: Leibe, B., Matas, J., Sebe, N., Welling, M. (eds.) ECCV 2016. LNCS, vol. 9909, pp. 350–365. Springer, Cham (2016). https://doi.org/10.1007/978-3-319-46454-1_22
21. Krähenbühl, P., Koltun, V.: Geodesic object proposals. In: Fleet, D., Pajdla, T., Schiele, B., Tuytelaars, T. (eds.) ECCV 2014. LNCS, vol. 8693, pp. 725–739. Springer, Cham (2014). https://doi.org/10.1007/978-3-319-10602-1_47
22. Li, Y., Liu, L., Shen, C., van den Hengel, A.: Image co-localization by mimicking a good detector's confidence score distribution. In: Leibe, B., Matas, J., Sebe, N., Welling, M. (eds.) ECCV 2016. LNCS, vol. 9906, pp. 19–34. Springer, Cham (2016). https://doi.org/10.1007/978-3-319-46475-6_2
23. Lin, T.Y., et al.: Microsoft COCO: common objects in context. In: Fleet, D., Pajdla, T., Schiele, B., Tuytelaars, T. (eds.) ECCV 2014. LNCS, vol. 8693, pp. 740–755. Springer, Cham (2014). https://doi.org/10.1007/978-3-319-10602-1_48
24. Liu, W., et al.: SSD: single shot multibox detector. In: Leibe, B., Matas, J., Sebe, N., Welling, M. (eds.) ECCV 2016. LNCS, vol. 9905, pp. 21–37. Springer, Cham (2016). https://doi.org/10.1007/978-3-319-46448-0_2
25. Long, J., Shelhamer, E., Darrell, T.: Fully convolutional networks for semantic segmentation. In: CVPR (2015)
26. Manen, S., Guillaumin, M., Van Gool, L.: Prime object proposals with randomized prim's algorithm. In: ICCV (2013)
27. Oquab, M., Bottou, L., Laptev, I., Sivic, J.: Learning and transferring mid-level image representations using convolutional neural networks. In: CVPR (2014)
28. Pinheiro, P.O., Collobert, R., Dollár, P.: Learning to segment object candidates. In: NIPS (2015)
29. Pinheiro, P.O., Lin, T.-Y., Collobert, R., Dollár, P.: Learning to refine object segments. In: Leibe, B., Matas, J., Sebe, N., Welling, M. (eds.) ECCV 2016. LNCS, vol. 9905, pp. 75–91. Springer, Cham (2016). https://doi.org/10.1007/978-3-319-46448-0_5
30. Rahtu, E., Kannala, J., Blaschko, M.: Learning a category independent object detection cascade. In: ICCV (2011)
31. Rantalankila, P., Kannala, J., Rahtu, E.: Generating object segmentation proposals using global and local search. In: CVPR (2014)
32. Redmon, J., Farhadi, A.: Yolo9000: better, faster, stronger. In: CVPR (2017)
33. Redmon, J., Divvala, S., Girshick, R., Farhadi, A.: You only look once: unified, real-time object detection. In: CVPR (2016)
34. Ren, S., He, K., Girshick, R., Sun, J.: Faster R-CNN: towards real-time object detection with region proposal networks. In: NIPS (2015)
35. Simonyan, K., Zisserman, A.: Very deep convolutional networks for large-scale image recognition. In: ICLR (2015)

36. Tang, P., Wang, X., Bai, X., Liu, W.: Multiple instance detection network with online instance classifier refinement. In: CVPR (2017)
37. Yu, J., Jiang, Y., Wang, Z., Cao, Z., Huang, T.: Unitbox: an advanced object detection network. In: ACMMM (2016)
38. Zitnick, C.L., Dollár, P.: Edge boxes: locating object proposals from edges. In: Fleet, D., Pajdla, T., Schiele, B., Tuytelaars, T. (eds.) ECCV 2014. LNCS, vol. 8693, pp. 391–405. Springer, Cham (2014). https://doi.org/10.1007/978-3-319-10602-1_26

Continuous-Time Stereo Visual Odometry Based on Dynamics Model

Xin Wang[1,2(✉)], Fei Xue[1,2], Zike Yan[1,2], Wei Dong[3], Qiuyuan Wang[1,2], and Hongbin Zha[1,2(✉)]

[1] Key Laboratory of Machine Perception (MOE), School of EECS,
Peking University, Beijing, China
{xinwang_cis,feixue,wangqiuyuan}@pku.edu.cn, zha@cis.pku.edu.cn
[2] Cooperative Medianet Innovation Center, Shanghai Jiao Tong University,
Shanghai, China
yanzike@hrbeu.edu.cn
[3] Robotics Institute, Carnegie Mellon University, Pittsburgh, USA
weidong@andrew.cmu.edu

Abstract. We propose a dynamics model to represent the camera trajectory as a continuous function of time and forces. Equipped with such a representation, we convert the classical visual odometry problem to analyzing the forces applied to the camera. In contrast to the classical discrete-time estimation strategy, the continuous nature of the camera motion is inherently revealed in the framework, and the camera motion can be simply modeled with only few parameters within time intervals. The dynamics model guarantees the continuous velocity, and hence assures a smooth trajectory, which is robust against noise and avoiding the pose vibration. Evaluations on real-world benchmark datasets show that our method outperforms other continuous-time methods.

1 Introduction

Visual odometry (VO) [25] estimates camera poses using image sequences captured by a camera. Camera pose is essential for many applications, e.g., autonomous driving and augmented reality. Most methods only estimate camera pose of each frame at the discrete timestamp [4,15]. While in the real world, camera trajectory can be continuous in space. Indeed, it can be modeled as a continuous function of time [11,17]. For simplicity, we denote the former method as 'discrete-time methods', and the latter as 'continuous-time methods'.

Camera motion abides by physical laws. The motion states and positions of neighbor frames are interrelated. Classical discrete-time methods ignore the dynamics constraints between adjacent frames and solve the camera poses separately. Solving the VO problem as a camera trajectory estimation problem is

This work is supported by the National Natural Science Foundation of China (61632003, 61771026), and National Key Research and Development Program of China (2017YFB1002601).

C. V. Jawahar et al. (Eds.): ACCV 2018, LNCS 11366, pp. 388–403, 2019.
https://doi.org/10.1007/978-3-030-20876-9_25

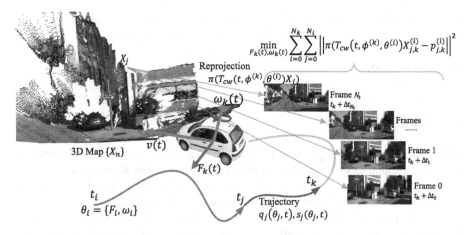

Fig. 1. The framework of our method. Camera trajectory is represented as continuous-time functions $q_j(\theta_j, t)$ to orientation and $s_j(\theta_j, t)$ to translation in a series time window, which illustrated as curves labeled as different colors. The motion of camera in a time window is described by physical parameters such as velocity, angular velocity, forces etc. The parameters are estimated via minimizing reprojection error in current time window. (Color figure online)

one intuitive way to encourage the continuous-time property. As a rigid-body object, the motion of camera is affected by forces and torques, which usually change slowly in a short time window. Considering the fact that the resultant force on an object is proportional to the second derivative of the displacement, camera trajectory estimation problem can be converted to analyzing the forces applied to the camera. Dynamics based methods can fully take the advantages of such methods by incorporating temporal consistency constraints.

In this paper, we introduce a dynamics model to represent the camera trajectory in a continuous-time way. By detecting the change of forces, the trajectory is segmented into pieces. In each segment, the dynamics parameter is assumed to be constant. The camera pose is not stored explicitly but represented as a function that can be evaluated at any timestamp. This representation not only generates a smooth and continuous camera motion, but also requires only few parameters within each small segment. As our method smooths the trajectory, it can be regarded as a low-pass filter with valid physical explanations. The inertia of the system prevents abrupt jumps and forbids physically irrational movements. This guarantees the continuous velocity, and hence assures a smooth and physically reasonable trajectory. These constraints can reduce error in VO, and enhance the stability of the systems, especially beneficial to autonomous driving and mixed reality rendering. As illustrated in Fig. 1, a batch-wise optimization is applied to update the constant parameters, where the camera trajectory can be easily modeled.

The rest of the paper is organized as follows: In Sect. 2, we discuss the methods that are relevant to our estimation strategy. In Sect. 3, we introduce our dynamics model of camera trajectory. In Sect. 4, we present our estimation strategy for the VO problem with the aforementioned dynamics model. In Sect. 5, we present the quantitative and qualitative analysis to validate the feasibility and robustness of our proposed method for VO problem. Finally, we conclude the paper in Sect. 6.

2   Related Works

Visual odometry is a subproblem of the simultaneous localization and mapping (SLAM) problem [25]. Most of the previous methods solve it as a discrete-time state problem by registering two consecutive frames. According to the visual information used in the front-end, VO methods can be divided into feature-based and direct methods. Feature-based methods extract feature correspondences between two views and compute the camera pose according these correspondences [3,10,12,14,15,21]. Direct methods, on the other hand, enforce the photometric consistency without specifying feature correspondences [2,5,6,16,24]. Besides, LSD-SLAM [2,4,6] proposes a semi-dense method to balance the pros and cons of each kind.

Apart from the visual information used in these methods, different optimization strategies are applied in back-end. Filter based methods use filters, such as Extended Kalman Filter (EKF), to estimate the pose of current frame [3,26]. Though maintaining a motion state in the filter, they don't consider the temporal consistency between frames. To obtain better precision and robustness, the poses of multiple frames are estimated in a batch form to integrate the abundant information. Graph based methods [15] construct a graph between frames to explore the relationship between frames, while sliding window based methods [5,18] estimate the pose of current frame by jointly optimizing the poses within a sliding window. However, the pose of each frame is still modeled in a discrete way.

Continuous-time SLAM [7] draws public attention these days by modeling the camera trajectory with a continuous function, which shares the similar concern with our method. Some researchers [13,17] model the camera trajectory with the B-spline curve. Kerl et al. [11] estimate the continuous-time trajectory to handle the rolling shutter issue. Although these methods leverage the continuous-time function, they focus more on the pose interpolation rather than the temporal consistency constraint. We, on the other hand, leverage the power of dynamics model to represent the camera trajectory, and handle the VO problem in a more robust way.

3   Dynamics Model

To represent the camera trajectory as a continuous-time function, we model the camera motion using a dynamics model. The pose of a camera in the world coordinate $\mathbb{C}_w$ includes an orientation component and a position component, where the orientation component denotes the optical axis direction, and the position component is defined as the original point of the body frame. As illustrated in Fig. 2(b), the change of the camera status induces the corresponding translation and rotation for a moving camera.

Camera orientation is modeled using a function of quaternion $\mathbf{q}(t)$ for its close relationship with angular velocity $\omega(t)$, while camera translation is modeled as a vector $\mathbf{s}(t) \in \mathbb{R}^3$. t denotes the time stamp, $\mathbf{R}(\mathbf{q}(t))$ denotes the rotation matrix parameterized by the quaternion function $\mathbf{q}(t)$, and $\mathbf{T}_{cw}(t)$ denotes the transformation of a 3D point $\mathbf{X}$ from world frame to camera frame as:

$$\mathbf{T}_{cw}(t) = \mathbf{T}_{wc}^{-1}(t) = \left[\mathbf{R}[\mathbf{q}(t)] \mid \mathbf{s}(t)\right]^{-1}. \tag{1}$$

where the subscripts cw and wc denote the camera-to-world and the world-to-camera mapping respectively.

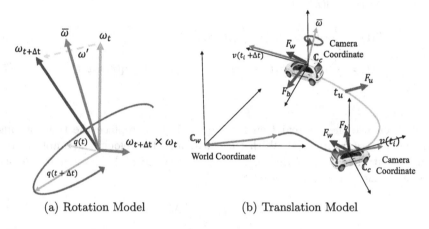

(a) Rotation Model	(b) Translation Model

Fig. 2. The illustration of rotation and translation models. (a) The rotation of camera is represented as a function of quaternion $\mathbf{q}(t)$, which changes according to the angular velocity $\omega(t)$. (b) The camera trajectory is represented as a piecewise smooth curve. The translation is jointly caused by a constant force in the world coordinate $\mathbf{F}_w$, a constant force in the camera coordinate $\mathbf{F}_b$, and an abruptly emerging force $\mathbf{F}_u$.

3.1   Model of Camera Orientation

The quaternion function $\mathbf{q}(t)$ describes the 3D rotation of a camera in the world coordinate. The change of $\mathbf{q}(t)$ depends on the angular velocity $\omega(t)$ of the camera, which follows the differential equation:

$$\mathbf{q}'(t) = \frac{1}{2}\mathbf{q}(t) \circ \omega(t), \tag{2}$$

where $\circ$ denotes the quaternion multiplication. $\omega(t)$ denotes the time-varying function of the angular velocity.

The relationship between angular velocity and torque $\tau(t)$ can be represented by an Euler equation as:

$$\omega'(t) = \mathbf{I}^{-1}[-\omega_\times(t)\mathbf{I}\omega(t) + \tau(t)]. \tag{3}$$

There is not a general analytical solution for most cases. For simplicity, we assume that the angular velocity is linear, which can be represented as:

$$w(t + \Delta t) = w(t) + w'(t)\Delta t. \tag{4}$$

Following [22], we apply Taylor expansion to approximate $\mathbf{q}(t)$ as:

$$\mathbf{q}(t + \Delta t) = \mathbf{q}(t) + \mathbf{q}'(t)\Delta t + \frac{1}{2!}\mathbf{q}''(t)\Delta t^2 + \cdots, \tag{5}$$

where the successive derivatives of $\mathbf{q}(t)$ are obtained repeatedly using Eq. (2) by assuming $\omega^{(n)}(t) = 0(n > 1)$ as:

$$\mathbf{q}''(t) = \frac{1}{2^2}\mathbf{q}(t) \circ \omega^2(t) + \frac{1}{2}q(t) \circ \omega' \tag{6}$$

$$\mathbf{q}^{(3)}(t) = \frac{1}{2^3}\mathbf{q}(t) \circ \omega^3(t) + \frac{1}{4}\mathbf{q}(t) \circ \omega'(t)\omega(t) + \frac{1}{2}\mathbf{q}(t) \circ \omega(t)\omega'(t) \tag{7}$$

$$\vdots$$

We then use the abbreviation form $\mathbf{q}_t$ and w_t to replace the time-varying variables like $\mathbf{q}(t)$ and $\omega(t)$. With the linear angular velocity assumption, the mean velocity from time t during a small interval Δt and the angular velocity at time $t + \Delta t$ can be represented as:

$$\bar{\omega}_t = \omega_t + \frac{1}{2}\omega'\Delta t \tag{8}$$

$$\omega_{t+\Delta t} = \omega_t + \omega'\Delta t. \tag{9}$$

Equation (5) then turns to:

$$\mathbf{q}_{t+\Delta t} = \mathbf{q}_t \circ (1 + \frac{1}{2}\bar{\omega}_t\Delta t + \frac{1}{2!}(\frac{1}{2}\bar{\omega}_t\Delta t)^2 + \cdots) \tag{10}$$

$$+ \mathbf{q}_t \circ (\frac{\Delta t^3}{48}(\bar{\omega}_t\omega' - \omega'\bar{\omega}_t)) \tag{11}$$

$$+ \mathbf{q}_t \circ (\cdots)\Delta t^4 + \cdots \tag{12}$$

Finally, the model of camera orientation can be approximated as:

$$\mathbf{q}(t + \Delta t) \approx \mathbf{q}_t \circ (e^{\frac{\Delta t}{2}\bar{\omega}_t} + \frac{\Delta t^2}{24}\begin{bmatrix} 0 \\ \omega_t \times \omega_{t+\Delta t} \end{bmatrix}), \tag{13}$$

where the first term in Eq. (10) is the Taylor series of $e^{\frac{\Delta t}{2}\bar{\omega}_t}$ as:

$$e^{\frac{\Delta t}{2}\bar{\omega}} = \begin{bmatrix} \cos(\|\bar{\omega}\|\frac{\Delta t}{2}) \\ \frac{\bar{\omega}}{\|\bar{\omega}\|}\sin(\|\bar{\omega}\|\frac{\Delta t}{2}) \end{bmatrix}. \tag{14}$$

3.2 Model of Camera Velocity

The velocity $\mathbf{v}(t)$ can be represented with an initial velocity parameter $\mathbf{v}_0$ and a acceleration parameter as:

$$\mathbf{v}(t_0 + \Delta t) = \mathbf{v}(t_0) + \int_0^{\Delta t} \frac{\mathbf{F}(t_0 + t)}{m} dt, \tag{15}$$

where $\mathbf{F}$ is the resultant force, and m is the mass of the camera. $\mathbf{v}(t_0 + \Delta t)$ is composed of an initial value $\mathbf{v}(t_0)$ and a variation term related to Δt.

In the real world, the resultant force itself is complex and hard to model. As illustrated in Fig. 2(b), we assume that, within a small time interval, the resultant force $\mathbf{F}$ can be decomposed into three components: a constant force $\mathbf{F}_w$ in the world frame, a constant force $\mathbf{F}_b$ in the camera coordinate, and a force $\mathbf{F}_u$ which describe an abruptly changing force. $\mathbf{F}_w$ denotes the major force in the world coordinate, and $\mathbf{F}_b$ models the centripetal force which acts as a compensation that is relevant to the orientation. We assume that trajectory can be approximated well using $\mathbf{F}_w$ and $\mathbf{F}_b$ in a short time window and the remaining components of resultant force can be approximated using force $\mathbf{F}_u$ start from time t_u. $\mathbf{F}_u$ is involved to detect the changing status. If a new force component constantly act on the camera, the consistency within the time interval is broken, and the dynamics model needs to be modified.

Specifically, as the only concern is the camera acceleration for its relationship with the trajectory, the absolute scale of the force is not important. Here, we assume a unit mass as $m = 1$, and the velocity model can then be represented as:

$$\mathbf{v}(t_0 + \Delta t) = \mathbf{v}(t_0) + \int_0^{\Delta t} \mathbf{F}(t_0 + \Delta t) d\Delta t \tag{16}$$

$$= \mathbf{v}(t_0) + \int_0^{\Delta t} \mathbf{F}_w d\Delta t + \int_0^{\Delta t} \mathbf{R}[\mathbf{q}(t_0 + \Delta t)]\mathbf{F}_b \, d\Delta t + \int_{t_u}^{\Delta t} \mathbf{F}_u d\Delta t. \tag{17}$$

Here, we neglect the second term in Eq. (13) for simplification considering that Δt and cross product of ω_t and $\omega_{t+\Delta t}$ are always small when compared to the resultant force. The velocity component induced by $\mathbf{F}_b$ can then be represented as:

$$\mathbf{v}_{\mathbf{F}_b}(t_0 + \Delta t) = \int_0^{\Delta t} \mathbf{R}[\mathbf{q}(t_0 + \Delta t)]\mathbf{F}_b \, d\Delta t \tag{18}$$

$$\simeq \mathbf{R}[\mathbf{q}(t_0)](\mathbf{A}_0^v \mathbf{F}_b + \mathbf{A}_1^v \mathbf{F}_b \Delta t) \tag{19}$$

$$\mathbf{A}_0^v = \frac{\mathbf{Q}_v \bar{\omega}_\times + \|\bar{\omega}\| \bar{\omega}_\times}{\|\bar{\omega}\|^3} \tag{20}$$

$$\mathbf{A}_1^v = \mathbf{I} - \frac{\bar{\omega}_\times \bar{\omega}_\times^T}{\|\bar{\omega}\|^2} \tag{21}$$

$$\mathbf{Q}_v = -[\bar{\omega} \sin(\|\bar{\omega}\| \Delta t)]_\times - \mathbf{I}\|\bar{\omega}\| \cos(\|\bar{\omega}\| \Delta t), \tag{22}$$

where $\|\bar{\omega}\|$ is the L2-norm of $\bar{\omega}$, $\mathbf{I}$ is identity matrix, $[\cdot]_\times$ is the skew-symmetric matrix form of the cross production of a vector.

3.3   Model of Camera Transition

With the model of camera velocity, the position $\mathbf{s}(t_0 + \Delta t)$ can be modeled as:

$$\mathbf{s}(t_0 + \Delta t) = \mathbf{s}(t_0) + \int_0^{\Delta t} \mathbf{v}(t_0 + \Delta t) d\Delta t \tag{23}$$

$$= \mathbf{s}(t_0) + \mathbf{v}(t_0)\Delta t + \frac{1}{2}\mathbf{F}_w \Delta t^2 + \frac{1}{2}\mathbf{F}_u (\Delta t - t_u)^2 + \mathbf{s}_{F_b}(t_0 + \Delta t), \tag{24}$$

where $\mathbf{s}_{F_b}(t_0 + \Delta t)$ denotes the displacement caused by $\mathbf{F}_b$, which can be represented by the integral of $\mathbf{v}_{F_b}$ according to Eq. (18) as:

$$\mathbf{s}_{F_b}(t_0 + \Delta t) \simeq \mathbf{R}[\mathbf{q}(t_0)](\mathbf{A}_0^s \mathbf{F}_b + \mathbf{A}_1^s \mathbf{F}_b \Delta t + \mathbf{A}_2^s \mathbf{F}_b \Delta t^2) \tag{25}$$

$$\mathbf{A}_0^s = \frac{\mathbf{Q}_s \bar{\omega}_\times - \bar{\omega}_\times^2}{\|\bar{\omega}\|^4} \tag{26}$$

$$\mathbf{A}_1^s = \frac{\bar{\omega}_\times}{\|\bar{\omega}\|^2} \tag{27}$$

$$\mathbf{A}_2^s = \frac{1}{2}(\mathbf{I} - \frac{\bar{\omega}_\times \bar{\omega}_\times^T}{\|\bar{\omega}\|^2}) \tag{28}$$

$$\mathbf{Q}_s = [\bar{\omega} \cos(\|\bar{\omega}\| \Delta t)]_\times - \mathbf{I}\|\bar{\omega}\| \sin(\|\bar{\omega}\| \Delta t). \tag{29}$$

Considering the fact that the translation component $\mathbf{s}(\cdot)$ is actually the position of camera center in the world coordinate, Eq. (23) can be viewed as the continuous-time incremental function of camera trajectory.

4   Visual Odometry Framework

In this section, we first introduce our trajectory representation given the dynamics model, and then demonstrate the way how dynamics parameters and states are updated. Finally, we introduce our velocity bootstrap strategy to acquire the initial velocity in the first frame.

4.1   Trajectory Representation

Based on the dynamics models described in Sect. 3, the visual odometry is solved as a camera trajectory estimation problem with a continuous-time function, which is illustrated in Fig. 3. The entire trajectory is represented as a set of trajectory segments, where each segment $S^{(i)}$ can be parametrized by the starting time point $t^{(i)}$ of the segment and a set of dynamics parameters $\theta^{(i)} = \{\mathbf{F}_w, \mathbf{F}_b, \omega, \omega'\}$. The dynamics model guarantees the continuous velocity in each segment, and hence, it assures a smooth and continuous trajectory.

For any time point t on the ith trajectory segment, we need to first determine the starting time point $t^{(i)}$ of this segment. The dynamics parameters $\theta^{(i)} = \{\mathbf{F}_w, \mathbf{F}_b, \omega, \omega'\}$ for $S^{(i)}$ are gradually updated through the optimization, where the updated dynamics parameters at time t determine the current state

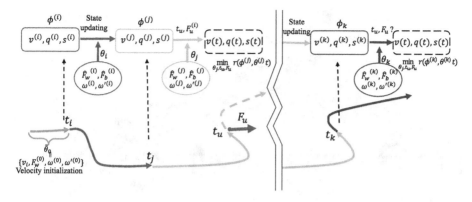

Fig. 3. The illustration of the camera trajectory representation. The entire trajectory is divided as a set of trajectory segments. Each segment can be represented by a set of constant motion parameters θ, and ϕ denotes the initial state of each segment. The segment is ended when a stable $\mathbf{F}_u$ is detected with a new trajectory segment created.

parameters $\phi_t = \{\mathbf{v}(t), \mathbf{s}(t), \mathbf{q}(t)\}$ incrementally (c.f. Sect. 3) through a small time interval Δt till time t.

As mentioned in Sect. 3.2, the abrupt updating force $\mathbf{F}_u$ models the change of the state of forces. Intuitively speaking, a stable $\mathbf{F}_u$ component is related to a new dynamics model, which implies the need to start a new trajectory segment. In our implementation, if the translation $\mathbf{s}_{F_u}(t_i + \Delta t) = \frac{1}{2} F_u (\Delta t - t_u)^2$ caused by $\mathbf{F}_u$ is larger than a threshold η_u, the current trajectory will be ended and a new segment will be created.

4.2   Updating Dynamics Parameters

The pose of camera at time t in the world coordinate can be represented with $\mathbf{s}(t, \phi^{(i)}, \theta^{(i)})$ and $\mathbf{q}(t, \phi^{(i)}, \theta^{(i)})$, where the initial state of ith trajectory segment $\phi^{(i)}$ is derived from the ending state of the last segment $S^{(i-1)}$. As depicted in Fig. 4, the camera pose at time t can be acquired using Eq. (1). By minimizing the reprojection error of a set of 3D-2D correspondences, the camera pose is optimized, and the optimal parameters $\phi^{(i)}$ and $\theta^{(i)}$ can be acquired.

Feature-Based Correspondences. We use a feature-based framework to build sparse correspondences. The framework is similar with the front-end in [15] by first extracting FAST corners [19] and then computing the ORB descriptor [20] around the keypoints. Thanks to the continuous-time representation of our trajectory, we predict the camera pose using the current dynamics variables. For a 3D map point $\mathbf{X}$ in the world coordinate, the projection from the 3D world coordinate to the image plane can be represented as:

$$\pi(T_{cw}(t, \phi^{(i)}, \theta^{(i)})\mathbf{X}_w), \tag{30}$$

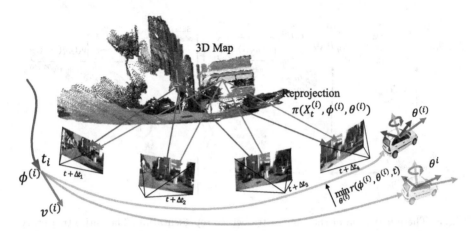

Fig. 4. The illustration of our visual odometry framework. The initial state $v(t_i)$ of current trajectory segment is drawn as blue arrow at time t_i. The pose of each frame can be derived using parameters θ_t. Then the map points are reprojected to each frame and reprojection error $r(\phi^{(i)}, \theta_t, t)$ is minimized to find the correct trajectory. (Color figure online)

where $\pi(\cdot)$ projects a 3D point in camera coordinate to camera plane.

Then the map points are projected to the current frame according to the predicted pose, and correspondences are searched near the projected map point. In this way, the search space can be reduced with robustness increased.

Optimization. The aforementioned time t is a continuous variable, while in the optimization section, the time refers to each discrete frame index. Here we denote $t_k^{(i)}$ as the kth frame on the ith trajectory segment. Assuming that the current time is Nth frame on the ith segment, and the number of matched pairs is m_k for kth frame, with the estimated correspondences, the jth matched map point $\mathbf{X}_{j,k}^{(i)}$ at time $t_k^{(i)} < t_N^{(i)}$ is reprojected to the image plane to calculate the reprojection error along with its corresponding feature pixel $p_{j,k}^{(i)}$. The parameters $\{\theta^{(i)}, \mathbf{F}_u^{(i)}, t^{(i+1)}\}$ are optimized by minimizing the energy function as follows:

$$\min_{\theta^{(i)}, \mathbf{F}_u^{(i)}, t^{(i+1)}} \sum_{k=0}^{N-1} \sum_{j=1}^{m_k} \|\pi(T_{cw}(t, \phi^{(i)}, \theta^{(i)})\mathbf{X}_{j,k}^{(i)}) - p_{j,k}^{(i)}\|_h + \alpha\|F_b\|^2 + \beta\|F_u\|^2 + \varphi\|\omega'\|^2$$

$$s.t. \quad \begin{cases} \mathbf{F}_{min} < \mathbf{F}_w, \mathbf{F}_b, \mathbf{F}_u < \mathbf{F}_{max} \\ \omega_{min} < \omega, \omega' < \omega_{max} \end{cases}$$

$$(31)$$

where α, β and φ are the weight of each term respectively, and $\|\cdot\|_h$ is the Huber norm.

In our implementation, $\alpha\|F_b\|^2$ is added to imply the assumption that F_b should be no more than a small compensation but not a major force component.

With the help of it, the major contribution to the resultant force is from F_w. $\beta \|F_u\|^2$ is used to penalize abrupt merging force. In addition, the regularization term $\|\omega'\|^2$ is used to encourage a stable angular velocity.

4.3 Bootstrap of Velocity

To estimate the initial velocity $\mathbf{v}(0)$, the first three frames are used. Different from Sect. 3, we assume that the change of velocity is only induced by the constant force $\mathbf{F}_w$ in world coordinate, and the dynamics parameters $\theta^{(0)} = \{\mathbf{v}_0, \mathbf{F}_w, \omega, \omega'\}$. Since the initial pose parameters $\mathbf{s}(0)$ and $\mathbf{q}(0)$ have no impact on the dynamics model, we assume that the camera starts from the original point of world coordinate.

The rotation model is the same as Eq. (4). According to the Eq. (23), in this simplified situation, the position function is a second-order polynomial as:

$$\mathbf{s}(t, \theta^{(0)}) = \mathbf{v}_0(t)t + \frac{1}{2}\mathbf{F}_w t^2. \tag{32}$$

The initial parameters $\theta^{(0)}$ are then estimated simply by minimizing the reprojection error of the first three frames as:

$$\min_{\theta^{(0)}} \sum_{k=0}^{3} \sum_{j=0}^{m_k} \|\pi_0(\mathbf{X}_j, \theta^{(0)}, t_k) - p_{j,k}\|_h. \tag{33}$$

5 Experiments

Our approach is evaluated on the public KITTI benchmark [8] which has been used in state-of-the-art VO/SLAM methods [14,23]. The KITTI dataset consists of 22 sequences captured by stereo cameras on a moving car in urban and highway environments. The first 11 sequences (Seq 00–10) provide raw sensor data along with ground-truth camera trajectory recorded by accurate GPS/INS while the rest (Seq 11–21) are without ground-truth. Low frame rate (10 fps), fast motion (up to 90 km/h), and dynamic objects such as cars and pedestrians make the dataset very challenging for VO algorithms.

In our experiments, we use rectified stereo image pairs in Seq 03–08 for quantitative evaluation. The standard VO/SLAM error metrics, i.e., averaged Root Mean Square Errors (RMSEs) of the translational and rotational errors are adopted for all the sequences with trajectory lengths ranging from 100 to 800 m.

5.1 Implementation Details

For each input stereo frame, we first extract ORB features as implemented in [14], and then search matches between left and right images along epipolar lines. All matched features are triangulated to generate 3D points used for building

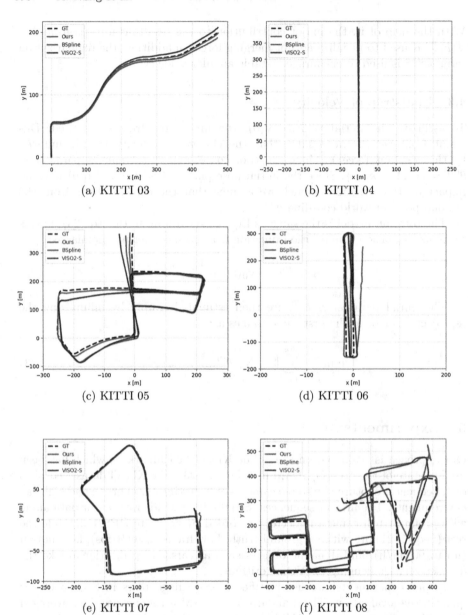

Fig. 5. Quantitative trajectory comparisons on the KITTI dataset.

correspondences between frames in trajectory segments. Newly generated 3D points are added to map according the camera pose computed from the optimized trajectory parameters.

We test our prototype algorithm on a PC with a Core i7 CPU and 8 G memory. We use the well-known Ceres Solver [1] for non-linear optimizations. The threshold η_u is set to 0.1 to control the time interval when a new trajectory segment should be generated. To constrain the computational cost, as many as 12 frames are allowed to be inserted into a trajectory segment.

Table 1. Results on the KITTI dataset.

Method	Sequence											
	03		04		05		06		07		08	
	t_{rel}	r_{rel}	t_{rel}	r_{rel}	t_{rel}	r_{rel}	t_{rel}	r_{rel}	t_{rel}	r_{rel}	t_{rel}	r_{rel}
VISO2-S [9]	3.21	3.25	2.12	2.12	1.53	1.60	1.48	1.58	1.85	1.91	2.83	1.33
LSD-VO [4]	1.16	0.32	0.42	0.34	0.90	0.34	1.28	0.43	1.25	0.79	1.24	0.38
DSO-S [23]	0.92	0.16	0.65	0.15	0.68	0.19	0.67	0.20	0.83	0.36	0.98	0.25
B-Spline	1.02	0.68	0.84	0.36	0.94	0.56	2.02	0.79	1.12	1.06	6.00	1.68
Ours	0.84	0.32	0.60	0.27	0.66	0.34	0.61	0.23	1.05	0.60	1.47	0.57

t_{rel}: average translational RMSE drift (%) on length from 100, 200 to 800 m.
r_{rel}: average rotational RMSE drift ($^\circ$/100 m) on length from 100, 200 to 800 m.

5.2 Qualitative Visualization of Dynamics Parameters

We first visualize the dynamics parameters estimated in our method in Fig. 6 for better understanding. In the figures, camera poses are visualized by green hexcones. The trajectory segments are represented by curves with various colors.

Intuitively, forces and velocities estimated by our approach are consistent with the real world:

1. During the velocity bootstrap stage, we only optimize the force F_w and the velocity. In Fig. 6(a), we can observe that the real motion coincides with the velocity.
2. When the car turns right in reality, the constant force F_b can be computed via our model. The force illustrated in Fig. 6(b) explains the physical reason how the car changes its direction.
3. Figure 6(c) shows the angular velocity, corresponding to the real motion of the car in the scene.

Generally, the car runs in a flat straight road and the forces are horizontal. Yet bumps on the road may cause vertical disturbances and affect the smoothness of the trajectory. These situations can be described by the abruptly emerging forces F_u and F_w, as depicted in Fig. 7(a). In addition, the car motion can be visually reflected in images, where feature flows in Fig. 7(b) indicate the fluctuations.

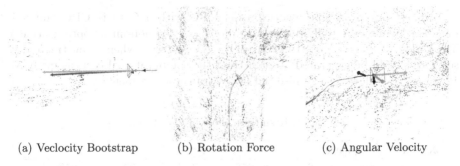

(a) Veclocity Bootstrap   (b) Rotation Force   (c) Angular Velocity

Fig. 6. Visualization of dynamics parameters. The cyan in (a–c), black in (c), and red in (a) vectors are velocity, angular velocity, and F_w in the world coordinate system, respectively. The green vector in (c) is the constant force F_b in the camera coordinate system. (Color figure online)

(a) Abruptly Emerging Force   (b) Feature Flow

Fig. 7. Visualization of the estimated abrupt force F_u and the observed feature flows caused by the bumpy road.

5.3 Quantitative Evaluation

To evaluate the effectiveness of our model, we compare our method both with frame-based and continuous-time stereo VO methods. We use the stereo version of VISO2 [9] as the baseline method of discrete-time frame-based method, which utilizes SURF descriptor and optimizes camera poses via minimizing the reprojection error. In addition, we compare against the stereo version of LSD-SLAM [6] and DSO [23], the state-of-the-art stereo VO methods, with loop closure module disabled.

As for continuous-time methods, we implement a B-Spline based trajectory representation. In detail, we use a fixed step B-Spline function, which is described in [11,13]. For fairness in comparison, we use the same feature-based front-end as our method rather than the direct front-end in [11].

The comparisons of trajectories in the X-Y plane are shown in Fig. 5. Our method outputs competitive results on all the sequences, and outperforms baselines on Seq 03, 05, 06, and 08 regarding the similarity between trajectories generated by our method and the GT. From the figures we can observe that the drift problem is alleviated using our method.

For further comparisons, we provide Table 1 showing the RMSE in terms of rotations and translations. In most sequences, our method outperforms frame-based LSD-SLAM and VISO2. Specifically, comparing to B-Spline continuous-time trajectory representation, our method achieves higher accuracy and robustness, while B-Spline outputs trajectories with less precision. Comparing to stereo DSO, we achieve competitive results in terms of translation errors, which are better for sequences 03, 04, 05, 06. But in our method, the orientation is approximated using a linear model, which is sufficient for most situations and guarantees the continuous property of the trajectory model, but may sacrifice certain precision compared to stereo DSO.

5.4 Failure Cases

Our physics-based model is mainly designed for cars and robots currently, which with high inertia. But for light camera systems such as hand-held cameras, the possible dynamic changes between consecutive camera frames will violate our assumptions. One typical case is unexpected fluctuations of motion direction between consecutive frames, as illustrated in the Fig. 8. It may lead to incorrect velocity even with correct pose estimations. When the vibration of camera is small, the result trajectory may be only over-smoothed. Besides, a higher frame-rate will be helpful to avoid these situations.

(a) Wrong velocity   (b) Over-smoothed trajectory

Fig. 8. Failure cases. In case (a), same camera poses may refer to different trajectories. In case (b), the result trajectory may be over-smoothed.

6 Conclusions

We present a continuous-time camera trajectory representation based on the physical dynamics model of the camera motion. Upon the representation, we propose a visual odometry approach which naturally considers the dynamics constraints and motion consistency between frames in a time interval. The experimental results on real-world datasets demonstrate the advantages of physically modeled trajectory by reducing the drift error in long sequences. In the future, equipped with the clear physical meanings of parameters, we may integrate data from IMU sensors and control signals from robot motions into our system. A complete SLAM framework will be finished where all the trajectory segments are optimized jointly.

References

1. Agarwal, S., Mierle, K., et al.: Ceres Solver (2012). http://ceres-solver.org
2. Caruso, D., Engel, J., Cremers, D.: Large-scale direct SLAM for omnidirectional cameras. In: Proceedings of IEEE/RSJ International Conference on Intelligent Robots and Systems, pp. 141–148 (2015)
3. Davison, A.J., Reid, I.D., Molton, N.D., Stasse, O.: MonoSLAM: real-time single camera SLAM. IEEE Trans. Pattern Anal. Mach. Intell. **29**(6), 1052–1067 (2007)
4. Engel, J., Schöps, T., Cremers, D.: LSD-SLAM: large-scale direct monocular SLAM. In: Fleet, D., Pajdla, T., Schiele, B., Tuytelaars, T. (eds.) ECCV 2014. LNCS, vol. 8690, pp. 834–849. Springer, Cham (2014). https://doi.org/10.1007/978-3-319-10605-2_54
5. Engel, J., Koltun, V., Cremers, D.: Direct sparse odometry. IEEE Trans. Pattern Anal. Mach. Intell. **40**(3), 611–625 (2018)
6. Engel, J., Stückler, J., Cremers, D.: Large-scale direct SLAM with stereo cameras. In: Proceedings of IEEE/RSJ International Conference on Intelligent Robots and Systems, pp. 1935–1942 (2015)
7. Furgale, P., Barfoot, T.D., Sibley, G.: Continuous-time batch estimation using temporal basis functions. In: Proceedings of IEEE International Conference on Robotics and Automation, pp. 2088–2095 (2012)
8. Geiger, A., Lenz, P., Urtasun, R.: Are we ready for autonomous driving? The KITTI vision benchmark suite. In: Proceedings of IEEE Conference on Computer Vision and Pattern Recognition, pp. 3354–3361 (2012)
9. Geiger, A., Ziegler, J., Stiller, C.: StereoScan: dense 3D reconstruction in real-time. In: Intelligent Vehicles Symposium (2011)
10. Kerl, C., Sturm, J., Cremers, D.: Dense visual SLAM for RGB-D cameras. In: Proceedings of IEEE/RSJ International Conference on Intelligent Robots and Systems, pp. 2100–2106 (2013)
11. Kerl, C., Stückler, J., Cremers, D.: Dense continuous-time tracking and mapping with rolling shutter RGB-D cameras. In: Proceedings of IEEE International Conference on Computer Vision, pp. 2264–2272 (2015)
12. Klein, G., Murray, D.: Parallel tracking and mapping for small AR workspaces. In: Proceedings of IEEE International Symposium on Mixed and Augmented Reality, pp. 225–234. IEEE (2007)
13. Lovegrove, S., Patron-Perez, A., Sibley, G.: Spline fusion: a continuous-time representation for visual-inertial fusion with application to rolling shutter cameras. In: Proceedings of British Machine Vision Conference, pp. 1–12 (2013)
14. Mur-Artal, R., Montiel, J.M.M., Tardos, J.D.: ORB-SLAM: a versatile and accurate monocular SLAM system. IEEE Trans. Rob. **31**(5), 1147–1163 (2015)
15. Mur-Artal, R., Tardós, J.D.: ORB-SLAM2: an open-source slam system for monocular, stereo, and RGB-D cameras. IEEE Trans. Rob. **33**(5), 1255–1262 (2017)
16. Newcombe, R.A., Lovegrove, S.J., Davison, A.J.: DTAM: dense tracking and mapping in real-time. In: Proceedings of IEEE International Conference on Computer Vision, pp. 2320–2327 (2011)
17. Ovrén, H., Forssén, P.E.: Spline error weighting for robust visual-inertial fusion. In: Proceedings of IEEE Conference on Computer Vision and Pattern Recognition, pp. 1–12 (2018)
18. Qin, T., Li, P., Shen, S.: VINS-mono: a robust and versatile monocular visual-inertial state estimator. arXiv preprint arXiv:1708.03852 (2017)

19. Rosten, E., Porter, R., Drummond, T.: Faster and better: a machine learning approach to corner detection. IEEE Trans. Pattern Anal. Mach. Intell. **32**(1), 105–119 (2010)
20. Rublee, E., Rabaud, V., Konolige, K., Bradski, G.: ORB: an efficient alternative to SIFT or SURF. In: Proceedings of IEEE International Conference on Computer Vision, pp. 2564–2571 (2011)
21. Schops, T., Engel, J., Cremers, D.: Semi-dense visual odometry for AR on a smartphone. In: Proceedings of IEEE International Symposium on Mixed and Augmented Reality, pp. 145–150 (2014)
22. Sola, J.: Quaternion kinematics for the error-state Kalman filter. arXiv preprint arXiv:1711.02508 (2017)
23. Wang, R., Schworer, M., Cremers, D.: Stereo DSO: large-scale direct sparse visual odometry with stereo cameras. In: Proceedings of IEEE International Conference on Computer Vision, pp. 3923–3931 (2017)
24. Yang, N., Wang, R., Stückler, J., Cremers, D.: Deep virtual stereo odometry: leveraging deep depth prediction for monocular direct sparse odometry. In: Ferrari, V., Hebert, M., Sminchisescu, C., Weiss, Y. (eds.) ECCV 2018. LNCS, vol. 11212, pp. 835–852. Springer, Cham (2018). https://doi.org/10.1007/978-3-030-01237-3_50
25. Younes, G., Asmar, D., Shammas, E., Zelek, J.: Keyframe-based monocular SLAM: design, survey, and future directions. Rob. Auton. Syst. **98**, 67–88 (2017)
26. Zhou, H., Zou, D., Pei, L., Ying, R., Liu, P., Yu, W.: StructSLAM: visual SLAM with building structure lines. IEEE Trans. Veh. Technol. **64**(4), 1364–1375 (2015)

A2A: Attention to Attention Reasoning for Movie Question Answering

Chao-Ning Liu[1], Ding-Jie Chen[2], Hwann-Tzong Chen[1(✉)], and Tyng-Luh Liu[2]

[1] Department of Computer Science, National Tsing Hua University,
Hsinchu, Taiwan
htchen@cs.nthu.edu.tw
[2] Institute of Information Science, Academia Sinica, Taipei, Taiwan

Abstract. This paper presents the Attention to Attention (A2A) reasoning mechanism to address the challenging task of movie question answering (MQA). By focusing on the various aspects of attention cues, we establish the technique of attention propagation to uncover latent but useful information to the underlying QA task. In addition, the proposed A2A reasoning seamlessly leads to effective fusion of different representation modalities about the data, and also can be conveniently constructed with popular neural network architectures. To tackle the out-of-vocabulary issue caused by the diverse language usages in nowadays movies, we adopt the GloVe mapping as a teacher model and establish a new and flexible word embedding based on character n-grams learning. Our method is evaluated on the MovieQA benchmark dataset and achieves the state-of-the-art accuracy for the "Video+Subtitles" entry.

1 Introduction

We aim to address a specific problem of Visual Question Answering (VQA) that is coined as Movie Question Answering (MQA). For a model to deal with a question answering (QA) task, it is expected to have the ability of analyzing visual and textual contents and inferring the most plausible answer to a given question. The MQA task is deemed to be challenging in that the correct answering requires a comprehensive understanding of not only the recognition sub-task (who, where, and when) but also the reasoning sub-task (what, why, and how) via associating the visual content with the textual and vice versa. So far, the popular content analysis approaches mainly comprise word embedding [20,24] and image embedding [9,28], and the inferring approaches usually are based on memory networks [16,18,21,23,25,29,31–33] and attention models [2,6,15,19]. We instead design a new attention based model that is able to propagate attention across different segments in a movie sequence to address the MQA problem.

The MovieQA dataset provides online testing for benchmark evaluation of VQA models. We compare our model with others on this collection. The dataset contains 408 movies with standard subtitles, and 140 of them are accompanied with video clips. To analyze and understand such long video sequences,

© Springer Nature Switzerland AG 2019
C. V. Jawahar et al. (Eds.): ACCV 2018, LNCS 11366, pp. 404–419, 2019.
https://doi.org/10.1007/978-3-030-20876-9_26

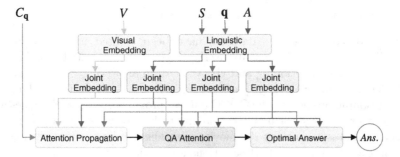

Fig. 1. An overview of the proposed network architecture for MQA. With the provided video data V and subtitle data S, our model leverages the A2A reasoning mechanism, namely, "Attention Propagation" and "QA Attention" to decide, from a set A of five candidate answers, the best answer to question $\mathbf{q}$.

previous strategies commonly rely on adopting the per-frame visual content, successive-frame temporal dependencies, and the subtitles. In contrast, the proposed model of attention-to-attention (A2A) reasoning focuses on exploring higher-level attention information about the questions and answers for QA video analysis.

The proposed method aims to explore high-level and multimodality attention mechanisms for addressing QA tasks of movie understanding. We illustrate the overall network architecture of our method in Fig. 1 and characterize the main contributions as follows.

- We propose the attention-to-attention (A2A) reasoning mechanism to distill more attention information for answering questions. The implications are twofold. First, it enables attention propagation to uncover neglected information that may be useful for MQA. Second, the distilled attention aggregates and associates the visual with the textual information from subtitles, questions, and answers.
- We adopt the GloVe mapping [24] as the teacher model to design a new word embedding approach for tackling the out-of-vocabulary issue in MQA.
- We establish a joint embedding approach that simplifies the association learning between the visual and textual modalities.
- Our model achieves the state-of-the-art performance on the "Video+ Subtitles" entry of MovieQA benchmark.

2   Related Work

We start with an overview of several popular datasets for visual captioning and question answering, and then briefly discuss the two main trends of solving QA tasks, *i.e.*, memory network and attention model.

2.1 Visual Captioning and Question Datasets

A number of comprehensive datasets have been created for evaluating the machine learning methods that are designed to tackle integrated visual-textual tasks such as visual captioning and visual question answering.

COCO [17] and LSMDC [27] are two widely used datasets for studying the visual captioning problems. The COCO dataset provides up to 330 K images with five captions per image for image captioning tasks. For video description tasks, the LSMDC dataset contains 200 movies with aligned description sentences for exploring the way to generate descriptions for movies.

There exist several datasets for studying the question answering tasks concerning text, image, or video. Regarding question answering tasks of pure text, bAbI [32] contains various tasks for evaluating the performance of a question answering system, and SQuAD [25] consists of hundred thousand QAs and 500 articles for studying the reading comprehension. For question answering tasks conducted on images, CLEVR [14], VQA-v1.0 [1], and VQA-v2.0 [8] can be considered. The CLEVR dataset comprises many questions that are explicitly relational, and hence it requires rich relational reasoning to analyze the data. VQA-v1.0 and VQA-v2.0 include images and their corresponding QAs from COCO dataset. The VQA-v1.0 dataset provides evaluation in a multiple-choice setting with additional candidate answers per question. VQA-v2.0 balances the answers to each question for minimizing the effects of dataset-prior learning.

TGIF-QA [13] and MarioQA [22] are conducted for studying video question answering tasks that require temporal reasoning to answer the questions. TGIF-QA dataset provides question answering tasks concerning not only single-image inputs but also spatio-temporal frames. The data are collected from animated Tumblr GIFs. MarioQA dataset is built upon Super Mario video gameplays. The dataset provides videos with multiple events and event-centric questions. There is no extra information to reason answers while analyzing temporal relationship between events in the MarioQA dataset.

This work focuses on another video question answering dataset, MovieQA [30], which provides several data modalities such as video clips, questions, subtitles, descriptive video service (DVS), plot synopsis, and scripts. The tasks in MovieQA is challenging because several questions are about the story and it needs the ability of long-term temporal reasoning, natural language understanding, and scene understanding. Table 1 illustrates a QA example from the MovieQA dataset.

2.2 Memory Network

Storing long sequential information is one key factor for dealing with the MQA problem. Memory networks usually perform read-write operations on an internal representation. Instead of using the traditional recurrent neural networks (RNNs) [10] that store and update the given information into fixed-size hidden units, another solution is to leverage an external memory network [21,29,33]

Table 1. Example of MovieQA benchmark. The answer marked in green is the ground truth. The first row presents example images from the movie, the second row shows the corresponding subtitles, and the third row lists the corresponding question, candidate answers, and the answer-required frame barcode $C_\mathbf{q}$.

| You can see here the Death Star.... | the Death Star does have a strong defense mechanism. | The shield must be deactivated... |

| q: How is the Death Star protected from attack?
 $\mathbf{a_1}$: By an army of soldiers.
 $\mathbf{a_2}$: *By nuclear weapons.*
 $\mathbf{a_3}$: By an energy shield.
 $\mathbf{a_4}$: By starfighters.
 $\mathbf{a_5}$: By Emperor Palpatine's army. | $C_\mathbf{q}$: a Boolean vector indicating the video frames (subtitles) that are relevant to the task of question answering w.r.t $\mathbf{q}$. |

that directly "memorizes" much earlier temporal information. Several state-of-the-art approaches, such as bAbI [32], SQuAD [25], and GMemN2N [18] have adopted memory networks to address pure-text question answering tasks.

The approaches LMN [31], DEMN [16], RWMN [23], and SC-MemN2N [4] show the state-of-the-art accuracy on the task of video question answering, LMN proposes static word memory and dynamic subtitle memory. The static word memory stores visual word with static size, and the dynamic subtitle memory use static word memory to generate clips-level representation with subtitle. They also use multiple computational steps (hops) mechanism [29] to refine the memory. DEMN uses a long-term memory component to embed both visual and textual features for storing, and query the features with respect to the question and the answers sequentially. RWMN adopts a convolution based read-write network for allowing highly-capable and flexible read-write operations to construct the long-term memory. Its visual features come from the last average pooling layer of ResNet-152 [9]. SC-MemN2N includes an end-to-end memory network that leverages visual, textual, and acoustic modalities with several grammatical and acoustic constraints in a unified optimization framework.

Notice that, the dynamic subtitle update rule of LMN [31] is similar to the attention mechanism of our approach. The difference is that we use both question and answer for guiding the attention of subtitle, while LMN uses clip-level semantic representation to do the refinement.

2.3 Attention Model

When global features are used to represent the visual contents, irrelevant or noisy information may affect the reasoning. It is possible to use an attention model to address this issue by assigning different importance weights to local features corresponding to partial contents.

Attention models are widely adopted in the task of image question answering [2,6,15,19]. Lu *et al.* [19] design a co-attention model to reason the attention of image and question jointly. The co-attention model hierarchically reasons the important part of both image and question via a one-dimensional convolutional neural network. Fukui *et al.* [6] propose to use multimodal compact bilinear (MCB) pooling to combine multimodal features. For visual question answering, the MCB module is adopted twice, one for predicting attention over spatial features and the other for combining the question representation with attended representation. Kazemi *et al.* [15] embed image via a ResNet and embed tokenized question via a multi-layer LSTM. The embedded image features and question are then concatenated to predict multiple attention distributions over image features. Anderson *et al.* [2] propose a mechanism that combines bottom-up and top-down attention for calculating object-level attention and salient-region attention. The bottom-up mechanism extracts image regions with associated feature vectors, and the top-down decides the feature weightings.

Attention mechanisms can be used to identify *where to notice* before further reasoning to answer questions in VQA task. The proposed A2A reasoning mechanism guides our question answering model to notice not only inter-segment relations in the spatial-temporal domain but also the association between questions and answers in sentence domain.

3   Our Method

This study considers the MovieQA dataset [30], comprising a set of movies, for evaluating the QA performance. Since for each particular movie the analysis of our method to perform question answering is the same, it is sufficient to restrict the discussion of the proposed formulation and notations for an arbitrary movie, unless explicitly stated otherwise. To begin, the following notations are used to express the various aspects about the data. We decompose a given movie into a set of video clips, $V = \{v_1, v_2, \ldots, v_{|V|}\}$ where the collection of corresponding subtitle sets is denoted as $S = \{s_1, s_2, \ldots, s_{|S|}\}$ and $|S| = |V|$. For a presented question $\mathbf{q}$ about the movie, the QA task is to choose the *best* answer from a set of five candidates, denoted as $A = \{\mathbf{a}_1, \mathbf{a}_2, \ldots, \mathbf{a}_5\}$. In addition, a Boolean mask $C_{\mathbf{q}}$ is provided to indicate those video clips (and hence the corresponding subtitle sets) that are relevant to carry out the task of question answering with respect to the specific question $\mathbf{q}$.

3.1   Visual and Linguistic Embedding

We represent visual information of each frame with its B most "salient" objects. To do so, we use Faster-RCNN [26] with the ResNet-101 [9] pre-trained model from TensorFlow object detection API [12] to select those object bounding boxes with the B highest scores among all detected candidates, and extract a feature vector of dimension $d_v = 2048$ for each bounding box from the last average pooling layer in the second stage of Faster-RCNN. The derivation yields $V \in$

$\mathbb{R}^{d_v \times N \times B}$ where N is the total number of frames (also subtitles) over all the video clips of a particular movie, and our current implementation assumes $B = 6$.

To model the linguistic input, we leverage the technique of word embedding to achieve the intended mapping. However, in tackling question answering with movies, out-of-vocabulary (OOV) could be a legitimate concern as the provided subtitles may contain slangs, special names and terms. We resolve the OOV issue by learning a more flexible word embedding based on character n-grams, using GloVe [24] as a teacher model. Denote the collection of words in GloVe as Ω. For each word $\mathbf{w} \in \Omega$, the resulting set of character n-grams is denoted as $G_{\mathbf{w}} = G_{\mathbf{w}}^1 \cup G_{\mathbf{w}}^3 \cup G_{\mathbf{w}}^6$, where 1-gram, 3-gram, and 6-gram tokens are considered in our formulation. Notice that in constructing $G_{\mathbf{w}}^3$ and $G_{\mathbf{w}}^6$, $\mathbf{w}$ is first augmented by adding the special token "<" at the beginning and ">" at the end. Thus assuming $\mathbf{w}$ is of length ℓ, we have $|G_{\mathbf{w}}^3| = \ell$ and $|G_{\mathbf{w}}^6| = \ell - 3$.

Now let the proposed word embedding be ϕ and the one by GloVe be $\tilde{\phi}$. Using the latter as a teacher model, we train a multi-layer perceptron to realize ϕ by minimizing the following loss function:

$$L(\phi) = \sum_{\mathbf{w} \in \Omega} D\left(\tilde{\phi}(\mathbf{w}), \phi(\mathbf{w})\right) \tag{1}$$

$$= \sum_{\mathbf{w} \in \Omega} D\left(\tilde{\phi}(\mathbf{w}), \sum_{\mathbf{g} \in G_{\mathbf{w}}} \phi(\mathbf{g})\right) \tag{2}$$

where D is defined to be the cosine distance function, *i.e.*, $D(\mathbf{x}, \mathbf{y}) = 1 - \cos(\mathbf{x}, \mathbf{y})$ and $\mathbf{g} \in G_{\mathbf{w}}$ is any of the n-gram tokens yielded by $\mathbf{w}$. From (1) and (2), we see that the new embedding $\phi(\mathbf{w})$ is obtained by summing over the embeddings of all n-gram tokens of $\mathbf{w}$. For $\mathbf{w} \in \Omega$, the proposed word embedding ϕ behaves like the GloVe embedding $\tilde{\phi}$. More importantly, it alleviates the OOV problem by integrating the embeddings of n-gram tokens via (2). To achieve sentence embedding, we simply divide each sentence in all provided $S, \mathbf{q}, A$ from the MovieQA dataset to words, and apply ϕ to each of those words. We can then employ *Smooth Inverse Frequency Weighting* scheme [3] to obtain sentence embeddings. With the embedding (linguistic) dimension d_ℓ set to 300, we have $S \in \mathbb{R}^{d_\ell \times N}$, $\mathbf{q} \in \mathbb{R}^{d_\ell \times 1}$, $A \in \mathbb{R}^{d_\ell \times 5}$, and $C_{\mathbf{q}} \in \{0, 1\}^{N \times 1}$, where $C_{\mathbf{q}}$ is a mask indicating those frames of the video clips relevant to $\mathbf{q}$.

3.2   Joint Embedding

Once we have respectively obtained the visual and linguistic representations, it is useful to investigate the association between the two modalities for more effectively solving the QA task. To this end, we reduce exploring the two embeddings to learning the relatedness of the representations in a *common space*, where a similar idea can be found in addressing image captioning [34] or VQA [11]. Using the notation "dnormal2" to represent taking "L_2-normalization" and then "dropout," we design the following *normalized affine transform* $\mathcal{J} : \mathbb{R}^{d_1} \to \mathbb{R}^{d_2}$ such that

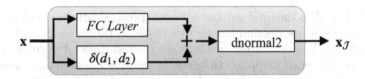

Fig. 2. Normalized affine transform $\mathcal{J}$: The dropout layer is performed after the $L2$-normalization in the "dnormal2" block. We denote the normalized affine mapping by $\mathbf{x} \overset{\mathcal{J}}{\longmapsto} \mathbf{x}_{\mathcal{J}}$ and therefore $X \overset{\mathcal{J}}{\longrightarrow} X_{\mathcal{J}}$.

$$\mathcal{J}(\mathbf{x}; d_1, d_2) = \text{dnormal2}((\delta(d_1, d_2)I + W_{\mathbf{x}}) \cdot \mathbf{x} + \mathbf{b}_{\mathbf{x}}) \tag{3}$$

where $\mathbf{x} \in \mathbb{R}^{d_1 \times 1}, \mathbf{b}_{\mathbf{x}} \in \mathbb{R}^{d_2 \times 1}, W_{\mathbf{x}} \in \mathbb{R}^{d_2 \times d_1}$ and $\delta(d_1, d_2)$ is the Kronecker delta, namely, $\delta(d_1, d_2) = 1$ when $d_1 = d_2$ and 0, otherwise. We implement the transform $\mathcal{J}$ as a single fully-connected layer. In particular, when $d_1 = d_2$, $\mathcal{J}$ does not alter the feature dimension so we can add a short-cut connection in the network to boost the performance. Also note that in (3), dropout and L_2-normalization are used to regularize the transform $\mathcal{J}$. Fig. 2 shows the network architecture of the affine transform $\mathcal{J}$.

With $\mathcal{J}$ in (3), the joint embedding of visual and linguistic representations can be achieved by transforming the visual dimension from $d_v = 2048$ to $d_\ell = 300$. We first apply $\mathcal{J}$ to each visual feature $\mathbf{v}$ of the visual tensor V and obtain the transformed visual tensor as

$$\mathbf{v}_{\mathcal{J}} = \mathcal{J}(\mathbf{v}; d_v, d_\ell) \Rightarrow V_{\mathcal{J}} = \mathcal{J}(V; d_v, d_\ell) \in \mathbb{R}^{d_\ell \times N \times B} \tag{4}$$

where the parameters of $\mathcal{J}$ to be learned are $W_{\mathbf{v}}$ and $\mathbf{b}_{\mathbf{v}}$. On the other hand, the transform $\mathcal{J}$ (now with a short-cut connection) can be applied to the linguistic data S, $\mathbf{q}$ and A, respectively. That is, we consider in turn the three types of linguistic data. For each $\mathbf{x} \in \{\mathbf{s}\,(\text{subtitle}), \mathbf{q}\,(\text{question}), \mathbf{a}\,(\text{answer})\}$, the transformed linguistic tensors are derived as follows:

$$\mathbf{x}_{\mathcal{J}} = \mathcal{J}(\mathbf{x}; d_\ell, d_\ell) \Rightarrow X_{\mathcal{J}} = \mathcal{J}(X; d_\ell, d_\ell). \tag{5}$$

The above mappings would yield $S_{\mathcal{J}} \in \mathbb{R}^{d_\ell \times N}$, $\mathbf{q}_{\mathcal{J}} \in \mathbb{R}^{d_\ell \times 1}$, and $A_{\mathcal{J}} \in \mathbb{R}^{d_\ell \times 5}$. Analogously, for transforming the linguistic representations with (3), the parameters to be learned in each case are $W_{\mathbf{x}}$ and $\mathbf{b}_{\mathbf{x}}$, for $\mathbf{x} \in \{\mathbf{s}, \mathbf{q}, \mathbf{a}\}$.

The transformed visual tensor $V_{\mathcal{J}} \in \mathbb{R}^{d_\ell \times N \times B}$ accounts for B objects in each image frame. To obtain the final visual representation, denoted as $U_{\mathcal{J}} \in \mathbb{R}^{d_\ell \times N}$, we compute the attention cue $\alpha_{\mathbf{q}}^o$ for each detected object o by

$$\alpha_{\mathbf{q}}^o[j, k] = \text{drelu}(\mathbf{q}_{\mathcal{J}}^{\top} \cdot V_{\mathcal{J}}[j, k]), \quad \text{for } 1 \leq j \leq N, \ 1 \leq k \leq B \tag{6}$$

where we use the notation "drelu" to denote the application of two consecutive operations, namely, first taking "relu" and then "dropout". Then, by weighted summing the B object features in each frame according to the resulting attention $\alpha_{\mathbf{q}}^o$, we have

$$U_{\mathcal{J}}[i, j] = \sum_{k=1}^{B} V_{\mathcal{J}}[i, j, k] \times \alpha_{\mathbf{q}}^o[j, k]. \tag{7}$$

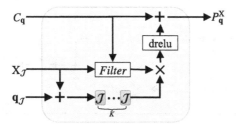

Fig. 3. A2A scheme: Attention propagation is applied to uncover latent but useful information from the data to help answer question **q**. *"Filter"* means the operation to select the subset of the input indicating by mask $C_{\mathbf{q}}$. $X \in \{V, S\}$

We now give an interpretation of (7). The attention matrix $\alpha_{\mathbf{q}}^o[j, k]$ reflects the relatedness of the detected object o_k in image frame j to the given question **q**. Thus, the final visual representation $U_{\mathcal{J}}[i, j]$ highlights the association between feature i and frame j concerning **q**.

3.3 Attention Propagation

For each question **q** pertaining to a specific movie in the MovieQA dataset, the provided mask $C_{\mathbf{q}} \in \{0, 1\}^{N \times 1}$ indicates those image frames relevant to answering the question **q**. We observed that $C_{\mathbf{q}}$ might not always yield sufficient information to answer the question. It is constructive to augment the provided clues by including other useful information from those neglected by $C_{\mathbf{q}}$. We thus propose an effective A2A scheme called *attention propagation* to augment $C_{\mathbf{q}}$. Without loss of generality, the following discussion focuses on the subtitle information in that the steps for dealing with visual information are similar.

Attention propagation for the linguistic information takes as input a specific transformed question $\mathbf{q}_{\mathcal{J}}$, the transformed subtitles $S_{\mathcal{J}}$, and the clue mask $C_{\mathbf{q}}$ to uncover the propagated subtitle mask $P_{\mathbf{q}}^S$. The propagation process starts by incorporating $\mathbf{q}_{\mathcal{J}}$ into $S_{\mathcal{J}}$. The affine transform $\mathcal{J}$ in (3) is then repeatedly applied to the question-augmented subtitle tensor so that a more flexible representation can be learned, which will be used to compute $P_{\mathbf{q}}^S$. We illustrate the mechanism of attention propagation in Fig. 3, and summarize the steps as follows.

1. Initialize and iterate the question-augmented subtitle tensor with

$$\hat{S}_{\mathbf{q}}^1 = S_{\mathcal{J}} + \mathbf{q}_{\mathcal{J}} \cdot \mathbf{1}^{1 \times N} \text{ and } \hat{S}_{\mathbf{q}}^k = \mathcal{J}(\hat{S}_{\mathbf{q}}^{k-1}; d_\ell, d_\ell), \ k = 2, \ldots, K.$$

To simplify the notation, the resulting $\hat{S}_{\mathbf{q}}^K$ will be written as $\hat{S}_{\mathbf{q}}$, while the iteration parameter K will be discussed in the experiments.

2. Let $N_{\mathbf{q}}$ be the number of relevant subtitles (frames) filtered by $C_{\mathbf{q}}$, and $S_{\mathbf{q}}^+ \in \mathbb{R}^{d_\ell \times N_{\mathbf{q}}}$ be the collection of relevant subtitles. We define the relatedness $F_{\mathbf{q}} \in \mathbb{R}^{N \times N_{\mathbf{q}}}$ of each subtitle to the relevant ones by $F_{\mathbf{q}} = \text{drelu}(\hat{S}_{\mathbf{q}}^\top \cdot S_{\mathbf{q}}^+)$.

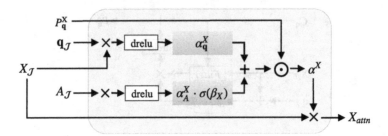

Fig. 4. A2A scheme: QA attention can be obtained via fusing multimodality attention and exploring the augmented mask P_q^X yielded by attention propagation.

3. The propagated mask $P_q^S \in \mathbb{R}^{N \times 1}$ can now be computed by

$$P_q^S[i] = \min\left\{1, C_q[i] + \frac{1}{N_q}\sum_{j=1}^{N_q} F_q[i,j]\right\} \text{ for } 1 \leq i \leq N. \quad (8)$$

The propagated visual mask $P_q^V \in \mathbb{R}^{N \times 1}$ for the given q and C_q can be obtained analogously. With the two propagated masks we are now ready to complete our method based on the augmented visual and linguistic information.

3.4 QA Attention

With the visual tensor $U_{\mathcal{J}}$, we can evaluate its question attention $\alpha_q^V \in \mathbb{R}^{N \times 1}$ and the answer attention $\alpha_A^V \in \mathbb{R}^{N \times 5}$. Similarly, we could also compute the question attention α_q^S and the answer attention α_A^S for the subtitle tensor $S_{\mathcal{J}}$. Specifically, we have

$$\alpha_q^V = \text{drelu}(U_{\mathcal{J}}^\top \cdot q_{\mathcal{J}}), \qquad \alpha_A^V = \text{drelu}(U_{\mathcal{J}}^\top \cdot A_{\mathcal{J}}), \quad (9)$$

$$\alpha_q^S = \text{drelu}(S_{\mathcal{J}}^\top \cdot q_{\mathcal{J}}), \qquad \alpha_A^S = \text{drelu}(S_{\mathcal{J}}^\top \cdot A_{\mathcal{J}}). \quad (10)$$

We add up the tiled question attention and the answer attention, scaled by the sigmoid output of a learnable variable, and then element-wise multiply the aggregated attention by the respective propagated mask P_q. Thus, we can obtain the visual attention $\alpha^V \in \mathbb{R}^{N \times 5}$ and subtitle attention $\alpha^S \in \mathbb{R}^{N \times 5}$ by

$$\alpha^V = (\alpha_q^V \cdot \mathbf{1}^{1 \times 5} + \sigma(\beta_V) \cdot \alpha_A^V) \odot (P_q^V \cdot \mathbf{1}^{1 \times 5}) \quad (11)$$

$$\alpha^S = (\alpha_q^S \cdot \mathbf{1}^{1 \times 5} + \sigma(\beta_S) \cdot \alpha_A^S) \odot (P_q^S \cdot \mathbf{1}^{1 \times 5}) \quad (12)$$

where $\odot$ is the element-wise multiplication operator for tensors, β_V and β_S are two learnable variables, and $\sigma(\cdot)$ is the sigmoid function. (See Fig. 4 for illustration of the architecture.) Finally, we can derive the attention-weighted visual representation V_{attn} and subtitle representation S_{attn} by

$$V_{attn} = U_{\mathcal{J}} \cdot \alpha^V \in \mathbb{R}^{d_\ell \times 5}, \quad (13)$$

$$S_{attn} = S_{\mathcal{J}} \cdot \alpha^S \in \mathbb{R}^{d_\ell \times 5}. \quad (14)$$

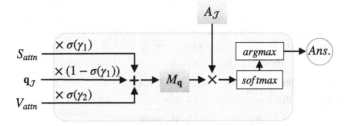

Fig. 5. Illustration of the network architecture to output the MQA responses.

3.5 Optimal Answer Response

By fusing the two modalities of visual and linguistic information, we obtain the overall movie representation $M_{\mathbf{q}} \in \mathbb{R}^{d_\ell \times 5}$ with respect to a specific question $\mathbf{q}$. (Also see Fig. 5 for the network architecture.) We then use "dnormal2" specified in formulating (3) to compute $M_{\mathbf{q}}$ as follows.

$$M_{\mathbf{q}} = \mathrm{dnormal2}(\sigma(\gamma_1) \cdot S_{attn} + (1 - \sigma(\gamma_1)) \cdot \mathbf{q}_{\mathcal{J}} \cdot \mathbf{1}^{1 \times 5} + \sigma(\gamma_2) \cdot V_{attn}) \quad (15)$$

where γ_1 and γ_2 are both learnable variables. Finally, the answer $\mathbf{a}_{j*} \in A$ to the question $\mathbf{q}$ by our method is given by finding the highest response $R[j^*]$, where

$$j^* = \arg \max_{1 \leq j \leq 5} R[j] = \sum_{i=1}^{d_\ell} M_{\mathbf{q}}[i, j] \times A_{\mathcal{J}}[i, j]. \quad (16)$$

4 Experiments and Discussions

All our experiments are carried out on the MovieQA benchmark dataset [30]. The evaluation of our method contains four parts, including *key components ablation*, *leader board comparison*, *model selection*, and *question types comparison*. Visualization examples of question answering are also included in the results.

Dataset Specification. The MovieQA dataset contains 14,944 multi-choice questions related to 408 movies. Each question has five candidate answers of which only one is correct. We focus on the task of "Video+Subtitels," which contains 6,462 QAs. These QAs are further split into 4,318, 886, and 1,258 for training, validation, and testing, respectively. All the results are measured in accuracy.

Implementation Details. To train our model, we use softmax cross entropy as our loss function between response R and one-hot vector $\mathbf{a}_{gt}$. For general hyperparameter setting, we set the dropout keep rate to 0.9 and the scale of L2-regularizer to 0.01. We use "powersign-ld" [5] as our neural optimizer with 128 decay epochs and a batch size of 1. All model parameters are initialized with Glorot normal initialization [7] and the learning rate is 10^{-3} with linear cosine decay [5]. In validating and testing our method, we use the same ensemble strategy as RWMN [23], which independently trains multiple models for answering,

Table 2. Ablation comparison for key components of our A2A method on the validation and test sets of MovieQA benchmark. For validation set, we report accuracy results within the 95% confidence interval. A variant that is not evaluated is marked by (-). Details of the model abbreviations are described in Sect. 4.1.

Method	Validation (%)	Method	Validation (%)	Test (%)
A2A-noJE	26.44 ± 0.78	A2A-noDropout	41.19 ± 0.40	-
A2A-noProp	40.58 ± 0.30	A2A-noSacle	40.01 ± 0.52	-
A2A-noQAattn	33.71 ± 0.31	A2A-noSubtProp	40.28 ± 0.41	-
A2A-noVis	41.22 ± 0.14	A2A-noVisProp	41.05 ± 0.69	41.65
A2A-noSubt	28.53 ± 0.28	A2A	41.66 ± 0.25	41.97
A2A-noL2norm	20.00			

to mitigate the potential overfitting issue on MovieQA due to relatively small dataset size and highly difficult task. To report our results, we average the best accuracy of 10 models with different random initializations on the validation set. As for the test set, we use majority voting by 20 models with different random initializations as an ensemble model, and submit our result to the official test server[1]. Both validation and test set are held out from training.

4.1 Ablation Study on Key Components

We perform an in-depth ablation study on the key components in our method, and report the results in Table 2. The experiment includes 11 variants of A2A.

  (i) (A2A-noJE) model: replacing normalized affine transformation with identity transformation in joint embedding.
 (ii) (A2A-noProp) model: replacing propagated attention with mask C_q.
(iii) (A2A-noQAattn) model: skipping the use of QA attention.
 (iv) (A2A-noVisual) model: skipping the visual input.
  (v) (A2A-noSubtitle) model: skipping the subtitle input.
 (vi) (A2A-noL2norm) model: skipping L_2-normalization after each layer.
(vii) (A2A-noDropout) model: skipping dropout after L_2-normalization.
(viii) (A2A-noScale) model: skipping the use of sigmoid scaling.
 (ix) (A2A-noSubtProp) model: attention propagation using only visual input.
  (x) (A2A-noVisProp) model: attention propagation using only subtitle input.
 (xi) (A2A) model: using all components described in our method.

In Table 2, we find that the full A2A model achieves the best performance on both the validation and test sets among all the other variants. It implies that all of our model components are essential. For instance, A2A-noJE has a performance gap in comparison with A2A model. A reasonable explanation is that the normalized affine transform $\mathcal{J}$ plays a key role in jointly embedding different modalities to the same semantic space, and enables the subsequent model

---

[1] http://movieqa.cs.toronto.edu/new_submission/.

Table 3. Performance comparison among the proposed A2A method, others from MovieQA leader board, and the two baselines, SSCB and MemN2N, in the original MovieQA paper [30]. "−" means the method is not evaluated.

Methods	Validation	Test	Methods	Validation	Test
A2A (ours)	41.66%	**41.97%**	RWMN [23]	38.67%	36.25%
A2A-noVisProp	41.05%	**41.65%**	DEMN [16]	44.70%	29.97%
LMN [31]	42.50%	39.03%	SSCB [30]	21.90%	−
SC-MemN2N [4]	−	38.16%	MemN2N [30]	34.20%	−

Table 4. Comparison with 4 implementation variants of A2A.

Variants	Validation
A2A-GloVe	$41.12 \pm 0.594\%$
A2A-U+SAttn	$41.06 \pm 0.318\%$
A2A-SoftmaxAttn	$28.32 \pm 0.087\%$
A2A-FeatRelu	$31.92 \pm 0.410\%$
A2A	$41.66 \pm 0.406\%$

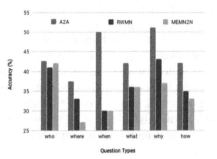

Fig. 6. Performance comparison on different question types.

components to explore correlations among inputs. Further, A2A-noQAattn also has a large gap in performance which indicates the QA attention mechanism is crucial to the localization of the most relevant content in video context.

We further investigate the outcome of source ablation. While A2A-noVis is the second best among all variants, we notice that it is better than A2A-noVisProp and A2a-noSubtProp. A possible reason is that the propagated attention of single modality of either the visual or subtitle input may impinge on the QA attention due to the connection between the two is left out.

Last but not least, we observe from the performance of A2A-noL2norm that L_2-normalization on features is critical to training our method for solving the MQA task. Without using L_2-normalization, the training would eventually fail. The phenomenon is caused by gradient vanishing due to small output values. On the other hand, A2A-noDropout and A2A-noScale are slightly inferior to A2A model, which suggests dropout operation and sigmoid scaling are needed.

4.2 Leader Board Comparison

In Table 3, we compare the A2A models with those from the MovieQA leader board[2] and the baselines used in Tapaswi *et al.* [30]. Our method achieves the best performance on the test set among all others. Compared with LMN [31],

---

[2] http://movieqa.cs.toronto.edu/leaderboard/.

A2A-noVisProp improves by 2.62% in accuracy and A2A improves by 2.94%. The results also indicate that our visual attention propagation is effective.

4.3   Model Selection

To search the best combination for MovieQA benchmark, we experiment on different parameter settings and implementation variants. Due to the limited space allowed, we omit the detailed experimental results and discuss our findings. The model selection is examined by varying different combinations of the number of layers in the normalized affine transform, visual propagated attention layers, and subtitle propagated attention layers. First, we observe that increasing the number of normalized affine transform layers in joint embedding does not yield performance gain, and indeed one layer is sufficient to achieve relatively good performance. Second, increasing the numbers of subtitle and visual propagated attention layers is beneficial to the performance. However, it becomes worse when the number of layers is over three/five for visual/subtitle propagated attention. The reason might be due to model overfitting while increasing the parameters. We next compare four implementation variants of A2A as reported in Table 4.

 (i) (A2A-GloVe) model: using GloVe [24] for word embedding. Each unknows token is mapped to the average vector of whole GloVe embedding.
 (ii) (A2A-U+SAttn) model: constructing V_{attn} and S_{attn} with the summation of visual α^V attention, and subtitle α^S attention.
(iii) (A2A-SoftmaxAttn) model: replacing relu with softmax to yield attention.
(iv) (A2A-FeatRelu) model: adding relu function to every fully-connected layer.

From Table 4, we find A2A-GloVe is slightly worse than the full A2A model. It suggests that the advantage of using our new word embedding is noticible but subtle. Presumably, the main reason might be that only a small proportion of movies (e.g. fiction movies which usually have characters with unusual names.) incurs the OOV problem. For A2A-U+SAttn, it performs a bit worse than A2A. It is because the summation of both attention cues may cause the final representation M_q to get some irrelevant information from visual and subtitle representations. Moreover, A2A-softmaxAttn and A2A-FeatRelu models degrade drastically, due to the use of softmax to account for attention fusion (Table 5).

4.4   Question Types Comparison

In MovieQA benchmark [30], questions can be classified into six different question types: *Who, Where, When, What, Why,* and *How.* Usually, answering *Where, When, What* questions (*e.g.*, "Where does Bruce go after revealing himself to Vicki as batman?, When does Forrest discover that he can run really fast for the first time?, What does Gandalf retrieve from Saruman?") requires localizing relevant information in context, and answering *Why* and *How* questions (*e.g.*, "Why does Gollum ask Frodo to leave Sam behind?, How does Bruce

Table 5. The examples of our results. The answer with green color is the ground truth, and one with Italic style is the predicted answer.

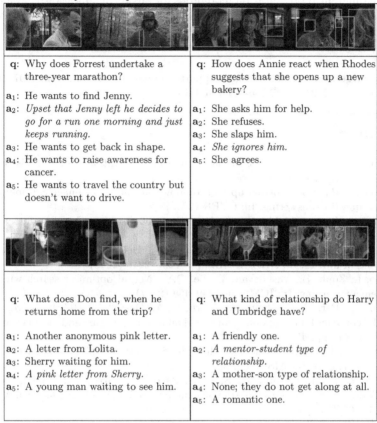

q: Why does Forrest undertake a three-year marathon? **a₁**: He wants to find Jenny. **a₂**: *Upset that Jenny left he decides to go for a run one morning and just keeps running.* **a₃**: He wants to get back in shape. **a₄**: He wants to raise awareness for cancer. **a₅**: He wants to travel the country but doesn't want to drive.	**q**: How does Annie react when Rhodes suggests that she opens up a new bakery? **a₁**: She asks him for help. **a₂**: She refuses. **a₃**: She slaps him. **a₄**: *She ignores him.* **a₅**: She agrees.
q: What does Don find, when he returns home from the trip? **a₁**: Another anonymous pink letter. **a₂**: A letter from Lolita. **a₃**: Sherry waiting for him. **a₄**: *A pink letter from Sherry.* **a₅**: A young man waiting to see him.	**q**: What kind of relationship do Harry and Umbridge have? **a₁**: A friendly one. **a₂**: *A mentor-student type of relationship.* **a₃**: A mother-son type of relationship. **a₄**: None; they do not get along at all. **a₅**: A romantic one.

survive the Joker's bullets?") requires abridging the context and relational reasoning. As for *Who* questions(*e.g.*, "Who attacks Zachry, Adam, and Zachry's nephew?"), it needs name entity matching.

Figure 6 compares the accuracy of A2A, RWMN [23], and MeMN2N [30] on different question types. We find that A2A outperforms all the other methods on every question type. For *Who* questions, A2A works slightly better than the others. The performance improvement of A2A on every question type except *Who* is over 4.5%. It indicates that our method is quite capable of summarizing and reasoning in *How* and *Why* questions. Furthermore, our method can extract the key part of context in *Where, When,* and *What* questions.

5   Conclusions

We have shown that the proposed Attention to Attention (A2A) reasoning effectively addresses the problem of movie question answering. With the A2A reasoning mechanism, our method distills attention cues to aggregate and to associate the different representation modalities for answering questions. Besides, we establish a flexible n-grams word embedding for tackling the out-of-vocabulary issue. The experimental results show the state-of-the-art performance on the "Video+Subtitles" entry of MovieQA benchmark dataset.

Acknowledgement. This work was supported in part by MOST Grants 107-2634-F-001-002 and 106-2221-E-007-080-MY3 in Taiwan.

References

1. Agrawal, A., et al.: VQA: visual question answering. Int. J. Comput. Vis. **123**(1), 4–31 (2017). www.visualqa.org
2. Anderson, P., et al.: Bottom-up and top-down attention for image captioning and visual question answering. In: CVPR (2018)
3. Arora, S., Liang, Y., Ma, T.: A simple but tough-to-beat baseline for sentence embeddings. In: ICLR (2017)
4. Azab, M., Wang, M., Smith, M., Kojima, N., Deng, J., Mihalcea, R.: Speaker naming in movies. In: NAACL-HLT, pp. 2206–2216 (2018)
5. Bello, I., Zoph, B., Vasudevan, V., Le, Q.V.: Neural optimizer search with reinforcement learning. In: ICML, pp. 459–468 (2017)
6. Fukui, A., Park, D.H., Yang, D., Rohrbach, A., Darrell, T., Rohrbach, M.: Multimodal compact bilinear pooling for visual question answering and visual grounding. In: EMNLP, pp. 457–468 (2016)
7. Glorot, X., Bengio, Y.: Understanding the difficulty of training deep feedforward neural networks. In: AISTATS, pp. 249–256 (2010)
8. Goyal, Y., Khot, T., Summers-Stay, D., Batra, D., Parikh, D.: Making the V in VQA matter: elevating the role of image understanding in Visual Question Answering. In: CVPR (2017)
9. He, K., Zhang, X., Ren, S., Sun, J.: Deep residual learning for image recognition. arXiv preprint arXiv:1512.03385 (2015)
10. Hochreiter, S., Schmidhuber, J.: Long short-term memory. Neural Comput. **9**(8), 1735–1780 (1997)
11. Hu, H., Chao, W.L., Sha, F.: Learning answer embeddings for visual question answering. In: CVPR (2018)
12. Huang, J., et al.: Speed/accuracy trade-offs for modern convolutional object detectors. In: CVPR, pp. 3296–3297 (2017)
13. Jang, Y., Song, Y., Yu, Y., Kim, Y., Kim, G.: TGIF-QA: toward spatio-temporal reasoning in visual question answering. In: CVPR (2017)
14. Johnson, J., et al.: Inferring and executing programs for visual reasoning. In: ICCV, pp. 3008–3017 (2017)
15. Kazemi, V., Elqursh, A.: Show, ask, attend, and answer: a strong baseline for visual question answering. CoRR abs/1704.03162 (2017)
16. Kim, K., Heo, M., Choi, S., Zhang, B.: DeepStory: video story QA by deep embedded memory networks. In: IJCAI, pp. 2016–2022 (2017)
17. Lin, T.-Y., et al.: Microsoft COCO: common objects in context. In: Fleet, D., Pajdla, T., Schiele, B., Tuytelaars, T. (eds.) ECCV 2014. LNCS, vol. 8693, pp. 740–755. Springer, Cham (2014). https://doi.org/10.1007/978-3-319-10602-1_48
18. Liu, F., Perez, J.: Gated end-to-end memory networks. In: EACL (2017)

19. Lu, J., Yang, J., Batra, D., Parikh, D.: Hierarchical question-image co-attention for visual question answering. In: NIPS, pp. 289–297 (2016)
20. Mikolov, T., Chen, K., Corrado, G., Dean, J.: Efficient estimation of word representations in vector space. CoRR (2013)
21. Miller, A.H., Fisch, A., Dodge, J., Karimi, A., Bordes, A., Weston, J.: Key-value memory networks for directly reading documents. In: EMNLP, pp. 1400–1409 (2016)
22. Mun, J., Seo, P.H., Jung, I., Han, B.: MarioQA: answering questions by watching gameplay videos. In: ICCV, pp. 2886–2894 (2017)
23. Na, S., Lee, S., Kim, J., Kim, G.: A read-write memory network for movie story understanding. In: ICCV (2017)
24. Pennington, J., Socher, R., Manning, C.D.: Glove: global vectors for word representation. In: EMNLP, pp. 1532–1543 (2014)
25. Rajpurkar, P., Zhang, J., Lopyrev, K., Liang, P.: Squad: 100, 000+ questions for machine comprehension of text. In: EMNLP, pp. 2383–2392 (2016)
26. Ren, S., He, K., Girshick, R.B., Sun, J.: Faster R-CNN: towards real-time object detection with region proposal networks. IEEE Trans. Pattern Anal. Mach. Intell. **39**(6), 1137–1149 (2017)
27. Rohrbach, A., et al.: Movie description. Int. J. Comput. Vis. (2017)
28. Simonyan, K., Zisserman, A.: Very deep convolutional networks for large-scale image recognition. In: ICLR (2015)
29. Sukhbaatar, S., Szlam, A., Weston, J., Fergus, R.: End-to-end memory networks. In: NIPS (2015)
30. Tapaswi, M., Zhu, Y., Stiefelhagen, R., Torralba, A., Urtasun, R., Fidler, S.: MovieQA: understanding stories in movies through question-answering. In: CVPR (2016)
31. Wang, B., Xu, Y., Han, Y., Hong, R.: Movie question answering: remembering the textual cues for layered visual contents. In: AAAI (2018)
32. Weston, J., Bordes, A., Chopra, S., Mikolov, T.: Towards AI-complete question answering: a set of prerequisite toy tasks. CoRR abs/1502.05698 (2015)
33. Weston, J., Chopra, S., Bordes, A.: Memory networks. CoRR abs/1410.3916 (2014)
34. Wu, Q., Teney, D., Wang, P., Shen, C., Dick, A.R., van den Hengel, A.: Visual question answering: a survey of methods and datasets. Comput. Vis. Image Underst. **163**, 21–40 (2017)

TraMNet - Transition Matrix Network for Efficient Action Tube Proposals

Gurkirt Singh$^{(\boxtimes)}$, Suman Saha, and Fabio Cuzzolin

Visual Artificial Intelligence Laboratory (VAIL),
Oxford Brookes University, Oxford, UK
`gurkirt.singh-2105@brookes.ac.uk`

Abstract. Current state-of-the-art methods solve spatio-temporal action localisation by extending 2D anchors to 3D-cuboid proposals on stacks of frames, to generate sets of temporally connected bounding boxes called *action micro-tubes*. However, they fail to consider that the underlying anchor proposal hypotheses should also move (transition) from frame to frame, as the actor or the camera do. Assuming we evaluate n 2D anchors in each frame, then the number of possible transitions from each 2D anchor to the next, for a sequence of f consecutive frames, is in the order of $O(n^f)$, expensive even for small values of f.

To avoid this problem we introduce a **Transition-Matrix-based Network** (TraMNet) which relies on computing transition probabilities between anchor proposals while maximising their overlap with ground truth bounding boxes across frames, and enforcing sparsity via a transition threshold. As the resulting transition matrix is sparse and stochastic, this reduces the proposal hypothesis search space from $O(n^f)$ to the cardinality of the thresholded matrix. At training time, transitions are specific to cell locations of the feature maps, so that a sparse (efficient) transition matrix is used to train the network. At test time, a denser transition matrix can be obtained either by decreasing the threshold or by adding to it all the relative transitions originating from any cell location, allowing the network to handle transitions in the test data that might not have been present in the training data, thus making detection translation-invariant. We show that our network is able to handle sparse annotations such as those available in the DALY dataset, while allowing for both dense (accurate) or sparse (efficient) evaluation within a single model. We report extensive experiments on the DALY, UCF101-24 and Transformed-UCF101-24 datasets to support our claims.

This project has received funding from the European Union's Horizon 2020 research and innovation programme under grant agreement No. 779813 (SARAS).

Electronic supplementary material The online version of this chapter (https://doi.org/10.1007/978-3-030-20876-9_27) contains supplementary material, which is available to authorized users.

C. V. Jawahar et al. (Eds.): ACCV 2018, LNCS 11366, pp. 420–437, 2019.
https://doi.org/10.1007/978-3-030-20876-9_27

1   Introduction

Current state-of-the-art spatiotemporal action localisation works [1–3] focus on learning a spatiotemporal, multi-frame 3D representation by extending frame-level 2D object/action detection approaches [4–11]. These networks learn a feature representation from pairs [1] or chunks [2,3] of video frames, allowing them to implicitly learn the temporal correspondence between inter-frame action regions (bounding boxes). As a result, they can predict micro-tubes [1] or tubelets [2], i.e., temporally linked frame-level detections for short subsequences of a test video clip. Finally, these micro-tubes are linked [1–3] in time to locate action tube instances [11] spanning the whole video.

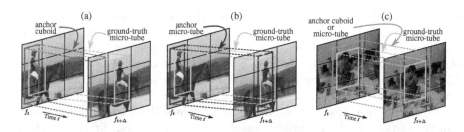

Fig. 1. Illustrating the key limitation of anchor cuboids using a "dynamic" action such as "horse riding". **(a)** A horse rider changes its location from frame f_t to $f_{t+\Delta}$ as shown by the ground truth bounding boxes (in green). As anchor cuboid generation [1,2] is constrained by the spatial location of the anchor box in the first frame f_t, the overall spatiotemporal IoU overlap between the ground-truth micro-tube and the anchor cuboid is relatively low. **(b)** In contrast, our anchor micro-tube proposal generator is much more flexible, as it efficiently explores the video search space via an approximate transition matrix estimated according to a hidden Markov model (HMM) formulation. As a result, the anchor micro-tube proposal (in blue) generated by the proposed model exhibits higher overlap with the ground-truth. **(c)** For "static" actions (such as "clap") in which the actor does not change location over time, anchor cuboid and anchor micro-tubes have the same spatiotemporal bounds. (Color figure online)

These approaches, however, raise two major concerns. Firstly, they [1–3] generate action proposals by extending 2D object proposals (anchor/prior boxes for images) [7,8] to 3D proposals (anchor cuboids for multiple frames) (cf. Fig. 1(a)). This cannot, by design, provide an optimal set of training hypotheses, as the video proposal search space ($\mathcal{O}(n^f)$) is much larger than the image proposal search space ($\mathcal{O}(n)$), where n is the number of anchor boxes per frame and f is the number of video frames considered. Furthermore, 3D anchor cuboids are very limiting for action detection purposes. Whereas they can be suitable for "static" actions (e.g. "handshake" or "clap", in which the spatial location of the actor(s) does not vary over time), they are most inappropriate for "dynamic" ones (e.g. "horse riding", "skiing"). Fig. 1 underscores this issue. For "horse riding", for instance, allowing "flexible" anchor micro-tubes (as those generated

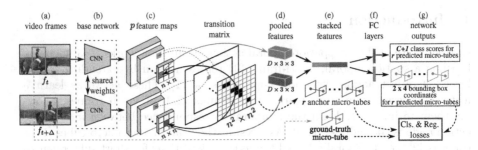

Fig. 2. Overview of our proposed TraMNet at training time. The diagram is described in the text.

by our approach, Fig. 1(b)) much improves the spatio-temporal overlap with the ground-truth (Fig. 1(a)). *Designing a deep network which can effectively make use of the video search space to generate high-quality action proposals, while keeping the computing cost as low as possible,* is then highly desirable. To this end, we produced a new action detection dataset which is a "transformed" version of UCF-101-24 [12], in which we force action instances to be dynamic (i.e., to change their spatial location significantly over time) by introducing random translations in the 2d spatial domain. We show that our proposed action detection approach outperforms the baseline [1] when trained and tested on this transformed dataset.

In the second place, action detection methods such as [2,3] require dense ground-truth annotation for network training: bounding-box annotation is required for k consecutive video frames, where k is the number of frames in a training example. Kalogeiton *et al.* [2] use $k = 6$ whereas for Hou *et al.* [3] $k = 8$. Generating such dense bounding box annotation for long video sequences is highly expensive and impractical [13,14]. The latest generation action detection benchmarks DALY [13] and AVA [14], in contrast, provide sparse bounding-box annotations. More specifically, DALY has 1 to 5 frames bounding box annotation per action instance, irrespective of the duration of an instance, whereas AVA only has one frame annotation per second. *This motivates the design of a deep network capable of handling sparse annotations, while still being able to predict micro-tubes over multiple frames.*

Unlike [2,3], Saha *et al.* [1] recently proposed to use *pairs* of successive frames $(f_t, f_{t+\Delta})$, thus eliminating the need for dense training annotation when Δ is large (e.g., $\Delta = \{5, 10, 21\}$) or arbitrary DALY [13]. If the spatio-temporal IoU (Intersection over Union) overlap between ground-truth micro-tube and action proposal could be improved (cf. Fig. 1), such a network would be able to handle sparse annotation (e.g., pairs of frames which are $\Delta = 21$ apart). Indeed, the use of pairs of successive frames $(f_t, f_{t+\Delta})$ in combination with the flexible anchor proposals introduced here, is arguably more efficient than any other state-of-the-art method [1,3,15] for handling sparse annotations (e.g. DALY [13] and AVA [14]).

Concept. Here we support the idea of constructing training examples using pairs of successive frames. However, the model we propose is able to generate a rich set of action proposals (which we call *anchor micro-tubes*, cf. Fig. 1) using a transition matrix (cf. Sect. 3.3) estimated from the available training set. Such transition matrix encodes the probability of a temporal link between an anchor box at time t and one at $t + \Delta$, and is estimated within the framework of discrete state/continuous observation hidden Markov models (HMMs, cf. Sect. 3.2) [16]. Here, the hidden states are the 2D bounding-box coordinates $[x_{min}, y_{min}, x_{max}, y_{max}]'$ of each anchor box from a (finite) hierarchy of fixed grids at different scales. The (continuous) observations are the kindred four-vectors of coordinates associated with the ground truth bounding boxes (which are instead allowed to be placed anywhere in the image). Anchor micro-tubes are not bound to be strictly of cuboidal (as in [1–3]) shape, thus giving higher IoU overlap with the ground-truth, specifically for instances where the spatial location of the actor changes significantly from f_t to $f_{t+\Delta}$ in a training pair. We thus propose a novel configurable deep neural network architecture (see Fig. 2 and Sect. 3) which leverages high-quality micro-tubes shaped by learnt anchor transition probabilities.

We quantitatively demonstrate that the resulting action detection framework: **(i)** is suitable for datasets with temporally sparse frame-level bounding box annotation (e.g. DALY [13] and AVA [14]); **(ii)** outperforms the current state-of-the-art [1, 2, 11] by exploiting the anchor transition probabilities learnt from the training data. **(iii)** is suitable for detecting highly 'dynamic' actions (Fig. 1), as shown by its outperforming the baseline [1] when trained and tested on the "transformed" UCF-101-24 dataset.

Overview of the Approach. Our network architecture builds on some of the architectural components of [1, 2, 8] (Fig. 2). The proposed network takes as input a pair of successive video frames $f_t, f_{t+\Delta}$ (where Δ is the inter-frame distance) (Fig. 2(a)) and propagates these frames through a base network comprised of two parallel CNN networks (Sect. 3.1 Fig. 2(b)), which produce two sets of p conv feature maps K_p^t and $K_p^{t+\Delta}$ forming a pyramid ((c)). These feature pyramids are used by a configurable pooling layer (Sect. 3.4 and Fig. 2(d)) to pool features based on the transition probabilities defined by a transition matrix $\mathbf{A}$ (Sect. 3.3, Fig. 2). The pooled conv features are then stacked (Sect. 3.4 and Fig. 2(e)), and the resulting feature vector is passed to two parallel fully connected (linear) layers (one for classification and another for micro-tube regression, see Sect. 3.5 and Fig. 2(f)), which predict the output micro-tube and its classification scores for each class C (g). Each training mini-batch is used to compute the classification and micro-tube regression losses given the output predictions, ground truth and anchor micro-tubes. We call our network *"configurable"* because the configuration of the pooling layer (see Fig. 2(d)) depends on the transition matrix $\mathbf{A}$, and can be changed by altering the threshold applied to $\mathbf{A}$ (cf. Sect. 3.3). or by replacing the transition matrix with a new one for another dataset.

Contributions. In summary, we present a novel deep learning architecture for spatio-temporal action localisation which:

- introduces an efficient and flexible anchor micro-tube hypothesis generation framework to generate high-quality action proposals;
- handles significant spatial movement in dynamic actors without penalising more static actions;
- is a scalable solution for training models on both sparse and dense annotations.

2   Related Work

Traditionally, spatio-temporal action localisation was widely studied using local or figure centric features [17–21]. E.g., inspired by Oneata *et al.* [18] and Jain *et al.* [19], Gemert *et al.* [17] would use unsupervised clustering to generate 3D tubelets using unsupervised frame level proposals and dense trajectories. As their method is based on dense-trajectory features [22], however, it fails to detect actions characterised by small motions [17]. More recently, motivated by the record-breaking performance of CNNs based object detectors [7,8,23] scholars [4,5,9–11,24,25] have tried to extend object detectors to videos for spatio-temporal action localisation. These approaches, however, fail to tackle spatial and temporal reasoning jointly at the network level, as spatial detection and temporal association are treated as two disjoint problems. Interestingly, Yang *et al.* [26] use features from current, frame t proposals to 'anticipate' region proposal locations in $t + \Delta$ and use them to generate detections at time $t + \Delta$, thus failing to take full advantage of the anticipation trick to help with the linking process.

More recent works try to address this problem by predicting micro-tubes [1] or tubelets [2,3] for a small set of frames taken together. As mentioned, however, these approaches use anchor hypotheses which are simply extensions of the hypothesis in the first frame, thus failing to model significant location transitions. In opposition, here we address this issue by proposing anchor regions

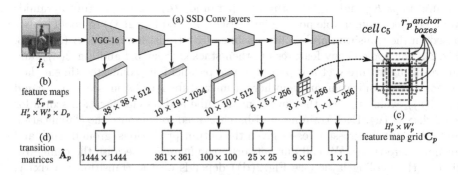

Fig. 3. Base network architecture. **(a)** SSD convolutional layers; **(b)** the corresponding conv feature maps outputted by each conv layer; **(c)** r anchor boxes with different aspect ratios assigned to cell location c_5 of the 3×3 feature map grid; **(d)** transition matrices for the P feature map grids in the pyramid, where $P = 6$.

which move across frames, as a function of a transition matrix estimated at training time from anchor proposals of maximal overlap.

Advances in action recognition are always going to be helpful in action detection from a general representation learning point of view. For instance, Gu et al. [14] improve on [2,10] by plugging in the inflated 3D network proposed by [27] as a base network on multiple frames. Although they use a very strong base network pre-trained on the large "kinetics" [15] dataset, they do not handle the linking process within the network as the AVA [14] dataset's annotations are not temporally linked.

Temporal association is usually performed by some form of "tracking-by-detection" [4,5,11] of frame level detections. Kalogeiton et al. [2] adapt the linking process proposed by Singh et al. [11] to link tubelets, whereas Saha et al. [1] build on [4] to link micro-tubes. Temporal trimming is handled separately either by sliding window [10,13], or in a label smoothing formulation solved using dynamic programming [9,28]. For this task we adopt the micro-tube linking from [2,11] and the online temporal trimming from [11]. We demonstrate that the temporal trimming aspect does not help on UCF101-24 (in fact, it damages performance), while it helps on the DALY dataset in which only 4% of the video duration is covered by action instances.

3 Methodology

In Sect. 3.1, we introduce the base network architecture used for feature learning. We cast the action proposal generation problem in a hidden Markov model (HMM) formulation (Sect. 3.2), and introduce an approximate estimation of the HMM transition probability matrix using a heuristic approach (Sect. 3.3). The proposed approximation is relatively inexpensive and works gracefully (Sect. 4). In Sect. 3.4, a configurable pooling layer architecture is presented which pools convolutional features from the regions in the two frames linked by the estimated transition probabilities. Finally, the output layers of the network (i.e., the micro-tube regression and classification layers) are described in Sect. 3.5.

3.1 Base Network

The base network takes as inputs a pair of video frames $(f_t, f_{t+\Delta})$ and propagates them through two parallel CNN streams (cf. Fig. 2(b)). In Fig. 3(a), we show the network diagram of one of the CNN streams; the other follows the same design.

The network architecture is based on Single-Shot-Detector (SSD) [8]. The CNN stream outputs a set of P convolutional feature maps K_p, $p = \{1, 2, ..., P = 6\}$ (feature pyramid, cfr. Fig. 3(b)) of shape $[H'_p \times W'_p \times D_p]$, where H'_p, W'_p and D_p are the height, width and depth of the feature map at network depth p, respectively. For $P = 6$ the conv feature map spatial dimensions are $H' = W' = \{38, 19, 10, 5, 3, 1\}$, respectively. The feature maps at the lower depth levels (i.e., $p = 1, 2$ or 3) are responsible for encoding smaller objects/actions, whereas feature maps at higher depth levels encode larger actions/objects. For each cell location c_{ij} of $[H'_p \times W'_p]$ feature map grid $\mathbf{C_p}$, r anchor boxes (with different aspect ratios) are assigned where $r_p = \{4, 6, 6, 6, 4, 4\}$. E.g. at each cell location of the 3×3 grid in the pyramid, 4 anchor boxes are produced (Fig. 3(c)), resulting in a total of $3 \times 3 \times 4 = 36$ anchor boxes. These anchor boxes, assigned for all $P = 6$ distinct feature map grids, are then used to generate action proposal hypotheses based on the transition probability matrix, as explained below.

Note that the proposed framework is not limited to any particular base network architecture, and is flexible enough to accommodate any latest network [27, 29].

3.2 HMM-Based Action Proposal Generation

A *hidden Markov model* (HMM) models a time series of (directly measurable) *observations* $\mathbf{O} = \{\mathbf{o}_1, \mathbf{o}_2, ..., \mathbf{o}_T\}$, either discrete or continuous, as randomly generated at each time instant t by a *hidden state* $\mathbf{q}_t \in \mathbf{Q} = \{\mathbf{q}_1, \mathbf{q}_2, ..., \mathbf{q}_N\}$, whose series form a Markov chain, i.e., the conditional probability of the state at time t given $\mathbf{q}_1, ..., \mathbf{q}_{t-1}$ only depends on the value of the state $\mathbf{q}_{t-1}$ at time $t-1$. The whole information on the time series' dynamics is thus contained in a *transition probability matrix* $\mathbf{A} = [p_{ij}; i, j = 1, .., n]$, where $p_{ij} = P(\mathbf{q}_j | \mathbf{q}_i)$ is the probability of moving from state i to state j, and $\sum_{j=1}^{N} p_{ij} = 1 \; \forall i$.

In our setting, a state $\mathbf{q}_n$ is a vector containing the 2D bounding-box coordinates of one of the anchor boxes $[x^a_{min}, y^a_{min}, x^a_{max}, y^a_{max}]'$ in one of the grids forming the pyramid (Sect. 3.1). The transition matrix encodes the probabilities of a temporal link existing between an anchor box (indexed by i) at time t and another anchor box (indexed by j) at time $t + \Delta$. The continuous observations $\mathbf{o}_t$, $t = 1, ..., T$ are the ground-truth bounding boxes, so that $\mathbf{O}$ corresponds to a ground-truth action tube.

In hidden Markov models, observations are assumed to be Gaussian distributed given a state $\mathbf{q}_i$, with mean $\mathbf{o}^i_\mu$ and covariance $\mathbf{Q}^i_\Sigma$. After assuming an appropriate distribution for the initial state, e.g. $P(\mathbf{q}_0) \sim \mathcal{N}(0, I)$, the transition model $A = [P(\mathbf{q}_j | \mathbf{q}_i)]$ allows us to predict at each time t the probability $P(\mathbf{q}_t | \mathbf{O}_{1:t})$ of the current state given the history of previous observations, i.e., the probability of each anchor box at time t given the observed (partial) ground-truth action tube. Given a training set, the optimal HMM parameters (A, $\mathbf{o}^i_\mu$ and $\mathbf{Q}^i_\Sigma$ for $i = 1, ..., N$) can be learned using standard expectation maximisation (EM) or the Baum-Welch algorithm, by optimising the likelihood of the predictions $P(\mathbf{q}_t | \mathbf{O}_{1:t})$ produced by the model.

Once training is done, at test time, the mean $\mathbf{o}^{\hat{q}_t}_\mu$ of the conditional distribution of the observations given the state associated with the predicted state $\hat{\mathbf{q}}_t \doteq \arg\max_i P(\mathbf{q}_i | \mathbf{O}_{1:t})$ at time t can be used to initialise the anchor boxes for each of the P CNN feature map grids (Sect. 3.1). The learnt transition matrix $\mathbf{A}$ can be used to generate a set of training action proposals hypotheses (i.e., anchor micro-tubes, Fig. 1). As in our case the mean vectors $\mathbf{o}^i_\mu$, $i = 1, ..., N$ are known a-priori (as the coordinates of the anchor boxes are predefined for each feature map grid, Sect. 3.1), we do not allow the M-step of EM algorithm to update $\mathbf{Q}_\mu = [\mathbf{o}_\mu^i, i = 1, ..., N]$. Only the covariance matrix $\mathbf{Q}_\Sigma$ is updated.

3.3   Approximation of the HMM Transition Matrix

Although the above setting perfectly formalises the anchor box-ground truth detection relation over the time series of training frames, a number of computational issues arise. At training time, some states (anchor boxes) may not be associated with any of the observations (ground-truth boxes) in the E-step, leading to zero covariance for those states. Furthermore, for a large number of states (in our case $N = 8732$ anchor boxes), it takes around 4 days to complete a single HMM training iteration.

In response, we propose to approximate the HMM's transition probability matrix $\mathbf{A}$ with a matrix $\hat{\mathbf{A}}$ generated by a heuristic approach explained below.

The problem is to learn a transition probability, i.e., the probability of a temporal link (edge) between two anchor boxes $\{b_t^a, b_{t+\Delta}^a\}$ belonging to two feature map grids $\mathbf{C}_p^t$ and $\mathbf{C}_{p'}^{t+\Delta}$. If we assume that transitions only take place between states at the same level $p = p'$ of the feature pyramid, the two sets of anchor boxes $\mathcal{B}_p^t = \{b_{t_1}^a, ..., b_{t_N}^a\}$ and $\mathcal{B}_p^{t+\Delta} = \{b_{(t+\Delta)_1}^a, ..., b_{(t+\Delta)_N}^a\}$ belonging to a pair of grids $\{\mathbf{C}_p^t, \mathbf{C}_p^{t+\Delta}\}$ are identical, namely: $\mathcal{B}_p^t = \mathcal{B}_p^{t+\Delta} \doteq \mathcal{B}_p = \{b_i^a, i = 1, ..., N\}$, allowing us to remove the time superscript. Recall that each feature map grid C_p has spatial dimension $[H_p' \times W_p']$.

We compute a transition probability matrix $\hat{\mathbf{A}}_p$ *individually for each grid level* p, resulting in p such matrices of shape $[(H_p')^2 \times (W_p')^2]$ (see Fig. 3(d)).

For example, at level $p = 5$ we have a 3×3 feature map grids, so that the transition matrix $\hat{\mathbf{A}}_p$ will be $[3^2 \times 3^2]$. Each cell in the grid is assigned to r_p anchor boxes, resulting in $n = H_p' \times W_p' \times r_p$ total anchor boxes per grid (Sect. 3.1).

Transition Matrix Computation. Initially, all entries of the transition matrix are set to zero: $\hat{\mathbf{A}}[i, j] = 0$. Given a ground-truth micro-tube $\mathbf{m}^g = \{b_t^g, b_{t+\Delta}^g\}$ (a pair of temporally linked ground-truth boxes [1]), we compute the IoU overlap for each ground-truth box with all the anchor boxes $\mathcal{B}_p$ in the considered grid, namely: $IoU(b_t^g, \mathcal{B}_p)$ and $IoU(b_{t+\Delta}^g, \mathcal{B}_p)$. We select the pair of anchor boxes $\mathbf{m}^a = \{b_i^a, b_j^a\}$ (which we term *anchor micro-tube*) having the maximum IoU overlap with $\mathbf{m}^g$, where i and j are two cell locations. If $i = j$ (the resulting anchor boxes are in the same location) we get an anchor cuboid, otherwise a general anchor micro-tube.

This is repeated for all P feature map grids $\mathbf{C}_p$ to select the anchor micro-tube $\mathbf{m}_p^a$ with the highest overlap. The best match anchor micro-tube $\mathbf{m}_{\hat{p}}^a$ for a given ground-truth micro-tube $\mathbf{m}^g$ is selected among those P, and the transition matrix is updated as follows: $\hat{\mathbf{A}}[i, j] = \hat{\mathbf{A}}[i, j] + 1$. The above steps are repeated for all the ground-truth micro-tubes in a training set. Finally, each row of the transition matrix $\hat{\mathbf{A}}$ is normalised by dividing each entry by the sum of that row.

Figure 4 plots the transition matrix $\hat{\mathbf{A}}_p$ for $p = 4$ (a feature map grid 5×5), for different values of Δ. As explained in the following, the configurable pooling layer employs these matrices to pool conv features for action proposal classification and regression.

Although our approach learns transition probabilities for anchor boxes belonging to the same feature map grid $\mathbf{C}_p$, we realise that the quality of the resulting action proposals could be further improved by learning transitions between anchors across different levels of the pyramid. As the feature dimension of each map varies in SSD, e.g. 1024 for $p = 2$ and 512 for $p = 1$, a more consistent network such as FPN [29] with Resnet [30] would be a better choice as base architecture. Here we stick to SSD to produce a fair comparison with [1,2,11], and leave this extension to future work.

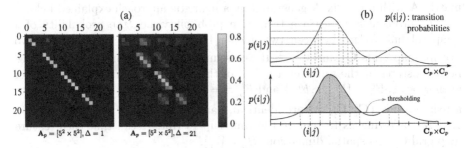

Fig. 4. (a) Transition matrix for a 5×5 feature map grid ($p = 4$) for different Δ values. As Δ increases, off-diagonal probability values also increase, indicating a need for anchor micro-tubes rather than anchor-cuboids. (b) Top - Monte Carlo sampling of transition hypotheses $(i, j) \in \mathbf{C}_p \times \mathbf{C}_p$ based on uniformly sampling the $[0, 1]$ range. Bottom - our anchor micro-tube sampling scheme, based on thresholding the transition probabilities $p(i|j)$, is also stochastic in nature and emulates Monte Carlo sampling. The blue line denotes the threshold and the shaded area above the threshold line shows the sampling region, a subset of the product grid $\mathbf{C}_p \times \mathbf{C}_p$. (Color figure online)

3.4   Configurable Pooling Layer

The SSD [8] network uses convolutional kernels of dimension $[3 \times 3 \times D]$ as classification and regression layers (called *classification* and *regression heads*). More specifically, SSD uses $r \times 4$ kernels for bounding box regression (recall r anchor boxes with different aspect ratios are assigned to each cell location (Sect. 3.1)) and $(C+1) \times r$ kernels for classification over the p conv feature maps (Sect. 3.1). This is fine when the number of proposal hypotheses is fixed (e.g., for object detection in images, the number of anchor boxes is set to 8732). In our setting, however, the number of proposals varies depending upon the cardinality $|\hat{\mathbf{A}}_p|$ of the transition matrix (Sect. 3.3). Consequently, it is more principled to implement the classification and regression heads as fully connected layers (see Fig. 2(**f**)). If we observe consistent off-diagonal entries in the transition matrices (e.g. lots of cells moving one step in the same direction), we could perform pooling as convolution feature map stacking with padding to allow spatial movement. However, transition matrices are empirically extremely sparse (e.g., there are only 25 and 1908 off-diagonal non-zero entries in the transition matrices at Δ equal to 4 and 20, respectively, on the UCF101-24 dataset).

Anchor Micro-tube Sampling. Each transition matrix is converted into a binary one by thresholding, so that the cardinality of the matrix depends not only on the data but also on the transition probability threshold. Our transition matrix-based anchor micro-tube sampling scheme is stochastic in nature and emulates Monte Carlo sampling techniques (Fig. 4(b)). A thresholding on the transition matrix allows us to sample a variable number of anchors rather than a fixed one. We empirically found that a 10% threshold gives the best results in all of our tests. We discuss the threshold and its effect on performance in Sect. 3.3.

The pooling layer (see Fig. 2(d)) is configured to pool features from a pair of convolutional feature maps $\{K_p^t, K_p^{t+\Delta}\}$, each of size $[H_p' \times W_p' \times D]$. The pooling is done at cell locations i and j, specified by the estimated (thresholded) transition matrix $\hat{\mathbf{A}}_p$ (Sect. 3.3). The pooling kernel has dimension $[3 \times 3 \times D]$. Pooled features are subsequently stacked (Fig. 2(e)) to get a single feature representation of size $[2 \times 3 \times 3 \times D]$ per anchor micro-tube.

3.5 Classification and Regression Layers

After pooling and stacking, we get M conv features of size $[2 \times 3 \times 3 \times D]$, for each M anchor micro-tube cell regions, where $M = \sum_{p=1}^{P=6} |\hat{\mathbf{A}}_p|$ is the sum of the cardinalities of the P transition matrices. We pass these M features to a classification layer $((18 \times D), ((C+1) \times r))$, and a regression layer $((18 \times D), ((2 \times 4) \times r))$ (see Fig. 2(f)). The classification layer outputs $C+1$ class scores and the regression layer outputs 2×4 bounding-box coordinates for r anchor micro-tubes per anchor micro-tube cell region (see Fig. 2(g)). The linear classification and regression layers have the same number of parameters as the convolutional heads in the SSD network [8].

3.6 Online Action Tube Generation and Temporal Trimming

The output of the proposed network is a set of detection micro-tubes and their class confidence scores (see Fig. 2(g)). We adapt the online action tube generation algorithm proposed by Singh et al. [11] to compose these detection micro-tubes into complete action paths (tracklets) spanning the entire video. Note that, Singh et al. [11] use their tube generation algorithm to temporally connect frame-level detection bounding-boxes, whereas our modified version of the algorithm connects video-level detection micro-tubes. Similarly to [11], we build action paths incrementally by connecting micro-tubes across time. As the action paths are extracted, their temporal trimming is performed using dynamic programming [9,28]. In Sect. 4 we show that temporal segmentation helps improve detection performance for datasets containing highly temporally untrimmed videos, e.g., DALY [13], where on average only 4% of the video duration is covered by action instances.

Fusion of Appearance and Flow Cues. We follow a late fusion strategy [2,11] to fuse appearance and optical flow cues, performed at test time after all the detections are extracted from the two streams. Kalogeiton *et al.* [2] demonstrated that *mean* fusion works better than both *boost* fusion [9] and *union-set* fusion [11]. Thus, in this work we produce all results (cf. Sect. 4) using *mean* fusion [2]. We report an ablation study of the appearance and flow stream performance in the supplementary material.

4   Experiments

We first present datasets, evaluation metrics, fair comparison and implementation details used in Sect. 4.1. Secondly, we show how TraMNet is able to improve spatial-temporal action localisation in Sect. 4.2. Thirdly, in Sect. 4.3, we discuss how a network learned using transition matrices is able to generalise at test time, when more general anchor-micro-tubes are used to evaluate the network. Finally, in Sect. 4.4, we quantitatively demonstrate that TraMNet is able to effectively handle sparse annotation as in the DALY dataset, and generalise well on various train and test Δ's.

4.1   Datasets

We selected UCF-101-24 [12] to validate the effectiveness of the transition matrix approach, and DALY [13] to evaluate the method on sparse annotations.

UCF101-24 is a subset of 24 classes from the UCF101 [12] dataset, which contains 101 classes. Initial spatial and temporal annotations provided in THUMOS-2013 [31] were later corrected by Singh *et al.* [11] – we use this version in all our experiments. UCF101 videos contain a single action category per video, sometimes multiple action instances in the same video. Each action instance covers on average 70% of the video duration. This dataset is relevant to us as we can show how the increase in Δ affects the performance of TraM-Net [1], and using transition matrices helps us recover from that performance drop. **Transformed-UCF101-24** was created by us by padding all images along both the horizontal and the vertical dimension. We set the maximum padding values to 32 and 20 pixels, respectively, as 40% of the average width (80) and height (52) of bounding box annotations. A uniformly sampled random fraction of 32 pixels is padded on the left edge of the image, the remaining is padded on the right edge of the image. Similar random padding is performed at the top and bottom of each frame. The padding itself is obtained by mirroring the adjacent portion of the image through the edge. The same offset is applied to the bounding box annotations. The **DALY** dataset was released by Weinzaepfel *et al.* [13] for 10 daily activities and contains 520 videos (200 for test and the rest for training) with 3.3 million frames. Videos in DALY are much longer, and the action duration to video duration ratio is only 4%, compared to UCF101-24's

70%, making the temporal labelling of action tubes very challenging. The most interesting aspect of this dataset is that it is not densely annotated, as at max 5 frames are annotated per action instance, and 12% of the action instances only have one annotated frame. As a result, annotated frames are 2.2 s apart on average ($\Delta = 59$). **Note.** THUMOS [32] and Activity-Net [33] are not suitable for spatiotemporal detection, as they lack bounding box annotation. Annotation at 1 fps for AVA [14] was released in week 1 of March 2018 (to the best of our knowledge). Also, AVA's bounding boxes are not linked in time, preventing a fair evaluation of our approach there.

Evaluation Metric. We evaluate TraMNet using video-mAP [1,2,10,11,34]. As a standard practice [11], we use *"average detection performance"* (avg-mAP) to compare TraMNet's performance with the state-of-the-art. To obtain the latter, we first compute the video-mAPs at higher IoU thresholds (δ) ranging [0.5 : 0.05 : 0.95], and then take the average of these video-mAPs. On the DALY dataset, we also evaluate at various thresholds in both an untrimmed and a trimmed setting. The latter is achieved by trimming the action paths generated by the boundaries of the ground truth [13]. We further report the video classification accuracy using the predicted tubes as in [11], in which videos are assigned the label of the highest scoring tube. One could improve classification performance on DALY by taking into consideration other tube scores. Nevertheless, in our tests we adopt the existing protocol.

For ***fair comparison*** we re-implemented the methods of our competitors [2,9,11] with SSD as the base network. As in our TraMNet network, we also replaced SSD's convolutional heads with new linear layers. The same tube generation [11] and data augmentation [8] methods were adopted, and the same hyperparameters were used for training all the networks, including TraMNet. The only difference is that the anchor micro-tubes used in [2,9] were cuboidal, whereas TraMNet's anchor micro-tubes are generated using transition matrices. We refer to these approaches as SSD-L (SSD-linear-heads) [11], AMTnet-L (AMTnet-linear-heads) [1] and as ACT-L (ACT-detector-linear-heads) [2].

Network Training and Implementation Details. We used the established training settings for all the above methods. While training on the UCF101-24 dataset, we used a batch size of 16 and an initial learning rate of 0.0005, with the learning rate dropping after $100K$ iterations for the appearance stream and $140K$ for the flow stream. Whereas the appearance stream is only trained for $180K$ iterations, the flow stream is trained for $200K$ iterations. In all cases, the input image size was $3 \times 300 \times 300$ for the appearance stream, while a stack of five optical flow images [35] ($15 \times 300 \times 300$) was used for flow. Each network was trained on 2 1080Ti GPUs. More details about parameters and training are given in the supplementary material.

Table 1. Action localisation results on untrimmed videos from UCF101-24 split1. The table is divided into 4 parts. The first part lists approaches which have single frames as input; the second part approaches which take multiple frames as input; the third part contemplates the re-implemented versions of approaches in the second group; lastly, we report our TraMNet's performance.

Methods	Train Δ	Test Δ	$\delta = 0.2$	$\delta = 0.5$	$\delta = 0.75$	$\delta = .5:.95$	Acc %
T-CNN [3]	NA	NA	47.1	–	–	–	–
MR-TS [10]	NA	NA	73.5	32.1	02.7	07.3	–
Saha *et al.* [9]	NA	NA	66.6	36.4	07.9	14.4	–
SSD [11]	NA	NA	73.2	46.3	15.0	20.4	–
AMTnet [1] rgb-only	1,2,3	1	63.0	33.1	00.5	10.7	–
ACT [2]	1	1	76.2	49.2	19.7	23.4	–
Gu *et al.* [14] ([10] + [27])	NA	NA	–	**59.9**	–	–	–
SSD-L with-trimming	NA	NA	76.2	45.5	16.4	20.6	92.0
SSD-L	NA	NA	76.8	48.2	17.0	21.7	92.1
ACT-L	1	1	77.9	50.8	19.8	**23.9**	91.4
AMTnet-L	1	1	**79.4**	**51.2**	19.0	23.4	**92.9**
AMTnet-L	5	5	77.5	49.5	17.3	22.5	91.6
AMTnet-L	21	5	76.2	47.6	16.5	21.6	90.0
TraMNet (ours)	1	1	79.0	50.9	**20.1**	**23.9**	92.4
TraMNet (ours)	5	5	77.6	49.7	18.4	22.8	91.3
TraMNet (ours)	21	5	75.2	47.8	17.4	22.3	90.7

4.2 Action Localisation Performance

Table 1 shows the resulting performance on UCF101-24 at multiple train and test Δs for TraMNet versus other competitors [2,3,9–11]. Note that Gu *et al.* [14] build upon MS-TS [10] by adding a strong I3D [27] base network, making it unfair to compare [14] to SSD-L, AMTnet-L, ACT-L and TraMNet, which all use VGG as a base network.

ACT is a dense network (processin 6 consecutive frames), which shows the best performance at high overlap (an avg-mAP of 23.9%). AMTnet-L is slightly inferior (23.4%), most likely due to it learning representations from pairs of consecutive frames only at its best training and test settings ($\Delta = 1$). TraMNet is able to match ACT-L's performance at high overlap (23.9%), while being comparatively more efficient.

The evaluation of AMTNet-L on Transformed-UCF101-24 (Sect. 4.1) shows an avg-mAP of 19.3% using the appearance stream only, whereas TraMNet records an avg-mAP of 20.5%, a gain of 1.2% that can be attributed to its estimating grid location transition probabilities. It shows that TraMNet is more suited to action instances involving substantial shifts from one frame to the next. A similar phenomenon can be observed on the standard UCF101-24 when the train or test Δ is greater than 1 in Table 1.

We cross-validated different transition probability thresholds on transition matrices. Thresholds of 2%, 5%, 10%, 15% and 20% yielded an avg-mAP of 21.6%, 22.0%, 22.4%, 21.9% and 21.2%, respectively, on the appearance stream. Given such evidence, we concluded that a 10% transition probability threshold was to be adopted throughout all our experiments.

4.3   Location Invariance at Test Time

Anchor micro-tubes are sampled based on the transition probabilities from specific cells (at frame f_t) to other specific cells (at frame $f_{t+\Delta}$) (Sect. 3.3) based on the training data. However, as at test time action instances of a same class may appear in other regions of the image plane than those observed at training time, it is desirable to generate additional anchor micro-tubes proposals than those produced by the learnt transition matrices. Such *location invariance* property can be achieved at test time by augmenting the binary transition matrix (Sect. 3.4) with likely transitions from other grid locations.

Each row/column of the transition matrix $\hat{\mathbf{A}}$ (Sect. 3.3) corresponds to a cell location in the grid. One augmentation technique is to set all the diagonal entries to 1 (i.e., $\hat{\mathbf{A}}[i,j] = 1$, where $i == j$). This amounts to generating anchor cuboids which may have been missing at training time (cfr. Fig. 4(a)). The network can then be evaluated using this new set of anchor micro-tubes by configuring the pooling layer (Sect. 3.4)) accordingly. When doing so, however, we observed only a very minor difference in avg-mAP at the second decimal point for TraMNet with test $\Delta = 1$. Similarly, we also evaluated TraMNet by incorporating the transitions from each cell to its 8 *neighbouring* cells (also at test time), but observed no significant change in avg-mAP.

A third approach, given a pyramid level p, and the initial binary transition matrix for that level, consists of computing the relative transition offsets for all grid cells (offset $= i - j \; \forall i, j$ where $\hat{\mathbf{A}}[i,j] = 1$). All such transition offsets correspond to different spatial translation patterns (of action instances) present in the dataset at different locations in the given video. Augmenting all the rows with these spatial translation patterns, by taking each diagonal entry in the transition matrix as reference point, yields a more dense transition matrix whose anchor micro-tubes are translation invariant, i.e., spatial location invariant. However, after training TraMNet at train $\Delta = 1$ we observed that the final avg-mAP at test $\Delta = 1$ was 22.6% as compared to 23.9% when using the original (sparse) transition matrix. As in the experiments (i.e., added diagonal and neighbour transitions) explained above, we evaluated the network that was trained on the original transition matrices at train $\Delta = 1$ by using the transition matrix generated via relative offsets, observing an avg-mAP consistent (i.e., 23.9%) with the original results.

This shows that the system should be trained using the original transition matrices learned from the data, whereas more anchor micro-tube proposals can be assessed at test time without loss of generality. It also shows that UCF101-24 is not sufficiently realistic a dataset from the point of view of translation invariance, which is why we conducted tests on Transformed-UCF101-24 (Sect. 4.1) to highlight this issue.

Table 2. Action localisation results (video-mAP) on the DALY dataset. SSD-L without trimming refers to when action paths are not trimmed and the network is SSD.

Methods	Test Δ	Untrimmed videos			Trimmed videos			
		$\delta = 0.2$	$\delta = 0.5$	Acc%	$\delta = 0.5$	$\delta = .5:.95$	Acc%	CleaningFloor
weinzaepfel *et al.* [13]	NA	13.9	–	–	63.9	–	–	–
SSD-L without-trimming	NA	06.1	01.1	61.5				
SSD-L	NA	**14.6**	**05.7**	58.5	63.9	38.2	75.5	80.2
AMTnet-L	3	12.1	04.3	62.0	63.7	39.3	76.5	83.4
TraMNet (ours)	3	13.4	04.6	**67.0**	**64.2**	**41.4**	**78.5**	**86.6**

4.4   Handling Sparse Annotations

Table 2 shows the results on the DALY dataset. We can see that TraMNet significantly improves on SSD-L and AMTnet-L in the trimmed video setting, with an average video-mAP of 41.4%. TraMNet reaches top classification accuracy in both the trimmed and the untrimmed cases. As we would expect, TraMNet improves the temporal linking via better micro-tubes and classification, as clearly indicated in the trimmed videos setting. Nevertheless, SSD-L is the best when it comes to temporal trimming. We think this is because each micro-tube in our case is 4 frames long as the test Δ is equal to 3, and each micro-tube only has one score vector rather than 4 score vectors for each frame, which might render temporal segmentation mute.

DALY allows us to show how TraMNet is able to handle sparse annotations better than AMTNet-L, which uses anchor cuboids, strengthening the argument that learning transition matrices helps generate better micro-tubes.

TramNet's performance on 'CleaningFloor' at δ equal to 0.5 in the trimmed case highlights the effectiveness of general anchor micro-tubes for **dynamic classes**. 'CleaningFloor' is one of DALY's classes in which the actor moves spatially while the camera is mostly static. To further strengthen the argument, we picked classes showing fast spatial movements across frames in the UCF101-24 dataset and observed the class-wise average-precision (AP) at δ equal to 0.2. For 'BasketballDunk', 'Skiing' and 'VolleyballSpiking' TraMNet performs significantly better than both AMTnet-L and ACT-L; e.g. on 'Skiing', the performance of TraMNet, AMTNet-L and ACT-L is 85.2, 82.4 and 81.1, respectively. More class-wise results are discussed in the supplementary material.

Training and Testing at Multiple Δ's. To test whether TraMNet can handle sparse annotation we introduced an artificial gap (Δ) in UCF101's training examples, while testing on frames that are far away (e.g. $\Delta = 30$). We can observe in Fig. 5(b) that performance is preserved when increasing the training Δ while keeping the test Δ small (e.g. equal to 5, as shown in plot (a)). One could think of increasing Δ at test time to improve run-time efficiency: we can observe from Fig. 5(a) that performance drops linearly as speed linearly increases. In both cases TraMNet consistently outperforms AMTNet. When Δ is large TraMNet's improvement is large as well.

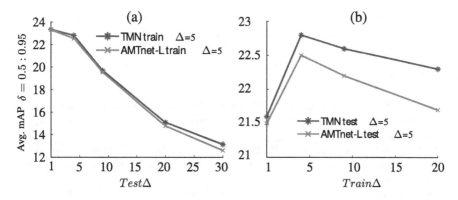

Fig. 5. Avg mAP ($\delta = 0.5 : 0.95$) performance of TraMNet vs the competitor AMTnet-L, (a) when tested at increasing Δ from 1 to 30 and trained at constant Δ equal to 5, (b) when tested at constant Δ equal to 5 and trained on increasing Δ from 1 to 20.

Temporal labelling is performed using the labelling formulation presented in [11]. Actually, temporal labelling hurts the performance on UCF101-24, as shown in Table 1 where 'SSD-L-with-trimming' uses [11]'s temporal segmenter, whereas 'SSD-L' and the other methods below that do not. In contrast, on DALY the results are quite the opposite: the same temporal labelling framework improves the performance from 6.1% to 14.9% at $\delta = 0.2$. We think that these (superficially) contradictory results relate to the fact that action instances cover on average a very different fraction (70% versus 4%) of the video duration in UCF101-24 and DALY, respectively.

Detection Speed: We measured the average time taken for a forward pass for a batch size of 1 as compared to 8 by [11]. A single-stream forward pass takes 29.8 ms (i.e. 33 fps) on a single 1080Ti GPU. One can improve speed even further by evaluating TraMNet with Δ equal to 2 or 4, obtaining a 2× or 4× speed improvement while paying very little in terms of performance, as shown in Fig. 5(a).

5 Conclusions

We presented a TraMNet deep learning framework for action detection in videos which, unlike previous state-of-the-art methods [1–3] which generate action cuboid proposals, can cope with real-world videos containing "dynamic" actions whose location significantly changes over time. This is done by learning a transition probability matrix for each feature pyramid layer from the training data in a hidden Markov model formulation, leading to an original configurable layer architecture. Furthermore, unlike its competitors [2,3], which require dense frame-level bounding box annotation, TraMNet builds on the network architecture of [1] in which action representations are learnt from pairs of frames rather than chunks of consecutive frames, thus eliminating the need for dense annotation.

An extensive experimental analysis supports TraMNet's action detection capabilities, especially under dynamic actions and sparse annotations.

References

1. Saha, S., Singh, G., Cuzzolin, F.: AMTnet: action-micro-tube regression by end-to-end trainable deep architecture. In: IEEE International Conference on Computer Vision (2017)
2. Kalogeiton, V., Weinzaepfel, P., Ferrari, V., Schmid, C.: Action tubelet detector for spatio-temporal action localization. In: IEEE International Conference on Computer Vision (2017)
3. Hou, R., Chen, C., Shah, M.: Tube convolutional neural network (T-CNN) for action detection in videos. In: IEEE International Conference on Computer Vision (2017)
4. Gkioxari, G., Malik, J.: Finding action tubes. In: IEEE International Conference on Computer Vision and Pattern Recognition (2015)
5. Weinzaepfel, P., Harchaoui, Z., Schmid, C.: Learning to track for spatio-temporal action localization. In: IEEE International Conference on Computer Vision and Pattern Recognition (2015)
6. Girshick, R., Donahue, J., Darrel, T., Malik, J.: Rich feature hierarchies for accurate object detection and semantic segmentation. In: IEEE International Conference on Computer Vision and Pattern Recognition (2014)
7. Ren, S., He, K., Girshick, R., Sun, J.: Faster R-CNN: towards real-time object detection with region proposal networks. In: Advances in Neural Information Processing Systems, pp. 91–99 (2015)
8. Liu, W., et al.: SSD: Single shot multibox detector. arXiv preprint arXiv:1512.02325 (2015)
9. Saha, S., Singh, G., Sapienza, M., Torr, P.H.S., Cuzzolin, F.: Deep learning for detecting multiple space-time action tubes in videos. In: British Machine Vision Conference (2016)
10. Peng, X., Schmid, C.: Multi-region two-stream R-CNN for action detection. In: Leibe, B., Matas, J., Sebe, N., Welling, M. (eds.) ECCV 2016. LNCS, vol. 9908, pp. 744–759. Springer, Cham (2016). https://doi.org/10.1007/978-3-319-46493-0_45
11. Singh, G., Saha, S., Sapienza, M., Torr, P., Cuzzolin, F.: Online real-time multiple spatiotemporal action localisation and prediction. In: IEEE International Conference on Computer Vision (2017)
12. Soomro, K., Zamir, A.R., Shah, M.: UCF101: a dataset of 101 human action classes from videos in the wild. Technical report, CRCV-TR-12-01 (2012)
13. Weinzaepfel, P., Martin, X., Schmid, C.: Human action localization with sparse spatial supervision. arXiv preprint arXiv:1605.05197 (2016)
14. Gu, C., et al.: AVA: a video dataset of spatio-temporally localized atomic visual actions. arXiv preprint arXiv:1705.08421 (2017)
15. Kay, W., et al.: The kinetics human action video dataset. arXiv preprint arXiv:1705.06950 (2017)
16. Elliott, R.J., Aggoun, L., Moore, J.B.: Hidden Markov Models: Estimation and Control, vol. 29. Springer, Heidelberg (2008). https://doi.org/10.1007/978-0-387-84854-9
17. van Gemert, J.C., Jain, M., Gati, E., Snoek, C.G.: APT: action localization proposals from dense trajectories. In: BMVC, vol. 2, p. 4 (2015)

18. Oneata, D., Verbeek, J., Schmid, C.: Efficient action localization with approximately normalized fisher vectors. In: Proceedings of the IEEE Conference on Computer Vision and Pattern Recognition, pp. 2545–2552 (2014)

19. Jain, M., Van Gemert, J., Jégou, H., Bouthemy, P., Snoek, C.G.: Action localization with tubelets from motion. In: 2014 IEEE Conference on Computer Vision and Pattern Recognition (CVPR), pp. 740–747. IEEE (2014)

20. Sapienza, M., Cuzzolin, F., Torr, P.H.: Learning discriminative space-time action parts from weakly labelled videos. Int. J. Comput. Vis. **110**, 30–47 (2014)

21. Sultani, W., Shah, M.: What if we do not have multiple videos of the same action? - video action localization using web images. In: IEEE International Conference on Computer Vision and Pattern Recognition (2016)

22. Wang, H., Kläser, A., Schmid, C., Liu, C.: Action recognition by dense trajectories. In: IEEE International Conference on Computer Vision and Pattern Recognition (2011)

23. Redmon, J., Farhadi, A.: Yolo9000: better, faster, stronger. arXiv preprint arXiv:1612.08242 (2016)

24. Weinzaepfel, P., Martin, X., Schmid, C.: Towards weakly-supervised action localization. arXiv preprint arXiv:1605.05197 (2016)

25. Zolfaghari, M., Oliveira, G.L., Sedaghat, N., Brox, T.: Chained multi-stream networks exploiting pose, motion, and appearance for action classification and detection. In: IEEE International Conference on Computer Vision, pp. 2923–2932. IEEE (2017)

26. Yang, Z., Gao, J., Nevatia, R.: Spatio-temporal action detection with cascade proposal and location anticipation. In: BMVC (2017)

27. Carreira, J., Zisserman, A.: Quo vadis, action recognition? A new model and the kinetics dataset. In: 2017 IEEE Conference on Computer Vision and Pattern Recognition (CVPR), pp. 4724–4733. IEEE (2017)

28. Evangelidis, G.D., Singh, G., Horaud, R.: Continuous gesture recognition from articulated poses. In: Agapito, L., Bronstein, M.M., Rother, C. (eds.) ECCV 2014. LNCS, vol. 8925, pp. 595–607. Springer, Cham (2015). https://doi.org/10.1007/978-3-319-16178-5_42

29. Lin, T.Y., Goyal, P., Girshick, R., He, K., Dollár, P.: Focal loss for dense object detection. arXiv preprint arXiv:1708.02002 (2017)

30. He, K., Zhang, X., Ren, S., Sun, J.: Deep residual learning for image recognition. In: Proceedings of the IEEE Conference on Computer Vision and Pattern Recognition, pp. 770–778 (2016)

31. Idrees, H., et al.: The THUMOS challenge on action recognition for videos "in the wild". Comput. Vis. Image Underst. **155**, 1–23 (2017)

32. Gorban, A., et al.: Thumos challenge: action recognition with a large number of classes (2015)

33. Caba Heilbron, F., Escorcia, V., Ghanem, B., Carlos Niebles, J.: ActivityNet: a large-scale video benchmark for human activity understanding. In: IEEE International Conference on Computer Vision and Pattern Recognition, pp. 961–970 (2015)

34. Yu, G., Yuan, J.: Fast action proposals for human action detection and search. In: Proceedings of the IEEE Conference on Computer Vision and Pattern Recognition, pp. 1302–1311 (2015)

35. Brox, T., Bruhn, A., Papenberg, N., Weickert, J.: High accuracy optical flow estimation based on a theory for warping. In: Pajdla, T., Matas, J. (eds.) ECCV 2004. LNCS, vol. 3024, pp. 25–36. Springer, Heidelberg (2004). https://doi.org/10.1007/978-3-540-24673-2_3

Shape-Conditioned Image Generation by Learning Latent Appearance Representation from Unpaired Data

Yutaro Miyauchi[✉][iD], Yusuke Sugano[iD], and Yasuyuki Matsushita[iD]

Graduate School of Information Science and Technology,
Osaka University, Osaka, Japan
{miyauchi.yutaro,sugano,yasumat}@ist.osaka-u.ac.jp

Abstract. Conditional image generation is effective for diverse tasks including training data synthesis for learning-based computer vision. However, despite the recent advances in generative adversarial networks (GANs), it is still a challenging task to generate images with detailed conditioning on object shapes. Existing methods for conditional image generation use category labels and/or keypoints and are only give limited control over object categories. In this work, we present SCGAN, an architecture to generate images with a desired shape specified by an input normal map. The shape-conditioned image generation task is achieved by explicitly modeling the image appearance via a latent appearance vector. The network is trained using unpaired training samples of real images and rendered normal maps. This approach enables us to generate images of arbitrary object categories with the target shape and diverse image appearances. We show the effectiveness of our method through both qualitative and quantitative evaluation on training data generation tasks.

1 Introduction

Generating realistic images is a central task in both computer vision and computer graphics. Despite recent advances in generative adversarial networks (GANs), it is still challenging to fully control how the target object should appear in the output images. There have been several approaches for conditional image generation which introduce additional conditions to GANs such as class labels [23,31] and keypoints [21,25]. However, previous approaches still suffer from an inability to control detailed object shapes and lack generalizability to arbitrary object categories.

Training data synthesis is one of the most promising applications of conditional image generation. Since recognition performance of machine learning-based methods heavily depends on the amount and quality of training images,

This work was supported by JST CREST Grant Number JPMJCR1781, Japan, and partly by the New Energy and Industrial Technology Development Organization (NEDO).

C. V. Jawahar et al. (Eds.): ACCV 2018, LNCS 11366, pp. 438–453, 2019.
https://doi.org/10.1007/978-3-030-20876-9_28

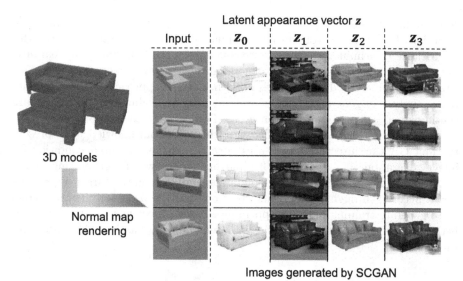

Fig. 1. The proposed shape-conditioned image generation network (SCGAN) outputs images of an arbitrary object with the same shape as the input normal map, while controlling the image appearances via latent appearance vectors.

there is an increasing demand for methods and datasets for training recognition models using synthetic data [12,24,26,33]. However, when synthetic training images are rendered with off-the-shelf computer graphics techniques, the trained estimators still suffer from an appearance gap from actual, often degraded test images. GANs have also been used to modify synthetic data to more realistic training images, and it has been shown that such data can improve the performance of learned estimators [2,27,28]. These methods use synthetic data as a condition on image generation so that output images remain visually similar to the input images and therefore keep their original ground-truth labels. In this sense, the aforementioned limitation of conditional image generation severely restricts the application of such training data synthesis approaches. If the method allows for more fine-grained control of object shapes, poses, and appearances, it can open a way for generating training data for, *e.g.*, generic object recognition and pose estimation.

In this work, we propose SCGAN (Shape-Conditioned GAN), a GAN architecture for generating images conditioned by input 3D shapes. As illustrated in Fig. 1, the goal of our method is to provide a way to generate images of arbitrary objects with the same shape as the input normal map. The image appearance is explicitly modeled as a latent vector, which can be either randomly assigned or extracted from actual images. Since we cannot always expect paired training data of normal maps and images, the overall network is trained using the cycle consistency loss [39] between the original and back-reconstructed images. In addition, the proposed architecture employs an extra discriminator network to examine whether the generated appearance vector follows the assumed distribution. Unlike prior work using a similar idea for feature learning [7], this appearance discriminator allows us to not only control the image appearance, but also to improve the quality of generated images. We demonstrate the effectiveness of our method in comparison with baseline approaches through qualitative analysis of generated images, and quantitative evaluation of training data synthesis performance on appearance-based object pose estimation tasks.

Our contributions are twofold. First, to the best of our knowledge, we present the first GAN architecture which uses normal maps as the input condition for image generation. This provides a flexible and generic way for generating shape-conditioned images without relying on any assumption on the target object category. Second, through experiments, we show that the proposed method allows us to generate training data for appearance-based object pose estimation, with better performances than synthetic data generated by baseline GAN architectures.

2   Related Work

Our method aims at generating shape-conditioned images with realistic appearances, related to prior methods on conditional image generation GANs. One of the potential applications of our method is generating realistic training data, and hence our method is further related to methods applying GANs for bridging the gap between synthetic training data and real images.

2.1   GANs for Conditional Image Generation

Generative Adversarial Networks (GANs) have made considerable advances in recent years [9,17,18,22], and have been successfully applied to various tasks such as image super-resolution [16,20], inpainting [15], and face aging [37]. GANs consist of mainly two networks, generator and discriminator, which are trained in an adversarial manner. The generator generates images so that they are recognized as real ones, while the discriminator learns to discriminate generated images from real images from a training dataset. The generator usually receives a vector of random numbers sampled from an arbitrary probability distribution as input, and outputs an image through the network. However, as discussed earlier, most of the standard GAN architectures do not allow for fine-grained control of the output images.

To address this limitation, much research has been conducted on GAN architectures for conditional image generation. There have been several approaches to use class labels as a condition on generated images and to specify which object category to be drawn in the output image [23]. Similarly, some prior work proposed to control the generated images by conditioning them on human-interpretable feature vectors built in an unsupervised manner [5,29]. To increase the flexibility of image generation, some works further used input features indicating where and how the target object should be drawn, such as bounding box [25] and keypoints [21]. Alternatively, iGAN [38] and the Introspective Adversarial Network [3] take an approach to use user drawings as a condition for image generation. However, the conditions used in these methods still have a limitation that precise 3D shape control is only possible with specific object categories with hand-designed keypoint locations. In contrast, our method allows for direct control on arbitrary object shapes using normal map rendering, without requiring paired training data.

2.2 Learning with Simulated/Synthesized Images

Due to the limited availability of fully-labeled training images for diverse computer vision tasks, there is an increasing attention on synthetic training data. Computer graphics pipelines have been employed to synthesize images with desired ground-truth labels. Such a learning-by-synthesis approach is especially efficient for tasks whose ground-truth labels require costly manual annotation, such as semantic segmentation [24,26] and eye gaze estimation [33]. However, synthetic images still suffer from a large gap from real images in terms of object appearance and often degraded imaging quality, and hence the learned estimator cannot directly achieve desired performance on real-world input images.

To fill the gap between training (synthetic) and test (real) image domains, there have been proposed many domain adaptation techniques. In addition to research attempts on the learning process [1,8,30,32,36], GANs have been also shown as promising tools for bridging the domain gap. Shrivastava *et al.* proposed the SimGAN that modifies the input synthetic images to be visually similar to real images, and showed that such an approach improves the baseline performances on tasks like hand pose and gaze estimation [27]. RenderGAN [28] takes a similar approach to convert simple barcode-like input images into realistic images. CycleGAN [39] architecture provides a way to mutually convert images from two different domains without requiring paired images, and also be applicable to the domain adaptation task. Bousmalis *et al.* proposed the pixel-level domain adaptation (PixelDA) approach which transfers source images to the target domain under the pixel-level similarity constraint. Essentially, synthetic images were used as a strong constraint on output images in these methods, and GANs were restricted only to modify the imaging properties of the target object. In contrast, since our method uses texture-less normal maps to provide purely shape-related information to the generator, it allows for a full flexibility to control object and background appearances.

3 SCGAN: Shape-Conditioned Image Generation Network

The goal of SCGAN is to generate images of arbitrary object categories, with the same shape as the input normal map. While the training process requires an access to both normal maps and real images of the target object, in practice it is almost impossible to assume paired training data. To this end, SCGAN adopts

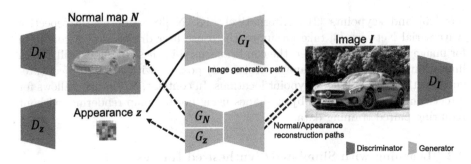

Fig. 2. Overview of the proposed architecture. G_I, G_N, and G_z are generators, and D_I, D_N, and D_z are discriminators. G_N and G_z share weights at the first few layers, and simultaneously output N and z from the input real image I.

the idea of cycle-consistency loss [39] and the whole network is trained using unpaired training images. Furthermore, to maximize the flexibility of object appearances, the image generator also takes an appearance vector as input, in addition to the normal map. By training the network so that appearance-related information is represented only with the appearance vector, our method realizes the shape-conditioned image generation task more efficiently and accurately.

3.1   Network Architecture

As illustrated in Fig. 2, the proposed architecture consists of five convolutional neural networks. G_I is an image generator that takes an appearance vector $z \in \mathbb{R}^n$ and a normal map $N \in \mathbb{R}^{m \times m}$ as input, and outputs an image $I \in \mathbb{R}^{m \times m}$. Conversely, G_N and G_z correspond to the normal map and appearance vector generators with partially shared network weights that converts an image I to an appearance vector z and a normal map N. Each data modality has their own discriminators D_I, D_N, and D_z. While D_I and D_N judge whether the input image and normal map are real or generated, D_z judges whether the input appearance vector is the one sampled from a Gaussian distribution or not.

As described earlier, the proposed network is designed to be trained on unpaired training samples using the cycle-consistency loss [39]. While the main goal of our approach is to train the image generator G_I, normal map and appearance generators (G_N and G_z) are also trained and used to back-reconstruct each modality and compare with the original input. However, if we only consider generators and discriminators of images and normal maps, generators tend to satisfy the cycle-consistency loss by *embedding* hidden information to intermediate data. For example, if the image generator learns to embed input information to the output image, the normal map generator can recover the original normal map without taking into account the object shape in the intermediate image. To avoid such situations, we also enforce the network to learn to separate shape and appearance information by introducing the appearance generator and discriminator. The proposed network effectively generates shape-conditioned images by modeling the appearance variation in the training data as a Gaussian appearance vector, while also allowing us to explicitly sample appearance information from actual images using the appearance generator G_z.

3.2 Training Loss

We train discriminators and generators using the WGAN-GP loss [10] which is based on the Wasserstein-1 distance between real and generated data distributions. The loss functions L_d and L_g for discriminators and generators, respectively, are defined as:

$$L_d(D) = \mathbb{E}_{x \sim P_x}[D(G(x))] - \mathbb{E}_{\hat{x} \sim P_{\hat{x}}}[D(\hat{x})] + \lambda_p \mathbb{E}_{\dot{x} \sim P_{\dot{x}}}[(\|\nabla_{\dot{x}} D(\dot{x})\|_2 - 1)^2], \quad (1)$$
$$L_g(G) = -\mathbb{E}_{x \sim P_x}[D(G(x))], \quad (2)$$

where x is real data (image, normal map, appearance vector), $\hat{x}$ is generated data from their corresponding generators, and $\dot{x} = \epsilon G(x) + (1 - \epsilon)\hat{x}$. $\epsilon \sim \mathscr{U}[0, 1]$ is random-weighted sum of input and generated data. P_x, $P_{\hat{x}}$, and $P_{\dot{x}}$ indicate distributions of each data, and $\mathbb{E}$ represents the mean of the distribution. The third term of Eq. (1) has an effect of stabilizing the adversarial training [10].

In our implementation, while three discriminators are trained using the individual discriminator losses, all generators are jointly trained as:

$$G_I, G_N, G_z = \underset{G_I, G_N, G_z}{\arg\min} L(G_I, G_N, G_z), \quad (3)$$

where $L(G_I, G_N, G_z)$ is the joint loss function also taking into account the cycle-consi-stency losses:

$$L(G_I, G_N, G_z) = L_g(G_I) + L_g(G_N) + L_g(G_z) + \lambda_N \|N - G_N(G_I(N, z))\|_F^2$$
$$+ \lambda_I \|I - G_I(G_N(I), G_z(I))\|_F^2 + \lambda_z \|z - G_z(G_I(N, z))\|_2^2. \quad (4)$$

λ_I, λ_N, and λ_z are weights for each cycle-consistency loss term which are defined as the distance between the input and the back-reconstructed output. These weights are required to take balance between discriminator and cycle-consistency losses in each domain, and they control how strictly the model should maintain the input shapes. Image I and normal map N are sampled from the distribution of real data P_I and P_N, and z are an appearance vector sampled from a zero-mean Gaussian distribution $\mathscr{N}(0, \sigma^2)$.

3.3 Implementation Details

Figure 3 shows the details of generator/discriminator networks. The architecture of the generator network follows Zhu *et al.* [39] and the network mainly consists of convolution (*Convolution-Pixelwise normalization-ELU*) block, deconvolution (*Deconvolution-Pixelwise normalization-ELU*) block, and ResNet block [11]. As described earlier, parameters of the first six convolution blocks of the normal map generator G_N and the appearance vector generator G_z are shared.

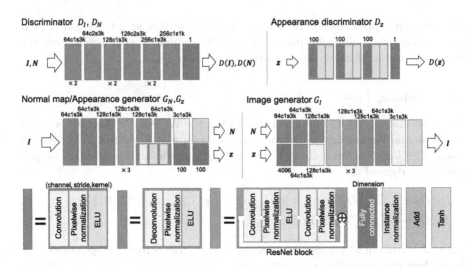

Fig. 3. Details of the generator/discriminator networks. N, I, and z indicate normal map, real image, and appearance vector. Parameters of the convolutional layers are indicated as $CcSsKk$, *i.e.*, a feature map is convolved into C channels with stride S and kernel size K.

The discriminator network for images and normal maps also consists of the convolution block and outputs a scalar value indicating discrimination results through a fully connected layer. The appearance discriminator network consists of a fully connected layer followed by a *Instance normalization-ELU* block, and also outputs a scalar value through a fully connected layer. The size of input images and normal maps are set to 64×64 pixels, and is downsampled to 16×16 before the ResNet blocks.

During training, each discriminator was trained independently with respect to the corresponding discriminator losses. Then the generators were trained as Eq. (4), with the discriminator parameters fixed. Following [10], discriminators were updated five times as much as generators. The networks are optimized using the Adam algorithm [19] ($\alpha = 0.001, \beta_1 = 0.5, \beta_2 = 0.9$), with the batch size of 16. We fixed hyper-parameters in Eq. (4) as $\lambda_I = 1.0, \lambda_N = 1.0$, and $\lambda_z = 10.0$. The variance of the Gaussian distribution was set to $\sigma^2 = 0.5$.

4   Experiments

We demonstrate the performance of the proposed SCGAN architecture through both qualitative analysis and quantitative evaluation. As a qualitative analysis, we compare shape-conditional generated images from the proposed method and other baseline methods in terms of both accuracies of object shape and diversity of object appearances. In addition, we show some ablation studies to analyze the efficiency of the proposed network design. As a quantitative evaluation, we

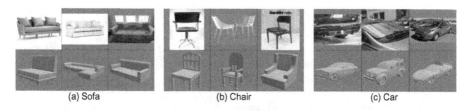

| (a) Sofa | (b) Chair | (c) Car |

Fig. 4. Examples of the training data taken from the LSUN dataset [35] and the ShapeNet dataset [4]. The top row is real images from the LSUN dataset after post-processing, and the bottom row is normal maps rendered using models from the ShapeNet dataset.

Table 1. Training detail about the number of real data, 3D model, normal map, and the range of camera angles. When azimuth and elevation are 0, it means the camera is located in front of the object. The camera moves in increments of $5°$.

	Num. images	Num. 3D models	Camera angle [degrees]			Num. normal maps
			Azimuth	Elevation	Num. angles	
Sofa	83,765	3,173	$-45\sim45$	$10\sim25$	36	114,228
Car	386,370	3,385	$-90\sim90$	$0\sim15$	76	257,260
Chair	151,758	6,778	$-90\sim90$	$10\sim25$	76	515,128

further compare the performance of appearance-based object pose estimator using these generated images from different methods as training data.

Training Datasets. In both qualitative and quantitative experiments, we take three object classes as examples: cars, sofas, and chairs. Table 1 shows details of the training datasets. Each dataset consists of both real images and normal maps. Real images were sampled from the LSUN dataset [35] with a simple filtering process to select images showing a single and sufficiently large target object. Using a pre-trained object detector [14], we accepted images with only one bounding box of the target class whose area is larger than 25% of the whole image. After the filtering process, there were in total 83,765, 151,758, and 386,370 images for sofa, chair, and car, respectively. These images were extended to 1:1 aspect ration by filling the borders by zero padding. Figures 4(a), (b), and (c) show samples of the sofa, chair, and car images used for training. The top row is real images from the LSUN dataset after post-processing, and the bottom row is normal maps rendered using models from the ShapeNet dataset. As can be seen in the cases such as the top-middle example in Figs. 4(b) and the top-left example in (c), the real images still contain some occlusions and mismatched object poses compared to the normal maps even after the automatic filtering, which illustrates the fundamental difficulty of handling unpaired data.

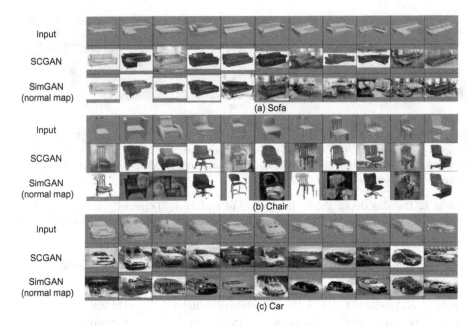

Input

SCGAN

SimGAN
(normal map)

(a) Sofa

Input

SCGAN

SimGAN
(normal map)

(b) Chair

Input

SCGAN

SimGAN
(normal map)

(c) Car

Fig. 5. Comparison with SimGAN and PixelDA for each object class. In each figure, the first row is input normal maps. The second and third rows are output from SCGAN and SimGAN using these normal maps.

We used 3D models taken from the ShapeNet dataset [4] to render normal maps. Using 3,173, 6,778, and 3,385 models for sofa, chair, and car, the normal maps were rendered so that the pose distribution roughly resembles the real image dataset. Table 1 lists the ranges of camera poses for each object, where the virtual camera was placed with increments of 5°. In total, there were 114,228, 515,128, and 257,260 normal maps for sofa, chair, and car. Since the position of the object also differs in the real images, during training we also applied random shifting and scaling to these normal maps.

Baseline Methods. Although there is no other method directly addressing the same task of shape-conditioned image generation, we picked two closely related approaches as baseline methods: SimGAN [27] and pixel-level domain adaptation (PixelDA) network [2]. The network architectures, discriminator losses, and training hyper-parameters of these baseline methods were set to the same as our method (SCGAN) for fair comparison, while method-specific losses stayed the same as the original papers. Following the original method, SimGAN does not have the input appearance vector and there is no mechanism to change the appearance of generated images. Since these methods were designed to modify rendered images of textured 3D models, we also evaluated them using textured rendering as input condition. The textured images were rendered in the same settings as the normal maps.

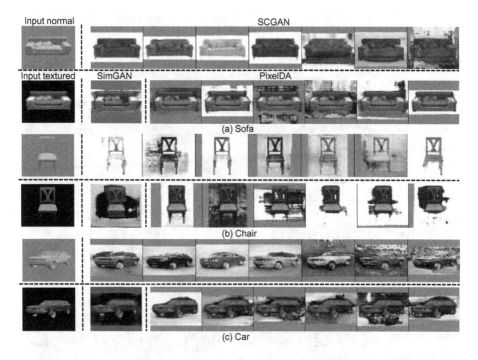

Fig. 6. Examples of generated images using the same normal map with several different appearance vectors. Each image shows the input normal map and textured image in the first column, the rest shows generated images with SCGAN, SimGAN, and PixelDA.

4.1 Comparison of Generated Images

Figure 5 shows examples of generated images from each method. Figures 5(a), (b), and (c) correspond to the cases of sofa, chair, and car, respectively. In each figure, the first row shows the input normal maps, and the second and third rows show the output from SCGAN and SimGAN using these normal maps as input.

It can be seen that SCGAN generates more naturalistic images than baseline methods. SimGAN could not successfully modify normal maps and failed to generate realistic images in most cases. In addition, there are many cases where the baseline methods failed to generate realistic background in Fig. 5(a). This illustrates the advantage of our method which does not rely on a strong constraint unlike baseline methods minimizing the distance between the generated and input images.

Figure 6 further shows more output examples of SCGAN, using the same normal map but with different appearance vectors. Figures 6(a), (b), and (c) are the input normal map and generated images of sofa, chair, and car, respectively. In each figure, the first column shows the input normal map and textured image. The remaining first row shows the generated images from the normal map using SCGAN, and the second row shows the output images from the textured image using both SimGAN and PixelDA. Since SimGAN cannot control the output

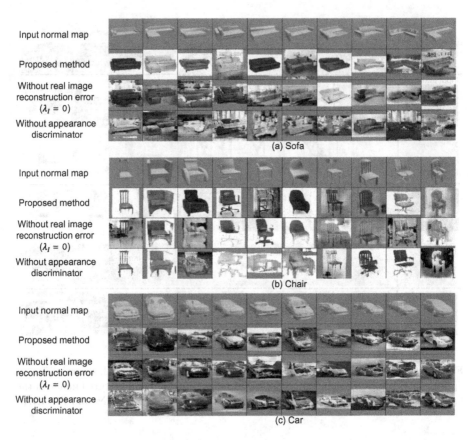

Input normal map

Proposed method

Without real image
reconstruction error
($\lambda_I = 0$)

Without appearance
discriminator

(a) Sofa

Input normal map

Proposed method

Without real image
reconstruction error
($\lambda_I = 0$)

Without appearance
discriminator

(b) Chair

Input normal map

Proposed method

Without real image
reconstruction error
($\lambda_I = 0$)

Without appearance
discriminator

(c) Car

Fig. 7. Generated images without real image reconstruction error and appearance discriminator. The first rows show input normal maps, and the rest shows output images generated by SCGAN, without the real image reconstruction loss, without the appearance discriminator loss.

image appearance, it only shows one example. While the baseline methods cannot control object shapes separately from the appearance, SCGAN can generate images with the same shape and diverse appearances. It is noteworthy that in Fig. 6(a) the output images also keep the cushion placed on the sofa, which is not an easy case for keypoint-based methods.

Ablation Study. In Fig. 7, we further show the effectiveness of individual loss terms in Eq. (4). To demonstrate the effect of the proposed architecture using the separate appearance modeling and the cycle-consistent real image reconstruction loss, we evaluated models trained without real image reconstruction error and appearance discriminator. Figures 7(a), (b), and (c) correspond to the cases of sofa, chair, and car, respectively. In each figure, the first row shows the input normal maps. The second row shows the output using all losses in Eq. (4).

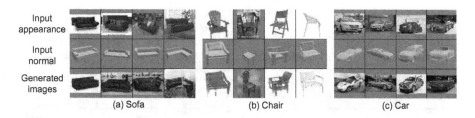

Input
appearance

Input
normal

Generated
images

(a) Sofa   (b) Chair   (c) Car

Fig. 8. Generated images with sampled appearances from real images. The first and second rows are input source images for appearance vectors and normal maps, and the third row shows the generated images.

The third row corresponds to the training result without the real image reconstruction error (λ_I was set to zero), and the fourth row corresponds to the case trained without the appearance discriminator.

These examples show that the proposed approach improves the overall image quality by using these losses. The real image reconstruction error significantly contributes to the realism of generated images, and the results without image reconstruction error mostly failed to generate object appearances. When the network was trained without the appearance discriminator, the generated images sometimes become highly distorted as can be seen in middle columns of Fig. 7(a).

Appearance Representation. As an consequence of the cycle-consistent training, the appearance generator G_z can also be used to extract appearance vectors from real images for generating new images. Figure 8 shows some examples of images generated using appearances sampled from real images. Figures 8(a), (b), and (c) correspond to the cases of sofa, chair, and car, respectively. As can be seen in these examples, SCGAN can generate shape-conditioned images with the similar appearance with the source images. This illustrates the potential of SCGAN for modifying pose and shape of objects in existing images.

Handling Unknown 3D Shapes. Another advantage of our method is that it can take an arbitrary normal map as input, even ones rendered using hand-crafted objects. In Fig. 9, we further show the output from the sofa image generator using hand-crafted sofa objects and shapes from the other object classes. The hand-crafted models were created by a person who has never experienced 3D modeling, and consists of basic 3D shapes without any texture.

Each block corresponds to the result of one 3D model, with the same three appearances. The first rows are input normal maps, and the second rows are generated images. Even when the object shape is significantly different from ordinary sofa shapes, SCGAN successfully generates their corresponding images. As can be seen in the bottom-right blocks, the proposed method tries to map the object texture to the input shape even when the shape comes from completely different object categories.

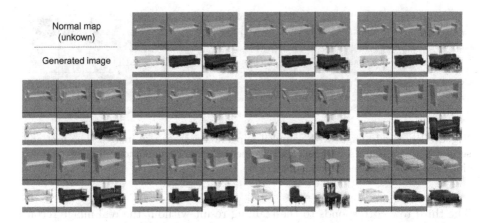

Fig. 9. Examples of generated images from unknown 3D shapes. Each block corresponds to one 3D model. The first rows are input normal maps, and the second rows are generated images.

4.2 Training Data Generation for Object Pose Estimation

Since SCGAN also keeps the object pose as the same as the input normal maps, the generated images can serve as a training data for appearance-based object pose estimation. In this section, we compare the effectiveness of SCGAN as training data generation framework, by comparing the accuracy of trained pose estimator with the cases using generated images from baseline methods. The architecture of the pose estimation network follows the DenseNet [13], while the last fully connected layer is modified to output 3-dimensional pose parameters. The network weights were pre-trained on the ImageNet [6], and the whole network including the last layer was trained on each target object dataset. Object poses are represented as Euler angles (azimuth, elevation, theta), and the loss function is set to be the Euclidean distance between ground-truth and estimated poses.

Test data were taken from the ObjectNet3D dataset [34] which consists of images annotated with pose-aligned 3D models. We selected images with the corresponding object annotations, and whose object poses stay within the pose range set for the training data. In total, we used 886, 2,547, and 3,939 test images for sofas, chairs, and cars, respectively.

We compare the performance of the pose estimator with the ones trained using data generated by SimGAN [27] and PixelDA [2]. As in the training of image generators, random shifting and scaling were also applied to the normal maps. As an indicator of the upper-bound accuracy of this task, we also trained the same pose estimator using the test data via 5-fold cross-validation. In addition, we evaluated the pose estimator directly using the textured images to show the estimator performance without any domain adaptation. Similarly, to show the baseline performance of each task we also evaluated a naive estimator which always output the mean pose in each object category.

Table 2. Mean pose error for ObjectNet3D dataset when the pose estimator is trained using dataset generated by SimGAN, PixelDA, and textured images. Naive baseline means that all predictions are an average of the target data.

	Target data	Normal map		Textured			Naive baseline
		SCGAN	SimGAN [27]	SimGAN [27]	PixelDA [2]	No op.	
Sofa	21.1	**23.9**	27.1	**23.8**	24.9	28.7	30.0
Chair	21.5	**26.0**	33.8	35.2	28.2	41.3	47.9
Car	16.9	**18.2**	26.0	22.4	20.4	33.6	38.9

Table 2 lists pose estimation errors for each method and object category. The estimation error was evaluated as the geodesic distance between the ground-truth rotation matrix R_t and the estimated rotation matrix R as $\frac{1}{\sqrt{2}}\|\log(R^T R_t)\|$ [34]. The first column (*Target data*) shows the upper-bound performance obtained via cross-validation. The second and third columns show the result using the dataset generated from normal maps, with SCGAN and SimGAN, respectively. Similarly, the third and fourth columns show the result using the dataset generated from textured images, with SimGAN and PixelDA, respectively. The fifth column (*No op.*) additionally shows the result directly using the original textured images. The sixth column shows the naive baseline performance of the average predictor.

The result shows that SCGAN achieved better pose estimation performances than SimGAN-based training results using normal maps, and better or close performance in comparison with SimGAN and PixelDA based training using textured 3D model images. SCGAN significantly improved the pose estimation performance especially in the case of the chair dataset. This is mainly because chair images have larger appearance gaps from the textured images, and SCGAN successfully generated training images closer to the actual test images.

5   Conclusion

In this work, we proposed SCGAN, a GAN architecture for shape-conditioned image generation. Given a normal map of the target object category, SCGAN generates images with the same shape as the input normal map. The network can be trained without relying on paired training data with cycle-consistency losses, and it is able to generate images with diverse appearances through the latent modeling of image appearances. Unlike prior work on conditional image generation, our method does not rely on any object-specific keypoint design and can handle arbitrary object categories. The proposed method therefore provides a flexible and generic framework for shape-conditioned image generation tasks.

We demonstrated the advantage of SCGAN through both qualitative and quantitative evaluations. SCGAN not only improves the quality of generated images while maintaining the input shape, but also efficiently handles the training data synthesis task for appearance-based object pose estimation. In future work, we will further investigate applications of the proposed method including a wider range of learning-by-synthesis approaches, together with more detailed human evaluation on generated images.

References

1. Baktashmotlagh, M., Harandi, M.T., Lovell, B.C., Salzmann, M.: Unsupervised domain adaptation by domain invariant projection. In: Proceedings of the ICCV, pp. 769–776 (2013)
2. Bousmalis, K., Silberman, N., Dohan, D., Erhan, D., Krishnan, D.: Unsupervised pixel-level domain adaptation with generative adversarial networks. In: Proceedings of the CVPR, pp. 95–104 (2017)
3. Brock, A., Lim, T., Ritchie, J.M., Weston, N.: Neural photo editing with introspective adversarial networks. In: Proceedings of the ICLR (2017)
4. Chang, A.X., et al.: ShapeNet: an information-rich 3D model repository. arXiv preprint arXiv:1512.03012 (2015)
5. Chen, X., Duan, Y., Houthooft, R., Schulman, J., Sutskever, I., Abbeel, P.: Info-GAN: interpretable representation learning by information maximizing generative adversarial nets. In: Proceedings of the NIPS, pp. 1–14 (2016)
6. Deng, J., Dong, W., Socher, R., Li, L.J., Li, K., Fei-Fei, L.: ImageNet: a large-scale hierarchical image database. In: Proceedings of the CVPR, pp. 248–255 (2009)
7. Donahue, J., Krähenbühl, P., Darrell, T.: Adversarial feature learning. In: Proceedings of the ICLR (2017)
8. Ganin, Y., et al.: Domain-adversarial training of neural networks. JMLR **17**, 1–35 (2015)
9. Goodfellow, I., Pouget-Abadie, J., Mirza, M.: Generative adversarial networks. In: Proceedings of the NIPS, pp. 2672–2680 (2014)
10. Gulrajani, I., Ahmed, F., Arjovsky, M., Dumoulin, V., Courville, A.: Improved training of Wasserstein GANs. In: Proceedings of the NIPS, pp. 5769–5779 (2017)
11. He, K., Zhang, X., Ren, S., Sun, J.: Deep residual learning for image recognition. In: Proceedings of the CVPR, pp. 770–778 (2016)
12. Hinterstoisser, S., et al.: Model based training, detection and pose estimation of texture-less 3D objects in heavily cluttered scenes. In: Lee, K.M., Matsushita, Y., Rehg, J.M., Hu, Z. (eds.) ACCV 2012. LNCS, vol. 7724, pp. 548–562. Springer, Heidelberg (2013). https://doi.org/10.1007/978-3-642-37331-2_42
13. Huang, G., Liu, Z., Van Der Maaten, L., Weinberger, K.Q.: Densely connected convolutional networks. In: Proceedings of the CVPR, pp. 2261–2269 (2017)
14. Huang, J., et al.: Speed/accuracy trade-offs for modern convolutional object detectors. In: Proceedings of the CVPR, pp. 3296–3305 (2017)
15. Iizuka, S., Simo-Serra, E., Ishikawa, H.: Globally and locally consistent image completion. ACM Trans. Graph. **36**(4), 1–14 (2017). https://dl.acm.org/citation.cfm?id=3073659
16. Johnson, J., Alahi, A., Fei-Fei, L.: Perceptual losses for real-time style transfer and super-resolution. In: Leibe, B., Matas, J., Sebe, N., Welling, M. (eds.) ECCV 2016. LNCS, vol. 9906, pp. 694–711. Springer, Cham (2016). https://doi.org/10.1007/978-3-319-46475-6_43
17. Junbo Zhao, M.M., LeCun, Y.: Energy-based GAN. In: Proceedings of the ICLR, pp. 32–48 (2015)
18. Karras, T., Aila, T., Laine, S., Lehtinen, J.: Progressive growing of GANs for improved quality, stability, and variation. In: Proceedings of the ICLR, pp. 1–25 (2018)

19. Kingma, D.P., Ba, J.: Adam: a method for stochastic optimization. In: Proceedings of the ICLR (2015)
20. Ledig, C., et al.: Photo-realistic single image super-resolution using a generative adversarial network. In: ACM Multimedia, pp. 4681–4690 (2016)
21. Ma, L., Jia, X., Sun, Q., Schiele, B., Tuytelaars, T., Van Gool, L.: Pose guided person image generation. In: Proceedings of the NIPS, pp. 405–415 (2017)
22. Mao, X., Li, Q., Xie, H., Lau, R.Y.K., Wang, Z., Smolley, S.P.: Least squares generative adversarial networks. In: Proceedings of the ICCV, November 2017
23. Odena, A., Olah, C., Shlens, J.: Conditional image synthesis with auxiliary classifier GANs. In: Proceedings of the ICML (2017)
24. Qiu, W., Yuille, A.: UnrealCV: connecting computer vision to unreal engine. In: Hua, G., Jégou, H. (eds.) ECCV 2016. LNCS, vol. 9915, pp. 909–916. Springer, Cham (2016). https://doi.org/10.1007/978-3-319-49409-8_75
25. Reed, S., Akata, Z., Mohan, S., Tenka, S., Schiele, B., Lee, H.: Learning what and where to draw. In: Proceedings of the NIPS, pp. 217–225 (2016)
26. Ros, G., Sellart, L., Materzynska, J., Vazquez, D., Lopez, A.M.: The SYNTHIA-Dataset: a large collection of synthetic images for semantic segmentation of urban scenes. In: Proceedings of the CVPR, pp. 3234–3243 (2016)
27. Shrivastava, A., Pfister, T., Tuzel, O., Susskind, J., Wang, W., Webb, R.: Learning from simulated and unsupervised images through adversarial training. In: Proceedings of the CVPR, p. 6 (2017)
28. Sixt, L., Wild, B., Landgraf, T.: RenderGAN: generating realistic labeled data. Front. Rob. AI **5**, 66 (2018)
29. Springenberg, J.T.: Unsupervised and semi-supervised learning with categorical generative adversarial networks. In: Proceedings of the ICLR (2016)
30. Sun, B., Saenko, K.: From virtual to reality: fast adaptation of virtual object detectors to real domains. In: Proceedings of the BMVC, pp. 82.1–82.12 (2014)
31. Tan, W.R., Chan, C.S., Aguirre, H., Tanaka, K.: ArtGAN: artwork synthesis with conditional categorial GANs. In: Proceedings of the ICIP, p. 10 (2017)
32. Vazquez, D., Lopez, A.M., Marin, J., Ponsa, D., Geronimo, D.: Virtual and real world adaptation for pedestrian detection. In: IEEE TPAMI, pp. 797–809 (2014)
33. Wood, E., Baltrušaitis, T., Morency, L.P., Robinson, P., Bulling, A.: Learning an appearance-based gaze estimator from one million synthesised images. In: ACM Symposium on Eye Tracking Research & Applications, pp. 131–138 (2016)
34. Xiang, Y., et al.: ObjectNet3D: a large scale database for 3D object recognition. In: Leibe, B., Matas, J., Sebe, N., Welling, M. (eds.) ECCV 2016. LNCS, vol. 9912, pp. 160–176. Springer, Cham (2016). https://doi.org/10.1007/978-3-319-46484-8_10
35. Yu, F., Seff, A., Zhang, Y., Song, S., Funkhouser, T., Xiao, J.: LSUN: construction of a large-scale image dataset using deep learning with humans in the loop. arXiv preprint arXiv:1506.03365 (2015)
36. Zhang, Y., David, P., Gong, B.: Curriculum domain adaptation for semantic segmentation of urban scenes. In: Proceedings of the ICCV, pp. 2039–2049 (2017)
37. Zhang, Z., Song, Y., Qi, H.: Age progression/regression by conditional adversarial autoencoder. In: Proceedings of the CVPR, pp. 5810–5818 (2017)
38. Zhu, J.-Y., Krähenbühl, P., Shechtman, E., Efros, A.A.: Generative visual manipulation on the natural image manifold. In: Leibe, B., Matas, J., Sebe, N., Welling, M. (eds.) ECCV 2016. LNCS, vol. 9909, pp. 597–613. Springer, Cham (2016). https://doi.org/10.1007/978-3-319-46454-1_36
39. Zhu, J.Y., Park, T., Isola, P., Efros, A.A.: Unpaired image-to-image translation using cycle-consistent adversarial networks. In: Proceedings of the ICCV (2017)

Dense In Dense: Training Segmentation from Scratch

Tao Hu[✉]

University of Amsterdam, Amsterdam, The Netherlands
taohu620@gmail.com

Abstract. In recent years, training image segmentation networks often needs fine-tuning the model which comes from the initial training upon large-scale classification datasets like ImageNet. Such fine-tuning methods are confronted with three problems: (1) domain gap. (2) mismatch between data size and model size. (3) poor controllability. A more practical solution is to train the segmentation model from scratch, which motivates our Dense In Dense (DID) network. In DID, we put forward an efficient architecture based on DenseNet to further accelerate the information flow inside and outside the dense block. Deep supervision also applies to a progressive upsampling rather than the traditional straightforward upsampling. Our DID Network performs favorably on Camvid dataset, Inria Aerial Image Labeling dataset and Cityscapes by training from scratch with less parameters.

Keyword: Image segmentation

1 Introduction

Convolutional Neural Networks (CNNs) are driving major advances in many computer vision tasks, such as image classification [16], object detection [7] and semantic image segmentation [19]. Recently, more and more network architectures [9,12] are proposed to be applied in those basic tasks, which are trained on large scale standard benchmarks such as ImageNet [4]. For instance, Szegedy *et al.* [28] propose an "Inception" module which concatenates feature maps produced by various sized filters. He *et al.* [9] propose the residual learning blocks with skip connections, which makes it possible to train *very deep* networks with more than 100 layers. Huang *et al.* [12] propose the DenseNet with dense layer-wise connections. Reasonable model architectures and large-scale data simultaneously push forward the frontier results of basic computer vision tasks step by step.

In the field of image semantic segmentation, many works [2,11] are pretrained on large scale datasets such as ImageNet to utilize the big data to obtain an initial feature extractor and then fine-tune on their own specific dataset. The fine-tuning process which comes from transfer learning owns several advantages.

© Springer Nature Switzerland AG 2019
C. V. Jawahar et al. (Eds.): ACCV 2018, LNCS 11366, pp. 454–470, 2019.
https://doi.org/10.1007/978-3-030-20876-9_29

Firstly, it enables better learning of low-level features representation by the large-scale data and high-level features based on specific task. Secondly, fine-tuning costs much less training time compared with training the classification task on ImageNet from scratch. In the end, less annotation data is needed for fine-tuning because some basic features can be shared from the source model.

However, there are also several serious limitations when fine-tuning is adopted in image segmentation. (1) *domain gap.* There are one thousand data distributions in one thousand datasets, which varies in lighting, scene, distance, etc. Directly fine-tuning sometimes tends to cause a poor result due to the domain gap between the source dataset and target dataset. (2) *mismatch between data size and model size.* As *"no free lunch theorem"* indicates, model size should correspond with data size. Too large data size would cause under-fitting, inversely overabundant model size would give rise to over-fitting. In the fine-tuning process, the mismatch between source dataset and target dataset data size often leads to inappropriate fitting. (3) *poor controllability.* The main network structure trained from the source dataset is often reserved when fine-tuning, which greatly limits the network design space.

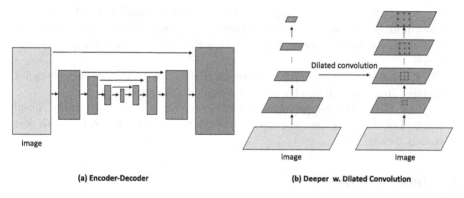

(a) Encoder-Decoder   (b) Deeper w. Dilated Convolution

Fig. 1. Two typical network structures in image segmentation. (a) Encoder-Decoder with U-shape. (b) Deeper network enlarging the receptive field without reducing the image resolution.

We here restate some normal cases under which we have to train segmentation from scratch. At first, most pre-trained models are trained on large-scale RGB image dataset such as ImageNet. It's very difficult to alter the model for the application in domains of depth images (with R-G-B-D four channels), multi-spectrum images in remote sensing field, medical images, etc. Secondly, to make the segmentation model efficiently work in the embedded system which is very resource-limited, it's unrealistic to use a model with large parameter number and heavy computing load. Training from scratch is an inevitable method in those embedded applications. Last but not least, data is precious in some fields such as medical diagnosis, which seriously need highly experienced physician to annotate medical data. Under these circumstances, utilizing large models such as resnet50 and resnet101 to pretrain on those small datasets will inevitably lead to over-fitting. The generalization ability will be seriously influenced.

Motivated by the above limitations of fine-tuning, we propose our DID Network architecture which can train image segmentation task from scratch and reach a better result than fine-tuning. Xie *et al.* [31] proposed a holistically-nested structure for edge detection named HED, which contains side-output layers from diverse scale context for explicit multi-scale fusion. Same with HED, the key point of our DID structure is to further enhance the information flow based on the DenseNet and simultaneously fuse the multi-scale context information to progressively refine the segmentation performance. Notably, as DenseNet only guarantees that the information flows sufficiently inside the dense block, our DID Network both accelerates the information flow **inside and outside** the dense block, which is where the name of Dense In Dense (DID) Network comes from.

Our main contributions are summarized as follows:

- (1) We put forward Dense In Dense (DID) Network, which not only explicitly fuses multi-scale context to realize progressive upsampling but also sufficiently facilitates the neural network information flow inside and outside the dense block.
- (2) We validate some factors to design efficient segmentation networks for training from scratch though step-by-step ablation studies.
- (3) Our DID Network performs favorably on Camvid dataset, Inria Aerial Image Labeling dataset and Cityscapes by training from scratch with less parameters.

2   Related Work

2.1   Image Segmentation

In the early period, the CNN is only employed in the classification task due to GPU memory limitation. Most of them [16,28] are composed of convolution layers and fully connected layers. Fully Convolutional Network (FCN) [19] firstly applies CNN into image segmentation, which makes it a fundamental architecture for segmentation. FCN is the first one to build "fully convolutional" network that takes the input of arbitrary size and produces correspondingly-sized output with efficient inference and learning. A skip connection that combines semantic information between a deep, coarse layer and a shallow, fine layer is deployed to produce both accurate and detailed segmentation result. Many different structures are proposed based on FCN, most of which can be divided into (1) Encoder-Decoder. (2) Deeper with Dilated Convolution, as shown in Fig. 1. Our DID network takes advantage of both structures to realize a progressive decoder based on a deep network with Dilated Convolution.

Encoder-Decoder: The architecture is composed of two parts: (a) encoder. The spatial dimension of feature maps is reduced gradually to a minimal size. Multiscale context can be extracted from this part. (b) decoder. The spatial dimension of feature maps is increased gradually to the original image size. In addition, skip layers from encoder can be also utilized at multiscale. For instance, SegNet [1] reuses the pooling indices from the encoder and adds extra convolutional layers to recover the image size. Meanwhile skip connections are widely applied in the decoder parts in U-net [25] to further fuse the multi-context.

Deeper with Dilated Convolution: In Deeplab [2], Dilated Convolutions are introduced as an alternative to CNN pooling layers in deep part to capture larger context without reducing the image resolution. A module named atrous spatial pyramid pooling (ASPP) is also included in Deeplab where parallel Dilated Convolution layers with different rates capture multi-scale information. Following the same spirit, Yu *et al.* [32] propose to provide FCNs with a context module built as a stack of dilated convolutional layers to enlarge the field of view of the network. Recently, Pyramid Scene Parsing Net (PSPNet) [33] performs spatial pooling at several grid scales and demonstrates outstanding performance on several semantic segmentation benchmarks.

Post Processing: DenseCRF [15] is a typical post processing method in segmentation. Position, color based pairwise potential and segmentation probability based unary potential are incorporated in DenseCRF. In another aspect, RNN has been introduced to approximate mean-field iterations of CRF optimization, allowing for an end-to-end training of both the FCN and the RNN [34]. Recently, Spatial Propagation Networks (SPN) [18] is proposed to directly learn the affinity matrix of pixels in a purely data-driven manner.

Devils in Decoder: In the work of Deeplab [2], by application of Dilated Convolution, the features are bilinearly upsampled by a factor of 8, which can be considered as a naive decoder module. Because of the diversity of object scale, this naive decoder module may not successfully recover object semantic details. Meanwhile, great memory cost caused by larger deep feature map size will do harm to the architecture performance. To mitigate this problem, Dense Upsampling Convolution (DUC) [30] is designed to generate a pixel-level prediction, which is able to capture and decode more detailed information that is generally missing in bilinear upsampling. However, DUC misses the global spatial information which is critical for segmentation task. In our work, we progressively upsample the feature map based on cascaded multi-scale context rather than directly upsample to original image size. Our architecture significantly saves large memory cost and widely refines the result.

2.2   Training Neural Network from Scratch

About training neural network from scratch in classification, there exist some methods in semantic segmentation [13] and object detection [26]. DSOD [26] proposes a framework based on DenseNet that can learn object detectors from scratch, meanwhile deep supervision is also applied in their model. Jegou et al. [13] demonstrate that a well-designed network structure FC-DenseNet can outperform state-of-the-art solutions without using the pre-trained models. It extends DenseNet to fully convolutional networks by adding an upsampling path to recover the full input resolution. Our DID architecture demonstrates better result than FC-DenseNet by refining semantic result step by step.

3   Method

Our DID architecture is composed of Dense Encoder and DID Decoder. The structure of Dense Encoder is based on DenseNet. DID Decoder takes the multi-scale context of Dense Encoder as input and progressively decodes the feature map to the original image size.

In this section, we introduce the detailed structure of DID network. As the baseline of our work, we review the DenseNet architecture in a glance. Then we introduce our DID network from different aspects.

3.1   Review of DenseNet

DenseNet [12] design a sophisticated connectivity pattern that iteratively concatenates all feature outputs in a feed-forward fashion. Thus, the output of the lth layer is defined as

$$x_l = H_l(concat(x_{l-1}, x_{l-2}, ..., x_0)) \tag{1}$$

where "concat" represents the concatenation operation. In this case, H is defined as Batch Normalization (BN), followed by ReLU, a convolution, and Dropout [27]. Such connectivity pattern strongly encourages the reuse of features and makes all layers in the architecture receive direct supervision signal. The output dimension of each layer l has k feature maps where k, hereafter referred to *growth rate*, is typically set to a small value (*e.g.* k = 12). Thus, the number of feature maps in DenseNet grows linearly with the depth.

Dense Block. *dense block* represents the concatenation of the new feature maps created at a given resolution. A *dense block* with 4 units is demonstrated in Fig. 2.

Transition Layer. A *transition layer* is introduced to reduce the spatial dimensionality of the feature maps. Such transformation is composed of a 1×1 convolution followed by a 2×2 pooling operation.

Compression Rate. To further improve model compactness, we can reduce the number of feature-maps at transition layers. If a dense block contains m feature-maps, we let the following transition layer generate $\theta \times m$ output feature maps, where $0 \leq \theta \leq 1$ represents the compression factor.

Difference Between Our DID Network and DenseNet. Our Dense Encoder architecture is based on DenseNet while differs from DenseNet in the following aspects: (a) Dilated convolution is adopted in Dense Block (3) and (4) to further enlarge the receptive field without downsampling the feature map, whose effect will be validated in the later experiment. (b) Transition layer after dense block (3) doesn't include 2×2 pooling to reduce feature map size. (c) Our dense block number varies from the official implementation because we believe the block number should coordinate well with dataset scale. (d) Larger growth rate(48) is adopted. (e) We set compression factor as 1 instead of 0.5 in official DenseNet. (f) Most importantly, our DID Decoder accelerates information flowing inside and outside dense block and progressively refines the semantic result though multi-context fusion.

Table 1. Dense Encoder in DID architecture for Camvid Dataset. We demonstrate it as image size is 312×321. dense{m}-k{n}-d{p} means m dense units, growth rate is n, max dilation is p. dense30-k48-d4 is chosen as our final model structure, dense30-k48-d2 and dense58-k24-d2 are network structures for later ablation study in Sect. 4.1. B-R-C means "Batch Normalization-ReLU-Convolution" combination. The output of dense block (1), dense block (2), dense block (3) are blended by DID Decoder which is depicted in Fig. 2.

Layers	Output size	dense30-k48-d2	dense30-k48-d4	dense58-k24-d2
Convolution	161×161		3×3 conv, stride 2	
Convolution	161×161		3×3 conv, stride 1	
Convolution	161×161		3×3 conv, stride 1	
Pooling	81×81		3×3 max pool, stride 2	
Dense Block (1)	81×81	$\begin{bmatrix} 1 \times 1 \text{ B-R-C} \\ 3 \times 3 \text{ B-R-C} \end{bmatrix} \times 6$	$\begin{bmatrix} 1 \times 1 \text{ B-R-C} \\ 3 \times 3 \text{ B-R-C} \end{bmatrix} \times 6$	$\begin{bmatrix} 1 \times 1 \text{ B-R-C} \\ 3 \times 3 \text{ B-R-C} \end{bmatrix} \times 6$
Transition Layer (1)	81×81		1×1 B-R-C	
	41×41		2×2 average pool, stride 2	
Dense Block (2)	41×41	$\begin{bmatrix} 1 \times 1 \text{ B-R-C} \\ 3 \times 3 \text{ B-R-C} \end{bmatrix} \times 8$	$\begin{bmatrix} 1 \times 1 \text{ B-R-C} \\ 3 \times 3 \text{ B-R-C} \end{bmatrix} \times 8$	$\begin{bmatrix} 1 \times 1 \text{ B-R-C} \\ 3 \times 3 \text{ B-R-C} \end{bmatrix} \times 12$
Transition Layer (2)	41×41		1×1 B-R-C	
	21×21		2×2 average pool, stride 2	
Dense Block (3)	21×21	$\begin{bmatrix} 1 \times 1 \text{ B-R-C} \\ 3 \times 3 \text{ B-R-C} \end{bmatrix} \times 8$ with dilation $= 2$	$\begin{bmatrix} 1 \times 1 \text{ B-R-C} \\ 3 \times 3 \text{ B-R-C} \end{bmatrix} \times 8$ with dilation $= 2$	$\begin{bmatrix} 1 \times 1 \text{ B-R-C} \\ 3 \times 3 \text{ B-R-C} \end{bmatrix} \times 24$ with dilation $= 2$
Transition Layer (3)	21×21		1×1 B-R-C	
Dense Block (4)	21×21	$\begin{bmatrix} 1 \times 1 \text{ B-R-C} \\ 3 \times 3 \text{ B-R-C} \end{bmatrix} \times 8$ with dilation $= 2$	$\begin{bmatrix} 1 \times 1 \text{ B-R-C} \\ 3 \times 3 \text{ B-R-C} \end{bmatrix} \times 8$ with dilation $= 4$	$\begin{bmatrix} 1 \times 1 \text{ B-R-C} \\ 3 \times 3 \text{ B-R-C} \end{bmatrix} \times 16$ with dilation $= 4$

3.2 Dense In Dense Network

In this subsection, we elaborate the DID architecture. The intention of the detail design in DID network can be found in Sect. 4.

Dense Encoder. We show our Dense Encoder structure in detail in Table 1. Dense30-k48-d4 is chosen as our final Dense Encoder in DID network architecture

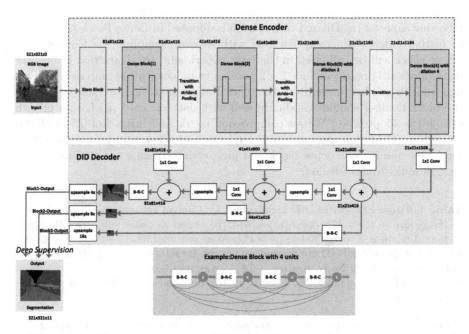

Fig. 2. Our network structure. Dense Encoder and DID Decoder make up our total architecture. Our Dense Encoder contains several combinations of dense block and transition block which is dense30-k48-d4 shown in Table 1 concretely. DID Decoder includes progressive refinement based on 1×1 convolution, bilinear upsampling. B-R-C means "Batch Normalization-ReLU-Convolution" combination. The feature map dimension is marked as $w \times h \times c$ after some operations. Our network structure finally outputs three probability map:block1-output, block2-output, block3-output (ranging from fine to coarse), only the finest output (block1-output) is used for our final inference. Best viewed in color.

based on the experiment in Sect. 4. In Dense Encoder we define the structure of dense block and the transition layer. Following pre-activation [10], our dense block layers are composed of BN, followed by ReLU, a 3×3 Convolution and dropout with $p = 0.2$. The growth rate of the layer is set to $k = 48$. The transition layer is composed of BN, followed by ReLU, a 1×1 Convolution, dropout with $p = 0.2$. Notably, In the deeper part, we do not downsample the feature map in transition layer and apply Dilated Convolution in the deeper dense block. Inspired by DSOD [26], we define *stem block* as a stack of three 3×3 convolution layers followed by a 2×2 max pooling layer. The first convolution layer works with stride $= 2$ and the other two with stride $= 1$.

DID Decoder. Details of our DID decoder are demonstrated in Fig. 2. All of the Convolutions in DID Decoder is 1×1 Convolution without BN and ReLU, except for the final convolution before upsampling. For 321×321 input images, four scales of feature maps are applied for segmentation. The largest feature maps are from the dense block (1) which owns the finest resolution (81×81) in order to handle small objects in an image. The remaining feature maps are from the output of dense block (2), (3) respectively. For short, we call these feature maps as block1-output, block2-output, block3-output accordingly.

Deep Supervision. Deep supervised learning has been successfully utilized in GoogLeNet [28], HED [31], etc. The core idea is to provide integrated objective function as direct supervision for the earlier hidden layers, rather than only for the output layer. We adopt deep supervision in our DID Network based on the following points: (1) These "auxiliary" objective functions at multiple hidden layers can mitigate the "vanishing" gradients problem. By deep supervision, it enables the precious gradient to keep propagating in the shallow parts of DID Network. (2) This deep supervised pattern greatly facilitates the multi-context fusion. In contrast, DenseNet only guarantees that the information flows sufficiently in the dense block. our DID Network both accelerates the information flow **inside and outside** the dense block. Sufficient information flow will make the network easier to be trained from scratch.

Wide DenseNet. As the original implementation of DenseNet is not memory efficient, wide DenseNet is adopted in our DID Network for better memory utilization. We set growth rate as $k = 48$. Interestingly, we also find that wide DenseNet leads to better accuracy than deep DenseNet on basis of nearly same parameter number. We conclude that wide structure is superior to a deep structure in the task of segmentation because far-ranging semantic features are essential for segmentation, which can only be extracted by wide DenseNet.

Loss Function. As we adopt the deep supervision in our DID Network, three cross entropy losses will be generated as indicated in Fig. 2. Our final loss is the average of three losses. Compared to previous fuse strategies [31], only the finest probability map (block1-output) will be used for inference. Our progressive refinement strategy is proved to be effective.

3.3 Training Setting

We implement our code based on the tensorflow framework. All our models are trained from scratch with Adam [14] solver on NVidia TitanX GPU. We initialize our models using Xavier [8] and train with an initial learning rate of 1e−3 and divide learning rate by 10 until we reach 2/3 of the total training process. All models are trained on data augmented with random crops and vertical flips. Following the method in Deeplabv3 [3], we fine-tune on the trainval set for another 100 epochs with a smaller base learning rate = 1e−4 after training. We regularize our models with a weight decay of 1e−4 and a dropout rate of 0.2. For Batch Normalization, we employ current batch statistics at training and use the moving average statistics of Batch Normalization during validation and test time.

4   Experimental Results

To better evaluate our model in the domain that owns different distribution from ImageNet, we conduct experiments on the Camvid Dataset and Inria Aerial Image labeling dataset [20]. The performance is measured by standard mean Intersection-over-Union (IoU).

Camvid is a dataset of fully segmented videos for urban scene understanding. We use the split and image resolution from [1], which consists of 367 frames for training, 101 frames for validation and 233 frames for testing. Each frame has a size of 360×480 and its pixels are labeled with 11 semantic classes.

Inria Aerial Image labeling dataset [20] owns images with coverage of $810 \, \text{km}^2$ ($405 \, \text{km}^2$ for training and $405 \, \text{km}^2$ for testing). Its ground truth contains two semantic classes: building and not building. The original dataset image size is 5000×5000, we crop it into 473×473 randomly.

4.1   Ablation Study on Camvid Dataset

We mainly investigate the basic improvement in cascade dilation, stem, compression rate, wide DenseNet, DID structure, deep supervision, etc. The overall result is shown in Table 2.

Table 2. Various design result on Camvid Dataset. Please refer to Table 3 for more details.

				DID				
Baseline	✓	✓	✓	✓	✓	✓	✓	✓
Cascade dilation?		✓	✓	✓	✓	✓	✓	✓
Stem?			✓	✓	✓	✓	✓	✓
Need compression?				✓	✓	✓	✓	✓
Wider or deeper?					✓	✓	✓	✓
Dense in dense?						✓	✓	✓
Deep supervision?							✓	✓
More iteration?								✓
Camvid test mIoU	54.9	56	58.8	60	61.3	64.5	65.7	68.3

Cascade Dilation. Dilated Convolution plays an important role in segmentation task. Without Dilated Convolution, the final output feature map size will be only $1/32$ of the original image size, which greatly does harm to the performance. Therefore, we adopt Dilated Convolution in transition layer (3), (4) and regard it as our baseline. In Table 3 (row 4, 5, 6), we mainly compare the different dilation rate (2, 4, 8) in transition block (4). We find that dilation rate = 4 performs 1.1% mIoU better than dilation rate = 2, while dilation rate = 8 nearly shows the same mIoU with dilation rate $= 4$. Therefore, we use the dilation rate $= 4$ dense block for our later experiment.

Stem Block in DenseNet. As DSOD [26] states, stem block is important in detection whose architecture is based on DenseNet. Motivated by this, we set stem block as a stack of three 3×3 convolution layers followed by a 2×2 max pooling layer. Our result (row 6, 7 in Table 2) could obtain 3.2% extra gain in our segmentation task. We conclude that 7×7 convolution is difficult for Camvid such small size dataset to train a good result. Instead, a stack of 3×3 convolution is much more convenient for training especially when the dataset scale is not so huge as ImageNet.

Compression Rate. We compare two compression rates (0.5, 1) in the transition layer of DenseNet. Results are shown in Table 3 (row 7 and 8). Compression rate $= 1$ means that there is no feature map number reduction in the transition layer, while compression rate $= 0.5$ means half of the feature map number is reduced. Results show that compression rate $= 1$ yields 1.2% higher mIoU than compression rate $= 0.5$ with extra 2.5M parameters. On the other hand, the wide DenseNet could also mitigate the memory efficiency problem in DenseNet so that we can fit larger batch size into the GPU memory. In the remaining ablation study, we mainly adopt the wide DenseNet architecture.

Wider or Deeper. We mainly increase the growth rate while reducing the depth on the basis of keeping nearly same parameter numbers. As shown in Table 3(row 3, 8), we mainly compare dense58k24 and dense30k48. Dense30k36 achieves slightly 0.1% better mIoU than dense58k24 with 1.9M less parameters.

Table 3. Ablation Study Result on Camvid Dataset. did3 means DID Network with 3×3 convolution, did1 means DID Network with 1×1 convolution, dense30k48.did1.ds means DID Network with 1×1 convolution and deep supervision.

Row	Pre-train	Input size	Backbone network	Stem	Dilation	Compression	# parameters (M)	Iterations	Test mIoU
1	✓	321 × 321	ResNet50	✗	2	–	23.7	9.9K	61
2	✗	321 × 321	ResNet50	✗	2	–	23.7	44.8K	59.8
3	✗	321 × 321	dense58k24	✓	4	1	7.6	73.6K	59.9
4	✗	321 × 321	dense30k36	✗	2	0.5	2.9	32K	54.9
5	✗	321 × 321	dense30k36	✗	4	0.5	2.9	32K	56
6	✗	321 × 321	dense30k36	✗	8	0.5	2.9	32K	55.6
7	✗	321 × 321	dense30k36	✓	4	0.5	3.2	38.4K	58.8
8	✗	321 × 321	dense30k36	✓	4	1	5.7	44K	60
9	✗	321 × 321	dense30k48	✓	4	1	9.6	60.8K	61.3
10	✗	353 × 353	dense30k48	✓	4	1	9.6	67.2K	61.3
11	✗	385 × 385	dense30k48	✓	4	1	9.6	83.2K	59.2
12	✗	321 × 321	dense30k48	✓	4	1	9.6	171K	63.4
13	✗	321 × 321	dense30k48.did3	✓	4	1	14.4	67.2K	63.7
14	✗	321 × 321	dense30k48.did1	✓	4	1	11.6	67.2K	64.5
15	✗	321 × 321	dense30k48.did1.ds	✓	4	1	11.6	67.2K	65.7
16	✗	321 × 321	dense30k48.did1.ds	✓	4	1	11.6	182K	68.3

Furthermore, when we make the DenseNet wider (growth rate as 48), wider DenseNet brings us extra 1.3% mIoU (row 8, 9). This result makes us firmly believe that wide structure is more important than deep structure in the task of segmentation, for it owns a better utilization of the total parameter space.

Dense In Dense (DID). Our DID structure mainly fuses the larger scale context with refined context recursively. Multi-scale context feature from different dense blocks is smoothened by 1×1 convolutions. Neighbor context features are fused by adding operation. As indicated in Table 3(row 9, 13), our DID structure (row 13) outperforms 2.4% mIoU than naive wide DenseNet baseline (row 9).

DID with 1×1 Convolution. Even though DID structure discussed above can bring large gain for the segmentation task, it brings extra 4.8M parameter overload. After analysis, we find the parameter burden is mainly caused by the convolution operation after the add operation in DID structure. After replacing the 3×3 convolution into 1×1 convolution, interestingly, we achieve 0.7% better mIoU than the 3×3 convolution with nearly less 2.8M parameters (row 13, 14).

Deep Supervision. Inspired by the wide application of deep supervision in dense pixel tasks [33], we creatively append deep supervision in every level of our DID structure output, which is depicted in Fig. 2. Three cross entropy losses are finally averaged for back propagation. 1.2% extra mIoU gain is obtained after applying the deep supervision as shown in Table 3(row 14, 15). We also try to blend the three probability maps in inference, the result is worse than using the finest probability map, which inversely demonstrates our refinement strategy really works.

Image Size and Iteration Number. Image size is an easily missed factor which greatly dominates the performance. We compare four image sizes: $321 \times 321, 353 \times 353, 385 \times 385, 360 \times 480$. We try our best to make the image input with spatial dimensions that fits $16n+1$, $n \in \{0, 1, 2, ...\}$ to facilitate alignment of the features to image. 321×321 and 353×353 demonstrates nearly the same better result that other image size choice. In order to make the batch size larger, we choose 321×321 as our final image size. As row 9, 12 in Table 3 indicates, larger iteration number leads a 2.1% better mIoU than the basic dense30k48. In order to save time, we conduct main ablation studies in small iteration number, after fixing the final architecture, training with a relative larger iteration number will be conducted. In the end, based on our best model structure dense30k48.did1.ds, we retrain it with a larger iteration number and obtain 68.3% mIoU (row 16).

Comparing with Traditional Fine-Tuning Method. By the analysis of disadvantage in fine-tuning in Sect. 1, mismatch problem between data size and model size obviously exists on our Camvid Dataset. Our DID Network demonstrates nearly 4% mIoU better than the fine-tuning method with 12M fewer parameters, the result of which is shown in Table 3(row 1, 16).

Final Result on Camvid Dataset. The overall design result is shown in Table 2. With larger iteration numbers, our DID Network could achieve the final 68.3% mIoU. Compared with the recent work FC-DenseNet [13], our result surpasses about 1.4% mIoU with slightly more parameters. On the other hand, Some approaches such as [5] utilize the temporal information, while our method only consider single-frame information, we don't compare with those methods for fairness.

It's worth noting that our DID Network training from scratch also performs favorably against some methods based on pretraining, such as deeplabv1-res50. To prove the progressive refinement, we try to calculate the mIoU that comes from the probability maps of Block3-output, Block2-output, Block1-output. The mIoU results are 67%, 67.9%, 68.3% accordingly. This observation shows that fine feature map will obtain a better result than a coarse result. Therefore it quantitatively proves our progressive refinement strategy in DID.

Some visualization results on Camvid Dataset are shown in Fig. 3. We demonstrate the Block3-Output, Block2-Output, Block1-Output which accordingly correspond to the probability map from coarsest to finest. Block3-Output (finest result) will be adopted in our final inference, the detailed structure can be found in Fig. 2. From the visualization result, we can easily observe that our progressive refinement mainly occurs in semantic boundary (tree, building boundary) or tiny objects (pole). These phenomena qualitatively prove that our step-by-step refinement based on DID Network functions well as our assumption (Table 4).

Table 4. Test result on Camvid Dataset

Model	Pretrained	#params(M)	Building	Tree	Sky	Car	Sign	Road	Pedestrian	Fence	Pole	Pavement	Cyclist	mIoU	Acc
SegNet[1]	✓	29.5	68.7	52.0	87.0	58.5	13.4	86.2	25.3	17.9	16.0	60.5	24.8	46.4	62.5
DeconvNet[21]	✓	252						n/a						48.9	85.9
Visin et al.[29]	✓	32.3						n/a						58.8	88.7
FCN8s[19]	✗	134.5	77.8	71.0	88.7	76.1	32.7	91.2	41.7	24.4	19.9	72.7	31.0	57.0	88.0
deeplabv1-res50[2]	✓	24	80.9	75.1	89.8	81.6	36.5	94	45.5	34.6	7.8	78.3	46.9	61.0	90.35
Dilation8[32]	✓	140.8	82.6	76.2	89.0	**84.0**	**46.9**	92.2	56.3	35.8	23.4	75.3	**55.5**	48.9	85.9
FC-DenseNet103 (k=16)[13]	✗	9.4	83.0	77.3	93.0	77.3	43.9	94.5	59.6	37.1	**37.8**	82.2	50.5	66.9	91.5
our DID Network	✗	11.2	**85.1**	**79.4**	**93.8**	83.5	46.4	**94.9**	**62.5**	**37.8**	33.5	**84.8**	49.8	**68.3**	**92.6**

4.2 Result on Inria Aerial Image Labeling Dataset

In Aerial Image Labeling dataset (IAIL), we crop the large image evenly into 500 × 500, then randomly crop out 473 × 473 as the input of neural network. 20% of the images are used as validation data. The total number of training iterations is 200K.

Table 5. Test result on Inria aerial image labeling dataset

Method	Bellingham		Bloomington		Innsbruck		San Francisco		East Tyrol		Overall	
	IoU	Acc	IoU	Acc	IoU	Acc	IoU	Acc	IoU	Acc	IoU	Acc
Inria1	52.91	95.14	46.08	94.95	58.12	95.16	57.84	86.05	59.03	96.40	55.82	93.54
DukeAMLL	66.90	96.69	58.48	96.15	69.92	96.37	75.54	91.87	72.34	97.42	70.91	95.70
NUS	**70.74**	97.00	66.06	96.74	73.17	96.75	73.57	91.19	76.06	97.81	72.45	95.90
ENPC – Singh2	64.28	96.00	65.84	96.52	**77.11**	**97.31**	75.86	**92.01**	**78.68**	**98.12**	73.30	95.99
Deeplabv1-ResNet101 pretrained	68.62	96.81	66.06	96.82	76.43	97.24	74.68	91.58	77.92	98.05	73.41	96.10
Our DID network	70.73	**97.10**	**69.75**	**97.15**	76.58	97.26	**76.10**	91.80	78.63	98.11	**74.95**	**96.29**

Results are summarized in Table 5. Some of the methods are from the official benchmark who didn't reveal their detail method. Notably, our DID Network achieves 74.95% mIoU on the test set, which exceeds the ResNet101-pretrained result with a large margin.

Figure 4 shows some qualitative segmentation examples on IAIL Dataset with our DID Network. We can get the following finding: when the buildings in the IAIL Dataset are closely adjacent to each other, our DID network is able to gradually separate each single building through our step-by-step refinement. Our refining upsampling strategy obviously benefits from the DID Decoder to perform favorably against other methods.

4.3   Result on Cityscapes Dataset

We also conducted experiment about DID Network in Cityscapes Dataset in Table 6. Compared with other methods training segmentation from scratch, our method obtains a better result 73.7 mIoU with much less parameters. Noticeably, the FC-DenseNet [13] only experiment with Camvid Dataset except Cityscapes Dataset, our method reaches state of the art in Cityscapes compared with other methods of the same type. Therefore, our method has more generality in dataset than FC-DenseNet [13].

Table 6. mIoU scores from the Cityscapes test set

Model	Coarse	Pretrained	#params(M)	Road	Sidewalk	Building	Wall	Fence	Pole	Traf. Light	Traf. Sign	Vegetation	Terrain	Sky	Person	Rider	Car	Truck	Bus	Train	Motorcycle	Bicycle	Class IoU	Category IoU
ENet[22]	✗	✗	0.36	96.3	74.2	75.0	32.2	33.2	43.4	34.1	44.0	88.6	61.4	90.6	65.5	38.4	90.6	36.9	50.5	48.1	38.8	55.4	58.28	80.39
Adelaide[17]	✗	✓	–	98.0	82.6	90.6	44.0	50.7	51.1	65.0	71.7	92.0	72.0	94.1	81.5	61.1	94.3	61.1	65.1	53.8	61.6	70.6	71.6	–
ERFNet[24]	✗	✓	–	97.9	82.1	90.7	45.2	50.4	59.0	62.6	68.4	91.9	69.4	94.2	78.5	59.8	93.4	52.3	60.8	53.7	49.9	64.2	69.7	87.3
FRRN[23]	✗	✗	17.7	98.2	83.3	91.6	45.8	51.1	62.2	69.4	72.4	92.6	70.0	94.9	81.6	62.7	94.6	49.1	67.1	55.3	53.5	69.5	71.8	–
LRR[6]	✓	✓	–	97.9	81.5	91.4	50.5	52.7	59.4	66.8	72.7	92.5	70.1	95.0	81.3	60.1	94.3	51.2	67.7	54.6	55.6	69.6	71.8	–
our DID Network	✗	✗	11.2	98.4	84.6	92.1	48.0	54.1	63.9	70.4	74.9	93.1	68.4	95.6	84.2	66.4	95.2	47.6	62.7	68.4	60.6	72.0	**73.7**	**89.66**

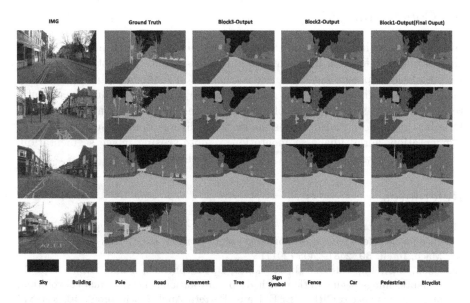

Fig. 3. Camvid Dataset result. Block3-Output, Block2-Output, Block1-Output accordingly correspond to the probability map from coarsest to finest, Block3-Output (finest probability map) will be adopted for our inference. Best viewed in color.

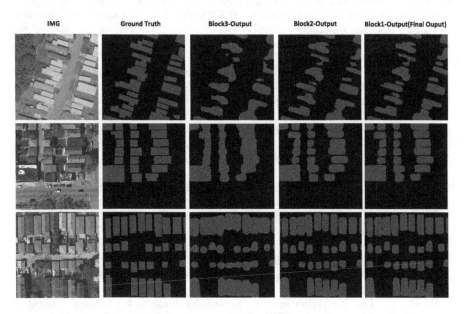

Fig. 4. Inria Aerial Image labeling Dataset result. Blue means buildings, black means non-buildings. Block3-Output, Block2-Output, Block1-Output accordingly correspond to the probability map from coarsest to finest, Block3-Output (finest probability map) will be adopted for our inference. Best viewed in color.

5   Conclusion

In this paper, we have presented Dense In Dense (DID) Network, a simple yet efficient framework for training segmentation from scratch. DID not only can realize progressive upsampling for better segmentation refinement, but also greatly facilitate the gradient flow inside and outside the dense block. Our experimental results show the salient effects of parameters and less redundancy of features. DID has great potential on the scenario with diverse domain such as medical segmentation, aerial image segmentation, remote sensing image segmentation, etc. Our future work is trying to apply DID in those fields.

References

1. Badrinarayanan, V., Kendall, A., Cipolla, R.: SegNet: a deep convolutional encoder-decoder architecture for image segmentation. IEEE Trans. Pattern Anal. Mach. Intell. **39**, 2481–2495 (2017)
2. Chen, L.C., Papandreou, G., Kokkinos, I., Murphy, K., Yuille, A.L.: DeepLab: semantic image segmentation with deep convolutional nets, atrous convolution, and fully connected CRFs. IEEE Trans. Pattern Anal. Mach. Intell. **40**, 834–848 (2018)
3. Chen, L.C., Papandreou, G., Schroff, F., Adam, H.: Rethinking atrous convolution for semantic image segmentation. arXiv preprint arXiv:1706.05587 (2017)
4. Deng, J., Dong, W., Socher, R., Li, L.J., Li, K., Fei-Fei, L.: ImageNet: a large-scale hierarchical image database. In: IEEE Conference on Computer Vision and Pattern Recognition (2009)
5. Gadde, R., Jampani, V., Gehler, P.V.: Semantic video CNNs through representation warping. CoRR (2017)
6. Ghiasi, G., Fowlkes, C.C.: Laplacian pyramid reconstruction and refinement for semantic segmentation. In: Leibe, B., Matas, J., Sebe, N., Welling, M. (eds.) ECCV 2016. LNCS, vol. 9907, pp. 519–534. Springer, Cham (2016). https://doi.org/10.1007/978-3-319-46487-9_32
7. Girshick, R.: Fast R-CNN. In: International Conference on Computer Vision (2015)
8. Glorot, X., Bengio, Y.: Understanding the difficulty of training deep feedforward neural networks. In: International Conference on Artificial Intelligence and Statistics, pp. 249–256 (2010)
9. He, K., Zhang, X., Ren, S., Sun, J.: Deep residual learning for image recognition. In: IEEE Conference on Computer Vision and Pattern Recognition (2016)
10. He, K., Zhang, X., Ren, S., Sun, J.: Identity mappings in deep residual networks. In: Leibe, B., Matas, J., Sebe, N., Welling, M. (eds.) ECCV 2016. LNCS, vol. 9908, pp. 630–645. Springer, Cham (2016). https://doi.org/10.1007/978-3-319-46493-0_38
11. Hu, T., Wang, Y., Chen, Y., Lu, P., Wang, H., Wang, G.: SOBEL heuristic kernel for aerial semantic segmentation. In: International Conference on Image Processing (2018)
12. Huang, G., Liu, Z., Weinberger, K.Q., van der Maaten, L.: Densely connected convolutional networks. In: IEEE Conference on Computer Vision and Pattern Recognition (2017)
13. Jégou, S., Drozdzal, M., Vazquez, D., Romero, A., Bengio, Y.: The one hundred layers tiramisu: fully convolutional DenseNets for semantic segmentation. In: IEEE Conference on Computer Vision and Pattern Recognition Workshop Papers (2017)

14. Kingma, D.P., Ba, J.: Adam: a method for stochastic optimization. International Conference on Learning Representations (2016)
15. Krähenbühl, P., Koltun, V.: Efficient inference in fully connected CRFs with Gaussian edge potentials. In: Advances in Neural Information Processing Systems (2011)
16. Krizhevsky, A., Sutskever, I., Hinton, G.E.: ImageNet classification with deep convolutional neural networks. In: Advances in Neural Information Processing Systems (2012)
17. Lin, G., Shen, C., Van Den Hengel, A., Reid, I.: Efficient piecewise training of deep structured models for semantic segmentation. In: IEEE Conference on Computer Vision and Pattern Recognition (2016)
18. Liu, S., De Mello, S., Gu, J., Zhong, G., Yang, M.H., Kautz, J.: Learning affinity via spatial propagation networks. In: Advances in Neural Information Processing Systems (2017)
19. Long, J., Shelhamer, E., Darrell, T.: Fully convolutional networks for semantic segmentation. In: IEEE Conference on Computer Vision and Pattern Recognition, pp. 3431–3440 (2015)
20. Maggiori, E., Tarabalka, Y., Charpiat, G., Alliez, P.: Can semantic labeling methods generalize to any city? The Inria aerial image labeling benchmark. In: IEEE International Geoscience and Remote Sensing Symposium (IGARSS) (2017)
21. Noh, H., Hong, S., Han, B.: Learning deconvolution network for semantic segmentation. In: International Conference on Computer Vision (2015)
22. Paszke, A., Chaurasia, A., Kim, S., Culurciello, E.: ENet: a deep neural network architecture for real-time semantic segmentation (2016)
23. Pohlen, T., Hermans, A., Mathias, M., Leibe, B.: Full-resolution residual networks for semantic segmentation in street scenes. In: IEEE Conference on Computer Vision and Pattern Recognition (2017)
24. Romera, E., Alvarez, J.M., Bergasa, L.M., Arroyo, R.: ERFNet: efficient residual factorized ConvNet for real-time semantic segmentation. IEEE Trans. Intell. Transp. Syst. (2018)
25. Ronneberger, O., Fischer, P., Brox, T.: U-net: convolutional networks for biomedical image segmentation. In: Navab, N., Hornegger, J., Wells, W.M., Frangi, A.F. (eds.) MICCAI 2015. LNCS, vol. 9351, pp. 234–241. Springer, Cham (2015). https://doi.org/10.1007/978-3-319-24574-4_28
26. Shen, Z., Liu, Z., Li, J., Jiang, Y.G., Chen, Y., Xue, X.: DSOD: learning deeply supervised object detectors from scratch. In: International Conference on Computer Vision (2017)
27. Srivastava, N., Hinton, G., Krizhevsky, A., Sutskever, I., Salakhutdinov, R.: Dropout: a simple way to prevent neural networks from overfitting. J. Mach. Learn. Res. **15**, 1929–1958 (2014)
28. Szegedy, C., et al.: Going deeper with convolutions. In: IEEE Conference on Computer Vision and Pattern Recognition (2015)
29. Visin, F., et al.: ReSeg: a recurrent neural network-based model for semantic segmentation. In: IEEE Conference on Computer Vision and Pattern Recognition Workshop Papers (2016)
30. Wang, P., et al.: Understanding convolution for semantic segmentation. In: IEEE Winter Conference on Applications of Computer Vision (2018)
31. Xie, S., Tu, Z.: Holistically-nested edge detection. In: International Conference on Computer Vision (2015)
32. Yu, F., Koltun, V.: Multi-scale context aggregation by dilated convolutions. In: International Conference on Learning Representations (2016)

33. Zhao, H., Shi, J., Qi, X., Wang, X., Jia, J.: Pyramid scene parsing network. In: IEEE Conference on Computer Vision and Pattern Recognition (2017)
34. Zheng, S., et al.: Conditional random fields as recurrent neural networks. In: IEEE Conference on Computer Vision and Pattern Recognition (2015)

Single Image Super-Resolution Using Lightweight CNN with Maxout Units

Jae-Seok Choi and Munchurl Kim[✉]

School of EE, Korea Advanced Institute of Science and Technology, Daejeon, Korea
{jschoi14,mkimee}@kaist.ac.kr

Abstract. Rectified linear units (ReLU) are well-known to obtain higher performance for deep-learning-based applications. However, networks with ReLU tend to perform poorly when the number of parameters is constrained. To overcome, we propose a novel network utilizing maxout units (MU), and show its effectiveness on super-resolution (SR). In this paper, we first reveal that MU can make the filter sizes halved in restoration problems thus leading to compaction of the network. To the best of our knowledge, we are the first to incorporate MU into SR applications and show promising results. In MU, feature maps from a previous convolutional layer are divided into two parts along channels, which are compared element-wise and only their max values are passed to a next layer. Along with interesting properties of MU to be analyzed, we further investigate other variants of MU. Our MU-based SR method reconstructs images with comparable quality compared to previous SR methods, even with smaller parameters.

Keywords: Super-resolution (SR) ·
Convolutional neural network (CNN) · Maxout unit (MU) ·
Lightweight

1 Introduction

Super-resolution (SR) methods aim to reconstruct high-resolution (HR) image or video contents from their low-resolution (LR) versions. The SR problem is known to be highly ill-posed, where an LR input can lead to multiple degraded HR versions without proper prior information [39]. As the role of SR becomes crucial recently in various areas such as up-scaling full-high-definition (FHD) to 4K [6], it is important to develop SR algorithms that are capable of generating HR

This research was supported by Basic Science Research Program through the National Research Foundation of Korea (NRF) funded by the Ministry of Science, ICT & Future Planning (No. 2017R1A2A2A05001476).

Electronic supplementary material The online version of this chapter (https://doi.org/10.1007/978-3-030-20876-9_30) contains supplementary material, which is available to authorized users.

C. V. Jawahar et al. (Eds.): ACCV 2018, LNCS 11366, pp. 471–487, 2019.
https://doi.org/10.1007/978-3-030-20876-9_30

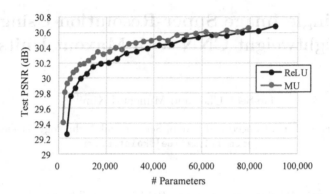

Fig. 1. Comparison on PSNR performance versus the number of filter parameters for two toy SR networks with ReLU [29] and maxout units (MU) [15], respectively. The network with MU shows higher performance than the conventional network with ReLU, especially when the number of parameter is small. This makes MU a suitable unit for application platforms with limited resources, such as mobile platforms.

contents with superior visual quality while maintaining reasonable complexity and moderate amounts of parameters.

1.1 Related Work

SR methods can be divided into two families according to their input types: single image SR (SISR) and video SR. While both spatial and temporal information can be used in video SR, SISR utilizes only spatial information within given LR images, making the SR problem more difficult [12,31]. In this paper, we mainly focus on SISR.

Various SR methods employed the following techniques in reconstructing HR images of high quality: sparse-representation [20,22,39], linear mappings [6,8,36,41,42], self-examples [12–14,38], and neural networks [7,10,11,21,25,26, 31,34,35]. Sparse-representation-based SR methods [20,22,39] undergo heavy computations to calculate sparse-representation of an LR patch from a pre-trained and complex LR dictionary. The resultant sparse-representation is then applied to a corresponding HR dictionary to reconstruct its HR version. Some SR methods [12–14,38] extracted LR-to-HR mappings by searching for similar patches (self-examples) to the current patch inside its self-dictionary. Linear-mapping-based SR methods [6,8,36,41,42] (LMSR) have been proposed to obtain HR images of comparable quality but with much lower computational complexity. The adjusted anchored neighborhood regression (A+, APLUS) [36] method searches for the best linear mapping for each LR patch, based on the correlation with pre-trained dictionary sets from [39]. Choi [6,8] employs simple edge classification to find suitable linear mappings, which are applied directly to small LR patches to reconstruct their HR version.

Recently, SR methods using convolutional neural networks (CNN) [7,10,11, 21,25,26,31,34,35] have shown high PSNR performance. Dong et al. [10] first utilized a 3-layered CNN for SR (SRCNN), and reported a remarkable performance jump compared to previous SR methods. Recently, Kim *et al.* [21] proposed a very deep 20-layered CNN (VDSR) with gradient clipping and residual learning, yielding the reconstructed HR images of even higher PSNR compared to SRCNN. Shi *et al.* [31] proposed a network structure where features are extracted in LR space. The feature maps at the last layer are up-scaled to HR space using a sub-pixel convolution layer. Recursive convolutions were also used in [34] to lower the number of parameters. Ledig *et al.* [25] presented two SR network structures: a network using residual units to maximize PSNR performance (SRResNet), and a network using generative adversarial networks for perceptual improvement (SRGAN). Lately, some SR methods using very deep networks [7,26,35] with large parameters have been proposed in NTIRE2017 Challenge [35], achieving the state-of-the-art PSNR performance.

In these deep learning-based SR methods, rectified linear units (ReLU) [29] are used to obtain nonlinearity between two adjacent convolutional layers. ReLU is a simple function, which has an identity mapping for positive values and 0 for negative. Unlike a sigmoid or hyperbolic tangent, ReLU does not suffer from gradient vanishing problems. By using ReLU, networks can learn piece-wise linear mappings between LR and HR images, which results in the mapping with high visual quality and faster training convergence. There are other nonlinear activation functions such as leaky ReLU (LReLU) [27], parametric ReLU [16] and exponential linear units (ELU) [9], but they are not often used in regression problems unlike ReLU. While LReLU replaces the zero part of ReLU with a linearity with certain small gradient, parametric ReLU parameterizes this gradient value so that a network can learn it. ELU has been designed so that it pushes mean unit activations closer to zero for faster learning.

1.2 Motivations and Contributions

One major reason for such high performance of neural networks in many applications [7,10,11,21,25,26,31,34,35] would be the use of ReLU [29] and its successors [27]. These nonlinear units were first introduced in classification papers [2,9,16,18,19,24,27,29], which were subsequently reused for regression problems such as SR. It can be easily noticed that while ReLU and LReLU functions have been frequently used in SR, it is hard to find other types of activation functions [9]. This is because they tend to distort scales of input values (more in Sect. 3.3), and thus networks with these functions generate HR results with lower quality compared to those with ReLU. This phenomenon can also be observed in normalization layers such as batch normalization [18] and layer normalization [2], and there have been some reports that these normalization layers degrade performance when used in regression problems [7,26].

In this paper, we try to tackle some limitations of ReLU: (i) ReLU produces feature maps with many zeros whose number is not controllable; (ii) therefore, learning with ReLU tends to collapse in a network with very deep layers without some help such as identity mappings [17]; and (iii) there could be a way to make use of those empty zero values so that we may be able to reduce number of channels for lower memory consumption and less computations.

Maxout units (MU) [15] are activation units which could overcome the aforementioned limitations. MU were first introduced in various classification problems [5,15,33]. Goodfellow *et al.* [15] proposed MU and used them in conjunction with dropout [32] in a multi-layer-perceptron (MLP), and showed competitive classification results, compared to those of using conventional ReLU [29]. In [33], MU were used for speech recognition, and it is stated that networks with MU were about three times faster to converge in training with comparable performance. In addition, Chang *et al.* [5] reported a network-in-network structure using MU for classification, which was able to mediate the problem of vanishing gradients that can occur when using ReLU. Although networks using MU were known to work well in high-level vision areas, only a few works [4] employed MU for regression problems. In this paper, we develop and present a novel SR network incorporating MU. Our contributions are as follows:

- Contrary to common thought that the number of parameters needs to be doubled when using MU, we first reveal that MU can effectively be incorporated into restoration problems. We show our SR network with MU that the number of channels of input feature maps is halved, even showing good results and thus resulting in a less memory usage and lower computational costs.
- We show a deep analysis on networks using basic MU, and further investigate other MU variants, showing their effectiveness on the SR application.

Various experiment results show that our SR networks that incorporate MU as activation functions are able to reconstruct HR images of competitive quality compared to those of ReLU. Figure 1 shows comparison on PSNR performance versus the number of parameters for two toy network examples with ReLU and MU, respectively. Both networks share the same 6-layered SR structure, except the type of activation functions used.

2   Maxout Units

First, let us denote the outputs of the l-th convolution layer as $\mathbf{x}^l$, where a network has L convolutional layers. Also, we denote the outputs of an activation function for $\mathbf{x}^l$ as $\mathbf{a}^l$.

2.1   Conventional Nonlinear Activation Functions

Many SR methods [7,10,11,21,25,26,31,34,35] often use ReLU [29] for activation functions between every two convolutional layers to obtain high nonlinearity between LR and HR. After each ReLU, the negative part of feature maps $\mathbf{x}^l$ becomes zero as

$$\mathbf{a}^l = max(\mathbf{x}^l, 0), \tag{1}$$

where $max()$ is a function that calculates maximum values between two inputs in element-wise fashion. The negative parts where inputs become zero ensure nonlinearity, while the positive parts allow for fast learning as its derivative is

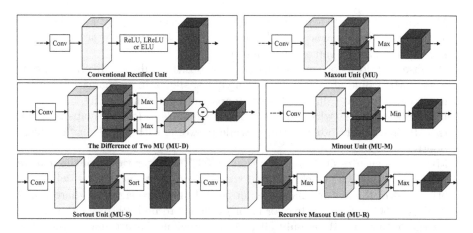

Fig. 2. Block diagrams for various activation functions used in networks: conventional units (ReLU [29], LReLU [27], ELU [9]), MU [15], MU-D [15], MU-M, MU-S and MU-R.

a unity. However, very deep or narrow networks may have some difficulty in learning when too many values fall into negative and become zero. While other ReLU variants such as LReLU [27] and ELU [9] try to overcome this limitation by modifying the negative parts, these ReLU variants still have little control over a ratio of the number of negative values.

2.2 Maxout Unit

To overcome the limitations, we come up with an SR network structure incorporating the MU.

Maxout. MU [15] computes the maximum of a vector of any length. Here, we use a special case of MU, where the feature maps $\mathbf{x}^l$ are halved along channel into two parts $\mathbf{x}_1^l$ and $\mathbf{x}_2^l$, and element-wise maximum of these two parts is calculated as:

$$\mathbf{a}^l = max(\mathbf{x}_1^l, \mathbf{x}_2^l). \tag{2}$$

Difference of Two MU. In [15], a difference of two MU was also introduced with a proposition that any continuous piece-wise linear function can be expressed as a difference of two convex piece-wise linear functions. In this paper, we use the form of:

$$\mathbf{a}^l = max(\mathbf{x}_1^l, \mathbf{x}_2^l) - max(\mathbf{x}_3^l, \mathbf{x}_4^l), \tag{3}$$

where $\mathbf{x}^l$ is equally divided into four parts $\mathbf{x}_1^l$, $\mathbf{x}_2^l$, $\mathbf{x}_3^l$ and $\mathbf{x}_4^l$. Note after this activation function, the input feature maps are reduced to quarter. We denote this MU variant as MU-D. Incorporating a simple max function between two sets of feature maps provides nonlinearity with various properties as follow:

- MU simply transfers feature map values from the input layer to the next, acting as the linear parts of ReLU. In backpropagation, error gradients simply flow to the selected values (maximum).
- Because MU does not consider negative or positive values unlike ReLU, outputs of MU would always have certain values, alleviating a chance of creating many close-to-zero values in feature maps and failing in learning.
- In narrow networks where the number of channels of feature maps is small, the MU allows for stable learning, while networks with ReLU may converge poorly.
- MU always ensures 50% sparsity: that is, 50% of larger values of the feature maps would always be selected and transmitted to the next layer, while the other 50% of the feature maps are not used. In backpropagation, there would be always 50% of paths alive for error gradients to be back-propagated.
- As the output of MU is only 50% of the previous feature map values, the number of convolutional filter parameters in the next layer can be reduced by half, lowering both computation time and memory consumption. Similarly, unlike ReLU, MU is able to compress the given feature maps by stopping the transmission of close-to-zero values in the feature maps. In doing so, the network compactness is improved by preserving needed information.

We demonstrate the effectiveness of MU through various experiments in Sect. 3. Based on the properties of MU, we further investigate other variants of MU.

2.3 MU Variants

From MU, its variants can be designed while preserving similar properties: minimum, recursive and sorting.

Minimum. Instead of using the max function, one can design activation functions with the min function as

$$\mathbf{a}^l = min(\mathbf{x}_1^l, \mathbf{x}_2^l), \tag{4}$$

where $min()$ is a function that calculates minimum values between two inputs in element-wise fashion. In training, this variant works similar to the original MU. We denote this MU variant as MU-M.

Sorting. If we are to maintain the size of feature maps as ReLU does, we can employ both max and min functions into one activation function as

$$\mathbf{a}^l = cat(max(\mathbf{x}_1^l, \mathbf{x}_2^l), min(\mathbf{x}_1^l, \mathbf{x}_2^l)), \tag{5}$$

where $cat()$ is a function that concatenates all inputs along channels. We denote this MU variant as MU-S.

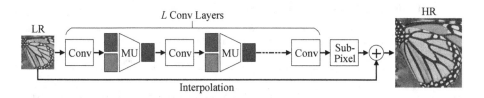

Fig. 3. Our proposed SR network, which incorporates MU for activation functions, residual learning between an interpolated image and a target HR image, and a sub-pixel convolution layer for up-scaling.

Recursive. By using MU recursively for n times before applying convolutions in the next layer, we can further enforce more sparsity, e.g. 75%, resulting reduced feature maps as outputs. This can be expressed as

$$\mathbf{a}^l = f^n(\mathbf{x}_1^l, \mathbf{x}_2^l), \tag{6}$$

where f^n indicates n-times repeated MU, whose output channels are reduced by $1/2^n$. We denote this MU variant as MU-R.

Figure 2 illustrates the various activation functions, including MU and MU variants. Through additional experiments using the MU variants, we confirmed that networks with the variants could be trained well as shown in Sect. 3.

2.4 Network Details

By incorporating MU and its variants, we propose multiple network structures as shown in Fig. 3, and show their performance for SR applications.

Toy Networks. In order to conduct many and quick validations for comparing effects of multiple activation function variants including MU, we present a baseline toy network structure that is shared for testing all types of activation functions. The toy networks were trained using a smaller training dataset from [39]. Our toy networks includes three types of layers: 6 layers of 3×3 convolutions, one type of activation function, and one sub-pixel convolution layer [31] at the end for up-scaling purpose. For convolutional layers, we simply use the kernel size of 3×3, where input feature maps are padded with zero before convolution, so that the size of feature maps is preserved until the last sub-pixel convolution layer. The experimental results obtained using the toy networks are presented throughout Figs. 1, 6, 7 and Table 2.

ESPCN-MU. For comparison, several state-of-the-art SR network structures [21,31] are implemented as stated in the papers but using MU and some modifications. Our first SR network using MU is based on ESPCN [31]. We replace all ReLU layers in [31] with MU. A 5-3-3 model [31] is also used in our network

Table 1. Average performance comparison for various SR methods.

Methods		Bicubic		SRCNN [11]		ESPCN [31]		ESPCN [31]		VDSR [21]		SRResNet [25]	
# of Params		-		57K		25K		25K		665K		923K	
Training Sets		-		ImageNet		91		ImageNet		291		ImageNet	
Testing	Scale	PSNR	SSIM	PSNR	SSIM	PSNR	SSIM	PSNR	SSIM	PSNR	SSIM	PSNR	SSIM
Set5	3	30.40	0.8687	32.75	0.9095	32.39	-	33.00	0.9121	33.66	0.9213	-	-
	4	28.43	0.8109	30.49	0.8634	-	-	30.76	0.8679	31.35	0.8838	32.06	0.8927
Set14	3	27.55	0.7741	29.30	0.8219	28.97	-	29.51	0.8247	29.77	0.8314	-	-
	4	26.01	0.7023	27.50	0.7517	-	-	27.75	0.7580	28.01	0.7674	28.59	0.7811
B100	3	27.21	0.7389	28.41	0.7867	-	-	-	-	28.82	0.7976	-	-
	4	25.96	0.6678	26.90	0.7107	-	-	-	-	27.29	0.7251	27.60	0.7361

*Results for the 9-5-5 model of SRCNN and results of ESPCN using ReLU are reported.

Methods		**ESPCN-MU**		**VDSR-MU**		**DNSR**	
# of Params		13K		338K		133K	
Training Sets		91		291		291	
Testing	Scale	PSNR	SSIM	PSNR	SSIM	PSNR	SSIM
Set5	3	32.85	0.9118	33.92	0.9231	33.80	0.9224
	4	30.57	0.8667	31.61	0.8861	31.57	0.8858
Set14	3	29.40	0.8222	29.99	0.8346	29.95	0.8338
	4	27.61	0.7547	28.21	0.7713	28.21	0.7714
B100	3	28.40	0.7853	28.87	0.7989	28.82	0.7980
	4	26.91	0.7114	27.31	0.7262	27.30	0.7260

with 64 filters for the first convolution layer and 32 filters for the second convolution layer. Note that due to MU's characteristics where the number of channels is halved after activation, the number of filter parameters of ours is reduced almost in half compared to that of ESPCN [31]. In addition, we aim to learn the residual between original HR images and interpolated LR images as in [21], but we use nearest-neighbor interpolation instead of bicubic to make SR problem harder and thus mainly focus on capability of types of activation functions. In doing so, networks converge faster. Due to its small number of parameters, we utilize a small training data set [39], but still produce comparable SR results to [31].

VDSR-MU. In addition, we propose another SR network using MU based on 20-layered VDSR [21]. Similar to [21], 20 convolutional layers with 3×3-sized filters are used in our network. We replace all ReLU layers in [21] with

MU. Similar to that of ESPCN-MU, the number of filters parameters of ours is reduced almost in half compared to that of VDSR [21]. Also, we use nearest-neighbor interpolation instead of bicubic, and a sub-pixel convolution layer [31] for faster computation speed. Due to its large number of parameters, our VDSR-MU network was trained using a larger data set combining [39] and [28] as in VDSR [21].

DNSR. We also present a deeper and narrower version of VDSR-MU, called DNSR. While VDSR-MU has 20 layers with 64 channels, our DNSR has 30 layers (deeper) with 32 channels (narrower). Due to its deeper structure, we also employ residual units [17] into DNSR for stable learning. Our DNSR holds a smaller number of total filter parameters, which is about 1/5 of that of VDSR [21], and about 1/2.6 of that of VDSR-MU, while showing PSNR performance similar to VDSR-MU.

3   Experiment Results

We now demonstrate the effectiveness of MU and its variants in SR framework on popular image datasets, compared to conventional SR deep networks with common nonlinear activation functions, including ReLU.

3.1   Experiment Settings

Datasets. Two popular datasets [28,39] were used for training networks. Images in the datasets were used as original HR images. Before given into networks, LR-HR training images are normalized between 0 and 1, and then LR training images are subtracted by 0.5 to have a zero mean. LR input images were created from these HR images by applying nearest-neighbor interpolation. SR process is only applied on Y-channel of YCbCr color space, and the chroma components, Cb and Cr, are up-scaled using simple bicubic interpolation. When comparing SR output images with original HR images, performance measures such as PSNR were done in Y-channel.

The training set of 91 images [39] has frequently been used in various SR methods [10,21,31,39]. The dataset consists of small resolutions but with a variety of texture types. In our experiments, this smaller training set was used for various toy networks in order to conduct fast and many experiments, and was also used for our ESPCN-MU.

The Berkeley Segmentation Dataset [28] has also been often used in SR works [21,31]. This dataset includes 200 training images and 100 testing images for segmentation. As used in VDSR [21], we utilize 200 training images of BSD and 91 images from [39] from training. This larger set was used for training VDSR-MU and DNSR.

For testing, three popular benchmark datasets including Set5 [3], Set14 [40] and BSD100 [28] were used.

Training. We trained all the networks using ADAM [23] optimization with an initial learning rate of 10^{-4} and the other hyper-parameters as defaults. We employed a uniform weight initialization technique in [19] for training. All the networks including our proposed networks with MU were implemented using TensorFlow [1], which is a deep learning toolbox for Python, and were trained/tested on GPU Nvidia Titan Xp.

The toy networks were trained for 10^5 iterations, where a learning rate was lowered by a factor of 10 after 5×10^4 iterations. The mini-batch size was set to 2, weight decay was not used, and simple data augmentation with flip and rotation was used. For sub-images, LR-HR training image pairs were randomly cropped for the size of 40×40 for a scale factor of 4.

Our ESPCN-MU, VDSR-MU and DNSR networks were trained for 10^6 iterations, where a learning rate was lowered by a factor of 10 after 5×10^5 iterations. The mini-batch size was set to 4, and weight decay was not used. To create sub-images for training, LR-HR training image pairs were randomly cropped for the size of 75×75 and 76×76 in HR space, respectively, for a scale factor of 3 and 4. We apply various data augmentations to the HR images such as flipping, rotating, mirroring, and randomly multiplying their intensities by a value in a range from 0.8 and 1.2. Data augmentations are done on the fly for every epoch in training to reduce overfitting.

3.2   SR Results

First, we show SR results using our three proposed SR networks, including ESPCN-MU, VDSR-MU and DNSR, and compare them with the state-of-the-art methods, including SRCNN [11], ESPCN [31], VDSR [21] and SRResNet [25]. Table 1 summarizes performance details for all the SR methods, including their numbers of filter parameters, their used training sets, and PSNR and SSIM [37] values for scale factors of 3 and 4, tested on three popular testing datasets. For SRCNN [11], the reported results of the 9-5-5 model are shown. For ESPCN [31], the reported results using ReLU for two different training datasets are shown in Table 1. The PSNR/SSIM values for the conventional SR methods in Table 1 are either the ones reported in their respective papers, or directly calculated from their publically available result images online. Figures 4 and 5 show reconstructed HR images and their magnified portions of *baby* and *zebra*, respectively, using various SR methods for a scale factor of 4.

SR Performance. As shown in Table 1, SRResNet [25], an SR network of the largest number of filter parameters (about 900K) that was trained using ImageNet [30], shows the highest PSNR and SSIM performance among various SR methods. Our proposed VDSR-MU and DNSR show the second and third highest performance with only 338 K and 133 K parameters, respectively, outperforming most of the conventional SR methods except SRResNet. It can be seen that our networks using MU have good efficiency with much less parameters, compared to other SR methods, while showing reasonable PSNR performance. As shown in

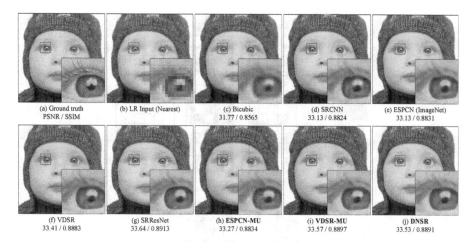

Fig. 4. Reconstructed HR images of *baby* using various SR methods for a scale factor of 4.

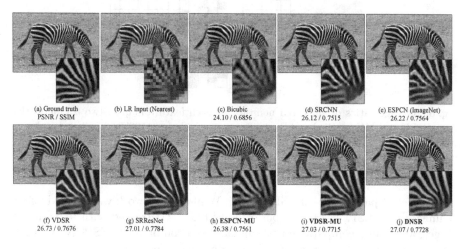

Fig. 5. Reconstructed HR images of *zebra* using various SR methods for a scale factor of 4.

Figs. 4 and 5, the quality of the reconstructed HR images using our VDSR-MU and DNSR are comparable to that of SRResNet [25]. Especially, our VDSR-MU and DNSR were able to reconstruct clearly discerned stripes of *zebra* as shown in Fig. 5(i) and (j), which are comparable to Fig. 5(g) of SRResNet, while other SR methods fail to do so.

ESPCN-MU. In order to show the effectiveness of using MU in SR, we compare two similar networks: ESPCN [31] and our ESPCN-MU. As shown in Table 1, the number of parameters of ESPCN-MU is only about 13K, which is almost half

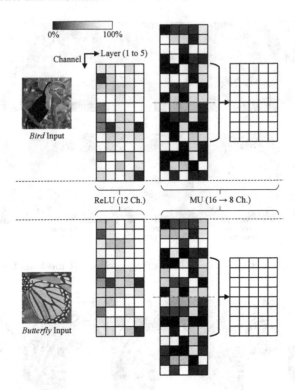

Fig. 6. Average ratios of activated neurons for each feature map in two toy networks using ReLU and MU for Bird and Butterfly, respectively (e.g. 100% activation is colored in white, while 0% in black and 50% in gray). Here, rows and columns indicate channels and layers, respectively.

the number of parameters of ESPCN [31]. While our network was trained using 91 images, our ESPCN-MU outperforms ESPCN [31] trained with 91 training images, and shows comparable performance even compared to ESPCN [31] that was trained using a larger set of images from ImageNet [30].

VDSR-MU. Similar to our ESPCN-MU, our VDSR-MU outperforms VDSR [21] in terms of PSNR and SSIM, but with a much lower number of parameters. Our VDSR-MU networks has about 338K parameters, which is about half the number of parameters of VDSR [21]. Note both networks were trained using the same 291 images [28,39].

DNSR. Our deeper and narrower version of VDSR-MU, DNSR, has an almost 2/5 times the number of filter parameters compared to our VDSR-MU, which is about 1/5 of VDSR [21] and 1/7 of SRResNet [25]. Even with a low number of parameters, our DNSR network was able to reconstruct HR images comparable to VDSR-MU, and outperforms most of the conventional SR methods.

Table 2. Training and testing PSNR (dB) performance after the first 10^5 iterations for networks with various activation functions.

Activation function	Size of conv filters	Number of params	Training PSNR	Testing PSNR
ReLU [29]	$3 \times 3 \times 12 \times 12$	7.1K	28.22	29.81
LReLU [27]	$3 \times 3 \times 12 \times 12$	7.1K	28.19	29.78
ELU [9]	$3 \times 3 \times 12 \times 12$	7.1K	27.91	29.30
MU [15]	$3 \times 3 \times 8 \times 16$	6K	28.42	30.07
MU-D [15]	$3 \times 3 \times 6 \times 24$	6.4K	28.46	30.07
MU-M	$3 \times 3 \times 8 \times 16$	6K	28.43	30.05
MU-S	$3 \times 3 \times 12 \times 12$	7.1K	28.46	30.08
MU-R	$3 \times 3 \times 6 \times 24$	6.4K	28.38	29.98

3.3   Discussions

We also conducted experiments on toy networks using various activation functions including ReLU, MU and MU variants. We show potential properties of MU compared to units used in conventional SR methods, by analyzing parameter-vs.-PSNR performance and by showing activation rates in feature maps.

MU Versus ReLU. Figure 1 shows comparison on PSNR performance versus the number of parameters for two toy networks with ReLU and MU, respectively. Both networks share the same 6-layered SR structure, except the type of activation functions used. The number of parameters for each subtest is controlled by adjusting the number of convolution filters. As shown, the PSNR performance gap between networks using ReLU and MU becomes larger as the number of parameters decreases. This indicates that in narrow networks where the number of channels of feature maps is small, MU allows for stable learning, while ReLU converges towards a worse point. We can argue that because MU does not consider negative or positive values unlike ReLU, the outputs of MU would always have certain values, alleviating a chance of creating many close-to-zero values in feature maps and failing in learning.

Figure 6 shows the average ratios of activated neurons for each feature map in two toy networks using ReLU and MU for *Bird* and *Butterfly*, respectively (e.g. 100% activation is colored in white, 0% in black and 50% in gray). The rows and columns indicate channels and layers, respectively. It is interesting to see that activations after MU are sparser than those of ReLU, which supports the effectiveness of MU in SR. Note that since the maximum values between two feature maps are always passed to the next layer, the feature maps after MU would always be 100% activated with half the number of feature maps. Note that Fig. 6 may suggest that MU can be related to network pruning, and this remains as our future work.

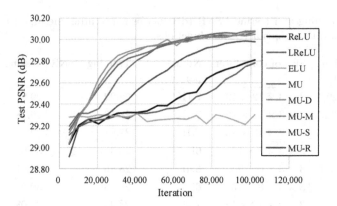

Fig. 7. A PSNR-versus-iteration plot for networks with various activation functions from Table 2.

MU Variants. Table 2 shows training and testing PSNR performance after the first 10^5 iterations for toy networks with various activation functions. Note that the size of convolutional filters has been adjusted for each network to yield a similar number of total parameters. Figure 7 presents a PSNR-versus-iteration plot for networks with various activation functions from Table 2. It can be seen in Fig. 7 that the networks with MU and MU variants enable faster convergence compared to those with ReLU and ReLU variants. Note that the network with ELU has a training difficulty in the SR problem, contrary to its performance in other classification papers. This may be due to the fact that ELU tend to distort scales of input values, which is undesirable in regression problems such as SR. Overall, the networks with MU and its variants show higher PSNR values with less parameters.

4   Conclusion

The proposed SR networks showed superior PSNR performance compared to the base networks using ReLU and other activation functions. The SR networks using MU tend to produce higher PSNR results with a smaller number of convolution filter parameters, which is desirable for computational platforms with limited resources. We showed that MU can be used in regression problems especially SR, and they have some potential with further extension to new types of activation functions for other applications.

References

1. Abadi, M., Barham, P., Chen, J., et al.: TensorFlow: a system for large-scale machine learning. In: OSDI, vol. 16, pp. 265–283 (2016)
2. Ba, J.L., Kiros, J.R., Hinton, G.E.: Layer normalization. arXiv preprint arXiv:1607.06450 (2016)

3. Bevilacqua, M., Roumy, A., Guillemot, C., Alberi-Morel, M.L.: Low-complexity single-image super-resolution based on nonnegative neighbor embedding (2012)
4. Cai, B., Xu, X., Jia, K., Qing, C., Tao, D.: DehazeNet: an end-to-end system for single image haze removal. IEEE Trans. Image Proc. **25**(11), 5187–5198 (2016)
5. Chang, J.R., Chen, Y.S.: Batch-normalized maxout network in network. arXiv preprint arXiv:1511.02583 (2015)
6. Choi, J.S., Kim, M.: Super-interpolation with edge-orientation-based mapping kernels for low complex 2× upscaling. IEEE Trans. Image Proc. **25**(1), 469–483 (2016)
7. Choi, J.S., Kim, M.: A deep convolutional neural network with selection units for super-resolution. In: Proceedings of the IEEE Conference Computer Vision Pattern Recognition Workshops, pp. 1150–1156 (2017)
8. Choi, J.S., Kim, M.: Single image super-resolution using global regression based on multiple local linear mappings. IEEE Trans. Image Proc. **26**(3), 1300–1314 (2017)
9. Clevert, D.A., Unterthiner, T., Hochreiter, S.: Fast and accurate deep network learning by exponential linear units (ELUS). arXiv preprint arXiv:1511.07289 (2015)
10. Dong, C., Loy, C.C., He, K., Tang, X.: Learning a deep convolutional network for image super-resolution. In: Fleet, D., Pajdla, T., Schiele, B., Tuytelaars, T. (eds.) ECCV 2014. LNCS, vol. 8692, pp. 184–199. Springer, Cham (2014). https://doi.org/10.1007/978-3-319-10593-2_13
11. Dong, C., Loy, C.C., He, K., Tang, X.: Image super-resolution using deep convolutional networks. IEEE Trans. Pattern Anal. Mach. Intell. **38**(2), 295–307 (2016)
12. Freedman, G., Fattal, R.: Image and video upscaling from local self-examples. ACM Trans. Graph. **30**(2), 12 (2011)
13. Freeman, W.T., Jones, T.R., Pasztor, E.C.: Example-based super-resolution. IEEE Comput. Graph. Appl. **22**(2), 56–65 (2002)
14. Glasner, D., Bagon, S., Irani, M.: Super-resolution from a single image. In: IEEE International Conference Computer Vision, pp. 349–356 (2009)
15. Goodfellow, I.J., Warde-Farley, D., Mirza, M., Courville, A., Bengio, Y.: Maxout networks. arXiv preprint arXiv:1302.4389 (2013)
16. He, K., Zhang, X., Ren, S., Sun, J.: Delving deep into rectifiers: surpassing human-level performance on imagenet classification. In: Proceedings of the IEEE International Conference Computer Vision, pp. 1026–1034 (2015)
17. He, K., Zhang, X., Ren, S., Sun, J.: Identity mappings in deep residual networks. In: Leibe, B., Matas, J., Sebe, N., Welling, M. (eds.) ECCV 2016. LNCS, vol. 9908, pp. 630–645. Springer, Cham (2016). https://doi.org/10.1007/978-3-319-46493-0_38
18. Ioffe, S., Szegedy, C.: Batch normalization: accelerating deep network training by reducing internal covariate shift. In: International Conference on Machine Learning, pp. 448–456 (2015)
19. Jia, Y., Shelhamer, E., Donahue, J., et al.: Caffe: convolutional architecture for fast feature embedding. In: Proceedings of the ACM International Conference Multimedia, pp. 675–678 (2014)
20. Jianchao, Y., Wright, J., Huang, T., Ma, Y.: Image super-resolution as sparse representation of raw image patches. In: Proceedings of the IEEE Conference Computer Vision Pattern Recognition, pp. 1–8 (2008)
21. Kim, J., Kwon Lee, J., Mu Lee, K.: Accurate image super-resolution using very deep convolutional networks. In: Proceedings of the IEEE Conference Computer Vision Pattern Recognition, pp. 1646–1654 (2016)
22. Kim, K.I., Kwon, Y.: Single-image super-resolution using sparse regression and natural image prior. IEEE Trans. Pattern Anal. Mach. Intell. **32**(6), 1127–1133 (2010)

23. Kingma, D.P., Ba, J.: Adam: a method for stochastic optimization. arXiv preprint arXiv:1412.6980 (2014)
24. Krizhevsky, A., Sutskever, I., Hinton, G.E.: ImageNet classification with deep convolutional neural networks. In: Advances in Neural Information Processing Systems, pp. 1097–1105 (2012)
25. Ledig, C., Theis, L., Huszár, F., et al.: Photo-realistic single image super-resolution using a generative adversarial network. In: Proceedings of the IEEE Conference on Computer Vision Pattern Recognition, vol. 2, p. 4 (2017)
26. Lim, B., Son, S., Kim, H., Nah, S., Lee, K.M.: Enhanced deep residual networks for single image super-resolution. In: Proceedings of the IEEE Conference Computer Vision Pattern Recognition Workshops, vol. 1, p. 3 (2017)
27. Maas, A.L., Hannun, A.Y., Ng, A.Y.: Rectifier nonlinearities improve neural network acoustic models. In: Proceedings of the International Conference on Machine Learning, vol. 30, p. 3 (2013)
28. Martin, D., Fowlkes, C., et al.: A database of human segmented natural images and its application to evaluating segmentation algorithms and measuring ecological statistics. In: Proceedings of the IEEE International Conference on Computer Vision, vol. 2, pp. 416–423 (2001)
29. Nair, V., Hinton, G.E.: Rectified linear units improve restricted Boltzmann machines. In: Proceedings of the International Conference on Machine Learning, pp. 807–814 (2010)
30. Russakovsky, O., et al.: Imagenet large scale visual recognition challenge. Int. J. Comput. Vis. **115**(3), 211–252 (2015)
31. Shi, W., Caballero, J., Huszár, F., et al.: Real-time single image and video super-resolution using an efficient sub-pixel convolutional neural network. In: Proceedings of the IEEE Conference on Computer Vision Pattern Recognition, pp. 1874–1883 (2016)
32. Srivastava, N., Hinton, G., Krizhevsky, A., Sutskever, I., Salakhutdinov, R.: Dropout: a simple way to prevent neural networks from overfitting. J. Mach. Learn. Res. **15**(1), 1929–1958 (2014)
33. Swietojanski, P., Li, J., Huang, J.T.: Investigation of maxout networks for speech recognition. In: IEEE International Conference on Acoustics, Speech and Signal Processing, pp. 7649–7653 (2014)
34. Tai, Y., Yang, J., Liu, X.: Image super-resolution via deep recursive residual network. In: Proceedings of the IEEE Conference Computer Vision Pattern Recognition Workshops, vol. 1 (2017)
35. Timofte, R., Agustsson, E., Van Gool, L., et al.: Ntire 2017 challenge on single image super-resolution: methods and results. In: Proceedings of the IEEE Conference on Computer Vision Pattern Recognition Workshops, pp. 1110–1121 (2017)
36. Timofte, R., De Smet, V., Van Gool, L.: A+: adjusted anchored neighborhood regression for fast super-resolution. In: Cremers, D., Reid, I., Saito, H., Yang, M.-H. (eds.) ACCV 2014. LNCS, vol. 9006, pp. 111–126. Springer, Cham (2015). https://doi.org/10.1007/978-3-319-16817-3_8
37. Wang, Z., Bovik, A.C., Sheikh, H.R., Simoncelli, E.P.: Image quality assessment: from error visibility to structural similarity. IEEE Trans. Image Proc. **13**(4), 600–612 (2004)
38. Yang, C.-Y., Huang, J.-B., Yang, M.-H.: Exploiting self-similarities for single frame super-resolution. In: Kimmel, R., Klette, R., Sugimoto, A. (eds.) ACCV 2010. LNCS, vol. 6494, pp. 497–510. Springer, Heidelberg (2011). https://doi.org/10.1007/978-3-642-19318-7_39

39. Yang, J., Wright, J., Huang, T.S., Ma, Y.: Image super-resolution via sparse representation. IEEE Trans. Image Proc. **19**(11), 2861–2873 (2010)
40. Zeyde, R., Elad, M., Protter, M.: On single image scale-up using sparse-representations. In: Boissonnat, J.-D., et al. (eds.) Curves and Surfaces 2010. LNCS, vol. 6920, pp. 711–730. Springer, Heidelberg (2012). https://doi.org/10.1007/978-3-642-27413-8_47
41. Zhang, K., Gao, X., Tao, D., Li, X.: Single image super-resolution with non-local means and steering kernel regression. IEEE Trans. Image Proc. **21**(11), 4544–4556 (2012)
42. Zhang, K., Tao, D., Gao, X., Li, X., Xiong, Z.: Learning multiple linear mappings for efficient single image super-resolution. IEEE Trans. Image Proc. **24**(3), 846–861 (2015)

AVID: Adversarial Visual Irregularity Detection

Mohammad Sabokrou[1(✉)], Masoud Pourreza[2], Mohsen Fayyaz[3],
Rahim Entezari[4], Mahmood Fathy[1], Jürgen Gall[3], and Ehsan Adeli[5]

[1] Institute for Research in Fundamental Sciences (IPM), Tehran, Iran
sabokro@ipm.ir
[2] AI & ML Center of Part, Tehran, Iran
[3] University of Bonn, Bonn, Germany
[4] Complexity Science Hub, Vienna, Vienna, Austria
[5] Stanford University, Stanford, USA

Abstract. Real-time detection of irregularities in visual data is very
invaluable and useful in many prospective applications including surveillance, patient monitoring systems, *etc.* With the surge of deep learning
methods in the recent years, researchers have tried a wide spectrum of
methods for different applications. However, for the case of irregularity or
anomaly detection in videos, training an end-to-end model is still an open
challenge, since often irregularity is not well-defined and there are not
enough irregular samples to use during training. In this paper, inspired
by the success of generative adversarial networks (GANs) for training
deep models in unsupervised or self-supervised settings, we propose an
end-to-end deep network for *detection* and *fine localization* of irregularities in videos (and images). Our proposed architecture is composed of
two networks, which are trained in competing with each other while col-
laborating to find the irregularity. One network works as a pixel-level
irregularity $\mathcal{I}$npainter, and the other works as a patch-level $\mathcal{D}$etector.
After an adversarial self-supervised training, in which $\mathcal{I}$ tries to fool $\mathcal{D}$
into accepting its inpainted output as regular (normal), the two networks
collaborate to detect and fine-segment the irregularity in any given testing video. Our results on three different datasets show that our method
can outperform the state-of-the-art and fine-segment the irregularity.

1 Introduction

In the recent years, intelligent surveillance cameras are very much exploited for
different applications related to the safety and protection of environments. These
cameras are located in sensitive locations to encounter dangerous, forbidden or
strange events. Every moment vast amounts of videos are captured by these
cameras, almost all of which comprise normal every-day events, and only a tiny

---

M. Sabokrou, M. Pourreza and M. Fayyaz–Contributed equally.

© Springer Nature Switzerland AG 2019
C. V. Jawahar et al. (Eds.): ACCV 2018, LNCS 11366, pp. 488–505, 2019.
https://doi.org/10.1007/978-3-030-20876-9_31

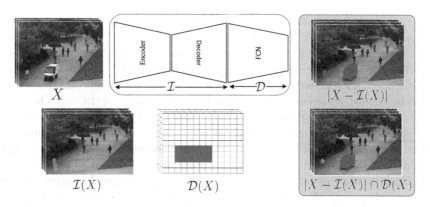

Fig. 1. The two networks $\mathcal{I}$ and $\mathcal{D}$ are trained jointly in an adversarial manner. $\mathcal{I}$ is an encoder-decoder convolutional network, which is trained to inpaint its input, X, *i.e.*, remove the irregularity. Therefore, $|X - \mathcal{I}(X)|$ indicates the pixel-level segmentation of the irregularity, from $\mathcal{I}$'s point-of-view. Whereas, $\mathcal{D}$ is a fully convolutional network (FCN), which identifies if different regions of its input are normal or irregular (patch-level). The intersection of the pixels denoted as irregularity in both $\mathcal{I}$ and $\mathcal{D}$ are labeled as the fine-segmentation of irregularity.

portion might be irregular events or behaviors. Accurate and fast detection of such irregular events is very critical in designing a reliable intelligent surveillance system. Almost in all applications, there is no clear definition of what the irregularity can be. The only known piece is whatever that deviates from the normal every-day activities and events in the area should be considered as irregularity [1]. This is a subjective definition that can include a wide-range of diverse events as irregularity and hence makes it hard for automated systems to decide if an event in the scene is really an irregularity. Therefore, systems are generally trained to learn the regularity, and rigorously tag everything else as irregularity [2].

Several different methods are used in the literature for learning the normal concept in visual scenes. Low-level visual features such as histogram of oriented gradients (HOG) [3] and histogram of optical flow (HOF) [4,5] were the first feature subsets explored for representing regular scenes in videos. Besides, trajectory features [6] are also used for representing and modeling the videos, although they are not robust against problems like occlusion [3,7]. Both low-level and trajectory features achieved good results while imposing a relatively high complexity to the system. Recently, with the surge of deep learning methods, several methods are proposed for detecting and localizing irregular events in videos [5,7–10].

Although these deep learning-based methods effectively advanced the field, they fell short of learning end-to-end models for both detecting the irregularities and localizing them in spatio-temporal sequences, due to several challenges: (1) In applications like irregularity detection, there are little or no training data from the positive class (*i.e.*, irregularity), due to the nature of the application. Hence, training supervised models, such as convolutional neural networks (CNNs), is nearly impossible. Therefore, researchers (*e.g.*, in [10]) have usually utilized pre-trained networks to extract features from the scenes, and the decision is surrendered to another module. (2) To train end-to-end models for this task, just recently [11–14] used generative adversarial networks (GANs) and adopted unsupervised methods for learning the positive class (*i.e.*, irregular events). In these methods, two networks (*i.e.*, generator and discriminator) are trained. The generator generates data to compensate for the scarcity of the positive class, while the discriminator learns to make the final decision making on whether its input is a normal scene or irregularity. Although they are trained with a very high computational load, the trained generator (or discriminator) is discarded at the testing time. Besides, most of these previous methods are patch-based approaches, and hence are often very slow. Note that these end-to-end models can only classify the scenes and do not precisely localize the irregularities. (3) Accurate pixel-level spatio-temporal localization of irregularities is still an ongoing challenge [9].

In addition to the above issues, as a general and ongoing challenging issue in video irregularity detection, detecting and localizing the irregularity in a pixel-level setting leads to models with many true positives while usually suffering from many false positive errors. On the contrary, some other methods operate on large patches (*e.g.*, [3]) and overcome the problem of high false positive error, with the price of sacrificing the detection rate. This motivated us to design a method that takes advantage from both pixel-level and patch-level settings, and come up with a model with high true positive rate while not sacrificing the detection rate. We do this by proposing an architecture, composed of two networks that are trained in an adversarial manner, the first of which is a pixel-level model and is trained to $\mathcal{I}$npaint its input by removing the irregularity it detects. The second network is a patch-level detector that $\mathcal{D}$etects irregularities in a patch level. The final irregularity detection and fine-segmentation is, then, defined as a simple intersection of the results from these two networks, having the benefits of both while discarding the pixels that result in high false positive errors (see Fig. 1).

According to the discussions above, in this paper, we propose an end-to-end method for joint detection and localization of irregularities in the videos, denoted as *AVID (Adversarial Visual Irregularity Detection)*. We use an adversarial training scheme, similar to those used in generative adversarial networks (GANs) [15]. But in contrast to previous GAN-based models (*e.g.*, [11,13,14,16]), we show how the two networks ($\mathcal{I}$ and $\mathcal{D}$) can help each other to conduct the ultimate task of visual irregularity detection and localization. The two networks can be efficiently learned against each other, where $\mathcal{I}$ tries to inpaint the image such that $\mathcal{D}$ does not detect the whole generated image as irregularity. By regulating each other, these two networks are trained in a self-supervised manner [12,17,18]. Although, $\mathcal{I}$ and $\mathcal{D}$ compete with each other during training, they are trained to detect the video irregularity from different aspects. Hence, during testing, these two networks collaborate in detection and fine-segmentation of the irregularity.

In summary, the main contributions of this paper are three-fold: (1) We propose an end-to-end deep network for detection and localization of irregularities in visual data. To the best of our knowledge, this is the first work that operates on a video frame as a whole in an end-to-end manner (not on a patch level). (2) Our method can accurately localize the fine segments of the video that contain the irregularity. (3) Our proposed adversarial training of the two networks (one pixel-level and one patch-level) alleviates the high false positive rates of pixel-level methods while not suffering from high detection error rate of patch-level models.

2 Related Works

Detection of visual irregularities is closely related to different methods in the literature (including one-class classifiers, anomaly detection, outlier detection or removal methods). These approaches search for an irregularity, which is hardly and scarcely seen in the data. Traditional methods often learn a model for the normal class, and reject everything else (*i.e.*, identify as irregularity). Learning under a constraint (such as sparsity and compressed sensing) or statistical modeling are two common methods for modeling the normal class. For the case of visual data, feature representation (from videos and images) is an important part. Low-level features (such as HOG and HOF) and high-level ones (*e.g.*, trajectory) are widely used in the literature. In the recent years, similar to other computer vision tasks, deeply learned features are vastly utilized for irregularity detection. In this section, a brief review of the state-of-the-art methods for irregularity detection and related fields is provided.

Video Representation for Irregularity Detection. As one of the earliest representations for irregularity detection, trajectory were used [6,19], such that an event not following a learned normal trajectory pattern is considered as anomaly. Optical-flows [4,20–22], social forces (SF) [23], gradient features [3,24], mixture of dynamic textures [2], and mixture of probabilistic PCAs (MPPCA) [25] are types of low-level motion representations used to model regular concepts. Deep learned features, using auto-encoders [26,27], pre-trained networks [9], or PCAnet [28,29] have recently shown great success for anomaly detection.

Constrained Reconstruction as Supervision. Representation learning for the normal (*i.e.*, regular) class under a constraint has shown effective to detect irregular events in visual data. If the new testing data does not conform to the constraint, it can potentially be considered as an irregularity. Learning to reconstruct normal concepts with sparse representation (*e.g.*, in [30]) and minimum effort (*e.g.*, in [1]) are widely exploited for this task. Boiman and Irani [1] consider an event as irregular if its reconstruction using the previous observations is nearly impossible. In [31], a scene parsing approach is proposed by Antic *et al.* in which all object hypotheses for the foreground of a frame are explained by normal training. Those hypotheses that cannot be explained by normal training are considered as anomaly. In [7,12,30] the normal class is learned through a model by reconstructing samples with minimum reconstruction errors. A high reconstruction error for a testing sample means this sample is irregular. Also,

[7,30] introduced a self-representation technique for video anomaly and outlier detection through a sparse representation, as a measure for separating inlier and outlier samples.

Deep Adversarial Learning. Recently, GANs [15] are widely being used for generating data to learn specific models. They are extended for prediction tasks, in which there are not enough data present for training (*e.g.*, in [11,13,14]). GANs are based on a game between two different networks, one generator (G) and one discriminator (D). G aims to generate sensible data, while D tries to discriminate real data from the fake data generated by G. A closely related type of GANs to our work is the conditional GANs [32]. In conditional GANs, G takes an image X as the input and generates a new image X', whereas, D tries to distinguish X from X'. Isola *et al.* [33] proposed an 'Image-to-image translation' framework based on conditional GANs, where both G and D are conditioned on the real data. Using a U-Net encoder-decoder [34] as the generator and a patch-based discriminator, they transformed images with respect to different representations. In another work, [16] proposed to learn the generator as the reconstructor for normal events, and tag chunks of the input frame as anomaly if they cannot be properly reconstructed. In our work, $\mathcal{I}$ learns to inpaint its input and make it free from irregularity in pixel-level, and $\mathcal{D}$ regulates it by checking if its output is irregular or not. This self-supervised learning scheme leads to two networks that improve the detection and fine-segmentation performance for any given testing image. Liu *et al.* [35] proposed to learn an encoder-decoder GAN to generate the future video frame using optical-flow features, used for irregularity detection, *i.e.*, if the prediction is far from the real future frame, it is counted as irregularity. Similar to all other works, the work in [35] ignores the discriminator in the testing phase. Also they suffer from high false positive rates.

3   AVID: Adversarial Visual Irregularity Detection

The proposed method for irregularity detection and localization is composed of two main components: $\mathcal{I}$ and $\mathcal{D}$. $\mathcal{I}$ learns to remove the pixel-wise irregularity from its input frame (*i.e.*, $\mathcal{I}$npaint the video), while $\mathcal{D}$ predicts the likelihood of different regions of the video (patches) being an irregularity. These networks are learned in an adversarial and self-supervised way in an end-to-end setting. In the following, we outline the details of each network. An overall sketch of the proposed method is illustrated in Fig. 1. In summary, $\mathcal{I}$ learns to $\mathcal{I}$npaint its input X to fool $\mathcal{D}$ that the inpainted version does not have any irregularities. For $\mathcal{I}$ to learn to reconstruct skewed images, $\mathcal{I}$ is exposed to noisy versions of the videos in the data set and therefore it implicitly learns not only to remove the irregularity but also to remove the noise in the data. Besides, $\mathcal{D}$ knows the distribution of original data $\mathcal{P}_d$, as it has access to the data set containing all normal videos (or with a tiny portion of irregularities present in the data). Having access to $\mathcal{P}_d$, $\mathcal{D}$ simply rejects poorly inpainted or reconstructed data. These two networks self-supervise each other and are trained through this bilateral game.

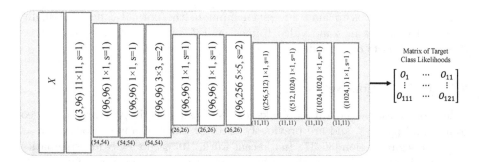

Fig. 2. Structure of $\mathcal{D}$, a FCN that scores video regions on how likely they are irregularities. All layers are convolutional layers and are described in this form $((C_1, C_2), K, s)$, with C_1 and C_2 as the number of channels of the input and output, K as the size of the applied kernel, and s as the stride for convoluted. Underneath each layer, the size of the feature maps are provided. Matrix $\mathcal{O}$, output of $\mathcal{D}$, defines regularity likelihood for each region.

This structure is inspired by GAN models, although our model does not generate from scratch and only enhances its input tailored for detection of irregularities.

After the adversarial training, $\mathcal{I}$ will be an expert to inpaint its input (and make it devoid of noise), which successfully fools $\mathcal{D}$. Module $\mathcal{I}$ is a pixel-level irregularity detector and $\mathcal{D}$ a patch-level one, hence, $|X - \mathcal{I}(X)| \cap \mathcal{D}(X)$ can define the fine-segmentation and the precise location of the irregularity in any input testing video frame X. Note that each of the two networks $\mathcal{I}$ and $\mathcal{D}$ can be exploited for detecting and localizing the irregularity, but by aggregating them, we show a great improvement in the results. Detailed descriptions of each module along with the training and testing procedures are explained in the following.

3.1 $\mathcal{I}$: Inpainting Network

In some recent previous works [5,7,12], it is stated that when an auto-encoder is trained only on the inlier or normal class, the auto-encoder will be unable to reconstruct outlier or anomaly samples. Since parameters of auto-encoder are optimized to reconstruct samples from the normal (regular) class, as a side-effect, the reconstruction error of outliers (irregularities in our case) will be high. Also, in [12] in an unsupervised GAN-style training, a patch-based CNN is proposed that decimates outliers while enhancing the inlier samples. This makes the separation between the inliers and outliers much easier. In this paper, we use a similar idea, but in contrast: (1) $\mathcal{I}$ (analogous to the generator in GANs) is not directly used as an irregularity detector; (2) Instead of decimating outliers (irregularities in our case), our network inpaints its input by removing the irregularity from it. Implicitly, $\mathcal{I}$ operates similar to a de-noising network, which replaces the irregularity in the video with a dominant concept (*e.g.*, dominant textures).

Architecturally, $\mathcal{I}$ is an encoder-decoder convolutional network (implemented identical to U-Net [34]), which is trained only with data from the normal (regular) class. It learns to map any given input to the normal concept. Usually, irregularity occurs in some video frames, and $\mathcal{I}$ acts by reconstructing those deteriorated parts of the videos.

3.2 $\mathcal{D}$: Detection Network

Fully convolutional neural networks (FCNs) can effectively represent video frames and patches, and are previously used for different applications, such as semantic segmentation [36,37]. In a recent work, [10] used a FCN for irregularity detection in videos, in which the authors used a pre-trained FCN just for describing the video patches. Their method was not capable to detect (or score) the irregularity in the frames. Inspired by this idea, we use a FCN for the detection phase, but train it in an adversarial manner (along with $\mathcal{I}$). Our model is, hence, an end-to-end trainable network. We train the FCN (*i.e.*, $\mathcal{D}$ network) to score (and hence detect) all irregular regions in the input frame all at once.

Unlike conventional discriminator networks in a GAN, where the discriminator just provides a judgment about its input as a whole, $\mathcal{D}$ is capable to judge about different regions of its input. Consequently, its output is a matrix of likelihoods, which imply if the regions of its input follow the distribution of the normal (regular) data or not (*i.e.*, $\mathcal{P}_d$). Figure 2 shows the architecture of $\mathcal{D}$, which includes several convolutional layers. For this application, since local spatial characteristics are crucial, we do not use any pooling or fully connected layers, which ignore the spatial characteristics. On the other hand, to preserve the locality and enrich the features, several 1×1 convolutional layers are used.

3.3 Adversarial Training of $\mathcal{I}+\mathcal{D}$

Goodfellow *et al.* [15] proposed an efficient way for training two deep-neural networks (Generator (G) and Discriminator (D), in their terminology) through adversarial training, called GAN. GANs aim to learn the distribution of training data $\mathcal{P}_d$, and simultaneously generate new samples based on the same distribution $\mathcal{P}_d$. Therefore, G maps a vector of random variables (say Z) from a specific distribution $\mathcal{P}_Z$ to a sample from real data distribution and D seeks to discriminate between the actual data and the fake data generated by G. Generator and Discriminator are learned in a two-player mini-max game, formulated as:

$$\min_{G} \max_{D} \left(\mathbb{E}_{X \sim \mathcal{P}_d}[\log(D(X))] + \mathbb{E}_{Z \sim \mathcal{P}_z}[\log(1 - D(G(Z)))] \right). \tag{1}$$

Similarly, $\mathcal{I}+\mathcal{D}$ can be adversarially trained. Unlike conventional GANs, which map a latent space Z to a sample from $\mathcal{P}_d$, $\mathcal{I}$ maps a very noisy sample $X + \eta$ to a noise-less one that can fool $\mathcal{D}$ into identifying it as a normal scene *i.e.*,

$$\tilde{X} = (X \sim \mathcal{P}_d) + \gamma \left(\eta \sim \mathcal{N}(0, \sigma^2 \mathbf{I}) \right) \longrightarrow X' \sim \mathcal{P}_d, \tag{2}$$

where η is a Gaussian noise sampled from the normal distribution with standard deviation σ, *i.e.*, $\mathcal{N}(0, \sigma^2 \mathbf{I})$. γ is a hyperparameter that defines how severely to

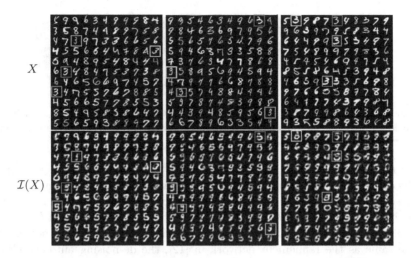

Fig. 3. Examples of images (X) and their inpainted versions using $\mathcal{I}$ (*i.e.*, $\mathcal{I}(X)$). The network is trained on images containing 0–9 digits, except digit '3'. These images are created from images in the MNIST dataset [38], to show how $\mathcal{I}$ and $\mathcal{D}$ operate. When digit '3' appears in a test image, it is considered as an irregularity. For clarity, several irregularity regions are marked in X and $\mathcal{I}(X)$.

contaminate X with noise. Note that the addition of η forces $\mathcal{I}$ to learn how to restore X from $\tilde{X}$, *i.e.*, in absent of irregularity.

On the other hand, $\mathcal{D}$ has access to the original pool of training data, hence, knows $\mathcal{P}_d$, and is trained to identify the normal class. In our case, $\mathcal{D}$ decides which region of $\mathcal{I}(\tilde{X})$ follows from $\mathcal{P}_d$. To fool $\mathcal{D}$, $\mathcal{I}$ is implicitly forced to inpaint its input. As mentioned above, $\mathcal{D}$ (*i.e.*, our discriminator network) judges on the regions of its input and not the whole image (which is the case for the GAN discriminators). Consequently, output of $\mathcal{D}(X)$ is a matrix, $\mathcal{O} \in \mathbb{R}^{n_1 \times n_2}$, in which each cell $\mathcal{O}(i,j)$ corresponds to the ith and j^{th} image region. Therefore, the joint training aims to maximize $\sum_{i=1,j=1}^{i=n_1,j=n_2} \mathcal{O}(i,j)$ (*i.e.*, maximize the likelihood of $\mathcal{I}$'s output to be normal). $n_1 \times n_2 = n$ is the total number of regions judged by $\mathcal{D}$. Accordingly, $\mathcal{I}+\mathcal{D}$ can be jointly learned by optimizing the following objective:

$$\min_{\mathcal{I}} \max_{\mathcal{D}} \left(\mathbb{E}_{X \sim \mathcal{P}_d}[\log(\|\mathcal{D}(X)\|^2)] + \mathbb{E}_{\tilde{X} \sim \mathcal{P}_d + \mathcal{N}_\sigma}[\log(\|\mathcal{Y} - \mathcal{D}(\mathcal{I}(\tilde{X}))\|^2)] \right), \quad (3)$$

where $\mathcal{Y} \in \mathbb{R}^{n_1 \times n_2} := \mathbf{1}^{n_1 \times n_2}$. Based on the above objective function, $\mathcal{I}$ learns to generate samples with the distribution of normal data (*i.e.*, $\mathcal{P}_d$). Hence, the parameters of this network, $\theta_{\mathcal{I}}$, are learned to restore a noisy visual sample. So, $\mathcal{I}(\tilde{X}, \theta_{\mathcal{I}})$ would be an irregularity-free version of $\tilde{X}$. For better understanding, suppose each frame of the video X is partitioned into $n = n_1 \times n_2$ non-overlapping regions (blocks), $B_{i \in 1:n}$. The proposed algorithm looks to find which of these regions are irregular. After the joint training of $\mathcal{I}+\mathcal{D}$, the modules can be interpreted as follows:

Fig. 4. Examples of the output of $\mathcal{D}$, *i.e.*, matrix $\mathcal{O}$, mapped on the original frames. The colored areas on the image are the low-scored regions in $\mathcal{O}$. (Color figure online)

- $\forall i;\ B_i \sim \mathcal{P}_d + \mathcal{N}_\sigma;\ \mathcal{I}(\tilde{X} = B_{i\in 1:n}) \Rightarrow X' = B'_{i\in 1:n}$, where $\forall i;\ B'_i \sim \mathcal{P}_d$. This is the case if the input is free from irregularity and is already following $\mathcal{P}_d$. X' is the output of $\mathcal{I}$, and hence $\|X - X'\|$ is minimized (will be near zero). This is because of the fact that $\theta_\mathcal{I}$ is optimized to reconstruct its input (all B_i regions) while the output also follows $\mathcal{P}_d$. Note that $\mathcal{I}$ works similar but not exactly the same as the refinement network in [12], the de-noising auto-encoder in [7], or de-nosing convolutional neural network in [39]. Consequently, if the input frame is already free from irregularity, $\mathcal{I}$ acts only as an enhancement function.
- $\exists j;\ B_j \not\sim \mathcal{P}_d;\ \mathcal{I}(\tilde{X} = B_{i\in 1:n}) \Rightarrow X' = B'_{i\in 1:n}$, where $\forall i;\ B'_i \sim \mathcal{P}_d$. This is the case if at least one of the regions in $\tilde{X}$ is irregular. Then, it is expected from $\mathcal{I}$ that $\mathcal{I}(B_j \not\sim \mathcal{P}_d) \Rightarrow B'_j \sim \mathcal{P}_d$. The irregular region is forced to follow the normal data distribution, as $\mathcal{I}$ is trained to restore a normal region contaminated with strong noise ($\gamma(\eta \sim \mathcal{N}(0, \sigma^2 \mathbf{I}))$) to a clean noise-free normal-looking region. In the testing phase, an irregular region, in $\mathcal{I}$'s point-of-view, is consider as strong noise. Note that in our experiments, $\gamma < 0.4$ is considered as weak and $\gamma \geq 0.4$ is considered as strong noise. Strong noise added to the training samples (inputs of $\mathcal{I}$) is considered as concepts that should be removed from the output of $\mathcal{I}$, for it to be able to fool $\mathcal{D}$. See Fig. 3, as a proof-of-concept example. Digit '3' is considered as an irregular concept in this example, and $\mathcal{I}+\mathcal{D}$ have never seen any '3' during training. So, $\mathcal{I}$ tries to replace it with a dominant concept from the normal concepts, which can be any digit between 0–9 except '3'. Consequently those B_is that follow $\mathcal{P}_d$ are not touched (or are enhanced), while those not following the normal data distribution are converted to a dominant concept (*i.e.*, inpainted).
- $\mathcal{D}(X = B_{i\in 1:n}) \Rightarrow \mathcal{O}_{i\in 1:n}$ where each element of matrix $\mathcal{O}$, output of $\mathcal{D}$, indicates the confidence for the corresponding region to be normal (regularity). Note that here $\mathcal{O}_i$ is analogous to $\mathcal{O}(a, b)$ with $i = b + (a-1)\cdot n_1$. Let's consider $\exists j;\ B_j \not\sim \mathcal{P}_d$; we expect that $\mathcal{O}_j \leq \mathcal{O}_{i\neq j}$. Parameters of $\mathcal{D}$, $\theta_\mathcal{D}$, are learned to map normal regions (*i.e.*, following $\mathcal{P}_d$) to 1, and 0 otherwise. Figure 4 shows the results of $\mathcal{D}$, in which the locations with an irregularity have lower scores.

With a modification on the objective function and the structure of GANs, our two proposed deep networks are adversarially trained. They learn to identify irregularities from two different aspects (pixel-level and patch-level) in a self-supervised manner. The equilibrium point as the stopping criterion for the two networks is discussed in Sect. 4.3.

3.4 Irregularity Detection

In the previous subsections, detailed structures and behaviours of the two networks are explained. As mentioned, $\mathcal{I}$ acts as a pixel-level inpainting network, and $\mathcal{D}$ as a patch-level irregularity detector. The difference between the input and outputs of $\mathcal{I}$ for any testing frame X (*i.e.*, $|X - \mathcal{I}(X)|$) can be a guideline for where pixels of the input frames are irregular. On the other hand, $\mathcal{D}(X = B_{i \in 1:n})$ shows which regions of X are irregular (*i.e.*, those with $\mathcal{O}_j \leq \zeta$). As discussed earlier, the detection based on $\mathcal{I}$ leads to high false positive rate, and the detection solely based on $\mathcal{D}$ leads to high detection error rates. Therefore, outputs of these two networks are masked by each other and the intersection is considered as the irregularity localization.

To identify the regions of irregularities from the output of $\mathcal{D}$ (*i.e.*, matrix $\mathcal{O}$), we can consider all regions with $\{B_i | (\mathcal{O}_i \leq \zeta)\}$, where B_i is respective field of $\mathcal{O}_i$ on the input. As mentioned above, $\mathcal{I}$ will reconstruct its whole input image, except for the irregularities, which are inpainted. Consequently, pixels where $|X - \mathcal{I}(X)| \geq \alpha$ can be considered as potential pixels containing an irregularity. To alleviate the high false positive rate, we just mask these pixels with the above regions. Consequently, final irregularity fine-segmentation on X can be defined as

$$\mathcal{M} = \{|X - \mathcal{I}(X)| \geq \alpha\} \cap \{B_i | (\mathcal{O}_i \leq \zeta)\}. \tag{4}$$

3.5 Preprocessing of the Videos

Irregular events in visual data (especially in videos) are defined in terms of irregular shapes, motion, or possibly a combination of both. Therefore, to identify the motion properties of events, we require a series of frames. Two strategies can be adopted for this purpose: (1) Adding a LSTM sequence at the end of the proposed network [40]; (2) Using 3D kernels, instead of 2D ones in the same architectures we proposed (such as in [41]). However, these methods increase the number of parameters and the computational complexity of the model. [10] proposed a simple preprocessing step to feed videos instead of images to a CNN without any modification on the structures of a 2D CNN. To interpret both shape and motion, we consider the pixel-wise *average* of frame I_t and previous frame I_{t-1}, denoted by I'_t (not to be confused with a derivative): $I'_t(p) = \frac{1}{2}(I_t(p) + I_{t-1}(p))$, where I_t is the tth frame in the video. For detecting irregularities on I_t, we use the sequence $X = \langle I'_{t-4}, I'_{t-2}, I'_t \rangle$, and input it to the three channels (similar to R, G, and B channels) of the networks.

4 Experimental Results

We evaluate the performance of the proposed method on two standard benchmarks for detecting and localizing irregular events in videos. Also, we create a dataset, called IR-MNIST, for evaluating and analyzing the proposed method to better showcase the abilities of the network modules, as a proof-of-concept.

Fig. 5. Examples of the output of $\mathcal{I}$ on the UCSD dataset. Bottom row shows output of $\mathcal{I}$. Top row shows the original frames.

The proposed method is implemented using PyTorch [42] framework. All reported results are from implementations on a GeForce GTX 1080 GPU. Learning rate of $\mathcal{I}$ and $\mathcal{D}$ are set to be the same and is equal to 0.002. Also, momentum of both is equal to 0.9, with a batch size of 16. The hyperparameter γ, which controls the scale of added Gaussian noise for the training samples (in $\mathcal{I}$) is equal to 0.4.

4.1 Datasets

UCSD: This dataset [2] includes two subsets, Ped1 and Ped2. Videos are from an outdoor scene, recorded with a static camera at 10 fps. The dominant mobile objects in these scenes are pedestrians. Therefore, all other objects (*e.g.*, cars, skateboarders, wheelchairs, or bicycles) are considered as irregularities.

UMN: The UMN dataset is recorded for three different scenarios. In each scenario, a group of people walk in normal pace in an area, but suddenly all people run away (*i.e.*, they escape). The escape is considered to be the irregularity.

IR-MNIST (Available at http://ai.stanford.edu/~eadeli/publications/data/ IR-MNIST.zip**):** To show the properties of the proposed method, we create a simple dataset using the images from MNIST [43]. To create each single image, randomly 121 samples are selected from the MNIST dataset and are put together as a 11×11 puzzle. Some samples are shown in Fig. 3. We create as much images to have 5000 training data and 1000 test samples. Training samples are created without using any images of the digit '3'. Hence, '3' is considered as an irregular concept. We expect that our method detects and localizes all patches containing '3' in the testing images, as irregularity.

4.2 Results

Results on UCSD. Figure 5 visualizes the outputs of network $\mathcal{I}$ on several examples of UCSD frames. As can be seen, irregular objects such as bicycles

Table 1. Frame-level accuracy (FL) and pixel-level accuracy (PL) comparisons on the UCSD dataset. The last column shows if the methods are (1) based on Deep learning or not, (2) End-to-end deep networks or not, and finally (3) Patched based methods or not.

Method	Ped1 (FL/PL)	Ped2 (FL/PL)	($\mathbb{D}/\mathbb{E}/\mathbb{P}$)
IBC [1]	(14/26)	(13/26)	(✗/✗/✓)
MDT [2]	(25/58)	(24/54)	(✗/✗/✗)
Bertini *et al.* [3]	(31/70)	(30/–)	(✗/✗/✓)
Xu *et al.* [44]	(22/–)	(20/42)	(✗/✗/✗)
Li *et al.* [45]	(16/–)	(18/29)	(✗/✗/✗)
RE [7]	(–/–)	(15/–)	(✓/✗/✓)
Xu *et al.* [26]	(16/40)	(17/42)	(✓/✗/✓)
Sabokrou *et al.* [27]	(–/–)	(19/24)	(✓/✗/✓)
Deep-Cascade [9]	(9.1/15.8)	(8.2/19)	(✓/✗/✓)
Deep-Anomaly [10]	(–/–)	(**11/15**)	(✓/✗/✗)
Ravanbakhsh *et al.* [14]	(**7**/34)	(**11**/–)	(✓/✗/✓)
ALOCC [12]	(–/–)	(13/–)	(✓/✓/✓)
$\mathcal{D}(X)$	(–/16.7)	(–/17.2)	(✓/✓/✗)
$\mathcal{I}(X)$	(17.3/–)	(17.8/–)	(✓/✓/✗)
AVID	(12.3/**14.4**)	(14/**15**)	(✓/✓/✗)

Table 2. EER and AUC performance metrics on UMN dataset.

	Chaotic invariant [46]	SF [2]	Cong [30]	Saligrama [47]	Li [45]	Ours (AVID)
EER	5.3	12.6	2.8	3.4	3.7	**2.6**
AUC	99.4	94.9	**99.6**	99.5	99.5	**99.6**

and cars disappear in the output of $\mathcal{I}(X)$, and the regular regions are approximately reconstructed. Although $\mathcal{I}$ is trained to reconstruct regular regions with minimum loss, loss of quality is unavoidable, as a consequence of the strong noise applied to the inputs of $\mathcal{I}$ during training. This shortage, however, does not adversely affect our final decision, because maximum difference between X and $\mathcal{I}(X)$ happens in the pixels when an irregularity occurred. Figure 4 also shows several output samples of the proposed detector $\mathcal{D}$ for detecting irregularity in videos. It confirms that irregular blocks can be appropriately detected. For a quantitative analysis, similar to [2], two standard measures on this dataset are considered. In frame level (FL) each of the frames is considered to be anomaly if at least one pixel is detected as irregularity. In pixel-level (PL) analysis, the region identified as anomaly should have an overlap of at least 40% with the ground-truth irregular pixels to be considered as irregularity. PL is a measure for evaluating the accuracy of the localization in a pixel-level. A comparison between the performance of the proposed and the state-of-the-art methods is provided in Table 1. The proposed method for detecting the irregular frames is comparable to state-of-the-art methods, but the localization performance outperforms all other methods by a large margin. As can be seen, [9,12,14] achieve a better performance by a narrow margin in a frame-level aspect compared to us, but unlike ours, these methods are not able to process images as a whole in an end-to-end fashion. They require to split a frame into a set of patches and feed them to the network one-by-one. The last column of Table 1 shows which methods are not patch-based and end-to-end. Furthermore, the performances of $\mathcal{I}$ and $\mathcal{D}$ as independent baselines are also reported in this table, which show that each single one of them can preform as well as previous state-of-the-arts, while our final end-to-end model, AVID, outperforms all of these methods.

Results on UMN. Table 2 shows the irregularity detection performance in terms of equal error rate (EER) and area under the ROC curve (AUC). As discussed earlier, this dataset has some limitations, as there are only three types of abnormal scenes in the dataset with very high temporal-spatial abrupt changes between normal and abnormal frames. Also, there are no pixel-level ground truth for this dataset. Based on these limitations, to evaluate the

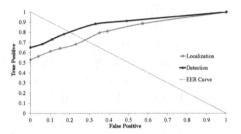

Fig. 6. ROC curves for detection and localization performance on IR-MNIST.

method, EER and AUC are reported in frame-level settings. Since this dataset is simple, and irregularity localization is not important, only the global detector is used to evaluate the results. Because of the simplicity of this dataset, previous methods already performed reasonably good on this dataset. AUC of our method is comparable with the other best results and EER of our approach is better (by 0.2%) than the second best.

Results on IR-MNIST as a Toy Data-Set. Figure 3 confirms that the network $\mathcal{I}$ can properly substitute irregular regions with a (closest) normal concept. Since '3' is considered as an irregular concept, $\mathcal{I}$ converted it to another digit, which is most similar to '3'. Several samples of irregular regions in Fig. 3 are marked (on both the original and inpainted version of the same samples). Similarly, we evaluate $\mathcal{D}$ in detecting irregular regions on an image. Figure 7 shows the heat-map of $\mathcal{D}$'s output for several samples, where blue is 1 and yellow indicates 0, and other colors are in between (in a parula colormap). Note that the output is resized to have the same size as the original images. Figure 6 shows the localization and detection performance on the IR-MNIST dataset using the receiver operating characteristic (ROC) curve. This curve is drawn by repeatedly changing the two thresholds in Eq. (4) and recording the results. Detection is just based on if a frame contains an irregular concept ('3' digits) or not (checked over 1000 different testing samples). For localization all 11 × 11 regions of an images are considered, and if the region is correctly detected, it is counted as a true

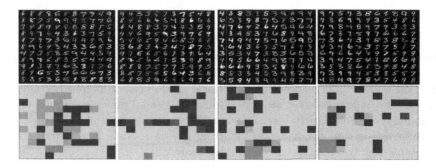

Fig. 7. Examples outputs of $\mathcal{D}$ on IR-MNIST. Bottom row shows (resized version of) the heat-map, for input testing images (in the top row). Here, '3' is intended as an irregular concept. (Color figure online)

localization. So, $11 \times 11 \times 1000$ regions are evaluated. The EERs of the detection and localization are equal to 21% and 29%, receptively.

4.3 Discussion

Added Noise to the Input of $\mathcal{I}$ in Training Phase. In some cases similar to de-nosing auto-encoder [48], de-nosing CNN [39] or one-class classification tasks [12], researchers added noise to the training data to make their network robust against noise. We also contaminated our training data with a statistical noise, with γ indicating its intensity. This hyperparameter actually plays a very interesting role for training the model. Using this hyperparameter, we can control the learning pace between $\mathcal{I}$ and $\mathcal{D}$. Since, $\mathcal{I}$ sees only normal samples during training, in the noise-free case, it can easily reconstruct them so that $\mathcal{D}$ is fooled. The added noise actually makes $\mathcal{I}$ to learn how to inpaint and remove the irregularity to a pixel-level. Therefore, a very small value for γ leads to a task, which is very easy for $\mathcal{I}$ and a very large value will mislead $\mathcal{I}$ from seeing the actual normal data distribution (*i.e.*, $\mathcal{P}_d$). Based on our experiments, $\gamma = 0.4$ leads to good results. From another point-of-view, γ is a very good means to create a proper scheduling between $\mathcal{I}$ and $\mathcal{D}$, which is a very interesting and recent topic on for GANs [49].

Stopping Criterion. In conventional GANs, the stopping criterion is defined as when the model reaches a Nash equilibrium between G and D. However, for our case, the optimum point for $\mathcal{I}$ and $\mathcal{D}$ is not often obtained at the same time. During learning of these two networks, when they are competing with each other, different conditions may occur. At a time that $\mathcal{D}$ is capable to efficiently classify between fake and real data (*i.e.*, work as an accurate classifier on the validation data), we save its parameters, $\theta_{\mathcal{D}}$. Also, when $\mathcal{I}$ generates samples as well as the normal class (*i.e.*, $\|X - \mathcal{I}(X)\|^2$ is in the minimum point), the parameters of $\mathcal{I}$, $\theta_{\mathcal{I}}$, are also saved. So, at different time spans $\theta_{\mathcal{I}}$ and $\theta_{\mathcal{D}}$ are saved, during the training procedure. Similar to other GAN-style models, finding the optimum point for stopping adversarial training of $\mathcal{I}+\mathcal{D}$ is a hard task.

Mode Collapse. One of the major concerns in GANs is the mode collapse issue, which often occurs when the generator only learns a portion of the real-data distribution and outputs samples from a single mode (*i.e.*, ignores other modes). For our case, it is a different story as $\mathcal{I}$ directly sees all possible samples of the normal class and implicitly learns the manifold spanned by them. Reconstructing the training samples, instead of starting from a random latent space, is an acceptable way to avoid the mode collapse issue [50].

5   Conclusions

In this paper, we proposed an efficient method for irregularity detection and localization in visual data (*i.e.*, images and videos). Two proposed deep networks, $\mathcal{I}$ and $\mathcal{D}$ are adversarially trained in a self-supervised setting. $\mathcal{I}$ learns to efficiently reconstruct normal (regular) regions and implicitly inpaints irregular ones. $\mathcal{D}$ learns to score different regions of its input on how likely they are irregularities. Integrating the outputs of the pixel-level results from $\mathcal{I}$, and the patch-level results from $\mathcal{D}$ provides a promising irregularity detection metric, as well as fine-segmentation of the irregularity in the visual scene. The results on several synthetic and real datasets confirm that the proposed adversarially learned network is capable of detecting irregularity, even when there are no irregular samples to use during training. Our method benefits from the advantages of both pixel-level and patch-level methods, while not having their shortcomings.

Acknowledgements. This research was in part supported by a grant from IPM (No. CS1396-5-01). Mohsen Fayyaz and Juergen Gall have been financially supported by the DFG project GA 1927/4-1 (Research Unit FOR 2535) and the ERC Starting Grant ARCA (677650).

References

1. Boiman, O., Irani, M.: Detecting irregularities in images and in video. Int. J. Comput. Vis. **74**, 17–31 (2007)
2. Mahadevan, V., Li, W., Bhalodia, V., Vasconcelos, N.: Anomaly detection in crowded scenes. In: 2010 IEEE Conference on Computer Vision and Pattern Recognition (CVPR), pp. 1975–1981. IEEE (2010)
3. Bertini, M., Del Bimbo, A., Seidenari, L.: Multi-scale and real-time non-parametric approach for anomaly detection and localization. Comput. Vis. Image Underst. **116**, 320–329 (2012)
4. Colque, R.V.H.M., Caetano, C., de Andrade, M.T.L., Schwartz, W.R.: Histograms of optical flow orientation and magnitude and entropy to detect anomalous events in videos. IEEE Trans. Circ. Syst. Video Technol. **27**, 673–682 (2017)
5. Xia, Y., Cao, X., Wen, F., Hua, G., Sun, J.: Learning discriminative reconstructions for unsupervised outlier removal. In: Proceedings of the IEEE International Conference on Computer Vision, pp. 1511–1519 (2015)

6. Morris, B.T., Trivedi, M.M.: Trajectory learning for activity understanding: unsupervised, multilevel, and long-term adaptive approach. IEEE Trans. Pattern Anal. Mach. Intell. **33**, 2287–2301 (2011)
7. Sabokrou, M., Fathy, M., Hoseini, M.: Video anomaly detection and localisation based on the sparsity and reconstruction error of auto-encoder. Electron. Lett. **52**, 1122–1124 (2016)
8. You, C., Robinson, D.P., Vidal, R.: Provable self-representation based outlier detection in a union of subspaces. In: 2017 IEEE Conference on Computer Vision and Pattern Recognition (CVPR) (2017)
9. Sabokrou, M., Fayyaz, M., Fathy, M., Klette, R.: Deep-cascade: cascading 3D deep neural networks for fast anomaly detection and localization in crowded scenes. IEEE Trans. Image Process. **26**, 1992–2004 (2017)
10. Sabokrou, M., Fayyaz, M., Fathy, M., Moayedd, Z., et al.: Deep-anomaly: fully convolutional neural network for fast anomaly detection in crowded scenes. Comput. Vis. Image Underst. **172**, 88–97 (2018)
11. Lawson, W., Bekele, E., Sullivan, K.: Finding anomalies with generative adversarial networks for a patrolbot. In: Proceedings of the IEEE Conference on Computer Vision and Pattern Recognition Workshops, pp. 12–13 (2017)
12. Sabokrou, M., Khalooei, M., Fathy, M., Adeli, E.: Adversarially learned one-class classifier for novelty detection. In: CVPR (2018)
13. Schlegl, T., Seeböck, P., Waldstein, S.M., Schmidt-Erfurth, U., Langs, G.: Unsupervised anomaly detection with generative adversarial networks to guide marker discovery. In: Niethammer, M., et al. (eds.) IPMI 2017. LNCS, vol. 10265, pp. 146–157. Springer, Cham (2017). https://doi.org/10.1007/978-3-319-59050-9_12
14. Ravanbakhsh, M., Sangineto, E., Nabi, M., Sebe, N.: Training adversarial discriminators for cross-channel abnormal event detection in crowds. arXiv preprint arXiv:1706.07680 (2017)
15. Goodfellow, I., et al.: Generative adversarial nets. In: Advances in Neural Information Processing Systems, pp. 2672–2680 (2014)
16. Ravanbakhsh, M., Nabi, M., Sangineto, E., Marcenaro, L., Regazzoni, C., Sebe, N.: Abnormal event detection in videos using generative adversarial nets. arXiv preprint arXiv:1708.09644 (2017)
17. Odena, A.: Semi-supervised learning with generative adversarial networks. In: Data Efficient Machine Learning workshop, ICML (2016)
18. Do-Omri, A., Wu, D., Liu, X.: A self-training method for semi-supervised GANs. In: ICLR (2018)
19. Piciarelli, C., Foresti, G.L.: On-line trajectory clustering for anomalous events detection. Pattern Recogn. Lett. **27**, 1835–1842 (2006)
20. Adam, A., Rivlin, E., Shimshoni, I., Reinitz, D.: Robust real-time unusual event detection using multiple fixed-location monitors. IEEE Trans. Pattern Anal. Mach. Intell. **30**, 555–560 (2008)
21. Cong, Y., Yuan, J., Tang, Y.: Video anomaly search in crowded scenes via spatio-temporal motion context. IEEE Tran. Inf. Forensics Secur. **8**, 1590–1599 (2013)
22. Benezeth, Y., Jodoin, P.M., Saligrama, V., Rosenberger, C.: Abnormal events detection based on spatio-temporal co-occurences. In: IEEE Conference on Computer Vision and Pattern Recognition, CVPR 2009, pp. 2458–2465. IEEE (2009)
23. Mehran, R., Oyama, A., Shah, M.: Abnormal crowd behavior detection using social force model. In: IEEE Conference on Computer Vision and Pattern Recognition, CVPR 2009, pp. 935–942. IEEE (2009)

24. Kratz, L., Nishino, K.: Anomaly detection in extremely crowded scenes using spatio-temporal motion pattern models. In: IEEE Conference on Computer Vision and Pattern Recognition, CVPR 2009, pp. 1446–1453. IEEE (2009)

25. Kim, J., Grauman, K.: Observe locally, infer globally: a space-time MRF for detecting abnormal activities with incremental updates. In: IEEE Conference on Computer Vision and Pattern Recognition, CVPR 2009, pp. 2921–2928. IEEE (2009)

26. Xu, D., Ricci, E., Yan, Y., Song, J., Sebe, N.: Learning deep representations of appearance and motion for anomalous event detection. In: BMVC (2015)

27. Sabokrou, M., Fathy, M., Hoseini, M., Klette, R.: Real-time anomaly detection and localization in crowded scenes. In: Proceedings of the IEEE Conference on Computer Vision and Pattern Recognition Workshops, pp. 56–62 (2015)

28. Feng, Y., Yuan, Y., Lu, X.: Learning deep event models for crowd anomaly detection. Neurocomputing **219**, 548–556 (2017)

29. Fang, Z., et al.: Abnormal event detection in crowded scenes based on deep learning. Multimed. Tools Appl. **75**, 14617–14639 (2016)

30. Cong, Y., Yuan, J., Liu, J.: Sparse reconstruction cost for abnormal event detection. In: 2011 IEEE Conference on Computer Vision and Pattern Recognition (CVPR), pp. 3449–3456. IEEE (2011)

31. Antić, B., Ommer, B.: Video parsing for abnormality detection. In: 2011 IEEE International Conference on Computer Vision (ICCV), pp. 2415–2422. IEEE (2011)

32. Mirza, M., Osindero, S.: Conditional generative adversarial nets. arXiv preprint arXiv:1411.1784 (2014)

33. Isola, P., Zhu, J.Y., Zhou, T., Efros, A.A.: Image-to-image translation with conditional adversarial networks. In: CVPR (2017)

34. Ronneberger, O., Fischer, P., Brox, T.: U-net: convolutional networks for biomedical image segmentation. In: Navab, N., Hornegger, J., Wells, W.M., Frangi, A.F. (eds.) MICCAI 2015. LNCS, vol. 9351, pp. 234–241. Springer, Cham (2015). https://doi.org/10.1007/978-3-319-24574-4_28

35. Liu, W., Luo, W., Lian, D., Gao, S.: Future frame prediction for anomaly detection-a new baseline. arXiv preprint arXiv:1712.09867 (2017)

36. Long, J., Shelhamer, E., Darrell, T.: Fully convolutional networks for semantic segmentation. In: Proceedings of the IEEE Conference on Computer Vision and Pattern Recognition, pp. 3431–3440 (2015)

37. Nie, D., Wang, L., Adeli, E., Lao, C., Lin, W., Shen, D.: 3-D fully convolutional networks for multimodal isointense infant brain image segmentation. IEEE Trans. Cybern. (2018)

38. LeCun, Y., Cortes, C., Burges, C.J.: MNIST handwritten digit database. AT&T Labs, vol. 2 (2010). http://yann.lecun.com/exdb/mnist

39. Divakar, N., Babu, R.V.: Image denoising via CNNs: an adversarial approach. In: New Trends in Image Restoration and Enhancement, CVPR Workshop (2017)

40. Sutskever, I., Vinyals, O., Le, Q.V.: Sequence to sequence learning with neural networks. In: Advances in Neural Information Processing Systems, pp. 3104–3112 (2014)

41. Ji, S., Xu, W., Yang, M., Yu, K.: 3D convolutional neural networks for human action recognition. IEEE Trans. Pattern Anal. Mach. Intell. **35**, 221–231 (2013)

42. Paszke, A., et al.: Automatic differentiation in pytorch (2017)

43. LeCun, Y., Bottou, L., Bengio, Y., Haffner, P.: Gradient-based learning applied to document recognition. Proc. IEEE **86**, 2278–2324 (1998)

44. Xu, D., Song, R., Wu, X., Li, N., Feng, W., Qian, H.: Video anomaly detection based on a hierarchical activity discovery within spatio-temporal contexts. Neurocomputing **143**, 144–152 (2014)

45. Li, W., Mahadevan, V., Vasconcelos, N.: Anomaly detection and localization in crowded scenes. IEEE Trans. Pattern Anal. Mach. Intell. **36**, 18–32 (2014)
46. Wu, S., Oreifej, O., Shah, M.: Action recognition in videos acquired by a moving camera using motion decomposition of Lagrangian particle trajectories. In: 2011 IEEE International Conference on Computer Vision (ICCV), pp. 1419–1426. IEEE (2011)
47. Saligrama, V., Chen, Z.: Video anomaly detection based on local statistical aggregates. In: 2012 IEEE Conference on Computer Vision and Pattern Recognition (CVPR), pp. 2112–2119. IEEE (2012)
48. Vincent, P., Larochelle, H., Bengio, Y., Manzagol, P.A.: Extracting and composing robust features with denoising autoencoders. In: Proceedings of the 25th International Conference on Machine Learning, pp. 1096–1103. ACM (2008)
49. Liu, S., Bousquet, O., Chaudhuri, K.: Approximation and convergence properties of generative adversarial learning. In: Advances in Neural Information Processing Systems, pp. 5551–5559 (2017)
50. Makhzani, A., Shlens, J., Jaitly, N., Goodfellow, I., Frey, B.: Adversarial autoencoders. In: International Conference on Learning Representations (2016)

Localization-Aware Active Learning
for Object Detection

Chieh-Chi Kao[1], Teng-Yok Lee[2(✉)], Pradeep Sen[1], and Ming-Yu Liu[2]

[1] University of California, Santa Barbara, Santa Barbara, CA 93106, USA
[2] Mitsubishi Electric Research Laboratories, Cambridge, MA 02139, USA
`tlee@merl.com`

Abstract. Active learning—a class of algorithms that iteratively searches for the most informative samples to include in a training dataset—has been shown to be effective at annotating data for image classification. However, the use of active learning for object detection is still largely unexplored as determining informativeness of an object-location hypothesis is more difficult. In this paper, we address this issue and present two metrics for measuring the informativeness of an object hypothesis, which allow us to leverage active learning to reduce the amount of annotated data needed to achieve a target object detection performance. Our first metric measures "localization tightness" of an object hypothesis, which is based on the overlapping ratio between the region proposal and the final prediction. Our second metric measures "localization stability" of an object hypothesis, which is based on the variation of predicted object locations when input images are corrupted by noise. Our experimental results show that by augmenting a conventional active-learning algorithm designed for classification with the proposed metrics, the amount of labeled training data required can be reduced up to 25%. Moreover, on PASCAL 2007 and 2012 datasets our localization-stability method has an average relative improvement of 96.5% and 81.9% over the baseline method using classification only.

Keywords: Object detection · Active learning

1 Introduction

Prior works have shown that with a large amount of annotated data, convolutional neural networks (CNNs) can be trained to achieve a super-human performance for various visual recognition tasks. As tremendous efforts are dedicated into the discovery of effective network architectures and training methods for further advancing the performance, we argue it is also important to investigate into effective approaches for data annotation as data annotation is essential but expensive.

Electronic supplementary material The online version of this chapter (https://doi.org/10.1007/978-3-030-20876-9_32) contains supplementary material, which is available to authorized users.

Data annotation is especially expensive for the object-detection task. Compared to annotating image class, which can be done via a multiple-choice question, annotating object location requires a human annotator to specify a bounding box for an object. Simply dragging a tight bounding box to enclose an object can cost 10-times more time than answering a multiple-choice question [22,32]. Consequently, a higher pay rate has to be paid to a human labeler for annotating images for an object detection task. In addition to the cost, it is more difficult to monitor and control the annotation quality.

Active learning [28] is a machine learning procedure that is useful in reducing the amount of annotated data required to achieve a target performance. It has been applied to various computer-vision problems including object classification [6,13], image segmentation [4,16], and activity recognition [8,9]. Active learning starts by training a baseline model with a small, labeled dataset, and then applying the baseline model to the unlabeled data. For each unlabeled sample, it estimates whether this sample contains critical information that has not been learned by the baseline model. Once the samples that bring the most critical information are identified and labeled by human annotators, they can be added to the initial training dataset to train a new model, which is expected to perform better. Compared to *passive learning*, which randomly selects samples from the unlabeled dataset to be labeled, active learning can achieve the same accuracies with fewer but more informative labeled samples.

Multiple metrics for measuring how informative a sample is have been proposed for the classification task, including maximum uncertainty, expected model change, density weighted, and so on [28]. The concept behind several of them is to evaluate how uncertain the current model is for an unlabeled sample. If the model could not assign a high probability to a class for a sample, then it implies the model is uncertain about the class of the sample. In other words, the class of the sample would be very informative to the model. This sample would require human to clarify.

Since an object-detection problem can be considered as an object-classification problem once the object is located, existing active learning approaches for object detection [1,30] mainly measure the information in the classification part. Nevertheless, in addition to classification, the accuracy of an object detector also relies on its localization ability. Because of the importance of localization, in this paper we present an active learning algorithm tailored for object detection, which considers the localization of detected objects. Given a baseline object detector which detects bounding boxes of objects, our algorithm evaluates the uncertainty of both the classification and localization.

Our algorithm is based on two quantitative metrics of the localization uncertainty.

1. *Localization Tightness (LT)*: The first metric is based on how tight the detected bounding boxes can enclose true objects. The tighter the bounding box, the more certain the localization. While it sounds impossible to compute the localization tightness for non-annotated images because the true object locations are unknown, for object detectors that follow the propose-then-

classify pipeline [7,26], we estimate the localization tightness of a bounding box based on its changes from the intermediate proposal (a box contains any kind of foreground objects) to the final class-specific bounding box.

2. *Localization Stability (LS)*: The second metric is based on whether the detected bounding boxes are sensitive to changes in the input image. To evaluate the localization stability, our algorithm adds different amounts of Gaussian noise to pixel values of the image, and measures how the detected regions vary with respect to the noise. This one can be applied to all kinds of object detectors, especially those that do not have an explicit proposal stage [20,21,24,37].

The contributions of this paper are two-fold:

1. We present different metrics to quantitatively evaluate the localization uncertainty of an object detector. Our metrics consider different aspects of object detection in spite that the ground truth of object locations is unknown, making our metrics suited for active learning.
2. We demonstrate that to apply active learning for object detection, both the localization and the classification of a detector should be considered when sampling informative images. Our experiments on benchmark datasets show that considering both the localization and classification uncertainty outperforms the existing active-learning algorithm works on the classification only and passive learning.

2 Related Works

We now review active learning approaches used for image classification. For more detail of active learning, Settles's survey [28] provides a comprehensive review. In this paper, we use the maximum uncertainty method in the classification as the baseline method for comparison. The uncertainty based method is used for CAPTCHA recognition [31], image classification [12], automated and manual video annotation [15], and querying samples for active decision boundary annotation [11]. It also has been applied to different learning models including decision trees [17], SVMs [34], and Gaussian processes [14]. We choose uncertainty-based method since it is efficient to compute.

Active learning is also applied for object detection tasks in various specific applications, such as satellite images [1] and vehicle images [30]. Vijayanarasimhan *et al.* [36] propose an approach to actively crawl images from the web to train part-based linear SVM detector. Note that these methods only consider information from the classifier, while our methods aim to consider the localization part as well.

Current state-of-the-art object detectors are based on deep-learning. They can be classified into two categories. Given an input image, the first category explicitly generates region proposals, following by feature extraction, category classification, and fine-tuning of the proposal geometry [7,26]. The other category directly outputs the object location and class without the intermediate

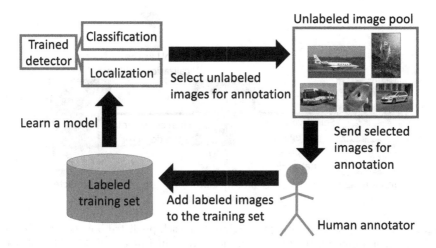

Fig. 1. A round of active learning for object detection.

proposal stage, such as YOLO [24], YOLO 9000 [25], SSD [20], R-FCN [3], Focal Loss [18], and Single-Shot Refinement [38]. This inspires us to consider localization stability, which can be applied to both categories.

Besides active learning, there are other research directions to reduce the cost for annotation. Temporal coherence of the video frames are used to reduce the annotation effort for training detectors [23]. Domain adaptation [10] is used to transfer the knowledge from an image classifier to an object detector without the annotation of bounding boxes. Papadopoulos *et al.* [22] suggest to simplify the annotation process from drawing a bounding box to simply answering a Yes/No question whether a bounding box tightly encloses an object. Russakovsky *et al.* [27] integrate multiple inputs from both computer vision and humans to label objects.

3   Active Learning for Object Detection

The goal of our algorithm is to train an object detector that takes an image as input and outputs a set of rectangular bounding boxes. Each bounding box has the location and the scale of its shape, and a probability mass function of all classes. To train such an object detector, the training and validation images of the detector are annotated with an bounding box per object and its category. Such an annotation is commonly seen in public datasets including PASCAL VOC [5] and MS COCO [19].

We first review the basic active learning framework for object detection in Sect. 3.1. It also reviews the measurement of classification uncertainty, which is the major measurement for object detection in previous active learning algorithms for object detection [1,28,30]. Based on this framework, we extend the uncertainty measurement to also consider the localization result of a detector, as described in Sects. 3.2 and 3.3.

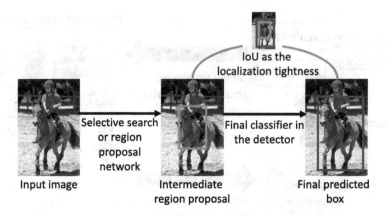

Fig. 2. The process of calculating the tightness of each predicted box. Given an intermediate region proposal, the detector refines it to a final predicted box. The IoU calculated by the final predicted box and its corresponding region proposal is defined as the localization tightness of that box. (Color figure online)

3.1 Active Learning with Classification Uncertainty

Figure 1 overviews our active learning algorithm. Our algorithm starts with a small training set of annotated images to train a baseline object detector. In order to improve the detector by training with more images, we continue to collect images to annotate. Other than annotating all newly collected images, based on different characteristics of the current detector, we select a subset of them for human annotators to label. Once being annotated, these selected images are added to the training set to train a new detector. The entire process continues to collect more images, select a subset with respect to the new detector, annotate the selected ones with humans, re-train the detector and so on. Hereafter we call such a cycle of data collection, selection, annotation, and training as a *round*.

A key component of active learning is the selection of images. Our selection is based on the uncertainty of both the classification and localization. The classification uncertainty of a bounding box is the same as the existing active learning approaches [1,28,30]. Given a bounding box B, its classification uncertainty $U_B(B)$ is defined as $U_B(B) = 1 - P_{max}(B)$ where $P_{max}(B)$ is highest probability out of all classes for this box. If the probability on a single class is close to 1.0, meaning that the probabilities for other classes are low, the detector is highly certain about its class. To the contrast, when multiple classes have similar probabilities, each probability will be low because the sum of probabilities of all classes must be one.

Based on the classification uncertainty per box, given the i-th image to evaluate, say I_i, its classification uncertainty is denoted as $U_C(I_i)$, which is calculated by the maximum uncertainty out of all detected boxes within.

(a)   (b)

Fig. 3. Images preferred by LT/C. Top rows show two figures are two cases that will be selected by LT/C, which are images with certain category but loose bounding box (a) or images with tight bounding box but uncertain about the category (b).

3.2 Localization Tightness

Our first metric of the localization uncertainty is based on the *Localization Tightness* (LT) of a bounding box. The localization tightness measures how tight a predicted bounding box can enclose true foreground objects. Ideally, if the ground-truth locations of the foreground objects are known, the tightness can be simply computed as the IoU (Intersection over Union) between the predicted bounding box and the ground truth. Given two boxes B^1 and B^2, their IoU is defined as: $IoU(B^1, B^2) = \frac{B^1 \cap B^2}{B^1 \cup B^2}$.

Because the ground truth is unknown for an image without annotation, an estimate for the localization tightness is needed. Here we design an estimate for object detectors that involves the adjustment from intermediate region proposals to the final bounding boxes. Region proposals are the bounding boxes that might contain any foreground objects, which can be obtained via the selective search [35] or a region proposal network [26]. Besides classifying the region proposals into specific classes, the final stage of these object detectors can even adjust the location and scale of region proposals based on the classified object classes. Figure 2 illustrates the typical pipeline of these detectors where the region proposal (green) in the middle is adjusted to the red box in the right.

As the region proposal is trained to predict the location of foreground objects, the refinement process in the final stage is actually related to how well the region proposal predicts. If the region proposal locates the foreground object perfectly, there is no need to refine it. Based on this observation, we use the IoU value between the region proposal and the refined bounding box to estimate the localization tightness between an adjusted bounding box and the unknown ground truth. The estimated tightness T of j-th predicted box B_0^j can be formulated as following: $T(B_0^j) = IoU(B_0^j, R_0^j)$, where R_0^j is the corresponding region proposal fed into the final classifier that generates B_0^j.

Once the tightness of all predicted boxes are estimated, we can extend the selection process to consider not only the classification uncertainty but also the tightness. Namely, we want to select images with inconsistency between the classification and the localization, as following:

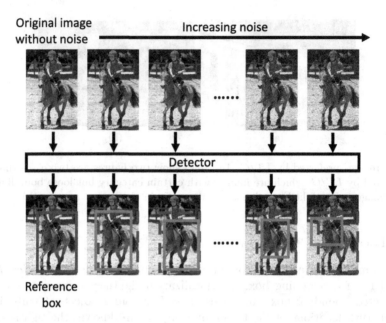

Fig. 4. The process of calculating the localization stability of each predicted box. Given one input image, a reference box (red) is predicted by the detector. The change in predicted boxes (green) from noisy images is measured by the IoU of predicted boxes (green) and the corresponding reference box (dashed red). (Color figure online)

- Given a predicted box that is absolutely certain about its classification result ($P_{max} = 1$), but it cannot tightly enclose a true object ($T = 0$). An example is shown in Fig. 3(a).
- Reversely, if the predicted box can tightly enclose a true object ($T = 1$) but the classification result is uncertain (low P_{max}). An example is shown in Fig. 3(b).

The score of a box is denoted as J, which is computed per Eq. 1. Both conditions above can get value close to zero.

$$J(B_0^j) = |T(B_0^j) + P_{max}(B_0^j) - 1| \qquad (1)$$

As each image can have multiple predicted boxes, we calculate the score per image as: $T_I(I_i) = min_j J(B_0^j)$. Unlabeled images with low score will be selected to annotate in active learning. Since both the localization tightness and classification outputs are used in this metric, later we use LT/C to denotes methods with this score. Another way to approach this problem is using the objectiveness score of intermediate bounding boxes. It's not explored in this paper since it does not explicitly encode the localization information.

3.3   Localization Stability

The concept behind the localization stability is that, if the current model is stable to noise, meaning that the detection result does not dramatically change even if the input unlabeled image is corrupted by noise, the current model already understands this unlabeled image well so there is no need to annotate this unlabeled image. In other words, we would like to select images that have large variation in the localization prediction of bounding boxes when the noise is added into the image. This is similar to the idea of distributional smoothing with virtual adversarial training [33], which uses KL-divergence based robustness of the model distribution against local perturbation around the datapoint to ensure local smoothness. Our localization stability method selects images from where the model distribution has low local smoothness. Adding these images with annotation to the training set may ensure local smoothness.

Figure 4 overviews the idea to calculate the localization stability of an unlabeled image. We first detect bounding boxes in the original image with the current model. These bounding boxes when noise is absent are called reference boxes. The j-th reference box is denoted as B_0^j. For each noise level n, a noise is added to each pixel of the image. We use Gaussian noise where the standard deviation is proportional to the level n; namely, the pixel value can be changed more for higher level. After detecting boxes in the image with noise level n, for each reference box (the red box in Fig. 4), we find a corresponding box (green) in the noisy image to calculate how the reference box varies. The corresponding box is denoted as $C_n(B_0^j)$, which has the highest IoU value among all bounding boxes that overlap B_0^j.

Once all the corresponding boxes from different noise levels are detected, we can tell that the model is stable to noise on this reference box if the box does not significantly change across the noise levels. Therefore, the localization stability of each reference box B_0^j can be defined as the average of IoU between the reference box and corresponding boxes across all noise levels. Given N noise levels, it is calculated per Eq. 2:

$$S_B(B_0^j) = \frac{\sum_{n=1}^{N} IoU(B_0^j, C_n(B_0^j))}{N}, \tag{2}$$

With the localization stability of all reference boxes, the localization stability of this unlabeled image, says I_i, is defined based on their weighted sum per Eq. 3 where M is the number of reference boxes. The weight of each reference box is its highest class probability in order to prefer boxes with high probability as foreground objects but high uncertainty to their locations.

$$S_I(I_i) = \frac{\sum_{j=1}^{M} P_{max}(B_0^j) S_B(B_0^j)}{\sum_{j=1}^{M} P_{max}(B_0^j)}. \tag{3}$$

4 Experimental Results

Reference Methods: Since no prior work does active learning for deep learning based object detectors, we designate two informative baselines that show the impact of proposed methods.

- **Random (R):** Randomly choose samples from the unlabeled set, label them, and put them into labeled training set.
- **Classification only (C):** Select images only based on the classification uncertainty U_c in Sect. 3.1.

Our algorithm with two different metrics for the localization uncertainty are tested. First, the localization stability (Sect. 3.3) is combined with the classification information (**LS+C**). As images with high classification uncertainty and low localization stability should be selected for annotation, the score of the i-th image (I_i) image is defined as follows: $U_C(I_i) - \lambda S_I(I_i)$, where λ is the weight to combine both, which is set to 1 across all the experiments in this paper. Second, the localization tightness of predicted boxes is combined with the classification information (**LT/C**) as defined in Sect. 3.2.

We also test three variants of our algorithm. One uses the localization stability only (**LS**). Another is the localization tightness of predicted boxes combined with the classification information but using the localization tightness calculated from ground-truth boxes (**LT/C(GT)**) instead of the estimate used in LT/C. The other is combining all 3 cues together (**3in1**).

For the easiness of reading, data for LS and 3in1 are shown in the supplementary result. Our supplementary result also includes the mAP curves with error bars that indicate the minimum and maximum average precision (AP) out of multiple trials of all methods. Furthermore, experiments with different designs of LT/C are included in the supplementary result.

Datasets: We validated our algorithm on three datasets (PASCAL 2012, PASCAL 2007, MS COCO [5,19]). For each dataset, we started from a small subset of the training set to train the baseline model, and selected from the remained training images for active learning. Since objects in training images from these datasets have been annotated with bounding boxes, our experiments used these bounding boxes as annotation without asking human annotators.

Detectors: The object detector for all datasets is the Faster-RCNN (FRCNN) [26], which contains the intermediate stage to generate region proposals. We also tested our algorithm with the Single Shot multibox Detector (SSD) [20] on the PASCAL 2007 dataset. Because the SSD does not contain a region proposal stage, the tests for localization tightness were skipped. Both FRCNN and SSD used VGG16 [29] as the pre-trained network in the experiments shown in this paper.

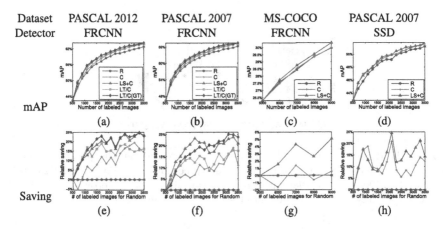

Fig. 5. Result on PASCAL 2012, PASCAL 2007, MS-COCO, and SSD, from left to right, respectively. (Top) Mean average precision curve of different active learning methods. Each point in the plot is an average of 5 trials. (Bottom) Relative saving of labeled images for different methods.

4.1   FRCNN on PASCAL 2012

Experimental Setup: We evaluate all the methods with the FRCNN model [26] using the RoI warping layer [2] on the PASCAL 2012 object-detection dataset [5] that consists of 20 classes. Its training set (5,717 images) is used to mimic a pool of unlabeled images, and the validation set (5,823 images) is used for testing. Input images are resized to have 600 pixels on the shortest side for all FRCNN models in this paper.

The numbers shown in following sections on PASCAL datasets are averages over 5 trails for each method. All trials start from the same baseline object detectors, which are trained with 500 images selected from the unlabeled image pool. After then, each active learning algorithm is executed in 15 rounds. In each round, we select 200 images, add these images to the existing training set, and train a new model. Each model is trained with 20 epoches.

Our experiments used Gaussian noise as the noise source for the localization stability. We set the number of noise level N to 6. The standard deviations of these levels are $\{8, 16, 24, 32, 40, 48\}$ where the pixels range from $[0, 255]$.

Results: Figure 5(a) and (e) show the mAP curve and the relative saving of labeled images, respectively, for different active learning methods. We have three major observations from the results on the PASCAL 2012 dataset. First, LT/C(GT) outperforms all other methods in most of the cases as shown in Fig. 5(e). This is not surprising since LT/C(GT) is based on the ground-truth annotations. In the region that achieves the same performance as passive learning with a dataset of 500 to 1,100 labeled images, the performance of the proposed LT/C is similar to LT/C(GT), which represents the full potential of LT/C. This

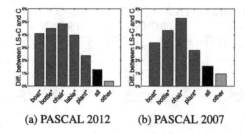

(a) PASCAL 2012   (b) PASCAL 2007

Fig. 6. The difference in difficult classes (blue bars) between the proposed method (LS+C) and the baseline method (C) in average precision on (a) PASCAL 2012 dataset (b) PASCAL 2007 dataset. Black and green bars are the average improvements of LS+C over C for all classes and non-difficult classes. (Color figure online)

implies that LT/C using the estimate of tightness of predicted boxes (Sect. 3.2) can achieve results close to its upper bound.

Second, in most of the cases, active learning approaches work better than random sampling. The localization stability with the classification uncertainty (LS+C) has the best performance among all methods other than LT/C(GT). In terms of average saving, LS+C and LT/C have 96.5% and 36.3% relative improvement over the baseline method C.

Last, we also note that the proposed LS+C method has more improvements in the difficult categories. We further analyze the performance of each method by inspecting the AP per category. Table 1 shows the average precision for each method on the PASCAL 2012 validation set after 3 rounds of active learning, meaning that every model is trained on a dataset with 1,100 labeled images. For categories with AP lower than 40% in passive learning (R), we treat them as difficult categories, which have a asterisk next to their name. For these difficult categories (blue bars) in Fig. 6a, we notice that the improvement of LS+C over C is large. For those 5 difficult categories the average improvement of LS+C over C is 3.95%, while the average improvement is only 0.38% (the green bar in

Table 1. Average precision for each method on difficult categories of PASCAL 2012 validation set after 3 rounds of active learning (number of labeled images in the training set is 1,100). Each number shown in the table is an average of 5 trials and displayed in percentage. Numbers in bold are the best results per column, and underlined numbers are the second best results. Categories with AP lower than 40% in passive learning (R) are defined as difficult categories and marked by asterisk.

Method	boat*	bottle*	chair*	table*	plant*	mAP
R	28.4	32.0	25.8	36.4	21.6	52.9
C	25.5	30.8	26.4	36.7	22.5	54.0
LS+C	**29.6**	**35.2**	**31.3**	_40.7_	**24.8**	**55.3**
LT/C	_29.5_	_33.8_	_29.5_	41.8	_23.2_	_54.7_

Fig. 6a) for the rest 15 non-difficult categories. This 10× difference shows that adding the localization information into active learning for object detection can greatly help the learning for difficult categories. It is also noteworthy that for those 5 difficult categories, the baseline method C performs slightly worse than random sampling by 0.50% in average. It indicates that C focuses on non-difficult categories to get an overall improvement in mAP.

4.2   FRCNN on PASCAL 2007

Experimental Setup: We evaluate all the methods with the FRCNN model [26] using the RoI warping layer [2] on the PASCAL VOC 2007 object-detection dataset [5] that consists of 20 classes. Both training and validation sets (total 5,011 images) are used as the unlabeled image pool, and the test set (4,952 images) is used for testing. All the experimental settings are the same as the experiments on the PASCAL 2012 dataset as mentioned Sect. 4.1.

Results: Figure 5(b) and (f) show the mAP curve and relative saving of labeled images for different active learning methods. In terms of average saving, LS+C and LT/C have 81.9% and 45.2% relative improvement over the baseline method C. Table 2 shows the AP for each method on the PASCAL 2007 test set after 3 rounds of active learning. The proposed LS+C and LT/C are better than the baseline classification-only method (C) in terms of mAP.

It is interesting to see that LS+C method has the same behavior as shown in the experiments on the PASCAL 2012 dataset. Namely, LS+C also outperforms the baseline model C on difficult categories. As the setting in experiments on the PASCAL 2012 dataset, categories with AP lower than 40% in passive learning (R) are considered as difficult categories. For those 4 difficult categories, the average improvement in AP of LS+C over C is 3.94%, while the average improvement is only 0.95% (the green bar in Fig. 6b) for the other 16 categories.

Table 2. Average precision for each method on PASCAL 2007 test set after 3 rounds of active learning (number of labeled images in the training set is 1,100). The other experimental settings are the same as shown in Table 1

Method	boat*	bottle*	chair*	plant*	mAP
R	40.0	33.6	34.5	25.9	57.3
C	36.8	34.4	34.0	24.9	57.8
LS+C	40.2	**38.7**	**39.6**	27.7	**59.4**
LT/C	**41.1**	38.4	36.4	**28.0**	58.6

4.3   FRCNN on MS COCO

Experimental Setup: For the MS COCO object-detection dataset [19], we evaluate three methods: passive learning (R), the baseline method using classification only (C), and the proposed LS+C. Our experiments still use the FRCNN model [26] with the RoI warping layer [2]. Compared to the PASCAL datasets, the MS COCO has more categories (80) and more images (80k for training and 40k for validation). Our experiments use the training set as the unlabeled image pool, and the validation set for testing.

The numbers shown in this section are averages over 3 trails for each method. All trials start from the same baseline object detectors, which are trained with 5,000 images selected from the unlabeled image pool. After then, each active learning algorithm is executed in 4 rounds. In each round, we select 1,000 images, add these images to the existing training set, and train a new model. Each model is trained with 12 epoches. We followed the same training parameters in [2] for MS COCO, but we reduced the number of GPUs from 8 to 1 in order to run more comprehensive experiments with limited GPU resources. The consequence is that our mini-batch size is essentially reduced too.

Results: Figure 5(c) and (g) show the mAP curve and the relative saving of labeled images for the testing methods. Figure 5(c) shows that classification-only method (C) does not have improvement over passive learning (R), which is not similar to the observations for the PASCAL 2012 in Sect. 4.1 and the PASCAL 2007 in Sect. 4.2. By incorporating the localization information, LS+C method can achieve 5% relative saving in the amount of annotation compared with passive learning, as shown in Fig. 5(g).

4.4   SSD on PASCAL 2007

Experimental Setup: Here we test our algorithm on a different object detector: the single shot multibox detector (SSD) [20]. The SSD is a model without an intermediate region-proposal stage, which is not suitable for the localization-tightness based methods. We test the SSD on the PASCAL 2007 dataset where the training and validation sets (total 5,011 images) are used as the unlabeled image pool, and the test set (4,952 images) is used for testing. Input images are resized to 300×300.

Similar to the experimental settings in Sects. 4.1 and 4.2, the numbers shown in this section are averages over 5 trails. All trials start from the same baseline object detectors which are trained with 500 images selected from the unlabeled image pool. After then, each active learning algorithm is executed in 15 rounds. A difference from previous experiments is that each model is trained with 40,000 iterations, not a fixed number of epochs. In our experiments, the SSD takes more iterations to converge. Consequently, when the number of labeled images in the training set is small, a fixed number of epochs means training with fewer number of iterations and the SSD cannot converge.

Results: Figure 5(d) and (h) show the mAP curve and the relative saving of labeled images for the testing methods. Figure 5(d) shows that both active learning method (C and LS+C) have improvements over passive learning (R). Figure 5(h) shows that in order to achieve the same performance of passive learning with a training set consists of 2,300 to 3,500 labeled images, the proposed

Table 3. Overlapping ratio between 200 images chosen by different active learning methods on the PASCAL 2012 and 2007 datasets after the first round. Each number represents the average over 5 trials.

	PASCAL 2012				PASCAL 2007			
C	3.5%				4.1%			
LS	4.0%	2.7%			4.2%	3.5%		
LS+C	4.4%	34.7%	34.6%		4.3%	34.0%	39.7%	
LT/C	5.0%	5.9%	2.4%	5.2%	5.6%	5.9%	4.5%	5.7%
Method	R	C	LS	LS+C	R	C	LS	LS+C

method (LS+C) can reduce the amount of image for annotation (12–22%) more than the baseline active learning method (C) (6–15%). In terms of average saving, LS+C is 29.0% better than the baseline method C.

5   Discussion

Estimate of Localization Tightness: Our experiment shows that if the ground truth of bounding box is known, localization tightness can achieve best accuracies, but the benefit degrades when using the estimated tightness instead. To analyze the impact of the estimate, after we trained the FRCNN-based object detector with 500 images of PASCAL2012 training set, we collected the ground-truth-based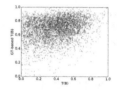
tightness and the estimated values of all detected boxes in the 5,215 test images. Figure in the right shows a scatter plot where the coordinates of each point represents the two scores of a detected box. As this scatter plot shows an upper-triangular distribution, it implies that our estimate is most accurate when the proposals can tightly match the final detection boxes. Otherwise, it could be very different from the ground-truth value. This could partially explain why using the estimated cannot achieve the same performance as the ground-truth-based tightness.

Relation Among the Metrics: As both proposed metrics LS+C and LT/C show improvement than random sampling and classification-only active learning, we also evaluate whether the selected images of both metrics are similar or different. We measured the overlapping ratio between images chosen by different active learning methods, as listed in Table 3. It clearly shows that the three metrics (C, LS, LT/C) not just select very different images from random sampling, but the overlapping among them are also low. This indicates that these three active learning metrics select very different types of images. We also tested combining the three metrics into a single metric, which nevertheless did not outperform LS+C. More detail discussions can be seen in the supplementary materials.

Computation Speed: The computation overhead of our evaluation metrics is small, which adds 21% of time to the forward propagation through the FRCNN model. The calculation of localization stability S_I is slowest, as it needs to run the detector multiple times. Since these metrics are automatic to calculate, nevertheless, using our approach to reduce the number of images to annotate is still cost-efficient, as one bounding box needs 20 s to draw in average [32], especially that we can reduce 20–25% of images to annotate.

6 Conclusion

In this paper, we present an active learning algorithm for object detection. When selecting unlabeled images for annotation to train a new object detector, our algorithm considers both the classification and localization results of the unlabeled images. With two metrics to quantitatively evaluate the localization uncertainty, our experiments show that by considering the localization uncertainty, our active learning algorithm can outperform existing active learning with the classification outputs alone. As a result, we can train object detectors to achieve the same accuracy with fewer annotated images.

Acknowledgments. This work was conducted during the first author's internship in Mitsubishi Electric Research Laboratories. This work was sponsored in part by National Science Foundation grant #13-21168.

References

1. Bietti, A.: Active learning for object detection on satellite images. Technical report, California Institute of Technology, January 2012
2. Dai, J., He, K., Sun, J.: Instance-aware semantic segmentation via multi-task network cascades. In: CVPR (2016)
3. Dai, J., Li, Y., He, K., Sun, J.: R-FCN: object detection via region-based fully convolutional networks. In: NIPS (2016)
4. Dutt Jain, S., Grauman, K.: Active image segmentation propagation. In: CVPR (2016)
5. Everingham, M., Van Gool, L., Williams, C.K.I., Winn, J., Zisserman, A.: The PASCAL Visual Object Classes (VOC) challenge. Int. J. Comput. Vis. **88**(2), 303–338 (2010)
6. Freytag, A., Rodner, E., Denzler, J.: Selecting influential examples: active learning with expected model output changes. In: Fleet, D., Pajdla, T., Schiele, B., Tuytelaars, T. (eds.) ECCV 2014. LNCS, vol. 8692, pp. 562–577. Springer, Cham (2014). https://doi.org/10.1007/978-3-319-10593-2_37
7. Girshick, R.: Fast R-CNN. In: ICCV (2015)
8. Hasan, M., Roy-Chowdhury, A.K.: Continuous learning of human activity models using deep nets. In: Fleet, D., Pajdla, T., Schiele, B., Tuytelaars, T. (eds.) ECCV 2014. LNCS, vol. 8691, pp. 705–720. Springer, Cham (2014). https://doi.org/10.1007/978-3-319-10578-9_46
9. Hasan, M., Roy-Chowdhury, A.K.: Context aware active learning of activity recognition models. In: ICCV (2015)

10. Hoffman, J., et al.: LSDA: large scale detection through adaptation. In: NIPS (2014)
11. Huijser, M., van Gemert, J.C.: Active decision boundary annotation with deep generative models. In: ICCV (2017)
12. Islam, R.: Active learning for high dimensional inputs using Bayesian convolutional neural networks. Master's thesis, Department of Engineering, University of Cambridge, August 2016
13. Kapoor, A., Grauman, K., Urtasun, R., Darrell, T.: Active learning with Gaussian processes for object categorization. In: ICCV (2007)
14. Kapoor, A., Grauman, K., Urtasun, R., Darrell, T.: Gaussian processes for object categorization. Int. J. Comput. Vis. **88**(2), 169–188 (2010). https://doi.org/10.1007/s11263-009-0268-3
15. Karasev, V., Ravichandran, A., Soatto, S.: Active frame, location, and detector selection for automated and manual video annotation. In: CVPR (2014)
16. Konyushkova, K., Sznitman, R., Fua, P.: Introducing geometry in active learning for image segmentation. In: ICCV (2015)
17. Lewis, D.D., Catlett, J.: Heterogeneous uncertainty sampling for supervised learning. In: ICML (1994)
18. Lin, T.Y., Goyal, P., Girshick, R., He, K., Dollar, P.: Focal loss for dense object detection. In: ICCV (2017)
19. Lin, T.Y., et al.: Microsoft COCO: common objects in context. In: Fleet, D., Pajdla, T., Schiele, B., Tuytelaars, T. (eds.) ECCV 2014. LNCS, vol. 8693, pp. 740–755. Springer, Cham (2014). https://doi.org/10.1007/978-3-319-10602-1_48
20. Liu, W., et al.: SSD: single shot multibox detector. In: Leibe, B., Matas, J., Sebe, N., Welling, M. (eds.) ECCV 2016. LNCS, vol. 9905, pp. 21–37. Springer, Cham (2016). https://doi.org/10.1007/978-3-319-46448-0_2
21. Najibi, M., Rastegari, M., Davis, L.S.: G-CNN: an iterative grid based object detector. In: CVPR (2016)
22. Papadopoulos, D.P., Uijlings, J.R.R., Keller, F., Ferrari, V.: We don't need no bounding-boxes: training object class detectors using only human verification. In: CVPR (2016)
23. Prest, A., Leistner, C., Civera, J., Schmid, C., Ferrari, V.: Learning object class detectors from weakly annotated video. In: CVPR (2012)
24. Redmon, J., Divvala, S., Girshick, R., Farhadi, A.: You only look once: unified, real-time object detection. In: CVPR (2016)
25. Redmon, J., Farhadi, A.: YOLO9000: better, faster, stronger. In: CVPR (2017)
26. Ren, S., He, K., Girshick, R., Sun, J.: Faster R-CNN: towards real-time object detection with region proposal networks. In: NIPS (2015)
27. Russakovsky, O., Li, L.J., Fei-Fei, L.: Best of both worlds: human-machine collaboration for object annotation. In: CVPR (2015)
28. Settles, B.: Active learning literature survey. Univ. Wis. Madison **52**(55–66), 11 (2010)
29. Simonyan, K., Zisserman, A.: Very deep convolutional networks for large-scale image recognition. arXiv preprint arXiv:1409.1556 (2014)
30. Sivaraman, S., Trivedi, M.M.: Active learning for on-road vehicle detection: a comparative study. Mach. Vis. Appl. **25**(3), 599–611 (2014). https://doi.org/10.1007/s00138-011-0388-y
31. Stark, F., Hazirbas, C., Triebel, R., Cremers, D.: Captcha recognition with active deep learning. In: GCPR Workshop on New Challenges in Neural Computation, Aachen, Germany (2015)

32. Su, H., Deng, J., Fei-Fei, L.: Crowdsourcing annotations for visual object detection. In: Workshops at the Twenty-Sixth AAAI Conference on Artificial Intelligence (2012)
33. Miyato, T., Maeda, S.I., Koyama, M., Nakae, K., Ishii, S.: Distributional smoothing with virtual adversarial training. In: ICLR (2016)
34. Tong, S., Koller, D.: Support vector machine active learning with applications to text classification. J. Mach. Learn. Res. **2**, 45–66 (2002)
35. Uijlings, J.R.R., van de Sande, K.E.A., Gevers, T., Smeulders, A.W.M.: Selective search for object recognition. Int. J. Comput. Vis. **104**(2), 154–171 (2013)
36. Vijayanarasimhan, S., Grauman, K.: Large-scale live active learning: training object detectors with crawled data and crowds. Int. J. Comput. Vis. **108**(1–2), 97–114 (2014)
37. Yoo, D., Park, S., Lee, J., Paek, A.S., Kweon, I.: AttentionNet: aggregating weak directions for accurate object detection. In: ICCV, pp. 2659–2667 (2015)
38. Zhang, S., Wen, L., Bian, X., Lei, Z., Li, S.Z.: Single-shot refinement neural network for object detection. In: CVPR (2018)

Deep Inverse Halftoning via Progressively Residual Learning

Menghan Xia[1,2] and Tien-Tsin Wong[1,2(✉)]

[1] The Chinese University of Hong Kong, Sha Tin, Hong Kong
{mhxia,ttwong}@cse.cuhk.edu.hk
[2] Shenzhen Key Laboratory of Virtual Reality and Human Interaction Technology,
SIAT, Shenzhen, China

Abstract. Inverse halftoning as a classic problem has been investigated in the last two decades, however, it is still a challenge to recover the continuous version with accurate details from halftone images. In this paper, we present a statistic learning based method to address it, leveraging Convolutional Neural Network (CNN) as a nonlinear mapping function. To exploit features as completely as possible, we propose a Progressively Residual Learning (PRL) network that synthesizes the global tone and subtle details from the halftone images in a progressive manner. Particularly, it contains two modules: Content Aggregation that removes the halftone patterns and reconstructs the continuous tone firstly, and Detail Enhancement that boosts the subtle structures incrementally via learning a residual image. Benefiting from this efficient architecture, the proposed network is superior to all the candidate networks employed in our experiments for inverse halftoning. Also, our approach outperforms the state of the art with a large margin.

Keywords: Inverse halftoning · Progressive learning

1 Introduction

Halftoning is the rendering of continuous-tone pictures on media where only two levels can be displayed. The problem arose in the late 19th century when printing machines attempted to print images on paper. This was accomplished by adjusting the size of the dots according to local image intensity, called analog halftoning. And digital halftoning, as a kind of image processing technique, transforms a continuous-tone image with discrete gray levels into a bi-level halftone image. It has been used in bi-level output devices such as printers, copiers, fax machines, and even in plasma display panels, for example, the inkjet printers use halftone image to determine the spatial position of the ink that drops on paper

Electronic supplementary material The online version of this chapter (https://doi.org/10.1007/978-3-030-20876-9_33) contains supplementary material, which is available to authorized users.

© Springer Nature Switzerland AG 2019
C. V. Jawahar et al. (Eds.): ACCV 2018, LNCS 11366, pp. 523–539, 2019.
https://doi.org/10.1007/978-3-030-20876-9_33

by the heating and localized vaporization of liquid in a jet chamber [14]. The commonly used halftoning methods are the clustered-dot dithering, blue-noise dithering, error diffusion, and direct binary search [4, 25, 28, 32].

Inverse halftoning, the counter process of digital halftoning, reconstructs a continuous-tone image with 255 levels or more levels from its halftoned version [23]. As a kind of important image restoration, there are a wide range of applications of inverse halftoning. First, working with effective inverse halftoning techniques, digital halftoning might be used as an image compression method by representing images with lower bits. In addition, photos printed on books, magazines showing halftone patterns can be scanned and transformed into a continuous-tone image, which is especially meaningful for those historically important photos on old newspapers. Further, continuous-tone images also need to be reconstructed for image manipulations, such as sharpening, resizing, rotation, or tone correction to obtain much better results [31]. However, due to the inevitable information loss during the halftoning process, inverse halftoning of image is an ill-posed problem. Anyway, it is still possible to approximate a continuous-tone image from its bi-level origins since the uniform dot patterns could give a visual impression of gray. This indicates that a simple low-pass filter is applicable to halftoning inverse, but the results by such a simple operation are prone to blur and artifacts. Thus, one reasonable solution for inverse halftoning is to provide enough prior information to guide the reconstruction of continuous-tone images, which is just the reason why the look up table (LUT) based approach [22] has been the state-of-the-art among all the conventional methods. However, this heuristic strategy that continuous-tone patch is used to replace the halftone patch based on the neighboring information can only achieve results of limited quality.

Inspired by the powerful representation ability of CNN, we propose to address this problem through training a CNN model as a nonlinear function in supervised manner. That is to say, by learning the corresponding pairs of halftone and continuous-tone images, the trained CNN would be embedded with prior knowledge and be able to reconstruct any continuous-tone image from its halftone input because of its generalization ability. Generally, recovering the continuous tone from a halftone image involves two tasks: the one is to synthesize the global tone, and the other is to extract the structural details. Considering this nature, we specifically design a PRL network that consists of two corresponding modules: Content Aggregation and Detail Enhancement. Under an end-to-end training scheme, the content aggregation module synthesizes an initial continuous-tone images firstly, and the detail enhancement module further extracts fine structures by learning a residual image. Convincing experimental results illustrates the superiority of PRL over several candidate networks with typical architectures, especially in recovering subtle structures. In addition, running on the inverse halftoning benchmark, our approach set a new state-of-the-art performance.

2   Related Works

As our approach exploits CNN to address the classic problem of inverse halftoning, we review on the conventional inverse halftoning algorithms and typical/relevant CNN works.

2.1   Conventional Inverse Halftoning

Over the last decades, a variety of inverse halftoning methods have been proposed. Although a simple low-pass filtering can remove most of the halftoning noise but it also removes edge information. Thus, most of works have been focused on developing an edge preserving filter while suppressing the visible dot patterns. Given the prior knowledge about a specific halftone pattern, customized filters are proposed to compute continuous grayscale values [12,33] based on neighboring dot patterns. Without requiring prior information, Analoui et al. [1] propose a method of projection onto convex sets for halftone images produced by ordered dithering. This method has also been successfully applied for the tone restoration of error diffused halftones [9]. Another method for inverse halftoning of error diffused images is introduced by Kite et al. [15], which exploits space varying filtering based on gradients on the halftone images. Leveraging the overcomplete wavelet expansions, Xiong et al. [35] propose to separate the halftoning noises from the original image through edge detection, which outperforms all the other competing methods at that time.

Different from those aforementioned methods, Mese et al. [22] creatively propose to precompute a look up table (LUT) first and all the continuous-tone values are assigned depending on the neighborhood distribution of pixels in template. As reported in [24], the LUT based method is extremely fast and has a reconstructed quality comparable to the state-of-the-art methods of that time. This is reasonable since plenty of prior statistic information is provided for inverse halftoning in LUT. Attracted by this merit, most of recently proposed methods have taken the strategy of dictionary learning for inverse halftoning [5,30,31].

2.2   Convolutional Neural Networks

Recent deep CNNs have become a common workhorse behind a wide variety of image transformation problems. These problems can be formulated as per-pixel classification or regression by defining low level loss. Semantic segmentation methods [2,21,27] use fully convolutional neural networks trained by per-pixel classification loss to predict dense scene labels. End-to-end automatic image colorization techniques [16,19] try to colorize grayscale image based on low level losses. Other works for depth [3] and edge detection [34] are also similar to transform input images to meaningful output images through CNN, which are trained with per-pixel classification or regression loss. Denoise [36] and super-resolution [11,17] networks use CNNs to remove noise and generate fine structures respectively, which can be roughly regarded as two subtasks of inverse halftoning. Thus, some useful architecture elements of such networks might be used as reference, such as residual learning. Besides, most networks for image transformation use high-level feature spaces defined by pretrained CNN or generative adversarial networks (GAN) [7] to guarantee their output within the photo-realistic domain.

The outstanding ability of representing complex mappings makes deep CNN popular in various application. However, many works show that they are difficult to train because of the notorious vanishing gradient problem. To address problem, He et al. [8] propose the concept of residual blocks that use an "identity shortcut connection" to relieves the vanishing gradient issue. Models based on residual blocks have shown impressive performance in generative networks. However, some other works for image generation tasks [18,26] find that the batch normalization (BN) [20] used in residual block impedes the flexibility of the network, and they use the residual block with BN removed. These experimental conclusions are well absorbed in our network architecture.

3   Methodology

We formulate the inverse halftoning as image transformation problems and employ deep CNN as a nonlinear function to map halftone images to their continuous-tone version. The network architecture and loss function are presented in Sects. 3.1 and 3.2 respectively.

3.1   Network Architecture

As shown in Fig. 1, the proposed PRL network consists of two modules: content aggregation and detail enhancement. The content aggregation module begins with a normal convolutional layer and a residual block [8], followed by two downscaling blocks to spatially compress and encode the global information of

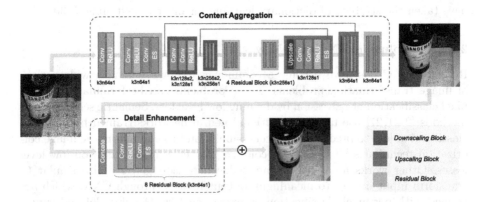

Fig. 1. Architecture of the proposed PRL network, where k is the kernel size, n is the number of feature maps and s is the stride in each convolutional layer, and ES denotes elementwise adding layer for feature maps.

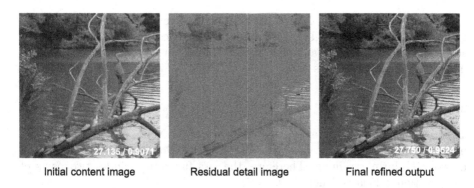

| Initial content image | Residual detail image | Final refined output |

Fig. 2. Output illustration of each module in the PRL network. For quantitative reference, the PSNR/SSIM against the groundtruth are annotated along.

the image. Then four residual blocks [8] with identical layout are used to construct the content and tone features, followed by two upscaling blocks bring the feature maps back to the input resolution. In detail enhancement module, we sequentially lay eight residual blocks to extract structural details in an incremental way. Such a simple yet effective strategy of using residual blocks is firstly adopted in the state-of-the-art super-resolution network [17] which majors in extracting fine structures from low-resolution images. Besides, providing auxiliary contextual cue, the output of content aggregation module is fed into the detail enhancement module along with the halftone input through a concatenation layer. Some readers might notice that the residual blocks used in our network use no batch normalization, which benefits in maintaining a higher flexibility of CNN [18,26]. The detailed parameters of each convolutional layer are annotated aside them in Fig. 1.

Residual learning framework facilitates the learning efficiency of CNN. However, we can not employ the normal residual learning architecture directly because of the large gap between the input and the output in inverse halftoning problem. The key idea of PRL is to first generate an initial result which is roughly the same as the groundtruth and then focus on extracting those subtle information by learning a residual image of the initial result and the groundtruth. For inverse halftoning, the first task is relatively easier, and even a simple CNN with several layers is enough to remove halftone noise. Nonetheless, a more advanced architecture contributes to generating more details. The real challenge lies in how to recover those subtle structures from halftone patterns as accurate as possible. In our PRL network, an initial continuous-tone image is firstly synthesized by the content aggregation module, and then the residual image between the initial image and the groundtruth is learned incrementally by the detail enhancement module. Through this way, much richer details could be recovered on the final reconstructed continuous-tone image that is the sum of the initial image and the optimized residual image. The output examples of each component are illustrated in Fig. 2. As we can observe, the residual image mainly contains tiny boundaries and subtle textures. Even though the output with refined details only outperforms the initial image slightly in quantitative metrics, those further enhanced structural and texture details play an very importance role in contributing to more photo-realistic results.

3.2 Loss Function

To strengthen the feature extraction efficiency of CNN, we provide supervising information for the output of both content aggregation module G and the full network F during training. Therefore, the loss function includes two parts of computation, which is denoted as:

$$\mathcal{L}(F) = \mathcal{L}_{content}(G) + \omega\mathcal{L}_{full}(F), \tag{1}$$

where ω is a weight to balance the two terms and $\omega = 1.5$ is used in all of our experiments. Obviously G is a part of F.

Let $\mathcal{P} = \{(\mathbf{I}_h^i, \mathbf{I}_c^i)\}_{i=1}^n$ be the whole training pairs of halftone image $\mathbf{I}_h$ and its continuous-tone version $\mathbf{I}_c$. $\mathcal{L}_{content}$ describes the difference between the predicted initial image $G(\mathbf{I}_h^i)$ and its ground truth $\mathbf{I}_c^i$. Considering this term only involves recovering the global information of the continuous-tone image, we employ the Mean Square Error (MSE) to compute its loss, expressed as:

$$\mathcal{L}_{content} = \mathbb{E}_{(\mathbf{I}_h^i, \mathbf{I}_c^i) \in \mathcal{P}}\{||G(\mathbf{I}_h^i) - \mathbf{I}_c^i||_2\} \tag{2}$$

where $||\bullet||_2$ denotes the L_2 norm (MSE). $\mathbb{E}$ denotes to compute the average loss over all the training set $\mathcal{P}$. Although achieving particularly high PSNR, the optimization results under MSE loss often lack high-frequency details which shows perceptually unsatisfying effects with overly smooth textures. Therefore, to compute the loss of the final output $F(\mathbf{I}_h^i)$, we use a measure metric that is closer to perceptual similarity together with pixel-wise L_1 loss. To define the perception loss, we adopt the high-level feature maps of the pretrained VGG network [29] which has been demonstrated to have good object preservation ability. Accordingly, $\mathcal{L}_{full}$ is formulated in Eq. 3.

$$\mathcal{L}_{full}(F) = \mathbb{E}_{(\mathbf{I}_h^i, \mathbf{I}_c^i) \in \mathcal{P}}\{\alpha||VGG_l(F(\mathbf{I}_h^i)) - VGG_l(F(\mathbf{I}_c^i))||_2 + ||\mathbf{I}_h^i - \mathbf{I}_c^i||_1\} \tag{3}$$

where $||\bullet||_1$ denotes the L_1 norm. l refers to the feature maps of a specific VGG layer. Alike to [6], $l = conv4\_4$ is used. $\alpha = 2.0 \times 10^{-6}$ is used to balance the magnitude difference between deep feature space and pixel value space.

3.3 Data Preparation and Training

There are lots of image halftoning algorithms, such as ordered dithering, error diffusion, etc. In this paper, we take the most popular one, Floyd Steinberg error diffusion, as an example for inverse halftoning experiments. Applying it to the others would the same story. Particularly, the publicly available VOC2012

Dataset[1] is used in experiment, of which over 13,000 images are randomly selected as our training images. We crop and resize them to 256 × 256 without aspect distortion as the continuous-tone groundtruth, and then employ the error diffusion algorithm on them to get the corresponding halftone images. Note that our network can process images of any size during testing phase since it is a fully convolutional network.

We implement our network with TensorFlow in Python language. All experiments are performed on an PC with one GPU of NVIDIA GeForce GTX 1080 Ti. We train our network end-to-end for 150 epochs. The learning rate is set as 0.0002 initially and linearly decreases to 0.0002/100 in the end. Adam [13] is employed to optimize the network parameters.

4   Results and Discussion

We perform experiments on two testing datasets, of which the one (*dataset-1*) contains 3000 images from VOC2012 dataset that has no overlap with the training part, the other (*dataset-2*) contains 5000 images that are randomly picked from PLACE205 Dataset[2]. For quantitative evaluation, we employ PSNR and SSIM to measure the similarity between the reconstructed images and the groundtruth. For color image, they are calculated in every channel of RGB color space independently and the average values are used. However, as presented in [17] by mean opinion score testing, PSNR and SSIM fail to capture and accurately assess image quality with respect to the human visual system. The focus of this paper is the perceptual quality of the reconstructed continuous-tone images, so we recommend readers to pay more attention to the qualitative evaluation.

Particularly, to concentrate on the essential problem of inverse halftoning, the gray version of the two datasets are used for evaluation and analysis. The code is available at: https://github.com/MenghanXia/InverseHalftoning.

Table 1. PSNR and SSIM obtained by the plain-architecture network and our PRL network.

Network	*dataset-1*		*dataset-2*	
	PSNR	SSIM	PSNR	SSIM
Plain architecture	29.676	0.8807	29.567	0.8912
PRL architecture	29.705	0.8797	29.567	0.8919

4.1   Effect of the PRL Architecture

To show the superiority of the proposed PRL architecture, we compare it with a plain version of our network that sequentially joints the content aggregation

---

[1] VOC2012: http://host.robots.ox.ac.uk/pascal/VOC/voc2012/.
[2] PLACE205: http://places.csail.mit.edu/index.html.

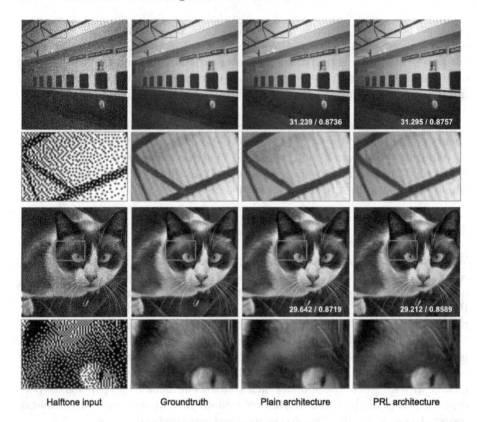

| Halftone input | Groundtruth | Plain architecture | PRL architecture |

Fig. 3. Results of networks of plain architecture and the proposed PRL architecture. For detail observation, typical regions within blue box are enlarged below each image. (Color figure online)

module and detail enhancement module without residual learning scheme. As the comparative results shown in Fig. 3, the PRL network has an superiority over the plain one in generating more accurate structural lines and richer details. This can be explained by that residual learning can ease the difficulty of learning the transformation from the input to the output, because it only need to synthesize a residual image instead of the whole output. Since there is obvious gap between the input and the output in inverse halftoning problem, it is not reasonable to directly apply the normal residual learning architecture that is widely used in denoise network or super-resolution network. Instead we propose a progressively residual learning strategy that is especially suitable for the inverse halftoning task. Quantitative results are listed in Table 1. Even the superiority in PSNR and SSIM is minor, it dose have some visually observable benefits on the reconstructed images.

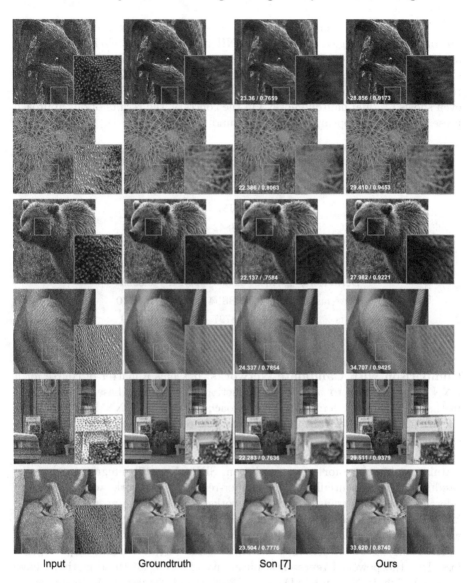

| Input | Groundtruth | Son [7] | Ours |

Fig. 4. Results of the state of the art [31] and our approach on the benchmark images. For quantitative comparison, PSNR and SSIM of each image are annotated along. The average values of [31] and ours are 23.002/0.7762 and 30.680/0.9232 respectively.

4.2 Comparative Evaluation

Comparison with State of the Art: The latest inverse halftoning work [31] that exploits local learned dictionaries for edge optimization has been the state-of-the-art approach so far. Here, we compare it with our CNN based approach on six benchmark images. The benchmark images and the results of [31] are downloaded from the website provided on their paper. The comparative results are illustrated in Fig. 4, where the PSNR and SSIM of each image are also annotated for reference. As we can observe, our approach have a great superiority over the state of the art in both qualitative and quantitative evaluation. The results of [31] are overly smooth and lack of texture details, and some regions even shows residual halftone noise. On the contrary, the results of our approach present very close appearance to the groundtruth.

Table 2. Comparison on PSNR and SSIM obtained by different methods.

Method	dataset-1		dataset-2	
	PSNR	SSIM	PSNR	SSIM
DnCNN	**29.967**	0.8842	29.865	0.8961
VDSR	29.763	0.8822	29.791	0.8948
SRResNet	29.708	0.8763	29.608	0.8890
DeHalftone	29.404	0.8809	29.247	0.8929
Ours(mse)	29.914	**0.8854**	**29.915**	**0.8970**
Ours	29.705	0.8797	29.567	0.8919

Comparison with Candidate Networks: It seems a matter of course for a CNN based method to outperform a dictionaries learning based conventional method. We further compare our approach with other CNN based state-of-the-art methods of relevant tasks, like denoise and super resolution, which are extended for inverse halftoning here. DnCNN [36] exploits the residual learning idea for image noise removal. VDSR [11] employs a network with residual learning architecture for super resolution. SRResNet [17] integrates a seres of residual block sequentially in their super-resolution network, which is widely referenced in image transformation networks. Note that the upscaling layers of VDSR and SRResNet are removed in order to make them fit to our task. Besides, we also compare our approach with an unpublished method of inverse halftoning (DeHalftone) [10] that combines a normal U-Net architecture with perception loss. Due the powerful representation ability of CNN, all these methods have achieved high PSNR and SSIM on *dataset-1* and *dataset-2*, as illustrated in Table 2. Moreover, the quantitative differences is quite small, which might be explained by that all the methods are flexible enough to cover the transformation from halftone to continuous tone but their performances are just limited to the information capacity carried by the halftone input. Anyway, DnCNN and VDSR have the relatively higher PSNR and SSIM among all the methods, because they only employ MSE loss that conforms to the computation of PSNR and SSIM. We also provide the result of our approach with using MSE loss only, which shows improved PSNR and SSIM as well.

However, the higher PSNR and SSIM do not necessarily means the better visual quality, since the MSE loss benefits to a higher PSNR and SSIM but tends to cause perceptually unsatisfying effects with overly smooth textures. As illustrated in Figs. 7 and 8, we present comparatively qualitative results of difference methods on representative images from *dataset-1* and *dataset-2* respectively. Observing as a whole, the continuous-tone version of halftone images are recovered by all the methods equally in quality. When we take a close look at local details, as presented in those enlarged regions, some reconstruction differences among the results of different methods can be further observed, which are not well reflected by PSNR and SSIM. Thanks to the PRL architecture that works on both global and subtle features, our approach achieves the best reconstruction accuracy, especially in those slight but semantically important structure lines. This well illustrates the effectiveness of residual learning. Anyhow, for inverse halftoning, the PRL architecture outperforms the normal residual learning architecture used in DnCNN, VDSR and SRResNet.

4.3 Extended Applications

Providing corresponding training data, our method can be employed for several exciting applications. Ordered dithering is widely used for printing media, which transforms normal photos into halftone before printed on books or newspapers. Training our model with such halftone categories, we can transform those printed

Printing halftone   Reconstructed results

Fig. 5. Reconstruction results from printing halftone: ordered dithering.

GIF halftone   Reconstructed results

Fig. 6. Reconstruction results from GIF halftone: error diffusion.

halftone photos back to their original continuous-tone version. This is especially meaningful for those historically important photos that only exist on printed materials now. In Fig. 5, we present two examples demonstrating this application. With a continuous-tone image, we can further apply all kinds of image editing and processing on them, while they are impossible for halftone images.

Besides, storing a digital image in Graphics Interchange Format (GIF) also employs error diffusion, where only 256 colors are sampled to rendering the whole image based on its color distribution. Because of information loss, images of GIF often present annoying visual artifacts. Training our model with such halftone images, we can transform such quantized images back to the visually pleasing continuous version. Two examples of this application are demonstrated in Fig. 6. In addition, we also provide a video demo displaying the dynamic effect of our processed results in the supplementary file.

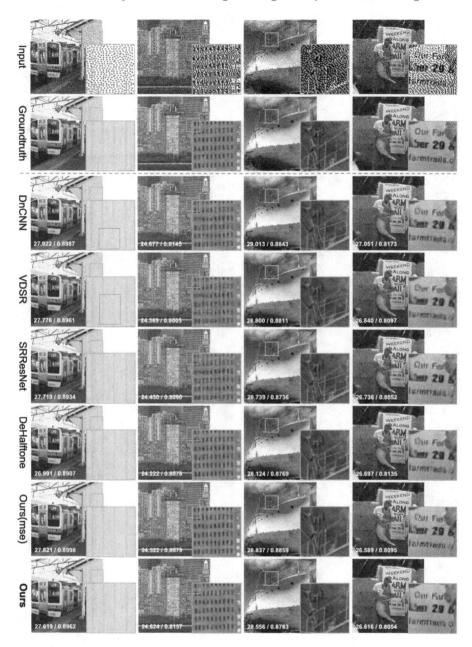

Fig. 7. Qualitative comparisons among different methods on selected images of *dataset-1*. Typical region marked with blue box are enlarged for detail observation (red dash box indicates reconstruction of low accuracy). For quantitative reference, the PSNR and SSIM of each image are annotated. (Color figure online)

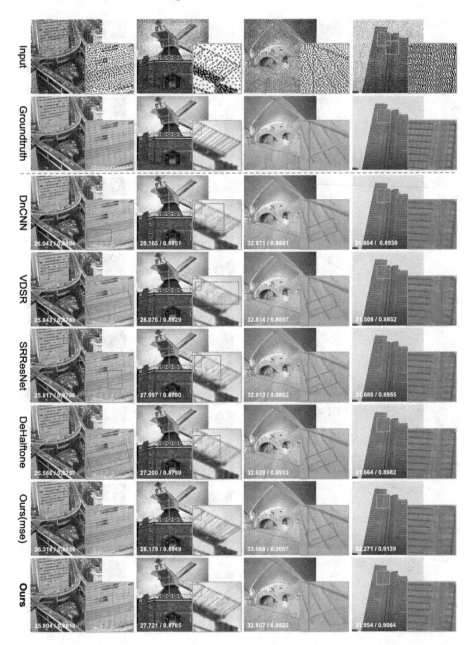

Fig. 8. Qualitative comparisons among different methods on selected images of *dataset-2*. Typical region marked with blue box are enlarged for detail observation (red dash box indicates reconstruction of low accuracy). For quantitative reference, the PSNR and SSIM of each image are annotated. (Color figure online)

5   Conclusion

We proposed a PRL network that shows outstanding performance in accurately reconstructing continuous-tone images from halftone images. Running on the benchmark dataset, our approach outperforms the state of the art with a significant margin both qualitatively and quantitatively. In addition, comparing our network with other candidate networks shows that all the methods have obtained a very close PSNR and SSIM but they have significantly different performances on details recovery. It means the widely used PSNR and SSIM could not effectively reflect the perceptual quality of the results. Anyway, comparative results on enlarged regions illustrate the superiority of our approach in accurately recovering structural details. Besides, applying our approach to other halftone categories enables two practical applications successfully.

Acknowledgement. This project is supported by Shenzhen Science and Technology Program (No. JCYJ20160429190300857) and Shenzhen Key Laboratory (No. ZDSYS201605101739178), and the Research Grants Council of the Hong Kong Special Administrative Region, under RGC General Research Fund (Project No. CUHK14201017).

References

1. Analoui, M., Allebach, J.: New results on reconstruction of continuous-tone from halftone. In: Proceedings of the IEEE International Conference on Acoustics, Speech, and Signal Processing (ICASS) (1992)
2. Eigen, D., Fergus, R.: Predicting depth, surface normals and semantic labels with a common multi-scale convolutional architecture. In: Proceedings of the IEEE International Conference on Computer Vision (ICCV) (2015)
3. Eigen, D., Puhrsch, C., Fergus, R.: Depth map prediction from a single image using a multi-scale deep network. In: the Advances in Neural Information Processing Systems (NIPS) (2014)
4. Floyd, R.W.: An adaptive algorithm for spatial gray-scale. In: Society of Information Display (1976)
5. Freitas, P.G., Farias, M.C., Araujo, A.P.: Enhancing inverse halftoning via coupled dictionary training. Sig. Process.: Image Commun. **49**, 1–8 (2016)
6. Gatys, L., Ecker, A.S., Bethge, M.: Texture synthesis using convolutional neural networks. In: Advances in Neural Information Processing Systems (NIPS) (2015)
7. Goodfellow, I., et al.: Generative adversarial nets. In: Advances in Neural Information Processing Systems (NIPS) (2014)
8. He, K., Zhang, X., Ren, S., Sun, J.: Deep residual learning for image recognition. In: Proceedings of the IEEE Conference on Computer Vision and Pattern Recognition (CVPR) (2016)
9. Hein, S., Zakhor, A.: Halftone to continuous-tone conversion of error-diffusion coded images. Sigma Delta Modulators **213**, 133–154 (1993)
10. Hou, X., Qiu, G.: Image companding and inverse halftoning using deep convolutional neural networks. arXiv preprint arXiv:1707.00116 (2017)
11. Kim, J., Lee, J.K., Lee, K.M.: Accurate image super-resolution using very deep convolutional networks. In: Proceedings of the IEEE Conference on Computer Vision and Pattern Recognition (CVPR) (2016)

12. Kim, Y.T., Gonzalo, R.A., Nikolai, G.: Inverse halftoning using binary permutation filters. IEEE Trans. Image Process. (TIP) **4**(9), 1296–1311 (1995)
13. Kingma, D.P., Ba, J.: Adam: a method for stochastic optimization. arXiv preprint arXiv:1511.06349 (2014)
14. Kipphan, H.: Handbook of Print Media. Springer, Heidelberg (2001). https://doi. org/10.1007/978-3-540-29900-4
15. Kite, T.D., Niranjan, D.V., Brian, L.E., Alan, C.B.: A high quality, fast inverse halftoning algorithm for error diffused halftones. In: Proceedings of the IEEE International Conference on Image Processing (ICIP) (1998)
16. Larsson, G., Maire, M., Shakhnarovich, G.: Learning representations for automatic colorization. In: Leibe, B., Matas, J., Sebe, N., Welling, M. (eds.) ECCV 2016. LNCS, vol. 9908, pp. 577–593. Springer, Cham (2016). https://doi.org/10.1007/ 978-3-319-46493-0_35
17. Ledig, C., et al.: Photo-realistic single image super-resolution using a generative adversarial network. In: Proceedings of the IEEE Conference on Computer Vision and Pattern Recognition (CVPR) (2017)
18. Lim, B., Son, S., Kim, H., Nah, S., Lee, K.M.: Enhanced deep residual networks for single image super-resolution. In: Proceedings of the IEEE Conference on Computer Vision and Pattern Recognition Workshops (2017)
19. Lizuka, S., Simo-Serra, E., Ishikawa, H.: Let there be color!: joint end-to-end learning of global and local image priors for automatic image colorization with simultaneous classification. ACM Trans. Graph. (TOG) **35**(4), 110–121 (2016)
20. Loffe, S., Szegedy, C.: Batch normalization: accelerating deep network training by reducing internal covariate shift. In: IEEE International Conference on Machine Learning (ICML) (2015)
21. Long, J., Shelhamer, E., Darrell, T.: Fully convolutional networks for semantic segmentation. In: Proceedings of the IEEE Conference on Computer Vision and Pattern Recognition (CVPR) (2015)
22. Mese, M., Palghat, P.V.: Look-up table (LUT) method for inverse halftoning. IEEE Trans. Image Process. (TIP) **10**(10), 1566–1578 (2001)
23. Mese, M., Vaidyanathan, P.P.: Recent advances in digital halftoning and inverse halftoning methods. IEEE Trans. Circ. Syst. **49**(6), 790–806 (2002)
24. Mese, M., Vaidyanathan, P.P.: Recent advances in digital halftoning and inverse halftoning methods. IEEE Trans. Circ. Syst. I: Fundam. Theory Appl. **49**(6), 790–805 (2002)
25. Mitsa, T., Parker, K.J.: Digital halftoning technique using a blue-noise mask. JOSA A **9**(11), 1920–1929 (1992)
26. Nah, S., Kim, T.H., Lee, K.M.: Deep multi-scale convolutional neural network for dynamic scene deblurring. In: Proceedings of the IEEE Conference on Computer Vision and Pattern Recognition (CVPR) (2017)
27. Noh, H., Hong, S., Han, B.: Learning deconvolution network for semantic segmentation. In: Proceedings of the IEEE International Conference on Computer Vision (ICCV) (2015)
28. Seldowitz, M.A., Allebach, J.P., Sweeney, D.W.: Synthesis of digital holograms by direct binary search. Appl. Opt. **26**(14), 2788–2798 (1987)
29. Simonyan, K., Zisserman, A.: Very deep convolutional networks for large-scale image recognition. arXiv preprint arXiv:1409.1556 (2014)
30. Son, C.H.: Inverse halftoning based on sparse representation. Opt. Lett. **37**(12), 2352–2354 (2012)
31. Son, C.H., Choo, H.: Local learned dictionaries optimized to edge orientation for inverse halftoning. IEEE Trans. Image Process. (TIP) **23**(6), 2542–2557 (2014)

32. Ulichney, R.A.: Dithering with blue noise. In: Proceedings of the IEEE (1988)
33. Wong, P.W.: Inverse halftoning and kernel estimation for error diffusion. IEEE Trans. Image Process. (TIP) **4**(4), 486–498 (1995)
34. Xie, S., Tu, Z.: Holistically-nested edge detection. In: IEEE International Conference on Computer Vision (ICCV) (2015)
35. Xiong, Z., Michael, T.O., Kannan, R.: Inverse halftoning using wavelets. IEEE Trans. Image Process. (TIP) **8**(10), 1479–1483 (1999)
36. Zhang, K., Zuo, W., Chen, Y., Meng, D., Zhang, L.: Beyond a Gaussian denoiser: residual learning of deep cnn for image denoising. IEEE Trans. Image Process. (TIP) **26**(7), 3142–3155 (2017)

Dynamic Random Walk for Superpixel Segmentation

Lei Zhu, Xuejing Kang$^{(\boxtimes)}$, Anlong Ming, and Xuesong Zhang

Beijing University of Posts and Telecommunications, Beijing, China
kangxuejing@bupt.edu.cn

Abstract. In this paper, we present a novel Random Walk model called Dynamic Random Walk (DRW) for superpixel segmentation. The proposed DRW adds a new type of node called dynamic node to enrich the features of labels and reduce redundant calculation. By greedily optimizing the Weighted Random Walk Entropy (WRWE), our DRW can consider the features of both seed nodes and dynamic nodes, which enhances the boundary adherence. In addition, a new seed initialization strategy, which can evenly distribute seed nodes in both 2D and 3D space, is proposed to extend our DRW for superpixel segmentation. With this strategy, our DRW can generate superpixels in only one iteration without updating seed nodes. The experiment results show that our DRW is faster than existing RW models, and better than the state-of-the-art superpixel segmentation algorithms in both efficiency and the performance.

1 Introduction

Image segmentation is a basic technic in computer vision. It focuses on partitioning an image into multiple regions. Superpixel segmentation, a branch of image segmentation, is proposed to segment the image into compact small regions. Comparing with the single pixel, superpixel can carry the features of region such as histogram features and reduce the calculation. Therefore, it has been used in many computer vision tasks as a preprocessing step, such as image segmentation [15], object tracking [22], object detection [21] and depth ordering [3,8].

Many superpixel segmentation algorithms are proposed in the last decade. These algorithms can be divided into two types: the gradient-based algorithms such as the SLIC [1], the SNIC [2], the MSLIC [12] and the SEEDS [4]; the graph-based algorithms such as the ERS [11] and the LRW [17]. However, both of them have their own advantages and drawbacks. The gradient-based algorithms usually have satisfactory time complexity, but lack of boundary adherence. This means the superpixels will carry features of different objects, which will confuse the following processes. In contrast to the gradient-based algorithms, graph-based algorithms work well in adhering boundaries but suffer from inefficiency, which makes them inappropriate for real-time tasks. Few superpixel algorithms

© Springer Nature Switzerland AG 2019
C. V. Jawahar et al. (Eds.): ACCV 2018, LNCS 11366, pp. 540–554, 2019.
https://doi.org/10.1007/978-3-030-20876-9_34

can make a balance between efficiency and performance. In this paper, we aim to propose a superpixel algorithm which can partly solve this problem.

In this paper, we propose a novel Random Walk model called Dynamic Random Walk (DRW), which is more suitable for superpixel segmentation. Comparing with the original RW [7], our DRW adds a new type of node called dynamic node to enrich the features of labels and reduce the redundant calculation. By optimizing the Weighted Random Walk Entropy (WRWE), our DRW can be appropriately solved. This solution not only uses the features of dynamic nodes but also concerns the significance of different nodes. When using the WRWE, we judge the nodes rather than the edges, which can improve the weak-boundary adherence and omit the redundancy seed nodes. Then a seed initialization strategy, which can evenly distribute seed nodes in both 2D and 3D space, is proposed to our DRW for superpixel segmentation. With this strategy, our DRW can generate superpixels in one iteration, which improves the efficiency.

2   Related Work

The existing superpixel segmentation algorithms can be divided into two main types: the gradient-based algorithms and the graph-based algorithms. The former usually base on iteratively clustering the pixels into some groups with high efficiency. The most popular one is the SLIC [1], which firstly adopts the thought of limiting search range to the superpixel segmentation. This method uses k-means cluster in a limited scope to generate superpixels, which greatly improves its efficiency. But, its boundary adherence is not good enough due to the limited scope and it still need almost 7 iterations to update the cluster centers. To further speed up the SLIC algorithm, Achanta [2] proposes the SNIC to greedily generate superpixels in only one iteration with a priority queue and a cluster center update strategy. However, its time efficiency is not improved a lot, because the logarithm of priority queue length $log(n)$ is similar to the iteration times of SLIC, which makes the SNIC's time efficiency $O(log(n) * N)$ not always lower than the SLIC's $O(iter * N)$. Moreover, the center update strategy makes the boundary adherence of the SNIC rather worse. The MSLIC [12] is another SLIC-based algorithm, which uses the gradient information to convert the fixed search range of the SLIC into a dynamic one. This strategy can make superpixels small in the complex texture area and big in the smooth area, which generates a better boundary adherence, but it still only uses the features of pixel. The SEEDS [4] is another famous gradient-based algorithm which considers the features of region rather than pixel's. It randomly changes the boundary pixels' label in the initial superpixels and use hill-climbing algorithm to optimize an energy function formed by the histogram features. This method can finish in real time and has a relatively good boundary adherence. But due to its randomness, its superpixels usually have irregularity shape, which is inconvenient to be used.

The other branch of superpixel segmentation algorithms are the graph-based algorithms which use a graph model to represent an image. Majority of them come from the graph-based image segmentation algorithms, such as the RW [17] and the NCut [16], so they usually have a great boundary adherence. The ERS [11] is a typical graph-based superpixel segmentation method which uses the Random Walk Entropy to generate superpixels. It adds edges into a new graph by greedy strategy to maximize the new graph's entropy, which avoids generating the initial seeds and improves the efficiency. Like the SNIC, the ERS also uses a priority queue, but the length of this queue is the same as the number of edges in graph, so its time complexity is $O(Nlog(N))$. The LRW [17] is another graph-based superpixel segmentation algorithm derived from the RW [7] model. It adds a self-loop on the model to concern the global relationship and extends the model for the superpixel task by proposing an energy function to update the seed node in each iteration. This function makes the LRW superpixels more compact but weaken the boundary adherence. Comparing with gradient-based algorithms, graph-based algorithms often cost a lot time due to the complexity of the graph model and their superpixels usually have irregular shape.

Like the LRW, our DRW model is also based on the RW, it is essential for us to review some related works about it. The RW [7] is a famous segmentation algorithm which acts perfectly in detecting weak-boundary, but it cannot segment twigs well. So, a series of RW derivation algorithms are developed to deal with this problem. The PARW [20] adds a self-loop for every node to catch global structure. Different from that in the LRW, this self-loop is used to absorb walk process. Benefitting from it, the PARW can use the absorbing probability to judge the unseed nodes' label, which concerns the global structure. The RWR [9] generates a return probability for every unseed node by adding edges between every unseed node and seed node. This return probability allows the RWR using the steady probability to judge the label of unseed nodes, so that more graph structures can be explored. To combine these different type of RW models, the SubRW [6] gives a framework and uses it to create a new type RW model with the Gaussian Mixture Model. Those RW models are all created for capturing the global structure. Although they can improve the performance, their graph models are statical, which makes seed nodes search the whole graph and makes unseed nodes labeled after finishing all searches. So, those models depend too much on the initial seeds and suffer from inefficiency. When the number of seed nodes is small, the segmentation performance will be bad. What's more, an inverse matrix must be computed to solve these models costing at least $O(kN^2)$ time complexity with the QR deposition [19], where k is the number of different labeled seeds. Those drawbacks will be magnified when facing superpixel segmentation, which need to efficiently segment the image with only a single seed node for each label. Our DRW is proposed to deal with these problems so as to efficiently generate better segmentation with a small number of seeds.

3   The Dynamic Random Walk

In this section, a new type of RW model called Dynamic Random Walk is firstly proposed, which can reduce the calculation and collect more features. Then, the solution of our DRW using the WRWE and the greedy strategy is given. Finally, we discuss the advantages of our DRW in efficiency and boundary adherence.

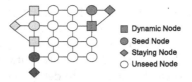

Fig. 1. The Dynamic Random Graph Model. Different color means different label. In this graph, we omit the killing node. (Color figure online)

3.1   The Model of DRW

When given an input image, a directed graph $G = (V, E)$ is constructed, where V represents the node set formed by pixels of image and E represents the edges which only connect the 4 neighbor nodes. Figure 1 shows the graph model of our DRW. A matrix $W(w_{ij})$ is defined to represent the weight of edges:

$$w_{ij} = exp(-\|I_i - I_j\|/\sigma) \tag{1}$$

where I_i and I_j are the intensity of node i and node j, σ is a parameter.

Different from the existing RW algorithms in [6,7,9,17,20], we add dynamic nodes into the graph model, which can catch some features because each of them has a label as seed nodes. Therefore, the node set V are further divided into three types: seed node set V_m, unseed node set V_u, and dynamic node set V_d, where $V_m \cup V_u \cup V_d = V$. The seed node set V_m is the set of the prelabeled nodes, and the unseed node set V_u is the set of unlabeled nodes.

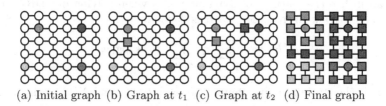

(a) Initial graph   (b) Graph at t_1 (c) Graph at t_2 (d) Final graph

Fig. 2. The process of the Dynamic Random Walk.

During the random walk process, dynamic nodes are progressively added into the graph model. At the begining there is no dynamic node in G as Fig. 2(a). When an unseed node generates the maximal increment of the Weight Random Walk Entropy, it will be labeled and converted into a dynamic node as Fig. 2(b) and (c). This process will continue until all unseed nodes are labeled. Our transition probability of G is defined as:

$$p_{ij} = \begin{cases} (1 - c_i)\frac{w_{ij}}{d_i} & i \in V_u \text{ and } j \in V_u \cup V_m \cup V_d \\ (1 - c_i)\frac{w_{ij}}{d_i} & i \in V_m^{l_k} \cup V_d^{l_k} \text{ and } j \in V_m^{l_k} \cup V_d^{l_k} \\ (1 - c_i)(1 - \sum_{l \in V^{l_k}} \frac{w_{il}}{d_i}) & i \in V_m^{l_k} \cup V_d^{l_k} \text{ and } j \in S^{l_k} \\ c_i & i \in V_u \cup V_m \cup V_d \text{ and } j \in \triangle \\ 1 & i, j \in \triangle \text{ or } i, j \in S^{l_k} \\ 0 & \text{others} \end{cases} \tag{2}$$

where V^{l_k} means the node set whose label is l_k, and c_i is a parameter for node i. Two types of auxiliary nodes: staying nodes S and killing node $\triangle$ are also added into G to make the degree $D(d_i)$ of each node satisfy: $d_i = \sum_j p_{ij} = 1$, as in [6].

From (2), we can see that different from the transition matrix of the RW [7], our DRW model isolates every labeled area to determine that labeled nodes can not walk into different labeled areas. By this means, low probability walks or redundancy calculation can be avoided, e.g., an unseed node walks cross some same labeled nodes and reach an different labeled seed. The parameter c_i is used to control the probability to deactivate an random walk, which can improve the boundary adherence like the self-loop in the LRW [17].

3.2 The Solution of DRW

The solution of the RW can be seen as labeling every unseed node by its first arrival probabilities to seed nodes. This process can be quantified and solved in a matrix way costing at least $O(N^2)$ time complexity, more detail of it can be seen in [6,7]. However, our DRW cannot be solved in this way because the structure of our graph is changing every moment, which means that the matrix can not be constructed. Here we propose a solution to solve our DRW model based on the WRWE and the greedy strategy.

The Weighted Random Walk Entropy. The Random Walk Entropy defined in [5] can reflect the similarity of the area by the features of all nodes in this area, so it can utilize the features of dynamic nodes when solving our DRW model. The Random Walk Entropy of area R is defined:

$$H(R) = - \sum_{i \in V_R} \pi_i \sum_{j \in Nb(i)} p_{ij} * \log(p_{ij}) \tag{3}$$

where π_i is the stationary distribution probability of i and $Nb(i)$ is the neighbor node set of i.

Due to the property of transition probability matrix $P(p_{ij})$ in our DRW model ($\sum_j p_{ij} = 1$) and the definition of stationary distribution: $\pi P = \pi$, we can get $\pi_i = 1/|V|$, which means π_i is a constant for every node i. To evaluate the different influence of each node, we give a weight function $\omega(i)$ for $H(R)$ and use $g(i)$ to merge the weight function with the constant stationary distribution π_i, i.e., $g(i) = \omega(i)/|V|$. The WRWE of R is defined as:

$$H_w(R) = - \sum_{i \in V_R} g(i) \sum_{j \in Nb(i)} p_{ij} * \log(p_{ij}) \tag{4}$$

From the transformation probability in (2), every labeled area is isolated to others. If the graph G has k isolated labeled areas, the WRWE of G can be defined as:

$$H_w(G) = \sum_{i=1}^{k} H_w(R_i) \tag{5}$$

In this way, our DRW model can be solved by progressively labeling the unseed nodes and converting them into dynamic nodes to maximize the WRWE of G until all unseed nodes have been labeled. When converting an unseed node, all its labeled neighbor nodes will bring variation to H_w. According to (2) and (4), the variation of H_w at the labeled area R_k can be calculated by:

$$\triangle H_w^k(i) = \sum_{j \in V^{l_k}} [\Omega(j)E(a_j) - \Omega(i)E(1 - p_{ij}) - \Omega(j)E(a_j - p_{ji})$$
$$- \Omega(i)E(p_{ij}) - \Omega(j)E(p_{ji})] \tag{6}$$

where $a_j = 1 - \sum_{j \in V^{l_k}} p_{im}$, $\Omega(x) = (1 - c_x)g(x)$, $E(x) = x * log(x)$.

Greedy Strategy. In our DRW, with some restriction for Ω, the WRWE in (5) has two mathematical properties: **Monotonically increasing** and **Submodularity**. This means the H_w is increasing when an unseed node i is labeled, and the increment is greater than labeling this unseed node later. Next, we will prove these properties and give the pseudocode of the greedy strategy.

Theorem 1. *A set function H_w is monotonically increasing if $H_w(R_1) \leqslant H_w(R_2)$ for all $R_1 \supseteq R_2$.*

Proof. When an unseed node i is added into the labeled area R_k, the increment of H_w is defined in (6). We can reformulate (6) with $b_i = 1 - p_{ij}$, $b_j = a_j - p_{ji}$, obviously $b_i \geq 0$, $b_j \geq 0$. Note that $E(b_i + p_{ij}) = E(1) = 0$, we can also add it into (6). Then, with the help of the monotonically increasing of $f(x) = log(x)$, which makes $log(p_{ij} + b_i) \geq log(p_{ij})$ and $log(p_{ij} + b_i) \geq log(b_i)$, we can get $\triangle H_w^k(i) \geq 0$, so H_w is monotonically increasing.   □

Theorem 2. *Let V be a finite set. A set function H_w is submodularity if $H_w(R \cup i) - H_w(R) \geqslant H_w(R \cup j, i) - H_w(R \cup j)$ for all $R \supseteq V$, $i, j \in V$ and $i, j \notin R$.*

Proof. From the definition of our DRW model, there is an unseed node labeled every time, so we can use the time t to represent for the labeled node's number. When the number of the nodes in labeled area increases (t increases), p_{ij} will not change, so the variables are a_j and Ω in (6). Thus $d\triangle H_w^k/dt$ can be calculated. Then with the property that a_j decreases as t rises, we can easily prove that $d\triangle H_w^k/dt \leq 0$ when $d\Omega/dt \leq 0$, which means H_w is submodularity.   □

So, greedy strategy can be used to solve our model with these two properties, when $d\Omega/dt \leq 0$. Algorithm 1 shows the pseudocode of this greedy solution.

Algorithm 1. DRW solution

```
INPUT: image I, probability matrix P, seed set S, priority queue Q
OUTPUT: assigned label map L
1 :    FOR s in S DO
2 :        push element e (pos_s, l_s, MAX) in Q
```

```
 3 :   WHILE Q is not empty DO
 4 :       pop Q to get e_i(pos_i, l_k, dH_w(i))
 5 :       IF pos_i has not been labeled
 6 :       L[pos_i] = l_k
 7 :           update transport probability of i and i's neighbors
 8 :           FOR each connected neighbor pos_j of pos_i Do
 9 :               IF pos_j has not been labeled
10:                   calculate the entropy increasing dH_w(j)
11:                   push element e_j(pos_j, l_k, dH_w(j)) in Q
12:   RETURN L
```

3.3 Advantages of the Proposed DRW

Time Complexity. Our DRW algorithm has 3 main steps: initializing the weight matrix, choosing the unseed node and labeling unseed nodes. First, in the initializing step, the weight matrix between every pixel and its 4-neighbour pixels can be calculated in $O(4N)$ complexity, where N is the number of pixels. Second, in the step of choosing the unseed node, the greedy strategy can be done with a priority queue, which costs $O(logn)$ to add the element and $O(1)$ to find the maximal element, where n is the maximal length of the queue. Finally, in the labeling step, one unseed node is labeled at every moment, so it takes $O(N)$ to label all unseed nodes. Thus, the time efficiency of our algorithm is $O(4N + Nlogn)$. In experiments, the number n is much more less than N, so the time complicity of our DRW is nearly $O(N)$, which is much lower than the $O(N^2)$ time complexity of other RW models [6,7,9,17,20].

Lack-Seed Segmentation. Considering that our DRW labels an unseed node every moment, which keeps enriching the features during the solving process, our DRW can collect more features than other RW algorithms whose features are only provided by the seed nodes. These abundant features are also utilized by the WRWE to constitute the labeled region's features, which can also reflect the importance of each labeled nodes by the weight function $\Omega(i)$.

Benefitting from this characteristic, our DRW can deal with the lack-seed problem (the amount of same labeled seed nodes is too small to represent the object's features). From Fig. 3, we can see that when encountering this problem, other RW models perform worse than our DRW, or even have a wrong result.

Seed Filtering. Seed filter is useful for the non-supervision segmentation task whose seed nodes are generated by algorithm. Redundancy seeds are the different labeled seed pairs which are in close and similar areas. Our DRW enlarges the optimal seed's region which is similar to its neighbors first. So when the walk reaches the unseed node around other seeds, the unseed node prefer being labeled by the optimal seed. What's more, the filter strength can be controlled by setting Ω. This characteristic also brings our DRW the adaptivity to get more superpixels for the complex texture image and less for the smooth one.

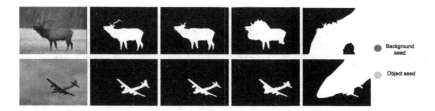

Fig. 3. Lack-seed segmentation of RW-based algorithms. From left to right is the original picture, result of our DRW, the RW [7], the RWR [9] and the LRW [17].

Figure 4(a) shows the mechanism of seed filter in our DRW. Because of the greedy strategy (discussed in Sect. 3.2), our DRW prefers firstly labeling the unseed node which is more similar to the seed. So if there are two seeds in a similar small region, our DRW expands the optimal one. For the unseed nodes in this small region like u in Fig. 4(a), our DRW concerns more edges of seed a than the redundancy seed d, so u prefers to have the same label as a.

Weak-Boundary Adherence. Weak-boundary means that the pixels around boundary is similar to those out of this boundary. Weak-boundary adherence is a characteristic of RW algorithm, our DRW inherits it by considering the WRWE increment of nodes rather than that of edges. From Fig. 4(b) we can see that the entropy increment of weak boundary pixel u is affected by the edges of its three labeled neighbor nodes a, b, c. So u has more probability to have the same label with a and b rather than c.

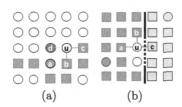

(a)   (b)

Fig. 4. (a) Seed filter of our DRW. (b) Weak-boundary adherence of our DRW. The thick full line means the boundary and the thick imaginary line means weak-boundary.

4   Dynamic Random Walk for Superpixel Segmentation

In this section, we use our DRW model for superpixel segmentation. Comparing with the RW-based algorithms whose efficiency and performance are not very satisfactory for superpixel segmentation, our DRW outperform the other state-of-the-art superpixel algorithms. What's more, our algorithm also has the adaptivity to automatically control the number of superpixels for different images. The DRW superpixel segmentation algorithm has three steps: initializing the seed nodes, creating the graph model of our DRW and solving this model to generate superpixels. In this algorithm we propose a new seed initialization strategy to generate superpixels in only one iteration. A suitable weight function of the WRWE is also defined for our DRW superpixel segmentation algorithm.

4.1   Seed Initialization Strategy

We propose an initialization method to generate seed nodes for our DRW superixels segmentation algorithm. First, the area of a 2-manifold camber $A(p)$ is calculated to represent the gradient information for every pixel p as the MSLIC [12]. Then seeds are produced by averaging the distribution of area in both 2D and 3D space. Given an maximum number of superpixel k, we can get the 2D and the 3D average area S_{2D}, S_{3D} by the function:

$$S_{2D} = N/(4k), \quad S_{3D} = \sum_{i \in V} A(i)/k \tag{7}$$

where N is the number of pixels in image. Figure 5 shows the principle of seed initialization strategy. First, grid seeds are produced by choosing the centre pixel of grids whose 2D area is equal to $S_{2D}/4$ as in Fig. 5(a). Then, we only select the seed s which satisfies $\sum_{i \in grid(s)} A(i) > S_{3D}$ to be the final seed as in Fig. 5(b). Algorithm 2 (lines 2 to 7) shows the pseudocode of this strategy.

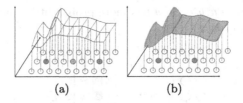

(a)   (b)

Fig. 5. (a) The 2D average generation. (b) The 3D average generation.

4.2   Weight Function of the WRWE

A weight function Ω is created for the DRW superpixel task. Considering the seed nodes in superpixel segmentation are generated by the algorithm rather than labeled by human, the feature of seed nodes is not more significant than that of dynamic nodes. Besides, due to the greedy strategy, the early labeled dynamic node is more important than the later labeled one. Therefore, for superpixel segmentation task, the weight function Ω of the WRWE in (6) is defined as:

$$\Omega(i) = (1 - c_i)g(i) = (1 - c_i)\omega(i)/N = (1 - 10^{-5}) * e^{-\beta * C(i)}/A(i) \tag{8}$$

where $C(i)$ means i is the $C(i)th$ labeled pixel in its labeled area, N is the number of pixels, β is a parameter, which can indirectly decide the seed filter intensity of our DRW. The weight function Ω also takes account of the gradient information by the term $A(i)$, which means pixels of smooth areas play a dominant role in the entropy. Obviously, $d\Omega/dt < 0$, greedy strategy can be used to solve the DRW from the discussion in Sect. 3.2.

4.3 DRW Superpixel Segmentation Algorithm

Now, we introduce our superpixel segmentation algorithm with the DRW model and a big root priority queue Q. First, we initialize the adjacency matrix W. Then we calculate the initial probability matrix P by (2). After that we use the strategy in Sect. 4.1 to initialize the seed nodes and then apply the DRW model to segment superpixels with the priority queue. Algorithm 2 shows the detail of DRW superpixel algorithm.

Algorithm 2. DRW superpixel segmentation algorithm

```
INPUT: image I, number K, probability matrix P, feature graph A
OUTPUT: Assigned label map L
1 :    initialize L[N*N] = 0, S = NULL, sum_3D = 0
2 :    calculate average area S_2D = N / (4*k), S_3D = sum(A)/k
3 :    FOR every center node of 2D grid s
4 :        sum_3D += S_3D(grid)
5 :        IF sum_3D > S_3D
6 :            s --> S, sum_3D = 0
7 :    Use Algorithm 1 to get L
8 :    RETURN L
```

5 Experimental Result

In this section, we compare our DRW superpixel algorithm to other state-of-the-art superpixel algorithms on the Berkeley 500 dataset with the benchmark toolbox proposed by Neubert [14]. The parameter σ is set 50 and β is set 10^{-3}. We use the original code released online for all methods, including SLIC [1], SNIC [2], SEEDS [4], ERS [11], LRW [17], NCut [16], PB [13], DBSCN [18]. The results show that our algorithm performs better than all these algorithms.

Adherence and Shape. The graph-model of our DRW guarantees the boundary adherence of superpixels as described in Sect. 3. And the weight function of the WRWE limits the search range of each seed node, which makes superpixels have a relatively regular shape and improves the efficiency. From Fig. 6, we can see that comparing with other superpixel algorithms, our DRW has a relative regular shape and a good boundary adherence. While the regular shape superpixels generated by SLIC, SNIC, LSC cannot adhere the boundary well, and the better adherence superpixels generated by ERS, SEEDS have irregular shape. However, our DRW can get a balance between this two properties.

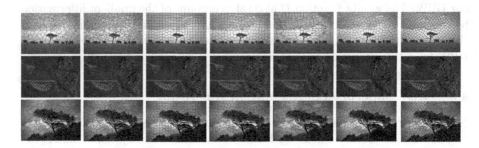

Fig. 6. Superpixel segmentation results with nearly 300 superpixels. From left to right is our DRW, the ERS [11], the SLIC [1], the LSC [10], the SEEDS [4], the LRW [17] and the DBSCN [18].

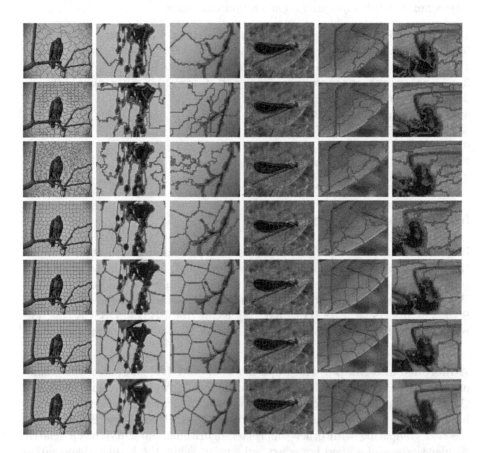

Fig. 7. Trigs segmentation results with nearly 300 superpixels. From top to down is the result of our DRW, the SEEDS [4], the ERS [11], the LSC [10], the SLIC [1], the SNIC [2], the LRW [17].

Fig. 8. The results of adaptivity. From left to right the beta is $10^{-3}, 10^{-4}, 10^{-5}, 0.?$

Twig Segmentation. Our DRW takes account of all edges that combine the unseed nodes and labeled areas, so it can better segment the weak-boundary and trig parts. Figure 7 shows the segmentation result of different algorithms with 300 superpixels. Our DRW performs better in the thin strip areas such as twigs and legs. Only our DRW and the ERS perform well in those strip areas, and our segments have more regular shape than that of the ERS.

Adaptivity. Another characteristic of our algorithm is that our DRW can control the superpixels compactness in smooth areas by the parameter β. Figure 8 shows the result about difference β, all those segmentations have nearly 500 superpixels. We can see that our DRW can get different number of superpixls for the smooth areas by setting different parameter without lower the adherence of complex areas. This characteristic makes our DRW have the ability to control the number of background superpixels for the smooth areas without weaken the performance and it also brings the adaptivity for our DRW to generate different number superpixels for different texture complexity images.

Boundary Recovery. Boundary Recall (BR) and Boundary Precision (BP) are the evaluation criterions which measure the percentage of the natural boundaries recovered by the superpixel boundaries, more detail of these criterions can be seen in [2]. We use the precision-recall curve (BP-BR) and F-Measure to evaluate boundary recovery of our DRW superpixel algorithm. F-Measure is a combination of BR and BP, we define F-Measure as: $F = \frac{2*BR*BP}{BR+BP}$. From Fig. 9(a) and (b), we can see that DRW have a much higher F-Measure and BP-BR curve, which means our DRW can well balance the recall and precision in adhering boundaries.

Undersegmentation Error. Undersegmentation error (UE) is another evaluation criterion for superpixel algorithm. The UE is used to measure how much the superpixels flood over the ground truth segmentation borders. The UE and the BR are the standard benchmark for superpixel segmentation. Due to the adaptivity (seed filter) of our DRW, we cannot compare the BR and the UE by increasing the superpixels number. So, we compare them for the non-adaptive DRW, which restrains the adaptivity of our DRW by judging the mean WRWE increment of the neighbor nodes. Therefore, the non-adaptive DRW can generate the accurate number superpixels. From Fig. 9(c) and (d) we can see that the BR and the UE of the non-adaptive DRW is better than most of the other algorithms which means that our DRW can generate superpixels with good performance (Table 1).

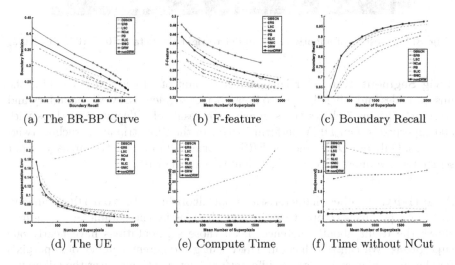

(a) The BR-BP Curve   (b) F-feature   (c) Boundary Recall

(d) The UE   (e) Compute Time   (f) Time without NCut

Fig. 9. Quantitative result of our DRW compared with other superpixel algorithms.

Compute Time. Comparing the solution process of our DRW shows in Fig. 2 and original RW algorithm discussed in [7], we can see that our DRW can be viewed as a semi-parallel algorithm which can simultaneously consider all seed nodes. While original RW in [7] only considers one labeled seed node set in each traversal. What's more, for every seed node, its search region in our DRW is the same as the number of dynamic nodes in its labeled region, while in the RW is the whole graph. We compare the compute time of our DRW with other superpxiel algorithms. From Fig. 9(e) and (f), we can see that our DRW has an

Table 1. The results of the BSDS500 with 1500 superpixels corresponding to Fig. 9.

	Graph-Based				Gradient-Based		
	Ours	NCut	LRW	ERS	SNIC	LSC	DBS
F ↑	0.418	0.362	0.302	0.345	0.341	0.374	0.349
BP ↑	0.280	0.231	0.193	0.214	0.220	0.237	0.219
BR ↑	0.961	0.904	0.846	0.961	0.877	0.948	0.922
UE ↓	0.062	0.065	0.078	0.053	0.058	0.052	0.070
T(s)	0.464	25.67	344.0	2.532	0.091	0.675	0.033

outstanding efficiency than the graph-based algorithms such as the ERS, the Ncut, and the LRW, and close or faster than the gradient-based algorithms. The runtime of the LRW algorithm is more than a few minutes (nearly 250 s for 300 superpixels in our experiment), so we do not add it to our figures.

6 Conclusions

We have proposed a novel Dynamic Random Walk model which is more suitable for the superpixel segmentation task. The DRW have two main advantages over original RW model: great efficiency and abundant feature. It can be solved by greedily optimizing the Weighted Random Walk Entropy. Our method also brings the property of seed filter, which can omit redundancy seed nodes. What's more, a superpixel segmentation algorithm is proposed based on our DRW model, in which a novel seed initialization strategy is applied to further speed up the DRW.

Further work will contribute to propose an unsupervised segmentation algorithm based on our DRW. Different from the existing RW-based segmentation algorithm which depend heavily on the pre-labeled seed node, our DRW can take account of both the seed node and the dynamic node. This trait will make our DRW more robust for unsupervised segmentation task.

Acknowledgement. This work was supported in part by the National Natural Science Foundation of China (61701036, 61871055), Fundamental Research Funds for the Central Universities (2018RC54).

References

1. Achanta, R., Shaji, A., Smith, K., Lucchi, A., Fua, P., Süsstrunk, S.: Slic superpixels compared to state-of-the-art superpixel methods. IEEE Trans. Pattern Anal. Mach. Intell. **34**(11), 2274–2282 (2012)
2. Achanta, R., Susstrunk, S.: Superpixels and polygons using simple non-iterative clustering. In: IEEE Conference on Computer Vision and Pattern Recognition, pp. 4895–4904 (2017)

3. Amer, M.R., Yousefi, S., Raich, R., Todorovic, S.: Monocular extraction of 2.1D sketch using constrained convex optimization. Int. J. Comput. Vis. **112**(1), 23–42 (2015)

4. Bergh, M.V.D., Boix, X., Roig, G., Capitani, B.D., Gool, L.V.: Seeds: superpixels extracted via energy-driven sampling. Int. J. Comput. Vis. **111**(3), 298–314 (2013)

5. Cover, T.M., Thomas, J.A.: Elements of Information Theory. Wiley, Tsinghua University Press (1991)

6. Dong, X., Shen, J., Shao, L., Gool, L.V.: Sub-Markov random walk for image segmentation. IEEE Trans. Image Process. **25**(2), 516–527 (2015)

7. Grady, L.: Random Walks for Image Segmentation. IEEE Computer Society (2006)

8. Jia, Z.: A learning-based framework for depth ordering. In: IEEE Conference on Computer Vision and Pattern Recognition, pp. 294–301 (2012)

9. Kim, T.H., Lee, K.M., Lee, S.U.: Generative image segmentation using random walks with restart. In: Forsyth, D., Torr, P., Zisserman, A. (eds.) ECCV 2008. LNCS, vol. 5304, pp. 264–275. Springer, Heidelberg (2008). https://doi.org/10. 1007/978-3-540-88690-7_20

10. Li, Z., Chen, J.: Superpixel segmentation using linear spectral clustering. In: Computer Vision and Pattern Recognition, pp. 1356–1363 (2015)

11. Liu, M.Y., Tuzel, O., Ramalingam, S., Chellappa, R.: Entropy rate superpixel segmentation. In: Computer Vision and Pattern Recognition, pp. 2097–2104 (2011)

12. Liu, Y.J., Yu, C.C., Yu, M.J., He, Y.: Manifold SLIC: a fast method to compute content-sensitive superpixels. In: Computer Vision and Pattern Recognition, pp. 651–659 (2016)

13. Martin, D.R., Fowlkes, C.C., Malik, J.: Learning to detect natural image boundaries using local brightness, color, and texture cues. IEEE Trans. Pattern Anal. Mach. Intell. **26**(5), 530–549 (2004)

14. Neubert, P.: Superpixels and their application for visual place recognition in changing environments (2015)

15. Arbelaez, P., Maire, M., Fowlkes, C., Malik, J.: Contour detection and hierarchical image segmentation. IEEE Trans. Pattern Anal. Mach. Intell. **33**(5), 898–916 (2011)

16. Ren, X.: Learning a classification models for segmentation. In: Proceedings of the IEEE International Conference Computer Vision (2003)

17. Shen, J., Du, Y., Wang, W., Li, X.: Lazy random walks for superpixel segmentation. IEEE Trans. Image Process. **23**(4), 1451–1462 (2014)

18. Shen, J., Hao, X., Liang, Z., Liu, Y., Wang, W., Shao, L.: Real-time superpixel segmentation by DBSCAN clustering algorithm. IEEE Trans. Image Process. Publ. IEEE Sig. Process. Soc. **25**(12), 5933–5942 (2016)

19. Trefethen, L.N., Bau, D.: Numerical Linear Algebra. Society for Industrial and Applied Mathematics (1997)

20. Wu, X.M., Li, Z., So, M.C., Wright, J., Chang, S.F.: Learning with partially absorbing random walks. In: Advances in Neural Information Processing Systems, pp. 3086–3094 (2012)

21. Yan, J., Yu, Y., Zhu, X., Lei, Z., Li, S.Z.: Object detection by labeling superpixels. In: Computer Vision and Pattern Recognition, pp. 5107–5116 (2015)

22. Yeo, D., Son, J., Han, B., Han, J.H.: Superpixel-based tracking-by-segmentation using Markov chains. In: Computer Vision and Pattern Recognition, pp. 511–520 (2017)

BAN: Focusing on Boundary Context for Object Detection

Yonghyun Kim[1]([✉])[ID], Taewook Kim[1][ID], Bong-Nam Kang[2][ID], Jieun Kim[1][ID], and Daijin Kim[1][ID]

[1] Department of Computer Science and Engineering, POSTECH, Pohang, Korea
{gkyh0805,taewook101,rlawldmsk,dkim}@postech.ac.kr
[2] Department of Creative IT Engineering, POSTECH, Pohang, Korea
bnkang@postech.ac.kr

Abstract. Visual context is one of the important clue for object detection and the context information for boundaries of an object is especially valuable. We propose a boundary aware network (BAN) designed to exploit the visual contexts including boundary information and surroundings, named boundary context, and define three types of the boundary contexts: side, vertex and in/out-boundary context. Our BAN consists of 10 sub-networks for the area belonging to the boundary contexts. The detection head of BAN is defined as an ensemble of these sub-networks with different contributions depending on the sub-problem of detection. To verify our method, we visualize the activation of the sub-networks according to the boundary contexts and empirically show that the sub-networks contribute more to the related sub-problem in detection. We evaluate our method on PASCAL VOC detection benchmark and MS COCO dataset. The proposed method achieves the mean Average Precision (mAP) of 83.4% on PASCAL VOC and 36.9% on MS COCO. BAN allows the convolution network to provide an additional source of contexts for detection and selectively focus on the more important contexts, and it can be generally applied to many other detection methods as well to enhance the accuracy in detection.

Keywords: Visual context · Boundary context · Object detection · Convolutional neural network

1 Introduction

Object detection is one of the core problem among computer vision tasks because of its extensiveness of applicable areas, such as robotics, visual surveillance and autonomous safety. In recent years, there have been outstanding achievements in objects detection by successfully deploying a convolutional neural network [12, 15,16,19,21–23]. Despite its success, there is still a gap between current state-of-the-art performance and perfectness, and many challenging problems remain unsolved.

Visual context is a powerful clue for object detection and the context around boundaries of an object such as the surroundings and the shape of the object is

© Springer Nature Switzerland AG 2019
C. V. Jawahar et al. (Eds.): ACCV 2018, LNCS 11366, pp. 555–570, 2019.
https://doi.org/10.1007/978-3-030-20876-9_35

1. Additional Information for Accurate Detection   **2. Not all areas are equally important**

3. In/Excluding the Relationship with Nearby Objects

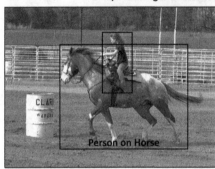 

Fig. 1. Three advantages of boundary contexts: (1) The boundary contexts provide information that could be lost due to mis-aligned proposals for more accurate classification and localization. (2) Depending on the sub-problem, the importance of the context may be differently weighted. The detector can localize more accurately by focusing on a specific area. (3) As the nearby objects are included or excluded by the context, the relationship between the object of the proposal and the nearby objects can be considered. For example, a person on a horse has a valid relationship, but a horse on a chair has a invalid relationship.

especially valuable. Many advantages can be expected by exploiting the boundary contexts in addition to a given proposal for detection (Fig. 1). The detection frameworks search the objects across the proposals generated from region proposal algorithms such as selective search [26], edge boxes [29] and region proposal network [23]. However, mis-aligned proposals with large differences in the location and size of objects may cause difficulties in detection due to the lack of information. The boundary context can be an additional source of information for detection and this contexts allow the detector to selectively focus on more important contexts depending on the sub-problem. The entire network includes and excludes the relationship of the surrounding context, thereby focusing on the partial detail of the object or considering the relationships between objects.

We propose a boundary aware network (BAN) designed to consider the boundary contexts and empirically prove the effectiveness of BAN. BAN efficiently represents the relationship between the boundary contexts by implementing the contexts as different sub-networks and improves the accuracy in detection. We use a total of 10 boundary contexts from the three different types of pre-defined boundary contexts: side, vertex and in/out-boundary context. Our BAN consists of 10 corresponding sub-networks for the area belonging to the boundary contexts. The detection head of BAN is defined as an ensemble of these sub-networks with different contributions depending on the sub-problem. We prove the validity of our methods by visualizing the activation of BAN and measuring the contribution of BAN's sub-networks.

We conduct experiments on two different datasets of object detection and experiments for the strategies for BAN such as a combination of boundary contexts, a feature resolution of sub-networks and sharing of features. TODO The proposed BAN shows the improvement of 3.2 mean Average Precision (mAP) with a threshold of 0.5 IoU from R-FCN [15] and 1.2 mAP from Deformable R-FCN [4] on PASCAL VOC [10], and the improvement of 4.5 COCO-style mAP from R-FCN and 2.4 COCO-style mAP from Deformable R-FCN on MS COCO [18]. The experiments verify that BAN improves the accuracy in detection and each boundary context have a distinct meaning for detection.

We make three main contributions:

- We develop the boundary aware network to consider the boundary contexts around the given proposal and study empirically the influence of the boundary context on classification and bounding box regression. Our BAN makes it possible to detect objects more accurately by combining sub-networks of different importance according to the detection head.
- We empirically demonstrate the effectiveness of BAN for object detection. We visualize the activation of the sub-networks according to the boundary contexts and empirically prove that the boundary contexts of BAN contribute more strongly to the detection head if they are intuitively related to each other. These related contributions suggest that BAN implies distinct meanings than naive ensemble of sub-networks.
- BAN allows the convolution network to provide an additional source of contexts for detection and selectively focus on more important contexts, and it can be generally applied to many other detection method as well to enhance the accuracy in detection.

This paper is organized as follow. We review the related works in Sect. 2. We demonstrate the proposed BAN and show the effectiveness of BAN in Sect. 3. We conduct experiments on two object detection datasets and also present several experiments on the strategies for BAN in Sect. 4. We conclude in Sect. 5.

2 Related Works

Classic Object Detectors. The sliding-window paradigm, in which a classifier is applied on a dense image pyramid [1,13], have been used for a long time to localize objects of various sizes. Viola and Jones [27] used adaptive boosting with Haar features and a decision stump as a weak classifier primarily for face detection. Dalal and Triggs [5] constructed human detection framework with HOG descriptors and a support vector machine. Dollár *et al.* [9] developed integral channel features, which extract features from channels such as LUV and gradient histogram with integral images, with a boosted decision tree for pedestrian detection. They expanded it to aggregated channel features and a feature pyramid [8] for fast and accurate detection framework. Deformable parts model (DPM) [11,28] extend conventional detectors to more general object categories by modelling an object as a set of parts with spatial constraints. While the sliding-window based approaches had been mainstream for many years, the advances in deep learning lead CNN-based detectors, described next, to dominate object detection.

Modern Object Detectors. The dominant paradigm in modern object detection is a two-stage object detection approach that generates candidate proposals in the first stage and classifies the proposals to the background and foreground classes in the second stage. The first-stage generators should provide high recall and more efficiency than a sliding window and directly affect the detection accuracy of the second-stage classifiers. The representative region proposal approaches are selective search [26], edge boxes [29] and region proposal network (RPN) [23]. As the representative two-stage object detection framework, Fast and Faster R-CNN [12,23] proposed the standard structure of CNN-based detection and show good accuracy in detection. These methods extract RoI-wise convolutional features by RoI pooling and classify RoIs of the proposals to the background and foreground classes using RoI-wise sub-networks. Region-based fully convolutional networks (R-FCN) [15] improved speed by designing the structure of networks as fully convolutional by excluding RoI-wise sub-networks. However, two-stage decision makes the detectors not practical enough. One-stage detectors such as SSD [19] and YOLO [22] showed practical performance by focusing on the speed/accuracy trade-off. These detectors have a 5–20% lower accuracy in detection with 30–100 FPS. We experiment our BAN with R-FCN and show the improvement in the detection accuracy.

Residual Network. The residual network [14], one of the most widely used backbone networks in recent years, was proposed to solve the problem that learning becomes difficult as the network becomes deeper. Against the expectation that stacking more layers increases accuracy with more capacity, deeper networks exposed to a degradation of both training and test accuracy. The degradation of training accuracy implies that the difficulty of learning from deep structures, rather than over-fitting, causes the degradation. The residual learning prevents the deeper networks from having a higher training error than the shallower networks by adding shortcut connections that are identity mapping. It is easier for the residual block to learn the residual to zero than to learn the desired mapping function directly. By designing the desired mapping as a residual function, the residual block makes learning easier for deeper networks.

Detection with Context. Context is an important clue in the applications of computer vision such as detection [6,7], segmentation [2] and recognition [3]. Ding *et al.* [6] designed the contextual cues in spatial, scaling and color spaces and developed an iterative classification algorithm called contextual boost. AZ-Net [20] accurately localizes an object by dividing and detecting the region recursively. Because the divided regions quite differ from the object area at first, it uses the inner and surrounding contexts to iteratively complement the imperfectness of the regions. Deformable R-FCN [4] is a generalization of atrous convolution. It partially includes the effect of the visual context by exploring the surrounding at the cell level. FPN [16]/RetinaNet [17] exploit the contexts for scale by aggregating multi-scale convolutional blocks. These methods try to consider the contextual cues in various ways, however, they partially exploit the visual context. BAN provides the distinct context more directly for surroundings and can improve the performance of various detectors easily.

3 Boundary Aware Network

We propose a boundary aware network (BAN) to exploit the contexts for boundary information and surroundings, named boundary context, and define three types of the boundary contexts: side, vertex and in/out-boundary context. Visual context [2,3,6,7] is one of the important clue for object detection. Because most of the detection frameworks pool convolutional features only from the proposal area, it is difficult to directly consider the areas not included exactly in the proposal and the relationship with the surroundings. The proposed BAN enhance the accuracy in detection by ensembling sub-networks that directly use boundary context of the proposal as additional information.

Here, $\mathcal{R}$ is one of the proposals for a given image $\mathbf{x}$ and $\mathcal{C}$ is a set of the boundary contexts c. $g(\mathcal{R}|c)$ denotes a generator that provides the boundary region related to $\mathcal{R}$. The classifier and regressor f, that are the aggregation of detection f_0 for the original proposal and detection h for BAN that integrates corresponding sub-networks f_c of each boundary context, are defined in the following form:

$$f(\mathbf{x}, \mathcal{R}) = f_0(\mathbf{x}, \mathcal{R}) + h(\{f_c(\mathbf{x}, g(\mathcal{R}|c))|c \in \mathcal{C}\}). \tag{1}$$

h is empirically built according to pooling methods such as RoI pooling and PSRoI pooling. In PSRoI pooling based implementation, each of f_c is a detection head and h is a simple aggregation of the detection heads, and f is defined as the aggregation of baseline and sub-networks of BAN in Eq. 1. Thus, the propagated errors are equally transferred to each sub-network in the back-propagation:

$$\frac{\partial E}{\partial f} = \frac{\partial E}{\partial f_0} = \frac{\partial E}{\partial f_c}. \tag{2}$$

Because the error of the upper layer is propagated equally to each sub-network, sub-networks are learned in a balanced manner considering the importance of each context for the same goal. In Sect. 3.3, we show that each sub-network of BAN actually contributes more to the related sub-problem.

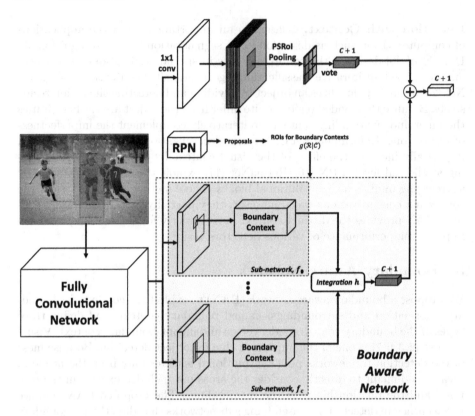

Fig. 2. Overview of the proposed BAN with a classifier head for C classes. Our detection architecture classifies and localizes an object from a proposal by integrating subnetworks representing difference boundary contexts.

3.1 Architecture

We use a fully convolutional network that excludes the average pooling, 1000-d fully connected and softmax layers from ResNet-101 [14] as backbone. Each subnetwork in BAN takes a prediction map by stacking 1×1 convolution from the backbone network and uses PSRoI pooling [15] to calculate the objectiveness and bounding box of the given proposals. We employ 10 different sub-networks to deal with different boundary regions generated from g for the boundary contexts. BAN classifies and regresses a objectiveness and a bounding box of the proposal through a detection head that is an ensemble of 11 sub-networks' predictions including a sub-network for the original proposal (Fig. 2). In the learning process, each sub-network is not learned to have the same importance, but is learned to have different magnitudes of contribution according to the sub-problems such as classification of person and relative regression of width, although it is a simple aggregation.

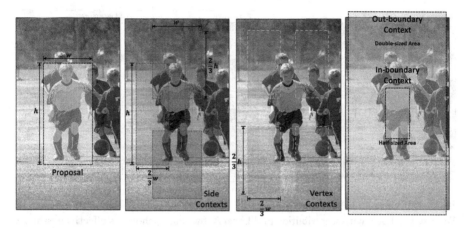

Fig. 3. Three types of boundary contexts: (1) Side contexts represent areas centered on each side of the proposal and imply the relationship with the nearby objects and localization in the vertical and horizontal direction, (2) Vertex contexts represent areas centered on each vertices of the proposal and imply the relationship with the nearby objects and localization in the diagonal direction, (3) In and Out-boundary contexts represent the inner or outer region around the boundaries of the proposal and imply the detail or the relationship with surrounding objects.

3.2 Boundary Context

We use a total of 10 boundary contexts from three different types of pre-defined boundary contexts: side, vertex and in/out-boundary context (Fig. 3). The RoIs for side contexts are defined as regions having the same height and 2/3 width of the proposal, centered at each left and right side of the proposal and regions having 2/3 height and same width of the proposal, centered at the other parallel sides. The RoIs for the vertex contexts are defined as the regions having 2/3 of height and width of the proposal and are centered at each vertex of the proposal. The RoIs for the in and out-boundary contexts are defined as a half-size region and a double-size region, respectively, sharing center point with the proposal.

3.3 Visualization of BAN

We visualize the response of feature map that is activated on the closer area to the related object (Fig. 4) to show the effectiveness of BAN. Contribution shows that BAN is weighted more strongly to the related instance rather than backgrounds and Local Activation shows that the context is activated closer to the target. We also measured the classification contribution of BAN's sub-networks (Table 1). The contributions are almost uniformly distributed due to large variations of the objects, but the boundary contexts of ↑ and In, which can include the representative part such as head and detail, show a slightly larger contribution. The localizations contributions demonstrate that BAN works faithfully in considering the boundary context (Table 2). The regression in vertical

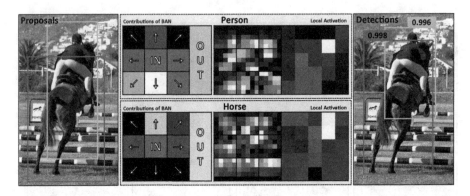

Fig. 4. Illustration of BANs for two related objects (person and horse) in a given image. We visualize BAN with Contribution and Local Activation to show it's effectiveness more directly.

Table 1. Contribution of BAN's sub-networks for classification in PASCAL VOC. Base represents the sub-network representing the original proposal, each arrows represent the side and vertex context located in the corresponding direction, and In and Out represent the in/out-boundary contexts

	Base	↑	↓	←	→	↘	↘	↗	↙	In	Out
bkgd	0.070	**0.138**	0.056	0.061	0.059	0.038	0.034	0.042	0.035	**0.328**	**0.140**
aero	0.069	0.112	0.082	0.103	0.101	0.056	0.062	0.047	0.075	**0.137**	**0.156**
bike	0.110	**0.157**	**0.112**	0.082	0.071	0.043	0.054	0.048	0.060	**0.207**	0.056
bird	0.131	**0.121**	0.094	0.101	0.095	0.062	0.054	0.060	0.055	**0.172**	0.054
boat	0.105	**0.130**	0.086	0.098	0.097	0.064	0.045	0.062	0.064	0.116	**0.133**
bottle	0.124	0.093	0.083	0.076	0.106	0.051	0.048	0.055	0.049	**0.227**	0.089
bus	0.074	**0.127**	0.084	0.089	0.078	0.054	0.053	0.053	0.059	**0.209**	**0.121**
car	0.095	**0.128**	0.081	0.099	0.111	0.063	0.071	0.056	0.075	**0.157**	0.063
cat	0.187	0.119	0.076	0.072	0.081	0.056	0.042	0.047	0.053	**0.209**	0.058
chair	0.112	**0.120**	0.115	0.104	0.105	0.058	0.057	0.055	0.060	**0.144**	0.070
cow	0.079	**0.163**	0.077	0.084	0.093	0.058	0.043	0.048	0.044	**0.255**	0.056
table	0.093	0.108	0.103	0.093	0.099	0.060	0.057	0.053	0.053	**0.222**	0.058
dog	0.088	0.108	0.088	0.079	0.085	0.060	0.045	0.049	0.057	**0.233**	0.107
horse	0.085	**0.137**	0.072	0.082	0.074	0.058	0.039	0.054	0.047	**0.256**	0.097
mbike	0.124	0.115	0.072	0.088	0.092	0.051	0.059	0.048	0.066	**0.225**	0.060
person	0.138	**0.148**	0.080	0.114	0.117	0.061	0.066	0.062	0.063	0.105	0.046
plant	0.096	**0.149**	0.092	0.095	0.093	0.059	0.067	0.050	0.073	**0.148**	0.078
sheep	0.109	**0.142**	0.112	0.107	0.118	0.065	0.053	0.051	0.059	**0.130**	0.054
sofa	0.107	**0.144**	0.080	0.088	0.086	0.068	0.040	0.066	0.046	**0.154**	**0.120**
train	0.075	0.097	0.083	0.090	0.084	0.058	0.060	0.055	0.069	**0.141**	0.190
tv	0.100	**0.134**	0.116	0.104	0.106	0.063	0.060	0.058	0.057	0.111	0.091

Table 2. Contribution of BAN's sub-networks for localization in PASCAL VOC

	Base	↑	↓	←	→	↖	↘	↗	↙	In	Out
cx	0.181	0.088	0.077	**0.118**	**0.137**	0.058	0.062	0.053	0.058	0.077	0.090
cy	0.094	**0.123**	**0.096**	0.046	0.046	0.037	0.041	0.033	0.045	0.055	**0.384**
$width$	0.118	0.065	0.071	**0.123**	**0.132**	0.068	0.070	0.059	0.089	0.100	0.104
$height$	0.089	**0.131**	**0.105**	0.051	0.044	0.038	0.042	0.034	0.044	**0.212**	**0.209**

direction such as cy and *height*, are highly contributed by ↑ and ↓. In/Out-boundary contexts do not have a specific tendency but show a high contribution. We infer that the redundancy of the regions for base, in and out makes them play a similar role. We construct both visualization and contributions using PSRoI pooling based BAN for intuitive comparison.

4 Experiments

We conduct experiments on two different datasets of object detection and experiments with the strategies for BAN such as a combination of boundary contexts, a feature resolution of sub-networks and sharing of features. Our BAN shows the improvement of 3.2 mAP with a threshold of 0.5 IoU from R-FCN [15] and 1.2 mAP from Deformable R-FCN [4] on PASCAL VOC [10], and the improvement of 4.5 COCO-style mAP from R-FCN and 2.4 COCO-style mAP from Deformable R-FCN on MS COCO [18]. The experiments show that BAN improves the detection accuracy of object detection and implies that the boundary contexts has a distinct meaning for detection among each other.

4.1 Implementation

Baseline. We use a fully convolutional network [15] that excludes the average pooling, 1000-d fully connected and softmax layers from ResNet-101 [14]. The last convolution block *res5* in ResNet-101 has a stride of 32 pixels. Many detection and segmentation methods employ a modified ResNet-101 that increases the receptive fields by changing the stride from 2 to 1. To compensate this modification, the dilation is changed from 1 to 2 for all 3 × 3 convolution in the last layer. The last convolution block *res5* in modified ResNet-101 has a stride of 16 pixels and we use this as backbone. We fine-tune the model from the pre-trained ResNet-101 model on ImageNet [24].

Structure. BAN can be implemented using any pooling methods such as RoI pooling and PSRoI pooling (Fig. 5). We empirically determine the structure of BAN according to each pooling method. BAN with PSRoI pooling integrates the sub-networks that are detection heads by aggregating them. BAN with RoI pooling extracts 256-d convolutional features from the sub-networks and builds a single detection head using the concatenated features. Both structures improve the detection accuracy. However, the former is easy to analyze the contributions

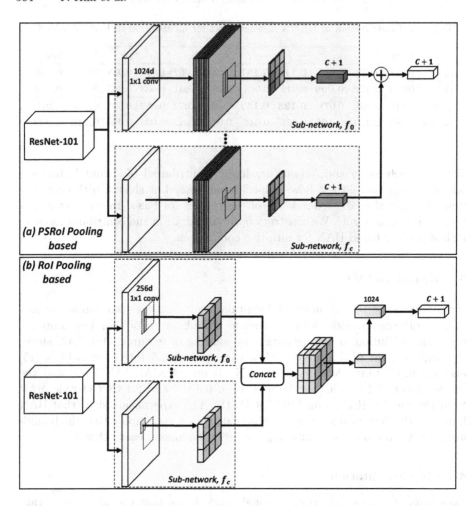

Fig. 5. Detail structure of BAN for a classifier head of C classes (a regression head of B offsets is also similarly defined). The structure of BAN is empirically determined according to pooling methods (PSRoI pooling and RoI pooling).

of contexts because all detectors, including the baseline, were structurally identical, and the latter contributes to higher improvement in accuracy because it generates more distinct features for R-FCN based detectors.

Learning. We use a weight decay of 0.0001 and a momentum of 0.9 with stochastic gradient descent (SGD). We train the network for 29k iterations with a learning rate of 10^{-3} dividing it by 10 at 20k iterations for PASCAL VOC and for 240k iterations with a learning rate of 10^{-3} dividing it by 10 at 160k iterations for MS COCO. A mini-batch consists of 2 images, which are resized such that its shorter side of image is 600 pixels. In training, the online hard example mining (OHEM) [25] selects 128 RoIs of hard examples among 300 RoIs per image.

Table 3. Cost analysis

	Inference time	Memory consumption
R-FCN [15]	70 ms	0.8 GB
R-FCN-BAN	97 ms	1.2 GB
Deformable R-FCN [4]	96 ms	0.9 GB
Deformable R-FCN-BAN	120 ms	1.2 GB

Table 5. Feature Resolution

	$mAP_{@.5}$	$mAP_{@.7}$
- 1 × 1	79.39	61.36
- 3 × 3	80.15	63.45
- 5 × 5	80.75	64.66
- 7 × 7	80.10	63.76

Table 6. Feature Sharing

	$mAP_{@.5}$	$mAP_{@.7}$
- Unshared	80.05	62.80
- Shared	80.75	64.66

Table 4. Boundary Context

	$mAP_{@.5}$	$mAP_{@.7}$
None	79.54	61.95
$\mathcal{S}$ (Sides)	80.23	62.84
$\mathcal{V}$ (Vertices)	80.01	62.13
$\mathcal{B}$ (In/Out-boundary)	79.80	63.23
$\mathcal{S}, \mathcal{V}$	80.39	63.36
$\mathcal{S}, \mathcal{V}, \mathcal{B}$	80.75	64.66

Table 7. Pooling Method

	$mAP_{@.5}$	$mAP_{@.7}$
- PSRoI pooling	80.75	64.66
- ROI pooling	82.72	67.84

OHEM evaluates the multi-task loss of all proposals then discard the proposals with the small loss to make the detector more focus on difficult samples. The detection network is trained with 4 synchronized GPUs: each GPU holds 2 images. We use 300 RoIs per image, which is obtained from RPN and post-processed by non-maximum suppression (NMS) with a threshold of 0.3 IoU, for both learning and inference.

Loss function. The loss function is defined as a sum of the classification loss and the box regression loss. The classification loss is defined as a cross-entropy loss, $L_{cls}(p, u) = -\log p_u$, where p is a discrete probability distribution over $K + 1$ categories and u is a ground-truth class. The regression loss is defined as a smooth L_1 loss [12], $L_{reg}(t^u, v) = \sum_{i \in \{x,y,w,h\}} \text{smooth}_{L_1} [t_i^u - v_i]$, where t^k is a tuple of bounding-box regression for each of the K classes, indexed by k, and v is a tuple of a ground-truth bounding-box regression.

Cost Analysis. We perform the cost analysis on the inference time and the memory consumption (Table 3). The analysis is performed using ResNet-101 and RoI pooling based BAN. Our BAN easily improves various detection methods with a reasonable increase in memory and computing time.

4.2 Comparison with Strategies for BAN

We experiment the strategies for BAN such as different combinations of boundary contexts, various feature resolutions of sub-networks, feature sharing and pooling method to construct effective BAN. The experiments are performed using ResNet-101 and PSRoI pooling based BAN on PASCAL VOC.

Table 8. Evaluation on PASCAL VOC 2007 and MS COCO test-dev

| | VOC 2007 | | MS COCO test-dev | | | | |
	mAP@.5	mAP@.7	mAP	mAP@.5	mAP@S	mAP@M	mAP@L
Faster RCNN [23]	76.4	-	30.3	52.1	9.9	32.2	47.4
YOLOv2 [22]	79.5	-	21.6	44.0	5.0	22.4	35.5
SSD513 [19]	76.8	-	31.2	50.4	10.2	34.5	49.8
R-FCN [15]	79.5	62.0	29.9	50.8	11.0	32.2	43.9
R-FCN-BAN	82.7	67.8	34.4	58.5	17.8	37.7	46.0
Deformable R-FCN [4]	82.2	67.6	34.5	55.0	14.0	37.7	50.3
Deformable R-FCN-BAN	83.4	70.0	36.9	58.5	15.8	40.0	53.6

Boundary Context. We conduct experiments on the types of boundary contexts (side, vertex and in/out-boundary contexts) and the combinations of the types (Table 4). All boundary contexts shows the meaningful improvement in the detection accuracy and the combination of the all three types of boundary contexts improves mAP@0.5 by 1.21 and mAP@0.7 by 2.71. This experiment shows that each boundary context have a distinct meaning for detection.

Feature Resolution. We conduct experiments on the feature resolution $k \times k$ of sub-networks from 1×1 to 7×7 (Table 5). The feature resolution of 5×5 shows the highest improvement and 1×1 degrades the detection accuracy as it crushes the boundary contexts.

Feature Sharing. Each sub-network consists of a 1024 dimensional 1×1 convolution and the following relu for feature extraction and a $(C + 1)k^2$ dimensional 1×1 convolution as classification and a $8k^2$ dimensional 1×1 convolution as regression for detection heads (Table 6). The different use of 1×1 convolution for feature extraction lead to the improvement of 0.73 point in mAP. This experiment implies that the boundary context transfers a distinctive influence to the feature level as well as the detection head in learning.

Pooling. The implementation of BAN is slightly different depending on the pooling method for extracting the visual context. We conduct experiments on two pooling methods: RoI pooling and PSRoI pooling. PSRoI pooling requires a small amount of resources because it is fully convolutional. RoI pooling highly improves the accuracy in detection because it is easy to extract the fundamental convolutional features for the boundary context (Table 7).

4.3   Experiments on PASCAL VOC

We evaluate the proposed BAN on PASCAL VOC [10] that has 20 object categories (Fig. 6). We train the models on the union set of VOC 2007 and VOC 2012 trainval, 07+12, (16,551 images), and evaluate on VOC 2007 test set (4,952 images). Detection accuracy is measured by mean Average Precision (mAP). BAN improves 3.2 mAP with a threshold of 0.5 IoU and 5.8 mAP with a threshold of 0.7 from R-FCN [15] and 1.2 mAP with a threshold of 0.5 IoU and 2.4 mAP with a threshold of 0.7 from Deformable R-FCN [4] (Tables 8 and 9).

Fig. 6. Examples of object detection results on PASCAL VOC 2007 test set using our method (83.4% mAP). The network is based on ResNet-101 and the training data is 07+12 trainval.

4.4   Experiments on MS COCO

We evaluate the proposed BAN on MS COCO dataset [18] that has 80 object categories. We train the models on the union set of 80k training set and 40k validation set (`trainval`), and evaluate on 20k `test-dev` set. The COCO-style metric denotes mAP, which is the average AP across thresholds of IoU from 0.5 to 0.95 with an interval of 0.05. Our BAN improves 4.5 COCO-style mAP and 7.7 mAP with a threshold of 0.5 IoU from R-FCN [15] and 2.4 COCO-style mAP and 3.5 mAP with a threshold of 0.5 IoU from Deformable R-FCN [4] (Table 8). We obtain the higher improvement in the detection accuracy for MS COCO with various classes and challenging environments, than PASCAL VOC.

Table 9. Detailed detection results on PASCAL VOC 2007 test set

Method	mAP	aero	bike	bird	boat	bottle	bus	car	cat	chair	cow	table	dog	horse	mbike	person	plant	sheep	sofa	train	tv
Faster R-CNN	76.4	79.8	80.7	76.2	68.3	55.9	85.1	85.3	89.8	56.7	87.8	69.4	88.3	88.9	80.9	78.4	41.7	78.6	79.8	85.3	72.0
R-FCN [15]	79.5	82.5	83.7	80.3	69.0	69.2	87.5	88.4	65.4	65.4	87.3	72.1	87.9	88.3	81.3	79.8	54.1	79.6	78.8	87.1	79.5
R-FCN-BAN	82.7	89.1	88.4	80.7	76.9	73.3	89.6	88.8	89.5	69.5	88.0	74.5	90.0	89.3	86.8	80.5	57.6	84.3	84.7	88.5	84.5
DR-FCN [4]	82.2	85.9	89.3	80.7	74.8	72.4	88.2	88.8	89.5	69.0	88.2	75.4	89.7	89.4	84.5	83.4	57.3	84.9	82.3	87.6	82.7
DR-FCN-BAN	83.4	88.0	89.5	80.6	77.0	73.4	88.8	89.0	89.8	70.7	88.4	77.3	90.2	89.4	87.5	84.6	58.2	85.6	85.3	88.2	85.9

5   Conclusions

We propose a boundary aware network (BAN) designed to exploit the boundary contexts and study empirically the influence of the boundary context on classification and bounding box regression. To show the effectiveness of BAN, we visualize the activation of the sub-networks according to the boundary contexts and empirically show that the boundary contexts of BAN contributes more strongly to the detection head intuitively related to the boundary context. These related contribution suggests that BAN implies distinct meanings than naive ensemble of sub-networks. We evaluate our method on PASCAL VOC detection benchmark dataset, which has 20 object categories and MS COCO dataset, which has 80 object categories. Our BAN improves mAP by 3.2 point from R-FCN and 1.2 point from Deformable R-FCN on PASCAL VOC and improves the COCO-style mAP by 4.5 point from R-FCN and 2.4 point from Deformable R-FCN on MS COCO. BAN allows the convolution network to provide an additional source of contexts for detection and selectively focus on more important contexts, and it can be generally applied to many other detection method as well to enhance the accuracy in detection.

As a future study, we will improve the detection accuracy by applying BAN to the entire network including RPN. In addition, we plan to develop a general version of BAN based on this study of the influence and relationship among the boundary contexts.

Acknowledgments. This work was supported by IITP grant funded by the Korea government (MSIT) (IITP-2014-3-00059, Development of Predictive Visual Intelligence Technology, IITP-2017-0-00897, SW Starlab support program, and IITP-2018-0-01290, Development of Open Informal Dataset and Dynamic Object Recognition Technology Affecting Autonomous Driving).

References

1. Adelson, E.H., Anderson, C.H., Bergen, J.R., Burt, P.J., Ogden, J.M.: Pyramid methods in image processing. RCA Eng. **29**, 33–41 (1984)
2. Avidan, S.: SpatialBoost: adding spatial reasoning to adaboost. In: Leonardis, A., Bischof, H., Pinz, A. (eds.) ECCV 2006. LNCS, vol. 3954, pp. 386–396. Springer, Heidelberg (2006). https://doi.org/10.1007/11744085_30
3. Carbonetto, P., de Freitas, N., Barnard, K.: A statistical model for general contextual object recognition. In: Pajdla, T., Matas, J. (eds.) ECCV 2004. LNCS, vol. 3021, pp. 350–362. Springer, Heidelberg (2004). https://doi.org/10.1007/978-3-540-24670-1_27
4. Dai, J., et al.: Deformable convolutional networks. In: IEEE International Conference on Computer Vision (2017)
5. Dalal, N., Triggs, B.: Histograms of oriented gradients for human detection. In: IEEE Computer Society Conference on Computer Vision and Pattern Recognition (CVPR) (2005)
6. Ding, Y., Xiao, J.: Contextual boost for pedestrian detection. In: IEEE Computer Society Conference on Computer Vision and Pattern Recognition (CVPR) (2012)
7. Divvala, S.K., Hoiem, D., Hays, J.H., Efros, A.A., Hebert, M.: An empirical study of context in object detection. In: IEEE Computer Society Conference on Computer Vision and Pattern Recognition (CVPR) (2009)
8. Dollár, P., Appel, R., Belongie, S., Perona, P.: Fast feature pyramids for object detection. IEEE Trans. Pattern Anal. Mach. Intell. (TPAMI) **36**, 1532–1545 (2014)
9. Dollár, P., Tu, Z., Perona, P., Belongie, S.: Integral channel features. In: British Machine Vision Conference (BMVC) (2009)
10. Everingham, M., Van Gool, L., Williams, C.K., Winn, J., Zisserman, A.: The pascal visual object classes (VOC) challenge. Int. J. Comput. Vis. (IJCV) **88**, 303–338 (2010)
11. Felzenszwalb, P.F., Girshick, R.B., McAllester, D., Ramanan, D.: Object detection with discriminatively trained part-based models. IEEE Trans. Pattern Anal. Mach. Intell. (TPAMI) **32**, 1627–1645 (2010)
12. Girshick, R.: Fast R-CNN. In: IEEE International Conference on Computer Vision (ICCV) (2015)
13. Gonzalez, R.C.: Digital Image Processing. Pearson Education India, Bengaluru (2009)
14. He, K., Zhang, X., Ren, S., Sun, J.: Deep residual learning for image recognition. In: IEEE Computer Society Conference on Computer Vision and Pattern Recognition (CVPR) (2016)
15. Li, Y., He, K., Sun, J., et al.: R-FCN: object detection via region-based fully convolutional networks. In: Advances in Neural Information Processing Systems (NIPS) (2016)
16. Lin, T.Y., Dollár, P., Girshick, R., He, K., Hariharan, B., Belongie, S.: Feature pyramid networks for object detection. In: IEEE Computer Society Conference on Computer Vision and Pattern Recognition (CVPR) (2017)
17. Lin, T.Y., Goyal, P., Girshick, R., He, K., Dollar, P.: Focal loss for dense object detection. In: IEEE International Conference on Computer Vision (2017)
18. Lin, T.Y., et al.: Microsoft COCO: common objects in context. In: Fleet, D., Pajdla, T., Schiele, B., Tuytelaars, T. (eds.) ECCV 2014. LNCS, vol. 8693, pp. 740–755. Springer, Cham (2014). https://doi.org/10.1007/978-3-319-10602-1_48

19. Liu, W., et al.: SSD: single shot multibox detector. In: Leibe, B., Matas, J., Sebe, N., Welling, M. (eds.) ECCV 2016. LNCS, vol. 9905, pp. 21–37. Springer, Cham (2016). https://doi.org/10.1007/978-3-319-46448-0_2
20. Lu, Y., Javidi, T., Lazebnik, S.: Adaptive object detection using adjacency and zoom prediction. In: IEEE Conference on Computer Vision and Pattern Recognition (2016)
21. Redmon, J., Divvala, S., Girshick, R., Farhadi, A.: You only look once: unified, real-time object detection. In: IEEE Computer Society Conference on Computer Vision and Pattern Recognition (CVPR) (2016)
22. Redmon, J., Farhadi, A.: Yolo9000: better, faster, stronger. In: IEEE Computer Society Conference on Computer Vision and Pattern Recognition (CVPR) (2017)
23. Ren, S., He, K., Girshick, R., Sun, J.: Faster R-CNN: towards real-time object detection with region proposal networks. In: Advances in Neural Information Processing Systems (NIPS) (2015)
24. Russakovsky, O., et al.: Imagenet large scale visual recognition challenge. Int. J. Comput. Vis. (IJCV) **115**, 211–252 (2015)
25. Shrivastava, A., Gupta, A., Girshick, R.: Training region-based object detectors with online hard example mining. In: IEEE Computer Society Conference on Computer Vision and Pattern Recognition (CVPR) (2016)
26. Uijlings, J.R., Van De Sande, K.E., Gevers, T., Smeulders, A.W.: Selective search for object recognition. Int. J. Comput. Vis. (IJCV) **104**, 154–171 (2013)
27. Viola, P., Jones, M.J.: Robust real-time face detection. Int. J. Comput. Vis. (IJCV) **57**, 137–154 (2004)
28. Yang, Y., Ramanan, D.: Articulated human detection with flexible mixtures of parts. IEEE Trans. Pattern Anal. Mach. Intell. (TPAMI) **35**, 2878–2890 (2013)
29. Zitnick, C.L., Dollár, P.: Edge boxes: locating object proposals from edges. In: Fleet, D., Pajdla, T., Schiele, B., Tuytelaars, T. (eds.) ECCV 2014. LNCS, vol. 8693, pp. 391–405. Springer, Cham (2014). https://doi.org/10.1007/978-3-319-10602-1_26

Rethinking Planar Homography Estimation Using Perspective Fields

Rui Zeng$^{(\boxtimes)}$ ⓘ, Simon Denman ⓘ, Sridha Sridharan ⓘ, and Clinton Fookes ⓘ

Queensland University of Technology, Brisbane, Australia
{r5.zeng,s.denman,s.sridharan,c.fookes}@qut.edu.au

Abstract. Planar homography estimation refers to the problem of computing a bijective linear mapping of pixels between two images. While this problem has been studied with convolutional neural networks (CNNs), existing methods simply regress the location of the four corners using a dense layer preceded by a fully-connected layer. This vector representation damages the spatial structure of the corners since they have a clear spatial order. Moreover, four points are the minimum required to compute the homography, and so such an approach is susceptible to perturbation. In this paper, we propose a conceptually simple, reliable, and general framework for homography estimation. In contrast to previous works, we formulate this problem as a perspective field (PF), which models the essence of the homography - pixel-to-pixel bijection. The PF is naturally learned by the proposed fully convolutional residual network, PFNet, to keep the spatial order of each pixel. Moreover, since every pixels' displacement can be obtained from the PF, it enables robust homography estimation by utilizing dense correspondences. Our experiments demonstrate the proposed method outperforms traditional correspondence-based approaches and state-of-the-art CNN approaches in terms of accuracy while also having a smaller network size. In addition, the new parameterization of this task is general and can be implemented by any fully convolutional network (FCN) architecture.

Keywords: Homography · Autoencoder · Perspective field · PFNet

1 Introduction

Planar homography estimation, which is a fundamental task in computer vision, aims to provide a non-singular linear relationship between points in two images. It has gained much attention since efficiently computing homographies is invaluable for many practical applications, such as image rectification [4,20,28], image registration [7,18], and camera calibration [8,24].

A well-known framework for this task is to use a hand-crafted key point detector to determine the transformation between two images. This typically consists

Electronic supplementary material The online version of this chapter (https://doi.org/10.1007/978-3-030-20876-9_36) contains supplementary material, which is available to authorized users.

© Springer Nature Switzerland AG 2019
C. V. Jawahar et al. (Eds.): ACCV 2018, LNCS 11366, pp. 571–586, 2019.
https://doi.org/10.1007/978-3-030-20876-9_36

of three steps: key point detection, correspondence matching, and a direct linear transformation (DLT). First, a hand-crafted detector, such as SIFT [17], ORB [22], KLT [9], SURF [2] etc., is used to extract key points using local invariant features from each image. Correspondence matching aims to match the two detected key point sets by a heuristic criterion (e.g. euclidean distance, correlation, etc.). Then outliers in the initial correspondence set are further eliminated using RANSAC [9]. In the last step, the transformation between two images can be established by making use of a direct linear transform (DLT), which takes as input the correspondence set. While such frameworks have achieved success to some extent, their performance is largely dependent on the accuracy of the key point detector and the correspondence matching. When the correspondences are misaligned, this framework may fail. This situation often happens when hand-crafted features perform poorly in the presence of large variations in perspective, illumination, etc.

To alleviate the dependence on key-point detection and matching performance, estimating homographies in a end-to-end fashion using convolutional neural networks (CNNs) has been widely studied in the last two years. Most existing works [5,12,21] aim to regress the 4-point homography directly, i.e., the offsets of the four corners are embedded into a vector and then predicted by a CNN through a dense layer preceded by a fully-connected layer. Unfortunately, the strategy of formulating this task has three drawbacks:

1. The vector representation of the four corners via a dense layer breaks their spatial structure and hence results in a loss of spatial information.
2. Four points are the minimum to estimate the homography. Perturbation of any one predicted corner may significantly affect the accuracy of the estimate. In other words, a 4-point homography is not robust.
3. Fully-connected layers are frequently used in these architectures, which increases the computation requirement and decreases the representation power of the network. For example, the fully-connected layers in networks such as VGGNet [23], AlexNet [13], etc., occupy nearly 20% (i.e., less representation capacity) for the weights but require 80% of the computation.

Aiming to address the aforementioned issues, we propose a conceptually simple, reliable, and general framework for homography estimation. Our approach parametrizes the bijective pixel-to-pixel linear mapping described by a homography using the perspective field, which encodes every pixels' offsets while retaining their spatial information. Subsequently, this new formulation is naturally learned by the perspective field network (PFNet), which contains a novel deconvolution block designed in a residual fashion.

The contribution in this paper is two-fold:

1. We propose a new parameterization for homography estimation which can be easily applied to any existing FCN.
2. We introduce the PFNet for homography estimation, endowed with the proposed novel deconvolution blocks, that allows for upsampling and predicting

homographies efficiently. Thanks to the proposed fully convolutional architecture, the network has fewer hyper-parameters while greatly boosting the performance compared with existing state-of-the-art methods.

2   Related Works

Approaches for homography estimation can be divided into two groups: feature-based and end-to-end deep-learning-based approaches.

Feature-Based Homography Estimation. Prior to the advent of deep learning, the standard approach for homography estimation consisted of three stages: (1) detecting a set of distinctive points using hand-crafted features (e.g. SIFT [17], ORB [22], SURF [2]), (2) finding matching detections using the distance between points according to a descriptor and a random sampling method (such as RANSAC [9]), and (3) estimating the homography via a direct linear transformation (DLT) [9]. Despite the prevalence of this style of approach, its performance is largely dependent on the accuracy of feature point detection and matching. It may fail when correspondences cannot be detected accurately due to the large variances in illumination, perspective, and clarity. In addition, designing effective features for new data or tasks typically requires new domain knowledge, which is often unavailable for new scenes. Regarding the properties of existing local invariant features, we refer readers to [19].

Homography Prediction with CNNs. Due to the remarkable advances of deep learning in the field of computer vision, research into homography estimation has been driven towards the use of CNNs. Detone *et al.* [5] was the first to use a CNN for regressing four corners offsets from a pair of image in a VGG-like network with 14 layers. Their technique was shown to outperform traditional feature-based methods, such as SITF, ORB, SURF, etc., when sufficient features could not be detected. Inspired by this work, [12] proposed a twin CNN module, which processes two images in parallel in the first 4 convolutional layers and concatenates feature maps to generate estimates using another 4 convolutional layers and 2 fully-connected layers. Subsequently, they arrange the proposed module in a stacked manner and trained them in a hierarchical fashion to reduce estimation error bounds. While this iterative architecture significantly outperforms [5], it increases both the model and computational complexity significantly.

Alternatively, to improve the quality of the predicted homography, [21] develops a hybrid approach that combines the strengths of both a deep learning and a conventional feature-based method. Specifically, it relies on features to compute the homography estimates using a 4-point parameterization in the first half of the network and then optimizes the pixel-wise photometric loss of the two images in the second half.

These three approaches have two key commonalities: (1) they design a dedicated network which lacks flexibility and so cannot benefit from existing the state-of-the-art CNN architectures, and (2) the 4-point parameterization does not model the bijective pixel-wise linear mapping and breaks the spatial information among four corners' offsets.

Unlike these existing methods, we formulate this task as predicting a perspective field, and then adapt the proposed fully convolutional network (FCN) to learn it simply and efficiently from a pair of images. Moreover, this new parameterization does not rely on any specific network and as such it has great generalization. It can be easily learned by any existing FCN to estimate homographies.

3   Homography Parameterization

The standard way to parameterize a homography is to find a 3×3 non-singular matrix which can establish a bijective projection between every pixel in two images. Suppose that we have a point $\mathbf{p} = (x_{\mathbf{p}}, y_{\mathbf{p}})$ on image I_A and its corresponding point on image I_B is denoted as $\mathbf{q} = (x_{\mathbf{q}}, y_{\mathbf{q}})$. Thus, the homography $\mathbf{H}$ that maps $\mathbf{p}$ to $\mathbf{q}$ can be expressed as,

$$
\begin{bmatrix} x_{\mathbf{q}} \\ y_{\mathbf{q}} \\ 1 \end{bmatrix} \sim \begin{bmatrix} \mathbf{H}_{11} & \mathbf{H}_{12} & \mathbf{H}_{13} \\ \mathbf{H}_{21} & \mathbf{H}_{22} & \mathbf{H}_{23} \\ \mathbf{H}_{31} & \mathbf{H}_{32} & \mathbf{H}_{33} \end{bmatrix} \begin{bmatrix} x_{\mathbf{p}} \\ x_{\mathbf{p}} \\ 1 \end{bmatrix}.
\tag{1}
$$

Since the transformation is defined up to a scaling factor, it can be normalized by scaling $\mathbf{H}_{33} = 1$, and as such $\mathbf{H}$ can be parameterized by 8 parameters.

While this straightforward parameterization has been widely used in computer vision, it may be problematic when we employ it as the learning objective of a CNN. This is because $\mathbf{H}$ implicitly encodes the rotation, translation, focal length, skew, and optical center parameters; and the value range of each parameter has high variance. Typically, the magnitude of translation, focal length, and optical center are much greater than that of rotation, as such it is very hard to balance (normalize) all parameters' contribution to the loss function.

To address this issue, we parameterize $\mathbf{H}$ between I_A and I_B using a PF, F_{AB}. F_{AB} has two channels F_{AB_x}, F_{AB_y}, where each channel represents the pixel offset caused by the homography in the x and y directions. Let W and H represent the width and height of I_A and I_B respectively. The displacement of $\mathbf{p}$ in terms of the x-axis is denoted $\Delta x_{\mathbf{p}} = x_{\mathbf{p}} - x_{\mathbf{q}}$. Similarly, $\Delta y_{\mathbf{p}} = y_{\mathbf{p}} - y_{\mathbf{q}}$ is the displacement of $y_{\mathbf{p}}$. Thus F_{AB_x}, F_{AB_y} can be expressed as follows,

$$
F_{AB_x} = \begin{bmatrix} \Delta x_{\mathbf{p}11} & \Delta x_{\mathbf{p}12} & \cdots & \Delta x_{\mathbf{p}1W} \\ \Delta x_{\mathbf{p}21} & \Delta x_{\mathbf{p}22} & \cdots & \Delta x_{\mathbf{p}2W} \\ \vdots & \vdots & \ddots & \vdots \\ \Delta x_{\mathbf{p}H1} & \Delta x_{\mathbf{p}H2} & \cdots & \Delta x_{\mathbf{p}HW} \end{bmatrix},
\tag{2}
$$

Fig. 1. Illustration of the PF between a pair of images. From left to right: the original image, the warped image (using a random homography), the PF. The PFs are plotted on a green gird at a 10 pixel interval. The red quiver on the pixel represents the direction and length of the pixel offset. By combining this PF with the warped image, we can easily recover the original image and obtain the homography. (Color figure online)

and

$$
F_{\mathrm{AB}_y} = \begin{bmatrix} \Delta y_{\mathbf{p}_{11}} & \Delta y_{\mathbf{p}_{12}} & \cdots & \Delta y_{\mathbf{p}_{1W}} \\ \Delta y_{\mathbf{p}_{21}} & \Delta y_{\mathbf{p}_{22}} & \cdots & \Delta y_{\mathbf{p}_{2W}} \\ \vdots & \vdots & \ddots & \vdots \\ \Delta y_{\mathbf{p}_{H1}} & \Delta y_{\mathbf{p}_{H2}} & \cdots & \Delta y_{\mathbf{p}_{HW}} \end{bmatrix}. \tag{3}
$$

To convert the PF back to the homography, we first simply restore the correspondences between two images by,

$$
\{\mathbf{p}_i, \mathbf{q}_i\}_{i=1}^{HW} = \{\mathbf{p}_i, \mathbf{p}_i - \Delta \mathbf{p}_i\}_{i=1}^{HW}, \tag{4}
$$

where i is the index of the correspondence, and $\Delta \mathbf{p}_i = (\Delta x_{\mathbf{p}_i}, \Delta y_{\mathbf{p}_i})$. Once the correspondences have been established by Eq. 4, RANSAC is applied to further filter out outliers and then we use a DLT to solve the homography from a set of equations,

$$
\begin{bmatrix} \mathbf{0}^\top & -\mathbf{q}_i^\top & y_{\mathbf{p}_i}\mathbf{q}_i^\top \\ \mathbf{q}_i^\top & \mathbf{0}^\top & -x_{\mathbf{p}_i}\mathbf{q}_i^\top \end{bmatrix} \mathbf{h} = 0. \quad i = 1, \ldots, HW \;, \tag{5}
$$

where $\mathbf{h} \in \mathbb{R}^{9\times 1}$ is the vectorized homography $\mathbf{H}$. Figure 1 visualizes the PF generated by a pair of images.

4   Methodology

In Sect. 4.1, we describe the architecture of the proposed fully convolutional residual network in detail. Then in Sects. 4.2 and 4.3, the strategies of building the loss function and optimization are introduced respectively. Figure 2 visualizes the proposed architecture.

4.1   FCN Architecture

Our objective is to design an end-to-end architecture that outputs the PF between a pair of images. Thus choosing an appropriate CNN backbone is crucially important. In this paper, ResNet-50 [10] is employed as our FCN backbone

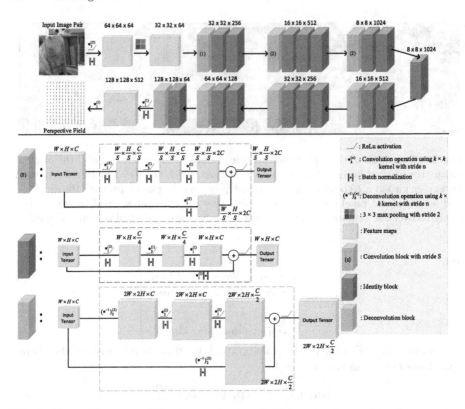

Fig. 2. The architecture of the proposed network. This network consists of two parts: encoder (the top row) and decoder (the bottom row). In the encoder, the network takes as input a pair of images and encodes its information into a set of feature maps through a series of convolutions. In the decoder, the PF information embedded in the feature maps is recovered progressively. In the second last layer, we use 512 filters to expand the width to enhance the representation ability of the network. The last layer outputs F_{AB_x} and F_{AB_y} respectively.

for its state-of-the-art performance in many computer vision tasks. In addition, ResNet-50 does not have high computational complexity when compared to many deep networks such as ResNet-101, DenseNet, VGG, etc., while having an acceptable level of performance.

The proposed fully convolutional residual network consists of two parts: the encoder and the decoder. In the encoder, we strictly use the first 4 stages of ResNet-50, where each stage is constructed by a specific number of residual blocks [10] (including identity blocks and convolution blocks), and we remove the 5th stage and following fully-connected layer to enable the connection between the encoder and decoder. The encoder takes as input a $W \times H \times 2$ gray image pair and gives rise to a tensor of features of shape $W_m \times H_m \times C_m$ for stage $m = \{3, 4\}$, where $W_m = \frac{W}{2^m}$, $H_m = \frac{H}{2^m}$, and $C_m = 2^{6+m}$. The output of the encoder captures the spatial correlation of the image pair at a set of uniformly sampled pixel locations, and forms the input to the decoder.

The decoder aims to learn how to generate the PF given the spatial correlations learned by the encoder. To achieve this goal, it progressively upsamples the feature maps through a series of identity blocks and the proposed deconvolution block, to ensure the output has the same size as the input image. The decoder is symmetrical to the encoder. It also consists of 4 stages, where each stage (denoted as $n = \{1, \ldots, 4\}$) has the same number of residual blocks but replaces the convolution block with the proposed deconvolution block. The output tensor generated from stage n is of shape $W_n \times H_n \times C_n$, where $W_n = \frac{W}{2^{4-n}}$, $H_n = \frac{H}{2^{4-n}}$, and $C_n = 2^{10-n}$. The deconvolution block embedded in each stage provides the ability to propagate low-resolution feature maps to high-resolution feature maps. More details are introduced in following discussion.

Once the encoder and decoder have been set up, we convolve the last layer of the decoder with a $1 \times 1 \times 512$, and a $1 \times 1 \times 2$ filters successively to enable the prediction of the PF, as such the output size is $W \times H \times 2$. It is worth noting that our model does not have any long skip connections between m and the corresponding n, which are heavily used in segmentation tasks [16]. Skip connections aim to propagate pixel-wise information from low stages to high stages to assist segmentation. However, homographies have significantly distorted pixel-to-pixel spatial relationships between two images and as such we omit long skip connections from our architecture. Moreover, we do not use drop out to further regularize our architecture because we want to enable fair comparison with other baselines.

Deconvolution Block. The structure of the deconvolution block is depicted in the bottom half of Fig. 2. The deconvolution block is the last residual-like block in each decoder stage. It receives an input tensor, and increases the spatial resolution using a deconvolution operation. The design of the deconvolution block is inspired by the philosophy of ResNet and as such we follow two simple rules: (1) the input tensor is added directly to the end of the block by being only convolved once to enable the residual operation, and (2) The block doubles the feature map size while halving the number of the filters. More specifically, we first adopt two 2×2 deconvolutional kernels with stride 2 to convolve the input tensor to obtain two data streams. In the first data stream, the number of filters is the same as that of the input tensor. The second data stream halves the number of filters of the input tensor to enable a direct add operation between the output of the first data stream and the second.

4.2 Loss Function

A standard loss for dense prediction problems is the l_2 loss, which minimizes the Euclidean distance between predictions and the ground truth. However, this commonly used loss is not suitable for PFNet because the l_2 loss places emphasis on outliers, i.e., the optimization objective focuses on minor outliers rather than major inliers in the PF. As mentioned in Sect. 3, we further use RANSAC to filter out outliers predicted by PFNet, this operation means that PFNet is robust to any outliers. Thus what really determines the performance of PFNet is the inliners in the estimated PF. To make use of this property, we choose a smooth-l_1 loss, which is robust to outliers, to optimize this network as follows,

$$\text{loss} = \begin{cases} 0.5 \times (F_{AB_*}^{\text{pred}} - F_{AB_*})^2, & \text{if } \left| F_{AB_*}^{\text{GT}} - F_{AB_*} \right| \leq 1 \\ \left| F_{AB_*}^{\text{pred}} - F_{AB_*} \right| - 0.5, & \text{otherwise} \end{cases} \tag{6}$$

where $*$ denotes x or y, and superscript *pred* represents the predictions in terms of F_{AB_*}. More details and a comparison of the smooth-l_1 and l_2 loss on PFNet are provided in supplementary materials.

4.3 Training and Inference

We have implemented our system using Keras [3] and TensorFlow [1]. The full network is trained in an end-to-end fashion. We train this network from scratch, where all weights are initialized using the method of [6]. We choose NAdam [25] as our optimizer because it generally acts well for many datasets and has a favorable convergence speed. The parameters used for NAdam are set to the defaults, with momentum 0.9, $\beta_1 = 0.9$, and $\beta_2 = 0.99$. We use a learning rate of 1×10^{-3} in the first 40 epochs, and divide it by 10 after each 40 epochs. Each epoch contains 1000 steps in which the batch size is set to 64. The model has finished when training reaches 80 epochs. One batch takes approximately 2s on a NVIDIA Tesla M40 GPU and it takes about 44 h of training for the model to converge. Once a PF has been obtained from a given image pair in the inference stage, we use Eq. 4 to recover dense correspondences and then adopt RANSAC to further filter outliers within. It is important to note that RANSAC is not contained within the network, and is used as a post processing step to improve the quality of the homography extracted from PFNet. In the last step, a DLT is applied on the refined dense correspondences to obtain the homography.

5   Experiments

In this section, we introduce the dataset used in our experiments and the strategy for generating samples (see Sect. 5.1). The baseline models including CNN-based and standard feature-based methods are outlined in Sect. 5.2. Section 5.3 evaluates the proposed network thoroughly with respect to CNN-based approaches to demonstrates the capacity of the proposed architecture and the contribution of the novel deconvolution block. Furthermore, a robustness analysis of our network and traditional feature-based methods, such as SIFT, and SURF, is examined in an extreme image contamination environment (see Sect. 5.4).

Fig. 3. Visualization of training dataset generation. **Left:** we randomly generate the red square in the original image (I_A) and then perturb it's four corners in $(-\rho, \rho)$ to get the green quadrilateral. The ground truth **H** can be computed from the red and green box using 4-point DLT. **Middle:** The warped image (I_B) obtained by applying the inverse of **H** on I_A. The blue square has the exact same position as that of the red box. **Right:** the F_{AB} generated from I_A and I_B. The magenta box has the same position as the blue box. Therefore, we stack the gray-scaled red patch and blue patch to form the input tensor with shape $128 \times 128 \times 2$. To obtain the $128 \times 128 \times 2$ output tensor, we stack F_{AB_x} and F_{AB_y} together in the magenta square. (Color figure online)

5.1   Synthetic Dataset Generation

The availability of large scale datasets is crucially important for the performance of CNNs. Unfortunately, there is no public dataset for this task and as such previous works use synthetic datasets to train and evaluate the approaches. By strictly following previous works' dataset generation rules [5], we trained our network using the Microsoft Common Objects in Context (MSCOCO) 2014 dataset [15], which contains 82,081 training images and 40,137 testing images. All images in the dataset have been transformed to gray scale and resized to 320×240 prior to further processing.

In the training phase, we generate the pair of input and output tensors by applying a random homography to an image. More specifically, we first randomly generate a 128×128 square of I_A with a random left top corner $\mathbf{p}_{ltc} = (x_{\mathbf{p}_{ltc}}, y_{\mathbf{p}_{ltc}})$. Secondly, we perturb each corner of this square (four corners in total) using a random value in the range of $(-\rho, \rho)$. Then the ground truth homography can be obtained from the original corners and the perturbed corners. Please note that we set ρ to 32 and limit $32 < x < 224$ and $32 < y < 80$ to ensure that the four perturbed corners do not fall outside the image. Therefore, the warped image I_B can be computed using the randomly generated homography. To create the input of the proposed network, we crop two 128×128 patches from I_A and I_B at $\mathbf{p}_{ltc}$ and then stack them together to form the input tensor whose shape is $128 \times 128 \times 2$. With respect to output, we crop two patches of the same size at $\mathbf{p}_{ltc}$ from F_{AB_x} and F_{AB_y}, such that the shape of the output tensor is $128 \times 128 \times 2$. Figure 3 visualizes our dataset generation strategy.

5.2 Baseline Models

To thoroughly evaluate the performance of the proposed network on this task, we select previous state-of-the-art CNN-based works [5,12,14] and the feature-based methods SIFT and SURF as the baseline models for comparison.

HomographyNet [5] uses a VGG-like network for this task which heavily uses fully-connected layers. HCN-x [12] stacks the proposed twin convolutional regression networks in a hierarchical way to estimate the homography between a pair of images, where x stands for the number of stacked modules. HomographyNet and HCN-x both make use of the traditional homography parameterization. While FCRN [14] is proposed for depth estimation, which is another dense prediction task, its architecture is similar to ours. Both PFNet and FCRN are built upon ResNet-50. The difference between FCRN and PFNet is that FCRN uses the upsampling block [14] to do deconvolution and does not use any identity block in the deconvolution stage. To demonstrate the effect of the identity block in the architecture, we add identity blocks to FCRN in the same way as ours and refer this method to as FCRN-IB. Furthermore, the performance of the proposed deconvolution block is validated by comparing PFNet with FCRN-IB. To maximize the performance of PFNet, we train PFNet again using 300 epochs, where the learning rate is divided by 10 after each 100 epochs, and other parameters remain the same. We denote this method as PFNet-300. Besides applying the PF to FCRN and FCRN-IB, to testify the generalization of this parameterization, we also apply the PF on the state-of-the-art FCN-DenseNet [11,26,27], which has been successfully applied to many dense prediction problems.

Regarding SIFT and SURF, we directly employ them using their OpenCV implementations with default parameter settings to detect key points and extract local descriptors on the input patch. Subsequently, correspondences are established using a standard matching and RANSAC scheme to estimate the homography.

5.3 Evaluation

We evaluate the performance of our approach and CNN-based methods on test data generated using the strategy of [5,12]. Specifically, we generate test samples from 5000 randomly selected images from the test dataset of MS COCO 2014 by following the data generation process described in Sect. 5.1. To evaluate the baseline models fairly, we employ the mean average corner error (MACE) as the metric, which is widely used in previous research [5,12]. MACE averages the Euclidean distance between the ground truth and the estimated positions of the four patch corners. Table 1 reports the results of each method in terms of MACE and also reports the network size.

Focusing on the first two columns of Table 1, we find that PFNet consistently outperforms baseline models with respect to MACE. Specifically, compared with the previous state-of-the-art, HCN-4, we have reduced MACE from 3.91 pixels to 0.92. The performance of HomographyNet is the worst among learning-based methods because of the shallow architecture and 4-point parametrization.

Table 1. Mean average corner error (MACE) comparison between our method and various baselines.

Method	MACE	Computation complexity	
		Architecture depth	Parameters
HomographyNet [5]	9.20	14	34M
HCN-1 [12]	13.04	14	17M
HCN-2 [12]	6.39	28	34M
HCN-3 [12]	4.46	42	51M
HCN-4 [12]	3.91	56	68M
FCN-DenseNet [11]	4.20	121	20M
FRCN [14]	1.86	72	28M
FRCN-IB	1.72	96	31M
PFNet	**1.63**	96	31M
PFNet-300	**0.92**	96	31M

It is worth noting that FCRN performs worse than FCRN-IB, which adds the identity blocks in the decoder. The hypothesis is that the extra layers brought by identity block increases the representative capacity of the decoder in the network, and as such the decoder can recover the PF distribution from the output of the encoder. In particular, we obtain performance improvements when we replace the upsampling block [14] with the proposed deconvolution block in FCRN-IB to form PFNet, which suggests that the deconvolution block can avoid losing information while upsampling the input feature maps by a 2X ratio when compared to the upsampling block. This is because the input tensors in the upsampling block are convolved with an extra convolutional layer before it propagates information to the end of the block. The extra convolutional layer closes the shortcut between the input and output tensor, and as such it obstructs the information flow used to learn the residual function. The lower validation loss and MACE of PFNet in Fig. 4 also demonstrates aforementioned analysis. For more details and comparisons between these three networks, readers are referred to the supplementary material. All four networks, i.e., FCN-DenseNet, FRCN, FRCN-IB, PFNet, have comparable performance with previous works and as such we claim the new homography parametrization for learning homographies has a good generalization ability.

Observing the last two columns of Table 1, one may see that HomographyNet and HCN-x have a significantly larger hyper parameter space. This is because when they formulate homography estimation as needing to estimate 8 parameters, they have to use at least two fully-connected layers to regress the homography. Therefore, the architectures have a huge numbers of parameters when compared to FCNs with the same depth. Please note that HCN-x progressively improves the performance by stacking the modules one by one. As a consequence of this hierarchical approach, a network with only 56 layers depth

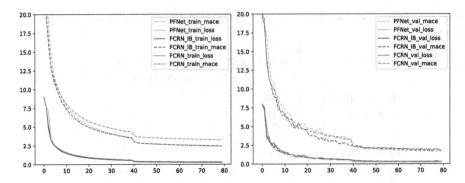

Fig. 4. The MACE and the loss value in the training and validation phases for FCRN, FCRN-IB, and PFNet.

contains 68M parameters. However, the depth of a deep learning architecture is crucially important for computer vision tasks as demonstrated in many studies [10].

Qualitative Results. We show example predictions of PFNet in Fig. 5. The model generates the PF from given image pairs and the predicted homography is recovered from the generated PF. Please note that the predicted PF is very similar to the ground truth. The same is true for the warped images. Additional qualitative experiments can be found in supplementary materials.

5.4   Evaluation on Noisy Data

In this section, we compare the proposed method with two feature-based methods, SIFT and SURF, in an extremely noise-contaminated environment to test the robustness of the algorithms. To simulate the noise contamination, we first create a image contaminator list which contains four contaminators: Gaussian blur (GB), dropout (DO), salt and pepper noise (SP), and Gaussian noise (GN); where their parameters are set in a range of (0, 4), (0, 0.4), (0, 0.4), and (0, 150) respectively according to the ImgAug toolbox[1].

To enable estimation of the PF in noise-contaminated images, we retrained our network by creating the dataset following the steps described in Sect. 5.1 but randomly select 0 to 4 contaminators to contaminate I_A and I_B separately. To analyze the robustness of the algorithms thoroughly, we split the testing experiments into 7 groups: 1. **N** (normal): the dataset is uncontaminated. 2–5. **GB** (Gaussian blur), **DO** (dropout), **SP** (salt and pepper noise), **GN** (Gaussian noise): only use one selected contaminator. 6. **M** (mix): mix 2 to 4 contaminators in a random order. 7. **HA** (heavy augmentation): mix 2 to 4 contaminators in a random order where each contaminator uses the maximum parameter. Testing

---

[1] ImgAug toolbox: https://github.com/aleju/imgaug.

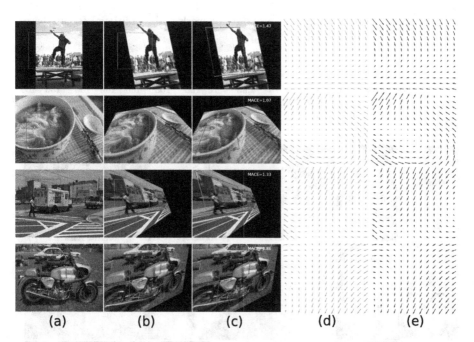

Fig. 5. Example PF generated by PFNet and the predicted homography. (a) The original 320 × 240 gray image. The red box is used to generate input. (b) The warped image transformed by the ground truth homography. A green square is placed in the same position as that of red box to form the input image patch pairs. (c) The warped image transformed by the predicted homography. MACE error is annotated in the top right corner of the image. The blue quadrilateral represents the ground truth homography, and yellow is the predicted homography. (d) The ground truth PF. (e) The predicted PF. (Color figure online)

samples in which MACE is less than 38.40 (30% × 128) are marked as successfully estimated samples. Using this, a success rate is employed to evaluate the robustness of each algorithm.

Table 2 reports the performance of the algorithms. We see that our method significantly outperforms feature-based methods in all cases. A 100% success rate in all cases means that our method has a high robustness when confronted with a noisy dataset. The significant drop in performance of SIFT and SURF when evaluating **DO** and **SP** contaminated images suggests that feature-based methods do not work when a large proportion of pixels are missing. It is worth noting that our method works acceptably for extremely contaminated image pairs, i.e., **HA**. However, SIFT, ORB, etc does not work at all in these conditions. Figure 6 shows example images and computed homography for the **HA** case.

Table 2. Comparison between the proposed network with traditional feature-based methods regarding robustness analysis.

Method	MACE							Success rate (%)						
	N	GB	DO	SP	GN	M	HA	N	GB	DO	SP	GN	M	HA
PFNet	**2.87**	**2.81**	**3.31**	**3.78**	**2.75**	**4.53**	**9.51**	100	100	100	100	100	100	100
SIFT	25.35	25.54	25.80	26.18	25.28	25.78	fail	42.45	19.44	7.98	5.21	42.01	1.4	0
SURF	25.43	25.43	26.19	25.86	25.33	27.21	fail	40.13	21.22	4.49	2.5	38.67	0.4	0

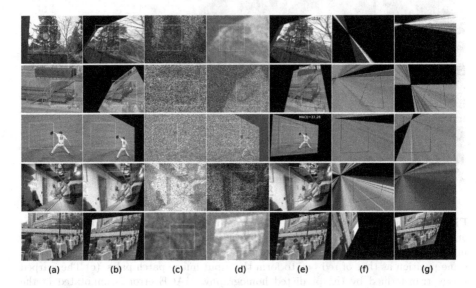

    (a)   (b)   (c)   (d)   (e)   (f)   (g)

Fig. 6. Visualization of estimating homographies in heavily contaminated image pairs. (a) Input image I_A. The red square shows the patch we extracted for training (b) The warped image I_B. The green square has the same location as the red one. (c) We randomly select two contaminators from the list and use the highest value in the value range to corrupt I_A. (d) I_B is contaminated in the same way as I_A but separately. (e)–(g) The results obtained from our method, SIFT, and SURF respectively. To improve visualization, we draw the ground truth homography using a blue square. The yellow squares are the predicted homographies. (Color figure online)

5.5   Conclusions

In this work, we introduced a new parameterization for homography estimation, i.e., the perspective field, which models the nature of the homography - pixel-to-pixel bijection. Unlike previous CNN approaches that require fully-connected layers for regressing, the PF can be easily learned by FCN architectures to significantly reduce computational complexity. To address this parameterization, we developed the PFNet architecture, which can naturally learn the PF and enables end-to-end training. The proposed deconvolution block follows the residual function fashion, and as such input information can be passed to the output directly by a shortcut connection for the upsampling. Our experiments demonstrate the power and robustness of our model with respect to baselines and previous state-of-the art works. The qualitative experiments also show visually pleasing results.

References

1. Abadi, M., et al.: TensorFlow: a system for large-scale machine learning. In: OSDI, vol. 16, pp. 265–283 (2016)
2. Bay, H., Tuytelaars, T., Van Gool, L.: SURF: speeded up robust features. In: Leonardis, A., Bischof, H., Pinz, A. (eds.) ECCV 2006. LNCS, vol. 3951, pp. 404–417. Springer, Heidelberg (2006). https://doi.org/10.1007/11744023_32
3. Chollet, F., et al.: Keras (2015)
4. Chum, O., Matas, J.: Planar affine rectification from change of scale. In: Kimmel, R., Klette, R., Sugimoto, A. (eds.) ACCV 2010. LNCS, vol. 6495, pp. 347–360. Springer, Heidelberg (2011). https://doi.org/10.1007/978-3-642-19282-1_28
5. DeTone, D., Malisiewicz, T., Rabinovich, A.: Deep image homography estimation. arXiv preprint arXiv:1606.03798 (2016)
6. Glorot, X., Bengio, Y.: Understanding the difficulty of training deep feedforward neural networks. In: Proceedings of International Conference on Artificial Intelligence and Statistics, pp. 249–256 (2010)
7. Gong, M., Zhao, S., Jiao, L., Tian, D., Wang, S.: A novel coarse-to-fine scheme for automatic image registration based on sift and mutual information. IEEE Trans. Geosci. Remote Sens. **52**(7), 4328–4338 (2014). https://doi.org/10.1109/TGRS.2013.2281391
8. Ha, H., Perdoch, M., Alismail, H., Kweon, I.S., Sheikh, Y.: Deltille grids for geometric camera calibration. In: Proceedings of IEEE Conference on Computer Vision and Pattern Recognition, pp. 5344–5352 (2017)
9. Hartley, R., Zisserman, A.: Multiple View Geometry in Computer Vision. Cambridge University Press, Cambridge (2003)
10. He, K., Zhang, X., Ren, S., Sun, J.: Deep residual learning for image recognition. In: Proceedings of IEEE Conference on Computer Vision and Pattern Recognition, pp. 770–778 (2016)
11. Huang, G., Liu, Z., van der Maaten, L., Weinberger, K.Q.: Densely connected convolutional networks. In: Proceedings of IEEE Conference on Computer Vision and Pattern Recognition (2017)
12. Japkowicz, N., Nowruzi, F.E., Laganiere, R.: Homography estimation from image pairs with hierarchical convolutional networks. In: 2017 IEEE International Conference on Computer Vision Workshops (ICCVW), pp. 904–911, October 2017. https://doi.org/10.1109/ICCVW.2017.111
13. Krizhevsky, A., Sutskever, I., Hinton, G.E.: ImageNet classification with deep convolutional neural networks. In: Advances in Neural Information Processing Systems, pp. 1097–1105 (2012)
14. Laina, I., Rupprecht, C., Belagiannis, V., Tombari, F., Navab, N.: Deeper depth prediction with fully convolutional residual networks. In: Proceedings of IEEE International Conference on 3D Vision, pp. 239–248. IEEE (2016)
15. Lin, T.Y., et al.: Microsoft COCO: common objects in context. In: Fleet, D., Pajdla, T., Schiele, B., Tuytelaars, T. (eds.) ECCV 2014. LNCS, vol. 8693, pp. 740–755. Springer, Cham (2014). https://doi.org/10.1007/978-3-319-10602-1_48
16. Long, J., Shelhamer, E., Darrell, T.: Fully convolutional networks for semantic segmentation. In: Proceedings of IEEE Conference on Computer Vision and Pattern Recognition, pp. 3431–3440 (2015)

17. Lowe, D.G.: Distinctive image features from scale-invariant keypoints. Int. J. Comput. Vis. **60**(2), 91–110 (2004)
18. Ma, J., Zhou, H., Zhao, J., Gao, Y., Jiang, J., Tian, J.: Robust feature matching for remote sensing image registration via locally linear transforming. IEEE Trans. Geosci. Remote Sens. **53**(12), 6469–6481 (2015). https://doi.org/10.1109/TGRS.2015.2441954
19. Mikolajczyk, K., Schmid, C.: A performance evaluation of local descriptors. IEEE Trans. Pattern Anal. Mach. Intell. **27**(10), 1615–1630 (2005)
20. Monasse, P., Morel, J.M., Tang, Z.: Three-step image rectification. In: Proceedings of British Machine Vision Conference, p. 89-1. BMVA Press (2010)
21. Nguyen, T., Chen, S.W., Shivakumar, S.S., Taylor, C.J., Kumar, V.: Unsupervised deep homography: a fast and robust homography estimation model. IEEE Rob. Autom. Lett. **3**(3), 2346–2353 (2018). https://doi.org/10.1109/LRA.2018.2809549
22. Rublee, E., Rabaud, V., Konolige, K., Bradski, G.: ORB: an efficient alternative to sift or surf. In: Proceedings of International Conference on Computer Vision, pp. 2564–2571. IEEE (2011)
23. Simonyan, K., Zisserman, A.: Very deep convolutional networks for large-scale image recognition. arXiv preprint arXiv:1409.1556 (2014)
24. Staranowicz, A.N., Brown, G.R., Morbidi, F., Mariottini, G.L.: Practical and accurate calibration of RGB-D cameras using spheres. Comput. Vis. Image Underst. **137**, 102–114 (2015). https://doi.org/10.1016/j.cviu.2015.03.013. http://www.sciencedirect.com/science/article/pii/S1077314215000703
25. Sutskever, I., Martens, J., Dahl, G., Hinton, G.: On the importance of initialization and momentum in deep learning. In: Proceedings of International conference on Machine Learning, pp. 1139–1147 (2013)
26. Zhang, H., Patel, V.M.: Densely connected pyramid dehazing network. arXiv preprint arXiv:1803.08396 (2018)
27. Zhu, Y., Newsam, S.: DenseNet for dense flow. arXiv preprint arXiv:1707.06316 (2017)
28. Zitova, B., Flusser, J.: Image registration methods: a survey. Image Vis. Comput. **21**(11), 977–1000 (2003)

Multivariate Attention Network
for Image Captioning

Weixuan Wang, Zhihong Chen, and Haifeng Hu$^{(\boxtimes)}$ (iD)

School of Electronics and Information Technology, Sun Yat-sen University,
Guangzhou 510006, China
{wangwx25,chenzhh45}@mail2.sysu.edu.cn, huhaif@mail.sysu.edu.cn

Abstract. Recently, attention mechanism has been used extensively in computer vision to deeper understand image through selectively local analysis. However, the existing methods apply attention mechanism individually, which leads to irrelevant or inaccurate words. To solve this problem, we propose a Multivariate Attention Network (MAN) for image captioning, which contains a content attention for identifying content information of objects, a position attention for locating positions of important patches, and a minutia attention for preserving fine-grained information of target objects. Furthermore, we also construct a Multivariate Residual Network (MRN) to integrate the more discriminative multimodal representation via modeling the projections and extracting relevant relations among visual information of different modalities. Our MAN is inspired by the latest achievements in neuroscience, and designed to mimic the treatment of visual information on human brain. Compared with previous methods, we apply diverse visual information and exploit several multimodal integration strategies, which can significantly improve the performance of our model. The experimental results show that our MAN model outperforms the state-of-the-art approaches on two benchmark datasets MS-COCO and Flickr30K.

Keywords: Image captioning · Attention mechanism ·
Multimodal combination

1 Introduction

Image captioning, which involves Computer Vision and Natural Language Processing, has recently attracted increasingly interests. Indeed, it is difficult for machine because not only does the machine need to have deep understanding on the objects and scenes in images, but also it needs to automatically generate a semantically and syntactically correct sentence to describe the relationship between them. However, image captioning has significant applications, ranging from helping visually impaired people to human-computer interaction to personal assistants, etc.

© Springer Nature Switzerland AG 2019
C. V. Jawahar et al. (Eds.): ACCV 2018, LNCS 11366, pp. 587–602, 2019.
https://doi.org/10.1007/978-3-030-20876-9_37

C: a table topped with plates bowls of food.

C+P: a table topped with plates of food and drinks.

C+P+M: a donut and a cup of coffee on a table.

(a)

C: a woman walking down the street with suitcase.

C+P: a woman standing on a sidewalk in the street.

C+P+M: a woman standing on a skateboard next to a store.

(b)

C: a desk with a computer and a keyboard.

C+P: a desk with a laptop and a monitor.

C+P+M: a desk with two monitors and two laptops on it.

(c)

Fig. 1. The illustration of captions generated by different attention mechanisms. C, P and M indicate the content, position and minutia attention mechanism respectively.

Recently, various kinds of attention mechanisms have been proposed in image captioning models. [7,28,30] propose a semantic attention mechanism to selectively focus on semantic concepts through soft attention. [15,27,29] generate a spatial map highlighting image patches associated with the generated words. [1] extracts bounding boxes via using an object detector and selectively preserves minutia information. These attention mechanisms are applied to refine the better content, position and minutia information respectively. However, just like a coin has two sides, each attention mechanism has its own advantages and disadvantages: content attention (or semantic attention) combines semantic concepts into sentences but discards visual information, position attention (or spatial attention) focuses on global relation but ignores the minutia information of objects, minutia attention (or object attention) preserves object details but lacks the global information. We illustrate the captions generated via different attention mechanisms in Fig. 1. In (a), it's obvious that the caption generated by content attention only describes there is food in image. After we add the position attention, the drink is also described. When applying content, position and minutia attention synchronously, our model enables to identify the types of food and drink.

The recent researches indicate that the above mentioned attention mechanisms may be similar to the visual information process on human brain. [23] demonstrates that the neurons in areas along the content pathway (areas Vl, V2, V4, and inferior temporal areas TEO and TE) respond selectively to relevant object identification (i.e. what). The neurons in areas along the position pathway (areas Vl, V2, V3, middle temporal area, medial superior temporal area, and further stations in inferior parietal and superior temporal sulcal cortex) respond selectively to spatial aspects of stimuli (i.e. where). Moreover, the latest research [17] indicates that there is a neural clustering in the V4 area for preserving the

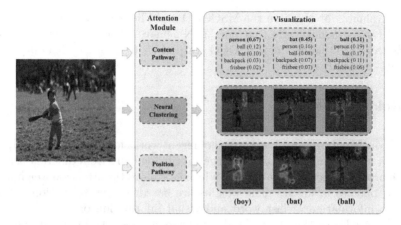

Fig. 2. The illustration of the visualization of content pathway, neural clustering and position pathway when predicting the words 'boy', 'bat' and 'ball'. The red and blue color represent the highest and lowest score respectively. (Color figure online)

fine-grained visual information of the primary visual cortex, which verifies the importance of preserving minutia information for visual tasks. In summary, the brain needs to synthesize diverse visual information to deeper understand images. Inspired by the above studies, in this paper, we propose a Multivariate Attention Network (MAN) for combining diverse attention mechanisms into a unified model to mimic the treatment of visual information on human brain. Specially, we construct content attention network, position attention network and minutia attention network, which are related to content pathway, position pathway and neural clustering respectively. Content attention network is applied to select the most relevant object concepts, position attention network is to select the areas that are most relevant to the current word and minutia attention is to preserve details of the most relevant objects. Figure 2 illustrates the visualization of each structure. Compared with the existing methods, MAN can not only focus on the specific object concepts and spatial patches but also preserve the details of objects, which results in generating more informative captions.

Since the features from different attention networks belong to different modalities, we need a multimodal embedding strategy to combine them. However, most existing image captioning models such as [18,22,30], directly integrate features of different modalities via addition or concatenation, which may be unable to fully capture the complex correlations between features of different modalities. Motivated by the researches [2,11,12] in Visual Question Answer (VQA), in this paper, we propose a novel Multivariate Residual Network (MRN) to model the richer multimodal representation. MRN is able to project feature of each modality into the target space and exploit the relevant relations among source spaces. Compared with the traditional methods, the MRN preserves the valuable information of each modality and extract more discriminative multimodal features.

We evaluate our MAN on the MSCOCO and Flickr30k datasets. The experimental results demonstrate that our MAN achieves BLEU-1 score of 80.5 and CIDEr score of 118.6 on the MSCOCO Karpathy's test split, which outperform the state-of-the-art models.

2   Related Works

Attention Mechanism. A great deal of recent works focus on exploring diverse attention mechanisms and solving image captioning tasks from different aspects. Xu [29] proposes the spatial attention which calculates the attention weights over different patches in images. The weights are based on the correlation between semantic information of last word and visual information of patches. On the basis of spatial attention, Chen [3] dynamically assesses the importance of each channel in the feature map, and obtains more discriminative information through weighted summation of different channels. You [30] constructs a visual attribute classifier for generating semantic concepts that are selectively attended and fused into the hidden state and the output of recurrent neural network. Peter [1] proposes a combined bottom-up and top-down attention mechanism which is able to calculate the attention weights of objects proposed by object detector. Although these attention mechanisms are effective, they are applied individually, which results in the inability to use the position information, concept information and minutia information synchronously.

Multimodal Embedding. Multimodal embedding is the important part in image captioning. Most existing image captioning models, such as [18,22,30], directly fuse features of different modalities via addition or concatenation. However, several studies have carried out in-depth research on multimodal embedding strategies in the Visual Question Answering (VQA) task. Inspired by ResNet [9], Kim [11] presents Multimodal Residual Network (MRN) for multimodal residual learning, whose idea is to use Hadamard multiplication for the joint residual mappings exploiting the residual learning of attentional model. Kim [12] also proposes a Multimodal Low-rank Bilinear Attention Networks (MLB) to approximate full bilinear pooling in order to learn the multimodal embedding features, which decomposes the three-dimensional weight tensor into a two-dimensional matrix. Ben-younes [2] proposes a more generalized multimodal framework Multimodal Tucker Fusion (MUTAN) for more efficient parameterized bilinear interactions between visual and textual representations. Therefore, it's benefit to transfer these achievements to image captioning.

3   Multivariate Attention Network

In order to integrate multiple attention mechanisms into a unified model, we propose a MAN for image captioning, which consists of language module, visual module, attention module and multimodal module, as illustrated in Fig. 3. The language module extracts textual features of input words and predicts the next

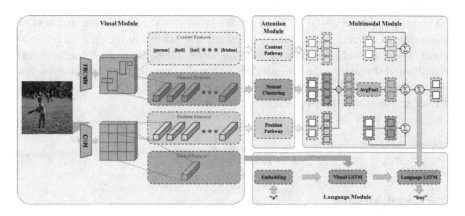

Fig. 3. The illustration of the overall structure of MAN, which is mainly composed of language module, visual module, attention module and multimodal module. The content pathway, neural clustering and position pathway in attention module refer to the content attention network, the minutia attention network and the position attention network respectively.

word. The visual module uses a Faster RCNN [21] to detect objects and identify their categories, and applies a ResNet to extract patch information and global information. The attention module selectively focuses on the most relevant contents, positions, and target objects at each time step. The multimodal module projects features of different modalities into high dimensional space and models the projection and relation among them. The language module and visual module are described in Sects. 3.1 and 3.2 respectively. In Sects. 3.3 and 3.4, we outline the architecture of our attention module and multimodal module, and in Sect. 3.5 we describe our objective function.

3.1 Language Module

The language module is designed to encode input words and decode the next word. In order to decouple the attention guide and caption generation, we construct a cascaded Long Short-Term Memory [8] (LSTM) structure including a visual LSTM and a language LSTM. The former perceives the global information in images and guides various attention, and the latter predicts words based on multimodal features.

The input of visual LSTM includes word embedding feature E_t, output of language LSTM h_{t-1}^L and global feature of input images V_g. Different from [1], we feed global feature into visual LSTM rather than the average of objects feature, so that the model has a preliminary understanding of scene, positions, objects and relationship in images. The output of visual LSTM is defined as:

$$h_t^V = LSTM_V(x_t) \tag{1}$$

$$x_t = [h_{t-1}^L, V_g, E_t] \tag{2}$$

The output h_t^V of visual LSTM encodes both global information and textual information of current word, which can lead the attention module to generate content, position and minutia attention features. Then, they are integrated into the multimodal features M via our MRN. Finally, we delivery multimodal features to language LSTM to generate semantic features, which are input into Softmax to calculate the probability of the next word:

$$Word_{t+1} \sim Softmax(h_t^L) \tag{3}$$

$$h_t^L = LSTM_L(M, h_{t-1}^L) \tag{4}$$

3.2 Visual Module

The visual module, a parallel structure consisting of Resnet101 and Faster RCNN, is designed for extracting diverse visual information. ResNet101 is adopted to obtain position representation $V_p \in R^{r \times r \times d}$ and global representation $V_g \in R^d$. The position representation $V_p = [V_{p(1)}, V_{p(2)}, ..., V_{p(r \times r)}]$ are extracted from the last convolution layer in ResNet101. Specially, $V_{p(i)} \in R^d$ is the d dimensional visual representation, which is corresponding to patch i in images. $V_g \in R^d$ is a high-level visual representation, which contains global information such as scene, positions, objects and relationship.

Faster RCNN is adopted to obtain content representation $C \in R^N$ and minutia representation $V_m \in R^{M \times d}$. The content representation C refers to the semantic concepts on the basis of each object, where N indicates the number of content representation. In practice, Faster RCNN is used to identify the categories of objects and record the N categories as the content representation according to their confidence. It is noted that we replace the phrase concepts with a single word for word embedding. For example, the concept 'sports ball' is replaced by 'ball'. The minutia representation $V_m \in R^{M \times d} = [V_{m(1)}, V_{m(2)}, ..., V_{m(M)}]$ refers to objects information detected by the Faster RCNN, where M indicates the number of objects. In practice, when an image is fed to the Faster RCNN, anchors boxes are placed on the image and predict the offset of region proposals. Then, we apply RoI pooling to map the top M region proposals to fixed-size feature vectors, which are delivered to the average pooling to obtain minutia representation.

3.3 Attention Module

The attention module is designed to selectively focus on the most relevant information. In traditional image captioning models [1,22,29,30], they mostly use single attention mechanism, whereas image captioning requires multiple types of visual information to generate captions. Inspired by [17,23] in neuroscience, we introduce content attention, position attention and minutia attention into a unified model to mimic content pathway, position pathway and neural clustering in human brain respectively. These attention mechanisms provide complementary information and produce more discriminative visual features.

Position Attention. Position attention corresponds to the position pathway for extracting the location information. We define the patch of image as the minimum calculation unit, and use the output of visual LSTM to guide the network in highlighting the most important patches at each time step. This attention mechanism can generate a weight mask related to the current word and provide the position information.

Given position features $V_p = [V_{p(1)}, V_{p(2)}, ..., V_{p(r \times r)}]$ and the output $h_t^V \in R^d$ of visual LSTM, a neural network is designed to fuse them. The output is delivered to a Softmax function in order to compute the $r \times r$ weight mask:

$$z_p(t) = W_\alpha^T tanh(W_p V_p + W_{hp} h_t^V) \tag{5}$$

$$\alpha(t) = softmax(z_p(t)) \tag{6}$$

where $W_p, W_{hp} \in R^{d \times o}$ and $W_\alpha \in R^o$ are the trainable matrices and $\alpha_t \in R^{r \times r}$ are the weights of position attention. Based on the weight matrix, the attention features can be calculated by weighted sum:

$$att_p(t) = \sum_{i=1}^{r \times r} \alpha_i(t) V_{p(i)}(t) \tag{7}$$

It's noted that the above Eqs. (5), (6), (7) can also be applied in the following content attention and minutia attention.

Content Attention. [30] points out that conceptual level information about the image content can effectively improve the performance of the captioning model. Similarly, we introduce content attention to mimic the content pathway, which selects the semantic concepts that are most relevant to current word to guide the next word generation. These concepts are the highly generalization of the objects, and can avoid generating a wrong word that is irrelevant to the input image.

Given the concepts $C = [C_1, C_2, ..., C_N]$ extracted by the Faster RCNN, we first use the Embedding layer to encode the concepts into content features $V_c = [V_{c(1)}, V_{c(2)}, ..., V_{c(N)}]$. The output h_t^V of the visual LSTM is combined with content features to calculate the weight of each concept at different time step.

Minutia Attention. Minutia attention corresponds to the neural clustering for preserving fine-grained information. Minutia attention attends the objects which are detected by Faster RCNN and selects the objective feature most relevant to current word. This attention mechanism can effectively preserve details of objects, and discard the information irrelevant to objects.

Given minutia features $V_m = [V_{m(1)}, V_{m(2)}, ..., V_{m(N)}]$ and the output h_t^V of visual LSTM, we are able to calculate the weight of each object feature at different time step.

3.4 Multimodal Module

In the previous image captioning works, researchers are devoted to exploiting how to extract better visual features and construct stronger language models.

However, image captioning involves information in diverse modalities but the existing models simply combine these information by addition, multiplication or concatenation operators. Therefore, we draw on the researches in [2,11,12] in the VQA task and propose an novel Multivariate Residual Network (MRN) for multimodal information combination. MRN is able to model the projections and extract relevant relations among different modalities.

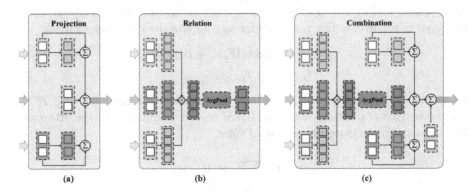

Fig. 4. The illustration of three multimodal combination strategies. (a) and (b) show the projection network and relation network respectively. (c) indicates our MRN, which is a combination of projection network and relation network.

Projection. Inspired by [9], we design the projection network (show in Fig. 4(a)) to learn the relationship between nonlinear residual function and the input data x, rather than directly learn the desired mapping $H(x)$. We define the nonlinear residual mapping as $F(x) = H(x) - x$ and the output of this network is $H(x) = F(x) + x$, which is obtained by a shortcut connection. Compared with the content space and the minutia space, the position space contains the spatial information, and we regard it as the target space. Two independent residual networks are constructed to project the content attention feature and the minutia attention feature into the target space:

$$H_c = att_c + ReLU(W_{mc}att_c) \tag{8}$$

$$H_m = att_m + ReLU(W_{mm}att_m) \tag{9}$$

where att_c and att_m are the content attention feature and minutia attention feature respectively. $ReLU$ is a nonlinear activation function and the overall projected feature H defined as

$$H = att_p + H_c + H_m \tag{10}$$

where att_p is the position attention feature.

Relation. Projecting the features of source space into the target space preserves the parallel component information of source space but loses the orthogonality component information. Therefore, we introduce the multimodal bilinear strategy to extract the latent relationship among the three source spaces.

Given the feature $x \in R^m$ and $y \in R^n$, multimodal bilinear strategy is defined as follows:

$$Z_i = x^T W_i y \tag{11}$$

where $W_i \in R^{m \times n}$ is the weight matrix, Z_i is the output of bilinear model. In order to obtain the output $Z \in R^o$, we need to learn o matrices $W = [W_1, ..., W_o] \in R^{m \times n \times o}$. Similar to [12], we can rewrite the above formula to reduce the dimensions of parameter matrices:

$$Z_i = x^T W_i y = x^T U_i V_i^T y = U_i^T x \circ V_i^T y \tag{12}$$

$$Z = U^T x \circ V^T y \tag{13}$$

where $U = [U_1, ..., U_o] \in R^{m \times o}$, $V = [V_1, ..., V_o] \in R^{n \times o}$, and $\circ$ represents the Hadamard product. In practice, in order to preserve the latent relation between different spaces, we map features into the high dimensional space. Further, we can extend this strategy to merge the features of three modalities and rewrite it as follows:

$$Z = U^T att_p \circ V^T att_c \circ W^T att_m \tag{14}$$

where $att_p, att_c, att_m \in R^d$ respectively represent position attention feature, content attention feature and minutia attention feature. $U, V, W \in R^{o \times d}$ are weight matrices that need to be learned. In order to reduce the amount of parameters, we introduce a average pooling layer to decrease the dimensions of the relation features:

$$R = AvgPool(Z, k) \tag{15}$$

where $R = AvgPool(Z, k)$ denotes a non-overlapping window of size k for average pooling. The relation network is shown in Fig. 4(b).

Combination. Given projection features H (refers to the Eq. (10)) and relational features R (refers to the Eq. (15)), the output of our multivariate residual network is defined as:

$$M = H + R \tag{16}$$

where the first item is the projection feature, and the second is the relation feature. The MRN is shown in Fig. 4(c).

3.5   Objective

Given the ground truth captions $\{w_1^*, ..., w_T^*\}$, we optimize the parameters θ of our model by maximizing the likelihood of the observed captions of given image. In practice, the goal is to minimize the cross entropy loss (XE):

$$L(\theta) = -\sum_{t=1}^{T} \log(p_\theta(w_t^* | w_1^*, ..., w_{t-1}^*)) \tag{17}$$

where $p_\theta(w_t^*|w_1^*, ..., w_{t-1}^*)$ is the probability of next word given the previous ground-truth words.

However, due to the inconsistency between the evaluation criterion and the objective function, the above optimization approach limits the performance of our model. In order to alleviate this problem, reinforcement learning strategy is introduced into MAN and the CIDEr is taken as the objective function of optimization for fair comparison. In practice, we use XE to optimize the model and then minimize the negative expectation score as followed:

$$L(\theta) = -E_{w^s \sim p_\theta}[CIDEr(w^s)] \tag{18}$$

According to [22], the expected gradient for single sample $w^s \sim p_\theta$ is:

$$\triangledown_\theta L(\theta) \approx -(CIDEr(w^s) - CIDEr(w)) \triangledown_\theta \log p_\theta(w^s) \tag{19}$$

where $w^s = (w_1^s, ..., w_T^s)$, w_t^s is the word sampled at time t and $CIDER(w)$ is the baseline score obtained by greedily decoding the current model.

4 Experiment

4.1 Datasets and Evaluation Metrics

We validated the effectiveness of MAN with two benchmark datasets: MSCOCO [13] and Flickr30k [31], which contains 123,287 images and 31,783 images respectively. Each images in these datasets has five reference captions. For fair validation and offline testing, we use the Karpathy's splits [10] which have been used extensively for reporting results in prior works. This split contains 113,287 training images, and 5 K images for validation and testing on MSCOCO. On Flickr30k, this split includes 29 K training images, and 1 K images for validation and testing. We also report the results on the online MSCOCO testing server. To evaluate caption quality, we adopt several evaluation criterions widely applied in recent image captioning works: BLEU [19], ROUGEL [5], METEOR [4] and CIDEr [24].

4.2 Comparison with State-of-the-arts

For offline evaluation, we compare our method with the current state-of-the-art models: Adaptive [15], Att2in [22], Updown [1] and NeuralBabyTalk [16] on MSCOCO, and ATT-FCN [30], RA-SS [6] and Adaptive [15] on Flickr30k. Table 1 shows the results on two datasets using Karpathy's test split.

On MSCOCO, we find that our method achieves state-of-the-art performance on all evaluation metrics with XE objective, outperforming the Adaptive by 2.6 and 5.5 on BLEU1 and CIDEr respectively. When adopting the CIDEr as objective, our method significantly outperforms previous models. Compared with Att2in that only introduces spatial attention mechanism, our method improves 6.0 on CIDEr, which demonstrates that our extra content pathway and neural

Table 1. The performance of MAN on the MSCOCO and Flickr30k Karpathy's test split. The XE is the cross entropy objective and the RL is the reinforcement learning objective. * uses better object features, and are thus not directly comparable.

Dataset	Objective	Models	B1	B2	B3	B4	M	R	C
MSCOCO		Att2in	-	-	-	31.3	26.0	54.3	101.3
		Adaptive	74.2	58.0	43.9	33.2	26.6	-	108.5
	XE	NBT	75.5	-	-	34.7	27.1	-	107.2
		Updown*	**77.2**	-	-	**36.2**	27.0	56.4	113.5
		ours	76.8	**60.7**	**46.6**	35.5	**27.5**	**56.4**	**114.0**
		Att2in	-	-	-	33.3	26.3	55.3	111.4
	RL	Updown*	79.8	-	-	36.3	**27.7**	56.9	**120.1**
		ours	**80.5**	**63.8**	**48.9**	**36.8**	27.5	**57.6**	118.6
Flickr30k		ATT-FCN	64.7	46.0	32.4	23.0	18.9	-	-
	XE	RA-SS	64.9	46.2	32.4	22.4	19.4	-	-
		Adaptive	67.7	49.4	35.4	25.1	20.4	-	53.1
		ours	**68.3**	**50.7**	**36.9**	**26.8**	**20.8**	**48.0**	**55.5**
	RL	ours	**73.3**	**53.7**	**38.6**	**27.9**	**19.6**	**47.6**	**48.9**

clustering are able to guide the model to generate infrequent and difficult words. It is unfair to directly compare our MAN with the Updown model, because the object detector of Updown is trained on Visual Genome [25] (VG) dataset which contains 1,600 categories and 400 attribute categories. Our detector is trained on MSCOCO dataset which only contains 80 categories, which means Updown model uses better object features. However, the experimental results indicate that our method is similar to the Updown model by using XE and CIDEr objectives. This further illustrates the superiority of our mimic strategy. On Flickr30k, our method significantly outperforms RA-SS and Adaptive by using XE objective, which demonstrates that our strategy can also achieve superior results on small dataset. After using the CIDEr objective, the BLEU scores increase but the CIDEr score decreases. It indicates that the CIDEr objective is not suitable for Flickr30k.

We also submit the results of our single model (MAN) to the official MSCOCO evaluation server and compare with several state-of-the-art approaches. As shown in Table 2, the models in first row are trained by XE objective and the models in second row adopt reinforcement learning to train. From Table 2, we can find that our MAN outperforms other models and achieves a state-of-the-art result.

4.3 Ablation Study

In order to better demonstrate the effectiveness of our mimic strategy and multimodal embedding strategy, we conduct several ablation experiments.

Table 2. Comparison with the state-of-the-art methods on the online MSCOCO test server. † indicates the results of ensemble models.

Models	B1		B2		B3		B4		M		R		C	
	c5	40	c5	40	c5	40	c5	40	c5	40	c5	40	c5	40
SCA [3]	72.5	89.2	55.6	80.3	41.4	69.4	30.6	58.2	24.6	32.9	52.8	67.2	91.1	92.4
NIC [26]	71.3	89.5	54.2	80.2	40.7	69.4	30.9	58.7	25.4	34.6	53.0	68.2	94.3	94.6
ATT [30]	73.1	90.0	56.5	81.5	42.4	70.9	31.6	59.9	25.0	33.5	53.5	68.2	94.3	95.8
Adaptive [15]	74.8	92.0	58.4	84.5	44.4	74.4	33.6	63.7	26.4	35.9	55.0	70.5	104.2	105.9
MIXER [20]	74.7	90.9	57.9	82.7	43.1	71.8	31.7	60.0	25.8	34.0	54.5	68.6	99.1	101.2
SPIDEr [14]	75.4	91.8	59.1	84.1	44.5	73.8	33.2	62.4	25.7	34.0	55.0	69.5	101.3	103.2
AC [32]	77.8	92.9	61.2	85.5	45.9	74.5	33.7	62.5	26.4	34.4	55.4	69.1	110.2	112.1
SCST† [22]	78.1	93.1	61.9	86.0	47.0	75.9	35.2	64.5	27.0	35.5	56.3	70.7	**114.7**	**116.7**
MAN	**79.8**	**94.2**	**63.0**	**87.3**	**48.0**	**77.3**	**35.8**	**66.0**	**27.2**	**35.8**	**56.9**	**71.5**	112.7	115.1

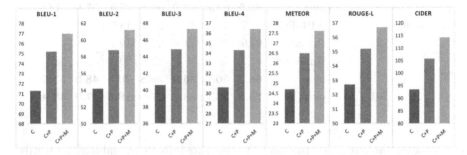

Fig. 5. The illustration of the effectiveness of three structures. C means the only content attention, C+P means the content attention and position attention, and C+P+M indicates that we apply the content attention, position attention and minutia attention synchronously.

To understand the effect of each structure in attention network, we design a series of ablation study, and the results are shown in Fig. 5. The content pathway achieves the BLEU-1 score of 71.3 and the CIDEr score of 93.5 on the Karpathy's validation split. Combining the content pathway with the position pathway, our model achieves a better performance, improving BLEU-1 to 75.2 and CIDEr to 105.7. When applying three attention mechanisms into the unified framework, the BLEU-1 and CIDEr are further promoted to 77.0 and 114.2. The success of our model may indicate that content, position and minutia attention mechanisms can provide complementary information, and generate more informative captions.

We further analyze the effectiveness of our MRN through ablation experiments and the results are shown in Fig. 6. Compared with the traditional embedding strategy which adopts addition operation to combine features of different modalities, our projection network achieves an improvement of CIDEr from 111.0 to 112.1. This demonstrates that it is effective to apply the residual network for feature combination. The relation network further promotes the CIDEr score to 112.8, because it can provide the latent relationship among different modali-

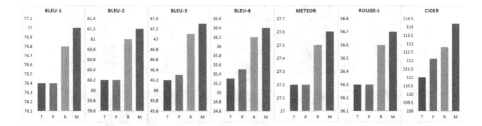

Fig. 6. The illustration of the effectiveness of our multimodal embedding strategies. T means the traditional embedding method, P means our projection network, R means our relation network and M means our MRN.

	a	group	of	people	playing	baseball	on	the	beach
person	0.2	0.22	0.23	0.6	0.08	0.02	0.2	0.21	0.23
ball	0.07	0.1	0.06	0.08	0.3	0.2	0.16	0.16	0.08
bat	0.16	0.15	0.18	0.06	0.28	0.56	0.08	0.1	0.11
glove	0.1	0.12	0.2	0.11	0.19	0.13	0.02	0.05	0.04
racket	0.04	0.03	0.05	0	0.08	0.01	0.01	0.02	0.01
handbag	0.02	0.13	0.04	0.02	0.01	0	0.03	0.03	0.02
backpack	0.03	0	0.03	0	0.02	0.02	0.02	0.01	0
boat	0.09	0.11	0.03	0	0	0	0.09	0.1	0.19
bird	0.1	0.01	0.03	0.07	0	0.02	0.19	0.06	0.04
surfboard	0.15	0.08	0.1	0.01	0	0	0.18	0.24	0.25

Fig. 7. The visualization of content attention.

ties. After integrating the projection network and the relation network into the unified framework, our MRN achieves the best CIDEr score of 114.2.

4.4 Qualitative Analysis

In order to qualitatively analyze the role of content pathway, position pathway and neural clustering, we visualize the attended image in caption generation. The visualizations are shown in Figs. 7, 8 and 9. In Fig. 7, when the input words are 'of' and 'playing', the content attention gives the highest weights to the content concepts 'person' and 'bat', to guide the generation of the next words 'people' and 'baseball' respectively. In Fig. 8, when generating the words 'beach', our position pathway focuses on the sand and the sea effectively. However, when generating object words (e.g. 'baseball'), the attention masks contain plenty of redundant information and discard details of objects. In Fig. 9, minutia attention focuses on the objects and their details, but discards the background information. Therefore, the position attention and the minutia attention provide complementary information and should be integrated into a unified framework.

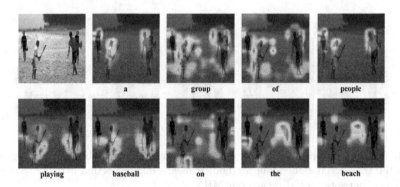

Fig. 8. The visualization of position attention. The red and blue color represent the highest and lowest score respectively. (Color figure online)

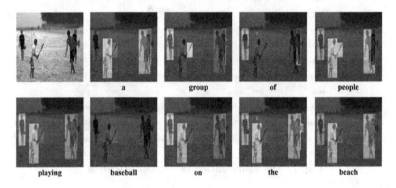

Fig. 9. The visualization of minutia attention.

5   Conclusions

Inspired by the latest research in neuroscience, we propose the Multimodal Attention Network for image captioning. Content attention, position attention and minutia attention are introduced to mimic position pathway, content pathway, and neural clustering, which are applied to locate attended positions, identify object categories and preserve details of objects respectively. Additionally, we propose a novel MRN to model the projection and extract the relevant relations among different modalities. We verify our model on the benchmark datasets MSCOCO and Flickr30k, and achieve the state-of-the-art results.

Acknowledgement. This work was supported in part by the NSFC (61673402), the NSF of Guangdong Province (2017A030311029), the Science and Technology Program of Guangzhou (201704020180), and the Fundamental Research Funds for the Central Universities of China.

References

1. Anderson, P., He, X., Buehler, C., Teney, D., Johnson, M.: Bottom-up and top-down attention for image captioning and visual question answering. In: Computer Vision and Pattern Recognition, pp. 6077–6086 (2018)
2. Benyounes, H., Cadene, R., Cord, M., Thome, N.: Mutan: multimodal tucker fusion for visual question answering. In: International Conference on Computer Vision, pp. 2612–2620 (2017)
3. Chen, L., et al.: SCA-CNN: spatial and channel-wise attention in convolutional networks for image captioning. In: Computer Vision and Pattern Recognition, pp. 5659–5667 (2017)
4. Denkowski, M., Lavie, A.: Meteor 1.3: automatic metric for reliable optimization and evaluation of machine translation systems. In: Proceedings of the Sixth Workshop on Statistical Machine Translation, pp. 85–91. Association for Computational Linguistics (2011)
5. Flick, C.: ROUGE: a package for automatic evaluation of summaries. In: The Workshop on Text Summarization Branches Out, p. 10 (2004)
6. Fu, K., Jin, J., Cui, R., Sha, F., Zhang, C.: Aligning where to see and what to tell: image captioning with region-based attention and scene-specific contexts. IEEE Trans. Pattern Anal. Mach. Intell. **39**(12), 2321–2334 (2017)
7. Gan, Z., et al.: Semantic compositional networks for visual captioning. In: Computer Vision and Pattern Recognition, pp. 5630–5639 (2017)
8. Graves, A.: Long short-term memory. In: Graves, A. (ed.) Supervised Sequence Labelling with Recurrent Neural Networks. Studies in Computational Intelligence, vol. 385, pp. 37–45. Springer, Heidelberg (2012). https://doi.org/10.1007/978-3-642-24797-2_4
9. He, K., Zhang, X., Ren, S., Sun, J.: Deep residual learning for image recognition. In: Computer Vision and Pattern Recognition, pp. 770–778 (2016)
10. Karpathy, A., Fei-Fei, L.: Deep visual-semantic alignments for generating image descriptions. In: Computer Vision and Pattern Recognition, pp. 3128–3137 (2015)
11. Kim, J.H., et al.: Multimodal residual learning for visual QA. In: Advances in Neural Information Processing Systems, pp. 361–369 (2016)
12. Kim, J.H., On, K.W., Lim, W., Kim, J., Ha, J.W., Zhang, B.T.: Hadamard product for low-rank bilinear pooling. arXiv preprint arXiv:1610.04325 (2016)
13. Lin, T.-Y., et al.: Microsoft COCO: common objects in context. In: Fleet, D., Pajdla, T., Schiele, B., Tuytelaars, T. (eds.) ECCV 2014. LNCS, vol. 8693, pp. 740–755. Springer, Cham (2014). https://doi.org/10.1007/978-3-319-10602-1_48
14. Liu, S., Zhu, Z., Ye, N., Guadarrama, S., Murphy, K.: Improved image captioning via policy gradient optimization of spider. In: International Conference on Computer Vision, pp. 873–881 (2017)
15. Lu, J., Xiong, C., Parikh, D., Socher, R.: Knowing when to look: adaptive attention via a visual sentinel for image captioning. In: Computer Vision and Pattern Recognition, pp. 375–383 (2017)
16. Lu, J., Yang, J., Batra, D., Parikh, D.: Neural baby talk. In: Computer Vision and Pattern Recognition, pp. 7219–7228 (2018)
17. Lu, Y., et al.: Revealing detail along the visual hierarchy: neural clustering preserves acuity from v1 to v4. Neuron **98**(2), 417–428 (2018)
18. Mao, J., Xu, W., Yang, Y., Wang, J., Huang, Z., Yuille, A.: Deep captioning with multimodal recurrent neural networks (m-RNN). arXiv preprint arXiv:1412.6632 (2014)

19. Papineni, K., Roukos, S., Ward, T., Zhu, W.J.: BLEU: a method for automatic evaluation of machine translation. In: Proceedings of the 40th Annual Meeting on Association for Computational Linguistics, pp. 311–318. Association for Computational Linguistics (2002)

20. Ranzato, M., Chopra, S., Auli, M., Zaremba, W.: Sequence level training with recurrent neural networks. arXiv preprint arXiv:1511.06732 (2015)

21. Ren, S., He, K., Girshick, R., Sun, J.: Faster R-CNN: towards real-time object detection with region proposal networks. In: International Conference on Neural Information Processing Systems, pp. 91–99 (2015)

22. Rennie, S.J., Marcheret, E., Mroueh, Y., Ross, J., Goel, V.: Self-critical sequence training for image captioning. In: Computer Vision and Pattern Recognition, pp. 7008–7024 (2017)

23. Ungerleider, L.G., Haxby, J.V.: 'what' and 'where' in the human brain. Curr. Opin. Neurobiol. **4**(2), 157–165 (1994)

24. Vedantam, R., Zitnick, C.L., Parikh, D.: CIDEr: consensus-based image description evaluation. In: Computer Vision and Pattern Recognition, pp. 4566–4575 (2015)

25. Krishna, R., Zhu, Y., Groth, O., Johnson, J., Hata, K., Li, F.F., et al.: Visual genome: connecting language and vision using crowdsourced dense image annotations. Int. J. Comput. Vis. **123**(1), 32–73 (2017)

26. Vinyals, O., Toshev, A., Bengio, S., Erhan, D.: Show and tell: a neural image caption generator. In: Computer Vision and Pattern Recognition, pp. 3156–3164 (2015)

27. Wang, Y., Lin, Z., Shen, X., Cohen, S., Cottrell, G.W.: Skeleton key: image captioning by skeleton-attribute decomposition. In: Computer Vision and Pattern Recognition, pp. 7272–7281 (2017)

28. Wu, Q., Shen, C., Liu, L., Dick, A., Hengel, A.V.D.: What value do explicit high level concepts have in vision to language problems? In: Computer Vision and Pattern Recognition, pp. 203–212 (2016)

29. Xu, K., Ba, J.L., Kiros, R., Cho, K., Courville, A., Salakhutdinov, R., et al.: Show, attend and tell: neural image caption generation with visual attention. In: International Conference on Machine Learning, pp. 2048–2057 (2015)

30. You, Q., Jin, H., Wang, Z., Fang, C., Luo, J.: Image captioning with semantic attention. In: Computer Vision and Pattern Recognition, pp. 4651–4659 (2016)

31. Young, P., Lai, A., Hodosh, M., Hockenmaier, J.: From image descriptions to visual denotations: new similarity metrics for semantic inference over event descriptions. Trans. Assoc. Comput. Linguist. **2**, 67–78 (2014)

32. Zhang, L., et al.: Actor-critic sequence training for image captioning. arXiv preprint arXiv:1706.09601 (2017)

Age-Puzzle FaceNet for Cross-Age Face Recognition

Yangjian Huang, Wendong Chen, and Haifeng Hu$^{(\boxtimes)}$ (iD)

School of Electronics and Information Technology, Sun Yat-Sen University,
Guangzhou 510006, China
{huangyj56,chenwd7}@mail2.sysu.edu.cn, huhaif@mail.sysu.edu.cn

Abstract. Cross-Age Face Recognition (CAFR) has drawn increasing attention in recent years. Technically however, due to the nonlinear variation of face aging and insufficient datasets covering a wide range of ages, it remains a major challenge in the field of face recognition. To address this problem, we propose a novel model called Age-Puzzle FaceNet (APFN) based on adversarial training mechanism. The model we propose can be subdivided into two networks consisting of three elementary parts: (a) a Generator G: our core part for generating age-invariant identity features; (b) an Identity Classifier which forms the first identity recognition network (namely IRN) with the generator G to enhance identity recognition performance; (c) an Age Discriminator which attempts to retrieve age information from the generated features and forms the second network (namely Age Verification network AVN) with the same generator. Our extracted features achieve improvement on age invariance via adversarial training in AVN while remaining identity discriminative utilizing joint training in IRN. Apart from achieving state-of-the-art performance, APFN has demonstrated two other distinct characteristics as follows. First, identity-labeled dataset and age-labeled dataset are used respectively for above two networks such that no more effort to search for training data labeled by both age and identity. As a consequence, more training data is available to give a better recognition performance. Second, the strategy we adopt to handle age and identity attributes can provide a new insight on other robust recognition domain with respect to multi-attributes or attributes separation. We conducted comprehensive experiments on two publicly available datasets called Cross-Age Celebrity and Cross-Age LFW. The results of our proposed architecture demonstrate a better performance and effectiveness.

Keywords: Cross-age face recognition ·
Generative adversarial networks · Multi-attribute recognition

1 Introduction

Face recognition has always been a hot topic in computer vision area. Much relative work focus on improving recognition performance under real-life conditions

© Springer Nature Switzerland AG 2019
C. V. Jawahar et al. (Eds.): ACCV 2018, LNCS 11366, pp. 603–619, 2019.
https://doi.org/10.1007/978-3-030-20876-9_38

such as occlusion, illumination, expression and age, etc. Among them, aging variation is a challenging factor to consider since facial appearance often changes dramatically with age, as shown in Fig. 1. Besides, cross-age face recognition (CAFR) has various practical applications such as finding missing children or outlaws years later. Although a great progress has been made in face recognition task, cross-age face recognition still lacks satisfactory solutions.

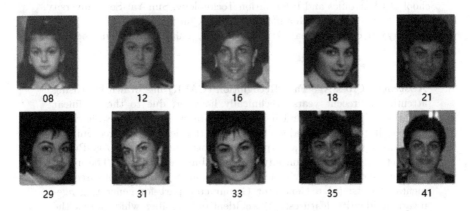

Fig. 1. The cross-age face images which show the significant intra-personal variations for one of the subjects in the FG-NET database

To address cross-age face recognition task, the previous study falls into two categories including generative approaches and discriminative approaches. The typical generative approaches first synthesize aged face images and then conduct recognition task. However, because of the high complexity in modeling aged face, these methods not only are at high computational cost but also fail to achieve stable performance. On the other hand, discriminative approaches [3,12,15,16] attempt to handle cross-age face recognition by employing age-invariant classifiers to distinguish preprocessed features. However, these features still contain age-related information due to the strong model assumption, which limits the accuracy of recognition. Some recent work is conducted to extract age-invariant discriminative features based on the assumption that the whole face features are combined by age-related factor and age-invariant factor [9,14,28].

Recently, due to the great classification power of deep convolutional neutral network (CNN), many new models based on CNN are established [14,28,33]. These models achieve great improvement compared with traditional methods due to the end-to-end training scheme. With end-to-end training, deep networks can learn features directly from raw materials which avoids error accumulation, strong model assumption and manual feature selection, leading to great improvement on the discriminative ability of the extracted features.

Although the existing CAFR methods mentioned above achieve promising results, they still have two major problems. Firstly, they fail to provide an end-to-end training network for both identity and age learning. Instead, these methods above try to separate the age information and identity information from a certain feature layer. To do a more thorough separation, more age-related information is extracted for removal before the feature layer. However, it is hard to remove all age-related information through models based on strong assumptions, like probability models. Hence these features include more age-related information and cannot provide age invariance in some cases. Besides, the performance of these networks heavily depend on specific training dataset for CAFR tasks. Under this circumstance, only dataset that both labeled by identity and age can be used for robust training, which however is rare in existing baseline datasets. Even for a dataset that satisfies above requirement, there are not enough samples covering different age stages for each person in most cases.

Inspired by the adversarial training mechanism in Generative Adversarial Nets (GAN) [11], in this paper, we consider obtaining age-invariant deep features based on an adversarial procedure to tackle these problems from a new perspective. Instead of explicitly separating age-related factor from the whole face feature, we aim to obtain a robust feature generator G whose extracted features have the following two requirements. The first is it should contain sufficient identity information for identification task. The second is that it can remain invariant with respect to age. In short, our ultimate goal is to obtain a generator which can extract age-invariant but identity-discriminative features. To achieve this, we devise an Age-Puzzle FaceNet (APFN) consisting of two networks: an Identity Recognition network (namely IRN) formed by a Generator G and an Identity Classifier I for satisfying the first requirement, and another Age Verification Network (namely AVN) formed by an Age Discriminator D with the same G for meeting the second requirement. To sum up, the contributions of our work are listed as follows:

(1) We devise a new robust cross-age face recognition model, APFN specifically for addressing CAFR tasks. The model is based on an IRN, followed by an AVN. Typically, the Generator G is a part of sharing, and it can extract features used to discriminate identity via identity-labeled datasets trained in IRN. Meanwhile, with age-labeled dataset, the features generated remain age-invariant via separate training in AVN. Additionally, we employ a cross-layer implementation to achieve better feature extraction in AVN.

(2) Our new model exploits the adversarial training mechanism to assist for age-invariant feature extraction. This method adopts an auxiliary age verification discriminator to guide age-invariant features extraction through adversarial process. To the best of our knowledge, it is the first attempt to introduce adversarial process into CAFR tasks. Furthermore, the processing method we use here for identity and age attributes provides a new insight into multi-attributes or attributes separation tasks and is equally applicable for these problems.

(3) Extensive experiments have shown that the proposed APFN outperforms previous studies such as HFA [9], LF-CNNs [28] and AFJF-CNN [14] on some public face aging datasets, including CACD-VS [3] and CALFW [34].

The remainder of the paper is organized as follows. Section 2 discusses the related works. Section 3 introduces the formulation and details of the proposed APFN. Section 4 presents the experimental results. In the end, Sect. 5 concludes this paper.

2   Related Works

The researches on age related face image analysis has only been studied in recent years. Existing methods on CAFR fall into two categories: generative approaches and discriminative approaches.

Generative methods try to synthesise face images that match the target age and then perform recognition tasks [5,8,21]. However, these methods fail to achieve a stable performance due to their inherent defect like strong parametric assumptions and high computational expense. The recent proposed generative method [19] devises a deep aging-aware denoising auto-encoder model (a2-DAE) combined with traditional aging pattern synthesis module to achieve face synthesis and recognition. The a2-DAE trains four parallel CNNs based on the synthesized faces of different age groups, and then predict the verification score. However a2-DAE still suffers the inherent constraint as above and even adds extra computational cost for more face synthesis.

Discriminative approaches typically employ classifiers to distinguish preprocessed age-invariant face features. For example, Ling et al. adopt gradient orientation pyramid (GOP) [18] as feature with the support vector machine (SVM) as classifier. Li et al. [17] combine SIFT [7] and Local Binary Pattern (LBP) [20] as features and use LDA approach (Random sampling LDA, RS-LDA) to do the classify task. Du et al. propose an alternating greedy coordinate descent (AGCD) algorithm [6] to balance features sharing and features exclusion between cross-age face verification (FV) and cross-face age verification (AV), thus to guide feature selection more precisely. Chen et al. introduce a novel coding method called Cross-Age Reference Coding (CARC) [3] which encodes the low-level feature of a face image with an age-invariant reference space. The Hidden Factor Analysis (HFA) [9] considers the facial image as linear combination of two independent factors: an identity factor and an age factor and extract the identity component to solve the cross-age face recognition. Gong et al. develop a new maximum entropy feature descriptor (MEFD) [10] together with a new matching method called identity factor analysis (IFA) to estimate the probability that two faces have the same underlying identity. These methods provide new ideas to obtain age-invariant features, but they require great manual effort to select sophisticated features without age priori. The above discriminative methods have proved to be effective in certain cases. However, without end-to-end training, the manual features cannot fit the complicated scene entirely. Besides, many methods above are based on strong model assumption of ageing which will limit the recognition performance such that the output may be unstable when the age gap is large.

Due to the great success of deep convolutional neutral network in the area of classification, researchers began to explore the potential of this useful tool in

CAFR tasks [14, 26, 28, 29]. With deep learned face representation, DeepFace [26] achieve human-level accuracy in face verification. Facenet [24] proposes a deep CNN trained to optimize the unified embedding and further achieves 99.63% verification accuracy on LFW. Wen et al. [29] combine a multi-patch deep CNN and deep metric learning together to achieve a new recording verification accuracy: 99.77% on LFW. Recently, deep CNN methods are also proposed for CAFR tasks. Wen et al. consider the facial representation as a liner combination of identity features and age features and propose a latent factor guided convolutional neutral network (LF-CNNs) [28]. Based on this assumption, they construct a latent identity analysis (LIA) module to guide the learning of the CNNs parameters thus to extract the age-invariant deep face features for CAFR tasks. Zheng et al. propose a new deep face recognition network to obtain age features by an age estimation task, namely age estimation guided convolutional neutral network (AE-CNN) [33]. Then the age features are used to remove age-related information of the identity feature layer. Although these methods greatly boost the verification accuracy, the lack of cross-age identity training dataset still extremely cumbers the improvement of performance.

To avoid the major constraint of training data, we attempt to find another solution. And recently proposed Generative Adversarial Nets (GANs) [11], to our knowledge, provides an idea to treat such multi-attributes tasks. GANs first proposed by Goodfellow et al. typically consist of two models: a generative model G and a discriminator model D. G tries to capture the training data distribution and maximize the probability of D making a mistake while D struggles to correctly distinguish the fake data from real distribution. By this adversarial training process, G finally recover the real data distribution. Marveled at the ability to generate plausible synthesis images of GANs, Antipov et al. [1] proposes an automatic face aging method based on GANs, but rather than using a conditional GANs, it employs a dependent face recognition network to learn the latent space thus achieve its emphasis on identity-preserving. Lample et al. introduce a new encoder-decoder architecture called Fader Network [13] by adding an adversarial component to generate different realistic versions of input image. By balancing both the discriminator objective and reconstruction objective, Fader network succeeds in learns attribute-invariant latent representation which could be used for image synthesis with different attribute values. Although GANs are usually performed to generate complete pictures, the potential of GANs on classification and recognition tasks is not well discovered.

3   Approach

CAFR means whether two face images of different ages can be identified as belonging to the same person, which is a challenging task in the field of face recognition. In this section, we propose a novel model named APFN for CAFR tasks. In the following, we first introduce the modeling problem about CAFR and the two independent networks about IRN and AVN. Then we present the whole deep architecture and describe cross-layer' implementation of APFN.

3.1 Modeling Problem

Let X be an image domain, Y be the identity domain and Z be the age domain associated with images in X.

$$Y = \{0, 1, 2, \ldots, max(identities)\} \tag{1}$$

$$Z = \{0, 1, 2, \ldots, max(age)\} \tag{2}$$

We have two training sets: $S1 = \{(x_1, y_1), (x_2, y_2), \cdots, (x_p, y_p)\}$ and $S2 = \{(x_1, z_1), (x_2, z_2), \cdots, (x_q, z_q)\}$ where p is the number of images in identity training set and q is the number of images in age training set.

The key for solving CAFR tasks is to obtain a model from $S1$ and $S2$ to generate feature vector which has strong discriminative ability on the identity domain Y but is irrelative to age domain Z. However, the previous models for CAFR can not get the age-invariant feature entirely since the age-invariant feature is latent and the feature they obtain often contains age-related component. Even though some methods have been proposed to extract person-specific feature for CAFR tasks, the performance of these methods heavily depend on specific training dataset labeled by both identity and age.

At the same time, considering the fact that there are rare dataset containing enough samples covering different age stages for each person, we propose a new method using the adversarial training mechanism to extract the person-specific features and get rid of age-related component from them. Our model can be trained with only identity-labeled data and only age-labeled data, solving the problem of lacking enough training data.

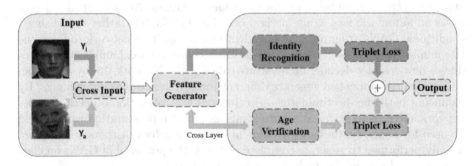

Fig. 2. The architecture of the proposed APFN and its training process. APFN is a combination of two networks: IRN and AVN. IRN consists of a feature generator and an identity discriminator while AVN includes the same feature generator and an auxiliary age discriminator. Y_i means the image with only identity label, Y_a means the image with only age label, Y_i and Y_a are used for training IRN and AVN respectively.

Figure 2 shows the architecture of our proposed APFN model, which is a combination of two networks: an Identity Recognition network (IRN) and an Age Verification network (AVN). The IRN consists of a feature generator and an Identity Classifier for identity recognition. The AVN includes the same feature generator and an auxiliary Age Discriminator to guide the optimization of IRN with age information. Overall, the formulation of our model can be represented as follow.

First, we construct a feature Generator $G(W_G) : X \to R^N$, a convolution neural network with parameter W mapping an input face image X into its corresponding N-dimensional feature vector $G(W_G, X)$. Then, the Identity Classifier $I(W_I) : R^N \to Y$ is a discriminator to capture identity information from $G(X)$ for verifying the true identity. At last, the Age Discriminator $A(W_A) : R^N \to Z$ is another discriminator predicting the age of input face image X by checking age information from $G(x)$. For convenience, we use G, I, A to denote $G(W_G)$, $I(W_I)$ and $A(W_A)$.

According to the design of the APFN's architecture, the AVN can provide enough age-related information by adversarial training for IRN. Because of the shared parameter W_G from the Generator G, the IRN can get both age robust and identity discriminative feature vector for solving the CAFR problems guided by age-related information. Hence, based on the adversarial training mechanism, our APFN model can extract age-invariant feature for improving the performance of CAFR tasks.

3.2 Identity Recognition Network (IRN)

In our model, IRN is used to train a discriminative generator G in order to reduce intra-class distance of and increase inter-class distance of generated features. IRN consists of a feature generator G and an identity discriminator I. Hence, the web-scale face datasets without age label can be used to train this network. In our implementation, we choose the triplet loss [22] as the loss function of I, which can be represented as:

$$J_{ide} = \sum_{i=1}^{N} ||I(G(x_i^a)) - I(G(x_i^p))||_2^2 - ||I(G(x_i^a) - I(G(x_i^n))||_2^2 + \alpha \qquad (3)$$

where $I(x)$ is the output of IRN, x_i^a, x_i^p and x_i^n mean the anchor image, positive image and negative image of subject i respectively for triplet loss, α is the margin of triplet loss.

In fact, if the training dataset S1 contains sufficient images for every person at different age states, we can make the feature vector satisfy the requirements of both age robust and identity discriminative by optimizing this network. However, in most cases, the collected identity datasets are on a relatively small span of age, where age information is more likely to serve as clues to assist in identification task, resulting in the difficulty to achieve age-sensitivity for a single network.

3.3 Age Verification Network (AVN)

In order to improve the performance of CAFR tasks, we propose the AVN to assist the IRN to extract age-invariant feature. Firstly, we attempt to learn age-invariant feature representation. The age-invariant feature can be represented as follow:

$$min \ ||G(x_i^m) - G(x_i^n)|| \tag{4}$$

G(x) means the generated feature from image x. x_i^m and x_i^n mean the two face images from the same subject i. m and n are the age variables meeting the condition that $m \ll n$.

In reality, it is difficult to collect a large number of photos of different ages for one person in dataset. So, in order to get age-invariant feature, we strength the constraint that the generated feature vectors cannot contain age information for a given picture in X. That is, neither can the true age of X be predicted through $G(x)$, nor can $G(x)$ be used to compare the age difference between images.

To meet this constraint, an auxiliary AVN is introduced in our method. In this network, we adopt the age discriminator $A(W_A)$ to predict true age from feature vector $G(x)$. Meanwhile, the generator $G(W_G)$ is updated by stochastic gradient ascent against the loss of $A(W_A)$ such that the discriminator is unable to identify the true age. Similar to GANs, G and A form a two-player game where A aims to maximize its ability for age verification while G struggles to prevent A by learning to extract features invariant with respect to age. By general setting, A can output probability of each candidate age group $P_{W_A}(z|G(x))$ given a picture X.

Because age is a continuous integer variable, if we use classification loss function directly, such as softmax may result in decrease in recognition performance level. So we propose a new age discriminative loss function called Regression Triple Loss (RTL) as follows:

$$\begin{cases} J_{age} = \sum_{j=1}^{M} ||A(G(x_j^a)) - A(G(x_j^p))||_2^2 - ||A(G(x_j^a)) - D(G(x_j^n))||_2^2 + \beta \\ | \ h(x_j^a) - h(x_j^p) \ | < k \ \& \ | \ h(x_j^a) - h(x_j^n) \ | > k \end{cases} \tag{5}$$

where $A(x)$ means the output of AVN and $h(x)$ means the age of image X. x_j^a , x_j^p and x_j^n mean the anchor image, positive image and negative image respectively, and β is the margin of triplet loss.

For better understanding, we may exemplify the objective of RTL as follows: for every three input images, when the age difference between two images is less than k but they both greater than k compared with the third counterpart, $A(W_A)$ attempts to minimize the distance between the first two feature vectors while maximizing their distances corresponding to the third one.

We have carefully designed a RTL function for continuous variables, with which AVN learns to make Generator G extract age-invariant features for the purpose of improving the CAFR's performance.

3.4   Cross-Layer APFN Implementation

According to [24] and [25], we apply Inception-ResNet-v1 model to our base network model, and apply the setting about IRN from [24]. The relationship between feature generator and IRN is shown in Fig. 3.

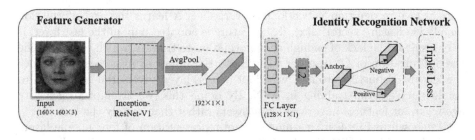

Fig. 3. The relationship between Feature Generator and IRN. APFN use the Inception-ResNet-v1 model as our base model for generate feature and triplet loss is used for loss function.

We use S, I_k, R_k to denote stem block [25], inception-resnet block and residual block respectively. Stem block consists of six convolution layers and a max-pooling layer.

In our model, $G(W_G)$, $I(W_I)$ can be set as follows: $Input \rightarrow S \rightarrow I_A \times 5 \rightarrow R_A \rightarrow I_B \times 10 \rightarrow R_B \rightarrow I_C \times 5 \rightarrow AvgPooling \rightarrow FC_{128} \rightarrow TripletLoss$.

For $A(W_A)$, it is set as follows: $S_{output} \rightarrow I_A \times 5 \rightarrow R_A \rightarrow I_B \times 10 \rightarrow R_B \rightarrow I_C \times 5 \rightarrow AvgPooling \rightarrow FC_{128} \rightarrow TripletLoss$.

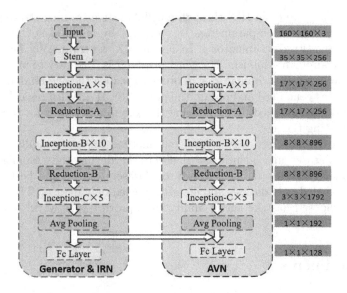

Fig. 4. An overview of the proposed APFN framework. By learning feature representation of four middle layers in G, AVN provides a direction for G to exclude age information, which will improve the ability of age-invariant recognition.

As shown above, I only adopts a triplet-loss to improve the identity discriminative power of G(x), so the training of IRN is equivalent to the process of a normal face recognition network. However, since A learns the age information merely via feature vector G(x), if the feature is adopted only in the last layer, it may result in the lack of enough age information to train A, which can not guide the optimization of G. In order to strength the power of A as well as enhance the features robustness to age, we adopt a cross-layer adversarial-connection to conduct adversarial training in AVN. By doing this, we attempt to generate age-invariant features in several lower layers rather than merely the last one.

As shown in Fig. 4, by learning feature representation of four middle layers in G, A provides a direction for G to exclude age information. Overall, G, on the one hand, needs to do co-train with I (in IRN) for improving the ability of discriminating identity, on the other hand, co-train with A (in AVN) to learn age invariance representation. To sum up, our model is divided into two subnetworks and trained in an alternative manner. We use identity-labeled datasets and age-labeled datasets for IRN and AVN respectively.

$$\min_{(W_G, W_I)} J_{ide} = \sum_{i=1}^{N} ||I(G(x_i^a)) - I(G(x_i^p))||_2^2 - ||I(G(x_i^a)) - I(G(x_i^n))||_2^2 + \alpha \quad (6)$$

$$\min_{W_A} \max_{W_G} J_{age} = \sum_{j=1}^{M} ||A(G(x_j^a)) - A(G(x_j^p))||_2^2 - ||A(G(x_j^a)) - A(G(x_j^n))||_2^2 + \beta \quad (7)$$

In Formula 6, we train IRN through a collaborative training strategy, which obtains the collaborative parameters W_G and W_I by minimizing the loss function of the identity discriminator I. In Formula 7, we train AVN by means of adversarial training mechanism. For generator G, it is necessary to maximize the loss function of age discriminator A in order to reduce the age-related information in features generated and obtain the parameter W_G. With regard to A, the parameter W_A is obtained by minimizing the loss function of it for the purpose of discriminating the age.

With the training strategy above, our method has successfully separated age-labeled dataset and identity-labeled dataset during the training phases, which effectively increases the capacity of datasets due to the best exploitation of age-labeled-only dataset and identity-labeled-only dataset. Therefore, the approach proposed has the better ability to improve the network's recognition performance.

4   Experiments

In this section, we conduct experiments to demonstrate the effectiveness of the proposed APFN on two challenging face aging databases, including CALFW [34] (the cross-age face verification dataset based on the LFW dataset) and CACD-VS [3] (the verification subset of the Cross-Age Celebrity Dataset).

4.1   Implementation Details

Preprocessing. For each face image, we use the recently proposed algorithm [32] to detect the facial landmarks in images. Then the face images are cropped to 160×160 according to the location of five facial points by similar transformation.

Training Datasets. The training data in this paper is composed of two parts: IRN training data Y_i (that only contains identity information) and AVN training data Y_a (that only contains age information), as shown in Fig. 5. For IRN training data Y_i, we use the large scale web-collected face dataset CASIA-WebFace [31], and for AVN training data Y_a, we use the IMDB dataset, which is a subset of the IMDB-WIKI dataset [23].

The CASIA-WebFace dataset is currently one of the largest available dataset with about $10\,K$ celebrities, and $500\,K$ images. The Imdb-Wiki dataset is the largest scale face aging dataset containing over $500\,K$ images with only age label. We set the time span of ten years for each age cluster, which is as the same as many previous studies [27,30].

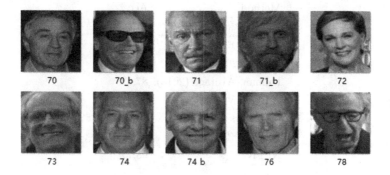

Fig. 5. Examples of face images with only age label in the IMDB-WIKI dataset

Detailed Setting in APFN Model. This paper implements FaceNet [24] and Inception-ResNet-v1 model [25] as the IRN and the feature generator respectively. FaceNet has been proved to be one of the most effective face feature descriptors in [24]. For improving the IRN's ability of extracting identity feature, we restore the pre-trained model provided by FaceNet as our IRN model and then fine-tuned by IRN training data.

Unless otherwise specified, the batch size is 90 and the epoch size is 540. We set different learning rates for IRN and AVN. For IRN, its learning rate is automatically changed from 10^{-3} to 10^{-6}. There is something noticeable that the AVN can not get real age information below enough training time, since the AVN's learning rate is set to 0 in 50 epochs and then the learning rate is changed from 5×10^{-2} to 5×10^{-5}.

In order to evaluate the performance of the proposed age-invariant features, our approach uses Euclidean distance and the nearest neighbor rule as the classifier.

4.2 Experiments on CACD Verification Subset

CACD-VS [3] is the subset of the Cross-Age Celebrity Dataset, which contains 163,446 images from 2,000 celebrities with labeled age. We test the APFN with CACD-VS which consists of 4,000 image pairs, including 2,000 positive pairs and 2,000 negative pairs, and has been annotated entirely. According to the ten-fold cross-validation rule, we calculate the Euclidean distance of each pairs and choose the best threshold with nine folds. We show the result of our module by verification rate compared with other baselines (including HD-LBP [4], HFA [9], CARC [3], LF-CNNs [28] and FaceNet [24]) on CACD-VS, and the comparative results are reported in Table 1 and Fig. 6.

Table 1. The verification rate of different methods on CACD-VS

Method	Acc
HD-LBP (2013) [4]	81.6%
HFA (2013) [9]	84.4%
CARC (2014) [3]	87.6%
Human, Average (2015)	87.6%
Human, Voting (2015)	87.6%
LF-CNNs (2016) [28]	98.5%
FaceNet (2015) [24]	97.6%
APFN	98.7%

As can be seen in Table 1, the performance of APFN outperforms other methods on CACD-VS dataset, which demonstrates the superiority of our method. However, as shown in the Fig. 6, since that the shooting time of photos from the same subject in CACD-VS are not span over nine years, our model surpasses the result of FaceNet with an inapparent margin, which means that the APFN model can not make great improvement in recognizing similar aged pairs of face images.

Figure 7 shows some failed retrievals in the CACD-VS dataset. While the positive pairs are not correct in these cases, the probe images or the false rejected images appear to be influenced by pose or expression.

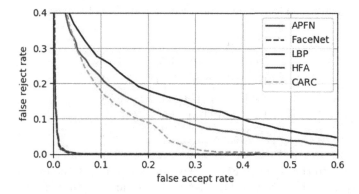

Fig. 6. ROC comparisons of APFN and baselines on CACD-VS

Fig. 7. Some examples of failed retrievals in CACD verification subset. The first row is the probe faces, the second row presents the false rejected faces using our approach.

4.3 Experiments on Cross Age LFW Dataset

CALFW is a newly proposed benchmark dataset which contains 4,025 individuals with 2 to 4 images for each persons. It selects 3,000 positive face pairs with age gaps to adding process intra-class variance. Negative pairs with same gender and race are selected to reduce the influence of attribute difference between positive or negative pairs and achieve face verification instead of attributes classification. Following the testing strategy as in Sect. 4.3, we compute the result of Equal Error Rate (EER) among our method and the baselines (including VGG-Face [22], Noisy Softmax [2], AFJT-CNN [14] and FaceNet) in this dataset, as shown in Fig. 8 and Table 2.

As can be seen from Table 2, our model achieves the lowest EER among all the results. The proposed APFN model significantly outperforms the published results in cross-age face recognition for the reason that much age-related information is removed during the process of training. It further demonstrates the effectiveness of the proposed age-invariant deep features.

Table 2. The resluts about EER on Cross-Age LFW dataset

Method	EER
VGG-face (2015) [22]	13.5%
Noisy softmax (2017) [2]	17.5%
AFJT-CNN (2018) [14]	14.8%
FaceNet (2015) [24]	10.8%
APFN	9.9%

Compared to the result in Fig. 6, as we can see in Fig. 8, the proposed APFN model surpasses the result of FaceNet with a clear margin, verifying the conclusion from Sect. 4.2 that our APFN model can make great improvement in recognizing pairs of face images with bigger age deviation rather than similar aged pairs.

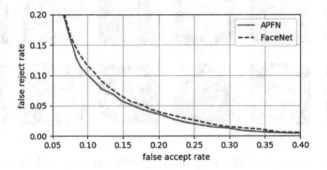

Fig. 8. ROC comparisons of APFN and FaceNet on CALFW

Finally, we show some failed verificatory pairs in the CALFW dataset in Fig. 9. These results confirm what we observed from Fig. 6: the face verification between probe images and false rejected images is influenced by pose or expression, and it limits the increase in verification rate.

Fig. 9. Some examples of failed retrievals in CALFW. The first row is the probe faces, the second row presents the false reject faces using our approach.

5 Conclusions

Based on the idea of GANs and the adversarial training mechanism, we propose a novel method called Age-Puzzle FaceNet (APFN) for CAFR task, which can be cross trained by dataset with only identity label or dataset with only age label. The extensive experimental results on face aging datasets (CACD-VS and CALFW) show that the APFN model outperforms other methods in cross-age face recognition, and our model provides a new insight into multi-attributes or attributes separation tasks and is equally applicable for these problems.

Acknowledgements. This work was supported in part by the NSFC (61673402), the NSF of Guangdong Province (2017A030311029), the Science and Technology Program of Guangzhou (201704020180), and the Fundamental Research Funds for the Central Universities of China.

References

1. Antipov, G., Baccouche, M., Dugelay, J.L.: Face aging with conditional generative adversarial networks. arXiv preprint arXiv:1702.01983 (2017)
2. Chen, B., Deng, W., Du, J.: Noisy softmax: improving the generalization ability of DCNN via postponing the early softmax saturation. arXiv preprint arXiv:1708.03769 (2017)
3. Chen, B.-C., Chen, C.-S., Hsu, W.H.: Cross-age reference coding for age-invariant face recognition and retrieval. In: Fleet, D., Pajdla, T., Schiele, B., Tuytelaars, T. (eds.) ECCV 2014. LNCS, vol. 8694, pp. 768–783. Springer, Cham (2014). https://doi.org/10.1007/978-3-319-10599-4_49
4. Chen, D., Cao, X., Wen, F., Sun, J.: Blessing of dimensionality: high-dimensional feature and its efficient compression for face verification. In: 2013 IEEE Conference on Computer Vision and Pattern Recognition (CVPR), pp. 3025–3032. IEEE (2013)
5. Du, J.-X., Zhai, C.-M., Ye, Y.-Q.: Face aging simulation based on NMF algorithm with sparseness constraints. In: Huang, D.-S., Gan, Y., Gupta, P., Gromiha, M.M. (eds.) ICIC 2011. LNCS (LNAI), vol. 6839, pp. 516–522. Springer, Heidelberg (2012). https://doi.org/10.1007/978-3-642-25944-9_67
6. Du, L., Ling, H.: Cross-age face verification by coordinating with cross-face age verification. In: Proceedings of the IEEE Conference on Computer Vision and Pattern Recognition pp. 2329–2338 (2015)
7. Geng, C., Jiang, X.: Face recognition using sift features. In: 2009 16th IEEE International Conference on Image Processing (ICIP), pp. 3313–3316. IEEE (2009)
8. Geng, X., Zhou, Z.H., Smith-Miles, K.: Automatic age estimation based on facial aging patterns. IEEE Trans. Pattern Anal. Mach. Intell. **29**(12), 2234–2240 (2007)
9. Gong, D., Li, Z., Lin, D., Liu, J., Tang, X.: Hidden factor analysis for age invariant face recognition. In: 2013 IEEE International Conference on Computer Vision (ICCV), pp. 2872–2879. IEEE (2013)
10. Gong, D., Li, Z., Tao, D., Liu, J., Li, X.: A maximum entropy feature descriptor for age invariant face recognition. In: Proceedings of the IEEE Conference on Computer Vision and Pattern Recognition, pp. 5289–5297 (2015)
11. Goodfellow, I., et al.: Generative adversarial nets. In: Advances in Neural Information Processing Systems, pp. 2672–2680 (2014)

12. Klare, B., Jain, A.K.: Face recognition across time lapse: on learning feature subspaces. In: 2011 International Joint Conference on Biometrics (IJCB), pp. 1–8. IEEE (2011)
13. Lample, G., Zeghidour, N., Usunier, N., Bordes, A., Denoyer, L., et al.: Fader networks: manipulating images by sliding attributes. In: Advances in Neural Information Processing Systems, pp. 5969–5978 (2017)
14. Li, H., Hu, H., Yip, C.: Age-related factor guided joint task modeling convolutional neural network for cross-age face recognition. IEEE Trans. Inf. Forensics Secur. 13(9), 2383–2392 (2018)
15. Li, Z., Gong, D., Li, X., Tao, D.: Learning compact feature descriptor and adaptive matching framework for face recognition. IEEE Trans. Image Process. 24(9), 2736–2745 (2015)
16. Li, Z., Gong, D., Li, X., Tao, D.: Aging face recognition: a hierarchical learning model based on local patterns selection. IEEE Trans. Image Process. 25(5), 2146–2154 (2016)
17. Li, Z., Park, U., Jain, A.K.: A discriminative model for age invariant face recognition. IEEE Trans. Inf. Forensics Secur. 6(3), 1028–1037 (2011)
18. Ling, H., Soatto, S., Ramanathan, N., Jacobs, D.W.: Face verification across age progression using discriminative methods. IEEE Trans. Inf. Forensics Secur. 5(1), 82–91 (2010)
19. Liu, L., Xiong, C., Zhang, H., Niu, Z., Wang, M., Yan, S.: Deep aging face verification with large gaps. IEEE Trans. Multimed. 18(1), 64–75 (2016)
20. Ojala, T., Pietikainen, M., Maenpaa, T.: Multiresolution gray-scale and rotation invariant texture classification with local binary patterns. IEEE Trans. Pattern Anal. Mach. Intell. 24(7), 971–987 (2002)
21. Park, U., Tong, Y., Jain, A.K.: Age-invariant face recognition. IEEE Trans. Pattern Anal. Mach. Intell. 32(5), 947–954 (2010)
22. Parkhi, O.M., Vedaldi, A., Zisserman, A., et al.: Deep face recognition. In: BMVC, vol. 1, p. 6 (2015)
23. Rothe, R., Timofte, R., Van Gool, L.: DEX: deep expectation of apparent age from a single image. In: Proceedings of the IEEE International Conference on Computer Vision Workshops, pp. 10–15 (2015)
24. Schroff, F., Kalenichenko, D., Philbin, J.: FaceNet: a unified embedding for face recognition and clustering. In: Proceedings of the IEEE Conference on Computer Vision and Pattern Recognition, pp. 815–823 (2015)
25. Szegedy, C., Ioffe, S., Vanhoucke, V., Alemi, A.A.: Inception-v4, inception-ResNet and the impact of residual connections on learning. In: AAAI, vol. 4, p. 12 (2017)
26. Taigman, Y., Yang, M., Ranzato, M., Wolf, L.: DeepFace: closing the gap to human-level performance in face verification. In: Proceedings of the IEEE Conference on Computer Vision and Pattern Recognition, pp. 1701–1708 (2014)
27. Wang, W., et al.: Recurrent face aging. In: Proceedings of the IEEE Conference on Computer Vision and Pattern Recognition, pp. 2378–2386 (2016)
28. Wen, Y., Li, Z., Qiao, Y.: Latent factor guided convolutional neural networks for age-invariant face recognition, pp. 4893–4901 (2016)
29. Wen, Y., Zhang, K., Li, Z., Qiao, Y.: A discriminative feature learning approach for deep face recognition. In: Leibe, B., Matas, J., Sebe, N., Welling, M. (eds.) ECCV 2016. LNCS, vol. 9911, pp. 499–515. Springer, Cham (2016). https://doi.org/10.1007/978-3-319-46478-7_31
30. Yang, H., Huang, D., Wang, Y., Wang, H., Tang, Y.: Face aging effect simulation using hidden factor analysis joint sparse representation. IEEE Trans. Image Process. 25(6), 2493–2507 (2016)

31. Yi, D., Lei, Z., Liao, S., Li, S.Z.: Learning face representation from scratch. arXiv preprint arXiv:1411.7923 (2014)
32. Zhang, K., Zhang, Z., Li, Z., Qiao, Y.: Joint face detection and alignment using multitask cascaded convolutional networks. IEEE Signal Process. Lett. **23**(10), 1499–1503 (2016)
33. Zheng, T., Deng, W., Hu, J.: Age estimation guided convolutional neural network for age-invariant face recognition. In: Proceedings of the IEEE Conference on Computer Vision and Pattern Recognition Workshops, pp. 1–9 (2017)
34. Zheng, T., Deng, W., Hu, J.: Cross-age LFW: a database for studying cross-age face recognition in unconstrained environments. arXiv preprint arXiv:1708.08197 (2017)

Video-Based Person Re-identification via 3D Convolutional Networks and Non-local Attention

Xingyu Liao[1(✉)], Lingxiao He[2], Zhouwang Yang[3], and Chi Zhang[4]

[1] School of Mathematical Sciences, University of Science and Technology of China, Hefei, People's Republic of China
`randall@mail.ustc.edu.cn`
[2] University of Chinese Academy of Sciences, Beijing, People's Republic of China
`lingxiao.he@nlpr.ia.ac.cn`
[3] School of Data Science, University of Science and Technology of China, Hefei, People's Republic of China
`yangzw@ustc.edu.cn`
[4] Megvii Inc. (Face++), Beijing, China
`zhangchi@megvii.com`

Abstract. Video-based person re-identification (ReID) is a challenging problem, where some video tracks of people across non-overlapping cameras are available for matching. Feature aggregation from a video track is a key step for video-based person ReID. Many existing methods tackle this problem by average/maximum temporal pooling or RNNs with attention. However, these methods cannot deal with temporal dependency and spatial misalignment problems at the same time. We are inspired by video action recognition that involves the identification of different actions from video tracks. Firstly, we use 3D convolutions on video volume, instead of using 2D convolutions across frames, to extract spatial and temporal features simultaneously. Secondly, we use a non-local block to tackle the misalignment problem and capture spatial-temporal long-range dependencies. As a result, the network can learn useful spatial-temporal information as a weighted sum of the features in all space and temporal positions in the input feature map. Experimental results on three datasets show that our framework outperforms state-of-the-art approaches by a large margin on multiple metrics.

1 Introduction

Person re-identification (ReID) aims to match people in the different places (time) using another non-overlapping camera, which has become increasingly popular in recent years due to the wide range of applications, such as public security, criminal investigation, and surveillance. Most deep learning approaches have been shown to be more effective than traditional methods. But there still remains many challenging problems because of human pose, lighting, background, occluded body region and camera viewpoints.

© Springer Nature Switzerland AG 2019
C. V. Jawahar et al. (Eds.): ACCV 2018, LNCS 11366, pp. 620–634, 2019.
https://doi.org/10.1007/978-3-030-20876-9_39

Video-based person ReID approaches consist of feature representation and feature aggregation. And feature aggregation attracts more attention in recent works. Although most of methods [24] (see Fig. 1(A)) propose to use average or maximum temporal pooling to aggregate features, they do not take full advantage of the temporal dependency information. To this end, RNN based methods [17] (see Fig. 1(B)) are proposed to aggregate the temporal information among video frames. However, the most discriminative frames cannot be learned by RNN based methods while treating all frames equally. Moreover, temporal attention methods [16] as shown in Fig. 1(C) are proposed to extract the discriminative frames. In conclusion, these methods mentioned above cannot tackle temporal dependency, attention and spatial misalignment simultaneously. Although there are a few methods [27] using the jointly attentive spatial-temporal scheme, it is hard to optimize the networks under severe occlusion.

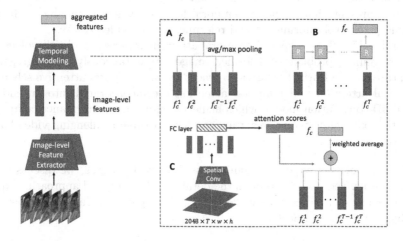

Fig. 1. Three temporal modeling methods (A: temporal pooling, B: RNN, C: temporal attention) based on an image-level feature extractor (typically a 2D CNN). For temporal pooling, average or maximum pooling is used. For RNN, hidden state is used as the aggregated feature. For attention, spatial conv + FC is shown.

In this paper, we propose a method to aggregate temporal-dependency features and tackle spatial misalignment problems using attention simultaneously as illustrated in Fig. 2. Inspired by the recent success of 3D convolutional neural networks on video action recognition [2,9], we directly use it to extract spatial-temporal features in a sequence of video frames. It can integrate feature extraction and temporal modeling into one step. In order to capture long-range dependency, we embed the non-local block [25] into the model to obtain an aggregate spatial-temporal representation.

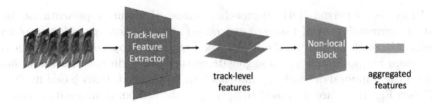

Fig. 2. The overall architecture of the proposed method. 3D convolutions are used for track-level feature extractor. Non-local blocks are embedded into aggregate spatial-temporal features.

We summarize the contributions of this work in three-folds.

1. We first propose to use 3D convolutional neural network to extract the aggregate representation of spatial-temporal features, which is capable of discovering pixel-level information and relevance among video tracks.
2. Non-local block, as a spatial-temporal attention strategy, explicitly solves the misalignment problem of deformed images. Simultaneously, the aggregative feature can be learned from video tracks by the temporal attentive scheme.
3. Spatial attention and temporal attention are incorporated into an end-to-end 3D convolution model, which achieves significant performance compared to the existing state-of-the-art approaches on three challenging video-based ReID datasets.

The rest of this paper is organized as follows. In Sect. 2, we discuss some related works. Section 3 introduces the details of the proposed approach. Experimental results on three public datasets will be given in Sect. 4. At last, we conclude this paper in Sect. 5.

2   Related Work

In this section, we first review some related works in person ReID, especially those video-based methods. Then we will discuss some related works about 3D convolution neural networks and non-local methods.

2.1   Person Re-ID

Image-based person ReID mainly focuses on feature fusion and alignment with some external information such as mask, pose, and skeleton, etc. Zhao *et al.* [29] proposed a novel Spindle Net based on human body region guided multi-stage feature decomposition and tree-structured competitive feature fusion. Song *et al.* [18] introduced the binary segmentation masks to construct synthetic RGB-Mask pairs as inputs, as well as a mask-guided contrastive attention model (MGCAM) to learn features separately from body and background regions. Suh *et al.* [20] proposed a two-stream network that consists of appearance map extraction stream and body part map extraction stream, additionally a part-aligned feature map is obtained by a bilinear mapping of the corresponding local appearance and body part descriptors. These models all actually solve the person misalignment problem.

Video-based person ReID is an extension of image-based methods. Instead of pairs of images, the learning algorithm is given pairs of video sequences. The most important part is how to fuse temporal features from video tracks. Wang *et al.* [24] aimed at selecting discriminative spatial-temporal feature representations. They firstly choosed the frames with the maximum or minimum flow energy, which is computed by optical flow fields. In order to take full use of temporal information, McLaughlin *et al.* [17] built a CNN to extract features of each frame and then used RNN to integrate the temporal information between frames, the average of RNN cell outputs are adapted to summarize the output feature. Similar to [17], Yan *et al.* [28] also used RNNs to encode video tracks into sequence features, the final hidden state is used as video representation. RNN based methods treat all frames equally, which cannot focus on more discriminative frames. Liu *et al.* [16] designed a Quality Aware Network (QAN), which is essentially an attention weighted average, to aggregate temporal features; the attention scores are generated from frame-level feature maps. In 2016, Zheng *et al.* [19] built a new dataset MARS for video-based person ReID, which becomes the standard benchmark for this task.

2.2 3D ConvNets

3D CNNs are well-suited for spatial-temporal feature learning. Ji *et al.* [9] first proposed a 3D CNN model for action recognition. Tran *et al.* [22] proposed a C3D network to be applied into various video analysis tasks. Despite 3D CNNs' ability to capture the appearance and motion information encoded in multiple adjacent frames effectively, it is difficult to be trained with more parameters. More recently, Carreira *et al.* [2] proposed the Inflated 3D (I3D) architecture which initializes the model weights by inflating the pre-trained weights from ImageNet over temporal dimension which significantly improves the performance of 3D CNNs and it is the current state-of-the-art on the Kinetics dataset [10].

2.3 Self-attention and Non-local

Non-local technique [1] is a classical digital image denoising algorithm that computes a weighted average of all pixels in an image. As attention models grow in popularity, Vaswani *et al.* [23] proposed a self-attention method for machine translation that computes the response at a position in a sequence (*e.g.,* a sentence) by attending to all positions and taking their weighted average in an embedding space. Moreover, Wang *et al.* [25] proposed a non-local architecture to bridge self-attention in machine translation to the more general class of non-local filtering operations. Inspired by these works, We embed non-local blocks into I3D model to capture long-range dependencies on space and time for video-based ReID. Our method demonstrates better performance by aggregating the discriminative spatial-temporal features.

3   The Proposed Approach

In this section, we introduce the overall system pipeline and detailed configurations of the spatial-temporal modeling methods. The whole system could be divided into two important parts: extracting spatial-temporal features from video tracks through 3D ResNet, and integrating spatial-temporal features by the non-local blocks.

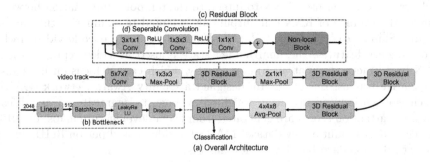

Fig. 3. Illustration of networks we propose in this paper; (a) illustrates the overall architecture that is consist of 3D convolutions, 3D pooling, 3D residual blocks, bottleneck and non-local blocks; (b) shows bottelneck; (c) illustrates residual blocks; Seperable convolutions are shown in (d).

A video tracet is first divided into consecutive non-overlap tracks $\{c_k\}$, and each track contains N frames. Supposing each track is represented as

$$c_k = \{x_t | x_t \in \mathbb{R}^{H \times W}, t = 1, \cdots, N\}, \tag{1}$$

where N is the length of c_k, and H, W are the height, width of the images respectively. As shown in Fig. 3(a), the proposed method directly accepts a whole video track as the inputs and outputs a d-dimensional feature vector f_{c_k}. At the same time, non-local blocks are embedded into 3D residual block (Fig. 3(c)) to integrate spatial and temporal features, which can effectively learn the pixel-level relevance of each frame and learn hierarchical feature representation.

Finally, average pooling followed by a bottleneck block (Fig. 3(b)) to speed up training and improve performance. A fully-connected layer is added on top to learn the identity features. A Softmax cross-entropy with label smoothing, proposed by Szegedy et al. [21], is built on top of the fully connected layer to supervise the training of the whole network in an end-to-end fashion. At the same time, Batch Hard triplet loss [7] is employed in the metric learning step.

During the testing, the final similarity between c_i and c_j can be measured by L2 distance or any other distance function.

In the next parts, we will explain each important component in more detail.

3.1 Temporally Separable Inflated 3D Convolution

In 2D CNNs, convolutions are applied on the 2D feature maps to compute features from the spatial dimensions only. When applied to the video-based problem, it is desirable to capture the temporal information encoded in multiple contiguous frames. The 3D convolutions are achieved by convolving 3D kernel on the cube formed by stacking multiple consecutive frames together. In other words, 3D convolutions can directly extract a whole representation for a video track, while 2D convolutions first extract a sequence of image-level features and then features are aggregated into a single vector feature. Formally, the value at position (x, y, z) on the j-th feature map in the ith layer V_{ij}^{xyz} is given by

$$V_{ij}^{xyz} = b_{ij} + \sum_m \sum_{p=0}^{P_i-1} \sum_{q=0}^{Q_i-1} \sum_{r=0}^{R_i-1} W_{ijm}^{pqr} V_{(i-1)m}^{(x+p)(y+q)(z+r)}, \qquad (2)$$

where P_i and Q_i are the height and width of the kernel, R_i is the size of the 3D kernel along with the temporal dimension, W_{ijm}^{pqr} is the (p, q, r)th value of the kernel connected to the m-th feature map in the previous layer V_{i-1}, and b_{ij} is the bias.

We adopt 3D ResNet-50 [5] that uses 3D convolution kernels with ResNet architecture to extract spatial-temporal features. However, C3D-like 3D ConvNet is hard to optimize because of a large number of parameters. In order to address this problem, we inflate all the 2D ResNet-50 convolution filters with an additional temporal dimension. For example, a 2D $k \times k$ kernel can be inflated as a 3D $t \times k \times k$ kernel that spans t frames. We initialize all 3D kernels with 2D kernels (pre-trained on ImageNet): each of the t planes in the $t \times k \times k$ kernel is initialized by the pre-trained $k \times k$ weights, rescaled by $1/t$. According to Xie *et al.* [26] experiments, temporally separable convolution is a simple way to boost performance on variety of video understanding tasks. We replace 3D convolution with two consecutive convolution layers: one 1D convolution layer purely on the temporal axis, followed by a 2D convolution layer to learn spatial features in Residual Block as shown in Fig. 3(d). Meanwhile, we pre-train the 3D ResNet-50 on Kinetics [10] to enhance the generalization performance of the model. We replace the final classification layer with person identity outputs. The model takes T consecutive frames (*i.e.* a video track) as the input, and the layer outputs before final classification layer is used as the video track identity representation.

3.2 Non-local Attention Block

A non-local attention block is used to capture long-range dependency in space and time dealing with occlusion and misalignment. We first give a general definition of non-local operations and then provide the 3D non-local block instantiations embedded into the I3D model.

Following the non-local methods [1] and [25], the generic non-local operation in deep neural networks can be given by

$$y_i = \frac{1}{C(x)} \sum_{\forall j} f(x_i, x_j) g(x_j). \tag{3}$$

Here x_i can be the position in input signal (image, sequence, video; often their features) and y_i is the position in output signal of the same size as x, whose response is to be computed by all possible input positions x_j. A pairwise function f computes a scalar between i and all j, which represents attention scores between position i in output feature and all position j in the input signal. The unary function g computes a representation in an embedded space of the input signal at the position j. At last, the response is normalized by a factor $C(x)$.

Because of the fact that all positions $(\forall j)$ are considered in the operation in Eq. (2), this is so-called non-local. Compared with this, a standard 1D convolutional operation sums up the weighted input in a *local* neighborhood (e.g., $i - 1 \le j \le i + 1$ with kernel size 3, and recurrent operation at time i is often based only on the current and the latest time step (e.g., $j = i$ or $i - 1$).

There are several versions of f and g, such as gaussian, embedded gaussian, dot product, etc. According to experiments in [25], the non-local operation is not sensitive to these choices. We just choose embedded gaussian as f function that is given by

$$f(x_i, x_j) = e^{\theta(x_i)^T \phi(x_j)} \tag{4}$$

Here x_i and x_j are given in Eq. (3), $\theta(x_i) = W_\theta x_i$ and $\phi(x_j) = W_\phi x_j$ are two embeddings. We can set $C(x)$ as a softmax operation, so we have a self-attention form that is given by

$$y = \sum_{\forall j} \frac{e^{\theta(x_i)^T \phi(x_j)}}{\sum_{\forall i} e^{\theta(x_i)^T \phi(x_j)}} g(x_j) \tag{5}$$

A non-local operation is very flexible, which can be easily incorporated into any existing architecture. The non-local operation can be wrapped into a non-local block that can be embedded into the earlier or later part of the deep neural network. We define a non-local block as:

$$z_i = W_z y_i + x_i \tag{6}$$

where y_i is given in Eq. (3) and "$+x_i$" means a residual connection [5]. We can plug a new non-local block into any pre-trained model, without breaking its initial behavior (e.g., if W_z is initialized as zero) which can build a richer hierarchy architecture combining both global and local information.

In ResNet3D-50, we use a 3D spacetime non-local block illustrated in Fig. 4. The pairwise computation in Eq. (4) can be simply done by matrix multiplication. We will talk about detailed implementation of non-local blocks in next part.

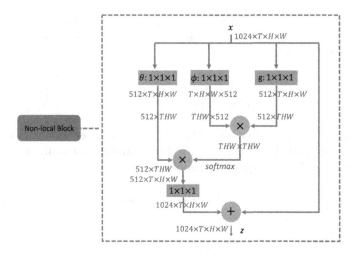

Fig. 4. The 3D spacetime non-local block. The feature maps are shown as the shape of their tensors, *e.g.*, $1024 \times T \times H \times W$ for 1024 channels (it can be different depending on networks). "$\otimes$" denotes matrix multiplication, and "$\oplus$" denotes element-wise sum. The softmax operation is performed on each row. The blue boxes denote $1 \times 1 \times 1$ convolutions. We show the Embedded Gaussian version, with a bottleneck of 512 channels. (Color figure online)

3.3 Loss Functions

We use triplet loss function with hard mining [7] and a Softmax cross-entropy loss function with label smoothing regularization [21].

The triplet loss function we use was originally proposed in [7], and named as Batch Hard triplet loss function. To form a batch, we randomly sample P identities and randomly sample K tracks for each identity (each track contains T frames); totally there are $P \times K$ clips in a batch. For each sample a in the batch, the hardest positive and the hardest negative samples within the batch are selected when forming the triplets for computing the loss $L_{triplet}$.

$$
L_{triplet} = \overbrace{\sum_{i=1}^{P} \sum_{a=1}^{K}}^{all\ anchors} [m + \overbrace{\max_{p=1\cdots K} D(f_a^i, f_p^i)}^{hardest\ positive} \\
- \underbrace{\min_{\substack{j=1\cdots P \\ n=1\cdots K \\ j \neq i}} D(f_a^i, f_n^j)}_{hardest\ negative}]_+
\tag{7}
$$

The original Softmax cross-entropy loss function is given by:

$$
L_{softmax} = -\frac{1}{P \times K} \sum_{i=1}^{P} \sum_{a=1}^{K} p_{i,a} \log q_{i,a}
\tag{8}
$$

where $p_{i,a}$ is the ground truth identity and $q_{i,a}$ is prediction of sample $\{i, a\}$. The *label-smoothing regularization* is proposed to regularize the model and make it more adaptable with:

$$L'_{softmax} = -\frac{1}{P \times K} \sum_{i=1}^{P} \sum_{a=1}^{K} p_{i,a} \log((1-\epsilon)q_{i,a} + \frac{\epsilon}{N}) \tag{9}$$

where N is the number of classes. This can be considered as a mixture of the original ground-truth distribution $q_{i,a}$ and the uniform distribution $u(x) = \frac{1}{N}$.

The total loss L is the combination of these two losses.

$$L = L'_{softmax} + L_{triplet} \tag{10}$$

4   Experiments

We evaluate our proposed method on three public video datasets, including iLIDS-VID [24], PRID-2011 [8] and MARS [19]. We compare our method with the state-of-the-art methods, and the experimental results demonstrate that our proposed method can enhance the performance of both feature learning and metric learning and outperforms previous methods.

4.1   Datasets

The basic information of three dataset is listed in Table 1 and some samples are displayed in Fig. 3.

Table 1. The basic information of three datasets to be used in our experiments.

Datasets	iLIDS-VID	PRID2011	MARS
#identities	300	200	1,261
#track-lets	600	400	21K
#boxes	44K	40K	1M
#distractors	0	0	3K
#cameras	2	2	6
#resolution	64×128	64×128	128×256
#detection	Hand	Hand	Algorithm
#evaluation	CMC	CMC	CMC & mAP

iLIDS-VID dataset consists of 600 video sequences of 300 persons. Each image sequence has a variable length ranging from 23 to 192 frames, with averaged number of 73. This dataset is challenging due to clothing similarities among people and random occlusions. **PRID-2011** dataset contains 385 persons in camera A and 749 in camera B. 200 identities appear in both cameras, consti-tuting of 400 image sequences. The length of each image sequence varies from 5 to 675. Following [19], sequences with more 21 frames are selected, leading to 178 identities. **MARS** dataset is a newly released dataset consisting of 1,261 pedestrians captured by at least 2 cameras. The bounding boxes are generated by classic detection and tracking algorithms (DPM detector), yielding 20,715 person sequences. Among them, 3,248 sequences are of quite poor quality due to the failure of detection or tracking, significantly increasing the difficulty of person ReID.

4.2   Implementation Details and Evaluation Metrics

Training. We use ResNet3D-50 [4] as our backbone network. According to the experiments in [25], five non-local blocks are inserted to right before the last residual block of a stage. Three blocks are inserted into res_4 and two blocks are inserted into res_3, to every other residual block. Our models are pre-trained on Kinetics [10]; we also compare the models with different pre-trained weights, and the details are described in the next section.

Our implementation is based on publicly available code of PyTorch. All per-son ReID models in this paper are trained and tested on Linux with GTX TITAN X GPU. In training term, eight-frame input tracks are randomly cropped out from 64 consecutive frames every eight frames. The spatial size is 256×128 pixels, randomly cropped from a scaled videos whose size is randomly enlarged by 1/8. The model is trained on an eight-GPU machine for about 8 h, and each GPU have 16 tracks in a mini-batch (so in total with a mini-batch size of 128 tracks). In order to train hard mining triplet loss, 32 identities with 4 tracks each person are taken in a mini-batch and iterate all identities as an epoch. Bot-tleneck consists of fully connected layer, batch norm, leaky ReLU with $\alpha = 0.1$ and dropout with 0.5 drop ratio. The model is trained for 300 epochs in total, starting with a learning rate of 0.0003 and reducing it by exponential decay with decay rate 0.001 at 150 epochs. Adaptive Moment Estimation (Adam) is adopted with a weight decay of 0.0005 when training.

The method in [6] is adopted to initialize the weight layers introduced in the non-local blocks. A BatchNorm layer is added right after the last $1 \times 1 \times 1$ layer that represents W_z; we do not add BatchNorm to other layers in a non-local block. The scale parameter of this BatchNorm layer is initialized as zeros. This ensures that the initialize state of the entire non-local block is an identity mapping, so it can be inserted into any pre-trained networks while maintaining its initial behavior.

Testing. We follow the standard experimental protocols for testing on the datasets. For iLIDS-VID, the 600 video sequences of 300 persons are randomly split into 50% of persons for testing. For PRID2011, only 400 video sequences of the first 200 persons, who appear in both cameras are used according to experi-ment setup in previous methods [17] For MARS, the predefined 8,298 sequences

Table 2. Component analysis of the proposed method: rank-1, rank-5, rank-10 accuracies and mAP are reported for MARS dataset. **ResNet3D-50** is the ResNet3D-50 pre-trained on Kinectis, **ResNet3D-50 NL** is added with non-local blocks.

Methods	CMC-1	CMC-5	CMC-10	mAP
Baseline	77.9	90.0	92.5	69.0
ResNet3D-50	80.0	92.2	94.5	72.6
ResNet3D-50 NL	84.3	94.6	96.2	77.0

of 625 persons are used for training, while the 12,180 sequences of 636 persons are used for testing, including the 3,248 low quality sequences in the gallery set.

We employ Cumulated Matching Characteristics (CMC) curve and mean average precision (mAP) to evaluate the performance for all the datasets. For ease of comparison, we only report the cumulated re-identification accuracy at selected ranks.

Fig. 5. Example of the behavior of a non-local block to tackle misalignment problems. The starting point of arrows represents one x_i, and the ending points represent x_j. This visualization shows how the model finds related part on different frames.

4.3   Component Analysis of the Proposed Model

In this part, we report the performance of different components in our models.

3D CNN and Non-local. Baseline method, ResNet3D-50 and ResNet3D-50 with non-local blocks on the MARS dataset are shown in Table 2. **Baseline** corresponds to ResNet-50 trained with softmax cross-entropy loss and triplet with hard mining on image-based person ReID. The representation of an image sequence is obtained by using the average temporal pooling. **ResNet3D-50** corresponds to ResNet3D-50 pre-trained on Kinetics discussed above. **ResNet3D-50 NL** corresponds to ResNet3D-50 with non-local blocks pre-trained on Kinetics. The gap between our results and baseline method is significant, and it is noted that: (1) ResNet3D increases from 77.9% to 80.0% under single query, which fully suggests ResNet3D-50 effectively aggregate the spatial-temporal features; (2) ResNet3D with non-local increase from 80.0% to 84.3% compared with

ResNet3D, which indicates that non-local blocks have the great performance on integrating spatial-temporal features and tackling misalignment problem. The results are shown in Fig. 5.

Table 3. Effect of different initialization methods: rank-1, rank-5, rank-10 accuracies and mAP are reported for MARS dataset. **ImageNet** corresponds to model pre-trained on ImageNet, **Kinetics** corresponds to model pre-trained on Kinetics and **ReID** corresponds to model pre-trained on ReID datasets.

Init Methods	CMC-1	CMC-5	CMC-10	mAP
ImageNet	78.4	91.5	93.9	69.8
ReID	79.9	92.6	94.5	71.3
Kinetics	84.3	94.6	96.2	77.0

Table 4. Comparisons of our proposed approach to the state-of-the-art on PRID2011, iLIDS-VID and MARS datasets. The rank1 accuracies are reported and for MARS we provide mAP in brackets. The best and second best results are marked by red and blue colors, respectively.

Methods	PRID2011	iLIDS-VID	MARS
AMOC+EpicFlow [15]	82.0	65.5	-
RNN [17]	40.6	58.0	-
IDE [30] + XQDA [13]	-	-	65.3 (47.3)
end AMOC+epicFlow [15]	83.7	68.7	68.3 (52.9)
Mars [19]	77.3	53.0	68.3 (49.3)
SeeForest [31]	79.4	55.2	70.6 (50.7)
QAN [16]	90.3	68.0	-
Spatialtemporal [11]	93.2	80.2	82.3 (65.8)
Ours	91.2	81.3	84.3 (77)

Different Initialization Methods. We also carry out experiments to investigate the effect of different initialization methods in Table 3. **ImageNet** and **ReID** corresponds to ResNet3D-50 with non-local block, whose weights are inflated from the 2D ResNet50 pre-trained on ImageNet or on CUHK03 [12], VIPeR [3] and DukeMTMC-reID [14] respectively. **Kinetics** corresponds to ResNet3D-50 with non-local blocks pre-trained on Kinetics. The results show that model pre-trained on Kinetics has the best performance than on other two datasets. 3D model is hard to train because of the large number of parameters and it needs more datasets to pre-train. Besides, the model pre-trained on Kinetics (a video action recognition dataset) is more suitable for video-based problem.

4.4   Comparision with State-of-the-Art Methods

Table 4 reports the performance of our approach with other state-of-the-art techniques.

Results on MARS. MARS is the most challenging dataset (it contains distractor sequences and has a substantially larger gallery set) and our methodology achieves a significant increase in mAP and rank1 accuracy. Our method improves the state-of-the-art by 2.0% compared with the previous best reported results 82.3% from Li *et al.* [11] (which use spatialtemporal attention). SeeForest [31] combines six spatial RNNs and temporal attention followed by a temporal RNN to encode the input video to achieve 70.6%. In contrast, our network architecture is straightforward to train for the video-based problem. This result suggests our ResNet3D with non-local is very effective for video-based person ReID in challenging scenarios.

Results on iLIDS-VID and PRID. The results on the iLIDS-VID and PRID2011 are obtained by fine-tuning from the pre-trained model on the MARS. Li *et al.* uses spatialtemporal attention to automatically discover a diverse set of distinctive body parts which achieves 93.2% on PRID2011 and 80.2% on iLIDS-VID. Our proposed method achieves the comparable results compared with it by 91.2% on PRID2011 and 81.3% on iLIDS-VID. 3D model cannot achieve the significant improvement because of the size of datasets. These two datasets are small video person ReID datasets, which lead to overfitting on the training set.

5   Conclusion

In this paper, we have proposed an end-to-end 3D ConvNet with non-local architecture, which integrates a spatial-temporal attention to aggregate a discriminative representation from a video track. We carefully design experiments to demonstrate the effectiveness of each component of the proposed method. In order to discover pixel-level information and relevance between each frames, we employ a 3D ConvNets. This encourages the network to extract spatial-temporal features. Then we insert non-local blocks into model to explicitly solves the misalignment problem in space and time. The proposed method with ResNet3D and non-blocks outperforms the state-of-the-art methods in many metrics.

References

1. Buades, A., Coll, B., Morel, J.M.: A non-local algorithm for image denoising. In: 2005 IEEE Computer Society Conference on Computer Vision and Pattern Recognition (CVPR 2005), vol. 2, pp. 60–65, June 2005. https://doi.org/10.1109/CVPR. 2005.38

2. Carreira, J., Zisserman, A.: Quo vadis, action recognition? A new model and the kinetics dataset. CoRR abs/1705.07750 (2017). http://arxiv.org/abs/1705.07750

3. Gray, D., Brennan, S., Tao, H.: Evaluating appearance models for recognition, reacquisition, and tracking. In: In IEEE International Workshop on Performance Evaluation for Tracking and Surveillance, Rio de Janeiro (2007)

4. Hara, K., Kataoka, H., Satoh, Y.: Can spatiotemporal 3D CNNs retrace the history of 2D CNNs and imagenet? CoRR abs/1711.09577 (2017). http://arxiv.org/abs/ 1711.09577

5. He, K., Zhang, X., Ren, S., Sun, J.: Deep residual learning for image recognition. In: 2016 IEEE Conference on Computer Vision and Pattern Recognition (CVPR), pp. 770–778, June 2016. https://doi.org/10.1109/CVPR.2016.90

6. He, K., Zhang, X., Ren, S., Sun, J.: Delving deep into rectifiers: surpassing human-level performance on ImageNet classification. CoRR abs/1502.01852 (2015). http://arxiv.org/abs/1502.01852

7. Hermans, A., Beyer, L., Leibe, B.: In defense of the triplet loss for person re-identification. CoRR abs/1703.07737 (2017). http://arxiv.org/abs/1703.07737

8. Hirzer, M., Beleznai, C., Roth, P.M., Bischof, H.: Person re-identification by descriptive and discriminative classification. In: Heyden, A., Kahl, F. (eds.) SCIA 2011. LNCS, vol. 6688, pp. 91–102. Springer, Heidelberg (2011). https://doi.org/ 10.1007/978-3-642-21227-7_9

9. Ji, S., Xu, W., Yang, M., Yu, K.: 3D convolutional neural networks for human action recognition. IEEE Trans. Pattern Anal. Mach. Intell. **35**(1), 221–231 (2013). https://doi.org/10.1109/TPAMI.2012.59

10. Kay, W., et al.: The kinetics human action video dataset. CoRR abs/1705.06950 (2017). http://arxiv.org/abs/1705.06950

11. Li, S., Bak, S., Carr, P., Wang, X.: Diversity regularized spatiotemporal attention for video-based person re-identification. In: The IEEE Conference on Computer Vision and Pattern Recognition (CVPR), June 2018

12. Li, W., Zhao, R., Xiao, T., Wang, X.: DeepReID: deep filter pairing neural network for person re-identification. In: 2014 IEEE Conference on Computer Vision and Pattern Recognition, pp. 152–159, June 2014. https://doi.org/10.1109/CVPR. 2014.27

13. Liao, S., Hu, Y., Zhu, X., Li, S.Z.: Person re-identification by local maximal occurrence representation and metric learning. In: 2015 IEEE Conference on Computer Vision and Pattern Recognition (CVPR), pp. 2197–2206, June 2015. https://doi. org/10.1109/CVPR.2015.7298832

14. Lin, Y., Zheng, L., Zheng, Z., Wu, Y., Yang, Y.: Improving person re-identification by attribute and identity learning. CoRR abs/1703.07220 (2017). http://arxiv.org/ abs/1703.07220

15. Liu, H., et al.: Video-based person re-identification with accumulative motion context. CoRR abs/1701.00193 (2017). http://arxiv.org/abs/1701.00193

16. Liu, Y., Yan, J., Ouyang, W.: Quality aware network for set to set recognition. In: The IEEE Conference on Computer Vision and Pattern Recognition (CVPR), July 2017

17. McLaughlin, N., Martinez del Rincon, J., Miller, P.: Recurrent convolutional network for video-based person re-identification. In: The IEEE Conference on Computer Vision and Pattern Recognition (CVPR), June 2016

18. Song, C., Huang, Y., Ouyang, W., Wang, L.: Mask-guided contrastive attention model for person re-identification. In: The IEEE Conference on Computer Vision and Pattern Recognition (CVPR), June 2018

19. Zheng, L., et al.: MARS: a video benchmark for large-scale person re-identification. In: Leibe, B., Matas, J., Sebe, N., Welling, M. (eds.) ECCV 2016. LNCS, vol. 9910, pp. 868–884. Springer, Cham (2016). https://doi.org/10.1007/978-3-319-46466-4_52

20. Suh, Y., Wang, J., Tang, S., Mei, T., Lee, K.M.: Part-aligned bilinear representations for person re-identification. CoRR abs/1804.07094 (2018). http://arxiv.org/abs/1804.07094

21. Szegedy, C., Vanhoucke, V., Ioffe, S., Shlens, J., Wojna, Z.: Rethinking the inception architecture for computer vision. In: The IEEE Conference on Computer Vision and Pattern Recognition (CVPR), June 2016

22. Tran, D., Bourdev, L., Fergus, R., Torresani, L., Paluri, M.: Learning spatiotemporal features with 3D convolutional networks. In: The IEEE International Conference on Computer Vision (ICCV), December 2015

23. Vaswani, A., et al.: Attention is all you need. In: Guyon, I., et al. (eds.) Advances in Neural Information Processing Systems, vol. 30, pp. 5998–6008. Curran Associates, Inc. (2017). http://papers.nips.cc/paper/7181-attention-is-all-you-need.pdf

24. Wang, T., Gong, S., Zhu, X., Wang, S.: Person re-identification by video ranking. In: Fleet, D., Pajdla, T., Schiele, B., Tuytelaars, T. (eds.) ECCV 2014. LNCS, vol. 8692, pp. 688–703. Springer, Cham (2014). https://doi.org/10.1007/978-3-319-10593-2_45

25. Wang, X., Girshick, R., Gupta, A., He, K.: Non-local neural networks. In: The IEEE Conference on Computer Vision and Pattern Recognition (CVPR), June 2018

26. Xie, S., Sun, C., Huang, J., Tu, Z., Murphy, K.: Rethinking spatiotemporal feature learning for video understanding. arXiv preprint arXiv:1712.04851 (2017)

27. Xu, S., Cheng, Y., Gu, K., Yang, Y., Chang, S., Zhou, P.: Jointly attentive spatial-temporal pooling networks for video-based person re-identification. In: The IEEE International Conference on Computer Vision (ICCV), October 2017

28. Yan, Y., Ni, B., Song, Z., Ma, C., Yan, Y., Yang, X.: Person re-identification via recurrent feature aggregation. CoRR abs/1701.06351 (2017). http://arxiv.org/abs/1701.06351

29. Zhao, H., et al.: Spindle Net: person re-identification with human body region guided feature decomposition and fusion. In: The IEEE Conference on Computer Vision and Pattern Recognition (CVPR), July 2017

30. Zheng, L., Zhang, H., Sun, S., Chandraker, M., Tian, Q.: Person re-identification in the wild. CoRR abs/1604.02531 (2016). http://arxiv.org/abs/1604.02531

31. Zhou, Z., Huang, Y., Wang, W., Wang, L., Tan, T.: See the forest for the trees: joint spatial and temporal recurrent neural networks for video-based person re-identification. In: 2017 IEEE Conference on Computer Vision and Pattern Recognition (CVPR), pp. 6776–6785, July 2017. https://doi.org/10.1109/CVPR.2017.717

Oral Session O6: Vision and Language, Semantics, and Low-Level Vision

ReCoNet: Real-Time Coherent Video Style Transfer Network

Chang Gao[1(✉)], Derun Gu[1], Fangjun Zhang[1], and Yizhou Yu[1,2]

[1] The University of Hong Kong, Pok Fu Lam, Hong Kong
{u3514174,greatway,u3514241}@connect.hku.hk
[2] Deepwise AI Lab, Beijing, China
yizhouy@acm.org

Abstract. Image style transfer models based on convolutional neural networks usually suffer from high temporal inconsistency when applied to videos. Some video style transfer models have been proposed to improve temporal consistency, yet they fail to guarantee fast processing speed, nice perceptual style quality and high temporal consistency at the same time. In this paper, we propose a novel real-time video style transfer model, ReCoNet, which can generate temporally coherent style transfer videos while maintaining favorable perceptual styles. A novel luminance warping constraint is added to the temporal loss at the output level to capture luminance changes between consecutive frames and increase stylization stability under illumination effects. We also propose a novel feature-map-level temporal loss to further enhance temporal consistency on traceable objects. Experimental results indicate that our model exhibits outstanding performance both qualitatively and quantitatively.

Keywords: Video style transfer · Optical flow · Real-time processing

1 Introduction

As a natural extension of image style transfer, video style transfer has recently gained interests among researchers [1,4,6,14,17,27,28]. Although some image style transfer methods [10,19] have achieved real-time processing speed, i.e. around or above 24 frames per second (FPS), one of the most critical issues in their stylization results is high temporal inconsistency. Temporal inconsistency, or sometimes called incoherence, can be observed visually as flickering between consecutive stylized frames and inconsistent stylization of moving objects [4]. Figure 1(a), (b) demonstrate temporal inconsistency in video style transfer.

To mitigate this effect, optimization methods guided by optical flows and occlusion masks were proposed [1,27]. Although these methods can generate smooth and coherent stylized videos, it generally takes several minutes to process each video frame due to optimization on the fly. Some recent models [4,14,17,28]

C. Gao, D. Gu and F. Zhang—Joint first authors.

© Springer Nature Switzerland AG 2019
C. V. Jawahar et al. (Eds.): ACCV 2018, LNCS 11366, pp. 637–653, 2019.
https://doi.org/10.1007/978-3-030-20876-9_40

improved the speed of video style transfer using optical flows and occlusion masks explicitly or implicitly, yet they failed to guarantee real-time processing speed, nice perceptual style quality, and coherent stylization at the same time.

In this paper, we propose ReCoNet, a real-time coherent video style transfer network as a solution to the aforementioned problem. ReCoNet is a feedforward neural network which can generate coherent stylized videos with rich artistic strokes and textures in real-time speed. It stylizes videos frame by frame through an encoder and a decoder, and uses a VGG loss network [19,30] to capture the perceptual style of the transfer target. It also incorporates optical flows and occlusion masks as guidance in its temporal loss to maintain temporal consistency between consecutive frames, and the effects can be observed in Fig. 1(c). In the inference stage, ReCoNet can run far above the real-time standard on modern GPUs due to its lightweight and feed-forward network design.

Fig. 1. Temporal inconsistency in video style transfer. (a) The style target *Edtaonisl* (Francis Picabia, 1913) and two consecutive video frames from Videvo.net [34] (b) Style transfer results by Chen *et al.* [4] (c) Style transfer results by ReCoNet. The circled regions show that our model can better suppress temporal inconsistency, while Chen *et al.*'s model generates inconsistent color and noticeable flickering effects (Color figure online)

We find that the brightness constancy assumption [16] in optical flow estimation may not strictly hold in real-world videos and animations, and there exist luminance differences on traceable pixels between consecutive image frames. Such luminance differences cannot be captured by temporal losses purely based on optical flows. To consider the luminance difference, we further introduce a luminance warping constraint in our temporal loss.

From stylization results of previous methods [4,14,17,27,28], we have also observed instability such as different color appearances of the same moving object in consecutive frames. With the intuition that the same object should possess the same features in high-level feature maps, we apply a feature-map-level temporal loss to our encoder. This further improves temporal consistency of our model.

In summary, there exist the following contributions in our paper:

- Our model highly incorporates perceptual style and temporal consistency in the stylized video. With a new feed-forward network design, it can achieve an inference speed over 200 FPS on a single modern GPU. Our model can reproduce various artistic styles on videos with stable results.
- We first propose a luminance warping constraint in the output-level temporal loss to specifically consider luminance changes of traceable pixels in the input video. This constraint can improve stylizing stability in areas with illumination effects and help suppress overall temporal inconsistency.
- We first propose a feature-map-level temporal loss to penalize variations in high-level features of the same object in consecutive frames. This improves stylizing stability of traceable objects in video scenes.

In this paper, related work for image and video style transfer will be first reviewed in Sect. 2. Detailed motivations, network architecture, and loss functions will be presented in Sect. 3. In Sect. 4, the experiment results will be reported and analyzed, where our model shows outstanding performance.

2   Related Work

Gatys et al. [11,12] first developed a neural algorithm for automatic image style transfer, which refines a random noise to a stylized image iteratively constrained by a content loss and a style loss. This method inspired many later image style transfer models [3,5,10,13,19,21,22,29,32]. One of the most successful successor is the feed-forward perceptual losses model proposed by Johnson et al. [19], using a pre-trained VGG network [30] to compute perceptual losses. Although their model has achieved both preferable perceptual quality and near real-time inference speed, severe flickering artifacts can be observed when applying this method frame by frame to videos since temporal stability is not considered. Afterwards, Anderson et al. [1] and Ruder et al. [27] introduced a temporal loss function in video stylization as an explicit consideration of temporal consistency. The temporal loss is involved with optical flows and occlusion masks and is iteratively optimized for each frame until the loss converges. However, it generally takes several minutes for their models to process each video frame, which is not applicable for real-time usage. Although Ruder et al. [28] later accelerated the inference speed, their stylization still runs far below the real-time standard.

To obtain a consistent and fast video style transfer method, some real-time or near real-time models have recently been developed. Chen et al. [4,6] proposed a recurrent model that uses feature maps of the previous frame in addition to the input consecutive frames, and involves explicit optical flows warping on feature maps in both training and inference stages. Since this model requires optical flow estimation by FlowNetS [9] in the inference stage, its inference speed barely reaches real-time level and the temporal consistency is susceptible to errors in optical flow estimation. Gupta *et al.* [14] also proposed a recurrent model which takes an additional stylized previous frame as the input. Although their model performs similarly to Chen *et al.*'s model in terms of temporal consistency, it suffers from transparency issues and still barely reaches real-time inference speed. Using a feed-forward network design, Huang *et al.* [17] proposed a model similar to the perceptual losses model [19] with an additional temporal loss. This model is faster since it neither estimates optical flows nor uses information of previous frames in the inference stage. However, Huang *et al.*'s model calculates the content loss from a deeper layer *relu4_2*, which is hard to capture low-level features. Strokes and textures are also weakened in their stylization results due to a low weight ratio between perceptual losses and the temporal loss.

Noticing strengths and weaknesses of these models, we propose several improvements in ReCoNet. Compared with Chen *et al.* [4]'s model, our model does not estimate optical flows but involves ground-truth optical flows only in loss calculation in the training stage. This can avoid optical flow prediction errors and accelerate inference speed. Meanwhile, our model can render style patterns and textures much more conspicuously than Huang *et al.* [17]'s model, which could only generate minor visual patterns and strokes besides color adjustment. Our lightweight and feed-forward network can run faster than all video stylization models mentioned above [1, 4, 14, 17, 27, 28].

3   Method

The training pipeline of ReCoNet is shown in Fig. 2. ReCoNet consists of three modules: an encoder that converts input image frames to encoded feature maps, a

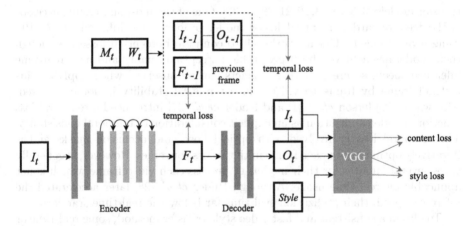

Fig. 2. The pipeline of ReCoNet. I_t, F_t, O_t denote the input image, encoded feature maps, and stylized output image at time frame t. M_t and W_t denote the occlusion mask and the optical flow between time frames $t - 1$ and t. *Style* denotes the artistic style image. The dashed box represents the prediction results of the previous frame, which will only be used in the training process. Red arrows and texts denote loss functions (Color figure online)

decoder that generates stylized images from feature maps, and a VGG-16 [30] loss network to compute the perceptual losses. Additionally, a multi-level temporal loss is added to the output of encoder and the output of decoder to reduce temporal incoherence. In the inference stage, only the encoder and the decoder will be used to stylize videos frame by frame.

3.1 Motivation

Luminance Difference. In real-world videos, the luminance and color appearances can be different on the same object in consecutive frames due to illumination effects. In such cases, the data does not satisfy the assumption known as brightness constancy constraint [16], and direct optical flow warping will ignore luminance changes in traceable pixels [9,18,35]. In animations, many datasets use the albedo pass to calculate ground-truth optical flows but later add illuminations including smooth shading and specular reflections to the final image frames, such as MPI Sintel Dataset [2]. This also results in differences on luminance and color appearances.

To further examine the illumination difference, we computed the absolute value of temporal warping error $I_t - W_t(I_{t-1})$ over MPI Sintel Dataset and 50 real-world videos download from Videvo.net [34], where W is the forward optical flow and I is the input image frame. We used *FlowNet2* [18] to calculate optical flows and the method of Sundaram *et al.* [31] to obtain occlusion masks for downloaded videos. Figure 3 demonstrates the histograms of temporal warping error in both RGB and XYZ color space. We can draw two conclusions based on the results. First, RGB channels share similar warping error distributions. There is no bias of changes in color channel. Second, despite changes in relative luminance channel Y, the chromaticity channels X and Z in XYZ color space also contribute to the total inter-frame difference. However, since there is no exact guideline of chromaticity mapping in a particular style, we mainly consider luminance difference in our temporal loss.

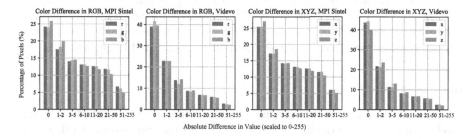

Fig. 3. Histograms of temporal warping error in different datasets and color spaces (Color figure online)

Based on our findings, we propose a novel luminance constraint in our temporal loss to encourage the stylized frames to have the same luminance changes as the input frames. This can reduce unstable color changes under illumination effects and improve temporal consistency of the stylized frames. Experiments in Sect. 4.3 show that this new constraint can bring significant improvements to the output perceptual quality and temporal stability.

Feature-Map-Level Temporal Loss. Another new loss function we propose for feature-map-level consistency is based on the intuition that the same object should preserve the same representation in high-level feature maps. Although warping frames directly at the output level may not be accurate due to illuminations, the same method can be very suitable at the feature-map level as examined by Chen *et al.* [4]. We use ground-truth optical flows and occlusion masks to calculate feature-map-level temporal loss between the warped feature maps and the current ones. Experiments in Sect. 4.3 show that this new loss can improve stylization consistency on the same object in consecutive frames.

3.2 Network Architecture

ReCoNet adopts a pure CNN-based design. Compared to feed-forward networks in literature [17,19], we separate the whole network to an encoder and a decoder for different purposes. The encoder is designed to encode image frames to feature maps with aggregated perceptual information, and the feature-map-level temporal loss is computed on its output. The decoder is designed to decode feature maps to a stylized image where we compute the output-level temporal loss. Table 1 shows our encoder and decoder design. There are three convolutional layers and four residual blocks [15] in the encoder, and two up-sampling convolutional layers with a final convolutional layer in the decoder. We use an up-sample layer and a convolutional layer instead of one traditional deconvolutional layer in the decoder to reduce checkerboard artifacts [25]. We adopt instance normalization [33] after each convolution process to attain better stylization quality. Reflection padding is used at each convolutional layer.

The loss network is a VGG-16 network [30] pre-trained on the ImageNet dataset [8]. For each iteration, the VGG-16 network processes each of the input image frame, output image frame and style target independently. The content and style losses are then computed based on the generated image features.

3.3 Loss Functions

Our multi-level temporal loss design focuses on temporal coherence at both high-level feature maps and the final stylized output. At the feature-map level, a strict optical flow warping is adopted to achieve temporal consistency of traceable pixels in high-level features. At the output level, an optical flow warping with a luminance constraint is used to simulate both the movements and luminance changes of traceable pixels. The perceptual losses design is inherited from the perceptual losses model [19].

Table 1. Network layer specification. Layer and output sizes are denoted as channel × height × width. *Conv, Res, InsNorm, ReLU, Tanh* denote convolutional layer, residual block [15], instance normalization layer [33], ReLU activation layer [24], and Tanh activation layer respectively

Layer	Layer size	Stride	Output size
Encoder			
Input			$3 \times 640 \times 360$
Conv + InsNorm + ReLU	$48 \times 9 \times 9$	1	$48 \times 640 \times 360$
Conv + InsNorm + ReLU	$96 \times 3 \times 3$	2	$96 \times 320 \times 180$
Conv + InsNorm + ReLU	$192 \times 3 \times 3$	2	$192 \times 160 \times 90$
(Res + InsNorm + ReLU) ×4	$192 \times 3 \times 3$	1	$192 \times 160 \times 90$
Decoder			
Up-sample		1/2	$192 \times 320 \times 180$
Conv + InsNorm + ReLU	$96 \times 3 \times 3$	1	$96 \times 320 \times 180$
Up-sample		1/2	$96 \times 640 \times 360$
Conv + InsNorm + ReLU	$48 \times 3 \times 3$	1	$48 \times 640 \times 360$
Conv + Tanh	$3 \times 9 \times 9$	1	$3 \times 640 \times 360$

A two-frame synergic training mechanism [17] is used in the training stage. For each iteration, the network generates feature maps and stylized output of the first image frame and the second image frame in two runs. Then, the temporal losses are computed using the feature maps and stylized output of both frames, and the perceptual losses are computed on each frame independently and summed up. Note again that in the inference stage, only one image frame will be processed by the network in a single run.

Output-Level Temporal Loss. The temporal losses in previous works [4,14,17,27,28] usually ignore changes in luminance of traceable pixels. Taking this issue into account, the *relative luminance* $Y = 0.2126R + 0.7152G + 0.0722B$, same as Y in XYZ color space, is added as a warping constraint for all channels in RGB color space:

$$\mathcal{L}_{temp,o}(t - 1, t) = \sum_c \frac{1}{D} M_t \| (O_t - W_t(O_{t-1}))_c - (I_t - W_t(I_{t-1}))_Y \|^2 \quad (1)$$

where $c \in [R, G, B]$ is each of the RGB channels of the image, Y the relative luminance channel, O_{t-1} and O_t the stylized images for previous and current input frames respectively, I_{t-1} and I_t the previous and current input frames respectively, W_t the ground-truth forward optical flow, M_t the ground-truth forward occlusion mask (1 at traceable pixels or 0 at untraceable pixels), $D = H \times W$ the multiplication of height H and width W of the input/output image. We apply the relative luminance warping constraint to each RGB channel equally based on the "no bias" conclusion in Sect. 3.1. Section 4.3 further discusses different choices of the luminance constraint and the output-level temporal loss.

Feature-Map-Level Temporal Loss. The feature-map-level temporal loss penalizes temporal inconsistency on the encoded feature maps between two consecutive input image frames:

$$\mathcal{L}_{temp,f}(t-1,t) = \frac{1}{D} M_t \| F_t - W_t(F_{t-1}) \|^2 \tag{2}$$

where F_{t-1} and F_t are the feature maps outputted by the encoder for previous and current input frames respectively, W_t and M_t the ground-truth forward optical flow and occlusion mask downscaled to the size of feature maps, $D = C \times H \times W$ the multiplication of channel size C, image height H and image width W of the encoded feature maps F. We use downscaled optical flows and occlusion masks to simulate temporal motions in high-level features.

Perceptual Losses. We adopt the content loss $\mathcal{L}_{content}(t)$, the style loss $\mathcal{L}_{style}(t)$ and the total variation regularizer $\mathcal{L}_{tv}(t)$ in the perceptual losses model [19] for each time frame t. The content loss and the style loss utilize feature maps at $relu3\_3$ layer and $[relu1\_2, relu2\_2, relu3\_3, relu4\_3]$ layers respectively.

Summary. The final loss function for the two-frame synergic training is:

$$\mathcal{L}(t-1,t) = \sum_{i \in \{t-1,t\}} (\alpha \mathcal{L}_{content}(i) + \beta \mathcal{L}_{style}(i) + \gamma \mathcal{L}_{tv}(i))$$
$$+ \lambda_f \mathcal{L}_{temp,f}(t-1,t) + \lambda_o \mathcal{L}_{temp,o}(t-1,t) \tag{3}$$

where $\alpha, \beta, \gamma, \lambda_f$ and λ_o are hyper-parameters for the training process.

4 Experiments

4.1 Implementation Details

We use Monkaa and FlyingThings3D in the Scene Flow datasets [23] as the training dataset, and MPI Sintel dataset [2] as the testing dataset. The Scene Flow datasets provide optical flows and motion boundaries for each consecutive frames, from which we can also obtain occlusion masks using the method provided by Sundaram *et al.* [31]. Monkaa dataset is extracted from the animation movie Monkaa and contains around 8640 frames, resembling MPI Sintel dataset. FlyingThings3D dataset is a large dataset of everyday objects flying along random 3D trajectories and contains around 20150 frames, resembling animated and real-world complex scenes. Same as the verification process of previous works [4,14,17], we use MPI Sintel dataset to verify the temporal consistency and perceptual styles of our stylization results.

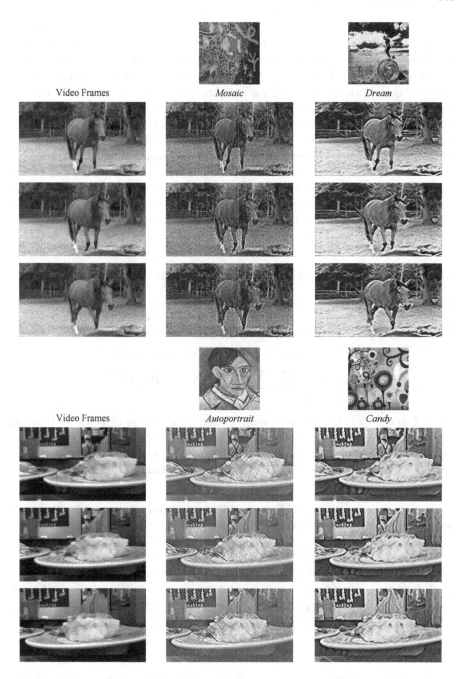

Fig. 4. Video style transfer results using ReCoNet. The first column contains two groups of three consecutive image frames in videos downloaded from Videvo.net [34]. Each video frames are followed by two style target images and their corresponding stylized results of the video frames. The styles are *Mosaic*, *Dream*, *Autoportrait* (Picasso, 1907), and *Candy* (Color figure online)

All image frames are resized to 640×360. We train the model with a batch size of 2 for 30,000 steps, roughly two epochs over the training dataset. We pair up consecutive frames for the two-frame synergic training and adopt random horizontal flip on each pair. The frame pairs are shuffled in training process. We use Adam optimizer [20] with a learning rate of 10^{-3}, and set the default training hyper-parameters to be $\alpha = 1, \beta = 10, \gamma = 10^{-3}, \lambda_f = 10^7, \lambda_o = 2 \times 10^3$. We implement our style transfer pipeline on PyTorch 0.3 [26] with cuDNN 7 [7]. All tensor calculations are performed on a single GTX 1080 Ti GPU. Further details of the training process can be found in our supplementary materials.

We also download 50 videos from Videvo.net [34] to verify our generalization capacity on videos in real world. Figure 4 shows style transfer results of four different styles on three consecutive video frames. We observe that the color, strokes and textures of the style target can be successfully reproduced by our model, and the stylized frames are visually coherent.

4.2 Comparison to Methods in the Literature

Quantitative Analysis. Table 2 shows the temporal error e_{stab} of four video style transfer models on five scenes in MPI Sintel Dataset with style *Candy*. e_{stab} is the square root of output-level temporal error over one whole scene:

$$e_{stab} = \sqrt{\frac{1}{T-1} \sum_{t=1}^{T} \frac{1}{D} M_t \|O_t - W_t(O_{t-1})\|^2} \tag{4}$$

where T is the total number of frames. Other variables are identical to those in the output-level temporal loss. This error function verifies the temporal consistency of traceable pixels in the stylized output. All scene frames are resized to 640×360. We use a single GTX 1080 Ti GPU for computation acceleration.

Table 2. Temporal error e_{stab} and average FPS in the inference stage with style *Candy* on different models. Five scenes from MPI Sintel Dataset are selected for validation

Model	Alley-2	Ambush-5	Bandage-2	Market-6	Temple-2	FPS
Chen *et al.* [4]	0.0934	0.1352	0.0715	0.1030	0.1094	22.5
ReCoNet	0.0846	0.0819	0.0662	0.0862	0.0831	235.3
Huang *et al.* [17]	0.0439	0.0675	0.0304	0.0553	0.0513	216.8
Ruder *et al.* [27]	0.0252	0.0512	0.0195	0.0407	0.0361	0.8

From the table, we observe that Ruder *et al.* [27]'s model is not suitable for real-time usage due to low inference speed, despite its lowest temporal error among all models in our comparison. Among the rest models which reach the real-time standard, our model achieves lower temporal error than Chen *et al.* [4]'s model, primarily because of the introduction of the multi-level temporal loss.

Although our temporal error is higher than Huang *et al.* [17]'s model, our model is capable of capturing strokes and minor textures in the style image while Huang *et al.*'s model could not. Please refer to the qualitative analysis below for details.

Another finding is that ReCoNet and Huang *et al.*'s model achieve far better inference speed than the others. Compared with recurrent models [4,14,28], feed-forward models are easier to be accelerated with parallelism since the current iteration do not need to wait for the previous frame to be fully processed.

Qualitative Analysis. We examine our style transfer results qualitatively with other real-time models proposed by Chen *et al.* 's [4] and Huang *et al.* 's [17].

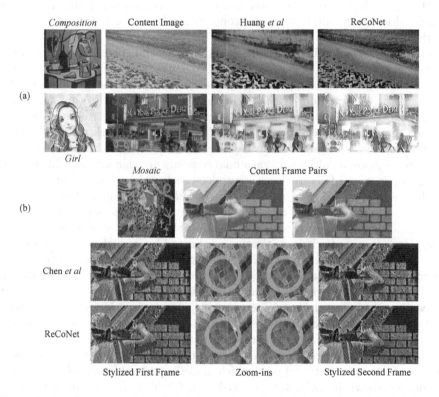

Fig. 5. Qualitative comparison of style transfer results in the literature. (a) Style transfer results between Huang *et al.* [17]'s model and ReCoNet on image frames. (b) Style transfer results between Chen *et al.* [4]'s model and ReCoNet on consecutive image frames with zoom-ins of flickering regions (Color figure online)

Figure 5(a) shows the stylization comparison between Huang *et al.* 's model and ReCoNet. Although Huang *et al.* 's model achieves low temporal error quantitatively and is able to capture the color information in the style image, it fails

Table 3. User study result. In each of the two comparisons, we aggregate the results of all four video clips for the three questions. "Same" means the voter find that results of both models are similar to each other or it is hard to support one against another

Models	Q1	Q2	Q3	Models	Q1	Q2	Q3
ReCoNet	64	162	152	ReCoNet	164	42	115
Chen et al. [4]	64	15	23	Huang et al. [17]	22	91	42
Same	72	23	25	Same	14	67	43

to learn much about the perceptual strokes and patterns. There are two reasons that may account for their weak perceptual styles as shown in the two examples in the figure. First, they use a low weight ratio between perceptual losses and temporal loss to maintain temporal coherence, which brings obvious reduction to the quality of output style. However, in ReCoNet, the introduction of the new temporal losses makes it possible to maintain temporal coherence with a larger perceptual to temporal losses ratio, leading to better preserved perceptual styles. As shown in the first example, our stylized image reproduces the distinct color blocks in the *Composition* style much better than Huang et al.'s result, especially on the uneven sand surfaces and the sea wave. Second, Huang et al.'s model uses feature maps from a deeper layer $relu4\_2$ in the loss network to calculate the content loss, which is difficult to capture low-level features such as edges. In the second example, although sharp bold contours are characteristic in the *Girl* image, their model fails to clearly reproduce such style. Unlike Huang et al. 's model, as shown in Figs. 1 and 5(b), Chen et al. 's work can well maintain the perceptual information of both the content image and the style image. However, from zoom-in regions, we can find noticeable inconsistency in their stylized results, which can also be quantitatively validated by its high temporal errors.

To further compare our video style transfer results with these two models, we conducted a user study. For each of the two comparisons (ReCoNet vs Huang et al. 's and ReCoNet vs Chen et al. 's), we chose 4 different styles on 4 different video clips downloaded from Videvo.net [34]. We invited 50 people to answer (Q1) which model perceptually resembles the style image more, regarding the color, strokes, textures, and other visual patterns; (Q2) which model is more temporally consistent such as fewer flickering artifacts and consistent color and style of the same object; and (Q3) which model is preferable overall. The voting results are shown in Table 3. Compared with Chen et al. 's model, our model achieves much better temporal consistency while maintaining good perceptual styles. Compared with Huang et al. 's model, our results are much better in perceptual styles and the overall feeling although our temporal consistency is slightly worse. This validates our previous qualitative analysis. Detailed procedures and results of the user study can be found in our supplementary materials.

4.3   Ablation Study

Temporal Loss on Different Levels. To study whether the multi-level temporal loss does help reduce temporal inconsistency and maintain perceptual style, we implement our video style transfer model on *Candy* style with three different settings: feature-map-level temporal loss only, output-level temporal loss only, and feature-map-level temporal loss plus output-level temporal loss.

Table 4. Temporal error e_{stab} with style *Candy* for different temporal loss settings in ReCoNet. Five scenes from MPI Sintel Dataset are selected for validation

Loss levels	Alley-2	Ambush-5	Bandage-2	Market-6	Temple-2	Average
Feature-map only	0.1028	0.1041	0.0752	0.1062	0.0991	0.0975
Output only	0.0854	0.0840	0.0672	0.0868	0.0820	0.0813
Both	0.0846	0.0819	0.0662	0.0862	0.0831	0.0804

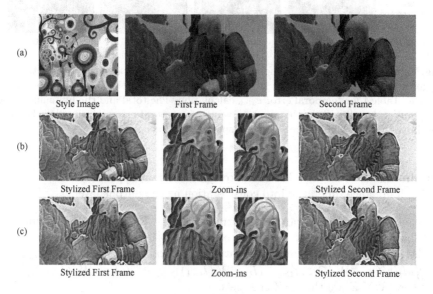

Fig. 6. Temporal inconsistency in traceable objects. (a) The style target and two consecutive frames in MPI Sintel Dataset. (b) Stylized frames generated without feature-map-level temporal loss. (c) Stylized frames generated with feature-map-level temporal loss. A specific traceable region is circled for comparison (Color figure online)

Table 4 shows the temporal error e_{stab} of these settings on five scenes in MPI Sintel Dataset. We observe that the temporal error is greatly reduced with the output-level temporal loss, while the feature-map-level temporal loss also improves temporal consistency on average.

Figure 6 demonstrates a visual example of object appearance inconsistency. When only using output-level temporal loss, the exactly same object may alter its color due to the changes of surrounding environment. With the feature-map-level temporal loss, features are preserved for the same object.

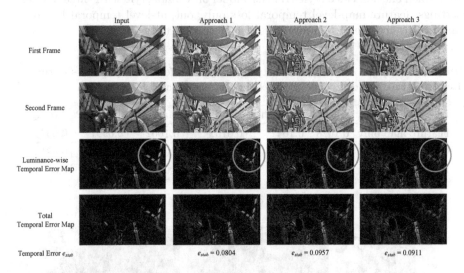

Fig. 7. Style transfer results using three different approaches described in Sect. 4.3 to target luminance difference. The style target is *Candy*, and the validation scenes are same as Table 4 for temporal error e_{stab} calculation. The total and the luminance-wise temporal error maps show the absolute value of temporal errors in all color channels and in the relative luminance channel respectively (Color figure online)

Luminance Difference. We compare three different approaches taking or not taking luminance difference into consideration at the output level:

1. A relative luminance warping constraint on each RGB channel (Formula 1);
2. Change color space of output-level temporal loss into XYZ color space, then add a relative luminance warping constraint to Y channel: $\mathcal{L}_{temp}^o = \frac{1}{D} M_t(\|(O_t - W_t(O_{t-1}))_Y - (I_t - W_t(I_{t-1}))_Y\|_2 + \|(O_t - W_t(O_{t-1}))_{X,Z}\|_2)$ where X, Y, Z are the XYZ channels;
3. No luminance constraint: $\mathcal{L}_{temp}^o = \frac{1}{D} M_t \|(O_t - W_t(O_{t-1}))_{R,G,B}\|_2$.

Other variables in approach 2 and 3 are identical to those in Formula 1. As shown in Fig. 7, all three approaches can obtain pleasant perceptual styles of *Candy* despite some variations in color. However, the first approach has a more similar luminance-wise temporal error map to the input frames compared with the other two methods, especially in the circled illuminated region. This shows the first approach can preserve proper luminance changes between consecutive frames as those in the input, and therefore leads to more natural stylizing outputs. Moreover, the total temporal error map of the first approach is also closer to zero than the results of other two approaches, implying more stable stylized results. This is also supported numerically by a much lower overall temporal error produced by the first approach in the validation scenes. Based on both qualitative and quantitative analysis, we can conclude that adding a relative luminance warping constraint to all RGB channels can generate smoother color change on areas with illumination effects and achieve better temporal coherence.

5 Conclusions

In this paper, we present a feed-forward convolutional neural network *ReCoNet* for video style transfer. Our model is able to generate coherent stylized videos in real-time processing speed while maintaining artistic styles perceptually similar to the style target. We propose a luminance warping constraint in the output-level temporal loss for better stylization stability under illumination effects. We also introduce a feature-map level temporal loss to further mitigate temporal inconsistency. In future work, we plan to further investigate the possibility of utilizing both chromaticity and luminance difference in inter-frame warping results for better video style transfer algorithm.

References

1. Anderson, A.G., Berg, C.P., Mossing, D.P., Olshausen, B.A.: DeepMovie: using optical flow and deep neural networks to stylize movies. arXiv preprint arXiv:1605.08153 (2016)
2. Butler, D.J., Wulff, J., Stanley, G.B., Black, M.J.: A naturalistic open source movie for optical flow evaluation. In: Fitzgibbon, A., Lazebnik, S., Perona, P., Sato, Y., Schmid, C. (eds.) ECCV 2012. LNCS, vol. 7577, pp. 611–625. Springer, Heidelberg (2012). https://doi.org/10.1007/978-3-642-33783-3_44
3. Champandard, A.J.: Semantic style transfer and turning two-bit doodles into fine artworks. arXiv preprint arXiv:1603.01768 (2016)
4. Chen, D., Liao, J., Yuan, L., Yu, N., Hua, G.: Coherent online video style transfer. In: Proceedings of the IEEE International Conference on Computer Vision, October 2017
5. Chen, D., Yuan, L., Liao, J., Yu, N., Hua, G.: StyleBank: an explicit representation for neural image style transfer. In: Proceedings of the IEEE Conference on Computer Vision and Pattern Recognition, pp. 1897–1906 (2017)
6. Chen, D., Yuan, L., Liao, J., Yu, N., Hua, G.: Stereoscopic neural styletransfer. In: CVPR (2018)
7. Chetlur, S., et al.: cuDNN: efficient primitives for deep learning. arXiv preprint arXiv:1410.0759 (2014)
8. Deng, J., Dong, W., Socher, R., Li, L.J., Li, K., Fei-Fei, L.: ImageNet: a large-scale hierarchical image database. In: Proceedings of the IEEE Conference on Computer Vision and Pattern Recognition, pp. 248–255. IEEE (2009)
9. Dosovitskiy, A., et al.: FlowNet: learning optical flow with convolutional networks. In: Proceedings of the IEEE International Conference on Computer Vision, pp. 2758–2766 (2015)

10. Dumoulin, V., et al.: A learned representation for artistic style. arXiv preprint arXiv:1610.07629 (2016)
11. Gatys, L.A., Ecker, A.S., Bethge, M.: A neural algorithm of artistic style. arXiv preprint arXiv:1508.06576 (2015)
12. Gatys, L.A., Ecker, A.S., Bethge, M.: Image style transfer using convolutional neural networks. In: Proceedings of the IEEE Conference on Computer Vision and Pattern Recognition, pp. 2414–2423. IEEE (2016)
13. Gatys, L.A., Ecker, A.S., Bethge, M., Hertzmann, A., Shechtman, E.: Controlling perceptual factors in neural style transfer. In: Proceedings of the IEEE Conference on Computer Vision and Pattern Recognition (2017)
14. Gupta, A., Johnson, J., Alahi, A., Fei-Fei, L.: Characterizing and improving stability in neural style transfer. In: Proceedings of the IEEE Conference on Computer Vision and Pattern Recognition, pp. 4067–4076 (2017)
15. He, K., Zhang, X., Ren, S., Sun, J.: Deep residual learning for image recognition. In: Proceedings of the IEEE Conference on Computer Vision and Pattern Recognition, pp. 770–778 (2016)
16. Horn, B.K.: Determining lightness from an image. Comput. Graph. Image Process. **3**(4), 277–299 (1974)
17. Huang, H., et al.: Real-time neural style transfer for videos. In: Proceedings of the IEEE Conference on Computer Vision and Pattern Recognition (2017)
18. Ilg, E., Mayer, N., Saikia, T., Keuper, M., Dosovitskiy, A., Brox, T.: FlowNet 2.0: evolution of optical flow estimation with deep networks. In: Proceedings of the IEEE Conference on Computer Vision and Pattern Recognition, vol. 2 (2017)
19. Johnson, J., Alahi, A., Fei-Fei, L.: Perceptual losses for real-time style transfer and super-resolution. In: Leibe, B., Matas, J., Sebe, N., Welling, M. (eds.) ECCV 2016. LNCS, vol. 9906, pp. 694–711. Springer, Cham (2016). https://doi.org/10.1007/978-3-319-46475-6_43
20. Kingma, D.P., Ba, J.: Adam: a method for stochastic optimization. In: International Conference on Learning Representations (2015)
21. Liao, J., Yao, Y., Yuan, L., Hua, G., Kang, S.B.: Visual attribute transfer through deep image analogy. arXiv preprint arXiv:1705.01088 (2017)
22. Luan, F., Paris, S., Shechtman, E., Bala, K.: Deep photo style transfer. In: Proceedings of the IEEE Conference on Computer Vision and Pattern Recognition, pp. 6997–7005. IEEE (2017)
23. Mayer, N., et al.: A large dataset to train convolutional networks for disparity, optical flow, and scene flow estimation. In: Proceedings of the IEEE Conference on Computer Vision and Pattern Recognition, pp. 4040–4048 (2016)
24. Nair, V., Hinton, G.E.: Rectified linear units improve restricted Boltzmann machines. In: Proceedings of the 27th International Conference on Machine Learning (ICML-10), pp. 807–814 (2010)
25. Odena, A., Dumoulin, V., Olah, C.: Deconvolution and checkerboard artifacts. Distill **1**, e3 (2016). https://doi.org/10.23915/distill.00003. http://distill.pub/2016/deconv-checkerboard
26. Paszke, A., et al.: PyTorch: tensors and dynamic neural networks in python with strong GPU acceleration (2017)
27. Ruder, M., Dosovitskiy, A., Brox, T.: Artistic style transfer for videos. In: Rosenhahn, B., Andres, B. (eds.) GCPR 2016. LNCS, vol. 9796, pp. 26–36. Springer, Cham (2016). https://doi.org/10.1007/978-3-319-45886-1_3
28. Ruder, M., Dosovitskiy, A., Brox, T.: Artistic style transfer for videos and spherical images. Int. J. Comput. Vis. **126**(11), 1199–1219 (2018)

29. Selim, A., Elgharib, M., Doyle, L.: Painting style transfer for head portraits using convolutional neural networks. ACM Trans. Graph. (ToG) **35**(4), 129 (2016)
30. Simonyan, K., Zisserman, A.: Very deep convolutional networks for large-scale image recognition. arXiv preprint arXiv:1409.1556 (2014)
31. Sundaram, N., Brox, T., Keutzer, K.: Dense point trajectories by GPU-accelerated large displacement optical flow. In: Daniilidis, K., Maragos, P., Paragios, N. (eds.) ECCV 2010. LNCS, vol. 6311, pp. 438–451. Springer, Heidelberg (2010). https://doi.org/10.1007/978-3-642-15549-9_32
32. Ulyanov, D., Lebedev, V., Vedaldi, A., Lempitsky, V.S.: Texture networks: feed-forward synthesis of textures and stylized images. In: International Conference on Machine Learning, pp. 1349–1357 (2016)
33. Ulyanov, D., Vedaldi, A., Lempitsky, V.S.: Instance normalization: the missing ingredient for fast stylization. arXiv preprint arXiv:1607.08022 (2016)
34. Videvo: Videvo free footage (2018). https://www.videvo.net/. Accessed 26 Feb 2018
35. Weinzaepfel, P., Revaud, J., Harchaoui, Z., Schmid, C.: DeepFlow: large displacement optical flow with deep matching. In: 2013 IEEE International Conference on Computer Vision (ICCV), pp. 1385–1392. IEEE (2013)

PIVTONS: Pose Invariant Virtual Try-On Shoe with Conditional Image Completion

Chao-Te Chou[✉], Cheng-Han Lee, Kaipeng Zhang, Hu-Cheng Lee, and Winston H. Hsu

National Taiwan University, Taipei, Taiwan
b03901096@ntu.edu.tw

Abstract. Virtual try-on – synthesizing an almost-realistic image for dressing a target fashion item provided the source human photo – has growing needs due to the prevalence of e-commerce and the development of deep learning technologies. However, existing deep learning virtual try-on methods focus on the clothing replacement due to the lack of dataset and cope with flat body segments with frontal poses providing the front view of the target fashion item. In this paper, we present the pose invariant virtual try-on shoe (PIVTONS) to cope with the task of virtual try-on shoe. We collect the paired feet and shoe virtual-try on dataset, Zalando-shoes, containing 14,062 shoes among the 11 categories of shoes. The shoe image only contains a single view of the shoes but the try-on result should show other views of the shoes depending on the original feet pose. We formulate this task as an automatic and labor-free image completion task and design an end-to-end neural networks composing of feature point detector. Through the numerous experiments and ablation studies, we demonstrate the performance of the proposed framework and investigate the parameterizing factors for optimizing the challenging problem.

Keywords: Virtual try-on · Generative model

1 Introduction

In recent years, the demands of online shopping for fashion items are increasing, and are predicted to increase in the future. When shopping online for fashion items, consumers will consider what they would look like in those fashion items. Therefore, virtual try-on systems for different fashion items are in need. These systems can assist consumers more effectively and precisely to find the fashion items they want and can also reduce the risk for the retailer to have an additional cost if the consumers want a return.

To use a virtual try-on system, a user should provide a *source image*, which is an image of a person or body parts intending to try a different fashion item, and an image of the target item. A virtual try-on system synthesizes a photo-realistic new image, a *target image*, by overlaying the given target fashion item seamlessly

C. V. Jawahar et al. (Eds.): ACCV 2018, LNCS 11366, pp. 654–668, 2019.
https://doi.org/10.1007/978-3-030-20876-9_41

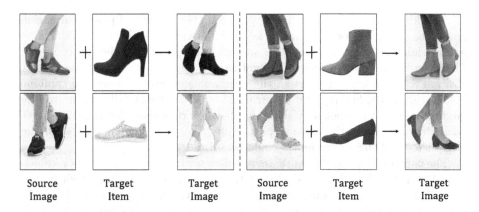

Source	Target	Target	Source	Target	Target
Image	Item	Image	Image	Item	Image

Fig. 1. Results generated by our PIVTONS. For our task of virtual-try on shoe, the inputs are a source image with feet wearing shoes and a target item, a single view of a single shoe. In this examples, we show that the poses of feet are diverse and only a single view of the target shoe is given. With this constraint, our virtual try-on method swaps the shoe onto the feet in the source image and generates the target images meeting the criteria for a virtual try-on system.

onto the corresponding region of body parts in the source image. Some examples are shown in Fig. 1. The generalized criteria for virtual try-on should include: (I) The fashion item in the target image should be the same as the target fashion item; (II) The region outside the fashion item in the target image should be the same as that of the source image; (III) The target image should be realistic and consistent.

Existing works using deep learning for virtual try-on have been focusing on virtual try-on clothing. Jetchev *et al.* [6] incorporate a cycle loss to replace the clothing texture. Han *et al.* [4] utilize the segmentation maps of human body part to guide the synthesis of target clothing onto human body. Both methods are designed for virtual try-on clothing providing the frontal-view human body and the frontal view of clothing. Virtual try-on systems using deep learning for other fashion items have not been developed but are still in need.

In this paper, we present a pose invariant virtual try-on shoe (PIVTONS) method with conditional image completion to address the virtual try-on shoe problem. We collect the images to conduct experiment from the Zalando website[1]. The task of virtual try-on shoe is challenging since the poses of human feet are diverse and the shoe, target fashion item, only shows the single view of a single shoe, which is a pose difference between the source image and the target shoe. Thus, we call our method pose invariant. To formulate our method into a conditional image completion problem, we first detect the bounding box of shoes in the source image. We hide the region inside bounding box and generate the target image considering the region outside bounding box and the conditioned target shoe.

---

[1] The images shown in this paper are collected from https://www.zalando.co.uk.

To address the problem of diverse poses and the missing of pose information inside the bounding box, we use a key-point detector to detect the four key-points, right toe, right heel, left toe, and left heel, of shoes in the source image. The detected key-points assist the synthesis of the target shoe to the correct position and size onto the feet in the source image. Furthermore, we combine $l2$ loss, perceptual loss [7], and adversarial loss [3] to realistically synthesize the target image that can not only show the shown part of shoe shown in the target image but also show the missing part. Thus, the pose difference between the target shoe and the source image could be solved.

The contributions of this work are as follows. First, to the best of our knowledge, this is the first work to deal with the problem of virtual try-on shoe with deep neural network. Second, we present a conditional image completion technique which is different from previous image completion problem to deal with virtual try-on shoe. Third, through numerous experiments conducting on the collected images, we show that our method can generate visually plausible results.

2   Related Work

Generative Adversarial Network. GAN [3] has been one of the most widely used deep generative models and shows promising results in image generation [16]. The generated image can be controlled by combining GAN with other conditional priors such as text [17,21], or discrete labels [13]. Some other works for image-to-image translation combine $l2$ or $l1$ loss with GAN to force the output to be conditioned on the input image. Isola *et al.* [5] use GAN in a conditional manner with $l1$ loss and propose a general framework for many tasks of image-to-image translation. The presented patchGAN is also used in our work. Ledig *et al.* [9] combine per-pixel loss, perceptual loss [7] and GAN for the task of super-resolution. In our work, we also apply these losses to generate realistic results for our task of virtual try-on shoe with conditional image completion. Zhu *et al.* [23] use a two-stage GAN to edit a fashion item a person wear on according to the given text description. It can be regarded as text-based virtual try-on task. Ma *et al.* [12] design a two stages network to generate person image of different view with the providing human image and key-points of target pose. In our work, we also provide the four key-points of shoes in the source image to compensate the pose information missing inside the bounding box.

Image Completion. Recently, deep learning and GAN-based approaches have been utilized to tackle image completion problem and show decent results. Rolf *et al.* [8] exploit the shape information of the missing regions and train a neuron network for denoising and inpainting of small regions. Pathak *et al.* [15] propose an unsupervised visual feature learning algorithm driven by context-based pixel prediction. Li *et al.* [10] propose an image completion algorithm using a deep generative based on GAN [3] by introducing a global and a local discriminator as adversarial losses and a semantic parsing network to provide face parsing loss. Different from these image completion tasks, our task needs not only to fill in the missing part with the surrounding information and the learned knowledge from the dataset but also to take target shoe as a prior into consideration to generate visually plausible results.

Virtual Try-On. VITON [4] is an image-based virtual try-on method utilizing only 2D information. Given a human try-on image and the image of target fashion item, it transfers the target fashion item onto the corresponding region of a person. It utilizes human segmentation maps to guide the generation of target fashion item onto the human body. With the state-of-the-art person pose detector [1] and human parser [2], this method can have good quality segmentation and key-points of the human body. CAGAN [6] use a cycle loss [22] to train a virtual try-on network. Therefore, it does not need segmentation or fashion item detection to swap a fashion item onto a human body. However, during training and testing, it needs the product images of both the target item and the original item in the human try-on image. This requirement is not convenient for users to try-on new fashion item with their own source image. Different from existing works, our method is designed for the task of virtual try-on shoe, which to the best of our knowledge has not been solved before utilizing deep neural network. We use the detection of a bounding box and four key-points in a person try-on image to dress the person in a new fashion item. Furthermore, our method does not need the image of the original fashion item the person wear to swap the new fashion item onto that human body, which is feasible for real-world applications as VITON [4].

3   Proposed Method

In this section, we present our PIVTONS for the virtual try-on shoe task. Given a source image I with feet wearing shoes, we aim to generate target image $\hat{I}$ with the feet in the source image wearing the target shoe I_s. To incorporate supervised learning, a solution is to collect training data of a person with fixed pose wearing different shoes and the corresponding target shoe images. However, it is expensive to collect this kind of data. Therefore, we use the source image as ground truth during training and both the source image and target shoe are the inputs of our pipeline following the general setting of virtual try-on system.

However, using the source image I as both the input and the ground truth to train the network would cause the network to output the source image I directly during testing, even if a different shoe is provided. Therefore, we formulate our problem as an image completion problem. We detect the bounding box and key-points (Sect. 3.1) of shoes in source image, hide the part inside the bounding box, and synthesize the full target image $\hat{I}$ (Sect. 3.2). With the region outside the bounding box and the target shoe provided to our pipeline, the proposed method could synthesize the target image satisfying the first and second virtual criteria described in Sect. 1. To make the generated target images consistent and realistic to meet the third criteria of virtual try-on described in Sect. 1, we combine the per-pixel loss, perceptual loss [7] and the adversarial loss [3] (Sect. 3.3). The proposed pipeline with the networks is shown in Fig. 2.

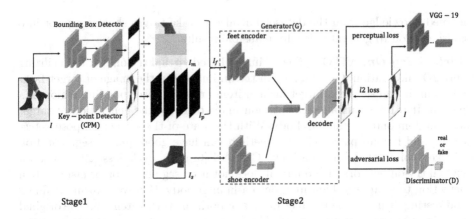

Fig. 2. Proposed pipeline. Our pipeline is composed of 2 stages. The first stage is composed of a bounding box detector and a key-point detector. Those networks are used to predict bounding box and key-points, which are used to prepare the masked source image I_m and the key-point maps I_p for the input of the next stage. The second stage is our conditional image completion virtual try-on network. It is used to fill in the missing part to generate the target image. Please refer to Sect. 3 for more details.

3.1   Stage-1: Detectors

Bounding Box Detector. For the task of virtual try-on, there is often a single person and a single fashion item to be swapped in a source image, so only a single bounding box is needed in our task. Therefore, we design a simple network for our task of bounding box detection. During training, we generate a binary mask by filling the region inside bounding box with ones and outside with zeros with respect to the ground truth bounding box. We then train a convolutional network for semantic segmentation with only two classes, foreground and background. During testing, our network predicts a mask indicating where the foreground is and then we can get the bounding box for the part of shoes in the source image through the boundary of that region. To provide more information of the target shoe that will be generated in this hiding region in the later stage, we fill the region inside the bounding box with the mean color of the shoe image I_s. We call the resulting image as a masked source image I_m.

Key-point Detector. I_m can provide the information of the pose the network need to generate. However, it often can not provide clear information. To preserve the feet pose inside the bounding box after swapping the shoe and generate more precise shoe size, we use key-points to help the generation of the target image. In our work, we use CPM [20] with six stages and use the belief map generated in the last stage as the final key-points detection result. After getting the belief maps for each key-point, we take the point with the maximum value as the center of the key-point. To leverage spatial layout, each key-point is then transformed into a Gaussian peak heatmap and the value at the location (x, y) on the heatmap is given by the following equation.

$$f(x, y) = exp(-\frac{(x - x_0)^2 + (y - y_0)^2}{\sigma^2}) \qquad (1)$$

where (x_0, y_0) is the position of the key-point. The four individual heatmaps are further stacked into 4-channel heatmaps I_p.

3.2 Stage-2: Conditional Image Completion

Given the masked source image I_m, key-point heatmaps I_p, and the image of the target shoe I_s, the network in stage-2 directly generates the full target image. The stage-2 network of our image completion virtual try-on consists of two encoders and one decoder. The architectures of both encoders are the same, but the parameters are not shared. For the sake of clarity, one encoder is called the feet encoder, and the other is called the shoe encoder. The input of feet encoder is I_f, which is the stack of I_m and I_p. This encoder extracts the feature and provides the information of the feature of pant and the pose of the feet. The input of the shoe branch is the target shoe image I_s. It can be regarded as a conditional branch to provide information of the shoe to try-on. It extracts the feature and provides the information of the texture, shape, and color of the target shoe. The features from feet encoder and shoe encoder are concatenated and fed into the decoder to predict the target image $\hat{I} = G(I_f, I_s)$.

3.3 Loss Function

Per-Pixel Loss. For image generation task with ground truth image, an intuitive method to train the network is using a per-pixel $l1$ or $l2$ loss. In our work, we choose to use $l2$ loss and its formula can be written as

$$L_{l2}(G) = \frac{1}{H \times W \times 3}||\hat{I} - I||_2^2 \qquad (2)$$

H and W are the height and width of the input three channels image, respectively.

Perceptual Loss. Since $l2$ loss generates smooth and blurred images, we add perceptual loss [7], which minimizes the difference between corresponding feature maps of the synthesized image and the ground truth image, computed by a pre-trained CNN network. The formula for perceptual loss can be written as

$$L_{perc}(G) = \sum_{i=1}^{i=5} \lambda_i ||\phi_i(\hat{I}) - \phi_i(I)||_2^2 \qquad (3)$$

ϕ is a VGG-19 network pre-trained on ImageNet for image classification. Therefore, $\phi_i(x)$ is the feature map of image x of the i-th layer in the network ϕ with shape $H_i \times W_i \times C_i$. We utilize 'conv1-2', 'conv2-2', 'conv3-2', 'conv4-2', 'conv5-2' of the VGG-19 model. Following perceptual loss [7], We choose $\lambda_i = \frac{1}{H_i \times W_i \times C_i}$.

Adversarial Loss. To make our generated images sharper and more realistic, the adversarial loss is added. In GAN [3], the generator is trained to produce realistic images and aims to deceive the discriminator to classify them as the real image. Therefore, the loss for the generator can be written as

$$L_{adv}(G) = log(1 - D(\hat{I})) \tag{4}$$

The discriminator is trained to distinguish between real images in the dataset and fake images generated by the generator. It would guide the generator to learn to generate realistic images similar to images in the distribution of real data. The loss for the discriminator can be written as

$$L_{adv}(D) = -[log(1 - D(\hat{I})) + log(D(I))] \tag{5}$$

Overall, our loss for the generator can be written as

$$L(G) = L_{l2}(G) + \alpha \cdot L_{perc}(G) + \beta \cdot L_{adv}(G) \tag{6}$$

α and β are constants controlling the ratio between these three losses. By simultaneous training generator and discriminator, the generator can learn to generate images in the distribution of real image.

4   Experiment

In this section, we first describe the details of how we collect the Zalando-shoes dataset (Sect. 4.1), and the implementation of our method (Sect. 4.2). Then, we construct a baseline method and compare with it (Sect. 4.3) as we are the first to tackle virtual try-on shoe. To demonstrate the effectiveness of the design of our method, we also conduct three analysis (Sect. 4.4). Since the task of virtual try-on is to try on a fashion item different from the original one in the source image, existing evaluation methods such as SSIM [19] and PSNR for image completion are not suitable for evaluating our experiment results owing to the lack of ground truth. The inception score (IS) [18] is usually used to evaluate the quality of the generated images synthesized by the generative models. However, it tends to reward sharper image content generated by adversarial training and fails to faithfully evaluate the generated target images of virtually try-on in VITON [4]. Therefore, in each separate experiments, we show some examples to qualitatively evaluate our method. All the examples shown in the experiments are from the test pairs described in Sect. 4.1. We draw the predicted bounding box and key-points in the source images shown in the following experiments. To quantitatively evaluate our method, a user study is conducted (Sect. 4.5). In the end, we show the situation in which our method may fail in Sect. 4.6.

Fig. 3. Example feet-shoe pairs in the collected Zalando-shoes dataset. The first row shows the human try-on feet images with the ground truth bounding box and key-points. The second row is the corresponding shoes in the source image. In these example, we can show that the feet poses are diverse and complicated. The shoe types also vary a lot with different shapes and sizes.

4.1   Zalando-Shoes Dataset

Existing dataset [11] provides images with human wearing shoes and shoes. However, the region of shoes in the human try-on image is small. Furthermore, it does not provide human-shoe pairs. Therefore, we collected the dataset, Zalando-shoes, from the website of Zalando. We first collected all the shoe and human try-on image pairs from the website. All images were then cropped and resized to 256×192. We manually removed image pairs including some part of shoes outside the human try-on images and annotated the remaining 14,062 pairs with bounding box and key-points. The bounding box is annotated such that the full pair of shoes is inside the bounding box and both ankles of human feet are inside bounding box. Some examples are shown in Fig. 3. Those remaining images were further randomly split into train set and test set with 11,877 and 2,185 pairs respectively. To test the feet to try on shoes different from the original one, we randomly shuffle the images of the shoe products to generate feet-shoe pairs for evaluation.

4.2   Implementation Details

Network Architecture. The encoders in stage-2 are composed of a series of convolution layers with a kernel size of 5 and a stride of 2, and their numbers of filters are 64, 128, 256, 512, 1024, respectively. After the feature maps extracted by feet encoder and shoe encoder are concatenated, the concatenated 2048 channels feature maps undergoes a convolution layer with a kernel size of 1, a stride of 1, and 1024 filters to perform dimension reduction. Since transpose convolution layer tends to introduce checkboard artifact [14], our decoder consists of a series of bilinear interpolation 2× upsample. Each 2× bilinear upsampling is followed by a convolution layer with a kernel size of 3 and a stride of 1, whose number of channels are 1024, 512, 256, 128, 64, respectively. All neurons use the *ReLU* as the activation function. In the end, a convolutional layer with a kernel size of 1, a stride of 1 and 3 filters with the *tanh* as the activation function is applied to the output of the encoder to generate a $256 \times 192 \times 3$ image. We use the same discriminator as that of patchGAN [5] and the setting of optimizer for training the discriminator is the same as the generator.

Training Step. We use the RMSProp optimizer with decay = 0.9, epsilon = $1e-10$ with an initial learning rate of 1e-4. We choose $\sigma = 3$ for the Gaussian peak in Eq. (1). For the generator loss in Eq. (6), we choose $\alpha = 1$ and $\beta = 1$. We train the network for 50 epochs with a batch size of 16. We use the ground truth bounding box and key-points to train our stage-2 network.

4.3 Compared Approach and Result

We compare our method with a modification of pix2pix [5] called pix2pix-m. The input of the generator is the concatenation of I_m, I_s and I_p. The input real data to the discriminator is the concatenation of I, I_s and I_p. We first modified the number of layers of the original network to fit image size of 256×192. We also add one convolutional layer with filter size 3 and stride 1 after each transpose convolutional layer and each convolutional layer in the generator. The number of channels for each added convolutional layer is the same as the convolutional or transpose convolutional layers before them. The λ of the loss is set to 0.001. The results are shown in Fig. 4.

4.4 Components Analysis

In this section, we conduct three analysis to analyze the design of our method. We first show the results of the combinations of different losses and conclude that we use the combinations of losses in an effective manner in Sect. 4.4.1. Second, we demonstrate that the key-points are import components for our method in Sect. 4.4.2. Third, we verify that using the source image I to replace I_m in the second stage of our pipeline will cause the network to output the source image during testing and ignore the different target shoes in Sect. 4.4.3. As a result, our design of hiding the part of shoes in the source image is an import technique in the proposed method.

4.4.1 Analysis of Different Combinations of Losses

Different losses have different properties, and will result in different target images, so we show some results in Fig. 5 to demonstrate the results for different combinations of losses. Our method using only $l2$ loss generates smooth and blurred results. Furthermore, when the target shoe is white as shown in column (f), $l2$ loss fails to generate a clear edge for the shoes in the target image. By adding perceptual loss [7], the target images show more details of shoes and

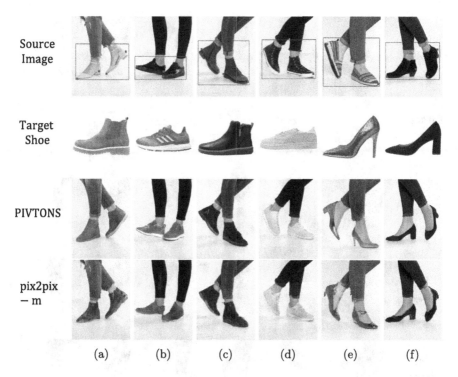

Source Image

Target Shoe

PIVTONS

pix2pix − m

(a)   (b)   (c)   (d)   (e)   (f)

Fig. 4. Compared with pix2pix-m. The results show that our method performs favorably against the compared method. See more details in Sect. 4.3

pants, which meets the feature provided in the target shoe and source image respectively, and it can clearly show the edge of white shoes in column (f). After adding the adversarial loss, the generated image become more realistic. In column (c), we show that adding adversarial can generate shoes with more precise color. It also generates the white shoelace, which is not clearly shown in the image of the target shoe, for the shoes in the target image shown in column (a). Furthermore, in column (b) (d) and (e), we see that adding adversarial loss can eliminate some defect and produce better target images.

4.4.2   Analysis of Key-Points

There are information losses about the feet pose in the cropped region. Therefore, the detected key-points are used to provide pose information in the missing region. In Fig. 6, we show the results with and without using key-points. In column (a), the left shoe generated by the without key-points setting is shorter than the left shoe in the source image. Another example is given in column (b), the right shoe generated without the guidance of key-points is shorter than the right shoe in the source image. Besides, column (c), (d) and (e) show that the the direction and shape of the shoes in the generated images may not be plausible without the assistance of the key-points. Column (f) shows that the setting of

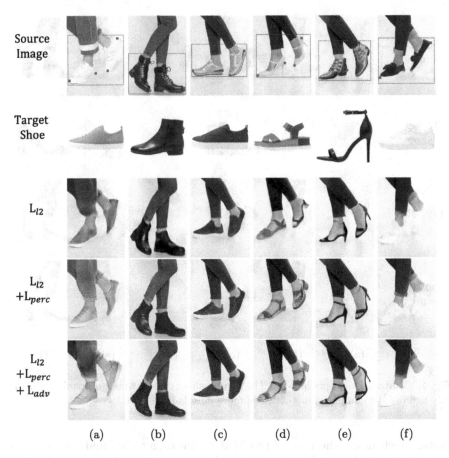

Fig. 5. Analysis – the combinations of losses. The results show that using all three losses performs favorably against using only L_{l2} or $L_{l2} + L_{perc}$. See more details in Sect. 4.4.1

not using key-points may not be able to generate a full shoe. As a result, the utilization of key-points is crucial to generate visually plausible results.

4.4.3 Analysis of Hiding the Region of Shoes in Source Image

To demonstrate that the masked source image I_m is a significant component, we compare between the generated target images of our original setting using masked source image I_m and the setting of replacing I_m with the source image I as input to our second stage. From the results shown in Fig. 7, we validate that using the original source image as input during training and testing will cause the network to ignore the target shoe when generating target image. In conclusion, hiding the part of shoes in the source image is an import technique for our method.

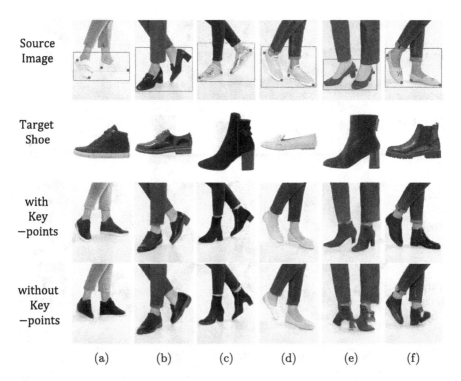

Source Image

Target Shoe

with Key−points

without Key−points

(a)   (b)   (c)   (d)   (e)   (f)

Fig. 6. Analysis – the importance of key-points. We compare the results between with key-points and without key-points. The setting of without key-points does not use key-points during training and testing. From the results, we demonstrate that the information of key-points are important components. Please see Sect. 4.4.2 for more details.

4.5   User Study

Since most evaluation metric fails to evaluate the results of generative models, we conduct the user study. A total of 20 volunteers participate in our user study. Two hundred try-on pairs are randomly selected from our test set and each pair is evaluated by 2 different workers. In each questions, the volunteers are provided with the source image, the target item, and 5 target images generated by pix2pix-m and other different settings at the same time. They rank those images according to which image is more similar to their expecting target image. Two target image are not allowed to be ranked equally. We further compare the rank between our method and the pix2pix-m, or other settings to get the pairwise comparison results. The results are shown in Table. 1. We show that our method with all three losses performs favorably against pix2pix-m and other settings.

4.6   Failed Cases

In Fig. 8, we show some failed cases. In column (a) and (b), our method sometimes fails to synthesize the target image properly when there are a big region

Source
Image

Target
Shoe

Target
Image
by I_m

Target
Image
by I

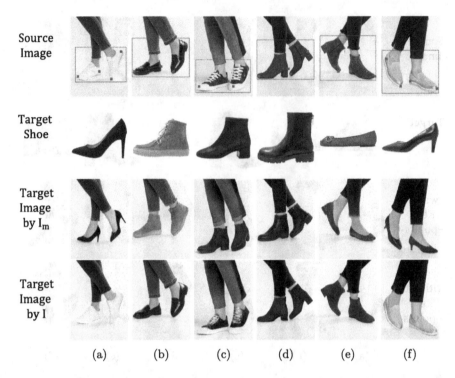

    (a)   (b)   (c)   (d)   (e)   (f)

Fig. 7. Analysis – the effectiveness of the masked source image I_m. In this figure, we compare the results of the generated target images between the original setting of using the masked source image I_m and using the source image I to replace I_m as input to our second stage. The results show that the network in the second stage will ignore the target shoe and generate image almost the same as the source image without using I_m for training. More discussions are shown in Sect. 4.4.3.

Table 1. User study – pairwise comparison. Each cell represents the fraction of the number of target images generated by PIVTONS (all three losses and with key-points) are ranked better than the baseline or different analysis settings. Please refer to Sect. 4.5 for more experimental details.

Method	pix2pix-m	L_{l2}	w/o key-points	$L_{l2} + L_{perc}$
v.s. PIVTONS	0.9675	0.9775	0.9775	0.52

of skin and toes needed to be generated. In column (c), the left feet is hard to generate properly because the left heel is not shown in the source image. Furthermore, our method fails to synthesize some kind of shoe onto non-proper feet pose as shown in column (d), (e), (f) since our method is designed to preserve the feet pose in source image when generating the target image. In column (d) and (e), when the source image is flat bottom shoes while the provided target image is high heels, our method fails to generate a feasible target image as the pose of

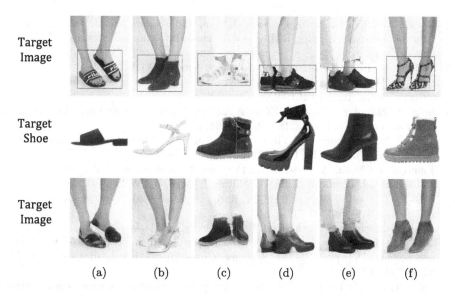

Fig. 8. Failed cases. In this figure, we show some examples that our method fails to generate perceptually realistic results. Please refer to Sect. 4.6 for more discussions.

the feet in source image is not suitable to wear shoes with heels. In column (f), we show that swapping a shoe with flat bottom to the feet wearing shoes with heels will result in an awkward image.

5   Conclusion

In this paper, we deal with the problem of pose invariant virtual try-on shoe. We collect a dataset, Zalando-shoes, and annotate bounding box and key-points annotations to address the limitation of existing dataset for virtual try-on shoe. We formulate our problem as a conditional image completion problem and use detected key-points of feet in the source image to assist the synthesis of target shoes onto the correct position. In the experiments, the presented method shows promising qualitative results meeting the criterion for virtual try-on.

Acknowledgement. This work was supported in part by the Ministry of Science and Technology, Taiwan, under Grant MOST 107-2634-F-002-007 and 105-2221-E-002-182-MY2. We also benefit from the grants from NVIDIA and the NVIDIA DGX-1 AI Supercomputer. We also appreciate the research grants from Microsoft Research Asia.

References

1. Cao, Z., Simon, T., Wei, S.E., Sheikh, Y.: Realtime multi-person 2D pose estimation using part affinity fields. In: CVPR (2017)

2. Gong, K., Liang, X., Zhang, D., Shen, X., Lin, L.: Look into person: self-supervised structure-sensitive learning and a new benchmark for human parsing. In: CVPR (2017)
3. Goodfellow, I., et al.: Generative adversarial nets. In: NIPS (2014)
4. Han, X., Wu, Z., Wu, Z., Yu, R., Davis, L.S.: VITON: an image-based virtual try-on network. In: CVPR (2018)
5. Isola, P., Zhu, J.Y., Zhou, T., Efros, A.A.: Image-to-image translation with conditional adversarial networks. In: CVPR (2017)
6. Jetchev, N., Bergmann, U.: The conditional analogy GAN: swapping fashion articles on people images. In: ICCV (2017)
7. Johnson, J., Alahi, A., Fei-Fei, L.: Perceptual losses for real-time style transfer and super-resolution. In: Leibe, B., Matas, J., Sebe, N., Welling, M. (eds.) ECCV 2016. LNCS, vol. 9906, pp. 694–711. Springer, Cham (2016). https://doi.org/10.1007/978-3-319-46475-6_43
8. Köhler, R., Schuler, C., Schölkopf, B., Harmeling, S.: Mask-specific inpainting with deep neural networks. In: Jiang, X., Hornegger, J., Koch, R. (eds.) GCPR 2014. LNCS, vol. 8753, pp. 523–534. Springer, Cham (2014). https://doi.org/10.1007/978-3-319-11752-2_43
9. Ledig, C., et al.: Photo-realistic single image super-resolution using a generative adversarial network. In: CVPR (2017)
10. Li, Y., Liu, S., Yang, J., Yang, M.H.: Generative face completion. In: CVPR (2017)
11. Liu, Z., Luo, P., Qiu, S., Wang, X., Tang, X.: DeepFashion: powering robust clothes recognition and retrieval with rich annotations. In: CVPR (2016)
12. Ma, L., Jia, X., Sun, Q., Schiele, B., Tuytelaars, T., Van Gool, L.: Pose guided person image generation. In: NIPS (2017)
13. Mirza, M., Osindero, S.: Conditional generative adversarial nets. arXiv (2014)
14. Odena, A., Dumoulin, V., Olah, C.: Deconvolution and checkerboard artifacts. Distill 1, e3 (2016). https://doi.org/10.23915/distill.00003. http://distill.pub/2016/deconv-checkerboard
15. Pathak, D., Krahenbuhl, P., Donahue, J., Darrell, T., Efros, A.A.: Context encoders: feature learning by inpainting. In: CVPR (2016)
16. Radford, A., Metz, L., Chintala, S.: Unsupervised representation learning with deep convolutional generative adversarial networks. arXiv (2015)
17. Reed, S., Akata, Z., Yan, X., Logeswaran, L., Schiele, B., Lee, H.: Generative adversarial text to image synthesis. arXiv (2016)
18. Salimans, T., Goodfellow, I., Zaremba, W., Cheung, V., Radford, A., Chen, X.: Improved techniques for training GANs. In: NIPS (2016)
19. Wang, Z., Bovik, A.C., Sheikh, H.R., Simoncelli, E.P.: Image quality assessment: from error visibility to structural similarity. TIP 13, 600–612 (2004)
20. Wei, S.E., Ramakrishna, V., Kanade, T., Sheikh, Y.: Convolutional pose machines. In: CVPR (2016)
21. Zhang, H., et al.: StackGAN: text to photo-realistic image synthesis with stacked generative adversarial networks. In: ICCV (2017)
22. Zhu, J.Y., Park, T., Isola, P., Efros, A.A.: Unpaired image-to-image translation using cycle-consistent adversarial networks. In: ICCV (2017)
23. Zhu, S., Urtasun, R., Fidler, S., Lin, D., Change Loy, C.: Be your own prada: fashion synthesis with structural coherence. In: ICCV (2017)

Dynamic Gated Graph Neural Networks for Scene Graph Generation

Mahmoud Khademi$^{(\boxtimes)}$ and Oliver Schulte

Simon Fraser University, Burnaby, BC, Canada
{mkhademi,oschulte}@sfu.ca

Abstract. We describe a new deep generative architecture, called Dynamic Gated Graph Neural Networks (D-GGNN), for extracting a scene graph for an image, given a set of bounding-box proposals. A scene graph is a visually-grounded digraph for an image, where the nodes represent the objects and the edges show the relationships between them. Unlike the recently proposed Gated Graph Neural Networks (GGNN), the D-GGNN can be applied to an input image when only partial relationship information, or none at all, is known. In each training episode, the D-GGNN sequentially builds a candidate scene graph for a given training input image and labels additional nodes and edges of the graph. The scene graph is built using a deep reinforcement learning framework: states are partial graphs, encoded using a GGNN, actions choose labels for node and edges, and rewards measure the match between the ground-truth annotations in the data and the labels assigned at a point in the search. Our experimental results outperform the state-of-the-art results for scene graph generation task on the Visual Genome dataset.

Keywords: Gated Graph Neural Networks · Scene graph generation

1 Introduction: Scene Graph Generation

Visual scene understanding is one of the most important goals in computer vision. Over the last decade, there has been great progress in related tasks such as image classification [10,14,29], image segmentation [19], object detection [24], and image caption generation [12,31,33,35]. However, understanding a scene is not just recognizing the individual objects in the scene. The *relationships* between objects also play an important role in visual understating of a scene.

To capture objects and their relationships in a given scene, previous work proposed to build a structured representation called scene graph [13,15,20]. A scene graph for an image is a visually-grounded labeled digraph, where the nodes represent the objects and the edges show the relationships between them (see Fig. 1). The visual information represented by a scene graph is useful in applications such as visual question answering [30] and fine-grained recognition [36]. This paper presents a new neural architecture that generates a scene graph for a given image.

© Springer Nature Switzerland AG 2019
C. V. Jawahar et al. (Eds.): ACCV 2018, LNCS 11366, pp. 669–685, 2019.
https://doi.org/10.1007/978-3-030-20876-9_42

An effective scene graph generation model needs to consider visual contextual information as well as domain priors. For example, if we know that a node has an incoming edge from another node which represents a man and the type of the edge is riding, then the type of the node is likely horse or bicycle. Clues from the relational context can be represented by leveraging models such as the recently proposed Gated Graph Neural Networks (GGNN) [16], which can learn a latent feature vector (embedding, representation) for each node from graph-structured inputs. However, to apply the GGNN model, the structure of the input digraph and the type of each edge must be known, whereas the structure and edge-types must be *inferred* in the scene graph generation task. In this work, we propose a new deep generative architecture, called Dynamic Gated Graph Neural Networks (D-GGNN), to perform this inference. Unlike GGNN, the D-GGNN can be applied to an input image to build a scene graph, without assuming that the structure of the input digraph is known.

In each training episode, the D-GGNN constructs a candidate graph structure for a given training input image by sequentially adding new nodes and edges. The D-GGNN builds the graph in a *deep reinforcement learning (RL) framework*. In each training step, the graph built so far is the current state. To encode the current graph in a state feature vector, the D-GGNN leverages the power of a GGNN to exploit the relational context information of the input image, and combines the GGNN with an attention mechanism. Given the current graph, and a current object, D-GGNN selects two actions: (i) a new neighbor and its type (ii) the type of the new edge from the current object to the new object. The reward for each action is a function of how well the predicted types measure the ground-truth labels. At the test time, the D-GGNN builds a graph for a given input by sequentially selecting the best actions with the greatest expected accuracies (Q-values).

In summary, the contributions of this paper are as follows: (i) We propose a new deep generative architecture that uses reinforcement learning to generate from unstructured inputs a heterogeneous graph, which represents the input information with multiple types of nodes and edges. Unlike the recently proposed Gated Graph Neural Networks (GGNN), the D-GGNN can be applied to an input without requiring that the structure of the scene graph is known in advance. (ii) We apply the D-GGNN to the scene graph generation task. The D-GGNN can exploit domain priors and the relational context of objects in an input image to generate more accurate scene graphs than previous work. (iii) Our model scales to predict thousands of predicates and object classes. The experiments show that our model significantly outperforms the state-of-the-art models for scene graph generation task on the Visual Genome dataset.

2   Related Work

Scene Graph Generation. In [28], the authors introduced a rule-based and a classifier based method for scene graph generation from a natural language scene description. [11] proposed a model based on a conditional random field that reasons about various groundings of potential scene graphs for an image. Recently, [20] proposed a model to detect a relatively large set of relationships using language priors from semantic word embeddings. In [32], the authors developed a model for scene graph generation which uses a recurrent neural network and learns to improve its predictions iteratively through message passing across the scene graph. After a few steps the learned features are classified. However, their model suffers from a class imbalance since for many pairs of objects, there is no edge between them.

More recently, [15] proposed a neural network model, called Multi-level Scene Description Network (MSDN), to address the object detection, region captioning, and scene graph generation tasks jointly. MSDN aligns object, phrase, and caption regions with a dynamic graph using spatial and semantic links. Then, it applies a feature refining schema to send messages across features of the phrase, objects, and caption nodes via the graph.

Most closely related to our work, [18] proposed a model for visual relationship and attribute detection based on reinforcement learning. In their method, as a state feature representation, they used the embedding of the last two relationships and attributes that were searched during the graph construction. This fixed-length representation will lead to limited representational power, since the resulting representation depends on the order of the actions, that is, the order that the algorithm selects node and edges. For example, this method may generate different representations using different order of actions for the same graph. In contrast, our state feature representation is based on a Gated Graph Neural Network (GGNN) which is tailored towards graph-structured input data and extracts features from the entire graph.

Graph Neural Networks. Several graph neural network models have been proposed for feature learning from graph-structured inputs [5,7,9,16,27]. [26] and [2] summarized recent work on graph neural networks in depth. Graph neural networks have been used for various range of tasks that need rich relational structure such as visual scene understanding [25] and learning to represent programs [1]. Recently, a few work proposed generative models of graphs [3,4,17,34]. To the best of our knowledge, our work is the first work that uses reinforcement learning to build a generative graph neural network architecture.

3   Background: Gated Graph Neural Networks

The state feature vectors in our RL framework encode an entire candidate graph. The first step in building the graph encoding is to encode node information by feature vectors (embedding, representations) such that each node feature vector takes into account contextual information from the neighbor nodes. For example, in scene graph prediction task, if we know that a node has an incoming edge from another node which represents a man and the type of the edge is riding, then the type of the node is likely horse or bicycle. There are various approaches for finding node embeddings which can be applied within our RL framework. In this work, we utilize the Gated Graph Neural Network (GGNN) [16], which is a recent state-of-the-art approach.

Formally, a GGNN takes as input a heterogeneous directed graph $\mathcal{G} = (\mathcal{V}, \mathcal{E})$. Each directed edge $e = (v, u) \in \mathcal{E}$ has an edge-type $\texttt{type}(e) \in \{1, \ldots, K\}$, where K is the number of edge-types (classes, labels). The given graph may also contain node-types $\texttt{type}(v) \in \{1, \ldots, M\}$ for each node v, where M is the number of node-types (classes, labels). Given the graph structure and the edge types, a GGNN iteratively computes a new node embedding $\mathbf{h}_v^{(t)} \in \mathbb{R}^d$, $t = 1, \ldots, T$, for each node v via a propagation model, where d is the embedding size.

For each node v, a node representation must take into account the information from every linked neighbor of v. Let E_k be the adjacency matrix for edge-type k. That is, $E_k(u, v) = 1$, if there is an edge with type k from node u to node v, otherwise $E_k(u, v) = 0$. The matrix E_k determines how nodes in the graph communicate with each other via edges of type k. We write $\mathbf{x}_v \in \mathbb{R}^M$ for the one-hot representation of node v's type.

The recurrence of the propagation for computing node embeddings $\mathbf{h}_v^{(t)} \in \mathbb{R}^d$ is initialized with the padded one-hot representation of node v's type, i.e. $\mathbf{h}_v^{(0)} = (\mathbf{x}_v, \mathbf{0}) \in \mathbb{R}^d$. The update equations are

$$\mathbf{a}_v^{(t)} = \sum_{k=1}^{K} W_k H^{(t-1)} E_{k:v} \tag{1}$$

$$\mathbf{h}_v^{(t)} = \text{GRU}\big(\mathbf{a}_v^{(t)}, \mathbf{h}_v^{(t-1)}\big). \tag{2}$$

The $H^{(t)} \in \mathbb{R}^{d \times |\mathcal{V}|}$ is a matrix with node representations $\mathbf{h}_v^{(t)}$, $v = 1, \ldots, |\mathcal{V}|$, as its column vectors, $W_k \in \mathbb{R}^{d \times d}$ is a weight matrix for edges of type k that we learn, and $E_{k:v}$ is the v'th column of E_k. The term $H^{(t-1)} E_{k:v}$ represents the sum of latent feature representations for all nodes u that are linked to node v by an edge of type k. Thus, $\mathbf{a}_v^{(t)}$ combines activations from incoming edges of all types for node v, aggregating *messages* from all nodes that have an edge to v. The GGNN first computes the node activations $\mathbf{a}_v^{(t)}$ for each node v. Then, a Gated Recurrent Unit (GRU) is used to update node representations for each node by incorporating information from the previous time-step.

The computation defined by the above equations are repeated for a fixed number of time steps T. The choice of T depends on the task. For each node the state vector from the last time step is used as the node representation. In many real-world applications, the edges and edge-types are not given as part of the input, which limits the applicability of the GGNN model. In this paper, we extend GGNN to infer edges and edge-types.

4   New Reinforcement Learning Architecture for Graph Structure Generation

Given an input image and a set of candidate bounding-boxes $\mathcal{P}$, our goal is to find a labelled graph $\mathcal{G} = (\mathcal{V}, \mathcal{E})$, where $\mathcal{V} \subseteq \mathcal{P}$, and assign the edge-types and node-types to it jointly such that $\mathcal{G}$ represents contextual information of the given input. The algorithm that we describe here can be applied for extracting relational information for a variety of input data sources. However, our presentation focuses on scene graph generation, the target application of this paper.

4.1   Initial Information Extraction

We extract initial information to constrain the reinforcement learning graph construction.

Global Type Information. We extract the following information from the training set to model type constraints in the target domain.

1. A set of M node types.
2. For each ordered pair of node-types i and j, a set of possible edge-types e-types(i,j). For example, we may find that e-types(man, horse) = {riding, next to, on, has}.

Image Node and Type Candidates. We extract the following information from each training image.

1. A set $\mathcal{P}$ of *candidate nodes*.
2. For each candidate node $v \in \mathcal{P}$:
    (a) A confidence score $s(v)$ that measures how likely v is to be a node in the scene graph.
    (b) A set of candidate node-types n-types$(v) \subseteq \{1, \ldots, M\}$.
    (c) A feature vector $\hat{\mathbf{x}}_v$.
    (d) A *vicinity* set vic(v) is given such that $u \notin$ vic(v) implies that $e = (v, u)$ is not an edge in the scene graph.

This information is extracted as follows. Objects (nodes) are represented by bounding-boxes. Each bounding-box v is specified by a confidence score $s(v)$ and its coordinates $(v_x, v_y, v_{x'}, v_{y'})$, where (v_x, v_y) and $(v_{x'}, v_{y'})$ are the top left and bottom right corners of the bounding-box, respectively. Given an image dataset with ground truth annotations, we train an *object detector*, using the Tensorflow Object Detection API from https://github.com/tensorflow/models/tree/master/research/object_detection. We use faster_rcnn_nas trained on MS-COCO dataset as the pretrained model. Also, we use default values for all hyper-parameters of the object detector API.

For each input image, the object detector outputs a set of object bounding-boxes with their objectness scores, classification scores, and bounding-box coordinates. We used 100 bounding-box per image with the highest objectness scores as the candidate nodes $\mathcal{P}$, and their objectness scores as the confidence scores. For each bounding box, the classification scores rank the possible node-types. The set of candidate object categories n-types(v) comprises the highest-scoring types. For example, n-types(v) can be {man, boy, skier}.

To extract a feature vector $\hat{\mathbf{x}}_v$ for each bounding-box $v \in \mathcal{P}$, we first feed the image to the 152-layer ResNet [10], pretrained on ImageNet [6], and obtain 1024 feature maps of size 14×14 from layer res4b35x. Then, we apply a Region of Interest pooling layer [8], based on the coordinates of the bounding-box, to get 1024 feature maps of size 7×7. Next, we use two fully-connected layers with ReLU activation function to get a 512-dimensional feature vector. Finally the set vic(v) is a subset of bounding-boxes in $\mathcal{P}$ which are spatially close to bounding-box v ($u_w = u'_x - u_x$ and $u_h = u'_y - u_y$):

$$\text{vic}(v) = \{u : u \neq v, |u_x - v_x| < 0.5(u_w + v_w), |u_y - v_y| < 0.5(u_h + v_h)\}$$

4.2 Dynamic Gated Graph Neural Networks

Figure 1 shows the architecture of a D-GGNN for scene graph generation task. The algorithm simultaneously builds the graph and assigns node-types and edge-types using Deep Q-Learning [21,22]. The full algorithm is presented in Algorithm 1. The Q-function maps a state-action pair to an expected cumulative reward value. Actions and states are defined as follows.

Actions. The node with the highest confidence score is the starting node v, and the type with the highest classification score its type l. At each time step t, given a current subject node $v \in \mathcal{P}$ with node type l, we expand the scene graph by adding a new object node and a new edge, and selecting the type of the new node and the type of the new edge. These choices represent two actions.

1. Select a node u_t and a node-type a_t from the pairs

$$\mathcal{A} = \{(a, u) : u \in \text{vic}(v) - \text{prv}(v), a \in \text{n-types}(u)\} \cup \{\text{STOP}\} \quad (3)$$

   where prv(v) denotes the set of previously selected nodes for neighbors of v, and STOP is a special action that indicates the end of searching for neighbors of node v. We first select the node type. If there are multiple nodes in $\mathcal{A}$ with the same type as the selected type, we randomly select one of them.
2. Select an edge-type b_t from

$$\mathcal{B} = \text{e-types}(l_t, a_t). \quad (4)$$

States. The current RL *state* is a (partial) scene graph denoted by s_t. The new state (graph) is obtained as $s_{t+1} = s_t + u_t + e_t$, where $s_t + u_t$ is obtained by adding node u_t with type a_t to graph s_t, and $s_t + u_t + e_t$ is obtained by adding edge $e_t = (v, u_t)$ with type b_t to graph $s_t + u_t$. A GGNN computes a state representation for state s_t. For each node v' of s_t, we initialize the node representation as $\mathbf{h}_{v'}^{(0)} = W(\mathbf{x}_{v'}, \hat{\mathbf{x}}_{v'})$, where $W \in \mathbb{R}^{d \times (512+M)}$ is a trainable matrix; so instead of padding the one-hot node type vector $\mathbf{x}_{v'}$ with 0, we concatenate it with the ResNet feature vector $\hat{\mathbf{x}}_{v'}$. Then, the state is represented by a vector GGNN(s_t) computed as follows

$$\text{GGNN}(s_t) = \tanh\left(\sum_{v'} \sigma\big(f(\mathbf{x}_{v'}, \mathbf{h}_{v'}^{(T)})\big) \odot \tanh\big(g(\mathbf{x}_{v'}, \mathbf{h}_{v'}^{(T)})\big)\right) \quad (5)$$

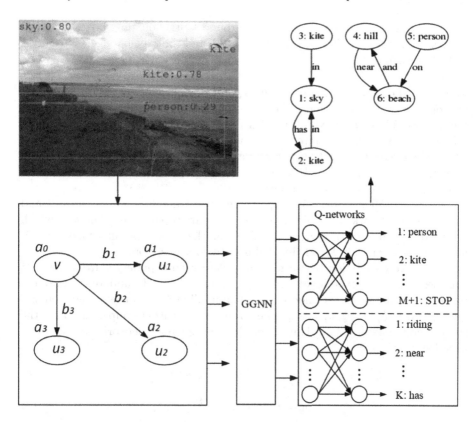

Fig. 1. Dynamic Gated Graph Neural Networks for scene graph generation task. Given an image and its candidate object bounding-boxes, we simultaneously build the graph and assign node-types and edge-types to the nodes and edges in a Deep Q-Learning framework. We use two separate Q-networks to select the actions, i.e. node-types and edge-types. We use two fully-connected layers with ReLU activation function to implement each Q-network. The input to the Q-networks is the concatenation of the GGNN representation of the current graph and a global feature vector from the image. The search for the scene graph continues with the next node in a breadth-first search order.

where, f and g are two neural networks, σ is the sigmoid function. The vector $\sigma\big(f(\mathbf{x}_{v'}, \mathbf{h}_{v'}^{(T)})\big)$ is a soft attention mechanism that decides which nodes are relevant to generate the vector representation for state s_t. Intuitively, $\sigma\big(f(\mathbf{x}_{v'}, \mathbf{h}_{v'}^{(T)})\big)$ represents the degree of importance of node v' to represent the current state, i.e. the contribution of node v' for selecting the next node-types and edge-types.

Rewards. Given the current object bounding-box v and the new object bounding-box u, the reward functions for taking actions a (non-STOP) and b at state s are defined as follows (IoU stands for Intersection over Union):

1. $r(a, u, s) = +1$ if there exists a ground truth bounding-box h with object category a such that $\text{IoU}(u, h) \geq 0.5$, otherwise $r(a, u, s) = -1$

2. $r'(b, v, u, s) = +1$ if there exists two ground truth bounding-boxes h and h' such that $\texttt{IoU}(v, h) \geq 0.5$, $\texttt{IoU}(u, h') \geq 0.5$ and the type of edge $e = (v, u)$ is b, otherwise $r'(b, v, u, s) = -1$.

Temporal-Difference Training of Q-networks. We use two separate Q-networks to select the actions: node-type Q-network and edge-type Q-network. We use two fully-connected layers with ReLU activation function to implement each Q-network. The input to each Q-network is $\phi_t = \phi(s_t) = \big(\texttt{GGNN}(s_t), \mathbf{x}\big)$, where $\mathbf{x}$ is a *global image feature vector* extracted from the last layer of the 152-layer ResNet [10]. The global feature vector adds contextual information of the image to the current state information.

After each 5000 steps, node-type Q-network trainable parameters $\theta^{(t)}$ and edge-type Q-network trainable parameters $\theta'^{(t)}$ are copied to $\hat{\theta}^{(t)}$ and $\hat{\theta}'^{(t)}$ which are used to compute the target Q-values for the node-type and edge-type Q-networks, respectively. This helps stabilize the optimization.

To reduce correlation between samples and keep experiences from the past episodes, we use an experience replay technique [21, 22]. To update the parameters of the Q-networks, we choose a random minibatch from the replay memory. Let $(\phi_j, s_j, a_j, b_j, r_j, r'_j, \phi_{j+1}, s_{j+1})$ be a random transition sample, and v_{j+1} the subject node in state s_{j+1}. The target Q-values for both networks are obtained as follows:

$$y_j = r_j + \gamma \max_{(a,u) \in \mathcal{A}_{j+1}} Q\big(\phi(s_{j+1} + u); \hat{\theta}^{(t)}\big) \tag{6}$$

$$y'_j = r'_j + \gamma \max_{b \in \mathcal{B}_{j+1}} Q\big(\phi(s_{j+1} + u^{\dagger}_{j+1} + e^{\dagger}_{j+1}); \hat{\theta}'^{(t)}\big) \tag{7}$$

where, $\mathcal{A}_{j+1}$ and $\mathcal{B}_{j+1}$ are actions that can be taken in state s_{j+1}, $u^{\dagger}_{j+1}$ is the node that maximizes 6, and $e^{\dagger}_{j+1} = (v_{j+1}, u^{\dagger}_{j+1})$.

Finally, the parameters of the model are updated as follows:

$$\theta^{(t+1)} = \theta^{(t)} + \alpha\Big(y_j - Q\big(\phi(s_j + u^{\dagger}_j); \theta^{(t)}\big)\Big)\nabla_{\theta} Q\big(\phi(s_j + u^{\dagger}_j); \theta^{(t)}\big) \tag{8}$$

$$\theta'^{(t+1)} = \theta'^{(t)} + \alpha\Big(y'_j - Q\big(\phi(s_j + u^{\dagger}_j + e^{\dagger}_j); \theta'^{(t)}\big)\Big)\nabla_{\theta'} Q\big(\phi(s_j + u^{\dagger}_j + e^{\dagger}_j); \theta'^{(t)}\big) \tag{9}$$

Search Strategy. The search for the scene graph continues with the next node in a breadth-first search order. The algorithm continues until all nodes that are reachable from the starting node have been visited. If some unvisited nodes are remained, we repeat the search for the next component, until the highest confidence score of the unvisited nodes is less than a threshold β, or a maximum number of steps n is reached. This allows the search to generate disconnected graphs. To train the RL model, we use ϵ-*greedy learning*, that is, with probability ϵ a random action is selected, and with probability $1 - \epsilon$ an optimal action is selected, as indicated by the Q-networks. For test images, we construct the graph by sequentially selecting the optimal actions.

Algorithm 1. Dynamic Gated Graph Neural Networks: Deep Q-learning

---

Hyperparameters are described in the text

Input: A set of bounding-boxes $\mathcal{P}$ of an image with their feature vectors

Input: A global feature vector $\mathbf{x}$ extracted from the image

Result: Updates the parameters of the model (the weight matrices of the
GGNN for each edge-type and parameters of both Q-networks)

$\mathcal{C} \leftarrow \mathcal{P}$ $\triangleright$ *Mark all nodes as unvisited ($\mathcal{C}$ is the set of all unvisited nodes)*

Let s_0 be an empty graph, $t \leftarrow 0$ $\triangleright$ *Initialize the state (graph)*

while $\mathcal{C}$ *is not empty* **do**

     From $\mathcal{C}$ select node v with the highest confidence score and its node-type l

     if $s(v) < \beta$ *or* $t > n$ **then** break

     Add node v to s_t, and compute $\phi(s_t) = \big(\text{GGNN}(s_t), \mathbf{x}\big)$ $\triangleright$ *Equation 5*

     $q = \text{Queue}(), q.\text{enqueue}((v, l))$ $\triangleright$ *Make an empty queue and add (v, l) to it*

     while q *is not empty* **do**

         $(v, l) = q.\text{dequeue}(), \text{prv}(v) \leftarrow \emptyset$ $\triangleright$ *Remove an element from the queue*

         repeat

             Generate a random number $z \in (0, 1)$ with uniform distribution

             if $z < \epsilon$ **then**

                 $\mathcal{A} \leftarrow \{(a, u) : u \in \text{vic}(v) - \text{prv}(v), a \in \text{n-types}(u)\} \cup \{\text{STOP}\}$

                 Select a random node-type a_t and its node u_t from $\mathcal{A}$

                 if a_t *is not STOP* **then**

                     Select a random edge-type b_t from $\mathcal{B} = \text{e-type}(l, a_t)$

                 end

             else

                 Select $(a_t, u_t) = \arg\max_{(a,u) \in \mathcal{A}} Q\big(\phi(s_t + u); \theta\big)$

                 if a_t *is not STOP* **then**

                     Select $b_t = \arg\max_{b \in \mathcal{B}} Q\big(\phi(s_t + u_t + e_t); \theta'\big)$

                 end

             end

             if a_t *is not STOP* **then**

                 Compute rewards r_t and r'_t

                 $s_{t+1} \leftarrow s_t + u_t + e_t$

             else

                 $s_{t+1} \leftarrow s_t$

             end

             $\phi_{t+1} \leftarrow \phi(s_{t+1}) = \big(\text{GGNN}(s_{t+1}), \mathbf{x}\big)$ $\triangleright$ *Equation 5*

             Store transition $(\phi_t, s_t, a_t, b_t, r_t, r'_t, \phi_{t+1}, s_{t+1})$ in replay memory $\mathcal{D}$

             Sample minibatch of transitions $(\phi_j, s_j, a_j, b_j, r_j, r'_j, \phi_{j+1}, s_{j+1})$ from replay memory $\mathcal{D}$

             Compute target Q-values y_j and y'_j $\triangleright$ *Equations 6 and 7*

             Update the parameters of the model $\triangleright$ *Equations 8 and 9*

             if u_t *is in* $\mathcal{C}$ **then**

                 $q.\text{enqueue}((u_t, a_t))$ $\triangleright$ *Add (u_t, a_t) to the queue*

             end

             $\text{prv}(v) = \text{prv}(v) \cup \{u_t\}, t \leftarrow t + 1$ $\triangleright$ *Add node u_t to the set prv(v)*

         until a_t *is STOP*

         $\mathcal{C} \leftarrow \mathcal{C} - \big(\{v\} \cup \text{vic}(v)\big)$ $\triangleright$ *Mark node v and its vicinity as visited*

     end

end

4.3 Optimization and Implementation Details

We used RMSProp with minibatch size of 100. The learning rate α was 0.00001. The number of iterations for the GGNN is set to $T = 2$. The maximum number of steps to construct a graph for an image is set to $n = 300$. The discount factor γ is set to 0.85 and ϵ is annealed from 1 to 0.05 during the first 50 epochs, and is fixed after epoch 50. The embedding size d is set to 512.

To avoid overfitting, we used a low-rank bilinear method [23] to reduce the rank of the weight matrix for each edge type. This technique effectively reduces the number of trainable parameters. We train our model for 100 epochs. Our model takes around two weeks to train on two NVIDIA Titan X GPUs.

5   Experiments

We introduce the datasets, baseline models and evaluation metrics that we use in our experiments. Then, the experimental results are presented and discussed.

5.1   Data, Metrics, and Baseline Models

Datasets. The Visual Genome (VG) dataset [13] contains $108,077$ images. We used Visual Genome version 1.4 release. This release contains cleaner object annotations [32]. Annotations provide subject-predicate-object triples. A triplet means that there is an edge between the subject and the object and the type of the edge is indicated by the predictate. We experiment with two variations of the VG dataset.

Following [32], we use the most frequent 150 object categories and 50 predicates for scene graph prediction task. We call this variation VG1.4-a. This results in a scene graph of about 11.5 objects and 6.2 relationships per image. The training and test splits contains 70% and 30% of the images, respectively.

Following [18], we use the most frequent 1750 object categories and 347 predicates for scene graph prediction task. We call this variation VG1.4-b. Following [18], we used 5000 images for validation, and 5000 for testing. This variation of the data allows large scale evaluation of our model.

Metrics. Top-K recall (Rec@K) is used as the metric, which is the fraction of the ground truth relationship triplets (subject-predicate-object) hit in the top-K predictions in an image. Predictions are ranked by the product of the objectness confidence scores and the Q-values of the selected predicates. Following [32], we evaluate our model on VG1.4-a based on three tasks as follows:

1. Predicate classification (PRED-CLS) task: to predict the predicates of all pairwise relationships of a set of objects, where the location and object categories are given.

2. Scene graph classification (SG-CLS) task: to predict the predicate and the object categories of the subject and object in all pairwise relationships, where the location of the objects are given.
3. Scene graph generation (SG-GEN) task: to detect a set of object bounding-boxes and predict the predicate between each pair of the objects, at the same time. An object is considered to be properly detected, if it has at least 0.5 Intersection over Union (IoU) overlap with a bounding-box annotation with the same category.

Following [18], we evaluate our model on VG1.4-b based on two tasks as follows:

1. Relationship phrase detection (REL-PHRASE-DET): to predict a phrase (subject-predicate-object), such that the detected box of the entire relationship has at list 0.5 IoU overlap with a bounding-box annotation.
2. Relationship detection (REL-DET): to predict a phrase (subject-predicate-object), such that detected boxes of the subject and object have at least 0.5 IoU overlap with the corresponding bounding-box annotations.

Baseline Models. We compare our model with several baseline models including the state-of-the-art models [18,32]. Faster R-CNN uses R-CNN to detect object proposals, while CNN+TRPN trains a separate region proposal network (RPN) on VG1.4-b.

[20] uses language priors from semantic word embeddings, while [32] uses an RNN and learns to improves its predictions iteratively through message passing across the scene graph. After a few steps the learned features are classified.

VRL [18] detects visual relationship and attributes based on a reinforcement learning framework. To extract a state feature, they used the embedding of the last two relationships and attributes that were searched during the graph construction.

5.2 Results and Discussion

Tables 1 and 2 report our experimental results on VG1.4-a and VG1.4-b datasets, respectively. CNN+RPN, Faster R-CNN, and CNN+TRPN train independent detectors for object and predicate classes. As a result, they cannot exploit relational information in the given image. D-GGNN outperforms the state-of-the art models (VRL [18] and [32]) for scene graph generation.

Both D-GGNN and the message passing approach [32] leverage the power of RNNs to learn a feature vector for each bounding-box. However, the message passing suffers from imbalanced classification problem (often there is no edge between many pairs of objects).

Table 1. Experimental Results of the predicate classification, scene graph classification, and scene graph generation tasks on the VG1.4-a dataset. We compare with visual relationship detection with language priors [20], and scene graph generation by iterative message passing [32]

Model	PRED-CLS		SG-CLS		SG-GEN	
	R@50	R@100	R@50	R@100	R@50	R@100
[20]	27.88	35.04	11.79	14.11	00.32	00.47
[32]	44.75	53.08	21.72	24.38	03.44	04.24
D-GGNN	**46.85**	**55.63**	**23.80**	**26.78**	**06.36**	**07.54**

Table 2. Experimental Results of the relationship phrase detection and relationship detection tasks on the VG1.4-b dataset.

Model	REL-PHRASE-DET		REL-DET	
	R@100	R@50	R@100	R@50
CNN+RPN [29]	01.39	01.34	01.22	01.18
Faster R-CNN [24]	02.25	02.19	-	-
CNN+TRPN [24]	02.52	02.44	02.37	02.23
[20]	10.23	09.55	07.96	06.01
VRL [18]	16.09	14.36	13.34	12.57
D-GGNN	**18.21**	**15.78**	**14.85**	**14.22**

Both D-GGNN and VRL use deep Q-learning to generate the scene graph. However, the representational power of VRL is limited, since it represents a state by the embedding of the last two relationships and attributes that were searched during the graph construction. In contrast, our state feature representation is based on a GGNN which exploits contextual clues from the entire graph to more effectively represent objects and their relationships.

Figures 2 and 3 illustrate some scene graphs generated by our model. The D-GGNN predicts a rich semantic representation of the given image by recognizing objects, their locations, and relationships between them. For example, D-GGNN can correctly detect spatial relationships ("trees behind fence", "horse near water", "building beside bus"), parts of objects ("bus has tire", "woman has leg"), and interactions ("man riding motorcycles", "man wearing hat").

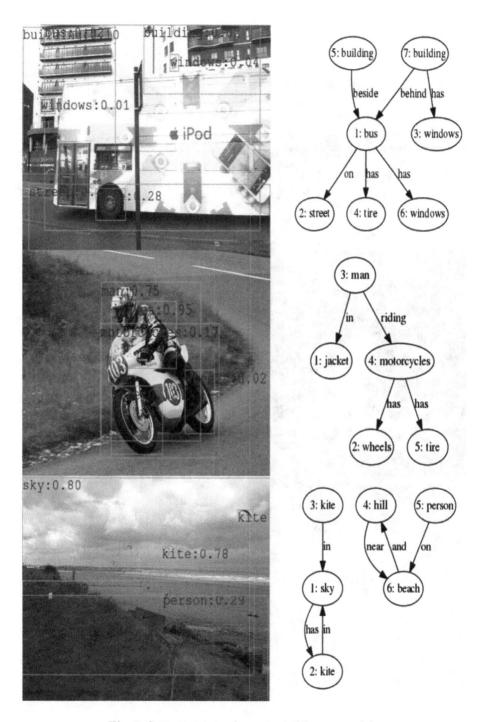

Fig. 2. Some scene graphs generated by our model.

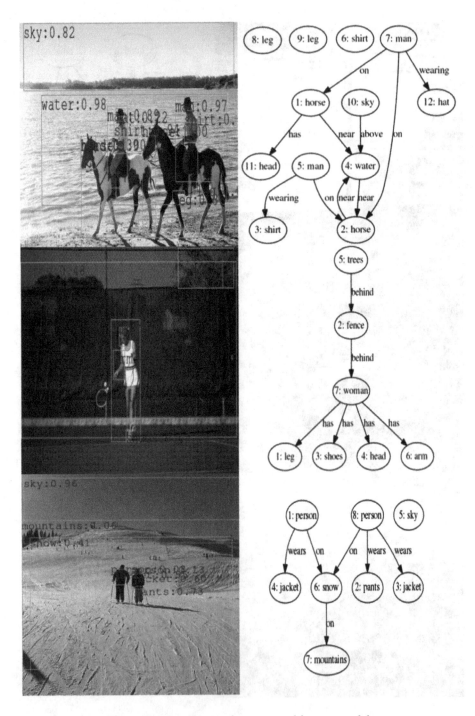

Fig. 3. Some scene graphs generated by our model.

6 Conclusions

We have presented a new model for generating a heterogeneous graph from unstructured inputs using reinforcement learning. Our model builds on the recently proposed GGNN model for computing latent node representations that combines relational and feature information. Unlike the recently proposed GGNN, the D-GGNN can be applied to an input when the structure of the input digraph is not known in advance. The target application in this paper was the scene graph generation task. The experiments on Visual Genome dataset show that D-GGNN significantly outperforms the state-of-the-art models for scene graph generation task.

Acknowledgements. This research was supported by a Discovery Grant to the senior author from the Natural Sciences and Engineering Council of Canada. The Titan X GPUs used for this research were donated by the NVIDIA Corporation.

References

1. Allamanis, M., Brockschmidt, M., Khademi, M.: Learning to represent programs with graphs. arXiv preprint arXiv:1711.00740 (2017)
2. Battaglia, P.W., et al.: Relational inductive biases, deep learning, and graph networks. arXiv preprint arXiv:1806.01261 (2018)
3. Bojchevski, A., Shchur, O., Zügner, D., Günnemann, S.: NetGAN: generating graphs via random walks. arXiv preprint arXiv:1803.00816 (2018)
4. De Cao, N., Kipf, T.: MolGAN: an implicit generative model for small molecular graphs. arXiv preprint arXiv:1805.11973 (2018)
5. Defferrard, M., Bresson, X., Vandergheynst, P.: Convolutional neural networks on graphs with fast localized spectral filtering. In: Advances in Neural Information Processing Systems, pp. 3844–3852 (2016)
6. Deng, J., Dong, W., Socher, R., Li, L.J., Li, K., Fei-Fei, L.: ImageNet: a large-scale hierarchical image database. In: IEEE Conference on Computer Vision and Pattern Recognition, CVPR 2009, pp. 248–255. IEEE (2009)
7. Gilmer, J., Schoenholz, S.S., Riley, P.F., Vinyals, O., Dahl, G.E.: Neural message passing for quantum chemistry. arXiv preprint arXiv:1704.01212 (2017)
8. Girshick, R.: Fast R-CNN. arXiv preprint arXiv:1504.08083 (2015)
9. Gori, M., Monfardini, G., Scarselli, F.: A new model for learning in graph domains. In: Proceedings of the 2005 IEEE International Joint Conference on Neural Networks, IJCNN 2005, vol. 2, pp. 729–734. IEEE (2005)
10. He, K., Zhang, X., Ren, S., Sun, J.: Deep residual learning for image recognition. arXiv preprint arXiv:1512.03385 (2015)
11. Johnson, J., et al.: Image retrieval using scene graphs. In: Proceedings of the IEEE Conference on Computer Vision and Pattern Recognition, pp. 3668–3678 (2015)
12. Karpathy, A., Fei-Fei, L.: Deep visual-semantic alignments for generating image descriptions. In: Proceedings of the IEEE Conference on Computer Vision and Pattern Recognition, pp. 3128–3137 (2015)
13. Krishna, R., et al.: Visual genome: connecting language and vision using crowd-sourced dense image annotations. arXiv preprint arXiv:1602.07332 (2016)

14. Krizhevsky, A., Sutskever, I., Hinton, G.E.: ImageNet classification with deep convolutional neural networks. In: Advances in Neural Information Processing Systems, pp. 1097–1105 (2012)
15. Li, Y., Ouyang, W., Zhou, B., Wang, K., Wang, X.: Scene graph generation from objects, phrases and region captions. In: Proceedings of the IEEE Conference on Computer Vision and Pattern Recognition, pp. 1261–1270 (2017)
16. Li, Y., Tarlow, D., Brockschmidt, M., Zemel, R.: Gated graph sequence neural networks. arXiv preprint arXiv:1511.05493 (2015)
17. Li, Y., Vinyals, O., Dyer, C., Pascanu, R., Battaglia, P.: Learning deep generative models of graphs. arXiv preprint arXiv:1803.03324 (2018)
18. Liang, X., Lee, L., Xing, E.P.: Deep variation-structured reinforcement learning for visual relationship and attribute detection. In: 2017 IEEE Conference on Computer Vision and Pattern Recognition (CVPR), pp. 4408–4417. IEEE (2017)
19. Long, J., Shelhamer, E., Darrell, T.: Fully convolutional networks for semantic segmentation. In: Proceedings of the IEEE Conference on Computer vision and Pattern Recognition, pp. 3431–3440 (2015)
20. Lu, C., Krishna, R., Bernstein, M., Fei-Fei, L.: Visual relationship detection with language priors. In: Leibe, B., Matas, J., Sebe, N., Welling, M. (eds.) ECCV 2016. LNCS, vol. 9905, pp. 852–869. Springer, Cham (2016). https://doi.org/10.1007/978-3-319-46448-0_51
21. Mnih, V., et al.: Playing atari with deep reinforcement learning. arXiv preprint arXiv:1312.5602 (2013)
22. Mnih, V., et al.: Human-level control through deep reinforcement learning. Nature 518(7540), 529 (2015)
23. Pirsiavash, H., Ramanan, D., Fowlkes, C.C.: Bilinear classifiers for visual recognition. In: Advances in Neural Information Processing Systems, pp. 1482–1490 (2009)
24. Ren, S., He, K., Girshick, R., Sun, J.: Faster R-CNN: towards real-time object detection with region proposal networks. In: Advances in Neural Information Processing Systems, pp. 91–99 (2015)
25. Santoro, A., et al.: A simple neural network module for relational reasoning. In: Advances in Neural Information Processing Systems, pp. 4967–4976 (2017)
26. Scarselli, F., Gori, M., Tsoi, A.C., Hagenbuchner, M., Monfardini, G.: Computational capabilities of graph neural networks. IEEE Trans. Neural Netw. 20(1), 81–102 (2009)
27. Scarselli, F., Gori, M., Tsoi, A.C., Hagenbuchner, M., Monfardini, G.: The graph neural network model. IEEE Trans. Neural Netw. 20(1), 61–80 (2009)
28. Schuster, S., Krishna, R., Chang, A., Fei-Fei, L., Manning, C.D.: Generating semantically precise scene graphs from textual descriptions for improved image retrieval. In: Proceedings of the Fourth Workshop on Vision and Language, pp. 70–80 (2015)
29. Simonyan, K., Zisserman, A.: Very deep convolutional networks for large-scale image recognition. arXiv preprint arXiv:1409.1556 (2014)
30. Teney, D., Liu, L., van den Hengel, A.: Graph-structured representations for visual question answering. CoRR, abs/1609.05600 3 (2016)
31. Vinyals, O., Toshev, A., Bengio, S., Erhan, D.: Show and tell: a neural image caption generator. CoRR abs/1411.4555 (2014). http://arxiv.org/abs/1411.4555
32. Xu, D., Zhu, Y., Choy, C.B., Fei-Fei, L.: Scene graph generation by iterative message passing. In: Proceedings of the IEEE Conference on Computer Vision and Pattern Recognition, vol. 2 (2017)
33. Xu, K., et al.: Show, attend and tell: Neural image caption generation with visual attention. arXiv preprint arXiv:1502.03044 (2015)

34. You, J., Ying, R., Ren, X., Hamilton, W., Leskovec, J.: GraphRNN: generating realistic graphs with deep auto-regressive models. In: International Conference on Machine Learning, pp. 5694–5703 (2018)

35. You, Q., Jin, H., Wang, Z., Fang, C., Luo, J.: Image captioning with semantic attention. CoRR **abs/1603.03925** (2016). http://arxiv.org/abs/1603.03925

36. Zhu, Y., Fathi, A., Fei-Fei, L.: Reasoning about object affordances in a knowledge base representation. In: Fleet, D., Pajdla, T., Schiele, B., Tuytelaars, T. (eds.) ECCV 2014. LNCS, vol. 8690, pp. 408–424. Springer, Cham (2014). https://doi. org/10.1007/978-3-319-10605-2_27

DOOBNet: Deep Object Occlusion Boundary Detection from an Image

Guoxia Wang[1], Xiaochuan Wang[1], Frederick W. B. Li[2], and Xiaohui Liang[1(✉)]

[1] State Key Lab of Virtual Reality Technology and Systems,
Beihang University, Beijing, China
mingzilaochongtu@gmail.com, {wangxc,liang_xiaohui}@buaa.edu.cn
[2] Department of Computer Science, University of Durham, Durham, UK
frederick.li@durham.ac.uk

Abstract. Object occlusion boundary detection is a fundamental and crucial research problem in computer vision. Solving this problem is challenging as we encounter extreme boundary/non-boundary class imbalance during the training of an object occlusion boundary detector. In this paper, we propose to address this class imbalance by up-weighting the loss contribution of false negative and false positive examples with our novel *Attention Loss* function. We also propose a unified end-to-end multi-task deep object occlusion boundary detection network (DOOBNet) by sharing convolutional features to simultaneously predict object boundary and occlusion orientation. DOOBNet adopts an encoder-decoder structure with skip connection in order to automatically learn multi-scale and multi-level features. We significantly surpass the state-of-the-art on the PIOD dataset (ODS F-score of .702) and the BSDS ownership dataset (ODS F-score of .555), as well as improving the detecting speed to as 0.037 s per image on the PIOD dataset.

Keywords: Boundary detection · Occlusion reasoning · Convolutional neural network

1 Introduction

A 2D image captures the projection of objects from a 3D scene, such that object occlusion appears as the depth discontinuities along the boundaries between different objects (or object and background). Figure 1 shows an example from the Pascal instance occlusion dataset (PIOD) [34], where one sheep is partially occluded by another one and each occludes part of the lawn background. Occlusion reasoning is both fundamental and crucial to a variety of computer vision research areas, including object detection [6] and segmentation [6,39], scene parsing [33]. Hoiem *et al.* [11] argue that it lies at the core of scene understanding and must be addressed explicitly. In computer vision, the study of occlusion reasoning has been largely confined to the context of stereo, motion and other multi-view imaging problems [5,10,31]. However, in single-view tasks, occlusion

© Springer Nature Switzerland AG 2019
C. V. Jawahar et al. (Eds.): ACCV 2018, LNCS 11366, pp. 686–702, 2019.
https://doi.org/10.1007/978-3-030-20876-9_43

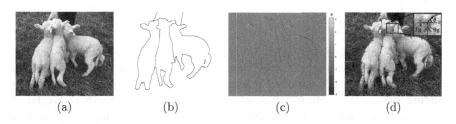

(a)   (b)   (c)   (d)

Fig. 1. A ground truth from the PIOD dataset. Given an image (a) PIOD provides two annotated maps, namely (b) object boundary map and (c) occlusion orientation variable $\theta \in (-\pi, \pi]$ map. (d) Object occlusion boundary is represented by red arrows, each indicating an orientation θ. By the "left" rule, the left side of each arrow indicates the foreground. (Color figure online)

reasoning becomes challenging due to the unavailability of multiple images. In this paper, we focus on detecting occlusion boundary and boundary ownership from a single image.

The problem of object occlusion boundary detection relies on having precise object boundary. We argue that it is key to improve the performance of object boundary detector. Recent CNN-based boundary detection methods [12,16,19–21,35,36] have demonstrated promising F-score performance improvements on the BSDS500 dataset [25]. However, it is still unsatisfactory for them to handle higher-level object boundary, leaving a large room for improvement. A primary obstacle is extreme boundary/non-boundary pixels imbalance. Despite this can be partially resolved by class-balanced cross entropy loss function [35] and focal loss [18], the easily classified true positive and true negative still constitute the majority of loss and dominate the gradient during training of object boundary detector. Recently, FCN [22], SegNet [1], U-Net [29] have been very successful for segmentation and related dense prediction visual tasks such as edge detection, which use an encoder-decoder structure to preserve precise localization and learn multi-scale and multi-level features. Meanwhile, dilated convolution [2,37] has been used to systematically aggregate multi-scale contextual information without losing resolution.

Motivated by these, we propose a novel loss function called *Attention Loss* tackling class imbalance. It is a dynamically scaled class-balanced cross entropy loss function, up-weighting the loss contribution of false negative and false positive examples. We also propose an encoder-decoder structure with skip connection and dilated convolution module, designing a unified end-to-end multi-task deep object occlusion boundary detection network (DOOBNet) by sharing convolutional features to simultaneously predict object boundary and occlusion orientation. Our model achieves a new state-of-the-art performance on both the PIOD and BSDS ownership dataset.

2   Related Work

Estimating the occlusion relationships from a single image is challenging. Early computer vision succeeded in simple domains, such as blocks world [28] and line drawings [3]. The 2.1D sketch [26] was a mid-level representation of images involving occlusion relations. Ren *et al.* [27] proposed a method for labeling occlusion boundaries in natural images on the BSDS border ownership dataset. They took a two-stage approach of image segmentation, followed by figure/ground labeling of each boundary fragment according to local image evidence and a learned MRF model. [17] addressed the border ownership problem based on the 2.1D model [26]. Teo *et al.* [32] embedded several different local cues (*e.g.* HoG, extremal edges) and semi-global grouping cues (*e.g.* Gestalt-like) within a Structured Random Forest (SRF) [4] to detect both boundaries and border ownership in a single-step. Maire *et al.* [23,24] also designed and embedded the border ownership representation into the segmentation depth ordering inference. Hoiem *et al.* [11] introduced an approach to recover the occlusion boundaries and depth ordering of free-standing structures in a scene using the traditional edge and region cues together with 3D surface and depth cues. However, these methods were segmentation dependent, and that their performance dropped significantly without perfect segmentation. Recently, DOC [34] proposed a deep convolutional network architecture to detect object boundaries and estimate the occlusion relationships, which adapted a two streams network to perform two tasks separately. To train and test the network, it introduced the PASCAL instance occlusion dataset (PIOD), comprising a large-scale (10k images) instance of occlusion boundary dataset constructed by PASCAL VOC images.

Similar to DOC [34], our method detects object boundaries and estimates the occlusion relationships from a single image, which is referred as the object occlusion boundary detection. Notably, we adapt a single stream network architecture simultaneously predicting both object boundary and occlusion orientation in a single step by sharing convolutional features.

3   Problem Formulation

We use the representation of object occlusion boundary as in [34]. Occlusion relations represented by a per-pixel representation with two variables: (I) a binary edge variable to flag an object boundary pixel, and (II) a continuous-valued occlusion orientation variable (at each edge pixel) to indicate the occlusion relationship using the "left" rule based on the tangent direction of the edge. As shown in Fig. 1, we visualize the object occlusion boundaries with these two variable by red arrows, where the left side of each arrow indicates the foreground.

Given an input image, our goal is to compute the object boundary map and the corresponding occlusion orientation map. Formally, for an input image $\mathbf{I}$, we obtain a pair of object boundary map and occlusion orientation map $\{\mathbf{B}, \mathbf{O}\}$, each having the same size as $\mathbf{I}$. Here, $\mathbf{B} = \{b_j, j = 1, ..., |\mathbf{I}|\}, b_j \in \{0, 1\}$ and

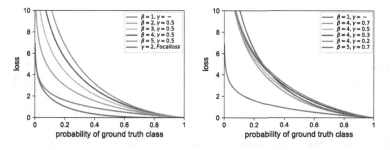

Fig. 2. Attention loss distribution curves by varying β and γ.

$\mathbf{O} = \{\theta_j, j = 1, ..., |\mathbf{I}|\}, \theta_j \in (-\pi, \pi]$. When $b_j = 1$ at pixel j, θ_j specifies the tangent of the boundary, where its direction indicates occlusion relationship using the "left" rule. We do not use the θ_j when $b_j = 0$. In addition, we denote the ground truth by a label pair $\{\bar{\mathbf{B}}, \bar{\mathbf{O}}\}$.

3.1 Class-Balanced Cross Entropy and Focal Loss

As described in Sect. 1, CNN-based methods encounter the extreme boundary/ non-boundary pixels imbalance during training an object boundary detector. As a priori knowledge, a typical natural image usually comprises not more than 0.97% boundary pixels[1]. CSCNN [13] proposed a cost-sensitive loss function with additional trade-off parameters introduced for biased sampling. HED [35] introduced a class-balancing weight α on a per-pixel term basis to automatically balance the loss between positive/negative classes. It is formulated as:

$$\mathrm{CCE}(p, \bar{b}_j) = \begin{cases} -\alpha\log(p) & \text{if } \bar{b}_j = 1 \\ -(1 - \alpha)\log(1 - p) & \text{otherwise} \end{cases} \tag{1}$$

where $\bar{b}_j \in \{0, 1\}$ specifies the ground truth (non-boundary/boundary pixel) and $p \in [0, 1]$ is the model's estimated probability for the boundary pixel, $\alpha = |\bar{\mathbf{B}}_-|/|\bar{\mathbf{B}}|$ and $1 - \alpha = |\bar{\mathbf{B}}_+|/|\bar{\mathbf{B}}|$. In addition, $\bar{\mathbf{B}}_-$ and $\bar{\mathbf{B}}_+$ denote the non-boundary and boundary ground truth label sets in a batch of images, respectively.

Recently, Lin *et al.* [18] introduced Focal Loss (FL) based on CE to object detection. FL is defined as $\mathrm{FL}(p) = -\alpha(1 - p)^\gamma\log(p)$, setting $\gamma > 0$ to reduce the relative loss for well-classified examples ($p > 0.5$) and putting more focus on hard, misclassified examples.

The CCE loss and FL can be seen as the blue and brown curve in Fig. 2, respectively, and the α weight relates to the number of boundary and non-boundary pixels. For the edge detection, CCE and FL can easily classify edge pixels. However, these loss curves change slowly and the penalization has a small difference for $p \in [0.3, 0.6]$, it is hard to discriminate both false negative and true

---

[1] The statistics come from PIOD dataset.

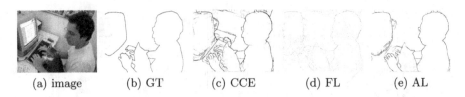

(a) image   (b) GT   (c) CCE   (d) FL   (e) AL

Fig. 3. The predicted boundary maps with different loss functions ($p \in [0,1]$). CCE and FL predict a large number of false negatives (edge pixels, but not boundary pixels). In contrast to CCE and FL, AL focuses the attention on class-agnostic object boundaries.

positive examples for object boundary detection, where most of the edge pixels do not belong to object boundary pixels and are false negative in object boundary detection. See Fig. 3.

3.2 Attention Loss for Object Boundaries

To address the problem, we propose a discriminating loss function motivated by FL, called the Attention Loss (AL), focusing the attention on class-agnostic object boundaries. Note that the true positive and true negative examples belong to well-classified examples after the loss are balanced by α weight and FL can continue to partially solve the class-imbalance problem. However, the number of false negative and false positive examples is small and that their loss are still overwhelmed during training. Meanwhile, training is insufficient and inefficient, leading to degeneration of the model. The attention loss function explicitly up-weights the loss contribution of false negative and false positive examples so that it is more discriminating.

Formally, we propose to add two modulating factors $\beta^{(1-p)^\gamma}$ and β^{p^γ} to the class-balanced cross entropy loss, with tunable parameters $\beta > 0$ and $\gamma \geq 0$. We define the attention loss as:

$$\text{AL}(p, \bar{b}_j) = \begin{cases} -\alpha\beta^{(1-p)^\gamma}\log(p) & \text{if } \bar{b}_j = 1 \\ -(1-\alpha)\beta^{p^\gamma}\log(1-p) & \text{otherwise} \end{cases} \tag{2}$$

The attention loss is visualized for several values of $\beta \in [1,5]$ and $\gamma \in [0.2, 0.7]$ in Fig. 2. The parameter β adjusts true positive (true negative) and false negative (false positive) loss contributions. The attention loss strongly penalizes misclassified examples and only weakly penalizes the correctly classified ones, being more discriminating. Notably, the parameter γ gives a free degree to smoothly adjust the loss contribution at certain β value. For instance, with $\beta = 4$, by reducing γ from 0.7 to 0.2, we can gradually enlarge the loss contribution. When $\beta = 1$, AL is equivalent to CCE. As our experiment results will show, we found setting $\beta = 4$ and $\gamma = 0.5$ works the best in our experiments.

AL shares many similarities with FL, but AL makes the network to accept more misclassified signals ($p \in [0.3, 0.6]$) and to sufficiently back propagate, while FL reduces the well-classified signals and predicts a large number of false negatives (edge pixels, but not boundary pixels), see Fig. 3. It is effective in terms of mAP metric ($p > 0.5$) for object detection but not for object boundary detection ($p \in [0,1]$).

3.3 Loss Function for Object Occlusion Boundary Detection

To perform occlusion orientation estimation, we adapt the L_1 loss function as defined in [7], which has demonstrated its simplicity yet effectiveness for regression task. Subsequently, our multi-task loss function for a batch of images is defined as:

$$\mathcal{L}(\mathbf{W}) = \frac{1}{N}\left(\sum_i \sum_j \text{AL}(p_j, \bar{b}_j) + \lambda \sum_i \sum_j \text{smooth}_{L_1}\left(f(\theta_j, \bar{\theta}_j)\right)\right) \qquad (3)$$

where N is mini-batch size, i is the index of an image in a mini-batch, j is the index of a pixel in an image, and

$$\text{smooth}_{L_1}(x) = \begin{cases} 0.5(\sigma x)^2 & \text{if } |x| < 1 \\ |x| - 0.5/\sigma^2 & \text{otherwise} \end{cases} \qquad (4)$$

$$f(\theta_j, \bar{\theta}_j) = \begin{cases} \theta_j + \bar{\theta}_j \text{ if } \theta_j > \pi, \bar{\theta}_j > 0 \text{ or } \theta_j < -\pi, \bar{\theta}_j < 0 \\ \theta_j - \bar{\theta}_j \text{ otherwise} \end{cases} \qquad (5)$$

where σ adjusts the L_1 loss contribution curve and we explicitly penalize the predicted occlusion orientation values $\theta_j \notin (-\pi, \pi]$ as we define the $\bar{\theta}_j \in (-\pi, \pi]$.

4 Network Architecture

DOOBNet Backbone. Encoder-decoder network structure has been successfully applied for semantic segmentation in [1,29]. Inspired by this, we adopt an encoder-decoder structure as the backbone network in our DOOBNet, as illustrated in Fig. 4. Typically, an encoder-decoder network comprises an encoder module and a decoder module. We use Res50 [9] (before *pool5* layer) as the encoder module and design a simple yet effective decoder module to gradually recover spatial information for obtaining sharper object occlusion boundaries. In contrast to typical image classification, object occlusion boundary detection requires relatively large spatial resolution and receptive field to obtain precise object boundaries localization. For this reason, we use dilated convolutions (*rate* $= 2$) [37] to increase the receptive field and remove sub-sampling (stride from 2 to 1) at *res5* stage to increase spatial resolution, where feature maps are 16 times smaller than the input image resolution now. Because using dilated convolutions can cause gridding artifacts [38], we add two *conv* block[2] at the end of *res5* to remove gradding artifacts. Besides, we reduce the number of channels to 256 for optimizing computation. Existing decoders [1,29] operate

---

[2] The *conv* block refers to convolution layer followed by batch normalization (BN) [14] and ReLU activation.

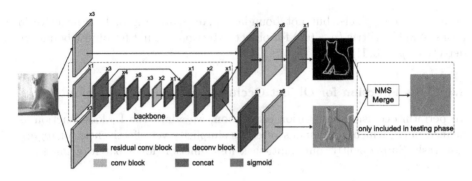

Fig. 4. DOOBNet architecture.

based on the features from encoder, which are gradually bilinearly upsampled by a factor of 2 up to full input resolution. However, this significantly increases network parameters and computation cost. We hence propose a simple yet effective decoder module. The encoder features are first bilinearly upsampled by a factor 4 and then concatenated with the corresponding mid-level features from the end of *res2*, which have the same spatial resolution (see Fig. 4). In this way, we explicitly learn multi-level (mid-level and high-level) features very effectively as our experiments will show. After the concatenation, we apply two *residual conv* blocks to refine the features followed by another simple bilinearly upsampling by a factor of 4.

Object Boundary Detection and Occlusion Orientation Estimation Subnet. In contrast to DOC [34], which relies on two separate stream networks, our DOOB-Net adapts a single stream network by sharing backbone features with two subnets: one for object boundary detection and the other for occlusion orientation estimation. For the object boundary detection subnet (see Fig. 4 top), we first apply three *conv* blocks to obtain low-level features, which have the same spatial resolution as the input image, and then concatenate them with the features from decoder. After concatenation, we add six extra *conv* blocks to learn specific task features. The final output feature is fed to a *sigmoid* classifier for pixel-wise classification. In parallel with the object boundary detection subnet, we attach the same subnet but exclude the *sigmoid* layer for occlusion orientation estimation (see Fig. 4 bottom). Notably, our object boundary detection subnet does not share low-features with the occlusion orientation estimation subnet. We particularly design these low-features to improve generalization on low-level perceptual edges. Table 1 depicts our proposed network architecture in details.

Training Phase. For each training image $\mathbf{I}$, the corresponding ground truth comprises a binary object boundary map and an occlusion orientation map $\{\bar{\mathbf{B}}, \bar{\mathbf{O}}\}$, as described above. We compute loss for object boundary detection subnet for every pixel but only compute occlusion orientation loss if $\bar{b}_j = 1$.

Table 1. DOOBNet architecture. Building blocks are in brackets, with the numbers of blocks stacked. Down-sampling is performed by res3_1, res4_1 with a stride of 2. We apply a dilated rate of 2 to res5_x. Finally, _b/_o refers to object boundary detection and occlusion orientation estimation subnets, respectively.

layer name	conv1	conv1_b/conv1_o	res2_x	res3_x	res4_x
setup	7×7, 64, stride 2	$\begin{bmatrix} 3 \times 3, 8 \\ 3 \times 3, 4 \\ 3 \times 3, 16 \end{bmatrix} \times 1$	3×3 max pool, stride 2 $\begin{bmatrix} 1 \times 1, 64 \\ 3 \times 3, 64 \\ 1 \times 1, 256 \end{bmatrix} \times 3$	$\begin{bmatrix} 1 \times 1, 128 \\ 3 \times 3, 128 \\ 1 \times 1, 512 \end{bmatrix} \times 4$	$\begin{bmatrix} 1 \times 1, 256 \\ 3 \times 3, 256 \\ 1 \times 1, 1024 \end{bmatrix} \times 6$

res5_x	conv6_x	deconv7/deconv9	res8_1	res8_2	conv10_b / conv10_o
$\begin{bmatrix} 1 \times 1, 512 \\ 3 \times 3, 512 \\ 1 \times 1, 2048 \end{bmatrix} \times 3$	$\begin{bmatrix} 3 \times 3, 256 \end{bmatrix} \times 2$	7×7, 256, stride 4	$\begin{bmatrix} 1 \times 1, 128 \\ 3 \times 3, 128 \\ 1 \times 1, 512 \end{bmatrix} \times 1$	$\begin{bmatrix} 1 \times 1, 8 \\ 3 \times 3, 8 \\ 1 \times 1, 16 \end{bmatrix} \times 1$	$\begin{bmatrix} 3 \times 3, 8 \end{bmatrix} \times 4$ $\begin{bmatrix} 3 \times 3, 4 \end{bmatrix} \times 1$ $\begin{bmatrix} 1 \times 1, 1 \end{bmatrix} \times 1$

Testing Phase. Given an input image **I**, we obtain an object boundary map **B** and an occlusion orientation map **O** by simply forwarding the image through the network. To obtain the final object occlusion boundary map, we first perform non-maximum suppression (NMS) [4] on the object boundary map and then obtain the occlusion orientation for each boundary pixel from the orientation map (see Fig. 4 right). Finally, similar to DOC [34], we adjust the orientation estimation to the direction of the tangent line estimated from the boundary map as we trust the accuracy of the estimated boundaries.

5   Experiments

5.1   Implementation

We implement DOOBNet by *Caffe* [15]. Our experiments initialize the encoder module with the pre-trained Res50 [9] model on ImageNet and the other convolutional layers with the "msra" [8] initialization. All experiments are run on a single NVIDIA TITAN XP GPU.

Evaluation Criteria. For object occlusion boundary detection, we use three standard measures: fixed threshold for all images in the dataset (ODS), per-image best threshold (OIS), and average precision (AP). In contrast to DOC [34], which evaluated occlusion relations by measuring occlusion accuracy w.r.t. boundary recall (AOR). Occlusion Accuracy (A) is defined as the ratio of the total number of correct occlusion orientation pixels on correctly labelled boundaries to the total number of correctly labelled boundary pixels, while boundary Recall (R) is defined as the fraction of ground truth boundaries detected. However, it only evaluates the occlusion relations but not for occlusion boundary. In this paper, we instead measure occlusion precision w.r.t. boundary recall (OPR) to evaluate object occlusion boundaries as the occlusion relationships estimation relies on object boundaries, where occlusion precision is only computed at the

Table 2. Varying β and γ for Attention Loss about object boundary detection on the PIOD.

β	1	2	2	2	2	3	3	3	3	4	4	4	4	5	5	5	5
γ	-	.2	.3	.5	.7	.2	.3	.5	.7	.2	.3	.5	.7	.2	.3	.5	.7
ODS	.633	.650	.679	.680	.687	.692	.698	.700	.706	.704	.710	**.716**	.712	.702	.713	.710	**.714**
OIS	.649	.666	.691	.692	.698	.704	.708	.716	.714	.715	.719	**.726**	.721	.714	.721	.721	**.726**
AP	.593	.511	.652	.644	.679	.680	.686	.696	.695	.699	.694	**.709**	.702	.695	.700	.611	**.713**

correctly detected boundary pixels. Note that a standard non-maximal suppression (NMS) [4] with default parameters is applied to obtain thinned boundaries and 99 thresholds are used to compute precision and recall for evaluation. We also refer readers to the original paper for the details about AOR curve.

Data Augmentation. Data augmentation has proven to be a crucial technique in deep networks. We augment the PIOD data by horizontally flipping each image (two times), and additionally augment the BSDS ownership data by rotating each image to {0, 90, 180, 270} different angles (eight times). To save training time and improve generalization, we randomly crop the image to 320×320 in every mini-batch during the training runtime. During testing, we operate on an input image at its original size.

Hyper-Parameters. We use a validation set from the PIOD dataset and the CCE [35] loss function to tune the deep model hyper-parameters, including mini-batch size (5), iter size (3), learning rate (3e−5), momentum (0.9), weight decay (0.0002), sigma (3) in the L_1 loss function, lambda (0.5) in Eq. 3. The number of training iterations for PIOD dataset (30,000; divide learning rate by 10 after 20,000 iterations) and BSDS ownership dataset (10,000; divide learning rate by 10 after every 4,000 iterations). In the following experiments, we set the values of these hyper-parameters as discussed above to explore DOOBNet variants.

Attention Loss. The attention loss introduces two new hyper-parameters, β and γ, controlling the loss contribution. To demonstrate the effectiveness of the proposed attention loss for object boundary detection as described in Sect. 3.2, we adapt the grid search method to find an optimal parameter combination. To save training time, we change the iter size to 1 and the learning rate to 1e−5. Results for various β and γ are shown in Table 2. When $\beta = 1$, our loss is equivalent to the CCE loss. AL shows large gains over CCE as β is increased and slight gains by varying γ. With $\beta = 4$ and $\gamma = 0.5$, AL yields 8.3% ODS, 7.7% OIS and 11.6% AP improvement over the CCE loss. One notable property of AL, which can be easily seen in Fig. 2(right), is that we can adjust β and γ to make two curves have similar loss contribution ($p > 0.4$). For example, $\beta = 4$, $\gamma = 0.5$ and $\beta = 5$, $\gamma = 0.7$ yield similar results as in Table 2. We use $\beta = 4$ and $\gamma = 0.5$ for all the following experiments.

To understand the attention loss better, we empirically analyse that the CCE loss accepts the pixels as edge pixels when $p > 0.5$. However, the object boundary

Table 3. Object occlusion boundary detection results on PIOD and BSDS ownership dataset. The term of MLF is multi-level features. SRF-OCC-BSDS trains on the BSDS ownership dataset and tests on the PIOD dataset. FL* achieves the best performance using 6e−5 learning rate. (Note: † refers to GPU running time.)

(a) PIOD dataset   (b) BSDS ownership dataset

Method	ODS	OIS	AP	FPS	Method	ODS	OIS	AP	FPS
SRF-OCC-BSDS	.268	.286	.152	1/55.5	SRF-OCC	.419	.448	.337	1/33.8
DOC-HED	.460	.479	.405	18.5†	DOC-HED	.522	.545	.428	20†
DOC-DMLFOV	.601	.611	.585	19.2†	DOC-DMLFOV	.463	.491	.369	21.5†
DOOBNet (w/o AL)	.624	.636	.611	27†	DOOBNet (w/o AL)	.510	.528	.487	26.3†
DOOBNet (w/o MLF)	.607	.617	.568	29.2†	DOOBNet (w/o MLF)	.443	.456	.324	29†
DOOBNet (VGG16)	.672	.683	.663	31.3 †	DOOBNet (VGG16)	.508	.523	.382	32.3†
DOOBNet (FL*)	.652	.661	.631	27†	DOOBNet (FL)	.536	.557	**.510**	26.3†
DOOBNet	**.702**	**.712**	**.683**	27†	DOOBNet	**.555**	**.570**	.440	26.3†

usually achieves a higher predicted probability, such as $p > 0.8$. We explicitly up-weight the loss contribution of false negative and false positive samples so that the model can focus on object boundaries. As the experiments shown, our design choices for AL is reasonable.

5.2   PIOD Dataset

We evaluate DOOBNet on the PIOD dataset [34] which is composed of 9175 training images and 925 testing images. Each image has an object instance boundary map and the corresponding occlusion orientation map. We compare our method with the structured random forests algorithm SRF-OCC [32], and the state-of-the-art deep learning methods DOC-HED and DOC-DMLFOV [34]. Results are shown in Table 3a and Fig. 5a. Notably, DOOBNet performs the best, achieving ODS = 0.702. It is 10.1%, 24.2% and 43.4% higher than DOC-DMLFOV, DOC-HED and SRF-OCC, respectively, with occlusion boundary precision being higher at every level of recall. On the other hand, we report the results of object boundary detection subnet in Table 4a and Fig. 6a. DOOBNet obtains 0.736 ODS, 0.746 OIS and 0.723 AP, which are 6.7%, 6.2% and 4.6% higher than DOC-DMLFOV. We also visualize some of our results in Fig. 7. It demonstrates DOOBNet has learned higher level features and can focus attention on class-agnostic object boundaries and estimate the corresponding occlusion orientations. For example, despite both the bird and the twig have similar color and texture, DOOBNet can correctly detect the bird boundaries and occlusion relationships.

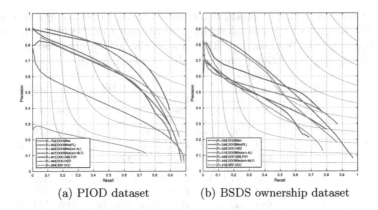

(a) PIOD dataset   (b) BSDS ownership dataset

Fig. 5. Occlusion precision/recall (OPR) curves on PIOD and BSDS ownership dataset.

Table 4. Object boundary detection results on PIOD and BSDS ownership dataset. The term of MLF is multi-level features. SRF-OCC-BSDS trains on the BSDS ownership dataset and tests on the PIOD dataset. FL* achieves the best performance using 6e−5 learnning rate.

	(a) PIOD dataset				(b) BSDS ownership dataset		
Method	ODS	OIS	AP	Method	ODS	OIS	AP
SRF-OCC	.345	.369	.207	SRF-OCC	.511	.544	.442
DOC-HED	.509	.532	.468	DOC-HED	**.658**	**.685**	**.602**
DOC-DMLFOV	.669	.684	.677	DOC-DMLFOV	.579	.609	.519
DOOBNet (w/o AL)	.655	.669	.646	DOOBNet (w/o AL)	.549	.598	.552
DOOBNet (w/o MLF)	.634	.643	.600	DOOBNet (w/o MLF)	.526	.541	.422
DOOBNet (VGG16)	.705	.717	.706	DOOBNet (VGG16)	.600	.617	.476
DOOBNet (FL*)	.673	.683	.659	DOOBNet (FL)	.596	.621	.583
DOOBNet	**.736**	**.746**	**.723**	DOOBNet	.647	.668	.539

5.3 BSDS Ownership Dataset

We also evaluate our model on the BSDS ownership dataset [27] although its small size makes it challenging to train. It contains 100 training images and 100 testing images. Table 3b and Fig. 5b show that DOOBNet can achieve the best performance but is lower than the one on PIOD. The main reason might be the case that there are only 100 training images, being insufficient for a complex deep network. We note that our DOOBNet is a more complex network (67-layer) and outperforms the complex model DOC-DMLFOV significantly by a margin of 9.2% ODS. DOOBNet is also 3.2% and 13.6% higher than DOC-HED and SRF-OCC, respectively. DOOBNet has a slightly low AP as setting $\beta = 4$ in AL leads to lower recall (see Fig. 5b). Reducing β in AL from 4 to 2

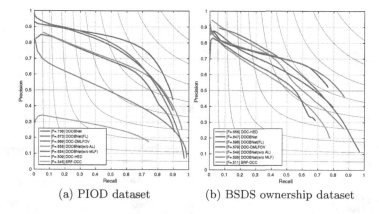

(a) PIOD dataset   (b) BSDS ownership dataset

Fig. 6. Object boundary detection precision/recall curves on PIOD and BSDS owner-ship dataset.

can further improve ODS, OIS and AP to 0.565, 0.585 and 0.481, respectively. Object boundary detection results are shown in Table 4a and Fig. 6b. DOOBNet is slightly lower than DOC-HED and still competitive with DOC-HED for recall below 0.65 (See Fig. 6b). While it obtains a large margin over DOC-DMLFOV. Qualitative results are shown in Fig. 8.

5.4   Ablation Study

An ablation study is performed on both the PIOD and BSDS ownership datasets to confirm our design choices for DOOBNet. Four DOOBNet variants are tested: (I) DOOBNet (w/o attention loss), which adapts CCE loss from [35] instead of AL for the object boundary detection subnet, (II) DOOBNet (w/o multi-level features), which removes the low- and mid-features concatenation by skip connection, (III) DOOBNet (VGG16), which uses VGG16 [30] as the encoder module and the decoder module as the same as DOOBNet, (IV) DOOBNet (FL), which adapts FL ($\alpha = 0.25, \gamma = 2$) from [18] instead of AL for the object boundary detection subnet. We report the results in Table 3 and Fig. 5. With AL, DOOBNet yields 7.8%/4.5% ODS, 7.6%/4.2% OIS, 7.2%/−4.7% AP improvements, while adding multi-level feature gives the gains of 9.5%/11.2% ODS, 9.5%/11.4% OIS, 11.5%/11.6% AP on the PIOD and BSDS ownership dataset, respectively. We observe that the improvement from AL on the PIOD dataset is higher than the one on the BSDS ownership dataset, especially to AP, but getting the opposite result for multi-level features learning. One of the main reasons is the PIOD dataset contains only object boundaries, while the BSDS ownership dataset includes many low-level edges. We also observe that DOOBNet(VGG16) is higher 7.1%/4.5% ODS, 7.2%/3.2% OIS, 7.8%/1.3% AP than DOC-DMLFOV on both datasets, while the later uses the same VGG16 as the encoder module. It demonstrates that the gains are come from our AL and decoder module design. DOOBNet with Res50 [9] improves performance

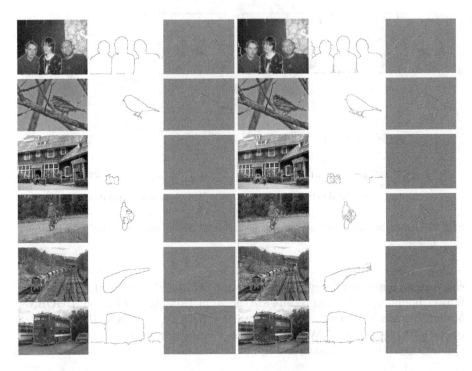

Fig. 7. Example results on PIOD dataset. Ground truth (Columns 1–3): visualization using "left" rule with arrows, object boundaries, and object occlusion boundaries by a 2.1D relief sculpture. DOOBNet results (Columns 4–6). Note for column 4: "red" pixels with arrows are correctly labelled occlusion boundaries; "cyan" pixels are correctly labelled boundaries but with incorrect occlusion; "green" pixels are false negative boundaries; "orange" pixels are false positive boundaries. (Best viewed in color)

Fig. 8. Example results on BSDS ownership dataset. (Best viewed in color)

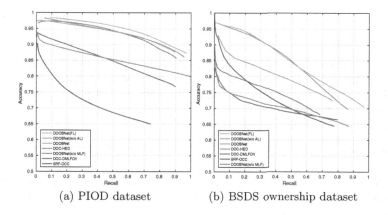

<table>
<tr><td>(a) PIOD dataset</td><td>(b) BSDS ownership dataset</td></tr>
</table>

Fig. 9. Occlusion accuracy/recall (AOR) curves on PIOD and BSDS ownership dataset.

by another 3.0%/4.7% ODS, 2.9%/4.7% OIS, 2.0%/5.8% AP over the DOOB-Net(VGG16). Further more, compare to FL, DOOBNet is higher 5.0%/1.9% ODS, 5.1%/1.3% OIS, 5.2%/−7.0% AP than DOOBNet(FL) on both datasets. It demonstrates that AL is more discriminating than FL. We also report object boundary detection subnet results in Table 4 and Fig. 6. All results of ablation study clearly show the effectiveness of our design choices for DOOBNet.

5.5 Additional AOR Curves

To demonstrate the effectiveness of our proposed DOOBNet and ensure a fair comparison, we also report the AOR curve results in Fig. 9. All our models outperform the methods under comparison. As described above, AOR curves only evaluate the accuracy of occlusion relations on correctly labelled boundaries so that a lower-performing object occlusion boundary detector may have a higher AOR curve. For example, the AOR curves of DOOBNet (FL) are higher than DOOBNet on both dataset. One of the reasons is that the lower-performing boundary detector have a smaller denominator when calculating the accuracy for two occlusion orientation estimators with the same performance.

6 Conclusion

In this paper, we propose the *Attention Loss* to address the extreme positive/negative class imbalance, which we have suggested it as the primary obstacle in object occlusion boundary detection. We also design a unified end-to-end encoder-decoder structure multi-task object occlusion boundary detection network that simultaneously predicts object boundaries and estimates occlusion orientations. Our approach is simple and highly effective, surpassing the state-of-the-art methods with significant margins. In the future, we plan to apply

Attention Loss to other tasks such as semantic edge detection and semantic segmentation in the future. Source code will be released.

Acknowledgement. This work is supported by National Key R&D Program of China (2017YFB1002702) and National Nature Science Foundation of China (61572058). We would like to thank Peng Wang for helping with generating DOC experimental results and valuable discussions.

References

1. Badrinarayanan, V., Kendall, A., Cipolla, R.: SegNet: a deep convolutional encoder-decoder architecture for image segmentation. IEEE Trans. Pattern Anal. Mach. Intell. **39**(12), 2481–2495 (2017)
2. Chen, L.C., Papandreou, G., Kokkinos, I., Murphy, K., Yuille, A.L.: DeepLab: semantic image segmentation with deep convolutional nets, atrous convolution, and fully connected CRFs. IEEE Trans. Pattern Anal. Mach. Intell. **40**(4), 834–848 (2018)
3. Cooper, M.C.: Interpreting line drawings of curved objects with tangential edges and surfaces. Image Vis. Comput. **15**(4), 263–276 (1997)
4. Dollár, P., Zitnick, C.L.: Fast edge detection using structured forests. IEEE Trans. Pattern Anal. Mach. Intell. **37**(8), 1558–1570 (2015)
5. Fu, H., Wang, C., Tao, D., Black, M.J.: Occlusion boundary detection via deep exploration of context. In: Proceedings of the IEEE Conference on Computer Vision and Pattern Recognition, pp. 241–250 (2016)
6. Gao, T., Packer, B., Koller, D.: A segmentation-aware object detection model with occlusion handling. In: 2011 IEEE Conference on Computer Vision and Pattern Recognition (CVPR), pp. 1361–1368. IEEE (2011)
7. Girshick, R.: Fast R-CNN. In: International Conference on Computer Vision (2015)
8. He, K., Zhang, X., Ren, S., Sun, J.: Delving deep into rectifiers: surpassing human-level performance on imagenet classification. In: Proceedings of the IEEE International Conference on Computer Vision, pp. 1026–1034 (2015)
9. He, K., Zhang, X., Ren, S., Sun, J.: Deep residual learning for image recognition. In: Proceedings of the IEEE Conference on Computer Vision and Pattern Recognition, pp. 770–778 (2016)
10. He, X., Yuille, A.: Occlusion boundary detection using pseudo-depth. In: Daniilidis, K., Maragos, P., Paragios, N. (eds.) ECCV 2010. LNCS, vol. 6314, pp. 539–552. Springer, Heidelberg (2010). https://doi.org/10.1007/978-3-642-15561-1_39
11. Hoiem, D., Stein, A.N., Efros, A.A., Hebert, M.: Recovering occlusion boundaries from a single image. In: IEEE 11th International Conference on Computer Vision, ICCV 2007, pp. 1–8. IEEE (2007)
12. Hu, X., Liu, Y., Wang, K., Ren, B.: Learning hybrid convolutional features foredge detection. Neurocomputing **313**, 377–385 (2018)
13. Hwang, J.J., Liu, T.L.: Pixel-wise deep learning for contour detection. arXiv preprint arXiv:1504.01989 (2015)
14. Ioffe, S., Szegedy, C.: Batch normalization: accelerating deep network training by reducing internal covariate shift. arXiv preprint arXiv:1502.03167 (2015)
15. Jia, Y., et al.: Caffe: convolutional architecture for fast feature embedding. arXiv preprint arXiv:1408.5093 (2014)

16. Kokkinos, I.: Pushing the boundaries of boundary detection using deep learning. arXiv preprint arXiv:1511.07386 (2015)
17. Leichter, I., Lindenbaum, M.: Boundary ownership by lifting to 2.1 d. In: 2009 IEEE 12th International Conference on Computer Vision, pp. 9–16. IEEE (2009)
18. Lin, T.Y., Goyal, P., Girshick, R., He, K., Dollár, P.: Focal loss for dense object detection. arXiv preprint arXiv:1708.02002 (2017)
19. Liu, Y., Lew, M.S.: Learning relaxed deep supervision for better edge detection. In: Proceedings of the IEEE Conference on Computer Vision and Pattern Recognition, pp. 231–240 (2016)
20. Liu, Y., Cheng, M.M., Bian, J., Zhang, L., Jiang, P.T., Cao, Y.: Semantic edge detection with diverse deep supervision. arXiv preprint arXiv:1804.02864 (2018)
21. Liu, Y., Cheng, M.M., Hu, X., Wang, K., Bai, X.: Richer convolutional features for edge detection. In: 2017 IEEE Conference on Computer Vision and Pattern Recognition (CVPR), pp. 5872–5881. IEEE (2017)
22. Long, J., Shelhamer, E., Darrell, T.: Fully convolutional networks for semantic segmentation. In: Proceedings of the IEEE Conference on Computer Vision and Pattern Recognition, pp. 3431–3440 (2015)
23. Maire, M.: Simultaneous segmentation and figure/ground organization using angular embedding. In: Daniilidis, K., Maragos, P., Paragios, N. (eds.) ECCV 2010. LNCS, vol. 6312, pp. 450–464. Springer, Heidelberg (2010). https://doi.org/10.1007/978-3-642-15552-9_33
24. Maire, M., Narihira, T., Yu, S.X.: Affinity CNN: learning pixel-centric pairwise relations for figure/ground embedding. In: Proceedings of the IEEE Conference on Computer Vision and Pattern Recognition, pp. 174–182 (2016)
25. Martin, D.R., Fowlkes, C.C., Malik, J.: Learning to detect natural image boundaries using local brightness, color, and texture cues. IEEE Trans. Pattern Anal. Mach. Intell. **26**(5), 530–549 (2004)
26. Nitzberg, M., Mumford, D.: The 2.1-d sketch. In: 1990 Proceedings of Third International Conference on Computer Vision, pp. 138–144. IEEE (1990)
27. Ren, X., Fowlkes, C.C., Malik, J.: Figure/ground assignment in natural images. In: Leonardis, A., Bischof, H., Pinz, A. (eds.) ECCV 2006. LNCS, vol. 3952, pp. 614–627. Springer, Heidelberg (2006). https://doi.org/10.1007/11744047_47
28. Roberts, L.G.: Machine perception of three-dimensional solids. Ph.D. thesis, Massachusetts Institute of Technology (1963)
29. Ronneberger, O., Fischer, P., Brox, T.: U-Net: convolutional networks for biomedical image segmentation. In: Navab, N., Hornegger, J., Wells, W.M., Frangi, A.F. (eds.) MICCAI 2015. LNCS, vol. 9351, pp. 234–241. Springer, Cham (2015). https://doi.org/10.1007/978-3-319-24574-4_28
30. Simonyan, K., Zisserman, A.: Very deep convolutional networks for large-scale image recognition. arXiv preprint arXiv:1409.1556 (2014)
31. Sundberg, P., Brox, T., Maire, M., Arbeláez, P., Malik, J.: Occlusion boundary detection and figure/ground assignment from optical flow. In: 2011 IEEE Conference on Computer Vision and Pattern Recognition, pp. 2233–2240. IEEE (2011)
32. Teo, C.L., Fermüller, C., Aloimonos, Y.: Fast 2D border ownership assignment. In: 2015 IEEE Conference on Computer Vision and Pattern Recognition (CVPR), pp. 5117–5125. IEEE (2015)
33. Tighe, J., Niethammer, M., Lazebnik, S.: Scene parsing with object instances and occlusion ordering. In: 2014 IEEE Conference on Computer Vision and Pattern Recognition (CVPR), pp. 3748–3755. IEEE (2014)

34. Wang, P., Yuille, A.: DOC: deep occlusion estimation from a single image. In: Leibe, B., Matas, J., Sebe, N., Welling, M. (eds.) ECCV 2016. LNCS, vol. 9905, pp. 545–561. Springer, Cham (2016). https://doi.org/10.1007/978-3-319-46448-0_33
35. Xie, S., Tu, Z.: Holistically-nested edge detection. In: Proceedings of the IEEE International Conference on Computer Vision, pp. 1395–1403 (2015)
36. Yang, J., Price, B., Cohen, S., Lee, H., Yang, M.H.: Object contour detection with a fully convolutional encoder-decoder network (2016)
37. Yu, F., Koltun, V.: Multi-scale context aggregation by dilated convolutions. arXiv preprint arXiv:1511.07122 (2015)
38. Yu, F., Koltun, V., Funkhouser, T.: Dilated residual networks. In: Computer Vision and Pattern Recognition, vol. 1 (2017)
39. Zhang, Z., Schwing, A.G., Fidler, S., Urtasun, R.: Monocular object instance segmentation and depth ordering with CNNs. arXiv preprint arXiv:1505.03159 (2015)

Spherical Superpixels: Benchmark and Evaluation

Liang Wan[1,2], Xiaorui Xu[1,2], Qiang Zhao[3(✉)], and Wei Feng[1,2]

[1] College of Intelligence and Computing, Tianjin University, Tianjin, China
{lwan,2016218015,wfeng}@tju.edu.cn
[2] Key Research Center for Surface Monitoring and Analysis of Cultural Relics (SMARC), SACH, Tianjin, China
[3] Institute of Computing Technology, Chinese Academy of Sciences, Beijing, China
zhaoqiang@ict.ac.cn

Abstract. Although a variety of superpixel algorithms have been developed and adopted as elementary tools in low-level computer vision and multimedia applications, most of them are designed for planar images. The quick growth of spherical panoramic images raises the urgent need of spherical superpixel algorithms and also a unifying benchmark of spherical image segmentation for the quantitative evaluation. In this paper, we present a general framework to establish spherical superpixel algorithms by extending planar counterparts, under which two spherical superpixel algorithms are developed. Furthermore, we propose the first segmentation benchmark of real-captured spherical images, which are manually annotated via a three-stage process. We use this benchmark to evaluate eight algorithms, including four spherical ones and the four corresponding planar ones, and discuss the results with respect to quantitative segmentation quality, runtime as well as visual quality.

Keywords: Superpixels · Spherical image · Panorama · Benchmark · Evaluation

1 Introduction

Superpixels group image pixels, which are perceptually similar in colors and close in space, to form visually meaningful entities. Since they heavily reduce the number of primitives to process, superpixels have gained great popularity as elementary tools in low-level computer vision and multimedia applications, such as image recognition [4], image parsing [17,24], object localization [14], saliency detection [12,21]. By today, a great number of superpixel algorithms have been developed for *planar* images [1,3,6,7,9]. As a key building block of many applications [8], the performance of superpixel algorithms may greatly affect the success of subsequent tasks. For the purpose of a fair performance comparison, several works [1,25] have focused on evaluating planar superpixel algorithms quantitatively from multiple aspects, including the adhesion to object boundaries and

© Springer Nature Switzerland AG 2019
C. V. Jawahar et al. (Eds.): ACCV 2018, LNCS 11366, pp. 703–717, 2019.
https://doi.org/10.1007/978-3-030-20876-9_44

shape regularity of superpixels. The evaluation is usually conducted on the BSD image segmentation dataset [2], which provides ground truth segmentations for multiple planar images.

Spherical superpixels, as a new type of superpixels, have received increasing attentions in recent years due to the quick growth of *spherical panoramas*, which cover 360° field of view and are widely used in recent applications [30]. The distinct difference between spherical superpixels from planar superpixels results from the fact that the underlying geometry of spherical images is a closed surface while that of planar images is an open domain. Directly applying planar superpixel algorithms on the unrolled spherical images or the transformed piecewise perspective images [4,16] would degrade the performance inevitably. Currently, there are only two spherical superpixel algorithms reported in the literature, namely spherical EGS (SphEGS) [28] and spherical SLIC (SphSLIC) [31]. Both extend the planar counterparts to the spherical domain.

Another dilemma that spherical superpixel algorithms are facing is the lack of spherical segmentation benchmark for the evaluation of their segmentation quality. To circumvent this situation, SphSLIC utilizes a transformed BSD segmentation dataset [31]. However, since the transformation from the planar to the spherical domain imposes assumptions on the field of view and the viewing direction for planar images, the transformed spherical images have large empty regions, and what's more, the evaluation is inevitably biased.

In this paper, we aim to bridge the planar superpixel algorithms with the spherical domain such that we can benefit from the rich development of planar superpixel algorithms, and obtain multiple spherical superpixel algorithms with as few costs as possible. Second, we plan to provide a high-quality segmentation dataset of real-captured spherical panoramas to fill the gap.

Specifically, inspired by the schemes of SphEGS [28] and SphSLIC [31], we first present a general framework (Sect. 3) on the establishment of spherical superpixel algorithms by extending planar counterparts, in which three main factors should be carefully concerned. Within the framework, we adapt two well-known planar superpixel algorithms, edge-augmented mean shift [6] and ETPS [29], to the spherical domain, and discuss the adaptions in detail. Next, we introduce the spherical segmentation dataset which is created by using an interactive image annotation tool (Sect. 4). With our tool, manual annotation for a spherical image can be conveniently obtained via a three-stage process. To our knowledge, this is the first benchmark for spherical image segmentation. Based on this dataset, we compare the performance of eight algorithms, including the two newly adapted ones, SphEGS [28], SphSLIC [31] and their planar counterparts, in terms of segmentation quality, runtime and visual quality (Sect. 5).

In the following, we first give a brief overview of the planar and spherical superpixel algorithms and existing superpixel evaluation works in Sect. 2. We then describe the general extension framework and the two new developed spherical superpixel algorithms in Sect. 3. Section 4 introduces the spherical segmentation dataset and the quantitative metrics, followed by experimental results reported in Sect. 5. Section 6 concludes the paper and gives the possible directions of future work.

2   Related Work

In this section, we introduce related works from three aspects: planar super-pixel segmentation algorithms, current spherical superpixel algorithms and the research on superpixel evaluation.

2.1   Planar Superpixels

In the literature, there are a variety of superpixel algorithms developed for planar images. According to their high-level approaches, those algorithms can be classified into several categories [1,25]. Density-based algorithms, e.g. edge-augmented mean shift [6], perform mode-seeking in the density image, where each pixel is assigned to the corresponding mode it falls into. Patch-based approaches, such as TPS [9], partition an image into superpixels by connecting seed points through pixel paths. Graph-based methods like normalized cut [23], graph based image segmentation [7] and entropy rate superpixels [16] treat the image as an undirected graph and cut the graph based on the edge weights. Clustering-based approaches borrow the idea from classic k-means algorithm. SLIC [1], preSLIC [20] and linear spectral clustering [15] are the well-known algorithms belonging to this category. Energy optimization-based methods, e.g. ETPS [29], SEEDS [3] and CCS [26], iteratively optimize a formulated energy. There are also contour evolution based algorithms, which represent superpixels as evolving contours starting from initial seed pixels [13]. By observing the shape of superpixels, the superpixel algorithms can also be classified into those generating regular primitives and those producing irregular primitives. For example, SLIC [1] and ETPS [29] can produce regular and compact superpixels, while the outputs of mean shift [6] and graph based image segmentation [7] are irregular.

2.2   Spherical Superpixels

To generate superpixels for spherical images, many works directly apply planar superpixel algorithms on the unrolled spherical images or the transformed piecewise perspective images [5,19]. Although this strategy works well for some applications, it would degrade the performance of the algorithms and produce superpixels with open contours. To deal with this problem, Yang and Zhang [28] presented a panoramic over-segmentation algorithm based on the graph based image segmentation method [7]. To make the original algorithm applicable to spherical images, additional neighborhood relationship is introduced when constructing the graph from the pixels of spherical images. This method gives irregular superpixels with closed contours. To generate more regular spherical superpixels, Zhao et al. [31] proposed an algorithm in the spirit of SLIC [1]. Their method explicitly considers the geometry for the spherical images and makes modifications to the initialization, assignment and update steps of SLIC algorithm. Based on these two works, we present the general framework that establishes spherical superpixel algorithms by extending planar ones.

2.3   Superpixel Evaluation

To assess the performance of superpixel algorithms, some works rely on application-dependent evaluation. For example, Koniusz and Mikolajczyk [11] proposed a segmentation-based method for interest point extraction, and they compared the quality of interest points that are extracted with different superpixel algorithms. Li et al. [14] presented a fast object localization method based on superpixel grid and gave the localization accuracy for different superpixel algorithms. Superpixel algorithms have also been evaluated in the application of image parsing [24].

As an over-segmentation technique, superpixel generation is also usually evaluated on the standard planar image segmentation dataset, i.e. BSD500 [2]. Achanta et al. [1] gave the first categorization of superpixel algorithms by comparing popular superpixel algorithms for the adherence to image boundaries, speed and memory efficiency. The compactness and regularity of superpixels produced by different algorithms are compared in [22] and [10]. Stutz et al. [25] presented an extensive evaluation of 28 state-of-the-art superpixel algorithms on 5 image segmentation datasets regarding visual quality, segmentation performance, runtime, robustness to noise, blur and affine transformations.

Zhao et al. [31] evaluated the performance of SphSLIC on a transformed BSD dataset, and presented the metrics for spherical superpixels. They assumed all the planar images in the BSD dataset have 90° field of view and the same viewing direction. Mapping the planar images to the spherical domain will lead to large empty regions in spherical panoramas. This indicates that the valid image information is defined on an open domain like a planar image. One real-captured spherical panorama, on the other hand, has image contents over the whole sphere, which means the image information is defined on a closed domain. Instead of relying on the transformed BSD dataset, we collect a new annotated segmentation dataset of real-captured spherical panoramas.

3   Spherical Superpixel Algorithms

Inspired by the schemes of SphEGS [28] and SphSLIC [31], we realize that one general way to establish spherical superpixel algorithms is to extend planar superpixel algorithms to make them applicable to spherical images. In this section, we first discuss the extension framework, and then give the extension details of two new spherical superpixel algorithms under this general framework.

3.1   Extension Framework

Our extension framework aims to bridge spherical images and planar superpixel algorithms. Note that the visual information of a spherical image is defined on a viewing sphere, but it has to be parameterized into 2D rectangular domain for storage. As we know, spherical parameterization schemes may suffer from geometric distortions, and different schemes may represent the sphere with a different number of 2D rectangular base faces, which always have discontinuity problem at patch boundaries. Hence the process of grouping pixels into superpixels

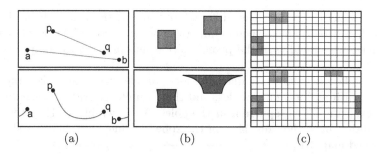

Fig. 1. The three terms that should be considered when extending planar superpixel algorithms to spherical ones: (a) spatial distance measure, (b) neighborhood range and (c) boundaries problem. The 1st and 2nd rows are the planar and spherical cases respectively, when the equirectangular map is used to represent the sphere. See text for more discussions.

needs to take into account both the spherical geometry and the parametrization scheme, focusing on three main factors including: (1) spatial distance measure, (2) neighborhood range and (3) boundaries problem (Fig. 1).

In our current work, we choose equirectangular map to represent the spherical image due to three reasons. First, equirectangular map is the most common way used by camera vendors and research communities to represent and store spherical panoramas. Second, it is used by both SphEGS [28] and SphSLIC [31]. Third, it has relatively simple neighborhood range and boundaries problem as compared to other spherical parameterization methods.

Spatial Distance Measure. In superpixel algorithms, perceptually similar pixels which are also close in space are grouped together. To measure the spatial distance between two pixels, the planar superpixel algorithms always use 2D Euclidean distance on spatial coordinates of pixels. For the spherical panorama, we need to reply on spherical distances, which measure the length of the great circle connecting the two pixels over the sphere.

As shown in Fig. 1(a), the shortest path between two pixels in an unrolled spherical image with 2D Euclidean distance is the line segment connecting them, while the shortest path becomes a curve when spherical distance measure is used. Another distance measure that considers the geometry for spherical panoramas is cosine dissimilarity [31]. Supposing that two arbitrary pixels on the panorama have spatial coordinates of $[X_1, Y_1, Z_1]$ and $[X_2, Y_2, Z_2]$, respectively, the cosine dissimilarity between them is computed as

$$D_s = 1 - \langle [X_1, Y_1, Z_1], [X_2, Y_2, Z_2] \rangle, \tag{1}$$

where $\langle \mathbf{a}, \mathbf{b} \rangle$ is the dot product of vector $\mathbf{a}$ and $\mathbf{b}$.

Neighborhood Range. Some density/clustering-based superpixel methods locate neighboring pixels or weight them in a local region. In planar algorithms, the neighborhood of a pixel is always defined as a square patch centered at that pixel. For spherical panoramas, different regions on the sphere have different levels of distortions. Thus, when defining the neighborhood for a pixel of spherical images, we should take the pixel position into account to compensate the distortions.

Let us take the equirectangular map for example. It parameterizes ray directions by zenith and azimuth angles, and then a uniform grid in the parametric domain oversamples the sphere near the poles. As shown in Fig. 1(b), the neighborhoods that have the same size on the sphere would have different shapes in the unrolled map [31].

Boundaries Problem. In the planar image (Fig. 1(c)), if a pixel p lies at the left (top) boundary, the neighboring pixels at the left (on the top) of it would be undefined. However, a sphere is a closed surface. When a sphere is parameterized into a set of 2D rectangular base faces, special attentions should be paid when we access the neighbors of a pixel lying near the boundaries of base faces [28].

In the equirectangular representation, the left and right boundaries correspond to the same meridian, while the top and bottom boundaries correspond to the north and south poles of a sphere respectively. Therefore, as shown in Fig. 1(c), if a pixel p is at the left boundary of the spherical image, the pixels at the right boundary with similar vertical coordinates are also neighbors. If p is at the top boundary, the pixels at the top boundary with horizontal coordinates as $x + \frac{w}{2}$ are also neighbors, where x is the horizonal coordinate of p and w is the width of the spherical image.

3.2   Two New Spherical Superpixel Algorithms

Under the above extension framework, we develop two new spherical superpixel algorithms by extending the planar mean shift [6] and ETPS [29]. These two methods are ranked as the fifth and the first best planar superpixel algorithms in a recent quantitative comparison [25].

Spherical Mean Shift (SphMS). Mean shift (MS) algorithm [6] is an iterative procedure for locating local maxima of a density function. It can be used to find modes in the joint spatial-color feature domain of an image. Pixels that converge to the same mode thus define the superpixels. The algorithm successively computes the mean shift vectors according to the kernel-weighted averages of pixel features, and translates the kernel windows. To develop the spherical mean shift, all the three terms in the extension framework should be considered. Specifically, we do the following modifications:

1. The original 2D spatial coordinates of a pixel in its feature representation are converted to a 3D unit vector, according to the equirectangular map computation. The cosine similarity (Eq. 1) is then adopted as the distance measure between a pixel and the mode's center.
2. Since the spherical panorama has different levels of distortions in the equirectangular map, the search window defined by the kernel should be modulated by the zenith angle.

3. When the mode's center goes near the boundaries of the equirectangular map, the search window is set to cross the boundaries.

It is also noted that the distance measure in MS is a combination of spatial distance and color distance. Since the color distance is kept intact, we need to weight the spherical spatial distance such that it has a similar magnitude as the planar spatial distance.

Spherical ETPS (SphETPS). Starting from an initial grid partitioning, ETPS [29] iteratively exchanges pixel blocks between neighboring superpixels, and uses a coarse-to-fine scheme. This algorithm encourages the color homogeneity, the shape regularization and the small boundary length within superpixels, and it enforces the superpixels to form a connected component. As the constraints of color coherence, boundary length and component connection can also work for spherical panoramas, we only need to consider the shape regularization and the boundaries problem. In more detail, three revisions are made to planar ETPS algorithm.

1. The shape regularization is formulated as the Euclidean distance between one pixel and the superpixel centroid. Given the equirectangular map, we map the 2D image coordinates of each pixel to the spherical domain, forming a 3D unit vector, and adopt the cosine dissimilarity (Eq. 1) as the spatial distance measurement.
2. To estimate the superpixel centroid over the sphere, we use an approximation scheme. We first calculate the centroid of pixels within a superpixel in 3D space, and then normalize it to a unit vector.
3. The equirectangular map has four boundaries. If a pixel block lies at the left boundary of the spherical image, the rightmost pixel block with the same vertical coordinate should be considered for potential exchange, and vice versa. If a pixel block lies at the top (bottom) boundary of the spherical image, the pixel block at the top (bottom) boundary with horizontal coordinate $x + \frac{w}{2}$ should be considered for potential exchange.

4 Dataset and Evaluation Metrics

In this section, we introduce the spherical segmentation dataset that we collected and the metrics used to evaluate the spherical superpixel algorithms.

4.1 Dataset and Annotation Process

The authors of SphSLIC [31] utilized a transformed BSD segmentation dataset to evaluate the performance of spherical superpixel algorithms. Although this strategy is relatively easier than collecting a spherical segmentation dataset, it has some disadvantages. First, each spherical image in the transformed BSD dataset has only a limited meaningful region, and the remaining regions are all empty. This indicates that the transformation scheme can not emulate all the

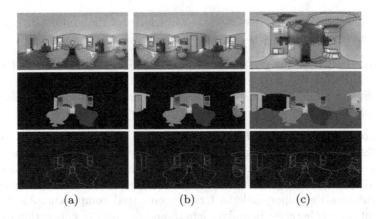

(a)   (b)   (c)

Fig. 2. Dataset preparation: manual annotation process (top), intermediate ground truth segmentation (middle) and boundaries (bottom). Our manual annotation process has three stages: (a) annotating the objects at the central part, (b) rotating the underlying sphere horizontally to annotate the objects that cross the left and right boundaries, (c) rotating the sphere vertically to annotate the objects that lie near the polar regions.

different levels of distortion in true spherical images. Second, when transforming the BSD dataset, all the planar images are assumed to have 90° field of view and the same viewing direction. Changing these two parameters will result in different transformed BSD dataset, and affect the evaluation performance. Therefore it is necessary to collect a dedicated dataset for spherical superpixel algorithm evaluation.

To construct the dataset, we choose 75 images from SUN360 spherical panorama database [27]. The selected images contain 50 indoor images and 25 outdoor images covering different categories. Each image is resized to 1024×512 pixels for manual annotation. The tool we used to annotate the spherical images is developed on the basis of the segmentation tool provided by Martin et al. [18], which is applied to acquire BSD image segmentation dataset. We made the modifications that allow the user to rotate the underlying image sphere in 3D space.

Our manual annotation process contains three basic stages, as illustrated in Fig. 2:

1. Since the central region of a spherical panorama in the format of equirectangular map is least distorted, we first label the objects in this region (see Fig. 2(a)).
2. Next, we rotate the underlying sphere horizontally due to the fact that some objects may be split by the left and right boundaries of the image. To make this rotation operation simple and efficient, we do the horizontal rotation by 180° such that the left and right boundaries of the original spherical image meet at the central region (see the top image in Fig. 2(b)). Then the two parts of split objects can be easily assigned to a common segment. The last two images in Fig. 2(b) show the possible segments for the input image.

Fig. 3. Sample images and ground truth annotations from spherical segmentation dataset: (top) spherical images, (middle) ground truth segmentations and (bottom) ground truth boundaries.

3. Finally, the sphere is rotated vertically by 90°. The objects at the polar regions of the original spherical image now appear at the central region, which can be conveniently annotated (the top image in Fig. 2(c)).

In the experiment, we trained three students to get familiar with the annotation tool, and each of them annotated 25 images. The final result is the spherical segmentation dataset[1]. The number of segments for each image ranges from 250 to 1085, with the average as 510. Some annotation examples are shown in Fig. 3.

4.2 Metrics

The most important properties of superpixels are adherence to image boundaries and structural regularity. In this paper, we use three standard metrics to evaluate boundary adherence, i.e. boundary recall, under segmentation error and achievable segmentation accuracy, and two metrics to evaluate structural regularity, i.e. compactness and size variation. The spherical metrics resemble their planar counterparts except that the pixel distortions are considered, usually by means of counting the solid angle of each pixel and the spherical distance. The detailed description of these metrics can be found in [31]. For the completeness, we give the brief introduction here.

Boundary recall measures the percentage of borders from the ground truth that coincide with those of the superpixels, given by

$$\frac{\sum_{p \in B(G)} A(p) I(\min_{q \in B(S)} d(p,q) < \varepsilon)}{A(B(G))}, \tag{2}$$

---

[1] The annotated dataset are available at http://scs.tju.edu.cn/~lwan/data/ spsdataset/spsdataset75.rar.

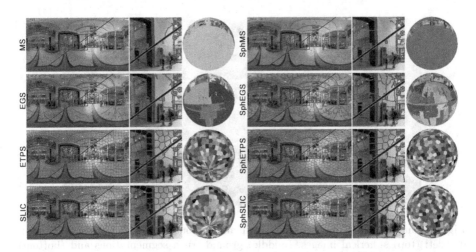

Fig. 4. Visual comparison of superpixels from different methods. For each method, we show the segmentation results with approximately 2000 and 670 superpixels, one zoom-in region, and the color-coded sphere for fewer superpxiels.

where $B(G)$ and $B(S)$ are the boundaries of ground truth $G = \{g_1, \cdots, g_m\}$ and superpixel segmentation $S = \{s_1, \cdots, s_n\}$, $d(p, q)$ is the spherical distance between p and q, $I(\cdot)$ is the indicator function and $A(\cdot)$ is the surface area of pixel or pixels set.

Under segmentation error evaluates how many pixels from superpixels leak across the boundary of ground truth segment. It is expressed as

$$\frac{\sum_i (\sum_{j|s_j \cap g_i \neq \emptyset} A(s_j)) - 4\pi}{4\pi}. \tag{3}$$

Achievable segmentation accuracy gives the best performance when taking superpixels as units for object segmentation. It is computed as

$$\frac{\sum_j \max_i A(s_j \cap g_i)}{4\pi}. \tag{4}$$

Compactness is a numerical quantity representing the degree to which a shape is compact. It is based on the isoperimetric quotient $Q(s_j) = \frac{4\pi A(s_j) - A^2(s_j)}{L^2(s_j)}$, where $L(s_j)$ is the perimeter of superpixel s_j. Then the compactness is the weighted mean of isoperimetric quotient of each superpixel, where weights are the areas of the superpixels, i.e.

$$\frac{\sum_j Q(s_j) A(s_j)}{4\pi}. \tag{5}$$

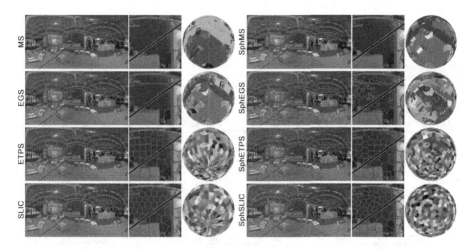

Fig. 5. Visual comparison of superpixels from different methods. For each method, we show the segmentation results with approximately 2000 and 670 superpixels, one zoom-in region, and the color-coded sphere for fewer superpxiels.

Size variation describes the uniformity of superpixel size. It can be defined as the variance of superpixel areas

$$\frac{n \sum_j A^2(s_j) - 16\pi^2}{n^2}. \tag{6}$$

5   Experimental Results

In the experiments, we evaluate eight superpixel algorithms based on our spherical segmentation dataset, including the four spherical superpixel algorithms, i.e. SphMS, SphETPS, SphEGS [28], SphSLIC [31], and the four planar counterparts. In order to make a fair comparison, we have determined the optimal parameter values for each algorithm separately.

5.1   Visual Comparison

Figures 4 and 5 shows the segmentation results for two spherical panoramas at two different numbers of superpixels. We can see that EGS and SphEGS generally produce superpixels that are more tightly adhesive to object boundaries, while SphSLIC ans SphETPS generate spherical superpixels with most regular shapes. It is also obvious that for all the superpixel algorithms, the more superpixels are created, the more object boundaries can be captured. In comparison, SphEGS captures more object boundaries than the other spherical superpixel algorithms. As shown in the blowups in Fig. 4, SphEGS grasps the lights and the edges of walls accurately, while SphETPS partitions those lights into separate segments, which is better than SphSLIC.

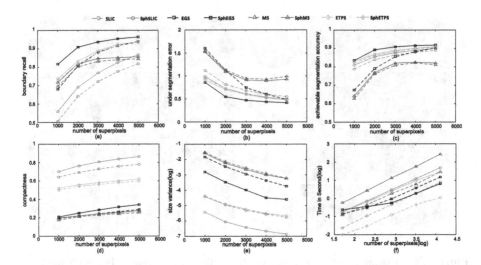

Fig. 6. The comparisons of different methods on the spherical segmentation dataset: (a) boundary recall; (b) under segmentation error; (c) achievable segmentation accuracy; (d) compactness; (e) size variation; and (f) running time.

By extending the adjacency relationship for boundary pixels, SphETPS, SphEGS, and SphSLIC overcome the discontinuity problem that can be obviously observed in the color-coded spheres for ETPS, EGS and SLIC. For better illustration, the equirectangular maps are rotated horizontally by 45°. The left and right image boundaries now meet together as the vertical red lines in the right parts of panoramas for EGS, ETPS and SLIC. Their spherical versions, on the other hand, are not subjected to this problem.

To observe the shape regularity on the spherical domain, we use color-coded spheres to illustrate the segments. By adopting the spherical distance, SphETPS is able to assign less superpixels near the polar regions, while ETPS has many small superpixels crowded together in the polar regions. As for SphMS, it improves the performance with respect to MS. For example, in Fig. 4, SphMS captures some salient object boundaries in the southern polar region.

5.2   Quantitative Evaluation

Figure 6 gives the performance of different algorithms in terms of boundary recall, under segmentation error, achievable segmentation accuracy, compactness and size variation. In comparison, we find that almost all the spherical superpixel algorithms get much better performance than their planar counterparts for the metrics under evaluation, while SphSLIC and SphEGS have much larger improvements than SphMS and SphETPS.

The boundary recall curves are plotted in Fig. 6(a). We can see that SphEGS achieves the best recall values for all the numbers of superpixels, followed by SphETPS and EGS, while SLIC reports the lowest values. For the under segmentation error as shown in Fig. 6(b), among the eight methods, SphEGS has the minimum under segmentation errors. SphETPS and SphSLIC achieve similar performance when the number of superpixels increases. In the term of the achievable segmentation accuracy, SphMS has the lowest values while SphETPS reports the second best performance (Fig. 6(c)). We notice that the increase of the superpixel number has relatively small impact on SphMS and MS, as they quickly converge after using 2000 superpixels. This may be because they are inclined to reach local minimum in the clustering.

As for compactness and size variation, which contribute to the structural regularity, SphSLIC and SphETPS significantly outperform the other spherical superpixel algorithms as shown in Fig. 6(d) and (e), because they start from uniformly distributed seeds or grids and explicitly consider the geometry for spherical image and superpixel regularity. On the other hand, EGS, MS and their spherical extensions do not constrain the compactness, and hence they generate superpixels with irregular shapes and less compactness.

5.3   Running Time

We evaluate the timing performance on a computer installed with Intel(R) Core (TM) i5-4590 CPU @ 3.30 GHz. Here, we use the authors' implementations for SphSLIC, SphEGS, and all the planar algorithms. Both SphMS and SphETPS are implemented by adapting the original codes of the planar versions. It is also noted that these algorithms cannot generate exactly the same number of superpixels as required, usually with a small variation. For a fair comparison, given each expected superpixel number, we run each algorithm for 10 times and count the average of the running times.

Figure 6(f) plots the running time for different superpixel algorithms. For most algorithms, their running time increases linearly with respect to the number of superpixels. However, SphEGS even spends less time than EGS for a larger superpixel number. Among all the methods, ETPS achieves the fastest performance, SphMS is the slowest algorithm, and SphETPS spends less time than SphSLIC when the number of superpixels increases.

6   Conclusion

In this paper, we have presented a general framework for establishing spherical superpixel algorithms, in which three main factors are considered to extend planar counterparts. By applying this framework, two well-known planar superpixel algorithms, i.e. mean shift and ETPS, are adapted to the spherical domain. We then collected a high-quality segmentation dataset of spherical images, and evaluate the performance of eight different algorithms, including the two newly adapted, two existing spherical superpixel algorithms, and their planar counterparts, in terms of quantitative performance, visual quality and running time.

Currently, our dataset contains 75 spherical panoramas, one groundtruth segmentation for each panorama. In the future, we would like improve the quality of the dataset by collecting multiple groundtruth segmentations for each individual panorama. Another direction is adapting more planar superpixel algorithms to the spherical domain, and making a more thorough comparison of spherical superpixel algorithms.

Acknowledgments. This work is supported by National Natural Science Foundation of China (61572354, 61671325, 61702479).

References

1. Achanta, R., Shaji, A., Smith, K., Lucchi, A., Fua, P., Süsstrunk, S.: SLIC superpixels compared to state-of-the-art superpixel methods. IEEE TPAMI **34**(11), 2274–2282 (2012)
2. Arbelaez, P., Maire, M., Fowlkes, C., Malik, J.: Contour detection and hierarchical image segmentation. IEEE TPAMI **33**(5), 898–916 (2011)
3. Van den Bergh, M., Boix, X., Roig, G., Van Gool, L.: Seeds: superpixels extracted via energy-driven sampling. IJCV **111**(3), 298–314 (2015)
4. Bu, S., Liu, Z., Han, J., Wu, J.: Superpixel segmentation based structural scene recognition. In: ACM MM, pp. 681–684 (2013)
5. Cabral, R., Furukawa, Y.: Piecewise planar and compact floorplan reconstruction from images. In: IEEE CVPR, pp. 628–635 (2014)
6. Comaniciu, D., Meer, P.: Mean shift: a robust approach toward feature space analysis. IEEE TPAMI **24**(5), 603–619 (2002)
7. Felzenszwalb, P., Huttenlocher, D.: Efficient graph-based image segmentation. IJCV **59**(2), 167–181 (2004)
8. Feng, W., Jia, J., Liu, Z.Q.: Self-validated labeling of markov random fields for image segmentation. IEEE TPAMI **32**(10), 1871–1887 (2010)
9. Fu, H., Cao, X., Tang, D., Han, Y., Xu, D.: Regularity preserved superpixels and supervoxels. IEEE TMM **16**(4), 1165–1175 (2014)
10. Giraud, R., Ta, V.T., Papadakis, N.: Robust shape regularity criteria for superpixel evaluation. In: IEEE ICIP (2017)
11. Koniusz, P., Mikolajczyk, K.: Segmentation based interest points and evaluation of unsupervised image segmentation methods. In: BMVC, pp. 1–11 (2009)
12. Lei, J., et al.: A universal framework for salient object detection. IEEE TMM **18**(9), 1783–1795 (2016)
13. Levinshtein, A., Stere, A., Kutulakos, K.N., Fleet, D.J., Dickinson, S.J., Siddiqi, K.: Turbopixels: fast superpixels using geometric flows. IEEE TPAMI **31**(12), 2290–2297 (2009)
14. Li, L., Feng, W., Wan, L., Zhang, J.: Maximum cohesive grid of superpixels for fast object localization. In: IEEE CVPR, pp. 3174–3181 (2013)
15. Li, Z., Chen, J.: Superpixel segmentation using linear spectral clustering. In: IEEE CVPR, pp. 1356–1363 (2015)
16. Liu, M.Y., Tuzel, O., Ramalingam, S., Chellappa, R.: Entropy rate superpixel segmentation. In: IEEE CVPR, pp. 2097–2104 (2011)
17. Liu, S., et al.: Fashion parsing with weak color-category labels. IEEE TMM **16**(1), 253–265 (2014)
18. Martin, D., Fowlkes, C., Tal, D., Malik, J.: A database of human segmented natural images and its application to evaluating segmentation algorithms and measuring ecological statistics. In: IEEE ICCV, pp. 416–423 (2001)

19. Micusik, B., Kosecka, J.: Piecewise planar city 3D modeling from street view panoramic sequences. In: IEEE CVPR, pp. 2906–2912 (2009)
20. Neubert, P., Protzel, P.: Compact watershed and preemptive SLIC: on improving trade-offs of superpixel segmentation algorithms. In: IEEE ICPR, pp. 996–1001 (2014)
21. Ren, Z., Hu, Y., Chia, L.T., Rajan, D.: Improved saliency detection based on super-pixel clustering and saliency propagation. In: ACM MM, pp. 1099–1102 (2010)
22. Schick, A., Fischer, M., Stiefelhagen, R.: An evaluation of the compactness of superpixels. PRL **43**, 71–80 (2014)
23. Shi, J., Malik, J.: Normalized cuts and image segmentation. IEEE TPAMI **22**(8), 888–905 (2000)
24. Strassburg, J., Grzeszick, R., Rothacker, L., Fink, G.A.: On the influence of super-pixel methods for image parsing. In: VISAPP (2), pp. 518–527 (2015)
25. Stutz, D., Hermans, A., Leibe, B.: Superpixels: an evaluation of the state-of-the-art. CVIU **166**, 1–27 (2017)
26. Tasli, H.E., Cigla, C., Gevers, T., Alatan, A.A.: Super pixel extraction via convexity induced boundary adaptation. In: IEEE ICME, pp. 1–6 (2013)
27. Xiao, J., Ehinger, K.A., Oliva, A., Torralba, A.: Recognizing scene viewpoint using panoramic place representation. In: IEEE CVPR, pp. 2695–2702 (2012)
28. Yang, H., Zhang, H.: Efficient 3D room shape recovery from a single panorama. In: CVPR, pp. 5422–5430 (2016)
29. Yao, J., Boben, M., Fidler, S., Urtasun, R.: Real-time coarse-to-fine topologically preserving segmentation. In: IEEE CVPR, pp. 2947–2955 (2015)
30. Zhao, Q., Wan, L., Feng, W., Zhang, J., Wong, T.: Cube2video: navigate between cubic panoramas in real-time. IEEE TMM **15**(8), 1745–1754 (2013)
31. Zhao, Q., Dai, F., Ma, Y., Wan, L., Zhang, J., Zhang, Y.: Spherical superpixel segmentation. IEEE TMM **20**(6), 1406–1417 (2018)

Neural Multi-scale Image Compression

Ken M. Nakanishi[1]($\boxtimes$)(iD), Shin-ichi Maeda[2](iD), Takeru Miyato[2](iD),
and Daisuke Okanohara[2]

[1] Graduate School of Science, The University of Tokyo,
7-3-1 Hongo, Bunkyo-ku, Tokyo 113-0033, Japan
`ken-nakanishi@g.ecc.u-tokyo.ac.jp`
[2] Preferred Networks, Inc.,
Otemachi Bldg., 1-6-1 Otemachi, Chiyoda-ku, Tokyo 100-0004, Japan
`{ichi,miyato,hillbig}@preferred.jp`
`https://www.preferred-networks.jp`

Abstract. This study presents a new lossy image compression method
that utilizes the multi-scale features of natural images. Our model consists of two networks: *multi-scale lossy autoencoder* and *parallel multi-
scale lossless coder*. The multi-scale lossy autoencoder extracts the multi-
scale image features to quantized variables, and the parallel multi-scale
lossless coder enables rapid and accurate lossless coding of the quantized
variables via encoding/decoding the variables in parallel. Our proposed
model achieves comparable performance to the state-of-the-art model on
Kodak and RAISE-1k dataset images, and it encodes a PNG image of
size 768×512 in 70 ms with a single GPU and a single CPU process and
decodes it into a high-fidelity image in approximately 200 ms.

1 Introduction

Data compression for video and image data is a crucial technique for reducing communication traffic and saving data storage. Videos and images usually
contain large redundancy, enabling significant reductions in data size via *lossy
compression*, where data size is compressed while preserving the information necessary for its application. In this work, we are concerned with lossy compression
tasks for natural images.

JPEG has been widely used for lossy image compression. However, the quality
of the reconstructed images degrades, especially for low bit-rate compression.
The degradation is considered to be caused by the use of linear transformation
with an engineered basis. Linear transformations are insufficient for the accurate
reconstruction of natural images, and an engineered basis may not be optimal.

In machine learning (ML)-based image compression, the compression model
is optimized using training data. The concept of optimizing the encoder and the
decoder model via ML algorithm is not new. The K-means algorithm was used

Electronic supplementary material The online version of this chapter (https://
doi.org/10.1007/978-3-030-20876-9_45) contains supplementary material, which is
available to authorized users.

© Springer Nature Switzerland AG 2019
C. V. Jawahar et al. (Eds.): ACCV 2018, LNCS 11366, pp. 718–732, 2019.
https://doi.org/10.1007/978-3-030-20876-9_45

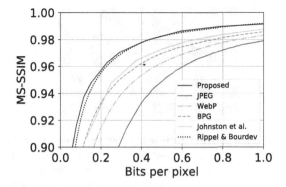

Fig. 1. Rate-distortion trade-off curves with different methods on Kodak dataset. The horizontal axis represents bits-per-pixel (bpp), and the vertical axis represents multi-scale structural similarity (MS-SSIM). Our model achieves better or comparable bpp with respect to the state-of-the-art results [12].

Fig. 2. Original and reconstructed images by our model.

for vector quantization [4], and the principal component analysis was used to construct the bases of transform coding [5]. However, their representation power was still insufficient to surpass the performance of the engineered coders. Recently,

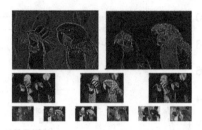

Fig. 3. Visualization of quantized features, $\tilde{z}$, at each resolution layer. Each panel represents the heatmap of $\tilde{z}$ at each resolution layer, where the top, middle, and bottom panels correspond to the map of the 1st, 2nd, and 3rd finest resolution layers. The value of $\tilde{z}$ in case of yellow-colored pixels is relatively high compared with the dark blue-colored pixels. (Color figure online)

several studies proposed to use convolutional neural networks (CNN) for the lossy compression, resulting in impressive performance regarding lossy image compression [2,6,9,12,14–16] by exerting their strong representation power optimized via a large training dataset.

In this study, we utilize CNNs, but propose different architectures and training algorithm than those of existing studies to improve performance. The performance targets are two-fold, 1. *Good rate-distortion trade-off* and 2. *Fast encoding and decoding.* To improve these two points, we propose a model that consists of two components: *multi-scale lossy autoencoder* and *parallel multi-scale lossless coder.* The former, multi-scale lossy autoencoder extracts the multi-scale structure of natural images via multi-scale coding to achieve better rate-distortion trade-off, while the latter, parallel multi-scale lossless coder facilitates the rapid encoding/decoding with minimal performance degradation. We summarize the core concepts of each component of the model below.

– **Multi-scale lossy autoencoder.** When we use a multi-layer CNN with pooling operation and/or strided convolution in this model, the deeper layers will obtain more global and high-level information from the image. Previous works [2,6,9,12,14–16] only used the features present at the deepest layer of such CNN model for encoding. In contrast, our lossy autoencoder model comprises of connections at different depths between the analyzer and the synthesizer, enabling encoding of multi-scale image features (See Fig. 5). Using this architecture, we can achieve a high compression rate with precise localization.
– **Parallel multi-scale lossless coder.** Existing studies rely on sequential lossless coder, which makes the encoding/decoding time prohibitively large. We consider concepts for parallel multi-scale computations based on the version of PixelCNN used in [11] to enable encoding/decoding $\tilde{z}$ in a parallel manner; it achieves both fast encoding/decoding of $\tilde{z}$ and a high compression rate.

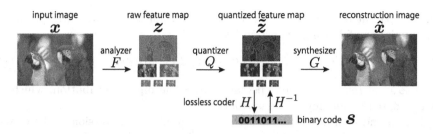

Fig. 4. Overall architecture of proposed model. Our model consists of a lossy auto-encoder and a lossless coder where the lossy autoencoder consists of analyzer F, quantizer Q, and synthesizer G. The analyzer F converts image $\boldsymbol{x}$ to a feature map $\boldsymbol{z}$. The quantizer module Q converts the feature map $\boldsymbol{z}$ to the quantized feature map $\tilde{\boldsymbol{z}}$. The synthesizer G converts the quantized feature map $\tilde{\boldsymbol{z}}$ to a reconstruction image $\hat{\boldsymbol{x}}$. The lossless coder H compresses the quantized feature map $\tilde{\boldsymbol{z}}$ to a binary code $\boldsymbol{s}$, losslessly. H^{-1} is the inverse function of the lossless coder H.

Our proposed model compresses Kodak[1] and RAISE-1k [3] dataset images into significantly smaller file sizes than JPEG, WebP, or BPG on fixed quality reconstructed images and achieves comparable rate-distortion trade-off performance with respect to the state-of-the-art model [12] on the Kodak and RAISE-1k datasets (See Figs. 1 and 8). Simultaneously, the proposed method achieves reasonably fast encoding and decoding speeds. For example, our proposed model encodes a PNG image of size 768×512 in 70 ms with a single GPU and a single CPU process and decodes it into a high-fidelity image with an MS-SSIM of 0.96 in approximately 200 ms. Two examples of reconstruction images by our model with an MS-SSIM of approximately 0.96 are shown in Fig. 2.

2   Proposed Method

2.1   Overview of Proposed Architecture

In this section we first formulate the lossy compression. Subsequently, we introduce our lossy auto-encoder and lossless coder. Let the original image be $\boldsymbol{x}$, the binary representation of the compressed variable be $\boldsymbol{s}$, and the reconstructed image from $\boldsymbol{s}$ be $\hat{\boldsymbol{x}}$. The objective of the lossy image compression is to minimize the code length (i.e., file size) of $\boldsymbol{s}$ while minimizing the distortion between $\boldsymbol{x}$ and $\hat{\boldsymbol{x}}$: $d(\boldsymbol{x}, \hat{\boldsymbol{x}})$ as much as possible. The selection of the distortion $d(\cdot, \cdot)$ is arbitrary as long as it allows differentiation with respect to the input image.

Our model consists of a lossy auto-encoder and a lossless coder as shown in Fig. 4. The auto-encoder transforms the original image $\boldsymbol{x}$ into the features $\boldsymbol{z}$ using the analyzer F as $\boldsymbol{z} = F(\boldsymbol{x}; \phi)$. Subsequently, the features are quantized using a quantizer Q as $\tilde{\boldsymbol{z}} = Q(\boldsymbol{z})$. Q quantizes each element of $\tilde{\boldsymbol{z}}$ using a multi-level uniform quantizer, which has no learned parameters. Finally, the synthesizer G of the auto-encoder, recovers the reconstructed image, $\hat{\boldsymbol{x}} = G(\tilde{\boldsymbol{z}}; \theta)$. Here, ϕ and

---

[1] http://r0k.us/graphics/kodak/.

θ are the parameters of F and G, respectively. Parameters θ and ϕ are optimized to minimize the following distortion loss:

$$L(\theta, \phi) := \mathbb{E}_{p(\boldsymbol{x})} \left[d(\boldsymbol{x}, G(Q(F(\boldsymbol{x}; \phi)); \theta)) \right], \tag{1}$$

where $\mathbb{E}_{p(\boldsymbol{x})}[\cdot]$ represents the expectation over the input distribution, which is approximated by an empirical distribution.

The second neural network is used for the lossless compression of the quantized features $\tilde{z}$. According to Shannon's information theory, the average code length is minimized when we allocate the code length, $\log_2 p(\tilde{z})$ bits, for the signal $\tilde{z}$ whose occurrence probability is $p(\tilde{z})$. Hence, we estimate the occurrence probability of $\tilde{z}$ as $p(\tilde{z}; \omega)$ where ω is a parameter to be estimated. In this study, ω is estimated via maximum likelihood estimation. Thus, we minimize cross entropy between $p(\tilde{z})$ and $p(\tilde{z}; \omega)$, using the fixed analyzer and synthesizer:

$$H(p, p_\omega) := -\mathbb{E}_{p(\tilde{z})}[\log_2 p(\tilde{z}; \omega)]. \tag{2}$$

Note that our objective function for ϕ, θ, and ω can be easily extended to the rate-distortion cost function, a weighted sum of distortion loss (1), and cross entropy (2). Using the rate-distortion cost function, we can jointly optimize ϕ, θ, and ω, as in previous studies [2,9,14]. Nevertheless, we separately optimize them by first optimizing the distortion loss with respect to ϕ and θ. Subsequently, we optimize the cross entropy with respect to ω. This two-step optimization simplifies the optimization of the analyzer F. Because the derivative of the rate-distortion function with respect to the parameter of the analyzer, ϕ depends on the occurrence probability $p(\tilde{z}; \omega)$, the computation of the derivative requires time and becomes complex. Furthermore, it may consume excessive memory for the computation of the derivative when we optimize the parameters with large number of images. Optimization with the rate-distortion cost function could be a future direction of research to pursue further performance improvements.

2.2   Multi-scale Auto-Encoder

In this section, we describe our proposed auto-encoder. Our multi-scale auto-encoder consists of an analyzer F, a synthesizer G, and a quantizer Q. Both the analyzer F and the synthesizer G are composed of CNNs similar to the existing studies. The difference between the proposed and existing models is that our auto-encoder encodes information of the original image in multi-scale features, as follows.

$$F : \boldsymbol{x} \mapsto \{z^{(i)}\}_{i=1}^{M}, \tag{3}$$

$$Q : \{z^{(i)}\}_{i=1}^{M} \mapsto \{\tilde{z}^{(i)}\}_{i=1}^{M}, \tag{4}$$

$$G : \{\tilde{z}^{(i)}\}_{i=1}^{M} \mapsto \hat{\boldsymbol{x}}, \tag{5}$$

$$z^{(i)} \in \mathbb{R}^{C^{(i)} \times H^{(i)} \times W^{(i)}}, \tag{6}$$

$$\tilde{z}^{(i)} \in \{0, \ldots, N-1\}^{C^{(i)} \times H^{(i)} \times W^{(i)}}, \tag{7}$$

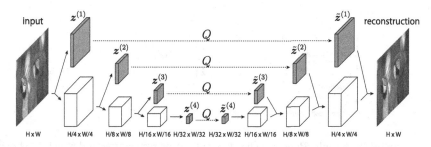

Fig. 5. Architecture of our multi-scale autoencoder. H and W are height and width of an input image, respectively. The left side of the network is the analyzer F, and the right side is the synthesizer G. Light and vivid red-colored boxes represent pre-quantized variables z, and quantized variables $\tilde{z}$. The analyzer F and synthesizer G are described in Sect. 2.2. Quantizer module Q is described in Sect. 2.2.

where $z^{(i)}$ and $\tilde{z}^{(i)}$ denote the i-th ($i = 1, \cdots, M$) resolution of features and its quantized version, whose spatial resolution is $H^{(i)} \times W^{(i)}$ and the number of channels is $C^{(i)}$. The spatial resolution becomes coarser as the layer i becomes deeper, such that both $H^{(i)} > H^{(i+1)}$ and $W^{(i)} > W^{(i+1)}$ hold. Each element of $\tilde{z}$ is quantized into $\{0, \ldots, N - 1\}$, $N \in \mathbb{N}$. Figure 5 shows an example of $M = 4$. Global and coarse information including textures, are encoded at the deeper layer, whereas local and fine information, such as edges, are encoded at the shallower layer. The parameters of F and G, ϕ and θ, are trained to minimize distortion loss (1).

Quantizer Module. Because quantization is not a differentiable operation, it makes optimization difficult. Recent studies [1,2,6,16] have used stochastic perturbations to avoid the problem of non-differentiability. They replace the original distortion loss with the average distortion loss where the distortion occurs owing to the injection of the stochastic perturbation to the feature maps, instead of the deterministic quantization. In general, however, the stochastic perturbation makes the training longer, because we require considering samples with large size to approximate the expected value.

To avoid complexity of optimization when injecting stochastic perturbation, we adopt deterministic quantization even during training, similar to the recent work [9]. The quantizer module we use is shown in Fig. 6.

Before quantization, we apply several preprocessing steps on z. First, to enhance the compression rate of the lossless coding, we apply batch normalization (BN) on z, which drives the statistics of the feature map to exhibit zero mean and unit variance. BN makes each channel of z possess similar statistics to each other, which is beneficial for estimating the probability of the discretized feature map $p(\tilde{z}; \omega)$ using CNN which shares internal layer except for the top layer. Additionally, the control of statistics via BN is advantageous for decreasing the entropy of $\tilde{z}$. Subsequently, we clip the normalized z into $[0, u]$ ($u > 0$) and expand its range into $[0, N - 1]$ via multiplying $\frac{N-1}{u}$. In this study, we set $u = 4$.

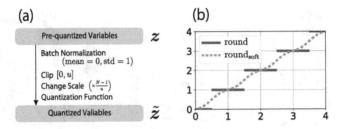

Fig. 6. Quantizer module. Panel (a) shows quantization procedures and panel (b) shows round(x) (blue dashed line) and the plot of round$_{\text{soft}}$(x) (red solid line), which are used as a hard quantization function and a soft quantization function, respectively. (Color figure online)

Following the above mentioned preprocessing, we apply multi-level quantization:

$$\text{round}(x) = \lceil x - 0.5 \rceil, \tag{8}$$

where $\lceil a \rceil$ is a ceiling function that yields the smallest integer, which is larger than or equal to a. This quantization function is not differentiable and does not allow conduction of the gradient-based optimization. To overcome this difficulty, we consider a similar strategy as [9]. We replace the quantization function with the "soft" quantization function when computing back-propagation, while the intact quantization function is used to compute forward propagation. The soft quantization function we used is written as

$$\text{round}_{\text{soft}}(x) = x - \alpha \frac{\sin(2\pi x)}{2\pi}, \tag{9}$$

where we used $\alpha = \frac{1}{2}$. Figure 6(b) shows round$_{\text{soft}}$(x) (Eq. (9)) overlaid on round(x) (Eq. (8)). Owing to this approximation, we can conduct conventional gradient-based optimization for the (approximate) minimization of the distortion loss (Eq. (1)) with respect to θ and ϕ as the usual training of the neural network. Although this gradient-based optimization uses improper gradient, the performance of our model is comparable or superior to the performance of existing models, as demonstrated in our experiment, implying that the side effect is not prominent.

2.3 Parallel Multi-scale Lossless Coder

In this section, we explain the construction of lossless coding, $H \colon \tilde{z} \mapsto s$, that transmits the multi-scale feature map $\tilde{z}$ into a one-dimensional binary sequence s.

To minimize average code length, we estimate the occurrence probability of $\tilde{z}$. Suppose $\tilde{z}$ is indexed in raster scan order as $\tilde{z} = (z_1, \cdots, z_I)$ where $I = \sum_{i=1}^{M} C^{(i)} \times H^{(i)} \times W^{(i)}$. Subsequently, the joint probability $p(\tilde{z})$ is represented as the product of the conditional distributions:

$$p(\tilde{z}) = p(z_1) \prod_{i=2}^{I} p(z_i|z_1, \cdots, z_{i-1}). \tag{10}$$

Conveniently, the problem of learning the conditional distribution can be formulated as a supervised classification task, which is successfully solved via neural networks. If z_i takes one of N-values, the neural network that contains N-output variables is trained to predict the value (i.e., label) of z_i. Subsequently, the output of the trained neural network mimics $p(z_i|z_1, z_2, \cdots, z_{i-1})$. The estimated probability is used for encoding z_i, as illustrated in Fig. 7(a).

Toderici et al. [16] used PixelRNN to estimate $p(z_i|z_1, \cdots, z_{i-1})$ $(i \geq 2)$, showing that it achieves a high compression rate in theory. In practice, however, it requires a long computation time for both encoding and decoding, proportional to the number of elements of $\tilde{z}$ because PixelRNN sequentially encodes z_i.

To reduce the computation time for both encoding and decoding, we use a parallel multi-scale PixelCNN [11]. The concept behind this model is to take advantage of conditional independence. We divide the elements of $\tilde{z}$ into K subsets $\boldsymbol{v}^{(k)}$ $(k = 1, 2, \cdots, K)$, where the k-th subset includes I_k elements. We subsequently assume the conditional independence among the elements of the subset. Namely, we assume that $p(\tilde{z})$ is represented as

$$p(\tilde{z}) \simeq p(\boldsymbol{v}^{(1)}) \prod_{k=2}^{K} \prod_{i=1}^{I_k} p(v_i^{(k)}|\boldsymbol{v}^{(1)}, \cdots, \boldsymbol{v}^{(k-1)}). \tag{11}$$

Although conditional independence does not hold in general, it significantly reduces the computation time, because the number of evaluations of neural networks is no longer proportional to the number of elements N, but is instead proportional to the number of subsets K, where, typically, $K \ll N$.

Specifically, we assume conditional independence in spatial and channel domain as conducted in [11], but with a slightly different implementation. Because we use CNN as the analyzer and the synthesizer of the autoencoder, the feature map $\tilde{z}$ preserves the spatial information. The spatial correlation between pixels of $\tilde{z}$ tends to decrease as the distance increases. Thus, we assume the conditional independence between the distant units in the feature map when conditioned on the relatively close units in the feature map. This is illustrated in Fig. 7(b)–(d), where the red units are assumed to be independent from each other under the condition that the dark-gray units are provided. We simply consider a single resolution case; the multi-resolution case is explained in the appendix. Encoding the red units given the dark-gray units, as in the order of Fig. 7(b) and (c), we can encode denser units, based on the given sparser units. Iterating this procedure, as shown in Fig. 7(d), we can encode all the units of $\tilde{z}$, given $\boldsymbol{v}^{(1)}$. To encode $\boldsymbol{v}^{(1)}$, we simply assume independence among the units in $\boldsymbol{v}^{(1)}$ and assume it obeys an identical distribution, irrelevant to the spatial position. Subsequently, we estimate the histogram to approximate the distribution.

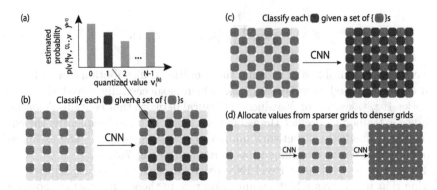

Fig. 7. Lossless coding with parallel multi-scale PixelCNN. (a) The conditional probability estimated by CNN is used to encode the i-th quantized feature $\boldsymbol{v}^{(i)}$; (b),(c) two types of conditional independence in spatial domain are assumed, and each distribution is estimated by solving the classification task with CNN; and (d) the values of dense grids are encoded by conducting procedures (b) and (c), iteratively.

3   Comparison with Existing CNN-Based Lossy Image Compression

In this section, we review recent studies regarding CNN-based image compression to elucidate the value of our contribution. CNN-based image compression exhibits high image compression performance. It also achieves better visual quality of reconstruction, especially on low bit-rate compression, compared with classic compression methods, such as JPEG.

For the entropy coding, [2] and [14] modeled $p(\tilde{z})$ using a factor of independent probability distributions (i.e., $p(\tilde{z}; \omega) := \prod_i p(z_i; \omega_i)$). However, this could result in poor accuracy regarding the entropy estimation, because spatial neighborhood pixels are generally highly correlated and independent assumption causes over-estimation of the entropy. To solve this problem, [8,9,12] constructed a model of probability distribution for each quantized variable, given their neighborhoods. This model is called *context model*. However, via construction, using such a context model requires sequential encoding/decoding over $\tilde{z}$, thus the encoding/decoding speed significantly slows down when a computationally heavy model, such as PixelCNN [10], is used for the context model. To reduce the computational cost for the encoding/decoding, [8,9] used learned *importance masks* models on $\tilde{z}$, to adaptively skip the encoding/decoding by observing each estimated importance mask on each element of $\tilde{z}$. [9] achieved state-of-the-art performance using PixelCNN as the context model. However, it still requires sequential encoding/decoding over $\tilde{z}$.

In contrast, our proposed model exhibits parallel encoding/decoding over a subset of $\tilde{z}$ assuming the conditional independence. Our assumption of the conditional independence reflects the property of the natural image statistics, i.e., the spatial correlation between pixels decreases as the pixels are distant from each other. The conditional independence allows to sample $\tilde{z}$ in a parallel manner, thus, our model can perform fast encoding/decoding with a GPU. [11] demonstrated that such a parallel multi-scale density model achieves comparative performance with respect to the original PixelCNN, thus we can expect our proposed model to achieve both fast encode/decoding and accurate entropy coding.

Regarding the architecture of lossy autoencoder, to the best of our knowledge, all the existing studies used variants of the autoencoder, which exhibits a bottleneck at the deepest layer of the encoder. Although the proposed architecture possesses a similar structure as in the existing studies [12,13] in the sense that the analyzer and the synthesizer exhibit symmetric structures, our model is specialized for lossy image compression where each feature map of the analyzer is quantized and stored to maintain the various resolutions of image features. This is not explored in existing studies where the quantization is applied to the deepest layer [2,6,9,14] or applied after taking the sum of multiple features [12]. [15,16] proposed a different architecture compared with the standard lossy autoencoder we have described here, to realize variable compression rate regarding neural compression. Their lossy compression model consists of recurrent neural network-based encoder and decoder. In each recurrence, the encoder considers the difference of each pixel between the original image and its reconstruction as an additional input to the originals, and the encoder and decoder are trained so as to minimize the distortion loss. Their proposed model, however, consumes significant computational time for encoding/decoding, compared with the standard lossy autoencoder model, owing to its nature of sequential recurrent computation.

4   Experiments

4.1   Experimental Setup

We conducted experiments to evaluate the image compression performance of our model regarding benchmark datasets.[2] We compared the performance with existing file formats, JPEG, WebP, BPG, and state-of-the-art neural compression methods [6,12].

For the training dataset, we used Yahoo Flickr Creative Commons 100M [7], which has been used in the study regarding the current state of the art method [12]. The original dataset consists of 100-million images. We selected portions of images whose both vertical and horizontal resolution were greater than or equal to 1,024 × 1,024. We used 95,205 selected images for training and 1,000 selected images for validation. For pre-processing of the lossy autoencoder training, we resized the images into those whose short sides were 512. Subsequently, we cropped the resized images to 512 × 512. For the lossless coder training, we performed the same pre-processing as for the lossy autoencoder,

---

[2] Our code used for the experiment is available at https://github.com/pfnet-research/nms-comp.

except that our resizing and cropping size was 1,024 × 1,024. We used (negative) MS-SSIM [17] for the distortion loss (1), which is observed to exhibit high correlation with human subjective evaluation. It is commonly used to evaluate the quality of the image compression. Please refer to the appendix for further details of the experiments.

4.2   Comparison of the Compression Performances

Figure 1[3] shows the RD curves with different compression methods on the Kodak dataset. Our proposed model achieved superior performance to the existing file formats, JPEG[4], WebP[5], and BPG[6].

Moreover, the proposed model achieved better performance than nearly all the existing neural compression methods [2,16]. It demonstrated comparable performance with respect to recent CNN-based compression [12]. When we compare the RD-curve carefully with [12], it seems that our method is advantageous in case of wide range of low bit-rates. Refer to appendix for certain reconstructed images on the Kodak dataset.

Figure 8 shows the RD curves on the RAISE-1k dataset. Our model also achieves superior performance over the other methods.

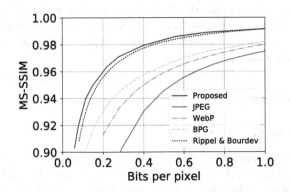

Fig. 8. Rate-distortion trade-off curves with different methods on the RAISE-1k dataset.

To evaluate the encoding and decoding speeds of our model, we compare the computation time for encoding and decoding against JPEG, WebP, and BPG.

---

[3] Regarding the RD curves of [12], we carefully traced the RD curve from the figure of their paper, because we could not obtain the exact values at each point. As for the RD curve of [6], we used the points provided by the authors via personal communication. The exact values of bpp and MS-SSIM on the RD curve of the proposed method are shown in Table 1 in appendix.

[4] http://www.ijg.org/.

[5] https://developers.google.com/speed/webp/.

[6] https://bellard.org/bpg/.

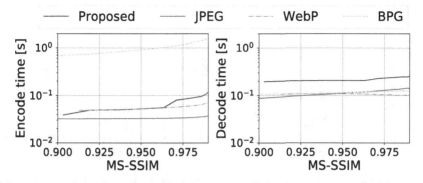

Fig. 9. Computational time vs. MS-SSIM plots on the RAISE-1k dataset. The left and right panel indicate the results of the encoding time and decoding time, respectively.

Unfortunately, we cannot implement the state-of-the-art DNN-based study [12] because the detail of the architecture and lossy compression procedures are not written in their paper.

As for the computational resources, our proposed model operated on a single GPU and a single CPU process, whereas JPEG, WebP, and BPG used a single CPU process. We used PNG file format as original images because it is a widely accepted file format and publicly available BPG codec, libbpg, only accepts either JPEG or PNG file format as the input. To achieve a fair comparison, we measured the computation time including the decoding of PNG-format image into Python array, and encoding process from Python array into the binary representations (encoding time), and the time required for decoding from the binary representations into the PNG-format image (decoding time). Note that the transformation between a PNG-format image and a GPU array was not optimized with respect to the computation time; we did not transform each PNG-format image into a cuda array on GPU directly[7]. The direct transformation, which would reduce the computation time of our model, is reserved for future study.

Figure 9 shows the computational times for encoding and decoding. For encoding, our proposed method takes approximately 0.1 s or less than 0.1 s for the region where the MS-SSIM takes less than 0.98. It is significantly faster than BPG, but inferior to JPEG and WebP. Note that a reconstructed image with an MS-SSIM of 0.96 is usually a high-fidelity image, which is difficult to distinguish from the original image by human eyes. Two examples of our reconstructed image are shown in Fig. 2. The MS-SSIM of the top and bottom reconstructed image are 0.961 and 0.964, respectively. The decoding time of our proposed method is approximately 0.2 s for the range of MS-SSIM between 0.9 to 0.99. It is nearly two times slower than the other file formats.

---

[7] We first transformed the PNG-format image into a numpy array on CPU with the python library 'Pillow', then transferred it to a cuda array on GPU.

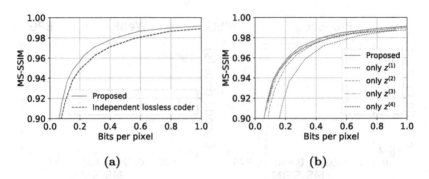

Fig. 10. (a) Entropy coding by proposed parallel multi-scale lossless coder vs. independent lossless coder. (b) Multi-scale vs. single-scale autoencoder. RD-curves of our proposed model (multi-scale autoencoder) are compared with that of single-scale autoencoders. Each single-scale autoencoder possesses architecture identical to the proposed model, but the quantization is applied to the units only at specific depth of the layer. "only $z^{(i)}$" in the legend refers to the single-scale autoencoder that is quantized only at the i-th layer units.

4.3   Analysis by Ablation Studies

We conducted ablation experiments to indicate the efficacy of each of our proposed modules: multi-scale lossy autoencoder and parallel multi-scale lossless coder.

Parallel Multi-scale Lossless Coder vs. Independent Lossless Coder. Here, we discuss the efficacy of our lossless coder against an *independent lossless coder* that conducts lossless coding of each element of $\tilde{z}$ by observing the histograms of each channel of $\hat{z}$. As for the lossy autoencoder model, we used architecture identical to the proposed model. Figure 10a shows the RD-curves with respect to our lossless coder and independent lossless coder [2,14]. We can observe that our lossless coder achieved significantly better performance than the independent lossless coder. Note that, evidently, the independent lossless coder can encode/decode faster compared with our lossless coder.

Multi-scale vs. Single-Scale Autoencoder. Figure 10b shows the RD-curves on multi-scale (i.e., proposed) and single-scale autoencoders. Each single-scale autoencoder possesses architecture identical to the proposed model, except it only possesses only one connection at specific depth of the layer. As for the structure of each single-scale autoencoder, we used the architecture identical to the proposed model, except that the quantization is applied at a specific depth of the layer. The deeper layers beyond the quantization were not used for both encoding and decoding. The training was separately conducted to achieve the best performance for each single-scale autoencoder. In this experiment, the quantization level was always fixed at 7. As can be observed from the figure, our model certainly achieves better performance than other single-resolution autoencoder models at any bitrate, although, the gains are not so large. This may be because we did not conduct the joint optimization of the parameters of the lossy autoencoder and the lossless coder. The separate optimization may hinder exploitation of the benefits of multi-resolution features, because the entropy of the feature map would be different at each resolution, and the separate optimization makes it difficult to exploit the property.

Figure 3 shows the quantized feature map at each layer, obtained via our lossy autoencoder. We observe that each quantized feature map extracts different scale of features. For example, the quantized feature maps at the high-resolution layer (top panels) encode the features in the high-frequency domain, including edges, whereas the quantized feature maps at the low-resolution layer encode the features in the low-frequency domain, including background colors and surfaces.

5   Conclusion

In this study, we propose a novel CNN-based lossy image compression algorithm. Our model consists of two networks: *multi-scale lossy autoencoder* and *parallel multi-scale lossless coder*. The multi-scale lossy autoencoder extracts multi-scale features and encodes them. We successfully obtained different features of images. Local and fine information, such as edges, were extracted at the relatively shallow layer, and global and coarse information, such as textures, were extracted at the deeper layer. We confirmed that this architecture certainly improves the RD-curve at any bitrate. The parallel multi-scale lossless coder encodes the discretized feature map into compressed binary codes, and decodes the compressed binary codes into the discretized feature map in a lossless manner. Assuming the conditional independence and the parallel multi-scale pixelCNN [11], we encoded and decoded the discretized feature map in a partially parallel manner, making the encoding/decoding times significantly fast without losing much quality. Our experiments with the Kodak and RAISE-1k datasets indicated that our proposed method achieved state-of-the-art performance with reasonably fast encoding/decoding times. We believe our model makes the CNN-based lossy image coder step towards the practical uses that require high image compression quality and fast encoding/decoding time.

References

1. Agustsson, E., et al.: Soft-to-hard vector quantization for end-to-end learning compressible representations. In: NIPS, pp. 1141–1151 (2017)
2. Ballé, J., Laparra, V., Simoncelli, E.P.: End-to-end optimized image compression. In: ICLR (2017)
3. Dang-Nguyen, D.T., Pasquini, C., Conotter, V., Boato, G.: RAISE: a raw images dataset for digital image forensics. In: ACM Multimedia Systems Conference, pp. 219–224 (2015)
4. Gersho, A., Gray, R.M.: Vector Quantization and Signal Compression, vol. 159. Springer, Heidelberg (2012)

5. Goyal, V.K.: Theoretical foundations of transform coding. IEEE Signal Process. Mag. **18**(5), 9–21 (2001)
6. Johnston, N., et al.: Improved lossy image compression with priming and spatially adaptive bit rates for recurrent networks. arXiv preprint arXiv:1703.10114 (2017)
7. Kalkowski, S., Schulze, C., Dengel, A., Borth, D.: Real-time analysis and visualization of the YFCC100M dataset. In: Workshop on Community-Organized Multimodal Mining: Opportunities for Novel Solutions, pp. 25–30 (2015)
8. Li, M., Zuo, W., Gu, S., Zhao, D., Zhang, D.: Learning convolutional networks for content-weighted image compression. arXiv preprint arXiv:1703.10553 (2017)
9. Mentzer, F., Agustsson, E., Tschannen, M., Timofte, R., Van Gool, L.: Conditional probability models for deep image compression. arXiv preprint arXiv:1801.04260 (2018)
10. van den Oord, A., Kalchbrenner, N., Kavukcuoglu, K.: Pixel recurrent neural networks. In: ICML, pp. 1747–1756 (2016)
11. Reed, S., et al.: Parallel multiscale autoregressive density estimation. In: ICML, pp. 2912–2921 (2017)
12. Rippel, O., Bourdev, L.: Real-time adaptive image compression. In: ICML, pp. 2922–2930 (2017)
13. Ronneberger, O., Fischer, P., Brox, T.: U-net: convolutional networks for biomedical image segmentation. In: Navab, N., Hornegger, J., Wells, W.M., Frangi, A.F. (eds.) MICCAI 2015. LNCS, vol. 9351, pp. 234–241. Springer, Cham (2015). https://doi.org/10.1007/978-3-319-24574-4_28
14. Theis, L., Shi, W., Cunningham, A., Huszár, F.: Lossy image compression with compressive autoencoders. In: ICLR (2017)
15. Toderici, G., et al.: Variable rate image compression with recurrent neural networks. arXiv preprint arXiv:1511.06085 (2015)
16. Toderici, G., et al.: Full resolution image compression with recurrent neural networks. In: CVPR, pp. 5435–5443 (2017)
17. Wang, Z., Simoncelli, E.P., Bovik, A.C.: Multiscale structural similarity for image quality assessment. In: Conference Record of the Thirty-Seventh Asilomar Conference on Signals, Systems and Computers, vol. 2, pp. 1398–1402. IEEE (2004)

Blur Detection via Phase Spectrum

Renyan Zhang[(✉)]

College of Electrical Engineering and Automation,
Shandong University of Science and Technology,
Qingdao, Shandong, China
zry@sdust.edu.cn

Abstract. The effectiveness of blur features is very important in blur detection from a single image and the most existing blur features are sensitive to the strong edges in the blurred image region which degrades the detection methods. We analyze the information carried by the reconstruction of an image from the phase spectrum alone (RIPS) and the influences of blurring on RIPS. We find that a clear image region has more intensity changes than a blurred one because the former has more high frequency components. And the local maxima of RIPS are at where these image components occur, which make the RIPS of the clear image regions are obviously bigger than that of the blurred ones. Based on this finding, we proposed a simple blur feature, called Phase Map (PM), generated by thresholding RIPS adaptively. And our blur detection method propagates PM to the final blur map only by filtering PM using the relative total variation (RTV) filter. Our proposed method is evaluated on challenging blur image datasets. The evaluation demonstrates that PM feature is effective for different blur types and our detection method performs better than the state-of-the-art algorithms quantitatively and qualitatively.

Keywords: Blur detection · Phase spectrum

1 Introduction

Blur regions caused by camera/object motion or defocus are common in digital images. Blur caused by motion and defocus are called motion blur and defocus blur, respectively. Although blur can degrade image quality, the intentional blur can also be used to make some specific object more prominent in the scene in some cases, for example Fig. 1(a).

In recent years, along with lots of research in connection with blurred images, such as image deblurring [7,18] and shape from defocus [6], the latent information in blurred images has been understood more deeply. It has been convinced of

Electronic supplementary material The online version of this chapter (https://doi.org/10.1007/978-3-030-20876-9_46) contains supplementary material, which is available to authorized users.

© Springer Nature Switzerland AG 2019
C. V. Jawahar et al. (Eds.): ACCV 2018, LNCS 11366, pp. 733–748, 2019.
https://doi.org/10.1007/978-3-030-20876-9_46

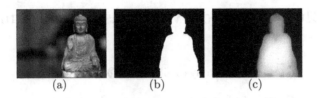

(a)   (b)   (c)

Fig. 1. An example result of our blur detection method. (a) Input image. (b) Ground-truth binary blur map. (c) Grayscale blur map generated by our proposed method.

that blur images have many positive applications in computer vision and graphics fields, such as image fusion [15], depth recovery [11], refocus [13] and 3D reconstruction [27], and so on. Distinguishing the blurred regions from the clear ones, i.e. blur detection, from a single blurred image is a challenging problem and can benefit these applications. In this paper, our objective is proposing a novel blur feature based on the phase spectrum of an image.

One key point of blur detection is finding effective blur features suitable for various blur types. Although many previous blur features perform well, such as local gradient histogram statistics [12], heavy-tailedness measure [19], absolute value of spectrum amplitude difference [22], blur features based on the steerable first and second derivative of Gaussian filters [5], these blur features are mostly based on the intensity magnitude or the amplitude spectrum of an image, which makes them sensitive to the strong edges of a blurred region. Especially, strong edges are common in the motion blurred regions, which makes these blur features degraded in motion blur detection.

In this paper, we analyze the function of the reconstruction of an image from the phase spectrum alone (RIPS) and the influences of blurring on the image intensity in Sect. 3. We find that: (1) The image intensity of a clear image region contains more changes than a blurred one because the clear region has more high frequency components than the blurred one. (2) The local maxima of RIPS occur at where the image components changes, which make the RIPS of a clear image region is bigger than that of a blurred one because the former has more intensity changes. In Sect. 4, based on these findings, we propose a novel blur feature, called Phase Map (PM), which is based on adaptively thresholding RIPS. And we also give a blur detection method based on PM, which employs the relative total variation (RTV) filter [25] for propagating the blur feature points in PM to the final blur map. Figure 1 shows one example result of our proposed method. The evaluations in Sect. 5 show that our proposed method performs better than the state-of-the-art methods qualitatively and quantitatively, and can handle images with different types of blur.

2 Related Work

Blur feature is very important for a blur detection method. According to the blur feature type, we can divide blur detection methods into statistics-based, transform-based, spectrum-based, and so on. In most methods, a single blur feature is not enough and several different features are combined together for better detection results.

Levin [12], Shi et al. [19] and Liu et al. [16] use image gradient histogram statistics for blur detection. Ferzli and Karam [8] point out that the relative changes in luminance are important rather than the absolute ones and propose a perceptual blur model based on the probability summation. Narvekar and Karam [17] improve the method of [8] based on the cumulative probability of blur detection (CPBD). Zhuo and Sim [29] re-blurred the input image by Gaussian kernel and get the defocus amount via the ratio between the gradient and the re-blurred edition of the input image. Chou et al. [4] take Structural Similarity (SSIM) [24] as the blur amount. Chakrabarti et al. [3] and Zhu et al. [28] get blur detection cues by local frequency component analysis. Elder and Zucker [5] estimate image blur by the steerable first and second derivative of Gaussian filters. Shi et al. [20] name the small defocus blurriness as just noticeable defocus blur (JNB) and learn a sparse blurry dictionary on images blurred slightly by Gaussian filters for blur detection. Bae and Durand [1] improves the method of [5] via nonhomogeneous optimization [14] and refine the defocus estimation by a cross bilateral filter. Tang et al. [22] use the spectrum contrast, i.e. the absolute value of spectrum amplitude difference between a pixel and its adjacent pixels at edge locations, as the blur feature. In [23] the image spectrum residual feature is used for blur detection, which is based on the real part of the Fourier spectrum of an image. The High-frequency multiscale Fusion and Sort Transform (HiFST) method [10] use the sorted absolute values of the high-frequency Discrete Cosine Transform (DCT) coefficients in blur detection. Su et al. [21] measure the blurry degree of an image by the singular value of the image singular value decomposition (SVD). Yi and Eramian [26] measure the amount of blur by Local Binary Patterns (LBP).

These previous methods mostly make use of the blur features based on the gradient or the amplitude spectrum of an image, and are mostly designed for the defocus blur detection. Different from these methods, our blur detection method uses our proposed PM feature based on RIPS. RIPS can capture the abundant fine changes in the clear image regions and is insensitive to the strong edges of a blurred region, which makes PM more robust than the previous blur features.

3 From Phase Spectrum to Blur Feature

The selection of blur features is very important for a blur detection method. In this section we investigate the information immersed in the phase spectrum that relates to the blur detection.

3.1 Phase Spectrum of Image

Given an image I, the 2D Fourier Transform of it is:

$$\mathcal{F}(I) = \mathcal{F}_{\mathcal{R}}(I) + i * \mathcal{F}_{\mathcal{I}}(I) \tag{1}$$

where $\mathcal{F}_\mathcal{R}(I)$ and $\mathcal{F}_\mathcal{I}(I)$ are the real part and the image part, respectively. To avoid the wraparound error, an $M \times N$ image is padded by adding $\frac{M}{2}$ and $\frac{N}{2}$ boarder pixels on both sides of the image in the column and the row directions, respectively, before the Fourier Transform.

The phase spectrum of I is:

$$P(I) = \arctan\left[\frac{\mathcal{F}_\mathcal{I}(I)}{\mathcal{F}_\mathcal{R}(I)}\right] \qquad (2)$$

The reconstruction of image I from the phase spectrum alone (RIPS) is:

$$R(I) = \mathcal{F}^{-1}\{\exp[i * P(I)]\} \qquad (3)$$

where $\mathcal{F}^{-1}$ denotes the 2D Inverse Fourier Transform.

3.2   Information Immersed in Phase Spectrum

The spectrum of a signal is composed of the amplitude spectrum and the phase spectrum. In computer vision field, the amplitude spectrum of an image has been used widely. The functionalities of the phase spectrum has been neglected for a long time, although it has been pointed out that the phase spectrum of an image is more critical than the amplitude spectrum to the integrity of an image long time ago [2,9]. Especially, Castleman [2] (Section 10.4.6 of the book) points out that the phase information specifies where each of the sinusoidal components resides within the images.

To demonstrate the functionalities of the phase spectrum of a signal, we give several 1D examples of RIPS in Fig. 2, and more theoretical explanations on RIPS are in our Supplementary. Figure 2 shows that:

(1) RIPS contains the position information of a signal, e.g. the local extremum of RIPS indicate where a signal starts and ends as shown in Fig. 2(a).
(2) RIPS can specify where each of the components of a signal changes, e.g. the changes of the component magnitudes and frequencies can result in the local extrema in RIPS as shown in Fig. 2(b) and (c), respectively.

In conclusion, the local maxima of RIPS indicate where the components of a signal occur and change, and the more local maxima RIPS contains, the more changes the signal contains.

3.3   Blur Feature PM Based on RIPS

To demonstrate the influences of blurring on the RIPS of an image, we give an example in Fig. 3. The faces of humanoid puppets in Figs. 3(a) and (b) are clear and blurred, respectively. Comparing the intensity curve of the clear face region (Fig. 3(a)) with that of the blurry face region (Fig. 3(b)), we find that the former has more details, i.e. fine intensity changes. So the rich changes can make an image clearer in some degree. And the clear image region contains more components, especially in high frequency region, than the blurred one, which results

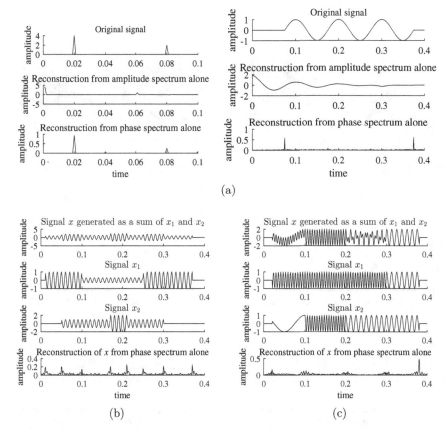

Fig. 2. 1D examples of RIPS. (a) RIPS of pulse signal and cosine signal. (b) and (c) RIPS of a synthetic signal generated as a sum of signal x_1 and x_2. In (b) the amplitudes of x_1 and x_2 change. In (c) the frequencies of x_1 and x_2 change.

in the blurred region have more intensity changes, as the amplitude spectrums in the bottom row of Fig. 3 show. Furthermore, the abundant components make the clear region containing more intensity changes, and these intensity changes make the RIPS of the clear region contains more local maxima, as Fig. 3(a) and (b) shown. And the most important to the blur detection is that RIPS is insensitive to the strong edges in the blurred region, which is because of that the foundation of RIPS is the location of the changes rather than the magnitude of the changes.

When the magnitude of the image intensity gradient is taken as the blur feature, the edges in the blurred regions will also be found, owing to the bigger gradients, together with the edges in the clear regions, as the gradient curves in Figs. 3(a) and (b) show. That means the image intensity gradient is not a good feature for blur detection. Many previous blur features based on the image intensity magnitude may suffer from this kind of shortcoming, such as spectrum residual [23] and power spectrum [19].

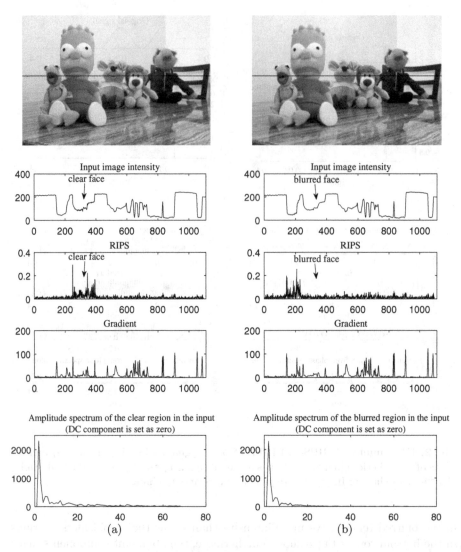

Fig. 3. Examples of the RIPS. In (a) and (b), from top to bottom: input image from [10], the intensity curve of a row in the input image indicated by the black line, the RIPS intensity curve of the row, the input image gradient of the row, the amplitude spectrum curves of the clear/blurred face region in the input image intensity curve.

The RIPS curves in Figs. 3(a) and (b) show that the RIPS of an image is sensitive to the fine intensity changes in a clear image region and is free from the drastic intensity changes on the image edges. We also find that the RIPS of a clear patch tends to be bigger than that of a blurred patch, as shown in Fig. 3, which makes RIPS a better feature compared with the gradient for blur detection.

Fig. 4. The example output for each step of our method. (a) Input Image I. (b) G: Gradient of I (c) R_G: RIPS of G. (d) P_τ: Phase Map of I. (e) B^{final}: our final blur map. (f) The edges of clear regions indicated by the red lines. (Color figure online)

But RIPS is not yet good enough for discriminating clear regions from blur ones. Actually, as Sects. 4.1 and 4.2 show, the local maxima of RIPS are better than RIPS for blur detection. That is because of the local maxima of RIPS are at where the image components change. In our method, we take PM (generated by thresholding RIPS) as the blur feature to locate these local maxima. And if the thresholding value is appropriate, PM could capture the local maxima of RIPS for specifying the key locations (or edges) of a clear region.

4   Proposed Blur Detection Method

Our proposed blur detection method is based on the RIPS. The example output for each step of our method on the image dataset [19] is shown in Fig. 4. In this section, we present our blur detection method in details.

4.1   Calculation of RIPS

Just as aforementioned in Sect. 3.3, the clear image regions contain more details, i.e. more fine changes of the image intensity. Because the relative changes in luminance are important rather than the absolute ones [8], in our proposed method, we use the gradient image G instead of the input image I for reinforcing the fine intensity changes in the input image. G is calculated by:

$$G = \sqrt{(I * h_x)^2 + (I * h_y)^2} \tag{4}$$

where $h_x = \begin{bmatrix} 1 & 0 \\ 0 & -1 \end{bmatrix}$, $h_y = \begin{bmatrix} 0 & 1 \\ -1 & 0 \end{bmatrix}$. G retains almost all of the intensity changes of an image, which may be fine or drastic, just as shown in Fig. 4(b).

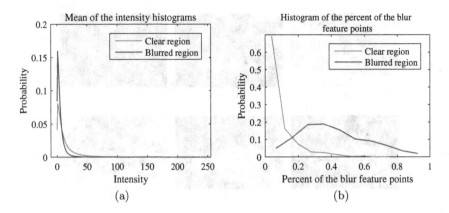

Fig. 5. Histogram analyses on images from the dataset [19]. (a) Mean of the intensity histograms of R_G. (b) Histogram of the percent of the blur feature points in P_τ.

According to Eqs. 1, 2 and 3, the 2D Fourier Transform of gradient image G is $G_\mathcal{F} = \mathcal{F}(G)$, the phase spectrum of G is $P_G = \mathcal{P}(G_\mathcal{F})$, and the RIPS of G is $R_G = \mathcal{R}(G)$. In R_G, the image intensity is in range of $[0, 255]$, which represents the blurry degree of an image pixel, i.e. the smaller R_G is, the more blurry the image pixel is, and vice versa. The comparison between Figs. 4(b) and (c) shows that R_G can retain the position information of the fine changes in the clear regions of G and can also effectively suppress the strong edges in the blurred regions of G.

We also analyze the means of the intensity histograms of the clear regions and the blurred regions in R_G of all the images in the dataset [19], respectively, as shown in Fig. 5(a). Figure 5(a) shows that the intensities of the clear regions in R_G are bigger than that of the blurred regions on the whole. But this difference between the clear and the blurred regions is obviously not enough for distinguishing them from each other.

4.2 Calculating Phase Map by Thresholding RIPS

There are more fine changes in the clear regions than the blurred ones in an image, and the local maxima of RIPS are at where the components of image change. So the locations of these local maxima contain the clues for differentiating the clear regions from the blurred ones. For capturing the local maxima of RIPS, we binarize R_G as denoted by:

$$P_\tau = \begin{cases} 1, & R_G > \tau \\ 0, & R_G \leq \tau \end{cases} \tag{5}$$

where P_τ is called Phase Map (PM), which is our final blur feature. In P_τ, the pixel with a value of one locates the neighbor regions of the local maxima of R_G, which is named as the blur feature point. Because the clear regions are full of fine

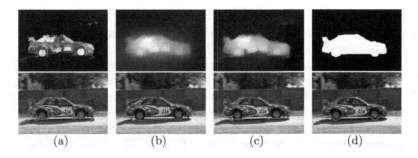

(a)   (b)   (c)   (d)

Fig. 6. Our blur maps with different scales. Images on the top are the blur maps. The bottom images indicate the edges between the clear regions and the blurred regions by the red lines. (a) B^3. (b) B^{63}. (c) B^{final}. (d) Ground truth. (Color figure online)

intensity changes resulting from abundant image components, if τ is appropriate, PM could capture the local maxima of RIPS and specify the key locations (or edges) of a clear region, as Fig. 4(d) shows. When τ is bigger, less blur feature points are captured, which results in incomplete clear regions in the final blur map. A smaller τ will results in more false blur feature points and make the blur region edges not clear. In our experiment, τ is generated by applying the Otsu algorithm on P_τ. Otsu's method is for finding the threshold to minimize the intraclass variance of the black and white pixels.

Figure 4(d) also confirms that there are more blur feature points in the clear regions than in the blurred regions in P_τ. Especially, P_τ has more blur feature points on edges than at other places, which conforms to what Bae et al. [1] have pointed out that the amount of blur can be estimated reliably only in areas of an image that has significant frequency content.

For evaluation the ability of P_τ as a blur feature, we calculate the histograms of the percent of the blur feature points in the clear regions and the blurred regions on all the images in the dataset [19], respectively, as shown in Fig. 5(b). Figure 5(b) shows that the percent of the blur feature points in clear regions are greater than that of in blurred regions on the whole.

4.3 Propagating Blur Feature Points to Blur Map

We propagate the blur feature points in P_τ to the raw blur map via the relative total variation (RTV) filter [25] as follows:

$$B^{\sigma,\lambda,t} = f_{rtv}\left(P_\tau, \sigma, \lambda, t\right) \tag{6}$$

where f_{rtv} represents the RTV filter. λ is the strength parameter controlling the degree of smooth. σ is the scale parameter specifying the maximum size of the texture elements. A bigger λ or σ makes a single scale blur map having completer blur regions, but too big λ or σ makes the blur region edges not clear and vice versa. The function of λ is similar to that of σ, so in our method λ is a constant set by hand and we only change σ. RTV filter is iterative, and t specifies the number of iterations. If $t > 1$, the blur map will be over smoothed, so $t = 1$ is used. We keep $\lambda = 1$ and $t = 1$ in our method, so $B^{\sigma,\lambda,t}$ is written as B^σ in the rest of the paper.

The reasons for using RTV are as follows. The windowed inherent variation in RTV is for recovering a surface from the similar-direction gradients generated by the major edges of the surface [25], and PM can just capture the major edges of a clear region, as Fig. 4(d) shows. We use the implementation of the RTV filter provided online by the author. Figure 4(e) shows that the RTV filter can reconstruct the scopes of the clear regions from the blur feature points in P_τ. Figure 6 demonstrates the effectiveness of our proposed method further.

4.4   Getting Final Multiscale Blur Map

We also analyze the influence of the scale parameter σ on the blur map B^σ. Just as Fig. 6 shows, comparing with B^σ with smaller σ, B^σ with larger σ is less sensitive to the strong edges in the blurred regions and the textures in the clear regions. And the clear region in B^σ with larger σ is more complete than that in B^σ with smaller σ. On the contrary, the edge of clear regions in B^σ with smaller σ is closer to the ground truth than that in B^σ with larger σ. To combine the advantages of the smaller σ and the larger σ, we generate our final blur map B^{final} at pixel (i, j) by the multiscale scheme:

$$B_{i,j}^{final} = \min \left(\bigcup_{k=1}^{n} B_{i,j}^{\sigma_k} \right) \tag{7}$$

where n specifies the number of scales. In our method, $n = 3$, $\sigma_k = 2^{2+k} - 1$. Figure 4(f) shows that B^{final} is effective. And Fig. 6 shows the edges in B^{final} accord with the ground truth better than other single scale blur maps.

5   Experiment Results

In our experiments, we evaluate our method on several synthetic blur images from [10], the blur image dataset [19] and dataset [20].

5.1   Adaptability to Different Blur Types

For demonstrating the adaptability of our method to different blur types, we test our method on the synthetic images from [10]. These images are with the blur types of Gaussian blur, lens blur, motion blur, radial blur, surface blur and zoom blur on the background, respectively. The test results in Fig. 7 show that our method can handle these common blur types well.

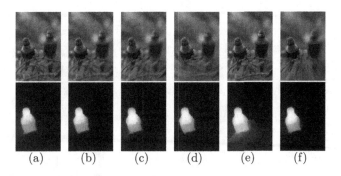

Fig. 7. Results of our method on images with different blur types. Top images are input images. Bottom images are the blur maps. (a) Gaussian blur. (b) Lens blur. (c) Motion blur. (d) Radial blur. (e) Surface blur. (f) Zoom blur.

5.2   Comparison with Previous Methods

We firstly compare quantitatively our method with the state-of-the-art algorithms [1,3,10,16,19–23,26,29] on the image dataset [19], which consists of 296 images with partial motion blur and 704 images with partial out-of-focus blur. The precision-recall curves on this dataset are in Fig. 8(a). The same as [10], the threshold value for binarizing the blur maps varies within the range [0, 255]. Figure 8(a) shows our proposed method achieves the highest precision within the recall range [0, 1]. We also compare the F_1-measure, $F_{0.3}$-measure and mean absolute error (MAE) on dataset [19], and the comparison result in Fig. 8(c) shows our method is better than these the state-of-the-arts. We secondly compare quantitatively our method with the state-of-the-art algorithms [1,3,10,16,19–21,23,26,28,29] on dataset [20], which consists of 8 images with just noticeable blur (JNB), i.e. small scale blur. Figure 8(d) shows that our method do better than most of the state-of-the-arts on dataset [20].

Our results are compared qualitatively with the results of several previous methods on the dataset [19] and dataset [20], as Fig. 9 shows. In Fig. 9, the images in Fig. 9(g) and (h) are from the homepage of Shi [19] and the result images of other previous methods are generated by the author's codes or provided by the authors. In all result images, the higher the intensity is, the clearer the pixel is. In other words, the blurred regions are blacker than the clear ones. As Fig. 9 shows, most of the previous methods can not handle images with motion blurs and perform badly on the image with strong edges in the out-of-focus regions. This is because of that these methods are mostly based on the image intensity magnitude, which is sensitive to the strong edges in the blur regions. Our method can do better than these methods because PM is insensitive to the big intensity changes in the blurred regions, but the other methods may take some strong edges in the blur regions as the clear ones. And the clear regions in our results are completer than those of other methods, e.g. there are more small black regions in the clear region of other method results.

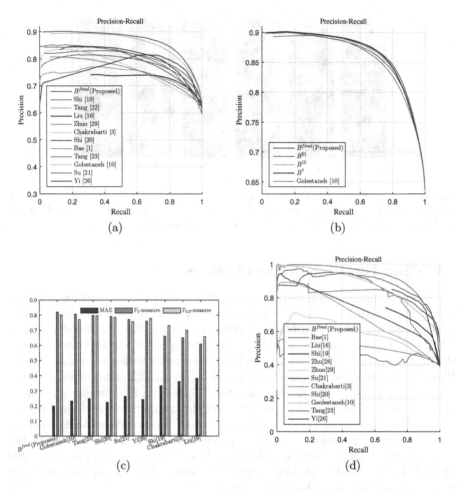

Fig. 8. Quantitative comparison. (a) and (b) are comparisons of Precision-Recall curves on dataset [19]. (c) Comparisons of the MAE, F_1-measure and $F_{0.3}$-measure on dataset [19]. (d) Comparison of Precision-Recall curves on dataset [20].

Moreover, our results accord with the ground truth more better than the best results of all the other methods, i.e. the results of [10], on dataset [19]. This is because of the binarization operation in our method for generating PM makes the position information of the clear regions be retained better.

5.3   Effectiveness of Our Multiscale Scheme

To demonstrate the effectiveness of our multi-scale scheme, we compare the B^{final} to several our single scale blur maps quantitatively.

As shown in Fig. 8(b), all of our single scale blur maps exceed the best one among all the previous methods, i.e. the method of [10]. And the multi-scale

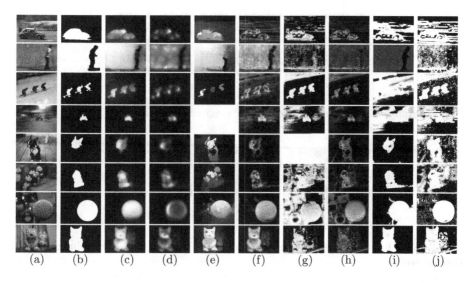

Fig. 9. Qualitative comparison for different blur detection methods. (a) Input image. (b) Ground-truth. (c) Ours. (d) Golestaneh [10]. (e) Tang [23]. (f) Shi [20]. (g) Liu [16]. (h) Su [21]. (i) Yi [26]. (j) Shi [19]. The input image in the last row is from dataset [20] and others are all from dataset [19].

Fig. 10. Application of our method to DFF. (a) and (c) are the input images from [10] with different focus regions. (b) and (d) are blur maps of (a) and (c), respectively.

B^{final} is better than all of our single scale blur maps. The comparison demonstrates our method based on PM feature is competitive and can get good results even by only one single scale blur map.

5.4 Applications

Depth from Focus. We apply our method to depth from focus (DFF). The results are in Fig. 10, which show that the changes of our blur maps are consistent with the changing of the camera focus.

Blur Magnification. We apply our method successfully to blur magnification, which increases the blur level of the blurred backgrounds in an image for simulating a shallow depth of field (DOF). The blur magnification result based on our blur map is in Fig. 11.

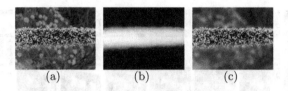

(a)   (b)   (c)

Fig. 11. Application of our method to blur magnification. (a) Input images. (b) Our blur map. (c) Blur magnification result.

(a)   (b)   (c)

Fig. 12. One failure example of our method. (a) Input image. (b) Our blur map. (c) Ground truth.

6   Conclusions

In this paper, we propose a novel blur feature for blur detection. Our proposed blur feature, called Phase Map (PM), is based on the reconstruction of the image from the phase spectrum alone (RIPS). PM is insensitive to the strong edges in the blur image regions and sensitive to the fine intensity changes in the clear image regions, which makes PM suitable for several different blur types. Our blur detection method based on PM achieves the state-of-the-art result on challenging image data. We also apply our method to DFF and blur magnification successfully. More explains of our proposed method are in the supplementary material.

The limitation of our method is the method will degrade when the clear image region is textureless, because flat texture regions have little intensity changes. As shown in Fig. 12, the clothes of several people are textureless and are detected as blurred regions by our method. In the future, we intend to improve our method for overcoming this limitation by combining the PM feature with the features used by other previous methods.

References

1. Bae, S., Durand, F.: Defocus magnification. Comput. Graph. Forum **26**(3), 571–579 (2007)
2. Castleman, K.R.: Digital Image Process. Prentice Hall Press, New Jersey (1996)
3. Chakrabarti, A., Zickler, T., Freeman, W.T.: Analyzing spatially-varying blur. In: 2010 IEEE Conference on Computer Vision and Pattern Recognition (CVPR), pp. 2512–2519. IEEE Press (2010)
4. Chou, Y.C., Fang, C.Y., Su, P.C.: Content-based cropping using visual saliency and blur detection. In: 10th International Conference on Ubi-Media Computing and Workshops (Ubi-Media), pp. 1–6. IEEE Press (2017)

5. Elder, J.H., Zucker, S.W.: Local scale control for edge detection and blur estimation. IEEE Trans. Pattern Anal. Mach. Intell. **20**(7), 699–716 (1998)
6. Favaro, P., Soatto, S.: A geometric approach to shape from defocus. IEEE Trans. Pattern Anal. Mach. Intell. **27**(3), 406–417 (2005)
7. Fergus, R., Singh, B., Hertzmann, A., Roweis, S.T., Freeman, W.T.: Removing camera shake from a single photograph. ACM Trans. Graph. **25**(3), 787–794 (2006)
8. Ferzli, R., Karam, L.J.: A no-reference objective image sharpness metric based on the notion of just noticeable blur (JNB). IEEE Trans. Image Process. **18**(4), 717–728 (2009)
9. Forsyth, D.A., Ponce, J.: Computer Vision: A Modern Approach. Pearson, London (2012)
10. Golestaneh, S.A., Karam, L.J.: Spatially-varying blur detection based on multiscale fused and sorted transform coefficients of gradient magnitudes. In: 2017 IEEE Conference on Computer Vision and Pattern Recognition (CVPR), pp. 596–605. IEEE Press (2017)
11. Ha, H., Im, S., Park, J., Jeon, H.G., Kweon, I.S.: High-quality depth from uncalibrated small motion clip. In: 2016 IEEE Conference on Computer Vision and Pattern Recognition (CVPR), pp. 5413–5421. IEEE Press (2016)
12. Levin, A.: Blind motion deblurring using image statistics. In: 2006 Advances in Neural Information Processing Systems (NIPS), vol. 19, pp. 841–848. MIT Press (2007)
13. Levin, A., Fergus, R., Durand, F., Freeman, W.T.: Image and depth from a conventional camera with a coded aperture. ACM Trans. Graph. **26**(3), 70 (2007)
14. Levin, A., Lischinski, D., Weiss, Y.: Colorization using optimization. ACM Trans. Graph. **23**(3), 689–694 (2004)
15. Li, S., Kang, X., Hu, J., Yang, B.: Image matting for fusion of multi-focus images in dynamic scenes. Inf. Fusion **14**(2), 147–162 (2013)
16. Liu, R., Li, Z., Jia, J.: Image partial blur detection and classification. In: 2008 IEEE Conference on Computer Vision and Pattern Recognition (CVPR), pp. 1–8. IEEE Press (2008)
17. Narvekar, N.D., Karam, L.J.: A no-reference image blur metric based on the cumulative probability of blur detection (CPBD). IEEE Trans. Image Process. **20**(9), 2678–2683 (2011)
18. Pan, J., Sun, D., Pfister, H., Yang, M.H.: Blind image deblurring using dark channel prior. In: 2016 IEEE Conference on Computer Vision and Pattern Recognition (CVPR), pp. 1628–1636. IEEE Press (2016)
19. Shi, J., Xu, L., Jia, J.: Discriminative blur detection features. In: 2014 IEEE Conference on Computer Vision and Pattern Recognition (CVPR), pp. 2965–2972. IEEE Press (2014)
20. Shi, J., Xu, L., Jia, J.: Just noticeable defocus blur detection and estimation. In: 2015 IEEE Conference on Computer Vision and Pattern Recognition (CVPR), pp. 657–665. IEEE Press (2015)
21. Su, B., Lu, S., Tan, C.L.: Blurred image region detection and classification. In: 19th International Conference on Multimedia, pp. 1397–1400. ACM Press (2011)
22. Tang, C., Hou, C., Song, Z.: Defocus map estimation from a single image via spectrum contrast. Opt. Lett. **38**(10), 1706–1708 (2013)
23. Tang, C., Wu, J., Hou, Y., Wang, P., Li, W.: A spectral and spatial approach of coarse-to-fine blurred image region detection. IEEE Sig. Process. Lett. **23**(11), 1652–1656 (2016)

24. Wang, Z., Bovik, A.C., Sheikh, H.R., Simoncelli, E.P.: Image quality assessment: from error visibility to structural similarity. IEEE Trans. Image Process. **13**(4), 600–612 (2004)
25. Xu, L., Yan, Q., Xia, Y., Jia, J.: Structure extraction from texture via relative total variation. ACM Trans. Graph. **31**(6), 139 (2012)
26. Yi, X., Eramian, M.: LBP-based segmentation of defocus blur. IEEE Trans. Image Process. **25**(4), 1626–1638 (2016)
27. Yu, F., Gallup, D.: 3D reconstruction from accidental motion. In: 2014 IEEE Conference on Computer Vision and Pattern Recognition (CVPR), pp. 3986–3993. IEEE Press (2014)
28. Zhu, X., Cohen, S., Schiller, S., Milanfar, P.: Estimating spatially varying defocus blur from a single image. IEEE Trans. Image Process. **22**(12), 4879–4891 (2013)
29. Zhuo, S., Sim, T.: Defocus map estimation from a single image. Pattern Recogn. **44**(9), 1852–1858 (2011)

Author Index